July 14–17, 2015
Bangalore, India

Association for
Computing Machinery

Advancing Computing as a Science & Profession

e-Energy'15

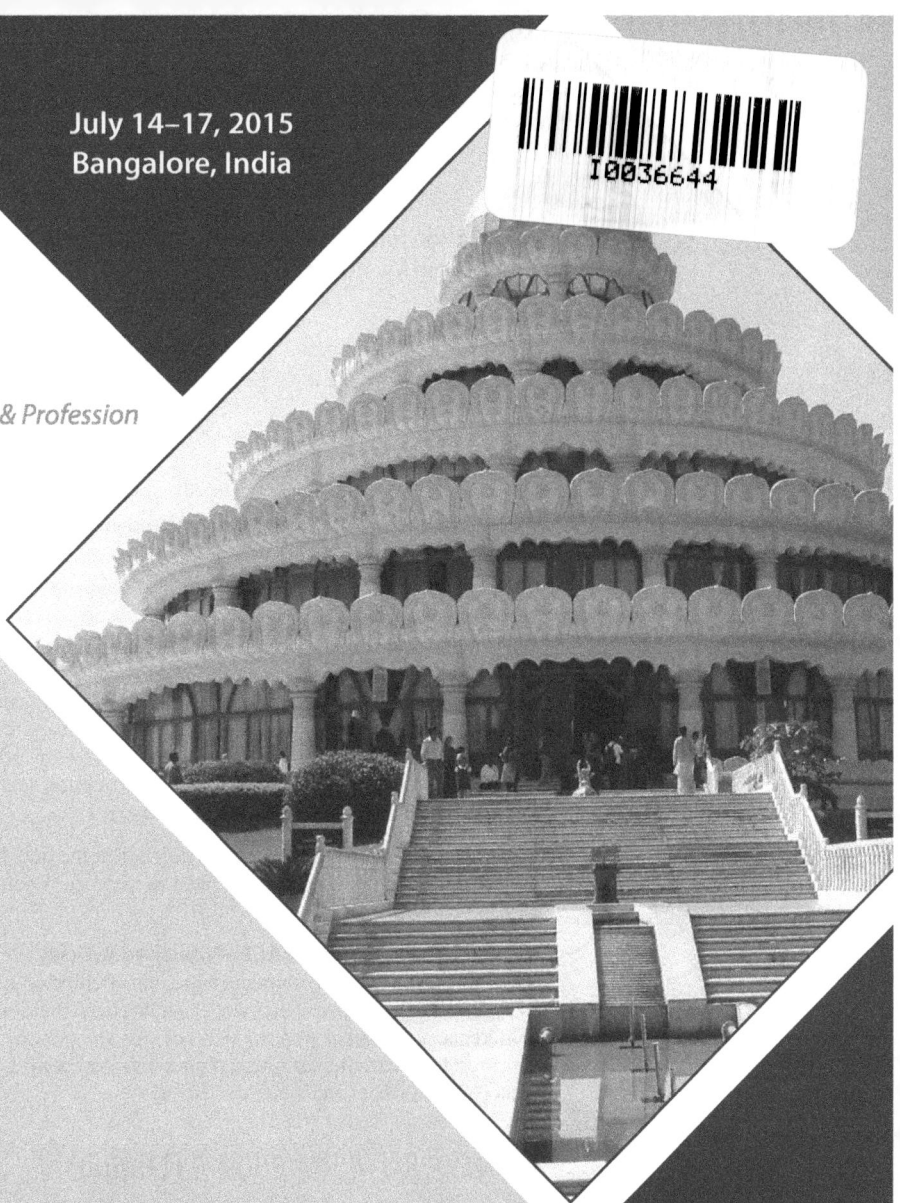

Proceedings of the 2015 ACM Sixth International Conference on

Future Energy Systems

Sponsored by:

ACM SIGCOMM

Supported by:

IBM, Rolta, Tata Consultancy Services, IIT Bombay, IIT Kharagpur, India Smart Grid Forum, IISc Bangalore, and IIID

The Association for Computing Machinery
2 Penn Plaza, Suite 701
New York, New York 10121-0701

ISBN: 978-1-4503-3609-3 (Digital)

ISBN: 978-1-4503-3884-4 (Print)

Additional copies may be ordered prepaid from:

ACM Order Department
PO Box 30777
New York, NY 10087-0777, USA

Phone: 1-800-342-6626 (USA and Canada)
+1-212-626-0500 (Global)
Fax: +1-212-944-1318
E-mail: acmhelp@acm.org
Hours of Operation: 8:30 am – 4:30 pm ET

Printed in the USA

ACM e-Energy 2015 Chairs' Welcome

These are the proceedings of the Sixth ACM International Conference on Future Energy Systems (ACM e-Energy 2015) hosted, for the first time in Asia, in Bangalore from July 15-17, 2015. The conference aims to be the premier venue for researchers working in the broad areas of computing and communication for smart energy systems, and in energy-efficient computing and communication systems.

Overall, over 85 papers were submitted to the regular and challenge tracks as well as 12 to the poster/demo track. The acceptance rate of the conference to the main track was 22.8%. To further improve upon last year's reviewing process the reviewing process was overseen by selected Senior Programme Committee members in specific thematic areas. This was punctuated by intense discussions during a live online PC meeting where final decisions were made on accepted papers. Furthermore, we introduced a new shepherding process to ensure that accepted papers would include all the recommendations of the reviewers. Despite this extra workload, all the members of the Programme Committee were diligent and extremely engaged in the reviewing process. We are extremely grateful to them in helping us shape a top quality program for the conference.

In addition to a single track of full papers and challenge papers, the program includes keynote addresses by eminent researchers, a panel discussion and a poster/demo session. The day (July 14th) before the main conference features three concurrent full-day workshops:

1. **Energy Efficient Data Centers (E^2DC):** The fourth international workshop on Energy Efficient Data Centers (E^2DC) represents the community of outstanding practitioners and researchers working in the fields of energy efficient and energy aware data centers, viewing data centers as active participants in smart grids and smart cities.

2. **Distributed Energy Networks (DEN):** The Distributed Energy Networks (DEN) workshop explores technologies that will shift the paradigm of energy networks from a conventional centralized top-down approach to a decentralized peer-to-peer one in which consumers, producers and prosumers can actively participate.

3. **Smart Grid Communication, Computation and Control (C3):** The C3 workshop brings together representatives from the communication, control and computation communities to discuss collaborative progress towards smart grid solutions, and to elucidate limitations and opportunities of emerging smart grid proposals.

Organizing an event of such breadth and depth entails a substantial amount of collaborative effort. We are fortunate to have a talented and dedicated committee that deftly executed the technical and non-technical tasks.

We thank the TPC Chairs (S. Ramchurn and Mani Srivastava), the Poster/Demo Chairs (Niranth Amogh, Sid Chi-Kin Chau and Minghua Chen), the DEN Workshop Chairs (Tanuja Ganu, Jay Taneja and George Thanos), the E^2DC chairs (Fabien Hermenier, Sonja Klingert and Gunnar Schomaker) and all the PC members for meticulously reviewing, selecting and shepherding the selected submissions.

We are grateful to Iven Mareels, P. R. Kumar and Julian De Hoog for organizing the C3 workshop based on a list of exciting invited papers.

We sincerely thank the conference keynote speakers: - Ashok Jhunjhunwala, Iven Mareels, Bruce Nordman – and the workshop keynote speakers: - S. Keshav (in DEN) and Amod Ranade (in E^2DC).

We acknowledge Sonja Klingert and Mathieu Sinn for working with the authors and the publisher to compile these proceedings.

We are grateful to Vincenzo Mancuso and Amarjeet Singh for publicizing the conference widely to attract a large number of submissions and attendees.

We acknowledge Sudipta Maitra for working with the supporting organizations to raise the required funds.

We thank Zainul Charbiwala and Sudipta Maitra for taking care of all the painstaking details of running this event in Bangalore.

We recognize Pandarasamy Arjunan and Sunil Ghai for maintaining the website that furnishes all the information pertinent to the conference community.

We acknowledge Anandhi Ramaswamy for providing administrative support to the organizing committee.

We thank the steering committee and ACM staff for their invaluable guidance and support.

We are grateful to ACM, Tata Consultancy Services, IBM Research and Rolta for providing generous financial support.

Most important of all, we thank the authors, speakers and attendees for validating the aforementioned efforts by participating in the conference.

We sincerely hope you find these proceedings and the conference informative and enjoyable.

Shivkumar Kalyanaraman
e-Energy 2015 General Chair
IBM Research,
India

Deva P. Seetharam
e-Energy 2015 Program Chair
DataGlen Technologies,
India

Rajeev Shorey
e-Energy 2015 Program Chair
TCS Innovation Labs,
USA/India

Table of Contents

DEN Workshop Session - Managing Grids

DEN Workshop Session - Deployment Experiences

ACM e-Energy 2015 Organization

General Chairs: Shivkumar Kalyanaraman *(IBM Research, India)*
Deva P. Seetharam *(DataGlen Technologies, India)*
Rajeev Shorey *(TCS Innovation Labs, USA/India)*

Program Chairs: Sarvapali Ramchurn *(University of Southampton, UK)*
Mani Srivastava *(UCLA, USA)*

Publicity Chairs: Vincenzo Mancuso *(IMDEA Networks, Spain)*
Amarjeet Singh *(IIIT Delhi, India)*

Sponsorship Chair: Sudipta Maitra *(Penny Lane Hospitality, India)*

Poster and Demo Chairs: Niranth Amogh *(Huawei, India)*
Sid Chi-Kin Chau *(Masdar Institute, Abu Dhabi, UAE)*
Minghua Chen *(The Chinese University of Hong Kong, China)*

Publication Chairs: Sonja Klingert *(University of Mannheim, Germany)*
Mathieu Sinn *(IBM Research, Ireland)*

Local Arrangement Chairs: Zainul Charbiwala *(IBM Research, India)*
Sudipta Maitra *(Penny Lane Hospitality, India)*

Local Arrangement Coordinator: Anandhi Ramaswamy *(IBM Research, India)*

Web Chairs: Pandarasamy Arjunan *(IIT Delhi, India)*
Sunil Ghai *(IBM Research, India)*

Workshop Chairs: Tanuja Ganu *(DataGlen Technologies, India)*
Fabien Hermenier *(University of Nice Sophia-Antipolis, France)*
Sonja Klingert *(University of Mannheim, Germany)*
P.R. Kumar *(Texas A&M University, USA)*
Iven Michiel Yvonne Mareels *(University of Melbourne, Australia)*
Gunnar Schomaker *(Software Innovation Campus Paderborn, Germany)*
Jay Taneja *(IBM Research, Kenya)*
George Thanos *(Athens University of Economics and Business, Greece)*

Steering Committee: Hermann de Meer *(University of Passau, Germany)*
David Hutchison *(Lancaster University, UK)*
Marco Ajmone Marsan *(Politecnico di Torino, Italy)*
S. Keshav *(University of Waterloo, Canada)*
Prashant Shenoy *(University Massachusetts Amherst, USA)*
Jon Crowcroft *(University of Cambridge, UK)*

Senior Technical Program Committee Members:

Mario Berges *(Carnegie Mellon University, USA)*
Aj Brush *(Microsoft Research, USA)*
Minghua Chen *(The Chinese University of Hong Kong, China)*
Mathijs De Weerdt *(Delft University of Technology, Netherlands)*
Julian De Hoog *(IBM Research / The University of Melbourne, Australia)*
Elena Gaura *(Cogent Computing Applied Research Centre, UK)*
Mike Hazas *(University of Lancaster, UK)*
David Irwin *(University of Massachusetts Amherst, USA)*
Karl Johansson *(Royal Institute of Technology, Sweden)*
Krithi Ramamritham *(IIT Bombay, India)*
George Thanos *(Athens University of Economis and Business, Greece)*
Dan Wang *(Hong Kong Polytechnic University, China)*
Kamin Whitehouse *(University of Virgina, USA)*

Technical Program Committee Members:

Yuvraj Agarwal *(Carnegie Mellon University, USA)*
Alberto Cerpa *(University of California Merced, USA)*
Keith Decker *(University of Delaware, USA)*
Longbo Huang *(Tsinghua University, China)*
Xiaofan (Fred) Jiang *(Columbia University, USA)*
Younghun Kim *(IBM Research, USA)*
Sebastian Lehnhoff *(OFFIS Institute for IT, Germany)*
Rahul Mangharam *(University of Pennsylvania, USA)*
Manish Marwah *(HP Labs, USA)*
Balakrishan Narayanaswamy *(UCSD, USA)*
Oliver Parson *(University of Southampton, UK)*
Sarvapali Ramchurn *(University of Southampton, UK)*
Alex Rogers *(University of Southampton, UK)*
Mani Srivastava *(UCLA, USA)*
Olle Sundstrom *(IBM Research, Switzerland)*
Dan-Cristian Tomozei *(Cisco Systems, Switzerland)*
Ting Zhu *(University of Maryland, USA)*

External Reviewers:

Tanuja Ganu
Jagabondhu Hazra
Harshad Khadilkar
Bruce Nordman
Deva P. Seetharam
Amith Singhee
George Stamoulis
Sebastian Stein
Rene Struik
Jay Taneja
Henry Truong

E2DC Workshop Organization

General Chairs: Sonja Klingert *(University of Mannheim, Germany)*
Gunnar Schomaker *(Software Innovation Campus Paderborn, Germany)*
Fabien Hermenier *(University of Nice, Sophia-Antipolis, France)*

Program Chairs: Marta Chinnici *(ENEA, Italy)*
Hermann de Meer *(University of Passau, Germany)*
Daniel Gmach *(HPLabs, USA)*
Jorjeta Jetcheva *(Fujitsu Laboratories of America, USA)*
Paul Kühn *(University of Stuttgart, Germany)*
Laurent Lefèvre *(Inria, France)*
Sebastian Lehnhoff *(Offis, Germany)*
Jean-Marc Menaud *(Ecole des Mines de Nantes, France)*
Wolfgang Nebel *(Offis, Germany)*
Barbara Pernici *(Politecnico di Milano, Italy)*
Jean-Marc Pierson *(University of Toulouse, France)*
Tomasz Siewierski *(Technical University of Lodz, Poland)*

DEN Workshop Organization

General Chairs: George Thanos *(Athens University of Economics and Business, Greece)*
Jay Taneja *(IBM Research, Kenya)*
Tanuja Ganu *(DataGlen Technologies, India)*

Program Chairs: Omid Ardakanian *(University of Waterloo, Canada)*
Costas Courcoubetis *(Singapore University of Technology and Design, Singapore)*
Zainul Charbiwala *(Tricog Health, India)*
Murali Narayanaswamy *(University of California, San Diego, USA)*
Anthony Papavasiliou *(Catholic University of Louvain, Belgium)*
Daniel Soto *(Sonoma State University, USA)*
George Stamoulis *(Athens University of Economics and Business, Greece)*
Taha Selim Ustun *(Carnegie Mellon University, USA)*

C3 Workshop Organization

General Chairs: P.R. Kumar *(Texas A&M University, USA)*
Iven Michiel Yvonne Mareels *(University of Melbourne, Australia)*

Associate Chair: Julian De Hoog *(IBM Research / University of Melbourne, Australia)*

ACM e-Energy 2015 Sponsor & Supporters

Sponsor:

Supporters:

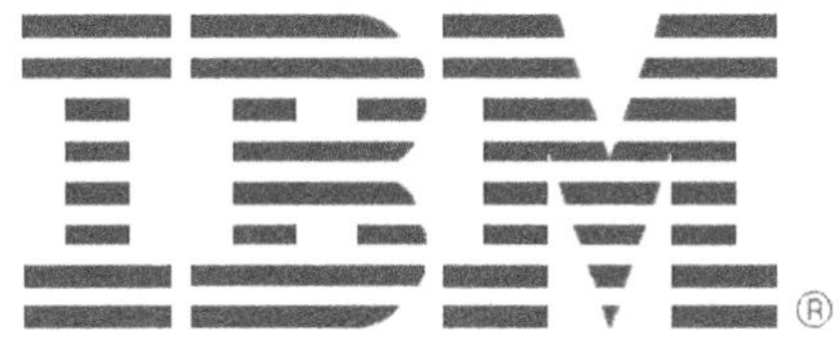

IIT Bombay

IIT Kharagpur

IISc Bangalore

Leveraging Decentralized Solar-DC towards Enable 24 x 7 Power to Indian Homes

Ashok Jhunjhunwala
IIT Madrasm Chennai, India

Abstract

Demand-supply gap in power has resulted in 2 to 20 hours power-cuts in most Indian homes especially in summer months, in addition to almost 80 million homes having no grid-connectivity. Using DC appliances as demand-side intervention and decentralized solar as a supply side intervention, the gap can be considerably reduced. Using an innovative UDC technology, the existing grid, with minimal change, could supply 24 x 7 but limited power to each home and at the same time create a demand pull for solar-DC. The paper presents steps to achieve this in near-term.

ACM Classification

J.7 COMPUTERS IN OTHER SYSTEMS

Keywords

Solar; rooftop solar; DC; decentralised solar; power grids; energy shortage.

BIO

Dr.Jhunjhunwala received his B.Tech degree from IIT, Kanpur, and his MS and Ph.D degrees from the University of Maine. From 1979 to 1981, he was with Washington State University and has been at IIT Madras ever-since, where he leads the Telecommunications and Computer Networks group (TeNeT). The group works with industry in the development of telecom, banking, IT and Power Systems (including solar) technologies relevant to India, and has a special focus on rural technologies. It has incubated more than fifty companies in the last twenty years. He chairs IITM Incubation cell, Health Technology Innovation Center (HTIC), co-chairs Rural Technology and Business Incubator (RTBI) at IIT Madras and is professor in-charge of IITM Research Park. He also chairs a MHRD committee called "Quality Enhancement of Engineering Education (QEEE)" focused on 500 Indian engineering colleges, other than IITs and NITs. He also chairs Mobile Payment Forum of India (MPFI).

Dr. Ashok Jhunjhunwala has been awarded Padma Shri in the year 2002. He has been awarded Shanti Swarup Bhatnagar Award in 1998, Dr.Vikram Sarabhai Research Award for the year 1997, Millennium Medal at Indian Science Congress in the year 2000 and H. K. Firodia for "Excellence in Science & Technology" for the year 2002, Shri Om Prakash Bhasin Foundation Award for Science & Technology for the year 2004, Awarded Jawaharlal Nehru Birth Centenary Lecture Award by INSA for the year 2006, IBM Innovation and Leadership Forum Award by IBM for the year 2006, awarded Bernard Low Humanitarian Award in 2009, awarded "Bharat Asmita Vigyaan-Tantragyaan Shresththa Award" for the best use of Science & Technology through Innovation in 2010, and awarded Honorary Doctorates by the Institute of Blekinge Institute of Technology, Sweden in 2008 and University of Maine, USA in 2010. In 2010, he was also awarded JC Bose Fellowship in 2010 by DST, Government of India, awarded Dronacharya (2011) by TiE and recently awarded Top Innovator of Top 11 in 2011 Innovators Challenge. He is a Fellow of World Wireless Research forum, IEEE and Indian academies including INAE, IAS, INSA and NAS.

Dr. Jhunjhunwala is a Director in the Board of Tata Teleservices (Maharashtra) Limited, Polaris, 3i-Infotech, Sasken, Tejas, Tata Communications, Exicom and Mahindra Reva Electrical Vehicles Pvt Ltd. He is also a board member of several educational institutes and section 25 companies including BIRAC. He is member of Prime Minister's Scientific Advisory Committee.

e-Energy'15, July 14-17, 2015, Bangalore, India.
ACM 978-1-4503-3609-3/15/07.
http://dx.doi.org/10.1145/2768510.2768511

Grid Futures – The View from the Last Mile

Prof Iven Mareels
Dean, Melbourne School of Engineering,
The University of Melbourne, Vic 3010, Australia
i.mareels@unimelb.edu.au

ABSTRACT

The original ideas underpinning the design and the management of the very first electricity grids of the early 20th century still define the power grid today. A typical large scale (continent size) electricity grid connects a small number of large power sources at discrete locations through a high voltage transmission grid followed by a low voltage distribution grid to a large number of spatially dispersed consumers. In the power grid, demand is king in that the consumers determine how much power they use, and the generated power must follow power demand, as there is little capacity for storage in the grid. As a consequence the entire power grid is designed around the notion of peak power (and safe operations). The control or management problem in the power grid is one of maintaining the voltages at the prescribed levels (quality of service), whilst delivering the power as requested by the consumers, within the physical transmission capacity of the grid's network infrastructure.

Today, this paradigm is being challenged.
(1) More and more solar power (solar thermal, wind or solar photovoltaic (PV)) derived electrical power is being deployed. These power sources are rather different from classical thermal power stations, as they have a far lower power intensity per square meter of installation, are spatially dispersed, and suffer from uncontrollable temporal variations in power supply as determined by the vagaries of the weather.
(2) For a variety of reasons, in well-established grids, peak-to-base power demand is increasing, creating the distinct impression that a vast resource is significantly underutilized.

At the same time, new technologies provide new opportunities and challenges:

(1) So-called smart metering is being deployed. It is now entirely feasible to conceive the grid as an intelligent, interconnected, infrastructure or an internet-of-things infrastructure. (More data, hence hopefully better control.)
(2) Transport is becoming more electrified, with electric vehicles (EV) entering the light vehicle market. (More demand, but not aligned with PV.)
(3) Battery energy storage at scale is becoming an economically realistic proposition. (Distributed energy storage allows for demand shaping.)

In this keynote we consider how in the last mile of the grid (the low voltage distribution network) demand and supply may be coordinated through a power matching strategy that respects the physical infrastructure's operational limits. We ask how much more PVs and EVs can be allowed using demand control strategies, as compared to the classical case, where supply follows demand. The proposed management strategy is a decentralized and distributed control strategy that approximately solves (a receding horizon) optimized demand-supply coordination that satisfies consumers' energy needs within distribution grid constraints. Demand shaping allows for significantly more PV and EV penetration than would be case without demand moderation.

Much of our experience, and the data used in the presentation, as well as the conclusions drawn, are Australia specific. Clearly, the energy mix and grid specifics will vary from region to region, and these will play a dominant role in the eventual approach taken to cater for EV and PV in the local distribution grids.

The talk will conclude with some observations about the technical feasibility, socio-economic and political dimensions of a grid infrastructure supplied entirely by renewable power sources.

Categories and Subject Descriptors

I6 Modelling and Simulation

General Terms

Algorithms, Management, Measurement, Theory

Keywords

Smart grids; distribution networks; distribution network modelling and simulation; distributed decentralized control; receding horizon optimization

e-Energy'15, July 14-17, 2015, Bangalore, India
ACM 978-1-4503-3609-3/15/07.
http://dx.doi.org/10.1145/2768510.2768512

Short Bio

Since July 2007, Iven Mareels is Dean of the School of Engineering, the University of Melbourne.

He obtained the (ir) Masters of Electromechanical Engineering from Gent University Belgium in 1982 and the PhD in Systems Engineering from the Australian National University in 1987. He became Professor of Electrical Engineering at the University of Melbourne in 1996, and held appointments at the Australian National University (1990-1996), the University of Newcastle (1988-1990) and the University of Gent (1986-1988). He is an honorary Professor at the National University of Defence Technology, China; and Shanghai Jiao Tong University, China.

For his work on smart large scale irrigation work he received in 2014 the IEEE CSS Control Technology Award, the 2008 Clunies Ross Medal, Academy of Technological Sciences and Engineering, Australia and the 2007 inaugural Vice-Chancellor's Knowledge Transfer Excellence Award. This work is executed in collaboration with Rubicon Water.

In 2013 he was the recipient of the *The Asian Control Association Wook Hyun Kwon Education Award.* In 2005, he was named *IEEE CSS Distinguished Lecturer*, and in 1994 he obtained the Vice-Chancellor's Award for Excellence in Teaching from the Australian National University.

He is Fellow of the Academy of Technological Sciences and Engineering, Australia, a Fellow of the Institute of Electrical and Electronics Engineers (USA), a Fellow of the Institute of Engineers Australia and a Foreign Member of the Royal Flemish Academy of Belgium for Science and the Arts (KVAB).

He received two civil honours for his work in engineering education and research, in 2013 he became a Commander in the Order of the Crown (Belgium), and in 2003 he received the Centenary Medal (Australia).

He is registered as a Corporate Professional Engineer and he is a member of the Engineering Executives chapter of Engineers Australia. He is a founding member of the Asian Control Association.

He is a Member of the Board of the Bionics Institute (since 1998), a Member of the Steering Committee for the Centre for Neural Engineering (since 2009) as well as a Member of the Steering Committee for the Melbourne based IBM Research Laboratory (Australia). He is a Life Advisor to the International Federation of Automatic Control.

Iven Mareels has extensive experience in consulting for both industry and government. He has strong interests in education and has taught a broad range of subjects in both mechanical and electrical engineering curricula.

His research interest focuses on the modelling and control of large scale systems, both engineered as well as natural systems, such as large scale water networks, smart grids and the brain (healthy and epileptic). He has a particular interest in adaptive or learning systems. He has published 5 books, in excess of 120 journal publications and 230 conference publications. He is a co-inventor of a portfolio of international patents dealing with open water channel management.

References

[1] De Hoog, J., Alpcan, T., Brazil, M., Thomas, D.A., Mareels, I. "Optimal charging of electric vehicles taking distribution network constraints into account" *IEEE Transactions on Power Systems*, 30 (1) 365-375, 2015

[2] De Hoog J, Muenzel V, Jayasuriya DC, Alpcan T, Brazil M, Thomas DA, Mareels I, Dahlenburg G, Jegatheesan R. "The importance of spatial distribution when analysing the impact of electric vehicles on voltage stability in distribution networks" *Energy Systems* **6**(1):63-84, 2014

[3] Iven Mareels, Julian de Hoog, Doreen Thomas, Marcus Brazil, Tansu Alpcan, Derek Jayasuriya, Valentin Muenzel, Lu Xia, Ramachandra Rao Kolluri, "On Making Energy Demand and Network Constraints Compatible in the Last Mile of the Power Grid", *Annual Reviews in Control*, 38 (2), 243-258, 2014

Rethinking Grids with Local Power Distribution

Bruce Nordman
Lawrence Berkeley National Laboratory
1 Cyclotron Road, 90-2000
Berkeley, California, USA
+1 510-486-7089
bnordman@lbl.gov

ABSTRACT

Increasing the reliability and power quality in electricity grids has been a focus since electricity distribution systems were first created. However, for a variety of technology, economic, and public policy reasons, it may be desirable to work towards utility systems standards that are lower than they are today. A network model of power at the local level can make local generation and storage – and hence local reliability – easier and less expensive to create. This paper summarizes how actual needs for power quality and reliability can be accomplished with new technology options and so lead to shifting substantial future capital investment from the utility grid to locally, within buildings.

Categories and Subject Descriptors

J.m [**Computer Applications**]: MISCELLANEOUS – *electricity distribution, networks, optimization.*

General Terms

Management, Performance, Design, Economics, Reliability, Security, Standardization, Theory, Legal Aspects.

Keywords

Electricity grid architecture; reliability; power quality; local power distribution; microgrids; nanogrids.

1. INTRODUCTION

Electrical systems have periodically failed, or operated outside of specifications, ever since they were created [3]. This can occur due to equipment failure, cable interruptions, large imbalances between supply and demand, natural disasters, or attacks by humans. For utility grids, the ideal is a system which provides power continuously, and always at specified levels of voltage and frequency. This is not feasible, but investments are made to increase reliability and quality, at least for some customers, and for some types of problems. A question always arises as to how much such investment should be done, considering whether utility generation transmission, and distribution are expanding, stable, or declining.

It has always been possible to generate power locally, and so not rely on quality or reliability from the utility grid, or to utilize both the grid and local resources. Doing so has become less expensive in recent years, and advances in communications and electronics technologies have created problems and opportunities that did not previously exist at all. Some of these, like cybersecurity, increase costs and risk within the utility grid; others, such as local renewable generation, increase the ease of creating local reliability. The result of these changes is to move the social optimum amount of grid reliability down, where more marginal investment is merited in local reliability, and less should be put into grid reliability. This proposition is from Chris Marnay of LBNL; this paper briefly summarizes it and explains how Local Power Distribution provides a practical path for implementing local reliability within buildings.

2. HETEREGENEOUS POWER QUALITY AND RELIABILITY

Marnay et al. [5, 6, 7] laid out the principle that individual electrical devices and end uses have widely varying requirements for power quality and reliability (PQR). Some are highly sensitive to any interruption, as devices for medical use, financial transactions, or communications; others can tolerate frequent or extended outages, such as pumping water into storage tanks; and most lie somewhere in between. Microgrids provide a basis for providing differential PQR to different electrical circuits within a building, and even to specific individual devices. They also are a frequent enabler of direct current (DC) power which can be an asset in providing high levels of reliability (and has much fewer power quality issues than does AC power). However, microgrids are currently custom deployments and so expensive.

The current model of providing the same level of PQR to all devices provides too little for some, and too much for many others. In many cases, hardware is installed to provide the higher PQR, such as Uninterruptible Power Supplies, or "power conditioning" devices, for individual devices or systems. For distribution through entire buildings, such as hospitals or data centers, standby generators (nearly) guarantee continuous operation. For all the end uses that don't need the PQR the utility provides, they must pay more than then should for electricity.

A key point from Marnay is that there is in principal a societal optimum level of PQR, even if its exact value is subject to debate. As reliability increases, the costs associated with unreliability decline. However, the costs to reach every higher reliability increases. The sum of these is a U-shaped curve with the optimal point at the minimum. Increasing use of local PQR as with microgrids increases total system costs, but will generally decrease costs of unreliability by more, since they are deployed where PQR is most valued. This shifts the total curve towards lower levels of utility grid reliability, at lower total societal cost.

3. UTILITY ECONOMICS

Electric utilities face an uncertain future in the U.S. For well over a century, demand for electricity rose on a consistent basis. However, in recent years, it has leveled off and talk of "peak

e-Energy'15, July 14-17, 2015, Bangalore, India.
ACM 978-1-4503-3609-3/15/07.
DOI: http://dx.doi.org/10.1145/2768510.2768513.

electricity" is on the rise. The technical ability to reduce buildings electricity use by about half is well-known, and recent technology advances make doing so easier and less expensive, e.g. with LED lighting and networked controls. The recent dramatic rise in photovoltaic generation shows the potential for most buildings electricity use to be generated locally. If efficiency reduced consumption by 40%, and local generation handled 75% of the rest, an amount of only 15% of today's use would need to be provided by utilities. Even increasing this to 20% to account for some buildings being net generators, at least at some time, would mean an 80% reduction in net sales. While vehicle electrification should provide some relief for utilities, the bottom line is that they may be in for some serious downsizing. The electricity grid in the U.S. has a capital investment of about $1 trillion, or about $3,000 per person. Proposals around the "smart grid" have called for investing well over another $100 billion more. Paying for this can only increase rates for utility grid power, particularly if sales drop substantially.

4. TECHNOLOGIES

Technology advancement is creating new options for hetergeneous PQR, beyond the simple use of UPSes and power conditioning noted above. The key to doing this is to *decouple* PQR of the grid to that experienced by end-use devices.

DC power inherently avoids the power quality issues present in AC power, and is readily coupled to a battery to ensure local reliability. DC is also easily segmented into many domains of power. In many contexts, use of DC distribution avoids multiple AC/DC conversions that increase cost, unreliability, and electricity losses [2].

Local Power Distribution (LPD) [8, 9, 10] is a technology to enable a *network model of power*, within buildings. In LPD, individual end-use devices are organized into domains of power are "nanogrids" that are then networked to other nanogrids, to local generation, and potentially to a building-wide microgrid; storage is internal to a nanogrid controller. This can enable commodity technology to be inexpensively deployed in a plug-and-play fashion. Power electronics in nanogrid controllers isolate PQR issues on power inputs from that experienced on outputs. In LPD, a local price is used to balance supply and demand and optimally direct power flows through a network of links. DC power and LPD are particularly suited to each other.

The Intelligent Universal Transformer project from the Electric Power Research Institute produced a prototype device that can convert grid AC power into multiple streams of AC or DC power of a variety of voltages [1, 4]. This could provide segmentation of the utility grid or of power distribution within buildings to isolate areas of low power quality from those that need higher quality.

5. SUMMARY

The long-standing assumption that increasing utility grid reliability is always good or necessary need not necessary hold for the future. We may be better off with a smaller, less reliable utility grid that serves mostly for bulk transfers of electricity, with most generation, storage, and provision of power quality and reliability done locally, as is done with Internet technology. This does not undermine the importance and value of the utility grid, but rather aligns it with the needs that future usages and technologies indicate. This is consistent with moving from a "unitary grid" paradigm, to a network model of power; quality and reliability are then provided at the edge of the network, not centrally. The key next steps are to postpone large capital investments in grid reliability, and quickly and deeply explore how a network model of power can be realized, to be able to better determine what balance among grid and local investment is appropriate.

For countries such as India, which lack the scale and reliability of the U.S. grid, plans could be made on the assumption that full grid development will be small compared to total electricity consumption, and that PQR need not be the priority it appears to be today.

6. ACKNOWLEDGMENTS

Much thanks to Chris Marnay for providing key inspiration on microgrids and creating the principle of heterogeneous power quality and reliability; to Ken Christensen for his consistent quality help in thinking, writing, and ideas; and to ACM e-Energy for inviting this presentation.

7. REFERENCES

[1] EPRI, 15KV Class 25KVA Single-Phase IUT Prototype Development, Testing, and Performance Verification, 2013. Palo Alto, CA December 2013. Product ID# 3002000661.

[2] Garbesi, K., Vossos, V., Sanstad, A., and Burch, G. *Optimizing Energy Savings from Direct-DC in US Residential Buildings*. LBNL-5193E, 2011.

[3] Hughes T.P., *Networks of Power: Electrification in Western Society, 1880-1930*. Johns Hopkins University Press, 1983.

[4] Maitra, A., Sundaram, A., Gandhi, M., Bird, S., and Doss, S., Intelligent Universal Transformer Design And Applications. C I R E D 20th International Conference on Electricity Distribution, Prague, 8-11 June 2009

[5] Marnay, C., Nordman, B., and Lai, J. Future Roles of Milli-, Micro-, and Nano- Grids. In *CIGRÉ International Symposium: The electric power system of the future - Integrating supergrids and microgrids*. Bologna, Italy.

[6] Marnay, C. Microgrids and Heterogeneous Power Quality and Reliability: Matching the Quality of Delivered Electricity to End-Use Requirements. *International Journal of Distributed Energy Resources*, vol 4(4),1 Oct-Dec 2008.

[7] Marnay, C., and Lai, J. Serving Electricity and Heat Requirements Efficiently and with Appropriate Energy Quality via Microgrids. *Electricity Journal*, vol. 25(9), Oct 2012.

[8] Nordman, B., Christensen, K., and Meier, A. Think Globally, Distribute Power Locally: The Promise of Nanogrids (Green IT column). *IEEE Computer,* Vol. 44, No. 9, pp. 89-91, September 2012.

[9] Nordman, B. and Christensen, K. Local Power Distribution with Nanogrids. *Proceedings of the International Green Computing Conference*, June 2013.

[10] Nordman, B., and Christensen, K. DC Local Power Distribution with Microgrids and Nanogrids. *First International Conference on DC Microgrids.* Atlanta, June 2015.

Consumer Targeting in Residential Demand Response Programmes

James C. Holyhead
Agents, Interaction and Complexity Group
Electronics and Computer Science
University of Southampton, UK
jch2g12@ecs.soton.ac.uk

Sarvapali D. Ramchurn
Agents, Interaction and Complexity Group
Electronics and Computer Science
University of Southampton, UK
sdr@ecs.soton.ac.uk

Alex Rogers
Agents, Interaction and Complexity Group
Electronics and Computer Science
University of Southampton, UK
acr@ecs.soton.ac.uk

ABSTRACT

Demand response refers to a family of techniques that are available to electricity suppliers to aid with balancing supply and demand, typically by calling on consumers of electricity to reduce consumption during periods of high demand. In this paper we propose a novel approach to residential demand response, in which incentives are targeted at the subset of consumers who are both relevant (likely to use shiftable appliances, such as washing machines and dishwashers during peak hours) and willing to reduce (likely to react positively to a reduction request from their electricity supplier). To this end, we present a mixed integer programming solution that finds the optimal subset of consumers to target with incentives. We show that our solution is capable of significantly reducing supplier costs and smoothing peaks in electricity demand by targeting only a subset of the consumer pool.

1. INTRODUCTION

Aging electricity distribution networks, increasing demand and ambitious CO_2 reduction targets have caused many developed countries to consider how to best upgrade their electrical networks to meet the demands of the 21st century [12]. The 'smart grid', a network that facilitates a two way flow of both electricity and information, is an emerging solution to this problem of next generation electricity distribution [13]. The introduction of smart grid technologies such as the smart meter have made it possible for the suppliers of electricity to communicate with consumers in real-time. These messages may be in the form of pricing signals, which are used to incentivise consumers to alter their electricity consumption as part of so-called 'demand response'. Demand Response is a family of approaches that call upon electricity consumers to curtail or to reschedule their electricity usage in response to requests from their electricity supplier [14] or from the grid operator. These consumers are typically offered incentives for compliance with these requests or penalties for failing to comply [2]. These requests are often issued at times of particularly high demand or as a response to shortfalls in generation caused by equipment failures on the grid. Customer responses to these requests alter the shape of the aggregate demand profile, often by reducing or smoothing peaks in demand.

e-Energy'15, July 14–17, 2015, Bangalore, India.

ACM 978-1-4503-3609-3/15/07 ...$15.00.
DOI: http://dx.doi.org/10.1145/2768510.2768531.

Existing demand response approaches targeted at residential consumers have been focussed on tariff based methods [11, 6]. These schemes make use of differential pricing, where the cost per unit of electricity varies periodically throughout the day in an attempt to nudge consumers into altering their consumption behaviour. For example, during periods of high load, the price of electricity will be increased to dissuade consumers from activating non-essential appliances. One subcategory of differential pricing is 'real-time pricing' (RTP). In an RTP scheme, the price of electricity is varied on an hourly or half hourly frequency with the prices being announced on a day ahead or hour ahead basis [2]. Economists typically consider RTP to be the most efficient differential price mechanism for use in demand response programs [1]. However, we argue that such schemes place a high information burden on consumers, which leads to poor consumer retention rates. In 2005, Rocky Mountain Power in Utah, USA evaluated the use of their differential pricing based tariffs. They found that in opt-out schemes, up to 98% of participating consumers chose to leave the programme after the mandatory period had been completed [9]. This indicates that the participants of differential pricing schemes do not feel that the inconvenience of resheduling their appliance usage is sufficiently compensated for by the cost savings they earn as participants.

The impact of this additional information burden can be seen in the prevalence of 'demand response fatigue' in residential demand response trials [8]. This fatigue results in a progressive disengagement from the scheme over time – as the novelty of a new tariff wears off, consumers begin to ignore the price signals and their consumption behaviour reverts to the behaviour expressed under static pricing, which often leads to a net increase in the costs incurred by the consumer when compared to static pricing. If a scheme cannot retain its participants, then it is not sustainable.

Several solutions have been proposed to the problem of residential demand response. Xiao et. al [17] model the problem as a task scheduling problem, but the authors find that their solution is intractable for non-trivial numbers of consumers. Ramchurn et.al. [11] aim to find a trade-off between the cost savings that a consumer can make by rescheduling appliances against a comfort cost' assigned to the rescheduling of appliances. However, they do not capture the full range of consumer behaviour in their model. In Chandan et. al. [3] the authors rank consumers according to the flexibility of their appliance usage in an attempt to target those consumers who would be the least inconvenienced by reduction requests, but the complexity of their algorithm means the number of consumers they can consider is limited.

To address these shortcomings, we propose a novel approach to demand response, where incentives are targeted at those electricity consumers who are both 'relevant' (likely to use shiftable appliances, such as washing machines and tumble dryers during peak hours) and 'flexible' (likely to react positively to an incentivised reduction request from their electricity supplier). We will show that the targeting of incentives to individual consumers reduces the costs incurred by the supplier, reduces peaks in demand. These individual requests may also reduce the information burden on the consumer, which in turn may lead to greater consumer retention rates.

We focus our attention on the shifting of 'shiftable static loads', such as dishwashers, washing machines and tumble dryers.[1] The shiftable static loads we concern ourselves with require direct consumer interaction; a dishwasher cannot be used before the consumer has filled it with dirty dishes and similarly, a washing machine cannot be used until the consumer has loaded it with dirty laundry. Further, there is evidence that consumers prefer to schedule the use of these appliances manually, even when a system is available to automate the process [5].

Thus, in this paper, we advance the state of the art in the following ways:

- We present a novel model of customer behaviour that captures the differences in how consumers respond to reduction requests, both in terms of their *willingness* to shift consumption, but also *how* the consumer will shift consumption (pre-emption or deferral).

- We propose a novel mixed integer programming solution to select the optimal subset of consumers that should be targeted with demand reduction requests and for which time period those reduction requests should be issued.

- We evaluate our solution using a dataset of real-world consumption data and show that our targeting algorithm and consumer response model lead to greater reductions in peak demand and lower supplier costs when compared to current models of consumer behaviour. We also show that our solution only requires participation by a portion of the consumer pool, reducing the impact of 'demand response fatigue', which could lead to improved retention rates.

The rest of this paper is organised as follows. In Section 2 we discuss related work in the field of residential demand response. Section 3 presents a formalisation of the demand response problem. Section 4 describes our novel consumer response model and our approach to finding the optimal subset of consumers to target with demand reduction requests. Section 5 provides an empirical evaluation of our model and our consumer targeting approach and Section 6 provides concluding remarks and a discussion of future work.

2. BACKGROUND

The problem of rescheduling appliance operation in order to effect peak reduction has been well studied. In this section we outline some of the different solutions that have been proposed to the problem of residential demand response.

Xiao et. al. [17] addressed the optimisation problem as a task scheduling problem where each load request is given an earliest start time and a deadline for completion. Their solution seeks to find the optimal mapping of appliance usage requests to timeslots in order to minimise the cost within an individual timeslot. The authors note that this task scheduling formulation is NP-hard and therefore intractable for large numbers of demand requests. By constrast, we show that the solution proposed in this paper is capable of scaling to communities of tens of thousands of consumers.

This in turn contrasts with Ramchurn et. al. [11], who propose a solution using a linear programming formulation to the deferrable load scheduling problem and include an explicit measure of consumer comfort. A scaling factor is used to denote a consumer's preference for comfort or cost saving. This measure of consumer comfort acknowledges that asking a consumer to reschedule their appliance usage carries some non-financial penalty in terms of convenience, but the authors stops short of defining a probabilistic measure of a user's willingness to shift. In addition, they scale this comfort cost by the size of the shift, acknowledging that consumers will often prefer to reschedule their consumption as little as possible, but this does not capture the full range of potential consumer responses to reduction requests. The consumer response model we propose in this paper allows for a much richer representation of consumer behaviour in demand response settings, which we show leads to greater reductions in peak reduction performance.

In Chandan et. al. [3], the appliance scheduling optimisation problem is formulated as a mixed integer non linear program (MINLP). Consumers are given a score that indicates how greatly they would be inconvenienced by a load shifting request. The consumers are ranked in order of their flexibility with the highest ranked being used as input for the MINLP solver, representing the consumers who would be least inconvenienced. The remaining consumers are discarded to reduce the complexity of the problem. Rather than ranking consumers in terms of their convenience, the solution we propose in this paper targets consumers whose expected behaviour leads to a reduction in the supplier's expected costs. Additionally, we do not need to pre-select the consumers we examine as our solution is capable of solving problems for tens of thousands of consumers.

Some commercial demand response schemes have tackled the problem of peak reduction by issuing reduction requests to their scheme participants for times of high demand [10]. We will benchmark the performance of our solution against this approach later in this paper.

None of these approaches take into consideration the full variety of potential consumer responses to a demand response event, whether it be triggered by a differential pricing scheme or other form of incentive. The unique socio-

[1]We omit any discussion of thermal loads or electric vehicle charging, as the scheduling of these loads may be automated by an intelligent agent without impacting on user comfort.

technical challenges posed by residential demand response programess are illustrated in the 'Agent B' field study [5], where an intelligent booking system was deployed to help consumers make efficient use of their washing machines in the presence of an RTP tariff. The authors discovered that even when the system offered to automate the booking process by finding the optimal operating times, the study participants preferred to carry out the scheduling manually, using the booking system in an advisory capacity only.

In the following section we formalise the problem of residential demand response.

3. THE DEMAND RESPONSE PROBLEM

Electricity is an unusual commodity in that it is not feasible to store it in large quantities due to the high cost of storage devices [4]. This means that electricity much be consumed at the same time it is generated and the supply must always match (be in balance with) the demand to prevent system instability and possible collapse.

The majority of energy is traded through bilateral contracts between the generators and the suppliers, which are often made far in advance of the time of consumption. Typically about half of the total volume of electricity traded within Great Britain is traded 'seasons ahead' [16].

The nature of electricity demand means it is impossible for a supplier to accurately predict their demand requirements months or even years ahead of time. Electricity markets enable suppliers to adjust the amount of electricity they are contracted to purchase through energy exchanges, where the various electricity suppliers can buy and sell electricity from one another. As the day the electricity has been contracted for approaches, the supplier can fine-tune their position through these exchanges.

We denote the volume of electricity that a supplier has contracted for as $\boldsymbol{\Gamma} = \{\Gamma_1 \cdots \Gamma_T\}$ and the total electricity demand consumed as $\boldsymbol{B} = \{B_1 \cdots B_T\}$.

We define any consumption above $\boldsymbol{\Gamma}$ to be a deficit, $\boldsymbol{d} = \{d_1 \cdots d_T\}$, where the deficit at time t, d_t is defined as follows:

$$d_t = \max(0,\ B_t - \Gamma_t) \tag{1}$$

Similarly, any consumption below $\boldsymbol{\Gamma}$ is defined as a surplus, $\boldsymbol{s} = \{s_1 \cdots s_T\}$ where the surplus at time t, s_t is defined as follows:

$$s_t = \max(0,\ \Gamma_t - B_t) \tag{2}$$

A deficit at time t, d_t, will incur a cost per kWH of ρ^t_{buy} where $\rho^t_{buy} > 0 \quad \forall t$ and a surplus at time t, s_t will be sold through the balancing market at a cost per kWh of $\hat{p}^t_{sell}$, where the penalty cost incurred by the supplier, ρ_{sell} is the difference between the price per kWh originally paid by the supplier for the electricity, ρ_t and $\hat{p}^t_{sell}$.

The prices set by the balancing mechanism, $\boldsymbol{\rho}_{buy}$ and $\hat{\boldsymbol{p}}_{sell}$ are set higher and lower than normal market rates respectively. This is to disincentivise suppliers from making use of the balancing mechanism as anything other than a last resort.

Given these market conditions, a supplier wishes to initiate a demand response event that leads to a reduced deficit or surplus and therefore a lower cost.[2] In the next section we

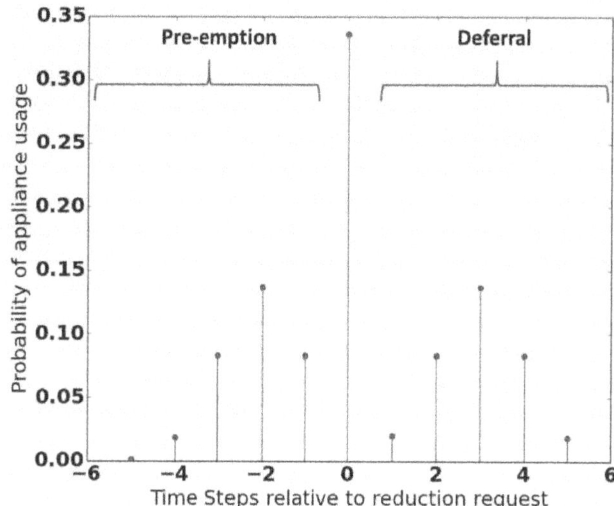

Figure 1: An example of a customer response profile. In this example we see the probability of the consumer ignoring the reduction request ($\tau = 0$) is approximately 0.35.

present an optimal solution to this problem that identifies which consumers to target with demand reduction requests in order to minimise the expected cost to the supplier.

4. AN OPTIMAL MILP SOLUTION TO THE DEMAND RESPONSE PROBLEM

In this section we provide details of our model of consumer response behaviour and present an optimal solution to the problem of targeting incentives to consumers.

4.1 Consumer Response Model

For a supplier of electricity, the ideal outcome of a demand response scheme is a smooth profile (one with no peaks). Achieving this goal is more complicated than simply incentivising consumers to reduce their electricity consumption during periods of high demand because large numbers of those consumers may activate their deferred appliances immediately after the reduction event has passed. This synchronisation of rescheduled appliances may lead to one or more secondary peaks that pose the same problems as the original peak [11]. The tendency for shifted loads to synchronise and form secondary peaks is known as the 'payback effect' [7]. A successful peak reduction programme must therefore account for the potential emergence of these secondary peaks. In this section we propose a model of consumer behaviour that takes into account how a user reschedules her consumption in the event a reduction request is issued. Rather than modelling a consumer's willingness to shift as a single probability value, we model a user's demand response behaviour by a probability mass distribution that describes the probability of when a shifted appliance activation has been rescheduled for. For example, a washing machine may be activated 2 hours after a demand response period (a deferral) or it may be activated 2 hours prior to the demand response period (a pre-emption). An example

[2]Although we use supplier cost minimisation as the motivating example in this paper, the same approach can be applied to any scenario where deviation from baseline Γ leads to some penalty being incurred. An alternative to a financial penalty may be increased CO_2 emissions.

of such a consumer response distribution is shown in Figure 1. By accounting for the variety in consumer responses, we are able to simulate aggregate consumer behaviour that results in a smoother consumption profile.

We represent a user's demand response behaviour by a probability mass distribution defined as:

$$p'_t(\tau) = P(z_{t+\tau} = 1) \quad (3)$$

where $z_{t+\tau} \in \{0,1\}$ indicates whether the consumer reschedules their shiftable appliance usage for the time period $t+\tau$ given that they received a reduction request from their supplier for time t. We represent the length of the shift by $\tau \in \{-T, ...T\}$. In the case that $\tau = 0$, the consumer has chosen not to shift or curtail their consumption and $\tau < 0$ indicates that the consumer has pre-empted their consumption and $\tau > 0$ indicates a deferral of consumption. A consumer's response distribution can be determined by analysing their behaviour during historical demand response events.[3]

We will use this probability distribution later when computing the consumer's updated demand following a demand reduction request.

This approach differs from current practice by modelling a consumer's behaviour in terms of *how* they shift their consumption. Existing approaches often assume that consumer's will always respond to price signals/incentives when doing so would lower the price of their appliance usage [11] or only consider whether a consumer's response in terms of accept/reject without considering how the rescheduled load may itself lead to unwanted system level behaviour, such as a secondary peak [3].

4.2 Optimal Consumer Selection

In what follows, we present an optimal solution to finding sets of consumer demand reduction recommendations that reduce the cost of the aggregate demand profile to the supplier. This solution takes the form of a mixed integer linear program.

In a demand response programme, the supplier aims to select a subset of consumers whose predicted behaviour during demand response events minimises the cost of the aggregate demand profile produced by its consumer's demand requirements.

The total cost to the supplier of balancing their demand can therefore be calculated as follows:

$$C = \sum_{t=0}^{T} s_t \; \rho^t_{sell} + d_t \; \rho^t_{buy} \quad (4)$$

Note that only one of the two clauses are non-zero at each time step because it is not possible for both d_t and s_t to be greater than zero (the supplier cannot simultaneously be experiencing a surplus and a deficit), so at least one of the clauses will be cancelled out at each timestep. The supplier wishes to initiate a demand response event that results in an aggregate demand profile that costs less than C.

Given a set of consumers $\mathcal{I}$ and a day split into T time slots, we define $\boldsymbol{B} = (B_1, B_2, \cdots, B_T)$ to represent the baseline consumption profiles of the consumer's within the supplier's customer pool and we define C_B to be the cost of the aggregate consumption profile to the supplier (see equation 4). We now compute $\boldsymbol{B}'$, a $(T+1)$x$|\mathcal{I}|$ matrix where $B'_{t,i} = \{B'_{t,i,1}, \cdots, B'_{t,i,T}\}$ represents the expected consumption profile for consumer i given that a reduction request for time period t was issued. $B'_{i,j,t}$ represents the updated consumer demand at time t given that consumer j received a reduction request for time period i. This expected profile is generated using the consumer's response profile p'_t (see equation 3).

The $(T+1)$th row in the matrix represents the case where no reduction request is issued to the consumer, i.e., $\boldsymbol{B}'_{T+1,i} = B_i$.

We introduce a $(T+1)$x$|\mathcal{I}|$ matrix of binary decision variables, $\boldsymbol{K}$, where $K_{t,i} \in \{0,1\}$. $K_{t,i} = 1$, indicates that consumer i will be issued a demand reduction request for time t, except for the case where $t = T+1$, where a value of 1 indicates that no reduction request will be issued for consumer i on the day in question. Our solution finds the optimal values of $\boldsymbol{K}$ that minimise the cost of the aggregate consumption profile to the supplier.

We define the updated deficit, $\boldsymbol{d}' = \{d'_1, \cdots, d'_T\}$ and the updated surplus $\boldsymbol{s}' = \{s'_1, \cdots, s'_T\}$ as the difference between the threshold Γ and the sum over all consumers and all time periods of the products of the decision variables K and the matrix of updated consumption profiles, $\boldsymbol{B}'$.

$$d'_t = \max(0, \sum_{i,j} K_{i,j} B'_{i,j,t} - \Gamma_t) \quad (5)$$

$$s'_t = \max(0, \; \Gamma_t - \sum_{i,j} K_{i,j} B'_{i,j,t}) \quad (6)$$

We now find the values of K that minimise the cost to the supplier, as defined in the following objective function:

$$\boldsymbol{K}^* = \arg\min_{K} \sum_{t}^{T} s'_t \; \rho^t_{sell} + d'_t \rho^t_{buy} \quad (7)$$

subject to the following constraints:

$$d'_t \geq 0 \quad \text{(constraint 1)}$$

$$d'_t \geq \sum_{i,j} K_{i,j} B'_{i,j,t} - \Gamma_t \quad \text{(constraint 2)}$$

$$s'_t \geq 0 \quad \text{(constraint 3)}$$

$$s'_t \geq \Gamma_t - \sum_{i,j} K_{i,j} B'_{i,j,t} \quad \text{(constraint 4)}$$

$$s'_t \leq \Gamma_t \; x_t \quad \text{(constraint 5)}$$

$$s'_t \leq \Gamma_t - \sum_{i,j} K_{i,j} B'_{i,j,t} + M(1 - x_t) \quad \text{(constraint 6)}$$

$$\sum_{t \in T} K_i \; = \; 1 \quad \text{(constraint 7)}$$

In order to formulate the problem as a mixed integer linear program, we must remove the non-linear *max* functions that appear in the definitions of d'_t and s'_t (see equations 5 and 6).

The definition for d'_t requires the variable to take a value greater than or equal to 0. Constraint 1 states this explicitly. Similarly constraint 2 states that the value of s'_t must take a value greater than or equal to the second argument in its *max* function, $\sum_{i,j} K_{i,j} B'_{i,j,t} - \Gamma_t$. We assume that the value of ρ_{buy} will always be positive (occasions where suppliers will be paid by the grid operator to use excess generation are extremely rare), these constraints are sufficient to guarantee that the value of d'_t will take the greater value of 0 or $\sum_{i,j} K_{i,j} B'_{i,j,t} - \Gamma_t$. Were it to take a value greater than

[3]The detail of the learning algorithm are beyond the scope of this paper and is left for future work.

this, the objective function could be minimised further by reducing the value of d'_t.

We begin the process for s'_t in the same way, with constraints 3 and 4 requiring the variable to take values are both greater than or equal to 0 and greater than or equal to $\Gamma_t - \sum_{i,j} K_{i,j} B'_{i,j,t}$. However, since the value of ρ_{sell} may take a negative value (the refund paid by the balancing mechanism to the supplier for their surplus was greater than the price the supplier originally paid for the electricity), we need to add further constraints to prevent the value of s'_t from inflating. This would happen whenever ρ_{sell} took a negative value because the objective function would be minimised when the value of $s'_t = \infty$. To prevent this inflation, we must also include constraints 5 and 6. These constraints introduce a new binary variable $\boldsymbol{x} = \{x_1 \cdots x_t\}$, where $x_t \in \{0, 1\}$. Constraint 5 states that the value of s'_t must be less than or equal to the value of $\Gamma_t x_t$ where Γ_t represents the upper bound on the value of $\Gamma_t - \sum_{i,j} K_{i,j} B'_{i,j,t}$ (when the total updated power demand = 0). Constraint 6 introduces a big-M coefficient (a very large number), where $-M$ represents the lower bound of $\Gamma_t - \sum_{i,j} K_{i,j} B'_{i,j,t}$ (where the updated power demand = ∞). The effect of these two constraints means that x_t will take the value 0 when $\Gamma_t - \sum_{i,j} K_{i,j} B'_{i,j,t} < 0$ and 1 otherwise and the value of s'_t cannot take a value larger than the greater of 0 or $\Gamma_t - \sum_{i,j} K_{i,j} B'_{i,j,t}$.

Constraint 7 requires that the sum of any row in the matrix $\boldsymbol{K}$ must be equal to 1 (a consumer can only receive a single reduction request per day or no request). We apply this constraint to limit the inconvenience caused to any one consumer.

In order to identify the subset of consumers who, when targeted, result in the lowest expected cost to the supplier, every combination of consumers must be evaluated. This means the size of the solution space grows exponentially in the number of consumers in the pool. However, as we will show in the next section, the algorithm can find optimal solutions for consumer pools that number in the tens of thousands.

In the following section we simulate, using real-world data, a community of residential electricity consumers engaged in a demand response programme to evaluate the performance of our solution.

5. EMPIRICAL EVALUATION

In this section we provide an empirical evaluation of our consumer selection algorithm. We first introduce the real-world consumption dataset that we use to evaluate our algorithm, before describing our experimental setup, including how we are simulating customer responses. We then provide results that shows our approach is capable of performing peak reduction on real world data and that we can achieve these reduction involving only a portion of the entire pool. Finally, we show that the algorithm is capable of scaling to communities of tens of thousands of consumers.

5.1 HES Dataset

The Household Electricity Use Study[4] (HES) was carried out on behalf of the Department for Environment, Food and Rural Affairs (DEFRA), the Department of Energy and Climate Change (DECC) and the Energy Saving Trust between April 2010 and April 2011. The study monitored the household appliance usage of 251 residential dwellings in the UK. 26 of these dwellings were monitored over a period of one year at a resolution of 10 minutes, whilst the remaining 225 dwellings were monitored over a rolling one month period at a 2 minute resolution. We evaluate our model on the dataset produced from this study.

5.2 Experimental Setup

In what follows, we will provide details of our experimental setup, including our pre-processing of the HES dataset, and our approach to synthesising consumer response profiles.

5.2.1 Processing of consumption data

For all of the experiments detailed in this section, we have divided each day into 12 two hour time steps. Time periods of 2 hours reflect a suitable granularity when dealing with human consumers and have been used for this purpose before [15].

In order to generate a large amount of unique real-world data, we have placed a sliding window on each household's profile and extracted the profiles for each weekday (including the 12 hours immediately before and after each weekday) as a separate consumer, i.e. for a household h we have extracted day 2 and day 3 and will consider them as separate consumers. By doing this we are able to perform experiments on sets of up to 10,000 unique days, where each day represents a consumer.[5] By splitting up a household's data in this way, we risk generating multiple consumers with similar underlying behaviour. However, since a consumer's contribution to a demand response event is a combination of both the consumer's consumption and response profile, consumers exhibiting similar consumption will still provide varied contributions to the demand response effort.

In order to account for the possibility of a consumer shifting consumption to an adjacent day, we extract consumption data in chunks of 48 hours. For this reason many of the consumption graphs have time axes starting at time step $t = -6$, corresponding to noon on day $d - 1$, and ending at $t = 17$, corresponding to noon on the day $d + 1$. As we are performing demand response for day d, we are only interested in reducing peaks in demand that fall in the interval $t = 0$ and $t = 11$, which correspond to the 12 time steps of day d. Figure 2 shows an example demand profile and highlights the area corresponding to day d.

5.3 Simulation of Customer Responses

In order to test our model's reaction to customer responses, we generate a number of synthetic response profiles. In order to generate the pre-emption probabilities, we select a value representing the most likely shift for the consumer by sampling from a normal distribution mean= -1, $\sigma = 1$. This biases this maximum probability to shifts near the reduction request timestep, to represent the tendency of consumers to shift their consumption immediately before or immediately after a demand response event [11]. In Figure 1, this maximum pre-emption probability is shown at $\tau = -2$. The re-

[4]https://www.gov.uk/government/collections/household-electricity-survey

[5]A disadvantage of this approach is that we are not able to show how show special events (such as major sporting events or days with cold temperatures) impact on the aggregate demand profile, but this is a minor concern.

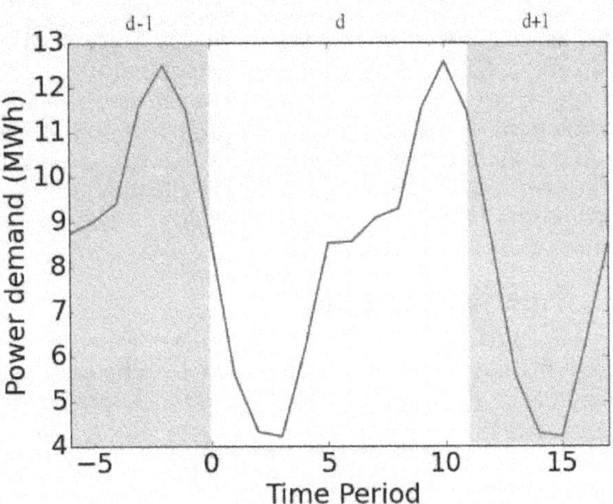

Figure 2: An example aggregate demand profile. The shaded areas show the days adjacent to the day that is undergoing demand response.

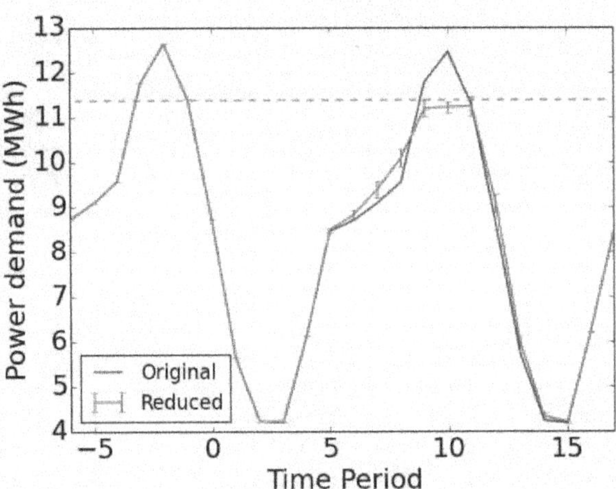

Figure 3: The performance of the 'Response Aware' reduction strategy. Forward market threshold, Γ is denoted by the dashed grey line. Performance was averaged over 20 runs and the error bars represent the 95% confidence interval.

maining pre-emption probabilities trail away from this value. A similar approach is taken to calculating the deferral probabilities, with the most likely shift being found by sampling from a normal distribution with mean$=1$, $\sigma = 1$.

There is currently insufficient data relating to consumer's responses to propose a detailed data-driven model. However, despite its simplicity, this model remains consistent with existing models of consumer convenience and with observations made during demand response field trials [11, 7].

In order to focus on the impact of our consumer response model on system performance, in the experiments detailed in this section, the consumer's willingness to shift was set to 1 for all consumers (the consumer pool always complies with reduction requests from the supplier). The results presented below therefore represent an upper bound on the algorithm's performance.

5.4 Simulation of an Electricity Market

We simulate an emergy market with a number of residential consumers. For the purposes of clarity we set uniform prices such that $\rho^t_{buy} = 6 \text{ x } \rho^t_{sell}\ \forall t \in T$. The value of ρ_{buy} is so much greater than ρ_{sell} because the value of ρ^t_{buy} represents the punitive price per kWh imposed by the balancing mechanism and ρ^t_{sell} represents the difference between the refund per kWh paid by the balancing mechanism and the original price paid for that electricity by the supplier. A more realistic price scheme may see the prices vary in line with the level of demand – high demand leading to higher values of ρ_{buy} and ρ_{sell}, however, we wish to show that the peak reduction performance our algorithm achieves is not dependent on an externally determined price scheme. Similarly, for clarity, we define a flat threshold, $\mathbf{\Gamma}$, where Γ_t is equal to 90% of the maximum demand on day d.

5.5 Reduction Strategies

To evaluate the performance of our targeting algorithm, we consider three reduction strategies:

- Response Aware ('Aware'): The algorithm utilises the consumers' response profiles when computing the optimal subset of consumers to target with demand reduction requests.
- Response Ignorant ('Ignorant'): The algorithm does not take consumers' response profiles into account when computing the optimal subset of consumers to target. The algorithm only takes into account the shiftable load the consumer has available at the timestep under evaluation. This strategy will demonstrate how our novel targeting algorithm works with current consumer modelling techniques.
- Peak Period Only ('Peak Only'): All consumers receive a demand reduction request for the time period with the highest load. This represents a classical approach to the problem of demand response, where a supplier will issue a blanket request to all participants in a demand response scheme [10]. No account is taken of a consumer's likely response and no consideration is given to the amount of shiftable load available to a consumer.

In what follows, we evaluate these three strategies in terms of peak reduction, supplier cost reduction and in terms of the percentage of the consumer pool who are recruited by the scheme.

5.6 Peak Reduction Performance

We measure the impact that our solution has in terms of peak reduction by considering the maximum power demand value on the day under reduction before and after reduction. We calculate a percentage peak reduction as follows:

$$P_{red} = \frac{max_t(B_t)}{max_t(\sum_{i,j} K_{i,j} B'_{i,j,t})} * 100 \quad (8)$$

Figure 3 shows the average performance of the response aware reduction strategy. It shows that the targeting algo-

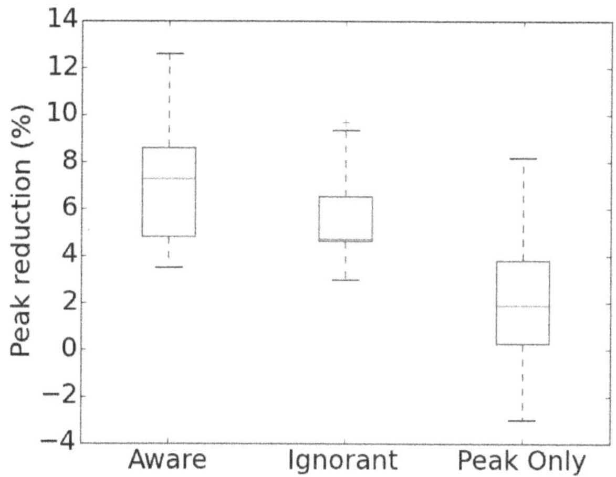

Figure 4: Peak reduction performance of the targeting algorithm for three different reduction strategies.

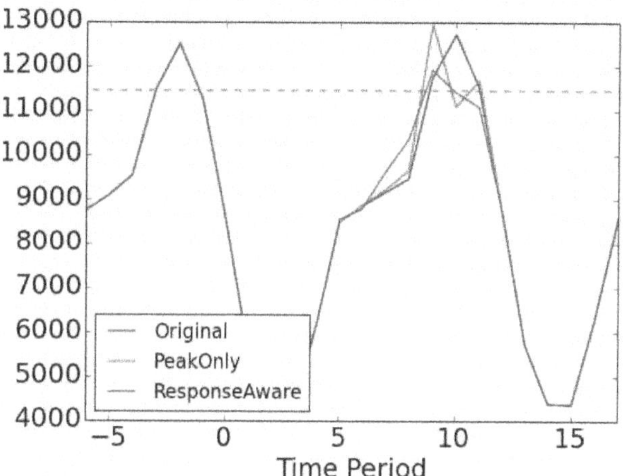

Figure 5: An example of the 'payback effect' generated by the 'peak period only' reduction strategy (red profile). The green profile represents the reduction performance of our 'response aware' solution on the same consumer pool. The forward market threshold, Γ is denoted by the dashed grey line

rithm consistently manages to reduce the peak in time slot 10. We show a comparison of peak reduction performance in Figure 4. This shows that the additional information provided by the consumer response profiles leads to increased peak reduction when compared to the 'response ignorant' and naïve 'peak period only' reduction. The increased performance of the 'response aware' strategy over the 'response ignorant' strategy is statistically significant at a 95% level of confidence. The 'peak period only' strategy also occasionally leads to negative peak reductions – that is, the peak in demand grew after the demand response event. Figure 5 shows how the 'peak period only' reduction strategy has successfully reduced the original peak, but it has led to the creation of a secondary peak in the preceding timestep that is larger than the original.

Figure 6 shows that in addition to significant peak reduction, both the 'response aware' and 'response ignorant' strategies lead to substantial cost savings for the supplier. The difference in cost reduction between the 'response aware' and 'response ignorant' strategies is not statistically significant, but this result shows that the inclusion of consumer response behaviour does not negatively impact the potential cost savings produced by our targeting algorithm and so a supplier would have no economic reason for choosing to use the simpler reduction strategy.

5.7 Consumer Recruitment

One of the benefits of the approach we outline in this work, is that incentives will only be targeted to those consumers whose expected behaviour leads to a reduction in the cost to the supplier. On average, our 'response aware' solution issues demand reduction requests to 56.4% of the consumer pool compared to the 'peak period only' reduction strategy, which sends requests to 100% of the consumer pool. The 'response ignorant' reduction strategy recruited an average of 57% of consumers showing that our targeting algorithm is capable of reducing the recruitment of consumers even when the consumer behaviour model is omitted. This means that our targeting algorithm results in fewer interruptions to the daily lives of the supplier's consumers, potentially minimising the onset of 'demand response fatigue', as well as leading to fewer incentives being paid to consumers whose behaviour following a reduction request actually leads to an increase in the supplier's costs.

In Figure 7 we show how our solution distributes recommendations among the different time periods. Where a traditional approach to demand response, such as that represented by the 'peak only period' strategy may only issue demand reduction requests to the period experiencing a peak in demand, our solution only issues slightly more than 50% of the recommendations to that peak period. This demonstrates that it is not only the selection of the right subset of consumers that contributes to the performance of the strategy, but the time periods that those requests specify also have a role to play.

5.8 Scalability

Finally, Figure 8 shows how the running time for the algorithm varies with an increasing number of consumers.[6] These results show that although the size of the solution space increases exponentially with the size of the consumer pool, solutions for problems involving tens of thousands of consumers can still be found in reasonable time. We make use of IBM ILOG CPLEX Optimization Studio (CPLEX), which is an industry standard software package for mathematical optimisation, to solve the consumer targeting problem. The CPLEX pre-solver makes use of the branch and cut algorithm to identify opportunities to reduce the size of the problem. The branch and cut method utilises the branch and bound algorithm to solve a continuous relaxation of the linear program and makes use of cutting planes (additional linear constraints) to progressively tighten those relaxations. The addition of these 'cuts' normally reduces the number of

[6]The experiments were executed on an Intel Core i7-2600 workstation with 3.40GHz cores and 16GB of RAM.

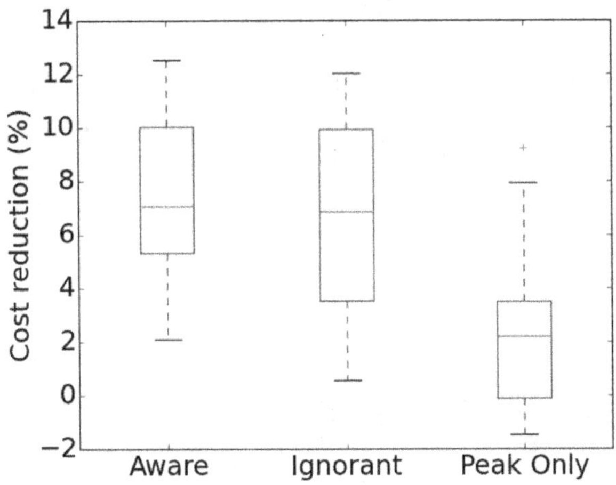

Figure 6: Cost reduction performance of the targeting algorithm for three different reduction strategies.

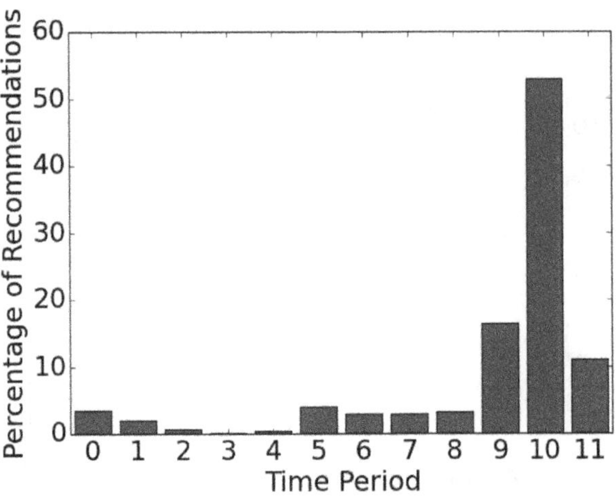

Figure 7: The distribution of recommendations to different timeslots.

branches requires to solve a MIP, enabling solutions to be found for larger scale problems.

The scalability of our algorithm means that it could potentially be used to coordinate all of a supplier's consumers across a localised area such as a town/city, enabling the supplier and the grid operator to more efficiently manage demand across that area.

6. DISCUSSIONS AND FUTURE WORK

In this work we presented a rich model of customer behaviour that describes how consumers will respond to reduction requests. We also proposed a mixed integer programming solution to select the optimal subset of consumers that should be targeted with demand reduction requests. We evaluated this solution using electricity usage data from residential dwellings within the United Kingdom. We have shown that our solution is capable of performing significant peak reductions whilst reducing supplier incurred costs. We demonstrated that our consumer response model leads to improved peak reduction without compromising on the costs incurred by the supplier when compared to a consumer behaviour model that ignored consumer responses. We also evaluated our algorithm against a classical approach that saw all consumers within the consumer pool being targeted with a reduction request for the time period with the maximum demand usage and showed that our solution showed greater peak reduction and increased cost savings for the supplier. Finally, we have shown it to be capable of coordinating the electricty usage of tens of thousands of consumers with only a few minutes of computing time.

In future work we will propose a method to learn a consumer's response profile using the system's previous interactions with the consumer and evaluate how the performance of our algorithm changes when the consumer response profile containts uncertainty. We will also introduce uncertainty to the input, by utilising predictions of appliance usage, such as those provided by [15].

Acknowledgements

We thank the anonymous reviewers and Dr AJ Brush for their comments, which lead to improvements in this manuscript. This work was carried out as part of the ORCHID project (EPSRC ref: EP/1011587/1) and received support from the EPSRC-funded International Centre for Infrastructure Futures (EP/K012347/1).

7. REFERENCES

[1] Assessment of customer response to real time pricing. Technical report, Edward J. Bloustein School of Planning and Public Policy, 2005.

[2] M. Albadi and E. El-Saadany. A summary of demand response in electricity markets. *Electric Power Systems Research*, 78(11):1989 – 1996, 2008.

[3] V. Chandan, T. Ganu, T. K. Wijaya, M. Minou, G. Stamoulis, G. Thanos, and D. P. Seetharam. idr: Consumer and grid friendly demand response system. In *Proceedings of The 5th ACM International Conference on Future Energy Systems (e-Energy" 14)*, number EPFL-CONF-198476, 2014.

[4] H. Chen, T. N. Cong, W. Yang, C. Tan, Y. Li, and Y. Ding. Progress in electrical energy storage system: A critical review. *Progress in Natural Science*, 19(3):291–312, 2009.

[5] E. Costanza, J. E. Fischer, J. A. Colley, T. Rodden, S. D. Ramchurn, and N. R. Jennings. Doing the laundry with agents: a field trial of a future smart energy system in the home. In *Proceedings of the 32nd annual ACM conference on Human factors in computing systems*, pages 813–822. ACM, 2014.

[6] R. de Sá Ferreira, L. A. Barroso, P. Rochinha Lino, M. M. Carvalho, and P. Valenzuela. Time-of-use tariff design under uncertainty in price-elasticities of electricity demand: A stochastic optimization approach. *Smart Grid, IEEE Transactions on*, 4(4):2285–2295, 2013.

[7] T. Ericson. Direct load control of residential water heaters. *Energy Policy*, 37(9):3502–3512, 2009.

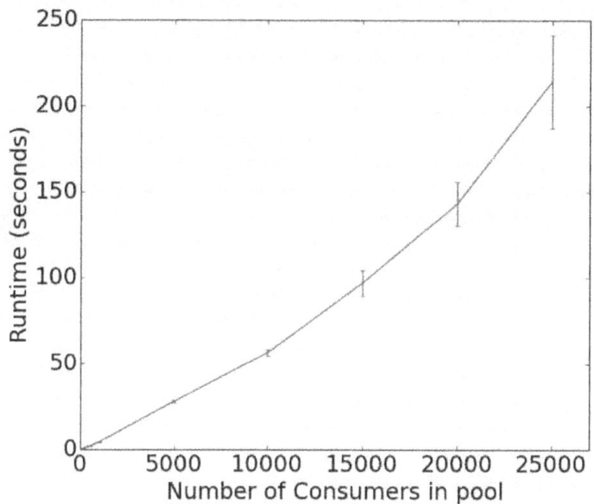

Figure 8: Running time of our targeting algorithm as the number of consumers varies. Error bars show a 95% confidence interval

[8] J.-H. Kim and A. Shcherbakova. Common failures of demand response. *Energy*, 36(2):873–880, Feb. 2011.

[9] J. K. Larsen. Correspondence regarding the rocky mountain power decision summary report on purpa time-based metering and communication standard. Technical report, 2007.

[10] K. P. Ltd. Kiwi power: our service. Website. Accessed On 2015-01-12.

[11] S. D. Ramchurn, P. Vytelingum, A. Rogers, and N. Jennings. Agent-based control for decentralised demand side management in the smart grid. In *The 10th International Conference on Autonomous Agents and Multiagent Systems-Volume 1*, pages 5–12. International Foundation for Autonomous Agents and Multiagent Systems, 2011.

[12] S. D. Ramchurn, P. Vytelingum, A. Rogers, and N. R. Jennings. Putting the'smarts' into the smart grid: a grand challenge for artificial intelligence. *Communications of the ACM*, 55(4):86–97, 2012.

[13] A. Rogers, S. Ramchurn, and N. R. Jennings. Delivering the smart grid: Challenges for autonomous agents and multi-agent systems research. In *Twenty-Sixth AAAI Conference on Artificial Intelligence (AAAI 2012), Toronto, CA, July*, pages 22–26, 2012.

[14] F. C. Schweppe, R. D. Tabors, J. L. Kirtley, H. R. Outhred, F. H. Pickel, and A. J. Cox. Homeostatic utility control. *Power Apparatus and Systems, IEEE Transactions on*, (3):1151–1163, 1980.

[15] N. C. Truong, J. McInerney, L. Tran-Thanh, E. Costanza, and S. D. Ramchurn. Forecasting multi-appliance usage for smart home energy management. In *Proceedings of the Twenty-Third international joint conference on Artificial Intelligence*, pages 2908–2914. AAAI Press, 2013.

[16] E. UK. Wholesale electricity market report: Winter season: to end of january 2014. Technical report, 2014.

[17] J. Xiao, J. Y. Chung, J. Li, R. Boutaba, and J.-K. Hong. Near optimal demand-side energy management under real-time demand-response pricing. In *Proceedings of Network and Service Management (CNSM), 2010 International Conference on*, pages 527–532, 2010.

Distributed Multi-Period Optimal Power Flow for Demand Response in Microgrids

Paul Scott
The Australian National University
NICTA
paul.scott@anu.edu.au

Sylvie Thiébaux
The Australian National University
NICTA
sylvie.thiebaux@anu.edu.au

ABSTRACT

The scalability and privacy preserving nature of distributed optimisation techniques makes them ideal for coordinating many independently acting agents in a microgrid setting. However, their practical applicability remains an open question in this context, since AC power flows are inherently non-convex and households make discrete decisions about how to schedule their loads. In this paper, we show that one such method, the alternating direction method of multipliers (ADMM), can be adapted to remain practical in this challenging microgrid setting. We formulate and solve a multi-period optimal power flow (OPF) problem featuring independent households with shiftable loads, and study the results obtained with a range of power flow models and approaches to managing discrete decisions. Our experiments on a suburb-sized microgrid show that the AC power flows and a simple two-stage approach to handling discrete decisions do not appear to cause convergence issues, and provide near optimal results in a time that is practical for receding horizon control. This work brings distributed control for microgrids several steps closer to reality.

Categories and Subject Descriptors

I.2.11 [**Computing Methodologies**]: Artificial Intelligence

Keywords

OPF; ADMM; demand response; distributed control; microgrid; multi-agent systems; scheduling

1. INTRODUCTION

The distinction between generators and loads is fading as households adopt distributed generation, storage and smart devices. We envisage a future where network operators provide a competitive electricity market that anyone can participate in, and where this distinction between generators and loads is removed. This will be of particular importance for the operation of microgrids, which require more finesse to ensure that demand and supply are balanced and that the network is in a safe operating state in each instance.

A different approach is needed from the traditional centralised markets as they were never designed to operate where every customer is an active participant, or to handle their unique time-coupled behaviours. In this new regime demand response (DR) techniques will play a central role in providing incentives, coordination and network support.

The goal of the network operator is to serve power at the lowest cost. Several works [22, 16, 24] have adopted distributed solving techniques in order to solve this problem for many participants. These distributed algorithms greatly parallelise the problem and help to preserve the privacy of participants. As a by-product, they provide a natural market mechanism for fairly allocating payments between consumers and producers. Theoretically, these algorithms require the problem to be convex in order to guarantee convergence to a globally optimal solution. However, the behaviour of many loads within households are discrete in nature [28], and the equations that govern how power physically flows on the network are non-convex.

In this paper, we show that these theoretical problems can in practice be dealt with in the context of microgrids. We show that for a distributed DR algorithm in a microgrid, exact non-convex power flow models perform well compared to inexact convex models, which makes them a valuable candidate in practice. Secondly, we identify that the non-convex nature of discrete household loads is a non-issue, and that in practice simple approaches to handling these discrete loads are effective at the microgrid level. By solving these problems, we show that the use of distributed algorithms for managing the balance of power on a microgrid is in practice not only possible, but also highly effective.

We formulate the problem as a multi-period optimal power flow (OPF) problem to account for multiple time steps over a day, which can be used as part of a day-ahead pricing scheme or, as we propose, a receding horizon control algorithm. We solve the multi-period OPF problems in a distributed manner by adapting the alternating direction method of multipliers (ADMM) approach presented in [22]. We experiment with a range of power flow models of varying degrees of accuracy, to compare their relative behaviour in a distributed algorithm. We then introduce and compare several approaches layered on top of ADMM which manage the introduction of discrete variables into the problem. Technically, our contributions can be summarised as:

e-Energy'15, July 14–17, 2015, Bangalore, India.

ACM 978-1-4503-3609-3/15/07 ...$15.00.
DOI: http://dx.doi.org/10.1145/2768510.2768534.

- A comprehensive experimental comparison of the convergence of five commonly used power flow models when used for distributed OPF in a microgrid context.
- The identification that the exact non-convex power flow model in practice not only converges in this context, but also finds near-optimal solutions in a timely fashion relative to other models.
- The introduction and comparison of three simple but effective approaches to managing the discrete shiftable loads that are typically found within households.

Combined, these results show that distributed DR using ADMM can achieve near optimal solutions in a time frame that is practical for receding horizon control in this challenging microgrid setting, regardless of the theoretical limitations. This work brings distributed DR closer to the point where it can be deployed in a real microgrid.

In the next section we discuss the related work and how our contribution is unique. In Sections 3–4 we formulate the problem and present the distributed algorithm we use to solve it. The test microgrid is introduced in Section 6 before presenting our results in Sections 7–8 on power flows and discrete decisions.

2. RELATED WORK

Much of the existing work on demand response (DR) has focused on using real-time pricing (RTP) as a control signal [28, 25, 7, 30, 32, 15]. In these methods, participants receive a RTP signal and individually optimise their own behaviour, so as to minimise a combination of monetary and discomfort costs. Other approaches have utilised non-pricing control signals, which are simpler to implement, but are limited in the types of loads that they can model [33, 31].

These approaches implement a form of open loop control, because the agent that sets the control signal (RTP or otherwise) at best can only estimate how consumers will respond to it. In order to reduce the amount of guesswork and improve solutions, a closed loop approach to RTP was presented by Gatsis et al. [16]. In this scheme, the prices are iteratively updated by a central agent, with consumers communicating their best responses to the price prior to acting. Mohsenian-Rad et al. [24] introduce an alternative iterative procedure not based on RTP, where consumers cooperate to reduce total generation costs in a distributed manner.

The approaches discussed so far do not model the electricity network, so cannot account for real power losses, reactive power, voltage limits or line thermal limits. Without these considerations, we cannot be sure that the DR outcome is efficient, safe or even possible. Many of the works on distributed algorithms which explicitly model the network have used ADMM as a solving technique, due to its ease in decomposition, and its convergence guarantees on a wide range of problems [6]. However, most of these works have focused on more traditional OPF problems rather than demand response in a microgrid context.

One of the first authors to apply ADMM to power networks was Kim et al. [21], who decomposed a convex approximation of the OPF problem into regions, and compared the results to two other approaches. They found it to have a significant speed improvement over a centralised approach, and that it preserved privacy between regions. Erseghe [12] also performed region-based decomposition of the network and found exact local solutions to the OPF problem. Instead of decomposing on the network structure, Phan et al. [27] decomposed across scenarios in a security-constrained OPF. The recent work by Magnússon et al. [23] decomposes the network to a greater extent than these other methods, and they solve the underlying non-convex OPF by taking sequential convex approximations. One thing all these works have in common is that they are focused on the more traditional OPF problem, whereas in our work we consider a microgrid where distributed participants act independently.

Region-based decomposition was also used by Dall'Anese et al. [9] to control distributed generation on radial feeders. They used ADMM to solve an unbalanced OPF problem using a semidefinite programming (SDP) relaxation. In our work we consider each customer to be independent, for privacy reasons, and we also allow for meshed microgrid topologies. Šulc et al. [34] use the relaxed DF (SOCP) equations to perform reactive power control on radial networks. For a similar problem, Peng et al. [26] provide closed-form solutions for ADMM subproblems, greatly reducing the computational requirements. Again these works focus on radial networks.

The work that is closest to ours is that presented by Kraning et al. [22], and indeed we build on their approach. They decompose all network components for a multi-period OPF problem using a quadratic power flow approximation. This procedure is effectively a principled method for settling RTPs for each bus, also known as locational marginal prices. Their experiments showed that very large problems could be solved efficiently in a parallel environment.

All these works have taken different approaches to modelling the power flows on the network. There is no comparison of the relative performance between these different power flow models in a distributed algorithm for microgrids, which is what we achieve in this paper for five different models. Our results in this area indicate that exact local methods can produce close to optimal solutions in a competitive number of iterations relative to other models. In addition, to the best of our knowledge, we are the first to incorporate discrete decisions into a distributed demand response mechanism that models the network. Our work brings ADMM to the point where it can be considered a practical approach for efficiently balancing power in a microgrid setting.

3. PROBLEM FORMULATION

The overall objective of the demand response problem is to minimise the average long-term cost of supplying electricity. We formulate this as a series of multi-period OPF problems embedded within a receding horizon control process, which enables time-coupled components to be accurately controlled in an uncertain environment. A multi-period OPF is first solved over a horizon of $n \in \mathbb{N}$ time steps, the decision in the first step is acted on, and then the process repeats with the window shifted forward by one. In this paper we focus on solving the multi-period OPF within a single horizon, and the actions that agents take to implement the first decision.

Note that the formulation that we use breaks away from the standard in power systems in order to decompose the network and distribute the problem. Fig. 1 highlights the difference between a standard line diagram and our formulation. In our model, a network N consists of a set of components C, terminals T and connections L. Each component

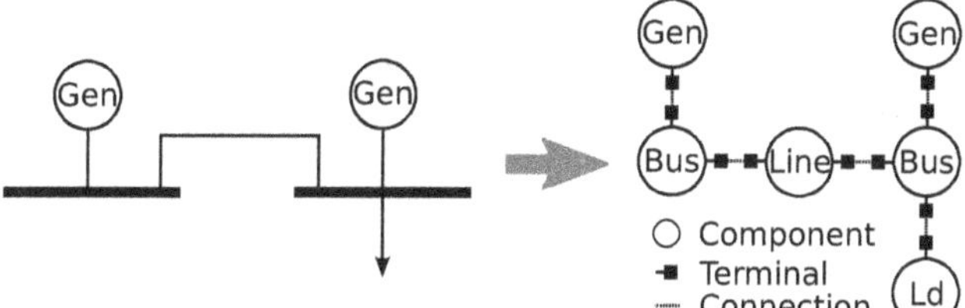

Figure 1: Conversion from a standard line diagram to the component orientated representation.

$c \in C$ (e.g., bus, line, generator, load) has a set of terminals $T_c \subseteq T$ which can be connected to the terminals of other components, where the T_c sets partition T. Each connection $l \in L$ is a pair of terminals, i.e. $L \subseteq T \times T$.

3.1 Connections

Connections exist between the terminals of two different components. We use the quantities of real power, reactive power, voltage and voltage phase angle ($p, q, v, \theta \in \mathbb{R}^n$ respectively) to model the flow of power into a component through a terminal. These are vectors in order to capture each time step in the horizon. For convenience, we use a parent vector $y_i \in \mathbb{R}^{4n}$ to represent all variables for a terminal $i \in T$, where $y_i := (p_i, q_i, v_i, \theta_i)^\mathsf{T}$. When two terminals are connected together, $(i,j) \in L$, we pose the following constraints:

$$p_i + p_j = 0, \quad q_i + q_j = 0, \quad v_i - v_j = 0, \quad \theta_i - \theta_j = 0$$

The first two constraints ensure that for a connected pair of terminals, at each time step, any power that leaves one terminal must enter the other. The second two constraints ensure that the connected terminals have the same voltage and phase angle. This duplication of variables is necessary in order to decompose the problem for our distributed algorithm. To avoid confusion, recall that connections and terminals are different from lines and buses (see Fig. 1).

We rewrite these constraints as $y_i + Ay_j = 0$ for y, where A is the appropriate $4n \times 4n$ diagonal matrix. Further, we define the connection function $h : \mathbb{R}^{4n} \times \mathbb{R}^{4n} \mapsto \mathbb{R}^{4n}$ as the LHS of this constraint for convenience: $h(y_i, y_j) := y_i + Ay_j$.

3.2 Components

At a high level, each component $c \in C$ has a variable vector $x_c \in \mathbb{R}^{a_c}$, an objective function $f_c : \mathbb{R}^{a_c} \mapsto \mathbb{R}$, and a constraint function $g_c : \mathbb{R}^{a_c} \mapsto \mathbb{R}^{b_c}$, where $g_c(x_c) \leq 0$. For a component $c \in C$, the vector x_c includes all terminal variables for that component: $y_i, \forall i \in T_c$.

The objective function is used to model any costs or preferences that a component may have other than the direct payments they make to the market for their consumption. For a generator this can be the fuel costs, for a house this might be temperature comfort preferences, and other components like a line will not have any costs.

In the following sections we describe at a lower level the models used for the components in our experiments. When necessary, we use $t \in \{0, \ldots, n\}$ to index vectors by time, otherwise we imply standard vector operations. The index where $t = 0$ is used to represent the value of the variable at the beginning of the current horizon, which we assume is known.

3.2.1 Bus

A bus has a variable number of terminals which depends on how many other components connect to it. For example, a bus might be connected to a generator, a load and 3 lines for a total of 5 terminals. Regardless of the number of terminals, the constraints take the form:

$$\sum_{i \in T_c} p_i = 0 \quad \sum_{i \in T_c} q_i = 0$$
$$\forall i, j \in T_c : v_i = v_j, \ \theta_i = \theta_j$$

The first two constraints are an expression of Kirchhoff's current law (KCL) in terms of power flows. The remaining constraints ensure that all terminal voltages and phase angles are the same.

3.2.2 Line

A line is a two terminal component which transports power from one location to another, typically from bus to bus. We model a line as having a constant conductance $g \in \mathbb{R}_+$, susceptance $b \in \mathbb{R}$ and maximum apparent power $s \in \mathbb{R}_+$. The AC power flow equations are derived from Ohm's law, where $\forall i, j \in T_c, i \neq j$:

$$p_i = gv_i^2 - gv_iv_j \cos(\theta_i - \theta_j) - bv_iv_j \sin(\theta_i - \theta_j) \tag{1}$$
$$q_i = -bv_i^2 + bv_iv_j \cos(\theta_i - \theta_j) - gv_iv_j \sin(\theta_i - \theta_j) \tag{2}$$
$$s^2 \geq p_i^2 + q_i^2, \quad \underline{v} \leq v_i \leq \bar{v}, \quad \theta_i - \theta_j \leq \bar{\theta} \tag{3}$$

These constraints are identical for each time step, so we have left out the indexing by time to improve clarity. These equations are non-convex, so they are often either approximated or relaxed, as we will discuss further in Section 7.

3.2.3 Generator

A generator is a single terminal component which produces real and reactive power. In our formulation the generator has a floating phase angle and voltage. A generator has lower and upper real and reactive power limits such that $p_{i,t} \in [\underline{p}, \bar{p}]$ and $q_{i,t} \in [\underline{q}, \bar{q}]$, a ramping rate $p^r \in \mathbb{R}_+$ and a quadratic cost function f for generation costs:

$$f(x) = p_i^\mathsf{T} \Psi p_i - \psi^\mathsf{T} p_i$$
$$\forall t \in \{1, \ldots, n\} : -p^r \leq p_{i,t} - p_{i,t-1} \leq p^r$$

where $\Psi \in \mathbb{R}_+^{n \times n}$ is a diagonal matrix and $\psi \in \mathbb{R}_+^n$. More advanced generator models with non-convex start up costs and minimum outputs can be modelled in this framework but are not considered here. They will be investigated in future work to see how they impact the distributed algorithm.

3.2.4 Shiftable Load

A shiftable load is a single terminal component used to model electrical loads like dish washers and clothes dryers. A household has some flexibility on when these loads can run, and will schedule them to minimise the costs they pay for the electricity. These loads must start running between an earliest and a latest start time: $t^e, t^l \in \mathbb{N}$. To model this we introduce binary variables $u \in \{0,1\}^n$ for the horizon. A value of 1 indicates that the component starts at the given time. A component runs for a duration of $d \in \mathbb{N}$ consecutive time steps, during which it consumes a load of $p^{\text{nom}} \in \mathbb{R}$.

$$p_{i,t} = p^{\text{nom}} \sum_{t'=t-d+1}^{t} u_{t'}, \qquad \sum_{t=t^e}^{t^l} u_t = 1$$

$$\forall t \notin \{t^e, \ldots, t^l\} : u_t = 0$$

A convex relaxation of this component can be obtained by relaxing the integrality requirement: $u \in [0,1]^n$. Shiftable loads with more complex time-varying power consumptions can be modelled as in [30]. We expect the results presented here will carry over to this more complicated model, but leave a thorough check to future work.

3.2.5 *Other Components*

A whole range of other components can easily be modelled within this framework, for example, batteries, inverters, solar PV, electric vehicles, HVACs and voltage regulators (see [30] for additional models). Indeed we have experimented with batteries and solar PV in our implementated algorithm, but in this paper we focus on the more difficult to handle shiftable loads.

3.3 Optimisation Problem

Now that we have the component models and the relations between them, we can write down the multi-period OPF problem for one horizon. The objective is to minimise the sum of all component cost functions, subject to component and terminal connection constraints. This is a utilitarian view of the problem.

$$\min_x \sum_{c \in C} f_c(x_c) \tag{4}$$

$$\text{s.t. } \forall c \in C : g_c(x_c) \leq 0 \tag{5}$$

$$\forall (i,j) \in L : h(y_i, y_j) = 0 \tag{6}$$

4. DISTRIBUTED ALGORITHM

The next step is to show how this multi-period optimisation problem can be solved in a distributed manner. The end result is an iterative algorithm where each component (household, generator and network device) selfishly optimises its own consumption/production profile for the currently standing prices. These profiles are then communicated amongst connected components and the prices are modified in order to encourage agreement and consistency.

In order to distribute and solve the problem in this way we use the alternating direction method of multipliers (ADMM) algorithm. ADMM is a variation of the standard augmented Lagrangian method that enables problem decomposition [6, 11, 14]. The augmented Lagrangian relaxation applied to the connection constraints (6) is:

$$\mathcal{L}(L, y, z, \lambda, \rho) := \sum_{c \in C} f_c(x_c) + \sum_{(i,j) \in L} \left[\frac{\rho}{2} \|h(y_i, z_j)\|_2^2 + \lambda_{i,j}^{\mathsf{T}} h(y_i, z_j) \right]$$

where $\rho \in (0, \infty)$ is a penalty parameter and $\lambda_{i,j} \in \mathbb{R}^{4n}$ are the dual variables for the connection constraints.

These dual variables represent the locational marginal prices in our problem, or put another way, connection dependent RTPs. These prices are used to charge (or pay) components for the power that they exchange through their terminals. For example, a component with a terminal i (connected to terminal j) will pay, or be paid an amount equal to:

$$\lambda_{i,j,p}^{\mathsf{T}} p_i + \lambda_{i,j,q}^{\mathsf{T}} q_i + \lambda_{i,j,v}^{\mathsf{T}} v_i + \lambda_{i,j,\theta}^{\mathsf{T}} \theta_i \tag{7}$$

Where we have split up the dual variables so that it is clear how they associate with each physical power quantity. These prices are based on not just the cost of generation, but also account for line losses and adjust to prevent congestion. They provide a natural market mechanism for the fair distribution of payments from consumers to producers.

4.1 Algorithm

A single iteration of the ADMM algorithm consists of two phases followed by a dual variable update. Components are each allocated to one of the two phases. The component sets C_1 and C_2, and the variable vectors x_1 and x_2 represent this allocation.

The connections are split into three parts: L_1, L_2 and $L_{1,2}$. The intra-phase connections L_1 (L_2) are those that are between components in C_1 (C_2). The inter-phase connections $L_{1,2}$ are those where one component is in C_1 and the other is in C_2. The augmented Lagrangian relaxation is only applied to the inter-phase connections.

The superscript $k \in \mathbb{N}$ is used to indicate the k-th iteration. At the start of the algorithm all terminal and dual variables are initialised to some values $y_i^{(0)}$ and $\lambda_{i,j}^{(0)}$. For the k-th iteration ADMM proceeds as follows:

1. Optimise for x_1, holding x_2 constant at its $k-1$ value
2. Optimise for x_2, holding x_1 constant at its k value
3. Update the dual variables λ

For our optimisation problem this becomes:

$$x_1^{(k)} = \arg\min_{x_1} \mathcal{L}(L_{1,2}, y, y^{(k-1)}, \lambda^{(k-1)}, \rho^k) \tag{8}$$

$$\text{s.t. } \forall c \in C_1 : g_c(x_c) \leq 0$$

$$\forall (i,j) \in L_1 : h(y_i, y_j) = 0$$

$$x_2^{(k)} = \arg\min_{x_2} \mathcal{L}(L_{1,2}, y^{(k)}, y, \lambda^{(k-1)}, \rho^k) \tag{9}$$

$$\text{s.t. } \forall c \in C_2 : g_c(x_c) \leq 0$$

$$\forall (i,j) \in L_2 : h(y_i, y_j) = 0$$

$$\forall (i,j) \in L_{1,2} : \lambda_{i,j}^{(k)} = \lambda_{i,j}^{(k-1)} + \rho^{(k)} h(y_i^{(k)}, y_j^{(k)}) \tag{10}$$

In the simple case when ρ is constant, f_c and g_c are convex, and h is affine, ADMM converges to a global optimum [6].

If a component has no intra-phase connections, then it can be separated from the optimisation problem for its phase, and can therefore be solved independently. We adopt the partitioning scheme where C_2 contains all buses and C_1 the rest of the network. This allows us to fully separate all components within phases, since buses will never connect to other buses ($L_2 = \emptyset$) and non-bus components will never connect to other non-bus components ($L_1 = \emptyset$). In this way each component acts as an independent agent and communicates only to other directly connected agents. As an additional benefit, some components are simple enough when separated that they have closed-form solutions that can be calculated at each iteration, instead of invoking an optimisation routine [26]. We adopt such closed-form solutions for buses as proposed in [22].

4.2 Residuals and Stopping Criteria

As in [22], we use primal and dual residuals to define the stopping criteria for our algorithm. The primal residuals represent the constraint violations at the current solution.

We combine the residuals of all connections into a single vector r_p. By indexing into the inter-phase connections $L_{1,2} = \{(i_1, j_1), (i_2, j_2), \ldots\}$, the primal residuals are:

$$r_p^{(k)} := (h(y_{i_1}^{(k)}, y_{j_1}^{(k)}), h(y_{i_2}^{(k)}, y_{j_2}^{(k)}), \ldots)^\mathsf{T}$$

The dual residuals give the violation of the KKT stationarity constraint at the current solution. We collect the dual residuals for each connection into the vector r_d. For ADMM, the dual residuals are (see [6] for derivation):

$$r_d^{(k)} := \rho(Ay_{j_1}^{(k)} - Ay_{j_1}^{(k-1)}, Ay_{j_2}^{(k)} - Ay_{j_2}^{(k-1)}, \ldots)^\mathsf{T}$$

These residuals approach zero as the algorithm converges to a KKT point. We consider that the algorithm has converged when the scaled 2-norms of these residuals are smaller than a tolerance ϵ: $\frac{1}{\sqrt{M}}\|r_p^{(k)}\|_2 < \epsilon$, $\frac{1}{\sqrt{M}}\|r_d^{(k)}\|_2 < \epsilon$. Here M is the total number of inter-phase terminal constraints $4n|L_{1,2}|$ minus the number of terminal constraints that are trivially satisfied (e.g., floating voltages and phase angles for generators). It is used to keep the tolerance independent of problem size.

5. IMPLEMENTATION

We developed an experimental implementation of the above approach in C++ using Gurobi [17] and Ipopt [35, 19] as backend solvers for subproblems. Gurobi is used for mixed-integer linear or quadratically constrained problems, and Ipopt for more general nonlinear problems. CasADi [1] was used as a modelling and automatic differentiation front end to Ipopt. This implementation was designed with flexibility in mind, so that a wide range of experiments could be conducted.

In a fully distributed real-world implementation every house, generator, bus, line, and other component could have its own collocated computational node. However, from a practical point of view it might make more sense to have the computational parts of the network located separately from their components and even grouped together. For example, all the buses and lines of a single feeder could be managed by a single node, which communicates to downstream houses and the upstream substation. A whole range of practical factors such as speed, communications, costs, robustness and maintenance would need to be considered before a decision could be made on the right architecture.

Our experimental setup is a sequential implementation of the ADMM algorithm, however we timed the slowest component at each iteration to get an idea of how long a fully distributed implementation would take.

The experiments were run on machines with 2 AMD 6-Core Opteron 4184, 2.8GHz, 3M L2/6M L3 Cache CPUs and 64GB of memory.

6. TEST MICROGRID

Our experiments are based around a modified 70 bus 11kV benchmark distribution network [10] (shown in Fig. 2), which was chosen because it has a comparable size to that of a suburb. We close all tie lines in the network in order to change it from a radial to a meshed configuration. We expect microgrids to take on more of a meshed network structure to improve reliability and efficiency, and to better utilise distributed generation.

The benchmark comes with a static PQ load at each bus, which we replace with a number of houses (around 50 on average) that depends on the size of the load. The houses are connected directly to the 11kV buses as we have no data on the low voltage part of the network. We assume that the power bounds we place on each household will be sufficient to prevent any capacity violation of the low voltage network.

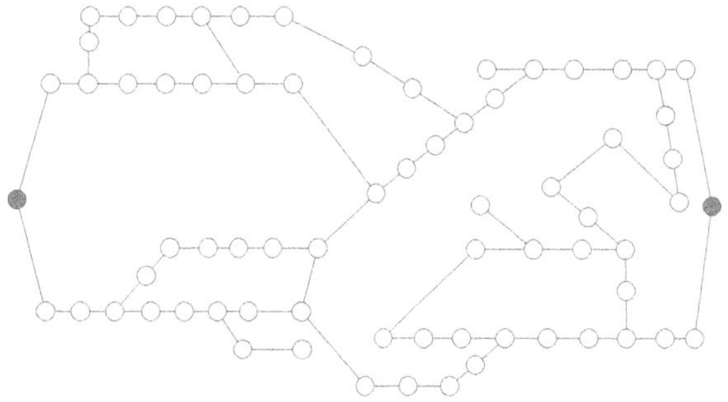

Figure 2: 70 bus network showing buses, lines and the generators/substations in grey.

A house is an independent agent that manages subcomponents. For our experiments these include an uncontrollable background power draw and two shiftable loads. A house has a single terminal through which it can exchange real and reactive power with the rest of the network. Each house has an apparent power limit of $s = 10$kVA.

We develop a typical house load profile l_t by modifying an aggregate Autumn load profile for the ACT region in Australia (data from [2]). We assume that households consume on average 20kWh per day. This provides the basis for all uncontrollable household background loads. For the purposes of these experiments, we assume that the static PQ loads in the benchmark were recorded when loads were at 75% of their peak. We divide the benchmark static real power at each bus by how much power a typical house consumes at 75% of its peak power (1.45kW). Rounding down this number gives us an estimate of the number of houses which would be located at a given bus. This approach produces a total of $h = 3674$ houses for the network, about the size of an Australian suburb.

We place two generators in the network where the distribution system connects to upstream substations. These can be thought of as either dispatchable microgenerators or as representing the cost of importing power into the microgrid.

We randomise some of the generator and household load parameters to produce different problem instances, as can be seen in Table 1. The time horizon spans 24 hours with 15 minute time steps, which produces a problem instance with over 2 million variables per horizon. The experiments were run with a primal and dual stopping tolerance of $\epsilon = 10^{-4}$ and a fixed penalty parameter of $\rho = 0.5$. To improve numerical stability, we scale the system to a per-unit representation with base values at 11kV and 100kVA. This means that a real power residual of 10^{-4} translates to 10W for a connection, or about 1% of the average household load.

The starting values for the distributed algorithm are the same for all terminals and all time steps. All are zero except for the voltage magnitudes $v_t = 1$ and the real power constraint dual variables $\lambda_t^p = 5$, which translates to a price of 200 \$/MWh. This is a naive (or cold) starting point as it uses no information about the particular network instance.

Table 1: Component parameters.

Comp	Param	Value	Units
Gen	ψ_t	$\max(4, \sim\mathcal{N}(40, 8^2))$	\$/MWh
Gen	$\Psi_{t,t}$	$\max(1, \sim\mathcal{N}(10, 2^2))$	\$/MWhMW
Gen	$\underline{p}, \bar{p}$	$-s \times h/2, 0$	kW
Gen	$\underline{q}, \bar{q}$	$0.2\underline{p}, -0.2\underline{p}$	kvar
House	p_t	$\sim\mathcal{N}(l_t, (0.2l_t)^2)$	kW
House	q_t	$0.3p_t$	kvar
Shift 1	d	$\max(15, \sim\mathcal{N}(90, 18^2))$	min
Shift 1	p^{nom}	$\max(0.3, \sim\mathcal{N}(3, 0.6^2))$	kW
Shift 2	d	$\max(15, \sim\mathcal{N}(60, 12^2))$	min
Shift 2	p^{nom}	$\max(0.1, \sim\mathcal{N}(1, 0.2^2))$	kW
Shift	t^e, t^l	$0, n-d$	

In addition to the 70 bus microgrid, we also ran a series of experiments on randomly generated networks similar to those described in [22]. These randomly generated networks ranged in size from 20 to 2000 buses, and were designed to be highly congested. We will occasionally mention some of the results from these random networks when they differ from those of our 70 bus microgrid.

7. IMPACT OF POWER FLOW MODELS

In this section we investigate how the ADMM method performs with different power flow models. We assess 5 different models, of varying degrees of accuracy and complexity, in order to establish the relative trade-offs when used as part of a distributed algorithm.

7.1 Power Flow Models

Due to their non-convex nature, the AC power flow equations (1–3) are often either relaxed or approximated. Convex relaxations include a quadratic constraint (QC) model [18], a semi-definite program (SDP) [3], the dist-flow (DF) relaxation [13, 4] and an equivalent SOCP relaxation [20, 5]. Approximations include the linear DC (DC) model that uses p and θ [29], the LPAC model [8] and the quadratic formulation (K) proposed by Kraning et al. [22].

The relaxations provide a lower bound on the globally optimal solution while the approximations can produce results with an objective higher or lower than the global optimal. Both the relaxations and approximations often produce solutions that are not feasible for the exact model. These alternative models, however, are often much simpler to compute and their solutions can be used as a heuristic or the bounds can be used for calculating optimality gaps. This is why they are often used with difficult network optimisation problems, for example, OPF, OPF with line switching, capacitor placement and expansion planing.

As shown in the related work section, some of these models have been used with the ADMM algorithm. What is lacking is a comparison of the relative strengths and weaknesses between the different models when used in this context. In this section we compare how the distributed ADMM algorithm performs when using the AC, QC, DF, DC, and K line models. We compare the differences in the solution quality, feasibility, processing time and number of iterations for our test network. What we find is that even though the AC equations are non-convex, in practice they converge and perform well compared to the other approaches. We also find that there is the potential to obtain faster convergence using the K model, but at the expense of accuracy.

Table 2: Iterations and parallel solve time for line models.

	Iterations (std.)	Time in sec (std.)
AC	1945 (17)	148 (12)
QC	1951 (14)	546 (33)
DF	1933 (26)	110 (8)
DC	4140 (50)	244 (8)
K	1027 (52)	15 (1)

We generate 60 random instances of our test microgrid with the binary variables for the shiftable devices relaxed. These are then solved using the distributed algorithm described in Section 4, for each of the 5 different power flow models. In the first part of this section we discuss the convergence, and in the second part we discuss the quality and accuracy of the solutions.

7.2 Convergence

For all 60 instances and all 5 power flow models the algorithm converged. This was expected for all the convex models, but we had no guarantee for the non-convex AC model. This gives us confidence that the exact AC model, even though non-convex, can in practice be used within distributed algorithms.

Table 2 provides the number of iterations and time taken to converge in the form of means and standard deviations. The parallel solve time is the amount of time required to solve the problem in a fully distributed implementation. This was measured by summing together the time of the slowest component at each iteration. In absolute terms, the parallel solve time is relatively small despite the fact that our implementation was designed with flexibility in mind, not performance. That said the K model is significantly faster relative to the other models. It converges in half the number of iterations required by the next fastest model, but as we will see in the next section, it gives us an inaccurate result.

The congested random networks produce similar results. One difference is that for a number of instances the K model was infeasible (would not converge) due to its tendency to exaggerate line losses, where we had a valid AC solution. It is expected that the DC model, and the relaxations to some degree, will exhibit the reverse effect: returning a solution when there is no feasible solution for the exact model. However, we did not come across such a scenario in our experiments with the microgrid and congested random networks.

Fig. 3 shows an example of the primal residual convergence for different line models (the dual residuals are similar). The AC, QC and DF models overlap. One unintuitive result is the fact that the DC model converges poorly when it is in fact a very simple linear model. Large oscillations build up during the solution process which slows the rate of convergence. We performed a series of experiments in order to get a better understanding of this effect. The explanation appears to be that the DC model behaves like an undamped system, as it has no line losses and only linear constraints. The DC model will have a stronger response for a given change in its terminal dual variables. The net effect is that oscillations build up across the network during the solving process. On the other hand the K model overestimates line

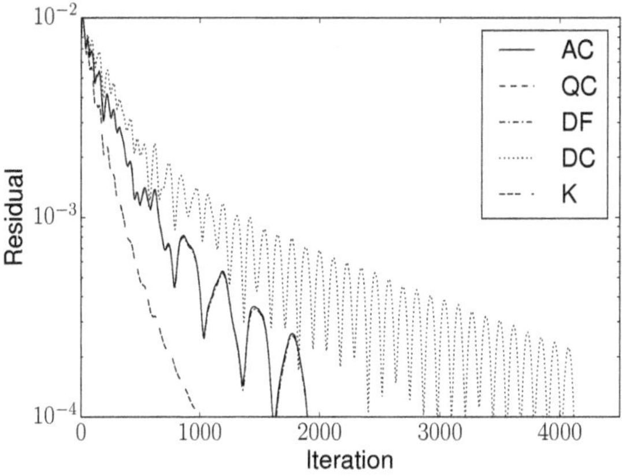

Figure 3: Convergence of primal residuals.

losses, which means it is much less sensitive and no oscillations form. The AC, QC and DF models are somewhere in between these two extremes.

7.2.1 *Warm Starting*

It is important to point out that we are giving the algorithm a naive starting point for both the primal and dual variables, as described in Section 6. In practice, the receding horizon control scheme will provide an excellent warm starting point, because the values from the previous horizon can be used for all but one time step. As a sanity check, we performed warm starting experiments for the AC model. Similar to what was done in [22], we duplicate a problem instance and then randomly resample the household background power and shiftable device power parameters according to the rule: $p \sim p\mathcal{N}(1, \sigma^2)$. We used the solution of the original instance as a starting point for the modified instance. For $\sigma = 0.2$ the warm started run only needed 11% of the original iterations on average. In a second experiment we fully correlated the resampling step, which could represent a correlated change in solar panel output for many households. With $\sigma = 0.2$, only 29% of the original iterations were required on average.

7.2.2 *Communication*

In reality, communication delay will play a major part in the total solve time for the algorithm. The communications could be done over existing internet infrastructure, or dedicated wired or wireless communications could be built for the system to enable more direct communications. Regardless of what technology is used, for each iteration messages need to be communicated from the first phase components to the second phase components and then back again. If we assume each of these hops takes 60ms, then 1000 iterations would require up to 2 minutes of communication time. For this reason, in certain circumstances it may be beneficial to cut down the total number of iterations, even if it requires more processing time per iteration.

We expect the mechanism can be designed to be quite robust to intermittent drops in communication. For example, if a component fails to receive a message from another connected component, then they can continue working by using the last received message. If a connection is dropped for an extended period, then the system could fall back to load predictions based on historical data and some conservative pricing scheme could come into place.

7.3 Solution Quality

Next we show the solution qualities for the different line models. For each model we calculate the percentage difference in objective value relative to the best known AC solution: $100 \cdot (f - f_{best})/f_{best}$. The means and standard deviations of the 60 instances are:

QC	-0.031% (0.008%)	DF	0.039% (0.018%)
DC	-3.541% (0.072%)	K	4.726% (0.090%)

Because the AC equations are non-convex, we don't have a guarantee that the solutions they produce are globally optimal. However, they provide a feasible upper bound on the global optimal. On the other hand, the QC and DF models are convex relaxations of the AC equations, so they provide a lower bound on the global optimal. Therefore the global optimal solution resides somewhere between the values of the AC solution and the QC and DF solutions.

With this in mind, we find that the AC, QC and DF models all produce solutions which are very close to each other. The difference is within the margin of error of the objective function afforded by our stopping criteria, which we estimate to be 1% (see Section 6). This indicates that the AC, QC and DF models produce solutions that are within 1% of the global optimal. They may in fact be closer than this, but we would need to run the experiments with tighter tolerances in order to check. On a limited number of instances we did just this, and found the gap between the objective of the AC model and its convex relaxations to further shrink into insignificance.

These results give us confidence that the non-convex AC model, which is the only one that guarantees Ohm's law is satisfied, produces solutions that are very close to optimal. The QC and DF models produce results with an objective that is very close to the AC model, but even with this small difference, there is the risk that the solutions violate constraints in the exact AC model. Other work has come to a similar conclusion, but in a more traditional OPF setting [18, 27, 12].

There is quite a different story for the approximate models. The DC model underestimates the optimal value by around 3.5% while the K model overestimates it by around 4.7%. Part of the reason for this is that the DC model completely ignores line losses while the K model overestimates them. Even though the K model has fast convergence, it is unlikely to useful on its own in a realistic setting due to its poor accuracy. However, it might be useful in hybrid approaches where line models are swapped, e.g., from K to AC, part way through the solution process in order to speed up convergence.

These results show the feasibility of using the non-convex AC power flow equations for solving a distributed OPF problem in a microgrid context. The K model adopted in [22] converges much faster, but it is unlikely to be usable in a realistic setting, as it ignores voltages and reactive power, and produces overly high costs.

8. DISCRETE DECISIONS

We now want to solve the multi-period OPF for the test microgrid where the binary variables in the shiftable loads are no longer relaxed. In order to do this we extend the algorithm so that it can manage discrete decisions. The focus here is on the scheduling of shiftable loads within households, but discrete decisions can also occur in some generator models and for network switching events.

We identify 3 different approaches to managing discrete decisions. Although they are quite simple, they are nonetheless very effective at managing the shiftable loads within households.

8.1 Methods

We investigate 3 tractable methods for dealing with integer variables which have no global optimality guarantees. Just as we did for the AC equations, we will compare our result to a lower bound in order to get an understanding of the optimality gap. We categorise these methods as:

- Relax and price (RP)
- Relax and decide (RD)
- Unrelaxed (UR)

The RP and RD approaches are broken up into 2 and 3 stages respectively. The first stage, called the negotiation stage, is common to both methods. All integer variables are relaxed and the distributed algorithm is run until convergence, just like what was done for the power flow experiments. At this point the integer variables may take on fractional values, and this solution gives a lower bound on the global optimal solution. In the second stage each component makes a local decision in order to force any fractional values to integers. Recall from Section 3.2.4 that shiftable devices have a binary variable u_t for each time step, only one of which can take on the value 1 to indicate the starting time.

8.1.1 Relax and Price

In the second stage of the RP method, each house performs a local optimisation to determine how to enforce integer feasibility of u_t. We designed a range of cost functions which penalise a component if it changes its terminal values from those that were negotiated in the first stage. For a given cost function each house solves a Mixed-Integer Program (MIP) to obtain an integer-feasible solution. The two most effective cost functions that we identified are:

$$f_0(y, \hat{y}, \hat{\lambda}) = \hat{\lambda}^{\mathsf{T}} y + \alpha h(y, \hat{y})^{\mathsf{T}} h(y, \hat{y}) \tag{11}$$

$$f_3(y, \hat{y}, \hat{\lambda}) = \hat{\lambda}^{\mathsf{T}} A\hat{y} + \alpha h(y, \hat{y})^{\mathsf{T}} \Lambda h(y, \hat{y}) \tag{12}$$

where, for a given house to bus connection, $\hat{y}$ is the negotiated terminal values for the bus and $\hat{\lambda}$ the negotiated dual variables. We use Λ to represent the diagonal matrix where $\Lambda_{i,i} := |\hat{\lambda}_i|$ and α is a penalty parameter.

The first function charges households at the negotiated price for what they *actually* consume, but they are also charged a quadratic penalty for operating away from the negotiated consumption. The second function requires the household to pay for all power that was negotiated in the first stage. As with the first function, a penalty is charged for operating away from the negotiated operating point, however the penalty is scaled by the dual variables, which can vary with time.

After this local optimisation step, we check that the solution is feasible and what the overall cost is. In order to do this we need to put some degrees of freedom back into the problem. In power networks the dispatch of generators are established in advance, in response to an estimated demand. This forecast is never perfect, so a certain number of generators are paid to perform frequency regulation in order to balance demand in real time. In our experiments we employ both our generators for this use by allowing them to adjust their output. For these experiments we assume the same cost function and prices for both dispatch and frequency regulation.

8.1.2 Relax and Decide

In the second stage of the RD method, the largest u_t value of each shiftable component is chosen to be fixed at 1 and the rest set to 0. In the third stage the distributed algorithm is restarted in order to converge to a new solution that is integer feasible.

8.1.3 Unrelaxed

The final approach, UR, consists of a single stage where it attempts to enforce integrality satisfaction at each iteration of the distributed algorithm. We have already foregone theoretical convergence guarantees by our adoption of the non-convex AC equations. Here we push the ADMM algorithm even further by allowing discrete variables into the algorithm (8–10), where Gurobi solves MIPs for houses, and Ipopt NLPs for lines.

We ran experiments on 60 random instances of our test microgrid for each of the three approaches. We use the AC line model for each experiment and a penalty of $\alpha = 10$ for the RP approach. In the following sections we discuss the convergence of the methods and the quality of the solutions.

8.2 Convergence

None of the approaches are guaranteed to find an integer feasible solution if one exists, however, in practice they all converged to feasible solutions for all experiments on our test microgrid.

The RP method only marginally increases the solve time above the results in Section 7. The RD method requires a small amount of extra time as it performs a warm restart of the distributed algorithm. The UR method takes 1.7 times longer on average, which is a result of the fact that it solves MIPs during each iteration.

8.3 Solution Quality

In order to assess the solution quality for each method, we compare the change in objective value relative to the relaxed version of the problem. The results are shown in Fig. 4, where we have separated the objective into terms for the cost of generation and the charge to households. The charge is the sum of household objective functions, which represents the amount of money they pay for their electricity. For the RP methods this is given by the cost functions in the previous section. For the RD and UR methods the charge is simply the final $\lambda^{\mathsf{T}} y$ for each house.

For the relaxed problem itself, the true cost of generation can be different from the amount households are charged, as we are dealing with marginal prices. In addition to this, network congestion typically generates additional revenue above the cost of generation itself. An increase in cost for the integer feasible solution relative to the relaxed problem is an indication of the additional cost to the generators for balancing supply. When household charge increases rela-

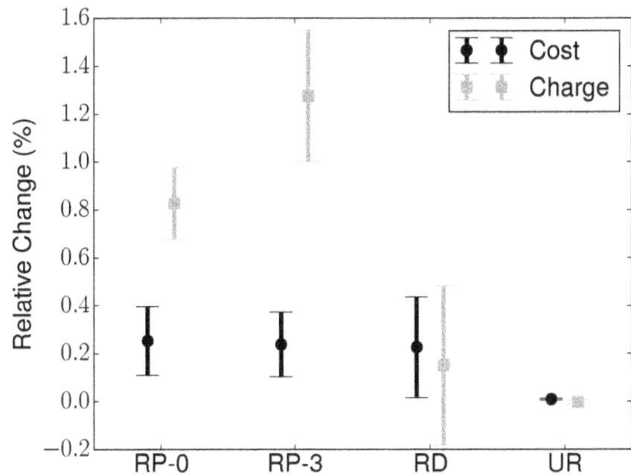

Figure 4: Change in generator cost and household charge relative to relaxed solution.

tive to the relaxed solution, this indicates that households were forced to change their consumption from the negotiated amount to ensure integer feasibility of the shiftable loads.

All methods produce costs that are within 1% of the relaxed problem, and hence also the global optimum. There is no significant difference between the methods as they reside within our estimated margin of error based on our stopping tolerance. What these results suggest is that we have a tight relaxation of the integer problem. A contributing factor is that each shiftable load only contributes a tiny amount to the overall power demand.

By artificially increasing the size of the shiftable loads by more than an order of magnitude, and heavily congesting the network, we do find instances where there is a significant gap between the relaxed solution and the candidate. However, for the realistically sized residential shiftable loads as utilised in our test microgrid, the relaxation was tight.

The charges to households are significantly higher for the RP method without gaining any benefit in terms of reduced costs. We ran the same experiments with a much smaller α, which all but eliminated charges without any increase to costs. When battery storage is introduced, we expect households will have even more flexibility in how they reach their negotiated consumptions, therefore further reducing incurred charges. This suggests that for the sole purpose of managing shiftable loads, there is no need to have a strong penalty. However, the penalty may serve a purpose for managing the effects of uncertainty in the network, and to prevent agents from lying during the negotiation stage.

All of the methods we have presented provide an efficient means for dealing with the discrete decisions in a household. Other factors such as the way they can handle uncertainty and the need for a penalty for agents gaming the system will affect the choice between these methods.

9. CONCLUSION AND FUTURE WORK

We have presented a distributed demand response mechanism for operating a microgrid. It can coordinate a whole range of distributed agents with time-coupled behaviours, whilst preserving network constraints. It also provides a natural way of pricing power in the network.

Using this mechanism we have successfully compared the performance of a range of power flow models in a meshed microgrid, and introduced simple but effective approaches to handling the shiftable loads within households. We developed a suburb-sized test microgrid, and found that the full non-convex AC equations produce close to optimal solutions in short solve times. All three of our methods for handling household shiftable loads produce close to optimal solutions with only a moderate increase in solve times.

Our work has shown that in practice distributed algorithms are not only feasible, but also highly effective at performing demand response within a microgrid context.

In future research we will investigate alternative distributed solving techniques with the aim of further improving the rate of convergence. There are opportunities for finding closed-form solutions for the exact AC equations, and to further parallelise the problem by decomposing certain components across time. It might also be possible to build a frequency regulation market into the distributed algorithm.

We need further experiments to investigate if our results carry over to larger discrete decisions, for example, those related to large industrial plant, generator start-up costs, and line switching. We also plan to answer the important question of how susceptible this mechanism is to gaming in practice, and if this is a problem, what can be done about it.

Acknowledgments

We would like to thank Hassan Hijazi for his helpful technical assistance. NICTA is funded by the Australian Government through the Department of Communications and the Australian Research Council through the ICT Centre of Excellence Program.

10. REFERENCES

[1] J. Andersson. *A General-Purpose Software Framework for Dynamic Optimization.* PhD thesis, Arenberg Doctoral School, KU Leuven, Department of Electrical Engineering (ESAT/SCD) and Optimization in Engineering Center, Kasteelpark Arenberg 10, 3001-Heverlee, Belgium, October 2013.

[2] Australian Energy Market Operator (AEMO). www.aemo.com.au.

[3] X. Bai, H. Wei, K. Fujisawa, and Y. Wang. Semidefinite programming for optimal power flow problems. *International Journal of Electrical Power & Energy Systems*, 30(6âĂŞ7):383 – 392, 2008.

[4] M. Baran and F. Wu. Optimal sizing of capacitors placed on a radial distribution system. *Power Delivery, IEEE Transactions on*, 4(1):735–743, 1989.

[5] S. Bose, S. H. Low, T. Teeraratkul, and B. Hassibi. Equivalent relaxations of optimal power flow. *CoRR*, abs/1401.1876, 2014.

[6] S. Boyd, N. Parikh, E. Chu, B. Peleato, and J. Eckstein. Distributed optimization and statistical learning via the alternating direction method of multipliers. *Foundations and Trends in Machine Learning*, 3(1):1–122, Jan 2011.

[7] Z. Chen, L. Wu, and Y. Fu. Real-time price-based demand response management for residential appliances via stochastic optimization and robust optimization. *Smart Grid, IEEE Transactions on*, 3(4):1822 –1831, dec. 2012.

[8] C. Coffrin and P. V. Hentenryck. A linear-programming approximation of ac power flows. *Informs Journal on Computing*, May 2014.

[9] E. Dall'Anese, H. Zhu, and G. B. Giannakis. Distributed optimal power flow for smart microgrids. *Smart Grid, IEEE Transactions on*, 4(3):1464–1475, 2013.

[10] D. Das. Reconfiguration of distribution system using fuzzy multi-objective approach. *International Journal of Electrical Power & Energy Systems*, 28(5):331 – 338, 2006.

[11] J. Douglas, Jim and J. Rachford, H. H. On the numerical solution of heat conduction problems in two and three space variables. *Transactions of the American Mathematical Society*, 82(2):pp. 421–439, 1956.

[12] T. Erseghe. Distributed optimal power flow using admm. *Power Systems, IEEE Transactions on*, 29(5):2370–2380, Sept 2014.

[13] M. Farivar, C. R. Clarke, S. H. Low, and K. M. Chandy. Inverter var control for distribution systems with renewables. In *SmartGridComm*, pages 457–462. IEEE, 2011.

[14] D. Gabay and B. Mercier. A dual algorithm for the solution of nonlinear variational problems via finite element approximation. *Computers & Mathematics with Applications*, 2(1):17 – 40, 1976.

[15] N. Gast, J.-Y. Le Boudec, and D.-C. Tomozei. Impact of demand-response on the efficiency and prices in real-time electricity markets. In *Proceedings of the 5th International Conference on Future Energy Systems*, e-Energy '14, pages 171–182, New York, NY, USA, 2014. ACM.

[16] N. Gatsis and G. Giannakis. Residential load control: Distributed scheduling and convergence with lost ami messages. *Smart Grid, IEEE Transactions on*, 3(2):770–786, June 2012.

[17] Gurobi Optimization, Inc. Gurobi optimizer reference manual, 2014.

[18] H. L. Hijazi, C. Coffrin, and P. Van Hentenryck. Convex quadratic relaxations for mixed-integer nonlinear programs in power systems. *NICTA Technical Report* `http://www.optimization-online.org/DB_HTML/2013/09/4057.html`, March 2014.

[19] HSL Archive. A collection of fortran codes for large scale scientific computation, 2014.

[20] R. Jabr. Radial distribution load flow using conic programming. *IEEE Transactions on Power Systems*, 21(3):1458–1459, Aug 2006.

[21] B. Kim and R. Baldick. A comparison of distributed optimal power flow algorithms. *Power Systems, IEEE Transactions on*, 15(2):599–604, 2000.

[22] M. Kraning, E. Chu, J. Lavaei, and S. Boyd. Dynamic network energy management via proximal message passing. *Foundations and Trends in Optimization*, 1(2), 2014.

[23] S. Magnússon, P. C. Weeraddana, and C. Fischione. A Distributed Approach for the Optimal Power Flow Problem Based on ADMM and Sequential Convex Approximations. *ArXiv e-prints*, Jan. 2014.

[24] A. Mohsenian-Rad, V. Wong, J. Jatskevich, R. Schober, and A. Leon-Garcia. Autonomous demand-side management based on game-theoretic energy consumption scheduling for the future smart grid. *Smart Grid, IEEE Transactions on*, 1(3):320 –331, dec. 2010.

[25] A.-H. Mohsenian-Rad and A. Leon-Garcia. Optimal residential load control with price prediction in real-time electricity pricing environments. *Smart Grid, IEEE Transactions on*, 1(2):120 –133, sept. 2010.

[26] Q. Peng and S. H. Low. Distributed Algorithm for Optimal Power Flow on a Radial Network. *ArXiv e-prints*, Apr. 2014.

[27] D. Phan and J. Kalagnanam. Some efficient optimization methods for solving the security-constrained optimal power flow problem. *Power Systems, IEEE Transactions on*, 29(2):863–872, March 2014.

[28] S. D. Ramchurn, P. Vytelingum, A. Rogers, and N. R. Jennings. Agent-based control for decentralised demand side management in the smart grid. In Tumer, Yolum, Sonenberg, and Stone, editors, *Proc. of 10th Int. Conf. on Autonomous Agents and Multiagent Systems - Innovative Applications Track (AAMAS 2011)*, pages 330–331, Taipei, Taiwan, May 2011.

[29] F. Schweppe and D. Rom. Power system static-state estimation, part ii: Approximate model. *power apparatus and systems, IEEE transactions on*, (1):125–130, 1970.

[30] P. Scott, S. Thiébaux, M. van den Briel, and P. Van Hentenryck. Residential demand response under uncertainty. In *International Conference on Principles and Practice of Constraint Programming (CP)*, pages 645–660, Uppsala Sweden, sep. 2013.

[31] M. Shinwari, A. Youssef, and W. Hamouda. A water-filling based scheduling algorithm for the smart grid. *Smart Grid, IEEE Transactions on*, 3(2):710–719, June 2012.

[32] H. Tischer and G. Verbic. Towards a smart home energy management system - a dynamic programming approach. In *Innovative Smart Grid Technologies Asia (ISGT), 2011 IEEE PES*, pages 1 –7, nov. 2011.

[33] M. van den Briel, P. Scott, and S. Thiebaux. Randomized load control: A simple distributed approach for scheduling smart appliances. In *International Joint Conference on Artificial Intelligence (IJCAI)*, Beijing, China, August 2013.

[34] P. Šulc, S. Backhaus, and M. Chertkov. Optimal Distributed Control of Reactive Power via the Alternating Direction Method of Multipliers. *ArXiv e-prints*, 2014.

[35] A. Wächter and L. T. Biegler. On the implementation of an interior-point filter line-search algorithm for large-scale nonlinear programming. *Mathematical Programming*, 106(1):25–57, 2006.

Peak-Aware Online Economic Dispatching for Microgrids

Ying Zhang
Information Engineering
The Chinese University of Hong Kong

Mohammad H. Hajiesmaili
Institute of Network Coding
The Chinese University of Hong Kong

Minghua Chen
Information Engineering
The Chinese University of Hong Kong

ABSTRACT

By employing local renewable energy sources and power generation units while connected to the central grid, microgrid can usher in great benefits in terms of cost efficiency, power reliability, and environmental awareness. Economic dispatching is a central problem in microgrid operation, which aims at effectively scheduling various energy sources to minimize the operating cost while satisfying the electricity demand. Designing intelligent economic dispatching strategies for microgrids, however, is drastically different from that for conventional central grids, due to two unique challenges. First, the erratic renewable energy emphasizes the need for online algorithms. Second, the widely-adopted peak-based pricing scheme brings out the need for new peak-aware strategy design. In this paper, we tackle these critical challenges and devise peak-aware online economic dispatching algorithms. For microgrids with fast-responding generators, we prove that our deterministic and randomized algorithms achieve the best possible competitive ratios $2-\beta$ and $e/(e-1+\beta)$, respectively, where $\beta \in [0,1]$ is the ratio between the minimum grid spot price and the local-generation price. Our results characterize the fundamental *price of uncertainty* of the problem. For microgrids with slow-responding generators, we first show that a large competitive ratio is inevitable. Then we leverage limited prediction of electricity demand and renewable generation to improve the competitiveness of the algorithms. By extensive empirical evaluations using real-world traces, we show that our online algorithms achieve near offline-optimal performance. In a representative scenario, our algorithm achieves 23% and 11% cost reduction as compared to the case without local generation units and the case using peak-oblivious algorithms, respectively.

Categories and Subject Descriptors

C.4 [**Performance of Systems**]: Modeling techniques; Design studies; F.1.2 [**Modes of Computation**]: Online computation; I.2.8 [**Problem Solving, Control Methods, and Search**]: Scheduling

Keywords

Microgrids, Online Algorithm, Peak-Aware Scheduling, Economic Dispatching

e-Energy'15, July 14 - 17, 2015, Bangalore, India.
 ISBN 978-1-4503-3609-3/15/07$15.00
DOI: http://dx.doi.org/10.1145/2768510.2768538.

1. INTRODUCTION

Microgrid represents a promising paradigm of future electric power systems that autonomously coordinate distributed renewable energy source (*e.g.*, solar PVs), local generation unit (*e.g.*, gas generators), and the external grid to satisfy time-varying energy demand of a local community. As compared to traditional grids, microgrid has recognized advantages in cost efficiency, environmental awareness, and power reliability. Consequently, worldwide installed microgrid capacity has witnessed a phenomenon growth, reaching 866 MW in 2014, and is expected to reach 4,100 MW by 2020 [4].

Energy generation scheduling in microgrid determines the power output level of local generation units and power to be procured from external grid, with the goal of minimizing the total cost over a pre-determined billing cycle. The scheduling plan should meet the time-varying energy demand and respect physical constraints of the generation units. Such problem has been studied extensively in the power system literature for large-scale traditional grids. Two main variants are unit commitment [13] and economic dispatching [10] problems. The unit commitment problem typically optimizes the start-up and the shut-down schedule of power generation units, whereas the economic dispatching problem optimally schedules the output levels given the on/off status as the input parameters. In this paper, we focus on economic dispatching problem in microgrid scenarios.

At first glance, economic dispatching in microgrid may appear to be a small-scale version of the classical urban-wide economic dispatching problem. However, the following two unprecedented challenges make the problem fundamentally different, thereby the previous solutions inapplicable.

▷ **Uncontrollable, intermittent, and uncertain energy sources.** Classical scheduling strategies rely on accurate prediction of future demand and dispatch-able supply [10]. In microgrids, however, the renewable sources are highly uncontrollable (not available on-demand), intermittent (irregular fluctuations), and uncertain (hard to predict accurately). Incorporating a large fraction of such renewable energy sources makes conventional strategies not applicable, and calls for new *online* scheduling strategies that do not rely on accurate prediction of demand and renewable generation [14,16].

▷ **Peak-based charging model of the external grid.** The real-world pricing scheme for consumers with large loads (such as universities or data centers) adopts a hybrid time-of-use and *peak-based* charging model where the electricity bill consists of both the total energy usage and the peak demand drawn over the billing cycle. The motivation is to encourage large customers to smooth their demand, thereby the utility provider can reduce its planned capacity obligations. The peak price is often more than 100 times higher than the maximum (on-peak) spot price, *e.g.*, 118 times for PG&E [5], and 227 times for Duke Energy Kentucky [3] [1]. Consequently, the contribution of peak charge in the electricity bill for a typical costumer can be considerable, *e.g.*, from 20% to 80% for several Google data centers [21]. These observations suggest that economic dispatching strategies with peak-based charging model taken into account (referred to as peak-aware economic dispatching) may substantially reduce the total operating costs for microgrids as compared to economic dispatching strategies oblivious to peak-based charging (referred to as peak-oblivious economic dispatching). This is indeed the case as verified by our real-world trace-driven evaluation in Sec. 5.

All previous researches on microgrid economic dispatching, that we are aware of and review in Sec. 6, adopt a peak-oblivious cost model, wherein the costumer bill is computed by total energy usage following a time-of-use pricing scheme. To the best of our knowledge, this work is the first that addresses the peak-aware economic dispatching problem using competitive online algorithms in microgrid scenario. The main contributions of the paper are summarized as follows:

▷ We identify and formulate the peak-aware economic dispatching problem of minimizing the operating cost for micro-grids under the hybrid time-of-use and peak-based pricing scheme in Sec. 2. Notably, two aforementioned challenges change the structure of the problem fundamentally (see the discussions in Sec. 3.4 for an example) and call for different online algorithm design.

▷ In Sec. 3, we focus on "fast-responding" generator scenario, where the *ramping* constraints (*i.e.*, the maximum change in output level over successive steps) of local generators are inactive. We follow a *divide-and-conquer* approach and decompose the problem into multiple sub-problems, solve the sub-problems by their "rent-or-buy" nature, and then combine the solutions to obtain a solution for the original problem. We then demonstrate that the competitive ratios of our algorithms are $(2-\beta)$ and $e/(e-1+\beta)$ for deterministic and randomized versions respectively, where $\beta \in [0,1]$ is the ratio between the minimum grid spot price and the generator price. We prove that the ratios are the best possible. As such, these results characterize the fundamental *price of uncertainty* for the problem.

▷ For "slow-responding" generator scenario in Sec. 4, where the ramping constraints are active, we firstly show that a large competitive ratio is inevitable without any future information. We then design an online algorithm with a small competitive ratio by taking the advantage of sufficient looking-ahead information. Our results suggest looking-head as a useful mechanism to neutralize the ramping constraints in online algorithm design.

▷ In Sec. 5, by extensive evaluations using real-world traces, we show that our online algorithms can achieve satisfactory empirical performance. Furthermore, our *peak-aware* online algorithms achieve near offline-optimal performance, and outperform the *peak-oblivious* designs [14,16] under various settings. The substantial cost reduction shows the benefit and necessity of designing peak-aware strategies for economic dispatching in microgrids.

Due to the space limitation, all the proofs can be found in our technical report [23].

[1]In practice, the unit of peak price is \$/KW while the unit of spot price is \$/KWh. This estimation is obtained by assuming the peak demand lasts one hour.

2. PROBLEM FORMULATION

In the microgrid economic dispatching problem, the objective is to orchestrate various energy sources to minimize the operating cost while satisfying the electricity demand.

We consider one billing cycle, which is a finite time horizon set $\mathcal{T} = \{1, \ldots, T\}$ with T discrete time slots. In practice, the duration of one cycle is usually one month and the length of each time slot is 15 minutes [5]. The key notations used in this paper are defined in Table 1.

Table 1: Key notations

Notation	Definition
T	The total number of time slots
$\mathcal{T}$	The time slot set
$e(t)$	The net electricity demand
$u(t)$	The electricity level obtained from local generators
$v(t)$	The electricity level obtained from electricity grid
$p_e(t)$	The spot price of the electricity from grid at time $t, p_e^{\min} \leq p_e(t) \leq p_e^{\max}$, (\$/KWh)
p_g	The unit cost of the electricity by local generators (\$/KWh)
p_m	The peak demand price of the electricity grid (\$/KWh)
R^{u}	The maximum ramping up rate of local generator
R^{d}	The maximum ramping down rate of local generator
C	Local generator capacity

Net electricity demand. We consider arbitrary renewable energy generation. Let $e(t)$ be the net electricity demand in time slot t, *i.e.*, the total electricity demand subtracted by the renewable generation. For ease of presentation and discussion, we assume $e(t)$ only takes nonnegative integer values. Note that we do not assume any specific stochastic model of $e(t)$.

Local generation. There are local generators deployed in the microgrid with C total generation capacity, *i.e.*, they can jointly satisfy at most C units of electricity demand. We consider a practical setting where the generator's incremental power output in two consecutive slots is limited by the *ramping-up* and *ramping-down* constraints R^{u} and R^{d}, respectively. Most microgrids today employ small-capacity generators that are powered by gas turbines or diesel engines. These generators are "fast-responding" in the sense that they have large ramping-up/-down rates. Meanwhile, there are also "slow-responding" generators with small ramping-up/-down rates. We denote p_g as the cost of generating unit electricity using local generation.

Electricity from the external grid. The microgrid can also obtain electricity supply from the external grid for unbalanced electricity demand in an on-demand manner. We denote the spot price at time t from the external grid as $p_e(t)$. We assume that $p_e(t) \geq p_e^{\min} \geq 0$ [2]. Again, we do not assume any stochastic model of $p_e(t)$. For ease of discussion later, we define $\beta \triangleq p_e^{\min}/p_g$ as the ratio between the minimum grid price and the unit cost of local generation.

Cost model. The microgrid operating cost in $\mathcal{T}$ includes the expense of purchasing electricity from the external grid and that of local generation. Let $v(t)$ be the amount of electricity purchased from the external grid and $u(t)$ be the amount of electricity generated locally.

The cost of grid electricity consists of volume charge and peak charge. The volume charge is simply the sum of volume cost in all the time slots, *i.e.*, $\sum_t p_e(t)v(t)$. In practice, the peak charge is based on the maximum single-slot power and the peak price unit is \$/KW [5], which is different from the spot price unit \$/KWh. Let the peak price in \$/KW be $\tilde{p}_m$ and the length of one time slot be δ (*e.g.*, 0.25 hour), we convert the peak price to \$/KWh as $p_m = \tilde{p}_m/\delta$. Consequently, the peak charge is $p_m \max_t v(t)$, *i.e.*, the peak demand over the billing cycle (in KWh) multiplied by p_m (in \$/KWh). This method is similar to the one used in [21]. We remark that p_m is usually more than 100 times larger than $p_e(t)$ [5].

For local generation, the cost of a generator to generate θ amount of electricity is commonly modeled as a quadratic function [13], *i.e.*, say, $a\theta^2 + b\theta + c$. The coefficient a is usually orders of magnitude smaller than b (*e.g.*, for a typical oil generator with capacity 15MW, $a = 0.007, b = 48.5$) [3]. Consequently, for small-capacity generators employed in microgrids, the quadratic term $a\theta^2$ is usually much smaller than the linear term $b\theta$ and is negligible. Let p_g be the unit generating cost. The total local generation cost is simply $\sum_t p_g u(t)$. In this study, we focus on the case where $p_g \geq p_e(t), \forall t \in \mathcal{T}$ [4].

Putting together all the components, the microgird total operating cost over a billing cycle is given by

$$\mathsf{Cost}(\boldsymbol{u}, \boldsymbol{v}) = \underbrace{\sum_{t\in\mathcal{T}} p_e(t)v(t) + p_m \max_{t\in\mathcal{T}} v(t)}_{\text{by external grid}} + \underbrace{\sum_{t\in\mathcal{T}} p_g u(t)}_{\text{by local generators}} . \tag{1}$$

Existing microgrid generation scheduling schemes [14, 16] did not consider the peak charge term $p_m \max_t v(t)$; we refer to these schemes as **Peak-Oblivious**. In this paper, we consider the **Peak-Aware Economic Dispatching (PAED)** problem as follows

$$
\begin{array}{lll}
\textbf{PAED} & \min\limits_{\boldsymbol{u},\boldsymbol{v}} & \mathsf{Cost}(\boldsymbol{u}, \boldsymbol{v}) \\
& \text{s.t.} & u(t) + v(t) \geq e(t), \quad t \in \mathcal{T}, \qquad \text{(2a)} \\
& & u(t) \leq C, \quad t \in \mathcal{T}, \qquad \text{(2b)} \\
& & u(t+1) - u(t) \leq R^{\mathsf{u}}, \quad t \in \mathcal{T}, \quad \text{(2c)} \\
& & u(t) - u(t+1) \leq R^{\mathsf{d}}, \quad t \in \mathcal{T}, \quad \text{(2d)} \\
& \text{var.} & u(t), v(t) \in \mathbb{R}^+, \quad t \in \mathcal{T}.
\end{array}
$$

The constraint in (2a) ensures that the electricity demand is satisfied. The constraint in (2b) is due to the generator capacity limitation. The constraints in (2c)-(2d) reflect the ramping up/down constraints, respectively.

The objective function $\mathsf{Cost}(\boldsymbol{u}, \boldsymbol{v})$ is convex and all the constraints are linear; hence **PAED** is a convex optimization problem. In the offline setting where the net demand in the entire time horizon, *i.e.*, $e(t)$ for all t in $\mathcal{T}$, is given (by for example accurate prediction), problem **PAED** can be solved easily using standard solvers. However, the net demand $e(t)$ in microgrid is hard to predict accurately as it inherits substantial uncertainty from renewable generation. This motivates the need of online strategies that do not rely on accurate net demand prediction to operate [14].

Denote an online algorithm for problem **PAED** by $\mathcal{A}$, we use competitive ratio (**CR**) as the metric to evaluate its performance. For an online algorithm, its competitive ratio is defined as the maximum ratio between the cost it incurs and the offline optimal cost over all inputs, *i.e.*,

$$\mathbf{CR}(\mathcal{A}) \triangleq \max_{\text{all inputs}} \frac{\mathsf{Cost\ incurred\ by\ } \mathcal{A}}{\mathsf{Offline\ optimal\ cost}}.$$

Clearly we have $\mathbf{CR} \geq 1$. It is desired to design online algorithms with small competitive ratios, since it guarantees that, for any input, the cost of the online algorithm is close to the offline optimal. The *price of uncertainty* (**PoU**) for problem **PAED** is defined as the minimum possible competitive ratio across all online algorithms, *i.e.*,

$$\mathbf{PoU} \triangleq \min_{\text{all } \mathcal{A}} \mathbf{CR}(\mathcal{A}).$$

3. FAST-RESPONDING GENERATOR CASE

In this section, we relax the ramping constraints (2c)-(2d) and consider the fast-responding generator scenario. Most generators employed in microgrids can ramp up/down very fast. For example, a diesel-based engine can ramp up/down 40% of its capacity per minute [18]. Considering the time scale of each slot (*e.g.*, 15 minutes), those generators can be thought as having no ramping constraints. That is, $R^{\mathsf{u}} = R^{\mathsf{d}} = \infty$. We note that even though we relax the ramping constraints, the relaxed problem, denoted as **FS-PAED**, still covers many practical scenarios in the current microgrids [14]. Moreover, the results in this section serves a building block for designing online algorithm for the original problem **PAED** with ramping constraints, which we will present in Sec. 4.

In the following, we first focus on a special version of problem **FS-PAED**, named as **FS-PAED**^{k}, where the net demand only takes value 0 or 1. We design optimal online algorithms for problem **FS-PAED**^{k} and then extend the algorithms to solve the general problem **FS-PAED**.

[2]We remark that the electricity spot price can sometime be negative in practice [8]. We restrict our attention to the case with $p_e(t) \geq 0$ in this study and leave the general case with negative price to future work.

[3]This can be further verified by more examples from http://pscal.ece.gatech.edu/archive/testsys/generators.html.

[4]It means generating one unit of electricity locally is no cheaper than purchasing it from the external grid. The approaches and results developed in this paper can be extended to the general case where p_g can be lower than $p_e(t)$.

3.1 Problem FS-PAED^k and An Optimal Offline Solution

We now consider a special version of problem **FS-PAED** as follows:

$$\begin{aligned} \textbf{FS-PAED}^k: \quad & \min \quad \mathsf{Cost}(\boldsymbol{u}^k, \boldsymbol{v}^k) \\ & \text{s.t.} \quad u^k(t) + v^k(t) \geq e^k(t), \quad t \in \mathcal{T}, \\ & \text{var.} \quad u^k(t), v^k(t) \in \mathbb{R}^+, \quad t \in \mathcal{T}, \end{aligned}$$

where $e^k(t)$ only takes value 0 or 1.

We first study the offline setting, where the net demand $e^k(t)$, $t \in \mathcal{T}$, is given ahead of time. We will reveal a useful structure of the optimal offline solution, which we exploit to design efficient online algorithms. Note that problem **FS-PAED**^{k} can be solved by dynamic programming, which however does not seem to bring significant insights for developing online algorithms. As such, in what follows, we study the offline optimal solution from another angle to reveal a useful structure.

Under the setting, the unit cost of local generation is more expensive than the spot price of the external grid, *i.e.*, $p_e(t) < p_g$. However, the expensive local generation can be leveraged to cut off the peak demand satisfied by the external grid and thus the prohibited peak charge from the external grid. Thus, the key in solving problem **FS-PAED** lies in balancing between the cost of using the expensive local generation and the peak charge of using the external grid. It turns out the optimal offline solution, as shown in Lemma 1, is developed by comparing the accumulated cost of using the local generation and the peak charge and leveraging the special structure of $e^k(t)$.

Lemma 1. *An optimal offline solution of* ***FS-PAED***^{k}, *denoted by* $\left\{\left((u^k(t))^*, (v^k(t))^*\right)\right\}_{\mathcal{T}}$, *only takes value 0 and 1 and is given by* $(u^k(t))^* = e^k(k) - (v^k(t))^*$ *and*

- *if* $\sigma > 1$, *then* $(v^k(t))^* = e^k(t)$, *for all* t *in* $\mathcal{T}$,
- *otherwise* $(v^k(t))^* = 0$, *for all* t *in* $\mathcal{T}$.

Here σ *is a critical peak-demand threshold defined by*

$$\sigma \triangleq \frac{1}{p_m}\left[\sum_{t\in\mathcal{T}} (p_g - p_e(t))\, e^k(t)\right]. \tag{3}$$

Remark: (i) Given that $e^k(t)$ is binary, certain mathematical derivation shows that it suffices to constrain the variables $u^k(t)$ and $v^k(t)$ to be 0 or 1, and there is no need to consider the cases where they take fractional values. This greatly simplify the offline solution. (ii) The optimal solution constructed in Lemma 1 is computed given that the critical peak-demand threshold σ is determined. Meanwhile, σ can only be computed in the offline setting where the net demand in the entire horizon is given, and it turns out it is the sufficient statistics of the net demand for characterizing the ratio between the cost of an online algorithm and the offline optimal cost.

3.2 Online Algorithms for Problem FS-PAED^k

The challenge for the online algorithm comes from the fact that it cannot determine the value of critical peak-demand threshold σ ahead of time. This brings out a dilemma in online decision making: *to suffer deficit of local generator and bypass the peak charge or to pay for the peak and enjoy cheaper electricity from the grid.* The most *aggressive* strategy acquires electricity from the grid from the very beginning, while the most *conservative* strategy uses local generation to satisfy all the net demands in the entire horizon, to avoid the peak charge.

An important observation in online decision making for problem **FS-PAED**^{k} is that after purchasing electricity from the grid once, meaning the peak charge has already been paid (and will not be charged again during the current billing cycle), the microgrid should continue to use the cheap electricity from the grid until the end of the billing cycle. It turns out that the key decision is to determine when to start to pay the peak-charge premium and buy electricity from the grid.

To pursue online algorithms with minimum competitive ratio, it turns out that it suffices to focus on online algorithms that switch from local generation to grid electricity procurement when the accumulated local generation deficit exceeds $s \cdot p_m$, where $s \in [0, \infty)$ is an algorithm-specific parameter. For deterministic algorithms, these are the ones switching to grid electricity procurement at time τ that satisfies the following condition for the first time in the entire horizon:

$$\sum_{t=1}^{\tau} (p_g - p_e(t))\, e^k(t) \geq s \cdot p_m.$$

The most aggressive strategy discussed above corresponds to $s = 0$, and the most conservative one corresponds to $s = \infty$. Randomized online algorithms can be then characterized by distributions of s.

3.2.1 An Optimal Deterministic Online Algorithm

For any deterministic online algorithm with parameter s, denoted by $\mathcal{A}_s$, the following proposition characterizes the ratio between its online cost and the offline optimal cost.

PROPOSITION 1. *The ratio between the cost of a deterministic online algorithm with parameter* s *and the offline optimal cost, denoted by* $h(\mathcal{A}_s, \sigma)$, *is given by:*
when $\sigma \leq 1$,

$$h(\mathcal{A}_s, \sigma) = \begin{cases} 1, & \text{if } s > \sigma, \\ 1 + \frac{1-\sigma+s}{\sigma}(1-\beta), & \text{otherwise;} \end{cases} \tag{4}$$

when $\sigma > 1$,

$$h(\mathcal{A}_s, \sigma) = \begin{cases} 1 + \frac{(\sigma-1)(1-\beta)}{(\sigma-1)\beta+1}, & \text{if } s > \sigma, \\ 1 + \frac{s(1-\beta)}{(\sigma-1)\beta+1}, & \text{otherwise.} \end{cases} \tag{5}$$

The competitive ratio for $\mathcal{A}_s$ *is then*

$$\mathbf{CR}(\mathcal{A}_s) = \max_{\sigma} h(\mathcal{A}_s, \sigma). \tag{6}$$

Based on the above proposition, we can design the best deterministic online algorithm by solving the following min-max optimization problem

$$\min_{s} \max_{\sigma} h(\mathcal{A}_s, \sigma). \tag{7}$$

The problem is non-convex and thus challenging on the first sight. However, given a deterministic online algorithm $\mathcal{A}_s$, it turns out the worst cost ratio is obtained when $\sigma = s$, in which case the online algorithm pays for the peak-charge

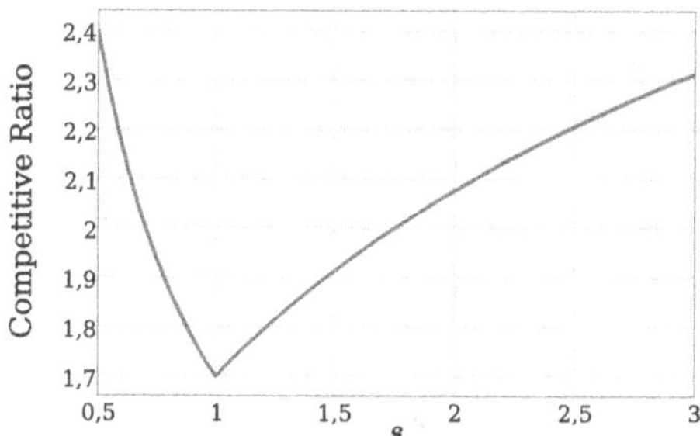

Figure 1: Competitive ratio of $\mathcal{A}_s$ as a function of s, with $\beta = 0.3$.

premium but there is no net demand to serve anymore. Thus we have

$$\max_{\sigma} h(\mathcal{A}_s, \sigma) = h(\mathcal{A}_s, s) = \begin{cases} 1 + \frac{1}{s}(1-\beta), & \text{if } s \leq 1, \\ 1 + \frac{s(1-\beta)}{(s-1)\beta+1}, & \text{otherwise.} \end{cases}$$

Leveraging this observation, the problem in (7) can be solved easily by studying the extreme points of the two functions of s, and the optimal value is obtained when $s = 1$. To visualize how the competitive ratio varies as s changes, we plot the competitive ratio for different values of s in Fig. 1 for the case where $\beta = 0.3$.

We obtain the optimal deterministic online algorithm by setting $s = 1$, named as Break-Even Economic Dispatching for problem **FS-PAED**^{k} (**BED-**k). The algorithm switches from local generation to grid electricity procurement when the accumulated local generation deficit seen so far just equals the peak charge, thus the name "break-even dispatching". We summarize the algorithm **BED-**k into Algorithm 1, and characterize its competitive ratio in the following theorem.

Theorem 1. *The competitive ratio of **BED-**k is given by*

$$\mathbf{CR}\,(\mathbf{BED}\text{−}k) = 2 - \beta.$$

This also gives the price of uncertainty suffered by all deterministic online algorithms, i.e.,

$$\mathbf{PoU}_{det} = \min_{\text{all deterministic } \mathcal{A}_s} \mathbf{CR}\,(\mathcal{A}_s) = 2 - \beta.$$

We remark that the optimal deterministic algorithm is easy to implement and achieves the minimum possible competitive ratio for problem **FS-PAED**^{k}. Next, we proceed to design optimal randomized algorithm for the problem.

3.2.2 An Optimal Randomized Online Algorithm

Recall that for the purpose of designing randomized online algorithms with the minimum competitive ratio for problem **FS-PAED**^{k}, it suffices to consider algorithm $\mathcal{A}_f$ where f represents the probability distribution by which we generate the algorithm-specific threshold s. Based on the analysis for deterministic online algorithms in Sec. 3.2.1, we can find the competitive ratio of $\mathcal{A}_f$ by solving the following optimization problem:

$$\mathbf{CR}\,(\mathcal{A}_f) = \max_{\sigma} \mathbf{E}_f\left[h(\mathcal{A}_f, \sigma)\right] = \max_{\sigma} \int_s h(\mathcal{A}_s, \sigma) f(s) ds. \tag{8}$$

Algorithm 1 BED-k: Optimal deterministic online algorithm for **FS-PAED**^{k}

Require: p_m,p_g,$p_e(t)$,$e^k(t)$
Ensure: $u^k(t)$,$v^k(t)$
$\zeta = 0,\ \tau = 1$
while $\tau \in \mathcal{T}$ **do**
  if $\exists \iota < \tau$ such that $v^k(\iota) = 1$ **then**
    $v^k(\tau) = e^k(\tau),\ u^k(\tau) = 0$
  else
    $\zeta = \zeta + (p_g - p_e(\tau))e^k(\tau)$
    if $\zeta < p_m$ **then**
      $u^k(\tau) = e^k(\tau),\ v^k(\tau) = 0$
    else
      $v^k(\tau) = e^k(\tau),\ u^k(\tau) = 0$
    end if
  end if
  $\tau = \tau + 1$
end while

In the following, we first design a randomized online algorithm by specifying a particular probability distribution and compute its competitive ratio. We then leverage *Yao's Principle* [22] to obtain a lower bound of the competitive ratio of any randomized algorithm. We will see the competitive ratio of our proposed online algorithm matches the lower bound, establishing its optimality. The result thus also characterizes the price of uncertainty suffered by all randomized online algorithms.

We propose a randomized online algorithm by choosing the distribution for s as

$$f^*(s) = \begin{cases} \frac{e^s}{e-1+\beta}, & \text{when } s \in [0,1]; \\ \frac{\beta}{e-1+\beta}\delta(0), & \text{when } s = \infty; \\ 0, & \text{otherwise.} \end{cases} \tag{9}$$

We summarize the resulting randomized online algorithm in to Algorithm 2, named as Randomized Economic Dispatching for problem **FS-PAED**^{k} (**RED-**k). Its competitive ratio is characterized in the following theorem.

Theorem 2. *With the distribution given by $f^*(s)$ in (9), the competitive ratio of **RED-**k is given by*

$$\mathbf{CR}\,(\mathbf{RED}\text{−}k) = \frac{e}{e-1+\beta}.$$

Now we leverage Yao's Principle [22] to obtain a lower bound for the competitive ratio of any randomized online algorithm. The idea is to choose a probability distribution for σ, denoted by $g(\sigma)$, and compute the competitive ratio of the best deterministic online algorithm for this input. Yao's Principle says that the computed ratio is a lower bound for any randomized online algorithm. The particular distribution we use is given by

$$g^*(\sigma) = \begin{cases} \frac{e}{e-1+\beta}\sigma e^{-\sigma}, & \text{when } \sigma \in [0,1], \\ \frac{e}{e-1+\beta}[(\sigma-1)\beta+1]e^{-\sigma}, & \text{otherwise.} \end{cases} \tag{10}$$

The lower bound is characterized in the following lemma.

Theorem 3. *For any randomized online algorithm $\mathcal{A}_f$ for problem **FS-PAED**^{k}, we have*

$$\mathbf{CR}\,(\mathcal{A}_f) \geq \frac{e}{e-1+\beta}.$$

Algorithm 2 RED-k: Optimal randomized online algorithm for **FS-PAED**^{k}

Require: p_m,p_g,$p_e(t)$,$e^k(t)$
Ensure: $u^k(t)$,$v^k(t)$

generate s according to the probability distribution specified in (9)
$\zeta = 0$, $\tau = 1$
while $\tau \in \mathcal{T}$ **do**
  if $\exists \iota < \tau$ such that $v^k(\iota) = 1$ **then**
    $v^k(\tau) = e^k(\tau)$, $u^k(\tau) = 0$
  else
    $\zeta = \zeta + (p_g - p_e(\tau))e^k(\tau)$
    if $\zeta < s \cdot p_m$ **then**
      $u^k(\tau) = e^k(\tau)$, $v^k(\tau) = 0$
    else
      $v^k(\tau) = e^k(\tau)$, $u^k(\tau) = 0$
    end if
  end if
  $\tau = \tau + 1$
end while

*The competitive ratio of algorithm **RED-k** achieves this lower bound and thus is optimal. Consequently, the price of uncertainty suffered by all randomized online algorithms is given by*

$$\mathbf{PoU}ran = \min_{all\ randomized\ \mathcal{A}_f} \mathbf{CR}\left(\mathcal{A}_f\right) = \frac{e}{e-1+\beta}.$$

Remark: (i) In the deterministic online algorithm, setting $s = 1$ means that the microgrid will start to buy electricity from the grid until the break-even condition is met. Similar to the ski rental problem [12], the break-even point turns out to be the best balance between being aggressive and conservative. (ii) The vigilant readers may notice that $f^*(s)$ is the same distribution that was adopted in solving the classic Bahncard problem [9], which is indeed similar to problem **FS-PAED**^{k} we study in this section. The basic version of **FS-PAED**^{k}, however, is different from Bahncard problem in the sense that the *discounted price* ($p_e(t)$ in this paper) is time varying. (iii) Different from the neat tricks used in [9] to prove the optimality of the proposed randomized online algorithm [9], we leverage *Yao's Principle* to prove the optimality of our proposed algorithm **RED-**k for problem **FS-PAED**^{k}. Exploiting the similarity of the two problems, our approach can also be applied to establish optimality of the proposed algorithm for the Bahncard problem in [9].

3.3 From Problem FS-PAED^k to Problem FS-PAED

In this section, we design online deterministic and randomized algorithms for **FS-PAED** based on those of **FS-PAED**^{k}.

3.3.1 Net Demand Layering

For each time slot t, we divide the demand $e(t)$ into multiple layers such that the demand of each layer is either 1 or 0, as shown in Fig. 2. Recall that $e(t)$ is assumed to take non-negative integer values. We denote the sub-problem of satisfying the demand of each layer as **FS-PAED**^{k}, $k = 1, 2, ...$, and we can apply the online algorithms **BED-**k and **RED-**k for each sub-problem.

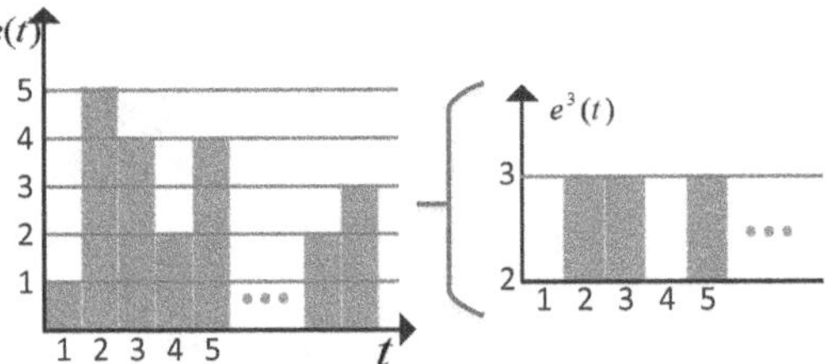

Figure 2: An example of decomposing the demand into multiple layers and a microscopic view of layer 3

3.3.2 Optimal Online Algorithms for FS-PAED

After layering, a bunch of sub-problems **FS-PAED**^{k} are obtained. However, unlike **FS-PAED**^{k}, the net demand of **FS-PAED** in some time slots can exceed the capacity of local generation, which makes it infeasible to ignore the whole picture when conquering each layer independently. For example, suppose the generation capacity is 4 for the case shown in Fig. 2. Even though the break even points are not reached for all the layers in time slot 2, it is infeasible to set $u^k(2) = 1$ for all the layers (A capacity of 5 is needed to do so). Thus by taking into account the capacity constraint, we need to determine for which layers the demand should be satisfied by the grid while still keeping the algorithm competitive.

An obvious but critical observation is that the demands in the lower layers are denser than those in the upper layers. In addition, after being charged for the peak, we expect more demands to come to enjoy the cheap grid electricity. Consequently, it is always more economic to use the grid electricity to satisfy the denser demands, *i.e.*, the lower layers. In other words, in the proper algorithm design, the layers below $(e(t) - C)^+$ should always be satisfied by the grid. Meanwhile, for the layers above $(e(t) - C)^+$, if the demand is already satisfied by the grid, the online algorithm continues to acquire the electricity from the grid; otherwise, Algorithm **BED-**k or **RED-**k is applied with the same value s for all layers to obtain the sub-solutions. The solution is finally obtained by combining the sub-solutions. We summarize the resulting deterministic an randomized online algorithms, named as **BED** and **RED**, in Algorithm 3 and 4, respectively.

Algorithm 3 BED: Optimal deterministic online algorithm for **FS-PAED**

Require: C,p_m,p_g,$p_e(t)$,$e(t)$
Ensure: $u(t)$,$v(t)$

while $\tau \in \mathcal{T}$ **do**
  A threshold: $\varsigma = (e(\tau) - C)^+$.
  For the layers below ς, $v^k(\tau) = 1$, $u^k(\tau) = 0$
  For the layers above ς, run **BED-**k to obtain $u^k(\tau)$ and $v^k(\tau)$.
  $u(\tau) = \sum_k u^k(\tau)$, $v(\tau) = \sum_k v^k(\tau)$
  $\tau = \tau + 1$
end while

We demonstrate a toy example of the solution given by **BED** in Fig. 3. For simplicity, we assume the break-even condition is firstly met when the third nonzero demands comes for all the layers, and the local capacity is 4. We

Algorithm 4 RED: Optimal randomized online algorithm for **FS-PAED**

Require: C,p_m,p_g,$p_e(t)$,$e(t)$
Ensure: $u(t)$,$v(t)$

while $\tau \in \mathcal{T}$ **do**
  A threshold: $\varsigma = (e(\tau) - C)^+$.
  For the layers below ς, $v^k(\tau) = 1$, $u^k(\tau) = 0$
  For the layers above ς, run **RED-**k with the same randomized parameter s to obtain $u^k(\tau)$ and $v^k(\tau)$.
  $u(\tau) = \sum_k u^k(\tau)$, $v(\tau) = \sum_k v^k(\tau)$
  $\tau = \tau + 1$
end while

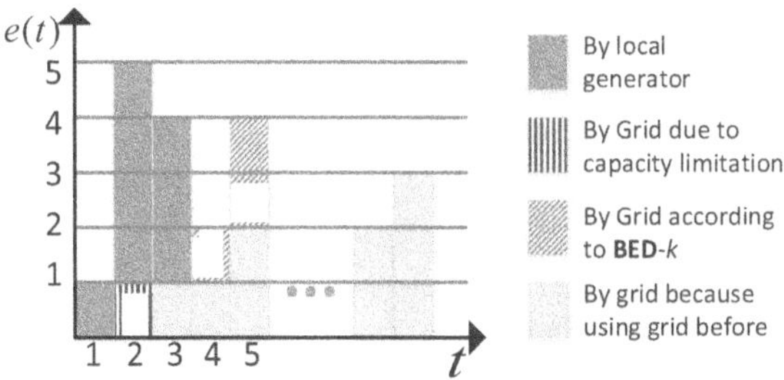

Figure 3: Demonstration of BED with $C = 4$, different colors denoting different strategies of the algorithm.

use different colors to demonstrate by which source and for what reason one unit of demand is satisfied. Even though the example is simple, it demonstrates two important and provable properties of **BED**: (i) For each layer, it will continue to use the grid after it uses it once, and (ii) when one layer uses the grid, all the layers below it use the grid too. The first property makes the solution and cost structure similar to that of **BED-**k, while the second property makes the peak of $v(t)$ equal to the sum of the peaks of $v^k(t)$, *i.e.*, $\max_t \sum_k v^k(t) = \sum_k \max_t v^k(t)$. The two properties allow us to leverage the results in Sec. 3.2 to establish the competitive ratios of **BED** and **RED**.

Theorem 4. *The competitive ratios of **BED** and **RED** are given by*

$$\mathbf{CR}(\mathbf{RED}) = 2 - \beta, \quad \text{and} \quad \mathbf{CR}(\mathbf{RED}) = \frac{e}{e - 1 + \beta}.$$

Further, no other deterministic and randomized online algorithm can achieve a smaller competitive ratio.

In the next subsection, we discuss an intriguing consequence of local generation capacity on the online algorithms' performance.

3.4 Critical Local Generation Capacity

The peak-aware economic dispatching aims at minimizing the sum of the peak charge (the term $p_m \max_{t \in \mathcal{T}} v(t)$ in (1)) and the volume charge (as the remaining part in (1)). The local generator provides the microgrid an option to use more expensive electricity (increase the volume charge) to reduce the peak (decrease the peak charge). An optimal solution is achieved with the best tradeoff between the two. Given an input, there is a threshold $\tilde{C}$, the demand below which should be satisfied by the grid and above which by the local generator. $\tilde{C}$ can be obtained by solving **FS-PAED** in an offline fashion without considering capacity constraint. It means that the optimal offline solution will not use the additional capacity even if it is larger than $\tilde{C}$.

We now discuss the impact of increasing local generation capacity C on the performance of offline and online algorithms. The offline algorithm will use full local capacity until C reaches $\tilde{C}$, and it will not use local capacity further beyond $\tilde{C}$. As such, one can expect that the operating cost of the offline algorithm is non-increasing as C increases. Meanwhile, the online algorithm, without knowing $\tilde{C}$ and with the tendency of reducing the peak with more expensive electricity, will try to exploit the whole capacity until it finds the break even point, which turns out to be less economic and deviates more from the optimal solution. As a result, for the online algorithm, larger capacity may incur higher operating cost. We provide a concrete case-study by real world traces to confirm the above observation in Sec. 5.

Overall, we believe the above insights are important for microgrid operators to (a) determine the amount of local generation to invest in order to maximize the economic benefit, and (b) understand the importance of demand/generation prediction when performing peak-aware economic dispatching in microgrids.

4. SLOW-RESPONDING GENERATOR CASE

This section considers the slow-responding generator scenario, in which the ramping up/down constraints in (2c)-(2d) are non-negligible. We remark that we can still optimally solve the problem **PAED** with these constraints in the offline manner by convex optimization techniques.

In the following analysis, we assume $R^{\mathrm{u}} = R^{\mathrm{d}} = R$ and define $\Gamma = \lceil \frac{C}{R} \rceil$. Then, it takes Γ time slots for the local generator's output to ramp up from zero to full capacity or down from full capacity to zero. Considering the time scale of our problem (say, 15 minutes for each time slot) and the microgrid scenario (high efficiency of local generators), Γ is conceivable to be small. We assume Γ is no larger than 5, meaning it roughly takes no more than 75 minutes for local generator to fully ramp up.

We first show a result highlighting the difficulty introduced by the ramping constraints in designing competitive online economic dispatching algorithms.

PROPOSITION 2. *Any online algorithm for problem **PAED** without future information,* i.e., *at time t the algorithm only have knowledge of $\{e(\tau), p_e(\tau)\}_{\tau=1}^{t}$, has a competitive ratio at least $\frac{p_m(C-R)+p_g R}{p_g(R\Gamma(\Gamma-1)+C)}$.*

When Γ is 5 and p_m is 100 times of p_g, a back-of-envelop calculation reveals that the lower bound of the competitive ratio can be as large as 20. This result shows that the ramping constraints will make any online algorithm design less attractive as the worst performance can be rather bad. The conventional method to address this problem is to put additional constraints on the input to obtain algorithms with reasonable performance guarantee [16]. In this paper, we propose to handle the challenge incurred by ramping constraints by a different approach; that is to empower the algorithm with a limited looking ahead window.

4.1 An Effective Online Algorithm by a Limited Looking-ahead Window

Motivated by the development of prediction algorithms [17,25], we assume that a limited looking ahead window with size of $\Delta = \Gamma - 1$ is available, which means that at time t we can know the input from $t+1$ to $t+\Delta$ in advance. In this section, we devise an online algorithm by leveraging such looking ahead information as well as the results in Sec 3. We name the proposed algorithm as NRBF (Neutralize Ramping constraint By Future information). We denote the online solutions we obtain for **PAED** by NRBF as $\tilde{u}(t), \tilde{v}(t)$.

In NRBF , we first solve problem **FS-PAED** by relaxing the ramping constraints from problem **PAED** and denote the solutions obtained by algorithms **BED** or **RED** as $u(t)$ and $v(t)$. We then adjust them to obtain online solutions for **PAED** that satisfy the ramping constraints. Specifically, we compute $\tilde{u}(t)$ as

$$\tilde{u}(t) = \max\{\tilde{u}(t-1) - R, u(t+i) - iR | i = 0, 1, .., \Delta\},$$

and $\tilde{v}(t) = \max(e(t) - \tilde{u}(t), 0)$.

The following lemma shows that the ramping constraints are respected by NRBF.

Lemma 2. *The solutions by NRBF satisfy the generator's ramping constraints, i.e.,*

$$|\tilde{u}(t+1) - \tilde{u}(t)| \leq R.$$

Meanwhile, we can have $\tilde{v}(t) \leq v(t)$, meaning the peak charge is upper bounded by that of the fast responding scenario. We leverage this observation to show the competitiveness of NRBF, as shown in Theorem 5.

Theorem 5. *The competitive ratio of NRBF satisfies*

$$\textbf{CR}(\mathsf{NRBF}) \leq \begin{cases} \Gamma(2-\beta), & \text{if } u(t), v(t) \text{ are obtained by } \textbf{BED}; \\ \Gamma\frac{e}{e-1+\beta}, & \text{if } u(t), v(t) \text{ are obtained by } \textbf{RED}. \end{cases}$$

Remark: Small values of Γ, which mean the ramping constraints are less strict, will lead to a small bound on the competitive ratio. Moreover, $\Gamma = 1$ indicates that the generator output can ramp up to its full capacity in one time slot and the ramping constraints vanish, thereby we do not need any future information ($\Delta = 0$) and the competitive ratio is exactly the same with that of the fast-responding generator scenario.

5. EXPERIMENTAL RESULTS

We carry out numerical experiments using real-world traces to scrutinize the performance of our online algorithms under various practical settings. Our purpose is to investigate (i) the competitiveness of online algorithms in comparison with the optimal offline one, (ii) the necessity of peak-awareness in economic dispatching of microgrids, and (iii) the performance of online algorithms under various parameter settings.

5.1 Experimental Setup

Electricity demand and renewable generation traces. We set the length of one billing circle as one month. We use the actual electricity demand of a college in San Francisco; its yearly demand is about 154GWh [1]. We inject renewable energy supply sources by a wind power trace

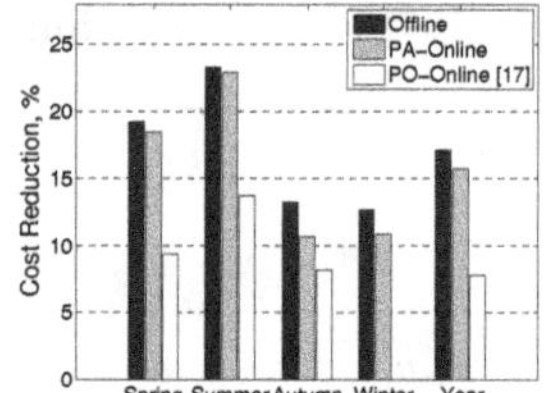

Figure 4: Cost reduction for different seasons and the whole year

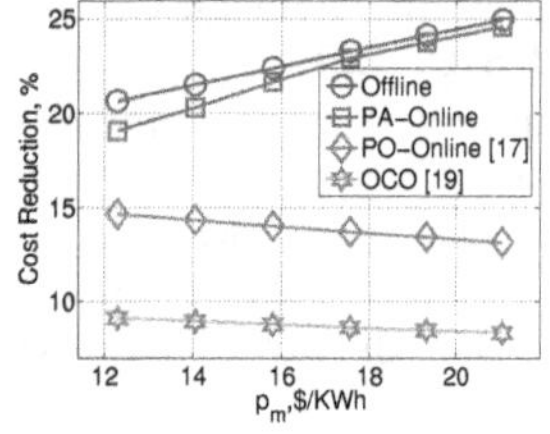

Figure 5: Cost reduction vs p_m

of a nearby offshore wind station outside San Francisco with a total installed capacity of 12MW [2]. We then construct the net demand by subtracting the output level of the wind from the college electricity demand.

Energy source parameters. The electricity price $p_e(t)$ and peak price p_m are set based on the tariffs from PG&E [5] and $p_m = 17.56\$/\text{KWh}$ while the electricity rate $p_e(t)$ varies from 0.056\$/KWh to 0.232\$/KWh for off-, mid-, and on-peak periods in different seasons. We set the unit cost of local generation p_g according to the monthly price of natural gas. Notably, the value of p_g could be less than $p_e(t)$ for some on-peak intervals. In such situations, generator plays its role not only by cutting off the peak but also by providing cheaper electricity as well. Finally, if not specified, the capacity of the local generator is set to be $C = 15\text{MWh}$, which is around 60% of the peak net demand.

Cost benchmark. We use the cost incurred by only procuring electricity from the external grid, *i.e.*, $v(t) = e(t)$, as the benchmark. We demonstrate cost reduction to show the benefit of employing local generation units and the effectiveness of algorithms. The cost reduction originates from the cheaper electricity (in some on-peak intervals) and peak cut-off by local generators.

Comparison of algorithms. We compare our proposed peak-aware online economic dispatching (PA-Online) algorithms with (i) the optimal peak-aware offline solution (OFFLINE) to evaluate the performance of the online algorithms, and (ii) the peak-oblivious online algorithms (PO-Online) in [14] and online convex optimization approach (OCO) in [16] to investigate the importance of peak-awareness.[5] We remark that both schemes in [14,16] are peak-oblivious as they only consider volume charge but ignore peak charge.

The results reported in Secs. 5.2- 5.4 cover the fast-responding generator scenarios and Sec. 5.5 is devoted to the slow-responding generator scenario.

5.2 Benefits of Employing Local Generators

Purpose. The purpose of this experiment is two-fold. First, compare the potential savings of microgrid in different seasons, in which the demand pattern, the wind output, and the cost parameters differ. Second, compare the cost

[5]We remark that in [14], the joint unit commitment and economic dispatching problem in peak-oblivious manner is addressed and in this paper we compare the economic dispatching part with our algorithms. OCO in [16] (without considering the peak charge) is designed deliberately to tackle the ramping constraints and may suffer performance loss in the fast responding generator scenario.

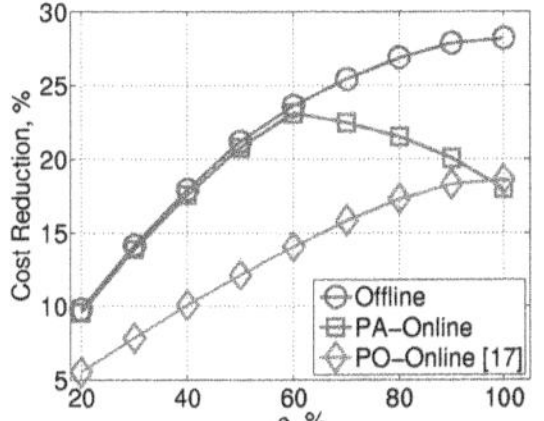

Figure 6: Cost reduction vs ρ

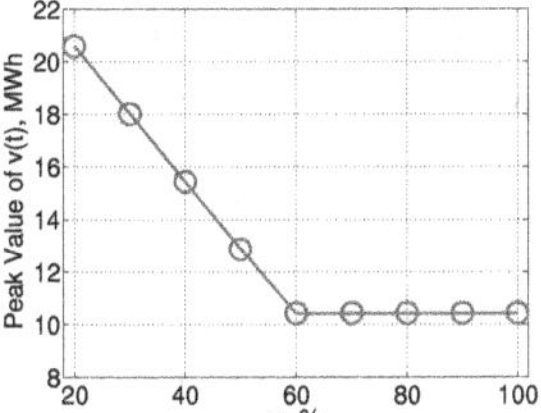

Figure 7: Peak value of $v(t)$ vs ρ

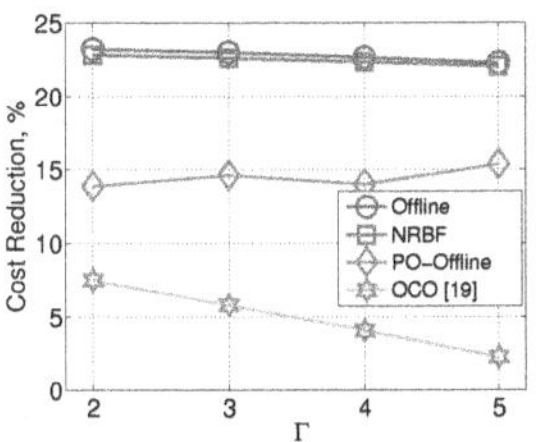

Figure 8: Cost reduction vs Γ

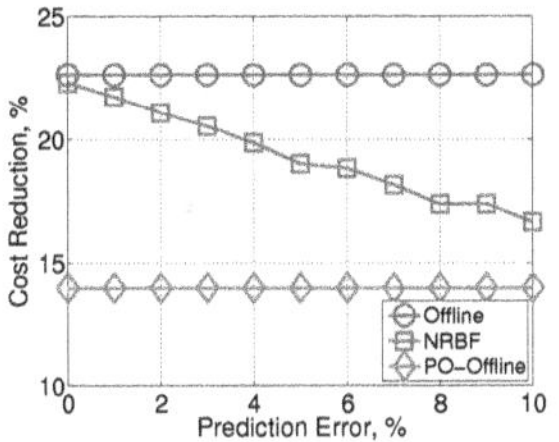

Figure 9: Cost reduction vs prediction error

reduction of peak-aware algorithms against peak-oblivious ones. The results are shown in Fig. 4.

Observations. The most notable observations from Fig. 4 are the following. First of all, the cost reduction varies over seasons and the most significant one occurs in the summer. This is because the gas price is lower and the grid electricity price is higher in the summer than those of the other seasons, thus employing local generators brings more benefit. Second, the performance of our proposed PA-Online is superior than PO-Online algorithm. In particular, PO-Online cannot reduce the cost in the winter, but our algorithm PA-Online can still achieve cost reduction. The reason is that, as $p_g > p_e(t)$ always holds in the winter, PO-Online algorithm always purchases cheaper electricity from the gird, which gives no cost reduction as compare to the benchmark strategy. In contrast, our PA-Online algorithm reduces the cost by exploiting (the expensive) local generation to reduce the peak demand served by the external grid, and consequently our algorithm can save operating cost. On average, PA-Online reduces the annual cost by 15.7%, while PO-Online reduces the cost only by 8.17%. *Third*, the performance of PA-Online in practice is close to that of the offline optimal.

5.3 The Performance of PA-Online under Different Peak Prices

Purpose. To validate the peak charge is non-negligible which motivates our study, we evaluate the performance of our peak-aware algorithm and that of the peak-oblivious one under different peak prices. In particular, in Fig. 5, we depict the cost reduction of different algorithms with the peak price p_m varying from 12.29\$/KWh to 21.07\$/KWh.

Observations. When p_m increases, the cost reduction of our PA-Online algorithm increases and is close to the offline optimal, while the reductions of the two peak oblivious algorithms decrease. This observation shows that our PA-Online algorithm is more effective and the cost reduction is more significant for microgrids with high peak prices.

5.4 The Performance of PA-Online under Different Local Generation Capacities

Purpose. At first glance, one may imagine that larger local generator leads to larger design space and thus larger cost reduction is expected. However, as discussed in Sec. 3.4, this is not the case for online algorithms that do not have the complete future knowledge of price and demand. We carry out an experiment to verify and elaborate the observation. For convenience, we define $\rho = C/\max e(t)$ as the ratio of local generation capacity over the peak net demand and change ρ from 20% to 100%. The result is shown in Fig. 6.

Observations. The results for OFFLINE and PO-Online algorithms follow the intuition that more local capacity brings more cost reduction. For PA-Online, however, we observe that the cost reduction increases when ρ increases from 20% to 60%, and degrades as ρ continues to increase from 60% to 100%. As we discussed in Sec. 3.4, there exists a critical local generation capacity $\tilde{C}$ beyond which the peak charge and the overall cost will not decrease further. In Fig. 7, we report the peak grid demand $\max v(t)$ versus ρ just for OFFLINE algorithm. Results show that the peak value of $v(t)$ does not decrease as ρ increases from 60% to 100%, evincing that $\tilde{C}$ is about 60% of the maximum demand in this case. The online algorithm, however, is unaware of $\tilde{C}$. As discussed in Sec. 3.4, $\tilde{C}$ can be computed by solving problem **FS-PAED** in an offline manner.

The online algorithm, without knowing $\tilde{C}$ and with the tendency of reducing the peak charge by using more expensive local generation, will try to exploit the entire local generation capacity until the cost-benefit break even point is reached, which turns out to be less economic and deviate from the offline optimal. As a result, for the online algorithm, larger capacity may incur higher operating cost, as shown in Fig. 6.

This experiment, together with the discussions in Sec. 3.4, show that it is important for the microgrid operator to set the local generation capacity right at $\tilde{C}$ to cope with online algorithms to achieve maximum cost reduction. A possible way to set $\tilde{C}$ is to use the historical data as the input to the offline algorithm and obtain the critical capacity.

5.5 The Impact of Ramping Constraints

Purpose. The experiment is devoted to explore the performance of our algorithm NRBF for slow-responding generators. We firstly change the ramping constraint such that Γ increases from 2 to 5 and evaluate the performance of the algorithms. We recall the meaning of Γ, as defined in Sec. 4, is that it takes Γ slots for local generators to ramp up from zero to full capacity or down from full capacity to zero. The result is demonstrated in Fig. 8.

Secondly, we relax the assumption that we can perfectly predict near future information. We add a zero mean gaussian noise to the net demand as the predicted input for our algorithm. Note that we can always satisfy unexpected demand by purchasing electricity from the external grid. We evaluate the performance of NRBF with standard deviation of the gaussian noise increasing from 0% to 10% of the actual demand. We use $\Gamma = 4$ for the experiment and NRBF utilizes 3-slot looking ahead demand and price information. The simulation results are shown in Fig. 9.

Observations. From Fig. 8, we observe that all cost reductions decrease as ramping constraints are more strict, while the performance of NRBF is always close to the offline optimal. This shows the effectiveness of using limited prediction in combating the difficulty in online scheduling caused by ramping constraints. Moreover, Fig. 9 shows that the prediction error will degrade the performance of NRBF . However, the performance is still significantly better than the peak-oblivious scheduling.

6. RELATED WORK

Microgrid is attracting substantial attention from both academic and industrial communities due to its economic and environmental benefits, evidenced by a number of real-world pilot microgrid projects [7].

With the penetration of renewable energy in microgrids, conventional economic dispatching approaches based on accurate demand prediction for power grid [10] are not applicable as the net demand inherits substantial uncertainty from the renewable generation and is hard to predict accurately. Online algorithm design is advocated by researchers to offer a paradigm-shrift alternative. Online convex optimization [16], Lyapunov optimization [11], and competitive analysis [14] are the main approaches adopted for online energy generation scheduling in microgrid. The authors in [14] study the unit commitment and economic dispatching problems of microgrid under the volume charging model. Our work considers economic dispatching under both the peak charging and volume charging model.

The cost minimization problem based on real-world peak charging scheme has been considered for microgird scenario in [15], by utilizing Energy Storage Systems to cut off the peak. In contrast, our work tackles the problem using local generators to shave the peak. The cost minimization with the same pricing mechanism taken into account is also studied for data centers in [19, 21], for EV charging in [24], and for content delivery in [6]. For fast-responding generator scenario, the economic dispatching problem we study in this paper can be considered as a generalization of the classic Bahncard problem [9]. The Bahncard problem and its solutions have also found application in the instance acquisition problem of cloud computing [20].

7. CONCLUSION AND FUTURE WORK

In this paper, we devised peak-aware online economic dispatching algorithms for microgrids, with peak charging model taken into account. In the fast-responding generator scenario, we developed both deterministic and randomized online algorithms with best possible competitive ratios following a divide-and-conquer approach. Our results not only characterized the fundamental price of uncertainty for the problem, but also served as a building block for designing online algorithms for the slow-responding generator scenario, where we proposed to tackle the ramping constraints using a limited look-ahead window. In addition to sound theoretical performance guarantees, the empirical evaluations based on real-world traces also corroborated our claim on the importance of peak-awareness in scheduling.

An interesting future direction is to study the microgrid economic dispatching problem under accurate or noisy prediction of future demand and renewable generation within a limited looking-ahead window.

Acknowledgement

The authors would like to thank Qi Zhu for the discussions on peak charging in the initial stage of the study. The first author wants to thank Shaoquan Zhang for proofreading the paper. The work described in this paper was supported by National Basic Research Program of China (Project No. 2013CB336700) and the University Grants Committee of the Hong Kong Special Administrative Region, China (General Research Fund Project No. 14201014 and Theme-based Research Scheme Project No. T23-407/13-N).

8. REFERENCES

[1] California commercial end-use survey, http://capabilities.itron.com/CeusWeb.

[2] National renewable energy laboratory, http://wind.nrel.gov.

[3] http://www.duke-energy.com/rates/kentucky/electric.asp.

[4] http://www.navigantresearch.com.

[5] http://www.pge.com/nots/rates/tariffs/rateinfo.shtml.

[6] M. Adler, R. K. Sitaraman, and H. Venkataramani. Algorithms for optimizing the bandwidth cost of content delivery. *Computer Networks*, 55(18):4007–4020, 2011.

[7] M. Barnes. Real-world microgrid-an overview. In *IEEE International Conference on System of Systems Engineering*, 2007.

[8] E. Fanone, A. Gamba, and M. Prokopczuk. The case of negative day-ahead electricity prices. *Energy Economics*, 35:22–34, 2013.

[9] R. Fleischer. On the bahncard problem. *Theoretical Computer Science*, 268(1):161–174, 2001.

[10] Z.-L. Gaing. Particle swarm optimization to solving the economic dispatch considering the generator constraints. *IEEE Trans. on Power Systems*, 18(3):1187–1195, 2003.

[11] Y. Huang, S. Mao, and R. Nelms. Adaptive electricity scheduling in microgrids. In *Proc. IEEE INFOCOM*, pages 1142–1150, 2013.

[12] A. R. Karlin, M. S. Manasse, L. Rudolph, and D. D. Sleator. Competitive snoopy caching. *Algorithmica*, 3(1-4):79–119, 1988.

[13] S. A. Kazarlis, A. Bakirtzis, and V. Petridis. A genetic algorithm solution to the unit commitment problem. *IEEE Trans. on Power Systems*, 11(1):83–92, 1996.

[14] L. Lu, J. Tu, C.-K. Chau, M. Chen, and X. Lin. Online energy generation scheduling for microgrids with intermittent energy sources and co-generation. In *Proc. ACM SIGMETRICS*, pages 53–66, 2013.

[15] A. Mishra, D. Irwin, P. Shenoy, and T. Zhu. Scaling distributed energy storage for grid peak reduction. In *Proc. ACM e-Energy*, pages 3–14, 2013.

[16] B. Narayanaswamy, V. K. Garg, and T. Jayram. Online optimization for the smart (micro) grid. In *Proc. ACM e-Energy*, pages 1–19, 2012.

[17] J. W. Taylor, L. M. de Menezes, and P. E. McSharry. A comparison of univariate methods for forecasting electricity demand up to a day ahead. *International Journal of Forecasting*, 22(1):1–16, 2006.

[18] A. Vuorinen. *Planning of optimal power systems*. Ekoenergo Oy Espoo, Finland, 2007.

[19] C. Wang, B. Urgaonkar, Q. Wang, and G. Kesidis. A hierarchical demand response framework for data center power cost optimization under real-world electricity pricing. In *Proc. IEEE MASCOTS*, 2014.

[20] W. Wang, B. Li, and B. Liang. To reserve or not to reserve: Optimal online multi-instance acquisition in iaas clouds. In *Proc. ICAC*, 2013.

[21] H. Xu and B. Li. Reducing electricity demand charge for data centers with partial execution. In *Proc. ACM e-Energy*, 2014.

[22] A. C.-C. Yao. Probabilistic computations: Toward a unified measure of complexity. In *IEEE 18th Annual Symposium on Foundations of Computer Science*, pages 222–227, 1977.

[23] Y. Zhang, M. H. Hajiesmaili, and M. Chen. Peak-aware online economic dispatching for microgrids. *CUHK, Tech. Rep., http://www.ie.cuhk.edu.hk/ mhchen/papers/PAED2015tr.pdf*.

[24] S. Zhao, X. Lin, and M. Chen. Peak-minimizing online EV charging. In *Proc. Allerton*, 2013.

[25] T. Zhu, A. Mishra, D. Irwin, N. Sharma, P. Shenoy, and D. Towsley. The case for efficient renewable energy management in smart homes. In *Proc. ACM BuildSys*, pages 67–72, 2011.

Integrating Energy Storage in Electricity Distribution Networks

Aditya Mishra*, Ramesh Sitaraman*, David Irwin*, Ting Zhu‡,
Prashant Shenoy*, Bhavana Dalvi§, and Stephen Lee*
*Univ. of Massachusetts Amherst, ‡Univ. of Maryland Baltimore County , § Carnegie Mellon University
{adityam,ramesh,irwin}@cs.umass.edu, zt@umbc.edu, shenoy@cs.umass.edu,
bbd@cs.cmu.edu, stephenlee@cs.umass.edu

ABSTRACT

Electricity generation combined with its transmission and distribution form the majority of an electric utility's recurring operating costs. These costs are determined, not only by the aggregate energy generated, but also by the maximum instantaneous peak power demand required over time. Prior work proposes using energy storage devices to reduce these costs by periodically releasing energy to lower the electric grid's peak demand. However, prior work generally considers only a single storage technology employed at a single level of the electric grid's hierarchy. In this paper, we examine the efficacy of employing different combinations of storage technologies at different levels of the grid's distribution hierarchy. We present an optimization framework for modeling the primary characteristics that dictate the lifetime cost of many prominent energy storage technologies. Our framework captures the important tradeoffs in placing different technologies at different levels of the distribution hierarchy with the goal of minimizing a utility's operating costs. We evaluate our framework using real smart meter data from 5000 customers of a local electric utility. We show that by employing hybrid storage technologies at multiple levels of the distribution hierarchy, utilities can reduce their daily operating costs due to distributing electricity by up to 12%.

Categories and Subject Descriptors

J.7 [**Computer Applications**]: Computers in Other Systems—*Command and control*

Keywords

Energy; Battery; Electricity; Grid; Peak shaving

1. INTRODUCTION

Nearly 40% of energy in the U.S. is consumed in the form of electricity [28]. Increasing the percentage of electrical energy is an important part of creating a clean and sustainable energy supply, as "green" energy, e.g., from solar and wind, is generally consumed in the form of electricity. In addition, transmitting and distributing electricity is significantly more efficient than transmitting and distributing other captive energy sources, e.g., via oil and gas pipelines or trucks. However, electricity transmission and distribution (T&D) costs are non-trivial, and, in some cases, such as New York and southern California, now dominate generation costs [34]. The cost and carbon footprint to generate electricity is a complex function of the electricity demand patterns, mix of generators and fuel sources, penetration of renewable energy, and T&D efficiency.

A significant fraction of these costs are determined by the electric grid's peak power demand. The peak demand influences capital costs by dictating the capacity (and number) of transmission lines, substations, transformers, etc., since utilities must size these to service the peak. In addition, since the "peaking" generators utilities activate to satisfy demand peaks are significantly less efficient and more expensive to operate than baseload generators that are continuously active, peak power demands also influence operational costs. Thus, satisfying even brief peak demand periods has a disproportionate affect on capital and operational expenses. For example, recent estimates attribute as much as 20% of the grid's generation costs in the U.S. to servicing only the top 100 hours of peak demand each year [32]. Finally, since energy lost in transmission and distribution is a function of the square of current, rising peak demand results in quadratically higher transmission losses.

The importance of reducing peak demand is one of the primary motivations for Demand Response (DR) programs, which attempt to coerce consumers into actively shifting their load from peak to off-peak periods. Since requiring consumers to actively change their behavior to shift load is often not effective, recent work has explored the use of energy storage to automatically shift load in the background, i.e., by storing energy during off-peak periods and using it during peak periods [22, 29, 30]. Prior work in this area has generally examined deploying energy storage devices (ESDs) in individual homes, where the approach can potentially reduce a consumer's electricity bill if electricity prices vary over time, e.g., such that peak prices are higher than off-peak prices. In fact, such energy arbitrage is an explicit use-case cited by Tesla for its new PowerWall battery, which is designed for deployment in homes [19].

While prior research, and now commercial products, target energy storage for homes, such storage can be deployed at any level of the grid's hierarchy from the lowest level (at homes) to the medium level (at distribution transformers) to the top level (at distribution and bulk power substations). The choice of where to deploy energy storage presents interesting tradeoffs. For example, using energy storage in individual homes to reduce the home's peak demand requires more aggregate storage capacity than employing storage at a higher level of the grid hierarchy, since each home's peak demand does not occur at the same time yielding some smoothing from statistical multiplexing at higher levels. Since prior research largely focuses on deploying energy storage in homes, it also generally focuses on only a single type of storage technology: in particular, batteries [22, 30]. However, while batteries are the only

e-Energy'15, July 14–17, 2015, Bangalore, India.

ACM 978-1-4503-3609-3/15/07 ...$15.00.
http://dx.doi.org/10.1145/2768510.2768543.

small-scale energy storage appropriate for homes at current price points, other ESDs become more feasible at higher levels of the grid hierarchy. Energy storage technologies differ in their cost, lifetime, energy-efficiency, etc. For example, flywheels exhibit a high energy-efficiency and lifetime, but have a high self-discharge rates and cost, while lead-acid batteries exhibit a low self-discharge rate and cost, but have a shorter lifetime and lower energy-efficiency.

Thus, our hypothesis is that intelligently employing hybrid combinations of different energy storage technologies at multiple levels of the grid's hierarchy has the potential to reduce costs relative to deploying only a single storage technology at a single level of the hierarchy. In evaluating our hypothesis, we make the following contributions.

- **ESD and Grid Modeling.** We extensively model important ESD operational characteristics, including energy density, self-discharge rate, cycle lifetime, power ramp time, etc., to capture their tradeoffs. We examine the deployment of different ESDs using a simple model of the grid's electricity distribution hierarchy, which includes the various costs associated with generating, transmitting, and distributing electricity.
- **Optimization Framework.** Using our above models, we develop an optimization framework that enables us to examine the benefit of using different combinations of ESDs at different levels of the hierarchy. The goal of our optimization framework is to minimize generation costs, including the capital, operational, and storage costs, for different configurations of ESDs.
- **Implementation and Evaluation.** We implement our optimization framework and then use it to evaluate in simulation the cost and benefit of different storage configurations using smart meter data from 5000 customers of a local utility. In doing so, we identify key insights into the benefits of different ESD technologies at different levels of the grid. We find that deploying hybrid ESDs at an individual level typically improves savings over any single-technology ESD deployment, while deploying multi-level hybrid ESDs typically provides the best savings. Overall, we find that ESDs can reduce distribution-related capital and operational costs by up to 12%.

2. BACKGROUND

2.1 Electric Grid

The electric grid is an interconnected network for delivering electricity from suppliers to consumers. Electricity is generated at power plants, often far from population centers, using different types of generators and fuels with different operational characteristics. Generated electricity exits the power plant and is stepped up to high voltages for long-distance transmission, since high voltages reduce transmission losses. At a substation near the final destination, a step-down transformer reduces the transmission voltage for distribution to both industrial and residential customers. At this point, distribution lines deliver electricity from the substation to end-consumers. In this work, we focus primarily on the large number of small-scale residential consumers in the grid, since they represent the vast majority of end-points in the distribution network.

2.1.1 Distribution Network

Figure 1 highlights the basic structure of electricity distribution in the grid. Electricity is fed into a bulk power substation, or a subtransmission station, which service a few "load areas" of customer demand. The bulk power substation routes the electricity to distribution substations. A distribution substation may then route the power to thousands of homes [1, 2]. Before being delivered to

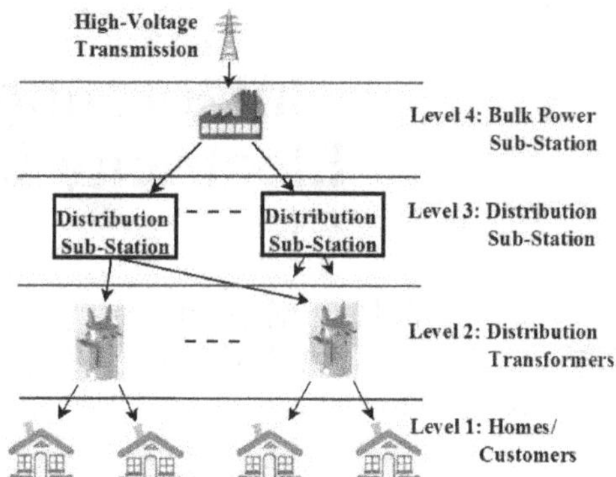

Figure 1: Typical electricity distribution hierarchy.

a building, distribution transformers near the building steps down the voltage of electricity. The number of consumers fed by a single distribution transformer varies: several homes may be fed off a single transformer in urban areas, or rural distribution may require one transformer per consumer [9].

In general, multiple distribution transformers may be connected in parallel. However, due to a lack of access to the distribution graph of an existing network and, for simplicity, in this paper, we assume the topology of the distribution network as shown in Figure 1. We base this simple model on information that is available in public domain [1, 2, 9], and use it in our experimental evaluation. Here, we assume each distribution transformer supports five homes, each distribution sub-station serves 500 transformers, and two distribution sub-stations are served by one bulk power substation. While our absolute results are specific to this simple model of a distribution network, we believe that many of our key insights are applicable to a range of real topologies, since we base our topology on publicly-available information. Importantly, our methodology and analyses extends to other types of distribution networks.

2.1.2 T&D Losses in the Grid

A fraction of electricity is lost in transmission and distribution. In the US, nationally, roughly 6% to 6.5% of the total electricity is lost each year [25]. Losses are generally divided equally between transmission and distribution. For example, in New York, transmission losses accounted for a total of 3.18% loss, while distribution losses accounted for the loss of 3.3% of the total annual electricity [5]. We use these loss values in our evaluation.

2.2 Electric Utility's Generation Costs

An electric utility generates, transmits, and distributes electricity for sale in the electricity market [10]. A consumer's electric bill is generally divided into three categories related to electricity's generation, transmission, and distribution, as listed below [18, 11, 7].

Energy Charge. Consumers are charged based on the total amount of energy, in kilowatt-hours (kWh), they consume over a billing period. This charge incorporates the cost for a utility to generate the energy or buy the energy on the open market.

Distribution Charge. Consumers are charged a fee to enable utilities to recover the cost of operating and maintaining the distribution system. This charge typically has two components: an energy component, based on the amount of kWh consumed over the billing period, and a peak power component, based on the highest peak power demand in kilowatts (kW) over the billing period [18].

Transmission Charge. Consumers are charged a fee to enable utilities to recover the costs related to the delivery of electricity over high-voltage transmission lines. This energy is generally purchased from a third-party and not generated by the local utility. As with the distribution charge, this charge has an energy component and a peak power component [18].

In some cases, consumers are not charged for energy, distribution, and transmission individually, but rather, the charges are included as part of the electricity rate. In addition to these costs, utilities also have expenditures related to the cost of materials and supplies and capital (including depreciation).

Expenses that are dependent on the total energy consumption are dictated by the pattern of end-user consumption, which cannot be controlled by a utility. However, the generation, transmission, and distribution costs incurred as a result of demand peaks can be reduced by curtailing the peaks. In addition, reducing demand peaks enables utilities to gain savings from avoided electricity costs, which include the marginal cost to produce and deliver one more unit of electrical energy. The avoided cost consists of two components—avoided energy costs ($/MWh) and avoided capacity costs ($/kW-month) [4]—which represent lower generation costs and the need for less peak capacity from lower peak demands.

2.3 Energy Storage to Lower Utility's Costs

Energy storage devices can be used to store energy during low demand periods, which can then be used later to satisfy customer demands during peak demand periods, thereby reducing the net peak on the higher levels of the grid. As capital and operational expenses of the grid are largely determined by the peaks, energy storage can cut these expenses for the grid.

2.3.1 Energy Storage Technologies

We examine the potential for the following energy storage technologies to reduce an electric utility's distribution costs.

Compressed Air Energy Storage (CAES): With Compressed Air Energy Storage, off-peak grid power is used to compress air underground. Later, when the energy is needed, this compressed air is released to power an electric generation and produce electricity. These systems are typically large, often requirings significant realestate for storing compressed air [23], e.g., underground tanks.

Ultra-capacitors (UC): Ultra-capacitors operate similarly to electrostatic capacitors, except that they can hold significantly more energy in a size similar to that of conventional capacitors [21]. UCs are now often being used for large-scale uninterruptible power supplies (UPS) in data centers, hospitals, industrial buildings, etc. [17].

Flywheels (FW): Flywheels store kinetic energy in rotating discs. These discs are made to turn a generator for producing electricity. Flywheels can be very efficient in storing energy over short durations; however, they have high self-discharge rates due to losses from friction [21, 12]. One example of a flywheel energy storage plant is the Beacon Power plant in New York [8].

Lead Acid batteries (LA): Lead-acid batteries are one of the most widely used energy storage devices. They have long been the primary technology for stationary energy storage at both grid-scales and in off-grid homes [15].

Lithium-Ion batteries (LI): Lithium Ion batteries are the most popular type of rechargeable batteries; they are known for their relatively high efficiency and energy density [16]. Lithium Ion batteries are the primary technology in mobile systems, e.g., electric vehicles, due to their light weight in comparison with lead acid batteries. However, these batteries are now being deployed in conjunction with renewable energy to provide energy storage for homes, as evidenced by Tesla's recent introduction of the PowerWall home battery based on lithium-ion technology [19].

While diesel generators, and other captive sources can also be considered energy storage devices, we do not consider them separately here. Pumped hydroelectric is another widely used storage technology in the grid; however, since it requires significant infrastructure, it is not readily deployable in the distribution networks.

ESD	CAES	UC	FW	LA	LI
Efficiency (%)	68	95	95	80	85
Discharge:Charge Rate	4	1	1	10	5
Self-discharge (%per day)	low	20	100	0.2	0.1
Energy Density (Wh/L)	6	30	80	80	150
Power Density (W/L)	0.5	30000	1600	125	450
Ramp Time (sec)	600	0.001	0.001	0.001	0.001
Max DoD (%)	100	100	100	80	80
Energy Cost ($/kWh)	50	500	1000	200	525
Cycle Lifetime	15000	100000	12000	2000	5000
Expected Lifetime (Years)	20	20	15	4	10

Table 1: ESD Parameters [23] [21] [39] [35]

2.3.2 Energy Storage Characteristics

Below we list key characteristics of the energy storage devices that are relevant to our optimizations. Table 1 list the default values of the parameters used in our study, which we derive from various scientific studies. Note that these parameters are inputs to our framework and while they vary significantly across technologies, we do not further consider the impact of varying them for a particular storage technology We are specifically interested in how these characteristics yield different trade-offs when placing various storage technologies at different levels of the distribution hierarchy to minimize a utility's distribution costs. We model the following characteristics:

Energy Storage Capacity: The energy storage capacity represents the total amount of energy that a device can store. Generally, the capacity is expressed in kilowatt-hours (kWh).

Maximum Charge and Discharge Rates: Usually expressed as E-rate, the maximum charge and discharge rates are a measure of the rate at which a battery can be charged or discharged relative to its total capacity [3]. For example, a 2E discharge rate is the discharge rate necessary to fully discharge the battery in half an hour.

Efficiency: Use of energy storage results in energy loss due to energy conversion. We employ a constant efficiency factor for each energy storage technology to capture these losses; e.g., typical lead-acid batteries are 80% efficient.

Self-Discharge Rate: The self-discharge rate is a phenomenon in energy storage by which the ESD loses stored energy merely with passage of time. The self-discharge rate can be significant for some technologies, such as flywheels. For energy storage technology k we model its self-discharge per unit time as a constant factor μ_k.

Cycle Lifetime: A ESD's lifetime is usually expressed in terms of number of charge-discharge cycles. Typically, ESD lifetime is measured based on the number of cycles as a function of the depth of discharge (DoD). For a given energy storage technology, we limit its DoD and the number of charge-discharge cycles at the given DoD over a given time horizon; thereby, we control the lifetime of an energy storage device, and capture its amortized per unit energy storage cost over its lifetime in our model.

Energy Density: The energy density is the nominal battery energy per unit volume (Wh/L). The energy density determines the battery size required to achieve a given energy output [3].

Power Density: Power density is defined as the maximum available power per unit volume (W/L). The power density determines the battery size required to achieve a given power output [3].

Power Ramp Time: The Power Ramp Time is the start-up latency associated with a given energy storage technology before it can start delivering its maximum power. This ramp-up is similar to the start-up acceleration in vehicles. Ramp times of most storage devices are very low, however for compressed air storage the ramp time may be several minutes.

3. PROBLEM STATEMENT

Although energy storage can reduce peaks and cut costs, the problem of storage deployment presents several interesting tradeoffs. Peak reduction at a given level of the grid's hierarchy enables provisioning the infrastructure at that level, as well as higher levels, for a lower peak. Therefore, storage deployment at lower levels of the hierarchy appears more beneficial than reducing the peak only at higher levels. However, in general, peaks at higher levels of the hierarchy are smaller than the sum of individual peaks at the lower levels, such as at homes; this occurs because individual homes peak at different times. The statistical multiplexing gains due to the spreading of individual peaks over time makes aggregate peaks at higher levels smaller. Therefore, deploying energy storage at the higher levels would require much less energy storage capacity, and hence lower aggregate energy storage costs.

In addition to deployment choices, the choice of storage technologies also presents tradeoffs in their cost, lifetime, efficiency, energy density, etc. For example, compressed air energy storage has a low energy cost and long expected lifetime, but a low energy efficiency and requires significant space for deployment. In contrast, lead-acid batteries have a higher energy-efficiency and a smaller form-factor, but also much higher energy costs and much shorter expected lifetime. Furthermore, different storage technologies are suitable for shaving different types of peaks: compressed air storage is suitable for wide peaks, lead-acid batteries work well for less frequent medium-width peaks, and ultra-capacitors are best for very narrow peaks (up to a minute). Since the nature of the peak demand depends on the level of the grid hierarchy—medium-width peaks are more likely at homes, whereas wide peaks are frequent higher in the hierarchy—the best choice may differ at each level.

In this work, we address the problem of deploying energy storage across a distribution grid hierarchy to cut a utility's distribution costs. As there are a number of variables involved, such as large distribution hierarchies, time varying demand profiles, different types of storage technologies, and a range of electricity pricing plans, it is not easy to formulate a heuristic solution for this problem. Therefore, we frame it as an optimization problem. We define the problem as follows: given an electricity distribution network, an estimate of power demands, and a set of available storage technologies, the problem is to find an optimal sizing and placement of energy storage devices across the distribution hierarchy so as to minimize a utility's expenses (Section 2.2) for distributing electricity. Our framework is general enough to provide storage provisioning solutions for a range of consumption profiles, electricity pricing plans, storage technologies, and distribution networks.

4. ENERGY STORAGE PROVISIONING AND CONTROL FRAMEWORK

We now present our optimization framework for energy storage provisioning. We intend the framework to provide storage deployment solutions for a distribution hierarchy with the goal of optimizing a utility's cap-ex and op-ex. Inputs to the framework include power demand, the distribution network topology, and cap-ex and op-ex costs. The framework solution then outputs the optimal choice, placement, and size of energy storage devices across the hierarchy, along with optimal energy storage control patterns.

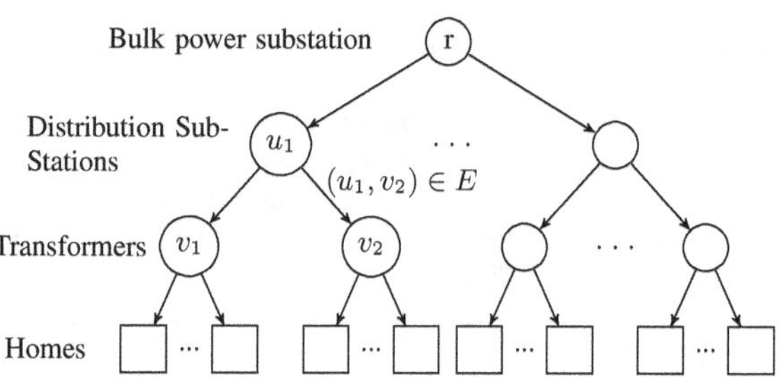

Figure 2: Illustrative graph depicting distribution hierarchy

Throughout the formulation we assume the grid distribution network is a directed graph $G = (V, E)$—as shown in Figure 2—where V is the set of nodes (i.e., homes, distribution transformers, substations, etc.) and E represents the directed edges between these nodes. In Figure 2, circles and squares represent the nodes, and arrows represent the edges. Two types of nodes are shown in the figure: squares are the leaf nodes and circles are the non-leaf nodes. In the distribution network, leaf nodes typically represent homes. In our formulation, all leaf nodes are represented by the set labeled LeafNodes. Node r (Figure 2) represents the root node. Finally, across the formulation, k represents the k-th energy storage technology (out of K) and t is the time interval (between 1 to T).

4.1 Inputs

Power Consumption (Demand): Broadly, there are two types of problems associated with energy storage deployments in the grid's distribution network. The first problem is determining the proper energy storage capacity and where in the hierarchy to deploy it. The second problem is determining how to charge-discharge the energy storage device to clip the peaks and realize cost savings. In this paper, we solve the first problem—the energy storage sizing and deployment problem, i.e., figuring out how much energy storage should be deployed and where. Therefore, we assume that historical power consumption traces are available, and we use these for future provisioning of storage in the distribution network. We assume that prior work can be employed to derive an accurate power demand time-series at each home (e.g., [20] [37]). Further, utilities have extensive power consumption logs over time for their customers, which can also be used as an input to our optimization framework. We divide time into T slots, each of length I. For home u we assume its power demand to be a time series $UsrDmnd_{u,t}$, where $t \in [1, T]$. We present results for both real and synthetic consumption power time series.

Capital Expenditure (Infrastructure Cost): We model two types of infrastructure costs: first, maintenance and upgrade cost, second, avoided (or marginal) capacity costs. These costs vary significantly between utilities and between locations within utilities: ranging from \$2.51/kW/month to \$46.34/kW/month [27, 26, 6]. In our experiments, we consider a cap-ex saving in the range of \$6/kW/month to \$30/kW/month resulting from peak reduction. These savings are obtained by reducing a watt of consumption from the maximum power draw $Peak_u^{max\_orig}$. At any time t, power draw at node u is given by the sum of power draws of all the nodes in the sub-tree with root at the node u at time t and net energy drawn by the energy storage devices at its vicinity; the sum is denoted by $Demand_{u,t}$. The corresponding size of the tallest shaved peak at u is denoted by $Peak_u^{shvd}$.

Operational Expenditure (Tariffs): Electricity tariffs are good indicators of the operational costs incurred in distribution of electricity. Most prevalent electricity tariff models charge customers for their total energy consumption, i.e., customers have to pay a flat $\$C_e^{unit}$/kWh of their consumption. Recently, to shave the peak demand on their grids, utilities have introduced a peak penalty on the tallest consumption peaks across the billing cycle. Typically, the peaks are computed as a sliding window of 30 minutes over the billing period. End users then pay a penalty of $\$b$/kW based on the tallest peak. For a utility, this peak penalty translates to the energy charged in generating the peak power and the cost incurred in routing the electricity to the distribution network (as in [14]). Note that our model for the value of peak reduction derives directly from the way electric utility companies charge for the peaks, therefore the marginal value of peak reduction is constant.

Our model for capital and operational expenditure for the utilities is derived from the information available in electricity bills and reports published by the utility companies, as reported in [4, 6, 7, 11, 18]. As utilities pass on their costs to the customers, we believe utility bills closely model the actual expenses of electric utility companies. In addition, several real-world factors, such as resource availability and market price, affecting utility expenses are accounted for while computing the avoided costs. For example, among other factors, [6] accounts for wholesale electric energy price, projections of natural gas prices, generation capacity costs, cost of controlling CO_2 emissions, and the effect of implementation of anticipated federal regulations.

4.2 Optimization Problem Formulation

Decision Variables: All notations used in the framework are summarized in Table 2. Our decision variables capture both the sizing and placement of energy storage and how to operate it to minimize the peak demand. The energy storage capacity of a storage technology of type k deployed at node u is denoted by $C_{k,u}$. The average power fed into and drawn out of an energy storage device at u during time slot t is denoted by $S_{k,u,t}$ and $D_{k,u,t}$.

Optimization Objective: Our optimization objective is:

$$\text{Minimize}(\text{CapEx} + \text{OpEx} + \text{StorageCost}) \tag{1}$$

The objective function has three components: capital expenditure (*CapEx*), operational expenditure (*OpEx*), and *StorageCost*. Each component is normalized to our experiment's time horizon.

CapEx includes the capital expenses due to infrastructure deployment for electricity distribution. Assuming α_u is the maintenance, upgrade, and marginal capacity costs for each watt of infrastructure provisioning at node u, *CapEx* is given by equation (2).

$$\text{CapEx} = \sum_{u \in V} Peak_u^{shvd} * \alpha_u \tag{2}$$

OpEx is the expected utility operational costs in electricity distribution and can be represented as in (3). The OpEx has three components, respectively: peak surcharge paid on the tallest demand peak served by the utility, electric energy cost paid on the total electricity served to the customers, and additional avoided costs of electricity incurred as a result of inefficiencies in energy storage devices.

$$\begin{aligned} OpEx = Peak_{root}^{shvd} * b + \sum_t Demand_{root,t} * I * a_t \\ + \sum_{k,u,t} (S_{k,u,t} - D_{k,u,t}) * I * \gamma \end{aligned} \tag{3}$$

In the above, b is the per unit surcharge (\$/kW) on the tallest peak and a_t is the unit cost of electricity at time t. $Peak_{root}^{shvd}$ is the tallest peak seen at the root node, which incurs the peak surcharge. γ is the avoided electric energy cost (AEEC in \$/MWh), as some energy is lost in the energy storage conversion process, this lost energy incurs extra avoided costs which is added to the utility operational costs.

Note that $Demand_{root,t}$ captures the total load including losses in transmission and storage charge-discharge.

StorageCost is the cost of energy storage deployment across the grid, given by (4), where $\beta_{k,u}$ is the amortized cost of the energy storage device k at node u per unit energy adjusted to its lifetime.

$$\text{StorageCost} = \sum_{u,k} C_{u,k} * \beta_{k,u} \tag{4}$$

The lifetime of an energy storage device depends on several factors such as the depth of discharge (DoD)—a battery lasts longer for smaller DoD. The value of $\beta_{k,u}$ is an input and is determined by the DoD and the set number of charge-discharge cycles over the time horizon. In this paper, in addition to the storage costs, $\beta_{k,u}$ includes the cost of the power conversion system, balance of plant, operation and maintenance [21].

Constraints: We assume that the state of charge in all storage devices at the end of the time horizon is same as their state at the beginning, as stated in (5).

$$E_{k,u,1} = E_{k,u,T+1}, \forall k, u \tag{5}$$

At any time, an energy storage device can only store energy between a lower threshold dictated by its allowed depth of discharge and a maximum capacity; this is captured by (6).

$$(1 - DoD_k^{max}) * C_{k,u} \le E_{k,u,t} \le C_{k,u}, \forall k, u, t \tag{6}$$

For each storage device, the rate at which energy can be drawn from and fed into the device is bounded by its discharge (r_k^{disch}) and charge (r_k^{charge}) rates, as determined by the underlying storage technology. This is captured in equations (7) and (8).

$$0 \le D_{k,u,t} \le C_{k,u} * r_k^{disch}, \forall k, u, t \tag{7}$$

$$0 \le S_{k,u,t} \le C_{k,u} * r_k^{charge}, \forall k, u, t \tag{8}$$

Equation (9) is the energy conservation constraint, which states that the total energy drawn out of the energy storage is never greater than the energy charged to the battery multiplied by the storage efficiency (e_k).

$$\sum_{t=1}^{T} D_{k,u,t} \le e_k * \sum_{t=1}^{T} S_{k,u,t}, \forall k, u \tag{9}$$

$$\begin{aligned} Demand_{u,t} = \frac{1}{\eta} \left(\sum_{v:(u,v) \in E} Demand_{v,t} \right) + \sum_k S_{k,u,t} \\ - \sum_k D_{k,u,t}, \forall u \in (V - \text{LeafNodes}), t \end{aligned} \tag{10}$$

Net power consumption at any non-leaf node u at time t, denoted by $Demand_{u,t}$, is determined by the sum of net power consumption at all its child nodes and the net power drawn/delivered by the energy storage devices deployed at the node, equation (10). (η takes care of the electricity lost due to transmission inefficiencies between node u and its children.) For example, in Figure 2, if transmission efficiency is 100%, the net power draw at node u_1 is given by the sum of net power drawn at its child nodes v_1, v_2 and the storage devices at u_1. On the other hand, net power draw at the leaf nodes, i.e., homes, is given simply by the sum of home's electricity demand and net electricity drawn/delivered by energy storage at the home, as in equation (11).

$$\begin{aligned} Demand_{u,t} = UsrDmnd_{u,t} + \sum_k S_{k,u,t} \\ - \sum_k D_{k,u,t}, \forall u \in \text{LeafNodes}, t \end{aligned} \tag{11}$$

Symbol	Notation
$C_{k,u}$	Capacity of the k-th energy storage device (ESD) at node u of the grid hierarchy
C_e^{unit}	Unit cost of energy
a_t	Unit cost of electricity in interval t
$D_{k,u,t}$	Average power drawn from the k-th energy storage at node u of the grid hierarchy in time interval t
DoD_k^{max}	Maximum depth of discharge for k-th type of storage
$E_{k,u,t}$	Energy stored in k-th storage device at node u of the grid hierarchy in interval t
e_k	Efficiency of storage type k
I	Length of each time interval
$Demand_{u,t}$	Net power demand on grid at node u in interval t
$UsrDmnd_{u,t}$	User consumption at home node u in interval t
$Peak_u^{shvd}$	Maximum shaved peak seen by the node u
$Peak_u^{max\_orig}$	Maximum original peak seen by the node u
b	\$/kW penalty on the tallest consumption peak
r_k^{charge}	Storage charging E-rate for the k-th energy storage
r_k^{disch}	Storage discharge E-rate for the k-th energy storage
R_k^{ramp}	Output power ramp up time of storage k
$S_{k,u,t}$	Average power fed into the k-th storage at node u in interval t
T	Total number of time intervals
ϕ_k^{energy}	Energy density of k-th storage technology; nominal energy per unit volume
ϕ_k^{power}	Power density of k-th storage technology; nominal power per unit volume
V_u^{max}	Maximum volume available for energy storage deployment at node u
α_u	Cost savings for each watt of under-provisioning at u
$\beta_{k,u}$	Amortized cost of storage k per unit energy adjusted to its lifetime
γ	Avoided electric energy cost (\$/MWh)
η	Electric transmission efficiency in the distribution
μ_k	Self discharge rate of storage technology type k

Table 2: Optimization framework notations

Equation (12) bounds the tallest peak ($Peak_u^{shvd}$) seen by u.

$$0 \leq Demand_{u,t} \leq Peak_u^{shvd}, \forall u, t \quad (12)$$

We also model the following energy storage characteristics in our framework, which are presented in the Appendix: the rate at which output power of a battery can increase, as some energy storages (such as compressed air) may take up to few minutes before delivering maximum rated power; battery self-discharge, as batteries lose some energy simply with passage of time; lifetime of the storage, as it affects the costs in the long term; volume needed for deploying energy storage, as some form of storages may need significant space, e.g., flywheels.

5. EXPERIMENTAL EVALUATION

5.1 Experimental Setup and Methodology

Configuration and Parameters: Our evaluation uses the grid distribution hierarchy shown in Figure 1. As explained in Section 2, we assume each distribution transformer supports five homes, each distribution substation serves 500 transformers, and two distribution substations are served by one bulk power substation. Storage devices can be placed at any of the levels in Figure 1. For simplicity, we present results at three levels: Homes, Transformers, and Substations, including distribution and bulk power substations.

Avoided Energy Cost (γ)	\$3.53/MWh [6]
CapEx(Low)	\$6/kW/month
CapEx(Medium)	\$15/kW/month
CapEx(High)	\$30/kW/month
Energy cost (Contract pricing)	\$ 0.05/kWh
Peak Penalty (Transmission + Energy)	\$20/kW/month
Volume V_{homes}^{max}	10L (~Car Battery)
Volume $V_{transformer}^{max}$	25L (~2.5X Car Battery)

Table 3: Experiment Parameter Values.

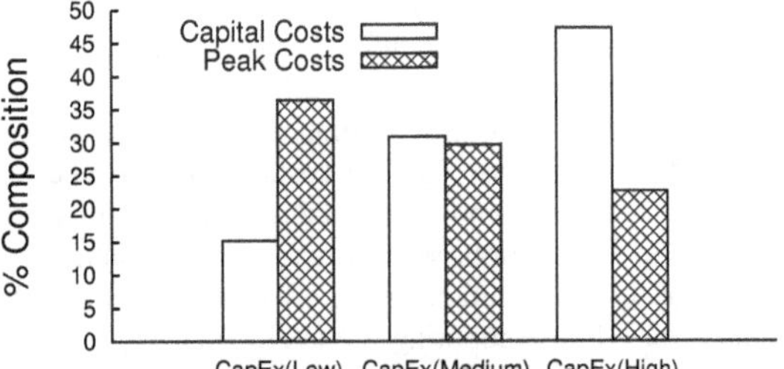

Figure 3: Composition of capex and peak penalty costs for Long-Term Contract.

We evaluate our framework with two op-ex cost models: a *long-term contract* and *day-ahead* model. *Long-term contract* represents the scenario where the utility either owns most of its generation or buys its energy from third parties under contracts. We adapt a real utility contract, available at [14], for evaluation. Since we include distribution costs as part of the distribution cap-ex costs, we subtract the distribution costs from the peak penalty and use the final values in Table 3. *Day-ahead* represents the case where a utility buys all of its electricity in day-ahead markets. However, the utility still incurs the peak penalty due to transmission. We use the day-ahead prices for March, 2014 from ISO New England [13]. We consider the cap-ex costs ranging from low to high, where *low* = \$6/kW/month, *medium* = \$15/kW/month, and *high* = \$30/kW/month ([27, 6, 26]).

The exact distribution of cap-ex, i.e., infrastructure cost (α), for the grid's distribution hierarchy is not available. Thus, in this paper, we assume these costs are equally split across all the levels. As the space available at homes and distribution transformers is limited, we use a conservative value of 0.01m^3 (or roughly the size of a car battery) for the energy storage volume at homes; for transformers we set the volume to 0.025m^3. Substations are built on large areas, so we do not constrain the available volume at substations. All results have been amortized to daily costs and savings, which includes the amortized cost of storage over its lifetime. We present results for the five ESDs, i.e., $K = 5$, discussed earlier.

We use the terms hybrid or multi-level energy storage to imply a combination of different storage technologies at a given node. Note that by using real-world day-ahead market prices and real utility consumption traces, we experiment with fine-grained time-varying prices and power consumption. Also, as we are solving an optimization problem, the computed storage values can be fractional. Although the computed numbers could differ from the actual storage capacity deployed in practice, we do not expect significant deviations from the computed values.

Workloads: For empirical evaluations, we use power consumption traces obtained from a local electric utility collected over one month (March 2014). Our traces are representative of consumption in a real electric grid. The traces contain power consumption data from 5000 homes at five minute granularity. In aggregate, we have

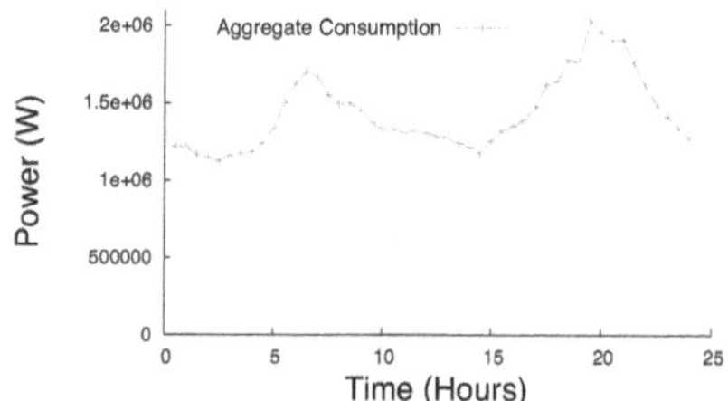

Figure 4: Electricity demand on a representative weekday.

more than 1.4 million unique power measurements. The average daily energy consumption of individual homes in our traces range from 15 kWh to 73 kWh.

Figure 4 shows the aggregate grid demand on a representative weekday. The figure shows that the homes peak between 6AM to 9AM (breakfast peak) and 6PM to 9PM, i.e., at dinner time. The pattern is expected based on typical work patterns, where home's electrical activity is concentrated after office hours. Throughout this paper, unless specified otherwise, we compute the peaks at a 30 minute granularity. To gain insights into the results, we present a detailed analysis of our results on a randomly picked weekday. Later, we present the results on traces for March, 2014.

5.2 Potential Savings from Storage

Can Energy Storage Reduce Distribution Costs? We first evaluate the savings from deploying only lead-acid batteries at a single level, i.e., either at homes, or transformers, or substations. Figure 5(a) shows the percentage distribution cost savings corresponding to a low, medium, and high capital expenditure for the long-term contract pricing plan. Figure 5(a) depicts the daily percentage cost savings for *long-term contract*, which shows that even a lead-acid deployment only at homes under a low cap-ex can cut costs by 3.75%. Savings increase as cap-ex increases. Also, note that for all single-level deployments, deployment at homes shows the maximum savings. This happens because peak shaving at the lowest level (homes) provisions the infrastructure at all levels for a lower peak, thereby saving significantly in cap-ex. In contrast, savings from deployments at the transformer-level are the lowest because of the limited volume availability, which is much smaller than at homes and substations.

Result: Deploying energy storage, in this case lead-acid batteries, at a single level of the hierarchy modestly reduces costs. Deploying at the lowest level, i.e., in homes, shows the greatest savings, since it also affects peak demands at higher levels.

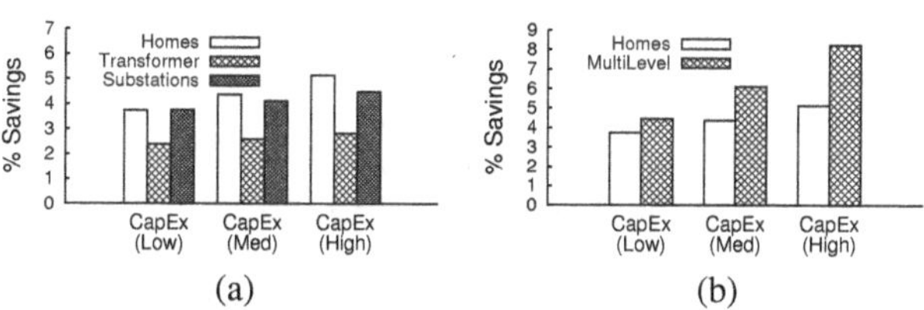

Figure 5: Savings from deploying lead-acid battery storage at (a) single level and (b) multiple levels under the long-term contract pricing plan.

Is Multi-Level Energy Storage Deployment Beneficial? Since related work suggests deploying lead-acid batteries only at homes, we next evaluate the impact of deploying lead-acid batteries across multiple levels of the hierarchy on savings. Figure 5(b) compares the savings from multi-level lead-acid deployment with its deployment only at homes (single-level). Savings are shown corresponding to low, medium, and high capital expenditures under the long-term contract pricing plan.

For all cap-ex values, savings from a multi-level deployment surpasses that of a single-level deployment at homes. In addition, for high cap-ex, the daily cost savings from multi-level lead-acid energy storage deployment shows an increase of more than 60% compared to single-level deployment at homes.

Result: Deploying one ESD type, in this case lead-acid batteries, at multiple levels of the grid's hierarchy further increases the cost savings up to an additional 60%.

Is Hybrid Energy Storage Deployment Beneficial? We next evaluate the additional savings possible from deploying multiple, i.e., hybrid, storage technologies at any given (single) level over a corresponding lead-acid storage deployment.

Figure 6 compares the percentage cost savings from hybrid energy storage deployment at single levels with the corresponding lead-acid deployment. Savings are shown for storage deployment at homes, transformers, and substations. Figure 6(a) and (b) shows results for the long-term contract, 6(a) is with low capex and 6(b) is with high capex.

We find that deploying hybrid energy storage boosts savings compared to lead-acid deployments, e.g., in Figure 6(a) hybrid energy storage at substations increases savings by 103%. Note that as opposed to our observation in Figure 5(a), in Figure 6(a), savings for hybrid deployment at substations is higher than that of homes. This occurs because under low cap-ex, substations can save more from greater peak shaving with hybrid energy storage, in large part, because there is no volume constraint at substations. However, as cap-ex increases, it becomes a greater component of the cost (as shown in Figure 3); as a result, the savings from deployment at homes is more than the substation's savings for high cap-ex.

Result: Employing multiple ESD technologies in hybrid further increases savings relative to only using lead-acid batteries at any single level to as much as ~10%. Hybrid deployments are able to best match the usage pattern at any given level with the characteristics of the energy storage device.

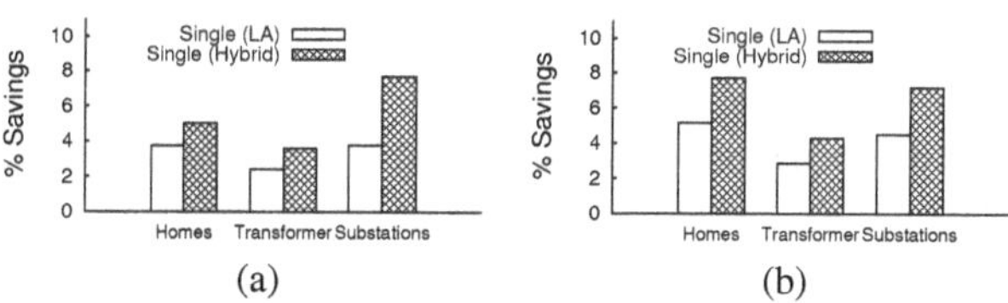

Figure 6: Savings from deploying hybrid storage technologies at a single-level for low and high cap-ex costs under long-term contract.

Is Multi-Level Hybrid Energy Storage Deployment worth it? Figure 7 shows how a multi-level multi-technology storage deployment can further increase savings over, first, any single level multi-technology deployment (7(a)), and second, any multi-level lead-acid (single storage technology) deployment (7(b)). Savings are shown for low, medium, and high values of cap-ex. Figure 7(a) shows that multi-level hybrid solution outperforms all the single-level hybrid solutions under all cap-ex values. For instance, 52% improvement over best single level solution under high cap-ex. We further find that a multi-level multi-technology storage deployment saves more than multi-level lead-acid deployment, as shown in Figure 7(b): for example, 83% increase in savings under low cap-ex. This increase in savings results from stringent volume constraints at lower levels, where multi-technology solutions gain an advantage by including storage technologies with higher power and/or energy density, as opposed to lead-acid storage.

Result: A hybrid, multi-level deployment results in the greatest savings, by as much as 12%, since it is able to exploit different energy storage device characteristics at each level of the grid hierarchy, which exhibits different usage patterns.

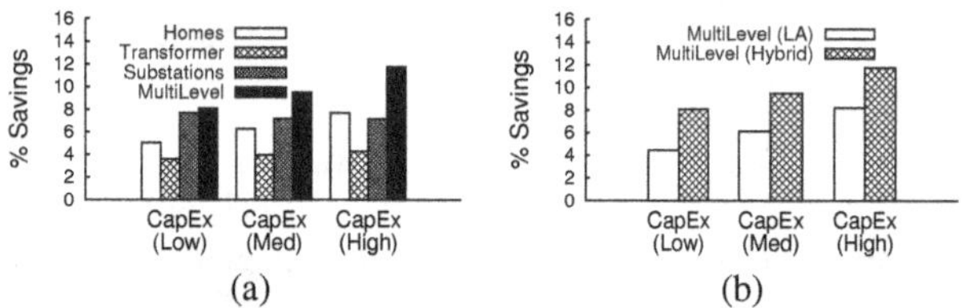

(a) (b)

Figure 7: Multi-Level Hybrid ESDs v/s: (a) Single-level Hybrid ESDs and (b) Multi-level lead-acid batteries under long-term contract.

How do the savings change under other pricing plans? While the above results depict savings for the long-term contract pricing plan, we have repeated all of the above experiments for the day-ahead pricing plan. In each case, we find similar cost savings for the day-ahead pricing when compared to the long-term contract plan. For example, Figure 8(a) and (b) depicts savings from a multi-level LA deployment and a multi-level hybrid deployment, respectively. As can be seen, the corresponding savings under long-term contract pricing, depicted in Figure 5(b) and 7(a), are similar to that depicted in Figure 8(a) and (b) under day ahead pricing. Since all experiments show similar results, we omit the remaining graphs for brevity (see [31] for detailed results). **Result:** Overall our experiments show that the savings due to energy storage are not specific to a pricing plan and hold for both long-term contract and day ahead pricing.

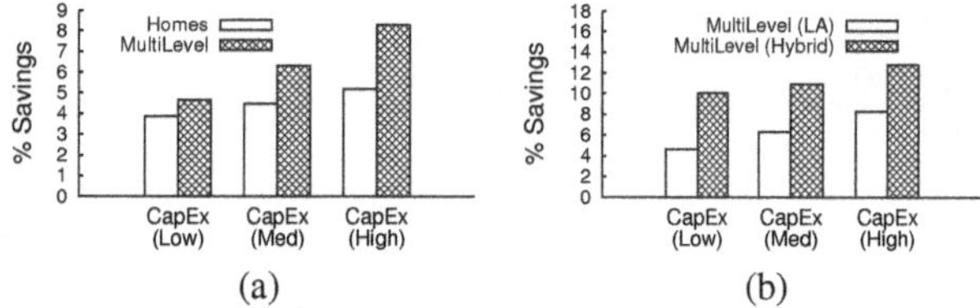

(a) (b)

Figure 8: Savings under day-ahead pricing for multi-level lead acid batteries and multi-level hybrid storage.

Peak Reduction: Figure 9 shows the aggregate percentage peak reduction across the grid with lead-acid only, and multi-technology storage deployments. For each of the cases, we present results for both single-level deployments at homes, transformers, substations, and multi-level deployment across the hierarchy. Results are presented for long-term contract (9(a)) and day-ahead pricing (9(b)). Only medium cap-ex numbers are shown, as the numbers for other cap-ex are similar. Figure 9(a) shows even a lead-acid deployment at homes achieve a peak reduction of 11.6%, which is further increased to 16.7% by a hybrid energy storage deployment.

As we have seen, hybrid solutions have the advantage of choosing storage technologies with greater power/energy density and discharge rates. In addition, note that peak reductions achieved by substation and multi-level deployments (both hybrid and lead-acid) are very close; however, the savings achieved by them are much different (e.g., 32% difference in Figure 7(a)). Although they get similar aggregate peak reductions, the multi-level approach saves more in cap-ex by deploying energy storage devices at the lower levels. Figure 9(b) shows equivalent results for day-ahead pricing.

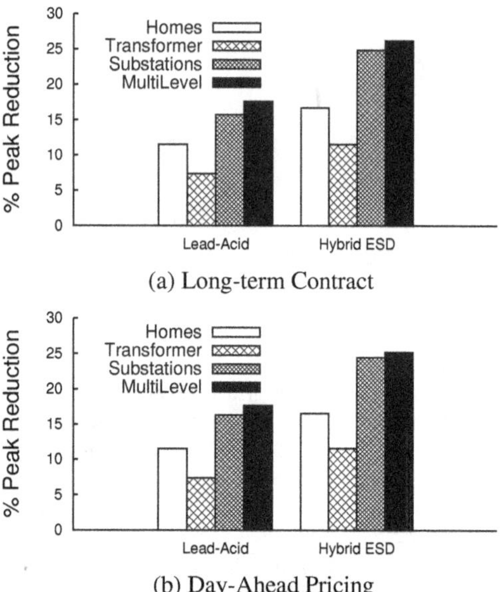

(a) Long-term Contract

(b) Day-Ahead Pricing

Figure 9: Aggregate Peak Reduction from Lead-Acid only and Hybrid ESDs for CapEx(Medium).

Result: Hybrid ESD deployments at multiple levels results in the greatest reduction in peak demand (by as much as 25%) compared to deploying hybrid ESD at individual levels or using only lead-acid batteries as the ESD.

Optimal Energy Storage Placement and Configuration: To give insight about the different types and configurations of storage technologies selected by our framework, Table 4 presents the energy storage configuration under the contract pricing for medium cap-ex. Configuration for the other cap-ex values and pricing are similar. To give an idea about absolute numbers, we include dollar savings and cost values. First, we see that if we are to use a single-level solution—just lead-acid batteries—deployment at homes does provide the best savings, because of the cap-ex gains at all levels. Second, volume constraints play an important role in limiting the benefits of lead-acid batteries in the lower level of the hierarchy; therefore, a single-level hybrid storage solution is able to increase savings by deploying a higher energy and power dense storage device, such as lithium-ion batteries, e.g., 42.5% increase at the homes. In addition, at substations where there is no volume constraint hybrid solutions employ a combination of lithium-ion, ultra-capacitors, and compressed air energy storage and further increases the savings by 15%.

Compressed air is the cheapest form of storage, however, it has a long start-up delay; ultra-capacitor and lithium-ion can be used to bridge this delay; ultra-capacitors have a very high power density, which helps in shaving tall narrow peaks, and their low energy density is complemented by lithium-ion energy storage. Finally, with the freedom of hybrid storage for multi-level deployment, we get maximum savings by deploying lithium-ion at lower levels and compressed air storage at the top level of the hierarchy.

Result: Using different ESDs at different levels of the grid's hierarchy result in significant differences in costs and savings.

Energy Storage Costs: As the numbers in Table 4 show, the cost of energy storage is a small fraction of the total daily costs without storage devices. For example, a hybrid storage solution at the substations is only 1.83% of the total daily cost. A hybrid storage deployment at lower levels costs more than deploying lead-acid

	LA Single ($ save, $ cost)	Hybrid Single ($ save, $ cost)	Hybrid MultiLevel ($ save, $ cost)
Substations	LA (880.25,416.74)	LI + UC + CAES (1544.73,394.27)	CAES
Transformer	LA (558.87,125.0)	LI (841.70,236.25)	LI
Homes	LA (940.06,249.77)	LI (1340.36,472.20)	LI (2039.53,766.21)

Table 4: Storage Configuration and Placement (Long-term Contract, Medium capex): (Savings($/day), Storage costs ($/day)). Total cost without storage is $21.5k/day.

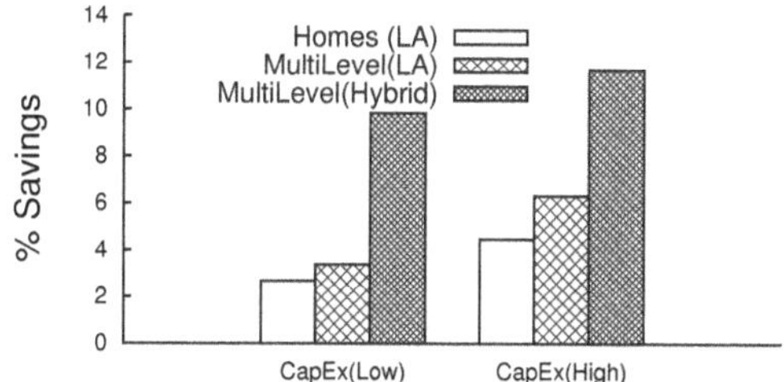

Figure 10: Average daily savings for March (Day-Ahead).

batteries because lithium-ion batteries are more expensive. However, due to their higher energy and power density they also save more. Even the most expensive energy storage deployment, i.e., multi-level hybrid, incurs less than 3.6% of the total costs; most of its costs are from the lithium-ion deployment at the lower levels.
Result: The cost of energy storage is a small fraction of the total daily distribution costs without any energy storage capacity.

5.3 Longer-term Savings

For computational tractability, so far, we have presented results on a single day. However, to show that the savings hold over longer periods, we conducted experiments oven an entire month. Figure 10 shows the average daily cost savings for the month of March, 2014 from our traces. Due to space constraints, savings are shown only for low and high cap-ex for day-ahead pricing; three types of deployments are shown: lead-acid at homes, multi-level lead-acid, and multi-level hybrid. Here, hybrid multi-level can save up to 11.7% for high cap-ex, and up to 9.8% for low cap-ex, which outperforms the multi-level lead-acid (low cap-ex) by 190%. The general trends in the figure are similar to what we have already seen. As peaks become taller, there is a greater opportunity for savings.

6. RELATED WORK

Much of the work on DR in the grid using ESDs has focused on cutting costs for customers with storage in presence of variable electricity pricing. For example, [24] presents an optimization approach to cut costs using ESDs in presence of spot electricity prices. Similarly, in [29] authors propose the use of energy storage in homes to cut their electricity bills under a variable prices [38], which they model as a Markov Decision Process. However, none of these approaches specifically look at cutting the costs for the utility. In fact, as noted in [22], such approaches can increase the peak demand on the grid and thereby increase its op-ex and cap-ex.

In contrast to the work above, the authors in [30] propose the use of ESDs for cutting peak demand on the grid and reducing its generation costs. Prior work has also proposed renewable energy integration to reduce consumption from the grid, e.g., [40, 36]. However, all of these consider ESD/renewable deployment only at customer premises (homes), and they evaluate their solutions only for a specific ESD technology. Finally, there has been considerable work in cost-aware provisioning and DR for datacenters, e.g., [33, 39]. The closest to our work is that done by Wang et al. [39]; here, the authors present a framework for modeling different ESDs, and the tradeoffs of placing them at different levels of datacenter power hierarchy. The authors evaluated the proposed framework using traces from real datacenters. As opposed to this, we have formulated and evaluated the solution for an electricity distribution network. We model several distribution network features which are absent in a datacenter, e.g., power losses in distribution.

7. CONCLUSIONS

In this paper, we study the novel problem of ESD deployment across distribution grid hierarchy for enabling automated Demand Response (DR). We present a generalized optimization framework for ESD deployment and control across the distribution grid hierarchy. Our framework can provide ESD provisioning solutions for a range of consumption profiles, electricity pricing plans, ESD technologies, and distribution networks. We showed that ESD provisioning can save up to 12% daily costs in distribution for the utility companies. In addition, we also present several key insights regarding ESD deployment in the distribution network.

Our work has some limitations, which we plan to address as part of future work. For example, our current model assumes the marginal value of reducing peak usage is constant, whereas in practice the marginal value varies with the magnitude of the peak. We also do not consider the impact of renewable generation, which may alter the cost of reducing peak demand. Our models assume linearity to keep the problem tractable, although there are many characteristics of ESDs, and particularly batteries, that are nonlinear, e.g., capacity as a function of discharge rate due to Peukert's law. Finally, while our capital and operational cost estimates are based on publicly available sources, and we evaluate our system over a wide range of possible costs, e.g., high, medium, and low cap-ex, these estimates may vary widely across utilities, which would effect the possible savings in the real world. However, our methodology is general and can be applied to utilities with different costs and distribution hierarchies.

8. ACKNOWLEDGEMENTS

We thank our shepherd, Mathijs de Weerdt, and reviewers for their comments. This research was supported by NSF grants CNS-1413998, CNS-1253063, CNS-1503590.

References

[1] Overview of CON EDISON System and LIC Network. http://bit.ly/1SB6YXA.

[2] Utilities. http://www.nyc.gov/html/sirr/downloads/pdf/final_report/Ch_6_Utilities_FINAL_singles.pdf.

[3] A Guide to Understanding Battery Specifications. http://web.mit.edu/evt/summary_battery_specifications.pdf, 2008.

[4] Biennial Report of the North Carolina Utilities Commission. http://www.ncuc.net/reports/CostAllocationReport09.pdf, 2009.

[5] Assessment of Transmission and Distribution Losses in New York. Technical Report PID071178 (NYSERDA 15464), EPRI, Palo Alto, CA, 2012.

[6] Avoided Energy Supply Costs in New England: 2013 Report. http://bit.ly/1LF0SzV, July 2013.

[7] Electric Bill Breakdown. http://bit.ly/1KyBhLT, 2013.

[8] Beacon Power. http://beaconpower.com/, 2014.

[9] Distribution Transformer. Wikipedia, 2014.

[10] Electric Utility. Wikipedia, 2014.

[11] Explanation of Unbundled Electricity Charges Residential Customers. http://bit.ly/1KyBhLT, July 2014.

[12] Flywheel. http://bit.ly/1FQbqwa, 2014.

[13] ISO New England - Hourly Data. http://www.iso-ne.com/markets/hrly_data/index.html, 2014.

[14] Large General Service Contract Schedule. http://www.hged.com/customers/payment-billing-rates/rates/electric-rates/183E%20-%20Large%20General%20Service.pdf, 2014.

[15] Lead-acid Battery. http://en.wikipedia.org/wiki/Lead%E2%80%93acid_battery, 2014.

[16] Lithium-Ion Battery. Wikipedia, 2014.

[17] Maxwell Ultracapacitor Uninterruptible Power Supply (UPS) Solutions. http://bit.ly/1BrzO1K, 2014.

[18] Summary of Rates for Public Service. http://bit.ly/1eA6QaZ, 2014.

[19] PowerWall: Tesla Home Battery. http://www.teslamotors.com/powerwall, June 2015.

[20] D. Akay and M. Atak. Grey prediction with rolling mechanism for electricity demand forecasting of turkey. *Energy*, 2007.

[21] K. Bradbury. Energy Storage Technology Review. http://people.duke.edu/~kjb17/tutorials/Energy_Storage_Technologies.pdf, August 2010.

[22] T. Carpenter, S. Singla, P. Azimzadeh, and S. Keshav. The impact of electricity pricing schemes on storage adoption in ontario. In *ACM e-Energy*, 2012.

[23] H. Chen, T. N. Cong, W. Yang, C. Tan, Y. Li, and Y. Ding. Progress in electrical energy storage system: A critical review. *Progress in Natural Science*, 2009.

[24] B. Daryanian, R. Bohn, and R. Tabors. Optimal Demand-side Response to Electricity Spot Prices for Storage-type Customers. *Power Systems, IEEE Transactions on*, 1989.

[25] U. S. EIA. How much electricity is lost in transmission and distribution in the united states? - FAQ, 2014. [July-2014].

[26] B. Horii and E. Cutter. Energy Efficiency Avoided Costs 2011 Update, December 2011.

[27] K. Knapp, J. Martin, S. Price, and F. Gordon. Costing Methodology for Electric Distribution System Planning, November 2000.

[28] L. L. N. Laboratory. U.S. Energy Flowchart 2013. https://flowcharts.llnl.gov/, August 2014.

[29] A. Mishra, D. Irwin, P. Shenoy, J. Kurose, and T. Zhu. Smartcharge: Cutting the Electricity Bill in Smart Homes with Energy Storage. In *ACM e-Energy*, 2012.

[30] A. Mishra, D. Irwin, P. Shenoy, and T. Zhu. Scaling Distributed Energy Storage for Grid Peak Reduction. In *ACM e-Energy*, 2013.

[31] A. Mishra, R. Sitaraman, D. Irwin, T. Zhu, P. Shenoy, B. Dalvi, and S. Lee. Integrating energy storage in electricity distribution networks. Technical Report UM-CS-2015-012, UMass Computer Science Tech Report, May 2015.

[32] A. T. C. on National Public Radio. Interview with Dan Delurey, President Demand Response Smart Grid Coalition. *How Smart is the Smart Grid?*, July 7th, 2010.

[33] S. Pelley, D. Meisner, P. Zandevakili, T. F. Wenisch, and J. Underwood. Power Routing: Dynamic Power Provisioning in the Data Center. In *ACM Sigplan Notices*, 2010.

[34] W. Pentland. Perverse Economics of the Electric Grid: As Generation Gets Cheaper, Transmission Costs Soar. http://onforb.es/1HJMsAP, 2013.

[35] S. M. Schoenung and W. V. Hassenzahl. Long-vs. Short-Term Energy Storage Technologies Analysis. A Life-Cycle Cost Study. A Study for the DOE Energy Storage Systems Program.

[36] J. Taneja, D. Culler, and P. Dutta. Towards Cooperative Grids: Sensor/Actuator Networks for Renewables Integration. In *SmartGridComm*, October 2010.

[37] G. K. Tso and K. K. Yau. Predicting electricity energy consumption: A comparison of regression analysis, decision tree and neural networks. *Energy*, 2007.

[38] P. Van de Ven, N. Hegde, L. Massoulie, and T. Salonidis. Optimal Control of Residential Energy Storage Under Price Fluctuations. In *Energy*, 2011.

[39] D. Wang, C. Ren, A. Sivasubramaniam, B. Urgaonkar, and H. Fathy. Energy Storage in Datacenters: What, Where, and How Much? *SIGMETRICS*, 2012.

[40] T. Zhu, A. Mishra, D. Irwin, N. Sharma, P. Shenoy, and D. Towsley. Efficient Renewable Energy Management for Smart Homes. In *BuildSys*, November 2011.

APPENDIX

Below are the additional constraints of the framework presented in section 4. Table-2 defines the notations. Constraint (13) limits the rate at which an energy storage's output power can increase, this is similar to acceleration of vehicles. Here $constant_k = \frac{r_k^{disch} * I}{R_k^{ramp}}$, and R_k^{ramp} is the power ramp-up time. As batteries lose some energy simply with passage of time, we model this battery self-discharge in constraint (14). constraint (15) bounds the lifetime of the storage. As the lifetime is primarily determined by the number of charge-discharge cycles and the depth of discharge, (15) bounds the number of times an energy storage can be discharged to its allowed depth of discharge in the given time horizon. Finally, we restrict the maximum volume for storage deployment that might be available at node u in (16) and (17).

$$D_{k,u,t} - D_{k,u,t-1} \leq C_{k,u} * Constant_k, \forall k, u, t \geq 2 \quad (13)$$

$$E_{k,u,t} = (1 - \mu_k) * E_{k,u,t-1} + e_k * S_{k,u,t-1} * I - D_{k,u,t-1} * I, \quad \forall k, u, t \geq 2 \quad (14)$$

$$\frac{I * \sum_{t=1}^{T} D_{k,u,t}}{DoD_k^{max} * C_{k,u}} \leq NumChDischCycles_k, \forall k, u \quad (15)$$

$$\sum_{k=1}^{K} \frac{C_{k,u}}{\phi_k^{energy}} \leq V_u^{max}, \forall u \quad (16)$$

$$\sum_{k=1}^{K} \frac{C_{k,u} * r_k^{disch}}{\phi_k^{power}} \leq V_u^{max}, \forall u \quad (17)$$

A Participatory Sensing Approach for Personalized Distance-to-empty Prediction and Green Telematics

Chien-Ming Tseng[†], Chi-Kin Chau[†], Sohan Dsouza[†] and Erik Wilhelm[‡]

[†]Masdar Institute of Science and Technology, UAE
[‡]Singapore University of Technology and Design, Singapore
{ctseng, ckchau, sdsouza}@masdar.ac.ae, erikwilhelm@sutd.edu.sg

ABSTRACT

Participatory sensing is an emerging concept that integrates crowd-sourced data collection and knowledge discovery of collective behavior. Capitalizing on the advent of abundant sensors and information collection systems in near-future vehicles, we develop a participatory sensing based system and its methodologies for driving energy efficiency applications. Distance-to-empty (DTE) is the distance an electric or internal-combustion engine (ICE) vehicle can reach before its energy/fuel is exhausted, which is determined by a variety of uncertain factors, such as driving behavior, terrain, types of road, traffic, and vehicle specification. Green telematics aims to optimize the route selection with lower energy consumption. In this paper, we explore an effective approach that integrates the vehicle data gathered from participatory sensing to provide more accurate personalized DTE prediction and green telematics. Our approach relies on extracting the driver/vehicle/route dependent features and discovering correlations from collective driving data. We also present concrete case studies of our results, such as (1) DTE prediction for EVs based on the data of ICE vehicles, (2) classification and recommendations of energy-efficient driving behavior, and (3) route-level energy consumption geo-fencing and planning.

Categories and Subject Descriptors

J.0 [**Computer Applications**]: General; K.4 [**Computing Milieux**]: Computers and Society

Keywords

Participatory sensing; Distance-to-empty; Green telematics

1. INTRODUCTION

While the in-vehicle information systems are increasingly sophisticated, the information presented in vehicles is not always accurate. One of the major features is *distance-to-empty* (DTE), which is the distance an electric or internal-combustion engine (ICE) vehicle can reach before its energy/fuel is exhausted. DTE is determined by a variety of factors, such as driver behavior, terrain, types of road, and traffic, as well as the vehicle specification (e.g., electric or gasoline power, tank capacity, engine load, vehicle weight).

The conventional approach of DTE prediction employed by car manufacturers is based on the projection of past long-term average vehicle energy efficiency (i.e., the total consumed energy/fuel over the total travelled distance). If there is perfect knowledge about the vehicle, driving behavior and the route to travel, future energy efficiency can be estimated with high accuracy. However, there are numerous uncertain factors, which make accurate prediction challenging.

On the other hand, the option of *green telematics* is being enabled by telematics providers, which aims to optimize the route selection decisions with lower fuel/energy consumption [5]. Green telematics systems are critical to optimal planning for recharging/refueling and fleet management. Like DTE prediction, green telematics is affected by the uncertain factors, such as driving behavior and routes.

These driving energy efficiency applications can be enhanced by exploring the historic data from other drivers. *Participatory sensing* is an emerging concept that integrates crowd-sourced data collection and knowledge discovery of collective behavior, enabling a variety of novel applications for pervasive computing systems [3]. The vehicles are becoming a vital platform for participatory sensing. First, there is a rise of advanced in-vehicle information systems, equipped with network connectivity and processing power, which can be turned into mobile sensing and information collection systems. Second, the wide availability of smartphones carried by passengers can extend the computing and sensing abilities of vehicles. Third, there are abundant off-the-shelf and after-market products for vehicle diagnostic tools to gather driving data and vehicle information. A participatory sensing platform for vehicles has been critical for a number of intelligent transportation applications (e.g., Google Map, Waze, real-time traffic alerts). Waze is a participatory App for traffic monitoring, which however does not have driving energy efficiency features.

In this paper, we focus on the applications of participatory sensing related to driving energy efficiency. In particular, there are a few example applications as follows.

1. *Vehicle Variable Applications*: Range anxiety is a critical issue for EVs, and accurate DTE prediction is highly desirable [12]. Since there are far many more ICE vehicles on the road than EVs, one can harness the data collected from ICE vehicles to improve the accuracy of DTE prediction for EVs. In particular, the data of taxis and buses on regular routes can shed light on the energy consumption of other vehicles.

e-Energy'15, July 14–17, 2015, Bangalore, India.

ACM 978-1-4503-3609-3/15/07 ...$15.00.
DOI: http://dx.doi.org/10.1145/2768510.2768530.

2. *Driver Variable Applications*: With the diverse data collected from various drivers, one can compare the driving behavior among drivers. By identifying the driver-specific characteristics from the data, one can analyze the driving behavior and make energy efficient driving recommendations. The insights gathered from driving behavior analytics are also relevant to safe driving and auto insurance, to the benefit of consumers (e.g., pay-as-you-drive plan [6]).
3. *Route Variable Applications*: Extensive green telematics can be enabled to compare different route options according to energy/fuel consumption. Route-level energy consumption geo-fencing can be constructed for EVs. Moreover, one can also optimize the route selection in order to refuel at cheaper gas stations.

In spite of the promising potential, there are several challenges of developing an effective participatory sensing system for driving energy efficiency applications:

1. *Automation*: With the availability of large amount of the data, an automated system is required to process and analyze data, with minimal human assistance.
2. *Flexibility*: The analytics synthesized from the data should be reusable to diverse applications, without the need for re-processing.
3. *Errors and Noise*: There exist considerable errors and noise in the participatory sensing data (e.g., due to synchronization, mechanic dumping, loss of data, differences in data sources). The system needs to resolve the inconsistency and maximize the integrality.
4. *Scalability and Efficiency*: Many applications require real-time processing, and the system needs to deliver the results efficiently in a scalable manner.

In this paper, we explore an effective approach that integrates the vehicle data gathered from participatory sensing to provide more accurate personalized applications. Our approach relies on extracting the driver/vehicle/route dependent features and discovering correlations from collective driving data. Furthermore, we present concrete case studies that utilize our results in diverse related applications, such as (1) DTE prediction for EVs based on the data of ICE vehicles, (2) classification and recommendations of energy-efficient driving behavior, and (3) route-level energy consumption geo-fencing and planning.

Outline: We present the related work in Sec. 2. The system framework is presented in Sec. 3. The methodology of energy consumption model and correlation discovery is presented in Sec. 4. We performed empirical evaluation on our methodology on electric and ICE vehicles, with results discussed in Sec. 5. Finally, the case studies that utilize our results are discussed in Sec. 6.

2. RELATED WORK

The problem of estimating DTE has been the subject of a significant number of academic publications, and is also a feature which vehicle manufacturers have been including in production vehicles for over two decades [2]. At its most basic level, the DTE, or range remaining can be estimated by observing the mean energy use over short and long distances as the authors describe in [12]. The same authors proceed to describe a system for estimating future travel profile using a Monte Carlo approach, which is a critical step in determining remaining energy. Estimates of stochastic effects which may impact travel velocity and acceleration profiles can be crowd-sourced for identifying traffic congestion [4].

The second step is using an accurate vehicle model to take the travel profile generated and turn it into future energy demands. Such model-based estimation can be performed as described in [7] for EVs. It is also possible for fuel consumption data shared between vehicles to be used without underlying physical profile and vehicle modeling to predict the energy consumption for a given route [5], although this approach is sensitive to much uncertainty and necessitates rigorous machine learning approaches – something which these authors have investigated for control applications, but which can easily be applied to the problem at the center of this work [11]. Early efforts at using social network participation to identify areas of fuel use reduction have been published [8]. Another participatory sensing system for improving fuel efficiency has been proposed in [10], and a simpler model for predicting fuel consumption across a driver-route matrix was proposed in [14].

This work differentiates from the previous work in several aspects: (1) We explicitly consider the features related to the driver, vehicle and route dependence in the energy consumption model. (2) We explore the correlations in driving data for personalized applications of individual drivers. (3) We present a unified study to diverse applications related to driving energy efficiency.

3. SYSTEM FRAMEWORK

We developed a system framework (depicted in Fig. 1) that consists of a number of components for data sensing and collection, data analytics, and information processing.

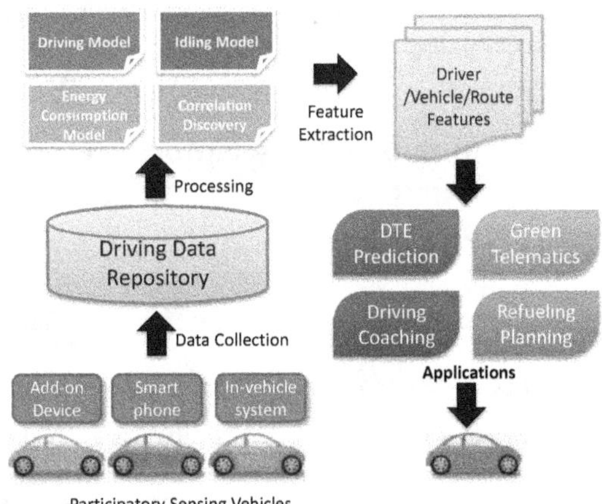

Figure 1: System framework.

3.1 Data Collection

The data sensing and collection system supports a range of methods. One method was based on a smartphone App. We developed an App for Android phone paired over a Bluetooth connection with a standard ELM327 dongle (depicted in Fig. 2), which is widely available online and in automotive electronic stores. The dongle plugs into the OBD port, and the ELM327 protocol is used by the App to query for data on specific engine and other vehicle parameters. The OBD data, supplemented with data from the phone's own positioning and accelerometer sensors, are accumulated within the device and, if configured and connected for this purpose, uploaded to a specific data server.

Another method is to rely on a tailor-made sensor-equipped electronic unit that plugs directly into the OBD port to draw power and query similar data, uploading the data over the cellular network. In future, when in-vehicle computers become more open to legal software customization, it would also be possible to develop user-level programs that can be installed on these computers and query data through APIs and use either the onboard connectivity or a paired mobile data device to support participatory sensing.

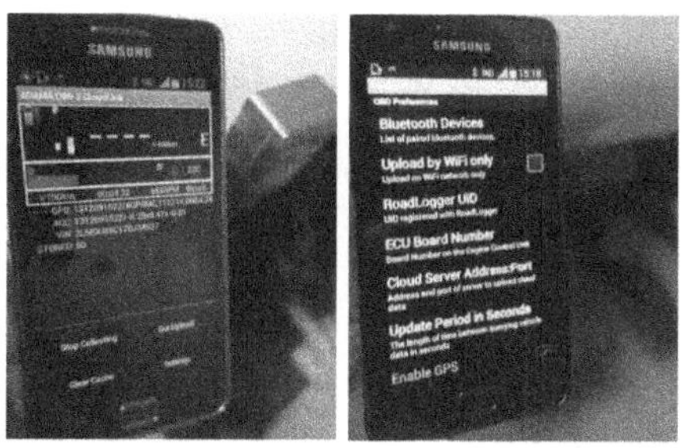

Figure 2: Android app and ELM327 dongle

3.2 Data Processing and Analytics

The data processing and analytics system receives data from the participatory sensing devices, stores it in databases, and processes it with analytic models for the applications. In a companion project, we develop CloudThink platform [1] as an open system for storing the data uploaded over Internet connections from the various in-vehicle data-gathering applications and devices, with a data access server allowing secure and traceable API service in multiple formats, and a web server to permit data visualization.

4. METHODOLOGY

In this section, we present a unified energy/fuel consumption model for both electric and ICE vehicles.

4.1 Basic Concepts

In order to perform the participatory sensing and subsequent estimation of DTE, features of the model must be defined. For this work, three categories of features important for the estimation will be described. The first relates vehicle speed and idle duration to the typical traffic conditions experienced on a road segment. The second enables the type of driver to be defined and parameterized. The third describes the physical characteristics of the vehicle which is the subject of the identification. The following subsections provide more details on how the model was constructed.

1. *Route*: The level of traffic which is expected for a road segment depends on a plethora of factors, including time of day, day of year, special events, etc., and is generally difficult to predict. For this work, the type of routes was used as the primary explanatory variable and was divided into three categories: small public or private roads with urban traffic, lower capacity "urban" highways, and higher capacity freeways.
2. *Driver*: The parameterization of the driver was enabled through the black-box statistical approach chosen for the model described in the next section. Different drivers are expected to behave according to preferences for stop/start accelerations, aggression in various scenarios, propensity for hypermiling, etc.
3. *Vehicle*: The extrinsic parameters capturing vehicle characteristics are only the weight of the vehicle. All other characteristics such as power, wheelbase, top speed are parametrized implicitly in the regression coefficients identified during the modeling process. This parameter is selected to be universal to both electric and ICE vehicles.

4.2 Energy Consumption Model

A tuple of driver-vehicle-route combination is denoted by $(\mathsf{D}, \mathsf{V}, \mathsf{R})$. The driving data repository is consisted of the data sets as a subset of $\{(\mathsf{D}, \mathsf{V}, \mathsf{R})\}$.

We divide a route R by a set of n segments[1]. The set of segments are denoted by $\{\mathsf{R}^i\}_{i=1}^n$.

The total energy consumption E of driver D with vehicle V on route R is given by:

$$E_{\mathsf{D},\mathsf{V},\mathsf{R}} = \sum_{i=1}^{n} (E^{\text{drv}}_{\mathsf{D},\mathsf{V},\mathsf{R}^i} + E^{\text{idl}}_{\mathsf{D},\mathsf{V},\mathsf{R}^i}) \tag{1}$$

where $E^{\text{drv}}_{\mathsf{D},\mathsf{V},\mathsf{R}^i}$ is the driving energy consumption and $E^{\text{idl}}_{\mathsf{D},\mathsf{V},\mathsf{R}^i}$ is the idling energy consumption of segment R^i. In this paper, we denote a symbol by $\hat{}$ for its estimated quantity. For example, $\hat{E}_{\mathsf{D},\mathsf{V},\mathsf{R}}$ denotes the estimated energy consumption.

4.2.1 Driving Energy Consumption Model

Considering a particular segment, the driving energy consumption of a moving vehicle E^{drv} has unit in liter or kWh. Here, we drop the subscript $_{\mathsf{D},\mathsf{V},\mathsf{R}^i}$ for brevity.

While there are more sophisticated approaches of estimating the driving energy consumption by detailed modelling of vehicle mechanics, this paper utilizes a black-box approach without the detailed knowledge of vehicle mechanics. This approach aims to maximize the applicability on a wide range of scenarios arising from participatory sensing.

In this paper, we estimate $\hat{E}^{\text{drv}}$ by a linear equation:

$$\begin{aligned} \hat{E}^{\text{drv}} &= \alpha_1 \bar{v} + \alpha_2 \bar{v}^2 + \vec{\alpha}_3 \vec{d} + \vec{\alpha}_4 \vec{a} + \vec{\alpha}_5 \vec{g} \\ &\quad + \alpha_6 \ell + \alpha_7 m + c \end{aligned} \tag{2}$$

where

- $\bar{v}$ is the continuous average speed (i.e., the average speed without idling);
- $\vec{d} = (\tau_d, \mu_d, \sigma_d)$ is the deceleration tuple, where
  - τ_d is the total duration of deceleration;
  - μ_d is the mean deceleration (i.e., the sum of deceleration values divided by the deceleration duration);
  - σ_d is the standard deviation of deceleration;
- $\vec{a}$ is the acceleration tuple (similar to the deceleration tuple);

[1]The length of each segment we choose currently is 100m. But we remark that it is possible to have dynamically variable lengths according to the road environments.

- $\vec{g} = (\bar{g}_x, \bar{g}_y, \bar{g}_z)$ is the gyroscope tuple, where
  - $\bar{g}_x, \bar{g}_y, \bar{g}_z$ are the mean absolute measurement values in $x/y/z$-axis along the moving vehicle;
- ℓ is the auxiliary load of idling, which the baseline reading when the vehicle is not moving;
- m is the vehicle weight;
- $\alpha_1, ..., \alpha_8, c$ are coefficients.

Remarks:

1. The deceleration tuple is critical to capture the energy consumption for EVs in the presence of regenerative braking, by which the vehicle's kinetic energy is converted to energy storage, during braking.
2. The deceleration duration τ_d can capture the dynamic of deceleration. For example, when a driver gradually releases gas pedal from high speed, the mean deceleration μ_d is small with a long deceleration duration, on the other hand, when a driver decelerates his vehicle for a short brake (e.g., avoiding speed camera), μ_d is also small with a short deceleration duration. In both cases, the mean deceleration will be similar, but the duration of deceleration can distinguish the difference.
3. The gyroscope tuple $\vec{g}$ can capture the curvature of a route. Normally, travelling a curve route consumes more energy than a straight route, in spite of equal distance. The gyroscope provides important information about the environments. The gyroscope may be available in smartphones.
4. The auxiliary load of idling ℓ is the *calculated engine load* when the vehicle is not moving, which is often available from On Board Diagnostic (OBD) port. The auxiliary load of idling provides the baseline energy consumption of a stationary vehicle, which is more affected by factors such as in-vehicle air-conditioning and stereo systems.

4.2.2 *Idling Energy Consumption Model*

Similarly, we rely on a black-box approach to estimate the idling energy consumption. Considering a particular segment, we estimate the idling energy consumption $\hat{E}^{\text{idl}}$ by a linear equation:

$$\hat{E}^{\text{idl}} = \beta_1 \tau^{\text{idl}} + \beta_2 \ell \tag{3}$$

where

- τ^{idl} is the total idle duration,
- ℓ is the auxiliary load of idling.

Here, we drop the subscript $_{\mathsf{D,V,R}^i}$ for brevity. The auxiliary load of idling ℓ provides the baseline energy consumption of a stationary vehicle.

4.3 Estimation of Coefficients

The coefficients $(\alpha_1, ..., \alpha_7)$, (β_1, β_2) and c in the linear equations (Eqns. (2)-(3)) can be estimated by the standard regression method, if provided a sufficiently large data set of driving data $(\bar{v}, \vec{d}, \vec{a}, \vec{g}, \ell, m, \tau^{\text{idl}})$ and energy consumption data $(\hat{E}^{\text{drv}}, \hat{E}^{\text{idl}})$. We assume that each driver-vehicle pair (D, V) has collected sufficient historic personal driving data, and the coefficients can be estimated in a-priori manner.

One notable advantage of regression method is that it is less susceptible to random noise, which can arise from various sources (e.g., due to synchronization, mechanic dumping, inaccurate measurements).

4.4 Dependence and Features

By participatory sensing, drivers can share their driving data (e.g., coefficients of Eqns. (2)-(3)) with each other. Next, we explore an effective approach that integrates the participatory sensing data to personalized applications.

In fact, the linear equations (Eqns. (2)-(3)) provide a convenient way to extract the features that are related to driver, vehicle, and route dependence. In Table 1, we heuristically assign the dependence of each parameter, according to the major effects from the driver, vehicle or route.

For the coefficients, it is assumed that their dependence is complementary to that of the respective parameters. For example, the average speed $\bar{v}$ is more likely affected by the driver and route, while to a less extent by the type of vehicle. Hence, coefficient α_1 is considered to be vehicle-dependent, such that the product $\alpha_1 \bar{v}$ will be specific to a particular tuple $(\mathsf{D}, \mathsf{V}, \mathsf{R}^i)$. For convenience, we assume that c is driver-dependent.

Parameters	Driver-dependent	Vehicle-dependent	Route-dependent
$\bar{v}, \vec{d}, \vec{a}, \vec{g}$	✓		✓
ℓ	✓	✓	
m		✓	
τ^{idl}			✓
$\alpha_1, ..., \vec{\alpha}_5$		✓	
α_6			✓
α_7	✓		✓
c	✓		
β_1	✓	✓	
β_2			✓

Table 1: Dependence of parameters and coefficients.

In light of dependence, we can specify each quantity by the respective subscripts when referring to a particular tuple $(\mathsf{D}, \mathsf{V}, \mathsf{R}^i)$. For example, we write $\bar{v}_{(\mathsf{D,V})}$ and $\alpha_{1(\mathsf{V})}$.

We denote a matrix of energy consumptions by $\mathbf{E} = (E_{\mathsf{D,V,R}^i})$. Each $E_{\mathsf{D,V,R}^i}$ can be computed by a linear equation:

$$E_{\mathsf{D,V,R}^i} = (\mathbf{c}_{\mathsf{V}}, \mathbf{c}_{\mathsf{R}^i}, \mathbf{c}_{\mathsf{D,R}^i}, \mathbf{c}_{\mathsf{D,V}}) \cdot (\mathbf{x}_{\mathsf{D,R}^i}, \mathbf{x}_{\mathsf{D,V}}, \mathbf{x}_{\mathsf{V}}, \mathbf{x}_{\mathsf{R}^i})^T + c \tag{4}$$

where

$$\mathbf{c}_{\mathsf{V}} = (\alpha_{1(\mathsf{V})}, \alpha_{2(\mathsf{V})}, \vec{\alpha}_{3(\mathsf{V})}, \vec{\alpha}_{4(\mathsf{V})}, \vec{\alpha}_{5(\mathsf{V})}) \tag{5}$$

$$\mathbf{x}_{\mathsf{D,R}^i} = (\bar{v}_{\mathsf{D,R}^i}, \bar{v}^2_{\mathsf{D,R}^i}, \vec{d}_{\mathsf{D,R}^i}, \vec{\mathcal{B}}_{,\mathsf{R}^i}, \vec{\mathcal{D}}_{,\mathsf{R}^i}) \tag{6}$$

$$\mathbf{c}_{\mathsf{R}^i} = (\alpha_{6(\mathsf{R}^i)}, \beta_{2(\mathsf{R}^i)}) \tag{7}$$

$$\mathbf{x}_{\mathsf{D,V}} = (\ell_{\mathsf{D,V}}, \ell_{\mathsf{D,V}}) \tag{8}$$

$$\mathbf{c}_{\mathsf{D,R}^i} = (\alpha_{7(\mathsf{D,R}^i)}) \tag{9}$$

$$\mathbf{x}_{\mathsf{V}} = (m_{\mathsf{V}}) \tag{10}$$

$$\mathbf{c}_{\mathsf{D,V}} = (\beta_{1(\mathsf{D,V})}) \tag{11}$$

$$\mathbf{x}_{\mathsf{R}^i} = (\tau^{\text{idl}}_{\mathsf{R}^i}) \tag{12}$$

To conveniently align with dependence, we refer the inputs as *features*, when they are grouped by the driver, vehicle or route dependence. The features we refer to are as follows.

- *Driver dependent features*: $\mathbf{x}_{\mathsf{D},\mathsf{R}^i}$, $\mathbf{x}_{\mathsf{D},\mathsf{V}}$, $\mathbf{c}_{\mathsf{D},\mathsf{R}^i}$, $\mathbf{c}_{\mathsf{D},\mathsf{V}}$.
- *Vehicle dependent features*: $\mathbf{c}_{\mathsf{V}}$, $\mathbf{x}_{\mathsf{D},\mathsf{V}}$, $\mathbf{x}_{\mathsf{V}}$, $\mathbf{c}_{\mathsf{D},\mathsf{V}}$.
- *Route dependent features*: $\mathbf{x}_{\mathsf{D},\mathsf{R}^i}$, $\mathbf{c}_{\mathsf{R}^i}$, $\mathbf{c}_{\mathsf{D},\mathsf{R}^i}$, $\mathbf{x}_{\mathsf{R}^i}$.

A number of applications can be enabled by flexibly substituting the proper features. We present several examples as follows.

1. To predict $E_{\mathsf{D},\mathsf{V},\mathsf{R}^i}$ by a different driver $(\mathsf{D}',\mathsf{V},\mathsf{R}^i)$, we can use the following equation:

$$\hat{E}_{\mathsf{D},\mathsf{V},\mathsf{R}^i} = (\mathbf{c}_{\mathsf{V}}, \mathbf{c}_{\mathsf{R}^i}, \mathbf{c}_{\mathsf{D}',\mathsf{R}^i}, \mathbf{c}_{\mathsf{D}',\mathsf{V}}) \cdot (\mathbf{x}_{\mathsf{D}',\mathsf{R}^i}, \mathbf{x}_{\mathsf{D}',\mathsf{V}}, \mathbf{x}_{\mathsf{V}}, \mathbf{x}_{\mathsf{R}^i})^T + c' \quad (13)$$

2. To predict $E_{\mathsf{D},\mathsf{V},\mathsf{R}^i}$ by a different vehicle $(\mathsf{D},\mathsf{V}',\mathsf{R}^i)$, we can use the following equation:

$$\hat{E}_{\mathsf{D},\mathsf{V},\mathsf{R}^i} = (\mathbf{c}_{\mathsf{V}}, \mathbf{c}_{\mathsf{R}^i}, \mathbf{c}_{\mathsf{D},\mathsf{R}^i}, \mathbf{c}_{\mathsf{D},\mathsf{V}'}) \cdot (\mathbf{x}_{\mathsf{D},\mathsf{R}^i}, \mathbf{x}_{\mathsf{D},\mathsf{V}'}, \mathbf{x}_{\mathsf{V}}, \mathbf{x}_{\mathsf{R}^i})^T + c \quad (14)$$

3. To predict $E_{\mathsf{D},\mathsf{V},\mathsf{R}^i}$ by a different route $(\mathsf{D},\mathsf{V},\mathsf{R}'^i)$, we can use the following equation:

$$\hat{E}_{\mathsf{D},\mathsf{V},\mathsf{R}^i} = (\mathbf{c}_{\mathsf{V}}, \mathbf{c}_{\mathsf{R}'^i}, \mathbf{c}_{\mathsf{D},\mathsf{R}'^i}, \mathbf{c}_{\mathsf{D},\mathsf{V}}) \cdot (\mathbf{x}_{\mathsf{D},\mathsf{R}'^i}, \mathbf{x}_{\mathsf{D},\mathsf{V}}, \mathbf{x}_{\mathsf{V}}, \mathbf{x}_{\mathsf{R}'^i})^T + c \quad (15)$$

4.5 Correlation Discovery in Driving Data Set

Let all the data sets in the repository be $\{\mathsf{D},\mathsf{V},\mathsf{R}^i\}$. Note that not every tuple is present in the repository. Next, we seek to identify the correlations in $\{\mathsf{D},\mathsf{V},\mathsf{R}^i\}$, such that one can identify the most similar $(\mathsf{D}',\mathsf{V},\mathsf{R}^i)$ to predict the energy consumption of $(\mathsf{D},\mathsf{V},\mathsf{R}^i)$.

In this paper, we characterize the correlation in the driving data between a pair (D,V) and $(\mathsf{D}',\mathsf{V}')$ with the same route using the concept of *dynamic time warping* (DTW) [13]. DTW is a widely used concept for determining the similarity among time series, and identifying the corresponding similar regions between two time series. DTW has been used in many applications, such as speech recognition, gesture recognition, robotics and bioinformatics.

The basic idea of DTW is to determine an optimal alignment between two time series. Consider two time series $X = (x[t])_{t=1}^{n_X}$ and $Y = (y[t])_{t=1}^{n_Y}$ of lengths n_X and n_Y respectively. A *warp path* is defined as $W = (w[k])_{k=1}^{n_W}$, where the kth element is $w_k = (i,j)$, such that i is an index from time series $x[t]$ and j is an index from time series $y[t]$. n_W is the length of the warp path W, such that $\max(n_X,n_Y) \le n_W < n_X + n_Y$.

The warp path W is subject to the following constraints:

1. $w[1] = (1,1)$;
2. $w[n_W] = (n_X, n_Y)$;
3. if $w[k] = (i,j)$ and $w[k+1] = (i',j')$, then $i \le i' \le i+1$ and $j \le j' \le j+1$.

An optimal warp path (illustrated in Fig. 3) is the one with the minimum distance $\mathsf{dist}(W^*)$, defined by:

$$\mathsf{dist}(W^*) = \arg\min_{w} \sum_{k=1}^{n_W} d(w[k]) \quad (16)$$

where $d(w[k])$ is the distance of the coordinates (i,j) of the kth element in W.

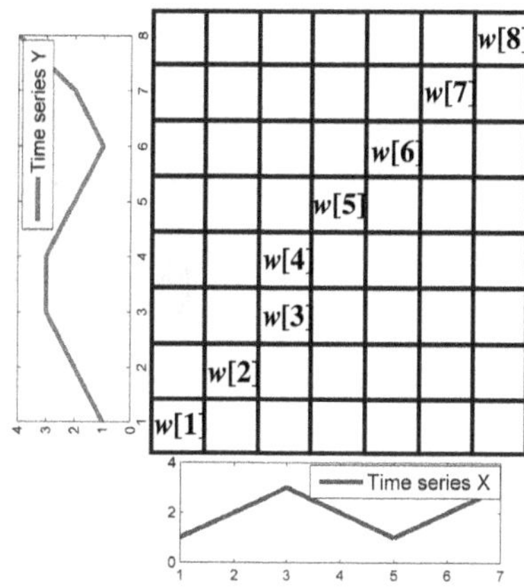

Figure 3: An illustration of warp path

A simple approach to determine an optimal warp path between two time series is to use dynamic programming. But there are other more efficient algorithms with linear running time [13].

Let $v_{\mathsf{D},\mathsf{V},\mathsf{R}^i}[t]$ be the time series of speed profile for tuple $(\mathsf{D},\mathsf{V},\mathsf{R}^i)$. For each pair of $(\mathsf{D},\mathsf{V},\mathsf{R}^i)$ and $(\mathsf{D}',\mathsf{V}',\mathsf{R}^i)$, let

$$\chi^{\mathsf{R}^i}_{(\mathsf{D},\mathsf{V}),(\mathsf{D}',\mathsf{V}')} = \mathsf{dist}(W^*) \quad (17)$$

where W^* is the minimum-distance warp path between the time series $v_{\mathsf{D},\mathsf{V},\mathsf{R}^i}[t]$ and $v_{\mathsf{D}',\mathsf{V}',\mathsf{R}^i}[t]$.

Let $\mathscr{R}(\mathsf{D},\mathsf{V})$ be a set of route segments that have speed profiles recorded with (D,V). Namely, if $\mathsf{R}^i \in \mathscr{R}(\mathsf{D},\mathsf{V})$, then the speed profile $v_{\mathsf{D},\mathsf{V},\mathsf{R}^i}[t]$ exists in the repository.

Define a correlation metric between each pair of (D,V) and $(\mathsf{D}',\mathsf{V}')$ by the average minimum warp path distance over all recorded segments:

$$\bar{\chi}_{(\mathsf{D},\mathsf{V}),(\mathsf{D}',\mathsf{V}')} = \frac{\sum_{\mathsf{R}^i \in \mathscr{R}(\mathsf{D},\mathsf{V}) \cap \mathscr{R}(\mathsf{D}',\mathsf{V}')} \chi^{\mathsf{R}^i}_{(\mathsf{D},\mathsf{V}),(\mathsf{D}',\mathsf{V}')}}{|\mathscr{R}(\mathsf{D},\mathsf{V}) \cap \mathscr{R}(\mathsf{D}',\mathsf{V}')|} \quad (18)$$

Note that $\bar{\chi}_{(\mathsf{D},\mathsf{V}),(\mathsf{D}',\mathsf{V}')} = \infty$, if $\mathscr{R}(\mathsf{D},\mathsf{V}) \cap \mathscr{R}(\mathsf{D}',\mathsf{V}') = \varnothing$.

In this paper, we will use $\bar{\chi}_{(\mathsf{D},\mathsf{V}),(\mathsf{D}',\mathsf{V}')}$ to characterize the similarity between each pair of (D,V) and $(\mathsf{D}',\mathsf{V}')$. We find the tuple $(\mathsf{D}',\mathsf{V}')$ with the smallest value $\bar{\chi}_{(\mathsf{D},\mathsf{V}),(\mathsf{D}',\mathsf{V}')}$ to estimate energy consumption of (D,V). We also employ k-nearest neighbors (k-NN) clustering to find the k most similar speed profiles of (D,V).

EXAMPLE 1. *In Fig. 4, the speed profiles of three drivers* $(\mathsf{D}_1,\mathsf{V}_1),(\mathsf{D}_2,\mathsf{V}_2),(\mathsf{D}_3,\mathsf{V}_3)$ *on the same route* R^1 *are plotted. Table 2 shows the minimum warp path distances between driver* $(\mathsf{D}_1,\mathsf{V}_1)$ *and other drivers. We observe that smaller minimum warp path distance indeed shows closer similarity in the speed profiles;* $(\mathsf{D}_1,\mathsf{V}_1)$ *is more similar with* $(\mathsf{D}_2,\mathsf{V}_2)$ *than* $(\mathsf{D}_3,\mathsf{V}_3)$.

	Minimum warp path distance
$\chi^{\mathsf{R}^1}_{(\mathsf{D}_1,\mathsf{V}_1),(\mathsf{D}_2,\mathsf{V}_2)}$	1.1385
$\chi^{\mathsf{R}^1}_{(\mathsf{D}_1,\mathsf{V}_1),(\mathsf{D}_3,\mathsf{V}_3)}$	1.3883

Table 2: Minimum warp path distance

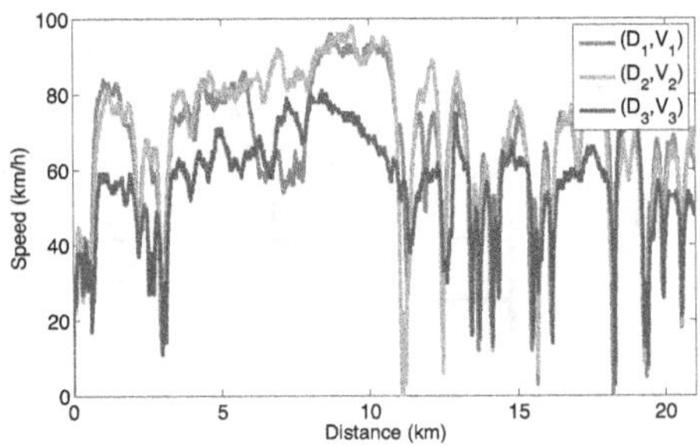

Figure 4: Speed profiles of three drivers on the same route.

5. EXPERIMENTS

We performed experiments to empirically evaluate the performance of our approach. The observations are reported in this section.

5.1 Experiment Setup

5.1.1 Routes

We select a range of different roads, as depicted in Fig. 5 and summarized in Table 3. R_1 has light traffic, consisting of both highway and suburban roads. R_2 has heavier traffic with traffic lights, and thus results in the much longer idle time seen in Table 3. R_3 and R_4 are similar in terms of traffic, with no need to stop. However, R_3 has a number of traffic signs and speed bumps, which force drivers to slow down, whereas R_4 has no restriction.

Route	Average Route Length (KM)	Average Driving Duration (sec)	Average Idle Duration (sec)
R_1	21.49	1356.4	10.4
R_2	10.36	761.8	398.6
R_3	6.78	412	0
R_4	8.18	450.8	0

Table 3: The routes in the experiments.

5.1.2 Vehicles

Four vehicles are used in the experiments, as summarized in Table 4, which consist of three ICE vehicles and one EV. The pictures of the vehicles are shown in Fig. 6.

Vehicle	Maker	Model	Year	Type	Displacement
V_1	Toyota	Yaris	2014	ICE	1.5
V_2	Hyundai	Veloster	2014	ICE	1.6
V_3	Nissan	LEAF	2013	EV	NA
V_4	BMW	650i	2014	ICE	5.0

Table 4: The vehicles in the experiments.

5.1.3 Data Collection

For ICE vehicles, we collected data through Bluetooth ELM327 dongles connected to the vehicles' onboard diagnostic (OBD) ports and paired with a smartphone App. The OBD data collected include mass air-flow, manifold absolute pressure, intake air temperature and engines' RPM, which are then utilized to compute the fuel consumption rate. Furthermore, the geo-location data, accelerometer and gyroscope measurements from the smartphone are also recorded. For EV (i.e., Nissan LEAF), we rely on Android App called "LEAF Spy Pro" to collect the EV's data. The sample rate of our smartphone App is 2 Hz, whereas the one for LEAF spy pro is 0.25 Hz.

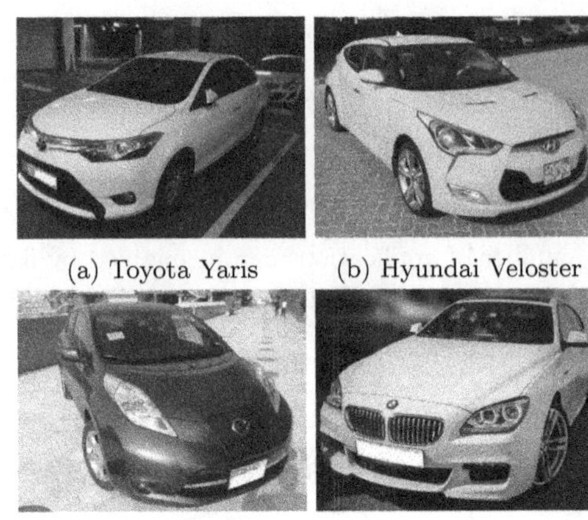

(a) Toyota Yaris (b) Hyundai Veloster (c) Nissan LEAF (d) BMW 650i

Figure 6: The vehicles in the experiments.

5.2 Data Sets

Fig. 7 shows some sample driving data. Fig. 7a shows the speed profiles of the EV and an ICE vehicle by the same driver on the same route. We can observe that both vehicles stopped several times due to traffic lights. Fig. 7b shows the energy consumption profiles of EV and ICE vehicles. Although the speed profiles are similar, there are remarkable differences in the energy consumption profiles. Notably, the energy consumption level decreases when the EV slows down, because of the regenerative braking that can convert kinetic energy into stored energy in battery.

Figs. 7c-7d show the driving data collected from the vehicles. The gyroscope data is used to determine the vehicle movement and orientation, which is gathered from smartphone. However, the gyroscope data is required to be aligned with vehicle's moving direction in order to obtain the corrected orientation. We use an automatic alignment algorithm to infer the vehicle's reference orientation [9,15].

5.3 Estimation Errors

To evaluate the accuracy of estimation, we measure the deviation error of the estimated energy consumption by the per segment error:

$$\varepsilon^i = \frac{|(E^{\rm drv}_{\rm D,V,R^i} + E^{\rm idl}_{\rm D,V,R^i}) - (\hat{E}^{\rm drv}_{\rm D,V,R^i} + \hat{E}^{\rm idl}_{\rm D,V,R^i})|}{E^{\rm drv}_{\rm D,V,R^i} + E^{\rm idl}_{\rm D,V,R^i}} \quad (19)$$

and the accumulative error:

$$\varepsilon^{\rm acc} = \frac{|E_{\rm D,V,R} - \hat{E}_{\rm D,V,R}|}{E_{\rm D,V,R}} \quad (20)$$

As an example, we plot the distribution of per-segment errors of one vehicle collected from three rounds of experiments in Fig. 8. It shows that the mean error is about 3.5% and the distribution is close to a normal distribution. Since we are interested in the energy consumption of the overall trip, the accumulative error is more relevant. Fig. 9

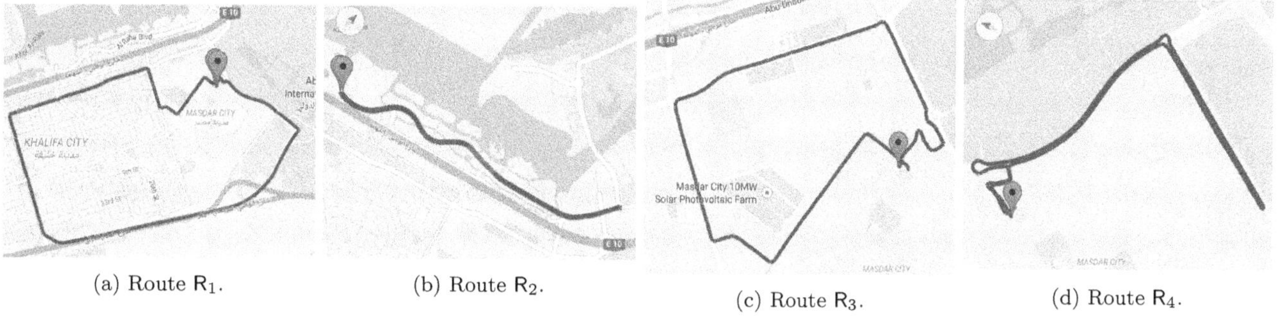

(a) Route R_1. (b) Route R_2. (c) Route R_3. (d) Route R_4.

Figure 5: The routes in the experiments.

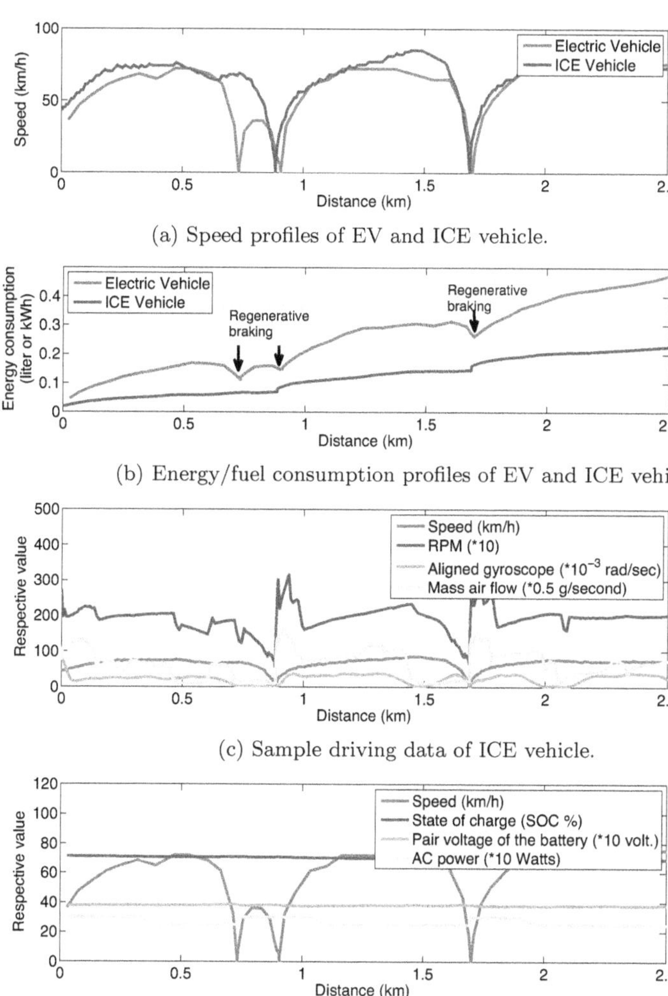

(a) Speed profiles of EV and ICE vehicle.

(b) Energy/fuel consumption profiles of EV and ICE vehicle.

(c) Sample driving data of ICE vehicle.

(d) Sample driving data of EV.

Figure 7: Sample driving data.

shows the accumulative error against travelled distance. We observe that the accumulative error fluctuates against travelled distance, but there is a general trend of decreasing error. This is due to the fact that the positive and negative deviations can offset each other over a longer distance. Therefore, the accumulative error reaches a lower value after a longer distance.

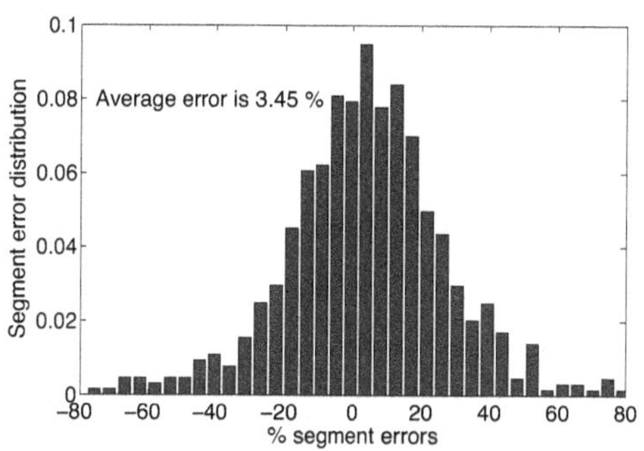

Figure 8: Distribution of per segment errors.

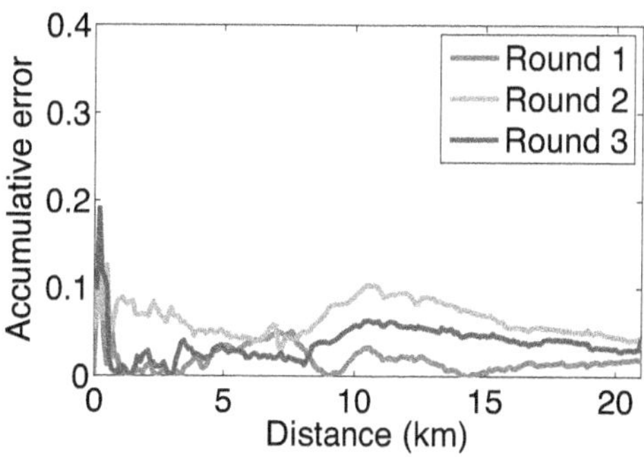

Figure 9: Accumulative error against travelled distance.

5.4 Energy Consumption Model Validation

We first use the data sets of R_1 and R_2 to obtain the coefficients of Eqns. (2)-(3). Next, we examine the accuracy of estimating the energy consumption using Eqns. (2)-(3) against the actual energy consumption. The respective accumulative error averaged over three rounds of experiments are shown in Table 5 and Fig. 10. We observe that the accumulative errors range from 0.1% to around 5%, which is sufficient to practical DTE prediction. In Fig. 11, we use other drivers' driving data to predict other drivers' energy consumption in the same route. The initial error is relatively large due to several reasons: 1) the prediction can overestimate or underestimate the accurate DTE, which creates short-term fluctuations. The prediction error will be offset by the positive and negative deviations in a long term. Therefore, the accumulative error can reach a lower value after a longer distance. 2) For vehicle D_3 (LEAF), the sample rate is relative low, therefore, the initial error is larger than others', because the driving behavior cannot be fully captured when sample rate is low. We are working on increasing the sample rate of the LEAF which will improve the initial error.

Route	Vehicle	Driver	Average accumulative error
R_1	V_1	D_1	3.6%
R_1	V_2	D_2	0.1%
R_1	V_3	D_2	3.2%
R_1	V_3	D_3	2.0%
R_1	V_4	D_4	0.1%
R_2	V_1	D_1	4.4%
R_2	V_2	D_2	3.7%
R_2	V_3	D_2	4.7%
R_2	V_3	D_3	5.4%
R_2	V_4	D_4	5.1%

Table 5: Estimation errors for route-vehicle-driver tuples.

5.5 Correlation Discovery

Next, we obtain the correlation metrics $\bar{\chi}_{(D,V),(D',V')}$ in Table 6. The two top-most similar pairs are highlighted in bold in each row. For example, (D_1, V_1) has a small value with (D_2, V_2) and (D_3, V_3). We use k-nearest neighbor method to choose the k most similar (D', V') for each (D, V), and use their respective driving data to estimate the energy consumption of (D, V).

$\bar{\chi}_{(D,V),(D',V')}$	(D_1, V_1)	(D_2, V_2)	(D_3, V_3)	(D_2, V_3)	(D_4, V_4)
(D_1, V_1)	0	**1.0799**	**1.0214**	1.1659	1.2319
(D_2, V_2)	**1.0799**	0	1.1022	**0.9872**	1.1895
(D_3, V_3)	**1.0214**	**1.1022**	0	1.1423	1.4211
(D_2, V_3)	1.1659	**0.9872**	**1.1423**	0	1.2169
(D_4, V_4)	1.2319	**1.1895**	1.4211	**1.2169**	0

Table 6: Correlation metrics.

6. CASE STUDIES

In this section, we apply our results to some concrete case studies: (1) DTE prediction, (2) characterization of driving behavior, (3) energy-efficient driving recommendations, and (4) route-level energy consumption geo-fencing and refueling planning.

6.1 DTE Prediction

Based on the correlation metrics, we can estimate the energy consumption using the driving data by the most similar driver-vehicle pairs. In particular, one can use the data of ICE vehicles (V_1, V_2, V_4) to predict the energy consumption of the EV (V_3).

In the following, five scenarios are considered:

1. Predicting (D_1, V_1) using estimators (D_2, V_2),(D_3, V_3)
2. Predicting (D_2, V_2) using estimators (D_1, V_1),(D_2, V_3)
3. Predicting (D_3, V_3) using estimators (D_1, V_1),(D_2, V_2)
4. Predicting (D_2, V_3) using estimators (D_2, V_2),(D_3, V_3)
5. Predicting (D_4, V_4) using estimators (D_2, V_2),(D_2, V_3)

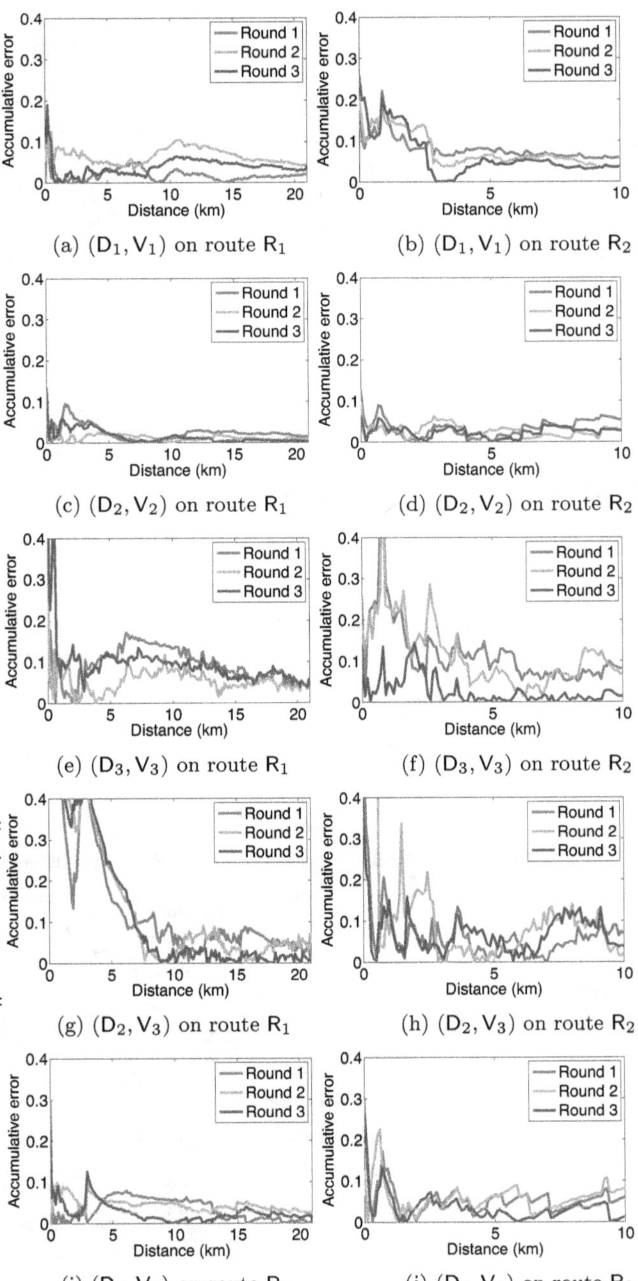

(a) (D_1, V_1) on route R_1 (b) (D_1, V_1) on route R_2 (c) (D_2, V_2) on route R_1 (d) (D_2, V_2) on route R_2 (e) (D_3, V_3) on route R_1 (f) (D_3, V_3) on route R_2 (g) (D_2, V_3) on route R_1 (h) (D_2, V_3) on route R_2 (i) (D_4, V_4) on route R_1 (j) (D_4, V_4) on route R_2

Figure 10: Estimation errors against traveled distance.

The respective accumulative errors for route R_1 are shown in Table 7, along with the prediction using its own data. Three rounds of data for each driver-vehicle pair are averaged and then used to predict others. For each driver-vehicle pair, we use the two most similar driver-vehicle pairs, as well as its own data. The diagonal entries of the Table 7 are the predictions based on the own data. Except driver (D_4), the estimation errors are observed to be low. Driver (D_4) drives much more aggressively compared to other drivers, and hence, its correlation metrics have larger values. Therefore, the estimation errors are larger for (D_4) using other drivers.

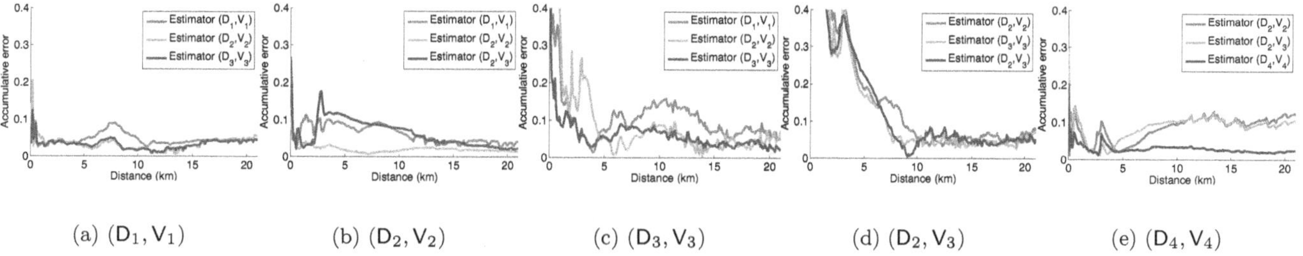

(a) (D_1, V_1) (b) (D_2, V_2) (c) (D_3, V_3) (d) (D_2, V_3) (e) (D_4, V_4)

Figure 11: Estimation errors against traveled distance.

Error	Estimator (D_1,V_1)	(D_2,V_2)	(D_3,V_3)	(D_2,V_3)	(D_4,V_4)
(D_1,V_1)	4.7%	5.8%	4.6%	..	..
(D_2,V_2)	4.3%	1.4%	..	2.4%	..
(D_3,V_3)	5.2%	7.4%	2.0%	..	..
(D_2,V_3)	..	5.9%	6.7%	5.3%	..
(D_4,V_4)	..	12.1%	..	10.3%	2.5%

Table 7: Estimation errors.

6.1.1 *DTE Prediction for EV*

In particular, we study the performance of DTE prediction for EV (i.e., Nissan LEAF). The data collected from EV includes:

1. State of charge (SOC), denoted by $\mathcal{S}$, indicates how much electricity remains in the battery.

2. Initial capacity of the battery, denoted by $\mathcal{B}_A$.

3. Battery pack voltage when driving, denoted by $\mathcal{B}_V$.

The remaining energy ($\Delta\mathcal{E}^t$) in battery at time t is given by:

$$\Delta\mathcal{E}^t = \mathcal{S}^t \times \mathcal{B}_A \times \mathcal{B}_V^t \qquad (21)$$

If the future average power intensity ($\bar{\mathcal{P}}$) is known, then DTE is given by:

$$\text{DTE} = \frac{\Delta\mathcal{E}^t}{\bar{\mathcal{P}}} \qquad (22)$$

We especially compare the DTE prediction based on our energy consumption model with the on board DTE meter on Nissan LEAF, which is captured by a camera mounted over the dashboard. Fig. 12 shows our estimated DTE and on board DTE meter readings in the experiment. The reference line in the Fig. 12 denotes the true DTE as the distance goes. We observe that our approach gives a considerably more accurate prediction than the onboard meter.

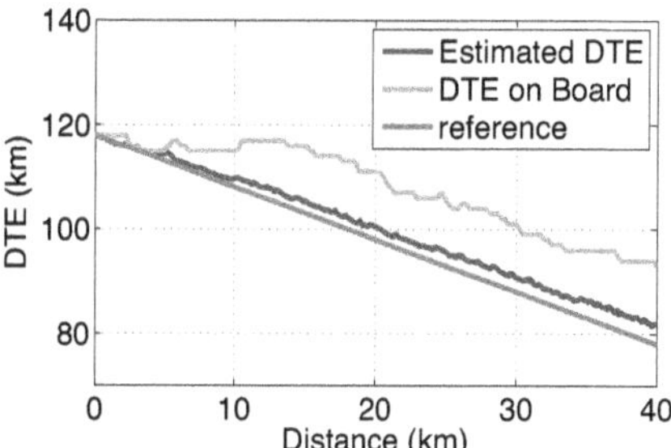

Figure 12: Comparison between our estimated DTE and onboard DTE meter reading.

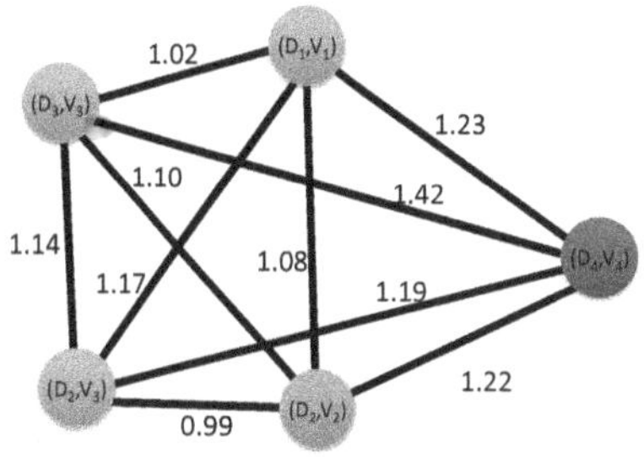

Figure 13: Clustering of driver-vehicle pairs based on correlation metrics. Green nodes are the energy-efficient driver, whereas the red node is energy-inefficient driver.

6.2 Classification of Driving Behavior

The correlation metrics between every pair of drivers can provide a distance matrix. One can apply standard clustering techniques on the set of driver-vehicle pairs in such a metric space. The clustered data set can classify energy-efficient driving behavior. Fig. 13 shows the clustered data set based on Table 6. We observe that energy-efficient driver-vehicle pairs (colored in green) tend to stay closer in the correlation metric space. Likewise, one can also obtain the cluster of energy-inefficient driver-vehicle pairs, and a complete classification of driving behavior.

6.3 Driving Recommendations

Our energy consumption model can be applied to provide recommendations of energy-efficient driving. Assuming other parameters are constant (e.g., acceleration, deceleration, and gyroscope data), the energy consumption is only dependent on the vehicle speed in our model. For example, Fig. 14 shows the energy intensity of several driver-vehicle pairs at different speeds. It is observed that there is a minimum point for ICE vehicles (namely, the least energy-consuming speed), and an energy intensity increasing with speed for EV (because electric motors operate more efficiency at low speeds). For ICE vehicles, we can recommend that the driver to maintain at the least energy-consuming speed obtained from the model. For EV, the optimal speed will be the smallest possible speed that can arrive at the destination before a deadline.

6.4 Geo-fencing and Planning

Geo-fencing depicts the geographical range before the energy of vehicle is exhausted. Traditionally, geo-fencing is estimated only considering the geographical distance. With the information from our model, more detailed route-level

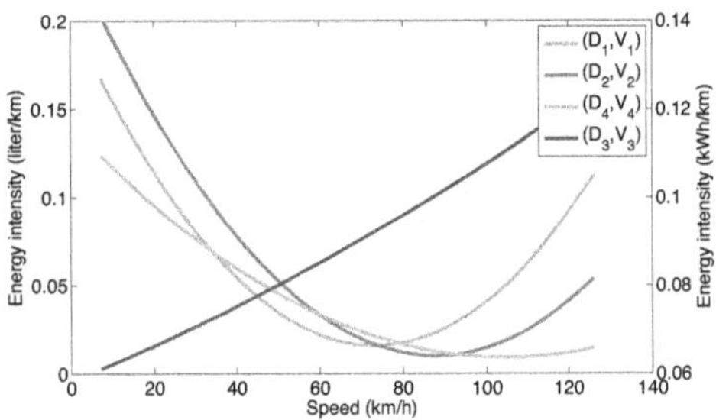

Figure 14: Energy intensity of vehicles at different speed according to our energy consumption model.

energy consumption geo-fencing can be constructed, for example, as seen in Fig. 15. The route-level energy consumption geo-fencing is constructed in the following manner. We first obtain the map data from OpenStreetMap (OSM). We employ our model to estimate the energy consumption at each point along a route. The least energy consumption required to reach a particular point can be estimated by A* algorithm, considering multiple route alternatives. The least energy consumption will be visualized on top of OSM data to provide route-level energy consumption geo-fencing. A critical application energy consumption geo-fencing is to enable informed decisions for refueling.

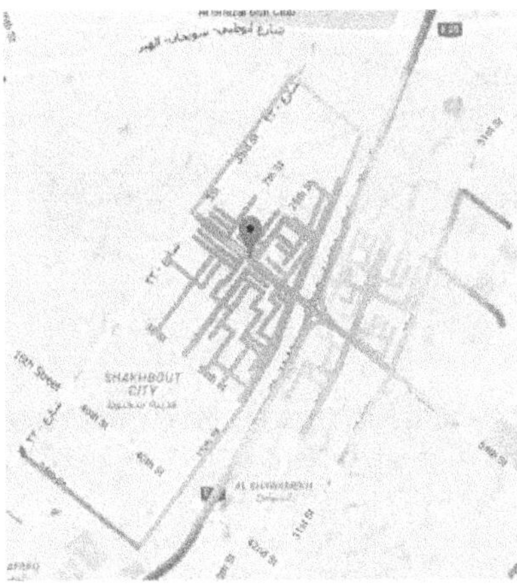

Figure 15: Route-level energy consumption geo-fencing.

7. CONCLUSION AND FUTURE WORK

An effective approach has been proposed to integrates the vehicle data gathered from diverse drivers and vehicles for personalized applications of improving driving energy efficiency. Our system provides a unifying approach for both ICE vehicles and EVs. The advantages include identifying the features according to the driver, vehicle and route dependence. The processed data can flexibly support diverse applications, such as DTE prediction, green telematics and energy-efficient route planning, and classification of energy efficient driving behavior.

Future work will include integration of extensive data from large-scale datasets such as those to be available from CloudThink [1] as well as from expanded GIS databases(e.g. the geometric of the roads). We are working to integrate our methodology to open platforms (e.g. OpenStreetMap). Moreover, hybrid vehicles or plug-in hybrid vehicles are not considered in this work, because of the lack of proper software to interoperate the proprietary data about battery state in these vehicles. Proper software will be sought in future to allow further experiments on these vehicles.

8. ACKNOWLEDGEMENT

We would like to thank the reviewers and the shepherd (Dr. Sarvapali D.(Gopal) Ramchurn) for helpful comments and suggestions.

9. REFERENCES

[1] CloudThink. http://cloud-think.com/, 2015. [Online; accessed 19-February-2015].

[2] Michael J Burke, Nick Sarafopoulos, and Viet Q To. Electronic system and method for calculating distance to empty for motorized vehicles, 1994. US Patent 5,301,113.

[3] Andrew T. Campbell, Shane B. Eisenman, Nicholas D. Lane, Emiliano Miluzzo, Ronald A. Peterson, Hong Lu, Xiao Zheng, Mirco Musolesi, Kristóf Fodor, and Gahng-Seop Ahn. The rise of people-centric sensing. *IEEE Internet Computing*, 12(4):12–21, July 2008.

[4] S. Dornbush and A. Joshi. StreetSmart traffic: Discovering and disseminating automobile congestion using VANET's. In *Vehicular Technology Conference, 2007. VTC2007-Spring. IEEE 65th*, pages 11–15, April 2007.

[5] Raghu K. Ganti, Nam Pham, Hossein Ahmadi, Saurabh Nangia, and Tarek F. Abdelzaher. Greengps: A participatory sensing fuel-efficient maps application. In *Proceedings of the 8th International Conference on Mobile Systems, Applications, and Services*, MobiSys '10, pages 151–164. ACM, 2010.

[6] Torsten J. Gerpott and Sabrina Berg. Explaining customers' willingness to use mobile network-based pay-as-you-drive insurances. *Int. J. Mob. Commun.*, 11(5):485–512, October 2013.

[7] J.G. Hayes, R.P.R. de Oliveira, S. Vaughan, and M.G. Egan. Simplified electric vehicle power train models and range estimation. In *Vehicle Power and Propulsion Conference (VPPC), 2011 IEEE*, pages 1–5, Sept 2011.

[8] Xiping Hu, Victor C.M. Leung, Kevin Garmen Li, Edmond Kong, Haochen Zhang, Nambiar Shruti Surendrakumar, and Peyman TalebiFard. Social drive: A crowdsourcing-based vehicular social networking system for green transportation. In *Proceedings of the Third ACM International Symposium on Design and Analysis of Intelligent Vehicular Networks and Applications*, DIVANet '13, pages 85–92. ACM, 2013.

[9] Prashanth Mohan, Venkata N. Padmanabhan, and Ramachandran Ramjee. Nericell: Rich monitoring of road and traffic conditions using mobile smartphones. In *Proceedings of the 6th ACM Conference on Embedded Network Sensor Systems*, SenSys '08, pages 323–336. ACM, 2008.

[10] Austin Louis Oehlerking. StreetSmart: modeling vehicle fuel consumption with mobile phone sensor data through a participatory sensing framework (master's thesis), 2011.

[11] Jungme Park, Zhihang Chen, L. Kiliaris, M.L. Kuang, M.A. Masrur, A.M. Phillips, and Y.L. Murphey. Intelligent vehicle power control based on machine learning of optimal control parameters and prediction of road type and traffic congestion. *Vehicular Technology, IEEE Transactions on*, 58(9):4741–4756, Nov 2009.

[12] L Rodgers, E Wilhelm, and D Frey. Conventional and novel methods for estimating an electric vehicle's "distance to empty". In *Proc. of the ASME 2013 International Conference on Advanced Vehicle Technologies*, 2013.

[13] Stan Salvador and Philip Chan. Toward accurate dynamic time warping in linear time and space. *Intell. Data Anal.*, 11(5):561–580, October 2007.

[14] Chien-Ming Tseng, Sohan Dsouza, and Chi-Kin Chau. A social approach for predicting distance-to-empty in vehicles. In *Proceedings of the 5th International Conference on Future Energy Systems*, e-Energy '14, pages 215–216. ACM, 2014.

[15] Yan Wang, Jie Yang, Hongbo Liu, Yingying Chen, Marco Gruteser, and Richard P. Martin. Sensing vehicle dynamics for determining driver phone use. In *Proceeding of the 11th Annual International Conference on Mobile Systems, Applications, and Services*, MobiSys '13, pages 41–54. ACM, 2013.

A Multi-Factor Battery Cycle Life Prediction Methodology for Optimal Battery Management

Valentin Muenzel*
Electrical and Electronic Eng.
University of Melbourne
Victoria, Australia

Julian de Hoog
IBM Research - Australia
Victoria, Australia

Marcus Brazil
Electrical and Electronic Eng.
University of Melbourne
Victoria, Australia

Arun Vishwanath
IBM Research - Australia
Victoria, Australia

Shiv. Kalyanaraman
IBM Research - Australia
Victoria, Australia

ABSTRACT

Affordability of battery energy storage critically depends on low capital cost and high lifespan. Estimating battery lifespan, and optimising battery management to increase it, is difficult given the associated complex, multi-factor ageing process. In this paper we present a battery life prediction methodology tailored towards operational optimisation of battery management. The methodology is able to consider a multitude of dynamically changing cycling parameters. For lithium-ion (Li-ion) cells, the methodology has been tailored to consider five operational factors: charging and discharging currents, minimum and maximum cycling limits, and operating temperature. These are captured within four independent models, which are tuned using experimental battery data. Incorporation of dynamically changing factors is done using rainflow counting and discretisation. The resulting methodology is designed for solving optimal battery operation problems.

Implementation of the methodology is presented for two case studies: a smartphone battery, and a household with battery storage alongside solar generation. For a smartphone that charges daily, our analysis finds that the battery life can be more than doubled if the maximum charging limit is chosen strategically. And for the battery supporting domestic solar, it is found that the impact of large daily cycling outweighs that of small more frequent cycles. This suggests that stationary Li-ion batteries may be well suited to provide ancillary services as a secondary function.

The developed methodology and demonstrated use cases represent a key step towards maximising the cost-benefit of Li-ion batteries for any given application.

*Please address all correspondence to this author at v.muenzel (at) student.unimelb.edu.au

e-Energy'15, July 14–17, 2015, Bangalore, India.

ACM: 978-1-4503-3609-3/15/07 ... $15.00
DOI: http://dx.doi.org/10.1145/2768510.2768532.

Keywords

Lithium-ion (Li-ion) batteries; cell degradation; cycle life prediction; battery value optimisation

1. INTRODUCTION

There is a growing need for affordable decentralised energy storage. The market for energy storage is predicted to grow by 50% in the six years to 2020 [7]. Rechargeable batteries, including lithium-ion, are promising candidates given their rapidly decreasing cost [10].

Rechargeable lithium-ion (Li-ion) batteries have been used in laptop computers, mobile phones, and other portable electronic devices since the 1990s. More recently, they are being implemented in much larger applications. These include hybrid-electric and pure electric vehicles, as well as stationary energy storage for domestic, industrial, and power grid-support applications. This transition to larger applications is not straightforward. The low power draw of portable electronics limits heat generation in battery cells, thereby facilitating battery management. Low power also means a low storage voltage is acceptable, allowing only one or a few cells to be used, which require only a very simple battery management system. Also, portable electronics are typically designed for a lifespan of three years or less.

Conversely, large battery systems typically have a large power draw, requiring a multitude of cells, as well as more complex battery and thermal management systems. They have significantly longer lifetimes, in many cases of more than ten years. And the high initial investment involved means that battery systems become strategic assets and the lifetime preservation is of critical importance.

Managing batteries for longer lifetimes, however, is not straightforward. In the literature, few long-term experiments lasting five or more years have been published [1]. Of these, many were based on early battery chemistries, since which point significant progress has been made [15]. Concurrently, estimation methods of battery cycle life remain a field with ample scope for improvement.

The battery cycle life prediction methodologies developed to date can be divided into electrochemical and empirical approaches. Electrochemical cycle life prediction uses physically-based models alongside chemical reaction equations [2]. This is fundamentally the most accurate and insightful modelling approach as it captures physical and chemical characteristics as part of the model. However, the vast number of physical and chemical parameters make fitting such models to any given cell a quite complicated and time-consuming process. This inhibits widespread use of such models.

Empirical approaches on the other hand use curve fitting to find general equations from discrete cycling measurement points. This reduces the complexity of model tuning notably. However, most empirical approaches focus on certain cells under a given range of conditions that entail only specific considered impact factors. This is done to limit the required amount of data and associated testing to a feasible volume. Ecker et al., for example, developed a life prediction model for pouch cells taking into account state-of-charge and temperature, but not charging or discharging currents [3]. And Ng et al. considered temperature, discharge current and depths-of-discharge, but does not consider charging currents or variations in the maximum state-of-charge [11].

The most encompassing empirically-based methodology, to the knowledge of the authors, was published by Omar et al. [13]. Their methodology uses separate models for four impact factors, all of which are modelled as independent from one-another. However, their methodology representing the state-of-the-art has room for improvement in several areas:

- It considers that for each cycle charging ends and discharging begins at 100% SOC. This may frequently be undesirable as high SOCs can lead to notable degradation during both cycling [4] and storage [3].
- Our attempts at replication found depth-of-discharge parameters that vary by several orders of magnitude from those published.
- The method of combining the various individual parameter models into a full model was demonstrated but not explained. It is based on fuzzy logic but is protected knowledge that the authors are not able to share (personal correspondence).
- The existing approach only predicts cycle life under static cycling conditions, in which cycling parameters such as currents and charging and discharging bounds do not change from cycle-to-cycle.

In this paper we present a battery life prediction model that addresses the above issues and is tailored towards usability as part of a battery management optimisation scheme. We make three main contributions to the literature:

1. We develop and demonstrate an empirically-supported model of how battery cycle life varies with interdependent average state-of-charge and depth-of-discharge[1].
2. We present a reproducible framework for combining numerous independent cycle life models considering different impact factors into a unified multi-factor cycle life model.
3. We develop and demonstrate a technique for enabling battery life prediction models to assess battery usage with dynamically changing cycling parameters.

We believe that the resulting model holds significant value for battery management and control optimisation for academic and commercial purposes alike.

[1]An explanation of domain-specific terminology is provided in Table 1.

Table 1: Domain-Specific Terminology

Notation	Meaning
CL	Cycle life; the number of cycles under certain conditions until the battery reaches its end-of-life of typically 70-80% of initial capacity.
DOD	Depth-of-discharge; the difference between minimum and maximum state-of-charge of a cycle.
nCL	Normalised cycle life; the cycle life of a battery under particular conditions divided by the cycle life under nominal conditions.
SOC	State-of-charge; the amount of charge stored in a battery at a given point of time divided by its nominal capacity. For the purpose of this paper we assume the battery voltage is fixed and the charge stored is directly proportional to energy stored.
SOC_{av}	Average state-of-charge; the mean of the maximum and minimum state-of-charge of a cycle.
SOC_{min}	The minimum state-of-charge reached during a given battery charge and discharge cycle.
SOC_{max}	The minimum state-of-charge reached during a given battery charge and discharge cycle.

2. METHODOLOGY

This section presents the combined cycle life algorithm, with following sections describing models for individual ageing factors for Li-ion batteries.

While the underlying methodology is valid for battery cells of any chemistry, the individual factor models and curve fitting are chemistry-dependent. The limited availability of suitable published Li-ion cell ageing data at present restricts us to taking a chemistry-agnostic approach here, but in future work this model is to be adjusted for specific Li-ion chemistries.

At the heart of the chosen approach, and as suggested in [13], is the assumption that the impacts that certain environmental and operational factors on lithium-ion battery cycle life are, or can be approximated as being, independent from one-another. Based on this independence assumption, it follows:

$$\frac{CL(x_1,...x_k)}{CL(x_{1,nom},...,x_{k,nom})} = \frac{CL(x_1)}{CL(x_{1,nom})} \times \cdots \times \frac{CL(x_k)}{CL(x_{k,nom})} \quad (1)$$

where CL is the predicted cycle life to a certain limit of degradation under given cycling parameters, x_k is the kth cycling parameter, and degradation impact factor, to be considered. In the case of interdependent ageing factors, the relevant factors need to be jointly included in one fraction on the right hand side. The index nom refers to nominal cycle life and cycling parameters, as found for example in a battery data sheet or gained from a cycling experiment for a single set of cycling parameters.

$$CL(x_1 \cdots x_k) = CL(x_{1,nom} \cdots x_{k,nom}) \times \frac{CL(x_1)}{CL(x_{1,nom})} \times \cdots \times \frac{CL(x_k)}{CL(x_{k,nom})} \quad (2)$$

In the case of lithium-ion battery ageing, among the most important impact factors are the operating temperature T, charging current I_{ch}, the discharging current I_d, as well as the minimum and maximum state-of-charge boundaries [4]. The following sections discuss and describe the development of impact factor models for these factors. The state-of-charge boundaries are transformed into depth-of-discharge DOD and average state-of-charge SOC_{av}.

The combined lithium-ion battery life cycle model, used in latter analysis and case studies, is formed by taking the product of the normalised individual models (Eqns. (7), (8, 9), and (18)) and the nominal cycle life:

$$CL(T, I_d, I_{ch}, SOC_{av}, DOD) = CL_{nom} \times nCL(T) \times nCL(I_d) \times nCL(I_{ch}) \times nCL(SOC_{av}, DOD) \quad (3)$$

where nCL is each associated normalised cycle life fraction, corresponding to terms on the right side of Eq. (1). This provides the underlying framework for predicting the cycle life of a given battery cell based on a single data cycle life data point. This data point can either come from manufacturer specifications, or from testing of a cell under a single set of cycling conditions.

2.1 Battery Currents and Temperature

For charging current, discharging current and working temperature of the cell, modified versions of the model published in [13] are used. In this model, cycle life is captured as a third order polynomial function of temperature:

$$CL(T) = aT^3 - bT^2 + cT + d \quad (4)$$

where a, b, c, and d are coefficients from fitting of experimental data on lithium iron phosphate based cells with values shown in Table 2. Note that the experiments in [13] used short-term cycling rather than as a simple constant current discharge, which is assumed here to have negligible impact.

The published model further approximates cycle life as a second-order exponential function of both discharging and charging current, respectively given as:

$$CL(I_d) = e \times exp(fI_d) + g \times exp(hI_d) \quad (5)$$

$$CL(I_{ch}) = m \times exp(nI_{ch}) + o \times exp(pI_{ch}) \quad (6)$$

where I_d and I_{ch} are the discharging and charging current, respectively, and e, f, g, h, m, n, o, and p are fit coefficients, the values of which are also listed in Table 2.

Eq. (3) requires each of the published models to be normalised. This normalisation is done as follows:

$$nCL(T) = \frac{aT^3 - bT^2 + cT + d}{aT_{nom}^3 - bT_{nom}^2 + cT_{nom} + d} \quad (7)$$

$$nCL(I_d) = \frac{e \times exp(fI_d) + g \times exp(hI_d)}{e \times exp(fI_{d,nom}) + g \times exp(hI_{d,nom})} \quad (8)$$

$$nCL(I_{ch}) = \frac{m \times exp(nI_{ch}) + o \times exp(pI_{ch})}{m \times exp(nI_{ch,nom}) + o \times exp(pI_{ch,nom})} \quad (9)$$

where nCL represents the normalised cycle life for each respective impact factor, T_{nom}, $I_{d,nom}$, and $I_{ch,nom}$, are nominal working temperature, nominal discharging current, and nominal charging current, respectively, as specified by the manufacturer for a given specified cycle life.

2.2 State-of-Charge and Depth-of-Discharge

By the nature of the coupling between the average state-of-charge, SOC_{av}, and depth-of-discharge, DOD, the respective impacts on cycle life are intuitively likely to be notably interdependent. For example, assume the life of a battery cell cycling between 40-60% (i.e. $SOC_{av} = 50\%$, and $DOD = 20\%$) is double that of a cell cycling from 30-70% ($SOC_{av} = 50\%$, and $DOD = 40\%$). This does not necessarily mean that a cell cycling between 10-30% SOC ($SOC_{av} = 20\%$, and $DOD = 20\%$) also has double the life of a cell cycling between 0-40% ($SOC_{av} = 20\%$, and $DOD = 40\%$). In fact, this is unlikely to give similar ageing, as discussed subsequently.

As a result an experimental dataset is required, in which both DOD and SOC_{av} are varied independently. Such a dataset was recently published by Ecker et al. [4]. It contains cycle life measurements for average SOC and DOD ranging from 10-90% and 10-100%, respectively. Obviously, the closer SOC_{av} is to either 0 or 100%, the lower the maximum DOD can be (a cell with an SOC_{av} of 10% can have at most a DOD of 20%, corresponding to cycling between 0-20% SOC).

Once digitised, a suitable fitting function is required for the dataset. [4] indicates that the cycle life of batteries decreases for cycling in both high and low SOC regions, while in mid-SOC regions less degradation occurs. This suggests a second-order polynomial function related to average SOC as a potentially suitable approach. The data further illustrates that as DOD increases, the cycle life reduces non-linearly. Having incorporated SOC_{av} as a second-order polynomial, a logical approach is to incorporate DOD as a multi-order polynomial also. Given the DOD and SOC_{av} are expected to be interdependent as discussed previously, there will also be one or more terms containing both variables.

Taking a second-order approach for DOD and SOC_{av}, the function to be fitted becomes:

$$CL^*(DOD, SOC_{av}) = q_0 + r_0 * DOD + s_0 * SOC_{av} + t_0 * DOD^2 + u_0 * DOD * SOC_{av} + v_0 * SOC_{av}^2 \quad (10)$$

where CL^* is the equivalent cycle life, and SOC_{av} and DOD are the average state-of-charge and depth-of-discharge over each cycle, respectively. Constants q_0, r_0, s_0, t_0, u_0, and v_0 are the fit coefficients. Curve fitting using the least-squares fitting method via the Matlab Curve Fitting Tool found these coefficients to have the values listed in Table 2.

As shown in left and centre of Fig. 1, this leads to a reasonably good fit, characterised by R-square and Root Mean Square Error values of 0.767 and 1220, respectively. Note that the figure shows all of the curve within the SOC_{av} and DOD range for which the cycle life is positive, including infeasible combinations of DOD and SOC_{av}. However, the fit has one problematic aspect. As shown in Fig. 1c, the maximum equivalent cycle life over SOC_{av} actually increases slightly when increasing DOD from around 85% upwards. This goes against the trend seen in experiments (e.g. [4]). A

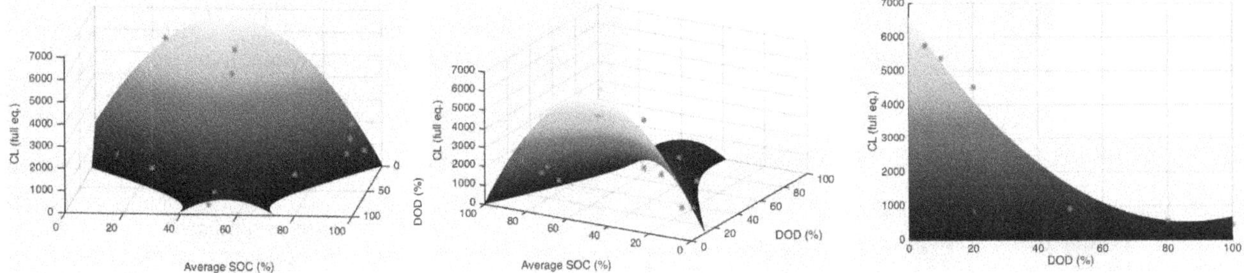

Figure 1: Two-variable second-order polynomial fit of cycle life as a function of average SOC and DOD. Figure on far right shows local minimum at $DOD < 100\%$, which is not consistent with practical findings.

Table 2: Values for tuning coefficients of models of lithium-ion degradation impact factors. Values for coefficients a···p are as published in [13]. Coefficients $q_0 \cdots v_0$, and $q \cdots v$ are deduced in Section 2.2.

Variable	a	b	c	d	e	f	g	h	m	n	o	p
Value	0.0039	1.95	67.51	2070	4464	-0.1382	-1519	-0.4305	5963	-0.6531	321.4	0.03168
Variable	q_0	r_0	s_0	t_0	u_0	v_0	q	s	t	u	v	
Value	1806	-160.8	207.7	0.7901	0.4425	-2.250	1471	214.3	0.6111	0.3369	-2.295	

local maximum at the 100% DOD boundary is problematic for use in optimisation of battery management as it would encourage batteries to be cycled to its maximum limits, leading in practice to particularly strong degradation.

One approach to avoid this is to force the cycle life to have its minimum over DOD at 100% DOD at all SOC_{av} points. However, doing so removes the expected interdependency between SOC_{av} and DOD.

A different approach is to specify that the minimum only falls on a specific single point where $DOD = 100\%$, thereby allowing flexibility everywhere else. A suitable choice of point is the cycle life has its maximum over SOC_{av} at 100% DOD. This point can be found by partially differentiating the cycle life from Eq. (10) over the SOC_{av} and setting to zero:

$$SOC_{av,100\%,max} = \frac{-s - 100 * u}{2 * v} \quad (11)$$

It is at this maximum point over the SOC that we want the minimum over DOD to occur. Therefore inserting this SOC_av value into Eq. (10) and setting $DOD = 100$:

$$\begin{aligned} r &= -200 * t - u * \frac{-s - 100 * u}{2 * v} \\ &= \frac{u}{2 * v} * (s + 100 * u) - 200 * t \quad (12) \end{aligned}$$

Reinserting into our original fitting function in Eq. (10), gives:

$$\begin{aligned} CL(DOD, SOC_{av}) = q + (&\frac{u}{2 * v} * (s + 100 * u) \\ &- 200 * t) * DOD + s * SOC_{av} + t * DOD^2 \\ &+ u * DOD * SOC_{av} + v * SOC_{av}^2 \quad (13) \end{aligned}$$

Recomputing the fit coefficients for this function using least-squares fitting gives the coefficient values listed in Table 2. It results in the function shown in Fig. 2. The only slightly worse R-square value of 0.7634, and slightly improved Root Mean Square Error of 1188 indicates that the imposed constraint does not significantly degrade the quality of fit.

For the fitted coefficient, the proposed function can analytically be shown to produce no partial minimum over DOD within the viable region characterised by the following four criteria:

$$0\% \leq SOC_{av} \leq 100\% \quad (14)$$

$$0\% \leq DOD \leq 100\% \quad (15)$$

$$DOD \leq 2 * SOC_{av} \quad (16)$$

$$DOD \leq 2 * (100 - SOC_{av}) \quad (17)$$

The result is a normalised model that predicts the normalised battery cycle life not just as a function of depth-of-discharge but also taking into account the average state-of-charge over a cycle.

Finally, the function in Eq. (13) can be normalised as follows:

$$nCL(SOC_{av}, DOD) = \frac{CL_4(DOD, SOC_{av})}{CL_4(DOD_{nom}, SOC_{av,nom})} \quad (18)$$

2.3 Verification of Developed Model

To ensure the developed DOD-SOC_{av} cycle life model is in line with expected results, it is compared to the DOD cycle life model based on [13]. Neither this model, nor associated data, was previously used to fit our model. Given difficulties in replicating the model's cycle life results directly using the published coefficients, the original data points are used to refit an exponential function as proposed, against which our model can then be compared. Least-squares fitting finds the model as:

$$CL^{+} = i \times exp(j \times DOD) \quad (19)$$

with coefficients i and j having values of 67560 and -0.03223, respectively.

Fig. 3 illustrates the comparison between this previously proposed DOD-only cycle life model and our DOD-SOC_{av} model.

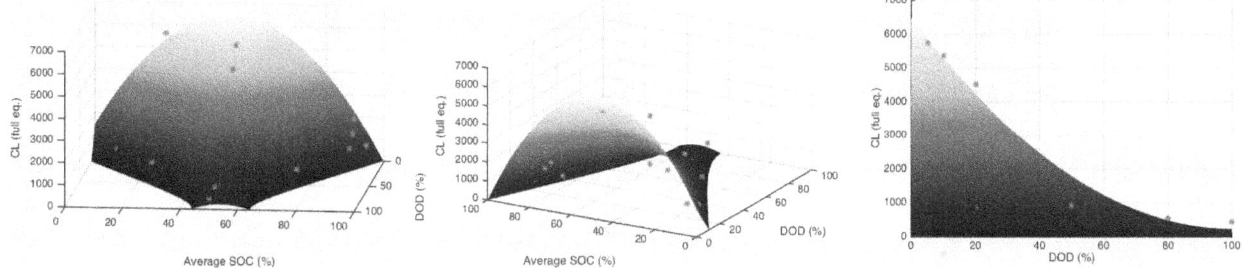

Figure 2: Modified two-variable second-order polynomial fit of cycle life as a function of SOC_{av} and DOD. The figure on far right confirms that local minimum for $DOD < 100$ is no longer visible.

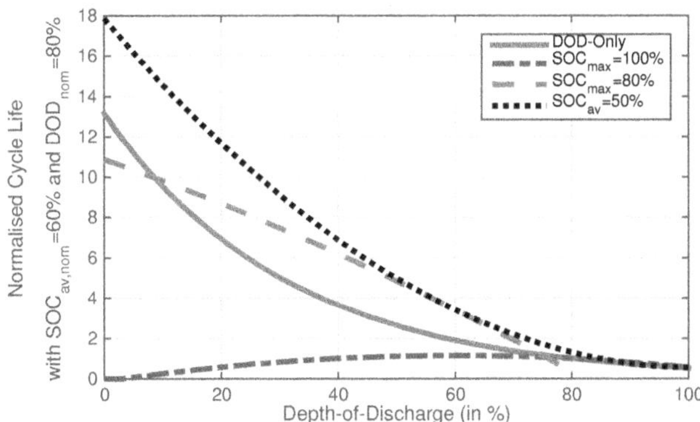

Figure 3: Verification of normalised cycle life models. The DOD-Only model based on [13] does not consider SOC. Our model considers SOC.

The closeness of results depends on both the SOC_av value chosen in our model, as well as the DOD region considered. The curve for $SOC_{max} = 100\%$, which corresponds to the conditions at which the DOD-Only data was collected, is a reasonable fit only above 70% DOD. This is because this choice of SOC represents the boundary case of feasible SOC-DOD behaviour (100% SOC is reached during very cycle) at which curve fitting seems to have its issues. With SOCs away from the edges, either by limiting SOC_{max} to 80%, or by fixing the average SOC to 50%, the resulting curves resemble the previously proposed model notably more closely. Remaining offsets are presumably the result of differences in the battery cells used for the experiments.

Table 3: Parameter limits of data points used for model fitting

Parameter	Minimum value	Maximum value
Temperature	-18°C	40°C
Discharge Current	1C	15C
Charge Current	C/8	4C
Average SOC[a]	10%	95%
DOD[a]	5%	100%

[a] Only part of the SOC-DOD region is feasible; see Eq. 14 - 17.

3. STATIC CASE STUDY: SMARTPHONE

To demonstrate the value of the static cycle life model developed thus far, we illustrate its use on a case study centred around smartphones. One of the suppliers of smartphone battery cells is Panasonic. Its NCA103450 battery, for example, is a prismatic Li-ion cell with a nominal capacity of 2350mAh, almost perfectly matching the 2300mAh offered by the batteries of Google 2013 Nexus 5 smartphone [5, 14]. The cell uses NCA cathodes, similar to those found in Tesla Motors electric vehicles.

Assuming one hour each of calling, browsing, and video watching per day, a new Nexus 5 battery has been shown to last 40 hours [6]. Under this assumption, a user has a wide range of charging options. We consider the following:

1. The battery is charged fully every 24 hours.
2. The battery is charged until full whenever it reaches a state-of-charge of 10%.
3. The battery is charged every 24 hours but only to the optimal level as determined as optimal by our battery ageing algorithm.

The obvious question is: what is the comparative battery life for each of these three charging options?

Using the developed life cycle prediction methodology, finding the answer to this question is quite straightforward. First, the nominal cycle life parameters of the cells need to be considered. The specifications listed in Table 4 are supplied by Panasonic in their associated data sheet [14].

Table 4: Battery cell specifications from Panasonic NCA103450 data sheet

Manufacturer spec	Variable	Value
Nominal capacity (Ah)	N/A	2.35
Nominal cycle life	CL_{nom}	649[a]
Measured at temp (deg C)	T_{nom}	25
Discharge current (C)	$I_{d,nom}$	1
Charging current (C)	$I_{ch,nom}$	0.7
Depth of discharge (%)	DOD_{nom}	100%
Average SOC (%)	SOC_{nom}	50%

[a] The cycle life was determined by digitising the cycle life graph, and linearly scaling forward the degradation seen at 100-500 cycles until the capacity falls below 80% of 2.35Ah.

Table 5: Smartphone cycling scenarios and cycling life outcomes

	Full charge from 10% SOC	Daily full charge	Daily optimal charge
$i_d(C)$	0.025		
$i_{ch}(C)$	0.7		
$T(dC)$	25		
DOD (%)	90	60	
SOC_{av}	55	70	51.09
$CL_{equiv.}$	963	1359	4040
CL_{actual}	1070	2265	6733
Life (years)	4.88	6.20	18.4

Assuming discharging at a steady rate, the current draw during its 40-hour battery life is:

$$I = \frac{2350Ah}{40h} = 58.75mA \tag{20}$$

Or:

$$I = \frac{58.75mA}{2350Ah} = 0.025C \tag{21}$$

The cycle life can then be estimated using our prediction methodology for the three use cases discussed previously, as defined by the parameters as listed in the upper part of Table 5.

As indicated in the final three rows of the table, the predicted cycle lives differ significantly. For the given assumptions, the smartphone battery is predicted to last around six years for daily full charging, versus five years for full charging only whenever 10% SOC is reached. However, an optimal daily charge approach, which is determined as having an average SOC of 51% (i.e. cycling between 21-81% SOC) more than doubles the expected life of the battery.

It should be noted that several of the assumptions mean that the predicted lifetimes are slightly optimistic. These include that battery cells always discharge at a steady rate and continuously operate at exactly $25°C$ working temperature. Better tailored assumptions would be likely to allow more accurate cycle life predictions. Nevertheless, it is clear that a strategic charging system has the potential to dramatically increase the expected lifetime of the battery.

4. MODELLING OF DYNAMIC CYCLES

The methodology presented thus far is able to predict the battery lifespan for all scenarios in which an identical charge-discharge cycle is repeated over the full life of the battery. However, in most applications, the cycles change dynamically over time. In electric vehicles, for example, the current input and output needs to change dynamically to provide timely vehicle acceleration and regenerative braking, respectively. And even in less variable application such as energy storage of surplus renewable generation, day-to-day variations in surplus generation lead to a variability in the cycling depth-of-discharge.

4.1 Rainflow Counting

To allow dynamic cycling, we have extended the prediction methodology using an approach called rainflow counting. This process combines a data set with non-uniform fluctuations in at least one variable into numerous data sets of uniform fluctuations by prioritising the most extreme fluctuations and discretising. In effect, rainflow counting screens a series of data for subsequent local maxima and minima indicating local cycle loops. Once found, these loops are recorded and removed from the data until the remaining loops become ever larger. It thereby preserves the most significant peaks and troughs to be considered last. The method is traditionally used for predicting material fatigue but has also been proposed for the prediction of battery ageing (e.g. [12]). In many battery applications such as electric cars with regeneration capability, batteries see notable short-term fluctuations in their state-of-charge, while at the same time following overall charge or discharge profiles. Previous experimental research has shown that deep cycling causes the most significant degradation whereas smaller cycles are

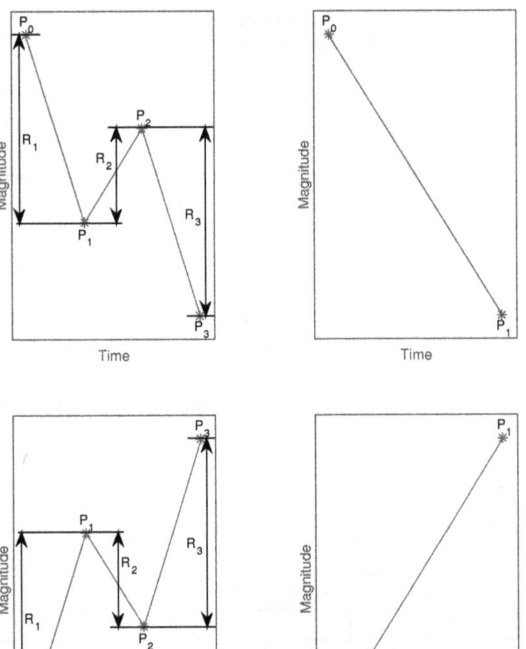

Figure 4: Rainflow counting algorithm illustrated on two profiles. Left and right shows the profiles before and after counting a local cycle, respectively.

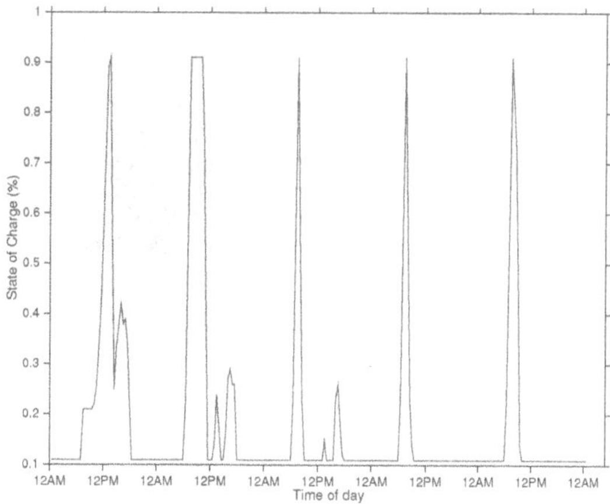

Figure 5: 5-day sample of battery SOC profile. The battery is found to cycle notably between 10% and 90% SOC with some smaller cycles occurring in-between.

less significant (e.g. [4]). As a result, rainflow counting is very suitable for modelling battery ageing.

Rainflow counting can be done in the form of either three- or four-point algorithms, which have been shown to be mathematically identical [8]. The three-point algorithm is faster as it only considers the two cycling ranges existing between three points in each iteration, as apposed to four points and three ranges for the four-point method. However, the three-point method requires an initial prearrangement of the data in order to start at either the global maximum or minimum. This inhibits real-time use of the method. To avoid this limitation, we have opted for the four-point approach.

The four-point rainflow counting method works as follows. It takes as input a set of data containing only the turning points. It then steps through this data from start to end, evaluating four turning points at a time. For each set of four points $P_0, ..., P_3$, three associated ranges are calculated:

$$R_k = |P_k - P_{k-1}| \tag{22}$$

where $k \in 1, 2, 3$. For a given set of four points, a local cycle is identified when the middle range has a smaller magnitude than the two outside ranges:

$$(R_k \geq R_{k-1}) \cap (R_{k-2} \geq R_{k-1}) = 1 \tag{23}$$

Following identification of a local cycle, the associated points P_1 and P_2 are recorded and removed from the dataset, and the algorithm continues. As shown in Fig. 4 this identification and removal approach works both when a local maximum is followed by a local minimum, and vice versa. Once the end of the data set is reached, the remaining cycles are accounted for through sequential repetition of the remaining points and rerunning the algorithm. When the end is reached the second time, all cycles have been accounted for. A more in-depth explanation of the algorithm as well as the pseudocode used as the basis for our programming code can be found in [8].

4.2 Dynamic Cycling Limits

Rainflow counting can be used to deal with variability in individual factor or multiple interlinked factors. An example of two interlinked factors, which we use in the demonstration case study in Section 5, are the maximum and minimum SOC points. As mentioned previously, variability in the depth-of-discharge of a battery is unavoidable for battery systems that are used to support the variable output from renewable generation, e.g. from solar and wind.

4.3 Combining Multiple Independent Factors

If only a single independent variable is considered (such as the temperature, or the charging current), the distribution will be one-dimensional. If multiple independent factors are considered to vary simultaneously, then this can be taken into account by recording not only cycles to be removed but also the other varying factors. Subsequently the cycles are then discretised in further dimensions (one for each varying independent factor), and the ageing map need to be conducted in an equally multi-dimensional form to allow matching up of cycles with corresponding ageing.

5. DYNAMIC CASE STUDY: STORAGE FOR DOMESTIC PV

To illustrate this algorithm, we have chosen to focus on the application of Li-ion battery storage for households that have solar panels. In countries where the feed-in tariff for solar generation has dropped below the typical electricity price, households have incentive to store surplus energy generated for subsequent use. The authors have previously conducted initial simulations to evaluate under which conditions battery storage becomes cost-effective in this context [9]. Here, we will use a randomly-selected simulation profile from the aforementioned paper to demonstrate the proposed ageing model.

5.1 Assumptions

The battery profile considers a $5kWh$ battery installed alongside an Australian household with a $2.5kW_p$ solar panel. The battery operation is optimised from a value-generating perspective that takes into account the electricity and feed-in price, but not the cost associated with battery degradation. It should also be noted that the battery was assumed to be limited to a DOD of 80% as is frequently done to avoid premature battery degradation. A five-day subset of the profile is shown in Fig. 5.

For this case study we have chosen the maximum and minimum state-of-charge to vary dynamically from cycle-

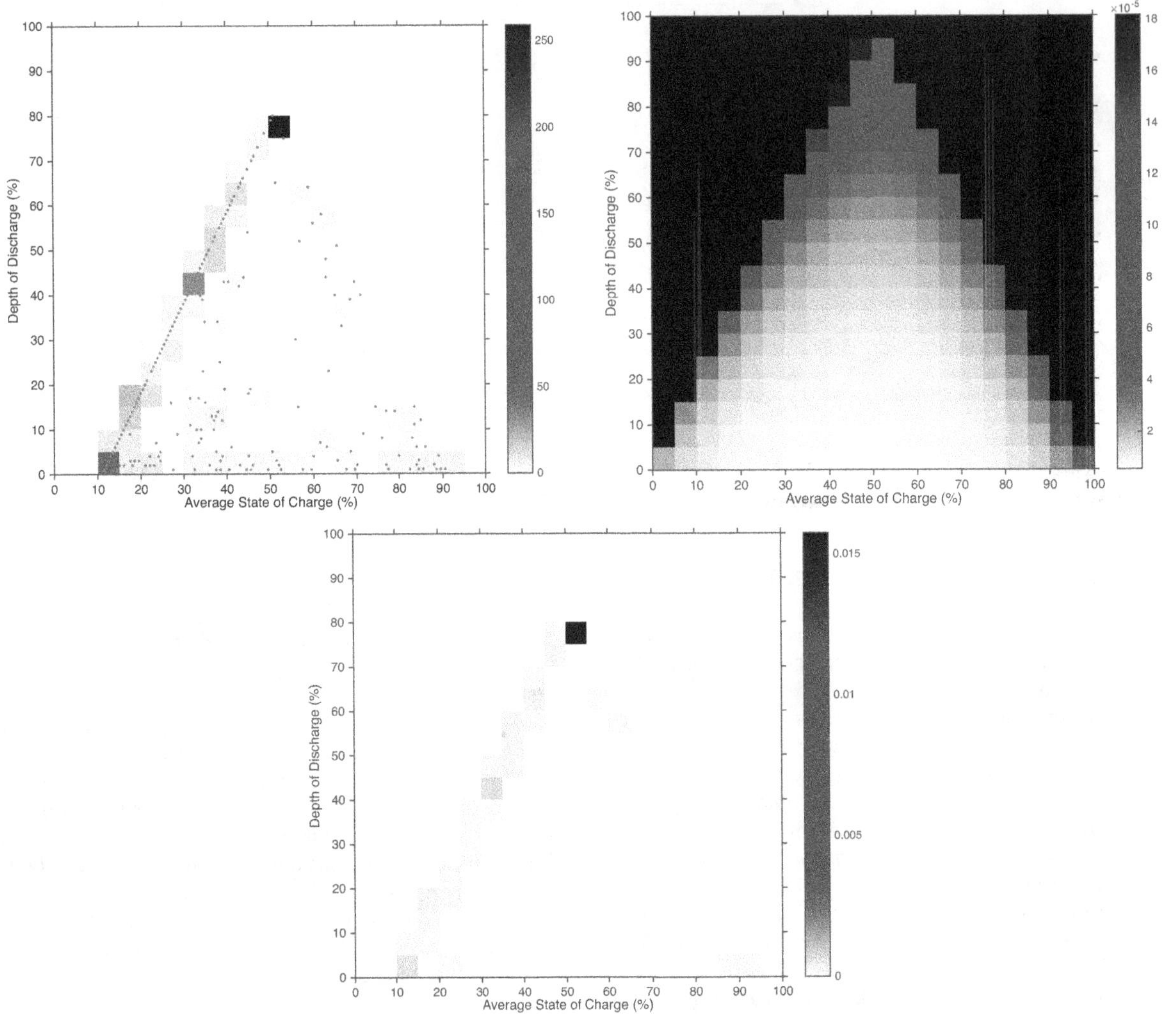

Figure 6: Top left: Cycle distribution after rainflow counting; the points represent individual cycles and the colour map indicates frequency of 5x5% sections. Top right: Fractional battery degradation per cycle for each 5x5% section. Bottom centre: Fractional degradation associated with each section for year-long profile.

Table 6: Domestic PV and storage assumptions. Top: application-specific cycling parameters; bottom: nominal battery parameters.

Battery capacity	5kWh
Operating temperature	25°C
Charge current	0.5C
Discharge current	1C
Maximum SOC	Dynamic (from profile)
Minimum SOC	Dynamic (from profile)
Nominal battery life	1200 cycles
@ Temperature	25°C
@ Charge current	0.5C
@ Discharge current	1C
@ Depth-of-discharge	80%
@ Average SOC	60%

to-cycle. The operating temperature, as well as the charge and discharge currents, are assumed to be fixed and have the values given in Table 6. the turning points fall at the times when the battery current changes direction. That is, the battery transitions either from charging to discharging, or vice versa.

5.2 Cycling Frequency

The first step is extracting the turning points from the data set. Next, the 4-point rainflow counting algorithm described in Section 4.1 is applied. The counted cycles are then discretised into segments, which we have chosen to be 5% SOC_{av} by 5% DOD.

The top left side of Figure 6 illustrates the cycle results. All individual extracted cycles are represented as points, whereas the colour map indicates the frequency of each discretised segment occurring in the one-year profile. It can be seen that by far the most frequent cycle is the maximum allowed battery cycle of 80% DOD and 50% SOC_{av}, corresponding to cycling between the boundaries 10% and 90% SOC.

5.3 Degradation

To calculate degradation, the cycling frequency matrix has to be matched with a matrix containing degradation per cycle for each segment. A matrix of cycle lives is found by evaluating ageing used the methodology presented Section 2 for the assumptions valid for each individual segment. This is converted to a matrix of degradation per cycle with elements D_k as follows:

$$D_k = \frac{1}{CL_k} \tag{24}$$

The resulting degradation map is shown on the top right side of Figure 6. It shows the analogous trend to Figure 2 in that the degradation per cycle increases with both increasing depth-of-discharge and when moving towards either extreme of the state-of-charge region.

The predicted battery degradation for the year-long data set can now be found by multiplying each sector frequency with its related degradation per cycle. This leads to the desired annual degradation matrix illustrated in Figure 6 bottom centre. The resulting degradation trends are similar to the frequency map, which is to be expected as many cycles of one type are likely to cause a notable degradation. By accumulating all points on the map, the total degradation over the year can be found. Assuming the profile is repeated year-after-year and that degradation occurs linearly, this can be used to estimate the lifetime of the battery cells until the capacity has reduced to a specific point. The results for the domestic PV with storage case study are listed in Table 7.

Table 7: Degradation result for storage alongside domestic PV generation

Degradation over one year	2.19%
Lifetime to 70%	13.72 years

6. CONCLUSIONS AND FUTURE WORK

6.1 Conclusions

In this paper we have presented a simple, yet powerful, methodology for predicting battery degradation rates and life spans that takes into account multiple impact factors. The methodology relies on a degree of independence between certain impact factors. For each independent factor, or set of factors, a normalised degradation model is developed based on curve-fitting of experimental data. In the paper this is demonstrated for lithium-ion batteries. The models are subsequently unified and combined with nominal battery information to allow prediction of cycle life under any given set of cycling conditions.

The developed static model was demonstrated on a static case study of a mobile phone. The case study found that daily charging to around 81% state-of-charge can prolong life significantly over both daily charging to 100% or charging fully only when the battery is nearly depleted. This suggests opportunities for charging solutions that improve battery management without requiring any user input or change in behaviour.

The paper further proposes a method to take into account dynamic variations in cycle parameters. A rainflow counting algorithm is used for determining and counting cycles, and discretisation is used to match cycles with degradation rates from our life prediction methodology.

The dynamic method is illustrated via a case study on batteries for households with PV generation. It identifies both the degradation caused by each discretised cycling interval, as well as the collective degradation caused by the applied cycling profile.

The resulting methodology provides a basis for conducting evaluations of battery life and optimisation of battery management for any battery-related applications.

6.2 Further Work

Future work to be done on this model is to extend the validation of the impact factor models against further experimental data. In particular, the individual factor models need to be evaluated for different cell chemistries to ensure suitability. Further factors should also be considered for inclusion in the methodology. One obvious such factor is the impact of resting periods between cycles, which over short times can lead to recovery effects but over long periods must include elements of calendar ageing.

7. ACKNOWLEDGMENTS

The first author would like to thank all members of Penn State University's Control Optimization Laboratory for the many stimulating discussions and collaborative work related to battery ageing, which form the basis on which this work is built. Particular thanks go to Michael Rothenberger and Ji Liu.

8. REFERENCES

[1] M. Broussely, P. Biensan, F. Bonhomme, P. Blanchard, S. Herreyre, K. Nechev, and R. Staniewicz. Main ageing mechanisms in li-ion batteries. *Journal of Power Sources*, 146:90–96, 2005.

[2] N. A. Chaturvedi, R. Klein, J. Christensen, J. Ahmed, and A. Kojic. Algorithms for advanced battery-management systems. *IEEE Control Systems*, 30(3):49–68, 2010.

[3] M. Ecker, J. B. Gerschler, J. Vogel, S. Käbitz, F. Hust, P. Dechent, and D. U. Sauer. Development of a lifetime prediction model for lithium-ion batteries based on extended accelerated aging test data. *Journal of Power Sources*, 215:248–257, 2012.

[4] M. Ecker, N. Nieto, S. Kaebitz, J. Schmalstieg, H. Blanke, A. Warnecke, and D. U. Sauer. Calendar and cycle life study of $Li(NiMnCo)O_2$-based 18650 lithiumion batteries. *Journal of Power Sources*, 248:839-851, 2014.

[5] Google. Nexus 5. http://www.google.com/nexus/5.

[6] GSMArena. LG Nexus 5 battery life test. http://blog.gsmarena.com/nexus-5-grinds-through-our-battery-test-routine.

[7] Lux Research. Energy storage market rises to $50 billion in 2020, amid dramatic changes. http://www.luxresearchinc.com/news-and-events/press-releases/read/energy-storage-market-rises-50-billion-2020-amid-dramatic.

[8] C. McInnes and P. Meehan. Equivalence of four-point and three-point rainflow cycle counting algorithms. *International Journal of Fatigue*, 30(3):547–559, 2008.

[9] V. Muenzel, J. de Hoog, I. Mareels, A. Vishwanath, S. Kalyanaraman, and A. Gort. PV generation and demand mismatch: Evaluating the potential of residential storage. In *Proceedings of IEEE PES ISGT 2015; in print.*

[10] V. Muenzel, I. Mareels, J. de Hoog, A. Vishwanath, and S. Kalyanaraman. Affordable batteries for green energy are closer than we think. https://theconversation.com/affordable-batteries-for-green-energy-are-closer-than-we-think-28772.

[11] S. S. Ng, Y. Xing, and K. L. Tsui. A naive bayes model for robust remaining useful life prediction of lithium-ion battery. *Applied Energy*, 118:114–123, 2014.

[12] A. Nuhic, T. Terzimehic, T. Soczka-Guth, M. Buchholz, and K. Dietmayer. Health diagnosis and remaining useful life prognostics of lithium-ion batteries using data-driven methods. *Journal of Power Sources*, 239:680–688, 2013.

[13] N. Omar, M. A. Monem, Y. Firouz, J. Salminen, J. Smekens, O. Hegazy, H. Gaulous, G. Mulder, P. Van den Bossche, T. Coosemans, and J. Van Mierlo. Lithium iron phosphate based battery – Assessment of the aging parameters and development of cycle life model. *Applied Energy*, 113:1575–1585, 2014.

[14] Panasonic. NCA103450 data sheet. https://www.master-instruments.com.au/cgi/ajax/get_file/63186/1.

[15] The Boston Consulting Group. Batteries for electric cars: Challenges, opportunities and the outlook to 2020. https://www.bcg.com/documents/file36615.pdf.

A Distributed Anytime Algorithm for Real-time EV Charging Congestion Control

Jose Rivera
Technische Universität München
j.rivera@tum.de

Christoph Goebel
Technische Universität München
christoph.goebel@tum.de

Hans-Arno Jacobsen
Technische Universität München
jacobsen@in.tum.de

ABSTRACT

A massive introduction of Electric Vehicles (EVs) will cause considerable load increase, and without proper control, can lead to congestion problems in the distribution of power. EV charging congestion control is the ability to control the EVs' charging rate to avoid the overloading of distribution grid elements while optimizing the use of the available infrastructure. We propose the implementation of a distributed anytime algorithm for real-time congestion control of EV charging in distribution feeders. The problem is formulated as a network utility maximization problem. An iterative distributed solution algorithm with feasible iterates is investigated. This paper shows the formulation of the proposed solution approach and also the formulation of the state-of-the-art dual decomposition solution. The resulting algorithms for the former approaches are evaluated under static and dynamic conditions. The results demonstrate that the proposed algorithm remains stable and retains its anytime property under dynamic conditions. Compared to the state-of-the-art solution, the proposed algorithm offers improved scalability and reliability for EV charging congestion control.

Categories and Subject Descriptors

I.2.8 [**Artificial Intelligence**]: Problem Solving, Control Methods, and Search—*control theory*

Keywords

Electric vehicle charging, congestion control, distributed control

1. INTRODUCTION

Many governments have identified Electric Vehicles (EVs) as a cornerstone of their sustainability strategies. EVs can reduce greenhouse gas emissions and serve as mobile storage units to provide balancing power [1]. The National EV targets of major economies call for there to be nearly 20 million vehicles by 2020, which represents a steep increase beyond the roughly one million EVs that were estimated to be in operation in 2013 [2]. This expected increase presents a series of challenges for system operators, who have to develop strategies for the efficient and reliable integration of large numbers of EVs.

One of the major obstacles to the large-scale deployment of EVs is that the current power distribution infrastructure is unable to handle the load increase: a typical household consumes on average 2 kW, while home EV chargers that require up to 22 kW can already be purchased. Since a 630 kVA transformer serving 250 households can handle an average load of up to 2 kW per house [2], we can see that the integration of EVs would exceed the capacity of the grid. A logical solution to this problem is to upgrade the distribution grid in order to handle the load increase. This, however, comes at a huge cost and could slow down adoption of EVs. A more practical solution is to use Information and Communication Technologies (ICT) to control EV charging. The challenge in this approach is the large number of expected EVs and their unknown spatial distribution. Furthermore, the distribution grid's state is highly dynamic and, if renewable energy is present, difficult to predict. Thus, there is growing interest in developing a distributed system for the control of EV charging that can adapt quickly to the fast dynamics of the grid, allows for local decisions of individual devices, and optimizes the global operation of the whole system. These efforts are part of a new research field known as Energy Informatics [3].

In this paper, we evaluate a distributed algorithm under dynamic conditions for real-time EV charging control. As in [4], we formulate the problem not as a time horizon scheduling problem, but as an instantaneous network utility maximization (NUM) problem. The goal herein is to maximize the utility of the EV chargers considering their individual constraints and the constraints of the grid for a particular state of the distribution system. The standard approach for solving NUM problems relies on using dual decomposition and subgradient methods, which through a dual price exchange mechanism yield algorithms that operate on the basis of local information (cf.[5]). This approach was applied to the EV charging problem in [4]. However, the drawback of the dual decomposition approach is that its iteration results are only feasible at optimality, i.e., the control values can only be used on convergence. In real-time EV charging control, a grid overload can only be avoided if the system is able to react within milliseconds, to avoid the triggering

e-Energy'15, July 14–17, 2015, Bangalore, India.
© 2015 ACM. ISBN 978-1-4503-3609-3/15/07...$15.00.
DOI: http://dx.doi.org/10.1145/2768510.2768544.

of protection devices. Thus, EV charging is a time critical application, where the iterative process of the optimization algorithm may need to be stopped before optimality is reached. Furthermore, the results produced for each iteration should be feasible, i.e., the control values produced should be usable at any time. Hence, we need an *anytime algorithm*. Anytime algorithms are defined as algorithms that return some answer for any allocation of computation time, and are expected to return better answers when given more time [6]. We expand our original work in [7], where we first introduced a distributed anytime algorithm for solving the NUM problem. In particular, the focus of this paper is the evaluation of the algorithm under dynamic conditions. In contrast to that, our previous work focuses on the convergence of the algorithm in a static setting. With this contribution, we show that the algorithm retains its anytime property under fast dynamic changes and can therefore actually be implemented for anytime EV charging congestion control. We define charging congestion control as the control of the EVs' charging current to avoid overloading the distribution grid elements while optimizing the use of the available infrastructure. Furthermore, we offer a comprehensive comparison with the state-of-the-art and show that our algorithm can offer better scalability and reliability than the state-of-the-art.

The paper is structured as follows: In Section 2, we discuss the work this paper builds on. The formulation of our problem, the state-of-the-art solution, as well as our novel approach are presented in Section 3. Section 4 provides algorithms for both solutions. Our evaluation in Section 5 shows the advantages of our approach over the state-of-the-art. Finally, in Section 6, we provide some concluding remarks and explain possible future extensions of this work.

2. RELATED WORK

The introduction of EVs offers several advantages. Once in large numbers, EVs could provide substantial, reliable system services with limited end-user disruption [8]. One of the main issues currently being investigated by the research community is the design of an EV control architecture [2, 9, 8, 1, 10, 11]. This question is linked with the type of grid support that EVs will need in the future. In [1], for example, the integration of EVs into the California Independent System Operator (CAISO) market for frequency reserves is considered. In [11], the use of EVs to level the demand curve of the whole system and the definition of a distributed control architecture to achieve this is discussed. The authors of [10] also study the direct coupling between EVs and renewable energy. A general framework that is able to cope with several control EV objectives was presented in [12]. However, all these approaches do not implicitly take the limitations of the distribution grid into account, which could limit their applicability in practice.

In [9], model predictive control is used to integrate the constraints for EV charging control. In [13], a simplified model of the power grid is used to speed up computation. A possible problem with these approaches is that all the computation is centralized. Hence, all EV chargers and protection devices need to send their data to a central location. For a large number of EVs and large distribution networks, this will cause an event shower [14]: frequent changes in the grid require the periodic updates of all control values, which translates into a very high control rate and in turn into a very high number of messages. Distributed optimization and control approaches could therefore reduce reaction times and communication requirements. In [4], such an approach is proposed. The proposed approach formulates the problem as a NUM and uses dual decomposition to solve the problem. However, this approach suffers from scalability problems, as the method can become unstable or in some situations may not adapt quickly enough to the grid dynamics. With this paper, we build on their work and use the same modelling and formulation style. However, our solution approach relies on primal decomposition which can cope with some of the mentioned challenges. We expand our initial work in [7] and analyse in this paper the behavior of our algorithm under static and dynamic conditions. The work in [7] focuses on the convergence of the algorithm in a static setting. However, there was no study on how the algorithm would behave in a dynamic setting and no guarantee that it would retain its anytime property under fast dynamic changes. The work in this paper fills this gap and demonstrates that the algorithm can actually be used for effective anytime EV charging congestion control.

3. REAL-TIME EV CHARGING CONGESTION CONTROL

We consider the problem of controlling the charging rate of EVs in a distribution network. The distribution network consists of several devices such as lines, transformers, and switches, all of which have a maximal loading rate. An overloading or congestion of the grid happens when the load demand at any of these devices is higher than the maximal allowed loading. Most of these devices are equipped with a protection device, which prevents equipment damage by opening the electric circuit whenever the maximal loading is reached. Protections have a reaction time of hundreds of milliseconds and many of them already have measuring, computation, and communication capabilities [15]. EV home chargers are also expected to have computation and communication capabilities. Hence, the overloading problem resulting from large EV populations can be solved using intelligent charging and by allowing chargers to communicate with protections.

We follow a best effort approach without considering predictions. With this approach, the problem becomes a time critical problem, in which fast reactions are required in order to prevent the overloading of grid devices or power outages. We divide time into control time slots of duration T_c. We assume that the state of the power system remains constant during each time slot. This also means that the time required for computation and communication has to be smaller than the triggering time of the protection devices. Furthermore, we assume that each EV wants to charge as fast as possible. During each control time slot an optimization problem needs to be solved. The objective of this problem is to maximize the charging rate of EVs, such that the capacity of the grid is optimally used and all EV chargers have access to the grid resources.

Although the real-time EV charging optimization problem can be solved centrally, we strive for a distributed solution.

In a centralized approach, the parameters of each EV charger and the parameters of each protection device would need to be communicated to a centralized location, where the optimization is performed. The result would then have to be sent back to the EVs. For a large distribution network, the communication and computation overhead of this procedure would not allow us to provide a solution within the required time frame: the control delay in a centralized solution would be too long to prevent locally triggered faults. Therefore, it is more suitable to keep the computation close to the data, i.e., to allow each device to make computations based on its local data and use message passing to coordinate them to solve the original optimization problem.

3.1 The optimization problem

We formulate the real-time EV charging control problem as a NUM problem (cf. [5]), where the objective is to maximize the utility of the network's users while respecting the users' and the network's constraints. In our case, the users are the EV chargers and the network constraints are set by the maximal available loading of the protection devices.

Let $\mathcal{V} = \{1, \ldots, N\}$ denote the set of EV chargers and $\mathcal{P} = \{1, \ldots, M\}$ the set of protection devices. Our optimization variables are the EV charging rates x_i for $i \in \mathcal{V}$. The energy flow to each EV charger traverses several protection devices before reaching its destination. We define this as the *route* to the EV charger. The set of protection devices in the route to charger $i \in \mathcal{V}$ is denoted by $\mathcal{P}_i$ and the set of charger routes leading through protection device $l \in \mathcal{P}$ is denoted by $\mathcal{V}_l$. With this, the real-time EV charging NUM problem is written as follows:

$$\begin{aligned} \underset{x}{\text{minimize}} \quad & \sum_{i \in \mathcal{V}} - w_i log(x_i) & (1)\\ \text{subject to} \quad & 0 \leq x_i \leq \overline{x}_i \quad \forall i \in \mathcal{V} & (2)\\ & \sum_{i \in \mathcal{V}_l} x_i \leq c_l \quad \forall l \in \mathcal{P}, & (3) \end{aligned}$$

where $\overline{x}_i$ is the maximal charging rate of EV charger i and c_l is the maximal available loading capacity of each protection device l. The value function (1) is the sum of the EV chargers' utility functions. The weighting parameters $w_i > 0$ can be used to set priorities, e.g., if an EV pays a higher price for charging it should have a higher priority, or if an EV is almost fully charged, its priority can be reduced.

The logarithmic utility function makes sure that no EV charger is denied service, i.e., $x_i \neq 0$. If this happened to any EV charger, its value function cost would be infinite. The first set of constraints (2) are the minimal and maximal charging rate for each EV charger. The second set of constraints (3) defines the maximal available loading of each protection device, i.e., the maximal loading that each device supports minus the current loading used to supply the customers with uncontrollable demand.

The objective function is separable, because each EV charger can compute its local objective using only its local optimization variable x_i. The constraints in (2) are also separable, because they also can be checked by each EV using only its local optimization variable. However, the constraints in (3) couple the local optimization variables of each EV charger, because one EV charger requires the local optimization variables of other EV chargers. These coupling constraints hinder us from distributing the computation across the EV chargers and protection devices. Hence, the problem is not separable.

The EV charging NUM problem is *convex*, since its cost function is convex and its constraint space is affine. Thus, there exists only one optimal point x^* that solves our problem [16].

3.2 State-of-the-art: Incentive-based control

The solution of the real-time EV charging NUM problem using dual decomposition has been studied in [4]. The goal therein is to allow each EV charger to optimize its charging rate independently using only local information and an incentive value generated by the protection devices. The result is an iterative distributed algorithm that generates the optimal incentives to solve the original problem described in Section 3.1. Since the EVs are controlled by these incentives, we refer to this approach as an *incentive-based control*. This work provides a derivation of the incentive-based algorithm that is an alternative to the one presented in [4].

To formulate the dual decomposition solution we use the dual ascent method [17]. The problem's Lagrangian is defined as:

$$L(x, \lambda) = \sum_{i \in \mathcal{V}} - w_i log(x_i) + \sum_{l \in \mathcal{P}} \{\lambda_l (\sum_{i \in \mathcal{V}_l} x_i - c_l)\}, \quad (4)$$

where $\lambda = [\lambda_1, \ldots, \lambda_M]^T$ is a vector of Lagrangian multipliers for each coupling constraint, also known as dual variables. By reordering the terms in the Lagrangian, we see that our Lagrangian is the sum of individual EV charger Lagrangians:

$$L(x, \lambda) = \sum_{i \in \mathcal{V}} L_i(x_i, \lambda) =$$

$$\sum_{i \in \mathcal{V}} \left\{ -w_i log(x_i) + \sum_{l \in \mathcal{P}_i} \{\lambda_l (x_i - c_l)\right\}. \quad (5)$$

The dual function of our problem is then defined as:

$$G(\lambda) = \sum_{i \in \mathcal{V}} \left\{ \min_{0 \leq x_i \leq \overline{x}_i} \{-w_i log(x_i) + \sum_{l \in \mathcal{P}_i} \{\lambda_l (x_i - c_l)\} \right\}. \quad (6)$$

With the dual function, the dual problem is written as:

$$\underset{\lambda \geq 0}{\text{maximize}} \quad G(\lambda). \quad (7)$$

Since our original problem is convex, strong duality holds [16]. This means, that the optimal values of the original problem and the dual problem are the same. To recover the optimal result x^* from the dual optimal point λ^*, we have to solve:

$$x^* = \min_{0 \leq x \leq \overline{x}} L(x, \lambda^*). \quad (8)$$

For this we use the gradient method. Since G is differentiable, its gradient, $\nabla G(\lambda)$, is evaluated as follows:

$$\nabla G(\lambda) = \sum\nolimits_{l \in \mathcal{P}} \{\lambda_l (\sum\nolimits_{i \in \mathcal{V}_l} x_i - c_l)\}. \quad (9)$$

We see in (4) and (5) that λ and x are both separable. Therefore, we can split the minimization with respect to x into N separable problems and the maximization with respect to λ into M separable problems. The dual ascent algorithm is then given as follows:

$$x_i(k+1) = \min_{0 \leq x_i \leq \overline{x}_i} L_i(x_i, \lambda(k)) \quad (10)$$

$$\lambda_l(k+1) = \left[\lambda_l(k) + \kappa(\sum_{i \in \mathcal{V}_l} x_i(k+1) - c_l)\right]^+, \quad (11)$$

where k is the iteration index, $\kappa \geq 0$ is the step size of the gradient method, and the function $f(a) = [a]^+ = \max\{a, 0\}$, is a projection onto the positive orthogonal. The first step (10) is an x minimization step and the second step (11) is a dual variable update. The dual variables can be interpreted as a vector of prices. Thus, step (11) is basically a price update.

The x minimization step (10) has an analytic solution. The solution is be obtained by setting the partial derivative of (5) with respect to x_i to zero, solving for x_i, and then projecting this value onto $0 \leq x_i \leq \overline{x}_i$. For more details on projections see [16]. With this solution, we write the dual decomposition algorithm for our problem as:

For each EV charger, $i = 1, \ldots, N$:

$$x_i(k+1) = \min\left\{\frac{w_i}{\sum_{l \in \mathcal{P}_i} \lambda_l(k)}, \overline{x}_i\right\}. \quad (12)$$

And for each protection device, $l = 1, \ldots, M$:

$$\lambda_l(k+1) = \max\left\{\lambda_l(k) + \kappa(\sum_{i \in \mathcal{V}_l} x_i - c_l), 0\right\}. \quad (13)$$

We see in (12) that each EV defines its charging rate based on the sum of the prices defined by the protections on its route. Thus, each protection along the EV charger's route needs to communicate this price to the EV charger. In (13), we see that each protection device does a price update based on the current available loading capacity, which is the maximal available capacity, c_l, minus the sum of the chargers loading. This can be measured by the protection device locally thus, there is no need for the EV chargers to communicate their charging rates to the protection devices. This property enables the one-way communication design proposed in [4].

The main drawback of the dual decomposition solution of the real-time EV optimization problem is that the coupling constraint $\sum_{i \in \mathcal{V}_l} x_i - c_l$ can be violated while the optimization algorithm is running: The constraint is sure to be satisfied only upon convergence, which means that the protection devices may already be triggered in the meantime. In [4] this is addressed by introducing an emergency response mode in which the charging of all EVs is interrupted if the protection device is about to be triggered. However, as we will later see, due to the highly dynamic nature of the fixed loads in the grid and the time scales on which the proposed control operates, the emergency response strategy may result in a prolonged time period during which EV charging is not possible. Another drawback of this algorithm is that its performance and convergence strongly depend on the step size κ. For certain values of κ, the algorithm may not converge or may become unstable. This instability leads to high oscillations in the computed EV charging rates and in turn to a fault in the protection devices.

Convergence: The convergence and stability of the dual decomposition algorithm for the NUM problem has been studied in [18]. In [4], it is confirmed for real-time EV charging control.
The incentive-based approach converges when a price equilibrium has been reached, i.e., when the prices don't change significantly in subsequent rounds:

$$||\lambda(k+1) - \lambda(k)||_2 \leq \epsilon_i, \quad (14)$$

where $\epsilon_i > 0$ is the convergence parameter. The convergence of the algorithm is guaranteed if:

$$0 < \kappa \leq \frac{2}{\overline{x}_{max} \overline{L} \overline{N}}, \quad (15)$$

where $\overline{x}_{max} = \max \overline{x_i}$, is the maximal charging rate across all EV chargers, $\overline{L} = \max_i \sum_l R_{li}$, is the maximal number of protection devices that any route to an EV charger goes through, and $\overline{N} = \max_l R_{li}$, which is equivalent to the number of EV chargers.

The evaluations in [4] showed that a higher value of κ leads to faster convergence. However, as seen in (15), the value of κ needs to be smaller the higher the number of EV chargers is and the larger the grid is. Hence, the larger the system, the longer the algorithm takes to converge.

3.3 Novel approach: Budget-based control

We propose a distributed anytime solution to the real-time EV charging NUM problem. The idea is to allow each EV charger to optimize its charging rate independently using local information, but to stay below a budget defined by the protection devices. When we modify the original problem to include budgets and apply primal decomposition to it, the result is an iterative distributed algorithm that generates the optimal budgets for each EV charger. The main advantage of this approach is that the resulting algorithm has the *anytime property*. This means that the charging rates produced by the algorithm with each iteration are always feasible. Moreover, the longer the algorithm runs, the closer the result gets to the optimal solution. Since the control of the EVs is based on setting maximal upper bounds on its charging rate or budgets, we call this approach *budget-based control*

We modify the original problem in Section 3.1 to include a budget for each EV charger. Let $b = [b_1, \ldots, b_N]^T$ denote a vector of the budgets for each EV charger $i \in \mathcal{V}$. Then, the problem is written as follows:

$$\begin{aligned}
\underset{x,b}{\text{minimize}} \quad & \sum_{i \in \mathcal{V}} -w_i log(x_i) && (16)\\
\text{subject to} \quad & 0 \leq x_i \leq \overline{x}_i \quad \forall i \in \mathcal{V} && (17)\\
& x_i \leq b_i \quad \forall i \in \mathcal{V} && (18)\\
& \sum_{i \in \mathcal{V}_l} b_i \leq c_l \quad \forall l \in \mathcal{P}. && (19)
\end{aligned}$$

In the formulation above we see that the budgets are included as optimization variables. Moreover, in Equation (18) we see that each EV budget represents an upper bound constraint for its corresponding EV charger. Since the budgets are to be defined by the protection devices, in Equation (19) the maximal available loading constraints have been modified to depend on the budgets instead of the EV charging rates. This formulation delivers the same optimal results as the original problem in Section 3.1, as proofed in [7]: if an EV charger cannot reach its maximal charging rate $\overline{x}_i$, the value for its charging rate becomes its budget, i.e., $x_i = b_i$.

In a distributed optimization scheme, each EV charger i optimizes using only its local decision variable, x_i. In Section 3.1, we explained that our original problem is not separable due to the coupling constraints. However, in our new formulation the coupling constraints depend only on the value of the budgets. Thus, if the budgets are fixed values, the problem becomes completely separable. Therefore, we can think of the budgets as interface variables between the individual problems of each EV charger.

Our new formulation can be represented as the sum of individual EV charger problems, which are coupled by the budget variables:

$$\begin{array}{lll} \min\limits_{b} & \sum\limits_{i \in \mathcal{V}} \left\{ \max\limits_{\mu_i \geq 0} \min\limits_{x_i} \{-w_i log(x_i) + \mu_i(x_i - b_i)\} \right\} & (20) \\ \text{subject to} & 0 \leq x_i \leq \overline{x}_i, \quad \forall i \in \mathcal{V} & (21) \\ & \sum\limits_{i \in \mathcal{V}_l} b_i \leq c_l, \quad \forall l \in \mathcal{P}, & (22) \end{array}$$

where μ_i is the Lagrangian variable from constraint $x_i \leq b_i$. The requirement $\mu_i \geq 0$, comes from the Karush Kuhn Tucker (KKT) conditions (cf. [16]). We separate this problem into a set of subproblems for each EV charger that optimizes the local variables x_i and a master problem that optimizes the interface variables b_i. Let $\phi_i(b_i)$ denote the optimal value for the following problem:

$$\max_{\mu_i \geq 0} \min_{0 \leq x_i \leq \overline{x}_i} \{-w_i log(x_i) + \mu_i(x_i - b_i)\}. \tag{23}$$

The master problem is defined as:

$$\begin{array}{lll} \min\limits_{b} & \sum\limits_{i \in \mathcal{V}} \phi_i(b_i) & \\ \text{subject to} & \sum\limits_{i \in \mathcal{V}_l} b_i \leq c_l, \quad \forall l \in \mathcal{P}, & (24) \end{array}$$

with $\phi_i(b_i) = -\mu_i b_i$.

In primal decomposition, the original problem is solved by solving the master problem with an iterative method, e.g., gradient projection. Each iteration requires solving the subproblems (23) in order to evaluate the master problem (24) (cf. [19]).

The subproblem of each EV charger (23) has an analytic solution. This solution is obtained by applying the KKT conditions and solving the equations after the optimization variables. The result for each EV charger $i = 1, \dots, N$ is:

$$x_i(k+1) = \min\{b_i(k), \overline{x}\} \tag{25}$$

$$\mu_i(k+1) = \begin{cases} 0 & \text{if } x_i(k+1) = \overline{x} \\ w_i/x_i(k+1) & \text{otherwise} \end{cases} \tag{26}$$

where k is the iteration index. These computations can be done in parallel by each EV charger once it knows its current budget $b_i(k)$. The resulting optimal value for the Lagrangian variable μ_i can be interpreted as the marginal benefit of the EV charger for the assigned budget. In Equation (26), we see that the marginal benefit is zero when $x_i(k+1) = \overline{x}$. This is because at this point the EV has achieved its maximal benefit. In turn, when the EV charger's maximal benefit cannot be achieved, its Lagrangian is the derivate of its utility function $U_i(x_i) = log(x_i)$. Hence, $\mu_i = \nabla U_i(x_i) = w_i/x_i$.

To update the budgets, we need to solve the master problem in (24). We could use the gradient projection method explained in [20]. However, this approach would require the current available loading c_l of all protection devices to be sent to a central location in each iteration. In a large distribution grid, this would cause a large communication overhead. Therefore, we propose using the *sequential projections method* described in [19] together with gradient descent, which results in a *gradient sequential projection method.* Our approach consists in projecting the budget updates onto the individual constraints of each protection device as they are communicated along the network back to the EVs.

For a sequential projection, we first need a communication node where the EVs send their current budgets $b_i(k)$ and their marginal benefits $\mu_i(k+1)$. In the following, we assume that this central communication node is located at the substation or the root node of the network. Then, we sequentially project the gradient updates of these budgets onto the individual constraint set of each protection device along the corresponding route. We formalize this as:

$$b(k+1) = \mathbf{P}_{\mathcal{C}_M}\{\dots \mathbf{P}_{\mathcal{C}_2}\{\mathbf{P}_{\mathcal{C}_1}\{b(k) + \alpha\mu(k+1),\}\}\dots\}, \tag{27}$$

where $\mathbf{P}_{\mathcal{C}_l}$ is the projection operator over the set:

$$\mathcal{C}_l = \{b | \sum_{i \in \mathcal{V}_l} b_i \leq c_l\}. \tag{28}$$

Equations (27) and (28) describe a procedure that updates the budgets as they are communicated along the protection devices back to the EV chargers. It loops over all protection devices, $l \in \{1, \dots, M\}$. We define the starting value of the budgets as the gradient update:

$$b^0 = b(k) + \alpha\mu(k+1). \tag{29}$$

Then, the problem to solve for each protection device is:

$$b^l = \mathbf{P}_{\mathcal{C}_l}\{b^{l-1}\}. \tag{30}$$

This projection is an optimization problem:

$$\begin{array}{ll} \min_{b^l} & ||b^l - b^{l-1}||_2^2 \\ \text{s.t.} & b^l \in \mathcal{C}_l. \end{array} \tag{31}$$

The problem above is solved using the KKT conditions. It represents a projection onto a halfplane, which has an analytic solution, (cf. [16]). Each protection device updates the budget of each EV charger route that goes through it, i.e., $\forall i \in \mathcal{V}_l$:

$$b_i^l = \begin{cases} b_i^{l-1}, & \text{if } \sum\limits_{i \in \mathcal{V}_l} b_i^{l-1} \leq c_l \\ b_i^{l-1} + \dfrac{(c_l - \sum_{i \in \mathcal{V}_l} b_i^{l-1})}{N_l}, & \text{otherwise} \end{cases}, \tag{32}$$

where N_l is the number of EV routes that go through protection device l, defined as $N_l = \sum_{i \in \mathcal{V}_l} 1$.

The resulting solution approach is a distributed algorithm, where the EV chargers define their charging rate and marginal benefit according to Equations (25) and (26). These values are then sent to the central communication node. There, the values are used to perform a gradient update of the budgets according to Equation (29). Afterwards, the updated budget values are propagated down through the protection devices back to the EVs. While they are propagated, each protection device projects them onto their individual constraint set (32). Once the budgets have been propagated through the network back to the EV chargers, a new iteration starts. This procedure guarantees that the resulting budgets are feasible for all protection devices in each iteration. Moreover, due to the gradient step update, we also close in on the optimal solution of the master problem in each iteration until it is finally reached.
Unlike the incentive-based approach, which requires only one-way communication from the protection devices to the EV chargers, the proposed dynamic budget approach requires two-way communication between protection devices and EV chargers. However, as we will later see, this drawback is more than compensated by its advantages.

Convergence: The convergence of this algorithm was proven in [7] for radial networks. It converges when the update of the budgets does not change significantly:

$$||b(k+1) - b(k)||_2 < \epsilon_b,$$

where $\epsilon_b > 0$ is the convergence parameter of our approach.

Our approach uses the gradient projection algorithm to solve the master problem (24) of the primal decomposition. As explained in [20], the gradient algorithm converges to the optimal solution if:

$$0 < \alpha \leq \frac{2}{K}, \tag{33}$$

where K is the Lipschitz constant, which is defined as the maximal absolute value of the master problem's cost function derivative: $|\sum_{\mathcal{V}} \nabla \phi_i(b_i)| = \sum_{\mathcal{V}} \mu_i \leq K$. From our definition of the marginal profit, $\mu_i = 1/x_i$, we see that if $x_i = 0$, then $\mu_i = \infty$. This means that our cost function is not Lipschitz. To overcome this, we can define an upper bound for the value of μ or we can avoid assigning zero budgets to any EV charger. For our evaluation, we assigned an upper bound value of $\overline{\mu} = 10^{10}$.

Even if $\alpha > 2/K$ our algorithm still converges to produce a feasible result. The convergence value is simply further away from the true optimal value.

Furthermore, the algorithm remains stable even when the weight of the utility function changes over time, provided that the changes take place after the algorithm has converged, i.e., when the time between weight changes is larger than the algorithm's convergence time. Changing the weight values over time is important for defining priorities between EVs. The weights can be used to give more or less priority to EVs based on their individual state, e.g., remaining connection time or battery state of charge.

4. ALGORITHMS

We now describe the algorithms that the protection devices and the EV chargers implement in the incentive- and dynamic budget-based approaches. As in [4], we define the control time slot duration as T_c = 20ms. We also assume that the algorithms perform one iteration with each clock tick. Therefore, the computation and the communication for one iteration has to be performed within this time period. This assumption results in the following requirement:

$$T_c > d, \tag{34}$$

where d is the delay caused by computation and communication.

4.1 Incentive-based algorithm

The algorithms for the incentive-based approach defined in [4] are based on the results discussed in Section 3.2. As defined by Equation (13), each protection device performs a price update based on its measured congestion states and sends this price to the EVs. It is assumed that all protection devices are synchronized and perform Algorithm 1 at the same time.

Algorithm 1: Congestion price update at each protection l with capacity c_l

```
input  : c_l, κ > 0

while true do
    Measure load
    congestion state ← c_l − load
    price ← max{price − κ × congestion state, 0}
    Send price along with all received prices to children
    Wait until the next clock tick
end
```

According to Equation (12), each EV charger receives the prices from the protection devices and updates its charging rate based on the sum of these prices. Again, it is assumed that all EVs are synchronized and perform Algorithm 2 at the same time.

Algorithm 2: Rate adjustment at EV charger i

```
input  : x̄_i, new congestion prices

while true do
    λ ← vector of new congestion prices
    aggregate price ← Σ_{l∈P_i} λ_l
    rate ← min{ w_i / aggregate price , x̄_i }
    Start charging the battery at rate
    Wait until the next clock tick
end
```

In our implementation of the incentive-based approach, we do not consider the emergency respond mode proposed in [4], where EV charging is stopped when a protection's maximal loading violation time gets close to its triggering time.

4.2 Budget-based algorithm

The algorithms for the budget-based approach are derived from the results obtained in Section 3.3. First, the substation receives the budgets and the marginal benefits of the

EV chargers. Based on Equation (29), Algorithm 3 is performed at the substation.

```
Algorithm 3: Budget update in substation
input : α, new marginal benefits, budgets

while true do
    μ ← vector of new marginal benefits
    budgets ← budgets + α × μ
    Send budgets to protection device l = 1
    Wait until the next clock tick
end
```

The updated budgets are propagated through the protection devices back to the EV chargers. As the budgets go through the protection devices, each protection device executes Algorithm 4, which is based on the sequence defined by Equation (32).

```
Algorithm 4: Budget projection onto protection l with capacity c_l
input : c_l, new budgets

while true do
    budgets ← new budgets ∈ V_l
    aggregate budgets ← Σ budgets
    if aggregate budgets > c_l then
        budgets ← budgets + (c_l − aggregate budgets) / length(budgets)
    end
    Send budgets to children
    Wait until the next clock tick
end
```

Once the budgets go through all protection devices back to the EVs chargers, each EV charger uses Algorithm 5 to update its charging rate. This algorithm is based on Equations (25) and (26). This computation can be performed in parallel and at the same time by each EV charger. We assume that all EVs are synchronized. This entails that all EVs must wait until all EVs have finished their computation.

```
Algorithm 5: Rate adjustment at EV charger i
input : x̄, budget

while true do
    rate ← min{budget, x̄}
    Start charging the battery at rate
    if budget < x̄ then
        marginal benefit ← w_i/budget
    end
    Send budget and marginal benefit to the substation
    Wait until the next clock tick
end
```

5. EVALUATION

We now evaluate the incentive- and the budget-based approach in a static and a dynamic setting. In the static setting, we assume that the parameters of the optimization problem do not change over time. This means that the fixed load consumed at each node does not change over time. In the dynamic setting we allow the fixed load to change with time. For both cases we assume that a constant number of EVs remain connected.

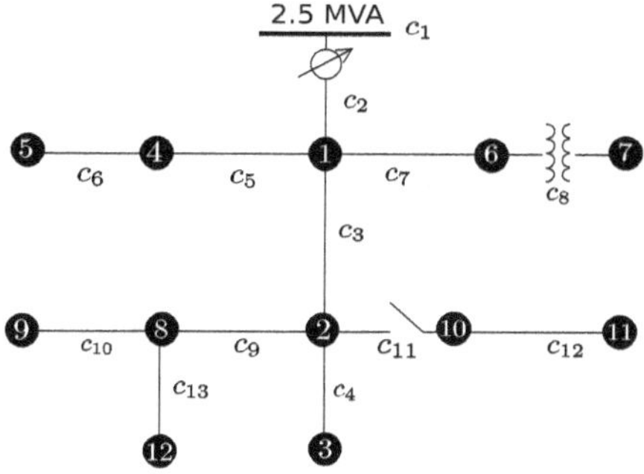

Figure 1: IEEE 13-node test feeder.

We consider the distribution network depicted in Fig. 1. This network is based on a simplification of the IEEE 13-bus test feeder [21]. As in [4], the network is assumed to be balanced, which allows for a single phase analysis. Moreover, the voltage is assumed to have a constant value of 4.16kV. Normally, this voltage level must be further reduced by field transformers for the consumers. However, this is ignored for the sake of simplicity. Based on these assumptions, we can focus on the currents that flow through the network and control the amount of current used by each EV charger.

In our evaluation, we consider a benchmark case of $N = 18$ EV chargers and $M = 13$ protection devices. Without loss of generality, we assume the same priority level for all EV chargers, $w_i = 1$, and a maximal charging current of 16 Amperes, $\overline{x}_i = 16$. The location of the EV chargers as well as the fixed load values of all nodes can be found in Table 1. With the position of the EV chargers and the topology of the grid shown in Fig. 1, we define our routing matrix as:

$$R = \begin{bmatrix} 1&1&1&1&1&1&1&1&1&1&1&1&1&1&1&1&1&1 \\ 1&1&1&1&1&1&1&1&1&1&1&1&1&1&1&1&1&1 \\ 1&1&0&0&0&0&0&0&0&0&1&1&1&1&1&1&1&1 \\ 1&1&0&0&0&0&0&0&0&0&0&0&0&0&0&0&0&0 \\ 0&0&1&1&1&1&0&0&0&0&0&0&0&0&0&0&0&0 \\ 0&0&0&0&1&1&0&0&0&0&0&0&0&0&0&0&0&0 \\ 0&0&0&0&0&0&1&1&1&1&0&0&0&0&0&0&0&0 \\ 0&0&0&0&0&0&0&0&1&1&0&0&0&0&0&0&0&0 \\ 0&0&0&0&0&0&0&0&0&0&1&1&0&0&0&0&1&1 \\ 0&0&0&0&0&0&0&0&0&0&1&1&0&0&0&0&0&0 \\ 0&0&0&0&0&0&0&0&0&0&0&0&1&1&1&1&0&0 \\ 0&0&0&0&0&0&0&0&0&0&0&0&0&0&1&1&0&0 \\ 0&0&0&0&0&0&0&0&0&0&0&0&0&0&0&0&1&1 \end{bmatrix}.$$

The vector of maximal available loading for the protections c_l is defined by their maximal load rating c_0, minus the capacity that is used to supply the fixed loads. In Table 1, we consider two static fixed load scenarios for which the maximal available loading vector c_A and c_B can be defined. In our evaluation parameters, these vectors are:

$$c_0 = \begin{bmatrix} 600.96 & 730730 & 730 & 140 & 140 & 340 & 340 & 230 & 230 & 340 & 340 & 230 \end{bmatrix}^T$$
$$c_A = \begin{bmatrix} 210.96 & 340 & 450 & 700 & 600 & 100 & 310 & 320 & 100 & 210 & 220 & 320 & 190 \end{bmatrix}^T$$
$$c_B = \begin{bmatrix} 210.96 & 340 & 450 & 700 & 60 & 100 & 310 & 320 & 10 & 210 & 310 & 320 & 190 \end{bmatrix}^T.$$

Table 1: Evaluation Parameters

Bus	3	4	5	6	7	8	9	10	11	12
Scenario A (static)										
Load [A]	30	40	40	10	20	70	20	100	20	40
18 EVs	2	2	2	2	2	0	2	2	2	2
Scenario B (static)										
Load [A]	30	40	40	10	20	160	20	10	20	40
18 EVs	2	2	2	2	2	0	2	2	2	2
Scenario real load data (dynamic)										
Load (2012- May-<day>.csv)	1, 2	3, 4	5, 6	7, 8	9, 10	11, 12	13, 14	15, 16	17, 18	19, 20
18 EVs	2	2	2	2	2	0	2	2	2	2

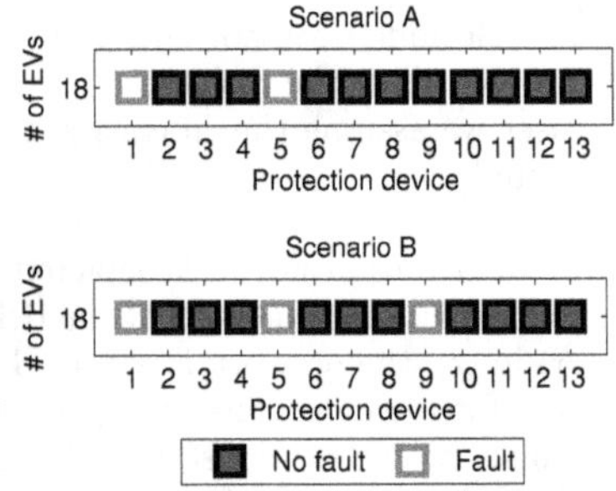

Figure 2: Overloaded protection devices at maximal EV charging rate.

The control time slot duration is defined as $T_c = 20$ms and the triggering time of the protection devices is defined as $T_f = 200$ms.

5.1 Static evaluation

We consider two scenarios: a low loading Scenario A and a high loading Scenario B in Table 1. In Fig. 2, we see the protection devices that would be triggered if we allowed all EVs to charge at their maximal rate. We observe that for load Scenario A Protection 1 and 5 would fault, and for load Scenario B Protection 9 would fault also.

The result of both optimization approaches in Scenarios A and B for the transformer are shown in Figures 3 and 4 for $\alpha = 1$ and $\kappa^* = 8.68 \times 10^{-5}$. As one can see, the budget-based approach outperforms the incentive-based approach, as fewer iterations are required to reach the optimal use of the infrastructure. Moreover, we see that the incentive-based approach causes a violation of the transformer's maximal loading rate in both scenarios. Since we assume that each iteration takes $T_c = 20$ms and we define the triggering time of the protections as $T_f = 200$ms, a violation of the maximal loading for more than 10 iterations would lead to a blackout. This is the case for the incentive-based approach in both scenarios. The performance of the incentive- and the dynamic budget-based approaches is mainly influenced by the respective step sizes, κ and α. The definition of the step size κ for the incentive-based approach was discussed in Section 3.2. As already discussed, if the value of κ is too high, the algorithm may become unstable, causing the charging rate of the EVs to oscillate. To avoid this, κ should be smaller than the maximal value for which stability is guaranteed, e.g., $\kappa^* = \frac{2}{16^2 \times 18 \times 5} = 8.68 \times 10^{-5}$. The stable step size becomes smaller as the number of EVs or the size of the grid increases. This leads to scalability problems.

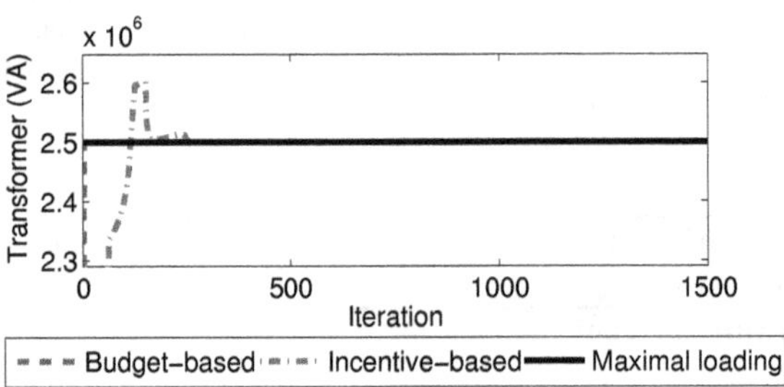

Figure 3: Scenario A loading.

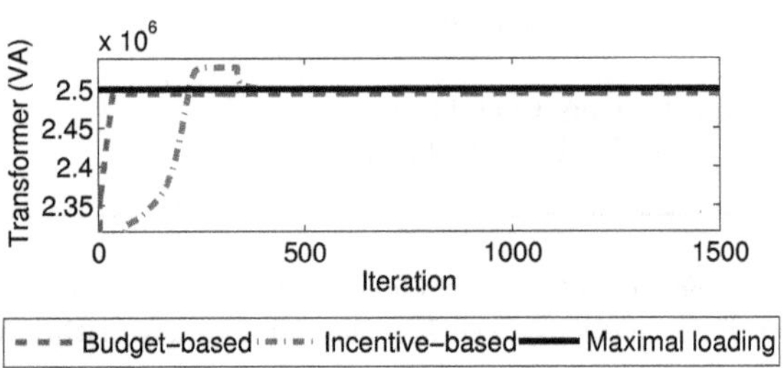

Figure 4: Scenario B loading.

For the budget-based approach, the definition of the step size α was discussed in Section 3.3. We established that the maximal value needed for reaching the optimal solution is $\alpha^* = \frac{18}{10^{10}}$. However, this approach remains stable even with a higher step size. The step size affects only the distance between the value to which we converge and the optimal solution.

We also studied the behavior of both approaches for different step size values using Scenario B. We allow the algorithms to run for 3,500 iterations and compare the number of iterations required to reach 95 % convergence to the optimal result. The optimal result was obtained by solving the problem with a centralized approach. We only consider the results that converged within the convergence criteria, $\epsilon_i = \epsilon_b = 10^{-3}$. As shown in Fig. 5, the higher the step size values, the faster the corresponding optimization algorithm's convergence. We see that the incentive-based approach of-

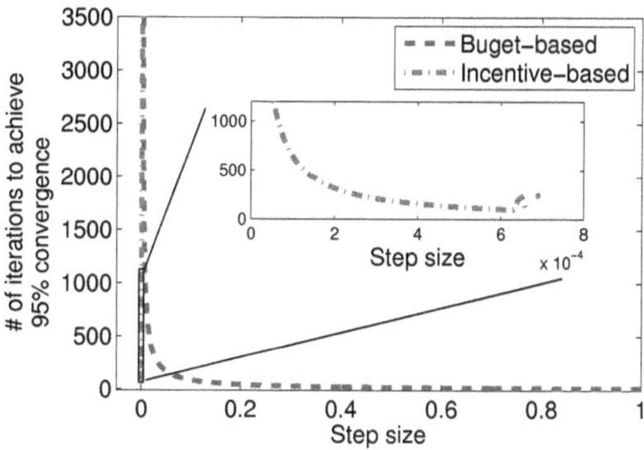

Figure 5: Number of iterations (Scenario B).

fers a faster solution for the same step size value. However, the incentive-based approach becomes unstable when the value of its step size is higher than $\kappa = 7 \times 10^{-4}$. In turn, our budget-based approach still converges to 95 % optimality even for high step sizes. This means that we can choose a higher step size than the incentive-based approach, thereby making our approach converge faster.

The static evaluation shows that our dynamic budget-based approach exhibits better reliability than the incentive-based approach. Under the defined assumptions, our approach guarantees that the maximal loading of the protection devices is not violated. Moreover, our evaluation reveals that our approach remains stable and can therefore offer better scalability than the incentive-based approach.

5.2 Dynamic evaluation

In this section, we analyse the behavior of the incentive and the dynamic budget-based approaches for loads changing over time. The changes in load cause changes in the maximal available capacity of the protection devices, c_l. Due to the highly dynamic changes of loads and the short available reaction time, it is important that any EV charging control approach remains stable and reacts quickly to the changing conditions of the grid.

We consider two scenarios. In the first, Scenario ABA, we iterate for 5 seconds between Scenarios A and B for a total period of 15 seconds (cf. [4]). The parameters can be found in Table 1. The second scenario uses real load measurements obtained from the `Smart*` data set [22]. This data set consists of the real load measurements of houses over several days with a resolution of 1 second. In our real load scenario, we use the measurements from the homeA-circuit. We assume that each node consists of two houses. Therefore, we use the measurements of the homeA circuit from two different days, dividing the measured power by 120V to obtain the currents (cf. Table 1). We focus on the time period between 4pm and 6pm, when the highest energy consumption is expected.

The results for Scenario ABA for the transformer and Line 9 are shown in Fig. 6. We see that both approaches remain stable and are able to reach the optimal point under load changes. However, for Line 9, the load change causes the incentive-based algorithm to violate the maximal line

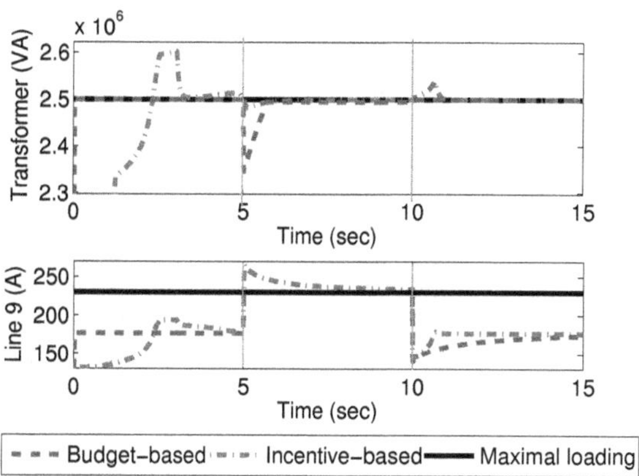

Figure 6: Loading in Scenario ABA.

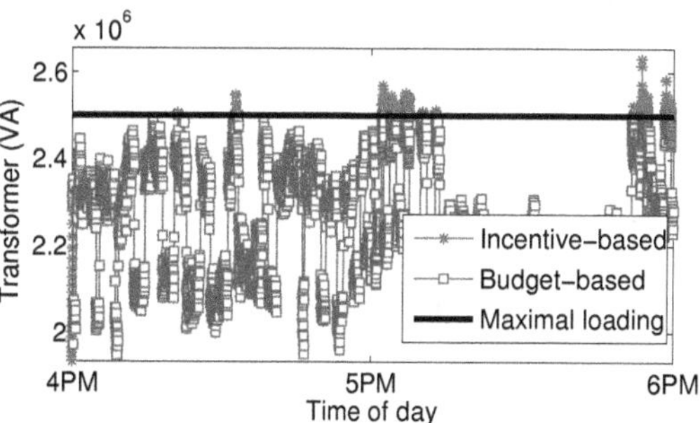

Figure 7: Loading in real load scenario.

loading. This line remains overloaded for several seconds, which would certainly lead to a blackout. This could be prevented by applying an emergency response mode as in [4], which would stop all EVs from charging and then resume the incentive-algorithm. However, if this is implemented, all EVs could be denied service. The advantage of the budget-based approach is that it does not need an emergency response mode because of the anytime property. We see in Fig. 6 that for the budget-based approach, the protection's maximal loading is never violated.

For the real load scenario, if we allowed all EV chargers to charge at their maximal rate, the only device that would fault is the transformer. In Fig. 7, we see the result of both approaches for the transformer: Around 5pm the incentive-based algorithm overloads the transformer for several minutes. Therefore, if an emergency response is implemented, the EVs would not be able to charge for several minutes. On the other hand, we can see that the budget-based approach retains its anytime property even under highly dynamic load changes.

The dynamic evaluation of both approaches revealed that the anytime property of the budget-based approach gives it a great advantage over the incentive-approach, especially when dealing with highly dynamic changes in the grid.

6. CONCLUSION AND FUTURE WORK

This work evaluates a distributed anytime algorithm for the real-time control of Electric Vehicle (EV) charging, considering distribution network constraints. We expanded our original work in [7], where a distributed anytime algorithm to solve the NUM problem was introduced, and in this paper we focus on the behavior of the algorithm under dynamic conditions. We show that the algorithm retains its anytime property under fast dynamic changes and can therefore actually be implemented for anytime EV charging congestion control.

The main advantage of our approach is that it provides a distributed method of EV charging control that has the anytime property. This means that the results of each iteration are feasible. Moreover, the longer the algorithm runs, the closer the result gets to the optimal solution.

We evaluated our algorithm against the distributed incentive-based approach proposed in [4]. Our simulation-based evaluation shows that the dynamic budget-based approach exhibits better reliability and can offer results faster than the incentive-based approach. Moreover, our dynamic load evaluation showed that the budget based approach is able to cope better with dynamic changes in the grid. However, this comes at the cost of greater message complexity than that of the incentive-based approach. Since the safe operation of the grid is the main concern in EV charging control, we believe that our distributed budget-based approach offers a good trade-off between performance and reliability for the control of EV charging. Furthermore, our algorithm appears to offer better scalability than the incentive-based approach, since it is not at risk of becoming unstable. Future work will focus on testing the scalability of our approach. We will also work on relaxing the assumptions made of the distribution grid modelling and reducing the message complexity.

7. REFERENCES

[1] C. Goebel and D. S. Callaway, "Using ICT-Controlled Plug-in Electric Vehicles to Supply Grid Regulation in California at Different Renewable Integration Levels," *IEEE Trans. Smart Grid*, vol. 4, no. 2, pp. 729–740, 2013.

[2] M. Bradley and Associates, "Electric vehicle grid integration in the U.S., Europe, and China," tech. rep., M.J Bradley and Associates, 2013.

[3] C. Goebel, H.-A. Jacobsen, V. Razo, C. Doblander, J. Rivera, *et al.*, "Energy Informatics," *Business & Information Systems Engineering*, pp. 1–7, 2013.

[4] O. Ardakanian, C. Rosenberg, and S. Keshav, "Distributed Control of Rlectric Vehicle Charging," in *Proceedings of the fourth International Conference on Future Energy Systems*, e-Energy '13, (New York, NY, USA), pp. 101–112, ACM, 2013.

[5] F. Kelly, A. Maulloo, and D. Tan, "Rate Control in Communication Networks: Shadow Prices, proportional Fairness and Stability," in *Journal of the Operational Research Society*, vol. 49, 1998.

[6] M. Boddy and T. Dean, "Solving Time-dependent Planning Problems," in *Proceedings of the 11th International Joint Conference on Artificial Intelligence*, vol. 2, 1989.

[7] J. Rivera and H.-A. Jacobsen, "A Distributed Anytime Algorithm for Network Utility Maximization with Application to Real-time EV Charging Control," in *53rd IEEE Conference on Decision and Control (CDC)*, 2014.

[8] D. Callaway and I. Hiskens, "Achieving Controllability of Electric Loads," *Proceedings of the IEEE*, vol. 99, no. 1, pp. 184–199, 2011.

[9] M. D. Galus, S. Koch, and G. Andersson, "Provision of Load Frequency Control by PHEVs, Controllable Loads, and a Cogeneration Unit," *IEEE Transactions on Industrial Electronics*, vol. 58, no. 10, pp. 4568–4582, 2011.

[10] O. Sundström and C. Binding, "Optimization Methods to Plan the Charging of Electric Vehicle Fleets," in *Proc. Int'l Conf. on Control, Communication and Power Engineering (CCPE)*, (San Diego, CA), pp. 323–328, 2010.

[11] L. Gan, U. Topcu, and S. H. Low, "Optimal Decentralized Protocol for Electric Vehicle Charging," *IEEE Trans. Power Systems*, vol. PP, no. 99, pp. 1–12, 2012.

[12] J. Rivera, P. Wolfrum, S. Hirche, C. Goebel, and H.-A. Jacobsen, "Alternating Direction Method of Multipliers for decentralized electric vehicle charging control," in *Decision and Control (CDC), 2013 IEEE 52nd Annual Conference on*, pp. 6960–6965, Dec 2013.

[13] O. Sundstrom and C. Binding, "Planning Electric-drive Vehicle Charging under constrained Grid Conditions," in *Power System Technology (POWERCON), 2010 International Conference on*, pp. 1–6, 2010.

[14] C. Doblander, T. Rabl, and H.-A. Jacobsen, "Processing Big Events with Showers and Streams," in *Specifying Big Data Benchmarks* (T. Rabl, M. Poess, C. Baru, and H.-A. Jacobsen, eds.), vol. 8163 of *Lecture Notes in Computer Science*, pp. 60–71, Springer Berlin Heidelberg, 2014.

[15] M. Chaturvedi, "Substation IED communications," in *Power Engineering Society Winter Meeting, 2002. IEEE*, vol. 1, pp. 596 vol.1–, 2002.

[16] S. P. Boyd and L. Vandenberghe, *Convex Optimization*. Cambridge University Press, 2004.

[17] S. Boyd, N. Parikh, E. Chu, B. Peleato, and J. Eckstein, "Distributed Optimization and Statistical Learning via the Alternating Direction Method of Multipliers," *Foundations and Trendsï£¡ in Machine Learning*, vol. 3, no. 1, pp. 1–122, 2011.

[18] S. Low and D. Lapsley, "Optimization flow control. I. Basic Algorithm and Convergence," *IEEE/ACM Transactions on Networking*, vol. 7, no. 6, pp. 861–874, 1999.

[19] S. Boyd, L. Xiao, A. Mutapic, J. Dattorro, and J. Mattingley, "Subgradient Methods, Decomposition Methods, Alternating Projections." Notes for EE364b, Stanford University, 2007.

[20] D. P. Bertsekas and J. N. Tsitsiklis, *Parallel and Distributed Computation: Numerical Methods*. Upper Saddle River, NJ, USA: Prentice-Hall, Inc., 1989.

[21] W. Kersting, "Radial Distribution Test Feeders," in *Power Engineering Society Winter Meeting, 2001. IEEE*, vol. 2, pp. 908–912 vol.2, 2001.

[22] S. Barker, A. Mishra, D. Irwin, E. Cecchet, J. Albrecht, and P. Shenoy, "Smart*: An Open Data Set and Tools for Enabling Research in Sustainable Homes," in *Proceedings Data Mining Applications In Sustainability*, 2012.

Challenge: Advancing Energy Informatics to Enable Assessable Improvements of Energy Performance in Buildings

Bo Nørregaard Jørgensen, Mikkel Baun Kjærgaard, Sanja Lazarova-Molnar, Hamid Reza Shaker, Christian T. Veje
Center for Energy Informatics
Mærsk Mc-Kinney Møller Institute
University of Southern Denmark
[bnj,mbkj,slmo,hrsh,veje]@mmmi.sdu.dk

ABSTRACT

Within the emerging discipline of *Energy Informatics* people are researching, developing and applying information and communication technologies, energy engineering and computer science to address energy challenges. In this paper we discuss the challenge of advancing energy informatics to enable assessable improvements of energy performance in buildings. This challenge follows a long-standing goal within the built environment to develop processes that enable predictable outcomes. Implementing this goal in the research framework of energy informatics creates a need for establishing a new underlying assumption, which states that *the impact of energy informatics solutions should be assessable.* This assumption applies to particular building contexts and when solutions act simultaneously. Research based on this assumption will enable new sound processes for the built environment facilitating informed decision for adding intelligent solutions to buildings compared to only favoring passive building improvements.

Categories and Subject Descriptors

C.3 [**Computer Systems Organization**]: Special-purpose and application-based systems.

General Terms

Management, Performance, Design, Human Factors.

Keywords

Energy informatics; energy efficiency; buildings; assessable methods

1. INTRODUCTION

Globally [1] and regionally, in Denmark [2], European Union [3], and United States [4], buildings account for approximately 40% of the total energy consumption. To reduce this percentage and thereby the associated greenhouse gas (GHG) emissions, the energy-performance of buildings has to be improved. Energy-performance of buildings is a focus area of the Danish and European building directives, the US better building initiative, and the IEA-EBC (International Energy Agency's Energy in Buildings and Communities) programme [5]. The Danish building directive's building-class 2020, aims at a 75% reduction relative to 2006 levels [6]. Therefore, society is facing an urgent need to find new innovative methodologies and tools to improve the energy-performance of buildings.

The emerging discipline of *Energy Informatics (EI)* covers research, development and application of, information and communication technologies, energy engineering and computer science to address energy challenges [7]. Existing work within EI broadly falls into two categories: solutions for improving energy efficiency and handling of renewable energy sources. EI solutions for buildings generally focus on adding various elements of intelligence to buildings covering diagnostic of building operation, feedback to occupants and control of equipment and building facilities as surveyed by Goebel et al. [7]. Existing research has approached the area with an assumption that each solution will be a silver bullet. However, to reach future energy efficiency goals, buildings will need to implement many EI solutions and, thereby, we need to be able to answer what the cumulative intelligence that several EI solutions add to a building, and be able to assess what the cumulative impact is on the energy performance when solutions act simultaneously. The problem is that the majority of current EI solutions are not assessable. This situation makes it difficult to integrate EI solutions in the workflows of the built environment and to argue for their benefits compared to passive building improvements.

The underlying community assumption that *ad-hoc silver bullet solutions with unpredictable impacts will satisfy future needs* has to be changed to assume *that the impact of solutions should be assessable in a particular building context also when solutions act simultaneously.* To consider the building context an impact assessment has to include relevant properties, such as occupant behavior, weather conditions, construction typologies, thermal properties, building systems and controls. Enabling EI solutions with an assessable impact creates the foundation for new sound building processes that facilitate making informed decisions for using EI solutions in building construction and improvements, compared to only favoring passive building improvements. In particular, we envision processes that can assess the impact of advancing the intelligence of a building using EI solutions or processes that evaluate for a particular building what combination of increased intelligence and passive-building improvements is

e-Energy'15, July 14 - 17, 2015, Bangalore, India
© 2015 ACM. ISBN 978-1-4503-3609-3/15/07…$15.00
DOI: http://dx.doi.org/10.1145/2768510.2770935

most effective for increasing the energy performance of a building.

The paper is structured as follows. In Section 2 we provide an overview of the challenges for EI to enable assessable improvements of the energy performance in buildings. In Section 3 we discuss the potential implications in the context of the processes of the built environment. Finally, in Section 4, we conclude the paper by summarizing the posed challenges and research directions.

2. ASSESSABLE ENERGY INFORMATICS

In this section we provide an overview of the challenges associated with advancing EI to provide assessable improvements to the energy performance of buildings. An impact assessment of an EI solution is an estimate, including risks, of the change in the energy performance of a building. The estimate includes changes in consumption of resources available in a building (E.g. heating, cooling, electricity and water) and impacts on occupant comfort and other relevant parameters. Therefore, to be assessable an EI solution requires an assessment method provided by a model or the solution itself that can provide accurate estimates for what the impact of using the solution will be in a given building context. Stakeholder tools will then utilize the assessments in building construction, operation processes or building systems to autonomously utilize the assessments and identify and recommend EI solutions to stakeholders that will improve a building's energy performance. EI solutions here span the broad range of individual solutions and combinations including diagnostic methods for building operation, hardware and software-based sensing and control infrastructures, feedback tools for occupants and managers, and software control algorithms for equipment and building facilities. Figure 1 illustrates the challenge for a given building, considering occupant behavior, weather conditions, thermal properties, construction typologies and building systems, to estimate if a given solution (building improvement) would improve or degrade the energy performance, and if they act simultaneously what the cumulative impact would be. In addition to energy performance other relevant goals, such as, cost, comfort and sustainability might also need to be considered.

2.1 Assessing the Building Context

An important aspect is how to enable assessment methods to take the particular building context into account. One could imagine that either models or data sets are provided that for a particular building describes occupant behavior, weather conditions, thermal properties, construction typologies and building systems. Therefore, an important prerequisite for following this research direction is to advance models and data availability by further developing building information models, building modeling methods and sensing infrastructures for collection of physical building data and occupant behavior data [8]. The community in this connection needs to answer at what level of granularity we need to model and monitor the different parameters including occupancy behavior, weather conditions, thermal properties and occupancy comfort to be able to make accurate assessment estimates.

2.2 Assessing an Energy Informatics Solution

When developing assessment methods the community has to address the broad area of EI solutions. As mentioned earlier this spans diagnostic methods for building operation, hardware and software-based sensing and control infrastructures, feedback tools for occupants and managers, and software control algorithms for equipment and building facilities. Therefore, a central question to answer is what assessment methods apply to the different solutions and what are the commonalities and differences across the solutions. A core challenge in this regard is also the impact of building occupants, which if unsatisfied with a control solution might change behavior in response to the solution, or for a diagnostic solutions might not have the resources or time to respond to alarms or recommendations [9]. Therefore, it is important that assessment methods not only focus on the impact estimates, but also on assessing the risks of a given solution in a

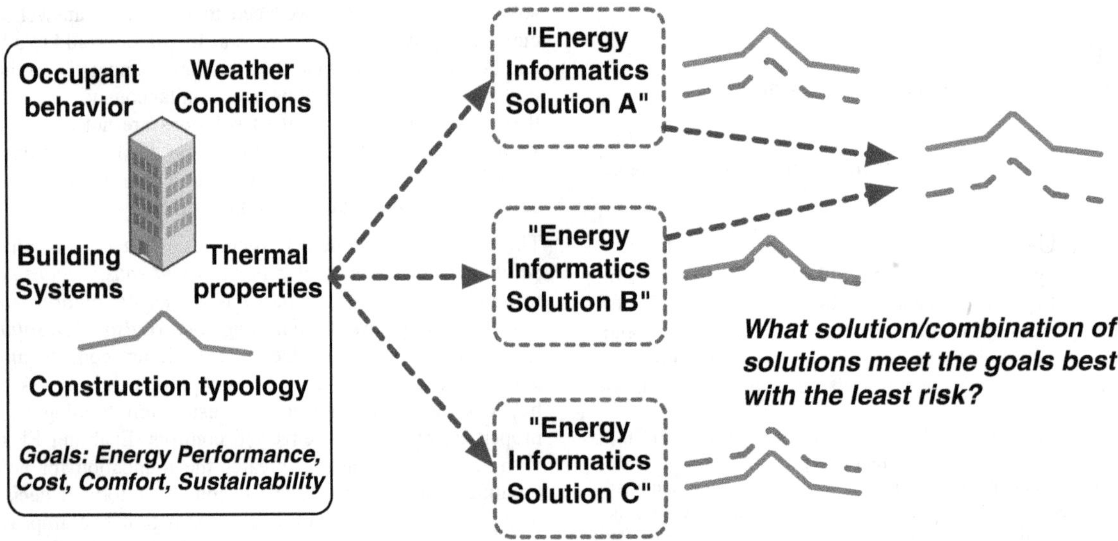

Figure 1. For a particular building we are given a set of goals for improving the energy performance. The performance for the particular building will be impacted by among others the occupant behavior, weather conditions, building systems, thermal properties and construction typology. To improve the energy performance we can consider a number of energy informatics solutions. However, how do we make the improvements of these energy informatics solutions assessable. Furthermore, it is relevant to consider what solution or combination of solutions will meet the goals best and with the least risk.

particular building context. In this regard, all risks might not be quantifiable, but still, even if only provided in a qualitative form, would be relevant to consider for stakeholders of building improvement processes. Another challenge is when solutions require modifications of a building including the placement of sensors or feedback devices. Here, physical properties of the building would be relevant to consider for securing wiring if needed or for esthetic considerations. Again, esthetic considerations are another issue that is impossible to properly quantify which would add to the list of qualitative risks instead.

2.3 Assessing Solutions Acting Simultaneously

As EI solutions cover many different aspects of building operation, a building will have to apply many solutions to improve its energy performance. Therefore, assessment methods have to be able to combine their results to quantify what happens when solutions act simultaneously. One approach would be to develop meta-assessment methods that would be able to combine the individual assessment methods or the models that the individual methods are built upon. However, such a choice would place strict requirements on the individual assessment methods. Therefore, other options should also be considered, including meta-assessment methods that build on knowledge databases, gathering statistics from different buildings for the resulting impacts of different EI solutions acting simultaneously. One might hope that from this data it would be possible to identify trends and quantify the impact given data from a significant amount of buildings and EI solutions. Therefore, a core question for the community is how to enable meta-assessment methods that enable the quantification of the combined impact or increased intelligence of a building when several solutions act simultaneously.

3. CLOSING THE ENERGY GAP: THREE IMPROVEMENT PROCESSES

Outcomes of the anticipated research could deeply affect the way buildings are constructed, operated and renovated and thereby have a large impact on their energy performance. To illustrate the challenge in the context of improvement processes of the built environment, we consider three categories of processes, as presented in the following subsections.

3.1 Closing the energy gap of new buildings by benchmarking and diagnostics

Evidence shows that public and commercial buildings certified according to energy efficiency and sustainability standards like ENERGY Star, LEED and Green Globes often perform worse than predicted and in some cases even worse than non-certified buildings [10]. This gap between actual and predicted energy-performance is typically revealed during building commissioning or as part of building re-commissioning [11, 12]. The main cause is often found to be unforeseen interference between a multitude of implicating factors such as occupant behavior, weather conditions, construction typologies, thermal properties, building systems and controls [12-14]. Hence, benchmarking a building's actual energy-performance with its predicted energy-performance provides an indicator of how well the construction and the specific use of the building matches its original design.

EI benchmarking solutions might be able to identify performance gaps and EI data-driven diagnostics tools might be able to discover their potential causes from model-based simulation of building energy-performance using fine-grained sensing of occupant behavior and building conditions. However, state of the art methods for sensing and modeling occupant behavior, as surveyed in [15], fall short on the types of activities and contexts they cover, and even though numerous building modeling and simulation tools exist [16] they lack support for prediction of building energy consumption based on measured observations of occupant behavior [17, 18]. Inclusion of real occupant behavior is essential as existing studies show that energy unaware behavior can add 33% to a building's predicted energy performance [15].

Therefore, assessable EI solutions are needed for stakeholders to close energy performance gaps of newly constructed buildings. The ability to predict impacts of building improvements allows in this process early identification of EI solutions to apply in commissioning that can help to close the gap for the particular building context. Solutions might also identify flaws in the original predictions for a given building as the use of materials might have changed during the construction phase due to lack of supply or change in stakeholder needs, leading to a change in the interior design of the building. Here, different solutions might be relevant in different building contexts or several solutions acting simultaneously.

3.2 Closing the energy gap by increasing the intelligence

It is commonly recognized by the building industry that increasing the intelligence level of building control has a positive impact on buildings' energy-performance. However, it is equally recognized that intelligent buildings are more difficult to handle correctly in commissioning and operation due to their higher complexity [12]. One way of defining building intelligence is based on the degree that building systems are integrated and coordinated intelligently compared to systems that operate independently without any building-wide coordination [19]. However, the idea of assessment enables another way of describing intelligence by the degree to which EI solutions complement each other when acting simultaneously to improve the energy performance of a building. Furthermore, assessable EI solutions with a predictable impact can enable accurate evaluations of the benefits of increasing the intelligence of buildings versus associated risks including increased complexity as already mentioned. Thereby, one can evaluate which solutions really improve the building intelligence and the energy performance. A promising direction for new EI solutions for control that enable assessable improvements is to work on multi-objective coordination frameworks to optimize building-wide operation of decentralized building systems based on simulation models for building energy performance that include relevant factors such as occupant behavior, weather conditions, construction typologies, thermal properties, and properties of building systems. By integrating simulation as a core component in the tool enables accurate assessment of the impact of such coordination frameworks.

3.3 Closing the energy gap by combining retrofits and intelligence

Leveraging the energy-performance of buildings built during the last decades to present day building standards requires a balanced mix of deep energy-retrofits and intelligent building control. Simply enhancing the building envelope and upgrading technical building equipment is not always the most cost-efficient approach to improve energy-performance of existing buildings. As energy performance of buildings is strongly dependent on occupants' behavior [15, 20, 21], it may be more cost-efficient to find a balanced tradeoff between the depth of energy-retrofits and increasing the building's intelligence. Existing work discusses tradeoffs for different retrofit methods [22, 23] and integration of

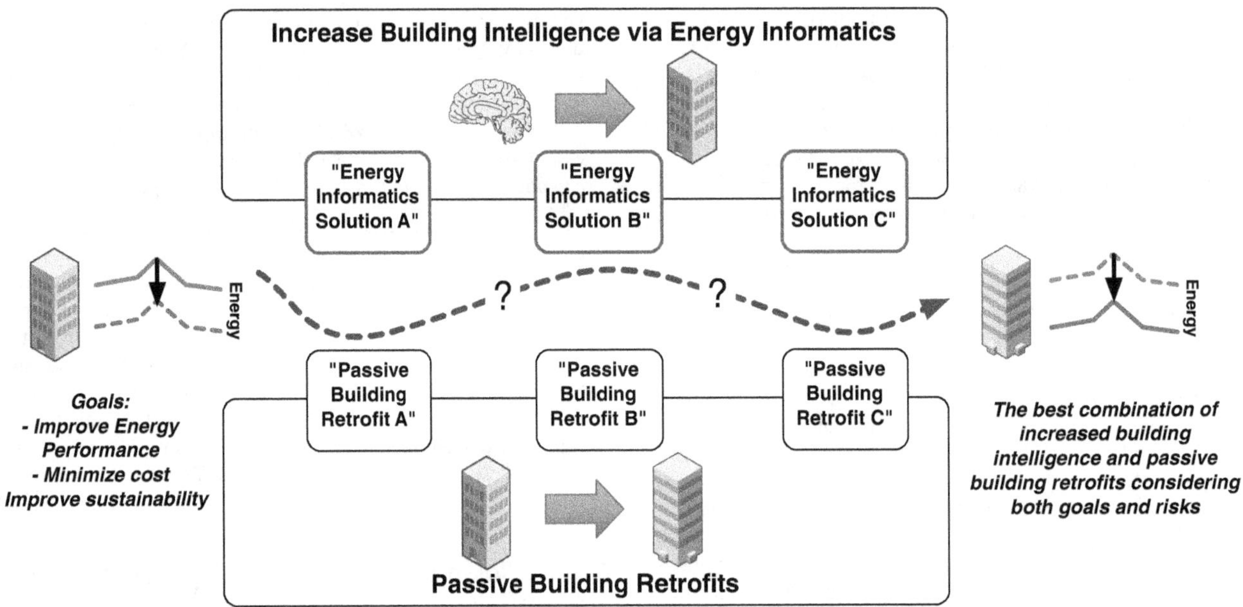

Figure 2. The challenge is to improve the support for walking the path from goals to the best combination of increased building intelligence and passive-building retrofits considering associated risks. Improving the support builds on the ability to assess the energy performance improvements via energy informatics solutions.

occupant behavior models [17], but there is a lack of work discussing tradeoffs between energy-retrofit methods and increasing the level of building intelligence. As stated, there are, typically, two approaches to improving the energy performance of existing buildings: retrofitting or enhancing building intelligence. Retrofitting is the process of upgrading an existing building after it has been built. This implies making changes to the building envelope or even the structure itself at some point after its initial construction and commissioning. The retrofit process is usually executed with the expectation that the availability of new technologies and materials will allow for significant reductions in energy or water consumption. Enhancing building intelligence, on the other hand, implies incorporating new and intelligent technologies that enable buildings to meet various goals, which typically include reduced energy consumption or other relevant goals. The question that further arises is which one of both available methods for improvement of the energy performance of a certain building is the better choice. The answer, however, is not a black-and-white one and it needs a more thorough analysis and introspection, as a more carefully chosen combination of both approaches could yield more favorable results in terms of predefined goals [24]. The challenge that sprouts from this is how to generate that optimal combination of retrofits and building intelligence, and how to assess the impact. Assessable EI solutions would enable the creation of tools for stakeholders to generate customized optimal solutions with predictable impacts to each and every building based on its properties and a set of predefined goals.

To describe what resulting tools might enable for stakeholders we use an illustrative example, presented in Figure 2, where a building in need of energy performance enhancement is presented. Building stakeholders need to define a number of goals to be considered, typically including maximizing energy performance, minimizing cost and maximizing sustainability. Here sustainability covers considerations about the resulting consumption and the resources used in the modification process. Given the availability of methods and tools developed to support the idea of assessable EI solutions, we could then generate an optimal combination of building adjustments to meet the set of predefined goals for a given building. Tools need to provide a careful analysis of all goals, as there are a number of goals that could influence a decision regarding energy performance optimization, typically including cost, time, and occupants' comfort during retrofitting, and sustainability (building materials, resource consumption and environmental effects). Therefore, to support these scenarios future EI tools have to support a holistic analysis of building energy-performance for the different tradeoffs between energy-retrofits and advancing building intelligence. The tools might be developed by combining building modeling, simulation platforms [25], thermal models of the building envelope, assessable EI solutions and concepts for recommendation and decision support systems

4. Conclusions

In this paper we have discussed the challenge of advancing energy informatics to enable assessable improvements of energy performance in buildings. The challenge follows a long-standing goal within the built environment to develop construction and operation processes that enable predictable outcomes. Implementing this goal in the energy informatics research framework creates a need for establishing a new underlying assumption, which states that *the impact of energy informatics solutions should be assessable.* This assumption applies to particular building contexts and when solutions act simultaneously with other solutions for increasing the total intelligence of a building. We have outlined several directions of research that are needed to address the challenge including how to assess different buildings contexts, individual EI solutions and EI solutions acting simultaneously. Research outcomes developed based upon the stated assumption will enable new sound processes for the built environment that facilitate informed decision for adding more intelligent solutions to buildings compared to only favoring passive building improvements. A recently funded US-DK research project named COORDICY managed by the Center for Energy Informatics at the University of Southern Denmark will work on the challenges in the coming years. We hope that the research community will help us address the challenges in future work to advance energy informatics to play an even larger role in improving the energy performance of buildings.

5. Acknowledgment

This work is supported by the Innovation Fund Denmark for the project COORDICY (4106-00003B).

6. REFERENCES

[1] "Facts&Trends Energy Efficiency in Buildings," World Business Council for Sustainable Development2008.

[2] "Danish Energy Agency."

[3] *Directive 2010/31/EU of the European Parliament and of the Council of 19 May 2010 on the energy performance of buildings,* E. Parliament, 2010.

[4] U.S. Energy Information Administration. *2015(January 22, 2015).* Available: http://www.eia.gov/tools/faqs/faq.cfm?id=86&t=1

[5] (January 22). *International Energy Agency's Energy in Buildings and Communities Programme.* Available: http://www.iea-ebc.org

[6] "Baggrundsrapport om bygningsklasse 2020," Erhvervs- og Byggestyrelsen2011.

[7] C. Goebel, H.-A. Jacobsen, V. del Razo, C. Doblander, J. Rivera, J. Ilg, *et al.*, "Energy Informatics," *Business & Information Systems Engineering,* vol. 6, pp. 25-31, 2014/02/01 2014.

[8] A. J. Ruiz-Ruiz, H. Blunck, T. S. Prentow, A. Stisen, and M. B. Kjaergaard, "Analysis methods for extracting knowledge from large-scale WiFi monitoring to inform building facility planning," in *Pervasive Computing and Communications (PerCom), 2014 IEEE International Conference on*, 2014, pp. 130-138.

[9] H. Blunck, N. O. Bouvin, J. Mose Entwistle, K. Grønbæk, M. B. Kjærgaard, M. Nielsen, *et al.*, "Computational environmental ethnography: combining collective sensing and ethnographic inquiries to advance means for reducing environmental footprints," in *Proceedings of the fourth international conference on Future energy systems*, 2013, pp. 87-98.

[10] J. H. Scofield, "Efficacy of LEED-certification in reducing energy consumption and greenhouse gas emission for large New York City office buildings," *Energy and Buildings,* vol. 67, pp. 517-524, 2013.

[11] "Initiativ Katalog," Netværk for Energirenovering2013.

[12] "Commissioning Tools for Improved Building Energy Performance," International Energy Agency2010.

[13] C. Nielsen and S. Hoeg, "Characterization and optimized control by means of multi-parameter controllers," 2009.

[14] T. Hong, W.-K. Chang, and H.-W. Lin, "A fresh look at weather impact on peak electricity demand and energy use of buildings using 30-year actual weather data," *Applied Energy,* vol. 111, pp. 333-350, 2013.

[15] T. A. Nguyen and M. Aiello, "Energy intelligent buildings based on user activity: A survey," *Energy and buildings,* vol. 56, pp. 244-257, 2013.

[16] January 30, 2015). Building Energy Software Tools Directory. Available: http://apps1.eere.energy.gov/buildings/tools_directory/

[17] J. Virote and R. Neves-Silva, "Stochastic models for building energy prediction based on occupant behavior assessment," *Energy and Buildings,* vol. 53, pp. 183-193, 2012.

[18] D. Robinson, "Some trends and research needs in energy and comfort prediction," in *Windsor conference,* 2006.

[19] C. B. Consortium, "Building Intelligence Quotient (BIQ)," *Continental Automated Buildings Association (CABA), Canada,* 2009.

[20] O. Masoso and L. Grobler, "The dark side of occupants' behaviour on building energy use," *Energy and Buildings,* vol. 42, pp. 173-177, 2010.

[21] S. Lazarova-Molnar, M. B. Kjærgaard, H. R. Shaker, and B. N. Jørgensen, "Commercial Buildings Energy Performance within Context: Occupants in Spotlight," in *SMARTGREENS 2015*, Lisbon, Portugal.

[22] G. Hillebrand, G. Arends, R. Streblow, R. Madlener, and D. Müller, "Development and design of a retrofit matrix for office buildings," *Energy and Buildings,* vol. 70, pp. 516-522, 2014.

[23] E. Asadi, M. G. Da Silva, C. H. Antunes, and L. Dias, "Multi-objective optimization for building retrofit strategies: a model and an application," *Energy and Buildings,* vol. 44, pp. 81-87, 2012.

[24] H. Doukas, C. Nychtis, and J. Psarras, "Assessing energy-saving measures in buildings through an intelligent decision support model," *Building and environment,* vol. 44, pp. 290-298, 2009.

[25] X. Li and J. Wen, "Review of building energy modeling for control and operation," *Renewable and Sustainable Energy Reviews,* vol. 37, pp. 517-537, 2014.

Challenge: Getting Residential Users to Shift Their Electricity Usage Patterns

Robert S. Brewer
Nervo Verdezoto
Department of Computer Science
Aarhus University, Denmark
[rbrewer, nervo]@cs.au.dk

Mia Kruse Rasmussen
Johanne Mose Entwistle
Alexandra Institute, Denmark
mia.kruse@alexandra.dk
johanne.mose@alexandra.dk

Kaj Grønbæk
Henrik Blunck
Thomas Holst
Department of Computer Science
Aarhus University, Denmark
[kgronbak, blunck, holst01]@cs.au.dk

ABSTRACT

Increased renewable electricity production, coupled with emerging sectors of electricity consumption such as electric vehicles, has led to the desire to shift the times of the day electricity is consumed to better match generation. Different methods have been proposed to shift residential electricity use from the less desirable times to more desirable times, including: feedback technology, pricing incentives, smart appliances, and energy storage. Based on our experience in this area, we present three challenges for residential shifting: getting users to understand the concept of shifting, determining when to shift and communicating that to users, and accounting for the dynamic nature of shifting. We argue that encouraging residential electricity shifting is much more challenging than electricity curtailment, and suggest an increased focus on understanding the everyday practices of users, which are crucial in order to shift electricity use.

Categories and Subject Descriptors

H5.m Information interfaces and presentation

General Terms

Measurement, Design, Human Factors

Keywords

Energy; shifting; curtailment; demand response; smart grid; practice theory; sustainability

1. INTRODUCTION

The modern electricity grid has become increasingly complex. Many countries are increasing the amount of electricity that is generated from renewable sources (both distributed and utility-scale) [11], which often produce variable amounts of electricity [2]. There is also growth in new sources of electricity demand, such as electric vehicles that may be connected to the grid to recharge at home or away [10]. These factors have exacerbated the degree to which demand for electricity is out of sync with production. For example, peak production from wind farms may not align with peak consumption periods [25]. Furthermore, the "cooking peak" of electricity use in the early evening requires utilities to ramp up production to meet demand, and then ramp it back down in a few hours [5:47].

In the absence of a way to scalably and affordably store electricity, these changes have led to a desire by utilities and policymakers to find ways to shift electricity demand to better match the increasingly variable renewable production. One way to accomplish this goal of shifting is to encourage residential users to make changes in their everyday activities in order to shift their electricity use, following the same path that has been used with some success in encouraging electricity curtailment [6, 9].

A variety of techniques have been attempted to encourage residential shifting, such as informational displays of grid CO_2 emissions [3, 15], time of use pricing [12, 16], smart meters, and smart appliances that can be scheduled to run at certain times [4, 17], or even putting appliances and infrastructure components like washing machines and ventilation under external smart grid control [8].

Based on our research on encouraging residential users to shift electricity use, we argue that such attempts are unlikely to succeed through awareness or persuasion alone (outside of isolated environments like the one described by Simm et al. [24]) because shifting is fundamentally different than curtailment, and techniques that have succeeded for encouraging curtailment fall short when applied to shifting. In this paper, we identify three main challenges related to encouraging residential users to shift:

1. Users find it difficult to understand what shifting is, and why it would be beneficial. Without this understanding, users are unlikely to consciously shift their behavior.
2. Even deciding which times are desirable for electricity use is challenging. There are multiple, potentially conflicting parameters such as CO_2 intensity per kilowatt-hour, grid capacity, percentage of renewable generation, and price. Further, these metrics must be communicated to users in a meaningful way.
3. Shifting is an inherently dynamic process: users must match their consumption to potentially ever-changing information about when it is desirable or undesirable (from a macro perspective) to use electricity. This unpredictability poses fundamental challenges in how users would change their habits to shift electricity use.

Our experiences come primarily from work on information-based shifting (i.e., providing feedback to encourage users to shift). It may be tempting to think that these challenges could be avoided

e-Energy'15, July 14 - 17, 2015, Bangalore, India

ACM 978-1-4503-3609-3/15/07...$15.00
DOI: http://dx.doi.org/10.1145/2768510.2770934

by removing the user from the loop through automation via smart appliances, or through economic incentives like time of use pricing. However, these three challenges stem from the process of shifting itself, so they must be addressed regardless of the specific intervention technique. Furthermore, there is no way to completely remove the user from the loop, so it is critical to understand users and their everyday practices.

Aligned with recent work in HCI [18], we use practice theory [23] to help us to understand the interwoven practices that make up everyday life, which consume electricity as a side effect. This understanding of how people go about the mundanities of residential life is crucial, since encouraging changes in one area (such as shifting when the laundry is washed) may imply changes to other areas such as exercise, personal hygiene, or an active social life, which people may find unacceptable.

In the following sections, we explain these three challenges in detail and discuss the need to understand users' everyday practices. Then, we describe how the challenges relate to automation and pricing-based solutions, ending with a set of recommendations for future research in this area.

2. CHALLENGE: UNDERSTANDING THE CONCEPT OF SHIFTING

The first barrier to getting residential users to shift their electricity use is getting them to understand the concept of shifting. To understand the underlying motivation for shifting, users need to grasp the challenges of the modern grid such as the variable output of renewable electricity generation, which are not widely appreciated by the general public. In contrast, curtailment is an easy concept to understand: using less electricity reduces the environmental impact of electricity generation, such as greenhouse gas emissions, and also saves money. In addition, the concept of curtailment also parallels other domains such as personal finance: an obvious way to save money is to spend less of it, whereas spending money at different times during a day will have no effect on the balance at the end of the day.

In order to consciously shift, users must be given some kind of information about when it is more or less desirable to use electricity. This information could take the form of variable pricing, or the "greenness" of current electricity generation. In order to shift effectively, users also need to be able to plan their more substantial electricity use, and such planning requires a forecast of electricity use desirability. In some cases, however, having information about electricity usage and consumption patterns could actually encourage shifting but at the same time increase consumption, and thus undermining the overall goal of shifting [20]. Thus, getting people to understand the concept of shifting is very complex, as there are many variables that play an important role while shifting electricity use.

Electricity feedback has frequently been used as a way to foster energy literacy [22] and encourage curtailment of electricity use [6, 9]. Therefore, it seems crucial that users trying to shift should also be able to see and understand their historical electricity use in comparison to the desirability metric. Consequently, a user trying to shift would potentially consult three different sources of data: a forecast of desirability, historical usage, and historical desirability. The addition of the desirability data makes shifting more difficult for users to understand than curtailment. For example, while conducting a pilot study of a casual mobile game intended to encourage players to reduce and shift their electricity usage by providing them with CO_2 intensity forecasts and feedback data on their usage, no player reported that they had attempted to shift [13]. Furthermore, 60% of questionnaire respondents (n=10) were unable to correctly answer a simple question about how well a particular day's usage matched a forecast of CO_2 intensity [13]. Players appeared to pursue a strategy of curtailment rather than shifting, in part because the concept of curtailment was easier and more familiar to them. This example reveals how difficult is for residential users to actually understand and shift their electricity use even if they are motivated to do so.

3. CHALLENGE: UNDERSTANDING WHEN TO SHIFT

In order to shift, there must be a way to signal and measure when the good and bad times are for electricity use. There are a variety of possible data sources to guide shifting:

- The CO_2 intensity per kilowatt-hour of electricity generated is an aggregated measure of how much greenhouse gas is emitted for electricity use. It can be affected by the amount of renewable generation, imports of electricity from other areas, and power plants being taken out of service due to scheduled or unscheduled maintenance.
- The percentage of renewable electricity generation in the grid is another measure of the environmental impact of electricity use.
- Grid utilization measures the logistics of transporting electricity from generators to consumers. This measure is important in the face of electric vehicle charging, which can potentially overwhelm existing residential subsystems [10].
- When time-of-use pricing is used, price is another factor to take into account.

Note that these data sources can potentially be in conflict over the best and worst times to use electricity. For example, a time of low CO2 intensity might not necessarily correspond to a time of low pricing, or low grid utilization, and vice versa. Those entities who are encouraging the shift of electricity use will need to pick one, or possibly a combination of these metrics in order to produce an appropriate forecast of the best and worst times for electricity use.

If we assume the metric has been normalized to a scale from 0 (worst time) to 1 (best time), it still must be communicated to users in some meaningful way. Should the forecast use an absolute threshold, where all time periods above some value are considered bad, and below some value are considered good? Or should all the time periods (such as hours in a day or days in a week) be compared only to each other, providing a relative indication of which are the best and worst times over the specific time interval? Absolute thresholds keep users in touch with the reality of the underlying metric, but leave open the possibility of long forecast periods that might be all good (any time is good for using electricity) or all bad (there is no time that is good for using electricity). Relative thresholds ensure that there is always some variation in the forecast, but only at the expense of exaggerating insignificant differences in the metric.

What is a person expected to do when faced with a forecast where all hours or days are bad for electricity use? It is not reasonable to expect people to defer all electricity use until some future point in time. One potential advantage of the shifting concept is that users can reduce the impact of frivolous electricity use by consulting the forecast and picking a desirable time. However, a forecast that shows that all times are good for electricity use could lead to a sense of impunity about electricity use. If the forecast shows the same value (in relation to the aforementioned scale 0–1) for a prolonged period of time, users may decide that consulting the forecast is pointless and cease to do so. Even when the forecast provides useful information, convincing users to check the forecast on a daily basis is challenging, as can be seen with longer term use of electricity feedback technology [14].

As with electricity usage feedback technology, researchers need to ensure that the forecasts are 'sticky' by providing reasons for users to continue to consult them over the long term [1].

4. CHALLENGE: THE DYNAMIC NATURE OF SHIFTING

A fundamental aspect of shifting is that the desired pattern of electricity usage is dynamic and not static. While there might be some fixed times when electricity usage is undesirable from a grid utilization perspective, such as the evening cooking peak, dynamic factors such as weather or generation failures will ensure some variety in the forecast over time. This variation poses a problem when attempting to encourage users to shift electricity usage, because it makes it more difficult for people to develop habits that will lead to shifting. A rule such as "avoid doing laundry in the evening" is much easier to follow than consulting the electricity forecast before doing the laundry, as it implies less cognitive and practical demands in our otherwise complex and busy everyday lives. Encouraging shifting stands in stark contrast to encouraging curtailment, where it is always better to use less electricity, and thereby much easier to develop habits and rules of thumb.

The dynamic nature of shifting means that there is no strong analogy to other areas of behavior change that users might be familiar with. If a person wants to save money, there is no constantly changing time of the day or week when reducing spending is more or less effective. If a person wants to lose weight, there is no constantly changing time of the week when calories are more or less additive to one's waistline. As mentioned previously, curtailment of electricity use does permit this very direct analogy to personal finance or weight loss. In contrast, the benefits of shifting might be perceived over a longer period of time, in which people's motivation as well as the dynamic aspects of shifting would play an important role to actually shift and reduce consumption.

The dynamic nature of the forecast also creates challenges for the forecast providers, who must decide how far into the future the period will stretch, the granularity of the forecast, and how frequently the forecast should be updated. A forecast duration that is too short (for example, only a few hours into the future) might not provide users with enough information on which to make decisions about shifting, because an appropriate time to shift might lie just beyond the current forecast. Forecasts can potentially be updated at a high frequency (for example, once every 5 minutes), but this frequently updated forecast can pose a problem if users have already made decisions about their activities based on a previous version of the forecast. To prevent users from becoming frustrated with the shifting process, a system might choose not to inform users of insignificant changes in the forecast.

Another curious property of shifting is that if an intervention is broadly successful in shifting residential electricity load from bad times to good times, then it is likely that the good times would then become bad times due to the increased load in the long term. Thus the progress towards the goal of shifting the load will actually affect the metric that measures that progress over time.

One solution to this problem would be to provide users with different individual forecasts that specify different good times for electricity use, thereby smoothing out peaks instead of just shifting them. However, this change adds additional complexity to the system, and also complicates any social encounters between users, who might discover that the system is recommending different times of day as most desirable for each user.

5. DISCUSSION

In this section, we cover the use of practice theory as a way to better understand the challenges of shifting, how the challenges apply to shifting through automation and pricing of electricity, and we end with our suggestions for future research in this area.

5.1 Understanding Practices

We have found practice theory to be helpful in uncovering these problems around shifting electricity use. One reason encouraging shifting is complex is because people generally do not see themselves as electricity consumers, instead they are simply going about the activities of daily life (cooking, eating, cleaning, washing, relaxing, exercising, etc.), which may have the side effect of consuming electricity [21]. These everyday practices are influenced by many factors, including societal structures like legislation and social norms, as well as physical things like the architecture of a building or the appliances installed in a home [23]. Therefore, when trying to encourage people to shift electricity use, practice theory can serve as a tool to understand the particularities of shifting in relation to people's everyday lives, pointing to solutions that should also consider the material and structural factors that affect practices rather than only counting on individuals to change their behaviors and schedules [7].

Moreover, people may also consider certain practices to be "non-negotiable", meaning they are unwilling or unable to consider changes to the schedule or duration of the activity [27] for various reasons, including social norms, personal preferences, or interconnections with other practices. For example, while conducting an investigation of the practices at a student dormitory, we found that residents were unwilling to consider shifting their dinner time later in the evening as part of an intervention, because dining was intertwined with other practices such as exercise and studying [7, 19]. In a longer field study of the mobile game described in [13], we found that while the game could help players to understand shifting, that understanding was not a gateway to actual shifting. Most players indicated that they felt that they had very limited opportunities to shift their electricity use because of the interplay between the various everyday practices in their lives.

In order to apply practice theory to design more sustainable technological interventions, it is necessary to understand the constitutive elements of practices. For example, we developed the Contextual Wheel of Practice as a way to remind researchers and designers about the important aspects of practice that goes beyond a focus solely on the individual [7], aiming to support people's sustainable intentions to actually reduce consumption.

While using the practice orientation does not ensure the success of an intervention intended to encourage shifting, failing to take practices into account makes success less likely due to the complicated and interconnected nature of activities in everyday lives and settings. However, it is precisely these practices that need to be understood and re-configured to enable shifting electricity consumption.

5.2 Automation and Pricing

Automation is another technique that has been proposed to shift residential electricity use: for example, introducing smart appliances that can be configured to run only when electricity use is most desirable. While automation is appealing because it seemingly removes users from the loop, in fact it suffers from all three of the challenges we have identified in this paper:

- Users still need to *understand the concept of shifting*, otherwise they will not upgrade to new smart appliances, and will not accept the delays that a smart appliance will introduce when it automatically delays operation to a future time.
- Smart appliances will need to decide *when to shift*, based on the factors we discussed previously (e.g., CO_2 emission, grid utilization, price). This decision is even more sensitive in the case of a smart appliance, due to the reduced user agency and potential for conflicts of interest: whose interests are being served by the shift?
- Similarly, automation cannot conceal the *dynamic nature of shifting*. Based on a dynamic forecast, the best time for a smart appliance to run might be in three hours, three days, or immediately. With automation, the situation is actually more complicated, because devices will need to explicitly negotiate with users to ensure that user needs are still met when shifting occurs: a fully-loaded smart dishwasher that decides to run in three days when electricity is expected to be very inexpensive may not be acceptable to the residential user.

Shifting through automation faces the additional challenge of getting users to upgrade their appliances to new, more expensive smart versions.

Pricing is also being used as a way to encourage shifting of residential electricity use, both through time of use pricing, and critical peak pricing where the price of electricity is raised dramatically when demand for electricity may exceed the supply. While pricing can be part of a shifting solution [12], it is unlikely to succeed by itself because people are not purely rational actors who seek optimal solutions based on the information available to them [26]. Indeed, as mentioned previously, people generally do not see themselves as resource consumers.

Therefore, while automation and pricing or a combination of the two may seem to remove the user (and the complexities that go with) from the loop, they actually need to understand and take users into account just as much as information-based systems do [28].

5.3 Research Directions

As we have shown, simply applying techniques, such as resource feedback, that have been used to encourage curtailment are unlikely to succeed in encouraging shifting (outside of specialized circumstances).

We propose that the best hope for success in residential shifting research lies in combining information, automation, and pricing techniques while targeting everyday practices. In particular, the targeted practices should meet two criteria: they can be shifted without extensive reconfiguration of other practices, and they use substantial amounts of electricity. In most homes, these criteria will probably limit the possibilities to heating/cooling, laundry, dishwashing, and electric vehicle charging.

There are some recent indications that residential electricity storage may become economically viable, such as the upcoming Tesla Powerwall [29]. If storage becomes viable, it will open a new area for research, because to be viable, the amount of storage capacity installed should be as small as possible, while still meeting the users' needs. Successfully integrating storage will also require a full understanding of the everyday practices that influence electricity use.

6. CONCLUSION

Based on our experiences investigating the everyday practices at a student dormitory, this paper shows how encouraging residential users to shift their electricity use to better match the changing needs of the modern electrical grid is a far greater challenge than encouraging curtailment of electricity use. This paper discusses major challenges including: getting users to understand the concept of shifting, deciding what shifting metric to use, how to communicate the shifting metric to users, and the inherent variability of forecasts. Based on our findings and experiences working in this area, we recommend researchers focus on understanding the everyday practices of residential users as a way of coping with the interconnectedness of the activities that must shift in time to shift electricity use.

Finally, the presented challenges may need further investigation and validation with other target groups such as families and in other settings. As the presented challenges are most likely far from complete, we encourage the e-Energy community to continue uncovering and understanding the particularities of everyday practices in order to support people to actually shift consumption.

7. ACKNOWLEDGEMENTS

This work has been supported by The Danish Council for Strategic Research as part of the EcoSense project (11-115331) and has been partly funded by the Danish Energy Agency project: Virtual Power Plant for Smartgrid Ready Buildings (no. 12019). We would also like to thank the EcoSense and VPP4SGR teams for their support in coming to an understanding of these challenges. Feedback from Yuka Nagashima and the anonymous reviewers was extremely helpful in improving this paper.

8. REFERENCES

[1] Brewer, R. S., Xu, Y., Lee, G. E., Katchuck, M., Moore, C. A. and Johnson, P. M. Three Principles for the Design of Energy Feedback Visualizations. *International Journal On Advances in Intelligent Systems, 3 & 4*, 6 (2013), 188-198.

[2] Brouwer, A. S., van den Broek, M., Seebregts, A. and Faaij, A. Impacts of large-scale Intermittent Renewable Energy Sources on electricity systems, and how these can be modeled. *Renewable and Sustainable Energy Reviews, 33* (2014), 443-466.

[3] Clausen, A.-M. *e-watch website*. 2012, http://newcow.dk/project/e-watch.

[4] Costanza, E., Fischer, J. E., Colley, J. A., Rodden, T., Ramchurn, S. and Jennings, N. R. Doing the laundry with agents: a field trial of a future smart energy system in the home. In *Proc. CHI* (2014), 813-822.

[5] Danish Energy Association. *Danish Electricity Supply 2008, Statistical Survey*. 2009, http://www.danishenergyassociation.com/~/media/English_site/Statistics/Statistik_08_UK.pdf.ashx.

[6] Darby, S. *The effectiveness of feedback on energy consumption.* Environmental Change Institute, University of Oxford, 2006, http://www.eci.ox.ac.uk/research/energy/downloads/smart-metering-report.pdf.

[7] Entwistle, J. M., Rasmussen, M. K., Verdezoto, N., Brewer, R. S. and Andersen, M. Beyond The Individual: The Contextual Wheel of Practice as a Research Framework for Sustainable HCI. In *Proc. CHI* (2015).

[8] Farhangi, H. The path of the smart grid. *Power and Energy Magazine, IEEE, 8*, 1 (2010), 18-28.

[9] Froehlich, J., Findlater, L. and Landay, J. The design of eco-feedback technology. In *Proc. CHI '10*, ACM Press (2010), 1999-2008.

[10] Green, R. C., II, Wang, L. and Alam, M. The impact of plug-in hybrid electric vehicles on distribution networks: A review and outlook. *Renewable and Sustainable Energy Reviews, 15*, 1 (2011), 544-553.

[11] Haas, R., Panzer, C., Resch, G., Ragwitz, M., Reece, G. and Held, A. A historical review of promotion strategies for electricity from renewable energy sources in EU countries. *Renewable and Sustainable Energy Reviews, 15*, 2 (2011), 1003-1034.

[12] Heberlein, T. A. and Warriner, G. K. The influence of price and attitude on shifting residential electricity consumption from on- to off-peak periods. *Journal of Economic Psychology, 4*, 1–2 (1983), 107-130.

[13] Holst, T. *ShareBuddy: A casual game for encouraging changes in electricity and water usage.* Aarhus University, 2014.

[14] Houde, S., Todd, A., Sudarshan, A., Flora, J. A. and Armel, K. C. Real-time Feedback and Electricity Consumption: A Field Experiment Assessing the Potential for Savings and Persistence. *The Energy Journal, 34*, 1 (2013), 87-102.

[15] Kluckner, P. M., Weiss, A., Schrammel, J. and Tscheligi, M. Exploring Persuasion in the Home: Results of a Long-Term Study on Energy Consumption Behavior. In J. C. Augusto, R. Wichert, R. Collier, D. Keyson, A. A. Salah and A.-H. Tan (eds.) *Ambient Intelligence, 8309*, (2013), 150-165.

[16] Newsham, G. R. and Bowker, B. G. The effect of utility time-varying pricing and load control strategies on residential summer peak electricity use: A review. *Energy Policy, 38*, 7 (2010), 3289-3296.

[17] Paetz, A.-G., Dütschke, E. and Fichtner, W. Smart Homes as a Means to Sustainable Energy Consumption: A Study of Consumer Perceptions. *Journal of Consumer Policy, 35*, 1 (2012), 23-41.

[18] Pierce, J., Strengers, Y., Sengers, P. and Bødker, S. Introduction to the special issue on practice-oriented approaches to sustainable HCI. *ACM Trans. Comput.-Hum. Interact., 20*, 4 (2013), 1-8.

[19] Rasmussen, M. K., Entwistle, J. M. and Nielsen, L. L. *Understanding Energy Consumption at the Grundfos Dormitory Lab as Situated Practices.* Alexandra Institute, 2014, http://alexandra.dk/sites/default/files/downloads/Sustainable_Transition/working_paper_1-energy-consumption-as-situated-practices.pdf.

[20] Robinson, J. *The Effect of Electricity-Use Feedback on Residential Consumption: A Case Study of Customers with Smart Meters in Milton, Ontario.* University of Waterloo, 2007.

[21] Røpke, I. Theories of practice — New inspiration for ecological economic studies on consumption. *Ecological Economics, 68*, 10 (2009), 2409-2497.

[22] Schwartz, T., Stevens, G., Jakobi, T., Denef, S., Ramirez, L., Wulf, V. and Randall, D. What People Do with Consumption Feedback: A Long-Term Living Lab Study of a Home Energy Management System. *Interacting with Computers* (2014).

[23] Shove, E., Pantzar, M. and Watson, M. *The dynamics of social practice: everyday life and how it changes.* Sage, 2012.

[24] Simm, W., Ferrario, M. A., Friday, A., Newman, P., Forshaw, S., Hazas, M. and Dix, A. Tiree Energy Pulse: Exploring Renewable Energy Forecasts on the Edge of the Grid. In *Proc. CHI* (2015), 1965-1974.

[25] Sinden, G. Characteristics of the UK wind resource: Long-term patterns and relationship to electricity demand. *Energy Policy, 35*, 1 (2007), 112-127.

[26] Strengers, Y. Smart Energy in Everyday Life: Are You Designing for Resource Man? *interactions, 21*, 4 (2014), 24-31.

[27] Strengers, Y. A. A. Designing eco-feedback systems for everyday life. In *Proc. CHI* (2011), 2135-2144.

[28] Sugarman, V. and Lank, E. Designing Persuasive Technology to Manage Peak Electricity Demand in Ontario Homes. In *Proc. CHI* (2015), 1975-1984.

[29] Tesla Motors. *Tesla Powerwall website.* 2015, http://www.teslamotors.com/powerwall.

Challenge: Resolving Data Center Power Bill Disputes: The Energy-Performance Trade-offs of Consolidation

Angelos Chatzipapas+, Dimosthenis Pediaditakis*, Charalampos Rotsos†, Vincenzo Mancuso+, Jon Crowcroft*, Andrew W. Moore*

*Computer Laboratory, University of Cambridge, UK {firstname.lastname}@cl.cam.ac.uk

+IMDEA Networks Institute, Universidad Carlos III de Madrid, Spain {firstname.lastname}@imdea.org

†School of Computing and Communications, Lancaster University, UK c.rotsos@lancaster.ac.uk

ABSTRACT

In this paper we challenge the common evaluation practices used in Virtual Machine (VM) consolidation, such as simulation and small testbeds, which fail to capture the fundamental trade-off between energy consumption and performance. We identify a number of over-simplifying assumptions which are typically made about the energy consumption and performance characteristics of modern networked systems. In response, we describe how more accurate models for data-center systems can be designed and used in order to create an evaluation framework that allows the exploration of the energy-performance trade-off in VM consolidation strategies with enhanced fidelity.

Categories and Subject Descriptors

C.4 [**Performance of systems**]: *Modeling techniques*

General Terms

Performance; Theory

Keywords

Virtualization; consolidation; energy modeling; emulation.

1. INTRODUCTION

In the last decade many large-scale services have migrated to cloud infrastructures, creating an equal increase in virtualized data centers. Data center infrastructures have become one of the largest and fastest growing consumers of electricity globally, surpassing the aviation industry both in terms of energy consumption and CO_2 emissions [1]. To put this into perspective, in 2013, U.S. data center's electricity consumption (91 TWh) was sufficient to power twice the number of all the households in New York City [2]. As a result, ICT energy consumption accounts for 3% of the global consumption and has an annual increase of ≈4.3% [3]. Consequently, there is a growing interest to improve energy efficiency in data center's design, with obvious environmental and financial motives.

A first approach towards building greener ICT was the development of *energy proportional* computing and networking infrastructures [4, 5]. This effort took advantage of energy efficient hardware, like CPU voltage/frequency scaling and sleep states, low-power Ethernet and power-efficient OS-level resource management (e.g. on demand Linux governor and PowerNap [6]). However, even at low utilization loads, in the order of 10%, the server power consumption can reach up to 50% of its peak demand [7], allowing room for further improvement.

To further reduce energy consumption, research has proposed workload consolidation algorithms which concentrate computation into a subset of the data center infrastructures. Numerous studies leverage live virtual machine (VM) migration, a modern virtualization functionality which allows seamless relocation of VMs between physical hosts, with relatively short down-times. In most cases, a consolidation strategy is encoded into a VM placement algorithm that maximize energy savings while fulfilling a minimum guaranteed level of performance, expressed in the form of service-level-agreements (SLA). The evaluation of the proposed approximation algorithms is typically based on custom simulation frameworks [8, 9] or small-scale testbeds [10, 11, 12].

In this paper we challenge the common evaluation practices as they frequently adopt over-simplified and unrealistic models for the estimation of the VM resource requirements and physical host resource availability. Hereafter, we identify a set of important system parameters, commonly ignored in favor of simplicity:

- the dynamic **energy consumption** profiles of servers;
- the complexity in **resource sharing** between VMs in a single host (*e.g.,* CPU, disk, network, memory), as well as the virtualization overheads;
- the performance characteristics of the underlying **network** infrastructure (topology, speed, configuration) and the employed network protocols;
- the **cost** of live **VM migration** in terms of energy, network traffic and application-level performance;
- complex performance behaviors of networked systems observed in **large scale** deployments.

We argue that underestimating the impact of the aforementioned system properties in the evaluation of VM consolidation algorithms introduces significant inaccuracies. The individual relocation decisions are based on inaccurate performance predictions for co-hosted VMs, as well as they overlook the overhead of large-scale VM migrations. As a result, the fundamental trade-off between energy consumption and application performance is not sufficiently captured, and

e-Energy'15, July 14 - 17, 2015, Bangalore, India

DOI: http://dx.doi.org/10.1145/2768510.2770933.

hence, the estimated power-bill savings of the proposed consolidation strategies have limited practical use.

In an effort to address the aforementioned issues, we point out how existing solutions can be reused, combined and extended in order to create an evaluation framework that allows the reliable exploration of the energy-performance trade-offs in VM consolidation strategies. Such a solution is particularly useful, since only few researchers can access a real-sized data center infrastructure for experimentation.

We initially present related work in the field (§ 2) and then highlight that many potential pitfalls exist in the methods used to model application performance and energy requirements of data center servers (§ 3). Furthermore, we propose a new evaluation methodology that comprises of two components: (i) the measurement-based characterization of physical servers, and (ii) the faithful emulation of the load that applications (running inside VMs) offer to the hosting servers under different configurations (§ 4). Finally, we conclude by summarizing this work (§ 5).

2. BACKGROUND AND RELATED WORK

Performing resource provisioning in a single data center infrastructure is a compound problem with multiple competing objectives (see Figure 1 for a brief taxonomy).

Firstly, *consolidation* aims to compress workloads into as few physical hosts as possible, and either turn off or leave idle the unused part of the infrastructure. During this step, the objective is to maximize the energy saving, at the cost of performance. Some approaches use live VM migration to implement consolidation [8, 13], while some others steeling of new workloads to different servers [14]. Secondly, the opposite to the process of consolidation, is the *elimination of performance hot-spots*, which spreads VMs across the data center, increasing the active physical hosts. Some techniques aim to remove network-related hot-spots [15], while others utilize end-host information to avoid high server utilization [12]. Lastly, a *load-balancing* process can run in the background and relocate VMs aiming to smoothen the load variations across the infrastructure, and therefore, better absorb the performance spikes of bursty workloads. Load-balancing solutions may be based on software proxies [16], proprietary hardware designs [17] or they can be built as software defined network applications [18].

Usually hot-spot removal and consolidation are used together, hand in hand. The two functionalities have opposing goals, but are equally necessary to achieve an equilibrium between performance and energy saving. Specifically, this is the most important aspect in designing greener data center solutions: *be in position to make informed decisions about the application-level performance which is sacrificed in trade for lower energy consumption, and vice versa.*

Energy-efficient VM placement algorithms: The energy/performance trade-off is controlled by the VM placement algorithms, which implement the decision-making logic for the followings:

- **Choose a source host** with average utilization above, in case of hotspot removal, or below, in a case of consolidation, a threshold.
- **Choose a VM** from the selected host based on its resource requirements. For example, during the evacuation of an under-utilized server, VMs are ordered based on their resource requirements.

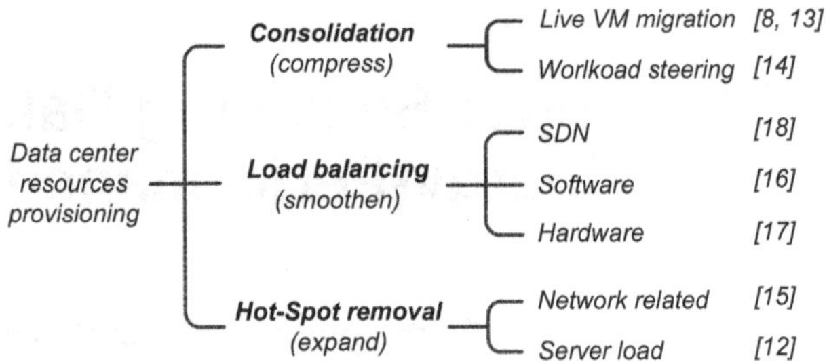

Figure 1: A brief taxonomy of resource provisioning functions for data center environments.

- **Choose a destination host** with sufficient available resources (*e.g.,* disk, network, CPU, memory) to fulfill the resource requirements of the previously selected VM, determined by its SLA.

Numerous research efforts transform this decision making process into a vectorized bin packing problem [8, 13]. VMs are represented as n-dimensional vectors of estimated resource demands, while each host is represented as an n-dimensional vector of available resources. VM placement aims to fulfill the minimum guaranteed resources, specified by the service SLAs, while minimizing the number of active hosts. Since the vector bin packing problem is NP-hard, a number of near-optimal solutions have been proposed using a variety of heuristics [19, 20] (*e.g.,* first-fit decreasing, best-fit decreasing, worst-fit decreasing, etc.). Alternative approaches towards the placement problem use genetic algorithms [21] and dynamic programming [9].

Unfortunately, the common methodology for evaluating the above solutions is simulation, which abstracts important properties of virtualized systems, discussed in detail in Section 3. As a result their applicability on real data center environments is limited. This observation is also supported by studies like [19, 12], that approach the problem from a more practical perspective. Other works like [10, 11], evaluate their systems using small testbeds with no more that few tens of machines, insufficient to capture the scalability of the resulting system in real-sized environments.

3. COMMON PITFALLS

The VM migration decisions use as inputs: (i) the resource requirements of a VM (given an SLA), (ii) the expected load increase in the destination host, (iii) the available resources of the physical hosts, and (iv) the expected level of performance for VM applications. The main argument of this paper states that the majority of the existing works does not accurately capture the aforementioned decision criteria.

In this section we elaborate on the aforementioned evaluation and design pitfalls, related to the specific properties of large-scale virtualized data centers which tend to ignore: (i) the dynamic of the underlying resource sharing model and the migration cost (§ 3.1) and (ii) the energy consumption profiles under mixed workloads (§ 3.2).

3.1 Modeling the availability of resources

Cloud providers have been refraining from using consolidation algorithms on their infrastructures mainly because it is not easy to predict the performance penalties on hosted applications. While the overhead of virtualization has been significantly reduced (*e.g., paravirtualized* I/O, hardware support), the interaction model with a host's physical resources has become more complex. For example, Wang *el al.* [22], exemplify some interesting artifacts in the perceived CPU and network resource availability by guest OS. Such performance variability has been measured to significantly affect large-scale time-sensitive services [23]. This performance variability is a direct consequence of the resource sharing functionality implementation between co-hosted VMs. Nevertheless, most of the heuristics used in VM placement algorithms, assume that the virtualization platforms provide perfect performance isolation.

The above assumption, however, can lead to incorrect VM placement decisions. The amount of the resources which each VM receives depends on three factors: the scheduling policy of the hypervisor, the available resources of the hosting platform, and the activity of co-hosted VMs. None of these three factors can be considered static, and moreover, they exhibit a high degree of interdependencies. For example, consider many highly-utilized VMs collocated on a server, each receiving a fair share of the CPU time. On a lower utilized server, the same VM would almost certainly reach a higher peak. Therefore, a typical hot spot removal algorithm would underestimate the peak CPU requirements of a VM, and could potentially make sub-optimal decisions.

Another over-simplifying assumption which is commonly made, is the inference of application SLA violations, based on VM or host-level utilization metrics. First, the poor resource sharing models which are used during evaluation, do not provide accurate utilization estimations. Second, it is fairly unreliable to employ only the CPU utilization to infer SLA violations, since this approach is susceptible to false negatives, especially for bursty workloads. This problem has been pointed out by *Wood et al.* in [12].

Finally, the available network resources is another important factor which also determines the application-level performance. This includes the available bandwidth at the end-hosts (including the CPU overheads of packet processing), the employed protocols, the topology of the data center's networking infrastructure, the speed of physical links, and the scheduling algorithms at intermediate devices. None of these important characteristics are sufficiently replicated in the majority of the VM consolidation studies. Relevant simulation frameworks use simplified network models, while small testbeds fail to reproduce the complex behaviors observed in large scale networked systems.

3.2 Accuracy of energy consumption models

Many of the VM placement approaches, covered in § 2, provide only gross insights on the resulting energy savings. The achieved accuracy in the estimated savings is usually limited at the level of accounting the number of powered-on servers over the unit of time. This reduced level of detail does not allow users to effectively evaluate the energy-performance trade-off.

Some research efforts, like [24, 8], consider the use of a more detailed energy model. Effectively, they are based on the observation that CPU utilization is highly correlated with the overall energy consumption of a server. As a result, they use linear models which are based on current utilization levels to estimate the energy consumption.

The importance of the above facts has been pointed out by several studies (*e.g.,* [25, 26]), showing that depending on the characteristics of a workload, the level of CPU-load alone might not be a very accurate metric. This is especially true for storage and network devices which implement energy saving features and have a wide and dynamic energy range. The system-level utilization is not modeled accurately in the simulation frameworks which are commonly used to evaluate VM consolidation algorithms. Hence, the input which is used in their linear energy/CPU-utilization models, is not reliable.

Ideally, we would like to have evaluation frameworks which can replicate with good accuracy the load of different system components over time with high accuracy, generated from custom scenarios of migrating VMs who execute a given workload. Thereafter, accurate heuristic models could be applied to estimate the energy consumption of servers using as input the collected measurements for the CPU-load as well as the disk, the network and the memory I/O operations.

3.3 Live VM migration does not come for free

Live VM migration is a first-class citizen in the data center energy consolidation problem because of the unprecedented level of flexibility it offers. While useful, it is a complex process with two main approaches. In the *pre-copy* [27] method, the hypervisor first copies all memory pages of the VM to the destination host, and while they change (become "dirty") they are re-copied until the dirtying rate slows down. The second method, post-copy [28], performs the inverse functionality; VM is first suspended temporarily, a minimal state (*e.g.,* CPU state, registers) is transferred and then resumed at the target host. At the same time memory pages are pushed to the target, and whenever a page fault occurs the missing page is fetched from the source on demand.

From the above it is clear that the live migration of a VM, introduces overheads at multiple levels. First, it increases the CPU load on the management domain of both the source and the target host, second, it creates extra network traffic and, finally, it temporarily degrades the performance of the applications which run on the migrating VM. The impact of these overheads heavily depend on the characteristics of the applications, the offered workload, and the available CPU and network resources. These facts have been pointed out from multiple empirical studies, like [29] and [30].

Unfortunately, very few of the existing VM consolidation studies take into consideration the aforementioned overheads. Even those who do (*e.g.,* [24, 8]), they use analytical models which not only are unrealistic, but they also rely on input which is not accurately replicated by the employed validation frameworks. As a result, such models commonly overlook the cost of migration (especially at scale) resulting in highly over-optimistic and unrealistic results.

4. PROPOSED METHODOLOGY

This section addresses the main points of criticism on past works by proposing practical solutions which provide an environment to faithfully evaluate energy-efficient VM placement algorithms. An accurate and effective experimentation framework should incorporate a unified model for the available resources of a virtualized server, the demands of hosted applications, the properties of network infrastructure and the energy consumption of devices based on the load. Ultimately, such a solution will allow users to benchmark their ideas and efficiently explore the important trade-offs between energy saving and application-level performance penalties.

Motivated by recent efforts in faithful network experiment replication (§ 4.1), we elaborate on ways to integrate energy consumption models (§ 4.2).

4.1 Data-center modeling platform

In recent years, a resurging interest for reproducible network experimentation has surfaced. This motivated the development of generic network experimentation platforms, which allow seamless replication of large scale systems. Mininet [31] was a pioneering emulation platform with support for dense topologies, using Linux containers and network namespaces. Overcoming the limitations of simulation, users could now reuse real applications and OS components to recreate topologies and experiment scenarios via a script-based automation interface. A more elaborate effort aiming to overcome Mininet's poor scalability, was SELENA [32]. SELENA's design employed *time dilation* [33] to improve the experimental fidelity at scale, while maintaining reproducibility.

Hereafter, we describe how SELENA can be used and extended, forming the basis for a data center modeling platform which fulfills the requirements set in the previous section. It should be emphasized that the proposed approach is not tightly coupled with SELENA and it is compatible with other emulation frameworks which rely on virtualization and provide resource management primitives.

Reusing applications, emulating VMs: SELENA is a Xen-based[1] emulation framework, thus supports the re-use of unmodified code and common OSes. VMs can be configured to form virtual networks (in-a-box) and recreate the properties of real networks (*e.g.,* topology, link speed, latency) and real hosts (*e.g.,* OS configuration, network protocols, resources, etc.). Nonetheless, SELENA employs a one-VM-per-host mapping, which can limit effective scaling of data center-scale experiments. This can be addressed by abstracting a subset of less important data center nodes, using more lightweight hybrid approach, such as running Mininet inside a time-dilated SELENA VM. A second extension is to create an abstraction to represent the entity of a VM instance which runs on a server. Instead of using a heavyweight approach such as nested virtualization, this can be implemented by using containers inside SELENA VMs.

Fidelity at scale: In order to faithfully emulate faster and larger computer networks, SELENA's technique of time-dilation transparently slows down the passage of time for guest operating systems. It effectively virtualizes the availability of hosting hardware resources and therefore, allows the recreation of scenarios with increased I/O and computational demands. Users can directly control the trade-off between fidelity and running-time via intuitive tuning knobs. To further improve SELENA's scalability, we could explore zero-copy inter-VM network connectivity [34] and also the distributed execution of experiments across multiple hosts.

Emulating resource utilization: SELENA relies on the Xen hypervisor which provides by-design fine resource resource share between hosted VMs. We identify four key virtual resources: CPU cycles, memory, disk and network I/O operations. The hypervisor allocates CPU resources between VMs using the *credit2* scheduler, a highly flexible and tunable scheduler. Memory resources are abstracted by the hypervisor using a grant table access control mechanism, which enables accurate memory allocation to each VM. The support of the Xen hypervisor for disk I/O rate control is limited to simple inter-VM prioritization. Nevertheless, Linux *cgroups* (via the *blkio* controller), allows users to regulate the rate of I/O operations allowed in a unit of time. In a Xen environment, a user can use *cgroups* based throttling from inside the guests. Network I/O rates can be controlled either from the VIF QoS primitives offered by the Xen *netback* driver, or from within the guest by using *tc* on a virtual interface's egress queue.

Using the above mechanisms, we can determine with a greater level of control the maximum amount of resources which are available to a VM, or to groups of VMs. The latter is particularly useful because many VMs will be grouped under the common abstraction of a host, hence, they need to share a common pool of resources. The maximum amount of available resources to each group, will be equal to the available resources of the real system's components we want to model. Time dilation, on the other hand, will help to virtually scale the resources of the emulation machine, and support larger experiments. With the described extensions and using different workloads, the utilization levels of emulated resources, and the performance of applications (running inside the regulated VMs), will approximate reality with substantially higher accuracy in comparison to a simulation.

Emulating the cost of live VM migration: Multiple studies have tried to analyze and model the impact of live VM migration in terms of application-perceived performance degradation, network resource requirements [30], as well as energy cost [29], migration duration and down time of a migrating VM [35]. Since our experiments execute on top of a single Xen hypervisor instance, it is not possible neither scalable to perform actual migrations. Therefore, our intention is to emulate the process of a pre-copy live VM migration inside SELENA in a lightweight way.

In order to emulate a migration, we can employ any of the aforementioned models and given the dirty page rate of a migrating VM, we can artificially recreate during runtime the followings: (i) the migration-specific network traffic volume, (ii) the VM downtime, and (iii) the extra CPU load. Since the resources which are available to each VM are regulated to match the real system (see above), the proposed methodology will accurately replicate the extra load introduced from migration. Consequently, the impact of a migration on the running application's performance will also be captured.

4.2 A system-load based energy model

Earlier measurement-based evaluations [36, 26] show that there is a huge impact of the energy management techniques on system power requirements. So far, this impact has not been addressed by VM migration or consolidation strategies. As an example, by reproducing the methodology proposed in [26] in our testbed, we show in Figure 2 the power consumption of the CPU of one of our data center servers, `quorum-102`, versus the load expressed in active cycles per second, namely ACPS. In the figure we observe that changing the number of cores and the CPU frequency produces rather different power consumption levels. More specifically, the authors of [26] have shown that energy consumption and efficiency of each server component can be accurately estimated upon a statistical characterization of baseline server energy consumption plus CPU utilization, disk I/O activity, and the network activity. Since CPU loads due to different server components operation are additive, the total energy

[1] http://www.xenproject.org/

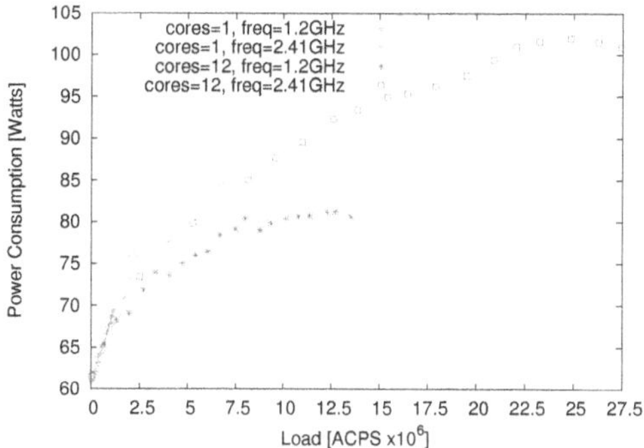

Figure 2: CPU performance bounds of `quorum-102`.

consumption of the server is the sum of the individual components' consumption, as experimentally shown in [26].

Therefore, collecting activity patterns of VMs is key to estimate the energy behavior of a modeled real system under VM consolidation and live migration strategy operation. As we discussed in § 3.2, to attain a reliable estimate of energy requirements for data center servers we need to obtain usage information for individual components. Indeed, we can access such information through the Xen hypervisor, which maintains fine grain accounting of the usage statistics for all computational resources: *i.e.*, CPU, disk I/O, memory I/O, and network I/O. However, it is important and challenging, to calibrate those statistics so that they refer to the load of a real system and not to the *virtual* load of the VM. This, though, is guaranteed through the resource utilization emulation model, discussed in § 4.1. Furthermore, such statistics can be emulated and used as input to a utilization-based energy estimation model. Like in [26], such model can be built using measurements from real server-grade machines, whereas emulation can be suitably used to estimate the load.

Energy model details. For the implementation of the utilization-based energy model, we follow the methodology described in [26]. We need, however, to extend it to include estimates for memory energy utilization (which was included in the *baseline* component in that work), and build an energy-performance model.

Our per-component energy model depends on a few activity parameters, which are the active CPU cycles per second, number of read/write disk and memory operations, and network utilization. Moreover, the effect of multicore processors and DVFS is not to be neglected, as can be seen in Figure 2, since both characteristics yields high variability in the energy consumption. Finally, we also consider a residual *baseline* energy consumption, which represents the activity of the server when no user-level process is active.

In what follows, since it is possible to characterize the CPU activity due to each different server component, we remove the energy consumption due to CPU activity in the estimate of each component's energy consumption. Thereby, energy requirements can be expressed as follows:

$$\begin{aligned} E_{cpu} &= \eta_{cpu}(T, f, c, a), & (1)\\ E_{disk} &= \eta_{dr}(T, f, c, cs, nc) + \eta_{dw}(T, f, c, cs, nc), & (2)\\ E_{net} &= \eta_{in}(T, f, c, s, l) + \eta_{out}(T, f, c, s, l), & (3)\\ E_{mem} &= \eta_{mr}(T, f, c, cs, nc) + \eta_{mw}(T, f, c, cs, nc); & (4) \end{aligned}$$

where $\eta_j, \forall j \in \{cpu, dr, dw, in, out, mr, mw\}$ is the efficiency of the CPU, the disk while reading or writing, the network while receiving or sending and the memory while reading or writing, respectively. T defines the duration of the experiment, f is the system frequency, c is the amount of cores used by the system, a is the CPU activity expressed in active cycles per second, cs is the chunk size used to read/write from/to the disk or memory, nc is the total number of chunks which has to be read/written from/to the disk or memory, s corresponds to the packet size flowing over the network and l is the network load. In the above model, we consider that network transmission and reception are independent processes. The same applies for the electro-mechanical operation of disks for *read* and *write*. Similarly, the behavior of memory is independent for *read* and *write* events. Since we do not account for CPU active cycles in all those events (the cost of CPU cycles is computed separately), we can safely assume that *read* and *write* operations of memory, disk and network are "energy-orthogonal", *i.e.*, they do not share energy consumption, and therefore we can simply sum up the respective energy consumptions for each component.

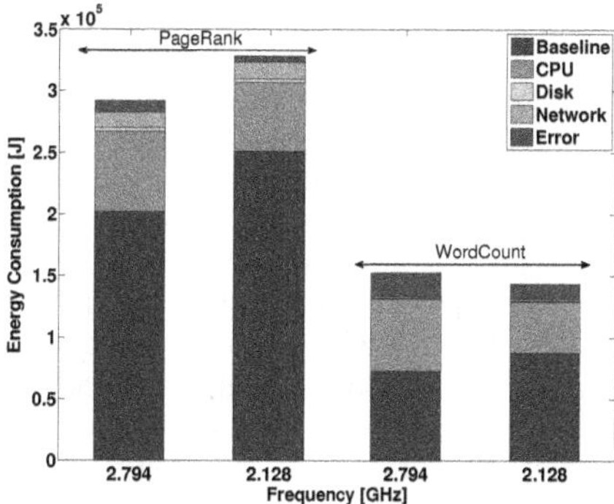

Figure 3: Energy consumption of our servers in a cloud-based scenario.

The resulting total energy estimation of the system is:

$$E_{total} = E_{base} + E_{cpu} + E_{disk} + E_{net} + E_{mem} \quad (5)$$

where $E_i, \forall i \in \{total, base, cpu, disk, net, mem\}$, corresponds to the energy requirements for the whole system, the baseline, the CPU, disk, network and memory respectively.

In order to use the proposed model in the evaluation of VM consolidation and, we also need to characterize the load of VMs on different machines, possibly using different hardware and configurations. Therefore, we need to emulate the activity of VMs and VM management software to estimate the correct amount of load caused to the host machines (*e.g.*, before and after migration). With SELENA, we can use the VM-activity statistics as input to the model described above. In addition, statistics of VMs which are grouped under the same "server" virtual entity (implemented as a common pool of resources), should be aggregated.

Preliminary evaluation. To evaluate the validity of the presented energy model, we set up a small scale experiment. We measure two similar servers, `quorum-101` and `quorum-102`, for consistency reasons. The servers are Dell PowerEdge R320 (Intel Xeon E5-2430L V2, 6 cores), two hard drives, a 100 *GB* SSD and a 1 *TB* HDD, two *Gigabit* and two 10 *Gigabit* ports. We installed Linux Ubuntu Server 14.04LTS and a recent version of Xen (v4.4).To monitor the instantaneous power consumption of the system we use the Sentry CDUs[2]. We collect our measurements every second via the `snmp` protocol and we store them locally.

In Figure 3 we show some preliminary results creating workloads on virtual machines. In the figure we can see the estimation of the per-component energy consumption

[2]Sentry Sw.Cabinet Distribution Unit CDW-24VEA458/C

(in *Joules*), for one of our servers considering the effect of DVFS. We use a cloud scenario with two servers, each one hosting a VM and running two Hadoop applications, WordCount and Pagerank algorithm. We keep track of the instantaneous power consumption and the overall utilization of CPU, disk and network for two different frequencies. As can be seen in the figure, the two applications have different utilization profiles for individual system components. It is worth mentioning that we have simplified our model, including the effect of memory within the other components (but it will be considered separately in later stages of our study).

Importing the utilization results into the model we estimate the accumulated energy consumption for the server which runs the application. From the power measurements we can extract the actual energy needs and finally, we observe that the estimation error is on average about 4% and never worse than 10%. We expect that this error can be reduced when we properly include the memory behavior.

5. CONCLUSION

This paper challenged common evaluation practices employed in past VM consolidation studies, such as simulation and small testbeds, which fail to capture the fundamental properties of real systems. Specifically, we identified a series of over-simplifying assumptions regarding energy consumption and performance characteristics with respect to virtualized infrastructures. To address this problem, we described the design of an evaluation framework which incorporates more accurate models for data center systems and their available resources. In addition, we proposed a measurement-based power characterization methodology for servers, which accepts as input the load of individual hardware components and estimates the energy consumption for different server configurations. The integration of the two solutions, allows us to achieve the envisioned goal of exploring the energy-performance trade-off in VM consolidation.

Acknowledgements

This work was jointly supported by MINECO (grant TEC2014-55713-R), the Greek State Scholarship Foundation, the EPSRC INTERNET Project EP / H040536/1, the EPSRC TOUCAN project EP / L020009/1 and the Defense Advanced Research Projects Agency (DARPA) and the Air Force Research Laboratory (AFRL), under contract FA8750-11-C-0249. The views, opinions, and/or findings contained in this article/presentation are those of the author/presenter and should not be interpreted as representing the official views or policies, either expressed or implied, of the Defense Advanced Research Projects Agency or the Department of Defense.

6. REFERENCES

[1] C. PETTEY. Gartner estimates for ICT industry CO_2 emissions. http://goo.gl/4KuOAi, 2007.

[2] P. DELFORGE. America's data centers consuming and wasting growing amounts of energy. http://goo.gl/HOLLBx, 2014.

[3] W. VAN HEDDEGHEM *et al.*. Trends in worldwide ICT electricity consumption from 2007 to 2012. *Computer Communications* (2014).

[4] D. ABTS *et al.*. Energy proportional datacenter networks. In *SIGARCH Computer Architecture News* (2010), vol. 38, ACM.

[5] L. A. BARROSO *et al.*. The case for energy-proportional computing. *IEEE computer* (2007).

[6] D. MEISNER *et al.*. PowerNap: eliminating server idle power. *SIGARCH Comp. Architecture News* (2009).

[7] G. CHEN *et al.*. Energy-aware server provisioning and load dispatching for connection-intensive Internet services. In *NSDI* (2008), USENIX.

[8] BELOGLAZOV, A., AND BUYYA, R. Energy efficient resource management in virtualized cloud data centers. In *MGC* (2010), IEEE.

[9] H. GOUDARZI *et al.*. SLA-based optimization of power and migration cost in cloud computing. In *CCGrid* (2012), IEEE.

[10] F. HERMENIER *et al.*. Entropy: a consolidation manager for clusters. In *VEE* (2009), ACM.

[11] R. NATHUJI *et al.*. VPM tokens: virtual machine-aware power budgeting in datacenters. In *Cluster comp.* (2009), Springer.

[12] T. WOOD *et al.*. Black-box and gray-box strategies for virtual machine migration. In *NSDI* (2007), USENIX.

[13] N. BOBROFF *et al.*. Dynamic placement of VM for managing SLA violations. In *IM* (2007), IEEE.

[14] WU, Q. Making Facebook's software infrastructure more energy efficient with Autoscale. https://goo.gl/69aZbd.

[15] D. KLIAZOVICH *et al.*. DENS: Data center energy-efficient network-aware scheduling. In *GreenCom, CPSCom, IEEE/ACM* (2010).

[16] WU, Q. HAProxy: The reliable, high performance TCP/HTTP load balancer, http://www.haproxy.org.

[17] PATEL, P., AND BANSAL, D. E. Ananta: Cloud scale load balancing. In *ACM SIGCOMM CCR* (2013).

[18] R. WANG *et al.*. Openflow-based server load balancing gone wild. In *Hot-ICE* (2011), USENIX.

[19] S. LEE *et al.*. Validating heuristics for virtual machines consolidation. *Microsoft Research TR* (2011).

[20] T. C. FERRETO *et al.*. Server consolidation with migration control for virtualized data centers. *Future Generation Computer Systems 27*, 8 (2011).

[21] J. XU, AND J. AB FORTES. Multi-objective virtual machine placement in virtualized data center environments. In *GreenCom* (2010), IEEE.

[22] G. WANG, AND T. S. E. NG. The impact of virtualization on network performance of amazon ec2 data center. In *INFOCOM* (2010), IEEE.

[23] J. DEAN, AND L. A. BARROSO. The tail at scale. *Commun. ACM 56*, 2 (Feb. 2013).

[24] A. VERMA *et al.*. pMapper: power and migration cost aware application placement in virtualized systems. In *Middleware*. Springer, 2008.

[25] A. GANDHI *et al.*. Optimal power allocation in server farms. In *SIGMETRICS Performance Evaluation Review* (2009), ACM.

[26] J. ARJONA AROCA *et al.*. A measurement-based analysis of the energy consumption of data center servers. In *e-Energy* (2014), ACM.

[27] C. CLARK *et al.*. Live migration of virtual machines. In *NSDI* (2005), USENIX.

[28] M. R. HINES *et al.*. Post-copy live migration of virtual machines. *ACM SIGOPS operating sys. review* (2009).

[29] H. LIU *et al.*. Performance and energy modeling for live migration of vm. *Cluster computing 16*, 2 (2013).

[30] R. BRADFORD *et al.*. Live wide-area migration of virtual machines including local persistent state. In *VEE* (2007), ACM.

[31] N. HANDIGOL *et al.*. Reproducible network experiments using container-based emulation. In *CoNEXT* (2012), ACM.

[32] D. PEDIADITAKIS *et al.*. Faithful reproduction of network experiments. In *ANCS* (2014), ACM.

[33] D. GUPTA *et al.*. To infinity and beyond: time-warped network emulation. In *NSDI* (2006), USENIX.

[34] L. RIZZO *et al.*. VALE, a Switched Ethernet for Virtual Machines. In *CoNEXT* (2012), ACM.

[35] S. AKOUSH *et al.*. Predicting the performance of VM migration. In *MASCOTS* (2010), IEEE.

[36] MCCULLOUGH, J. C., AND AGARWAL, Y. E. Evaluating the effectiveness of model-based power characterization. In *USENIX ATC* (2011).

Challenge
On Online Time Series Clustering For Demand Response
OPTIC - *A Theory to Break the 'Curse of Dimensionality'*

Ranjan Pal, Charalampos Chelmis, Chandra Tadepalli
Marc Frincu, Saima Aman, Viktor Prasanna
University of Southern California
{rpal, chelmis, ctadepal, frincu, saman, prasanna}@usc.edu

ABSTRACT

The advent of smart meters and advanced communication infrastructures catalyzes numerous smart grid applications such as dynamic demand response, and paves the way to solve challenging research problems in sustainable energy consumption. The space of solution possibilities are restricted primarily by the huge amount of generated data requiring considerable computational resources and efficient algorithms. To overcome this Big Data challenge, data clustering techniques have been proposed. Current approaches however do not scale in the face of the "increasing dimensionality" problem, where a cluster point is represented by the entire customer consumption time series. To overcome this aspect we first *rethink* the way cluster points are created and designed, and then devise OPTIC, an efficient online time series clustering technique for demand response (DR), in order to analyze high volume, high dimensional energy consumption time series data at scale, and on the fly. OPTIC is randomized in nature, and provides optimal performance guarantees (Section 2.3.2) in a computationally efficient manner. Unlike prior work we (i) study the consumption properties of the whole population simultaneously rather than developing individual models for each customer separately, claiming it to be a 'killer' approach that breaks the "curse of dimensionality" in online time series clustering, and (ii) provide tight performance guarantees in theory to validate our approach. Our insights are driven by the field of sociology, where collective behavior often emerges as the result of individual patterns and lifestyles. We demonstrate the efficacy of OPTIC in practice using real-world data obtained from the fully operational USC microgrid.

Categories and Subject Descriptors

I.5 [**Pattern Recognition**]: Clustering—*Algorithms*

Keywords

time series; clustering; demand response; online algorithm

1. INTRODUCTION

With the increased penetration of smart meters and advanced wireless network infrastructures, smart grids are becoming ubiquitous. Numerous practical smart grid applications, including Demand Response (DR) [1], are catalyzed by Advanced Metering Infrastructure. As a result, utilities need to dynamically adjust their DR strategy; this leads to Dynamic DR (D^2R) programs according to which the target, duration, and depth of curtailment is a dynamically changing function of customers' responsiveness, particularly in incentive-based DR programs. However, the capability of the cyber-infrastructure to support such applications efficiently is primarily limited by the Big Data deluge (i.e., high volume, velocity, variety, and veracity) coming from sensors. The large amount of high speed data coming from smart meters and other smart appliances such as thermostats, luminosity sensors, etc., pose significant challenges to real-time data processing and decision making by impacting the efficiency and speed at which information can be extracted from the data stream.

Traditional solutions for predicting energy consumption and curtailment analyze either individual or groups of customers by applying prediction techniques on the historical energy consumption time series. Individual customer predictions are challenging because different prediction methods give different results in terms of accuracy for distinct consumption trends [2]. Predicting consumption for each customer can become a computational bottleneck especially for large smart grids with millions of customers. i.e., the response time for consumer data processing is on the order of a few hours [2]. Clearly, such performance guarantees are inefficient for D^2R applications. In this regard, clustering techniques have the advantage of making predictions easier by (a) reducing the noise in the aggregate customer energy consumption time series [3], and (b) reducing the customer prediction time complexity by not being required to running prediction algorithms on individual customers. A good customer clustering can provide utilities with an optimal set of customers to target during D^2R.

While customer clustering has its benefits it does not come without a trade-off. Traditionally, each point in the cluster is represented by the time series of a single customer. In an online scenario such as D^2R, where the time series grows linearly, clustering techniques are faced with the problem of increasing dimensionality. Increasing dimensionality is a major issue to the space-time performance of existing time series clustering algorithms; such algorithms are designed to perform well for fixed-dimensional data sets [4], and give bad performance for online cases, where clustering needs to be recomputed on the fly as the number of dimensions increase. While one solution to the problem is to keep dimensionality constant by disregarding stale data, this approach may not always work because most consumption time series data show some periodicity, and that might get lost by dropping older data points.

In this paper we challenge the use of traditional approaches towards clustering consumption time series data for data *continually* coming from a massive number of smart sensors. We instead propose a novel clustering approach where we fix the dimensions to the number of customers. In our approach, each point denotes the energy consumption values for all customers at a given point in time. This enables the formation of clusters of points in time which encompass the consumption values of all smart meters simultaneously. The advantage of our proposed approach is twofold. First, clustering can be performed incrementally on "data-in-motion", i.e., new data points can be incrementally integrated as they arrive in a stream allowing the clustering configuration to be computed once and updated incrementally with the arrival of new observations. In contrast, traditional approaches require clustering

e-Energy'15, July 14 - 17, 2015, Bangalore, India
© 2015 ACM ISBN 978-1-4503-3609-3/15/07 $15.00.
DOI: http://dx.doi.org/10.1145/2578726.2578744

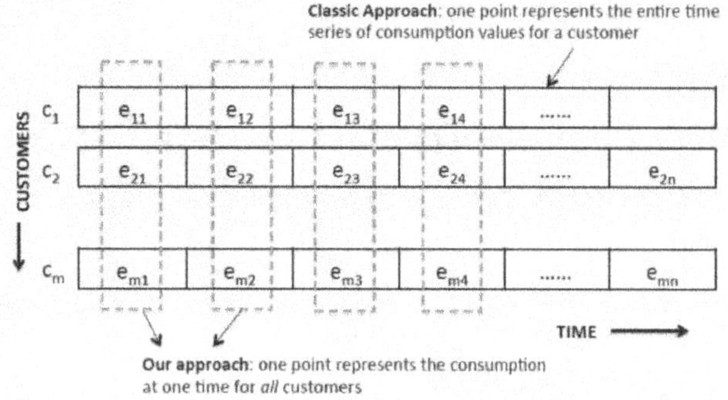

Figure 1: Classic vs. our proposed point representation.

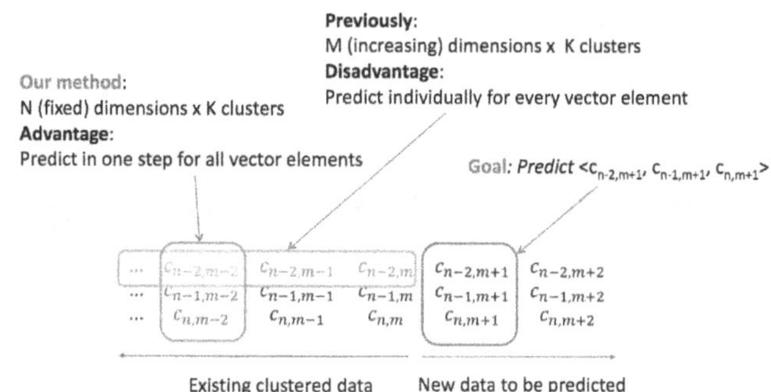

Figure 2: Advantage of our approach w.r.t clustering goal

points (time series) whose dimensionality increases with time; thus with increasing dimensions, clustering has to be recomputed from scratch. Second, by co-integrating customers' consumption values in a vector it is possible for emerging patterns to be mined.

Figure 1 depicts the two approaches. The consumption value for customer i at time j is denoted by e_{ij}. Our representation can be naturally obtained by *transposing* the original collection of time series. Instead of new columns being added with the arrival of new data points, the matrix grows in the rows dimension in our representation. The clustering goal and the advantages of our approach in this context are depicted in Figure 2

We make the following research contributions in this paper.

- We propose an intuitive idea to the 'dynamic customer time series segmentation' problem that is driven by the field of sociology, where collective behavior emerges as a result of individual patterns (See Section 2).
- We model this problem as an online clustering of time series data, which in turn is intractable, i.e., computationally expensive (See Section 2.3.3). To address this issue, we propose an online approximation algorithm with provable *performance guarantees* (See Section 2.3.2) to dynamically cluster energy consumption data points on the fly (See Section 3.1). Based on our online approximation algorithm, we design OPTIC, an online randomized algorithm with better provable performance guarantees to online clustering compared to the pure approximation version (See Section 3.2).
- We demonstrate the efficacy of OPTIC using experiments conducted on fine-grained '15-minute' interval energy consumption data for one year, of 115 buildings at the University of Southern California (USC), obtained from their Facility Management Services (FMS). In the process of practically showing the efficacy of OPTIC, we also compare OPTIC's performance with existing provable online clustering algorithms, and heuristics. (See Section 4).

To the best of our knowledge, OPTIC is the first time series clustering algorithm that is both dynamic and provably optimal. OPTIC is extendible to all scenarios and applications that require online time series clustering with provable performance guarantees.

2. PROBLEM SETUP AND BACKGROUND

In this section, we first state the importance of mining emerging behavior from individual consumer dynamics. We then describe our problem setting, which is followed by a description of the model preliminaries.

2.1 Mining Emerging Behavior

Intuitively, energy consumption is expected to be periodic, as it is governed by human activities that usually follow some schedule (e.g., daily or weekly). For example, in workplace and even residential settings, it is very likely that people are at the same place on Monday mornings, and therefore it is also likely that an emerging behavior can be recorded. In this case the energy consumption of a building will be similar on Monday mornings even if occupied by multiple tenants with different schedules or hosts hundreds of office spaces. As an example, we present daily consumption observations over a course of a year for four buildings of different types in Figure 3. From Figure 3, it can is seen that, despite the differentiation between consumption patterns among individual buildings, consumption is relatively stable for each of the buildings individually at a specific point in time over the course of a day throughout the year. Some variation is to be expected depending on the function of buildings (e.g., the second building from the left demonstrates a significant drop in consumption during summer). Similarly, usage is likely to differ by few half hours earlier or later due to natural irregularities in behavior (e.g., someone returned home at 6:30 p.m. instead of 6 p.m.). In our study, we are focusing on 15-minute intervals which even though can provide fine details on consumption, can be affected by small shifts in behavior (e.g., a tenant who overslept or worked at home on a Monday) can significantly impact the expected periodicity. Our premise is that such patterns can be detected and utilized efficiently both for consumer behavior analysis and load prediction. Typically utilities develop personalized models for each customer or rely on customer segmentation techniques, where individual models are made for each customer segment, to reduce their modeling and prediction uncertainty. *Our hypothesis is that using our representation of time series can lead to significant insights about customers' emerging behavior, and more importantly, to efficient very-short-term and medium-term prediction algorithms for electricity consumption forecasting.*

So, how does a utility go about uncovering such patterns for hundreds of thousands or millions of customers? In this work, we are venturing to address this question by appropriately arranging fine-grained streaming energy data and examining it holistically. Our approach is based on social theory, according to which individual human behavior often results in emerging collective behavior. Our assumption is that collective patterns should emerge as a result of individual patterns (as shown in Figure 3).

2.2 Problem Setting

We consider a fixed large number of customers in a metropolitan area, whose time series data of energy consumption for a given period of each day (e.g., starting at 12 AM) and sampled every 15 minutes or less is known to the local utility. The utility wants to make energy consumption predictions with the goal of achieving consumption reduction during DR. As such, as a first step, the utility adopts a time series clustering technique to group customers together based on consumption trends. This not only lowers the prediction error per cluster but also allows utilities to treat each cluster independently by customizing the DR program. Traditional clustering techniques require re-running the clustering every time a new consumption data point is available. This is however time consuming and unfeasible in a D^2R scenario. As a result a clustering technique that can update itself with the advent of new data points for a given day without *re-evaluating* the segmentation from scratch is preferred. The objective is to *dynamically* update the customer clusters efficiently with respect to space (memory) and time complexity. In this paper we propose an online time-series clustering approach with provable performance guarantees. Here, the

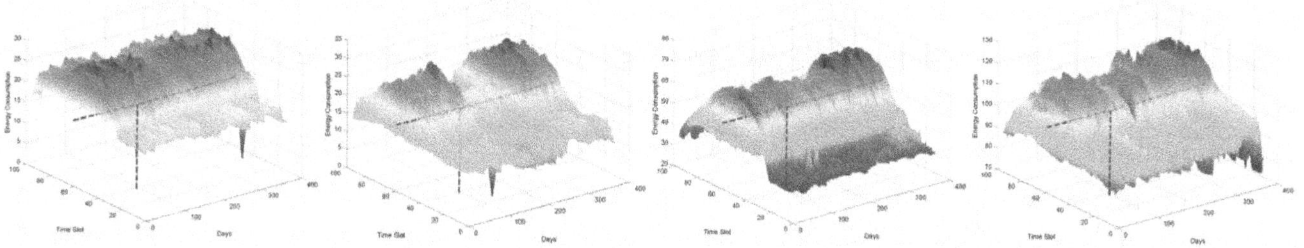

Figure 3: Smart meter data for four buildings of diverse functions, measured over a period of one year.

term "performance guarantee" refers to the clustering quality with respect to the optimal clustering possible on data points available currently.

2.2.1 *Related Work in Brief*

Several recent approaches have been proposed in the literature for time series clustering related to human patterns on different activities. These are driven by different end goals, such as to summarize information conveyed in temporal data, and to find representative consumption pattern for each cluster of time series. Chua et al. [5] have performed segmentation and clustering of time series of sensor data collected in smart homes for unsupervised learning of human behaviors. Hino et al. [6] have clustered daily household electricity patterns to find representative customer patterns. Martinez-Alvarez et al. [7] have performed time series clustering using similarity of pattern sequences for prediction.

Regarding the mechanism behind time-series clustering, many different approaches have been used. These include approaches based on Euclidean distance, Manhattan distance, shapelets, and dynamic time warping (DTW), etc. For more detailed information on time series clustering mechanims, see [4] [8]. All existing time series clustering approaches require appropriate selection of numerous variables, (e.g., the number of clusters, appropriate window length for time series data), are computationally expensive, etc., - but the common underlying properties characterizing all these approaches are that they are (a) *heuristics*, and not *provably optimal,* (b) static in nature, and (c) does not scale well to high dimensions (unless accompanied by dimensionality reduction techniques; one exception being the approach in [8])

In this work, we derive time-series clustering approaches that are provably optimal, dynamic, and suited for high-dimensional data.

2.2.2 *Challenging a Conventional Mechanism*

In this section, we first provide the rationale of why our given problem setting is subject to the 'increasing dimensionality' problem of the conventional application of time series clustering algorithms. We then provide a brief intuition of how this challenge can be resolved in an effective way so as to harness the power and simplicity of clustering mechanisms.

Challenge: Assume a time series clustering algorithm exists to dynamically update groups of users for efficient D^2R. Such an algorithm would need to deal with data that is increasing in dimensionality. Intuitively, the length of each vector $c(i,:), \forall i$ (i.e., vector of consumption values for customer i from Figure 2) increases with time because new data points are added as they are recorded. This strictly increasing dimensionality is a major road block to the space-time performance of existing time series clustering algorithms; *such algorithms are designed to perform well for fixed-dimensional data sets.* Windowing techniques can be applied to keep dimensionality constant, however this approach may lead to accuracy degradation; as important consumption patterns might be overlooked in favor of more recently added data points.

Solution Insight: Our main intuition behind solving the above-mentioned challenge is to change the conventional view of looking at time series data. More precisely, given a pre-specified number of customers, instead of considering each consumption value in a time series as a dimension, we fix the number of dimensions to be the number of customers. Then for each time point, we have a vector of consumption values of customers, where the length of the vector equals the number of consumers (see Figure 1). We obtain a data point which is not an increasing time series but a vector of fixed dimension. Our goal is to efficiently cluster these data points in an online fashion as they arrive with time.

2.3 Model Preliminaries

In this section we describe the principle behind our proposed clustering mechanism, formulate our clustering problem, and comment on its complexity.

2.3.1 *Clustering Principle*

Our clustering mechanism is based on the principle of *Hierarchical Agglomerative Clustering* (HAC) [9] [10]. The basic idea is: *initially assign n points to n distinct clusters; repeatedly merge pairs of clusters until their number is sufficiently small.* HAC computes hierarchy trees of clusters whose leaves are individual points and internal nodes correspond to clusters formed by merging clusters at the children. The *primary advantage* of HAC-based algorithms is that (i) in a dynamic setting (such as ours, where there is the advent of new data points, and we need to update the clustering accordingly in an efficient manner), it is desirable to retain the hierarchical structure while ensuring efficient update and high-quality clustering, (ii) experience shows that HAC performs extremely well, both in terms of efficiency, as well as in cluster quality [11] [12], and (iii) the applicability of HAC extends to arbitrary metric spaces, and thus can accomodate a large number of distance metrics.

2.3.2 *Problem Formulation*

Assume a general arbitrary metric space M, e.g., $\mathbb{R}^m$. Consider a set of n_1 points in M that have *already* been clustered into k clusters so as to minimize the maximum cluster diameter. Here, each point is a vector of energy consumption values for a consumer at a particular time instant, the *diameter* of a cluster is defined to be the maximum inter-point distance in it, and the the *distance* between points in M is given by a distance function on the metric space, e.g., l_2 distance in $\mathbb{R}^m$. Now consider a set of n_2 points in M that are yet to arrive. For each point arrival, we need to design an algorithm (say A) that maintains a collection of k clusters such that either the input point is assigned to one of the current k clusters, or it starts off as a new cluster while two existing clusters are merged into one. Clearly A in *online* in nature. We define the *performance ratio* of A as the maximum over all update sequences of the ratio of its maximum cluster diameter to that of the *optimal* clustering for the input points, where the optimal clustering refers to a configuration of clusters that minimizes the average dissimilarity of any input point towards its closest center . By formulating our problem in this way, we enforce the requirement that *at all times* algorithm A will maintain a HAC for the points presented up to that time. *Our main objective in this paper is to design A such that it is efficient in both computational time and space, and at the same time providing the best performance guarantee.*

We note here that it could have been the case that a newly arrived point could start off from a new cluster and we could allow the points of one old cluster to be re-distributed among the remaining clusters, rather than two clusters to be merged together. The problem with such formulations is that they do not lead to HACs. In the following section, we characterize the hardness of our proposed clustering problem.

2.3.3 Problem Intractability

The static version of our clustering problem falls into the group of problems known as *pairwise clustering* or *Bregman k-center* problems [13] [14]. Both these problem types are NP-Hard in nature [15] [16], and in fact hard to approximate to within factor 2 for arbitrary metric spaces. Even if we consider the specific case of Euclidean metric spaces, the problem types are NP-Hard for data point dimensionality greater than or equal to 2 (such as in our case), and for arbitrary distance metrics. It is evident that with the static clustering problem being hard, the online version is at least harder. Thus, in our work we will look to design efficient approximation algorithms for the online clustering problem. In this regard, we borrow techniques from [17] [18] to come up with an algorithm whose time complexity is solely a function of k.

3. THE OPTIC ALGORITHM DESIGN

In this section, we design our proposed online time series clustering algorithm, OPTIC. As mentioned earlier, due to to the inherent intractability of our clustering problem, we first resort to the design of an efficient approximation algorithm to address the online time series clustering problem. In order to ensure strong performance guarantees, we then construct a randomized online algorithm, i.e., OPTIC, for our clustering problem, the structure of which lies embedded in the non-randomized approximation online algorithm. We now describe this non-randomized algorithm.

3.1 The 'Pure' Approximation Algorithm

Our approximation online algorithm is mainly based on two parameters, α and β (to be described later), and thus we will term it as the '(α, β) - online time series clustering algorithm', or simply (α, β) - OTSC. The algorithm works in phases: at the start of phase i, it has a collection of $k+1$ clusters $C_1, C_2, ..., C_{k+1}$ and a lower bound d_i on the optimal clustering's diameter (denoted as OPT). Each cluster C_i has a center c_i which is one of the points in the cluster. The following algorithm *invariants* are assumed at the start of phase i: (a) for each cluster C_j, the radius of C_j defined as $max_{p \in C_j} d(c_j, p)$ is at most αd_i; (b) for each pair of clusters C_j and C_l, the inter-center distance $d(c_j, c_l) \geq d_i$; and (c) $d_i \leq$ OPT.

Algorithm 1: (α, β)-OTSC finds a time series clustering

Input: (a) *Dynamic* point set $S \subset \mathbb{R}^n$ of consumer energy consumption data at time instants. Let $n = |N|$ - number of consumers, (b) Number of desired clusters, k, (c) Given *dynamic* set T of k clusters of currently observed data points, each cluster having at least one point, (d) Given (α, β) pair such that $\frac{\alpha}{\alpha-1} \leq \beta$, and (e) d - smallest interpoint distance in T.

Output: A k clustering configuration, T

Repeat forever
while $|T| \leq k$ **do**
  Get new point x; $S \leftarrow S \cup \{x\}$
  if $D(x, T) > \beta d$ **then**
    $T \leftarrow T \cup \{x\}$
$T' \leftarrow \{\}$
while $\exists z \in T$ *such that* $D(z, T') > \beta d$ **do**
  $T' \leftarrow T' \cup \{z\}$
$T \leftarrow T'$
$d \leftarrow \beta d$
return T

Each phase consists of two stages: the first is the *merging stage* in which the algorithm reduces the number of clusters by merging certain pairs; the second is the *update stage* in which the algorithm accepts new updates and tries to maintain at most k clusters without increasing the radius of the clusters or violating the invariants. A phase ends when the number of clusters again exceeds k. We now explain in detail the merging and update stages of our algorithm.

3.1.1 Merging Stage

The merging stage works as follows: Define $d_{i+1} = \beta d_i$, and let G be the d_{i+1} - *margin* graph on the $k + 1$ cluster centers, $c_1, c_2, ..., c_{k+1}$. We define a d-margin graph on a set of points $P = \{p_1, p_2, ..., p_n\}$ as the graph $G = (P, E)$ such that $(p_i, p_j) \in E$ if and only if $d(p_i, p_j) \leq d$. The graph G is used to merge clusters by repeatedly performing the following steps while the graph is non-empty: pick an arbitrary cluster C_i in G and merge all neighbors into it; make c_i the new cluster's center; and remove C_i and its neighbors from G. Let $C'_1, C'_2, ..., C'_m$ be the new clusters at the end of the merging stage. Note that it is possible that $m = k + 1$ when the graph G has no edges, in which case the algorithm will be forced to declare the end of phase i without going through the update stage. *We have the following lemma regarding the merging stage, the proof of which is in the Appendix.*

LEMMA 1. *The pairwise distance between the cluster centers after the merging stage of phase i is at least d_{i+1}, and the radius of the clusters after the merging stage of phase i is at most $d_{i+1} + \alpha d_i \leq \alpha d_{i+1}$.*

3.1.2 Update Stage

The update stage continues while the number of clusters is at most k. When a new data point arrives, the algorithm attempts to place it in one of the current clusters without exceeding the radius bound αd_{i+1}: otherwise a new cluster is formed with the update as the cluster center. When the number of clusters reaches k + 1, phase i ends and the current set of k +1 clusters along with d_{i+1} are used for the $(i + 1)th$ phase. We have the following lemma on the invariant preservation after every phase of our deterministic clustering algorithm. *The proof of the lemma is in the Appendix.*

LEMMA 2. *The k + 1 clusters at the end of the ith phase satisfy the following conditions: (i) the radius of the clusters is at most αd_{i+1}, (ii) the pairwise distance between cluster centers is at least d_{i+1}, and (iii) $d_{i+1} \leq$ OPT, where OPT is the diameter of the optimal clustering for the current set of points.*

Algorithm 1 provides our algorithmic steps. We have the following theorem regarding the computational complexity of (α, β)-OTSC, *the proof of which is in the Appendix.*

THEOREM 1. *Algorithm (α, β)-OTSC has an optimal performance ratio of 8 in any metric space when both $\alpha = \beta$ equals 2, and can be implemented to run in $O(k \log k)$ amortized time per update.*

As mentioned above, the performance ratio of (α, β)-OTSC is 8, but we can do significantly better if we use this algorithm as the backbone to design a randomized algorithm, as shown next.

3.2 Randomized Algorithm (OPTIC) Design

The randomized algorithm remains essentially the same as the deterministic one, the main change being the value of d_1, which is the lower bound for phase 1. In the deterministic case we choose d_1 to be the minimum pairwise distance of the first $k + 1$ points, say x. We now choose a random value r from the closed interval $[\frac{1}{e}, 1]$ according to the probability density function $\frac{1}{r}$. We also set d_1 to rx, redefine $\beta = e$, and force α to be equal to $\frac{e}{e-1}$. We now state our randomized algorithm, OPTIC, that is based on the dynamic information retrieval theory in [19].

The following theorem regarding the computational complexity of (α, β)-OPTIC, *the proof of which is in the Appendix.*

THEOREM 2. *Algorithm (α, β)-OPTIC has an optimal performance ratio of 2e, i.e., approximately a factor of 5.43, in any metric space with $(\alpha, \beta) = (\frac{e}{e-1}, e)$, and can be implemented to run in $O(k \log k)$ amortized time per update.*

4. EXPERIMENTAL EVALUATION

In this section, we provide the details of our experimental setup and analyze our results.

Algorithm 2: (α, β)-OPTIC finds a time series clustering

Input: (a) *Dynamic* point set $S \subset \mathbb{R}^n$ of consumer energy consumption data at time instants. Let $n = |N|$ - number of consumers, (b) Number of desired clusters, k, (c) Given *dynamic* set T of k clusters of currently observed data points, each cluster having at least one point, (d) Given $(\alpha = \frac{e}{e-1}, \beta = e)$ pair such that $\frac{\alpha}{\alpha-1} \leq \beta$, and (e) $d = r\times$ smallest interpoint distance in T, where r is a random value chosen from $[\frac{1}{e}, 1]$ with probability density function $\frac{1}{r}$.

Output: A k clustering configuration, T

Repeat forever
while $|T| \leq k$ **do**
    Get new point x; $S \leftarrow S \cup \{x\}$
    if $D(x, T) > \beta d$ **then**
        $T \leftarrow T \cup \{x\}$
$T' \leftarrow \{\}$
while $\exists z \epsilon T$ *such that* $D(z, T') > \beta d$ **do**
    $T' \leftarrow T' \cup \{z\}$
$T \leftarrow T'$
$d \leftarrow \beta d$
return T

4.1 Experimental Setup

To test the performance our proposed randomized algorithm, we use building energy consumption data for the year of 2013, for 115 buildings in the University of Southern California's University Park campus. The data is fine-grained and captures energy consumption (in kilowatt hour- (kWh)) points for each of the 115 buildings at every 15-minute interval. Thus, we have 115 time series data elements at our disposal, for a time duration of an entire year. We obtain this data from USC's Facility Management Services (FMS). Mapping the data set to the OPTIC setting (See Figure 1) results in individual data points having 115 dimensions each. We use a single machine from USC's Center for High-Performance Computing (HPCC - `https://hpcc.usc.edu/`) to run our experiments.

As part of OPTIC's clustering performance, we study two metrics: (i) time to online clustering of the entire data set (ii) its corresponding online clustering cost, where the cost is computed using the l_2 Euclidean metric. For the given data set, we vary the number of clusters from 5 to 15, into which the data set is going to be segmented. Given k - the number of clusters, we assume that only k points are available to the OPTIC algorithm as initial input, and it subsequently clusters new data points in an online manner. The algorithm stops when all the data points from the data set are exhausted. This is when we record our time and cost values for the clustering task[1]. We compare the performance of OPTIC with three recent online clustering techniques available in the literature: (a) Online k-means (OKM) heuristic [20], (b) Smoothed Online k-means (SOKM) heuristic, [21] with $\alpha = 0.5$, and (c) Online Clustering with Experts (OCE) [22], where we adopt the OKM and the k-means ++ [23], as the experts. *For the purpose of comparison with k-means based methods, the cost for OPTIC in the plots is in reference to the k-means cost, whereas the cost in Theorems 1 and 2 reflect the Bregman's k-center metric.* While reporting the time and cost of clustering tasks on our data set, we consider the average values of 50 runs of each algorithm.

4.2 Results

The experimental results are shown in Figure 4. From Figure 4a., we observe that for a pre-specified $k > 5$, time to cluster our data set is the lowest for OPTIC when compared to existing k-means based online clustering algorithms, by a significant margin (nearly *one-fifth* on average, and better for higher k). To justify the lower bound of $k = 5$ for our experiments, we expect for demand response applications in a large locality such as Los Angeles that consumer consumption behavior will reflect at least 5 distinct types, at a given time. From Figure 4a., we infer that OPTIC scales to scenarios where new data points arrive in intervals of seconds, rather than in minutes, making it suitable for clustering high velocity data sets. From Figure 4b., we observe that OPTIC performs better than all the other online clustering techniques (nearly 60% lesser costs on average), except for OKM, in terms of clustering cost (even for increasing k). Thus, we recommend the use of OPTIC in BigData applications that focus on both speed and accuracy.

[1]Ideally, we would like to study the time curve to dynamically cluster data ranging from a single point to all the points in the 2013 data set; however, we are constrained by space requirements and wish to study such a plot, as part of future work.

5. CONCLUSION AND FUTURE WORK

In this paper, we studied the problem of dynamically clustering consumer energy consumption data for demand response purposes, as it arrives over time in a stream. Given that time series data is high dimensional, it is a big challenge in the Smart Grid to dynamically cluster consumer energy usage on the fly, with the continuous increase in streaming data dimensions. We resolve this challenge with an idea stemming from the field of sociology: *collective behavior often emerges as the result of individual patterns and lifestyles.* This idea motivated us to look at the time series clustering problem in an inverted manner, where each data point is a fixed dimensional vector of the energy consumption of all the consumers in the system, at a particular time instant. As a result the clustering problem is reduced to an online task of dynamically clustering points of fixed dimensions. In this regard, we designed OPTIC, a randomized online algorithm that provides optimal performance guarantees in a computationally efficient manner. Unlike prior work, (i) we studied the consumption properties of the whole population simultaneously rather than developing individual models for each customer separately, claiming it to be a 'killer' approach that breaks the 'curse of dimensionality' in online time series clustering, and (ii) we provided tight performance guarantees for the quality of our approach. *To the best of our knowledge, OPTIC is the first work on dynamic (online), and provably optimal time series clustering of high dimensional data points.*

As part of future work, we plan to develop a distributed version of the OPTIC algorithm, and use OPTIC to perform both, short-term, as well as long-term predictions for the entire population of consumers using real-world smart grid data.

Acknowledgement

This material is based upon work supported by the United States Department of Energy under Award Number number DE-OE0000192, the U.S. National Science Foundation under grant ACI-1339756, and the Los Angeles Department of Water and Power (LADWP). The views and opinions of authors expressed herein do not necessarily state or reflect those of the United States Government or any agency thereof, the LADWP, nor any of their employees.

6. REFERENCES

[1] F. Rahimi and A. Ipakchi, "Demand response as a market resource under the smart grid paradigm," *Smart Grid, IEEE Transactions on*, vol. 1, no. 1, pp. 82–88, 2010.

[2] M. Frincu, C. Chelmis, M. U. Noor, and V. K. Prasanna, "Accurate and efficient selection of the best consumption prediction method in smart grids," in *Proc. IEEE International Conference on Big Data*, IEEE, 2014.

[3] Y. Simmhan and M. Noor, "Scalable prediction of energy consumption using incremental time series clustering," in *Big Data, 2013 IEEE International Conference on*, pp. 29–36, Oct 2013.

[4] T. W. Liao, "Clustering of time series data - a survey," *Pattern Recognition*, vol. 38, no. 11, 2005.

[5] S.-L. Chua, S. Marsland, and H. Guesgen, "Unsupervised learning of human behaviors," in *AAAI*, 2011.

[6] H. Hino, H. Shen, N. Murata, S. Wakao, and Y. Hayashi, "A versatile clustering method for electricity consumption

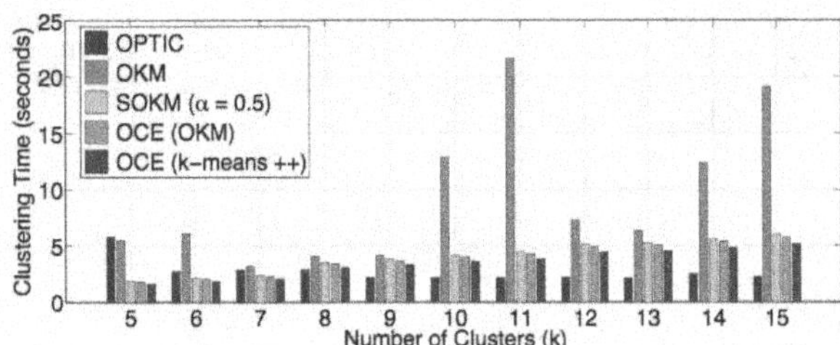

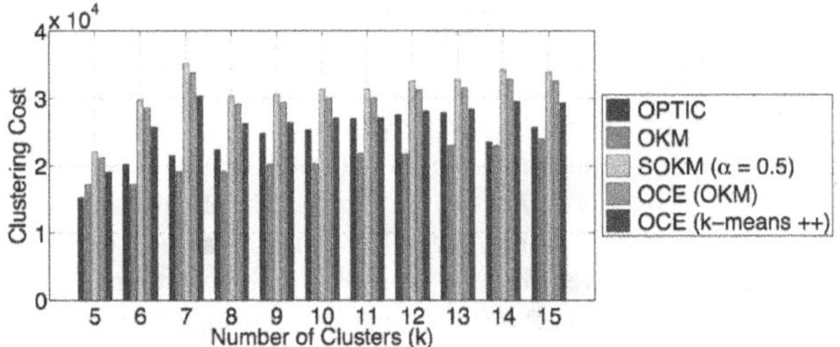

Figure 4: Comparison of Online Clustering Algorithms w.r.t. (a) Clustering Time Peformance (left), (b) Clustering Cost Performance (right)

pattern analysis in households," *IEEE Transactions on Smart Grid*, 2013.

[7] F. Martinez-Alvarez, A. Troncoso, J. C. Riquelme, and J. S. Ruiz, "Energy time series forecasting based on pattern similarity," *IEEE Transactions on Knowledge ad Data Engineering*, 2011.

[8] R. Ding, Q. Wang, Y. Dang, Q. Fu, H. Zhang, and D. Zhang, "Yading: Fast clustering of large-scale time series data," in *VLDB*, 2015.

[9] B. Everitt, *Cluster Analysis*. Heinemann Educational, 1974.

[10] C. J. van Rijsbergen, *Information Retrieval*. Buttersworth, 1979.

[11] G. Salton and M. J. Gill, *Introduction to Modern Information Retrieval*. McGraw-Hill Book Compnay, 1983.

[12] P. Willet, "Recent trends in hierarchical document clustering: A critical review," *Information Processing and Management*, vol. 24, 1988.

[13] M. Bern and D. Eppstein, *Approximation Algorithms for Geometric Problems*. PWS Publishing Company, 1996.

[14] D. Hochbaum, *Various Notions of Approximations: Good, Better, Best, and More*. PWS Publishing Company, 1996.

[15] M. R. Garey and D. Johnson, *Computers and Intractability: A Guide to the Theory of NP-Completeness*. W. H. Freeman and Company, 1979.

[16] O. Kariv and S. L. Hakimi, "An algorithmic approach to network location problems," *SIAM Journal of Applied Mathematics*, vol. 37, 1979.

[17] T. Feder and D. H. Greene, "Optimal algorithms for approximate clustering," in *STOC*, 1988.

[18] T. E. Gonzalez, "Clustering to minimize the maximum inter-cluster distance," *Theoretical Computer Science*, vol. 38, 1985.

[19] M. Charikar, C. Chekuri, T. Ferer, and R. Motwani, "Incremental clustering and dynamic information retrieval," *SIAM Journal on Computing*, vol. 33, no. 6, 2004.

[20] A. King, "Online k-means clustering of non-stationary data." Technical Report, Massachusetts Institute of Technology, May 2012.

[21] W. Barbakh and C. Fyfe, "Online clustering algorithms," *International Journal of Neural Systems*, vol. 18, no. 3, 2008.

[22] A. Choromanska and C. Monteleoni, "Online clustering with experts," *Journal of Machine Learning Research*, vol. 22, 2012.

[23] D. Arthur and S. Vassilvitskii, "k-means ++," in *SODA*, 2007.

7. APPENDIX

In this section, we provide detailed proofs of the lemmas and theorems proposed in Section 3.

Proof of Lemma 1. Prior to merging, the distance between two clusters which are adjacent in the margin graph is at most d_{i+1}, and their radius is at most αd_i. Therefore, the radius of the merged cluster is at most

$$d_{i+1} + \alpha d_i \leq (1 + \frac{\alpha}{\beta}) d_{i+1} \leq \alpha d_{i+1},$$

where the last inequality follows from our assumption choice that $\frac{\alpha}{\alpha-1} \leq \beta$. Now the distance between the cluster centers after the merging stage is d_{i+1}, and a new cluster is created only if a request point is at least d_{i+1} away from all current clusters. Therefore the cluster centers have pairwise distance at least d_{i+1}. Thus, we have proved Lemma 1. ■

Proof of Lemma 2. We have $k+1$ clusters at the end of the phase since that is the terminating condition. From Lemma 1, the radius of the clusters after the merging stage is at most αd_{i+1}, and from the definition of the update stage this bound is not violated by the insertion of new points. Now the distance between the cluster centers after the merging stage is d_{i+1}, and a new cluster is created only if a request point is at least d_{i+1} away from all current clusters. Therefore the cluster centers have pairwise distance at least d_{i+1}. Since at the end of the phase we have $k+1$ cluster centers that are d_{i+1} apart, the optimal clustering is forced to put at least two of them in the same cluster. It follows that $d_{i+1} \leq$ OPT. Thus, we have proved Lemma 2. ■

Proof of Theorem 1. Based on Lemmas 1 and 2, the algorithm (α, β)- OTSC ensures the invariant that $d_i \leq$ OPT at the start of phase i. The radius of the cluster during phase i is at most αd_{i+1}. Thus, the performance ratio at any time during phase i is at most $\frac{2\alpha d_{i+1}}{OPT} \leq \frac{2\alpha\beta}{OPT} \leq 2\alpha\beta$. Now the values of α, β that minimize $2\alpha\beta$ and at the same time satisfies the condition $\frac{\alpha}{\alpha-1} \leq \beta$, are $\alpha = 2, \beta = 2$. Thus, algorithm (α, β)- OTSC has a performance ratio of 8 in any metric space, and the ratio is tight.

Regarding the computational complexity of the algorithm, we first assume that there is a black-box for computing the distance between two points in the metric space, in unit time, and this is a reasonable assumption. We maintain the edge lengths of the complete graph induced by the current cluster centers in a heap. Since there are at most k clusters, the space requirement is $O(k^2)$. When a new point arrives, we compute the distance of this point to each of the current cluster centers, which requires $O(k)$ time. If the point is added to one of the current clusters, we are done. If, on the other hand the new point initiates a new cluster, we insert into the heap edges labeled with the distances between this new center and the existing cluster centers. This step takes $O(k \log k)$ time. For accounting purposes in the amortized analysis, we associate $\log k$ credits with each inserted edge. We will show that it is possible to charge the cost of implementing the merging stage of the algorithm to the credits associated with the edges. This implies the desired time bound.

We assume without loss of generality that the merging stage merges at least two clusters. Let d be the margin used during the phase. The algorithm extracts all the edges from the heap which have length less than d. Let m be the number of edges deleted from the heap. This deletion step costs $O(m \log k)$ time. The d-margin graph on the cluster centers is exactly the graph induced by these m edges. It is evident that finding new cluster centers usign the margin graph takes tie linear in the number of edges of the graph, assuming the edges are given in the form of an adjacency list. Forming the adjacency list from the edges takes linear time. Thus, the total cost of the merging phase is bounded by $O(m \log k + m) = O(m \log k)$ time. The credit of $\log k$ is placed with each edge when it is inserted into the heap accounts for this cost. Thus, we have proved Theorem 1. ■

Proof of Theorem 2. Let σ be the sequence of updates, and let the optimal cluster diameter for σ be γx, where x is the minimum pairwise distance of the first $k+1$ points. The optimal value is at least x, so $\gamma \geq 1$. Now suppose we choose $d_1 = rx$ for some $r \in (\frac{1}{e}, 1]$. Let ρ_r be the maximum radius of the clusters created for σ with this value of r. Using arguments similar to those in the proof of Theorem 1, we can show that ρ_r is at most $d_{i+1} + \alpha d_i = \frac{e^{i+1} d_1}{e-1}$, where i is the largest integer such that

$$d_i = e^{i-1} d_1 = e^{i-1} rx \leq OPT = \gamma x.$$

Let i^* be the integer such that $e^{i^*-1} \leq \gamma < e^{i^*}$, and $\delta = \frac{\gamma}{e^{i^*}}$. Then we have

$$\rho_r \leq \frac{rex\gamma}{(e-1)\delta}; r > \delta, \ \& \ \rho_r \leq \frac{re^2 x\gamma}{(e-1)\delta}; r \leq \delta.$$

Let X_r^- and X_r^+ be the indicator variables for the events $[r \leq \delta]$ and $[r > \delta]$ respectively. We claim that the expected value of ρ_r is bounded by

$$E[\rho_r] \leq \int_{\frac{1}{e}}^{1} \frac{re\gamma x(eX_r^- + X_r^+)}{\delta r(e-1)} dr, \ or \ E[\rho_r] \leq \frac{eOPT}{\delta(e-1)} \int_{\frac{1}{e}}^{1} (eX_r^- + X_r^+) dr,$$

therefore,

$$E[\rho_r \leq \frac{eOPT\delta(e-1)}{\delta(e-1)} = eOPT.$$

Thus, the expected diameter is at most $2eOPT$, thereby proving Theorem 2. ■

Bugs in the Freezer: Detecting Faults in Supermarket Refrigeration Systems Using Energy Signals

Shravan Srinivasan, Arunchandar Vasan, Venkatesh Sarangan
Innovation Labs – Chennai
Tata Consultancy Services
IIT Madras Research Park, Chennai, India
s.shravan1@tcs.com

Anand Sivasubramaniam
Dept. of Comp. Sci. & Eng.
Pennsylvania State University
University Park, PA 16802, USA
anand@cse.psu.edu

ABSTRACT

Refrigeration is a major component of supermarket energy consumption. Ensuring faultless operation of refrigeration systems is essential from both economic and sustainability perspectives. Present day industry practises of monitoring refrigeration systems to detect operational anomalies have several drawbacks: (i) Over-dependence on human skills; (ii) Limited help in identifying the root-cause of the anomaly; and (iii) Presumption about high degree of instrumentation – which prevents their usage in supermarkets in developing economies. Existing approaches in literature to detect anomalies in refrigeration systems either are done in controlled laboratory settings or assume the availability of sensory information other than energy. In this paper, we present an approach to detect anomalous behavior in the operation of refrigeration systems by monitoring their energy signals alone. We test the performance of our approach using data collected from refrigeration systems across 25 stores of a real world supermarket chain. We find that using energy signal, we can not only detect anomalies but also narrow down the possible root-cause of the anomaly to a reduced set. Further, using energy signal along with data collected from other sensors (if available) allows us to reduce the false positive rate while identifying the root-cause of the anomaly.

Categories and Subject Descriptors

G.3 [**Probability and Statistics**]: Time series analysis; J.2 [**Physical Sciences and Engineering**]: Engineering

Keywords

Refrigeration; Energy; Anomaly detection; Root-cause analysis

1. INTRODUCTION

Refrigeration in supermarkets: The annual energy intensity of supermarkets is around 50 kWh per sqft., which is more than twice the intensity of office buildings [2]. Reducing electricity costs by 10% can boost the (typically thin) profit margins of supermarkets by 16% [15]. Therefore, it is important to discover ways to reduce energy consumption of supermarkets. Refrigeration is a key contributor to supermarket energy consumption. Refrigerated systems (RS) are used to maintain produce, dairy, and meat that are perishable at a temperature well below the HVAC conditioned temperature. Unlike space cooling, RS consumes significant energy even during winter; for instance, frozen food needs to be maintained typically at $-6^\circ F$ even when the space (i.e., indoor ambient) temperature around refrigeration cases is maintained $70^\circ F$ in winter. Thus energy consumed by RS can even surpass that of the HVAC systems for space cooling of the overall supermarket [1,8]. Consequently, any optimization of supermarket electricity consumption necessarily needs to look at RS and that too throughout the year.

RS are subject to maintenance routines scheduled at regular intervals to address any wear and tear. As in any other physical asset, despite regular maintenance faults do occur. If a fault is critical, the entire RS can become unfit for use leading to a complete shut down necessitating an emergency maintenance. If the fault is non-critical, it will degrade the performance of the overall system while allowing it to be functional. An unattended non-critical fault may affect the energy consumption and can become a future critical fault.

Current maintenance practices and challenges: Refrigeration systems in large supermarket chains are increasingly being equipped with sensors to monitor various parameters. This sensory data is relayed to a centralized remote monitoring center. In these centers, human operators analyze the data either online or on demand basis when the sensor values exceed preset thresholds.

This present model of remote monitoring has several drawbacks: (i) It relies heavily on the ability of human operators to detect anomalies. If the operators do not have the necessary skill-sets, detection of anomalous behavior can get delayed, or even worse not happen at all; (ii) Typically, the operators pick up only the symptoms to trigger a maintenance work-order. It is up to the visiting technician to do the root-cause analysis on the ground and do the necessary fixes. Any guidance that can be given to help the technician's diagnostic process will reduce the time and hence the costs associated with the fix. (iii) It assumes the existence of a high degree of instrumentation. Refrigeration assets in small convenience stores and supermarkets in developing economies do not have such a high degree of instrumentation. At best, they may have only energy meters for the refrigeration assets. Hence, the present remote monitoring model cannot be used for these stores.

Given these drawbacks in terms of limited instrumentation and the need to reduce the time taken to identify anomalies even in such a scenario, the following questions arise:

- Is it possible to detect anomalous behavior in refrigeration systems by monitoring their energy signals alone (which are likely to be available only at coarse temporal resolutions)?

e-Energy'15, July 14–17, 2015, Bangalore, India.

DOI: http://dx.doi.org/10.1145/2768510.2768536.

- To what extent would it be possible to identify the possible components or reasons for the anomalous behavior using the energy signal alone?

- If additional sensors are available, can these be used in conjunction with the energy signal to detect faults and identify the root-cause automatically?

Existing models for detecting anomalies in refrigeration systems and diagnosing the root causes have mostly been done in controlled laboratory settings [3, 6, 7, 11–14, 17]. These may not be applicable in real world scenarios since the operating conditions may be different from a controlled environment. Consequently, the rules derived in laboratory may not be applicable. Further, not all sensors required by the laboratory models may be available in practise. There are also works which attempt to detect anomalies in refrigeration cases from the energy consumption signal [4]. However, these approaches require information pertaining to indoor and outdoor temperatures, indoor and outdoor humidity, and the loads imposed by the occupants to develop their energy models – all of which may not be available in all the stores. Further, the extent to which the root cause of the problem can be diagnosed has not been analyzed in these works.

In this paper, we attempt to address the above mentioned questions using data collected from refrigeration systems in real-world supermarket stores. Addressing these questions is non-trivial for the following reasons: (i) Typically, energy consumption of refrigeration units is measured at an aggregate level – i.e., several compressors and condenser units are grouped together in racks and it is this rack consumption that gets measured. In addition, this rack of compressors and condensers serve several refrigeration cases. Hence, a fault in one of the cases or compressor/condenser units may not manifest in the measured aggregate energy signal. (ii) Since energy consumption results from the aggregate performance of all refrigeration components, a single component's anomaly may not affect the overall energy significantly enough (or uniquely enough) to be traced back.

We overcome the challenges through **these contributions**.

- We develop an energy model that is sensitive enough to pick up even short-lived anomalies in the energy signal so that we maximize our likelihood to detect an anomaly. Simultaneously, our model also allows us place a bound on the false positives. We do this by integrating a statistical model and a physical model thereby overcoming the limitations of both.

- We use the direction of the anomaly as a signature to identify the anomaly root-cause as a group of components (rather than an individual component).

- If additional sensors are made available, we develop statistical models for the sensor data. By leveraging the anomalies detected by these statistical data models, we identify the individual component that is likely to be at fault.

These models have been developed and tested on real world sensory data and work-order logs obtained over a period of five months from refrigeration systems deployed across 25 stores from a supermarket chain[1]. The data was collected over every 15 minutes and included the energy consumption of the refrigeration systems and sensory information wherever available. In this period, we observed four different work-orders occurring across these 25 stores, at times even repeatedly. Our findings from this study include:

- The classification rules based on anomalies in the energy signal can detect between $80 - 95\%$ of all anomalies. The false positive rates in most stores is about 0.2%.

- Detecting anomalies using a set of sensors can classify individual anomaly types with a detection likelihood between $66 - 100\%$ across all types. The false positive ratio is again bounded by 0.2%.

- We note that if the supplementary sensors alone are used for detecting faults in individual components, the resulting false positive rate is higher than what would be possible when using the sensors along with the overall energy signal. This is due to the correlated nature of the energy and individual sensory signals.

- For the detected anomalies, the average detection time is $2.8 - 21$ days before the work-order is actually logged in the system. The model is able to pick up steady deterioration from the baseline over a period of time, well before the human operators notice the symptoms and log it.

To the best of our knowledge, ours is one of the first few papers to report on detecting and identifying faults in supermarket refrigeration systems using real-world data logs from an ensemble of stores. The rest of this paper is organized as follows. Section 2 presents a survey of related work. A background on supermarket refrigeration is presented in 3. We develop statistical and physical models for the energy consumption in Section 4. Section 5 gives a short introduction to the faults we had observed in the real world stores. Using the energy model as the baseline we predict if an observed energy sample can be classified as anomalous and if so of what type in Section 6. Section 7 discusses how additional sensor based information can help in reducing false positive rates of anomaly detection and identify the sub-type of the anomalies. Section 8 concludes the paper.

2. RELATED WORK

Work related to ours can be broadly categorized into two groups.

Fault diagnosis in refrigeration and air-conditioning systems: Works on detecting anomalies in refrigeration systems and diagnosing the root causes [3, 5–7, 12, 17] typically use simple sensor value based thresholding or techniques such as PCA and SVM to detect the anomalies. However, these have mostly been done in laboratory settings or as controlled one-off experiments. In real-world scenarios, the operating conditions and availability of sensors may be different from a controlled environment. Consequently, the rules derived in laboratory may not always be applicable in real world.

Some works attempt to detect anomalies (but not identify the root-cause) in refrigeration cases from the energy consumption signal [4]. However, unlike us, these approaches require additional information pertaining to indoor and outdoor temperature, indoor and outdoor humidity, and loads imposed by the occupants to develop the energy model – all of which may not be available in all the stores. Further, the extent to which the root cause of the problem can be diagnosed has not been quantified in these works.

Our work complements existing works in that we use time-series models such as ARIMA/SARIMA (which have not been reported earlier) with reasonable success to detect anomalies and identify the root-cause in refrigeration systems. Further, our approach works with limited existing sensor and metering infrastructure.

Domain model based approaches to detect faults and identify the root-causes have also been suggested in the literature [11, 14]. These approaches rely on the ability to develop a well-calibrated domain model that mimics the operations of a real world refrigeration system. While such an approach can be quite powerful,

[1]The identity of the chain is withheld due to confidentiality requirements.

the challenge is to calibrate the model to accurately reflect the real world behavior – this can become unwieldy due to two reasons: (i) the set of refrigeration systems across various stores can be different necessitating not one but several domain models; (ii) these models need to be re-calibrated periodically to keep pace with component aging.

Fault diagnosis in HVAC systems and operations: Though the underlying principle of refrigeration remains the same as that of a refrigerator/simple air-conditioner, centralized HVAC systems have a larger set of components and involve multiple heat exchangers. There have been several works that focus on detecting faults not only in HVAC systems but also in their operations (or control settings). Narayanaswamy et. al. [9] adopt a data-driven approach to detect faults in HVAC usage. Their focus is on detecting faults in variable air volume (VAV) control settings and use parameters which are very HVAC specific. Similarly, Zhou et. al [18] propose a regression based approach based on HVAC specific parameters to detect faults in HVAC sub-systems. On the other hand, the focus of our paper is on refrigeration systems and we use a different set of parameters. Consequently, the methodologies and classification rules proposed using HVAC specific parameters may not be applicable in our context. Reference [13] discusses about detecting refrigerant leaks in large chillers using artificial neural networks. They do a simulation based study and use temperatures gathered at various points in the refrigeration loop as feature vectors. Unlike them, we use the liquid level in the receiver as a feature, which is relatively simpler, to detect leaks and test their efficacy in real world systems. We also focus on identifying other kinds of faults.

Some work has been done to demonstrate that anomalous behavior of window air-conditioners in buildings can be detected from the aggregate energy consumption (more precisely, the current drawn) [10]. The anomaly is detected using the presence of high frequency current spikes drawn by a faulty air-conditioner. Consequently, these works assume that the energy/current signal is sampled at a finer temporal resolution (every few seconds). However, the energy data in real-world stores is typically available at a coarser granularity and hence such methods may not be applicable.

3. BACKGROUND

The refrigeration load in a typical supermarket consists of display cases that house beverages, produce, or perishable items in a refrigerated environment. These cases are typically at various internal temperatures depending on the kind of product: (1) Beverage coolers and dairy cases are typically maintained at around $36^{\circ}F$ - we refer to these as **coolers**; and 2) Frozen food needs to be maintained at around $-6^{\circ}F$ - we refer to these cases as **freezers.** Because there is an economy of scale in cooling systems (in terms of watts required to remove a unit heat-load), the heat loads of multiple display cases are typically aggregated into one compressor/condenser system.

3.1 System setup and operation

Figure 1 shows the configuration of a typical supermarket RS. It consists of a compressor rack and a condenser rack. A compressor/condenser rack may have one or more units of same or different capacities with a common inlet and outlet. Each compressor rack and its condenser unit serves multiple display cases where the set-point temperature is identical or similar. Typically, all freezer cases are served by one compressor-condenser system and all cooler cases are served by a different compressor-condenser system. Each display case has an individual evaporator with an evaporator coil through which cold refrigerant flows through picking up heat inside the case. The cases have fans that blow air across the cold evaporator coil to enhance heat exchange.

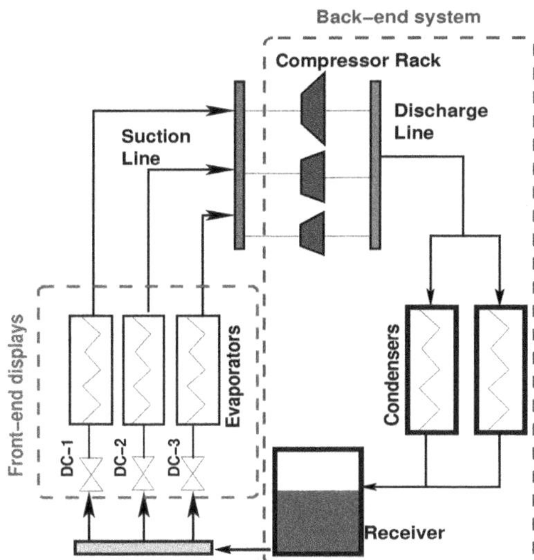

Figure 1: Schematic of a simplified Refrigeration System configuration indicating front-end and back-end components

The system operates in a typical refrigeration cycle as follows. One or more compressors are staged (i.e., scheduled ON) by the control system. These compressors pull in evaporated refrigerant gas from a common suction line. The hot gas is compressed by the compressors resulting in super-heated gas at very high pressure. This super-heated gas is discharged by the compressors on to a common discharge line. This discharge line feeds to the condenser(s) where because of the high pressure, the condensing temperature of the refrigerant is high. Because the condensing temperature of the gas is higher than the ambient temperature of the air outside the condenser (in air-cooled systems), the refrigerant rapidly loses heat (picked up from the evaporators) and undergoes a phase transition to become a high-pressure liquid.

The high-pressure liquid is stored in a receiver, from which the liquid enters the evaporators of the multiple display cases. Each evaporator has a locally controlled valve that regulates the flow of refrigerant through the evaporator. This expansion valve constricts the flow and thereby reduces the pressure, forcing the liquid refrigerant to evaporate to a gas. This evaporation causes cooling in the evaporator coil, which cools the refrigeration cases. Higher the heat-load of the evaporator, more would be the flow of the liquid refrigerant through the valve. If sufficient liquid refrigerant is not available, the pressure of the hot gas leaving the evaporator increases. The evaporator exit feeds the compressor's suction line. When the pressure on the suction line increases beyond a control threshold, the compressors are switched on (if they are off), and the entire cycle repeats.

4. ENERGY MODEL FOR ANOMALY DETECTION

Most supermarkets in developing economies are at best, likely to have energy meters. Typically, the back-end components including the compressor and condenser systems are physically separated from the front-end components in the store. Due to this spatial separation, they are on different electrical circuits. Typically, the front-end circuits (supplying to the display case lights, evaporator fans, and door heaters) are connected to the store's lighting supply, while the back-end (supplying to the compressors and condensers) has a standalone circuit which is metered. In this section, we discuss our approach to develop a model for the back-end refrigeration

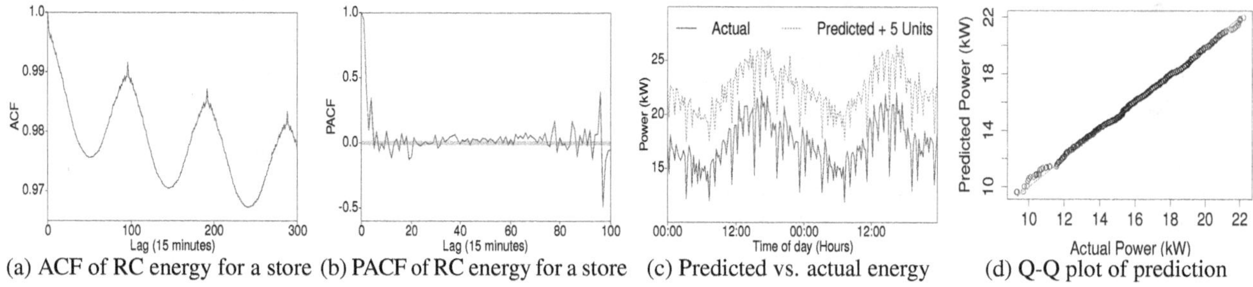

(a) ACF of RC energy for a store (b) PACF of RC energy for a store (c) Predicted vs. actual energy (d) Q-Q plot of prediction

Figure 2: SARIMA model for predicting energy consumption (best viewed in color)

energy consumption. We develop a baseline model for the energy consumption using energy data gathered from fault-free durations of the system. The actual consumption observed in the refrigeration system is then compared against this model in an on-line manner. Any significant deviations are flagged as anomalies.

The underlying hypothesis behind this approach is that a fault in any of the refrigeration system component would present itself in the energy signal. As per this hypothesis, we expect that problems in the backend system would result in increase in energy consumption of the backend system. In addition, any problem in the frontend system could *also* cause an increase in the backend energy consumption. For example, consider a refrigerated case (RC) door that is left open permanently; the compressor system would see an additional heat-load and consequently consume more energy. In sum, both front-end and back-end systems are expected to result in anomalies in the back-end energy consumption. Therefore, we focus on developing energy models for the back-end energy consumption so as to be able to detect a wider range of faults.

Ideally, to model the energy consumption, we need to capture the dynamics of the control system(s) of the refrigeration system, track the evolution of the compressor and condenser system states, and map the system operating states to the energy consumption. However, the control choices in the compressor and condenser systems are typically proprietary and tuned locally to a site by the installation vendor. Also, this approach would be prone to the drawbacks associated with a domain-based model discussed in Section 2. Further, even if one were to develop a model that tracks the system state in terms of the controlled variables, it is difficult to calibrate such a control system model (which runs every few seconds) from the sensory data that is typically logged every few minutes Therefore, we do not model the back-end at a control system level.

4.1 Statistical model - SARIMA

In the absence of an explicit control system model, our approach is to use a statistically-based SARIMA (Seasonal-ARIMA) model for predicting the energy consumption and implicitly tracking the system state. Essentially, the SARIMA model estimates the energy consumption as a regressed function of temporally adjacent samples as well as temporally well-separated samples. We adopted a SARIMA based approach to model the energy for the following reasons: (i) Because the SARIMA model uses temporally adjacent past energy samples to predict the next sample, any effect due to the control system actions are captured. (ii) Because the SARIMA model uses temporally well-separated samples as well (in the seasonal component), it implicitly captures the trends that may exist in the ambient weather conditions.

The energy data is available to us over every 15 minutes as the average power consumed over the interval [2]. Figure 2(a) shows the autocorrelation function (ACF) of the energy timeseries for a typical store, while Figure 2(b) shows the corresponding partial ACF. The X-axis shows the lag of the correlation function where each lag corresponds to 15 minutes, and the Y-axis shows the correlation coefficient at that lag. The figures indicate that a seasonal parameter is required to account for the trend in the ACF. We note the periodicity at every 96 samples (corresponding to one day). We used the Box–Jenkins methodology to arrive at the appropriate orders for the SARIMA model. For a typical store, the order of the parameters in the SARIMA model are as follows: Autoregressive (3), Moving Average (2), Seasonal Auto-regressive (1), Seasonal Moving Average (1), period of 96, and order of differencing 1. This indicates that to predict an power value given the past history, we need to look into local samples (order of hours) to non-local samples (order of days).

Figure 2(c) compares the predicted and actual power consumption time-series with prediction one-sample ahead with all past history known. The X-axis shows time in days and the Y-axis shows the power consumption over 15 minute intervals. The match is very good between the predicted and actual with a mean relative error of 6.7%. Figure 2(d) shows the Q-Q plot that compares the quantiles of the predicted and the actual time-series. We note that except for the upper and lower tails, the predicted matches very well the actual. The upper and lower tails can be used by one for detecting anomalous operations as explained later in Section 6. This SARIMA model is used as the baseline model for energy.

Limitation of the SARIMA model: Recall that the main goal of building a SARIMA model is to use it for detecting anomalous energy samples. Once an anomalous sample is detected say at t, that sample value should not be used for future predictions starting at $t+1$. This is to ensure that an anomalous sample does not pollute the subsequent predictions. The standard practice is to typically use the predicted estimate of the anomalous sample – which is typically the maximum likelihood estimate (MLE) of the sample's mean value, as the actual sample value for future predictions. When we correct an anomalous sample with the MLE of the sample mean expected at that time, the ensuing sample values predicted from the SARIMA model could diverge from the actual energy series. This is true especially when there is a burst of anomalous samples detected within a small time interval. SARIMA predicted energy values can diverge from the actual energy series because the SARIMA model would converge to the stationary mean of the time-series. Figure 4 shows a case when a series of anomalous samples are omitted, and the corresponding SARIMA mean MLE is used to continue prediction. As we can see, the predicted time-series diverges significantly from the actual series when a series of anomalous samples are detected. Therefore, we need a mechanism that can help us correct anomalous samples for a burst of errors, which is likely to happen when a malfunctioning equipment has not been repaired for a period of time.

[2]**Therefore, neglecting the semantics and abusing the terminology, we use energy and power interchangeably in this paper.**

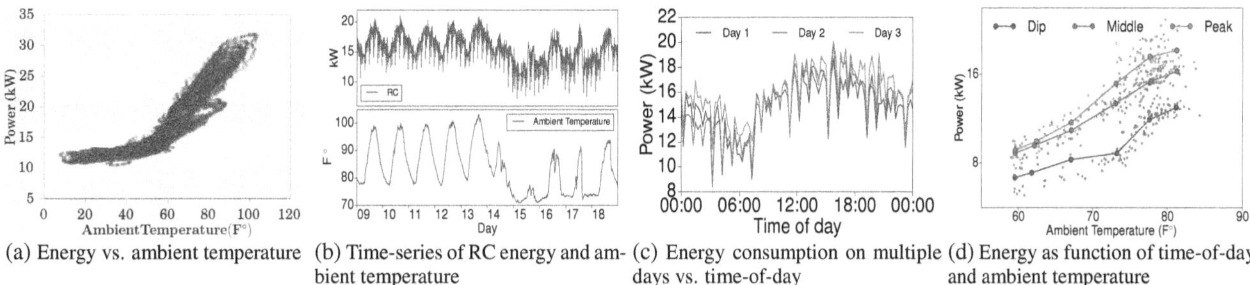

(a) Energy vs. ambient temperature (b) Time-series of RC energy and ambient temperature (c) Energy consumption on multiple days vs. time-of-day (d) Energy as function of time-of-day and ambient temperature

Figure 3: Development of physical model for back-end energy consumption as a function of time-of-day and ambient temperaure (best viewed in color)

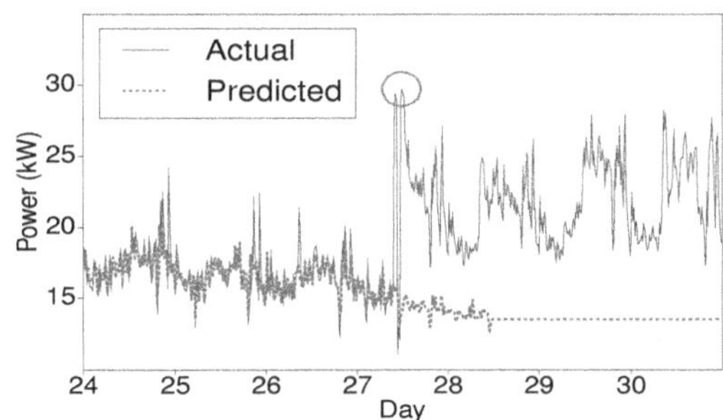

Figure 4: Correcting anomalous samples with MLE predicted samples for a burst of errors can cause the SARIMA model to diverge from the actual data. (best viewed in color).

4.2 Physical model

To create an alternate model that can be used to correct anomalous samples for SARIMA, we identify the physical parameters influencing energy and then fit a model.

As in the HVAC systems, ambient temperature is likely to a key driver for the energy consumption of a refrigeration system's back-end. Figure 3(a) shows a scatter plot of a store's average back-end consumption over 15 minutes in the Y-axis against the average ambient temperature over the same 15 minute interval on the X-axis. From the scatter plot, we see two distinct regimes of operation. Specifically, there is a knee in the trend at some critical value of the ambient temperature τ_C^* of $62°F$. When the ambient temperature T_A is greater than τ_C^*, the curve shows a clear increasing linear behavior, while for $T_A < \tau_C^*$ the curve is near flat to linear with a small slope. We explain these trends as follows.

Linear trend for $T_A > \tau_C^*$: Suppose the set-point temperature of the refrigeration cases is T_S, then the compressor-condenser system is moving heat from a low-temperature of T_S to an ambient temperature of T_A. Due to the physics of the heat flow, the work done is at least given by $H \times \frac{T_A - T_S}{T_S}$, where H is the freezer's heat load to be removed [16]. In the case of supermarket freezers (and coolers), the internal set-point, T_S, remains constant. Further, the heat loads induced in the freezers would also remain constant – since the freezers are in a space conditioned environment and the items that are stocked inside afresh will already be at a temperature comparable to T_S. Therefore, we expect the energy required to remove H from inside the freezer case to outside the store to vary as $H\left(\frac{T_A - T_S}{T_S}\right)$. This explains the linearly increasing trend with T_A when the ambient temperature $T_A > \tau_C^*$.

Flat trend for $T_A < \tau_C^*$: We now want to understand why the system does not behave as expected ideally, when the ambient temperature is less than some critical value. For any cooling to happen in the refrigeration cases, one needs a refrigeration cycle to take place (unless one is letting in air at ambient outdoor temperature through separate piping). For at least some compressor(s) to be working during the refrigeration cycle, we need to maintain some minimum load on the compressor. A compressor being driven by a motor cannot work with no pressure being maintained at the exit (this is akin to short-circuiting a battery by offering zero resistance). Therefore, the condenser system offers a minimum load to the compressor by switching the cooling fans off when the ambient temperature floats below a certain critical value. Consequently, the energy consumption trend remains close to flat when $T_A < \tau_C^*$, and this is true in most stores which have mostly one compressor turned on during low ambient temperatures. We confirmed this with the manufacturer's design specification for the compressors. The minimum design discharge pressure against which the compressor is supposed to operate is around 148 *psig* for the refrigerant type R-404A (which is used in the store under study); this corresponds to a condensing temperature of $70°F$. Therefore, we expect the condenser to maintain this minimum condensing temperature load at any ambient temperature below $60°F$, after accounting for the temperature differential of $10°F$ with respect to the ambient. Indeed, the control system for the fans maintains a differential of about $10°F$ between the condensing and the ambient temperatures.

Hidden variable: While the trends are quite clear, the spread in the graph for the same ambient condition indicates a potential hidden variable that needs to be accounted for. Consider Figure 3(b) which shows the energy consumption as a function of time along with the temperature for the same store. The X-axis is in days for both energy and temperature. Although the energy follows the ambient temperature as a trend, the instantaneous values show high frequency components that do not depend on the ambient temperature alone. Instead, these high frequency components occur at deterministic times-of-the-day. This is confirmed by the time-of-day aligned peaks and troughs of the energy signal at different days as seen in Figure 3(c). The X-axis in Figure 3(c) is the time-of-day over a 24 hour period. The Y-axis shows the energy consumption across three days. We see that across all three days the peaks and dips are aligned at the same times-of-the-day.

These sharp dips and spikes in the energy signal are due to defrost cycles. Specifically, RCs are defrosted according to a schedule fixed by the store. During a defrost, the energy consumption first dips because several refrigerated cases are taken offline and thus the compressor bank sees a steep reduction in the heat load. Post the defrost, the compressors see a sharp peak in the heat-load as the cases at room temperature need to be quickly cooled to the freezing temperature for maintaining food quality.

Figure 3(d) shows the RC energy consumption for a store as a function of the ambient temperature for varying times-of-day. The X-axis is the ambient temperature. The Y-axis shows a family of three curves. Each curve shows the energy consumption for varying ambient temperatures at a specific time-of-day. The three curves

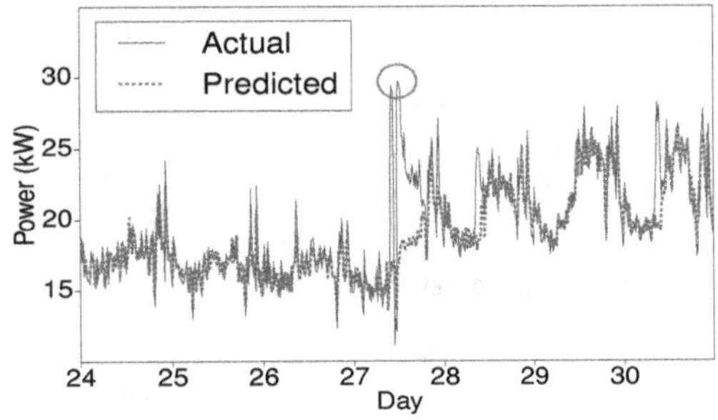

Figure 5: Time-series of RC energy and ambient temperature with an anomalous sample being substituted with the physical model prediction for that time-of-day and ambient temperature. Note that the model does not diverge from actual sample points unlike Figure 4.

are for three sequential times-of-day corresponding to normal operation, defrost dip, and defrost peak. The curve in the middle corresponds to the normal operation, while the other two curves correspond to the peak and the dip of the defrost cycle. We see that when parametrized by time-of-day the scatter plot seen in Figure 3(a) resolves into a family of curves as shown in Figure 3(d). Therefore, any physical model should consider the time-of-day as a parameter, in addition to ambient temperature, for predicting the instantaneous energy consumption of the compressors and condensers. Accordingly, to estimate the average energy consumption ($\hat{E}$) corresponding to a given ambient temperature (T), we first index into the time-of-day (t) for the prediction; and then use the ambient temperature to estimate the energy consumption. In other words, our model is of the form $\hat{E}(t,T) = \phi_t(T)$, where $\phi_t(.)$ is a regressor that relates the energy consumption and external temperature T at the time-of-day t.

We note here that the mean energy value predicted using $\phi_t(T)$ on any given day for a t will not factor the effects of any shock or disturbance seen earlier during preceding t's. In other words, the $\phi_t(T)$ model does not capture the temporal correlations between the energy samples as well as SARIMA. It is for this reason, we do not use $\phi_t(T)$ as the primary model for detecting energy anomalies. As an aside, it is also difficult to obtain a tight bound on the false positive rate of the $\phi_t(T)$ model while (as we will see shortly) it is possible to do so with a SARIMA model.

Overcoming SARIMA limitation: Figure 5 shows the effect of correcting the SARIMA sample using the average physical model prediction value for a given ambient temperature. This overcomes the limitation highlighted in Figure 4. While the SARIMA model starts diverging around the set of anomalous samples, because we use the physical model, it reconverges to normal operations and the predicted values once again match the normal values.

5. WORK-ORDERS: BACKGROUND

When a malfunctioning equipment is noticed (e.g., a condenser fan making noise) or an anomalous operation is observed (e.g., an RC not maintaining a cold environment), the store personnel log a *work-order*. A work-order log basically describes the problem symptoms, categorization, the day it was observed, the day it was fixed, and details of an eventual fix. Ideally, work-orders should be avoided through proactive maintenance. This is because a work-order indicates that there was disruption of service and food could potentially go bad entailing other losses.

Trivial work-orders are the ones that are readily detected by some sensors tripping the pre-determined level. For example, a typical compressor system would trip the compressor off if the discharge pressure becomes excessive and raises an alarm. In this paper, we focus on non-trivial work-orders. The non-trivial work-orders occurring in the system can be broadly categorized into those occurring in the front-end and back-end systems. Over the study period of five months, four types of work-orders occurred across our study sample of 25 stores. The work-orders we observed are as follows:

- **Leaky refrigerant:** As the name indicates, this occurs when the refrigerant leaks from system due to fatigue in pipe walls or valves. If left unattended, can lead to a complete system shut-down and no refrigeration (cooling) will take place. In certain instances, even the compressors can get damaged.
- **Malfunctioning EPR valve:** EPR valve is the element which throttles the refrigerant flow into the evaporator coils. A malfunctioning valve can flood the evaporator coils with more refrigerant than what is necessary. This can result in over-cooling of the stored items which can damage the quality. In extreme cases, even liquid refrigerant can enter the compressors permanently damaging them.
- **Iced evaporator:** This is the work-order in which thick ice or frost builds around the evaporator coils which decrease the refrigeration effect. Consequently, the refrigerated case becomes warm which can damage the food items.
- **Iced door:** This work-order results if the refrigerated case's glass door is all covered in frost/water vapour. This results in poor visibility of the case items which can annoy the end consumers. This work-order affects the sales.

Work-order type	Symptoms
Leaky refrigerant	Poor cooling in the coolers and freezers.
EPR valve malfunctioning	Excessive cooling in cases. Items are too cold.
Iced evaporator	Ice buildup across expansion coils in coolers and freezers. Poor cooling.
Iced door	Excessive condensation, frosting in case doors. Poor visibility into the case.

Table 1: Work-order types and their associated symptoms

These work-orders and the associated physical symptoms are summarized in Table 1. Depending on the work-order, the time to fix could vary from 9 to 83 days with an average of 29 days.

The work-orders are logged as soon as the symptoms become visible and are observed by the store personnel. Our goal, however, is to detect these work-orders as early as possible, or even anticipate them before these effects become visible thereby reducing/eliminating repair downtime through pro-active maintenance. It is also likely that sensory instrumentation associated for detecting some/all of these work-orders may not be available in smaller stores and stores in developing economies. Therefore, we are interested in early-detection/prediction of these work-orders by observing how the energy signal behaves during work-orders.

6. DETECTING WORK ORDERS USING ENERGY SIGNALS

As mentioned earlier, our underlying hypothesis is that any fault or a work-order in any refrigeration system component would present itself in the energy signal. We expect problems in both frontend and backend systems to create anomalies in energy consumption of the backend system.

Over the study period of 5 months, for each store, we identify a consecutive duration of 30 days in which no work-orders occur. To ensure that the data period corresponds to "normal" operations, we allow for an additional buffer window of three days around the end-points of the identified 30-day window. While this method cannot guarantee that no work-order points occur in the selection, we believe this to be a reasonable approximation of the same. Using the energy data over these 30 days, we train individual SARIMA and Physical energy models for each store. We then use this model the predict the energy samples for the rest of the days in our study period (which becomes our test set). We compare the predicted energy sample(s) with the actual energy sample(s) over an interval to flag something anomalous. Because we flag samples over an interval, any anomalous real sample cannot be used in future predictions. So we use the physical model for the average energy consumption to replace the anomalous energy sample in SARIMA prediction as explained in Section 4. Using the prediction model, we can identify anomalous samples and the associated deviations of the actual energy samples from the predicted.

6.1 Anomaly detection rule

Let $E_A(t)$ denote the actual energy consumption at t and $E_P(t)$, the predicted energy consumption. Let α be such that $0 \leq \alpha \leq 1$. Define $\epsilon(t) = \frac{(E_A(t)-E_P(t))}{E_P(t)}$. Over all t in the training set, let ϵ_H^* and ϵ_L^* respectively denote the α-th and $(1-\alpha)$-th percentile points of $\epsilon(t)$. The value of α is chosen such that ϵ_H^* corresponds to outliers that are positive (i.e., indicate increased energy consumption) and ϵ_L^* corresponds to outliers that are negative (i.e., indicate highly reduced energy consumption). Our rule for classifying an energy sample as anomalous and hence indicate the onset of a work-order is as follows:

- **Positive outliers:** If $\epsilon(t) > \epsilon_H^*$, then the sample at t is anomalous and work-order is flagged.
- **Negative outliers:** If $\epsilon(t) < \epsilon_L^*$, then the sample at t is anomalous and work-order is flagged.

Note that as per the above rules, the occurrence of even one outlier would be detected as a work-order. While one could potentially use two or more consecutive outliers to flag a work-order, we do not do so for the following reason. Consider a malfunctioning refrigerated case (RC) that presents a higher (lower) heat-load to the compressor. The impact of this RC on back-end energy would not be uniform throughout. It would depend on the relative loads of other RCs served by the same compressor. Therefore, if there is any front-end work-order in an RC, its effect on compressor energy may be quite short-lived (but not necessarily). Since energy is sampled every 15 minutes at our study stores, to capture such short-lived events, we have defined the classification rule to accommodate only one outlier. We note that, since the classification rules are based on the error percentiles observed, the false-positive rate of our classification is $(1 - \alpha)$.

6.2 Error direction as work-order signatures

Depending on the impact of the anomaly on the operations, the energy consumption could increase or decrease. Specifically, if the anomaly increases (reduces) the heat load seen by the compressor, it results in higher (lower) energy consumption. Among the work-orders we observed, a refrigerant leak shows an anomaly in the lower tail. Because refrigerant leaks from the system, lesser pressure builds up at the compressors' suction inlet, and so lesser number of compressors are scheduled to reduce the built-up pressure. This is demonstrated in Figure 6(a). Note that this will likely be accompanied by a loss in cooling capacity. Therefore, if there is a negative outlier in the energy signal, it can be construed as the onset of refrigerant leak. The other three work-orders, however, had anomalies which were all in the upper tail. *Thus, the direction of the anomaly can be used as a signature to identify the anomaly root-cause to be a subset of the refrigeration system components (if not to the degree of an individual component).*

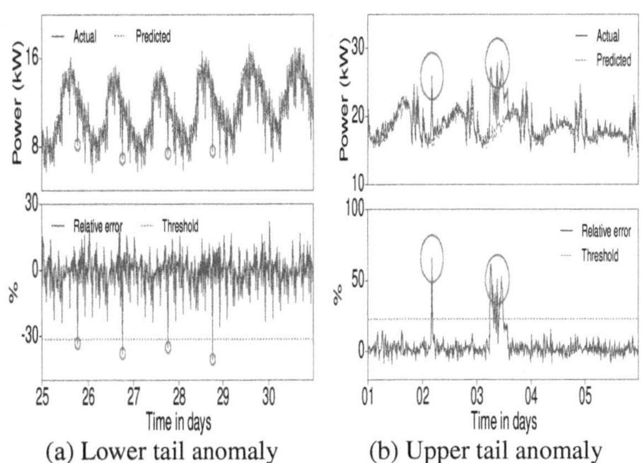

(a) Lower tail anomaly (b) Upper tail anomaly

Figure 6: Error direction based classification of anomalies

6.3 Performance

Choice of α: A low value of α would increase the likelihood of detecting a work order but also would increase the false positive rate. Suppose we have N samples per day from M data sources. Then, for upper-tail anomalies, the number of samples that would be classified as potentially anomalous is approximately $(1-\alpha) \times N \times M$. Note that human checks or interventions are typically dispatched by an external contracted agency in response to store personnel complaints. Thus to keep human intervention to a reasonable frequency, we assume a conservative estimate of the number of checks or visits by a technician to be one per week. For a typical store, $N = 96$ and $M >= 2$, and thus, the value of $1 - \alpha$ should be at most 0.00074. As a more conservative choice, we use $1 - \alpha = 0.002$.

Table 2 gives the detection likelihood and false positive rates of the energy based detection. While the detection likelihood is calculated over stores with work-orders as seen in the ground truth, the false positive rate is calculated over all stores. We note that the average false positive rates for the stores with work-orders is 0.06%, which is lesser than the method's expected 0.2%. For the stores with no work-orders, the false positive rates are around 0.2%. In sum, the detection likelihood is reasonable, and the false positive rates are low. We also note that using energy anomalies, we are able to detect the work-orders well in advance which can be quite useful in practice.

Tail	Work-orders	Detection Likelihood (%)	False positive (%)	Early detection (days)
Upper	Iced door, Iced evaporator, EPR valve	80	0.17	2.8
Lower	Leaky refrigerant	95	0.12	20.1

Table 2: Performance of energy based detection

6.4 Comparison with baseline

As a baseline for comparison, we use the current practice of setting a (static) threshold for the signal being measured; and using any violation of the threshold as a potential outlier. We proceed with the comparison as follows. For a given α, we identify the $(1 - \alpha)$-th percentile point as the (static) threshold for the baseline approach. For the same α, we use the $(1 - \alpha)$-th percentile point

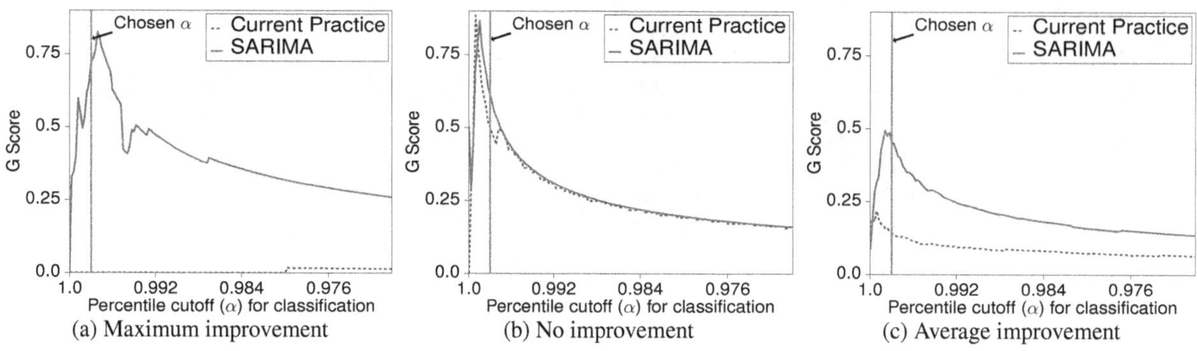

Figure 7: Comparison with a static threshold based approach across stores

of the error between our predicted value of the energy and the actual sample, as the (dynamic) threshold. For both approaches of classifying samples as outliers, we calculate the standard metrics of classification, i.e., precision and recall, and compose them using the G-score, which is defined as $\sqrt{(Precision \times Recall)}$.

Figure 7(a) compares the performance of our approach and the baseline approach for the best-performing store. The X-axis shows the cut-off percentile α for the classification. The Y-axis shows the G-score as a function of α as evaluated on the data-set for that store. As can be seen, our approach performs significantly better than the baseline approach for most values of α in this store. Further, for the value of α chosen to minimize the number of human interventions, the performance is close to the best performance.

Figure 7(b) shows a store where our approach performs very similar to a statically chosen threshold. In this store, the variation in energy is very low across time and temperature, that there is hardly any need to predict the current consumption as a function of time-of-day and temperature. Therefore, a simple static threshold identifies the same anomalies that any prediction-based approach identifies. The average improvement of our approach (average across all stores for each value of α) is shown in Figure 7(c). We find that the average improvement is significant enough to merit a model that accounts for modeling temporal variations in the energy signal.

7. IDENTIFYING WORK-ORDERS USING OTHER SENSORS

Having detected work-orders using anomalies in the energy signal, we now explore if the root-cause of the problem or the faulty component can be identified. This would help in stores where a reasonable set of sensors have been deployed. Typically, among others, sensors are deployed for: number of active compressors, number of active condenser fans, refrigerant temperature at condenser exit, level of the refrigerant in the receiver, temperature and pressure of the refrigerant at the suction end of the compressor, temperature and pressure of the refrigerant at the discharge side, and energy consumed by door heaters and evaporator fans.

7.1 Model fitting for sensory data

As with the energy time series, we fit a suitable statistical model for each individual sensor and identify anomalous samples. We hypothesize that a work-order will be identified by anomalies in one or more sensors. The goal is to identify one or more sensory streams that can be used as a feature vector. The training and testing set is taken from the same duration as done for the energy models. The value of α is taken to be 99.8.

Since the ambient temperature and energy consumption have daily patterns, several of these sensory variables (e.g., discharge pressure of a compressor)also follow a similar pattern. Thus, for all those sensors which have a statistically tractable model, we identify upper and lower tails as seen before for energy.

Some sensed parameters, on the other hand, are maintained at a steady level and can be treated as stationary processes. For example, the suction pressure at the inlet of compressors is maintained within a band typically by using PID based scheduling of compressors. If the heat load increases, the suction pressure goes up, and compressors are turned on to reduce the pressure by pulling the hot refrigerant in. For such sensors, the data can be treated as a stationary ARMA time-series and upper and lower tails of this stationary distribution can be obtained to see if there are any anomalies given the local history. As with the energy time series, anomalous samples are substituted with estimates obtained from appropriate alternative regression based models.

7.2 Mapping sensor readings to work-orders

Let K be the number of sensors deployed to monitor a refrigeration system in a store. Let $\mathbf{S}(t) =< S_1(t), S_2(t), \cdots, S_K(t) >$ be the array of sensor readings at time t corresponding to each of the k sensors deployed. Given the past history up to $t-1$, using either SARIMA or stationary models, we flag an anomaly at t if at least one of the sensors $S_i(t)$ is anomalous according to the individual time-series model. Admittedly, this approach does not consider combinations of sensor readings and does not explicitly use information that may be available in the joint distributions of the sensors. Nevertheless, we find that this approach is effective and can yield reasonably good results.

For the work-orders that we have observed in our dataset, we find that there is good correlation between the observed anomalies in the sensor data and the work-order being logged in the system. For each of the four work-orders observed in our study stores, there was one sensory signal whose anomaly uniquely identifies the work-order. In other words, the anomaly of the unique sensory signal acts as the feature vector for classifying the work-order.

The sensory parameter used as the feature for each work-order type is shown in Table 3. Figures 8(b), 8(a), 8(d), 8(c) show the sensor anomaly samples respectively for work orders corresponding to excessively cold refrigerated case, ice buildup in the evaporator, leaky refrigerant, and ice buildup on doors.

7.3 Sensors as features for work-orders

Sensor	Work-order
Liquid level	Leaky refrigerant
Suction temperature	Faulty EPR value
Active compressors	Evaporator ice buildup
Door heater energy	Frosting/condensation in doors

Table 3: Sensors features for work-orders

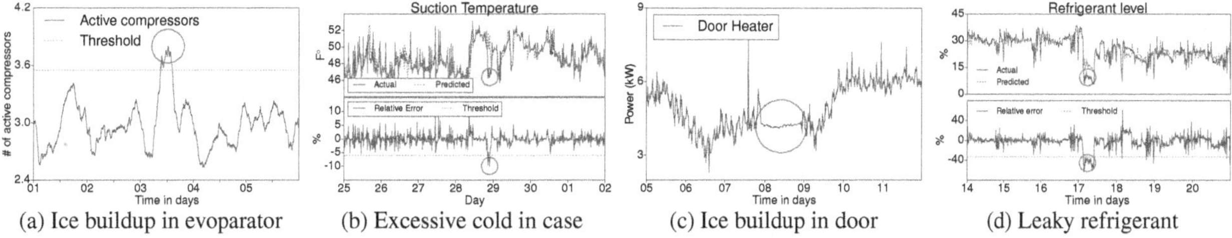

(a) Ice buildup in evoparator (b) Excessive cold in case (c) Ice buildup in door (d) Leaky refrigerant

Figure 8: Sensor based classification of work orders

We now explain why each type of work order manifests as an anomaly in the corresponding sensor reading. Recall Figure 1 that shows the refrigeration cycle in a RC. We expect that an anomaly in each component would show up as an anomaly in the sensor reading either in the inlet or the outlet of the component within a short period of time; the anomaly could also show up in another component after a significant period of time. For ease of presentation, we first highlight an example with anomalous sensor readings for each work-order type and summarize aggregate performance statistics later.

Ice buildup in evaporator: When ice builds up in the evaporator, the ice thermally insulates the evaporator from the rest of the refrigerated case. Therefore, the normal heat flow **rate** from the refrigerated case to the refrigerant (which carries it away as it flows) is reduced. Because the liquid refrigerant continues to flow, to maintain a set-point, the liquid refrigerant flow rate through the evaporator needs to increase. Thus, additional compressors need to be scheduled to increase the refrigerant flow rate as the compressors act in parallel. This also leads to an increase in the energy consumption. We expect to see this picked up in the number of compressors that are scheduled.

Figure 8(a) shows a smoothed (over 1 hour) version of the number of active compressors in the system. Between days 3 and 4, we see than the number of compressors exceeds the 99.9% percentile of all points during operation. The energy also picks up during this interval as seen in the corresponding upper tail anomaly graph in Figure 6(b). As explained later, using both the energy and sensor based thresholds could be used to reduce the false positive rate.

Excessive cooling in refrigerated cases: Excessive cooling in an RC implies that the flow rate of the refrigerant through the evaporator is higher than the heat load offered by the evaporator. This in turn would result in the refrigerant leaving the evaporator without picking up much-heat, i.e., a refrigerant with less super-heat. Consequently, this gets detected in the monitored suction temperature being lower than expected for that ambient condition.

Figure 8(b) shows the monitored suction temperature as a function of time for a store with a excessively cold refrigerated case. Between days 28 and 29, the monitored suction temperature dips significantly. The dip is observed with a corresponding increase in the energy consumption (i.e., an upper-tail energy anomaly).

Ice build up on case door: Whenever there is condensation or frosting in the door of a refrigeration case, the door heater gets turned on (by sensing the humidity level) and evaporates the condensate. Since this is a state dependent activity, it is non-periodic. When the door heater fails to get turned on, frost build-up happens. This non-turning of door heater can be detected as an anomaly in the front end energy consumption signal. Specifically, we expect to see that the signal has lesser "noise" than average, which we confirm by using a rolling deviation of the signal. Figure 8(c) shows that the *front-end* energy channel showing a flat consumption well before the period the work-order is actually noticed and logged.

Leaky refrigerant: Consider the receiver in Figure 1. The refrigeration loop tries to produce and maintain some level of liquid refrigerant in the receiver. Because the loop is closed, for a given ambient condition, we expect the time-average liquid level to be roughly constant, barring transient oscillations due to compressors and condensers turning on and off. However, when the refrigerant leaks from the system, we expect the average liquid level maintained in the receiver to go down significantly from the expected value. We have developed a statistical model for the liquid level, and we see that the average liquid level does go down when the work-order of refrigerant leak is logged in the system. Note that the work-order is logged in the system only when the liquid level is critically low and trips some sensor. Figure 8(d) shows the liquid level for a store with leak refrigerant. There is a progressive degradation is the maintained liquid level, and there is a sharp perturbation just before the work-order itself is logged around day 17-18.

7.4 Overall performance across work-orders

While a sensor reading can detect a particular work-order, it does so with some false positive rate. We find that while using both energy and sensor readings to identify and classify an anomaly, the false positive rate decreases in comparison to using the sensor alone for detection. This is because the energy signal is correlated with the sensory signals, especially around true anomalies which allows combining the two information streams with beneficial results. Table 4 shows the results of the detection using both the sensor and energy signals. On an average, the detection using energy and sensors has lesser false positives than the expected tail probability mass of 0.2%, indicating the robustness of the method. Further, the time of early detection is good and very significant in the case of liquid level work-orders. This is because the degradation in liquid level due to a refrigerant leak is a progressive event, the actual work order being logged only when the receiver fails to function due to to critically low refrigerant during operation. The impact on the detection likelihood is very little for three of the four work-orders. The detection likelihood decreases for the evaporator ice build-up work-order alone. This can be overcome by using a lower threshold value α for detecting the energy anomalies. The increase in false positives in energy anomalies will be toned down in the overall detection due to the supplementary sensory input (viz., # of active compressors).

Table 5 presents the confusion matrix using data from both energy and sensors. Each metric is first calculated for each store. For the sake of brevity, we present the average (across all stores) value of the metric averaged in each of the rows. While the precision and recall values for three types of work-orders are acceptable, the precision for the frosting work-order is low. This is because in our data-set we could detect only one true positive, while significant number of false positives were triggered due to a conservative choice of $\alpha = 0.98$ across all work-order types, whereas a higher α would improve the precision.

Features used	Energy		Sensor & Energy				
Work-order	Detection Likelihood (%)	False Positives (%)	Detection Likelihood (%)	False Positives (%)	# stores	# Events	Avg Early Detection (days)
Faulty EPR valve	100	0.13	66	0.05	4	6	4.9
Evaporator ice buildup	71	0.18	71	0.02	7	7	1.43
Leaky refrigerant	95	0.12	95	0.03	11	12	20.2
Frosting in doors	100	0.19	100	0.17	1	1	0.33

Table 4: Combining detection from energy and sensors improves the classification accuracy

Work-order	False Positive	False Negative	True Positive	True Negative	Precision	Recall
Faulty EPR valve	0.0005	0.0002	0.0007	0.9985	0.53	0.75
Evaporator ice buildup	0.0002	0.0005	0.0015	0.9979	0.90	0.75
Leaky refrigerant	0.0003	0.0011	0.0033	0.9953	0.82	0.77
Frosting in doors	0.0018	0.0001	0.0001	0.9981	0.06	0.67

Table 5: Details of the classification accuracy when using both energy and sensors. For each work-order type, the metrics are averaged across all the stores where that work-order occurs.

8. CONCLUSIONS

Refrigeration systems consume a significant portion of supermarket aggregate energy consumption. Because failure of such systems can have significant impact on store operation, it is important to identify any potential faults in their operation before critical failure. We presented a data-driven study of fault detection in 25 stores. Using the energy signal alone, we were able to identify faults with good detection likelihood and low false positive rates. The method could detect faults 2.8-21 days before the fault is noted in the database. Using additional sensors, we were able to further classify the faults into the four types that occurred during the duration of the study using a union of faults shown up by all sensors. Future directions of work include modeling dependencies between sensors to identify frequently occurring short-term anomalies that remain undetected with long-term modeling.

9. ACKNOWLEDGEMENTS

We thank our shepherd Mario Bergés and the anonymous reviewers; their comments have significantly improved the paper.

10. REFERENCES

[1] Commercial Buildings Energy Consumption Survey. http://www.eia.doe.gov/emeu/cbecs/cbecs2003.

[2] Energy Star Building Energy Manual - Facility Type Supermarkets. http://www.energystar.gov/buildings/sites/default/uploads/tools/EPA_BUM_CH11_Supermarkets.pdf.

[3] M. S. Breuker and J. Braun. Evaluating the performance of a fault detection and diagnostic system for vapor compression equipment. *International Journal of Heating, Ventilating, and Air Conditioning and Refrigerating Research*, 4(4):401–425, 1998.

[4] R. Fisera and P. Stluka. Performance monitoring of the refrigeration system with minimum set of sensors. *World Academy of Science, Engineering and Technology*, 6(7):396–401, 2012.

[5] H. Grimmelius, J. K. Woud, and G. Been. On-line failure diagnosis for compression refrigeration plants. *International Journal of Refrigeration*, 18(1):31–41, 1995.

[6] H. Han, Z. Cao, B. Gu, and N. Ren. Pca-svm-based automated fault detection and diagnosis (afdd) for vapor-compression refrigeration systems. *HVAC&R Research*, 16(3):295–313, 2010.

[7] M. Kim, S. H. Yoon, P. A. Domanski, and W. V. Payne. Design of a steady-state detector for fault detection and diagnosis of a residential air conditioner. *International Journal of Refrigeration*, 31:790–799, 2008.

[8] M. Leach, C. Lobato, A. Hirsch, S. Pless, and P. Torcellini. *Technical Support Document: Strategies for 50% Energy Savings in Large Office Buildings*. National Renewable Energy Laboratory, 2010.

[9] B. Narayanaswamy, B. Balaji, R. Gupta, and Y. Agarwal. Data driven investigation of faults in hvac systems with model, cluster and compare (mcc). In *Proceedings of the 1st ACM Conference on Embedded Systems for Energy-Efficient Buildings*, BuildSys '14, pages 50–59, 2014.

[10] K. Palani, N. Nasir, V. C. Prakash, A. Chugh, R. Gupta, and K. Ramamritham. Putting smart meters to work: Beyond the usual. In *Proceedings of the 5th International Conference on Future Energy Systems*, e-Energy '14. ACM, 2014.

[11] K. B. Rasmussen, A. Kieu, and Z. Yang. Fault detection and isolation for a supermarket refrigeration system. Master's thesis, Aalborg University, Denmark, 2009.

[12] N. Rena, J. Liang, B. Gua, and H. Han. Fault diagnosis strategy for incompletely described samples and its application to refrigeration system. *Mechanical Systems and Signal Processing*, 22:436–450, 2008.

[13] S. Tassou and I. Grace. Fault diagnosis and refrigeration leak detection in compression refrigeration systems. *International Journal of Refrigeration*, 28:680–688, 2005.

[14] C. Thybo and R. Izadi-Zamanabadi. Development of fault detection and diagnosis schemes for industrial refrigeration systems lessons learned. In *Proceedings ofthe 2004 IEEE International Conference on Control Applications*, 2004.

[15] U.S. Environmental Protection Agency. ENERGY STAR Certified Buildings and Plants. http://www.energystar.gov/buildings/.

[16] G. J. Van Wylen and R. E. Sonntag. *Fundamentals of classical thermodynamics*. Wiley Singapore, 1985.

[17] A. Wichman and J. E. Braun. Fault detection and diagnostics for commercial coolers and freezers. In *Proceedings of the International Refrigeration and Air Conditioning Conference*, 2008.

[18] Q. Zhou, S. Wang, and Z. Ma. A model-based fault detection and diagnosis strategy for hvac systems. *International Journal of Energy Research*, 33(10):903–918, 2009.

PIMM: Packet Interval-Based Power Modeling of Multiple Network Interface-Activated Smartphones

Jonghoe Koo, Wonbo Lee, Sunghyun Choi
Department of ECE and INMC,
Seoul National University, Seoul, Korea
{jhkoo,wblee}@mwnl.snu.ac.kr
schoi@snu.ac.kr

Yongseok Park
DMC R&D Center, Samsung Electronics,
Suwon, Korea
yongseok.park@samsung.com

ABSTRACT

State-of-the-art smartphones can utilize multiple network interfaces simultaneously, e.g., WiFi and LTE, to enhance the throughput and network connectivity in various use cases. In this paper, we present an accurate power modeling for the smartphones, especially, those capable of activating/utilizing multiple networks simultaneously. All kinds of traffic patterns are accurately converted into the estimated power consumption using our proposed algorithm by incorporating the variation of packet interval, packet length, and WiFi/LTE channel quality on a per-packet basis. The accuracy of our model is comparatively evaluated by comparing the estimated power with the measured power in various scenarios. We find that our model reduces estimation error by 7%–35% even for single network transmissions, and by 25% for multiple network transmissions compared with existing power models.

Categories and Subject Descriptors

C.4 [**Performance of systems**]: Modeling techniques

General Terms

Algorithm, Measurement, Performance

Keywords

Power Modeling; Energy Consumption; LTE; Wi-Fi; Smartphones

1. INTRODUCTION

Today's smartphones can activate and use multiple network interfaces, e.g., WiFi and LTE, simultaneously to achieve higher throughput or to maintain seamless connection to a server. The *download booster* of Samsung Galaxy S5[1] utilizes WiFi and LTE networks simultaneously to boost up the file download speed. Apple's *iOS 7* supports MPTCP (Multi-Path TCP) to enhance the reliability of *Siri* services by using WiFi as the primary TCP connection and cellular data as a backup connection. In addition, mobile hotspot service (a WiFi-based tethering service) and *Airplug*[2] (a video streaming application platform using both LTE and WiFi to provide stable video quality) are also the real-world applications which simultaneously utilize both LTE and WiFi at the same time. In this case, the energy consumption of a smartphone varies depending on the number of activated network interfaces and their usage.

Meanwhile, measuring the device power consumption using a power meter to evaluate the energy efficiency of a certain algorithm is a fairly burdensome job, thus motivating researchers to develop power consumption models. The previous efforts on wireless devices' power consumption modeling include the power-throughput curve [3], the airtime and packet rate-based model [2], and the state transition between the high and low power states according to the packet transmission and reception (tx/rx) rates [7, 8, 14]. The authors of [12, 13] group the packets with inter-packet times below a threshold into a burst of packets, and model the power levels of the burst, idle, and sleep modes of a device. Some of these models overlook the power saving operations of the network interfaces in a smartphone [2, 3], or the others model the power of an active state in a coarse manner, e.g., a single constant value [7, 8, 12–14], thus resulting in significant estimation error in certain scenarios. Most importantly, these power models are limited to single network-activated cases.

Being motivated by this, we propose a packet interval-based power modeling of multiple network interface-activated smartphones (PIMM), which is a generalized and extensible power model for state-of-the-art smartphones. The proposed power model features: 1) accurate estimation of the energy consumption of a smartphone for all kinds of traffic from packet traces, especially with varying packet lengths, intervals, and channel conditions, and 2) extensibility to combine multiple network interfaces' power models, estimating the power consumption when both WiFi and LTE are activated for data communication.

Two key contributions of this paper can be summarized as follows. First, we propose a 'packet interval-based power modeling' for smartphones which has the valuable features as described above. Second, using real-world applications and emulations, we validate PIMM shows quite good accuracy for both single and multiple network-activated scenarios. With these contributions, the PIMM can be used for the development and evaluation of energy-efficient smartphone operations. For example, it can help evaluate the performance of specific multiple network interface activation algorithms in the simulation tools so that the algorithm developers do not need to put much effort into measuring the device's power to evaluate the performance.

The rest of the paper is organized as follows. Section 2 presents the background of this work. Section 3 provides the proposed power modeling, PIMM, and practical issues are considered in Section 4. Section 5 comparatively evaluate the performance of PIMM in various scenarios. Finally, Section 6 concludes the paper.

[1]http://www.samsung.com/global/microsite/galaxys5/features.html
[2]http://www.airplug.com/solution.php

e-Energy'15, July 14–17, 2015, Bangalore, India.

ACM 978-1-4503-3609-3/15/07 ...$15.00.
http://dx.doi.org/10.1145/2768510.2768537.

2. BACKGROUND

2.1 Related work

Research on power modeling of network interfaces: The models in [7, 8] quantize the power consumption of network interfaces into several discrete constant values based on the packet rate, which are too simplified to accurately estimate the power consumption of network interfaces. Huang *et al.* [3] model the power used for data transfer via WiFi or cellular interface as a linear function of uplink and downlink throughput. Sun *et al.* [10] extend throughput-power linear fitting model considering the packet length and the transport layer protocol, but the model is limited to the WiFi power consumption. In [2], the authors model the power consumption of WiFi devices and investigate per-frame energy consumption, called 'cross-factor.' This work does not consider the power saving operation because it is the power model for the WiFi devices on laptop PCs, which is less sensitive to the power issue than smartphones. The authors of [12, 13] group packets of which the inter-packet time is less than a certain threshold into a burst of packets, and model the power levels of the burst (active), idle, and sleep modes of a device. Ding *et al.* [1] model the impact of 3G/WiFi signal strength on smartphone energy consumption based on measurement. The authors apply different tx/rx power consumption depending on the RSS of 3G/WiFi to incorporate the effect of the signal strength to the power consumption. The existing models have two kinds of shortcomings. One is overlooking the power saving operation of smartphones, and the other is modeling the active state power of network interfaces in a coarse manner, thus causing significant estimation error in certain scenarios.

Multi-homed device and MPTCP: ESPA [11] utilizes the multiple network interfaces of smartphones, i.e., WiFi and LTE, to enhance the user experience for FTP services. It considers the energy consumption and cellular data quota in addition to the file download completion time. In particular, ESPA experimentally characterizes the power consumption of the network interfaces and CPU to obtain the best network selection in terms of energy efficiency. MPMTP [4] exploits path diversity over multiple network interfaces to provide a seamless video streaming service by using Raptor coded multiple network interfaces simultaneously and Raptor coded UDP transmissions. Peng *et al.* [9] design an MPTCP algorithm by jointly considering the performance and energy consumption. They conducted simulation with the MPTCP power model given by $\sum_{r \in S} P_r(x_r)$, where $S \in \{$3G, 4G, WiFi$\}$. $P_r(x_r) = a_r x_r + b_r$, where x_r is the throughput over interface r, and a_r and b_r are the coefficients of the throughput-based power model in [3]. Lim *et al.* [6] develop an energy consumption model for MPTCP based on the experimental measurement using a smartphone. Through experimental measurement, the authors observed that the MPTCP energy consumption is less than the sum of energy consumed by each network interface, i.e., WiFi and LTE. The authors introduce the constant coefficient γ to make the estimated power by their model fit with the measurement. As evaluated in Section 5.3 in comparison with our model, the models in [6, 9] do not properly capture the characteristics of multiple network-activated smartphones.

2.2 Power saving operations of WiFi and LTE

WiFi network interface: IEEE 802.11 standard defines two power management modes, namely, **active mode (AM)** and **power save mode (PSM)**. The WiFi interface in **AM** always runs in the **awake state** in which it can transmit and receives the packets, while the WiFi interface in **PSM** toggles between the **awake state** and **doze state**, in which the interface is basically turned off. The AP informs the presence of the buffered packets via the traffic indication map (TIM) element in the beacons. The WiFi interface in **PSM** periodically wakes up, i.e., switching from **doze state** to **awake state**, for every delivery TIM (DTIM) period to receive beacons, and checks the TIM element in the beacon. If there exist buffered packets destined to the device, the WiFi interface sends a null data packet (NDP) in order to switch from **PSM** to **AM**, and then receives the buffered packets. The WiFi interface sets the inactivity timer which has a specific timeout value, called *PSM timeout*, and it resets the timer for every packet reception. When the inactivity timer expires, the WiFi interface switches back to **PSM** to save energy by sending an NDP to the AP.

LTE network interface: LTE has two radio resource control (RRC) states, namely, **RRC_connected** and **RRC_Idle**. Once an eNodeB (i.e., LTE base station) allocates resources to a user equipment (UE), the UE operates at **RRC_connected** state consuming high power. At **RRC_connected** state, the UE first stays in **continuous reception** mode and keeps monitoring physical downlink control channel (PDCCH). The UE starts **discontinuous reception (DRX) operation** and enters **short DRX** mode when *DRX inactivity timer* expires. The UE remains in *short DRX* until *short DRX cycle timer* expires and goes to **long DRX** when it expires. If the UE, which operates in **long DRX**, does not receive any packet until *RRC inactivity timer* expires, it enters **RRC_idle** state by releasing the allocated resources, and saves the energy consumption. When the UE operates in either **short DRX** or **long DRX**, it goes back to **continuous reception** if it receives/transmits a packet. During **RRC_idle** state, the UE sleeps for most of time and periodically wakes up to receive paging messages from eNodeB. Accordingly, it is awake for a few milliseconds every *RRC_idle DRX cycle* period, which is for example 1.28 seconds.

3. POWER CONSUMPTION MODELING

In this section, we propose a power consumption model for the smartphones, capable of activating/using multiple network interfaces simultaneously. The best way to estimate energy is integrating the instantaneous power consumption over time. However, it is impossible to obtain instantaneous power consumption without any external power/current measuring equipment with high granularity and precision. For this reason, the existing approaches have tried to approximate the energy consumption by converting certain representative factors, e.g., average-sense throughput and packet rate, network states (active/idle) given by system calls, into the modeled power values. These models have their own drawbacks and are not easily generalized to cover all kinds of traffic and network status. Moreover, the scenarios utilizing multiple network interfaces simultaneously have not been accurately modeled. Being motivated by this, we propose a generalized and extensible power model for smartphones, thus making it possible to incorporate as many situations as possible, including the number of simultaneously activated network interfaces, packet size, and channel conditions.

3.1 Modeling Methodology

3.1.1 Packet interval-based energy approximation

Our energy estimation methodology for data communication is based on the integration of the approximated power consumption over time. To approximately obtain the energy consumption, we divide the total time in consideration into a countable number of time partitions. Fig. 1(b) represents an example that imitates a smartphone's real power trace from a given packet trace and generates the approximated power trace. The power consumption is estimated with the rules as follows: 1) a packet interval becomes a

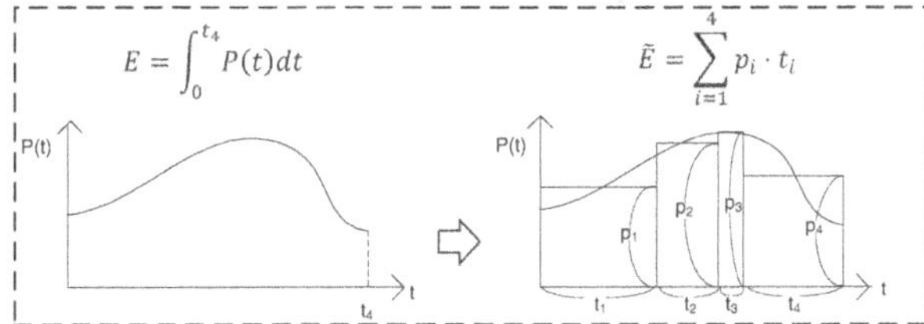

(a) The example of approximating the area of the region underneath the curve $P(t)$.

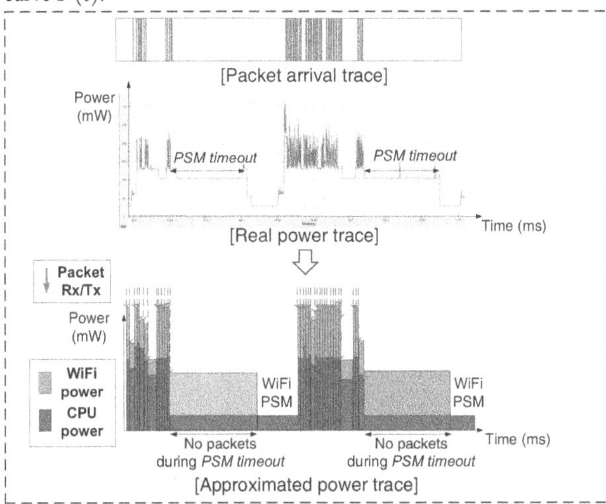

(b) The energy consumption approximation of a smartphone which communicates using a WiFi interface.

Figure 1: The area approximation methodology (a) and the power estimation approach from a given packet trace (b).

partition size, e.g., $t_i - t_{i-1}$ in Fig. 1(a), and 2) the average power consumption for the partition i is represented by a certain value that is equivalent to the average power for the partition, e.g., p_i in Fig. 1(a).

Dividing the total time into the packet intervals has two kinds of merit. First, the representative power value p_i for interval t_i, called *per-packet* power consumption, can be effectively obtained by measuring the power consumption of the smartphone that sends/receives packets periodically generated with interval t_i at the modeling stage without knowing the exact tx/rx artime of the packet. Second, the power saving operations of the network interfaces are highly related to the packet interval, and hence, the power saving operations can be easily considered by setting the packet interval as one of the modeling variables even if no system call-based finite state machine [8] is managed. With these advantages, our modeling approach accurately estimates the power consumption caused by the network operations irrespective of traffic pattern, and even provides the insight of the energy efficiency with respect to the traffic pattern, e.g., burst traffic results in higher energy efficiency [3]. In the following, the definition and characteristics of *per-packet* power consumption of the network interfaces are explained.

3.1.2 Per-packet power of network interface

The *per-packet* power consumption, P_{pp}, is defined as the average power consumption incurred by a packet until the corresponding network interface goes to the low power mode (**LPM**), i.e., **PSM** and **RRC_idle** for WiFi and LTE, respectively. Whenever a packet reception is completed, the network interface waits for a while in the active state, and enters the LPM when the *LPM timer* expires, where the *LPM timer* has a predefined timeout value, namely *LPM timeout*. Then, the tail time is defined as the time duration from the end of packet reception to the next packet arrival time, e.g, T^i_{tail} and T^{i+1}_{tail} in Fig. 2, or to the time when the *LPM timer* expires, e.g., T^{i+2}_{tail}. The **LPM**, *LPM timeout*, and power consumption for the tail time of the WiFi/LTE interface are summarized in Table. 1.

Table 1: Terminologies of power saving operations.

	LPM	*LPM timeout* (T_{to})	Tail power (P_{tail})
WiFi	**PSM**	*PSM timeout*	channel sensing power
LTE	**RRC_idle**	*RRC inactivity timer timeout*	**long DRX** state power

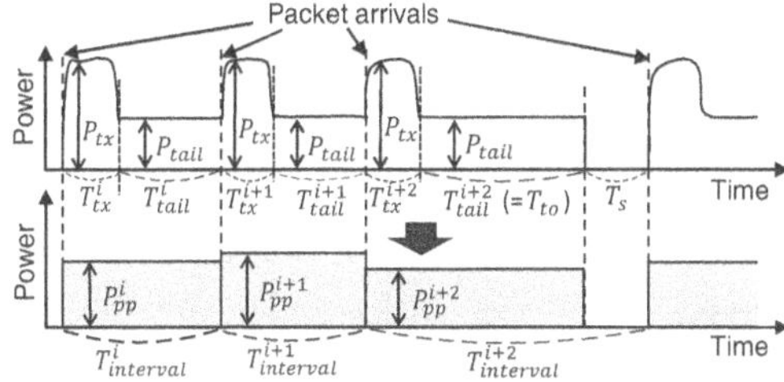

Figure 2: Per-packet power consumption model.

P_{pp} is the function of the packet interval, and is defined only for the packet intervals less than the *LPM timeout* of a network interface. Fig. 2 represents a simple example of P_{pp} for sending the packets via a network interface, i.e., $P_{pp} = \frac{P_{tx} \cdot T_{tx} + P_{tail} \cdot T_{tail}}{T_{tx} + T_{tail}}$, where P_{tx}/P_{tail} and T_{tx}/T_{tail} are the tx/tail power consumption and time durations, respectively. If the packet interval $T_{interval}$ is larger than $T_{tx} + T_{to}$, P_s is applied for $T_{s'}$ (= $T_{interval} - T_{tx} - T_{to}$). The energy consumption for $T_{interval}$ is calculated by $P_{pp} \cdot (\min(T_{interval}, T_{to} + T_{tx})) + P_s \cdot T_s \cdot u(T_{interval} - T_{tx} - T_{to})$, where $u(\cdot)$ is the unit step function. P_s in Fig. 2 is zero and normally $T_{to} + T_{tx} \simeq T_{to}$ since $T_{to} \gg T_{tx}$.

P_{pp} is mainly determined by the ratio of the tx/rx airtime to the tail time of the network interface. Without the tail time, e.g., sending an aggregate MAC protocol data unit (A-MPDU) of IEEE 802.11n, i.e., $T_{tail} = 0$ between the MAC frames, P_{pp} is equal to P_{tx}. In the case of a packet sent via the LTE interface, P_{pp} converges to the LTE **long DRX power**, called LTE tail power, if the packet interval is close to the LTE *RRC inactivity timer*, i.e., $T_{to} \gg T_{tx}$. In short, P_{pp} is a decreasing function of the packet interval but lower-bounded by P_{tail}. We highlight that the power model is extended to the cases that consider the impacts of the packet length and channel status, i.e., the channel quality and congestion. Fig. 3 summarizes how these factors affect P_{pp}. Congested channel, smaller available TCP window (due to long round trip time

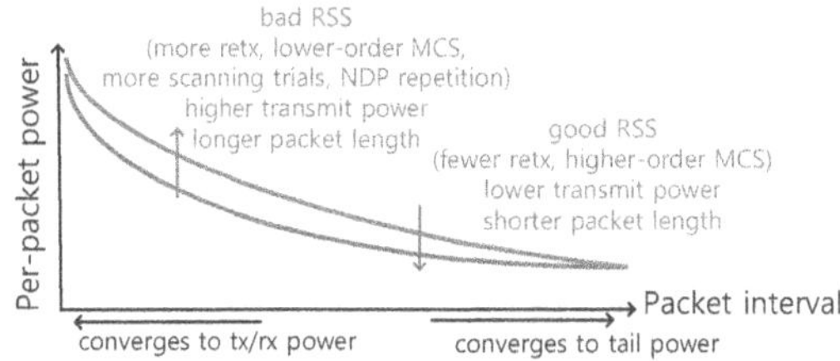

Figure 3: Summary of per-packet power characteristics.

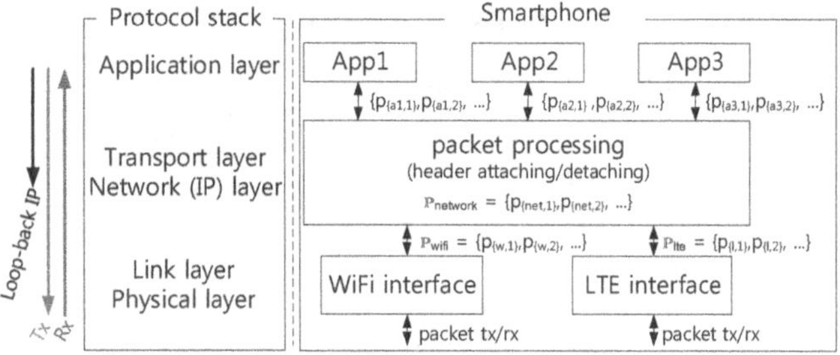

Figure 4: Packet flow procedure at a multiple network interface-activated smartphone.

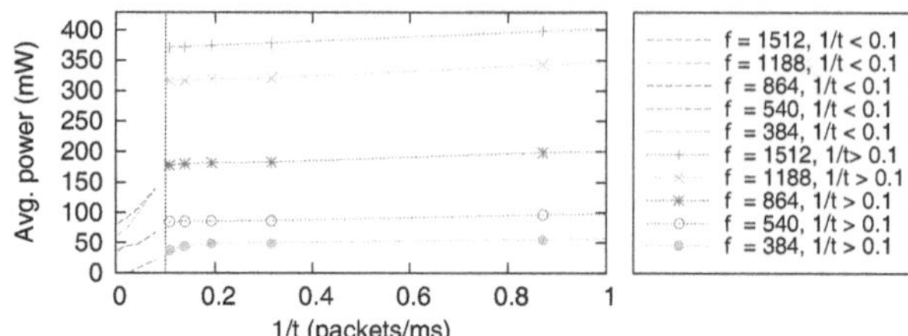

Figure 5: CPU packet processing power with respect to $1/t$ (packets/ms) according to the CPU clock frequency f (MHz).

(RTT)), and lower packet generation rate lead to the increase of the packet interval, thus resulting in lower P_{pp}. Otherwise, higher packet generation rate, less contention, and shorter RTT make the packet interval shorter, and hence, P_{pp} goes to high. Meanwhile, even for the same packet interval, bad quality channel, i.e., low received signal strength (RSS), and long packet length incur higher P_{pp} compared to the good quality channel and small packet length due to increased tx/rx time portion and retransmission (retx) rate. The details of the P_{pp} modeling are presented in Section 3.2.

3.1.3 Multiple network-activated smartphone

Even though multiple network interfaces of a smartphone are activated and operated independently, all the packets are processed at a common CPU of the smartphone after received or before transmitted. Accordingly, the power of the multiple network interface-activated smartphone is modeled as the sum of the power of each network interface and the CPU packet processing power for the aggregated packet rate. Fig. 4 shows the packet flow between the applications and the network interfaces. For the case of the packet reception, the set of data packets received by the network interfaces for time T is represented as $\mathbb{P}_{network} = \mathbb{P}_{wifi} \cup \mathbb{P}_{lte}$, where $\mathbb{P}_{wifi}$ and $\mathbb{P}_{lte}$ are the set of the packets received via the WiFi and LTE interfaces, respectively. The packets in $\mathbb{P}_{network}$ pass through the protocol stacks, incurring the packet processing power consumption at the CPU. Finally, the payloads are delivered to the corresponding applications. The packet transmission procedure is similar to the packet reception. On the other hand, if the destination address of a packet is set to the loop-back IP address, the packet is processed only upon the IP-layer and not delivered to the network interface, incurring only the packet processing power consumption.

With this overview, the power consumption is decomposed into two main parts, namely, 1) the power P_{wifi}/P_{lte} of the network interfaces when sending/receiving packets with their antennas and 2) the power P_{proc} of the CPU when processing the packets. Consequently, in terms of data communication, the power consumption of multiple network interface-activated smartphone is obtained by synthesizing each individual power model. We provide the details of the power models for CPU packet processing, WiFi, LTE, and their synthesis in the following section.

3.2 Packet interval-based power modeling

In this section, we provide the *per-packet* power modeling with the extensive measurement. We use Samsung Galaxy S2 (SHV-E120) and Galaxy S4 (SHV-E330) smartphones with Android OS 4.1.2 and Monsoon power monitor for modeling the power consumption. Due to the page limit, we only provide the results of SHV-E120 from Section 3.2 to Section 5.3 and summarize the part of the results of SHV-E330 in Section 5.4. The *tcpdump* is used to capture the packet traces of the smartphones. Moreover, for WiFi, the packets captured by *Airpcap* are also used to obtain the detailed information of the packets over the air.

3.2.1 Per-packet power model of CPU processing

We first analyze how much the CPU power is consumed for packet processing. The CPU packet processing power, P_{proc}, is related to the packet rate, γ, i.e., the reciprocal of packet interval t^{-1}, regardless of the packet length [2]. P_{proc} is affected by the CPU clock frequency, which is adaptively changed according to the CPU usage by DVFS (dynamic voltage and frequency scaling), one of the CPU power management techniques.

To measure the CPU power consumption for packet processing, we implement a simple socket program on the smartphone and sends the packets by setting the destination IP address to the loop-back IP address ('127.0.0.1'). Fig. 5 is the power consumption when the smartphone sends packets with the periodic packet interval t (ms) using the loop-back IP for various CPU clock frequencies. The higher CPU clock frequency, the higher power consumption even for the same number of packets. The packet processing power is well modeled as a discontinuous piecewise linear function of the inverse of packet interval t^{-1} with one step at $t^{-1} = 0.1$ (packets/ms). When the packet rate is low, i.e., the packet interval is longer than the CPU tail time, the CPU can switch to the low power state until the next packet arrives. Otherwise, the CPU continuously processes the packets in the high power state without switching to the low power state. Reflecting this observation, we summarize the coefficients of the discontinuous piecewise linear model for the CPU packet processing power, $P_{proc}(t^{-1}) = a{\cdot}t^{-1}+b$, in Table 2.

The modeling described above is valid only when any other applications using the CPU are not activated, e.g., the case that a smartphone transmits/receives packets in a background job. For real applications, the other processes may use the CPU at the same time. Therefore, the CPU remains at the high power state when the total CPU usage u_{cpu} exceeds the CPU usage corresponding to processing packets with 0.1 (packets/ms) packet rate, which is the discontinuous point of the function in Fig 5. To model the CPU power consumption for the general cases, we decompose the total CPU usage u_{cpu} $(= u_p + u_o)$ into two parts, i.e., u_p and u_o, which are the CPU usage by the processing packets and the other operations, respectively. Considering the base CPU power consumption, the CPU power consumption model is constructed as follows:

$$P_{cpu} = P_{base} + P_{proc} + P_{cpu\_o}(u_{cpu} - u_p), \tag{1}$$

where P_{cpu}, P_{base}, P_{proc} and P_{cpu_o} are the total CPU power, CPU base power, packet processing power, and the other operations' CPU power, respectively. u_p and P_{cpu_o} are modeled by linear functions of the packet rate and CPU usage, respectively. u^*_{cpu} is the CPU usage threshold to determine whether the CPU remains at the high power state or not, and it is equal to $u_p(0.1)$. The coefficients of the models are obtained by running a training application with varying CPU clock frequencies and summarized in Table 2.

Table 2: Coefficients of a linear model for the CPU packet processing power (unit: power (mW), t (ms)).

	$P_{proc}(t^{-1}) = a \cdot t^{-1} + b$ ($u_{cpu} < u^*_{cpu}$)		$P_{proc}(t^{-1}) = a \cdot t^{-1} + b$ ($u_{cpu} > u^*_{cpu}$)		u^*_{cpu}	$u_p(t^{-1}) = a \cdot t^{-1} + b$		$P_{cpu\_o}(u_o) = a \cdot u_o + b$		P_{base}
CPU clock frequency (f_c)	a	b	a	b		a	b	a	b	
384 MHz	398.1	32.7	16.2	106.9	16.8	4.3	16.4	1.5	106.6	105
540 MHz	361.8	34.9	12.1	127.1	13.4	4.3	12.9	2.4	127.1	107
864 MHz	385.1	55.1	18.0	178.2	10.5	7.9	9.8	4.0	198.1	130
1188 MHz	100.6	12.5	31.3	269.9	7.1	5.1	6.6	7.3	259.9	150
1512 MHz	762.7	11.5	33.4	303.0	6.3	9.7	5.3	10.2	292.8	170

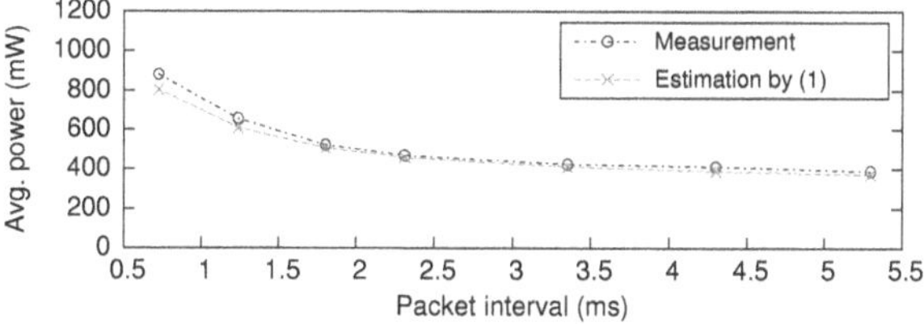

Figure 6: Measured and estimated power consumption of WiFi interface for 1400-byte UDP packet transmission over 5 GHz band.

3.2.2 *Per-packet power model of network interfaces*

Now, we propose a new power model for the WiFi/LTE network interface, i.e., *packet interval-based power function approximation model*. First of all, we experimentally investigate the relationship between the packet interval and average power consumption. We implement the socket programs on the smartphone and a laptop to configure the packet interval. The measured power consumption of the network interface with the packet interval t is obtained by subtracting the packet processing power, $P_{proc}(t^{-1})$ in Table 2 from the smartphone's overall power consumption measured by the power monitor. Through intensive measurement, we validate that the power consumption of the network interface P_{net} for the packet interval t, where t is smaller than the *LPM timeout* T_{to}, is well fitted to the *power function* ($f : x \mapsto \alpha \cdot x^\beta$, where $\alpha, \beta \in \mathbb{R}$) with respect to t as follows:

$$P_{net}(t) = \max(\alpha \cdot t^\beta, P_{tail}), \; t < T_{to}. \tag{2}$$

Fig. 6 shows the measured power when the smartphone sends 1400-byte UDP packets over 5 GHz WiFi with varying packet intervals, and estimated power by (2) with $\alpha = 723.44$ and $\beta = -0.373$. The estimated power and measured power quite well match. For the WiFi interface, *PSM timeout* is 210 ms and the channel sensing power is 300 mW for 5 GHz band and 180 mW for 2.4 GHz band from our measurement by sending the packets with increasing intervals. We find that **long DRX** power is 880 mW and *RRC inactivity timer timeout* is 10.8 s using the same approach as the WiFi interface case. (2) is lower bounded by P_{tail}, i.e., the channel sensing power for WiFi and **long DRX** state power for LTE, as explained in Section 3.1.2. To obtain the coefficients of the power model (2) empirically, we make the smartphone send and receive the packets via WiFi and LTE with various periodic packet intervals while measuring the power consumption. In Table 3, we summarize the coefficients of the *power function* approximation for the WiFi and LTE *per-packet* power models. The coefficient of determination, R^2, of the approximation is at least 0.95 ($R^2 = 1$ means the approximation is perfectly fitted), and hence, we confirm the feasibility of the *power function* approximated *per-packet* power model.

Table 3: Coefficients of power function approximation for the 1400-byte packet tx/rx power consumption of network interfaces.

(for t ms)	tx			rx		
$\alpha \cdot t^\beta$	α	β	R^2	α	β	R^2
WiFi 2.4	782.02	−0.408	0.97	446.56	−0.32	0.96
WiFi 5	723.44	−0.373	0.96	527.65	−0.24	0.95
LTE	1853.5	−0.189	0.96	1265.9	−0.125	0.99

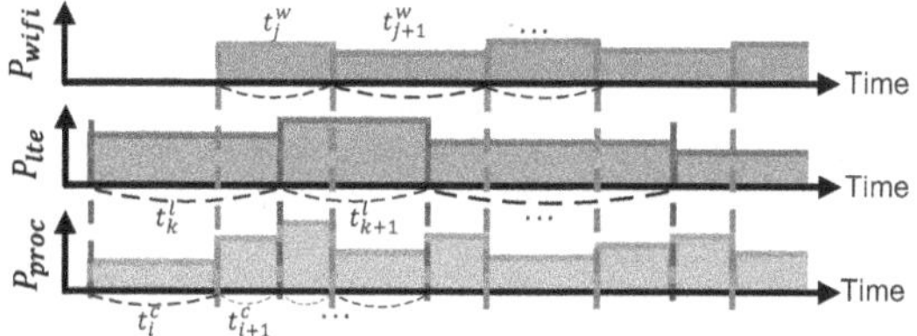

Figure 7: Packet interval-based power consumption anatomy for data communication using the multiple network interfaces.

3.2.3 *PIMM: Proposed power model*

As mentioned in Section 3.1.3, the power consumption of a multiple network interface-activated smartphone is obtained by combining the individual power models in Sections 3.2.1 and 3.2.2 using the modeling methodology explained in Section 3.1. When a data communication happens over time T, the average power consumption P for T is estimated as follows:

$$P = \frac{1}{T}\left(\sum_{i=1}^{n_w+n_l} P_{proc}(\tfrac{1}{t^c_i})t^c_i + \sum_{j=1}^{n_w} P_{wifi}(t^w_j)t^w_j + \sum_{k=1}^{n_l} P_{lte}(t^l_k)t^l_k\right), \tag{3}$$

where n_w and n_l are the total numbers of data packets received and transmitted via the WiFi and LTE interfaces, respectively. t^w and t^l are the packet intervals of the packets passing through the WiFi and LTE interfaces, respectively, and t^c are the packet intervals of all the packets processed by the CPU as shown in Fig 7. P_{proc}, P_{wifi}, and P_{lte} are the *per-packet* power consumption of the CPU, WiFi and LTE interfaces, respectively. (3) holds when t^w and t^l are less than the corresponding *LPM timeout* since P_{wifi} and P_{lte} are only defined by the packet interval less than *LPM timeout*. For example, if t^w is larger than *PSM timeout* t_{psm}, then $P_{wifi}(t^w_j)t^w_j$ is substituted by $P_{wifi}(t_{psm})t_{psm} + p_s t_s$ in order to reflect the energy reduction by **PSM**, where P_s is the WiFi sleep state power[3] and $t_s = t^w_j - t_{psm}$. We refer to (3) as PIMM, meaning Packet Interval-based power Modeling of Multiple net-

[3] We measure that the WiFi/LTE consume 0.8 mJ/7.2 mJ during beacon/downlink transmission reception, and hence, $P_s = \frac{0.8}{0.3072} = 2.6$ mW for WiFi and $P_s = \frac{7.2}{1.28} = 5.6$ mW for LTE when the DTIM period is 307.2 ms and the RRC_idle DRX cycle period is 1.28 s, respectively.

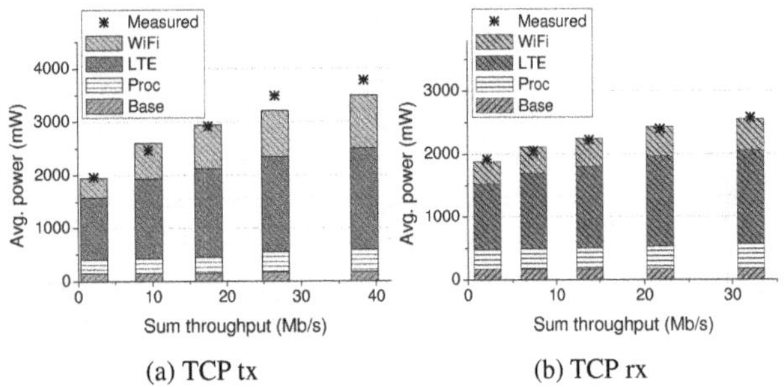

(a) TCP tx

(b) TCP rx

Figure 8: Model validation of PIMM for various source throughput.

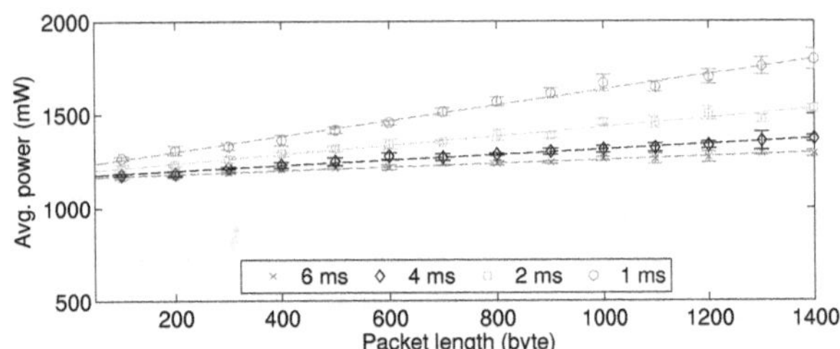

Figure 9: Impact of packet length to tx power consumption of LTE interface under periodic packet intervals, 6, 4, 2, and 1 ms. The points and bars represent the average and standard deviation of 10 iterations, respectively.

work interface-activated smartphones. PIMM synthesizes all the power models previously discussed, i.e., the packet processing power and WiFi and LTE interfaces power model. We validate PIMM by simultaneously activating TCP connections via WiFi and LTE. **Simultaneous activation of WiFi and LTE:** The default connectivity service of Android does not permit to activate both the WiFi and LTE data connections simultaneously, i.e., when the smartphone is associated with an AP, the LTE data connection is disabled and cannot be activated unless the WiFi link is disconnected. However, Android provides the API, called *ConnectivityManager*, with which a user can control the connections at the application layer.

With this API, we can activate both WiFi and LTE and selectively route specific packets via a desired network interface as follows. First, we make the smartphone connect to a WiFi AP, and then activate the LTE data connection by using *startUsingNetworkFeature* function with *TYPE_MOBILE* as the network type variable and *enableHIPRI* as the network feature variable. Second, we generate some traffic to the specified destination delivered via the specified network interface, i.e., the LTE interface, by using *requestRouteToHost* function with *TYPE_MOBILE_HIPRI* as the network type variable. *HIPRI* APN (access point name) type uses the mobile data connection to route specific traffic to mobile network until *HIPRI* timer expires, even if a WiFi connection is alive. Only the process that activates the mobile data connection with *HIPRI* type will have access to the mobile DNS server, and only the traffic having IP addresses requested via *requestRouteToHost* will be routed through the mobile network interface. Third, we set the DNS and add the default gateway for the LTE in addition to the WiFi DNS and WiFi gateway by using *setprop net.dns1* and *route add default gw* commands, respectively. After setting up the parallel TCP connections via WiFi and LTE, we make the smartphone send/receive packets via both of the interfaces at the same time.

PIMM model validation: We validate the accuracy of PIMM with various packet generation rates at the application-layer (app-

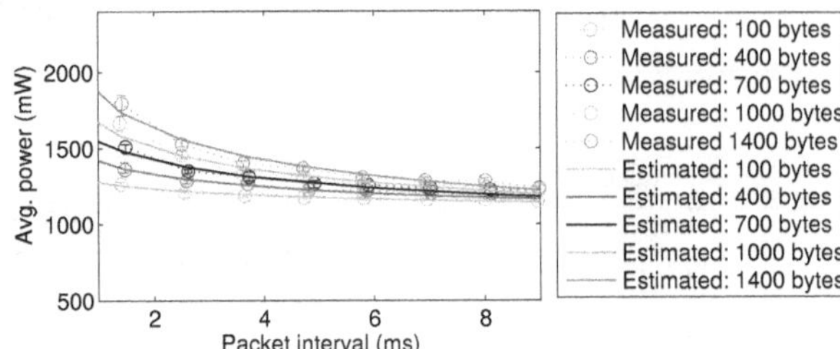

Figure 10: Measured and estimated tx power consumption of LTE interface with respect to the packet interval for $\{100, 400, 700, 1000, 1400\}$-byte packets.

layer) at the server side. Both WiFi and LTE TCP connections are activated and communicate with two local servers using each link. The packet length is 1400 bytes and the packet generation rates for two links are the same. Fig. 8 shows the average estimated power consumption by (3) for various packet generation rates. The x-axis represents the sum tx/rx throughput of the TCP connections via WiFi and LTE. The average estimated power consumption is composed of "WiFi" P_{wifi}, "LTE" P_{lte}, "Proc" P_{proc}. We add the CPU base ("Base") power to the estimated power in order to fairly compare with the measured power. PIMM shows quite accurate average power estimation with the estimation error of $4.5\pm3.1\%$ for TCP tx and $1.7\pm0.8\%$ for TCP rx. We further evaluate the performance of PIMM in various scenarios and compare the accuracy with other existing models in Section 5.

4. PRACTICAL ISSUES

4.1 Impact of packet length

Now, we investigate the impact of packet length to the network interface power consumption. In Section 3.2.2, all the packets have 1400-byte application layer payload. This assumption is quite reasonable for file transfer scenarios in which most packets have lengths similar to the maximum transmission unit (MTU), and hence, has been adopted in many existing power models [3, 5, 12, 13]. However, it is not appropriate for other types of traffic, e.g., the audio streaming and online gaming, of which the packet length are often variable. In addition, the packets of VoIP traffic mostly have small application payload, e.g., under 200 bytes.

To get the empirical result, we send UDP packets for 20 s with fixed packet length and interval, and measure the average power consumption during the packet transmission. We iterate this experiment 10 times and obtain the average and standard deviation of measured power consumption. Fig. 9 shows the LTE tx power consumption for each packet interval[4] in $\{1, 2, 4, 6\}$ (ms), with various packet lengths in $\{100, 200, \ldots, 1400\}$ (bytes). As expected, the power consumption linearly increases as the packet length increases for each packet interval under almost the same MCS (modulation and coding scheme) as we experiment at the same place at night when the traffic load is light.

From the linearity of the power consumption with respect to the packet length, we can estimate the power consumption of the network interfaces for the packet length l with the packet interval t, $P_{net}(t, l)$, by interpolating the two power functions of reference

[4] The packet interval in Fig. 9 is the time interval between the consecutive packet generations at the application layer, while the packet interval in the other figures and text means the time interval over the air.

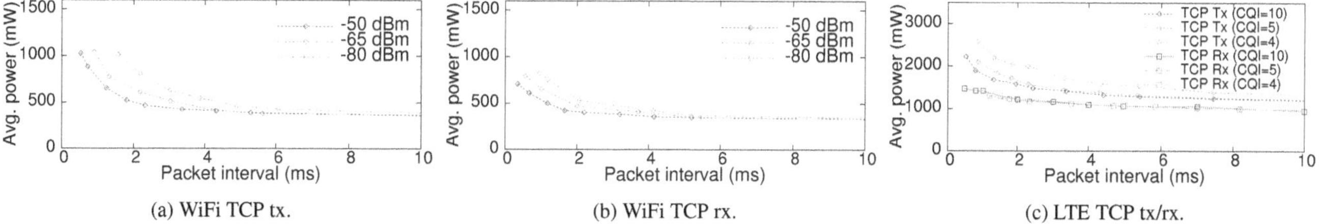

(a) WiFi TCP tx. (b) WiFi TCP rx. (c) LTE TCP tx/rx.

Figure 11: WiFi/LTE interface power consumption with respect to the packet intervals for three different levels of channel quality.

Table 4: Coefficients of power function approximation for the 100-byte packet tx/rx power consumption (mW) of network interfaces.

(for t ms)	tx			rx		
$\alpha \cdot t^{\beta}$	α	β	R^2	α	β	R^2
WiFi 2.4	459.54	−0.317	0.95	342.02	−0.213	0.95
WiFi 5	488.26	−0.134	0.96	455.98	−0.172	0.97
LTE	1275.8	−0.049	0.96	1248.2	−0.138	0.95

Table 5: Channel-aware power function coefficient compensation.

WiFi					LTE		
	tx		rx			tx	
RSS	α_c/α	β_c/β	α_c/α	β_c/β	CQI	α_c/α	β_c/β
−50	1	1	1	1	10	1	1
−65	1.28	1.31	1.21	1.3	5	1.07	1.11
−80	1.75	1.61	1.47	1.62	4	1.32	1.33

packet lengths, $P_{net}(t, L_1)$ and $P_{net}(t, L_2)$, as follows:

$$P_{net}(t, l) = \frac{(L_1 - l) \cdot P_{net}(t, L_2) + (l - L_2) \cdot P_{net}(t, L_1)}{(L_1 - L_2)}, \quad (4)$$

where L_1 and L_2 are reference packet lengths. In this paper, we set $L_1 = 1400$ and $L_2 = 100$, which represent reasonably long and short packet lengths, respectively. The parameters for WiFi and LTE power model with different packet lengths L_1 and L_2 are summarized in Tables 3 and 4, respectively.

Fig. 10 shows the measured power consumption for {100, 400, 700, 1000, 1400}-byte packet tx via LTE and the estimated power consumption using Tables 3 and 4, and (4). Furthermore, we additionally conduct the experiment for tx/rx with WiFi and LTE, and the MAPEs (mean absolute percentage error) of the estimated power for {200, 300, ..., 1200, 1300}-byte packet tx/rx via LTE, WiFi 2.4 GHz, and 5 GHz are calculated as 3.25%, 3.58%, and 3.40%, respectively. As a result, we validate the power consumption of arbitrary packet lengths can be properly estimated by interpolating the approximation functions of the reference packet lengths.

4.2 Impact of channel quality

As discussed in Section 3.1.2, poor channel quality causes higher energy consumption between consecutive packet interval, and hence, we introduce the parameters α_c and β_c instead of α and β in (2) to reflect the channel impact on power consumption as follows:

$$P_{net}(t) = \max(\alpha_c \cdot t^{\beta_c}, P_{tail}), \ t < T_{to}. \quad (5)$$

WiFi: With low RSS, the packets are transmitted with low-order MCS due to the rate adaptation, thus resulting in increased tx/rx airtime ratios, and the retransmitted packets incur additional energy consumption between consecutive successfully received data packets. Furthermore, much more MAC frame overheads arise when the RSS is below −80 dBm, e.g., active scanning for searching better APs and heavy retransmissions of NDPs due to the receive sensitivity difference between the antenna of APs and that of the smartphones. Figs. 11(a) and 11(b) present the increased per-packet power consumption at the locations of −65 dBm RSS and −80 dBm RSS compared to the location of −50 dBm RSS, which represents good channel quality.

LTE: We set the channel quality indicator (*CQI*)[5] as the metric of LTE channel quality. At low *CQI* region, the smartphone (UE) uses higher transmit power causing higher power consumption, and the data from eNodeB would be modulated by lower-order MCS. We select three spots where the different *CQI*s are measured, i.e., *CQI* = 10, 5, and 4.[6] We conduct the experiments at these three spots with 1400-byte packets by varying the packet generation interval. The smartphone (UE) and the local server are connected over TCP session to incorporate the retransmission effect for bad channel quality. Fig. 11(c) presents the LTE interface power consumption at the three spots with respect to the average TCP data packet intervals. In the case of TCP tx, the LTE interface consumes more power at the place where the lower *CQI* is reported, i.e, the power consumption at the *CQI* = 4 spot is the largest among the three spots, since the eNodeB commands the UE to transmit packets with higher transmit power level. On the other hand, the LTE rx power consumption negligibly varies according to the channel conditions since the eNodeB controls the downlink MCS to reduce retransmissions.

Summary: For both WiFi and LTE interfaces, the *per-packet* power consumption increases as the channel condition becomes poor while the maximum achievable TCP throughput decreases due to low-order MCS, retransmissions, and high transmit power. We generalize the network interface *per-packet* power model at different channel conditions by (5). Since the impact of channel quality on LTE rx *per-packet* power is not significant, the ratios of α_c and β_c to α and β (of Tables 3 and 4) only for WiFi tx/rx and LTE tx are summarized in Table 5.

5. PERFORMANCE EVALUATION

In this section, we evaluate the accuracy of PIMM in comparison with other existing models and measurement results. For this work, we implement an on-line power estimation algorithm for PIMM in

[5]The *CQI* is the UE feedback indicating downlink channel quality and UE's receive capability, and helps eNodeB determine the downlink data rate which can be supported. The UE determines the *CQI* corresponding to the MCS which allows the UE to decode the downlink data with less than 10% error rate.

[6] In our area, where LTE eNodeBs are seamlessly deployed, we hardly found places with *CQI* under 5.

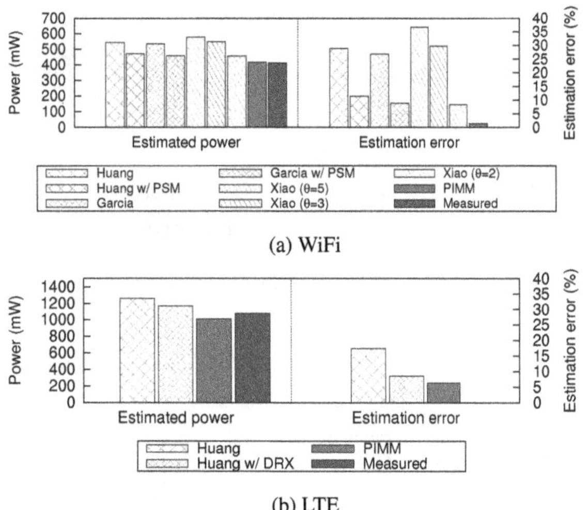

Figure 12: Estimated power and estimation error of PIMM and comparison models for 1400-byte UDP tx with random packet intervals using (a) WiFi and (b) LTE.

Algorithm 1 PIMM power estimation algorithm from packet trace

$T^w_{\text{last}} \leftarrow 0, T^l_{\text{last}} \leftarrow 0, T^c_{\text{last}} \leftarrow 0$
for all packets **do**
  $(T, N_{\text{type}}, l, ch) \leftarrow Get\_Packet\_Information()$
  $(t_{tail}, P_s) \leftarrow Set\_Network\_Parameters(N_{\text{type}})$
  if N_{type} = WiFi **then**
    $t^n \leftarrow T - T^w_{\text{last}}$
    $T^w_{\text{last}} \leftarrow T$
  else if N_{type} = LTE **then**
    $t^n \leftarrow T - T^l_{\text{last}}$
    $T^l_{\text{last}} \leftarrow T$
  $t^c \leftarrow T - T^c_{last}$
  $T^c_{\text{last}} \leftarrow T$
  $t^n_a \leftarrow \min(t^n, t_{tail}), t^n_s \leftarrow \max(0, t^n - t_{tail})$
  $P_{net} \leftarrow Cal\_Network\_P_{pp}(ch, l, N_{type}, t^n_a)$
  $P_{proc} \leftarrow Cal\_Proc\_P_{pp}(f_c, u_{cpu}, t^c)$
  $E \leftarrow E + P_{net} \cdot t^n_a + P_s \cdot t^n_s + P_{proc} \cdot t^c$
$P \leftarrow \frac{E}{total\ time}$

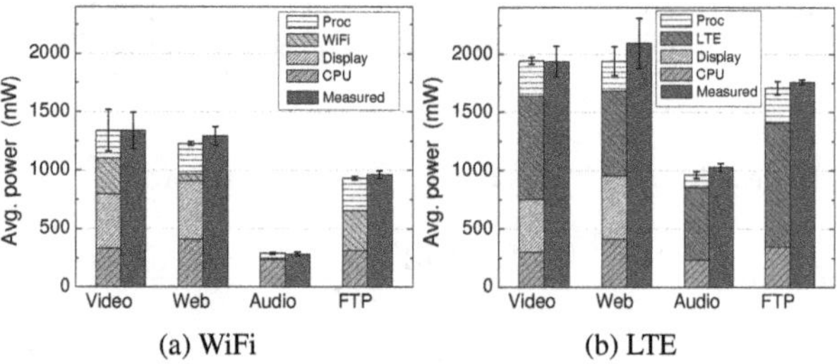

Figure 13: Estimated power consumption breakdown and measured power consumption for various real-world applications using (a) WiFi and (b) LTE.

the Android application based on packet traces. We recalibrate all the coefficients of the comparison models [2,3,12,13] fitted to the smartphone used in this validation for a fair comparison.

5.1 On-line power estimation

We propose the on-line algorithm for PIMM to estimate the average power consumption from packet traces. The timestamp (T), the type of a network interface where the packet passes (N_{type}, either WiFi or LTE), packet length (l), and channel quality (ch) of each packet are obtained from packet traces. Next, set the *LPM timeout* t_{tail} and the tail power P_s of N_{type} and calculate packet intervals t^n (equal to t^w for WiFi or t^l for LTE in Fig. 7) and t^c, where T^w_{last} and T^l_{last} are timestamps of the last packet of WiFi and LTE interface, respectively, and T^c_{last} is the timestamp of the last packet without distinction of N_{type}. t^n is then divided into t^n_a and t^b_s by comparing t^n and t_{tail} and P_{net} is applied for t^n_a and P_s for t^n_s. P_{net}, the *per-packet* power of N_{type}, is determined by (2), (4), and t^n with appropriate α and β using channel quality ch and packet length l. P_{proc} is determined by CPU clock frequency f_c, total CPU usage u_{cpu}, and t^c. The *per-packet* energy consumption is cumulatively added to the total energy consumption E, and the average power consumption is finally calculated by dividing E by the total time. The algorithm is described in Algorithm 1.

5.2 Single network data connections

Modeling validation: To validate the accuracy of PIMM for arbitrary traffic pattern, we send the 1400-byte UDP packets by regulating the app-layer packet intervals for 300 s. Every packet is sent with the interval (ms) selected within the range [0, 1000] via WiFi and [0, 15000] via LTE to generate burst traffic and sparse traffic alternately. The smartphone logs the packet intervals during transmission as the input trace of PIMM to estimate the average power consumption. We conduct the experiment in a clean channel at the 5 GHz band for WiFi to avoid interference and congestion. For comparison, we use the model proposed by Huang *et al.* [3] for both WiFi and LTE traffic, the models proposed by Xiao *et al.* [12, 13] and Garcia *et al.* [2] only for WiFi traffic. Even though [5] proposes an LTE power model, we do not compare with it because it needs the transmit power, received signal strength, and airtime of every packet, which are not available at the smartphone side.

Fig. 12 shows the estimated power and estimation error of each model for WiFi (a) and LTE (b). Both the throughput-based model [3] and airtime-based model [2] without considering the PSM/DRX overestimate the power. Although [3] and [2] additionally consider the PSM/DRX, they result in relatively high estimation errors because they do not consider the fact that the CPU packet processing power differs according to the CPU clock frequency. Xiao *et al.* [12, 13] always overestimate the power even though $\theta = 3$ ms is the best threshold in their paper. PIMM reflects the idle time between consecutive packets while Xiao *et al.* [12, 13] ignore the idle time within a packet burst. In summary, PIMM outperforms existing power models for WiFi and LTE by 1) effectively distinguishing active and idle states of network interface, and 2) accurately estimating the energy consumption for inter-packet time with *per-packet* power concept.

Real-world applications: We validate the performance of PIMM with four representative real-world applications, i.e., video streaming, web browsing, audio streaming, and file transfer protocol (FTP). The real-world applications utilize various components and the major power consuming components among them are CPU, display, and network interfaces. Before the model validation, we have run the benchmark application for display power modeling based on the modeling method described in [7] with a fixed brightness level for a simple model. The total smartphone power consumption model is constructed as follows:

$$P = P_{wifi} + P_{lte} + P_{proc} + P_{cpu} + P_{display}, \tag{6}$$

where P_{proc} is the packet processing power and P_{cpu} is the additional CPU power except for the packet processing power in Section 3.2.1.

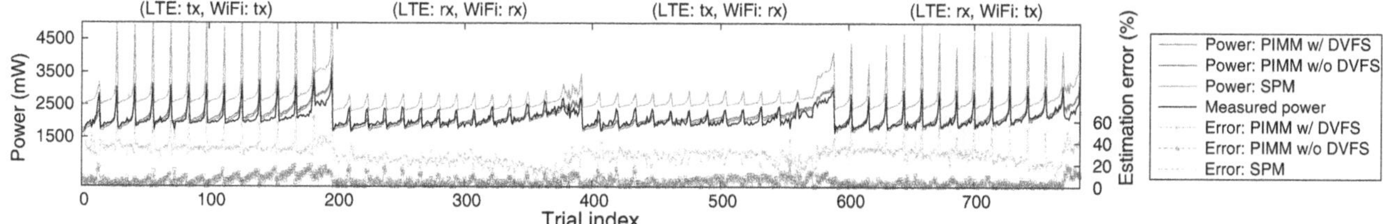

Figure 14: Estimated power and estimation error of each trial with parallel TCP connections via both WiFi and LTE.

We run each application with five trials, and each trial is executed for 60 s. The FTP and audio applications run as background processes, i.e., the display is turned off. For the FTP, the file size is 25 Mbytes, and the average bitrate of streamed videos is 1.4 Mb/s. The packet traces captured by *tcpdump* are used to estimate P_{wifi}, P_{lte}, and P_{proc} by Algorithm 1, and the CPU usage and the clock frequency are logged to estimate P_{proc} and P_{cpu}. For the foreground applications, the images displayed on the screen are captured every 3 s, and the display power model converts the pixel information of the captured image into $P_{display}$. The additional power consumption for logging and packet capturing is 85 mW including the image capture, and only 10 mW excluding the image capture. Fig. 13 shows the expectations and standard variations of the estimated power consumption by (6) and measured power consumption for various real-world applications, and breakdown of the average estimated power consumption, where "Proc" denotes the packet processing power.

In the case of video streaming over WiFi, 41.1% (559 mW) of total power is attributed by the network operation ("Proc"+"WiFi"), which are additionally required for video streaming compared with playing locally stored video. On the other hand, since the LTE consumes more power than WiFi for the same amount of traffic in addition to the longer tail time and higher tail power, 60.6% (1192 mW) of total power (1944 mW) is caused by the network operation ("Proc"+"LTE") in the case of video over LTE. In other words, 71% and 150%[7] more power are additionally consumed for video streaming over WiFi and LTE, respectively, compared with playing local video. In the case of audio streaming, the size of audio data is comparable small, and hence, "WiFi" takes only few portion of average power consumption, while "LTE" takes considerably higher portion for the same reason as the video streaming case. "WiFi" and "LTE" portions of web surfing can vary according to the users' web surfing pattern and the size of Java scripts and images in the web pages. For FTP, "WiFi" and "LTE" portions are related to the WiFi and LTE throughput. Low average power consumption for FTP does not indicate high energy efficiency since the file download completion time should be different according to the link throughput. Overall, PIMM with CPU and display model accurately estimates the power consumption for real-world applications with average estimation error of 6.1% for WiFi and 8.6% for LTE.

5.3 Multiple network data connections

Modeling validation: We evaluate the accuracy of PIMM for multiple interface-activated scenarios by setting the packet generation rates of two TCP connections to $(\gamma_{lte}, \gamma_{wifi}) \in \Gamma$ with 1400-byte packets. The set Γ is defined as $\Gamma = \Gamma_{lte} \times \Gamma_{wifi} = \{(x, y) | \ x \in \Gamma_{lte} \ \wedge \ y \in \Gamma_{wifi}\}$ by the cartesian product of Γ_{lte} and Γ_{wifi}, where $\Gamma_{lte} = \Gamma_{wifi} = \{10, 20, 50, 100, 111, 125, 143, 167, 200, 250, 333, 500, 1000, \text{full}\}$ (packets/s), such that $|\Gamma| = 196$. For $\gamma = $ full, the sender tries to send packets as fast as possible. The packet generation rates limit the maximum TCP throughput and the actual TCP throughput is determined by round trip time and packet loss pattern of that TCP link. We firstly let the smartphone act as TCP tx via WiFi and LTE, and then repeat the experiments after changing the direction of TCP at the smartphone to (LTE: rx, WiFi: rx), (LTE: tx, WiFi: rx) and (LTE: rx, WiFi: tx). Especially, (LTE: rx, WiFi: tx) and (LTE: tx, WiFi: rx) represent the case of smartphones providing a mobile hotspot, which is one of the most popular applications utilizing both WiFi and LTE interfaces simultaneously.

We compare the modeling accuracy of PIMM with SPM, representing the sum of WiFi and LTE power models, as proposed in [6, 9]. For SPM, the individual power model for data transfer via WiFi or LTE is obtained based on the linear fitting function of the WiFi and LTE throughput variables x_w and x_l, represented as $P_{WiFi} = (a_w x_w + b_w)$ and $P_{LTE} = (a_l x_l + b_l)$, where $\{a_w, b_w\}$ and $\{a_l, b_l\}$ are the linear fitting coefficients for the WiFi and LTE throughput-power curves, respectively. Each power model involves the packet processing power according to the throughput variable. Then, SPM is obtained as the sum of the two linear functions, i.e., SPM $= P_{WiFi} + P_{LTE}$.

Fig. 14 shows the estimated power and estimation error of the PIMM and SPM for the parallel TCP connections via WiFi and LTE. In summary, "PIMM with DVFS" shows the best result of the power estimation (4.9±3.7% MAPE). The estimation error slightly increases to 5.4 ± 4.3% MAPE without DVFS. However, "SPM" shows much higher estimation error (29.9 ± 9.0%) for the parallel TCP connections via WiFi and LTE. The reason is that the SPM is the sum of $P_{wifi} + P_{proc} (= P_{WiFi})$ and $P_{lte} + P_{proc} (= P_{LTE})$, thus incorrectly summing P_{proc} twice, and hence, results in the overestimation of the power by b in Table 2 compared to PIMM.

FTP using both WiFi and LTE: Here, we investigate the estimation accuracy of PIMM for the FTP scenarios, especially the smartphone downloads the segments of the file using both WiFi and LTE interfaces. We emulate the FTP for this evaluation by activating both WiFi and LTE TCP connections as presented in Section 3.2.3 with two local servers. 25 Mbyte-file download is considered with two downloading policies; with "Policy 1," the file is equally divided into two segments, and each segment is downloaded via WiFi and LTE. With "Policy 2," packets are downloaded via WiFi and LTE until the cumulative received data size becomes 25 Mbytes, i.e., the data transfer times for WiFi and LTE are the same for both.

Fig. 15 shows the measurement and estimation results at two locations, namely "−50 dBm" and "−80 dBm", where the LTE channels are good while the WiFi (2.4 GHz band) channels are

[7]The values can vary depending on the display brightness level, CPU governor policy, and video bitrate.

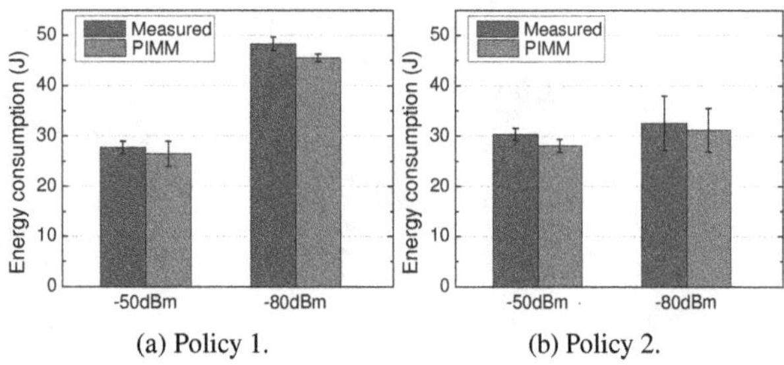

(a) Policy 1. (b) Policy 2.

Figure 15: Measured and estimated energy consumption of downloading 25 Mbtyes file using both WiFi and LTE TCP connections.

good (-50 dBm RSS) and bad (-80 dBm RSS), respectively. The average throughput of LTE is 12.8 Mb/s, and WiFi throughput at the good and the bad channels are 5.1 Mb/s and 1.4 Mb/s, respectively. PIMM estimates the energy consumption with the error of $5.7 \pm 1.7\%$. For "Policy 1", the energy consumption highly increases due to the low WiFi throughput at "-80 dBm" even though the LTE already finished the downloading. On the other hands, for "Policy 2", the results show the similar energy consumption since the downloaded data size via the LTE is dominant for the both locations. However, "-80 dBm" consumes slightly more energy than "-50 dBm" due to the increase of the LTE download time and the increased power consumption of WiFi at low RSS. For "-50 dBm" cases, "Policy 1" is more efficient than "Policy 2" due to short LTE download time since the LTE throughput is even higher than that of WiFi, but the lower energy efficiency (J/bit) of LTE.

To investigate the energy efficiency of FTP using both WiFi and LTE, we measure the energy consumption of downloading 25 Mbyte-file only via LTE ("Only LTE") and the averaged result is 32.9 J. The energy efficiency improvement ratios to "Only LTE" are 15.8% ("Policy 1") and 7.9% ("Policy 2") at "-50 dBm", and 1.1% ("Policy 2") at "-80 dBm", but the efficiency of "Policy 1" at "-80 dBm" decreases by 46.5% compared to "Only LTE". From these observations, we find that utilizing WiFi and LTE links with proper network selection policy and download file segment allocations enhances the energy efficiency of the smartphones, and PIMM helps estimate the performance with expected packet traces.

5.4 Model generation complexity

Let (N_n, N_l, N_q, N_i) be a 4-tuple denoting the cases to be modeled for network interface modeling, where the four elements are the numbers of network interfaces, packet lengths, signal quality levels, and packet intervals, respectively. The overall model generation complexity becomes $O(N_n \cdot N_l \cdot N_q \cdot N_i)$. In our modeling procedure, the measurements have been conducted for $N_n = 2$ (WiFi and LTE), $N_l = 2$ (1400 and 100-byte packets), $N_q = 3$ (-50,-65, and -80 dBm for WiFi and CQI $=$ 4, 5, and 10 for LTE), and $N_i = 10$ (from full-pumping to light load traffic). For CPU packet processing power modeling, $N_c \cdot N_i$ additional measurements are needed, where N_c is the number of CPU clock frequencies to be modeled.

We obtain the PIMM model of SHV-E330 smartphone with the same modeling procedure above, and the average R^2 (in Table 3) of the *power function* approximation of the network interfaces is $0.95(\pm0.02)\%$, and estimation errors for FTP scenarios in Sections 5.2 and 5.3 are 3.5% for WiFi, 4.2% for LTE, and 4.7% when both WiFi and LTE are activated. Accordingly, we validate that PIMM accurately estimates the power consumption of SHV-E330 in addition to that of SHV-E120 smartphone.

6. CONCLUSION

In this paper, we propose a packet interval-based power model for multiple network interface-activated smartphones, which estimates the average power consumption based on the packet interval. The proposed power model is constructed by combining *per-packet* power of the packet processing, WiFi, and LTE network intefaces. The accuracy of our model is evaluated in various scenarios including the real-world smartphone applications. We validate that our model outperforms other existing power models for single/multiple network transmissions in terms of the estimation error.

We prospect that PIMM will help estimate the future energy consumption as part of the energy-aware algorithm operation and develop energy-efficient protocols/algorithms especially utilizing multiple network interfaces. PIMM can be used in a simulator as a power model, which are not possible with measuring power consumption using a real hardware. As future work, we will further evaluate the *download booster* and *Airplug* with PIMM.

7. ACKNOWLEDGMENT

This work was supported by Digital Media & Communications R&D Center in Samsung Electronics and the Brain Korea 21 Plus Project.

8. REFERENCES

[1] N. Ding, D. Wagner, X. Chen, Y. C. Hu, and A. Rice. Characterizing and modeling the impact of wireless signal strength on smartphone battery drain. In *Proc. ACM SIGMETRICS*, pages 29–40, 2013.

[2] A. Garcia-Saavedra, P. Serrano, A. Banchs, and G. Bianchi. Energy consumption anatomy of 802.11 devices and its implication on modeling and design. In *Proc. ACM CoNEXT*, pages 169–180, 2012.

[3] J. Huang, F. Qian, A. Gerber, Z. M. Mao, S. Sen, and O. Spatscheck. A close examination of performance and power characteristics of 4G LTE networks. In *Proc. ACM MobiSys*, pages 225–238, 2012.

[4] O. C. Kwon, Y. Go, Y. Park, and H. Song. MPMTP: Multipath multimedia transport protocol using systematic Raptor codes over wireless networks. *IEEE Transactions on Mobile Computing*, 2014.

[5] M. Lauridsen, P. Mogensen, and L. Noël. Empirical LTE smartphone power model with DRX operation for system level simulations. In *Proc. IEEE VTC*, pages 1–6, 2013.

[6] Y.-S. Lim, Y.-C. Chen, E. M. Nahum, D. Towsley, and R. J. Gibbens. How green is multipath TCP for mobile devices? In *Proc. ACM AllThingsCellular*, pages 3–8, 2014.

[7] R. Mittal, A. Kansal, and R. Chandra. Empowering developers to estimate app energy consumption. In *Proc. ACM MobiCom*, pages 317–328, 2012.

[8] A. Pathak, Y. C. Hu, M. Zhang, P. Bahl, and Y.-M. Wang. Fine-grained power modeling for smartphones using system call tracing. In *Proc. ACM EuroSys*, pages 153–168, 2011.

[9] Q. Peng, M. Chen, A. Walid, and S. Low. Energy efficient multipath TCP for mobile devices. In *Proc. ACM MobiHoc*, pages 257–266, 2014.

[10] L. Sun, R. K. Sheshadri, W. Zheng, and D. Koutsonikolas. Modeling WiFi active power/energy consumption in smartphones. In *Proc. IEEE ICDCS*, pages 41–51, 2014.

[11] W. Lee, J. Koo, S. Choi, and Y. Park. ESPA: Energy, usage ($), and performance-aware LTE-WiFi adaptive activation scheme for smartphones. In *Proc. IEEE WoWMoM*, pages 1–9, 2014.

[12] Y. Xiao, P. Savolainen, A. Karppanen, M. Siekkinen, and A. Yla-Jaaski. Practical power modeling of data transmission over 802.11g for wireless applications. In *Proc. ACM e-Energy*, pages 75–84, 2010.

[13] Y. Xiao, M. Siekkinen, A. Wang, Y. Cui, P. Savolainen, L. Yang, S. Tarkoma, and A. Yla-Jaaski. Modeling energy consumption of data transmission over Wi-Fi. *IEEE Transactions on Mobile Computing*, 13(8):1760 – 1773, August 2014.

[14] L. Zhang, B. Tiwana, Z. Qian, Z. Wang, R. P. Dick, Z. M. Mao, and L. Yang. Accurate online power estimation and automatic battery behavior based power model generation for smartphones. In *Proc. IEEE/ACM/IFIP CODES+ISSS*, pages 105–114, 2010.

Individual and Aggregate Electrical Load Forecasting: One for All and All for One

Sambaran Bandyopadhyay, Tanuja Ganu, Harshad Khadilkar, Vijay Arya
IBM Research
{sambandy, tanuja.ganu, harshad.khadilkar, vijay.arya}@in.ibm.com

ABSTRACT

Electrical load forecasting is an important task for utility companies, in order to plan future production and to increase the efficiency of the distribution network. Although load forecasting at the aggregate level has been extensively studied in existing literature, forecasts for individual consumers have been shown to be prone to errors. This paper deals with the problem of electrical load forecasting at multiple scales, from individual consumers to the network as a whole. We use smart meter data from carefully selected sets of consumers for this purpose.

First, we consider the problem of forecasting the load for individual consumers at the outermost nodes of the distribution network. We propose an algorithm which considers external available information like calendar or weather contexts along with the energy consumption profiles of different consumers for accurate mid-term and short-term load forecasting. Multiple aggregation approaches are considered for utility level forecasting, in order to characterize their error properties. We show that careful clustering of consumers for aggregation can result in smaller errors. We experiment with two public data sets for demonstrating the advantages of the proposed method over the state-of-the-art approaches.

Categories and Subject Descriptors

H.4 [**Information Systems Applications**]: Miscellaneous; J.7 [**Computer Applications**]: Computer in Other Systems

General Terms

Algorithms, Experimentation

Keywords

Load Forecasting, Short and Medium Term, Individual time series, Clustering, Context Information

e-Energy'15, July 14–17, 2015, Bangalore, India.

DOI: http://dx.doi.org/10.1145/2768510.2768539.

1. INTRODUCTION

Electrical load forecasting has always been an important task for utility companies. Accurate prediction of future demand (from a few hours to a few months ahead) allows utilities to schedule the operation of their generation and distribution infrastructure in advance, thus reducing the chance of unexpected blackouts or brownouts. It also helps them to tackle supply shortfall by establishing contracts for energy purchase from other providers. The farther ahead these contracts are established, the lower the cost of the energy.

Load forecasting in different levels of the distribution network is important for optimal demand response and dynamic pricing schemes. Historical and real-time data may be readily available through the recent introduction of Advanced Metering Infrastructure (AMI), but the problem of forecasting future load is non-trivial. Methods for load forecasting typically use data generated from the smart meters of individual users. We can consider data from each user as a time series of electric consumption. Load forecasting can be done in different levels of the network, including (i) individual consumers, (ii) at the distribution transformer level, or (iii) for the entire network of a given utility. Forecasting can be done on different time granularity like, hourly energy forecasting, daily energy forecasting etc., where hourly (daily) energy forecasting for hour (day) t means to forecast the total consumption of the energy during the tth hour (day). Some of the algorithms and methods presented in this paper have focused mainly on the hourly load forecasting, but the same techniques can also be used for load forecasting at different granularity.

Forecasts of future load can be split not only by the level of aggregation, but also according to their look ahead periods. Short term forecasts relate to times from an hour up to a day in advance. Medium term forecasts are valid from a few days up to few months in the future, while long term forecasts relate to time scales of a few months or even years. In general for short and medium term forecasting, trend in the data is assumed to be fixed upto some range, but for long term forecasting, trend of the data can change significantly. It is not difficult to understand that obtaining accurate long term forecasts is more difficult than medium term forecasts, and by extension, accurate medium term forecasts are more difficult to obtain than short term forecasts. Intuitively, this happens because past and current data has stronger correlation with future demand in the near term rather than the longer term.

Load forecasting for individual users is difficult because of several factors. Hourly energy consumed by a single house

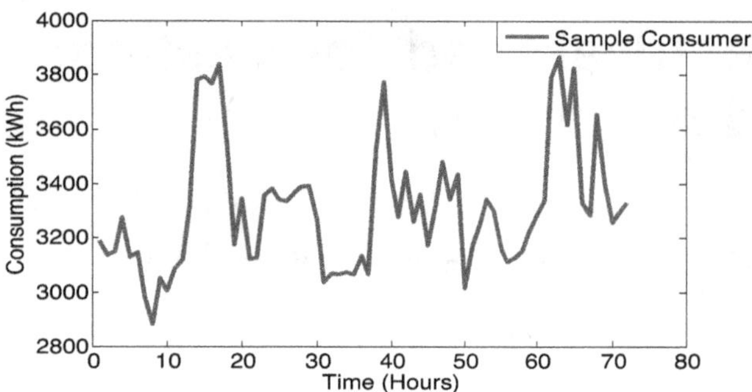

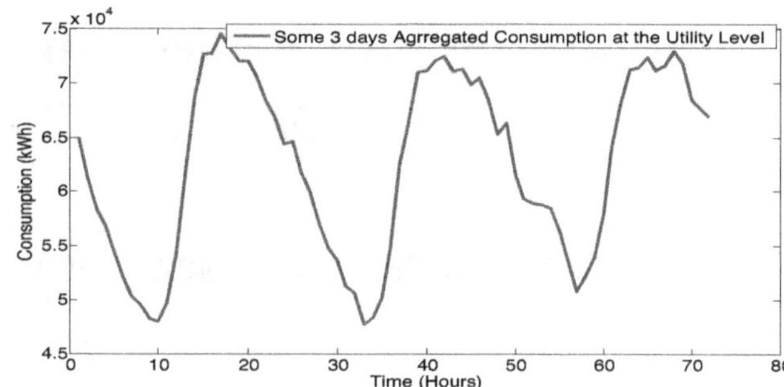

Figure 1: Three consecutive days of consumption for a Sample user and the corresponding aggregate consumption at the utility level in Enernoc Data Set

is small and highly variable, since it depends on the number of people staying in the home, the number and type of electrical appliances running at that particular time, and so on. That is why energy consumption at some home fluctuates heavily even in consecutive hours or in consecutive days from any regular pattern. The fluctuation is relatively low for small scale industry level consumers because of some fixed schedule of the industries.

The problem is comparatively easy when we forecast the energy at the utility level. This is because the fluctuations and the noise in the individual houses may cancel each other out while taking the sum. In this paper we deal with two real life data sets. First one is Enernoc data set where the individual consumers are small scale industries [1]. Second one is CER Ireland data set where individual consumers are different houses [2]. We assume there is only one utility company in each of the data sets who is supplying the electricity to all consumers. In Figure 1 and 2, we plot randomly selected three consecutive days of consumption for one sample consumer and the corresponding aggregate consumption for the utility company, for both of the data sets. It can be seen that in both of the figures, the aggregate consumption patterns are much more regular than individual consumption patterns. We explain the data sets in detail in Section 5.

Though the problem of load forecasting at an aggregate level has been studied extensively in literature, load forecasting for individual consumers is known to be a much more difficult problem. However, individual level load forecasting has become an important requirement in the context of upcoming schemes for demand response. It would also help consumers to plan accordingly in case of real-time and dynamic pricing. We address the problem of load forecasting at individual level in this paper. We also discussed the issues related to real-time load forecasting as required by some utility.

We also discuss the issue of aggregate level load forecasting in this paper. But our approach is significantly different from the traditional methods. Most of the existing aggregate level load forecasting methods only consider the aggregate level consumption data while forecasting. Our approach considers the individual level consumption data to give an accurate aggregate level forecasting. We design a novel clustering paradigm that aims to reduce the error in the aggregate forecast through suitable assignment of individuals to clusters. The main advantage of this method is that it intelligently uses the information from individual consumption patterns to get an accurate aggregate forecast. The details of this method is described in Section 4.

1.1 Contributions made in this paper

Following are the brief of the contributions made in this paper.

- We propose a context based medium term load forecasting technique for individual consumers. We have designed a novel short term forecasting algorithm by updating the medium term forecasts based on very recent past data. We also give a stylized real-time forecasting algorithm which uses the medium term and short term forecasting models proposed by us.

- We propose a novel clustering paradigm and propose a clustering algorithm which would cluster the consumers in such a way that when we forecast load for individual clusters and sum them up, we will get a better aggregate forecasting estimate.

- We implement our proposed algorithms on two publicly available real life data sets and show improvement in terms of both accuracy and running time over the existing state-of-the-art methods (details are given in section 5).

1.2 Paper Outlines

In the next section, we will briefly discuss some state-of-the-art load forecasting techniques. In Section 3, we will explain our load forecasting technique for individual consumers. In section 4, we will describe our clustering paradigm to forecast the load in the utility level. After that in section 5 we will experiment with two real life data sets and give the results of our proposed methods. In Section 6, we will conclude our work and discuss some possible future work in the same direction.

2. RELATED WORK

Load forecasting has been addressed in literature for a long time [3, 4]. With the invention of advanced metering infrastructure, the resolution of the available consumption data increases and it creates a new demand of forecasting in a high resolution. Many traditional approaches of forecasting have been applied on a utility or aggregate level consumption data directly. But they are not powerful enough

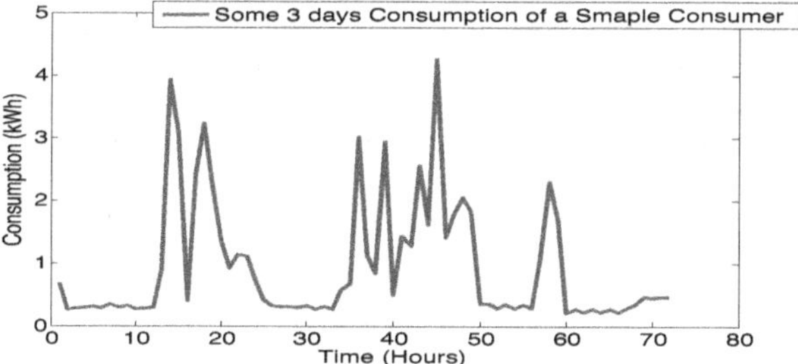

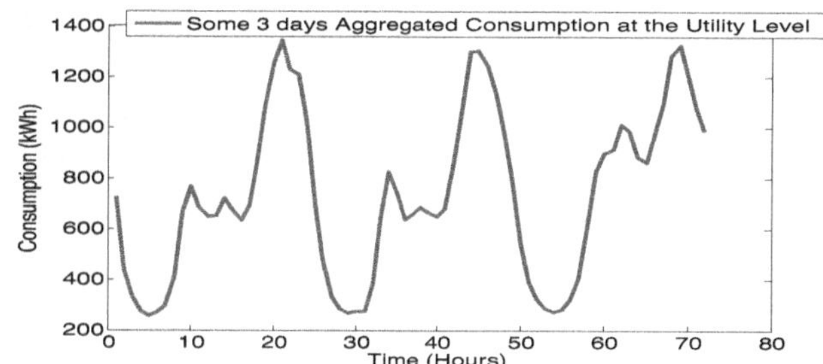

Figure 2: Three consecutive days of consumption for a Sample user and the corresponding aggregate consumption at the utility level in CER Ireland Data Set

to forecast the individual load due to high irregularity in individual consumption patterns. Recently algorithms have been developed for individual forecasting due to demand response and smart grids. In this section we discuss some of the forecasting methods for both aggregate and individual load prediction.

Different machine learning techniques have been used for electrical load forecasting. Multilayer perceptron and neural networks have been used extensively for load forecasting for a long time [3, 5]. Most of these techniques deal with short term forecasting. Use of support vector machine model [6, 7] for short term and medium term load forecasting has been used in [8] and [9] respectively. Gaussian process models have also been applied for short term forecasting [4]. Different types of time series analysis techniques including ARMA and ARIMA models have also been used for electricity load forecasting [10, 11]. Most of these machine learning algorithms and regression techniques tend to be increasingly complex [12]. This not only results in slow computational performance, but also makes it difficult to get intuitive insights into the results.

Recently specific models are being developed for home electricity prediction. Markovian models are used to model the home electricity consumption for studying demand response, transformer sizing, and distribution network simulation in [13]. Using different types of external context information to compute electrical baseline for contract based demand response has been implemented in [14]. A graphical model based appliance level load prediction algorithm for smart home management has been proposed in [15]. There are external changes that may be made to improve forecasting accuracy, including providing distributed storage [16].

Aggregate level load forecasting is also important for the utility to balance between the supply and demand of total energy. Traditional approaches use aggregate consumption data directly to forecast the load in aggregate level. Recently some approaches has been made to cluster individual consumption patterns and use prediction over cluster-level consumption data to forecast the aggregate load [17]. Some improvement for the aggregate level load forecasting via kernel spectral clustering of individual consumers has been shown in [18]. Experiments are conducted in [19] to assess the impact of smart meter grouping on the accuracy of forecasting algorithms for load prediction. But the proper justification of grouping individual consumers and a focused clustering mechanism with a goal to improve aggregate level forecasting is missing from most of the existing literature. We want to address this research gap in section 4 of this paper.

3. LOAD FORECASTING FOR INDIVIDUAL CONSUMERS

In this section, we develop a model for medium term load forecasting for individual consumers. We also demonstrate that the model can be extended for short term load forecasting through minor modifications.

3.1 Medium term forecasting

The medium term load forecasting model is similar in spirit to that developed in [14]. However, our algorithm selects the optimal context vector in an hourly basis (as opposed to a daily basis) and based on the minimum normalized variance (as opposed to simple variance) in past data corresponding to each context combination. We also give a detailed analysis of the algorithm in this section. The intuition behind this approach is explained below, and is summarized in Algorithm 1.

Algorithm 1 Context Based Medium Term Forecasting

Input: Consumption time series for individuals (y^1, y^2, ..., y^T), context variables $C_1, C_2, \cdots, C_r$
Output: Predicted Consumption values ($\bar{y}^{T+1}$, $\bar{y}^{T+2}$, ..., $\bar{y}^{T+L}$)
Take all possible combination of contexts, and call each combination as a context vector V_j, where $V_j \in V$
Assign consumption values corresponding to each of the context vectors V_j and the hour h. So, $CONS^h_{V_j} = \{y^t| \; V_j \subseteq contexts(t) \; and \; hour(t) = h\}$, $\forall V_j \in V$, and $h \in \{1, 2, \cdots, 24\}$
for $t \leftarrow (T+1) \rightarrow (T+L)$ **do**
  Assign, $h \leftarrow hour(t)$
  Consider each $V_j \subseteq contexts(t)$, and find the V_j for which the **normalized variance**[1]in $CONS^h_{V_j}$ is minimum. We call that context vector as V_{min}
  Find the mean of the set $CONS^h_{V_{min}}$ and assign it to $\bar{y}^{T+1}$
end for

The input to the algorithm is the time series of energy consumption for a single consumer. There is one consumption value y^{t_1} corresponding to each time stamp t_1 in the training data. We assume that there are T time stamps for each consumer in the training data. For the sake of simplicity we denote the consumption values as y^l instead of y^{t_l}, $\forall l = 1, 2, \cdots, T$. So the input to the algorithm is the time series $(y^1, y^2, \cdots, y^T)$. Based on this training data, we need to predict the consumption values for the consumer in the next L time stamps. Precisely, we need to estimate the values in the time series, $(y^{T+1}, y^{T+2}, \cdots, y^{T+L})$.

We introduce the set of context information corresponding to each time stamp present in the data. Context in general can be calendar context, weather context or any external meta information associated with the data. For example, if we consider the date January 04, 2015 in India, the set of context variables can be **Day Type** (weekday/ *weekend*), **Day of the Week** (*Sunday* to Saturday), **Month** (*January* to December), **Season** (Summer, *Winter*) etcetera. Clearly each context variable can take a specific value (specified in italic for the particular example) from the set of some possible values (mentioned within the parenthesis) for a particular time stamp. Let us denote these context variables by $C_1, C_2, \cdots, C_r$, where r is the total number of context variables we consider.

Clearly, corresponding to each date, there can be multiple context variables, and each of them will take some values. So we can take any combination of these context variables. For example, if we consider the date January 04, 2015, the context combinations can be {Sunday}, {Sunday, Winter}, {Weekend, Winter, Sunday} etcetera. We call each of these context combinations as one **Context Vector**. Therefore, {Sunday, Winter} is a specific context vector for the date January 04, 2015. Let us denote the set of all possible context vectors for any date as V. For any time stamp t, we assume that the function *contexts*(t) gives the set of values corresponding to all of the r contexts available. Similarly, the function *hour*(t) gives the hour (from the set $\{1, 2, \cdots, 24\}$) of the day associated with the time stamp t. With these preliminaries in place, we proceed to explain Algorithm 1.

This algorithm first constructs the set of all possible context vectors from the set of available context values. Then for each of the time stamps in the test set, we find the best hourly context vector which has lowest dispersion (measured by normalized variance) in the corresponding set of the consumption values in the input training data. As variance depends on the scale of the numbers, i.e., a set of large numbers tends to have a higher variance than a set of small numbers, we use normalized variance to select the best context vector. Using normalized variance would not prioritize context vectors corresponding to low consumption values over those having high consumption values. Once we get the best context vector for the time stamp t, we compute the estimate for the given time period by taking the mean of the consumption values corresponding to same context vector. Note that the set of consumption values corresponding to each context vector (the sets $CONS_{V_j}$, $CONS^h_{V_j}$ in Algorithm 1) can have repeated values, as a consumer can consume the same amount of energy at different time stamps.

[1]If X is a set of numbers, then $Normalized\ Variance(X) = Variance(X)/mean(X)$, if $mean(X) = 0$, we assume $Normalized\ Variance = \infty$

Typically, the number of context variables and their possible combinations is much smaller than the size of the training data set. If we assume that the number of context vectors is a constant, then the run **time complexity** of the algorithm is $O(T + L)$, which is linear in the total size of training and test sets. In summary, the proposed algorithm 1 exhibits the following benefits:

- It is simple to implement, and its run time complexity is linear in the total length of the time series.
- It can run efficiently with several classes of input, including cases where the time stamps are the only available context. The algorithm can also incorporate non-temporal information such as temperature, humidity in the form of other context variables.
- Sophisticated regression techniques over the filtered input set $CONS^h_{V_{min}}$, can be accommodated in step 8 of Algorithm 1 if required. We note that the algorithm exhibits superior performance in comparison with the state of the art, even with a simple mean estimate. A detailed analysis is provided in Section 5.

Since Algorithm 1 computes future estimates for one time series at a time, it is executed once for each consumer in the data set. We note that the current implementation assigns equal weight to each consumption reading in the training data. These weights may be modified in step 8 of Algorithm 1 to give different priorities to different time stamps in the training set. The (weighted) mean is used in this medium term algorithm, because we assume that the average consumption by a consumer will not change significantly in a period of a few days. This assumption is not valid for a forecast with a look-ahead of few years (when the value of L in algorithm 1 is very high).

3.2 Short Term Forecasting

In this paper, we refer to the short term as a time period of between 1 hour and a few days. In this section, we adapt the medium term forecasting algorithm for short term prediction. In a real-time set up, when data comes incrementally over time, the amount of data available for training also increases over time. Potentially, an hourly short term algorithm could be designed to include the new points in the training set after each hour and run Algorithm 1 to make predictions for the next few hours. This method would be analogous to the concept of model predictive control. However, such an algorithm would be inefficient because of the $O(T)$ time required for each run and cannot be used in real time when the size of the distribution network is very large. Hence in this section, we develop a novel method which will just update the forecast obtained by running algorithm 1 only once on the original training set, instead of running it on the updated training set again and again.

Let us assume that the medium term forecasting algorithm has been run on a data set that ends excluding the latest D days in the past. So there is additional data available for the latest D days of consumption, which have not been included in the training data. We call these D days as the **Validation interval**. The short term forecasting algorithm combines (i) the medium term forecast from the historical data set, and (ii) corrections of medium term forecasts based on consumption data in the validation interval, to produce short term predictions. This method balances the fast computational characteristics of training the algorithm on a fixed data set (the training interval) and then updating the forecasts based on latest consumption values (validation interval), with the accuracy of the medium term algorithm.

One simple way to update this will be subtracting the average of some m error terms in the validation interval from the medium term estimate. We assume that the set M consists of the lag of these time stamps corresponding to those m error terms. For example, to get a short term forecast at any time stamp t, if the error terms to be considered are at time stamp $t - t_1$, $t - t_2$ and so on, the set M will contain the values t_1, t_2 and so on. We propose algorithm 2 to construct the set M. We are going to explain it in the next few paragraphs. So at some time stamp t, where the medium term forecast $\bar{y}^t$ is available, we can calculate the **short term forecast** $\hat{y}^t$ as,

$$\hat{y}^t = \bar{y}^t - \sum_{t' \in M} (\bar{y}^{t-t'} - y^{t-t'})/m \qquad (1)$$

Figure 4 would help us to understand the intuition behind equation 1. In this figure, there is some gap (error) between the medium term forecasts and the original consumption, for a particular consumer from Enernoc data set. This happens as the medium term forecasting is based on the fixed training set which can be consumption data upto few months back. Now we want to capture this gap by the term $\sum_{t' \in M}(\bar{y}^{t-t'} - y^{t-t'})$ in RHS of eqation 1 and then adjust the medium term forecast $\bar{y}^t$ so that the expected gap can be reduced.

Algorithm 2 Finding the set M for a p-time stamps ahead Short Term Forecasting

1: **Input:** An individual consumption time series $(y^1, y^2, \cdots, y^{T_1}, y^{T_1+1}, \cdots, y^{T_2})$; Medium term forecasts $(\bar{y}^{T_1+1}, \cdots, \bar{y}^{T_2})$ using algorithm 1; Parameter h which is the length from which m time stamps should be chosen
2: **Output:** Compute the members in the set M, where the cardinality of M is m
3: Assume that the validation time interval is from time stamp $T_1 + 1$ to T_2 where $T_1 < T_2$.
4: Find the prediction error, where error = (predicted consumption − original consumption), occurred in each time stamp in the validation set.
5: **for** $k \leftarrow p \rightarrow p + h - 1$ **do**
6: Compute the correlation coefficient of the error occurred at time t to that at time $(t - k)$, $\forall t = T1 + k, \cdots, T2$, and insert the value in $(k-p+1)$th position of some array $Corr$.
7: **end for**
8: Take the highest m values from the array $Corr$. If jth term is selected from the array $Corr$, Insert $(j + p - 1)$ in M

We have used correlation analysis to construct the set M in algorithm 2. Intuitively, we check the auto-correlation of the error terms with different lags in the validation time interval. Then we are using those error values that are highly correlated (positive correlation) to compute the expected error between the actual consumption and the medium term forecast at the time stamp where the short term forecast is needed. The overall short term forecasting method we are proposing has several benefits as follows.

- The training set can be fixed for some long time even when the data is coming in real time. We just need to run the algorithm 1 only once to get the medium term forecasts and then at the time of short term prediction, we just need to update the medium term forecast based on the past error terms as in equation 1. In general m is a fixed quantity and very small compared to the size of the training interval. So we can get the short term forecast in $O(1)$ time complexity.

- Algorithm 2 is needed to get the set M. In real time set up, it is in general sufficient to run it only once per day. Run time complexity of algorithm 2 is $O(h(T_2 - T_1))$, which is linear on the size of validation interval.

3.3 Real-time Forecasting

We demonstrate the combination of the short term and medium term algorithms, by instantiating the procedure for a real time, one hour look ahead period, and present an online procedure in algorithm 3. We assume that the input time series also contains hourly consumption values. We also assume that the training set is updated after each day, and that the medium term algorithm is executed at the beginning of each day. The short term algorithm is executed every hour.

Algorithm 3 Real Time Forecasting

1: **Input:** An individual consumption time series $(y^1, y^2, \cdots, y^T)$; Set of Context Variables $C_1, C_2, \cdots, C_m$, The incoming real time actual consumption values
2: **Output:** Real Time consumption forecasts
3: Assume that the last 24 hours of the input time series is validation interval, and the rest is training interval
4: Run Algorithm 1 to get the forecasts $(\bar{y}^{T-23}, \bar{y}^{T-22}, \cdots, \bar{y}^T, \bar{y}^{T+1}, \bar{y}^{T+2}, \cdots, \bar{y}^{T+24})$
5: Compute the error terms $(\bar{y}^t - y^t)$ in validation interval
6: Run algorithm 2 to construct the set M
7: **while** (at each new hour t) **do**
8: Note the actual consumption y^t
9: Compute the error term $(\bar{y}^t - y^t)$
10: Compute the forecast (short term) $\hat{y}^{t+1}$ for the hour $t + 1$ from equation 1 and output it
11: **end while**

4. EFFECT OF CLUSTERING ON AGGREGATE LOAD FORECASTING

Building upon the individual load forecasting algorithm presented in the previous section, we now present a method for aggregate (multiple consumers) load forecasting. Throughout this paper, we perform aggregation over multiple consumers only (as opposed to aggregation over time). The utility level consumption at some point of time t is the sum of the consumption by all the consumers under consideration. We assume that there are n consumers supplied by the utility. Traditional methods for aggregate load forecasting directly use historical aggregate load data. However, this approach sometimes ignores useful relations between consumption of two or more consumers (referred to in this paper as *consumer segments*. In this section, we will discuss about

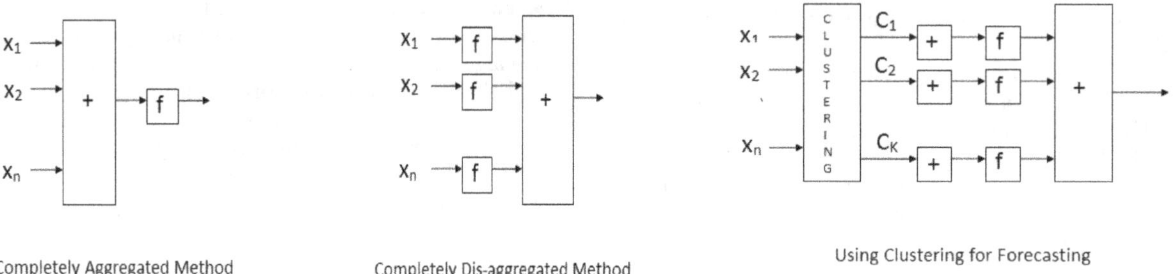

Figure 3: Different Level of Aggregation for aggregate level Load Forecasting. Here the blocks with symbol '+' take the sum of the input vectors and the blocks with symbol 'f' forecast the future values for its input vector. x_i's are individual consumption time series

a method which would use this information for aggregate level load forecasting.

The formal definition of the problem is as follows. Let us denote the set of n consumers as $y_1, y_2, \ldots, y_n$, and the consumption history of consumer i as $y_i = \{y_i^1, y_i^2, \ldots, y_i^T\}$, $\forall i = 1, 2, \ldots, n$. Here, y_i^t is the energy consumption of ith consumer during time period t. The total number of historical time periods is T. Since we are interested in predicting the energy consumption at the utility level, the total energy consumption can be represented by, $y_A = (y_A^1, y_A^2, \ldots, y_A^T)$, where $y_A^t = \sum_{i=1}^{n} y_i^t$. There are three possible approaches to compute load predictions at the utility level. One is to use the vector y_A as the feature and predict over this. We refer to this method for prediction as the *completely aggregated method.* The second method would be to perform load prediction for each y_i, $\forall i = 1, 2, \ldots, n$, and then take the sum of the individual predictions to get an overall estimate for the aggregate level. We call this method the *completely disaggregated method.* Finally, a third possible approach is using clustering for forecasting where, we (i) cluster the individual consumers into specific segments, (ii) estimate segment-level future consumption directly based on segment level consumption data, and (iii) combine the segment estimates to forecast utility level consumption. These three techniques are explained in the Figure 3. We would like to take the third approach in this work. We need to design the segmentation procedure based on the knowledge that the ultimate goal is to accurately predict the load at the utility level.

The intuition for clustering in this context is as follows. It is known that an accurate prediction for each individual consumer is difficult, due to the irregularity of individual consumption patterns. To overcome this problem, we attempt to group the consumers in our data set such that individual variations in their consumption tend to mutually cancel each other out. An illustration of this idea would be two factory buildings producing the same parts for a given manufacturer. Depending on the production load in each building, the individual consumption may vary. However, if they produce the same total number of parts for the manufacturer, their combined consumption will be smoother than their individual time series. Thus the objective is to put two or more consumers in the same cluster if their total consumption is easier to predict than their individual consumption.

The performance of the segment (group) based algorithm exceeds that for the aggregate method, when (i) consumers in a single cluster are highly similar, and (ii) different clusters are highly dissimilar. Consider a scenario where any single customer's time series belongs to one of two well defined types, each defined by a set of n parameters. The underlying functional structure is known, but the parameter values have to be estimated in the presence of noise. A direct utility-level (completely aggregated) forecasting method would have to compute $2n$ parameters simultaneously. However, the group based algorithm would only be required to compute n parameters at a time. As the data is limited, it would be easier to learn n parameters than $2n$ parameters and hence group-based forecasting would perform better than utility-level forecasting in this case.

Similarly, for another set of data, where the noise in the time series are highly negatively correlated, a completely disaggregated method would not use the negative correlation among the individual time series, and may not perform well for an aggregate level forecasting. But in our group-level approach (using clustering), we would cluster time series in such a way that total noise in each cluster gets minimized due to negative correlation, and hence it is likely that group-based approach would perform better than completely disaggregated method in this case.

The total error in the validation data set is frequently used as a measure of 'cost' associated with forecasting in a machine learning context. Formally, if $x = (x^1, x^2, \cdots, x^T)$ is the input time series to some forecasting algorithm and $Cost(x)$ is a measure of the quality of forecasting by the algorithm on the input x, then lesser the value of the cost, better would be the quality of forecasting. For some ML based forecasting techniques like LS or SVM regression, the objective functions used in the optimization to minimize, can also be used as the 'cost function' in equation 2. Given some definition of the cost function, the problem of clustering consumers to get a more accurate forecast for the aggregate level consumption can be formalized as follows.

Given the set of n individual consumption time series $y_1, y_2, \cdots, y_n$; where $y_i = (y_i^1, y_i^2, \cdots, y_i^T)$. We would like to solve the following optimisation problem,

$$\min_{K} \min_{C_1,\ldots,C_K} \sum_{k=1}^{K} Cost(y_{C_k})$$

subject to,

$$\begin{aligned} & y^t_{C_k} = \sum_{i \in C_k} y^t_i; \ \forall t = 1, 2, \cdots, T \\ & \bigcup_{k=1}^{K} C_k = \{1, 2, \cdots, n\} \\ & \bigcap_{k_1 \neq k_2} C_k = \emptyset; \ \forall k_1, k_2 = 1, 2, \cdots, K \end{aligned} \tag{2}$$

Instead of a direct solution of the problem formulated in equation 2, we propose a fast greedy algorithm which computes a local minimum of it.

Algorithm 4 Clustering of Consumers for aggregate Forecasting

1: **Input:** n individual consumption time series $y_1, y_2, \cdots y_n$; Number of clusters K
2: **Output:** K clusters $C_1, C_2, \cdots, C_K$
3: Take some random permutation of the set of consumers. Index the consumers as $(1, 2, \cdots, n)$ after the permutation
4: Initialize K clusters by $C_k \leftarrow y_k$, $\forall k = 1, \cdots, K$
5: Compute y_{C_k} as defined in equation 2, $\forall k = 1, \cdots, K$
6: Compute $Cost(y_{C_k})$, $\forall k = 1, \cdots, K$
7: **for** $i \leftarrow (K+1) \rightarrow n$ **do**
8: Computer $y_{\{C_k \cup \{y_i\}\}} = \sum_{t=1}^{T} (y^t_{C_k} + y^t_i)$, $\forall k = 1, \cdots, K$
9: Compute $Cost(y_{\{C_k \cup \{y_i\}\}})$, $\forall k = 1, \cdots, K$
10: Find $j = \underset{k}{\operatorname{argmin}} \{Cost(y_{\{C_k \cup \{y_i\}\}}) + \sum_{k', k' \neq k} Cost(y_{C_{k'}})\}$
11: Assign $C_j \leftarrow C_j \cup \{i\}$
12: **end for**

Algorithm 4 is a greedy algorithm which clusters the set of consumers into K groups. It initializes the clusters randomly with one consumer each. The remaining consumers are added one at a time in random order. Each consumer i is assigned to a cluster j such that the total cost of the K clusters, with $i \in j$, is minimised over all $j \in \{1, \ldots, K\}$.

The iterative loop at step 7 of Algorithm 4 runs $(n - K)$ times, and in each iteration, the steps 8 to 11 require $O(KT)$ operations (assuming that calculating the $Cost()$ function for a time series should not take more than $O(T)$ time). So the total run time complexity of the algorithm is $O(nKT)$. The number of clusters K is generally much smaller than the total number of consumers n. As the size of the input to the algorithm is $O(nT)$ (n consumers and T time stamps), so the run time complexity of the algorithm is linear in the size of its input. It is to be noted that the utility does not need to cluster consumers in real-time. They just need to cluster the consumers once in a relatively long time period (like once per 2-days/week) with the assumption that clustering would not change in that time period. Once the clustering is available, they just need to predict the total consumption over these fixed clusters in real-time and need to take the sum of all those estimates to get the utility-level prediction.

Now we will try to define such a 'cost function' for the proposed medium term forecasting algorithm 1, so as to able to use it as the forecasting module in algorithm 4. Algorithm 1 assigns the best context vector (in terms of least normalized variance) to each consumption value (step 7). Therefore, we define the quality of forecasting based on the total normalized variance over all time stamps. More precisely, we divide each consumption time series $x = (x^1, x^2, \cdots, x^T)$, of length T into training and validation intervals. Then we train algorithm 1 on the training interval and predict the consumption values in the validation interval to get the sum of total normalized variance of the sets $CONS^h_{V_{min}}$ over the validation interval ($T+1 \leq t \leq T+L$, as in the steps 5-9 in algorithm 1). We can consider this sum as $Cost(x)$, which is the cost of forecasting over the time series x. Clearly lesser the value of that sum, better should be the quality of forecasting by the forecasting algorithm 1.

5. EXPERIMENTAL RESULTS

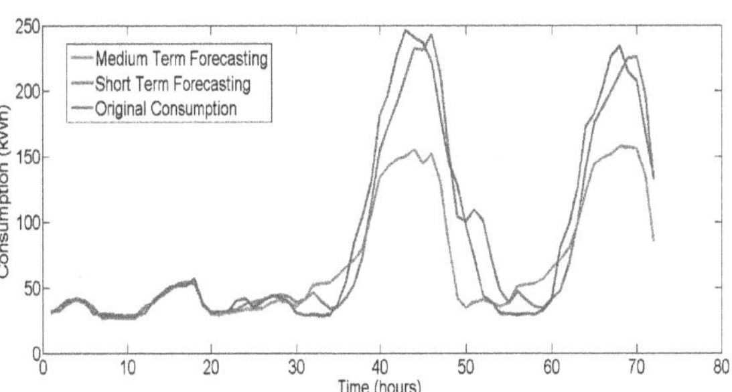

Figure 4: Original consumption and predicted consumption for a particular consumer from Enernoc data set

In this section, we have tested our algorithms and compare with other state-of-the-art methods on two publicly available real world consumption data sets. We evaluate the performance of both the approaches - (i) Individual level load forecasting, (ii) Aggregate level load forecasting. The goal of this evaluation is to explain the results of the proposed algorithms on real life data, demonstrate the scalability of them and show the efficiency by comparing with other state-of-the-art methods.

5.1 Description of Data Sets

The first data set we have used is is Enernoc data set [1], which consists of power consumption data from different industrial consumers. Second one is CER Ireland data set [2], which consists of power consumption data from residential consumers. As expected, consumption behavior of residential consumers are more irregular compared to industrial consumers. As discussed earlier in section 1, we have plotted some 3 day's hourly consumption of a randomly selected consumer and the total aggregate consumption from both the data sets in figure 1 and 2 respectively. We have chosen the data sets intentionally to check the performance of our proposed algorithms on two different types of consumers, i.e., industrial and residential.

For convenience of our analysis, we have used hourly consumption values in both the data sets. The Enernoc data set contains real time energy consumption of 100 different

Algorithms Used	Enernoc Data			CER Ireland Data		
	Medium Term (SMAPE)	Short Term (SMAPE)	Total Time (Sec.)	Medium Term (SMAPE)	Short Term (SMAPE)	Total Time (Sec.)
Linear LS Regression	14.95	9.297	13.431	33.957	33.61	105.433
SVM Regression (Linear Kernel)	15.084	9.33	1324.985	35.152	33.515	45157.109
SVM Regression (RBF Kernel)	15.083	9.312	4197.87	35.86	33.49	116077.079
Gaussian Process	18.47	9.214	20373.094	34.829	32.933	163926.485
Multilayer Perceptron	14.191	9.132	75.564	35.79	33.611	1055.104
Proposed Context Based Forecasting	**9.847**	**7.541**	**7.757**	**31.995**	**32.796**	**64.544**

Table 1: Performance of Different Algorithms for Individual Level Forecasting on Enernoc and CER Ireland Data Sets

industrial consumers from January 2012 to December 2012. For our experiments, we divide the one year data into two parts. We have used the first six months of data as training set and the next six months of data for testing set. In some of the cases, we have further used some parts of training data for validation purpose.

The CER Ireland data set contains real time energy consumption of 782 residential consumers (after removing missing values) from July 2009 to December 2010. The data was collected as a part of dynamic pricing trial. So we consider that subset of consumers who were in a single control group. After removing consumers with missing values, the total number of consumers used for our experiments is 782. Here we use the first one year of data for training purpose and last six months of data for testing purpose. For both of these data sets, measurements were obtained by using smart meters in the individual consumers level.

5.2 Performance Measurement

We have evaluated the performance of our algorithms both in terms of accuracy and run time. Checking the accuracy of forecasting algorithms is itself an important problem in the domain of machine learning and time series analysis. Thee are several measures of errors like Mean Absolute Error (MAE), Mean Absolute Percentage Error (MAPE), Mean Square Error (MSE) etc. [20]. But each of these measures have some drawbacks. For example, MAE, MSE are not scale invariant. Some of them like MAPE do not have alower or upper bound on the percentage error term. They are also very prone to outliers in the data. To overcome these problems, we use Symmetric Mean Absolute Percentage Error (SMAPE) [21, 22]. SMAPE is defined as,

$$SMAPE = \frac{\sum_{t=1}^{T} |f^t - y^t|}{\sum_{t=1}^{T} |f^t| + |y^t|} \quad (3)$$

Here $y^1, y^2, \cdots, y^T$ and $f^1, f^2, \cdots, f^T$ are respectively original and forecasted consumption time series over T time stamps. Clearly lesser the value of SMAPE, better would be the quality of forecasting.

To check the running time of our algorithm, we note the total running tine in seconds. All the experiments are done in a personal laptop with 8GB Ram and Intel(R) Core(TM) i5-3360M CPU @ 2.80GHz processor. IBM Informix Dynamic Server has been used to store the data into the database.

5.3 Results

Throughout all the experiments in this paper, for medium term forecasting, we train all the model only once on the training data. We use this trained model to forecast over all the testing interval. So the medium term forecast for Enernoc data can be *upto 6 months* (length of testing interval) ahead prediction and similarly for CER Ireland data, it can be *upto 12 months* ahead prediction. For short term forecasting, we have done a *24 hours ahead* prediction. The look ahead period for both medium term and short term forecasting will be same for the rest of this paper. To get the short term forecasts, we use equation 1 along with algorithm 2 to update the estimates obtained from medium term forecasting, as discussed in section 3.2. We run algorithm 2 to find the set M for both the data sets. We choose $m = 3$, i.e., we will update medium term forecast based on the three highest correlated error terms from the validation interval. It turns out that for majority of the consumers in both the data sets, the set M is $\{1, 2, 3\}$, i.e., the set of last three hours. So for the experiments in this section, we would use the update equation 1 as follows,

$$\hat{y}^t = \bar{y}^t - \sum_{t'=1}^{3} (\bar{y}^{t-t'} - y^{t-t'})/3 \quad (4)$$

We use different regression techniques like Linear Least Square Regression, SVM regression (with two different kernels), Gaussian Process and Multilayer Perceptron. We use the inbuilt function libraries available in Weka [23] to use these techniques. We divide each time stamp into two features, date (for example, January 17, 2012 in Unix time format) and hour (for example, 13th hour) and feed them along with consumption values to these regression techniques.

5.3.1 *Individual Forecasting results*

For individual forecasting, we consider each of the consumers from a data set separately. Then we feed the training interval of their consumption time series to different algorithms and present the performance in table 1. It can be seen easily that Our proposed Context based Forecasting techniques outperform all other state-of-the-art algorithms used for comparison, both in terms of quality of prediction (in SMAPE) and running time (in seconds). For Enernoc data set, the improvement is quite significant both in terms of SMAPE and seconds; where in CER Ireland data set, our algorithm performs slightly better than others in terms of SMAPE, but the time it takes to execute is significantly less than others. As the error values are always high (more than

Aggregation Methods	Enernoc Data set	CER Ireland Data Set
Completely aggregate method	3.452	2.834
Completely Dis-aggregate method	3.112	3.089
Using k-means (K=3)	3.098	2.741
Using k-means (K=4)	3.114	2.710
Using Proposed Clustering Algorithm 4	**2.99** (K=22)	**2.64** (K=12)

Table 2: Performance (in SMAPE) of Context Based Forecasting with different types of Aggregation Methods for 24 hours ahead aggregate Level Forecasting on Enernoc and CER Ireland Data Sets

30%) in CER Ireland data set, it can be concluded that the consumption patterns from individual houses in this data set are highly irregular, or it needs more external information like temperature, humidity, occupancy to correctly find the pattern in the consumption data.

In Figure 4, we have shown the medium term and short term forecasting along with original power consumption for 3 consecutive days (72 hours) of a randomly taken consumer from Enernoc data set. One can see that short term forecasting is closer to original consumption compared to that for long term prediction, which matches to our intuition.

5.3.2 Aggregate Forecasting Results

Here we want to evaluate the efficiency of our consumer segmentation framework for an accurate forecasting in aggregate level. We use our medium term forecasting algorithm 1 and define the *Cost*() function as discussed in the last paragraph of section 4. Then we apply the proposed clustering algorithm 4 to cluster the consumers into K segments. As the number of clusters is unknown here, we use multiple values of K and choose the one which gives the lowest sum of the *Cost*() function over all clusters. It turns out that the number of clusters in Enernoc data set is 22 and that in CER Ireland data set is 12. Then we find the segment-level consumption time series over each segment. We apply our medium term forecasting algorithm (1 and 2) for a 24 hours ahead forecasting over each of these segment-level time series. Finally we add these forecasts to get the utility level or aggregate level forecasting. We present the results in table 2. To compare the performance of our technique with other baselines, we use the same medium term forecasting with different aggregation techniques - (i)completely aggregated method (as discussed in section 4), (ii) completely disaggregated method, (iii) Clustering consumers using k-means algorithm [24]. We check the aggregate level forecasting performance with different number of clusters in k-means algorithm and presented the top two results in table 2.

There can be some interesting conclusions which can be drawn from the results obtained in table 2. From the first two rows of the table, we can say that completely dis-aggregate method outperforms completely aggregate method for Enernoc data set. But it is reverse for the CER Ireland data set. So it is not possible to compare the aggregate and dis-aggregate methods irrespective of any particular data set. We can also see that our proposed clustering algorithm 4 outperforms all other aggregation methods of table 2. This is because some general clustering algorithm like k-means may fail to catch the ultimate goal of an accurate aggregate forecasting in this case. But our proposed algorithm clusters the data with that specific goal and that is why it is outperforming other methods.

We also try to compare the performance of our medium term forecasting algorithm along with the proposed clustering algorithm 4 for aggregate level load forecasting with other state-of-the-art regression techniques. We use those regression techniques in a completely disaggregated fashion for aggregate level forecasting. The results are presented in table 3. Again it can be seen that the algorithm proposed by us outperforms other algorithms used for comparison, on both the data sets.

6. CONCLUSIONS AND FUTURE WORK

In this paper, we have proposed fast, scalable and efficient algorithms for electrical load forecasting for both individual and aggregate power consumption. We tackle the problems of medium term and short term forecasting in this paper. The forecasting algorithms proposed by us are easy to implement, but still outperforms many state-of-the-art forecasting techniques. The algorithms can work on minimum data (consumption values at different time stamps), but still different types of context information (like different calendar contexts, weather contexts etc.) can easily be used with them to improve the accuracy. We presented the algorithms with the format and constraints so that they can be applied in real online systems by some utility. We also give a framework for intelligently group the individual consumers to improve the aggregate level load forecasting accuracy. We evaluated our algorithms on two publicly available consumption data sets consisting of two different types of consumers.

Based on the work presented in this paper, we identified few more interesting problems to solve in future. As discussed, long term forecasting is another important and harder problem than medium term and short term forecasting. An accurate long term forecasting needs different types of social and economic information apart from the context information. It would be nice to check if it is possible to extend the algorithms presented in this paper for long term forecasting.

We have also dealt with the problem of different types of aggregation of consumers for an efficient utility (aggregate) level forecasting. It would be great to see some theoretical bound on the generalization error of the aggregate level load forecasting. Group-based approach may perform worse than completely aggregated approach in case when our choice of k (the number of clusters for group-based approach) is very bad. So one can also find analytical way to determine the value of k for this approach. It would also be interesting to find the relation between the cluster size and the accuracy of cluster-level forecasting. This types of studies are required for load forecasting in transformer level, or for the demand response systems for a group of consumers.

Algorithm	Enernoc Data set	CER Ireland Data Set
Linear LS Regression	5.168	5.06
SVM Regression (Linear Kernel)	5.243	4.819
SVM Regression (RBF Kernel)	5.231	4.698
Gaussian Process	5.031	4.731
Multilayer Perceptron	5.071	4.881
Context Based Forecasting with Proposed Clustering	**2.99**	**2.64**

Table 3: Performance (in SMAPE) of Different Algorithms for 24 hours ahead Aggregate Level Forecasting on Enernoc and CER Ireland Data Sets

7. REFERENCES

[1] EnerNOC, "2012 Commercial Energy Consumption Data," http://open.enernoc.com/data/.

[2] Electricity customer behaviour trial. The Commission for Energy Regulation (CER), 2012.

[3] D. Park, M. El-Sharkawi, R. Marks, L. Atlas, and M. Damborg, "Electric load forecasting using an artificial neural network," *IEEE Transactions on Power Systems*, vol. 6, no. 2, pp. 442–449, May 1991.

[4] H. Mori and M. Ohmi, "Probabilistic short-term load forecasting with gaussian processes," in *Intelligent Systems Application to Power Systems, 2005. Proceedings of the 13th International Conference on.* IEEE, 2005, pp. 6–pp.

[5] H. S. Hippert, C. E. Pedreira, and R. C. Souza, "Neural networks for short-term load forecasting: A review and evaluation," *Power Systems, IEEE Transactions on*, vol. 16, no. 1, pp. 44–55, 2001.

[6] C. J. Burges, "A tutorial on support vector machines for pattern recognition," *Data mining and knowledge discovery*, vol. 2, no. 2, pp. 121–167, 1998.

[7] D. Basak, S. Pal, and D. C. Patranabis, "Support vector regression," *Neural Information Processing-Letters and Reviews*, vol. 11, no. 10, pp. 203–224, 2007.

[8] Y.-c. LI, T.-j. FANG, and E.-k. YU, "Study of support vector machines for short-term load forecasting [j]," *Proceedings of the Csee*, vol. 6, p. 010, 2003.

[9] B.-J. Chen, M.-W. Chang, and C.-J. Lin, "Load forecasting using support vector machines: A study on eunite competition 2001," *Power Systems, IEEE Transactions on*, vol. 19, no. 4, pp. 1821–1830, 2004.

[10] S.-J. Huang and K.-R. Shih, "Short-term load forecasting via arma model identification including non-gaussian process considerations," *Power Systems, IEEE Transactions on*, vol. 18, no. 2, pp. 673–679, 2003.

[11] M. Cho, J. Hwang, and C. Chen, "Customer short term load forecasting by using arima transfer function model," in *Energy Management and Power Delivery, 1995. Proceedings of EMPD'95., 1995 International Conference on*, vol. 1. IEEE, 1995, pp. 317–322.

[12] W. Hong, "Electric load forecasting by seasonal recurrent SVR (support vector regression) with chaotic artificial bee colony algorithm," *Energy*, vol. 36, no. 9, pp. 5568–5578, September 2011.

[13] O. Ardakanian, S. Keshav, and C. Rosenberg, "Markovian models for home electricity consumption," in *Proceedings of the 2nd ACM SIGCOMM workshop on Green networking.* ACM, 2011, pp. 31–36.

[14] V. Chandan, T. Ganu, T. K. Wijaya, M. Minou, G. Stamoulis, G. Thanos, and D. P. Seetharam, "idr: Consumer and grid friendly demand response system," in *The 5th ACM International Conference on Future Energy Systems (e-Energy" 14)*, no. EPFL-CONF-198476, 2014.

[15] N. C. Truong, J. McInerney, L. Tran-Thanh, E. Costanza, and S. D. Ramchurn, "Forecasting multi-appliance usage for smart home energy management," in *Proceedings of the Twenty-Third international joint conference on Artificial Intelligence.* AAAI Press, 2013, pp. 2908–2914.

[16] D. Ilic, S. Karnouskos, and P. G. D. Silva, "Improving load forecast in prosumer clusters by varying energy storage size," in *Powertech Grenoble*, France, June 2013.

[17] M. Misiti, Y. Misiti, G. Oppenheim, J.-M. Poggi *et al.*, "Optimized clusters for disaggregated electricity load forecasting," *Revstat*, vol. 8, pp. 105–124, 2010.

[18] C. Alzate and M. Sinn, "Improved electricity load forecasting via kernel spectral clustering of smart meters," in *Data Mining (ICDM), 2013 IEEE 13th International Conference on.* IEEE, 2013, pp. 943–948.

[19] D. Ilić, P. G. da Silva, S. Karnouskos, and M. Jacobi, "Impact assessment of smart meter grouping on the accuracy of forecasting algorithms," in *Proceedings of the 28th Annual ACM Symposium on Applied Computing.* ACM, 2013, pp. 673–679.

[20] S. Makridakis, S. C. Wheelwright, and R. J. Hyndman, *Forecasting methods and applications.* John Wiley & Sons, 2008.

[21] B. E. Flores, "A pragmatic view of accuracy measurement in forecasting," *Omega*, vol. 14, no. 2, pp. 93–98, 1986.

[22] J. S. Armstrong and L.-R. Forecasting, "From crystal ball to computer," *New York ua*, 1985.

[23] M. Hall, E. Frank, G. Holmes, B. Pfahringer, P. Reutemann, and I. H. Witten, "The weka data mining software: an update," *ACM SIGKDD explorations newsletter*, vol. 11, no. 1, pp. 10–18, 2009.

[24] A. K. Jain, M. N. Murty, and P. J. Flynn, "Data clustering: a review," *ACM computing surveys (CSUR)*, vol. 31, no. 3, pp. 264–323, 1999.

Evaluating the Value of Flexibility in Energy Regulation Markets

Bijay Neupane
Aalborg University
bn21@cs.aau.dk

Torben Bach Pedersen
Aalborg University
tbp@cs.aau.dk

Bo Thiesson
Aalborg University
thiesson@cs.aau.dk

ABSTRACT

In this paper, we perform an econometric analysis on the benefits of introducing flexibility in the Danish/Nordic regulating power market. The paper investigates the relationships between market power prices and regulation volumes, in order to quantify the effects of flexibility on regulating power prices. Further, we analyze the benefit for various types of flexibility and market objectives, to detect the type of energy flexibility that maximizes the benefits. Results show that if 3.87% of total demand is flexible, the market can reduce the regulation cost by 49% and the regulation volume by 29.4%.

Keywords

Econometric analysis; flexibility; demand management.

1. INTRODUCTION

Nord pool is the common electricity market for the Nordic countries, with a history back to the 1990's. A major portion of the electricity demands in the Nordic region is fulfilled by Renewable Energy Sources (RES), with wind power accounting for 6% of the total power generation, increasing at the rate of 4 TWh per year [11]. Further, in 2014, wind power contributed $\approx$ 39% of total electricity demand in Denmark. This high dependence on weather conditions creates huge challenges in demand management, which would often result in market imbalances if not controlled by other means. In Denmark, the balancing is controlled by a separate, perhaps external, Balance Responsible Party (BRP). The BRP is financially responsible for imbalances, which have traditionally been handled by trading in the regulating power market. The total volume of regulating power market for the DK1 (West Denmark) price area was 395.4 GWh in 2013, with a maximum power imbalance of 750 MW [11].

In order to reduce the cost of regulation, the market adopts various approaches for bidding. One of them is using the power prediction for RES and bid accordingly. There has been improvements in the prediction techniques for RES [6] [14], but the prediction error remains too high. The higher prediction error causes higher imbalance in the market, consequently increasing the regulation cost. An experiment for estimating the cost associated with wind power prediction error has been performed in [5]. It shows that, depending on the prediction horizon and granularity, the prediction error can reduce the total revenue by up to 10%. However, improvement in prediction accuracy alone is not enough to confront the demand management challenges, since the weather condition can change rapidly and the demand may also change unexpectedly. Therefore, a market capable of providing rapid reaction is required to mitigate the imbalance caused due to a sudden change in supply and demand.

Further, various optimization techniques for bidding strategies considering the imbalance penalty has been studied in [7] [15] [3]. An optimal bidding strategy recognizing the imbalance penalty and allowed imbalance band has been discussed in [15]. Further, two different approaches for tuning the optimal bidding strategy to account the fluctuations of the generated power has been discussed in [7]. The study shows that, with the proposed approaches energy producer can increase their revenue by up to 28.7%. Most of the previous studies focus on the bidding strategy or improvement in the prediction, in order to reduce the penalty of imbalance. In addition, various techniques for integrating household devices into demand side management for leveling of fluctuating RES production has been discussed in [9] [4]. In contrast, this paper discusses a dynamic energy market that utilizes the *flexibility* in energy demand to confront demand management challenges, as well as to reduce the cost of imbalance (regulation cost). A flexibility can be considered as a two-dimensional object representing the time and the amount dimensions, detailed in Section 3.

In order to facilitate flexibility in a dynamic energy market, the TotalFlex [2] project, implements a mechanism to express and utilize the concept of the *flex-offer* proposed in the EU FP7 project MIRABEL [1]. This flex-offer framework addresses the challenges of balancing the variations in RES energy production and consumption by communicating a negotiation in the form of flexible consumption (or production) offers. The integration of flexibility into the energy market system is supported by advancements in the Danish/Nordic energy market and is of importance for accomplishing the Danish national power goal of complete independence of fossil fuels by 2050. To our knowledge, this paper is first to quantify the benefit of dynamic flexibility market that utilizes flex-offers for demand management.

e-Energy'15, July 14–17, 2015, Bangalore, India.

http://dx.doi.org/10.1145/2768510.2768540.

The minimum latency required for the realization of the flex-offer concept is a few minutes (5-10 Minutes), which includes time from the generation of flex-offers to the final scheduling of the flex-offers. Therefore, the concept is targeted at services that permit the required latency such as day-ahead market, regulation market, etc., rather than at services with very short latency times, e.g., typical ancillary services. Further, the concept reduces the imbalance problem ahead of the real time and hence helps the services with very short latency times. In this paper, we mainly focus on an econometric assessment of the benefits of introducing flexibility into the energy regulation market. Here, the benefit is measured in terms of the reduction in regulation cost and/or regulation volume that a BRP (market) can achieve. A positive result from experiments could motivate various market operators such as Transmission System Operator, Distribution System Operator, e.t.c. to implement, contribute, and adopt the flex-offer concept.

With the overall goal of quantifying the financial benefit and investigating the type and size of flexibility that maximizes the benefit, the paper offers the following contributions. First, it proposes a number of structural models. Second, it evaluates the models and selects the model which best capture the relationship between the market power prices and regulation volumes. The selected model is used to quantify the effect on the regulating power prices that are caused by the fluctuation in the market balance as a consequence of shifting flexible demand. Third, it evaluates the financial benefit obtained with various types of energy flexibility and market objectives. The overall financial benefit is further analyzed by decomposing it into the direct benefit and the benefit due to the side effects of shifting a flexible demand. Finally, the results from the various experiments are compared to determine the size and type of energy flexibility that maximizes the benefits of integrating flexibility in the market. The results show that the market can achieve up to 49% reduction in the average regulation cost and 29.4% reduction in regulation volume, with just 3.87% of average gross demand (2.58 GW) being flexible.

The remainder of the paper is organized as follows. Section 2 provides detailed information on the Nordic regulating power market. Section 3 describes our notation of flexibility. In Section 4 we analyze the impact of flexibility on energy regulating market. Section 6 presents the experimental results and the analysis. Finally, Sections 7 concludes the paper and provides directions for future research.

2. NORDIC REGULATING POWER MARKET

The Nordic energy market plays an important role in balancing the supply and demand in the spot market for electricity in the Nordic countries. This regulating power market is activated shortly before the time of the actual delivery and purchase of the power, when the market is anticipated to have any imbalance in supply or demand. The regulating power could be activated for any duration of time. For our experiment, we assume that the duration of activation of regulating power is in unit of an hour. This assumption is not essential for our analysis and could be changed if a more fine-grained control should be desired. Regulating power can be either up or down as a consequence of the following situations. If the supply is less than the demand, the BRP has to buy up-regulating power – at up-regulating power price – in order to maintain the energy balance in the market. The required amount of *up-regulating* power is fulfilled by other energy suppliers or by decreasing the demand by an amount equivalent to the difference. On the other hand, if the supply is greater than the demand, the BRP has to sell *down-regulating* power – at down-regulating power price – to maintain the energy balance in the market. The down-regulating power is sold to the reserve energy market or the demand is increased by an amount equivalent to the difference. The regulating power prices differ from the spot price, thus the BRP suffers financial loss when using the regulating power. The BRP may eventually settle the regulating loss with the energy suppliers that did not fulfill their commitment or the cost is transferred to the customers.

Regardless of the market situation, the regulating power market closes two hours before the actual deliveries and purchases take place. However, the clearance for the regulating power market is done only if needed to balance the market and take place 15 min before the actual deliveries and purchases of energy. The suppliers or buyers of energy in the regulating power market must therefore fulfill their bids within 15 min of being given notice. Here, we define various parameters associated with the regulating power market.

- Spot price, $p_s(t)$: Energy price at the spot market.
- Up-regulation volume, $v_u(t)$: The amount that is less than the actual demand in the spot market.
- Down-regulation volume, $v_d(t)$: The amount that exceed the actual demand in the spot market.
- Up-regulating power price, $p_u(t)$: Price paid for the up-regulating power.
- Down-regulating power price, $p_d(t)$: Price received for down-regulating power.

At any point in a time, one of the regulation volumes in the pair $(v_u(t), v_d(t))$ will be zero. For notational convenience, we will in the following represent the regulation volumes with a single notation.

- Up/Down-regulation volume, $v_{u/d}(t)$: denotes the non-zero regulating element, or zero if both elements in the pair are zero.

3. FLEXIBILITY

The term flexibility denotes a flexible energy demand and is represented in two dimensions. The first dimension is the *time flexibility*, which represent the possibility of preponing or postponing a portion of a demand for energy. The second dimension *amount flexibility*, is the range between maximum and minimum energy demand at a particular point in time. For example, if we consider a demand at device level, say for a dishwasher, a *time flexibility* represents the possibility of shifting the activation time to better match an anticipated surplus production from RES. Similarly, the *amount flexibility* represents the volume of power demand from, say, electric heating that can be scaled up or down according to the market requirement. The vision behind the TotalFlex is to analyse past usage patterns, operation correlations, and energy profiles of individual devices, and then predict available flexibilities. The potential of extracting flexibility from

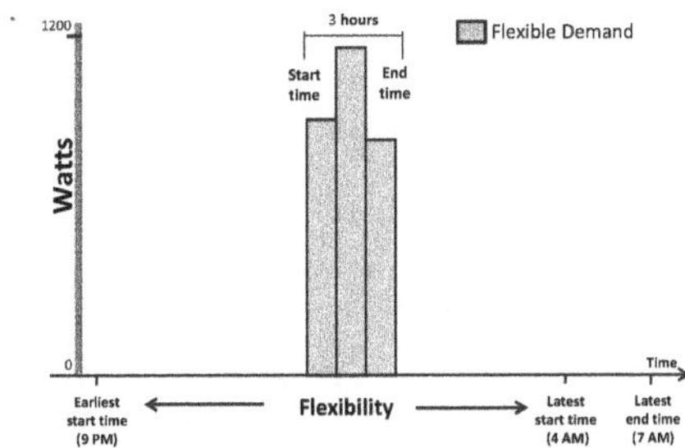

Figure 1: A sample flex-offer for dishwasher.

the usage of devices in a household is demonstrated in [10]. Still, this flexibility in demand depends on the consumers and their willingness to contribute to it. In this regard, the customers can be incentivized to contribute their flexibility in return for being offered better electricity prices.

The flexibilities extracted from individual devices such as EVs, heat pumps, dishwashers, freezers, industrial production, etc. are generalized to generate the so-called *micro flex-offers.* Figure 1 shows a simple example of a micro flex-offer generated from the extracted flexibility of a dishwasher. The flex-offer in the figure states that the dishwasher could be activated anytime between 9 PM - 4 AM and it operates for 3 time units. The figure also shows the energy profile for the dishwasher, which represents the flexible demand for each unit time of the dishwasher's operation. It further has a constraint that the energy profile of the dishwasher cannot be changed, i.e., once activated it should be operated continuously for 3 time units. The computational complexity of optimally utilizing the flexibility of each micro flex-offer derived from millions of individual devices is too high to make direct scheduling feasible. Thus, multiple micro flex-offers are aggregated into fewer larger flex-offers, known as *macro flex-offers.* The quantity of energy flexibility for each timestamp in a macro flex-offer will depend on the aggregation technique used, the profile of the individual micro flex-offers, and the market requirement.

Various techniques to aggregate micro flex-offers to macro flex-offers has been described in [13]. We will apply a simpler view on aggregation in this paper in order not to take the focus away from the investigation of the simple flexibility scenarios, as described below. First of all, we will only consider time flexibility and, second, we will assume that the energy profile of a flex-offer spanning multiple time units can be broken into multiple independent offers, one for each time unit. In this case, the aggregation simplifies as a simple grouping of the flex-offers (with the same time flexibility) at each time unit, resulting in the energy profile of a macro flex-offer being simply the sum of the values for the underlying micro flex-offers. For example, a macro flex-offer with an amount flexibility of 100 MWh could be aggregated from $50K$ micro flex-offers each with 2 KWh of amount flexibility. Although this simplified view may seem unrealistic at first, we emphasize that our analyses investigate the case of a huge amount of micro flex-offers, where far from all flex-offers need to be considered to sustain the market balance. The above assumptions are therefore reasonable for the selected smaller part of the flex-offers that are activated during the balancing.

We are going to investigate three types of time flexibility:

- *Forward Time Flexibility*: The flexible energy demand can only be shifted forward in time, to a time later than the initial planned start time for the demand.
- *Backward Time Flexibility*: The flexible energy demand can only be shifted backward in time, to a time before the initial planned start time for the demand.
- *Bi-directional Time Flexibility*: The flexible energy demand can be shifted in both directions of time.

4. ENERGY MARKET AND FLEXIBILITY

The utilization of flexibility for demand management involves shifting of some portion of demand from an originally planned timestamp to a new timestamp within a given *time flexibility.* This concept of demand management comes with side effects that change the market dynamics. A Lack of detailed information and dataset constraints the modelling of an experiment that could address all possible side effects. For example, the available dataset do not tell us detail information regarding the type of the device consuming the specific energy, this limits a model that can address the change in overall demand due to shifting of flexible demands. However, the paper will now go on to carefully model some of these side effects on the market in order to simulate a real world scenario of utilizing the energy flexibility and its side effects on the market. We will in the following use the convention that t refers to the original timestamp of an available flexible demand and use t' to denote the timestamp whereto the flexible demand is shifted.

4.1 Modeling the Effect of Flexibility on Energy Markets

We analyse the displacement in the market states (at both timestamps t and t') and the corresponding changes in the regulation prices as a consequence of shifting flexible demand. In addition to evaluating the models in the literature, we propose various new structural models to capture the dynamic pricing mechanism of the current electricity market, i.e., the relationship between the market power prices and regulation volumes. We evaluate the models and select the model with best performance as the final model to be used in the experiments.

4.1.1 Displacement of market balance

The shifting of flexible energy from one timestamp to another will displace the anticipated market balance for both timestamps. This displacement will change the regulation volumes in the market and might also reverse the market balance state (e.g., from *demand* > *supply* to *supply* > *demand*). At any timestamp the market will be in one of three different states $S = \{$*up-regulated, down-regulated, balanced*$\}$, and, as such, the configuration (t, t') of the two timestamps may be in any of the market state configurations from the Cartesian product $S \times S$, as detailed in Table 1. A shifting of flexibility may affect the anticipated market states at both times t and t'. Let us capture these state transitions by defining a shift of a flexible demand f as

$$a(t,t') \xrightarrow{f} b(t,t'),$$

where $a(t,t') \in S \times S$ and $b(t,t') \in S \times S$ are the market state configurations before and after the shift, respectively.

Table 1: Possible market state at timestamps t and t' (represented as pairs).

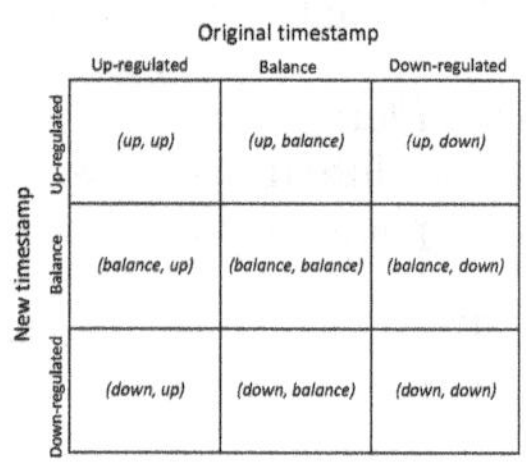

		Original timestamp		
		Up-regulated	Balance	Down-regulated
New timestamp	Up-regulated	(up, up)	(up, balance)	(up, down)
	Balance	(balance, up)	(balance, balance)	(balance, down)
	Down-regulated	(down, up)	(down, balance)	(down, down)

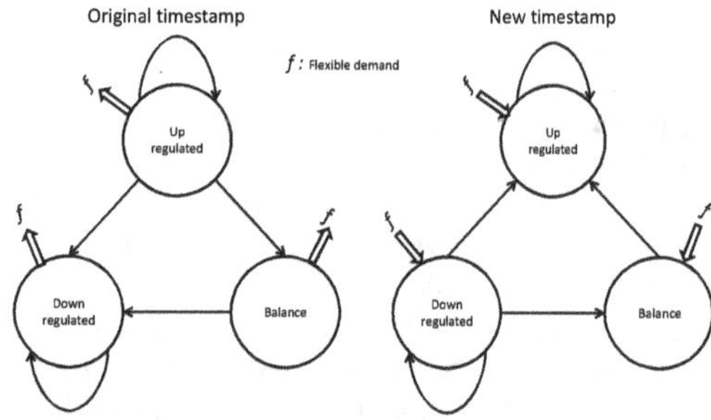

Figure 2: Possible market states transition for t and t' (arrows represent addition and removal of flexible demand).

With $|S \times S|$=9 market state configurations both before and after the shift, we would naively have to consider 81 different situations, when analyzing the effect of a shift of energy from t to t'. However, there are logical constraints that reduce this number of possible situations considerably. Namely, at time t, only the up-regulated state may shift to any of the three states in S, while for the remaining two states the shift of energy will result in a down-regulated state. Similarly, at time t', only the down-regulated state may result in any of the three states in S, while the remaining two states will be in the up-regulated state after the shift. For example, the initial pair of market states (up, down) can shift to one of many possible pairs such as (down, up), (balance, up), (down, down), etc., whereas, the (down, up) pair will always remain (down, up) irrespective of the size of the shifted flexible demand. These constraints reduce the number of possible situations to only 25 out of the 81, as illustrated in Figure 2.

Examples for 9 out of 25 possible situations, one example for each possible pair of initial market states, are shown in Figure 3. In each of the examples, the left–hand side of the figure shows the anticipated market states $a(t, t')$ before utilizing the flexibility, and the right–hand side represent the new market states $b(t, t')$ after utilizing flexibility, i.e., shifting the flexible demand from t to t'.

4.1.2 Changes in regulating power prices

Experiments on the relationships between the market power prices and regulation volumes, and the cost associated with a market imbalance has been discussed in [12]. Further, the effect of the level of the spot price and the volumes of regulation bid on regulating power prices has been analysed in [12] [8], respectively. The regulating power prices are generally affected by the market balance, i.e., supply and demand. A displacement in the market balance, due to the utilization of flexible energy, will consequently affect the regulating power

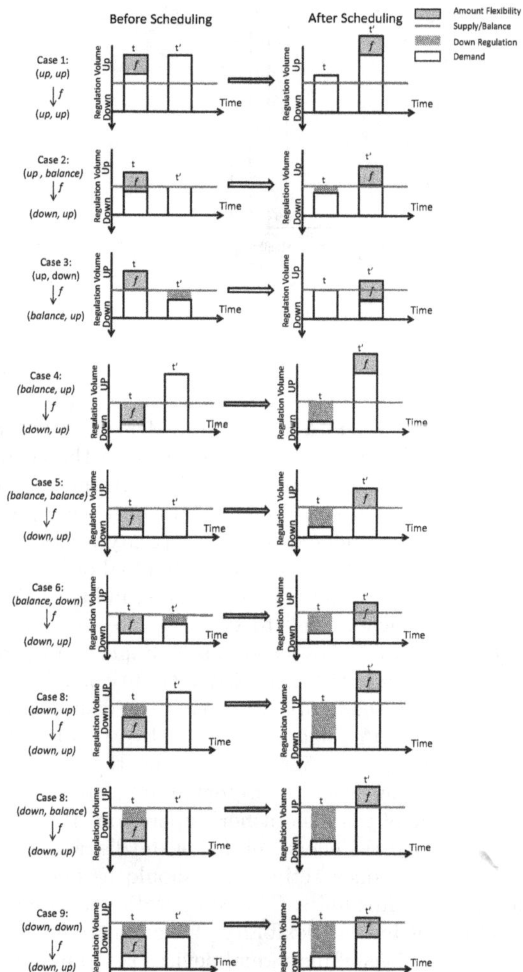

Figure 3: Example of changes in market states due to utilization of energy flexibility.

prices in the market. Our economic analysis of flexibility incorporates a model for this relationship between regulation volumes and regulating power prices that we have inferred from historical data (described in further detail below). All experiments are performed using the obtained model to estimate updated prices at the timestamps t and t' affected by a shift in demand.

Figure 4, illustrates the dependency of regulating power prices on the regulation volumes in the market. The regulating power prices are clearly seen to follow the spot price trend with a margin. The size of the margin depends on the regulation volume in the market, with a few outliers where the margin does not reflect the regulation volume. These outliers may occur due to the dependency of regulating power prices on additional exogenous factors such as hydrology - reservoir levels and inflow, temperature, wind speed, nuclear availability, etc. [11]. The figure further reveals some difference in the relationship between spot and regulating power prices according to the type of regulation (up or down) and, arguably, there seem to be some dependence on the regulation volume as well. In [12], it was found that the most predictive features of the regulating power price were, in fact, the spot price, the regulation volumes,

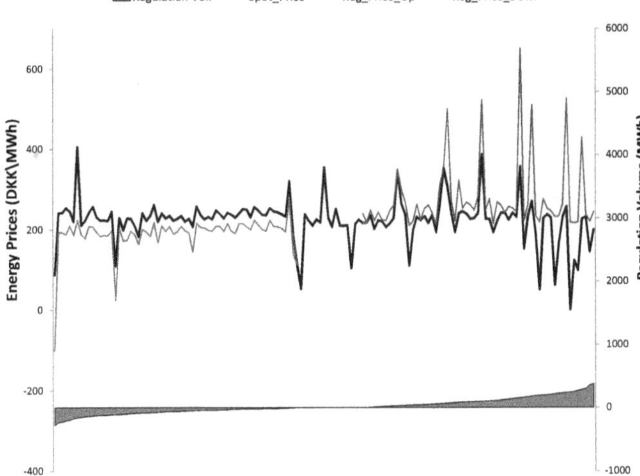

Figure 4: Dependency of energy prices on the regulation volumes

and the regulation type (up or down). Based on data from the Nordic energy market in 1999, the paper inferred a model that defines a linear relationship on spot price and regulation volume with a conditioning effect given by the type of regulation. The parameterized model in [12] (in the following referred to as Model 1) is as follows

$$\begin{aligned} p_{u/d}(t) &= 1 \cdot p_s(t) \\ &+ 1_{v_d(t)<0}(-0.069 \cdot p_s(t) + 0.023 \cdot v_d(t) - 4.3) \\ &+ 1_{v_u(t)>0}(0.028 \cdot p_s(t) + 0.042 \cdot v_u(t) + 13.07) \end{aligned} \tag{1}$$

Here, $1_{a<b}$ denotes the indicator function for the predicate $a < b$, and $p_{u/d}(t)$ is the predicted up-regulating power price $p_u(t)$ in case of up-regulation and the predicted down-regulating power price $p_d(t)$ in case of down-regulation. That is

$$p_{u/d}(t) = \begin{cases} p_u(t) & \text{for } v_u(t) > 0 \\ p_d(t) & \text{for } v_d(t) > 0 \\ p_s(t) & \text{otherwise (i.e. } v_u(t) = v_d(t) = 0) \end{cases}$$

Since this analysis, the market may have changed in certain aspects. To account for these potential changes, we consider two alternative models. The first model maintains the same structural relations as in [12], but with a parameterization that is re-estimated with our more current 2014 data. This model (in the following referred to as Model 2) is as follows

$$\begin{aligned} p_{u/d}(t) &= 1 \cdot p_s(t) \\ &+ 1_{v_d(t)<0}(-0.5101 \cdot p_s(t) - 0.0324 \cdot v_d(t) + 55.8372) \\ &+ 1_{v_u(t)>0}(0.0657 \cdot p_s(t) + 2.6157 \cdot v_u(t)) - 12.281) \end{aligned} \tag{2}$$

In order to account for the dramatic changes in the energy market since 1999, we created 14 different structural models which exhaustively defines all possible linear combinations of main effects and multiplicative interactions between the three predictive features: spot price, regulation volumes, and regulation type (up or down). Out of the 14 constructed structural models, we selected the model that best quantify the effect on regulating power prices that are caused by the fluctuation in the market balance. The search for the best structural model was performed as follows. We partitioned the data from 2012 - 2014 into three parts, with the data from Jan 2012 - June 2013 in a training set, data from July 2013 - Dec 2013 in a validation set, and the latest data from Jan 2014 - Feb 2014 set aside as a test set used for later evaluation/experiment. The alternative model structures – each with individually optimized parameterization obtained by using the Matlab curve fitting toolbox on the training dataset – are compared based on the Mean square Error (MSE) achieved on the validation set. The model with the least (MSE) is selected as the final structural model. Finally, with the model structure in place, the combined training and validation data was used for estimating the final parameterization of the model. The final learned model (in the following referred to as Model 3) resulting from the structural model selection and the associated parameter estimation is as follows:

$$\begin{aligned} p_{u/d}(t) &= 1 \cdot p_s(t) \\ &+ 1_{v_d(t)<0}(-0.3362 \cdot p_s(t) + 0.0005 \cdot (p_s(t) \cdot v_d(t))) \\ &+ 1_{v_u(t)>0}(0.2378 \cdot p_s(t) + 0.0034 \cdot (p_s(t) \cdot v_u(t))) \end{aligned} \tag{3}$$

As for the previous two models, we see that the prediction of the regulating power prices exhibits a direct relation on the spot price in the first term, with the following terms accounting for the price adjustment. In contrast, the price adjustment terms differ structurally from the previous models. Not surprisingly, all three models show that in the condition, where there is neither up- nor down-regulation the spot price equals the regulating power prices, i.e., $p_s = p_u = p_d$. Furthermore, the negative coefficients for the down-regulated market and positive coefficients for the up-regulated market constraint the market price to $p_u > p_s > p_d$, which is similar to the price trend obtained by [12].

4.2 Cost Calculation

At any point in time, the loss due to regulation is computed as the regulated volume times the price difference between the regulating and spot prices. Hence, under the normal energy market condition, i.e., without utilizing a flexibility shift from t to t', the combined regulation cost at the two time points is

$$\begin{aligned} R(t,t') &= v_{u/d}(t) * |p_{u/d}(t) - p_s(t)| \\ &+ v_{u/d}(t') * |p_{u/d}(t') - p_s(t')| \end{aligned} \tag{4}$$

Now, consider a flexible load $f(t)$ and let us define the resulting regulation volumes after this load has been shifted from time point t to t' as follows

$$\begin{aligned} \underline{v_{u/d}}(t) &= v_{u/d}(t) - f(t) \\ &= \begin{cases} v_u(t) - f(t) & \text{for } v_u(t) \geqslant f(t) \\ f(t) - v_u(t) & \text{for } 0 < v_u(t) < f(t) \\ v_d(t) + f(t) & \text{for } v_u(t) = 0 \text{ (and } v_d(t) \geqslant 0) \end{cases} . \end{aligned}$$

$$\begin{aligned} \overline{v_{u/d}}(t') &= v_{u/d}(t') + f(t) \\ &= \begin{cases} v_d(t') - f(t) & \text{for } v_d(t') \geqslant f(t) \\ f(t) - v_d(t') & \text{for } 0 < v_d(t') < f(t) \\ v_u(t') + f(t) & \text{for } v_d(t') = 0 \text{ (and } v_u(t') \geqslant 0) \end{cases} . \end{aligned}$$

Notice the notation, where underbar and overbar denotes a shift to, respectively, lower and higher volumes of the market demand due to a shift of the flexible load. In section 4.1.2

we saw that a change in regulation volume affects the regulating power price. After the flexible load is shifted, the expected combined regulation cost $E(t, t')$ is therefore computed in a similar way as in Equation 4, but with estimated prices taking the changed volumes into the account. That is,

$$E(t, t') = \underline{v_{u/d}}(t) * |\underline{p_{u/d}}(t) - p_s(t)| + \overline{v_{u/d}}(t') * |\overline{p_{u/d}}(t') - p_s(t')|, \quad (5)$$

where $p_{u/d}(t)$ and $p_{u/d}(t')$ are updated regulation price at timestamp t and t', respectively, calculated by using regulating power price prediction Model 3 from section 4.1.2.

The expected change in regulation cost due to shifting a flexible load is then

$$\Delta R(t, t') = R(t, t') - E(t, t') \quad (6)$$

A positive value for $\Delta R(t, t')$ represents a savings, i.e., decrease in the regulation cost, and a negative value represents an increase in a regulation cost. The decision regarding the shifting of flexible demand is therefore made based on the value obtained for $\Delta R(t, t')$, and is shifted only if $\Delta R(t, t')$ is positive. The details regarding the market objective and methods for selecting the best time for shifting the flexible demand are discussed in the next section.

5. MARKET OBJECTIVES

Let us define a data set $X = \{f_1, f_2, \ldots, f_n\}$ of n flexible demands. To ease notation, we will assume the same fixed time flexibility for all the demands, but this assumption is easily generalized to varying time flexibilities across demands. Let T denote the set of possible time flexibilities and $\tau \in T$ be a specific given flexibility. We will in the following analyses investigate flexibility ranges of all units (hours) of a day. That is, $\tau \in \{0, 1, \ldots, 24\}$, where, in particular, $\tau = 0$ corresponds to in-flexible demands.

Recall that a flexible demand $f_i(t)$ at time t can shift its load to any unit (hour) within the flexibility of τ. Hence, the new time t' for the flexible load of this demand can be any of

$$t' \in \begin{cases} t, \ldots, t+\tau \\ t-\tau, \ldots, t \\ t-\tau, \ldots, t+\tau \end{cases}.$$

Let $C(t_i, t_i'; \tau)$ denote the benefit (or negative cost) of moving the ith flexible load $f_i(t)$ at most τ time units to the new point in time t'. The objective is to maximize the total benefit of utilizing flexibility for all flexible demands in the data set X. In other words, we are optimizing the objective benefit criterion

$$C(X; \tau) = max_{(t_1', \ldots, t_n')} \sum_{i=1}^{n} C(t_i, t_i'; \tau) \quad (7)$$

We will be using a greedy procedure that optimizes the above benefit criterion for one flexible demand at a time and in this way lower bound the total benefit [1]. With a more sophisticated procedure the benefits could therefore be even bigger than what we demonstrate in the experimental section. Based on the requirement of a regulation market, the energy flexibility can be used to achieve various objectives such as minimizing regulation cost and volume, or even more elaborate objectives such as minimizing loss from underutilized wind energy. To demonstrate our approach, we will focus on minimizing regulation cost and volume, as follows

Minimizing regulation cost: The benefit criterion in Equation 7 will in this case maximize the savings that can be obtained in the regulation costs by time shifting the flexible demands. This benefit can be expressed by using the regulation change from Equation 6 on the right-hand side of Equation 7. That is,

$$C(t_i, t_i'; \tau) = \Delta R(t_i, t_i'; \tau),$$

where the τ in the regulation change expresses the maximal shift considered during the optimization. In more detail, the greedy optimization procedure proceeds as follows. We use Equation 6 to calculate the regulation cost of utilizing a flexible demand $f_i(t)$ at each possible load shift under the given time flexibility τ for the demand, and then select the most cost-saving shift as the optimal t_i' for this flexible energy demand. Following, the regulation volumes at the two affected time points are updated, as described in Section 4.2, and new estimated regulating power prices are calculated by using prediction Model 3 from Section 4.1.2. For example, if the flexible demand $f_i(t)$ is shifted forward by a duration of 3 units (hours), then the regulation volume and associated predicted regulating power prices are updated at both time points t and $t' = t + 3$. The next step in the greedy procedure will now consider one of the remaining flexible energy demands in X, but with the updated regulation volumes and prices.

Minimizing regulation volume: The benefit criterion in Equation 7 will in this case optimize the balance between the energy demand and supply. This benefit can be expressed by simply using the difference in regulation volume before and after each shift on the right-hand side of 7. That is,

$$C(t_i, t_i'; \tau) = (v_{(u/d)}(t) + v_{(u/d)}(t')) - (\underline{v_{(u/d)}}(t) + \overline{v_{(u/d)}}(t'))$$

The greedy optimization procedure will in this case proceed exactly as in minimization of the regulation cost above, except that there is no need for updating expected regulating power prices.

6. EXPERIMENTAL DESIGN AND ANALAYSIS

6.1 Data

In this paper, we evaluate the financial benefit of utilizing energy demand flexibility for the Nord Pool regulating market in the DK1 (West Denmark) region, the region which produces the largest part of the wind power production in Denmark. We obtained the time series dataset from the Danish TSO Energinet.dk[2]. For the cost evaluation, we uti-

[1]The lower bound will be tight if the optimal shifts for individual flexible loads are independent, which is, however, rarely the case. Consider, for example, $C(t_i, t_i'; \tau) = \Delta R(t_i, t_i')$, the change in regulation cost from Equation 6. Here, the move of a flexible demand may affect the benefit associated with shifting of other flexible demands and, therefore, the order of greedy optimization may matter.

[2]//www.energinet.dk/EN/El/Engrosmarked/Udtraek-af-markedsdata/Sider/default.aspx

Table 2: Sample Data

Date	Hour	Up Regulation Price	Down Regulation Price	Up Regulation Volume	Down Regulation Volume	Spot Price	Wind power production	Energy Demand
1/1/2014	0	222.43	113	200	0	113.01	1709.2	1893.8
-	-	-	-	-	-	-	-	-
-	-	-	-	-	-	-	-	-
1/1/2014	9	189.83	137.91	0	0	189.84	1359.6	1896.9
1/1/2014	10	183.71	164.6	0	-84	183.72	1413.3	2027

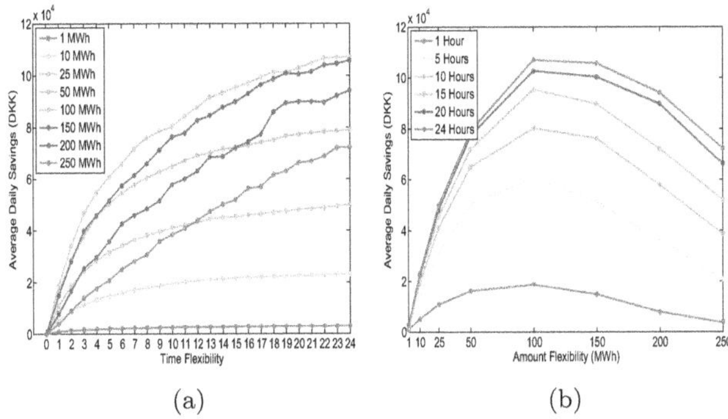

(a) (b)

Figure 5: Savings in regulation cost - averaged across days (forward time flexibility).

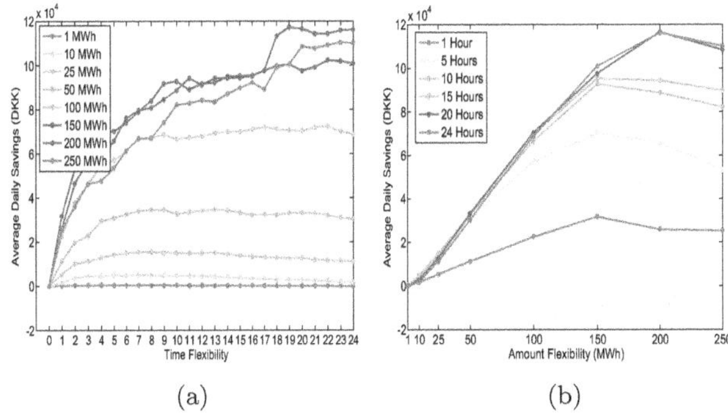

(a) (b)

Figure 9: Direct savings from the volume of flexible amount - averaged across days (forward time flexibility).

lize the market data set from Jan 2014 to Feb 2014 collected in an hourly resolution. An additional two year dataset for 2012-2013 was used to analyze the patterns of different prices in the regulating power market. The data set consists of 9 different attributes as shown in Table 2. For the 2 month period (1416 hours) in 2014, the market shows the need for up- and down-regulating power for 29.78% and 31.90% of the hours, respectively, while no regulation was needed for 38.32% of the hours. The maximum magnitude of up- and down-regulation volume was 457 MWh/h and 403 MWh/h, respectively, which represent 17.76% and 15.67% of the average energy demand for the region.

6.2 Minimizing Regulation Cost (First Experiment)

The first market objective we consider is to minimize the regulation cost paid by the BRP due to imbalance in the market. We analyze the reduction in the regulation cost that a market can achieve for each duration of time flexibility and a given amount flexibility.

Forward Time Flexibility: The average daily savings that can be achieved by utilizing the forward time flexibility in the energy demand is shown in Figure 5a and 5b. The figures show that with 24 hours of time flexibility and 100 MWh of amount flexibility available for each hour in a day, the market can achieve the highest average daily saving of 107K DKK. Further, we can see that savings in regulation cost generally grow with increasing time flexibility. However, a few drops in savings between the corresponding time flexibility can also be seen, such as in the case of 200 MWh of amount flexibility the saving for 22 hours is less than for 21 hours. This is mainly due the greedy approach we adopted to optimize the shifting of flexible demand (discussed in Section 5). In addition, the varying relationship between the market power prices and regulation volumes affects the savings based on the timestamp of the shifted flexible demand, e.g., if we have flexible demands at time t and $t+1$ and only one of them can be economically shifted to timestamp t', then the savings might differ based on the flexible demand we choose to shift. Further, we can see diminishing returns for the larger time flexibilities. We can see that the savings gradually grow with increasing amount flexibility up to a certain limit, in this case up to 100 MWh, after which it gradually decreases. This behavior is more clearly demonstrated by the bell shaped structure in Figure 5b. The saving decreases because for this particular market (DK1) with its average regulation volume of 63MWh, shifting of larger flexible demands (>100MWh) creates a higher fluctuation in the market and requires higher regulating power to balance the market. As a result, the cost paid for the side-effect is greater than the saving generated from the shifting of flexible demand, i.e., regulation cost increases and the shifting of flexible demand becomes uneconomical as it in some sense does more harm than good. This effect can be further seen in Figure 6, where we see a gradual decrease in the average percentage count of flexible demands that are shifted.

The daily relative savings/MWh of flexible energy demand is shown in Figure 7. The curve is similar to that of average daily savings, showing a gradual growth in the savings with increasing time flexibility. The maximum saving/MWh is achieved for 1 MWh of flexible demand with 24 hours of time flexibility, after which savings/MWh gradually decreases with increasing amount flexibility, which is further demonstrated in Figure 8. The savings in regulation cost come from two sources, first from the difference in the regulation cost paid for the volume of flexible demand at the original and new timestamps, i.e., direct savings. The second from the side effects, the change in the regulation cost for the remaining part of the regulation volumes at both timestamps. It is interesting to analyze the savings from these two sources separately. Thus, we disaggregate the average savings into direct savings and the savings from side effects, as shown in Figures 9a and 9b, respectively. The curves in Figure 9a show slightly different patterns in savings compared to that of total savings, i.e., for lower amount flexibilities (up to 100 MWh) direct savings are lower, whereas the savings are higher for larger amount flexibilities (> 100 MWh). Similarly, Figure 10b shows that the savings from side effects are positive for lower amount flexibilities, but negative for higher amount flexibilities. These differences are due to the effect of difference in market power prices on the over-

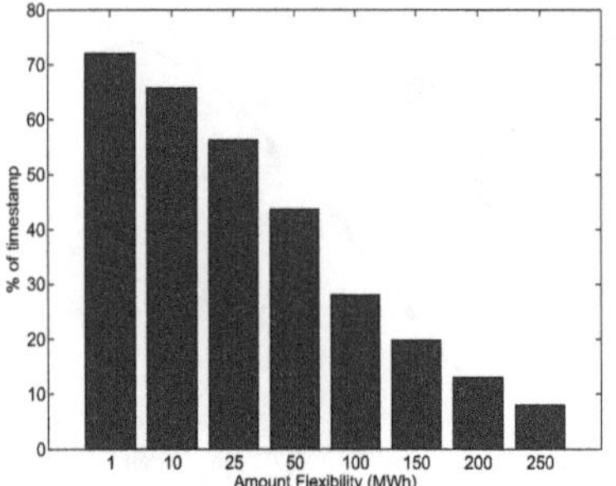

Figure 6: Percentage of shifted flexible demand - averaged over the entire time flexibility.

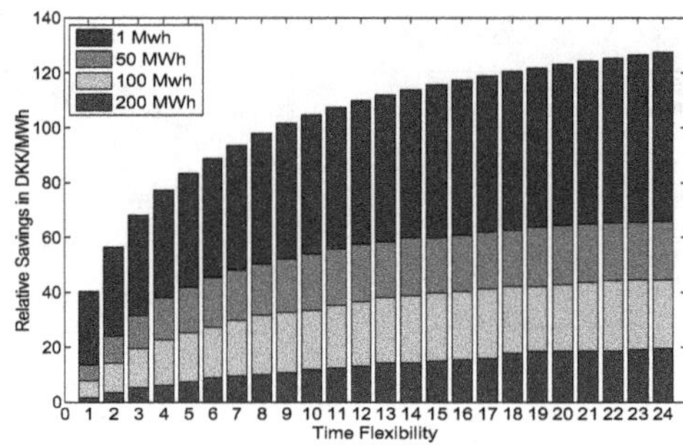

Figure 7: Savings in regulation cost per MWh - averaged over the days.

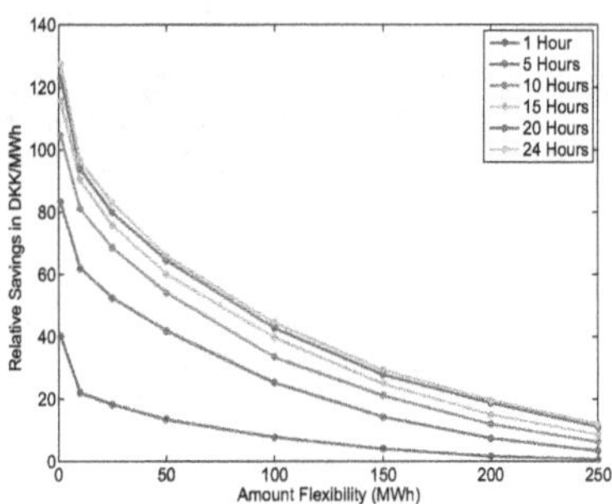

Figure 8: Savings in regulation cost per MWh - averaged over the days.

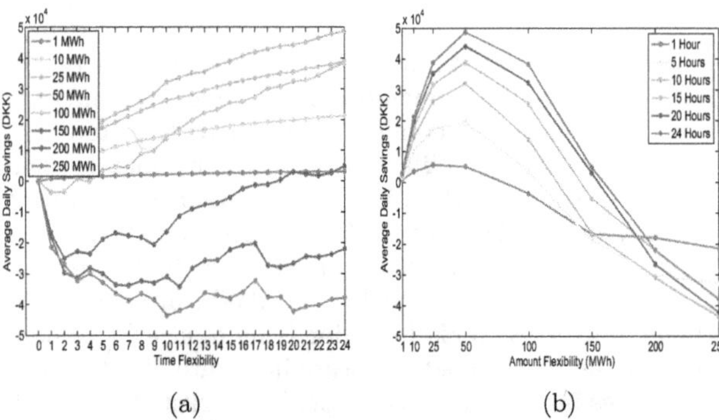

Figure 10: Savings from side effects of shifting flexible demand - averaged across days (forward time flexibility).

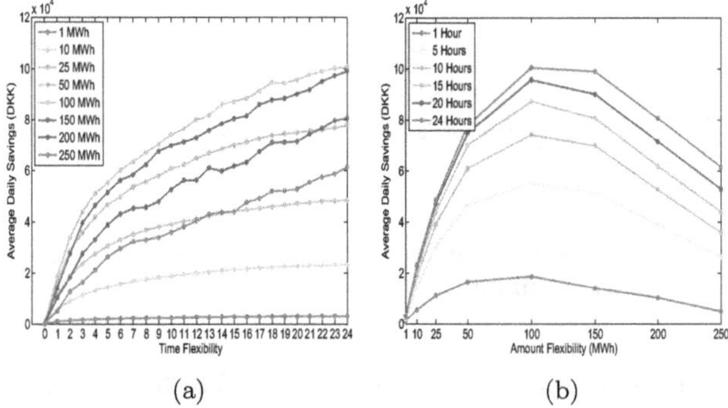

Figure 11: Savings in regulation cost - averaged across days (backward time flexibility).

all savings. The lower amount flexibilities has a dual benefit because they could be shifted to an up-regulated timestamp, if the difference in the market power prices is high enough to cover the loss due to changes in regulation volumes.

On the other hand, for the higher amount flexibilities the difference in market power prices cannot cover the loss due to a higher fluctuation in regulation volumes, which results in negative savings for side effects and lowers the total savings as shown in Figure 5a. Further, compared to Figure 5b, Figure 9b shows an increase in threshold values of amount flexibility by 50 MWh and 100 MWh for lower and higher time flexibilities, respectively. The threshold value of the amount flexibility that generates positive savings for the side effects of shifting flexible demand depends on the energy demand and the average regulation volumes of the market.

Backward Time Flexibility: The average daily savings that can be achieved by utilizing the backward time flexibility in the energy demand is shown in Figure 11a and 11b. The trends are similar to that of forward flexibility, but with slightly lower values, e.g., the best average daily saving is 6.1% less. This is due to the occurrence of a few consecutive up-regulations at the beginning of the time series, which decrease the possible shifting of flexible demand. Further, we see similar trends for direct savings and savings from side effects. Similarly, the relative savings/MWh also gradually decreases with growing amount flexibility. A detailed comparison of savings between various types of time flexibility and market objectives is shown in Table 3.

Bi-directional Time Flexibility: The average daily savings and trends obtained for the bi-directional time flexibility are very similar to that of forward flexibility, but with slightly lower values, e.g., the best average daily saving is 11% less. A comparison of savings between various types of time flexibility and market objective is shown in Table 3.

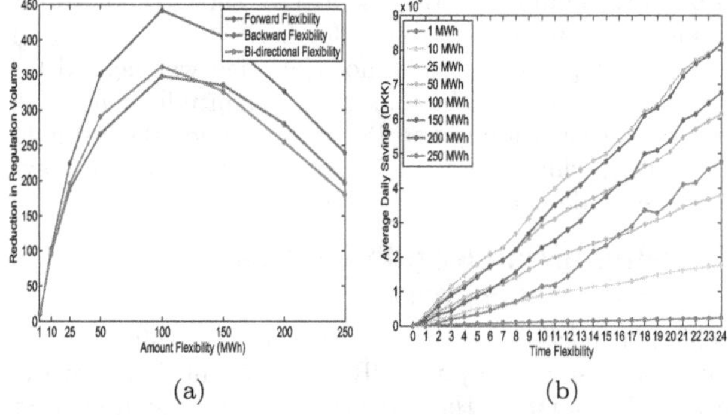

Figure 12: Savings in regulation volume (a) and regulation cost (b) - averaged across days (forward time flexibility).

6.3 Minimizing Regulation Volume (Second Experiment)

The second market objective, we consider, is to minimize the volume of energy traded in the regulating market, i.e., regulation volume. In addition, we also analyze the reduction in regulation cost in this case. As seen above, the result for forward, backward, and bi-directional flexibility are similar, so we now describe them jointly.

Amount Flexibility (MWh)	Regulation Cost						Regulation Volume					
	Forward		Backward		Bi-directional		Forward		Backward		Bi-directional	
	Direct	Side Effect	Direct	Side Effect	Direct	Side Effect	Direct	Side Effect	Direct	Side Effect	Direct	Side Effect
1	-10	3070	-6	3071	-181	2939	741	1600	642	1563	571	1450
10	1844	21327	2571	20739	-326	23003	6692	10997	5291	10597	4574	10172
50	30313	48671	37585	40194	22377	52457	23858	27511	13406	33578	14624	30051
100	68685	38303	78114	22351	54459	40803	41970	40026	26913	37416	28214	30187
200	116136	-21969	111981	-31369	84037	-12009	66018	1540	55600	-3370	48125	-7669

Table 3: Relative average daily savings (in DKK) for 24 hours time flexibility: compared over various market objective.

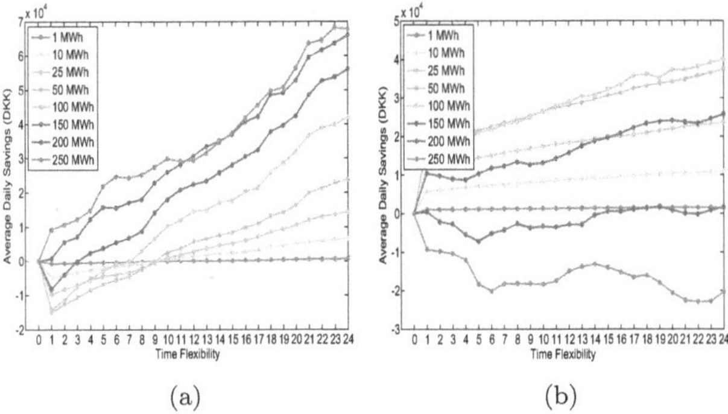

Figure 13: Direct Savings (a) and savings from side effect (b) - averaged across days (forward time flexibility).

Figure 12a shows the average daily reduction in the regulation volume utilizing the maximum time flexibility (24 hours). The figure shows that the regulation volume can be reduced by up to 442 MWh on average, which accounts for 29.4% of the average daily imbalance in the market. Further, the curves show that benefits for the market grows up to a certain value of amount flexibility, and then gradually decreases. In addition to the regulation volume, the regulation cost also reduces by up to 82K DKK on average, which is $\approx$ 24% less than for the first experiment. The most interesting of all, is the disaggregation of the total savings into direct savings and savings from the side effects, as shown in Figure 13a and 13b, respectively. For the small amount flexibilities, the trends are different from the first experiment: the direct savings are negative and become positive with the increasing time flexibility. On the other hand, for higher amount flexibilities the savings are positive from first flexible hour and increases gradually. Similarly, the savings from the side effect are positive for small amount flexibilities and negative for higher amount flexibilities. This contrasting trend is explained by the market objective, where the shifting of flexible demand is only possible from an up-regulated market to a down-regulated market. In addition, it is also due to the varying effects of flexibility on the market balance and market power prices, based on the size of shifted flexible demand, as discussed in Section 6.2. The complete comparison of savings can be seen in Table 3.

6.4 Analysis

The results above show that in general a market can increase its savings in regulation cost with increasing time flexibility, but the specific trend depends on the market objective. For the first experiment, the market has diminishing returns for increasing time flexibility. For example, for 100 MWh of amount flexibility, 8 hours of forward time flexibility give 71% of the benefit of 24 hours. In contrast, for the second experiment the savings grow steadily with increasing time flexibility, where 8 hours of forward time flexibility give approximately a third of the benefit of 24 hours. On the other hand, the size of the amount flexibility plays an important role in determining the benefits of flexibility in the market. The financial benefits of the market grow with the increasing amount flexibility up to a certain limit, after which it decreases and can be negative, e.g., the highest benefit with 100 MWh of amount flexibility is almost 48% higher than that for 250 MWh. Further, the relative savings/MWh gradually decreases with increasing amount flexibility, e.g., the best possible relative saving/MWh (127 DKK/MWh) for 1 MWh of amount flexibility is twice that for 50 MWh and six times that for 200 MWh.

In addition, until the threshold value of amount flexibility (100 MWh) is reached, the market has a dual benefit of utilizing the flexibility, i.e., the market benefits from both direct savings and savings from side effects, whereas, above the threshold value the market loses a huge amount in side effects due to higher imbalance in the market. This loss reduces the overall savings and diminish the benefit of utilizing flexibility in the energy market, e.g., in the first experiment, savings from side effects for 50MWh is 62% of the best possible saving, whereas for 200MWh it reduces to -52%. The higher the amount flexibility, the lower the possibility of gaining financial benefit from shifting it. This argument is supported by the fact that, on average flexible demand of size 10 MWh is shifted 65.2% of time, which reduces to 8% for 250 MWh. These results indicate the maximum size of energy flexibility that can be traded in an energy market with profitability. In addition, it also provides the guidelines for aggregating micro flex-offers to macro flex-offers.

A market with an objective to reduce regulation volume can achieve a best possible average daily reduction of 442 MWh along with a 37.5% reduction in regulation cost. These results show that, the time shifting of flexible demand can generate a substantial benefit regardless of the types of energy flexibility or market objectives. However, the geographical location, size of the market, and the type of RES will determine the optimal size of time and amount flexibility that maximizes the benefits, e.g., demand management for solar energy need flexible load to be shifted to day time, which requires higher time flexibility to maximize benefit. For the market in this study, forward time flexibility and objective to reduce regulation cost generates the best possible benefits for the market. Here, the market can achieve up to 49% (107K DKK) reduction in the average regulation cost, with 24 hours of forward time flexibility and just 3.87% of average gross demand (2.58 GW) being flexible.

Further, with just 1 hour of time flexibility, the market can achieve 17.6% of the savings for 24 hours. Finally, we can conclude that the flexibility has a positive financial impact on the regulation market and the market can trade-off between the available time and amount flexibility, to maximize their benefit and better map the demand with the surplus production from RES.

7. CONCLUSION AND FUTURE WORK

In this paper, we have quantified the benefits of introducing flexibility in the Danish/Nordic energy market and investigated the type and size of flexibility that maximizes the benefit. In particular, we analysed the reduction in regulation cost and volumes that a market can achieve with a time shift of flexible energy demand. We proposed a number of structural models and evaluated each of them to select the model that best quantify the effect on the regulating power prices caused due to shifting of flexible demand. Finally, we performed a number of experiments to evaluate the financial benefit for various flexibility types and market objectives. The experimental results have shown that with just 3.87% flexibility in the demand, the market can reduce the regulation cost by up to 49% (daily average of 107K DKK) and the regulation volume by up to 29.4% (daily average of 442 MWh). Further, the experiments showed that the savings in regulation cost grows with increasing time flexibility, whereas it only grows up to a certain value of amount flexibility, after which it decreases. Furthermore, all experiments shows that, regardless of the type of market objective and energy flexibility, a market can generate substantial economic benefit by introducing the flexibility. Indeed, with just 4 hours of time flexibility and 100 MWh of amount flexibility the market could reduce the regulation cost by 24.9%, and the regulation volume by 5.2%.

Important directions for future work are (1) considering a more complex flexibility market, such as introduce various market constraints during shifting of flexible demand, 2) a more optimized load shift strategy, (3) analyzing the benefit for various other market objectives, and (4) evaluating the financial benefit of introducing flexibility in other energy market areas.

8. ACKNOWLEDGMENTS

This work was supported in part by the TotalFlex project sponsored by the ForskEL program of Energinet.dk.

9. REFERENCES

[1] The *MIRABEL* project, 2013. `http://www.mirabel-project.eu`.

[2] The *TotalFlex* project, 2014. `http://www.totalflex.dk/Forside/`.

[3] G. Bathurst, J. Weatherill, and G. Strbac. Trading wind generation in short term energy markets. *Power Systems, IEEE Transactions on*, pages 782–789, 2002.

[4] T. Bigler, G. Gaderer, P. Loschmidt, and T. Sauter. Smartfridge: Demand side management for the device level. In *ETFA 2011*, pages 1–8, 2011.

[5] A. Fabbri, T. Román, J. Abbad, and V. Quezada. Assessment of the cost associated with wind generation prediction errors in a liberalized electricity market. *Power Systems, IEEE Transactions on*, pages 1440–1446, 2005.

[6] A. M. Foley, P. G. Leahy, A. Marvuglia, and E. J. McKeogh. Current methods and advances in forecasting of wind power generation. *Renewable Energy*, pages 1 – 8, 2012.

[7] A. Giannitrapani, S. Paoletti, A. Vicino, and D. Zarrilli. Bidding strategies for renewable energy generation with non stationary statistics. In *World Congress*, pages 10784–10789, 2014.

[8] I. Ilieva and T. F. Bolkesjø. An econometric analysis of the regulation power market at the nordic power exchange. *Energy Procedia*, pages 58 – 64, 2014.

[9] O. Lünsdorf and M. Sonnenschein. A pooling based load shift strategy for household appliances. In *EnviroInfo 2010*, pages 734–743, 2010.

[10] B. Neupane, T. Pedersen, and B. Thiesson. Towards flexibility detection in device-level energy consumption. In *Proceedings of the Second ECML/PKDD Workshop, DARE'14*, pages 1–16. 2014.

[11] N. E. R. (NordREG). Nordic market report 2014.

[12] K. Skytte. The regulating power market on the Nordic power exchange Nord Pool: an econometric analysis. *Energy Economics*, pages 295–308, 1999.

[13] L. Šikšnys, M. Khalefa, and T. Pedersen. Aggregating and disaggregating flexibility objects. In *SSDBM 2012*, pages 379–396. 2012.

[14] X. Wang, P. Guo, and X. Huang. A review of wind power forecasting models. *Energy Procedia*, pages 770 – 778, 2011.

[15] X. Zhang. Optimal wind bidding strategy considering imbalance cost and allowed imbalance band. In *Energytech, 2012 IEEE*, pages 1–5, 2012.

Recouping Energy Costs from Cloud Tenants: Tenant Demand Response Aware Pricing Design

Cheng Wang, Neda Nasiriani, George Kesidis, Bhuvan Urgaonkar, Qian Wang,
Lydia Y. Chen†, Aayush Gupta‡ and Robert Birke†
The Pennsylvania State University, †IBM Research Zurich, ‡IBM Research Almaden

ABSTRACT

As energy costs become increasingly greater contributors to a cloud provider's overall costs, it is important for the cloud to recoup these energy costs from its tenants for profitability via appropriate pricing design. The poor predictability of real-world tenants' demand and demand responses (DRs) make such pricing design a challenging problem. We formulate a leader-follower game-based cloud pricing framework with the goal of maximizing cloud's profit. The key distinguishing aspect of our approach is our emphasis on modeling both the cloud and its tenants as working with low predictability in their inputs. Consequently, we model them as employing myopic control with short-term predictive models. Our empirical evaluation using tenant trace from IBM production data centers shows that (i) cloud's profit and VM prices are sensitive to the tradeoffs between its energy costs, tenant's demand and DR, and (ii) the cloud's estimation of tenants' demands/DR may significantly affect its profitability.

Categories and Subject Descriptors

C.4 [**Performance of Systems**]: Design studies; Modeling techniques

General Terms

Design, Experimentation, Economics

Keywords

Cloud Tenant; Pricing Design; Game; Demand Response

1. INTRODUCTION

The electric utility bills of data centers make up significant portions of their overall expenses and are fast approaching the capital expenditure towards IT infrastructure itself. Studies from large cloud/IT providers such as Google [2] and Amazon [12] show that the electric utility bill amounts to 10-20% of the overall costs of their state-of-the-art data centers.

e-Energy'15, July 14–17, 2015, Bangalore, India.

DOI: http://dx.doi.org/10.1145/2768510.2768541.

More alarmingly, perhaps, it is likely that these energy bills will become even larger contributors to data center costs as energy prices increase in the future [27]. Consequently, the pricing mechanism employed by a cloud provider (or simply "cloud" henceforth) to recoup these energy costs from its customers (i.e., "tenants") has important implications for its profitability and has recently emerged as a topic of much interest [22, 18, 31].

Pricing design for a cloud is made challenging by uncertainty in tenant workloads as well as in electric utility prices. Although much related work in cloud pricing design makes assumptions of predictability in utility prices and tenant workloads for theoretic tractability (see discussions in Sections 2 and 5 for salient examples), many real-world prices and workloads exhibit poor predictability and are best considered non-stationary. Even in cases where utility prices or workloads can be reasonably predicted via higher-order predictors [9, 5], the resulting control problems (including pricing design) are likely to be computationally difficult to solve.

We envision that a whole new source of complexity in pricing design will arise in the near future due to the emergence (or increasing adoption) of *price sensitive tenant behavior.* Demand response (DR) has been recently identified as being important for the profitable operation of data centers [29], and we foresee even individual tenants (perhaps starting with large and sophisticated ones) similarly carrying out DR of their own. We use the phrase "tenant DR" (or simply DR when the meaning is clear) to describe strategic resource procurement by tenants in response to prices set by the cloud. Many enterprises and businesses are moving increasing portions of their IT needs to various cloud providers, a trend that is likely to continue in the foreseeable future [11]. As these tenants become increasingly invested into cloud computing, it is reasonable to expect that price sensitive DR will become increasingly important for their profitability. As a salient example, the video steaming giant Netflix already procures all of its vast computational needs from Amazon's EC2 cloud and employs certain forms of DR [21]. Generally speaking, *tenant DR will be a priori unknown to the cloud provider,* making the problem of price determination for the cloud even more complicated.

Using real-world data for tenant workloads and utility prices, we study the problem of *virtual machine (VM) pricing design for a cloud whose tenants engage in price-sensitive demand response.* Our approach involves modeling this ecosystem via a leader-follower game with the cloud being the leader and tenants the followers. Whereas some existing work has investigated cloud's pricing design assuming that tenants' workloads and DRs can be well predicted/inferred (see Section 5), a key feature of our approach is our emphasis on modeling various participants as working with low predictability. Specifically, we assume that the cloud and the tenants find long-term prediction difficult and instead choose to work with relatively short-term predictions (of cloud prices and workloads for tenants and of utility prices and tenant workloads/DRs for the cloud). In other words, the cloud and the tenants employ "myopic" control approaches with objectives of maximizing only their respective short-term profits.

Our contributions are along both analytical and empirical lines. On the analytical front, we formulate a leader-follower game-based cloud pricing framework with the goal of maximizing cloud's profit. In this model, the cloud employs short-term sequential decision making (VM pricing) with prediction models for estimating tenants' DRs. To the best of our knowledge, this is novel in the area of cloud pricing. Our most significant contributions are the following key findings of the empirical evaluation based on real-world utility prices and tenant demand workloads from production data centers run by IBM: (i) cloud's profit and VM prices are sensitive to the tradeoffs between its energy costs, tenant's demand and DR, and (ii) the cloud's estimation of tenants' demands/DR may significantly affect its profitability. Our analysis based on the cloud and the tenants carrying out decision-making restricted by short-term predictability yields non-trivial and surprising findings compared to those offered by existing work that simplifies input complexity for tractable analytical solutions. For example, optimal *long term* profitability is not achieved by the necessarily "myopic" framework (both in terms of revenue objectives and estimation techniques), even under otherwise ideal circumstances such as perfect forecasting of tenants' DRs; even without perfect knowledge of tenant's demand response, the cloud might still garner more profit by implementing the proposed pricing framework than applying a constant VM price.

2. BACKGROUND

2.1 System model and assumptions

A cloud provider procures various resources from different kinds of utility providers and/or renders and constructs virtualized IT resources from these for its tenants. E.g., a cloud provider might purchase electric power from an electric utility company, network bandwidth from an Internet Service Provider (ISP), and servers and storage once every few years from IT infrastructure retailers. The cloud provider then creates a variety of resources for its tenants such as virtual machines (VMs), storage, software services, etc., with a variety of pricing options such as on-demand pricing, reservation-based pricing, spot pricing (with tenants' bidding) [1].

We consider a system model that simplifies the above diversity significantly by considering a single resource - energy - procured by the cloud, and a single resource - a single type of VM - sold to the tenants. Figure 1 illustrates our model and helps compare it with a more general ecosystem. In the following, we describe key simplifying assumptions in our model.

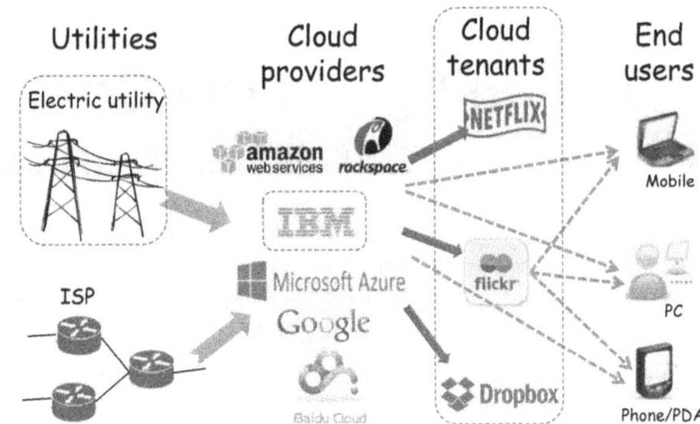

Figure 1: Illustration of a general cloud ecosystem. We highlight the elements we focus on in our simplified model.

Utility-Cloud: We assume that the cloud is charged by the electric utility company based on a time-varying electricity pricing scheme. Any DR the cloud does is accomplished *implicitly* via the behavior of tenants (as described next) incentivized by the VM prices set by the cloud. In future work we will also incorporate explicit DR by the cloud (in addition to and/or complementary to that carried out by the tenants). We further assume that the utility prices are unaffected by the power demands posed by the cloud. The goal of the cloud is to maximize its own profit by modulating VM prices based on its short-term predictions of tenants' demands/DRs.

Cloud-Tenant: The cloud charges its tenants using a time-varying VM pricing scheme. We assume VMs to have a fixed resource capacity. In practice VM resource capacity could be dynamic due to cloud's resource management actions such as VM consolidation, under-provisioning, etc. E.g., Netflix employs certain forms of control in response to such variations in the resource capacity of Amazon EC2 VMs [21]. Tenants are assumed to be price sensitive and carry out DR with the goal of maximizing their respective net utility. We assume that a tenant's DR is carried out by "delaying" its workload, i.e., by deferring (or suspending) VMs with a delay penalty that captures the tenant's revenue loss/performance degradation due to DR. Other forms of DR such as strategic VM procurement and workload consolidation, etc., are interesting future work.

2.2 Motivating myopic control based on short-term predictions

Plenty of evidence from real-world data centers shows that their workloads (and correspondingly power demands) can be very complex [24, 16, 5, 15]. In particular, data center workloads exhibit varying degrees of predictability. For example, the Facebook demand shown in Figure 2(a) lends itself to low complexity predictors, e.g., by subtracting the time-of-day effects from raw demand and modeling the residual demand as Markovian. On the other hand, job arrivals at a Google cluster (Figure 2(b)) exhibit poorer predictability: upon plotting the autocorrelation of the residue after detrending for time-of-day effects from Figure 2(b) (not shown here due to lack of space), we find that rather high-order predictors might be required that would result in computationally complex control formulations. As an example with even poorer predictability, in Figure 2(c) we observe an unexpected burst of VM arrivals on the 40-th day from the VM demand trace of a tenant belonging to an IBM production

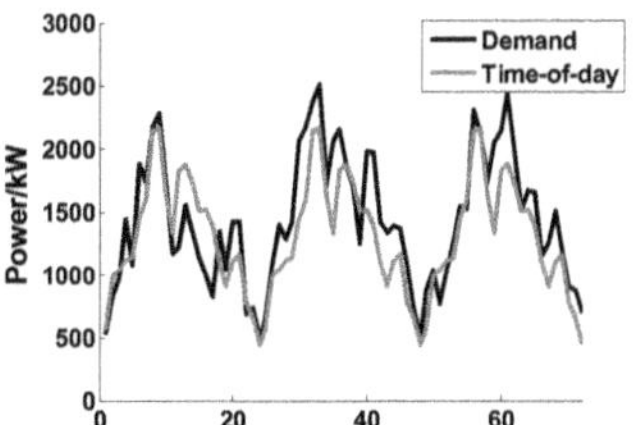

(a) Power demand from a facebook data center [6].

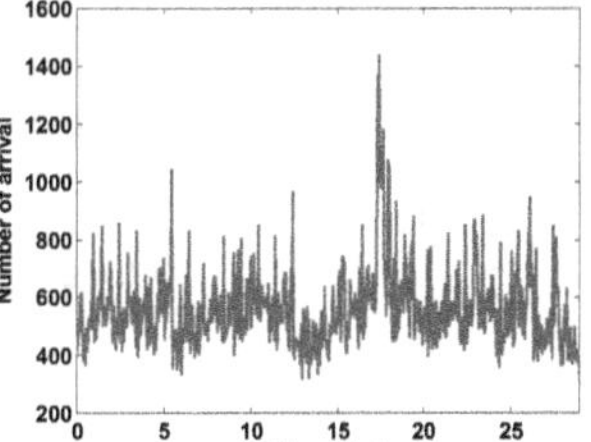

(b) Job arrivals at a Google cluster [10].

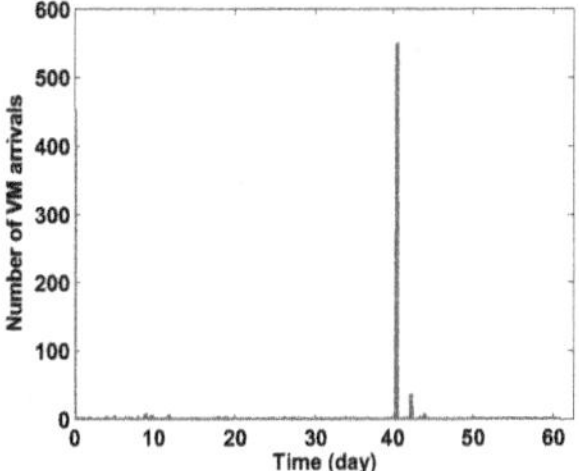

(c) VM arrivals for an IBM tenant.

Figure 2: Examples of real-world data center workloads with different degrees of predictability.

data center. Most existing work on cloud pricing design is suitable only for workloads like in Figure 2(a). In this work, we choose to focus on scenarios exemplified by Figures 2(b) and (c).

A whole new source of complexity arises in our problem domain due to the tenants' DRs and the cloud's lack of knowledge thereof. Different tenants could have different sensitivities to price changes. As an example, tenants that run performance-centric applications, e.g., Web services, might want guaranteed performance even at a high price (i.e., less price-sensitive) whereas some batch jobs could be scheduled with more flexibility (i.e., more price-sensitive). Furthermore, tenants' DRs could also be time-varying and/or depend on the tenant's own customers' demand. For example, when streaming a very popular event, a streaming video server tenant hosted on the cloud might be willing to procure more computing resources and be willing to pay a higher price to the cloud to satisfy the demands of the large number of clients with guaranteed QoS than when it streams a less popular event.

In the face of these complexities, optimal control techniques that rely upon effective predictors for inputs (e.g., based on Markov Decision Processes) might not work well. Therefore, we choose to work with "myopic" control for both the cloud and the tenants wherein (a) the cloud only maximizes its short-term profit and sets VM prices based on short-term prediction/estimation of tenant's VM demand and DR, and (b) the tenant also only optimizes its short-term net utility and defers VMs myopically by only considering the penalty (i.e., revenue loss) of deferring VMs in the short term.

An Important Warning. An implication of the complexity of workloads and DRs in our problem domain is that we will be unable to compare the quality of our solutions against an offline optimal (due to the computational complexity of such a formulation). Instead, our "baseline" would be a solution that is "optimal" only with respect to our myopically defined objective (i.e., short-term profit maximization) which does not necessarily maximize the long-term profit. It will be important to keep in mind that we use "optimal" in this sense when we present our empirical evaluation in Section 4.

Cloud's estimation of tenants' DR. Due to the aforementioned complexity in tenants' DRs, we assume that the cloud only estimates the tenants' **aggregate DR** for computational tractability. Extensions to consider different types of tenants whose behavior needs to be predicted separately form future work. We consider a time-slotted system wherein the cloud needs to determine the VM price θ_{t^-} at the beginning of time-slot t. Here t^- implies that θ_{t^-} is determined by the cloud *before* the actual VM demand during time-slot t is revealed by the tenants. Having clarified this causal order, we simply use θ_t instead of θ_{t^-} for notational simplicity in the following.

Denoting as x_t the aggregate VM demands from all tenants during time-slot t, the cloud employs predictive models to forecast x_t. As an example, if it uses a first-order auto-regressive estimator with exogenous input (ARX), i.e., $\hat{x}_t = A_t x_{t-1} + B_t\theta_t$ where A_t, B_t are model parameters that are updated online recursively by using historical data. The rationale behind the above prediction model is that (i) the tenants' aggregate admitted VM demand may depend significantly on that of the previous time-slot, which is reflected by the AR term $A_t x_{t-1}$, and (ii) VM demand is likely to decrease as price increases, which is captured by $B_t\theta_t$ with $B_t < 0$.

To see how the cloud's profitability might be affected by its estimation of tenant's aggregate DR, we consider several different predictors whose key properties are shown in Table 1. We report experiment results with all these predictors in Section 4.

Name	Predictor	DoF
ARX	$\hat{x}_t = A_t x_{t-1} + B_t\theta_t$	2
Affine	$\hat{x}_t = B_{1,t}\theta_t + B_{0,t}$	2
Quad (quadratic)	$\hat{x}_t = B_{2,t}\theta_t^2 + B_{1,t}\theta_t + B_{0,t}$	3
PW (piecewise linear)	$\hat{x}_t = \sum_{i=1}^{M}(B_{i,t}\theta_t + C_{i,t})$	$2M$

Table 1: Predictors for cloud's estimation of tenants' aggregate DR. "DoF": degrees of freedom.

Generally speaking, the cloud could be tempted to use more complex predictors instead of the prosaic predictors aforementioned. However, higher order predictors would rely on larger training sets to tune their parameters (and sometimes even hyper-parameters) adaptively. When the real-world tenants' DR models are (highly) time-varying, the cloud might not be able to find sufficiently informative prior training data for system identification (since outdated data might not be helpful). Furthermore, the real-world tenant's demand we consider has poor predictability, which further adds to the difficulty of applying complex high-order predictors. Therefore, we rely on the above parsimonious predictors in our design.

3. GAME-THEORETIC PRICING DESIGN

In this section, we design a leader/follower game-based cloud pricing framework with the goal of maximizing the cloud's profit. Figure 3 illustrates the sequential decision making process of our game. As shown, at the beginning of time-slot t, there are two steps: in step I (cloud's move), assuming that the cloud has perfect knowledge (or is reasonably well informed) of the future electricity prices in K future slots $\alpha_t, \alpha_{t+1}, ..., \alpha_{t+K}$, it determines VM prices $\theta_t, \theta_{t+1}, ..., \theta_{t+K}$ to maximize its profit during these $(K+1)$ slots using predictions of tenants' aggregate DR. Towards this, the cloud forecasts the tenants' aggregate VM demands for the next $K+1$ time-slots under the VM prices it sets. Since its prediction of tenant's demand will likely be increasingly less accurate as the cloud forecasts farther into the future, it only adopts θ_t as the VM price for time-slot t. Estimates of $\theta_{t+1}, ..., \theta_{t+K}$ are either discarded or sent to the tenants as guiding pricing signals, denoted as $\theta'_{t+1}, ..., \theta'_{t+K}$ to distinguish them from the prices actually used.

Step II (tenant's move) has two sub-steps: In step II.a, the tenants decide how many VMs to admit and how many VMs to defer based on their respective demands, delay costs, and cloud's VM price θ_t and pricing signals $\theta'_{t+1}, ..., \theta'_{t+K}$. In step II.b, the tenants choose which VMs to defer to future time-slots according to priority, deadline or any specific performance requirement (if any) of their VMs.

3.1 Step I: Cloud's control

We develop our formulation for $K = 1$, i.e., the cloud maximizes its profit over two consecutive time-slots, and note that it can be easily generalized to cases with larger K. The cloud would predict its revenue during time-slots t and $t+1$ as: $\theta_t \hat{x}_t + \theta'_{t+1}\hat{x}_{t+1}$.

Assuming that the fraction of cloud's overall costs that comes from its electricity bill is c ($c < 1$), and that the energy consumed by $\hat{x}_t$ VMs is $g(\hat{x}_t)$[1], the **cloud's cost** during time-slots t and $t+1$ can be written as: $\frac{1}{c}\{\alpha_t g(\hat{x}_t) + \alpha_{t+1} g(\hat{x}_{t+1})\}$.

At the beginning of time-slot t, the cloud takes the electricity prices α_t and α_{t+1} as inputs, and outputs the actual VM price θ_t and the estimated pricing signal θ'_{t+1} by solving the following profit maximization problem:

$$\max_{\theta_t, \theta'_{t+1}} \; (\theta_t \hat{x}_t + \theta'_{t+1}\hat{x}_{t+1}) - \frac{1}{c}\{\alpha_t g(\hat{x}_t) + \alpha_{t+1} g(\hat{x}_{t+1})\}$$

Subject to

$$0 \le \hat{x}_t = A_t x_{t-1} + B_t \theta_t$$
$$0 \le \hat{x}_{t+1} = A_t \hat{x}_t + B_t \theta'_{t+1}$$
$$\theta_t \hat{x}_t \ge \frac{1}{c}\alpha_t g(\hat{x}_t)$$
$$\theta'_{t+1}\hat{x}_{t+1} \ge \frac{1}{c}\alpha_{t+1} g(\hat{x}_{t+1})$$

where x_{t-1} and θ_{t-1} are known (to the cloud) at the beginning of time-slot t. The first two constraints represent the cloud's estimations of the tenants' aggregate demands during time-slots t and $t+1$ using an ARX model. The last two constraints imply that the cloud's profit should be non-negative. Whereas we show the formulation using an ARX predictor, it can be replaced by a different predictor (as we explored in Section 4).

3.2 Step II: Tenant's control

[1]In evaluation, we use $g(\hat{x}_t) = \delta \hat{x}_t$, which could be a reasonable model assuming fixed degree of VM consolidation (e.g., fixed number of VMs per physical machine).

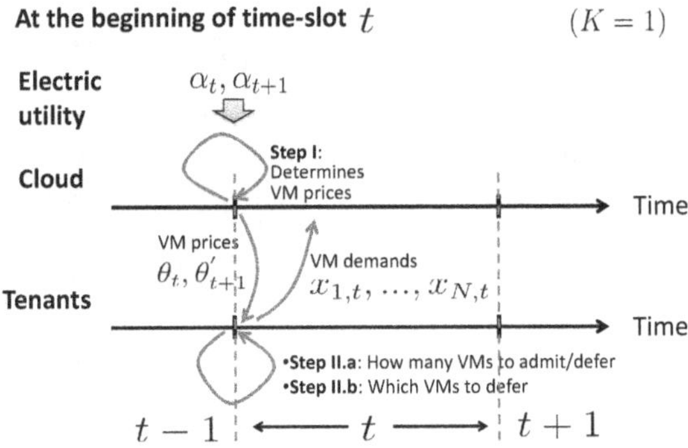

Figure 3: Illustration of our leader/follower game.

At the beginning of time-slot t, upon receiving θ_t and θ'_{t+1} from the cloud[2], tenant i has to determine the number of VMs to be admitted, denoted as $x_{i,t}$, and the number of VMs to be deferred (with certain delay cost) to the next time-slot, denoted as $\eta_{i,t}$, and choose from all VMs which to defer.

Step II.a: How many VMs to admit? (Determine the **control variable** $x_{i,t}$).

Each VM is characterized as a two-tuple: $\{a_{i,k}, l_{i,k}\}$ wherein $a_{i,k}$ denotes the arrival time (beginning of a time-slot) of tenant i's k-th VM, and $l_{i,k}$ is the lifetime of that VM. If we defer a VM from time-slot t to time-slot $t+1$, the lifetime of the VM will be increased such that $\tilde{l}_{i,k,t+1} = \tilde{l}_{i,k,t} + 1$, where $\tilde{l}_{i,k,t}$ denotes the lifetime of the VM at the beginning of time-slot t. Note that $l_{i,k} = \tilde{l}_{i,k,t}$ when $t = a_{i,k}$.

Define the **VM arrivals-minus-departures** at the beginning of time-slot t as follows:

$$\Delta x_{i,t} := \sum_k 1\{a_{i,k} = t\} - \sum_k 1\{a_{i,k} + \tilde{l}_{i,k,t} = t\}$$

If $x_{i,t}$ is the number of VMs that are active during time-slot t, and $X_{i,t}$ the total number of VMs in the system that are eligible for deferral/admittance at the beginning of time-slot t, then

$$X_{i,t} = x_{i,t-1} + \eta_{i,t-1} + \Delta x_{i,t}.$$

Since some of the VMs will continue to be active ($x_{i,t}$) while other VMs will be deferred to $t+1$ ($\eta_{i,t}$) at the beginning of time-slot t, we have

$$\eta_{i,t} = x_{i,t-1} + \eta_{i,t-1} + \Delta x_{i,t} - x_{i,t}$$

Figure 4 illustrates our model for tenant i's demand and control actions.

Define $f_i(.)$ as tenant i's utility function, which is assumed concave and increasing in number of VMs. Then we can express **tenant i's revenue** during time-slot t as $f_i(x_{i,t})$. Similarly, we can write **tenant i's costs** as $\theta_t x_{i,t} + \pi_{i,t}\eta_{i,t}$ where $\pi_{i,t}$ is the tenant-specific unit delay cost during time-slot t.

Now given θ_t and θ'_{t+1} from the cloud, tenant i can maximize its net profit over, e.g., two-consecutive time-slots, by

[2]Note that it is also possible that the cloud exposes electricity prices α_t to the tenants for better forecasting and DR. Naturally, in this case, the tenant could attempt to forecast the cloud's VM prices in deciding whether and which VMs to defer.

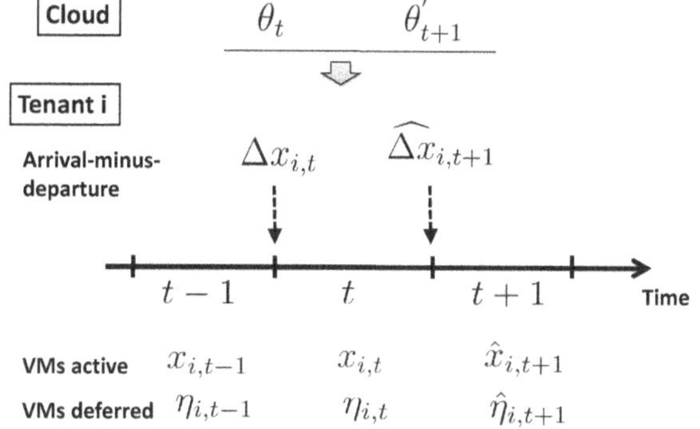

Figure 4: Illustration of tenant i's demand and control actions.

determining $x_{i,t}$ and $\hat{x}_{i,t+1}$ as follows:

$$\max_{x_{i,t},\hat{x}_{i,t+1}} \quad f_i(x_{i,t}) - (\theta_t x_{i,t} + \pi_{i,t}\eta_{i,t}) + f_i(\hat{x}_{i,t+1}) - (\theta'_{t+1}\hat{x}_{i,t+1} + \pi_{i,t+1}\hat{\eta}_{i,t+1})$$

Subject to

$$0 \le \eta_{i,t} = x_{i,t-1} + \eta_{i,t-1} + \Delta x_{i,t} - x_{i,t}$$
$$0 \le \hat{\eta}_{i,t+1} = x_{i,t} + \eta_{i,t} + \widehat{\Delta x}_{i,t+1} - \hat{x}_{i,t+1}$$

where $x_{i,t-1}, \Delta x_{i,t}, \eta_{i,t-1}$ are known at the beginning of t, and $\widehat{\Delta x}_{i,t+1}$ needs to be forecasted beforehand via predictive model, e.g., $\widehat{\Delta x}_{i,t+1} = \gamma_1 \Delta x_{i,t} + \gamma_2 \Delta x_{i,t-1}$. Here we adopt the idea of "receding horizon control" [19]: the tenant only implements $x_{i,t}$ and discards $\hat{x}_{i,t+1}$ assuming that its prediction (and control actions henceforth) can be further improved when time advances to time-slot $t+1$.

Step II.b: Which VMs to defer?

It is a design choice for the tenants to decide which VMs to defer. The tenant could cast a generic VM scheduling problem to minimize the average delay or deadline violation given information about the VMs' priority, deadline or specific performance requirement (if any). However, without the above information in our work, we have to defer VMs based on heuristics, e.g, deferring the VMs that have stayed in the system for least amount of time (assuming that those VMs might be short-lived and thus less important than others). That is, at the beginning of time-slot t, if $\eta_{i,t} = 1$, the tenant chooses VM k^* such that $k^* = \arg\min_k \{t - a_{i,k} \mid a_{i,k} \le t \le a_{i,k} + \tilde{l}_{i,k,t}\}$. Here $a_{i,k} \le t \le a_{i,k} + \tilde{l}_{i,k,t}$ implies that VM k enters the system before or at the beginning of t and does not leave at the end of t where $t - a_{i,k}$ is the number of time-slots that the VM has been in the system by time-slot t. If $\eta_{i,t} > 1$, then the tenant chooses the VMs that have been in the system for shortest amount of time by time-slot t.

Note that $\tilde{l}_{i,k,t}$ is generally not known at the beginning of time-slot t. However, for VM k, we do know the cumulative delay that it experiences at the beginning of t: $\tilde{l}_{i,k,t} - l_{i,k}$. Therefore, we can choose the VMs to defer based on $t - a_{i,k}$ or $\tilde{l}_{i,k,t} - l_{i,k}$ or alternatively a combination of them.

Remark 1. It is easy to check that the tenant's profit in time-slot $t+1$ does not depend on $x_{i,t}$ due to our assumption that the tenant's revenue is only a function of the number of VMs it admits in the current time-slot (and proportional to VM lifetime henceforth). Therefore, the above optimization problem reduces to the following "myopic" control that only maximizes tenant's profit over a single time-slot:

$$\max_{x_{i,t}} f_i(x_{i,t}) - (\theta_t x_{i,t} + \pi_{i,t}\eta_{i,t})$$

Subject to

$$0 \le \eta_{i,t} = x_{i,t-1} + \eta_{i,t-1} + \Delta x_{i,t} - x_{i,t}$$

Note that now the tenant does not need to know θ'_{t+1} in this myopic control. In addition, prediction of future demand is not needed since the tenant only maximize profit within the current time-slot. In evaluation, we will use this simplified myopic control for tenant's DR for simplicity.

Remark 2. In the real world, we can also have scenarios wherein the revenue is not proportional to the lifetime of the VM. In that case, one simple idea is to define the utility function $f_i(x_{i,t} + \beta\hat{x}_{i,t+1})$ for a parameter $0 < \beta < 1$. In this case, the tenant will have to take the guiding price signal θ'_{t+1} to maximize its profit. Intuitively this utility function implies that the tenant's revenue diminishes as the service time of a VM increases. One such example could be a Web search engine as a tenant, wherein the usefulness of additional search results (at the expense of larger response times) reduces [13]. Another example is a video streaming server wherein the extra benefit of increasing quality of video diminishes with bandwidth needs.

3.3 Understanding cloud-tenant interactions

Before carrying out our empirical evaluation, we try to get a preliminary understanding of cloud-tenant interactions in our model by making some simplifying assumptions about the players' knowledge of future inputs. Recall that all the "optimal solutions" discussed in this section are only optimal w.r.t. the "myopic" objective (short-term optimization horizon), which do not necessarily optimize the long-term profits.

The following claim reveals the tenant's optimal demand response behavior under our assumptions. Due to space limit, we present all the proofs in a technical report [28].

CLAIM 1. *Assuming that the tenant's utility function $f_i(\cdot)$ is strictly concave and non-decreasing, the tenant's control problem has the following closed-form optimal solution:*

$$x^*_{i,t} = \begin{cases} X_{i,t}, & \text{if } \theta_t \le \tilde{\theta}_t \\ (f'_i)^{-1}(\theta_t - \pi_{i,t}), & \text{otherwise} \end{cases}$$

where $X_{i,t} = x_{i,t-1} + \eta_{i,t-1} + \Delta x_{i,t}$, $(f'_i)^{-1}(\cdot)$ is the inverse function of the derivative $f'_i(\cdot)$, and $\tilde{\theta}_t$ is the solution of equation $(f'_i)^{-1}(\theta_t - \pi_{i,t}) = X_{i,t}$ with θ_t as variable[3].

In particular, if $f_i(x_{i,t}) = a\log(bx_{i,t}+1)$ with $a, b > 0$, then $x^*_{i,t} = \frac{a}{\theta_t - \pi_{i,t}} - \frac{1}{b}$. We show the tenant's optimal demand response behavior in Figure 5 assuming the above log-form utility function. When $\theta_t \le \pi_{i,t}$, i.e., the VM price is lower than unit delay cost, then the tenant can actually admit as many VMs as possible to gain more profit without delaying any VMs. Since the total number of VMs at the beginning of

[3]Note that $f'_i(\cdot)$ is monotonically decreasing since $f_i(\cdot)$ is concave and increasing. Thus there exists a unique solution for the equation $(f'_i)^{-1}(\theta_t - \pi_{i,t}) = X_{i,t}$.

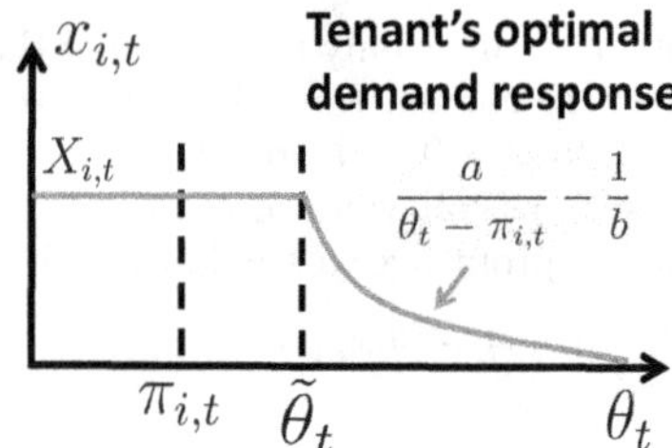

Figure 5: Illustration of tenant i's optimal demand response assuming $f_i(x_{i,t}) = a\log(bx_{i,t} + 1)$.

time-slot t is $X_{i,t}$, the tenant can only admit up to $X_{i,t}$ VMs. As the VM price increases, if $\pi_{i,t} < \theta_t \leq \tilde{\theta}_t$, the tenant can still make more profit by increasing number of VMs admitted as its revenue per VM outweighs the net loss of admitting a VM $(\theta_t - \pi_{i,t})$, so the number of VMs admitted is still $X_{i,t}$. $\tilde{\theta}_t$ is the break-even VM price where the tenant's revenue equals to the cost of admitting all VMs. When $\theta_t > \tilde{\theta}_t$, the net cost of admitting a VM increases, thus the tenant decides to reduce the number of VMs admitted.

Our next claim shows the optimal VM pricing decision of the cloud if it has perfect knowledge of the tenant's demand and DR.

CLAIM 2. *If the cloud has perfect knowledge of the tenants' optimal control decisions, $g(x) = \delta x$, $f_i(x) = f(x) = a\log(bx + 1)$, $\pi_{i,t} = \pi_t$, and $X_{i,t} = X_t, \forall i \in [1, N]$, then the cloud's optimal VM price is*

$$\theta_t^* = \begin{cases} \tilde{\theta}_t, & \text{if } \frac{1}{c}\alpha_t\delta \leq \pi_t \\ \max\{\tilde{\theta}_t, \frac{1}{c}\alpha_t\delta\}, & \text{if } \frac{1}{c}\alpha_t\delta > \pi_t, \max\{\tilde{\theta}_t, \frac{1}{c}\alpha_t\delta\} > \\ & \sqrt{ab(\frac{1}{c}\alpha_t\delta - \pi_t)} + \pi_t \\ \sqrt{ab(\frac{1}{c}\alpha_t\delta - \pi_t)} + \pi_t, & \text{otherwise} \end{cases}$$

where $\tilde{\theta}_t = \pi_t + f'(X_t) = \pi_t + \frac{ab}{bX_t+1}$.

Here $\frac{1}{c}\alpha_t\delta$ is the cloud's cost of serving one VM. We can make several useful observations from Claim 2. (i) If the cloud's cost per VM is low enough ($\frac{1}{c}\alpha_t\delta \leq \pi_t$), it can always have more profit by serving one more VM, so the best strategy is to set the highest VM price that does not result in tenant's back-off, i.e., tenants admit all of their demand. (ii) π_t reflects the tenant's intolerance to delay; the higher π_t is, the more VMs the tenant has to run, allowing the cloud to increase VM price without losing (too many) VMs. (iii) A tenant with higher a and b will have higher marginal revenue than another tenant with lower a and b. Hence, the cloud can set a higher price for the former tenant. (iv) Since $f'(X_t)$ is decreasing in X_t, $\tilde{\theta}_t$ is also decreasing in X_t, which implies that the cloud might have to reduce its VM price to encourage tenants to run VMs in order to have more profit when $\frac{1}{c}\alpha_t\delta \leq \pi_t$. A **key insight** from Claim 2 is that setting constant VM price or VM price proportional to energy price naively might not be a good choice for the cloud's profit maximization. *The cloud must be careful about exploring the tradeoffs between cloud's energy cost, tenant's demand and DR to optimize its profit.*

4. EVALUATION

We carry out our evaluation for three "scenarios" in increasing order of complexity. For our simplest scenario I, we

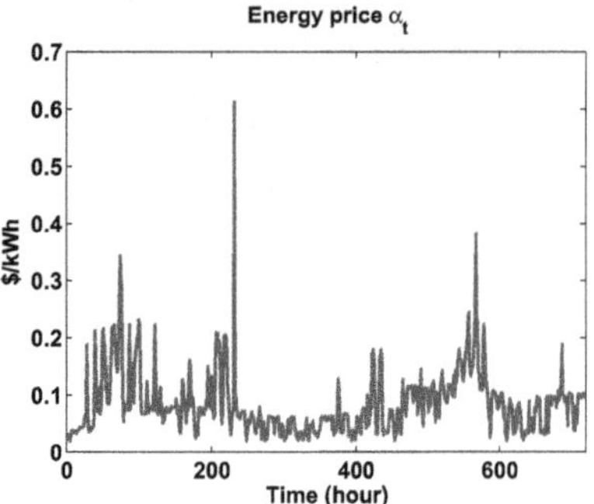

Figure 6: Hourly energy price from an electric utility in [14].

only work with a constant energy price and a constant tenant demand partly as a sanity check (Section 4.2). In scenario II, we use real-world energy prices and tenant's demand from an IBM production data center to show the impact of different predictors on cloud's profitability assuming constant delay penalty, i.e., time-invariant tenant DR (Section 4.3). Finally, in scenario III, we also vary tenant's DR over time (Section 4.4).

4.1 Experiment setup

In all the following experiments, we choose to work with "homogeneous" tenants (i.e., having identical DR behavior) from the IBM tenant trace and leave experiments with diverse tenants to future work. Even with this simplification, we still gather interesting insights upon which our future work can build.

Inputs: For scenario I, we work with a constant energy price $\alpha_t = 0.1\$/kWh, \forall t$ and constant tenant VM demand (400 VMs arrive at the beginning of the simulation and stay in the system forever). In scenarios II and III, we use the hourly energy prices in January, 2014 from an electric utility in [14] as shown in Figure 6. Our tenant VM demand trace comes from a production data center operated by IBM and is shown in Figure 2(c) wherein most of the VMs are long-lived and stay in the system during the entire simulation[4].

Parameters: Table 2 presents various parameters. We assume that the cloud can convert tenants' aggregate VM demand into power consumption as $g(x_t) = \delta x_t$, with the complementary assumption that the cloud consolidates ten VMs on each physical server which consumes 500 Watts on average. Then we can compute the power consumption of a single VM as $\delta = 500/(10*1000)*1.2 = 0.06kW/\text{VM}$ assuming the power usage effectiveness PUE = 1.2. We assume that the tenant's utility function has *log*-form: $f_i(x_{i,t}) = a\log(bx_{i,t} + 1)$. We explored many combinations of these parameters during our evaluation. Our final choice of the parameters values is based on the following **guiding rule**: all parameters should have non-negligible impact on cloud's and tenants' profitability, and all terms in all utilities are non-negligible. We conducted extensive experiments and present here interesting and representative results.

Cloud's predictors: We study the impact of four different predictors employing different degrees of freedom (DoF). Intuitively, predictors with higher DoF should yield higher profits for the cloud since they might provide better prediction of the tenant's aggregate demand for the cloud; how-

[4]We omit the results from Google trace since the insights are similar with those from the IBM tenant trace.

Sym.	Value	Definition
δ	0.06kW/VM	Power consump. of a single VM
c	17%	Frac. of cloud's costs as energy costs
a	10	Param. of tenant's utility function
b	5\$/VM	Param. of tenant's utility function
π	0.05\$/VM	Default delay cost in scenarios I & II

Table 2: Values chosen for our models.

ever, with higher uncertainty in utility pricing, tenant's demand and DR (particularly when tenant's DR is also time-varying as in Scenario III), it is possible that not all past data are equally valuable for the cloud to tune the parameters of the predictors. Therefore, we choose a "forgetting factor", denoted as λ, as a tuning parameter for the predictors which reflects how quickly the cloud forgets past sample observations of (demand, price) pairs[5]. Larger λ implies that the cloud forgets past data faster. We only show the results under different forgetting factors ($\lambda = 0, 0.1, 0.2$) for the piecewise linear predictor: "PW-M-λ" refers to a piecewise predictor with M line segments and forgetting factor λ.

Tenant's predictor: Generally speaking, tenants might want to predict both their respective VM demand and future VM prices. However, as discussed in Section 3, since we assume that tenant's revenue is only a function of the number of VMs it runs in the current time-slot, the tenant's control problem reduces to optimizing net utility within a single time-slot and thus prediction of future demand is not needed.

Baseline: We choose the case that the cloud has perfect knowledge of both tenant's demand and DR as our baseline to compare with, denoted as "Baseline". As discussed in Section 2, this baseline is sub-optimal w.r.t. long-term profits since it only optimizes the short-term objective. It is possible that some predictors might yield better long-term profits than this baseline for the cloud, however, only by chance, which is verified in our experiment results.

4.2 Constant energy price and tenant's demand

In this section, we assume a constant energy price ($\alpha_t = 0.1\$/kWh$) and constant tenant demand (400 VMs arrive at the beginning of the first time-slot and stay in the system within the entire simulation).

Performance expectations. We expect that the optimal VM price be a constant; all the past data are equally important for the predictors since all the inputs (including tenant's DR) are constant. We expect that the cloud's predictors for tenants' DR with smaller forgetting factors and higher DoF to offer better profits for the cloud.

Figure 7(a) shows the VM prices under different predictors with $\lambda = 0$. We observe that the VM price under simple predictors (ARX, Affine and Quad) with smaller DoF converges to a sub-optimal price (Baseline is optimal w.r.t. the above utilities) whereas error in estimate of aggregate tenant DR is minimized when the tenant demand (and DR) is time-invariant and the cloud knows this to be the case and simply tabulates past (price,demand) $=(\theta_t, x_t)$ observations and interpolates between them. As an example, the PW-40-0 performs much better than PW-5-0. We also observe that the steady-state VM price converges towards the optimal price very quickly as we increase DoF, i.e., the number

[5]A forgetting factor can be used to minimize weighted least square error in sample data, e.g., $\min \sum_{t=0}^{n} (1-\lambda)^{n-t}(x_t - \hat{x}_t)^2$, when out-dated data are less useful.

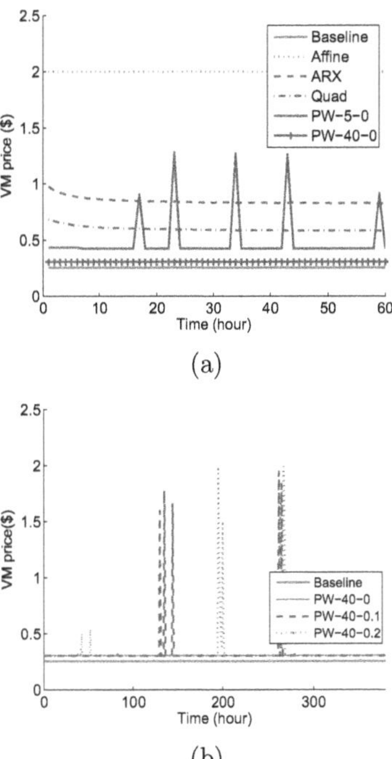

Figure 7: Scenario I: (a) VM prices under different predictors with $\lambda = 0$. (b) VM prices under piecewise linear predictors with different forgetting factors. PW-40-0 overlaps with others but without spikes.

of line segments (though results not shown here). However, when the aggregate tenant DR is time-varying (possibly due to tenant churn), system identification (to tune the parameters of the predictors) with aged-out data (i.e., forgetting factor larger than 0) is required.

We show the VM prices under the same piecewise linear predictor with different forgetting factors in Figure 7(b). We find that when $\lambda = 0$, the VM price converges very quickly to a sub-optimal price and stays stable. As λ increases from 0 to 0.2, the VM price exhibits more fluctuations. This is because all inputs (including tenant's DR) are time-invariant, and that all past data are important for the cloud's estimation of tenant's DR. Thus the performance of the predictor gets better as λ increases, but fluctuations also increase.

Key insights: (i) DoF affects the optimality of the predictors and higher DoF offers better performance. (ii) Convergence to sub-optimal price is faster for smaller forgetting factor. When inputs are constant and tenant's DR is time-invariant, larger forgetting factor results in oscillation/unstable behavior whereas smaller forgetting factor yields faster convergence and maintains stability.

4.3 Real-world energy prices and tenant demand

In this section we look at the scenario with real-world energy price and tenant's demand as introduced in Section 4.1.

Performance expectations. We expect to see that the cloud has better profits under predictors with higher DoF. However, due to the poor predictability of utility prices and tenants' demand, it is possible that not all past data are equally useful for the cloud's estimation of tenant and higher forgetting factor might offer better profit.

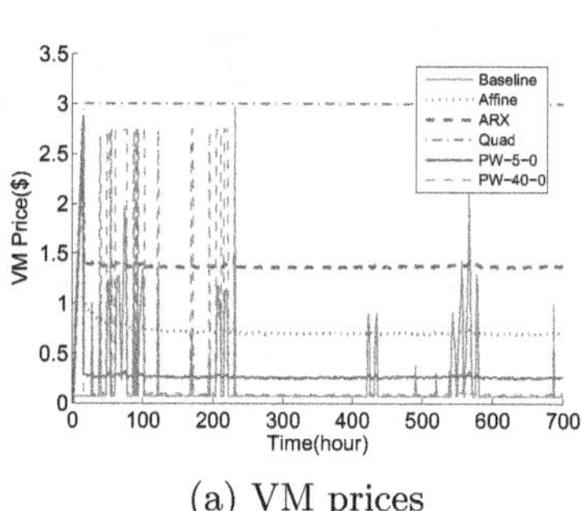

(a) VM prices

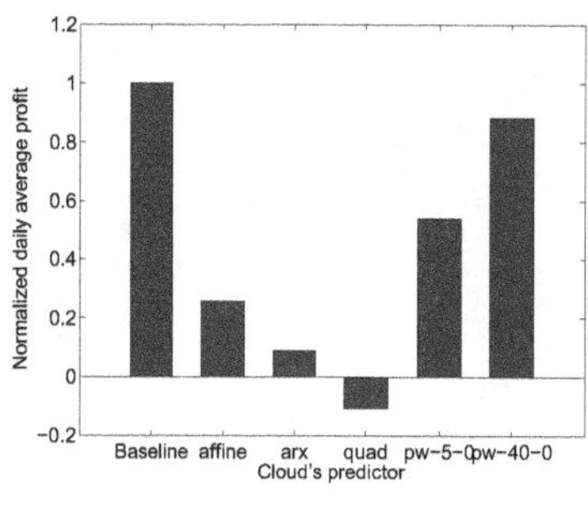

(b) Tenant's daily average profit.

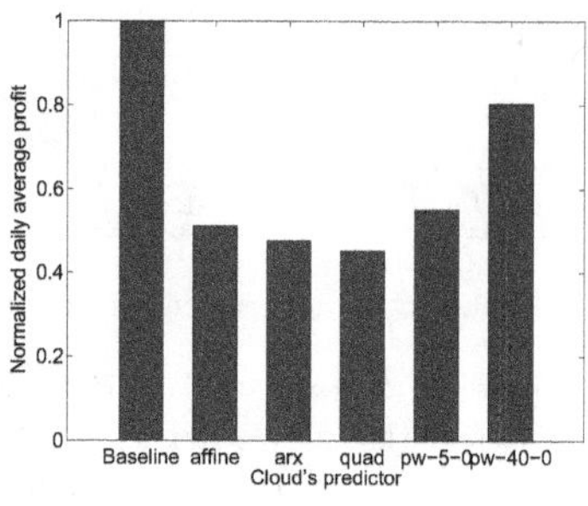

(c) Cloud's daily average profit.

Figure 8: Scenario II with different predictors and $\lambda = 0$. Profits normalized w.r.t. Baseline.

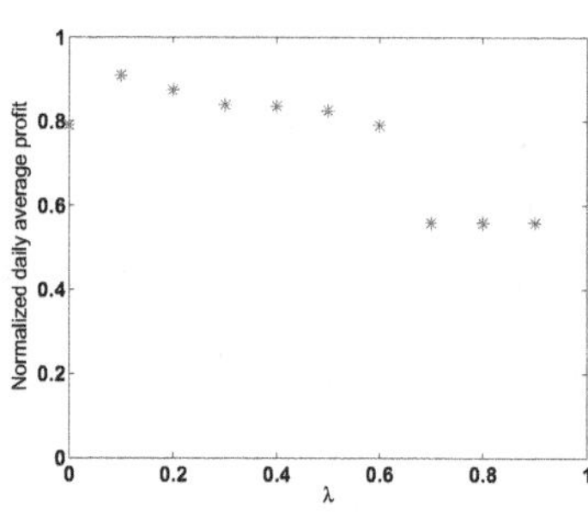

(a) Cloud's daily average profit.

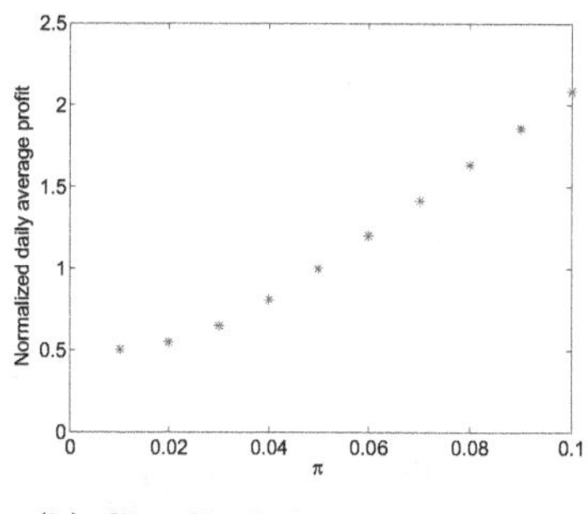

(b) Cloud's daily average profit.

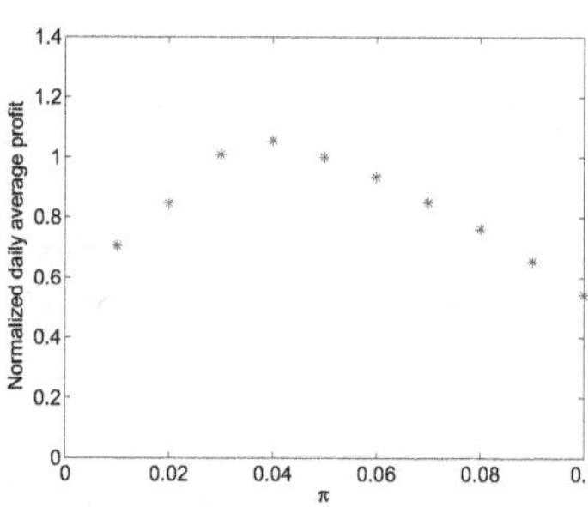

(c) Tenant's daily average profit.

Figure 9: Scenario II: (a) Cloud's daily average profit under PW-40-λ, $\lambda \in [0, 0.9]$, normalized w.r.t. Baseline. (b) Cloud's daily average profit under Baseline with $\pi \in [0.01, 0.1]$, normalized w.r.t. $\pi = 0.05$. (c) Tenant's daily average profit under Baseline with $\pi \in [0.01, 0.1]$, normalized w.r.t. $\pi = 0.05$.

Figure 8 shows the VM prices, cloud's daily average profit and tenant's daily average profit over a month with different predictors and $\lambda = 0$. First, we observe that the baseline assuming perfect knowledge of tenant's demand and DR offers dynamic VM prices which have similar fluctuation with the energy prices α_t. However, when the energy price is low, the VM price seems stable and does not depend on energy price. This is consistent with Claim 2 in Section 3 that only when energy price is high enough ($\frac{1}{c}\alpha_t\delta > \pi_t$), the optimal VM price is either proportional to energy price, or depends on the tradeoffs between energy price, tenant's utility and delay cost. Second, we find that VM prices generated under predictors with low DoF (such as ARX, Affine and Quad) converge to different constant VM prices and there is great gap between the cloud's profits with those predictors and the baseline profit. This justifies our motivation for DR-aware dynamic pricing: Simply setting **constant VM prices** cannot guarantee cloud's profitability. On the other hand, predictors with higher DoF (such as PW-40-0) offer much better profit for the cloud (higher than Affine by 30%), with VM prices closer to those of Baseline. Third, tenant's profit could be negative (as shown in Figure 8(b)) due to high VM price. As an extreme case, the VM price under Quad is so high that the tenant has to defer most of its VMs which results in high delay cost and even negative profit. In such cases, the tenant might have to switch to a different cloud provider (an action space beyond the scope of this paper).

Next, we evaluate the impact of different forgetting factors. As we expected, in Figure 9(a), PW-40-0.1 and PW-40-0.2 offer similar cumulative profit for the cloud, which is much higher than that of PW-40-0. This is due to the poor predictability in both the utility price and tenant's demand. In such cases, out-dated past samples of (price, demand) might not be so useful for the cloud to estimate tenant's DR, consistent with the choice of high forgetting factor. However, as λ keeps increasing, the cloud's profit starts to decrease. This is due to the fact that predictors with higher λ might be too responsive in estimating tenant's DR, and oscillating behavior (in the VM prices) might occur which may in turn hurt the cloud's profitability.

In addition, we explore the impact of delay cost π on both the cloud's and tenant's profits by varying $\pi \in [0.01, 0.1]$ while keeping all other parameters and inputs the same. In Figure 9(b), the cloud achieves higher profit when the tenant's delay cost is larger. This is consistent with our intuition: larger delay cost implies that the tenant is willing to pay higher price for the same amount of VMs to guarantee its workload performance, and thus the cloud could make more profit by charging higher price without losing much VM demand, whereas a tenant with less delay cost has more flexibility in its demand and thus the cloud's profit becomes less. Intuitively, the opposite should happen at the tenant-side: as delay cost increases and the cloud makes more profit, the tenant's profit should decrease. However, as shown in Figure 9(c), the tenant's profit increases as π increases before reaching $\pi = 0.04$. This is because when delay costs are low, the optimal VM price is also very low (see Claim 2); a tenant with relatively higher delay costs tends to admit more VM demand and thus has higher profit.

Key insights: (i) Similar to scenario I, predictors with higher DoF offer better profit for the cloud. (ii) However, forgetting factor has to be chosen carefully (instead of using $\lambda = 0$ in scenario I) due to the poor predictability of input-

s. (iii) Even without perfect knowledge of tenant's demand response, the cloud might still garner more profit by implementing the proposed pricing framework than applying a constant VM price.

Remark. In scenario II, the Baseline always offers more profit for the cloud than other predictors. However, recall that our myopic control only maximizes short-term profit as discussed in Section 2, which is not the way we assess the performance (i.e., long-term profit of the cloud) of different predictors. In fact, we can even create scenarios wherein the Baseline solution is not optimal w.r.t. the cloud's long-term profit. We show such results in Section 4.4.

4.4 Real-world data and time-varying DR

In this section we look at the scenario with assumptions in scenario II. We introduce more dynamic behavior at tenant side by imagining time-varying delay cost. We vary the tenant's delay cost π_t between $0.005\$/VM$ and $0.1\$/VM$ every 48 time-slots[6].

Performance expectations. Time-varying delay costs add to the complications of prediction at cloud side. Here based on insights from section 4.3, we expect to see better performance for predictors with higher DoF. Different λ values are used to see the effect of forgetting past data. In the next section, we study the non-trivial trade-off associated with the choice of forgetting factor λ.

We observe in our experiments that predictors with lower DoF convergence to a constant price which does not perform well in terms of cloud profit. This is consistent with what is observed in previous section. Therefore, we use the piecewise-linear predictor with 40 segments to predict the highly variable tenants' DR at cloud side. Additionally we study the effect of forgetting the past data to explore this effect in more complex and closer to real-world scenarios. The piecewise predictor which was observed to have the best performance in previous sections is chosen. In section 4.3 the myopic objective gives the best performance for the cloud but here we see that under highly variable situations (which is close to real-world cases) satisfying myopic objective does not guarantee the end goal which is cloud cumulative profit. In Figure 10, we show that the cloud's profit using PW-40-0 is higher than Baseline by around 40% - this is possible because the myopic objective of the cloud and tenant does not guarantee optimal long-term profit (as a longer-term objective would under standard Markovian assumptions).

Key insights: (i) Predictors with higher DoF perform better even in highly variable environments. (ii) Optimal solutions of myopic control does not guarantee long term optimal profit for the cloud.

5. RELATED WORK

Pricing design in the cloud. Pricing in the cloud has emerged as an active area of research, and various techniques including dynamic pricing [17, 30, 22], auction-based pricing [26, 20], Nash bargaining [7] with either single or federation among cloud providers [8, 3], have been proposed. However, a common assumption of existing work is the tenants' DRs/demands can be inferred by the cloud, generally for theoretic tractability reasons, which is not suitable in our work due to poor predictability of the real-world data we use and the complexity of tenant's DR. We do find one exception: in [23], the cloud designs pricing for bandwidth reservation without knowing tenants' DR and decentralized algorithms are proposed with optimality guarantees. However, such nice properties largely depend on the way that the problem is constructed, e.g., [23] maximizes the social welfare of the cloud and the tenants which is not a reasonable goal in our environment due to the assumed selfish nature of these entities.

[6]In the real world, it is possible that the tenants might have highly variable delay costs or utility parameters. For such cases, we can have a data collection system before applying the pricing framework for system identification. For example, we can filter the past samples and only look at the (price, demand) pairs at, e.g., the same time-of-day, energy price and delay penalty regime, to tune the parameters of the cloud's predictors. We leave this line of study to future work.

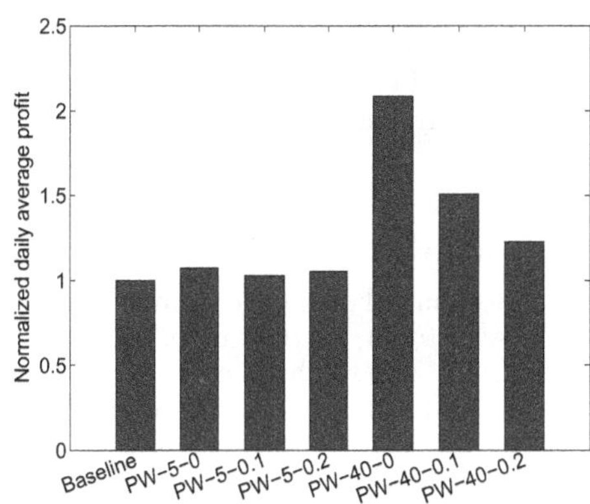

Figure 10: Scenario III: Normalized cloud's daily average profit under PW with different forgetting factors.

Game with incomplete information. Although not well-explored in cloud computing yet, in other areas (e.g., power systems) general incomplete-information game-theoretic frameworks include Bayesian games and hypergames, e.g., [25], have been explored. In both VCG and PSP auctions (e.g., [4] recently), issues of truthfulness in the disclosed bids are considered, i.e., reflecting actual demand response (by marginal valuation). More prosaic approaches simply interpolate and extrapolate from presumed honest bids (by (amount, price)) to obtain a complete estimate of other players' demand response. These frameworks are applicable to iterated (sequential) adversarial (non-cooperative) games with or without leaders. Generally, estimates are greatly simplified under the assumption that player strategies are time (play-action iteration) invariant. In future work, we will consider introducing such more complex/advanced techniques to our cloud pricing design.

DR in cloud computing. A large body of work now exists on DR for data centers that is complementary to our work. A comprehensive survey is offered in [29]. DR by individual tenants, as imagined in our work, is relatively less well-explored.

6. CONCLUSION AND FUTURE WORK

In this paper, we proposed a leader-follower game-based cloud pricing framework for cloud's profit maximization. In face of poor predictability of tenants' demand and DRs, we employed myopic control with short-term predictive models. Our empirical evaluation with real-world data showed useful insights on cloud's profitability affected by its predictive models. In our future work, we will explore enhancements to our models identified throughout our paper and carry out more comprehensive evaluation using benchmarks and realistic prototypes.

Acknowledgements

We would like to thank the anonymous reviewers and our shepherd, Dr. David Irwin, for their useful comments. This work was supported, in part, by the following: NSF CAREER award 0953541, NSF 1000699, NSF CNS 1228717, Swiss NSF 200021, 141002 and EU commission under FP7 GENiC 608826.

7. REFERENCES

[1] Amazon EC2 Pricing, 2014. `http://aws.amazon.com/ec2/pricing/`.

[2] L. André Barroso and U. Hölzle. *The Datacenter as a computer: an introduction to the design of warehouse-scale machines.* Morgan & Claypool, 2009.

[3] J. Anselmi, D. Ardagna, J. C. S. Liu, A. Wierman, Y. Xu, and Z. Yang. The economics of the cloud: price competition and congestion. *SIGMETRICS Perform. Eval. Rev.*, 41(4), Apr. 2014.

[4] S. Bhattacharya, K. Kar, J. H. Chow, and A. Gupta. Progressive second price auctions with elastic supply for pev charging in the smart grid. In *Proc. of NeTGCoop*, 2014.

[5] G. Chen, W. He, J. Liu, S. Nath, L. Rigas, L. Xiao, and F. Zhao. Energy-aware server provisioning and load dispatching for connection-intensive internet services. In *Proc. of NSDI*, 2008.

[6] Y. Chen, A. Ganapathi, R. Griffith, and R. H. Katz. The case for evaluating mapreduce performance using workload suites. In *Proc. of IEEE MASCOTS*, 2011.

[7] Y. Feng, B. Li, and B. Li. Bargaining towards maximized resource utilization in video streaming datacenters. In *Proc. of INFOCOM*, 2012.

[8] Y. Feng, B. Li, and B. Li. Price competition in an oligopoly market with multiple iaas cloud providers. *IEEE Trans. Computers*, 63(1), 2014.

[9] M. Ghorbani, Y. Wang, Y. Xue, M. Pedram, and P. Bogdan. Prediction and control of bursty cloud workloads: a fractal framework. In *Proc. of CODES*, 2014.

[10] Google cluster data, 2011. `https://code.google.com/p/googleclusterdata/`.

[11] D. Hamilton. Most US companies plan to increase public cloud spending 15 percent or more in 2015. `http://www.thewhir.com/web-hosting-news/us-companies-plan-increase-public-cloud-spending-15-percent-2015`.

[12] J. Hamilton. Internet-scale service infrastructure efficiency. *SIGARCH Comput. Archit. News*, 37(3):232–232, June 2009.

[13] Y. He, S. Elnikety, J. R. Larus, and C. Yan. Zeta: scheduling interactive services with partial execution. In *Proc. of SoCC*, 2012.

[14] Ontario electric utility, 2014. `http://www.ieso.ca/Pages/Power-Data/default.aspx#price`.

[15] D. Juan, L. Li, H. Peng, D. Marculescu, and C. Faloutsos. Beyond poisson: modeling inter-arrival time of requests in a datacenter. In *Advances in knowledge discovery and data mining.* Springer International Publishing, 2014.

[16] S. Kandula, S. Sengupta, A. Greenberg, P. Patel, and R. Chaiken. The nature of data center traffic: measurements & analysis. In *Proc. of ACM SIGCOMM*, 2009.

[17] V. Kantere, D. Dash, G. Francois, S. Kyriakopoulou, and A. Ailamaki. Optimal service pricing for a cloud cache. *IEEE Trans. Knowledge and Data Engineering*, 2011.

[18] R. T. Kaushik, P. Sarkar, and A. Gharaibeh. Greening the compute cloud's pricing plans. HotPower, 2013.

[19] W. Kwon and S. Han. *Receding horizon control.* Invited chapter for Green High-Performance Computing. SpringerLink, 2005.

[20] H. Li, C. Wu, Z. Li, and F. Lau. Profit-maximizing virtual machine trading in a federation of selfish clouds. In *Proc. of IEEE INFOCOM*, 2013.

[21] D. Link. Netflix and stolen time. `http://blog.sciencelogic.com/netflix-steals-time-in-the-cloud-and-from-users/03/2011`.

[22] Z. Liu, I. Liu, S. Low, and A. Wierman. Pricing data center demand response. In *Proc. of ACM SIGMETRICS*, 2014.

[23] D. Niu, C. Feng, and B. Li. Pricing cloud bandwidth reservations under demand uncertainty. In *Proc. of ACM SIGMETRICS*, 2012.

[24] C. Reiss, A. Tumanov, G. R. Ganger, R. H. Katz, and M. A. Kozuch. Heterogeneity and dynamicity of clouds at scale: google trace analysis. In *Proc. of ACM SoCC*, 2012.

[25] Y. Sasaki and K. Kijima. Hypergames and bayesian games: A theoretical comparison of the models of games with incomplete information. *J Syst Sci Complex*, 25:720–735, 2012.

[26] W. Shi, L. Zhang, C. Wu, Z. Li, and F. C. Lau. An online auction framework for dynamic resource provisioning in cloud computing. In *Proc. of ACM SIGMETRICS*, 2014.

[27] R. Vartabedian. US electricity prices may be going up for good. `http://www.latimes.com/nation/la-na-power-prices-20140426-story.html`.

[28] C. Wang and et. al. Recouping energy costs from cloud tenants: Tenant demand response aware pricing design. Technical report, CSE TR-15-001, Penn State University. `http://www.cse.psu.edu/~bhuvan/CSE-TR-15-001.pdf`.

[29] A. Wierman, Z. Liu, I. Liu, and H. Mohsenian-Rad. Opportunities and challenges for data center demand response. In *Proc. of IEEE IGCC*, 2014.

[30] H. Xu and B. Li. Maximizing revenue with dynamic cloud pricing: the infinite horizon case. In *Proc. of IEEE ICC*, 2012.

[31] J. Zhao, H. Li, C. Wu, Z. Li, Z. Zhang, and F. Lau. Dynamic pricing and profit maximization for the cloud with geo-distributed data centers. In *Proc. of IEEE INFOCOM*, 2014.

Auc2Charge: An Online Auction Framework for Electric Vehicle Park-and-Charge

Qiao Xiang[1], Fanxin Kong[1], Xue Liu[1], Xi Chen[1], Linghe Kong[1], Lei Rao[2]
[1]School of Computer Science, McGill University
[2]General Motors Research Lab
{qiao.xiang, xueliu}@cs.mcgill.ca,
{fanxin.kong, xi.chen11, linghe.kong}@mail.mcgill.ca, lei.rao@gm.com

ABSTRACT

The increasing market share of electric vehicles (EVs) makes large-scale charging stations indispensable infrastructure for integrating EVs into the future smart grid. Thus their operation modes have drawn great attention from researchers. One promising mode called park-and-charge was recently proposed. It allows people to park their EVs at a parking lot, where EVs can get charged during the parking time. This mode has been experimented and demonstrated in small scale. However, the missing of an efficient market mechanism is an important gap preventing its large-scale deployment. Existing pricing policies, e.g., pay-by-use and flat-rate pricing, would jeopardize the efficiency of electricity allocation and the corresponding social welfare in the park-and-charge mode, and thus are inapplicable. To find an efficient mechanism, this paper explores the feasibility and benefits of utilizing auction mechanism in the EV park-and-charge mode. The auction allows EV users to submit and update bids on their charging demand to the charging station, which makes corresponding electricity allocation and pricing decisions. To this end, we propose *Auc2Charge*, an online auction framework. *Auc2Charge* is truthful and individual rational. Running in polynomial time, it provides an efficient electricity allocation for EV users with a close-form approximation ratio on system social welfare. Through both theoretical analysis and numerical simulation, we demonstrate the efficacy of *Auc2Charge* in terms of social welfare and user satisfaction.

Categories and Subject Descriptors

C.4 [**Performance of systems**]: Modeling techniques; J.7 [**Computers in other systems**]: Industrial control

Keywords

smart grid, electric vehicles, mechanism design, auction

1. INTRODUCTION

The electric vehicle (EV) is visioned as a crucial component in the future intelligent transportation systems (ITS) [4]. Compared with gasoline-powered vehicles, EVs have the potential benefits of a lower carbon emission, a lower powering cost and a higher power efficiency. With these promising benefits, however, EVs also introduce a high penetration into the power grid by shifting the energy load from gasoline to electricity. As EVs' market share is increasing, the integration of EV into the future smart grid has drawn great interests of both academia and industry. Various charging facilities have been studied [4,8,9,12,15,17,18].

Among all charging facilities (e.g., home charging point, workplace charging facility and etc.), charging stations have become indispensable infrastructure to support the large-scale development of EVs [9,10]. Thus their operation mode requires a careful design. Recently, researchers propose a promising operation mode of charging station, which is called EV park-and-charge. In this mode, people can park their EVs at the parking lot equipped with charging points. These vehicles can then be charged during the period of parking. Potential application scenarios of this mode include parking-lot charging at workplace, shopping mall, airport and military base. Several field experiments have been done to explore the feasibility of this operation mode. For instance, several universities in Europe conduct the V-Charge project, which aims to design an automated valet parking and charging system to support autonomous local transportation [3]. General Motors (GM) and TimberRock perform a pioneering experiment [2], in which TimberRock uses the OnStar vehicle communication system to manage the charging schedule of a fleet of Chevrolet Volts parked in GM's E-Motor Plant. Its objective is to balance the stochastic arrival of charging demand and the intermittency of renewable energy supply at the park-and-charge station. And the U.S. Air Force works with the Lawrence Berkeley National Laboratory to conduct a similar experiment at its Los Angeles Base [19]. Though these experiments provide positive feedback on the potential of the park-and-charge mode, one important gap still exists between small-scale experiments and the large-scale deployment of this mode. This gap is the missing of an efficient market mechanism.

An efficient market mechanism for charging station should achieve two objectives: 1)to avoid overpricing and underpricing the electricity by quickly adapting to the change in demand-supply relation; and 2)to provide an explicit guarantee on social welfare by constructing an efficient electricity allocation between EV users. The social welfare is the monetary sum of the revenue from charging station and the utility gained by EV users. Regardless the differences on hardware and charging schedule, current charging stations mainly adopt either one of the following pricing policies as their market mechanism: pay-by-use pricing and flat-rate pricing. Though they are simple and helpful for the market expanding of EVs, they are not efficient market mechanisms. For instance, overpricing and underpricing could happen in both policies due to the fluctuation of electricity price from power distributors, thus harm the benefits of EV users and charging station, respectively. What is worse, the long charging time of EV and limited capacity of charging station would cause inefficient electricity allocation between

e-Energy'15, July 14–17, 2015, Bangalore, India.

DOI: http://dx.doi.org/10.1145/2768510.2768529 .

EV users and significantly prolong the total time (waiting time and actual charging time) spent by EV users. In extreme cases, some EVs would end up getting very little electricity charged after hours of waiting. And this inefficiency would become more severe as the market share of EV continues increasing.

To design an efficient market mechanism, we explore the feasibility and benefits of utilizing auction in the park-and-charge operation mode. In particular, we propose to design an online auction framework for this mode. Finding such an auction framework for this mode, however, is a non-trivial task because we need to address a series of challenges. 1)The proposed auction must be online to cope with the stochastic nature of system information in the park-and-charge mode. 2)The auction framework should be computationally efficient so that the electricity allocation and pricing decision can be quickly made in large-scale park-and-charge stations. 3)The auction framework should ensure truthfulness, individual rationality and an explicit guarantee on social welfare simultaneously.

To address these challenges, we propose *Auc2Charge*, a computationally efficient online auction framework, which leverages recent progress in mechanism design [5,6,16,23]. It involves a budget-based bid update process between any consecutive two time slots [6,23], which transforms the long-term total social welfare maximization problem(**PNC**) into a series of one-shot social welfare maximization problems $\mathbf{PNC_{one}(t)}$. For each $\mathbf{PNC_{one}(t)}$ problem, we design a greedy α-approximation algorithm using the classic primal-dual method [5], and translate it to a randomized one-shot auction mechanism, which is truthful and individual rational. It ensures an α-approximation ratio on social welfare of $\mathbf{PNC_{one}(t)}$ problem in polynomial time [16]. Different from auctions in cloud systems, where exists no constraint on users' capacity of receiving resources, we adopt a dropping process to drop bids violating maximal charging-capacity constraint in one-shot auction, without compromising social welfare. By integrating this one-shot auction with the budget-based bid update process, *Auc2Charge* provides an explicit approximation ratio on overall social welfare of park-and-charge while maintaining the property of truthfulness and individual rationality. Our **main contributions** are as follow:

1. We study the novel problem of utilizing auction in designing an efficient market mechanism for the EV park-and-charge mode. In particular, we propose *Auc2Charge*, a computationally-efficient online auction framework.

2. Through theoretical analysis, we show that *Auc2Charge* ensures the property of truthfulness and individual rationality, and provides a close-form competitive ratio on system social welfare.

3. Using numerical simulation, we demonstrate its efficacy under various settings in terms of social welfare and user satisfaction.

The remaining of this paper is organized as follows. In Section 2 we illustrate EV park-and-charge, discuss our motivation and identify the corresponding challenges. We present system settings and problem formulation in Section 3, and the design of *Auc2Charge* in Section 4. We study the performance of *Auc2Charge* in Section 5. We discuss related work in Section 6, and conclude our paper in Section 7.

2. PARK-AND-CHARGE: ILLUSTRATION, MOTIVATION AND CHALLENGES

In this section, we first illustrate the EV park-and-charge mode in Figure 1. In a large parking lot, every parking spot is equipped with a charging point. People drive to the parking lot, park their EVs, connect vehicles to charging points and leave for their personal arrangements, e.g., working, shopping and etc. During the parking period, charging points can charge electricity to the connected EVs. The detailed charging scheduling, e.g., charging speed and charging amount, is determined by a controller in the park lot.

The park-and-charge mode works in a dynamic environment, including fluctuate electricity supply, unpredictable arrival of EV charging demand and the ever-changing unit-time charging capacity of different EVs, all of which result in a stochastic demand-supply relation. To be deployed in large-scale, therefore, the park-and-charge mode needs an efficient market mechanism to quickly response to the change of demand-supply relation. However, existing pricing policies for charging stations, such as pay-per-use pricing and flat-rate pricing, fail to adapt to the rapid change of demand-supply relation in EV park-and-charge mode. For instance, when the available electricity supply is larger than the charging demand from parked EVs, both policies are overpricing electricity, which jeopardizes the benefit of EV users. On the contrary, when the available electricity supply is smaller than the charging demand from parked EVs, both policies are underpricing electricity as it is now a scarce resource. As a result, the benefit of charging station is jeopardized.

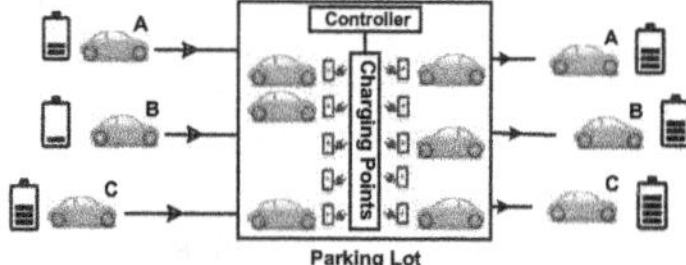

Figure 1: An overview of park-and-charge operation mode

What is worse, these pricing polices may yield an inefficient electricity allocation between EV users, and thus impair system social welfare, i.e., the monetary sum of revenue made by charging station and the utility gained by EV users. Take the scenario in Figure 2 as an example, where the park-and-charge station has an electricity supply of 30 kWh. When arriving at the parking-and-charge lot, EV user A has an SOC of 20kWh/40kWh=0.5 while user B has an SOC of 5kWh/25kWh=0.2. Only focusing on station's revenue, pay-per-use and flat-rate policies do not distinguish the utility difference under various allocation schemes as they yield the same revenue. Thus charging A and B by 15kWh each in Figure 2a) appears to be a fair allocation for these policies. However, the lower SOC of B, i.e., 0.2, implies that a unit amount of electricity would bring a higher utility to user B than A. To maximize total social welfare, an efficient electricity allocation should charge B as much as possible, i.e., charging B by 20kWh and A by 10kWh in Figure 2b). Thus charging each vehicle by 15kWh is an inefficient allocation. The inability to guarantee an efficient electricity allocation makes neither of these policies efficient market mechanisms for park-and-charge.

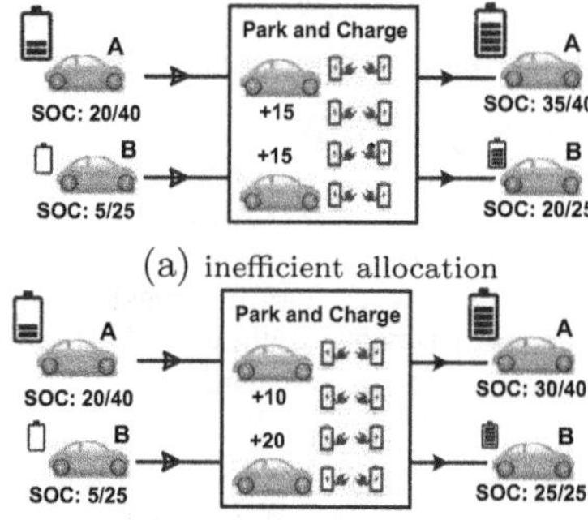

Figure 2: The utility difference between two allocations are not considered by pay-per-use and flat-rate pricing policies.

To overcome these shortcomings of existing pricing policies and thus design an efficient market mechanism for the EV park-and-charge mode, we propose to utilize auction as the market mechanism for this mode. An efficient auction can avoid overpricing and underpricing by adapting to the change of demand-supply relation, provide an efficient resource allocation by assigning resources to users who values them most, and thus improve system social welfare. Towards designing an efficient auction mechanism, we need to address the following challenges:

Challenge 1 *The auction framework must be online.* This is because in the EV park-and-charge mode, system information such as the electricity supply, the charging demand of EV users, and the unit-time charging capacity of every vehicle, are stochastic and unpredictable.

Challenge 2 *The auction framework should be computationally efficient.* A good auction should make allocation and pricing decisions in polynomial time so that it can be applied in large-scale facility, e.g., a parking lot with hundreds or thousands charging points.

Challenge 3 *The auction framework must be truthful, individual rational and achieve explicit guarantee on total social welfare.* For an auction, the truthfulness property can avoid speculative strategic action of EV users. The individual rationality ensures that participating users will not receive negative utility. And an explicit guarantees on system social welfare ensures the market efficiency. Directly applying existing auctions such as first-price and VCG auctions into dynamic scenarios of EV charging [13, 14, 24] cannot maintain these properties at the same time, and sometimes even lead to infeasible allocation, e.g., fractional VCG in combinatorial auctions.

To tackle these challenges, we leverage recent progress in mechanism design [5, 6, 16, 23] and propose our *Auc2Charge* online auction framework for park-and-charge in this paper.

3. PROBLEM FORMULATION

We consider an EV park-and-charge station operating in a discrete-time model. Time is divided into time slots of equal length, denoted by $t = 1, 2, \ldots, T$. Charging point is equipped at every parking spot. And we consider a set of M EV users, denoted by $j = 1, 2, \ldots, M$, who arrive at the station and park their vehicles for one or more time slots. Every EV user j has a budget limit B_j during her whole parking period, During their stay, EV users can submit and update their bids about their charging demand to the station using mobile devices or computers. For each time slot t, any user j can submit up to K bids, denoted by $k = 1, 2, \ldots, K$. We define the kth bid submitted by EV user j about charging demand for time slot t as a 2-tuple $(c_j^k(t), b_j^k(t))$, in which $c_j^k(t)$ represents the electricity demand of this bid, and $b_j^k(t)$ represents user j's *reported valuation* for getting charged for an amount of $c_j^k(t)$ electricity in slot t, in a monetary form. Other than the reported valuation, every user j also has a *real valuation* $v_j^k(t)$ for every electricity demand $c_j^k(t)$ submitted to the station. $v_j^k(t)$ is private to user j, which can be affected by many factors, e.g., personal agenda, risk preference and etc., and is also expressed in monetary form. For each user j, her reported valuations $b_j^k(t)$ are correlated across different t, and so are real valuations $v_j^k(t)$. These correlations are private to j. All we know is that $b_j^k(t)$ and $v_j^k(t)$ are monotone increasing functions of $c_j^k(t)$ in any t.

At the beginning of every time slot t, the charging station makes electricity allocation and pricing decisions for slot t based on all the submitted bids of charging demand for t. The total amount of allocated electricity in time slot t must not exceed $R(t)$, the available electricity supply at the station in slot t. For any EV user j, she can win at most one bid among all her submitted bids for every time slot t, and the electricity demand in the winning bids cannot exceed $C_j(t)$, the unit-time maximal charging capacity for EV j during time slot t. This capacity depends on the characteristics of EV battery, e.g., state of charge, lifetime and etc., and hence is stochastic and unpredictable. We use a set of binary decision variables $y_j^k(t) \in \{0, 1\}$ to denote the allocation decision for each bid $(c_j^k(t), b_j^k(t))$. $y_j^k(t) = 1$ means this bid is a winning bid and user j will receive a charging of $c_j^k(t)$ electricity by paying $\Gamma_j(t)$ to the station, and $y_j^k(t) = 0$ means user j does not win this bid and will pay nothing, i.e., $\Gamma_j(t) = 0$. We define $u_j(t)$, the utility for user j at slot t as follows:

$$u_j^t = \sum_{k=1}^{K} v_j^k(t) y_j^k(t) - \Gamma_j(t)$$

To avoid overpricing and underpricing, and to allocate the electricity to EV users who really value it, an good auction mechanism needs to achieve the following properties: 1) truthfulness, 2) individual rationally, and 3) social welfare maximization. An auction mechanism is *truthful* if reporting her *real valuation* as the *reported valuation* for any bid she submits is the dominant strategy for every user j. An auction ensures *individual rationally* if every participating user gets non-negative utility. And an auction achieve social welfare maximization by maximizing the total *real valuation* of all winning bids. When the truthfulness property is achieved, it can be written as $\sum_t \sum_j \sum_k b_j^k(t) y_j^k(t)$ since the reported valuation for each bid equals to the corresponding real valuation [16]. Then we can formulate the offline overall social welfare maximization problem for the park-and-charge system as the following binary integer programming model.

$$\textbf{PNC}: \quad \text{maximize} \quad \sum_{t=1}^{T} \sum_{j=1}^{M} \sum_{k=1}^{K} b_j^k(t) y_j^k(t) \tag{1}$$

subject to

$$\sum_{k=1}^{K} \sum_{t=1}^{T} b_j^k(t) y_j^k(t) \le B_j, \qquad \forall j, \tag{2a}$$

$$\sum_{j=1}^{M} \sum_{k=1}^{K} c_j^k(t) y_j^k(t) \le R(t), \qquad \forall t, \tag{2b}$$

$$\sum_{k=1}^{K} y_j^k(t) \le 1, \qquad \forall j \text{ and } t, \tag{2c}$$

$$\sum_{k=1}^{K} c_j^k(t) y_j^k(t) \le C_j(t), \qquad \forall j \text{ and } t, \tag{2d}$$

$$y_j^k(t) \in \{0, 1\}, \qquad \forall j,\ k \text{ and } t. \tag{2e}$$

In this model, constraint (2a) is the overall budget limit for every user j. Constraint (2b) ensures that the total amount of electricity allocated to the winning bids in time slot t does not exceed the total available electricity supply at the station in t. Constraint (2c) ensures that each EV user j can win at most one bid in every time slot. And constraint (2d) ensures that the electricity allocated to EV user j in time slot t does not exceed j's unit-time charging capacity in t. As we explained earlier, this unit-time maximal charging capacity is unpredictable in that it depends on the characteristics of EV battery, e.g., state of charge, lifetime and etc.

A linear program (LP) relaxation of problem **PNC** can be achieved by replacing the 0-1 integer constraint (2e) with $y_j^k(t) \in [0, 1]$, for any j, k and t. And the upper bound of 1 for each $y_j^k(t)$ can then be omitted because the lower bound 0 and constraint (2c) constitute a sufficient condition of this upper bound. We introduce dual variables x_j, $z(t)$, $s_j(t)$ and $q_j(t)$, for any j and t, to constraints (2a)-(2d) and get the dual problem of the LP relaxation of **PNC** as:

D-PNC^{lp} :

$$\text{minimize} \sum_{j=1}^{M} B_j x_j + \sum_{t=1}^{T} R(t) z(t) + \sum_{j=1}^{M} \sum_{t=1}^{T} C_j(t) q_j(t) + \sum_{j=1}^{M} \sum_{t=1}^{T} s_j(t), \tag{3}$$

subject to

$$b_j^k(t) x_j + c_j^k(t) z(t) + s_j(t) + c_j^k(t) q_j(t) \ge b_j^k(t), \forall j,\ k \text{ and } t, \tag{4a}$$

$$x_j,\ z(t),\ s_j(t),\ q_j(t) \ge 0, \forall j \text{ and } t. \tag{4b}$$

Solving the **PNC** problem requires the complete knowledge about the whole system over all time slots, which is practically impossible. In the park-and-charge mode, system information including the electricity supply of charging station, the arrival and leaving time of EV users, the bids submitted by EV users and the unit-time charging capacity of different EVs are all stochastic, and thus not known *a priori*. In addition, the overall budget constraint for every EV user makes the bidding decisions at different time slots all coupling together, which further complicates the problem. In addition, the objective function of **PNC** problem in Equation (1) is only valid when the truthfulness property is ensured in the auction mechanism. In the next section, therefore, we propose *Auc2Charge*, an online auction framework for the park-and-charge mode, which ensures the truthfulness and individual rationality and makes electricity allocation and pricing decisions with an explicit competitive ratio on the total system social welfare in polynomial time.

4. AUC2CHARGE: AN ONLINE AUCTION FRAMEWORK

In this section, we present our *Auc2Charge* online auction framework for the park-and-charge mode. This framework utilize the randomized mechanism design technique [5, 6, 16, 23]. Its basic idea is to first transform the offline **PNC** problem into a series of one-shot social welfare maximization problems $\mathbf{PNC_{one}(t)}$, one for each time slot t. During the transformation, the reported valuation $b_j^k(t)$ for the kth bid of EV user j for time slot t is adjusted to a reduced value $w_j^k(t)$ based on the budget limit B_j and the auction result for user j in last time slot $t-1$. In this way, bidding decisions at different time slots are successfully decoupled. For each $\mathbf{PNC_{one}(t)}$ problem, a one-shot randomized auction mechanism, Auc_{one}, is designed to provide a close-form approximation ratio on social welfare of the current time slot, while maintaining the truthfulness and individual rationality. In the following subsections, we first present the transformation from **PNC** to $\mathbf{PNC_{one}(t)}$, which is the basic structure of *Auc2Charge*. We then present the construction of one-shot randomized auction mechanism Auc_{one}. In each subsection, we also analyze the performance of the *Auc2Charge* framework and the Auc_{one} one-shot auction, respectively.

4.1 Basic Structure of Auc2Charge

Assuming all the bids from EV users are truthful bids, as discussed in Section 3, social welfare maximization for EV park-and-charge can be achieved by solving the offline **PNC** problem. To cope with the stochastic and unpredictable nature of system information in **PNC** problem, we propose to transform it into a series of social welfare maximization problem in single time-slot. At a first glance, directly decomposing **PNC** into smaller problems for each time slot seems a nature transformation. However, it is an inappropriate transformation method due to the existence of budget limit across all time slots for every EV user. In direct decomposing, EV users may deplete their budget in early time slots without getting fully charged. Without sufficient budget remaining, EV users will lose the chance to participate the auction in future time slots to get more electricity. This would result in inefficient electricity allocation and thus jeopardizing total social welfare. To avoid this situation, we adopt a *budget-based bid updating* approach, which was first proposed for budget-constraint Adwords auction [6], to perform our transformation. Based on auction results in time slot $t-1$ and the remaining budget of every user, this approach adjusts the reported valuation of each bid in the one-shot social welfare maximization problem in time slot t to a reduced value. In this way, users will not deplete their budget as early as they do in direct decomposing.

Algorithm 1 *Auc2Charge*: the Online Auction Framework for EV Park-and-Charge

1: $\eta_j(0) = 0, \forall j = 1, 2, \dots, M$
2: **for** $t \to 1, 2, \dots, T$ **do**
3:   **for all** j, k **do**
4:     **if** $\eta_j(t-1) \geq 1$ **then**
5:       $\omega_j^k(t) = 0$
6:     **else**
7:       $\omega_j^k(t) = b_j^k(t)\Big(1 - \eta_j(t-1)\Big)$
8:     **end if**
9:   **end for**
10:   Run a randomized one-shot auction Auc_{one}. Let $M_{win}(t)$ be the set of winning EVs and k_j be the index of corresponding winning bids for each EV $j \in M_{win}(t)$.
11:   **for** $j \to 1, 2, \dots, M$ **do**
12:     **if** $j \in M_{win}(t)$ **then**
13:       $\eta_j(t) = \eta_j(t-1)\Big(1 + \frac{b_j^{k_j}(t)}{B_j}\Big) + \frac{b_j^{k_j}(t)}{B_j(\varphi - 1)}$
14:     **else**
15:       $\eta_j(t) = \eta_j(t-1)$
16:     **end if**
17:   **end for**
18: **end for**

Using this bid updating approach, we are able to construct the *Auc2Charge* online auction framework as Algorithm 1. In Algorithm 1, we introduce auxiliary variables $\eta_j(t)$ for every EV user j with $\eta_j(0) = 0$. $\eta_j(t)$ is an indicator of the remaining budget of EV user j in time slot t. The more budget is used by user j, the higher value $\eta_j(t)$ becomes. When $\eta_j(t)$ reaches 1, it means user j has used up all her budget B_j. At the beginning of every time slot t, Algorithm 1 adjusts the reported valuation $b_j^k(t)$ to a reduced value $w_j^k(t)$ based on $\eta_j(t-1)$, i.e., Line 3-9. Then it executes a one-shot randomized auction Auc_{one}, which ensures truthfulness, individual rationality and provides an explicit approximation ratio on the one-shot problem $\mathbf{PNC_{one}(t)}$, i.e., Line 10. To not affect the integrity of our discussion on *Auc2Charge*, we leave the design of Auc_{one} auction in next subsection. After getting the result of Auc_{one} in time slot t, *Auc2Charge* accordingly adjusts $\eta_j(t)$, i.e., Line 11-17. If EV user j wins a bid in the auction at time slot t, then $\eta_j(t)$ is updated using the equation in Line 13. In this equation, the parameter φ is defined as $\varphi = (1 + R_{max})^{\frac{1}{R_{max}}}$, where R_{max} is the maximal per-timeslot bid-to-budget ratio, i.e., $R_{max} = \max\{\frac{b_j^k(t)}{B_j}\} \forall j, k$ and t. If user j does not win any bid, $\eta_j(t)$ stays unchanged. Note that the way how φ is defined was first proposed by Buchbinder for revenue maximization in budget-constrained Adwords auction [6]. It is later extended for designing auctions in broader areas [11, 23]. And φ approaches to e when $R_{max} \to 0$.

In Algorithm 1, the one-shot social welfare maximization problem $\mathbf{PNC_{one}(t)}$ for every time slot t is defined as:

$$\mathbf{PNC_{one}(t)}: \quad \text{maximize} \quad p(t) = \sum_{j=1}^{M} \sum_{k=1}^{K} \omega_j^k(t) y_j^k(t), \tag{5}$$

subject to

$$\sum_{j=1}^{M} \sum_{k=1}^{K} c_j^k(t) y_j^k(t) \leq R(t), \tag{6a}$$

$$\sum_{k=1}^{K} y_j^k(t) \leq 1, \qquad \forall j \tag{6b}$$

$$\sum_{k=1}^{K} c_j^k(t) y_j^k(t) \leq C_j(t), \qquad \forall j \tag{6c}$$

$$y_j^k(t) \in \{0, 1\}, \qquad \forall j \text{ and } k. \tag{6d}$$

There are two differences between **PNC** and $\mathbf{PNC_{one}(t)}$. The first one is that the constraint of total budget limit over all time slots, i.e., constraint (2a), is dropped in $\mathbf{PNC_{one}(t)}$. As explained earlier, this constraint is dealt with by the *budget-based bid update* process in Algorithm 1. The second one is that we use $\omega_j^k(t)$, a reduced value of $b_j^k(t)$, in $\mathbf{PNC_{one}(t)}$. Similar as problem **PNC**, we get the linear program (LP) relaxation of problem $\mathbf{PNC_{one}(t)}$ by replacing the 0-1 integer constraint (6d) with $y_j^k(t) \in [0,1]$, for any j and k, and dropping the upper bound 1. Then we define the dual problem of the LP relaxation of $\mathbf{PNC_{one}(t)}$ as:

$$\mathbf{D\text{-}PNC_{one}^{lp}(t)} : \text{minimize } d(t) = R(t)z(t) + \sum_{j=1}^{M} s_j(t) + \sum_{j=1}^{M} c_j(t)q_j(t) \tag{7}$$

subject to

$$c_j^k(t)z(t) + s_j(t) + c_j^k(t)q_j(t) \geq \omega_j^k(t), \quad \forall j \text{ and } k, \tag{8a}$$

$$z(t), s_j(t), q_j(t) \geq 0, \quad \forall j. \tag{8b}$$

$\mathbf{PNC_{one}(t)}$ is NP-hard via a reduction from the 0-1 knapsack problem. However, we can design an α-approximation algorithm for this problem via the greedy primal-dual approach [5], and translate it into a randomized one-shot auction mechanism Auc_{one}, which provides the same approximation ratio for $\mathbf{PNC_{one}(t)}$ and ensures truthfulness and individual rationality [16]. Before discussing how to design Auc_{one}, we propose and prove the following theorem on the performance of the *Auc2Charge* framework.

THEOREM 1. *If we can find a randomized one-shot auction* Auc$_{one}$ *which ensures truthfulness and individual rationality, provides feasible solutions to both* $\mathbf{PNC_{one}(t)}$ *and* $\mathbf{D\text{-}PNC_{one}^{lp}(t)}$*, and guarantees an approximation ratio of* α*, i.e.,* $\alpha p(t) \geq d(t)$*, in every time slot* t*, then the* Auc2Charge *online auction framework provides a* $(1+R_{max})(\alpha + \frac{1}{\varphi-1})$*-competitive ratio for the* **PNC** *problem.*

PROOF. We follow the sketch in [6,23] to prove this theorem. If we can find such a one-shot auction Auc_{one} satisfying the requirements specified in the theorem, we first prove that the following claims hold.

Claim 1. Let $x_j(t) = \eta_j(t)$ for any t, Algorithm 1 yields a feasible solution to the dual problem $\mathbf{D\text{-}PNC^{lp}}$.

It is straightforward to see that Lines 4-8 in Algorithm 1 ensure that $\omega_j^k(t) \geq b_j^k(t)(1-\eta_j(t-1))$. And the constraint (8a) is guaranteed in the feasible solution provided by Auc_{one}. Therefore, we have

$$c_j^k(t)z(t) + s_j(t) + c_j^k(t)q_j(t) \geq \omega_j^k(t) \geq b_j^k(t)(1-\eta_j(t-1)),$$

for j, k and t. Because $\eta_j(t)$ is non-decreasing with t, we also have $\eta_j(t) \leq \eta_j(T) = x_j$. Putting it into the right-hand-side (RHS) of the above inequality, we can get

$$c_j^k(t)z(t) + s_j(t) + c_j^k(t)q_j(t) \geq b_j^k(t)(1-x_j), \forall j, k, \text{ and } t$$

Rearranging its terms and we can see that it is exactly the constraint (4a). Therefore, Algorithm 1 provides a feasible solution to problem $\mathbf{D\text{-}PNC^{lp}}$.

Claim 2. Denote $P(t)$ and $D(t)$ as the values of objective functions in **PNC** and $\mathbf{D\text{-}PNC^{lp}}$, respectively, after the t-th iteration in Algorithm 1. Let $\Delta P(t) = P(t) - P(t-1)$ and $\Delta D(t) = D(t) - D(t-1)$. Algorithm 1 guarantees that:

$$\frac{\Delta D(t)}{\Delta P(t)} \leq \alpha + \frac{1}{\varphi - 1} \qquad \forall t. \tag{9}$$

To prove this claim, we first see that in the t-th iteration of Algorithm 1, the change in the value of problem $\mathbf{PNC_{ol}}$ is the sum of winning bids in time slot t, i.e., $\Delta P(t) = \sum_{j \in M_{win}(t)} b_j^{k_j}(t)$. Meanwhile, $D(t)$ can be transformed as:

$$\begin{aligned}\Delta D(t) &= \sum_{j=1}^{M_{win}(t)} B_j\Big(x_j(t) - x_j(t-1)\Big) + d(t) \\ &= \sum_{j=1}^{M_{win}(t)} \Big(b_j^{k_j}(t)x_j(t-1) + \frac{b_j^{k_j}(t)}{\varphi-1}\Big) + d(t) \\ &\leq \sum_{j=1}^{M_{win}(t)} \Big(b_j^{k_j}(t)x_j(t-1) + \frac{b_j^{k_j}(t)}{\varphi-1}\Big) + \alpha p(t).\end{aligned}$$

Since the only non-zero bids in one-shot auction at t are from EVs that has $x_j(t-1) < 1$, we can rewrite $p(t)$ as

$$p(t) = \sum_{j \in M_{win}(t)} b_j^{k_j}(t)\Big(1 - x_j(t-1)\Big).$$

Putting the rewritten $p(t)$ in the inequality above, we get:

$$\begin{aligned}\Delta D(t) &\leq \sum_{j=1}^{M_{win}(t)} \Big[b_j^{k_j}(t)x_j(t-1) + \frac{b_j^{k_j}(t)}{\varphi-1} + \alpha b_j^{k_j}(t)\Big(1 - x_j(t-1)\Big)\Big] \\ &= \sum_{j=1}^{M_{win}(t)} \Big(\alpha + \frac{1}{\varphi-1} - (\alpha-1)\Big) b_j^{k_j}(t) \\ &\leq \sum_{j=1}^{M_{win}(t)} \Big(\alpha + \frac{1}{\varphi-1}\Big) b_j^{k_j}(t) \leq \Big(\alpha + \frac{1}{\varphi-1}\Big)\Delta P(t).\end{aligned}$$

Hence we have proved this claim.

Claim 3. Let $x_j(t) = \eta_j(t)$ for any t. In Algorithm 1, given any EV user j, if time slot t_j^o is the first slot that $\sum_{k=1}^{K}\sum_{t=1}^{t_j^o} b_j^k(t)y_j^k(t) \geq B_j$, then we have $x_j(t_j^o) > 1$.

We prove this claim by showing that for any EV user j and any time slot $t' = 0, 1, 2, \ldots, T$,

$$x_j(t') \geq \frac{1}{\varphi - 1}\Big(\varphi^{\frac{\sum_{k=1}^{K}\sum_{t=1}^{t'} b_j^k(t)y_j^k(t)}{B_j}} - 1\Big). \tag{10}$$

When $t' = 0$, we can easily see that Inequality (10) holds. Assume it holds for $t'-1$. For time slot t', if $j \notin M_{win}(t)$, i.e., j wins no bid in t', this inequality still holds as both sides stay the same as in $t'-1$. If $j \in M_{win}(t)$, i.e., j wins one bid in slot t', $x_j(t')$ will be updated in Algorithm 1 as:

$$\begin{aligned}x_j(t') &= x_j(t'-1)\Big(1 + \frac{b_j^{k_j}(t')}{B_j}\Big) + \frac{b_j^{k_j}(t')}{B_j(\varphi-1)} \\ &\geq \frac{1}{\varphi-1}\Big(\varphi^{\frac{\sum_{k=1}^{K}\sum_{t=1}^{t'-1} b_j^k(t)y_j^k(t)}{B_j}} - 1\Big)\Big(1 + \frac{b_j^{k_j}(t')}{B_j}\Big) + \frac{b_j^{k_j}(t')}{B_j(\varphi-1)} \\ &= \frac{1}{\varphi-1}\Big(\varphi^{\frac{\sum_{k=1}^{K}\sum_{t=1}^{t'-1} b_j^k(t)y_j^k(t)}{B_j}}\Big(1 + \frac{b_j^{k_j}(t')}{B_j}\Big) - 1\Big).\end{aligned} \tag{11}$$

Leveraging the inequality $\frac{\ln(1+x)}{x} \geq \frac{\ln(1+y)}{y}$, $\forall 0 \leq x \leq y \leq 1$ and the definition of $R_{max} = \max \frac{b_j^k(t)}{B_j}, \forall j$, k and t, we get

$$1 + \frac{b_j^{k_j}(t')}{B_j} \geq \varphi^{\frac{b_j^{k_j}(t')}{B_j}}.$$

Plugging this conclusion into the RHS of Inequality (11), we have proved Inequality (10) by induction. When $t' = t_j^o$, the RHS of Inequality (10) is greater than or equal to 1 since $\sum_{k=1}^{K}\sum_{t=1}^{t_j^o} b_j^k(t)y_j^k(t) \geq B_j$, hence we have $x_j(t_j^o) \geq 1$, which completes the proof of this claim.

Claim 4. Algorithm 1 provides an almost feasible solution for the $\mathbf{PNC^{lp}}$ problem.

For any EV j, Algorithm 1 stops it from getting any electricity after t_j^o since its budget has been depleted. And we see that at $t_j^o - 1$, the budget of j is not used up yet. Thus

$$\begin{aligned}\sum_{k=1}^{K}\sum_{t=1}^{T} b_j^k(t)y_j^k(t) &= \sum_{k=1}^{K}\sum_{t=1}^{t_j^o-1} b_j^k(t)y_j^k(t) + \sum_{k=1}^{K} b_j^k(t_j^o)y_j^k(t_j^o) \\ &+ \sum_{k=1}^{K}\sum_{t=t_j^o+1}^{T} b_j^k(t)y_j^k(t)\end{aligned}$$

$$= \sum_{k=1}^{K}\sum_{t=1}^{t_j^o-1} b_j^k(t)y_j^k(t) + \sum_{k=1}^{K} b_j^k(t_j^o)y_j^k(t_j^o)$$
$$\le B_j + \max\{b_j^k(t_j^o)\} \le B_j(1+R_{max}),$$

for any user j. This indicates that Algorithm 1 ensures a slightly relaxed budget constraint compared to constraint (2a):

$$\sum_{k=1}^{K}\sum_{t=1}^{T} b_j^k(t)y_j^k(t) \le B_j(1+R_{max}), \qquad \forall j. \qquad (12)$$

Meanwhile, constraints (2b)(2d)(2e) are strictly guaranteed by Algorithm 1. Therefore, this algorithm yields an almost feasible solution to problem $\mathbf{PNC_{ol}}$.

Claim 4 implies that the total social welfare W_{total} is the minimum between the sum of users' valuation over winning bids and the sum of their budget. Hence we have:

$$\begin{aligned} W_{total} &= \sum_{j=1}^{M} \min\{B_j, \sum_{k=1}^{K}\sum_{t=1}^{T} b_j^k(t)y_j^k(t)\} \\ &\ge \sum_{j=1}^{M} \min\{\frac{\sum_{k=1}^{K}\sum_{t=1}^{T} b_j^k(t)y_j^k(t)}{1+R_{max}}, \sum_{k=1}^{K}\sum_{t=1}^{T} b_j^k(t)y_j^k(t)\} \\ &= \sum_{j=1}^{M}\sum_{k=1}^{K}\sum_{t=1}^{T} \frac{b_j^k(t)y_j^k(t)}{1+R_{max}} = \frac{P(T)}{1+R_{max}}. \end{aligned}$$

Summing Inequality (9) from Claim 2 over all t and recall that $P(0) = D(0) = 0$, we have $P(T) \ge \frac{D(T)}{\alpha + \frac{1}{\varphi-1}}$. Plugging it into the RHS of the above inequality, we have

$$W_{total} \ge \frac{D(T)}{(1+R_{max})(\alpha + \frac{1}{\varphi-1})} \qquad (13)$$

Therefore by duality, the approximation ratio of *Auc2Charge* is $(1+R_{max})(\alpha + \frac{1}{\varphi-1})$. □

4.2 Designing Randomized One-Shot Auction

Having built the basic structure of *Auc2Charge*, we next study how to design a randomized one-shot mechanism Auc_{one} which ensures truthfulness, individual rationality and provides an explicit approximation ratio on the social welfare in t. To this end, we apply the framework proposed in [16] and design the Auc_{one} auction shown in Algorithm 2.

The first step of Auc_{one} is to perform a fractional VCG auction (Line 1-4). This fractional auction follows the classic VCG mechanism to compute the optimal allocation and pricing decisions, and is truthful and individual rational [16,23]. Since its result is inapplicable in real-world, we further decompose this optimal factional solution into a combination of feasible integer solutions to $\mathbf{PNC_{one}(t)}$ (Line 5-6). We utilize the decomposition theory in [7,16] to achieve this. We first define the following linear programming model:

$$\mathbf{DC_P} \text{ minimize } \sum_{l\in I} \lambda_l \qquad (14)$$

subject to

$$\sum_{l\in I} \lambda_l y_j^k(t)^l = \frac{y_j^k(t)^F}{\alpha}, \qquad \forall j \text{ and } k, \qquad (15a)$$

$$\sum_{l\in I} \lambda_l \ge 1, \qquad (15b)$$

$$\lambda_l \ge 0, \qquad \forall l \in I, \qquad (15c)$$

In this problem, every vector $\mathbf{y(t)}^l = \{y_j^k(t)^l\}, \forall j, k$ represents a feasible integer solution to problem $\mathbf{PNC_{one}(t)}$, and α is the approximation ratio provided by the approximation algorithm for $\mathbf{PNC_{one}(t)}$. We notice that there are an exponential number of decision variables in $\mathbf{DC_P}$. Thus we look at its dual problem:

$$\mathbf{DC_D} \text{ maximize } \frac{1}{\alpha}\sum_{j\in M}\sum_{k=1}^{K} y_j^k(t)^F \mu_j^k(t) + \sigma \qquad (16)$$

subject to

$$\sum_{j\in M}\sum_{k=1}^{K} y_j^k(t)^l \mu_j^k(t) + \sigma \le 1 \qquad \forall l \in I, \qquad (17a)$$

$$\sigma \ge 0, \qquad (17b)$$

and find out that in problem $\mathbf{DC_D}$, there are only $MK+1$ decision variables but with an exponential number of constraints. Applying the decomposition theory in [7, 16], we have the following lemma:

LEMMA 1. *If there exists an α-approximation algorithm for problem $\mathbf{PNC_{one}(t)}$, a polynomial number of feasible integer solutions and the decomposition $\frac{y_j^k(t)^F}{\alpha} = \sum_{l\in I}\lambda_l \mathbf{y(t)}^l$ can be found within polynomial time by using this approximation algorithm as a separation oracle in the ellipsoid method, and the decomposition satisfies that $\sum_{l\in L}\lambda_l = 1$.*

PROOF. The proof of this lemma follows directly from the decomposition theory in [7,16], and thus is omitted due to the space constraint. □

Algorithm 2 Auc_{one}: The Randomized One-Shot Auction for EV Park-and-Charge

1: **Step 1: Simulate a fractional VCG auction**
2: Solve problem $\mathbf{PNC_{one}^{lp}}(t)$, the linear relaxation of $\mathbf{PNC_{one}(t)}$ and get the optimal fractional allocation decision $\mathbf{y(t)}^F = y_j^k(t)^F$, for any j and k.
3: For any user j, solve $\mathbf{PNC_{one}^{lp}}(t)$ by setting $w_j^k(t) = 0$ for every k, and denote the optimal value as $\widetilde{V}_j(t)^F$
4: Compute the corresponding payment rule as $\Gamma_j(t)^F = \widetilde{V}_j(t)^F - \sum_{j'\neq j,k} w_{j'}^k(t)y_{j'}^k(t)^F$
5: **Step 2: Decompose the optimal fractional solution**
6: Use the ellipsoid method to solve the primal-dual linear programming problems $\mathbf{DC_P}$ and $\mathbf{DC_D}$, in which an α-approximation algorithm for $\mathbf{PNC_{one}(t)}$ is used as a separation oracle, and get a polynomial number of feasible integer solutions to $\mathbf{PNC_{one}}(t)$. For each solution $\mathbf{y(t)}^l$, get the decomposition coefficient λ_l
7: **Step 3: Construct randomized electricity allocation and pricing decision**
8: Allocation decision: select $y(t)^l$ with probability λ_l
9: Pricing decision: $\Gamma_j(t)^l = \Gamma_j(t)^F \frac{\sum_k w_j^k(t)y_j^k(t)^l}{\sum_k w_j^k(t)y_j^k(t)^F}$

Lemma 1 indicates that in order to get the decomposition of the optimal fractional solution, all we need now is an α-approximation algorithm for problem $\mathbf{PNC_{one}(t)}$. To design such an algorithm, we first drop the constraint (6c) from $\mathbf{PNC_{one}(t)}$ by setting $w_j^k(t) = 0$ for all $c_j^k(t) > C_j(t)$. Correspondingly, dual variables $q_j(t)$ are also dropped from the objective function (7) and constraints (8) of problem $\mathbf{D\text{-}PNC_{one}^{lp}(t)}$. We see that this dropping will not affect the optimal solution to $\mathbf{PNC_{one}(t)}$ or the proof of Theorem 1 since no bids exceeding EV's unit-time maximal charging capacity can win. Combining this dropping process, we resort a classic primal-dual method [5] to design an approximation algorithm for $\mathbf{PNC_{one}(t)}$, as shown in Algorithm 3.

Algorithm 3 A Primal-Dual Approximation Algorithm For $\mathbf{PNC_{one}}(t)$

```
w_j^k(t) = 0 for all c_j^k(t) > C_j(t), drop constraint (6c) and all q_j(t)
y_j^k(t) = 0, s_j(t) = 0, ∀j, k
z(t) = 1/R(t), G(t) = max_{j,k}{c_j^k(t)}, θ = R(t)/G(t)
z_base = e^{θ-1}, M_win = ∅
while R(t)z(t) < z_base and M_win ≠ M do
    for all j ∈ M − M_win do
        k_j = arg max_k {w_j^k(t)}
    end for
    j_win = arg max_j { w_j^{k_j}(t) / (c_j^{k_j}(t) z(t)) }
    y_{j_win}^{k_{j_win}}(t) = 1, s_{j_win}(t) = w_{j_win}^{k_{j_win}}(t)
    r = c_{j_win}^{k_{j_win}}(t) / (R(t) − G(t)), z(t) = z(t) · (z_base)^r, M_win = M_win ∪ {j_win}
end while
```

After the dropping process and the initialization of prime and dual variables, Algorithm 3 adopts a greedy approach to find solutions to $\mathbf{PNC_{one}(t)}$. It iteratively selects the bid with the highest unit-value as a winning bid, one at a time, from EV users who have not yet won any bid in the current time slot. The iterative selection stops when every user has won one bid or the total electricity demand in winning bids exceeds the electricity supply at the park-and-charge station.

Next we analyze the performance of this approximation algorithm. Before deriving its approximation ratio, we first exam the feasibility of solutions computed by this algorithm. Given a $\mathbf{PNC_{one}(t)}$ problem, we assume Algorithm 3 stops at the L-th iteration. Let $s_j^{\rho}(t)$ and $z^{\rho}(t)$ be the value of $s_j(t)$ and $z(t)$ in the ρ-th iteration of Algorithm 3, where $\rho = 1, 2, \ldots, L$. And we denote the winning EV j_{win} in the ρ-th iteration as j_{ρ}. We propose the following two lemmas on the feasibility of this algorithm.

LEMMA 2. *After the termination of execution, Algorithm 3 yields a feasible solution to problem* $\mathbf{PNC_{one}(t)}$.

PROOF. The proof of this lemma is straightforward and hence omitted due to the space constraint. □

LEMMA 3. *Define a function*

$$f(z^{\rho}(t), k_j) \triangleq \frac{w_j^{k_j}(t)}{c_j^{k_j}(t) z^{\rho}(t)}$$

and $\epsilon = \max_{k',k''=1,\ldots,K, j\in M} \frac{c_j^{k'}(t)}{c_j^{k''}(t)}$. *If* $\{s_j^{\rho}(t), z^{\rho}(t)\}$ *for any* j *is a dual solution computed by Algorithm 3 at the end of the* ρ*-th iteration, then a feasible solution to the problem* $\mathbf{D\text{-}PNC_{one}^{lp}(t)}$ *can be computed as* $\{s_j^{\rho}(t), \epsilon f(z^{\rho}(t), k_j) z^{\rho}(t)\}$ *for any* j.

PROOF. By the end of the ρ-th iteration, it is easy to see that constraint (8a) is satisfied for any EV user $j \in \mathcal{M}_{win}$, since the winning bid of j is the highest bid of all its own bids. For any EV user $j \in M - \mathcal{M}_{win}$, we have

$$f(z^{\rho}(t), k_{j_{\rho}}) \geq \frac{w_j^{k_j}}{c_j^{k_j}(t) z^{\rho}(t)}. \tag{18}$$

From the definition of ϵ, we can find that for any two bids k^1 and k^2, we have $\epsilon c_j^{k^1}(t) \geq c_j^{k^2}(t)$. Thus the constraint (8a) can be satisfied for any EV user $j \in M - \mathcal{M}_{win}$ through substituting $c_j^{k_j}(t)$ by $\epsilon c_j^{k}(t)$ on the RHS of Inequality (18):

$$f(z^{\rho}(t), k_{j_{\rho}}) \geq \frac{w_j^{k_j}}{\epsilon c_j^{k}(t) z^{\rho}(t)} \Leftrightarrow c_j^{k}(t) \epsilon f(z^{\rho}(t), k_{j_{\rho}}) z^{\rho}(t) \geq w_j^{k_j} \geq w_j^{k},$$

for any $j \in \mathcal{M}_{win} - M$ and k, which proves this lemma. □

Using these two lemmas on the feasibility of Algorithm 3, we then propose the following theorem on the approximation ratio provided by this algorithm.

THEOREM 2. *For any slot* t*, Algorithm 3 provides an approximation ratio of* α *and an integrality gap of* α *to problem* $\mathbf{PNC_{one}}(t)$ *in polynomial time, where* $\alpha = 1 + \epsilon(e-1)\frac{\theta}{\theta-1}$*,* ϵ *is defined in Lemma 3, and* θ *is defined in Algorithm 3.*

PROOF. It is straightforward to see that Algorithm 3 terminates in polynomial time since the while loop is executed for at most M times and the corresponding loop body can also be finished in polynomial time. Let $p_{opt}(t)$ and $d_{opt}(t)$ be the optimal value of $\mathbf{PNC_{one}}(t)$ and $\mathbf{D\text{-}PNC_{one}^{lp}(t)}$, respectively. We also define $d_1^{\rho}(t) = \sum_{j=1}^{M} s_j^{\rho}(t)$ and $d_2^{\rho}(t) = R(t) z^{\rho}(t)$. We follows the sketch in [5] to prove the approximation ratio of α by considering three different cases..

Case 1: When Algorithm 3 stops at the L-th iteration, $\mathcal{M}_{win} = M$ and $R(t)z(t) < z_{base}$. In this case, every EV wins one bid. We also see that for each EV user j, only its highest bid $w_j^{k_j}(t)$ will be considered during the allocation process. Thus, we observe that 1) $p(t) = \sum_{j\in M} w_j^{k_j}(t)$, and 2) $s_j(t) = w_j^{k_j}(t) \geq w_j^{k}(t)$ for any EV j and its bid k. The second observation makes any non-negative $z(t)$ become a part of feasible solution to problem $\mathbf{D\text{-}PNC_{one}^{lp}(t)}$. By weak duality, we have $d(t) \geq p(t)$. When we let $z(t) = 0$, $d(t)$ reaches its optimal value $d_{opt}(t)$ and has the exactly the same value as $p(t)$, i.e., $\sum_{j\in M} w_j^{k_j}(t)$. In this way, Algorithm 3 provides an optimal solution to problem $\mathbf{PNC_{one}}(t)$.

Case 2: When Algorithm 3 stops at the L-th iteration, $R(t)z(t) \geq z_{base}$, and there exists an iteration $\rho \leq L$ such that $\alpha \geq \frac{d_{opt}(t)}{d_1^{\rho-1}(t)}$. In this case, we have $d_1^{\rho-1}(t) = p^{\rho-1}(t)$. And we also observe that $d_1^{\rho}(t)$ is non-decreasing as ρ increases. By weak duality, Algorithm 3 provides an approximation ratio of α in this case.

Case 3: When Algorithm 3 stops at the L-th iteration, $R(t)z(t) \geq z_{base}$, and for any iteration $\rho \leq L$, $\alpha < \frac{d_{opt}(t)}{d_1^{\rho-1}(t)}$. In this case, we first define two auxiliary variables:

$$\delta = (\frac{R(t)}{G(t)} - 1)\left(z_{base}^{1/(\frac{R(t)}{G(t)}-1)} - 1\right) \text{ and } \Delta = \frac{\delta R(t)}{R(t) - G(t)}.$$

Leveraging the update process of $z^{\rho}(t)$ in Algorithm 3 and the inequality $(1+a)^x \leq 1 + ax, \forall x \in [0.1]$, we have the following observation on $d_2^{\rho}(t)$:

$$\begin{aligned} d_2^{\rho}(t) &= R(t) z^{\rho-1}(t) z_{base}^{c_{j_\rho}^{k_{j_\rho}}(t)/(R(t)-G(t))} \\ &= R(t) z^{\rho-1}(t)\Big(1 + \frac{\delta}{\frac{R(t)}{G(t)} - 1}\Big)^{c_{j_\rho}^{k_{j_\rho}}(t)/G(t)} \\ &\leq R(t) z^{\rho-1}(t)\Big(1 + \frac{\delta}{\frac{R(t)}{G(t)} - 1} \cdot \frac{c_{j_\rho}^{k_{j_\rho}}(t)}{G(t)}\Big) \\ &= d_2^{\rho-1}(t) + \Delta c_{j_\rho}^{k_{j_\rho}}(t) z^{\rho-1}(t). \end{aligned} \tag{19}$$

From the execution of Algorithm 3, we also observe that

$$p^{\rho}(t) = p^{\rho-1}(t) + \omega_{j_\rho}^{k_{j_\rho}}(t), \text{for any } 0 < \rho \leq L.$$

Using the definition of function f and Inequality (18), we continue to transform the RHS of Inequality (19):

$$d_2^{\rho}(t) \leq d_2^{\rho-1}(t) + \frac{\Delta(p^{\rho}(t) - p^{\rho-1}(t))}{f(z^{\rho-1}(t), k_{j_\rho})}. \tag{20}$$

Lemma 3 shows that any set of dual solution $\{s_j^{\rho-1}(t), z^{\rho-1}(t)\}$, $\forall j$ during the execution of Algorithm 3 can be transformed to a feasible dual solution to $\mathbf{D\text{-}PNC_{one}^{pl}(t)}$. Thus we have

$$d_{opt}(t) \leq d_1^{\rho-1}(t) + \epsilon f(z^{\rho-1}(t), k_{j_\rho}) d_2^{\rho-1}(t),$$

which implies

$$f(z^{\rho-1}(t), k_{j_\rho}) \geq \frac{d_{opt}(t) - d_1^{\rho-1}(t)}{\epsilon d_2^{\rho-1}(t)}.$$

Since in this case we have $\alpha < \frac{d_{opt}(t)}{d_1^{\rho-1}(t)}$, we can further get

$$f(z^{\rho-1}(t), k_{j_\rho}) \geq \frac{(\alpha-1)d}{\epsilon \cdot \alpha d_2^{\rho-1}(t)}. \tag{21}$$

Plugging Inequality (21) into the RHS of Inequality (20) and utilizing $1 + x \leq e^x, \forall x \geq 0$, we get the following inequality

$$\begin{aligned} d_2^{\rho}(t) &\leq d_2^{\rho-1}(t)\Big(1 + \frac{\epsilon\cdot\alpha\cdot\Delta}{(\alpha-1)d_{opt}(t)}(p^{\rho}(t) - p^{\rho-1}(t))\Big) \\ &\leq d_2^{\rho-1}(t) e^{\frac{\epsilon\cdot\alpha\cdot\Delta}{(\alpha-1)d_{opt}(t)}(p^{\rho}(t) - p^{\rho-1}(t))}. \end{aligned} \tag{22}$$

Summing Inequality (22) over $\rho = 1, 2, \ldots, L$, we reach

$$d_2^{L}(t) \leq d_2^{0}(t) e^{\frac{\epsilon\cdot\alpha\cdot\Delta}{(\alpha-1)d_{opt}(t)} p^{L}(t)}.$$

Note that $d_2^0(t) = 1$, and when the algorithm stops at the L-th iteration under this case, we have $d_2^L(t) = R(t)z(t) \geq z_{base}$. Hence we have

$$\theta - 1 = \frac{R(t)}{G(t)} - 1 \leq \frac{\epsilon\cdot\alpha\cdot\Delta}{(\alpha-1)d_{opt}(t)} p^{L}(t) \Leftrightarrow \frac{d_{opt}(t)}{p^{L}(t)} \leq \frac{\epsilon\cdot\alpha\cdot\Delta}{(\alpha-1)(\theta-1)}.$$

Based on weak duality we know that

$$\frac{p_{opt}(t)}{p^L(t)} \leq \frac{d_{opt}(t)}{p^L(t)},$$

which means $\frac{d_{opt}(t)}{p^L(t)}$ is an upper bound of the approximation ratio. Through some simple mathematical transformation, we can obtain the following approximation ratio

$$\alpha = 1 + \epsilon(e-1)\frac{\theta}{\theta - 1}.$$

Denote the optimal value of the linear relaxation version of $\mathbf{PNC_{one}}(t)$ problem as $p_{opt}^{LR}(t)$. From the fact that $d_{opt}(t) \geq p_{opt}^{LR}(t)$ and $p_{opt}(t) \geq p^L(t)$ we can further get

$$\frac{p_{opt}^{LR}(t)}{p_{opt}(t)} \leq \frac{p_{opt}^{LR}(t)}{p^L(t)} \leq \frac{d_{opt}(t)}{p^L(t)} = \alpha$$

Hence, the integrality gap provided by Algorithm 3 is also α and we have finished our proof. □

Having proved the approximation ratio and the integrality gap provided by Algorithm 3, we can now plug it into the Auc_{one} one-shot auction as a separation oracle. In this way, Auc_{one} can derive a polynomial number of feasible integer solutions to the $\mathbf{PNC_{one}(t)}$ problem and the corresponding decomposition coefficient through ellipsoid method, as shown in Lemma 1. If the Auc_{one} mechanism is performed independently, i.e., in a scenario without any budget-based bid updating, it can achieve an α-approximation ratio on social welfare. This conclusion was proved in [16]. With the proposed budget-based bid updating process, however, the approximation ratio provided by Auc_{one} will be scaled up by a factor of $1 + R_{max}$. This is because the valuation $w_j^k(t)$ in problem $\mathbf{PNC_{one}(t)}$ is a reduced value from $b_j^k(t)$. Therefore, we propose the following theorem on the performance of Auc_{one} in our online auction framework.

THEOREM 3. Auc$_{one}$ *is computationally efficient, truthful, individual rational, and* $\alpha(1 + R_{max})$*-competitive.*

PROOF. The proof of this theorem follows the sketch in [16, 23], and is omitted due to the space constraint. □

Putting the conclusion in Theorem 1 and 3 together, we then propose the following theorem on the performance of *Auc2Charge* online auction framework.

THEOREM 4. *Integrating* Auc$_{one}$ *into Algorithm 1, our* Auc2Charge *framework is truthful, individual rational, computationally efficient and* $(1 + R_{max})(\alpha(1 + R_{max}) + \frac{1}{\varphi - 1})$*-competitive.*

PROOF. The proof of this theorem follows the sketch in [6, 23] and is omitted due to the space constraint. □

5. NUMERICAL SIMULATION

We conduct numerical simulation to demonstrate the efficacy of the *Auc2Charge* online auction framework. In our simulation, we define the length of one time slot as one-hour. We assume a parking-lot with 500 spots, each of which has a charging point, and the electricity source of this facility is from renewable energy. We use the hourly wind power generation capacity profile of a 24-hour period from a random location in New York City of the United Sates [1] as the electricity supply profile of this facility. We assume each EV has the same battery capacity of $40kWh$. In any simulation with T time slots, we assume all EVs arrive at the charging stations between time slot 1 and $T - 6$ in a uniformly random way. The SOC of each EV when arriving at the charging facility is uniform randomly chosen between 0 and 0.7. And the length of parking for each EV is uniformly chosen between 2 to 6 hours. The total budget of each EV user follows a uniform distribution between 8 and 12 dollars. At the beginning of each time slot, every EV user submits up to 5 bids in the form of *(valuation, charging demand)*. For every EV user j, the valuation and charging demand in her bids for a given time slot t are separately randomly generated. Then the valuations and charging demands are sorted respectively and reorganized based on the sorted order to ensure the monotonicity of valuation over charging demand. The unit-time maximal charging capacity for each EV at every time slot is set to be a random value between $6kWh$ and $8kWh$. We perform simulation of *Auc2Charge* under the setting of $T = 12, 18,$ and 24 hours, with 5 different numbers of EVs, i.e., 100, 200, 300, 400 and 500. simulation for 5 times and compute the average value.

5.1 Social Welfare

We first investigate the performance of *Auc2Charge* on social welfare. To this end, we first simulate *OffOptimal*, the offline optimal solution to the **PNC** problem. We then repeat the simulation of *Auc2Charge* framework under each combination of T and EV numbers for 5 times and derive its average approximation ratio for each setting.

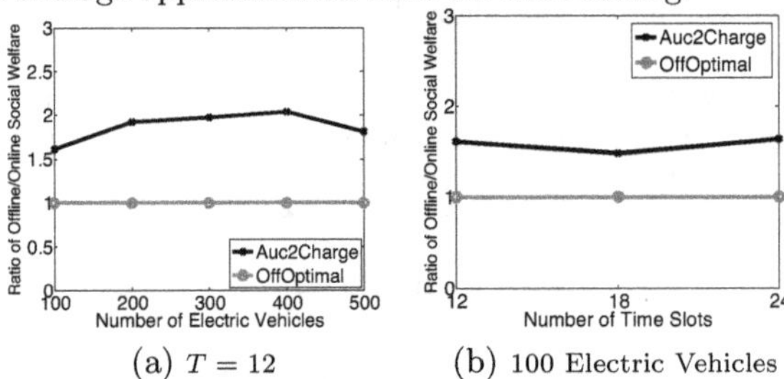

(a) $T = 12$ (b) 100 Electric Vehicles

Figure 3: Offline/Online Ratio of Social Welfare

Figure 3a) shows the approximation ratio of social welfare achieved by *Auc2Charge* under different numbers of participating EVs when the simulation period is 12 hours. We see that our *Auc2Charge* online auction achieves a stable offline/online ratio on social welfare under different density of electric vehicles. In Figure 3b) we plot the approximation ratio of *Auc2Charge* under different simulation periods when the number of EV is fixed at 100 . And we can observe a similar stable approximation ratio provided by *Auc2Charge*. Not only does these two observations indicate the existence of approximation ratio provided by our *Auc2Charge* auction, they also demonstrate the scalability of this online auction under various numbers of participating vehicles and arbitrary time period. It thus sheds some light for large-scale deployment of *Auc2Charge* in practice.

5.2 User Satisfaction

Next we study the performance of our *Auc2Charge* auction framework from the perspective of EV users. Note that we do not include results of *OffOptimal* because it is impractical in real world. We focus on the following metrics regarding the experience of EV users during the parking:

- *User Satisfaction Ratio*: The ratio between the total electricity allocated to an EV and the amount of electricity needed to fully charge this EV.
- *Unit Charging Payment*: The average payment made by an EV to charge one unit of electricity, i.e., 1kWh.
- *Total Charging Payment*: The total charging payment made by an EV during its parking.
- *Budget Utilization Ratio*: The ratio between the total charging payment of EV and its total bidding budget.

In what follows, we discuss the performance of *Auc2Charge* on these metrics. Figure 4a) shows the average user satisfaction ratio when executing the *Auc2Charge* framework. When the number of EVs are fixed, the average user satisfaction ratio increases as the number of time slots increases. Because the arrival of EVs are distributed between time slot 1 and $T - 6$ in our simulation. When T becomes larger, there are less EVs staying in the parking lot in a given time slot, resulting in abundant supply of electricity and a high user satisfaction ratio. On the contrary, for a fixed length of simulation time, this ratio decreases as the number of EVs increases. This is because with more vehicles arriving at the parking lot, the electricity becomes scarce. We then plot the unit charging payment of EV users under different simulation settings in Figure 4b). We can see that the average unit charging payment of EV users shows an opposite monotonicity from user satisfaction ratio, i.e., the unit charging payment increases as the number of EVs increases, and decreases as the simulation period T decreases. This monotonicity is desirable in an efficient market mechanism as it plays the role of *the indicator of electricity scarcity*. As a conclusion, both the monotonicity on user satisfaction ratio and unit charging payment demonstrate the ability of *Auc2Charge* to adapt to various demand-supply relations.

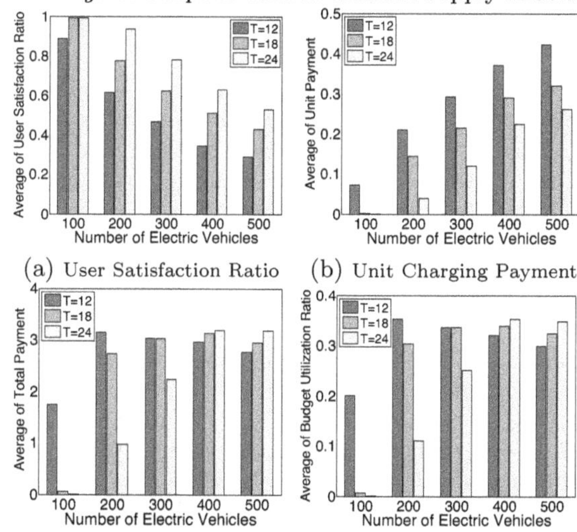

(a) User Satisfaction Ratio (b) Unit Charging Payment

(c) Total Charging Payment (d) Budget Utilization Ratio

Figure 4: Metrics of User Satisfaction

Figure 4c)-d) show the average total payment and the average budget utilization ratio of EV users in different simulation settings. Some interesting observations in these two figures are worth noting. The first one is that the total payment and budget utilization ratio does not show any monotonicity on simulation period or the number of EVs. For instance, the highest budget utilization ratio occurs when 200 EVs participate in the auction in a 12-hour period. This is because the expense of EV users is decided by both the total amount of electricity they received and the unit-price they pay. As we explained, these two factors have the opposite monotonicity, which leads to the lack of regular pattern in total payment and budget utilization ratio. The second observation is that when there are only 100 EVs in the simulation and the simulation time is large, i.e., 18 or 24 hours, the total payment of EV users decided by *Auc2Charge* online auction approaches to zero, and so is the budget utilization ratio. This is because under these two cases, the small number of EVs and the long simulation period cause the oversupply and under-demand of electricity, resulting in a less competition between EV users to get charged. Under this scenario, *Auc2Charge* is able to allocate electricity to fulfill all the charging demand of EV users, i.e., a 100% user satisfaction ration in Figure 4a), while charging a near-zero unit price to EV users as shown in Figure 4b). The near-zero total charging payment and budget utilization ratio are direct response from *Auc2Charge* on electricity oversupply and under-demand, and protects EV users from overpricing. When the electricity demand is much larger than the supply, on the contrary, *Auc2Charge* allocates limited electricity to EV users who really value the electricity with a higher pricing, which protects the charging station from underpricing. One example can be found in Figure 4b)-d) when $T = 12$ and the number of EVs is 500. Observations on user satisfaction metrics in these scenarios again demonstrate *Auc2Charge*'s ability to adapt to various supply-demand relations. And as we already showed in Figure 3, *Auc2Charge* achieves this adaptiveness with a social welfare guarantee simultaneously.

6. RELATED WORK

EV Charging Facilities. There has been a growing literature on the operation mode of EV charging facilities [2–4, 8, 9, 12, 17, 19]. Lopes *et al.* [17] explored the potential benefits and impact brought by the integration of EV into power grid. Chen *et al.* [9] designed a central controller to schedule the EV charging using renewable energy. The authors proposed an online scheduling algorithm that can achieve the maximum competitive ratio of an offline solution. Ardakanian *et al.* [4] designed a distributed charging algorithm to adjust EV charging rate based on available capacity of power network and ensure the proportional fairness between EV chargers. Gan *et al.* [12] proposed a distributed controller to capture the uncertainty and elasticity of EV charging and the intermittency of renewable energy. Chen *et al.* [8] studied a joint optimal power flow and EV charging problem. An online distributed controller was designed to enable efficient EV charging and maintain grid stability.

Recently, a promising operation mode called park-and-charge was proposed, and has drawn the interest of both academia and industry. It allows EVs to get charged during staying in a parking lot while the drivers are away for other agendas. Several experiments have been performed to explore the potential of this mode in integrating EVs into smart grid and ITS [2,3,19]. The V-charge project [3] proposed to design an automated valet park-and-charge system to support local autonomous transportation. And some prototypes have been built in several universities in Europe. GM and TimberRock built an park-and-charge station at GM's E-Motor Plant [2], where TimberRock manages the charging schedule of a fleet of EVs with the aim to balance the intermittent renewable energy supply and the stochastic EV charging demand. The U.S. Air Force is conducting an experiment at its Los Angeles Base [19], where the charging schedule of an EV fleet is controlled to minimize the total electricity cost. Though these experiments provide positive outcome, the missing of an efficient market mechanism prevents it from large-scale deployment. Existing pricing policies such as pay-per-use and flat-rate fail to adapt to the dynamic change of demand-supply relation in this mode. To fill this gap, we propose the *Auc2Charge* online auction framework as the market mechanism for park-and-charge

Auction Theory. Being a market mechanism, auction allocates resources to buyers who value them most, reduces the chance of overpricing and underpricing, and thus improves social welfare. Auction mechanisms have been widely used in areas such as online advertisement [6,11], wholesale electricity market [20,22] and cloud computing [23,25,26]. Recently some studies [13,14,21,24] focus on utilizing auction mechanisms into different scenarios of EV charging, with the hope of improving the efficiency of electricity allocation. For instance, Gerding *et al.* [14] proposed a two-side market with advanced reservation, in which EV users and the charging station can exchange their charging preference and cost. An online mechanism was designed for this market to ensure the truthfulness of EV users, but it does not provide any explicit guarantee on system social welfare. Robu *et al.* [21] designed an online mechanism, in which EV users bid for different charging speeds based on their arrival time, and cancel the charging allocation on departure. The authors analyzed the worst-case competitive ratio of social welfare under such cancellation scenario. Designing an auction with a close-form approximation ratio on social welfare while ensuring truthfulness and individual rationality has always been a major challenge in mechanism design. Lavi *et al.* [16] tackles this challenge by proposing a randomized auction framework, which could translate any α-approximation algorithm into truthful and individual rational mechanisms. In our paper, we leverage this framework together with techniques in Adwords auction [11, 23] and combinatorial auction [5], and propose the *Auc2Charge* online auction framework for electricity allocation in EV park-and-charge station. We show that *Auc2Charge* ensures truthfulness and individual rationality, and provides a close-form approximation ratio on total social welfare in polynomial time. *Auc2Charge* was motivated by the online auction mechanism for resource allocation in cloud computing [23]. One important difference is that in cloud systems, users do not have any constraint on the capacity of receiving resources. In EV charging systems, however, there exists a stochastic and unpredictable constraint on the unit-time maximal charging capacity for every EV due to battery characteristics. To the best of our knowledge, *Auc2Charge* is the first online auction mechanism that achieves truthfulness, individual rationality and explicit guarantee on social welfare for electricity allocation in EV park-and-charge.

7. CONCLUSION

As a promising operation mode for charging stations, park-and-charge allows EVs to get charged during their stay in a parking lot. To find an efficient market mechanism for large-scale deployment of this mode, we explore the feasibility and benefits of utilizing auction in EV park-and-charge. In an auction, every EV user can submit and update bids about their charging demand to the parking lot, which makes electricity allocation and pricing decisions based on the collected bids. We propose *Auc2Charge*, an online auction framework for park-and-charge. Our theoretical analysis indicates that *Auc2Charge* ensures truthfulness and individual rationality, computes electricity allocation and pricing solutions in a polynomial time, and guarantees an explicit approximation ratio of system social welfare. Results from numerical simulation demonstrate the efficacy of *Auc2Charge* in terms of social welfare and user satisfaction. The *Auc2Charge* auction framework fills the gap between small-scale experiment and large-scale real-world deployment of park-and-charge mode. Though it is designed for park-and-charge, the design rationale of *Auc2Charge* also applies to other modes for charging stations, e.g., the charging-point reservation system. As future work, we plan to extend the *Auc2Charge* framework by including other realistic constraints in both the electricity market, e.g., vehicle-to-grid electricity transmission and ramp-up/ramp-down cost of electricity generation, and intelligent transportation systems, e.g., the uncertainty of EV's mobility.

8. ACKNOWLEDGMENT

We thank eEnergy'15 reviewers and our shepherd Younghun Kim for helpful comments on our paper. This work was supported in part by the NSERC Collaborative Research and Development Grant CRDPJ418713, General Motors Research, and Canada Foundation for Innovation (CFI)'s John R. Evans Leaders Fund 23090.

9. REFERENCES

[1] National solar radiation data base. rredc.nrel.gov.

[2] Solar microgrid integrates solar pv, energy storage, smart grid functionality and advanced vehicle-to-grid capabilities. timberrockes.com/docs/TRES-MEA.pdf.

[3] The v-charge project. www.v-charge.eu.

[4] O. Ardakanian, C. Rosenberg, and S. Keshav. Distributed control of electric vehicle charging. In *ACM e-Energy*, 2013.

[5] P. Briest, P. Krysta, and B. Vöcking. Approximation techniques for utilitarian mechanism design. In *Proceedings of ACM STOC'05*.

[6] N. Buchbinder, K. Jain, and J. S. Naor. Online primal-dual algorithms for maximizing ad-auctions revenue. In *Algorithms–ESA'07*.

[7] R. Carr and S. Vempala. Randomized metarounding. *Random Struct. Algorithms*, 2002.

[8] N. Chen, C. W. Tan, and T. Quek. Electric vehicle charging in smart grid: Optimality and valley-filling algorithms. *Technical Report*, 2014.

[9] S. Chen and L. Tong. iems for large scale charging of electric vehicles: Architecture and optimal online scheduling. In *IEEE SmartGridComm*, 2012.

[10] C. Chung, J. Chynoweth, C. Qiu, C. Chu, and R. Gadh. Design of fair charging algorithm for smart ev charging infrastructure. In *2013 IEEE ICTC*.

[11] N. R. Devanur and T. P. Hayes. The adwords problem: online keyword matching with budgeted bidders under random permutations. In *ACM EC'09*.

[12] L. Gan, A. Wierman, U. Topcu, N. Chen, and S. H. Low. Real-time deferrable load control: handling the uncertainties of renewable generation. In *e-Energy'13*.

[13] E. H. Gerding, V. Robu, S. Stein, D. C. Parkes, A. Rogers, and N. R. Jennings. Online mechanism design for electric vehicle charging. In *AAMAS'11*.

[14] E. H. Gerding, S. Stein, V. Robu, D. Zhao, and N. R. Jennings. Two-sided online markets for electric vehicle charging. In *AAMAS'13*.

[15] L. He, L. Kong, S. Lin, S. Ying, Y. Gu, T. He, and C. Liu. Reconfiguration-assisted charging in large-scale lithium-ion battery systems. In *ACM ICCPS'14*.

[16] R. Lavi and C. Swamy. Truthful and near-optimal mechanism design via linear programming. *Journal of the ACM (JACM)*, 2011.

[17] J. A. P. Lopes, F. J. Soares, and P. M. R. Almeida. Integration of electric vehicles in the electric power system. *Proceedings of the IEEE*, 2011.

[18] Z. Ma, D. S. Callaway, and I. A. Hiskens. Decentralized charging control of large populations of plug-in electric vehicles. *Control Systems Technology, IEEE Transactions on*, 2013.

[19] C. Marnay. Los angeles air force base vehicle to grid pilot project. *ECEEE 2013*.

[20] J. Nicolaisen, V. Petrov, and L. Tesfatsion. Market power and efficiency in a computational electricity market with discriminatory double-auction pricing. *Evolutionary Computation, IEEE Transactions*, 2001.

[21] V. Robu, E. H. Gerding, S. Stein, D. C. Parkes, A. Rogers, and N. R. Jennings. An online mechanism for multi-unit demand and its application to plug-in hybrid electric vehicle charging. *JAIR*, vol 48, 2013.

[22] G. B. Sheblé. *Computational auction mechanisms for restructured power industry operation*. springer, 1999.

[23] W. Shi, L. Zhang, C. Wu, Z. Li, and F. C. Lau. An online auction framework for dynamic resource provisioning in cloud computing. In *SIGMETRICS'14*.

[24] S. Stein, E. Gerding, V. Robu, and N. R. Jennings. A model-based online mechanism with pre-commitment and its application to ev charging. In *AAMAS'12*.

[25] L. Zhang, S. Ren, C. Wu, and Z. Li. A truthful incentive mechanism for emergency demand response in colocation data centers. In *INFOCOM'15*.

[26] J. Zhao, X. Chu, H. Liu, Y.-W. Leung, and Z. Li. On-line procurement auctions for resource pooling in client-assisted cloud storage systems. In *INFOCOM'15*.

Timely Query Processing in Smart Electric Grids: Algorithms and Performance

Kedar Khandeparkar,
Krithi Ramamritham
IIT Bombay

Rajeev Gupta
IBM Research, India

Anil Kulkarni,
Gopal Gajjar,
Shreevardhan Soman
IIT Bombay

ABSTRACT

Smart-grid applications have widely varying data needs as well as bandwidth and latency requirements. The usual approach to collecting the available data (e.g., from Phasor Measurement Units) at a centralized site continuously and executing all the applications there leads to large latencies and requirements for high communication bandwidth. This paper proposes and evaluates, using real data, techniques wherein the data packets are disseminated based on the applications' data needs and semantics. These techniques systematically filter data in the dissemination network and reduce bandwidth requirements while resulting in low latency solutions. For example, based on the results from our testbed for the Indian Electric Grid, we show that the processing overheads decrease by at least 50% for the large PMU data sizes compared to the traditional centralized approach.

Keywords

Smart grid; Query processing; Latency; PMU; PDC

1. INTRODUCTION

1.1 The Grid Infrastructure

In power grids, there is an increased need for reliability, stability, distributed generation, and integration of renewable sources. A large number of monitoring and sensing devices, such as Phasor Measurement Units (PMUs), are being deployed throughout the network. They provide a continuous stream of informative data by measuring various electrical signals. These measurements are typically sampled and communicated at high rates – several 10s or 100s of times per second – to augment or even replace the conventional supervisory control and data acquisition (SCADA) in which measurements are done 4 times per second. Each PMU measures the voltage magnitude and angle at a substation (also known as a bus). The complex representation of the magnitude and angle of a voltage is called a phasor. These measurements are synchronized using a GPS clock, enabling a consistent snapshot of the system. Other high-frequency data measured at a substation can also be disseminated along with the PMU data. These provide the instrumentation necessary to assess grid performance and enhance the ability to control system operations and management. Typical PMU data measured at transmission lines have three voltage phasors, three current phasors, one frequency value, a GPS timestamp, and other analog and digital values [1]. Thus, a typical PMU data packet size is 100 bytes but larger packet sizes are expected to be the norm soon as more and more grid parameters get included for monitoring [15, 1]. Thus, with PMUs having 90 phasors and 45 analog values at 100 Hz of sampling frequency, data from a single PMU could exceed 700 kb. For India's grid, a total of 1600 PMUs is envisaged, making the total data size exceed 1 Gbps.

e-Energy'15, July 14–17, 2015, Bangalore, India.

ISBN 978-1-4503-3609-3/15/07$15.00.
DOI: http://dx.doi.org/10.1145/2768510.2768535.

1.2 Grid Applications and their Requirements

Various analytics tools and algorithms are used to aggregate and analyze the PMUs data from different geographical locations [16]. Phasor Data Concentrators (PDCs) at one or more levels aggregate and integrate the PMU data. Lower level PDCs (LPDCs) aggregate data from PMUs that are geographically located at different places, time align the data, and send the aggregated data to the applications running at higher level or super PDCs (SPDCs). These applications include angular stability monitoring, voltage monitoring, island detection, frequency monitoring, identification and monitoring coherent groups of generators, and power system state estimation.

This paper focuses mainly on three grid applications. We model the applications as continuous queries over PMU data and develop methods for distributed execution of these queries:

Angular Stability Monitoring (ASM): Phase angle differences across different buses in a system are a measure of static stress across the grid and its propensity to instability. Thus, phase angle differences are required to be monitored with respect to predetermined stability thresholds.

Monitoring Coherent Groups of Generators (MCGG): A group of generators is coherent if the difference between the centre of inertia of generators in the group from the global centre of inertia is within a given threshold. The difference beyond the thresholds is an alert to the system operator for possible islanding.

State Estimation (SE): Power system state estimation is a statistical technique to estimate the system state of a bus in the face of noisy and missing PMU data.

We define QoS requirements of these applications in terms of packets per second to be supported, data items required, criticality of the application, data latency tolerated, geographic movement of data and deadline for bulk data transfer [3]. Table 1 lists some of the QoS requirements for the three grid applications.

1.3 Timely Execution of the Applications

The straightforward way of executing these applications is to collect all the data from PMUs to a central site, say SPDC. In

Table 1: QoS Requirements of Grid Applications

Application	Latency (millisec)	Data items (Voltage: V, Current: I)	packets/sec
ASM	50	V angles	50
MCGG	50	V angles	50
SE	100	V, I magnitude and angles	$25-50$

this case, LPDCs forward all the data packets received from downstream PMUs to SPDC, irrespective of whether the data packets are relevant to the applications or not. Each PDC waits for the arrival of PMU packets associated with the same time-stamp till it times out. If a PDC does not receive all the data before the time-out, it sends whatever has been received to higher PDCs. Henceforth we refer to this scheme as ***C**entralized **E**xecution with **U**nfiltered data forwarding **T**echnique* (CEUT).

With PDCs at each level waiting for the arrival of all PMU data packets to be aggregated and sent to higher PDCs, a delay or drop of a PMU packet will cause the corresponding LPDC to wait until time-out. The overall delay, which we show in Section 5.2 to be above 100 msec, can ultimately affect the QoS of smart grid applications. Moreover, pushing all the data packets from downstream PMUs/PDCs to higher levels PDCs, irrespective of what data packets are required for applications, increases the bandwidth requirement as well. We need an alternative to CEUT. This paper proposes a semantics-aware distributed query processing approach to better utilizing the communication infrastructure. Semantics is of two kinds: data semantics (involving physical meaning of data and its characteristics) and application semantics (domain knowledge). Application semantics can be used to optimize the actual processing required. For example, if the angle difference threshold is 2 degrees, then for the application, it does not matter whether the angle difference is 0.5 or 1 degree (provided it is below the threshold). It also includes the data needs of the applications (voltage, current, frequency), the data rate required by the applications, whether the application is a monitoring, control or protection application, types of sub-queries (threshold or non-threshold based), etc.

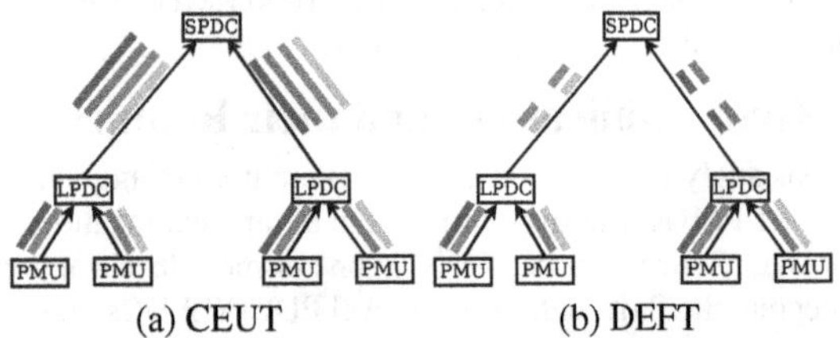

(a) CEUT (b) DEFT

Figure 1: CEUT vs. DEFT

We primarily focus on the question: *How do we design data dissemination techniques to efficiently process applications to meet their timeliness requirements?*

1.4 Contributions of this paper

Motivated by these considerations, we present ***D**istributed **E**xecution with **F**iltered data forwarding **T**echnique* (DEFT) as an alternative to CEUT. In this technique, only the data relevant to applications get delivered to the SPDC. We provide an application semantics-aware processing and communication solution in which the application is divided into coordinated sub-applications (sub-queries) executed in a distributed manner at LPDCs and the SPDC, but only application relevant filtered and aggregated data gets forwarded from LPDCs to SPDC, as shown in Figure 1b.

Grid applications over PMU data can be modeled as continuous threshold queries over multiple streams. In such queries, as long as the threshold condition holds, a user is not interested in any data. Authors of [6] describe various methods of dividing a continuous aggregation query into a number of sub-queries. These sub-queries are executed at different nodes in the network. While deriving the sub-queries from the query, we have to make sure that query threshold violation occurs only if the threshold of at least one of its sub-queries is violated. Otherwise, we may get into a situation where the application threshold is violated (e.g., indicating a possible onset of angular instability) and the application site is not getting the required data. This is a false negative case in which the sub-query improperly indicates no threshold violation when in reality it may be there. It is also possible that the SPDC, where the application query is executing, keeps on getting the data even when the threshold is not violated.These sub-queries, requiring only a sub-set of the data, can be executed at different PDCs. Thus, it is non-trivial to have zero false negative with minimum data transfer– so that the application gets all the data when needed and gets as little as possible when not needed. Significant contributions of this paper are:

- We categorize the smart grid applications along two dimensions: 1) Whether the sender node filters the data based on some condition, and 2) Whether different nodes executing the sub-queries share information about each other or not. For example, in the angular stability monitoring application, nodes, executing a sub-query, filter the data based on their local thresholds whereas, in distributed state estimation, the nodes executing sub-query communicate the boundary bus voltages.
- All the PMU measurements exhibit a certain dynamic behaviour. We model the data dynamics and use that for distributed execution of the grid applications modeled as continuous queries.
- We simulated a smart grid with more than 650 PMUs that cover the eastern and western regions of India. The proposed algorithms are shown to disseminate significantly lesser amount of data and incur considerably lower latency.
- We validated our results using PMU data, just before, during, and after a disturbance that occurred in the Indian grid on 30th July, 2012 which led to blackout in different parts of India.

Outline: We start with a discussion of three representative smart grid applications in Sections 2, 3, 4 and then discuss CEUT and DEFT realizations of each application. In Section 5, we present the performance evaluation of various algorithms, with simulated and real PMU data, along with a latency analysis. Section 6 presents the related work followed by conclusion in Section 7.

2. ANGULAR STABILITY MONITORING

2.1 Salient Details

Power flow in transmission lines of an electrical network depends on the difference between the phase angles of the voltages at the two ends of the transmission lines. Let V_s and V_d be the bus voltages across the two ends of a transmission line and let θ_s and θ_d be the corresponding phase angles. Then power flow in the line is proportional to $V_s V_d \sin(\theta_s - \theta_d)$. Quiescent angular separation should be low to ensure safe operations of the grid. After a disturbance, oscillations in angular difference occur but are usually damped and we get back to equilibrium. Angular instability occurs when the difference in phase angles between the ends of the transmission line increases uncontrollably [9]. Under these circumstances, the synchronization between the two areas is lost– resulting in separation of the two areas, loss of generation units in those areas, and ultimately a blackout occurs. Thus, if the fault can be identified and rectified within a reasonable amount of time, called *fault clearing time*, angular instability can be prevented. If θ_t^s and θ_t^d are PMU measurements at two ends of the bus s and d and $\theta_{\mathbf{Th}}^{\mathbf{sd}}$ is the maximum phase angle difference allowed before any action can be contemplated; application node does not need any data as long as:

$$|\theta_t^s - \theta_t^d| \leq \theta_{\mathbf{Th}}^{\mathbf{sd}} \quad \forall\, t \tag{1}$$

To ensure that the phase angles satisfy (1), PDC may need to get the PMU data from both ends of the bus continuously. Rather than getting all the PMU data, can we limit the data to get the angle values only if there is some *chance* of the difference crossing the threshold? The next section discusses approaches for the same.

2.2 DEFT approach

As explained in Sub-Section 2.1, we need to monitor multiple buses and send an alert if the difference in the phase angles is above the specified threshold (Equation 1). For monitoring $\theta_t^s - \theta_t^d$, rather than sending all the phase values of θ_t^s and θ_t^d, we can assign thresholds (θ_{Th}^s and θ_{Th}^d) to individual values of them such that the threshold θ_{Th}^{sd} is violated only if one or both of these thresholds are violated. But, unlike phase difference, the phase angles vary continuously with time. Hence, we need to model the phase angles and get the corresponding sub-queries with time-varying thresholds over individual phase angle values. Given the frequency of the electrical signal, phase angle is a linear function of time. Thus, we can model phase angle θ_t as:

$$\theta_t = f \times t \times 360° + \theta_0 \; (mod\, 360°)$$

where, f is the frequency offset from nominal frequency in Hz, t is measurement time in seconds, and θ_0 is the phase angle at time $t = 0$. Using this model, we have time varying threshold over individual values of phase angles which bounds the phase angles with an upper bound and a lower bound. Further, as per the data model, these two bounds should be linear with time, parallel to each other, and the distance between them should be less than or equal to the value of phase angle difference threshold (θ_{Th}) as in Figure 2.

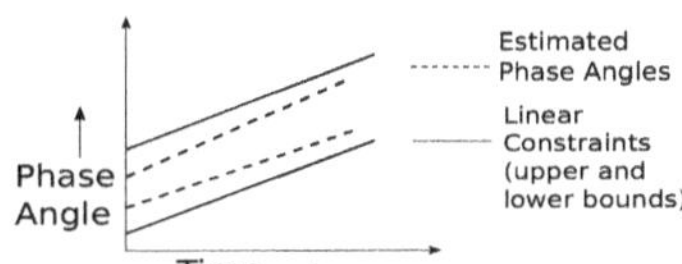

Figure 2: Angle Difference Threshold Monitoring Technique

We can derive the individual values of thresholds using various methods. If the frequencies for PMU_s and PMU_d, corresponding to θ^s and θ^d, are equal ($f_s = f = f_d$), individual values of phase angles will be parallel to each other. Let us assume that initially θ^s is greater than θ^d. If β_s is the distance of the upper bound from linear equation estimating θ_t^s and β_d is the distance of the lower bound from linear equation estimating θ_t^d, we get,

$$\beta_s + \beta_d = \theta_{\mathbf{Th}}^{\mathbf{sd}} - |(\theta_0^s - \theta_0^d)| \tag{2}$$

where $\beta_s \geq 0$ and $\beta_d \geq 0$. We can then set same or different values for β_s and β_d. Thus the linear constraints, for both θ^s and θ^d, would be,

$$\theta_0^d - \beta_d \leq (\theta^s - f \times t \times 360)\; (mod\, 360°) \leq \theta_0^s + \beta_s$$
$$\theta_0^d - \beta_d \leq (\theta^d - f \times t \times 360)\; (mod\, 360°) \leq \theta_0^s + \beta_s \tag{3}$$

The values of β_s and β_d can be dynamically obtained using the method outlined in [14]. If the frequencies at the two buses are different, the upper bound and lower bound on the phase angles of the buses will be not be same. Hence, we derive the equation of the linear bounding constraints based on the average frequency ($f_{avg} = (f^s + f^d)/2$), i.e., use f_{avg} in (3) while dividing the β values in proportion to the corresponding frequency values.

2.3 Data Model

Consider SPDC monitoring an angle difference query, $|\theta_t^s - \theta_t^d| <= 20$. At time $t = 0$, let the initial values of θ^s and θ^d be 50 and 40 degrees respectively. To create models at LPDC, SPDC obtains the angle and frequency values from both LPDCs and calculates the local monitoring conditions as given in (3). These conditions are then disseminated to both LPDCs to monitor the individual phasor angles. Thus, *Model Creation* requires a total of 90 bytes of data transfer, out of which 32 bytes are from LPDC to SPDC (meta info 16 bytes, statistics (2), phasor angle (4), frequency (4), PMU ID (2), application ID (2), sub-query ID (2)) and 58 bytes are from SPDC to LPDC (meta info (16), CMD (2), application ID (2), sub-query ID (2), phasor name (16), GPS time (8), line slope (4) and upper and lower bounds (8)). More details on Meta info and CMD are given in [1].

At time $t = t_n$, let θ^s and θ^d be 70 and 60 degrees respectively. Also, let the local thresholds for $\theta_0^d - \beta_d$ and $\theta_0^s + \beta_s$ be 65 and 75, respectively. We can see that though the actual angle difference is within 20, θ^s does not lie within its local conditions. This leads to a message transfer of 32 bytes, with θ^s and f_s values at time $t = t_n$ being sent from LPDC to SPDC. SPDC then pulls θ^d value from other LPDC corresponding to the timestamp for which θ^s experienced a *local violation*. This leads to a transfer of 2 messages between LPDC and SPDC. The request message from SPDC is 46 bytes, and data message from LPDC is 32 bytes. As SPDC detects no angle difference violation, it creates a new model with, possibly, modified local thresholds. The SPDC uses the newly obtained values of θ^s, θ^d, f^s and f^d to modify the local thresholds, and these modified queries are disseminated to individual LPDCs (58 bytes each). Thus, a local violation costs 226 bytes of data transfer. If there was a global violation, there is no model recreation. Thus, in case of global violation, 110 bytes are transmitted from LPDCs to SPDC. Table 2 summarizes the data transfer for each of the cases discussed above.

Table 2: Case Analysis for the Data Transfer in ASM

	Data Transfer between LPDCs and SPDC (bytes)
Model Creation	$90(32+58)$
Local violation at one LPDC	$226(32+46+32+2*58)$
Global violation	$110(32+46+32)$

2.4 Data Dissemination Strategies

We propose two data dissemination strategies for ASM:

DEFT-NSM : In DEFT with LPDC in *non-streaming* mode (DEFT-NSM), for each local violation, SPDC pulls data from other LPDCs. If the local violation is not a global violation, SPDC responds with new models. The data transfer for different cases of DEFT-NSM is already discussed in Section 2.3.

DEFT-SM : In DEFT with LPDC in *streaming* mode (DEFT-SM), SPDC pulls data from other LPDCs for the first global violation. From then on, LPDCs send their phasor angles continuously until the SPDC responds with new models.

Thus, in DEFT-SM, a first-time global violation for an angle difference pair leads to 110 bytes of data transfer in DEFT-SM. For all subsequent global violations, packets are sent from both LPDCs (32 bytes each). This leads to a transfer of 64 bytes of data for each angle difference pair.

3. MONITORING COHERENT GROUPS OF GENERATORS

3.1 Salient Details

Electric grids cover vast geographic areas. To study the stability of such systems, it is not practical to model the details of the entire grid. Rather, it is common practice to represent parts of the grid by equivalent models while preserving the general behavioural characteristics of the system. One step of creating these equivalent models is to identify coherent groups of generators. Coherency of generators implies that when a remote disturbance occurs coherent generators *swing* together and can, therefore, be represented by a single equivalent (generating) machine.

When a system is subjected to a sufficiently small magnitude of disturbance, it results in electromechanical oscillations (modes) in transmission lines. Engineering characteristics of a mode comprise of an oscillatory frequency, damping, and wave spectrum. The mode shape describes the amplitude and phasing of the oscillation throughout the system. Accurate estimates of the electromechanical modes are required for safe and reliable operation of the grid. Each mode is characterized by the coherent groups of generators swinging against another coherent groups of generators with an approximate phase difference of 180°. The modes and the group of generators in a mode can be determined by modal analysis [17].

A group of generators is coherent if all the generators in the group have similar response characteristics to changes in the operating conditions of a power system. When a system is steady, the difference between the centre of inertia (COI) of a coherent group i, δ_{COI_i} from the global centre of inertia, δ_{COI} should be within threshold [2]. From all the modes identified, only the groups of generators in inter-area swing modes having a low frequency of oscillation (0.2 - 0.8 Hz) are considered for monitoring at higher level PDCs. This is because, low-frequency modes indicate oscillations that occur across multiple regions of an electric grid. These modes can be identified and monitored at higher PDCs. High-frequency modes are observed within a small area and can be monitored at LPDCs. The monitoring query at higher PDC is:

$$\epsilon_l \leq \left|\delta_{COI_i} - \delta_{COI}\right| \leq \epsilon_u \tag{4}$$

where ϵ_l, ϵ_u are lower and upper bounds respectively. When a load trips, there is an imbalance between cumulative generation and cumulative load and COI shifts. The violation of condition (4) alerts the system operator for possible islanding. The phase angles from all generators need to be continuously obtained at higher PDC to monitor the deviation of group COI from global COI.

3.2 MCGG with DEFT

As discussed in Section 3, it is necessary to determine if, in the given set, generators are coherent or not âĂŤ within the given threshold bounds. Unlike a centralized approach, where group COIs and global COI are computed at SPDC, in DEFT, each LPDC computes COI of the group of generators from which it receives data. The group COI is then sent to SPDC to calculate global COI.

We formulate the sub-query for coherent groups of generators as follows: Suppose there are N groups in an inter-area swing mode with each group having $k_i, i \in [1, N]$ generators. Let there be N LPDCs corresponding to N groups that compute COI of respective groups. Each LPDC then sends only the computed group COI to SPDC. As given in [2], the sub-query at LPDC to compute group i COI with k_i generators is:

$$\delta_{COI_i} = \frac{\sum_{j=1}^{k_i} H_j * \delta_j}{G_i} \tag{5}$$

where H_j and δ_j are the inertia constant and rotor angle of generator j respectively and $G_i = \sum_{j=1}^{k_i} H_j$. Global COI is:

$$\delta_{COI} = \frac{\sum_{i=1}^{n} G_i * \delta_{COI_i}}{W} \tag{6}$$

where δ_{COI_i} is COI of group i and $W = \sum_{i=1}^{n} G_i$, G_i is the inertia constant of group i. The monitoring query at SPDC is:

$$\epsilon_l \leq \left|\delta_{COI} - \delta_{COI_i}\right| \leq \epsilon_u, \forall i \in [1, N] \tag{7}$$

To estimate the percentage drop in bandwidth (PDB) for MCGG with DEFT over CEUT, consider all LPDCs monitoring the m modes, with each mode having k generators. In CEUT, each LPDC sends $100mk$ bytes to SPDC during a cycle (20 msec), where 100 is the PMU data size in bytes. In DEFT, $18 + 4m$ bytes are sent by each LPDC to SPDC, that includes, meta info (16), statistics (2) and group COIs ($4m$). PDB is obtained as, $\frac{100mk-(18+4m)}{mk}$. For m = 3 and k = 20, PDB is 99.5%.

4. STATE ESTIMATION

4.1 Salient Details

State estimation is an essential tool for power system monitoring. The state of the system includes voltage magnitude and angle of buses which, as given in Section 2, can be used to get the real power transmission across buses. As shown in Figure 3, the

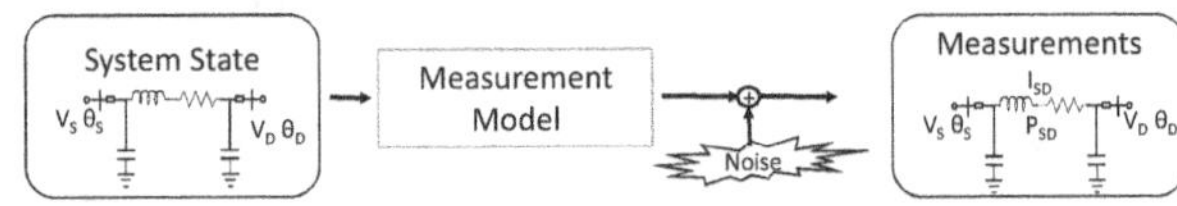

Figure 3: Schematic relationship between system state and measurements

measurement model for state estimation allows the calculation of various parameters of interest with high confidence by detecting, identifying and eliminating the measurement errors, which may be present due to the existence of bias or drift in measurements. If z is the measurement vector and x is current state vector then the model used in power system state estimation [11] is:

$$z = h(x) + e \tag{8}$$

where h is the vector of nonlinear measurement functions between x and z, and e is the measurement noise vector. State estimation, i.e., estimating x from z, is a statistical technique to estimate the system state of a bus. Function h depends on admittance values in various buses and, in general, is nonlinear. Performing state estimation involves solving non-convex optimization problems. But, typically, such models are iteratively linearized in the form of:

$$\mathbf{Z} = \mathbf{MV} + \epsilon \tag{9}$$

where Z is the measurement vector, *M*, the model matrix, which depends on admittance values, *V* is the vector of voltages at ends of buses and ϵ indicates the measurement errors.

Due to the synchronized measurements provided by the PMUs, the relation in (8) for an observable system is linear and can be solved in a single step. A system is observable if there are enough PMUs, such that the state estimator can estimate all the states of the grid. Linear state estimation (LSE) reduces the computational complexity unlike nonlinear state estimation, which may take many iterations to converge towards a solution. The solution of the LSE problem, $\min \frac{1}{2}\|\mathbf{Z} - \mathbf{M}\hat{\mathbf{V}}\|_2$, is:

$$\hat{\mathbf{V}} = \mathbf{M}^{+}\mathbf{Z} = (\mathbf{M}^{\mathbf{H}}\mathbf{M})^{-1}\mathbf{M}^{\mathbf{H}}\mathbf{Z} \tag{10}$$

where, $\mathbf{M}^{+}$ is also known as Penrose Moore inverse of M. Operator **H** is a Hermitian operator. It should be noted that **M** is a large and sparse complex matrix. Thus, computations in the state estimation application involve large sparse matrices *M* and its complexity increases with the size of the grid.

4.2 SE with DEFT

Algorithms for distributed state estimation (DSE) have been proposed in [18]. As a smart grid consists of many interconnected and geographically distributed sub-networks, each sub-network has local information about the state of the sub-network. Globally optimal control action requires knowing the global state of the system. In DSE, each sub-network shares estimates, PMU measurements, and corresponding weights of only boundary buses to the central node (SPDC). The SPDC can then use weighted least square (WLS) to obtain the new estimates of the boundary buses. In WLS, one tries to minimize the error between the measurements and the estimations of these measurements when using the state variables.

As given in [18], the benefits of DSE are threefold, 1) The communication channels are vulnerable to cyber-attacks and hence sending only boundary bus estimates will hide the data of the individual consumer and generator from out-of-network entities, 2) Distribution of computation on multiple processors at local sub-networks reduces the SPDC load and hence, the overall computation time is reduced, 3) communication network traffic is reduced due to less message transfer. To have better understanding of DSE, consider

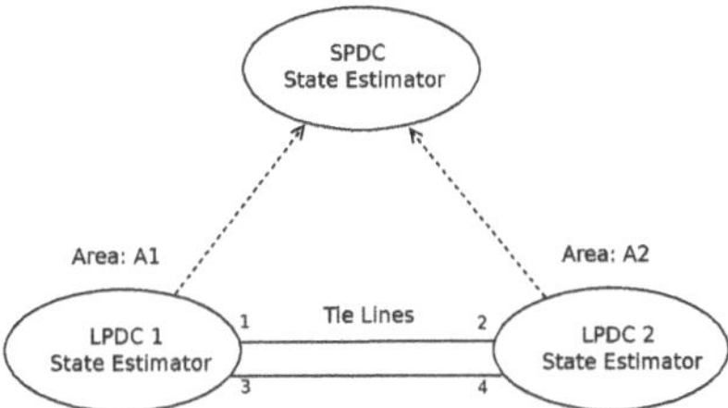

Figure 4: Two Area System

the two area system shown in Figure 4. Areas A1 and A2 are connected by two tie lines. LPDC 1 and LPDC 2 are the lower PDCs corresponding to A1 and A2 respectively. Let V_{b1}, V_{b2}, V_{b3} and V_{b4} be the voltage measurements corresponding to boundary buses 1, 2, 3 and 4 respectively. LPDC 1 and LPDC 2 estimate all the bus voltages including $\hat{V}_{b1}$, $\hat{V}_{b2}$, $\hat{V}_{b3}$ and $\hat{V}_{b4}$. The state estimators at LPDC 1 and LPDC 2 estimate voltages of A1 and A2 respectively. However, they send only the voltage estimates and actual PMU measurement of the boundary buses, the tie line currents and the weights corresponding to estimates and measurements to SPDC. SPDC re-estimates the boundary bus voltages using WLS.

In DSE, all LPDCs perform LSE given by (9). The solution of the weighted least square problem viz., min $\frac{1}{2}\|\mathbf{W_s}^{-\frac{1}{2}}(\mathbf{Z_s} - \mathbf{M_s}\hat{\mathbf{V}}_\mathbf{s})\|_2$ at SPDC is given by the following equation [13]:

$$\hat{\mathbf{V}}_\mathbf{s} = (\mathbf{M_s^H W_s M_s})^{-1}\mathbf{M_s^H W_s Z_s} \tag{11}$$

where, $\hat{\mathbf{V}}_\mathbf{s}$ are the boundary bus voltage estimates, $\mathbf{M_s}$ is a model matrix, and $\mathbf{W_s}$ is weight matrix. More details of deriving $\mathbf{W_s}$ can be found in [13]. As the amount of data transmitted from each LPDC to SPDC in DSE depends on the boundary buses of each electric region and the number of electric transmission lines connecting these regions, it varies for different grid topologies. To estimate the bandwidth used by SE with DEFT and CEUT, consider two regions r_1, r_2, both having n buses, b of which are the boundary buses and connected by b transmission lines. Also, let both r_1, r_2 have l transmission lines. Neglecting the meta info from PMU data, each LPDC in CEUT would send $8(n + l)$ bytes of data to SPDC, where 8 is the size of each phasor in bytes.

In DEFT, LSE of both regions would estimate the boundary bus voltages of r_1 and r_2, which would lead to a total of $2b$ voltage estimates. As each LPDC receives data from b boundary buses, considering phasor data of 8 bytes, the PMU measurement of b buses and $2b$ voltage estimates leads to $24b$ bytes of data. The tie line currents measurements and their estimates lead to $16b$ bytes of data. The weights associated with measurements and estimates lead to $20b$ bytes of data, where each weight requires 4 bytes. As the remaining $n - b$ voltage estimates of a region are also sent to SPDC, the total data sent by each LPDC is $52b + 8n$ bytes. The percentage drop in bandwidth (PDB) of DEFT over CEUT is $\frac{8l-52b}{8(n+l)} * 100$. For n = 662, b = 5 and l = 3006, PDB is 81%.

Our distributed algorithms are motivated by scalability issues connected with centralized schemes. The synchronization of PMU readings for all the distributed algorithms discussed above is achieved with GPS timestamps that is part of message exchanges between PMUs and PDCs. The algorithms mentioned in Section 3.2 and 4.2 are not new; however, the literature lacks performance analysis of these algorithms on system-level implementations concerning bandwidth and latency requirements.

5. PERFORMANCE ASSESSMENT OF THE ALGORITHMS

This section reports on the evaluation of the performance of the algorithms in a variety of scenarios, using real as well as simulated data on a testbed. Through these experiments, we show that DEFT approaches outperform CEUT in both latency and bandwidth reduction. For ASM, DEFT latency was 59% less of that for CEUT. Among the DEFT approaches, we show that DEFT-SM transfers much less data compared to DEFT-NSM when there are disturbances in the grid, whereas DEFT-NSM performs better if such disturbances are rare. We further show how latencies of individual applications get affected due to concurrent executions on the same PMU data.

First we discuss the experimental setup and then present the results and discuss the insights they provide.

5.1 Details of the Experimental Setup

We evaluated the performance of our algorithms for the eastern and the western regional grids of India with the data aggregated at their respective PDCs and, in turn, at SPDC.

Table 3: Grid Simulation Specifications

Total buses	662
Total transmission lines	3006
Buses in eastern region	363
Buses in western region	299
Packet generation rate of each PMU	50
Angle difference pairs	14
Number of tie lines	5

Table 3 shows the specifications of the simulation. The tie lines are the electric transmission lines connecting the two regions. Simulated data were generated by a transient stability program that enables modeling the power system dynamics and faults. Together the two regions had 662 buses with PMUs at each bus sending packets at 50 Hz. A three phase ground fault was injected at 0.1 sec on a boundary bus using a transient stability program. The time duration of the fault was 35 milliseconds.

The performance of some of our algorithms under fault conditions was also evaluated over real PMU data sampled at 25 Hz (from the time just before, during, and after a real disturbance in the Indian grid on 30th July, 2012). This data came from PMUs located at Kanpur, Moga, and Dadri substations, part of the northern regional grid of India.

Details of Scenarios Studied: We studied the three applications, ASM, SE and MCGG when executed individually as well as together. For ASM application, 14 pairs of buses were selected that directly or indirectly connect the two regional grids (eastern and western). These 14 pairs were monitored at SPDC. For MCGG application, in two of the three low-frequency oscillation modes monitored at SPDC, generators at the boundary of the eastern region were found to swing with generators of the western region and vice-versa. Hence, for the distributed query execution of MCGG application, to calculate group COI at LPDC, PMU data of a few generators of one region (say eastern) that formed a coherent group with the generators of the other region (say western) was sent to LPDC of that region (western). For the DSE application, each LPDC sent the phasor estimates, measurements, and weights of the boundary buses to SPDC.

Normally, when a system is stable, (i.e., before a fault), the thresholds for ASM and MCGG queries are almost constant. After a certain duration following the occurrence of a fault (known as fault clearing time), every system tries to regain its stability. The steady-state data of the system, after the fault, can give the maximum (in case of ASM and MCGG) and minimum (in case of MCGG) tolerated thresholds, such that the system still remains stable. Hence, for both ASM and MCGG applications, the query thresholds were derived using off-line analysis of pre-fault and post-fault steady-state data. For each of the fourteen angle difference pairs in ASM, the maximum angular difference obtained, from pre-fault and post-fault steady state data, was set to be the threshold for the pair. In MCGG, for each low-frequency mode, group COI and global COI were calculated. As the deviation of a group COI from global COI is a sub-query monitored at LPDC, the minimum and maximum deviation of a group COI from global COI in pre-fault and post-fault steady state data were set to be the thresholds on the sub-query.

Details of Grid Data Used: Figure 5 shows PDCs at three levels – state, regional and national. Of all the state PDCs, the Maharashtra state PDC receives data from the maximum number of PMUs (83). Furthermore, among regional PDCs, WR PDC receives aggregated data from the highest number of PMUs (483). As discussed in section 1, each PDC waits for the arrival of all data from its lower-level PDCs and PMUs. Hence, the sum of the processing latency at Maharashtra PDC, WR PDC and NLDC PDC gives the estimated PL from PMU to SPDC.

Details of the PMU and PDC Simulator: We simulated PMUs and PDCs using the open source grid simulator, iPDC. This simulator implements IEEE C37.118.2-2011 and IEEE C37.244 Standards for PMU and PDC respectively [12]. IEEE C37.118.2-2011 [1] standard defines four kinds of frames: *command, data, configuration*, and *header*.

Command frames are sent to PMUs or lower level PDCs to pull other types of frames. A data frame contains measured data. A *configuration* frame contains machine-readable data, having information and processing parameters for a synchrophasor data stream. A *header* frame has human-readable information about the PMU, the data sources, scaling, algorithms, filtering, or other related information. Each frame type has some meta-data fields along with bytes indicating the operational data. For example, each frame has SYNC information identifying the type of frame and FRAMESIZE information indicating the size of the frame in bytes. These meta-fields occupy 16 bytes. If a PMU measures p phasors along with a analog and d digital control information, the size of individual *data* frames in byte will be: meta info (16)+ statistics (2)+ phasors (8 $\times$ p)+ frequency (4)+ rate of change of frequency (4) + analogs (4 $\times$ a) + digital info (2 $\times$ d). Similarly, the size of a configuration frame depends on the number of PDCs sending the configuration information. We will be using similar calculations to measure the bandwidth requirement for our algorithms throughout the paper.

iPDC has three components- client, server (along with DBserver) and PMU simulator. iPDC client handles incoming data frames from PMUs and other PDCs that are compatible with IEEE C37.244 Standard; it time aligns and concatenates all the data frames with the same time-stamp into a single data frame. iPDC server handles requests from other PDCs and sends them the concatenated data. The DBServer archives all the data received by iPDC. The PMU simulator sends time-stamped measurements at user-specified rates to PDCs.

The Hardware Set-up: The hardware setup for the test bed consists of 3 Intel(R) Core(TM) i5-3230M CPU machines with 4 GB RAM and Ubuntu 12.04 installation. Processes that simulate PMUs of eastern and western region were deployed on two different machines, along with their respective LPDCs. SPDC was simulated on the third machine. All the machines were connected via a 100 Mbps LAN through a 100 Mbps router.

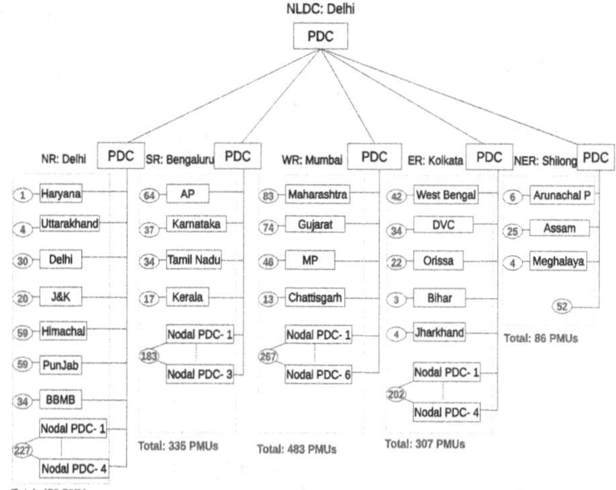

Figure 5: Planned Indian electric grid

Performance Metrics: The primary performance metrics are average response time and average bandwidth usage. The response time of a query is the time taken for the required PMU data to reach SPDC and produce the output that reflects the changes in the PMU data. Hence, response time is composed of *network latency (NL)* from PMU to LPDC, the *processing latency (PL)* at LPDC, the NL from LPDC to SPDC and the PL at SPDC. The PL *observed* in the testbed (PL_o) for the cases that were studied was used to derive expressions for the *estimated PL* (PL_e) at LPDC and SPDC for arbitrary grid configurations and also for the planned Indian electric grid. As it turned out, in the case of CEUT, PL by itself exceeded the required response time for most applications when PMU data sizes were large. So for purposes of comparison of algorithms we just use PL as the performance metric. Thus, *in the rest of the document, when we refer to latency or response time we are referring to just the PL.*

5.2 Expressions for PL at LPDC and SPDC

In this sub-section, we discuss the different latency components for the PL at the LPDC (D^{lpdc}) and SPDC (D^{spdc}). Using the PL_o, we develop a model for PL_e. The PL at a PDC is composed of two components, *parsing time* for the PMU data frames (D^{parse}) and time to create an *aggregated* data frame (D^{agg}).

$$D^{lpdc} = D^{parse}(X) + D^{agg}(N) \tag{12}$$

$$D^{spdc} = D^{parse}(X) \tag{13}$$

where N is the total number of PMUs at the leaf level. A PDC has a separate thread to parse data from each sender. For a PDC that receives data from N PMUs, $X = \lceil \frac{N}{n} \rceil$, where n is the number of processors. For an intermediate PDC or SPDC that receives data from other LPDCs, D^{parse} depends on the number of sender PDCs and the amount of the aggregated data sent by each. The parsing time of the largest sender PDC data frame is a lower bound on D^{parse}. X at an intermediate PDC or SPDC is considered to be the number of PMUs handled by the sender PDCs with the largest aggregated data size.

Modeling PL$_e$ at LPDC and SPDC from PL$_o$: Two sets of experiments were conducted: E1 to measure the LPDC PL (D^{parse}, D^{agg}) for different number of PMUs, and E2 to measure PL (D^{parse}, D^{agg}) under varying data sizes. The PL$_o$ of E1 was used to model the PL$_e$ of PDC to which PMU data packet is sent. Here, the PL$_e$ is dependent on the PMU data size and number of PMUs sending data to LPDC. Hence, the PL$_e$ for LPDC was modeled separately for each PMU data size. Table 4 gives the estimated parsing and PL at LPDC (D^{lpdc}) to which PMU data of varying sizes were sent. For a large X, N, the D^{parse} and D^{agg} for PL$_e$ at an intermediate PDC and SPDC is obtained from Table 4.

$$D^{parse}(X) = 5.97XK \tag{14}$$

$$D^{agg}(N) = 4.36NK \tag{15}$$

Table 4: D^{parse} and PL at LPDC for varying Data sizes ($100K$) and number of PMUs (N)

K	D^{parse} (microsec)		PL (microsec)	
	Observed for single PMU (E2)	Estimated for N PMUs (E1)	Observed for single PMU (E2)	Estimated for N PMUs (E1)
1	30.3	$31N$	41.1	$36.6N$
3	43.8	$75.6N$	64.1	$93.4N$
5	53.5	$72.4N$	81.5	$97.7N$
10	84.2	$90.1N$	126.6	$134.6N$
15	90.7	$101.8N$	155.3	$168.2N$
20	113.1	$119.4N$	203.5	$209.9N$
25	133.2	$141.1N$	223.2	$231.5N$

Validation of PL$_e$s for PDCs: The PL$_o$ for WR PDC and NLDC PDC were 13.3 msec and 1.8 msec respectively. The data sizes of most of the PMUs in the experiment varied from 80 bytes to 120 bytes. The Gaussian fit for the histogram of PMU data sizes had $\mu = 96$ and $\sigma = 22$. For simplicity, considering PMU data of 100 bytes and $N = X = 363$, the PL$_e$ for WR PDC and NLDC PDC is, 13.2 msec and 2.1 msec respectively. That is, the PL$_e$ and PL$_o$ for LPDC and SPDC are very close to each other.

PL$_e$ for the PDCs of the Indian Electric Grid: As given in [15], the nodal PDCs at some substations may receive data from 50-60 PMUs. For the PMU data of 50 bytes with 50 PMUs sending data to a nodal PDC, the aggregated data frame size is around 2500 bytes. For PMU data of 2500 bytes, the PL$_e$ at PDCs of Maharashtra, WR and NLDC are 19.2 msec, 65 msec, and 72 msec respectively. Further, the PL$_e$ from, 1) PMU to WR PDC, and 2) PMU to NLDC PDC are 84.2 msec and 156.2 msec respectively. Considering the nodal PDC as a representative for PMU, we observe for CEUT that, PL by itself exceeded the required response time for most applications at WR and NLDC PDC. In all further analysis of PLs for the Indian electric grid, we consider PMU data of 2500 bytes.

5.3 Results Pertaining to ASM

Having developed a simple latency model for PLs at the PDCs, we are in a position to discuss the latencies experienced by our three applications. In this sub-section, we present the PL$_o$ for ASM from the experiments discussed in Section 5.1. We further give PL$_e$ for ASM with DEFT followed by its implications for the Indian electric grid. We also present the plots showing data transferred with DEFT-NSM and DEFT-SM for real and simulated PMU data.

PL$_o$ for ASM: The benefits of DEFT are evident from Figure 6 that shows a significant reduction in the average latency for the applications with DEFT. It was observed that, during the fault duration of 35 msec, only 12 global violations happened whereas the rest of the time saw very few local violations. The total number of global and local violations accounted for 3% time of the entire simulation whereas the rest 97% of the time, the data were filtered at LPDCs. Hence, Figure 6 portrays the fact that 97% of the time, the latency of ASM with DEFT-NSM was just 2.8 msec as the query execution stopped at LPDC. Only 3% of the time, the latency for ASM with DEFT was 9.39 msec as data were pulled from peer LPDC for each local violation leading to 32 kb of data transfer for the entire period of simulation. This corresponded to 87% and 59% drop in average latency over CEUT when query result was delivered at LPDC (97% of the time) and SPDC (3% of the time) respectively. Even though the query result was delivered to SPDC for 3% of the time, the percentage drop is still considerable. As there were only 12 global violations of the fault duration, the average latency for ASM with DEFT-NSM and DEFT-SM approach was same. Hence, we do not distinguish between DEFT-NSM and DEFT-SM.

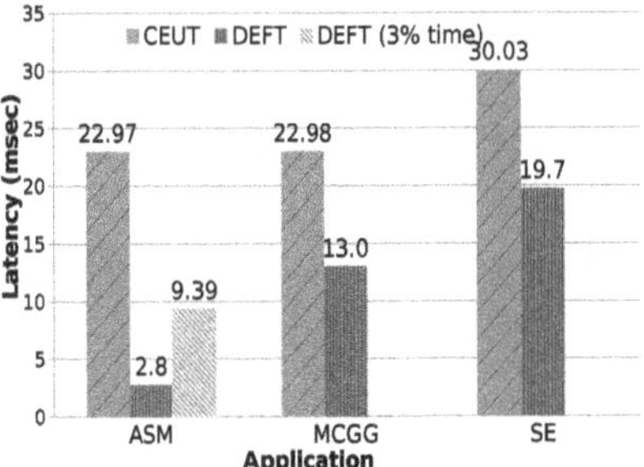

Figure 6: Latency reduction for each application

PL$_e$ for ASM with DEFT: Consider a three level grid hierarchy. The latency (D^{resp}_{ASM}) for ASM at SPDC is:

$$D^{resp}_{ASM} = D^{ntk_1} + D^{parse}(X) + D^{lpdc\_subquery} + D^{ntk_2} + D^{spdc\_subquery} \tag{16}$$

where $D^{lpdc\_subquery}$ and $D^{spdc\_subquery}$ are PLs for the queries at LPDC and SPDC respectively, X is the greatest of the PMUs for any of the LPDCs that monitor the angle difference sub-query and D^{ntk_1} and D^{ntk_2}, are the NLs' from PMU to LPDC and LPDC to SPDC respectively. The PL for the sub-query ($D^{lpdc\_subquery}$) is very small (a few microsecs) and is ignored. Normally, when the grid is steady, there are no local violations and PL$_e$ for ASM ($PL_{e_{ASM}}$) with no local violations is:

$$PL_{e_{ASM}} = D^{parse} \tag{17}$$

For local violations, the data are pulled from other LPDCs. Hence, the latency is:

$$D^{resp}_{ASM} = D^{ntk_1} + D^{parse}(X) + D^{ntk_2} + D^{spdc\_query} + D^{ntk_2} \tag{18}$$

where $D^{spdc\_query} = D^{ntk_2} + D^{queue} + D^{ntk_2}$ and D^{queue} is the delay to fetch data from peer LPDC. The sub-query arriving at LPDC can get queued due to parsing of X PMUs and in the worst case, $D^{queue} = D^{parse}$. The PL$_{e_{ASM}}$ during local violations is:

$$PL_{e_{ASM}} = 2D^{parse}(X) \tag{19}$$

PL$_e$ for ASM with DEFT on the Indian Electric Grid: To illustrate the implications of DEFT on the Indian electric grid, we consider (for ASM) the angle difference between the substations of Gujarat and Maharashtra states monitored at WR PDC. The sub-queries' conditions are then monitored at their respective state PDCs. For PMU data of 2500 bytes, the PL$_e$ for ASM with and without local violations from Table 4, (17) and (19) are 23.4 msec and 11.7 msec respectively. The query execution time for ASM at WR PDC with CEUT is very small (a few microsecs) and hence, ignored. Unlike CEUT, which has PL$_e$ of 84.2 msec at WR PDC, ASM with DEFT has 72% and 86% reduction in latency for the query result delivered at SPDC and LPDC respectively. We see that ASM with DEFT easily meets the 50 msec latency requirement of ASM.

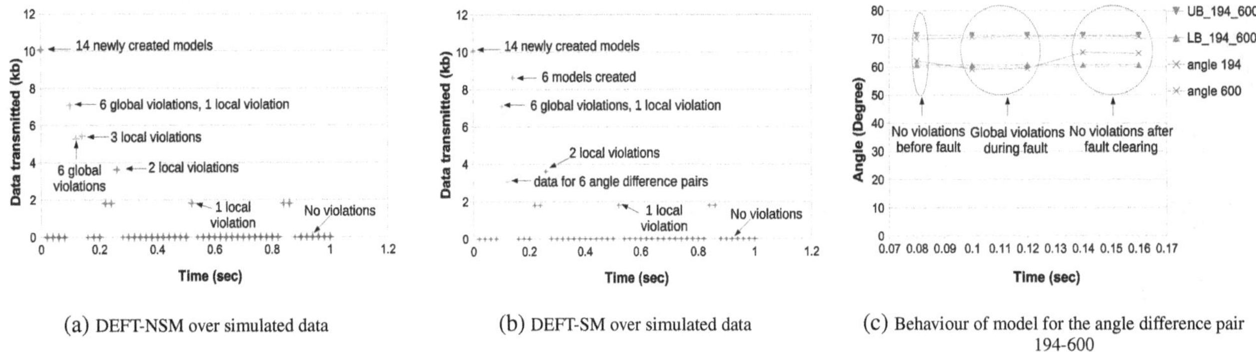

(a) DEFT-NSM over simulated data

(b) DEFT-SM over simulated data

(c) Behaviour of model for the angle difference pair 194-600

Figure 7: Comparison of data transmitted with DEFT-NSM and DEFT-SM for simulated data: Before, during and after the fault.

Comparison of DEFT-NSM and DEFT-SM over simulated data for ASM: Figures 7a and 7b show the data transferred in each cycle of 20 msec duration for DEFT-NSM and DEFT-SM respectively during the first 1 sec data transfer of simulation. These figures portray the behaviour of DEFT-NSM and DEFT-SM discussed in Section 2 for pre-fault and post-fault conditions of the grid. In both DEFT-NSM and DEFT-SM, 10.08 kb of data was transferred to create 14 data dynamics models (corresponding to 14 bus pairs) at LPDCs. As there were no local violations from 0.02 to 0.098 secs. of simulated time, no data was transferred between either of the LPDCs and SPDC.

As different buses are connected directly or indirectly to the faulty bus, after the fault (injected at 0.1 sec at bus 354), there were violations of local conditions for seven of fourteen angle difference pairs at only one LPDC. Out of these, six were global violations whereas one was a local violation. The buses corresponding to pairs with global violations were closer to the faulty bus. Hence, fault at bus 354 affected the power flow on transmission lines, which in turn led to the angular separation of the corresponding angle difference pairs. For the local violation experienced by the pair 155-455, the angle of bus 455 was unaffected by the fault as it was farther from the faulty bus. However, as there is a transmission line connecting buses 155 and 354, bus 155 was affected by the fault, which led to the local violation. Nevertheless, this local violation did not result in a global violation, and the new model was sent by the SPDC to both the LPDCs. As the global violations were detected for the first time, six global violations and one local violation led to a transfer of 7.088 kb data with both DEFT-NSM and DEFT-SM.

At 0.12 sec, there were global violations corresponding to six local violations at the LPDC for same six pairs as detected previously. As discussed in Section 2.4, in DEFT-NSM, a local violation leads to pulling of data from peer LPDC to SPDC, a total of 5.28 kb data were transferred. In contrast, in DEFT-SM, as both the LPDCs entered streaming mode after the first global violation, each LPDC sent corresponding angle pairs that had global violations without any request (46 bytes) for data from peer LPDC. Hence, only 3.072 kb of data were transferred.

At 0.14 sec, the system regained an equilibrium state. Hence, DEFT-NSM was expected to send data to create six new models. But surprisingly, only three local violations (with 5.424 kb data) happened. This is because, as Figure 7c shows, the phasor angles of the pair 194-600 did not experience local violations at 0.14 sec were within the threshold bounds of the model created before fault (0.08 sec). Similar behaviour was seen for the angle difference pairs 194-397 and 299-320. From this, we infer that, when the electric grid comes back to a stable operating point, not all dynamics, which lead to global violations in DEFT-NSM, need to be remodeled. In DEFT-SM, since the models that experienced global violations were already discarded by the LPDC, at 0.14 sec, phasor data associated with all the angle difference pairs were sent by the LPDCs to create six new models. Thus, 8.64 kb ($1.44 * 6$ kb) data were transferred compared to 5.424 kb in DEFT-NSM. The local violations observed 0.16 sec onwards were due to minor post-fault oscillations that eventually damp out without causing any instability in the grid.

The summarized observations from Figures' 7a and 7b are: 1) for the global violations detected at 0.12 sec, DEFT-SM transferred fewer messages compared to DEFT-NSM, 2) as the grid came back to stable equilibrium at 0.14 sec, not all dynamics that led to global violations in DEFT-NSM were re-modeled, and 3) after the fault was cleared (at 0.14 sec), there were very few local violations, resulting in data filtering with both, DEFT-NSM and DEFT-SM.

Comparison of DEFT-NSM and DEFT-SM over the real PMU data: Figure 8 shows data transmitted with DEFT-NSM and DEFT-SM, with real PMU data. DEFT-SM transmitted a total of 27% less data compared to DEFT-NSM for the duration of a real disturbance in the Indian grid. The reduction is chiefly attributed to the streaming mode of DEFT-SM with global violations which showed 30% reduction in data transfer over DEFT-NSM. For local violations, DEFT-SM showed marginal reduction in data transfer compared to DEFT-NSM. This is mainly because, there were few local violations, whose global violations had occurred in the previous time slot, which in turn led to LPDC enter the streaming mode.

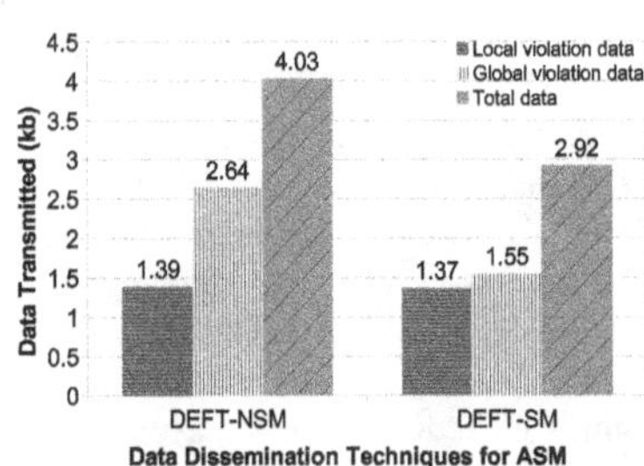

Figure 8: Comparison of data transferred with DEFT-NSM and DEFT-SM for real PMU data– for 2 angle difference pairs (Kanpur-Moga and Moga-Dadri substations).

The inference drawn from the two distributed approaches, SM and NSM, for ASM is that, with only local violations, the performance of DEFT-NSM and DEFT-SM for bandwidth requirement was almost the same. However, DEFT-SM used lesser bandwidth compared to DEFT-NSM for global violations.

5.4 Results Pertaining to MCGG

In this sub-section, we present the PL$_o$ for MCGG from the experiments discussed in section 5.1. We further describe PL$_e$ for MCGG with DEFT.

PL$_o$ for MCGG: Figure 6 shows that MCGG with DEFT saw a 43% reduction in average latency over CEUT and had more than 99% drop in bandwidth usage for the data transferred from LPDC to SPDC over CEUT. The reduction in average latency can be chiefly attributed to the distributed computation of application queries at LPDCs and very less PL of the sub-query results at SPDC. The drop in bandwidth with DEFT was because, both the LPDCs sent just 30 bytes in each cycle (20 msec) for the sub-query results executed at LPDCs unlike 15918 and 14782 bytes sent by the two respective LPDCs in CEUT.

PL$_e$ for MCGG with DEFT: Consider a three level grid hierarchy. The latency (D^{resp}_{MCGG}) for MCGG at SPDC with each LPDC computing group COI is:

$$D^{resp}_{MCGG} = D^{ntk_1} + D^{parse}(X) + D^{lpdc\_subquery} + D^{ntk_2} + D^{spdc\_query} \quad (20)$$

where $D^{lpdc\_subquery}$ and D^{spdc_query} are the PLs for the queries at LPDC and SPDC respectively, X is the largest number of the PMUs for any of the LPDCs that monitor the sub-queries and D^{ntk_1} and D^{ntk_2}, are the NLs' from PMU to LPDC and LPDC and SPDC respectively. The PL$_e$ for MCGG ($PL_{e_{MCGG}}$) is:

$$PL_{e_{MCGG}} = D^{parse}(X) + D^{lpdc\_subquery} + D^{spdc\_query} \quad (21)$$

As $D^{lpdc\_subquery} << D^{parse}(X)$, $PL_{e_{MCGG}}$,

$$PL_{e_{MCGG}} = D^{parse}(X) + D^{spdc\_query} \quad (22)$$

PL$_e$ for MCGG with DEFT for the Indian Electric Grid: To illustrate the implications of DEFT for the Indian electric grid, we consider for MCGG, that the coherent groups of generators belonging to Maharashtra and Gujarat state are monitored at WR PDC. The PL for MCGG with DEFT is the sum of, (1) parsing of 83 PMUs at Maharashtra PDC and (2) D^{spdc_query}. The observed D^{spdc_query} for ER-WR grid of India was 1.25 msec. If we consider WR PDC monitoring low-frequency modes, with generators of Maharashtra and Gujarat, D^{spdc_query} would be less than 1.25. Considering $D^{spdc\_query} = 1.25$, the PL$_e$ at WR PDC for MCGG with PMU data size of 2500 bytes, as given from Table 4 and (22) is, $(11.7 + 1.25) = 12.9$ msec. Thus, DEFT easily meets the 50 msec latency requirement of MCGG. The query execution time for MCGG at WR PDC with CEUT is very less (a few microsecs) and hence, ignored. Unlike CEUT, which has PL$_e$, 84.2 msec at WR PDC, DEFT has comparatively 84% lower PL.

5.5 Results Pertaining to SE

In this sub-section, we present the PL$_o$ for SE from the experiments discussed in section 5.1. We further give PL$_e$ for SE with DEFT.

PL$_o$ for SE: As Figure 6 shows, SE with DEFT had 34% reduction in average latency and had 81% drop in bandwidth usage for the data transferred from LPDC to SPDC over CEUT. The significant decrease in average latency is mainly attributed to the fact that the size of the model matrix at LPDCs was approximately half that of the one at SPDC in CEUT and very low PL to perform WLS on a smaller size model matrix at SPDC. Similarly, in DEFT, two LPDCs sent just 2256 and 3068 bytes respectively compared to 15918 and 14782 bytes with CEUT, resulting in reduced bandwidth.

PL$_e$ for SE with DEFT: The latency for SE with DEFT (D^{resp}_{DSE}) of a three level grid hierarchy is:

$$D^{resp}_{DSE} = D^{ntk_1} + D^{parse}(X) + D^{lpdc\_subquery} + D^{ntk_2} + D^{spdc\_query} \quad (23)$$

where $D^{lpdc\_subquery}$ and D^{spdc_query} are the PL for the queries at LPDC and SPDC respectively, X is the greatest of PMUs sending data to any LPDC and and D^{ntk_1} and D^{ntk_2}, are the NLs' from PMU to LPDC and LPDC to SPDC respectively. The PL$_e$ for SE with DEFT ($PL_{e_{DSE}}$) is:

$$PL_{e_{DSE}} = D^{parse}(X) + D^{lpdc\_subquery} + D^{spdc\_query} \quad (24)$$

PL$_e$ for SE on the Indian Electric Grid: To illustrate the implications of DEFT for the Indian electric grid, we assume that the five regional PDCs perform LSE and NLDC PDC performs WLS. The PL$_e$ and D^{parse} for the Maharashtra PDC and WR PDC respectively with PMU data of 2500 bytes as given from Table 4 is 19.2 msec and 12.3 msec respectively. As given in [13], the LSE solved with QR factorization for the North East West (NEW) Indian grid took 23 msec. The NEW grid includes the four regional grids of India. With the assumption that each regional PDC would take one fourth of the PL required for LSE at NLDC PDC, performing LSE at the regional PDC would take at most 6 msec ($D^{lpdc\_subquery}$). Since the size of the matrix at SPDC is comparatively smaller, the execution of WLS should not exceed 6 msec. Considering WLS PL ($D^{spdc\_subquery}$) as 6 msec, the PL$_e$ for DSE in the Indian electric grid is 43.5 msec.The PL$_e$ for CEUT with the time to perform LSE (23 msec) is 179.2 msec, whereas, DSE has 75% reduction in PL and is within the 100 msec latency requirement of SE. This demonstrates that DEFT based SE is better than CEUT based SE.

5.6 Latency under Concurrent Execution

Figure 9 shows the average latency in DEFT for each application when run singly and concurrently with other applications. It shows an increasing trend of average latency for each application when run singly and when run concurrently with other applications. The current PDC implementation does not pre-empt the threads that process PMU data based on applications priorities. Hence, if a PMU data packet is pertaining to, say, ASM arrival at PDC, and all the processors are busy processing the packets for MCGG or SE application, execution of ASM would be delayed. The same is also true for MCGG and SE. Hence, as Figure 9 shows, the concurrent execution of applications affects their individual latencies.

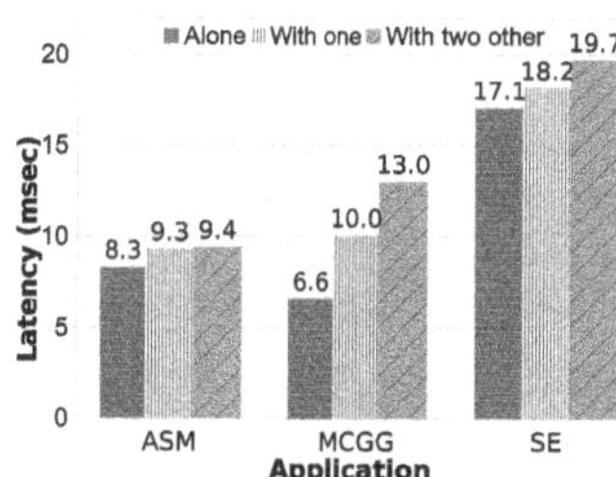

Figure 9: Average latency: running singly and concurrently with other applications.

The priority of executing the applications at a PDC depends on the time criticality of the application. ASM has higher execution priority over MCGG, as in ASM, control action needs to be taken quickly to prevent propagation of instability throughout the system. The lowest priority is assigned to SE. Though our implementation does not preempt the threads that process PMU data, it does preempt the applications with lower priorities that require the data from the same PMUs. In our case, some PMUs contain angular information common to both, MCGG and ASM. As ASM has higher priority over MCGG, ASM is executed before MCGG. The effect gets reflected in Figure 9.

6. RELATED WORK

In-network query processing, data filtering, and distributed execution with aggregation have been studied extensively in the literature. Authors of [4] use probabilistic models of sensor data for minimizing data acquisition for given user query. Model-based estimation of data values to filter data values that are not *very* different from the estimated values is presented in [5]. In comparison, our technique uses *application semantics* to perform in-network query processing for smart grid applications. Thus, our technique can be used for exact monitoring and not just probabilistic monitoring.

Data traffic reduction using filtering at the data sources is proposed in [7, 10, 14]. These filtering conditions are derived from sufficient conditions for providing *no-false-negative* guarantees for threshold queries. Authors of [6] use data aggregation from distributed sources. These techniques perform in-network query processing on sensor values. In comparison, we use data modeling and in-network processing to monitor the grid efficiently.

Techniques for timely and QoS guaranteed delivery of data have been studied in the literature. Gridstat [3] discusses the implementation of a data dissemination network with delivery guarantees in a smart grid. Our approach optimizes data dissemination and is orthogonal to Gridstat. Thus, our solution can be used with Gridstat or any other data delivery mechanism. We also retain the existing client-server framework for PMU-PDC communication that is currently adopted by the power system domain – unlike Gridstat, which is a new middleware paradigm. The use of stream computing based approach for optimizing the data transmission in [8] makes way for an easy development of applications and allows for graceful degradation during times of overload. Our work has some similarity with [8] in the use of partial computations to get the query results. However, the techniques discussed in [8] do not take into consideration application semantics. We also show the implications of our techniques on the topology of the Indian electric grid.

7. CONCLUSION AND FUTURE WORK

The high bandwidth requirements of critical real-time monitoring applications in the smart grid prompted us to design in-network query processing techniques that allow for flexible bandwidth sharing among smart grid applications. We achieved significant gains in latency reduction for critical applications. The techniques are semantics-aware – high data filtering when the grid is stable, and the application receiving almost all the data when the grid may move into instability.

In the future, we intend to do a wholistic evaluation of our technique for multiple applications running on the grid simultaneously based on their priority of execution and also study the effect of our technique on the latency of detecting the faulty events in the grid.

ACKNOWLEDGMENTS

We thank DeitY, Govt. of India, and TCS for their financial support; to PGCIL for sharing details of the Indian grid; to Swadesh Jain and Mayur Kale for helping in our work.

8. REFERENCES

[1] Ieee standard for synchrophasor data transfer for power systems. *IEEE Std C37.118.2-2011 (Revision of IEEE Std C37.118-2005)*, pages 1–53, 2011.

[2] H. Alsafih and R. Dunn. Identification of critical areas for potential wide-area based control in complex power systems based on coherent clusters. *Universities Power Engineering Conference (UPEC)*, September 2010.

[3] D. Bakken, A. Bose, C. Hauser, D. Whitehead, and G. Zweigle. Smart generation and transmission with coherent, real-time data. *Proceedings of the IEEE*, 99(6):928 –951, june 2011.

[4] A. Deshpande, C. Guestrin, S. R. Madden, J. M. Hellerstein, and W. Hong. Model-driven data acquisition in sensor networks. In *Proceedings of the Thirtieth international conference on Very large data bases-Volume 30*, pages 588–599. VLDB Endowment, 2004.

[5] P. Edara, A. Limaye, and K. Ramamritham. Asynchronous in-network prediction: Efficient aggregation in sensor networks. *ACM Trans. on Sensor Networks (TOSN)*, 4(4):25, 2008.

[6] R. Gupta and K. Ramamritham. Query planning for continuous aggregation queries over a network of data aggregators. *Knowledge and Data Engineering, IEEE Trans. on*, 24(6):1065–1079, 2012.

[7] R. Gupta, K. Ramamritham, and M. Mohania. Ratio threshold queries over distributed data sources. In *Data Engineering (ICDE), 2010 IEEE 26th International Conference on*, pages 581–584. IEEE, 2010.

[8] J. Hazra, K. Das, D. Seetharam, and A. Singhee. Stream computing based synchrophasor application for power grids. In *Proceedings of the first international workshop on High performance computing, networking and analytics for the power grid*, pages 43–50. ACM, 2011.

[9] D. Hu and V. Venkatasubramanian. New wide-area algorithms for detection and mitigation of angle instability using synchrophasors. In *Power Engineering Society General Meeting, 2007. IEEE*, pages 1–8. IEEE, 2007.

[10] Z. Ives, D. Florescu, M. Friedman, A. Levy, and D. Weld. An adaptive query execution system for data integration. 1999.

[11] K. D. Jones. Three-phase linear state estimation with phasor measurements. Master's thesis, Blacksburg, VA, 2011.

[12] K. Khandeparkar and N. Pandit. Design and implementation of IEEE c37.118 based phaser data concentrator and pmu simulator for wide area measurement system. *Technical Report, Dept. of Electrical Engg., IIT, Bombay.*, May, 2012.

[13] P. V. Navalkar. *Phasor Measurement Unit Based Linear State Estimate Or-Diagnostics And Application to Secure Remote Backup Protection of Transmission Lines*. PhD thesis, Dept. of Electrical Engg., IIT, Bombay, India, 2012.

[14] C. Olston, J. Jiang, and J. Widom. Adaptive filters for continuous queries over distributed data streams. In *Proceedings of the 2003 ACM SIGMOD international conf. on Management of data*, pages 563–574. ACM, 2003.

[15] PGCIL. Unified real time dynamic state measurement (urtdsm), Feb. 2012.

[16] A. Phadke. Synchronized phasor measurements in power systems. *Computer Applications in Power, IEEE*, 6(2):10–15, 1993.

[17] K. Shubhanga and Y. Anantholla. *A Multi-machine Small-signal Stability Programme*. Dept. of Electrical Engg. NITK, Surathkal, v1.0 edition.

[18] C. Wu, A.-H. Mohsenian-Rad, and J. Huang. *Distributed state estimation: a learning based framework*. Cambridge University Press, 2012.

HAMS: A Memory-Efficient Representation of Power Grids using Hierarchical and Multi-Scenario Graphs

Amith Singhee, Mark Lavin, Ulrich Finkler, Fook-Luen Heng
IBM T.J. Watson Research Center
Yorktown Heights, NY, USA
asinghe@us.ibm.com

Jun Mei Qu
IBM China Research Lab
Beijing, China

Steven Hirsch
IBM Systems and Technology Group
Burlington, VT, USA

ABSTRACT

Advanced analytical applications that will enable the smart grid need to analyze the connectivity of the power grid under multiple different operating scenarios, taking into account time-varying topology of the grid. This paper proposes a highly memory-efficient representation of the power grid that enables efficient construction of multiple topological and operational states in memory for high-performance graph analysis. The proposed representation exploits repeating patterns in the grid and uses a hierarchical graph as the core model. Time-varying topology and operational conditions are modeled as mapping functions on this hierarchical graph, so as to avoid construction of multiple graphs to represent multiple topologies. The efficiency and performance of the proposed representation is demonstrated on a large real-world distribution electrical grid.

Categories and Subject Descriptors

E.1 [**Data Structures**] Data Structures – *Graphs and networks*

General Terms

Algorithms.

Keywords

Smart grid, power grid, power systems, topological analysis.

1. INTRODUCTION

Any electrical power grid is an interconnected system of conducting equipment and can be modeled as a graph for representation in software applications. This enables applications to perform a variety of complex graph-based analyses on the representation of the power grid. Examples of such analyses are complex network-based risk analyses [1] and graph-tracing based reliability analysis [2]. In fact, the need for complex analyses of the connectivity of the electric grid will only increase going forward as grid operational and planning systems have to deal with the increased complexity from distributed energy resources and renewable energy, and exploit the flexibility provided by technologies such as demand response and increased sensing (smart meters, PMUs, etc.) [3].

There has been work in the community that represents a power grid as a graph [1][2] to support graph-based computation, however, two important aspects have not been addressed: 1) The grid topology is changing over time as equipment is installed and removed and advanced analytical applications will need to be able to reconstruct multiple network topologies very efficiently for historical analysis, multi-scenario analysis and also future planning. 2) Power grids can be extremely large in size with many millions of resources connected together. Flat graph representations of these large systems can have very large memory footprints. If multiple topologies have to be constructed in memory (as per the first aspect), the memory footprint can blow up significantly.

One option to circumvent the memory issue is to use disk storage, such as a relational database to represent the topology and not load the graph into memory. All graph analyses would then have to be run as queries on the database. This becomes intractable very quickly because such analyses, such as a depth-first search, tend to be sequential and result in very long sequences of database queries. For example, each edge traversal on the graph could result in a database query and it is very common to have many millions of edges in a single graph representing a distribution grid.

This paper proposes a highly memory-efficient representation of power grids that addresses both aspects aforementioned. The representation, called HAMS (Hierarchical and Multi-Scenario), uses a hierarchical graph representation of the grid network topology and couples that with dictionary-based representation of topological and operational scenarios.

1.1 Related Work

Hierarchical graphs have been used in the domain of electronic design automation (EDA) to represent static Very Large Scale Integration (VLSI) circuits [4]. The topology, however, is static. Dynamic topologies show up in the domains of social networks and dynamic mobile networks, where time-varying graphs are used, as summarized in [5]. However, the representation described in [5] is restricted to flat graphs and does not address conductivity and flow states that are relevant for power grids. The proposed HAMS model combines a hierarchical graph model with a multi-scenario model that addresses the dynamic nature of the power grid, to address the unique challenges and opportunities presented by power grids.

Graphs have been used for analyzing power grids too, but without exploiting hierarchy. In [2], the authors use a flat graph to represent a power grid, where every modeled piece of equipment is represented as an edge and graph traversals are used to evaluate a Monte Carlo simulation based measure of reliability. Topology iterators enable applications to traverse the graph data structure. [1] models the notion of electrical distance between nodes in a grid to construct an electrical graph representation for comparison with the topological representation (similar to bus-branch model). The Common Information Model (CIM)-based IEC 61970

e-Energy'15, July 14-17, 2015, Bangalore, India.
 ISBN 978-1-4503-3609-3/15/07…$15.00.
DOI: http://dx.doi.org/10.1145/2768510.2768542

standard [6] models the grid as a flat graph at the level of asset and physical connectivity. Each modeled piece of equipment has terminals on it, which are connected together at special nodes called connectivity nodes. This approach has some conceptual similarity with our proposed model, which also considers all modeled pieces of equipment as nodes, with terminals that are connected at connectivity nodes. However, we propose an actual data structure whereas the standard is an information model. In addition the standard does not exploit hierarchy or model dynamic topology as we do in this paper.

1.2 Outline

The rest of this paper is organized as follows. Section 2 describes some key characteristics of electrical power grids that present challenges and opportunities addressed by HAMS. Section 3 describes the HAMS model in detail and presents an overview of the implementation. Section 4 outlines an implementation of HAMS and discusses computational cost in terms of memory and runtime. Section 5 describes some experiments and results that demonstrate the performance of HAMS as implemented here and Section 6 provides concluding remarks.

2. POWER GRID CHARACTERISTICS

Let us look at some key characteristics of typical power grids that present challenges and opportunities that will be addressed by the HAMS model.

2.1 Electrical Connectivity

A power system, for transmission or distribution, is composed of conducting equipment (cables, transformers, switches, etc.) electrically connected together to enable and control the flow of electricity. We refer to each such piece of equipment as a *resource.* Each resource has a set of terminals and some internal electrical connectivity. The terminals are points of potential electrical interconnection between equipment. There might be more than two pieces of equipment that are connected together at a single node, for example, when a line branches out into two in a distribution feeder circuit.

2.2 Encapsulation

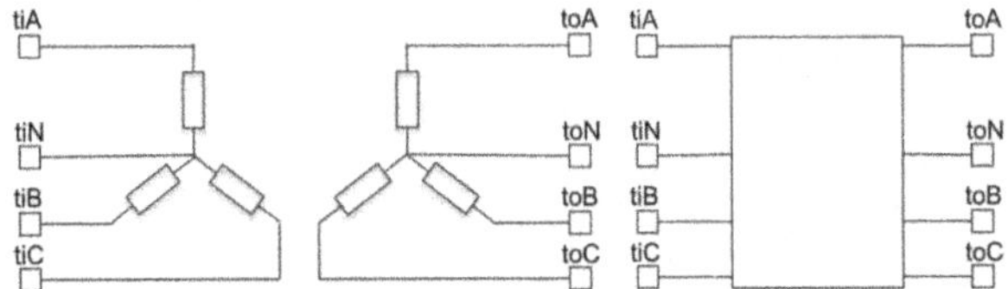

Figure 1 Internal connectivity of a YY-connected 2-winding transformer. Left: schematic. Right: encapsulation.

It is very often the case that multiple resources share the same internal electrical connectivity. For example, YY-connected 2-winding transformers can be represented with the same internal structure as shown in Figure 1. The connections between the transformer and other resources is determined by the terminals available on the transformer, and are independent of the internal connectivity, given that the terminal roles are clearly identified (e.g., which is the neutral terminal, etc.). Hence the terminals present an interface to the internal connectivity of the resource and we can *encapsulate* the internal connectivity into an abstract representation (Figure 1 right), while still maintaining the same connectivity with other resources. We will exploit this characteristic in our model to reduce memory usage.

2.3 Dynamic topology

Any resource has a finite lifetime that is less than the lifetime of the entire power grid. Resources are installed and removed frequently from the grid, as they reach the end of their life, or the system is upgraded or extended. At any given point in time, the grid has a certain connectivity topology, which can change over time because of these modifications to it. It is very important to model this dynamism in the topology of the grid to allow applications to analyze these different topologies for purposes such as historical event analysis and optimal planning of future grid enhancement.

2.4 Operational State

Even for a given topology, the grid can typically be operated in multiple different operational states. From the point of view of modeling the connectivity, there are two primary components of this operational state, as described below.

1) Conductivity state: The grid consists of several sectionalizing devices that can block or allow the flow of electricity, such as switches, fuses, breakers and reclosers. In addition, damages to the infrastructure from environmental and other impact can block the flow of electricity and cause power outages. In all these cases of blocking electricity, some resource in the grid stops conducting. The resource maybe conducting in one scenario and not in another. Many analyses, such as state estimation [7] and fault location, need to consider the conductivity state of entities in the grid to identify the energized part of the grid.
2) Flow state: The flow state denotes the direction of electricity flow through every resource in the grid. It is important to model it to enable topological analysis of the grid. For example, if we are interested to compute the loading history on a conducting equipment by aggregating downstream loads over time, we would need to know which loads are "downstream" to that equipment, and which ones are not. For this we have to know the direction of power flow through the connections of the grid. With the advent of distributed energy resources (DER) such as rooftop solar and storage, the direction of power flow can change frequently under different grid operating scenarios, different environmental conditions (sunny or not) and different energy usage profiles. These changes can have dramatic impacts on the reliability and efficiency of the power system and have to be carefully analyzed to drive planning and operational activities [8].

It becomes quite important to be able to model multiple different operating scenarios for the same grid to enable operational and planning applications to analyze and optimize across these scenarios. The next section describes the proposed model that captures all of the characteristics of power grids described in this section.

3. THE HAMS MODEL

The core of HAMS is a *Hierarchical Connected System* (HCS). The HCS models the connected topology of the grid as a hierarchical graph and can be coupled with representations of different topological and operational states that define different scenarios, to create a full HAMS model. The next two sections will describe the model and the scenario representation.

3.1 Hierarchical Connected System

A generic graph is an ordered pair (V, E), where V is a set of *entities* (vertices) and E is a set of pair-wise *connections* (edges) between these entities: each connection $e \in E$ is a 2-entity subset of V. We further refine this definition to define a *cell.*

A *cell* d is a graph (V_d, E_d), where

1. $V_d = I_d \cup T_d \cup C_d$. Here I_d is a set of *instances*, T_d is a set of *terminals* and C_d is a set of *connectivity nodes*. A cell models the common internal structure of physical entities that we are trying to model. Every instance $i \in I_d$ is a reference to a cell $d(i) \neq d$, and models a physical entity in the power grid (e.g. transformer, line, winding, etc.) that has the internal structure modeled by $d(i)$. Terminals mark connection points on the external interface of the cell. For example, a transformer may have a complex internal structure with multiple entities and connections internally, but it may receive external connections only on its terminals.
2. $E_d = E_{dT} \cup E_{dI}$. Let us define $T(I_d) = \{i,t | i \in I_d, t \in T_{d(i)}\}$ as all possible pairs of instances in d and terminals contained within their reference cells. Then we define *flat connections* $E_{dT} \subseteq T_d \times C_d$ and *jump connections* $E_{dI} \subseteq T(I_d) \times (T_d \cup C_d)$. Hence, a flat connection starts on a terminal and ends on a connectivity node in the same cell, while jump connections start on a terminal within an instance and ends either on a terminal or a connectivity node in the same cell as the instance. We define two functions that operate on connections: 1) $start(c)$ returns the starting entity (terminal) for a flat connection and the pair (i,t) for a jump connection, where (i,t) is the starting instance-terminal pair. 2) $end(c)$ returns the ending entity (connectivity node or terminal) for flat and jump connections. Each connection has an *inherent direction* as implied by these definitions. However, this direction does not imply the direction of power flow through the connection. We use flow states (described later) to capture the direction of power flow.
3. Any terminal can have no more than one flat connection and no more than one jump connection on it.

A cell represents the encapsulation that was described in Section 2.2, and allows this encapsulation to be hierarchical. $I(d')$ is the set of instances *of* a cell d': $I(d') = \{i | d(i) = d'\}$. Note that this is different from the set $I_{d'}$, which denotes the set of instances contained *in* a cell d'. $I(d')$ may contain instances that are contained in multiple cells, whereas $I_{d'}$ contains instances that are contained only within the cell d' but may be instances of multiple other cells. A *root cell* is a cell d with $|I(d)| = 0$.

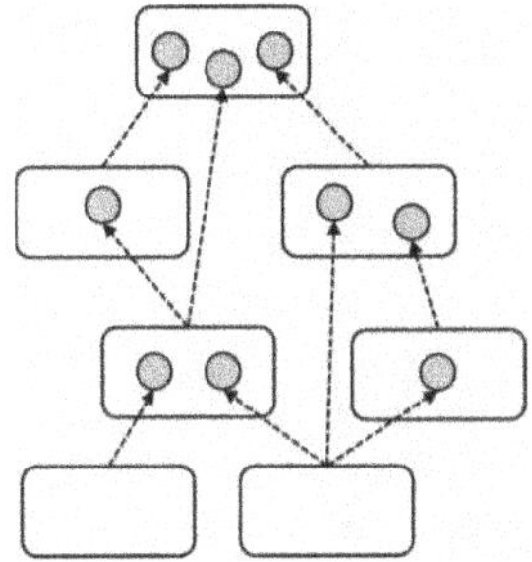

Figure 2 An instantiation graph with 4 levels of hierarchy, composed with a set of 7 cells. Cells: rectangles, Instances: shaded circles, Instantiation: dashed arrows. Connectivity nodes, terminals and connections are not shown.

An instance i has an *instantiation* relationship with its reference cell $d(i)$. Let us consider a set of cells $D = \{d\}$. These instantiation relationships result in an *instantiation graph* g_D, as illustrated by the example in Figure 2, where each edge indicates an instantiation relationship. It contains one root cell with three instances, one each of three other cells. There are two leaf cells, which contain only connectivity nodes and terminals (not shown) and no instances. We denote the set of root cells of D by D_r.

Figure 3 shows a simple example to illustrate all of the aforementioned concepts. It shows a system with five cells: Root, Busbar, Cable, Breaker and Transformer, where Root is the single root cell. Cable, Breaker and Transformer each have an internal structure containing one connectivity node and two terminals, while Busbar contains just one terminal. There are two instances of Breaker, s1 and s2, one instance of Transformer, x1, one of Busbar, b1, and three of Cable, c1, c2 and c3. All instances are in the Root cell. There are 10 jump connections in the Root cell. For example, the leftmost connection starts on terminal t1 in the Transformer instance x1 and ends on the connectivity node cn1. Breaker, Cable and Transformer each have two flat connections. Although this example only has two levels of hierarchy, the proposed model supports arbitrary depth in the hierarchy.

A *hierarchical entity path* (*hentity*) is an ordered set $h = (d_1, v_1, v_2, \ldots, v_k)$ where v_i are entities and d_1 is a cell, such that 1) $v_{i+1} \in V_{d(v_i)}$ for $i < k$, 2) $d(v_1) \in d_1$ and 3) $d_1 \in D_r$. It denotes a path through the instantiation graph of D that starts in a root cell. An example hentity from Figure 3 is (Root,s1,t1). This satisfies the requirements since $\text{t1} \in V_{d(\text{s1})} = V_{\text{Breaker}}$, $\text{s1} \in V_{\text{Root}}$ and Root is the root cell. The function $leaf(h) = v_k$ returns the *leaf entity* v_k of any hentity h.

A *hierarchical connection path* (*hconn*) is an ordered set $o = (h, c)$ where $h = (d_1, v_1, v_2, \ldots, v_k)$ is an hentity, v_k is an instance and c is a connection such that $c \in E_{d(v_k)}$ (c is contained in $d(v_k)$). An example hconn from Figure 3 is (Root,s1,c0).

Now we are ready to define the proposed hierarchical model. A *hierarchical connected system* (*HCS*) $D = \{d\}$ is a set of cells such that there exists no hentity $h = (d_1, v_1, v_2, \ldots, v_k)$ where $d(v_i) = d(v_j): i \neq j$. Such a hierarchical system can be used to represent a power grid, as illustrated by the simple example in Figure 3.

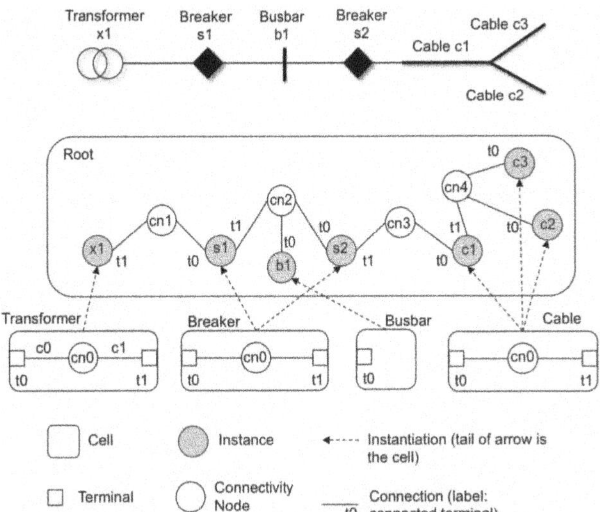

Figure 3 A hierarchical system representation of a simple power network topology.

3.1.1 Virtual Flat Graph

Any HCS can be viewed as a flat graph using the *virtual flat graph* of the system. The virtual flat graph of an HCS D is given by $G_F(D) = (V_F(D), E_F(D))$ where $V_F(D)$ is a set of vertices obtained by creating one *virtual vertex* for each hentity in D with a terminal or connectivity node as its leaf entity, and $E_F(D)$ is the set of edges obtained by creating one *virtual edge* for each hconn in D. Note that these virtual vertices and edges are not really created in memory, and are only conceptually defined here to aid our description.

For simplicity, we refer interchangeably to a virtual vertex and its hentity, and also to a virtual edge and its hconn. Let us consider any hconn $o = (h, c) \in E_F(D)$ where $h = (d_1, v_1, \ldots, v_k)$. Here, o defines a virtual edge between two hentities belonging to $V_F(D)$ as follows. If c is a flat connection, the virtual edge starts from the hentity $(d_1, v_1, \ldots, v_k, t)$, where $t = start(c)$. If c is a jump connection, the virtual edge starts from the hentity $(d_1, v_1, \ldots, v_k, i, t)$ where $(i, t) = start(c)$. The virtual edge always ends at the hentity $(d_1, v_1, \ldots, v_k, v)$, where $v = end(c)$ is a terminal or connectivity node. The resulting virtual flat graph is isomorphic to the flat graph obtained by physically flattening D by replacing every instance i with a copy of the graph contained in the cell $d(i)$ and updating all the jump connections accordingly.

We define extensions to the $start$ and end functions for any hconn (virtual edge) o: $start(o)$ returns the hentity at the start of the hconn and $end(o)$ returns the hentity at the end of the hconn, as defined in the preceding paragraph.

3.1.2 Alternative Abstractions

The proposed HCS model does not impose any constraints on the level of abstraction chosen for the representing the power grid and its resources. For example, Figure 4 and Figure 5 show three different cell definitions for the YY-connected 2-winding transformer of Figure 1. The choice of the representation would depend on the application using the model.

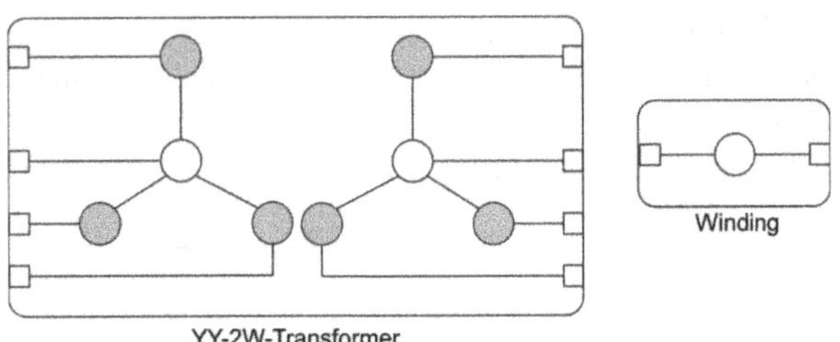

Figure 4 Physical representation of a YY-connected 2-winding transformer. The shaded circles are instances of the Winding cell.

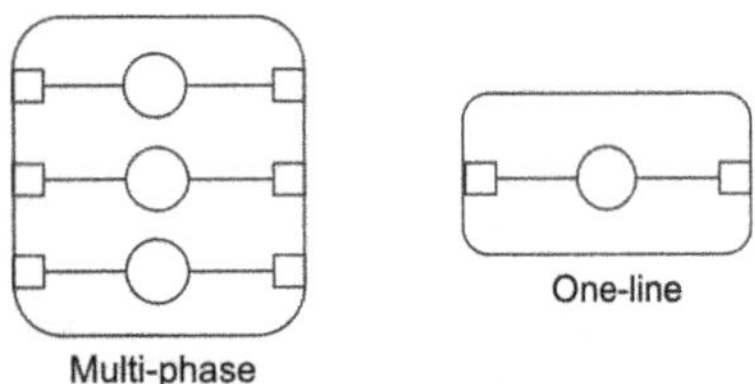

Figure 5 Left: Multi-phase representation of the transformer. Right: One-line style representation of the transformer.

3.1.3 Relationship with IEC 61970 CIM Standard

The notions of terminals and connectivity nodes also exist in the flat connectivity model of the IEC 61970 Common Information Model (CIM) standard [6]. We have further extended it here into a hierarchical graph representation that allows us to recognize repeating connectivity patterns, and model each such pattern as a cell. This gives us considerable savings in memory use because we do not need to replicate the same connectivity pattern multiple times in memory; instead we store each repeating pattern once as a cell and then store references to it, in the form of instances.

3.2 Scenario Representation

We now describe our approach for representing multiple scenarios on a hierarchical connected system to create a full HAMS representation. A scenario defines the three conditions of the system that were discussed in Sections 2.3 and 2.4: topological state, conductivity state and flow state.

3.2.1 Existence State

As described in Section 2.3, one may want to construct models for multiple topologies of the grid, for example, when reconstructing historical events, or when planning for future enhancements to the grid. A naïve approach would be to construct a HCS representation for each topology of interest. However, this will not exploit the fact the differences between these topologies are relatively much smaller than the size of topology and a large part of the topology remains the same. We propose an *existence state* model to enable highly efficient reconstruction of multiple topologies with minimal computation overhead.

The *existence state* of an entity v in cell d is given by a function $\rho(d, v) \in \{0,1\}$, where 1 indicates that the entity exists, while 0 indicates that it does not. The function ρ denotes an existence scenario for a given HCS D. In general, an application may be working with a set of multiple existence scenarios $P = \{\rho_1, \ldots, \rho_l\}$. For example, when reconstructing historical topologies of the grid, each scenario ρ_i provides the existence of entities at some time point t_i. When constructing alternative planning scenarios for potential changes to the grid, the existence scenarios correspond to the planning scenarios. Given an existence scenario ρ, we can naturally derive an extension for any hentity $h = (d_1, v_1, v_2, \ldots, v_k)$ as $\rho(h) = 0$ if $\rho(d_1, v_1) = 0$ or $\rho(d(v_{i-1}), v_i) = 0$ for $i > 1$, and $\rho(h) = 1$ otherwise.

It is important to note here that the HCS contains all entities that exist in any possible existence scenario. Combining this HCS with a specific existence scenario ρ marks a subset of the entities as not existing (and the rest as existing). The analysis application then must honor the existence states given by ρ while traversing the HCS: 1) if $\rho(d, v) = 0$ then consider v as non-existent, and 2) for any hentity h with $\rho(h) = 0$, consider h as non-existent.

3.2.2 Conductivity State

We propose a conductivity state model to overlay different conductivity scenarios on the HCS, enabling construction of multiple conductivity scenarios in memory. The *conductivity state* of an hentity $h = (d_1, v_1, v_2, \ldots, v_k)$ is given by a function $\sigma(h) \in \{0,1,?\}$, where 0 indicates that the hentity is not conducting (open), 1 indicates that the hentity is conducting (closed) and ? indicates that the state is unknown (e.g., in the case of missing data). Note that while existence state is defined on entities, conductivity state is defined on hentities. This is because existence is a topological condition and by definition, we require two instances of the same cell to have the same topology. However, conductivity is an instance specific condition: two instances of the same Breaker cell might have different conductivity states.

The function σ denotes a conductivity scenario for a given HCS D. Similar to existence scenarios, an application may be working with a set of multiple conductivity scenarios $\Sigma = \{\sigma_1, \sigma_2, \ldots, \sigma_m\}$

representing, for instance, historical switching configurations, planned switching configurations or different outage scenarios. The application must honor the conductivity states given by any chosen scenario while analyzing the HCS. An example of this is the topology processing typically performed as part of state estimation [7], where a physical model including all breakers is simplified to a branch/bus model by shorting all closed breakers and removing all parts of the grid that are de-energized by open breakers. In our proposed model, the underlying graph structure (HCS) does not change, but the conductivity states of the conductivity scenario are honored in any analysis, to achieve the same result.

3.2.3 *Flow State*

The *flow state* of an hconn $o = (h,c)$ is given by the function $\phi(o) \in \{0, F, R, FR\}$, where 0 indicates that there is no flow through o, F indicates flow in the forward direction (along the inherent direction), R indicates flow in the reverse direction (opposite the inherent direction) and FR indicates flow possible in either direction. Given that the set of hconns in an HCS has a bijective mapping to the set of edges in the corresponding flattened graph, assigning flow states to the hconns is equivalent to assigning flow states to the corresponding edges in the flattened graph. This is important because physical flows like power flow manifest at the fully flat physical system and we need to be able to represent them accurately on our hierarchical representation. Assigning flow states to hconns lets us do that.

The function ϕ denotes a flow scenario for a given HCS D. Similar to existence scenarios, an application may be working with a set of multiple flow scenarios $\Phi = \{\phi_1, \phi_2, \dots, \phi_n\}$ representing, for instance, different distributed generation scenarios such as a rainy day when rooftop solar generation is near zero versus a sunny day when rooftop solar generation is high and power flows from homes into the grid. The flow direction may be derived from a variety of different methods, for example, power flow analysis, discrete graph orientation or pre-configured scenarios. Typically the flow state ϕ would be dependent on a particular combination of ρ and σ, but it is possible to use ϕ is combination with different existence and conductivity states.

3.2.4 *Illustration*

Figure 6 shows an example analysis on a HAMS model consisting of an HCS H and a combination of existence, conductivity and flow scenarios (ρ, σ, ϕ). The analysis starts from a given hentity h and traverses in a depth-first fashion through the virtual flat graph. The traversal along a path terminates whenever any of the following conditions is satisfied:

1) the flow direction of any hconn (virtual edge) is 0 or does not match the direction of traversal,
2) the visited hentity is non-existent, or
3) the visited hentity is non-conducting.

It marks all reachable hentities as discovered. An hentity h' is reachable from h if there exists a path p in the virtual flat graph that starts at h and ends at h', such that 1) the flow state of every virtual edge in p is not 0 and matches the direction of traversal from h to h' along the path, 2) the conductivity state of every hentity on the path, excluding h', is 1, and 3) the existence of every hentity on the path, including h', is 1.

This is only an example to illustrate one possible application of the proposed model. A wide variety of analyses are possible and the relevance and interpretation of the existence, conductivity and flow states may change in different contexts. For example, if the flow state is derived based on the conductivity and existence states, the application may choose to use only the flow state and ignore the conductivity and existence states.

```
function VFDFS(H, h, ρ, σ, ϕ)
  if ρ(h) == 0
    return
  discovered[h] = true
  if σ(h) == 0
    return
  for each hconn o on h
    if ϕ(o) == 0
      return
    if start(o) == h and ϕ(o) == R
      continue
    if end(o) == h and ϕ(o) == F
      continue
    h' = OtherEnd(o,h)
    if discovered[h'] != true
      VFDFS(H, h', ρ, σ, ϕ)
 endfor
```

Figure 6 Pseudo-code for a virtually flat depth-first search that honors existence, conductivity and flow states. The search starts from a given hentity and marks all hentities in the virtual flat graph reachable from there, as discovered.

4. IMPLEMENTATION

Although the details of implementation of the entire model are beyond the scope of this paper, an outline is presented here.

Each cell holds a list of all entities contained in it, and handles to all instances of it. Each entity holds a list of all connections on it. Each connection holds handles to its start and end entities. Apart from these objects and handles, there is some bookkeeping information held by each object. The memory use breakdown is then as given in Table 1.

Table 1 Memory used by each type of element in the HAMS implementation.

Element Type	Size (bytes)
Cell	124
Instance	96
Conn. Nodes	84
Terminals	84
Connections	72

Each existence scenario function $\rho(d, v)$ is implemented as a two level dictionary: dictionary < cell, dictionary < entity, state > >. The outer dictionary maps from the identifier of the cell to the inner dictionary. The inner dictionary maps from the identifier of an entity to the value of the existence state for that entity. The entities in the key set of an inner dictionary are contained in the cell matching the key of the outer dictionary. Both dictionaries are implemented for constant-time access, using a radix tree [9] for the outer dictionary and an array for the inner one, where the array is indexed by a unique identifier for the entity. This inner array implementation is equivalent to a hash table [9] where the hash function is chosen to avoid any conflicts.

Each conductivity scenario function $\sigma(h)$ is implemented as a dictionary: dictionary < hentity, state >. Hentities that have the most common state are not inserted into the dictionary. All other hentities have an entry in the dictionary. This dictionary implementation allows specification of the most common state as the default value. This allows the application to minimize the memory used by the dictionary. This is a useful feature because the number of hentities can be extremely large and a large majority of them typically have the same state in any given scenario (for example, most equipment are conducting). The dictionary is implemented using a red-black tree [9] to hold the keys. This allows iteration over the keys, which can be useful in some applications, while still providing efficient $O(\log(N))$ access time.

Each flow scenario function $\phi(o)$ is implemented similarly to conductivity scenarios, using a dictionary: dictionary < hconn, state >. The same scheme of default state value as for conductivity scenarios is used to optimize memory use.

5. EXPERIMENTS AND RESULTS

5.1 Data Ingestion

An HCS can be created *ab initio* by invoking a series of API functions to create individual cells, instances, terminals, connectivity nodes and connections. Alternatively, we have defined an ASCII file format, named *Grid Description Format* (GDF) for describing the data for a HAMS model and a corresponding parser that can populate an in-memory representation. In addition, we also have a database representation for HAMS with an adapter to load the data from database into memory. The details of the GDF format and the database model are out of scope of this paper. However, it is worth noting that an HCS consisting of several million entities (further detailed below) can be read from a GDF file in approximately 7.6 seconds (real time), and reading from an IBM PureData System for Analytics data warehouse appliance takes approximately 38.4 seconds. These are results from running on a 4-core 2.3GHz Intel Xeon Linux virtual machine with 16 GB of RAM, using code compiled –O3 in g++.

Table 2 Hierarchical vs. Flattened HCS size (size in kilobytes, not including text labels for entities and some small baseline bookkeeping).

Element Type	Hier. Count	Hier. Size (kB)	Flat Count	Flat Size (kB)
Cells	27	3.3	1	0.1
Instances	2,166,875	203,145	0	0
Conn. Nodes	1,135,310	93,129	3,302,166	270,881
Terminals	72	5.9	3,233,303	265,232
Connections	2,723,749	191,514	5,956,980	418,850
Total		487,797		954,963

5.2 Data Flattening

To illustrate the storage benefits of the HCS hierarchical representation, we can compare the size of a hierarchical design vs. an equivalent flattened design. We use the distribution grid operated by DTE Energy as a test case. The grid serves 2.2 million customers. Table 2 shows the results for an HCS consisting of several million entities and connections representing the complete connectivity of the distribution grid. It can be seen that even for this limited (two-level) hierarchy, the counts and sizes nearly double for the flat design. For this design, the process of flattening took approximately 6.8 seconds (real time).

5.3 Existence State

To examine the storage benefits of using the existence state mechanism to represent multiple existence scenarios, we perform the following experiment: We construct a fabricated case where the existence state for 100,000 entities is set to 0. The storage cost of the resulting data structure is about 13,000 kilobytes, with a per entity cost of 4 bytes (plus some additional overhead for common bookkeeping). This can be compared to the incremental cost of 487,797 kilobytes to represent one additional "full" scenario explicitly.

Using the existence state mechanism incurs some execution time cost. This can be measured by comparing the run times for a graph operation that uses, or does not use, the Existence State mechanism. When using the example of the virtually flat breadth-first search shown in Figure 7, which does not honor existence, conductivity or flow states, it takes approximately 68.2 seconds to traverse the model detailed in Table 2. Existence state lookup operations for all entities traversed adds less than 1 second to the total runtime. To better estimate the overhead associate with the existence state mechanism, we performed another experiment: We observe that the difference between the two cases is the time to do a lookup in the existence scenario data structure; this is measured at approximately 37 ns per access.

```
function VFBFS(H, s)
  queue<hentity> q
  queue.push_back(s)
  while queue.notempty()
    h = queue.pop()
    discovered[h] = true
    for each hconn o on h
      h' = OtherEnd(o,h)
      if discovered[h'] != true
        q.push_back[h']
    endfor
  endwhile
```

Figure 7 Pseudo-code for a virtually flat breadth-first search. The search starts from a given hentity and marks as discovered, all hentities in the virtual flat graph reachable from there.

5.4 Conductivity State

To illustrate the storage benefits and execution time costs of using the conductivity state mechanism, we performed experiments analogous to those done for existence state in Section 5.2. The results were that an entry in the Conductivity State data structure costs approximately 141 bytes. It is worth noting that the existence scenario is represented by a dense associative array, while the conductivity scenario is represented by a sparse red-black tree. For this reason, the execution time overhead for using the conductivity state is larger, 271 ns per access.

5.5 Flow State

We repeated the experiments of sections 5.3 and 5.4, comparing breadth-first traversal without and with the use of the flow state mechanism. The resulting storage cost was 78 bytes per entry. The execution time overhead was 383 ns per access.

6. CONCLUSION

We presented a memory-efficient representation of power grids for use in in-memory graph-based analytics. The representation, called HAMS, is flexible enough to represent the connectivity of the grid at arbitrary levels of abstraction. It can represent multiple topologies of a time-varying grid along with multiple operational states very efficiently in memory. HAMS employs a hierarchical graph coupled with dictionaries that represent different existence, conductivity and flow states to optimize memory use. As the need for complex connectivity analysis of power grids increases with the advent of new smart grid technologies, such computationally efficient models and data structures will be critical to support the operational and planning applications needed to manage the grid of tomorrow.

7. ACKNOWLEDGEMENT

We would like to thank DTE Energy for providing data in support of this work.

8. REFERENCES

[1] Cotilla-Sanchez E., Hines P. D. H., Barrows C., Blumsack S. 2012. Comparing the Topological and Electrical Structure of the North American Electric Power Infrastructure. *IEEE Systems Journal* 6(4) (Dec. 2012), 616-626.

[2] Cheng D., Zhu D., Broadwater R. P., Lee S. 2009. A graph trace based reliability analysis of electric power systems with time-varying loads and dependent failures. *Electric Power Systems Research* 79 (2009), 1321-1328.

[3] Medina J., Muller N., Roytelman I. 2010. Demand response and distribution grid operations: opportunities and challenges. *IEEE Trans. Smart Grid* 1(2) (Sep. 2010), 193-198.

[4] Allen R. J., Finkler U., Lavin M. A., Sayah R. T. 2006. Framework for hierarchical VLSI design, US Patent 7,089,511 B2.

[5] Casteigts A., Flocchini P., Quattrociocchi W., Santoro N. 2011. Time-varying graphs and dynamic networks. *Proc. ADHOC-NOW* 2011.

[6] *IEC 61970 Energy management system application program interface (EMS-API) - Part 301: Common Information Model (CIM) Base*, IEC, Edition 1.0, November 2003.

[7] Monticelli A. 2000. Electric power system state estimation. *Proc. IEEE* 88(2) (Feb. 2000), 262-282.

[8] Walling R. A., Saint R., Dugan R. C., Burke J., Kojovic L. A. 2008. Summary of distributed resources impact on power delivery systems. *IEEE Trans. Power Delivery* 23(3) (Jul. 2008), 1636-1644.

[9] Cormen T. H., Leiserson C. E., Rivest R. L. 1990. *Introduction to Algorithms*. MIT Press.

Using Analytics to Minimize Errors in the Connectivity Model of a Power Distribution Network

Rajendu Mitra
IBM Research – India
rajendum@in.ibm.com

Vijay Arya
IBM Research – India
vijay.arya@in.ibm.com

Brian Sullivan
DTE Energy, USA
sullivanbj@dteenergy.com

Richard Mueller
DTE Energy, USA
muellerrj@dteenergy.com

Heather Storey
DTE Energy, USA
storeyh@dteenergy.com

Gerard Labut
DTE Energy, USA
labutg@dteenergy.com

ABSTRACT

The connectivity model of a power distribution network can easily become outdated due to system changes. Maintaining and sustaining an accurate connectivity model is a key challenge for most distribution utilities today. This work presents novel analytics techniques that can infer the connectivity model from measurements already available from a distribution network. Our techniques utilize voltage data from customer smart meters and circuit metering points to identify and correct errors in the connectivity model. We report analysis results based on data collected from multiple feeders of a large electric distribution network in North America. Our analysis shows that customer voltage measurements exhibit hierarchical correlations, which can be exploited to cluster customers under the same distribution transformer or same phase with high accuracy. To the best of our knowledge, this is the first large scale measurement study of voltage data collected from smart meters and its use in inferring customer to transformer and phase connectivity information.

Categories and Subject Descriptors

G.3 [**Mathematics of Computing**]: Time series analysis;
I.5.3 [**Pattern recognition**]: Clustering;
H.4 [**Information Systems Applications**]: Miscellaneous;
I.6.5 [**Model Development**]: Modeling methodologies

General Terms

Measurement, Experimentation, Algorithms, Design

Keywords

Power distribution grids, Topology Inference, Voltage data

e-Energy'15, July 14–17, 2015, Bangalore, India.

ACM 978-1-4503-3609-3/15/07 ...$15.00.
DOI: http://dx.doi.org/10.1145/2768510.2768533.

1. INTRODUCTION

The connectivity model (CM) of the physical distribution network specifies how the devices, assets, and customers are interconnected together downstream of a distribution substation. For example, which customer is powered by which distribution transformer, which customer is powered by which phase of the feeder, and so on. A common problem faced by distribution utilities worldwide is an inaccurate or unknown CM of their network when compared to the actual connectivity that exists on the field. The CM stored in the utility's database may not always be tracked or updated based on system changes occurring in the field. Therefore its accuracy deteriorates over time after maintenance, repairs, and restoration activities following faults or outages. Moreover during large scale outages, there is often a trade-off between expediting restoration versus tracking changes to the distribution network. As a consequence, utilities are seeking tools to keep the connectivity model in sync with the actual connectivity that exists in the field.

While CM is foundational to planning, operations, and maintenance of distribution networks, the key factors driving utilities to improve its accuracy are essentially faster restoration and the ability to accurately communicate with impacted customers during outages. The annual cost of power interruptions in US is estimated to be $79B with 106 ± 54 outage minutes per customer. Interruptions in electric service occur from time to time due to a number of different reasons including storms, aging assets, excess loading from heat waves, and other system disturbances. Any analysis following a fault in the distribution system uses the CM to identify the root causes and determine the appropriate course of action. An accurate CM minimizes the diagnostic time and the time spent by crew in the field, leading to reduced outage minutes and improved system availability [1, 2].

During outages, utilities seek to inform customers about the status of restoration and the expected downtimes. The CM is required to localise customers downstream of a faulted device and to map each fault with the right set of outaged customers for communication. An inaccurate CM increases the risk of erroneous communication and limits a utility's ability to provide customized and timely information to their customers, which can affect customer relationships negatively. Additionally, an accurate CM is required to localise losses, estimate loading at unmetered points such as distribution transformers, and ensure a balanced infusion of energy back into the distribution grid when customers have behind-the-meter resources such as distributed generation [3–6].

Existing techniques to maintain an accurate CM include the use of manual field inspections and power line communications (PLC). Manual inspections are expensive and unsustainable as field configurations change over time and therefore these need to be undertaken periodically. The PLC approach requires both customer and grid meters to be able to read and write signals onto the power-line and is capital intensive. Additionally, signals may not propagate over long distances or across assets.

Leading utilities are undertaking initiatives to modernize information management and data analytics capabilities to realize the benefits of smart grid deployments. This work focuses on the use of data already available from a distribution network to infer its connectivity model. We present techniques that can verify and correct customer to transformer and phase[1] mapping from voltage measurements already available from customer smart meters and circuit metering points. We report experimental results based on analyzing smart meter and SCADA data collected from multiple feeders of a large distribution network in North America. The data includes average RMS values of voltage recorded once every 5 minutes from more than 6K customers across 3 feeders and 2 substations for about 2 months. The performance of techniques is estimated by comparing the computed customer to transformer and phase mapping with the ground truth that was available before and after manual field inspections.

The main contributions of this work are as follows:

1. We show that customer voltage measurements exhibit hierarchical correlations which tend to be in agreement with the hierarchical connectivity relationships between customers, transformers, and phases of a distribution feeder. Customers are correlated based on same phase as well as same distribution transformer with transformer correlations being stronger when compared to phase correlations.

2. A novel approach is proposed that infers both customer to transformer and phase connectivity by clustering customers based on their voltage measurements. The voltage measurements are transformed into binary fluctuations and partitioned into groups so that customers powered by the same transformer or same phase are clustered into one group. The computed clusters may be used to verify and correct an existing customer to transformer and phase mapping that may be partially accurate. The methods are outlined along with accuracy results based on the analysis of real voltage measurements collected from multiple feeder circuits of a North American distribution network.

3. We compare different approaches to infer customer to transformer mapping by clustering customers within a feeder, its phases, or its individual branches. The clustering solutions are compared with the currently available mapping in the database which is known to be accurate. Our results indicate that clustering customers under each branch of the feeder introduces constraints that help improve the accuracy of clustering.

4. To infer customer to phase mapping, customer voltage measurements are clustered by using the per-phase feeder measurements as centroids of the initial clustering solution. We compare the computed solutions with the mapping that was available both before and after manual field inspections. Our results indicate that the proposed approach is able to correct most of the errors identified during field inspections and may be used as a low cost alternative to help maintain an accurate phase connectivity model.

The balance of the paper is organized as follows. Section 2 explains the topology of the distribution network and the mapping between customers, transformers, and phases of a feeder. Section 3 summarizes the voltage data used in this work and our observations on various correlations. Section 4 presents our techniques to infer customer to transformer and phase connectivity using clustering. Section 5 presents experimental results and performance of clustering approaches. Section 6 presents related work and we conclude with section 7 with directions of future work.

2. DISTRIBUTION NETWORK: PHASE AND TRANSFORMER CONNECTIVITY

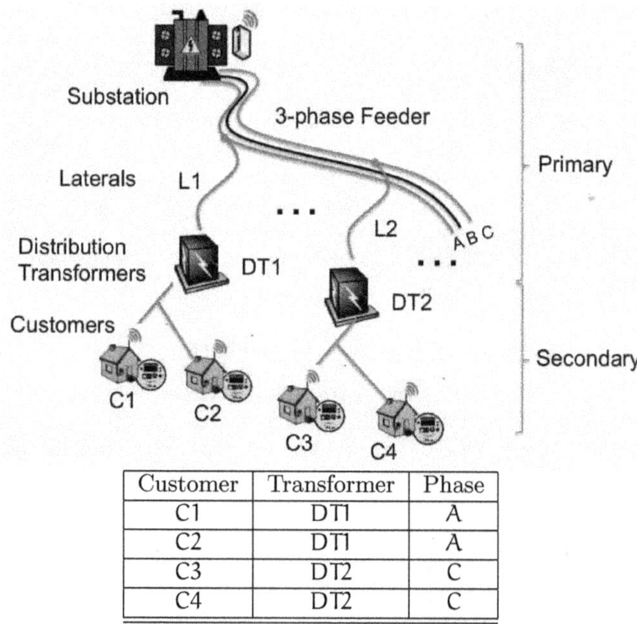

Customer	Transformer	Phase
C1	DT1	A
C2	DT1	A
C3	DT2	C
C4	DT2	C

Figure 1: Simplified view of a distribution network and the customer to transformer and phase mapping

The power delivery infrastructure consists of generation, transmission, and distribution systems. Electric power is generated in large power plants as 3-phase AC voltage and reaches distribution via a transmission system. The distribution system starts from the distribution substation and consists of primary and secondary networks. The primary network consists of 3-phase *feeders* which carry power at medium voltage from the substation to the *distribution transformers* (DTs). Depending on factors including the type and density of customers, a feeder may carry power at different voltages such as 33kV, 13.2kV, and 4.8kV and serve a few

[1]The concept of *phase* and the structure of the distribution network are explained in section II

Table 1: Information about the feeder circuits analyzed from the distribution network

Substation	Circuit	Voltage fed	Length (Miles)	Residential	non-Residential	1-phase transformers	1-phase customers	Missing data
SUBSTATION-I	CIRCUIT-I	13.2kV	34	80%	20%	221	1773	12%
SUBSTATION-II	CIRCUIT-II	13.2kV	38	97%	3%	342	2178	1%
SUBSTATION-II	CIRCUIT-III	13.2kV	39	91%	9%	306	2363	1%

hundred distribution transformers. The branches or line segments of a feeder are also known as *laterals*. The secondary network carries power from the distribution transformers to the customers at low voltage (e.g. 120V).

A 3-phase feeder consists of three transmission lines, usually labelled as A, B and C, which carry AC power with their voltage waveforms shifted by 120°. A DT receives power by tapping onto one of the 3 phases of a feeder and is generally single-phase (1-phase). On average a DT might serve about 8 single-phase residential customers. A few DTs that serve larger loads such as super-markets or office buildings may be 2 or 3-phase. Similarly a feeder branch or lateral may be single, two, or three-phase.

While the above grid structure is most common in North America, in countries such as Australia and in Europe, DTs are generally 3-phase and have a higher capacity, serving about 50-200 customers. However the residential customer is still single-phase and each customer is powered by one of the 3 phases of the transformer. The rest of the paper assumes a North American setting for ease of exposition, though our solutions are applicable to other settings as well [5, 6].

The CM specifies the connectivity between the devices, assets, and customers downstream of the substation. In this work, we primarily focus on inferring customer to distribution transformer and customer to phase connectivity information. With regards to this, the CM of the distribution system in Fig. 1 would record that: (i) customers C1, C2 are powered by distribution transformer DT1, while C3, C4 are powered by DT2 (ii) customers C1, C2 as well as DT1 are powered by phase A, while C3, C4 and DT2 are powered by phase C of the feeder. In the above example, since the distribution transformers are single-phase, customer phase is same as transformer phase. The CM also records other hierarchical relationships such as the mapping between a lateral and the set of transformers that it powers. While the set of customers under each feeder is known and remains unchanged, accurate knowledge about the connectivity relationships between the phases, DTs, and customers is variable.

3. DATA

Power measurements in a distribution network are generally available from customer smart meters and on-grid sensors. The primary network is monitored using a SCADA (supervisory control and data acquisition) system [7] that records feeder level measurements (per-phase voltage, current, active and reactive power, etc.) close to the substation. Consumer smart meters generally record periodic measurements of load (kWh) and voltage over small time intervals of 5-30 min as setup by the utility.

In this work, we consider voltage measurements from three anonymized feeder circuits from a North American distribution network: CIRCUIT-I, CIRCUIT-II, and CIRCUIT-III. Of these, CIRCUIT-I is powered by one substation while CIRCUIT-II and CIRCUIT-III are both powered by another substation. Each circuit is fed at 13.2kV and serves more than 2K residential, commercial and industrial customers (Table 1).

Low-voltage data from smart meters. We analyze two months of voltage measurements from customers which are powered by single-phase distribution transformers. The measurements have average RMS values of voltage in the 120V range. These are recorded once every 5 minutes up to a precision of one decimal place. The measurements also have missing values.

Medium-voltage data from scada system. The feeder circuits are instrumented with SCADA field devices which monitor the feeders close to the substation transformer and periodically report per-phase measurements of voltage, current, and power. We consider two months of voltage measurements from these devices. The measurements are averaged over 5 minute intervals and normalized to 120V range to compare them against the low-voltage data from the customers.

Customer to transformer mapping (Ground Truth). The existing CM holds the mapping between customers and the distribution transformers. While this mapping is known to have good accuracy for the 3 chosen circuits, it may not be 100% accurate. We use this mapping to estimate the performance of clustering algorithms.

Customer to phase mapping (Ground Truth). The transformer phase is available for all 1-phase distribution transformers (customer phase is same as transformer phase for 1-phase transformers). The phase of overhead (pole top) transformers is available before and after manual field inspections. In case of overhead distribution, field inspections are conducted by linemen using a combination visual inspections and specialized devices. The devices are reserved to check the phase at certain operating points in the feeder while walking down the line segments and visually inspecting the phase down to individual transformers or customers. The voltage data analyzed in this work was collected before commencing field inspections. The phasing information available during data collection and after field inspections is used to estimate the performance of algorithms and also identify errors in existing phasing information.

Transformer to lateral mapping. Accurate mapping from distribution transformers to laterals, i.e. the set of customers powered by each branch of the feeder, is available in the existing CM for each of the three circuits. This mapping is used to introduce spatial constraints in the inference of customer to transformer mapping.

3.1 Observations on Voltage Data

Figure 2 shows benchmark plots that give an overview of the voltage measurements obtained from customer smart meters and the SCADA system. Fig. 2 (left) plots the voltage measurements of 3 random customers on different phases and under different distribution transformers over a 7 day

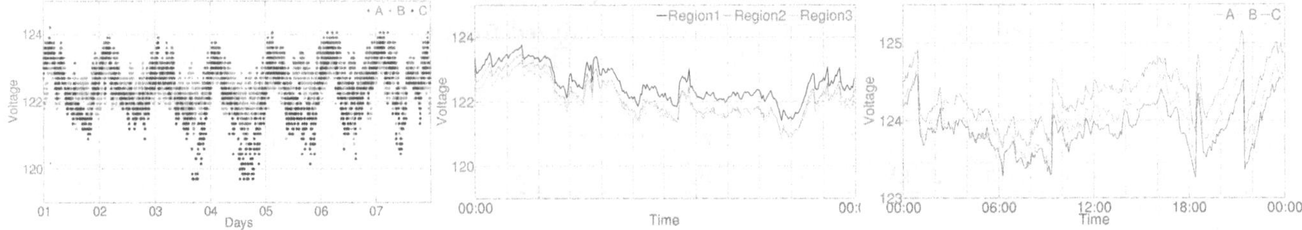

Figure 2: Voltage data from one of the feeders and its customers. (left):Voltage of 3 customers on phases A, B, and C over 7 days, (center): Average voltage of customers in 3 different sections of a feeder circuit over a day, (right): Per-phase feeder measurements taken close to substation over a day.

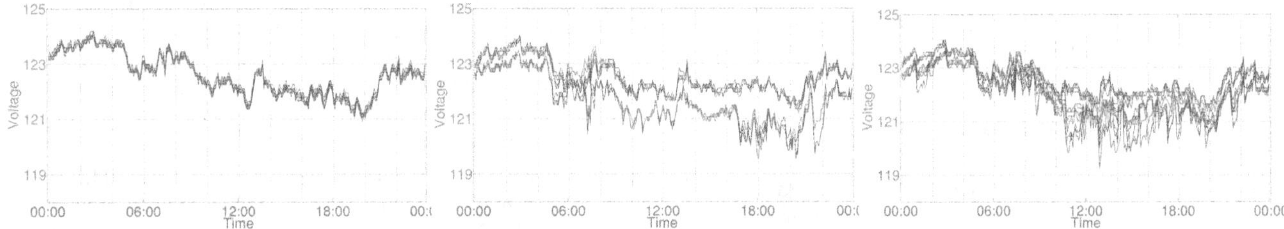

Figure 3: Different types of voltage measurements. Measurements of all customers under each distribution transformer.

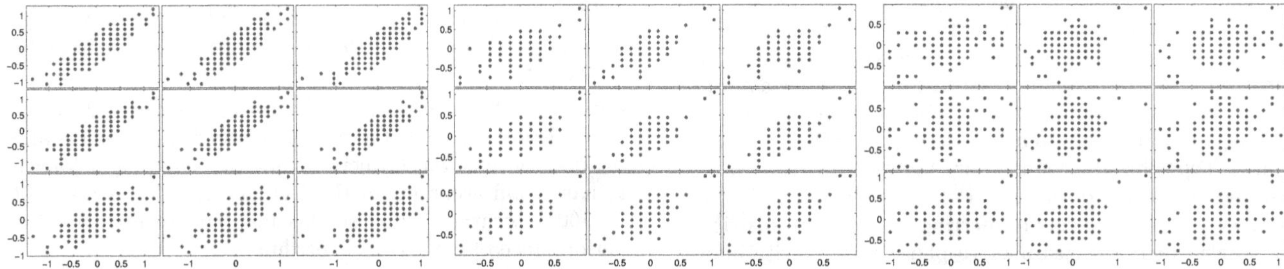

Figure 4: Correlations of customer voltage fluctuations using scatter plot matrices: (left): Two different sets of customers under the same transformer (hence same phase) (center): Two sets of customers under different transformers but same phase. (right): Two sets of customers under different phases (hence different transformers).

period. We observe the diurnal cycles of voltage based on energy consumed each day and differences in voltage across customers based on phase. In order to study the voltage observed in different regions of a feeder circuit, we divided the circuit into three sections based on deployed reclosers (circuit breakers). Figure 2(center) plots the average voltage of customers in each of these regions. Region 1 corresponds to customers which are closer to the distribution substation. These customers observe a slightly higher voltage irrespective of phase. Customers in regions 2 and 3 observe a small voltage drop as they are located further away from the substation. The plot demonstrates that customer voltage also depends on a number of factors other than phases or distribution transformers. Figure 2(right) plots the per-phase voltage measurements observed at the feeder normalized to 120V range for a day. We see that the voltages on the 3 phases vary together on larger time scales based on aggregate load while each phase shows distinct variations at smaller time scales. Although voltages on the 3 phases differ, the feeder voltage measurements showed low imbalances on average across all days.

Figure 3 shows voltage plots of customers under different distribution transformers. Figure 3 (left) shows an example where voltages of all customers under a transformer are very similar and vary together. Figure 3 (center) shows another transformer where the customer voltages vary within two groups. This may occur due to variable loading or distances of customers from their transformers. Figure 3 (right) shows a transformer where the voltages of customers show high variation. The plots show that deciphering customer voltage may be challenging as it depends on several factors in the electric network.

Figure 4 shows the benchmark correlations between voltage fluctuations of customers under a feeder using a matrix of scatter plots. Figure 4 (left) shows correlations between two different sets of random customers which are powered by the same single-phase transformer (hence same phase as well). Each scatterplot shows correlations between a pair of customers. We observe that voltage fluctuations of customers under the same transformer show high correlation and points lie closer to the X = Y line. The figure 4 (center) shows correlations between two sets of random customers powered by different transformers under the same phase of the feeder. We observe that correlations still exist but become weaker in comparison to the same transformer case. Lastly figure 4(right) shows correlations between two sets of random customers powered by different phases of the feeder (hence different transformers as well). We see that these customers are least correlated and points are spread over the $X = Y$ plane. Our goal is to differentiate between these three cases in order to identify customer to phase and transformer connectivity.

4. INFERENCE OF CUSTOMER TO TRANSFORMER AND PHASE MAPPING

A distribution system is effectively a large power circuit with a number of interconnected sub-circuits corresponding to different feeders, phases, and DTs. Therefore the voltage values at different locations are closely related according to the electrical interconnections in the system. Since conductors exhibit impedance, the voltage is not constant throughout the system and drops closer to the load or customer and is a function of the nature and spread of loads on the feeder. Our approach leverages the fact that the voltage variations observed by customers powered by the same transformer or same phase may be more "similar" (according to a measure of similarity), compared to those on different transformers or phases. We transform the voltage measurements into binary fluctuations and cluster these into groups in order to infer the transformer or phase of each customer.

Transformations. Let $v_{i,t}$ denote the raw RMS voltage measurements from customer i in the tth time step, $t \in \{1, \dots, m\}$. We compute the continuous voltage fluctuations as $\delta_{i,t} = v_{i,t} - v_{i,t-1}$. We also discretize these to obtain binary fluctuations, which we denote by $b_{i,t}$. Let $\mathbf{V}_i = [v_{i,t}]_{m \times 1}$ denote the m-dimensional *observation vector* that holds the time series of voltage measurements obtained from customer i. Similarly, let Δ_i and $\mathbf{B}_i$ denote the delta and binary observation vectors respectively. We assume that voltage measurements are approximately synchronised across customers, which infact holds true for our datasets as well.

Clustering voltage time series. We explain how clustering is performed over the raw observation vectors $\mathbf{V}_i$. A similar approach is used for Δ_i and $\mathbf{B}_i$. The three datasets are compared in section 5.

Let $\ell = \{\mathbf{V}_1, \dots, \mathbf{V}_n\}$ denote the set of observation vectors of customers under one feeder. ℓ is partitoned into k clusters $\{\ell_1, \dots, \ell_k\}$ using *correlation distance* d as a measure of similarity between the vectors ($d = 1 - r$, where $r \in [-1, 1]$ is the correlation coefficient). We use the K-MEANS algorithm [8] algorithm for clustering, which finds a solution that minimizes the within-cluster distances:

$$\arg\min_{\ell_1,\dots,\ell_k} \sum_{i=1}^{k} \sum_{\mathbf{V}_j \in \ell_i} d(\mathbf{V}_j - \mathbf{C}_i) \quad (1)$$

where $\mathbf{C}_i$ is the centroid of observation vectors in cluster ℓ_i. K-MEANS is an iterative algorithm that starts with a random initial solution and successively refines the solution to minimize the above objective function.

4.1 Inference of customer to phase mapping

In order to partition customers based on phases, we cluster the voltage observation vectors into three groups, *i.e.* $k = 3$ in (1), one coresponding to each phase A, B, and C. Although the clustering solution does not assign a phase to each cluster, it can still be used to verify if two customers belong to the same phase. Therefore it can identify inconsistencies in the existing customer to phase mapping solely from customer voltage measurements.

Labelling of clusters. In order to assign a phase to each cluster, we utilize the per-phase feeder measurements obtained from the SCADA system. Let $f_{A,t}$ denote the RMS voltage measurement from phase A of the feeder during time step $t \in \{1, \dots, m\}$ and let $\mathbf{F}_A = [f_{A,t}]_{m \times 1}$. Similarly let $\mathbf{F}_B$ and $\mathbf{F}_C$ correspond to phases B and C respectively. We pass feeder measurements $\{\mathbf{F}_A, \mathbf{F}_B, \mathbf{F}_C\}$ as centroids of the initial solution to the K-MEANS algorithm. Thus each centroid effectively has a phase. The algorithm iteratively updates the centroids and yields the final set of customer clusters. Each cluster is assigned the phase of its centroid. We test the performance of this approach in section 5.

4.2 Inference of customer to transformer mapping

Let x denote the total number of transformers under a feeder. In order to partition customers based on distribution transformers, we cluster the voltage observation vectors into x clusters *i.e.* $k = x$ in (1). As before, we have customer clusters, but without any transformer assigned to each cluster. The clustering solution as such can be used to verify if two customers belong to the same transformer and identify inconsistencies in the existing customer to transformer mapping solely from customer voltage measurements.

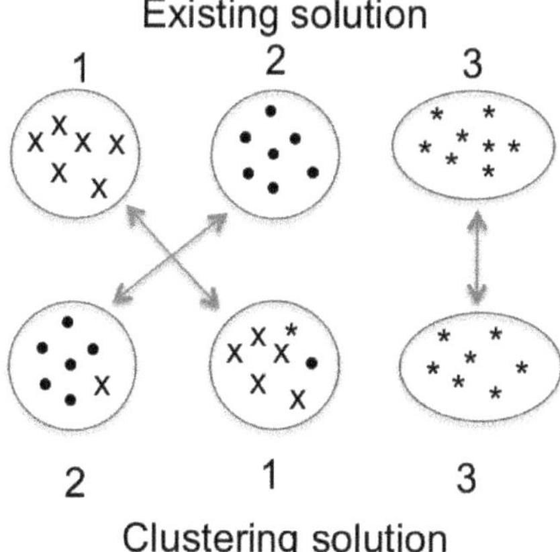

Figure 5: Labeling clusters in the computed solution using labels of an existing solution.

Labelling of clusters. In order to assign a transformer to each cluster, we use the existing customer to transformer mapping that may be partially accurate. The computed clusters are intersected with the clusters corresponding to the existing customer to transformer mapping and a one-to-one correspondence is established based on maximum match. Each cluster in the computed solution is assigned the transformer of its matching cluster in the existing solution. This approach may be used to assign a transformer to each cluster provided the accuracy of the existing mapping is not too low (figure 5).

In addition to the approach of clustering all customers under a feeder, we consider two other techniques: (i) We cluster

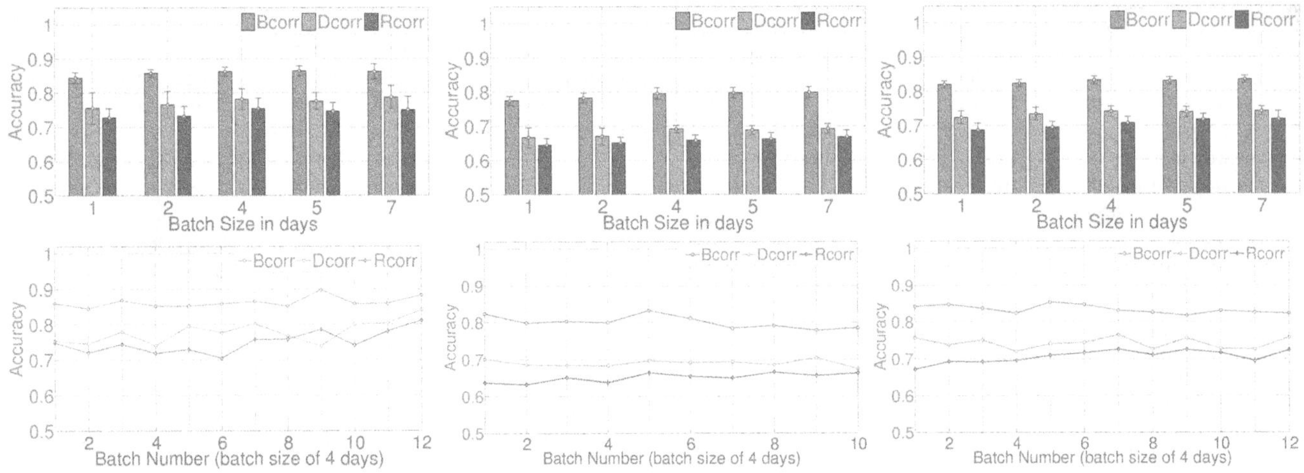

Figure 6: Customer to transformer Mapping: Accuracy of clustering all customers under the feeder. (left to right): circuit-i, circuit-ii, circuit-iii. (top): Average accuracy over different batch sizes (bottom): Accuracy for each batch of 4 days.

customers under each phase separately (ii) We cluster customers under each branch (lateral) of the feeder separately. These approaches are compared in section 5.

5. EXPERIMENTS

We process the customer and feeder voltage measurements and obtain 3 datasets per feeder circuit: (i) *Raw*: original data V_i's, (ii) *Delta*: continuous fluctuations Δ_i's, and (iii) *Binary*: discretized fluctuations $\mathbf{B}_i$'s. We use the K-MEANS algorithm to cluster the customer observation vectors using correlation distance as a measure of similarity. We divide the datasets into batches of 1 to 7 consecutive days and study the accuracy of clustering versus the number of measurements for the 3 feeder circuits. We denote the results by Rcorr, Dcorr, and Bcorr corresponding to solutions based on correlation distance over raw, delta, and binary datasets.

5.1 Customer to transformer mapping

We test the performance of clustering by considering all customers (i) under a feeder, (ii) within each phase, and (iii) within each lateral. In order to estimate the accuracy, we intersect the computed clusters with the clusters formed from ground truth based on maximum match and compute the fraction of customers present in correct clusters. Next, we randomly introduce errors in the ground truth so that its accuracy decreases to 60−80% and use the partially accurate solution to assign a transformer to each cluster (as described in section 4.2). We then compare the resulting solution with the ground truth.

(i) Clustering within a feeder. Figure 6 (top) shows the accuracy of clustering for the 3 datasets over different batch sizes of consecutive days when all customers under a feeder are considered. We observe that correlation distance on binary datasets (Bcorr) yields highest accuracy followed by Dcorr and Rcorr. The plots show that it is easier to separate customers under different transformers using their voltage fluctuations versus raw voltages. The plots also demonstrate that discretization helps, which means that the actual magnitude of fluctuation does not play a significant role and what counts is whether the fluctuations of customers increase or decrease simultaneously. Figure 6 (bottom) demonstrates how the accuracy varies across batches of 4 days. We observe that Bcorr shows lower variation and generally yields above 80% accuracy for all feeders (the accuracy also varies since missing measurements get eliminated in some batches).

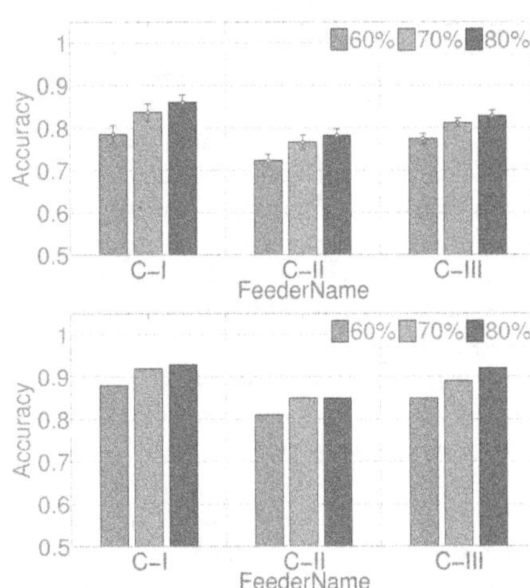

Figure 7: Customer to Transformer Mapping: Accuracy of assigning labels to clusters using a partially accurate customer to transformer mapping. (top): Average accuracy with a batch size of 4 days. (bottom): Accuracy of the majority solution across batches.

Utilizing a partially accurate mapping. Figure 7 demonstrates the performance of the cluster labelling technique, which assigns a transformer to each computed cluster with the help of a partially accurate customer to transformer mapping. The plot shows the results for case (i), wherein all customers under a feeder are clustered. Figure 7 (top) shows the average accuracy across 4 day batches using Bcorr, when the accuracy of the existing solution varies between 60−80%. Figure 7 (bottom) shows the accuracy of the majority solution across batches i.e. each customer is assigned a transformer based on the majority of assignments made across all batches. We see that this approach improves the accuracy further. The plots show that proposed labeling approach may be utilized when majority of the customers under each transformer in the existing mapping are accurately mapped. This is often the case in practice when errors in the existing mapping are not very high.

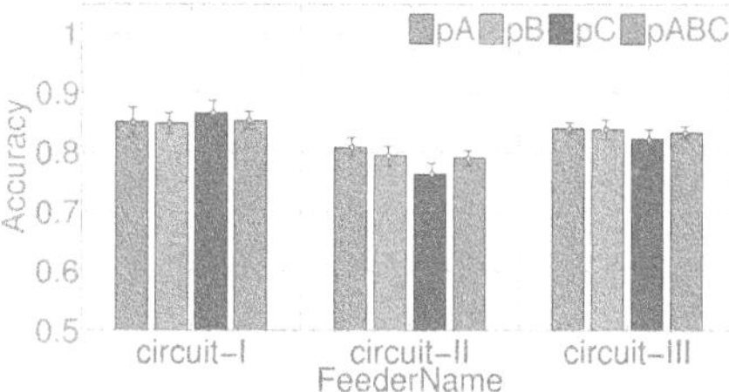

Figure 8: Customer to Transformer Mapping: Average accuracy of clustering customers within each phase using Bcorr with 4 days of voltage data.

(ii) Clustering within each phase. Figure 8 shows the clustering accuracy when customers within each phase are clustered separately. The plot shows the accuracy of Bcorr for individual phases (pA, pB, pC) and the overall accuracy for the full feeder(pABC) using a batch size of 4 days. We observe that the accuracy remains unchanged when compared to figure 6 corresponding to case (i). This implies that clustering customers under transformers of the same phase is in fact a more harder problem. This is because customers on two different transformers of different phases are the least correlated (figure 4(right)), while customers under two different transformers of same phase still exhibit phase-level correlations (figure 4 (center)).

(iii) Clustering within each lateral. Figure 9 shows the overall accuracy for the full feeder when customers within each lateral (branch of the feeder) are clustered separately. We observe that Bcorr yields the highest accuracy as before. We also observe that the accuracy improves compared to cases (i) and (ii) and generally remains above 90% for 4-7 days of measurements. The laterals or feeder branches introduce additional spatial constraints which prevent customers from getting clustered into wrong groups based on voltage alone.

5.2 Customer to phase mapping

We use both customer and per-phase feeder measurements in order to assign phases to customers. We use the raw, delta, and binary datasets and test the accuracy of the clustering approach described in section 4.1. We then compare clustering to manual field inspections.

As explained in section 3, we have two solutions of transformer to phase mapping for all 1-phase overhead distribution transformers: (a) *Database solution*: available before field inspections and (b) *Ground truth*: available after field inspections. For 1-ph transformers, since customer phase is same as transformer phase, we effectively have both customer to phase and transformer to phase mapping.

Performance of clustering. Figure 10 (top) plots the accuracy of the computed customer phase over different batch sizes (as compared against ground truth). As before, we observe that Bcorr yields the highest accuracy, which remains above 90% for $4-7$ days of measurements. The plots demonstrate that binary fluctuations in voltage can be used to partition customers into phase based groups effectively. Figure 10 (bottom) shows the variation in accuracy across different batches of 4 days. We observe that Bcorr exhibits least variance as well.

Analytics versus Field Inspections. We now compare clustering with manual field inspections to determine its effectiveness in identifying and correcting errors in the existing database solution. For this, we use the computed customer to phase mapping (using Bcorr) and assign a phase to each transformer based on the phases of all customers under it. We then compare transformer phases across the computed solution, database solution, and the ground truth. Table 2 shows the results of comparison. The second column lists the total number of single-phase transformers which were verified in the field and the last column shows the accuracy of the existing database solution (as compared with ground truth from field inspections). The *positive* and *negative* columns count transformers wherein the computed phase is same as ground truth. The *positive* column counts transformers whose phase remains unchanged after field inspections. The *negative* column counts transformers whose phase was erroneous in the database, but was identified and corrected in the computed solution. The *false positive* counts the transformers which had an erroneous phase in the database solution but were not corrected by the algorithm. The *false negatives* counts transformers which had a correct phase in the database solution, but were identified as incorrect by the algorithm. The table shows that analytics helped improve the accuracy of the database solution significantly in case of CIRCUIT-II and CIRCUIT-III. For CIRCUIT-I, there is a negligible drop in the accuracy. While field inspections can be used to obtain 100% accuracy, they are expensive. The analytics approach is a low-cost alternative, which may be used to improve the accuracy of the database solution.

While the above results are for a North American distribution system, in countries such as Australia and in Europe, the problem of phase inference arises beyond the distribution transformer as these are generally 3-phase. In these settings, higher accuracy is expected due to local imbalances of loads on the 3 phases of the distribution transformer.

6. RELATED WORK

We know of no prior work that infers customer to transformer mapping using data available in the distribution network. This section summarizes prior work on inferring customer phase. Caird [9] discloses a system and method for phase identification with suitably enhanced meters that can detect phases based upon a unique signal injected into the phase line. The disadvantage of signal injection methods or in general those that rely on power-line communication (PLC) is that they require enhanced hardware to transmit and receive signals at different points of the grid, increasing capital and maintenance costs. Moreover in North america, feeders from substations can run for several miles before reaching a customer. Therefore PLC-based solutions become impractical and expensive since the signal may not propagate over long distances or across DTs without repeaters. Our approach on the other hand simply relies on voltage measurements from customers and feeders and therefore does not require any additional hardware other than conventional meters.

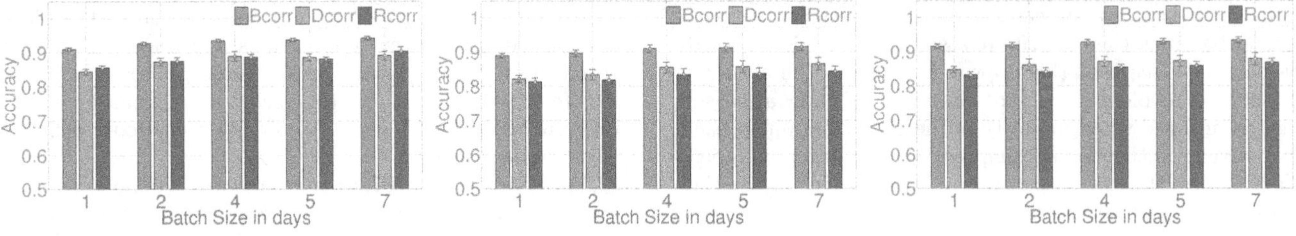

Figure 9: Customer to transformer Mapping: Average accuracy of clustering customers within each lateral. (left to right): circuit-i, circuit-ii, circuit-iii.

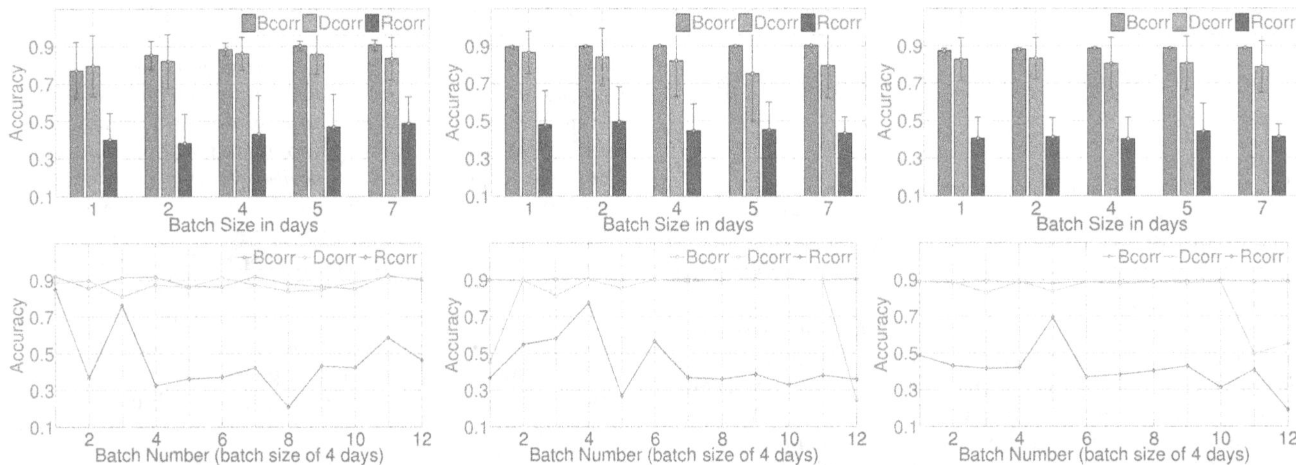

Figure 10: Customer to phase mapping: Performance of clustering. (left) circuit-i, (center) circuit-ii, (right) circuit-iii. (top): Average accuracy over different batch sizes (bottom): Accuracy for each batch of 4 days.

Our prior work [10] describes an optimization approaches to infer the connectivity model using a time series of customer and grid side load (kWh) measurements. The measurements are used to set up a system of linear equations based upon the principle of conservation of energy. The equations are analyzed to fit a customer to phase mapping that is consistent with the observed time series (i.e. it minimizes the error of fit). Dilek's [11] work on phase prediction in power circuits also uses interval consumption measurements, however the author employs a heuristic Tabu search to determine the phase of attached loads. Voltage-based techniques have two advantages over load-based techniques. Firstly, voltage-based clustering techniques may be used to verify and correct an existing customer to phase mapping solely from customer meter measurements. The load-based optimization approaches require both customer and feeder measurements. Secondly, since load-based optimization techniques are based on the principle of conservation, their accuracy may reduce in the presence of any non-AMI or unmetered loads. The voltage-based approaches however are insensitive to unmetered loads in the system.

In [12], authors analyse measurements from a low voltage network consisting of a 3-phase distribution transformer and its customers. Voltage measurements of individual customers are matched with the per-phase measurements taken at the transformer to determine customer phase. Our prior work [13, 14] studies voltage measurements from a microgrid and a feeder circuit respectively to infer phase relationship. We demonstrate that individually comparing the low voltage measurements from customers with the feeder measurements yields a lower accuracy when compared to clustering, which simultaneously compares customer measurements with each other as well as with the per-phase feeder measurements. This work on the other hand studies voltage data from multiple feeder circuits of a distribution network and reports accuracy results based on manual field inspections. We demonstrate the effectiveness of the clustering in comparison to field inspections for identifying and correcting phase errors. Furthermore we show that voltage measurements exhibit hierarchical correlations which can be exploited to infer customer transformer mapping in addition to customer phase.

7. CONCLUSIONS

An accurate connectivity model is required in the planning, operations, and maintenance of distribution networks. It enables faster restoration, accurate and timely communication with customers during outages, and is also needed to efficiently integrate distributed generation sources. Automated inference of customer-to-transformer and phase mapping using data that is already available from smart meters and feeder sensors allows utilities to periodically validate their connectivity and maintain a more accurate CM of their distribution network without the use of expensive manual inspections.

In this work, we show that customer voltage measurements exhibit hierarchical correlations which are consistent with the hierarchical connectivity relationships that exist

Table 2: Effectiveness of Analytics

Circuit	Verified Transformers	Positive	Negative	False Positive	False Negative	Flagged inaccurate but incorrectly assigned	Analytics Accuracy	Database Accuracy
CIRCUIT-I	119	100	6	5	7	1	89%	90%
CIRCUIT-II	200	110	78	3	8	1	94%	59%
CIRCUIT-III	233	161	48	13	5	6	90%	71%

Category	database solution = ground truth	database solution = computed solution	computed solution = ground truth
Positives	Yes	Yes	Yes
Negatives	No	No	Yes
False positives	No	Yes	No
False Negatives	Yes	No	No
Flagged Inaccurate but incorrectly assigned	No	No	No

between customers, transformers, and phases of a feeder in the distribution network. We present a novel analytics approach that can infer both customer-to-transformer and phase mapping with the help of customer voltage measurements in combination with feeder measurements and any existing but partially accurate customer-to-transformer mapping. We showed accuracy results based on analysis of low and medium voltage measurements collected from multiple feeder circuits with more than 6K single-phase customers. Our results indicate that voltage measurements spanning several days could be utilized to infer both customer to transformer and phase mapping with high accuracy.

Our experimental results indicate that spatial constraints can help improve the accuracy of customer to transformer connectivity. Future work will explore this direction and study the use of spatio-temporal techniques using a combination of voltage data and geospatial data from the geographical information system. We also plan to study the impact of distributed generation on customer voltage measurements. Behind-the-meter devices such as PV and storage may introduce voltage variations [15] that may work for or against the algorithms. The diversity of generation on different phases may help improve the accuracy. However, if the local generation masks the variations introduced by the aggregate load on a phase, it may negatively impact the clustering algorithms. A related issue is to study the impact of averaging instantaneous voltage measurements over larger time intervals as this may help reduce the volume of data sent from the meter to the utility. We will also develop approaches that combine both load (kWh) and voltage measurements to infer customer phase and study the applicability of other machine learning techniques such as support vector machines and label propagation.

8. REFERENCES

[1] G. Clark, "A changing map: Four decades of service restoration at alabama power," *Power and Energy Magazine, IEEE*, vol. 12, no. 1, pp. 64–69, Jan 2014.

[2] Kristina Hamachi LaCommare and Joseph H. Eto, "Understanding the Cost of Power Interruptions to U.S. Electricity Consumers," LBNL-55718, Sep 2004.

[3] J. Bouford and C. Warren, "Many states of distribution," *Power and Energy Magazine, IEEE*, vol. 5, no. 4, pp. 24–32, 2007.

[4] J. Fan and S. Borlase, "The evolution of distribution," *Power and Energy Magazine, IEEE*, vol. 7, no. 2, pp. 63–68, 2009.

[5] J. D. D. Glover and M. S. Sarma, *Power System Analysis and Design*, 3rd ed. Pacific Grove, CA, USA: Brooks/Cole Publishing Co., 2001.

[6] W. H. Kersting, *Distribution system modeling and analysis*, 2nd ed. Boca Raton :: CRC Press,, 2007.

[7] S. A. Boyer, *Supervisory Control and Data Acquisition*, 2nd ed. ISA, 1999.

[8] J. A. Hartigan and M. A. Wong, "A K-means clustering algorithm," *Applied Statistics*, vol. 28, pp. 100–108, 1979.

[9] K. Caird, "Meter Phase Identification," US Patent Application 20100164473, January 2010, Patent No. 12/345702.

[10] V. Arya, T. S. Jayram, S. Pal, and S. Kalyanaraman, "Inferring connectivity model from meter measurements in distribution networks," in *e-Energy*, 2013, pp. 173–182.

[11] M. Dilek, "Integrated Design of Electrical Distribution Systems: Phase Balancing and Phase Prediction Case Studies," Ph.D. dissertation, Virginia Polytechnic Institute and State University, 2001.

[12] H. Pezeshki and P. Wolfs, "Correlation based method for phase identification in a three phase lv distribution network," in *Universities Power Engineering Conference, 22nd Australasian*, 2012, pp. 1–7.

[13] V. Arya and R. Mitra, "Voltage-based clustering to identify connectivity relationships in distribution networks," in *SmartGridComm*, 2013, pp. 7–12.

[14] V. Arya, R. Mitra, R. Mueller, H. Storey, G. Labut, J. Esser, and B. Sullivan, "Voltage analytics to infer customer phase," in *IEEE PES Innovative Smart Grid Technologies(ISGT) Europe*, 2014.

[15] J. von Appen, M. Braun, T. Stetz, K. Diwold, and D. Geibel, "Time in the sun: The challenge of high pv penetration in the german electric grid," *Power and Energy Magazine, IEEE*, vol. 11, no. 2, pp. 55–64, March 2013.

OS|Plug: Open Platform for Smart Plugs

Muhammad Aftab, Amalfi Darusman, Israa A. Al Qassem, Majid Khonji, Chi-Kin Chau

Masdar Institute of Science and Technology, UAE
{muhaftab, aydarusman, ialqassem, mkhonji, ckchau}@masdar.ac.ae

ABSTRACT

We develop OS|Plug, an open-source smart plug platform that supports appliance energy consumption monitoring, remote control and future consumption prediction. The smart plug platform is based on popular hardware platform (Arduino). OS|Plug can communicate with smartphones and a back-end cloud computing system through web services for consumption analysis and prediction. We observe low power consumption of OS|Plug system. Our smart plug platform can be extended to support advanced features, such as classification of appliance energy consumption profiles, diagnosis of appliance anomaly, big data analysis, privacy and security controls.

Categories and Subjects: J.7 [COMPUTERS IN OTHER SYSTEMS]: *Consumer products*, B.0 [Hardware]: *Generals*

General Terms: Measurement, Reliability, Performance

Keywords: Smart Plug; Internet of Things

1. INTRODUCTION

Electric appliances can generate a large amount of energy consumption data that should be analyzed in an effective manner [2–4]. Managing and visualizing the energy consumption data appropriately can optimize the electricity costs and reduce idle power consumption, which gives rise to more effective energy conservation. The basic goals of a smart plug system are: (i) measuring the power consumption data of electric appliances accurately (including active, reactive power and power factor), (ii) predicting future energy consumption and cost for each appliance, (iii) controlling these appliances (e.g., automatic powering on and off) based on consumption budget, pre-set schedules, or intelligent computerized decisions. To these ends, we develop an open-source smart plug platform (called OS|Plug [1]) based on popular hardware platform (Arduino). OS|Plug can communicate with smartphones and a back-end cloud computing system through web services for consumption analysis and prediction. Our open platform can enable researchers and developers to integrate smart home applications.

e-Energy'15, July 14–17, 2015, Bangalore, India.
ACM 978-1-4503-3594-2/15/06.
http://dx.doi.org/10.1145/2768510.2770939.

2. COMPARISONS TO RELATED WORK

Various commercial proprietary smart plugs are available in the market to monitor and control electric appliances. There are two major types of smart plugs: (i) *active plugs* that can monitor and control appliances, and (ii) *passive plugs* that can only monitor appliances. Smart plugs can interoperate with mobile gadgets, and remote cloud computing systems.

In addition to the basic features of monitoring and controlling appliances in commercial proprietary smart plugs, our smart plug system offers more accurate energy measurement, by providing power factor measurements which differ between resistive, inductive, and capacitive appliances. Some electric utilities charge the customers of small power factor at a higher price, since small power factor generally indicates more energy loss in transmission/distribution systems. As such, additional correction devices are required to maintain acceptable power factor.

Our smart plug system also provides energy and cost prediction to assist users in managing their energy consumption effectively. Furthermore, our smart plug system supports control of multiple plugs and visualizes their aggregated consumption data simultaneously. Finally, we observe low power consumption of our smart plug system, as compared with other commercial smart plugs, because our system utilizes XBee protocol where sensors can be powered up only when communicating with the base station rather than relying on a continuous WiFi connection or other inefficient communication protocols.

3. ARCHITECTURE

The OS|Plug system consists of smart plugs that transmit power consumption data at periodic intervals to an Internet-connected base station via Zigbee radio link. The base station gathers and transmits the data received from smart plugs to a cloud computing server. The smart plugs can interoperate with smartphones, which enable users to visualize data and control the appliances. The high-level architecture of OS|Plug system is illustrated in Figure 1.

3.1 Hardware

OS|Plug is based on popular hardware platform (Arduino). Each smart plug contains sensors to measure the instantaneous AC voltage and current of the attached appliance.

AC voltage is measured by a standard AC-to-AC power adapter that can step down and shape the AC voltage wave-

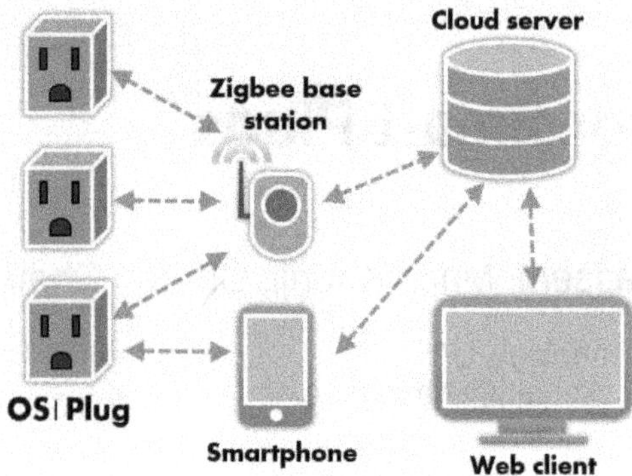

Figure 1: System architecture.

form. AC current is measured by a Hall effect based sensor. Knowing the instantaneous voltage and current, a variety of quantities can be computed, such as real power, apparent power, root-mean-square voltage, root-mean-square current, power factor, and other power quality parameters. Capturing these quantities will give a more accurate estimation of energy consumption.

The smart plug also has a relay to control the power to the attached appliance and an XBee module for radio communication with the base station. XBee is selected because of its lower power consumption compared to other protocols. The cases of smart plugs are created using a 3D printer. Figure 2 shows the hardware components of the smart plug.

We develop the base station based on Raspberry Pi, which supports a WiFi dongle to connect to the cloud, and Zigbee connections to the smart plugs. The smartphones can interoperate with the base station based (when both are in the same network) or through cloud server to remotely monitor and control the appliances.

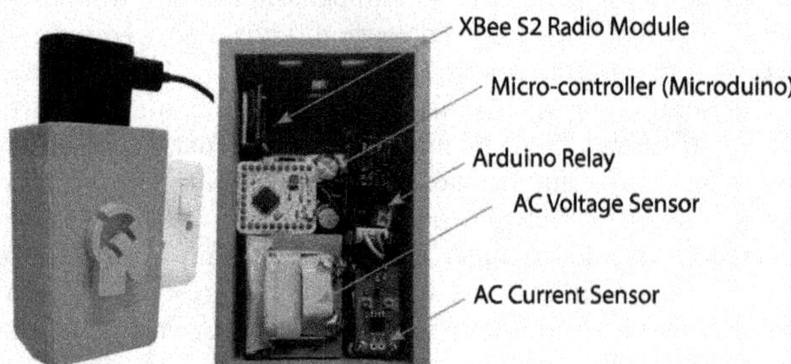

Figure 2: Hardware components of the smart plug.

3.2 Software

3.2.1 Server System

The smart plug server system hosts several services of the entire system. The server system consists of two parts: the cloud server and the base station (Raspberry Pi). Both entities handle the core system tasks:

- *Data Storage*: Since Raspberry Pi has limited storage capabilities, sensors energy consumption data are compressed and transmitted frequently from the base station to the remote server. The data is stored in MySQL database hosted in a cloud server.

- *Data Forwarding*: A base station is developed to collect data from multiple plugs and communicate their aggregated data to the cloud. It also distributes powering on and off commands (as received from cloud or from smartphones) to the smart plugs.

- *Web Service API*: A web server is deployed on cloud computing system that deploys a RESTfull web API. The API can provide data analysis and prediction services to users.

3.2.2 Mobile Application

The smart plug client application runs on android platform. It communicates with cloud server to obtain and visualize energy consumption data and to issue powering on and off commands. Figure 3 illustrates the user interface of the android application.

Figure 3: User interfaces of mobile application.

The mobile application supports the following features:

- *Control*: It allows users to power on and off the appliances remotely. Users can set schedules, and daily consumption budget, such that if an appliance exceeds its daily budget, the system will automatically shut down until the next day. All communications between the application and the cloud server follow a standard REST protocol.

- *Data Visualization*: In addition to real-time device monitoring, energy consumption is also visualized on daily, hourly, weekly, or monthly basis.

- *Prediction*: The mobile application can rely on a prediction model for each appliance. After the user has entered the electricity rates, the application can compute the exact current costs and future cost estimation.

4. CONCLUSION

This work presents OS|Plug, an open-source smart plug platform that can enable researchers and developers to integrate smart home applications. The system consists of smart plugs based on Arduino open hardware platform. The system supports appliance energy consumption monitoring, remote control and future consumption prediction. Our smart plug platform can be extended to support advanced features, such as classification of appliance energy consumption profiles, diagnosis of appliance anomaly, big data analysis, privacy and security controls.

5. REFERENCES

[1] OS|Plug. http://SustainableNetworks.org/smartplug.

[2] L. Atzori, A. Iera, and G. Morabito. The Internet of Things: A survey. *Computer Networks*, 54(15):2787–2805, Oct. 2010.

[3] J. Gubbi, R. Buyya, S. Marusic, and M. Palaniswami. Internet of Things (IoT): A vision, architectural elements, and future directions. *Future Generation Computer Systems*, 29(7):1645–1660, Sept. 2013.

[4] D. Miorandi, S. Sicari, F. De Pellegrini, and I. Chlamtac. Internet of things: Vision, applications and research challenges. *Ad Hoc Networks*, 10(7):1497–1516, Sept. 2012.

Demo Abstract: Demonstration of Using Sensor Fusion for Constructing a Cost-Effective Smart-Door

Vivek Chil Prakash   Anand Krishnan Prakash   Uddhav Arote
Vitobha Munigala   Krithi Ramamritham

Department of Computer Science and Engineering
Indian Institute of Technology, Bombay

ABSTRACT

As buildings get smarter they need to be aware of their spaces and occupants to improve prediction and management of energy consumption and environment customization based on user preference. User identification is crucial to this. However, accuracy of identification, intrusiveness and cost are important factors that one considers before installing such a system. Accounting for these factors, we built a Smart-Door that incorporates fusion of not-so-smart sensors, soft information available and learning algorithms to build an economical and accurate user identification system that requires no user intervention to monitor the occupant count and identities in a shared office space that can be scaled up to a building. It provides real-time occupancy status for the area and it can also learn to identify new users. In addition to energy management, such a user identification system has significant applications including evacuation procedures and localizing malfunctioning appliances.

General Terms

Occupancy Identification

Keywords

Smart Door; Smart Building; Energy Saving; User Comfort

1. INTRODUCTION

The ever increasing consumption of electric energy has resulted in wide spread research and initiatives to reduce and manage consumption of energy. In light of this ever increasing energy consumption smartmeters have become a boon in analysing and gaining new insights to power consumption patterns. Studies have shown that buildings consume 40% of total energy produced [3]. Hence it is important to focus on energy management of buildings. Though smartmeters provide information about total consumption, base consumption and patterns of usage, a new dimension of inferences can be made when information regarding occupancy of the building is added to the mix. This throws light on per capita consumption, contributors to base load, user device interactions, etc. Having inferred these, proactive steps to curb and reduce power consumption can be made in reducing base load, detecting anomalous devices, implementing energy quota system based on per capita consumption, customized setting of building spaces based on user preference, feedback systems to bring awareness to users about their consumption and hence in the process make users actively participate in reducing power consumption. The new dimension of user identity and count has been implemented by many systems with good accuracies but are expensive, require user intervention, have scalability issues, etc. These motivated us to come up with a smart door that identifies and counts the users, at the same time does not have the above drawbacks. The smartdoor is built using the sensor fusion of 'not so smart'cheap sensors which provides accurate identification of the users. Apart from saving energy a smartdoor can also aid in evacuation procedures during emergencies to pin point locations of children and senior citizens in a building for faster and efficient response of rescue team.

e-Energy'15, July 14–17, 2015, Bangalore, India.
ACM 978-1-4503-3609-3/15/07.
http://dx.doi.org/10.1145/2768510.2770938.

2. SETUP

2.1 Hardware

A Smart-Door [2] consists of a door frame with multiple sensors installed on it. Two laser-phototransistor pairs of the door have been installed to detect entry or exit. The change in voltage generated by the phototransistor detects the cut of the laser. An ultrasonic sensor has been placed on top of the door, in order to get height of a person as he walks through the door. A weight mat has been installed as well, which measures the weight of the person as he walks through the door when he steps on it. The height and weight sensors are connected to individual Arduinos which are connected to a Raspberry Pi installed on the door.

When either of the lasers is cut, it triggers an interrupt to the Raspberry Pi, which in turn triggers the height and weight sensors to start recording their respective readings. The order of the laser cut denotes an entry or an exit event. The sensors are reset after the second laser is cut. The Raspberry Pi assigns a unique session id to each entry/exit event and the recorded height and weight readings are tagged to this session id and stored in the database. During the training phase, each event is tagged with the ground truth - who the person is - using the two tablets installed at the door. After the training period, a classification algorithm runs on the recorded readings and the user identity is determined and displayed on the tablets again. This architecture is shown in Figure 1.

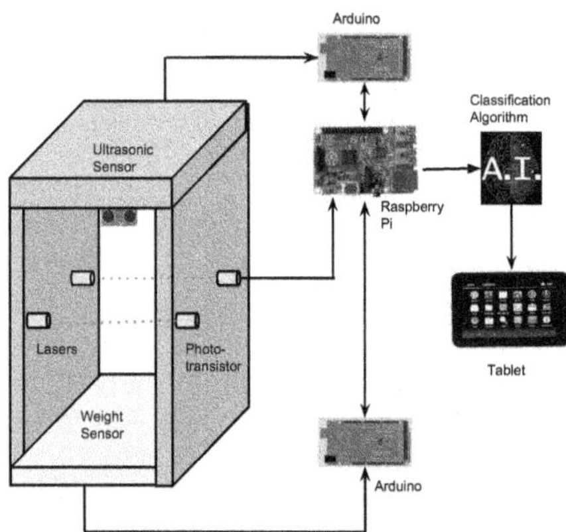

Figure 1: Smart-Door Architecture

2.2 Software

We use the Random Forest Classifier for learning and prediciting the user identity. Random Forest Classifier is an ensemble of decision trees [1]. In a Random Forest classifier many decision trees are built by taking the sample of data from the training set with replacement and a randomly selected subset of features is used to split at each node. To classify a new object, the classifier presents the object to each tree generated and makes the identification. The prediction of the object is the class which is predicted most number of time. We also use other soft information to improve the correctness of prediction. Soft information may include academic schedules or room schedules or knowledge of current occupants of the room, etc. Therefore for a person entering the room, from height + weight basd (hard sensor) information, we identify the set of possible occupants.
— For example, {A, B or C}.
We prune this set using soft sensors like user schedules or room schedules or current occupants of the room to identify who the person is.
— C has a meeting elsewhere, so person has to be {A,B}.
— B usually comes after lunch (that is, at the current time, B is usually not present), so has to be A.

3. ACCURACY AND EVALUATION

There are many ways for detecting and identifying a person as described by [2]. But, instead of using SVM, we have used a Random Forest Classifier. Similarly, as in [2], we also observed that the low cost height and weight sensors provided more insight into predicting the occupant with greater accuracy when compared to the body signatures obtained from the costly device Kinect. In order to justify this we trained an ensemble model Random Forest Classifier and observed the impact due to the different features on the accuracy of prediction, as can be seen in Figure 2.

The training data comprised around 2500 entries corresponding to 18 people and, the recorded data was used to train the machine learning algorithms in order to predict the person coming in or going out of the room. We employed both classifiers namely SVM and Random Forest Classifier to provide a valid comparison. Figure 2 shows the accuracies obtained by using different features and classifying using SVM and Random Forest Classifier.

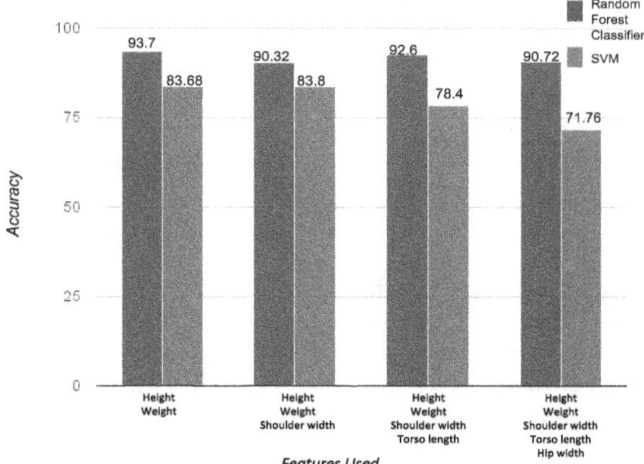

Figure 2: Performance of Classifiers Using Different Features

4. ON-SITE DEMONSTRATION

The on-site demonstration will have the Smart-Door set up to let visitors pass through and tag themselves on the tablets provided during the training period. After sufficient training data is obtained, each subsequent passing of the tagged participant will trigger identification of users on the tablets.

5. CONCLUSIONS

The demo will illustrate the Smart-Door: an economical, accurate and non-intrusive setup for tracking occupant count and user identification in an room. User identification is very crucial in customized environment management, evacuation procedures and in locating faulty appliances - especially if there is an appliance to user mapping. These features make the Smart-Door a very efficient and easy-to-deploy system in any building.

6. REFERENCES

[1] L. Breiman. Random forests. *Machine Learning*, 45(1):5–32, 2001.

[2] N. Nasir, K. Palani, A. Chugh, V. Prakash, U. Arote, A. Krishnan, and K. Ramamritham. Fusing sensors for occupancy sensing in smart buildings. In R. Natarajan, G. Barua, and M. Patra, editors, *Distributed Computing and Internet Technology*, volume 8956 of *Lecture Notes in Computer Science*, pages 73–92. Springer International Publishing, 2015.

[3] L. PĂl'rez-Lombard, J. Ortiz, and C. Pout. A review on buildings energy consumption information. *Energy and Buildings*, 40(3):394 – 398, 2008.

Brownout Energy Distribution Scheme for Mitigating Rolling Blackouts

Samrudha Kelkar
Department of Electrical Engineering
Indian Institute of Technology
Bombay
samrudh@ee.iitb.ac.in

Nimish Kothari
Department of Electrical Engineering
Indian Institute of Technology
Bombay
kothari@ee.iitb.ac.in

Krithi Ramamritham
Department of Computer Science
Indian Institute of Technology
Bombay
krithi@cse.iitb.ac.in

ABSTRACT
Large imbalance in energy generation and demand is usually handled through load shedding specific areas during different times of a day. Instead of a complete blackout, we have prototyped a brownout energy distribution scheme wherein a pre-determined guaranteed level of power required for essential loads is provided to all consumers. And consumers have the flexibility to choose which devices they want to power-up.

Keywords
Brownout; Load-shedding; Energy distribution scheme.

1. INTRODUCTION
Developing as well as developed economies struggle to fulfill increasing energy demands. In India, energy deficit estimated for the year 2014-2015 is 53,515 (MU) which is 5.1% of the total energy demand. Few states face energy deficit as large as 20%. Solving such critical energy crisis and simultaneously maintaining consumer comfort requires optimal energy distribution scheme. Currently, the distribution companies or power utilities handle this imbalance in demand-supply through load-shedding in specific areas. Specifically rolling blackout is implemented, in which different areas suffer from the blackout at different times of a day. Thus, one of the simplest ways in which demand-supply balance is maintained is to completely disrupt energy distribution in a particular area for a limited period of time.

Instead of imposing a complete blackout during different times of the day, we propose a brownout energy distribution scheme for such areas. Brownout is defined as a condition where sufficient power is delivered to run essential consumer loads. It is an intermediary condition between blackout and unconstrained regular power supply. Typically, such brownouts are implemented by changing supply voltage magnitude with the help of low voltage ratio transformers. This demands reinforcements in the power system network and escalates the infrastructure cost. The proposed scheme avoids the need for such reinforcements.

e-Energy'15, July 14-17, 2015, Bangalore, India.
ACM 978-1-4503-3609-3/15/07
http://dx.doi.org/10.1145/2768510.2770937

Instead, it exploits the benefits of information and communication techniques.

The paper proposes a system and method that empowers the power distribution companies to initiate a brownout during energy imbalance and distribute the optimum share of available power to cater to essential load requirements of the consumer. It also gives consumers the flexibility to classify the electrical loads at their premises into Essential (E) and Non-essential (N) loads. Utility ensures energy distribution to at least the Essential (E) loads and as much as possible of the Non-essential (N) loads during brownout situations, provided the total consumption (E as well as N) remains below the assigned power threshold. Non-essential (N) loads can be clubbed as a single entity or can be assigned priorities depending on consumer requirement. Priorities of N loads can be altered dynamically. Thus, only essential (E) or some combination of E and N loads are utilized during brownout condition.

2. BROWNOUT DISTRIBUTION ALGORITHM
During energy imbalances, the algorithm attempts to provide adequate energy to essential loads and maximizes power to non-essential loads. Energy imbalance is marked at the utility end when available instantaneous power (D_A) is less than instantaneous demand power (D_D). At the macro level for N consumers present in the utility, instantaneous demand power can be given by cumulative power consumed by all the consumers.

$$D_D = \sum_{i=1}^{N} P_T(i)$$

Here P_T is total power consumption by each consumer. It is further divided into multiple essential loads and non-essential loads as mentioned before. So for the ith consumer present in the area of utility, total power consumption is given by

$$P_T(i) = \sum_{j=1}^{K1} P_{Nj}(i) + \sum_{j=1}^{K2} P_{Ej}(i)$$

Where,

K1 = total number of Non-essential (N) loads for i[th] consumer

K2 = total number of Essential (E) loads for i[th] consumer

P_{Nj} = Power consumed by j[th] Non-essential load

P_{Ej} = Power consumed by j[th] Essential load

Initially, P_{Nj}'s are sorted in descending order of priority. During brownout emergency, each of the smart control unit (SCU) installed at the consumer receives a threshold value of instantaneous power (P_{TH}) from utility. For a critical case where $P_T(i) > P_{TH}(i)$, two approaches can be adopted.

A] In this simplistic approach, all the non–essential loads are disconnected or tripped off.
B] In consumer driven priority model, the least priority Non-essential (N) load is disconnected first and so the process continues till $P_T(i) < P_{TH}(i)$ is achieved.

$$P_{TH} > \max(\sum_{j=1}^{k} P_{Nj} + \sum_{j=1}^{K2} P_{Ej})$$

Where, $k \subset K1$
Consumer has the liberty of fixing the priority of all the (N) loads through a User Access Device (UAD) like cell phone, computer web interface etc

3. DEMO IMPLEMENTATION

In order to demonstrate the distribution scheme, we implemented it with a sample of electrical loads. A SCU is replicated by a laptop and energy meter, where the brownout algorithm is deployed. Multiple switch-boards with wireless connection interface are connected to the phase (P) - neutral (N) supply. Cumulative instantaneous power consumed by all the loads is measured from the energy-meter and given as an input to the algorithm.

3.1 Set-up

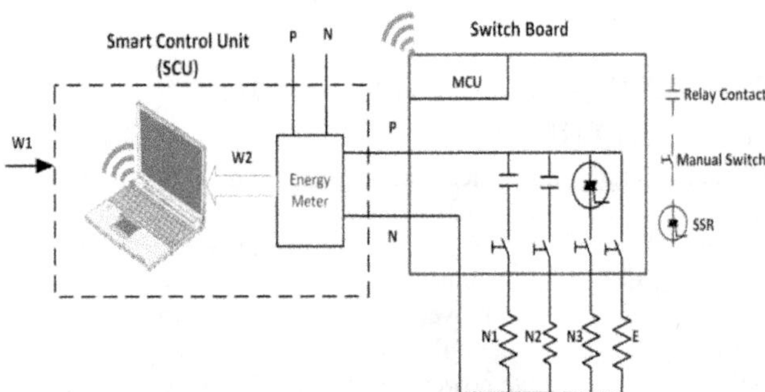

Figure 1. Prototype of brownout distribution system at consumer end.

All the switch-boards and energy meter are connected to the utility supply. Along with manual switches fitted on typical switchboards, a tiny micro-controller is mounted. Electric relays are connected in series with the manual switches as shown in figure 1. These relays can be controlled (switched ON/OFF) using the micro-controller. Wireless communication module is interfaced with micro-controller of the switch-board which enables communication with SCU. To replicate SCU, energy meter is connected to computer using MODBUS to USB connector. Our energy meter provides instantaneous power in watts using the MODBUS protocol. It is probed at 1 Hz.

3.2 Operation

Input to the algorithm:
W1= Instantaneous P_{TH} (in watts) received from utility
W2 = Instantaneous power consumption (in watts) obtained from energy meter

Brownout Alert: Boolean status to indicate initiation of brownout from utility.

Output of the algorithm:
Consumer Alarm: Boolean alarm to indicate if power consumption is above threshold

Switch Status arrays: One array for each of the switch-boards with length equal to number of switches present in that switch-board. Each array field has either ON or OFF state to indicate status of electrical relay. When Brownout Alert is activated, algorithm monitors W1 and W2. If W1 > W2, no action is initiated. If W1 < W2, Consumer Alarm is initiated. Based on the priority of loads maintained in the algorithm, Switch Status arrays are updated till the condition W1>W2 is met. After every modification, Switch Status array is communicated to corresponding switch-board. Switch-board receives modified Switch Status array and changes the status of relays based on the corresponding array fields.

Here priority of loads plays an important role in changing the switch status. In distribution systems like [1], flexibility to change priorities is not provided. Our system allows flexibility to the consumer to modify priority at any point of time using mobile/web application.

4. BEYOND– DEMO

Decisions such as assigning P_{TH}, scheduling time interval of brownout and choosing area boundaries of implementation are critical issues that need to be considered. Also, few extensions can be incorporated in the current scheme such as selecting time varying P_{TH}, penalizing the event of crossing P_{TH} with higher per unit rate of energy or ceasing the supply based on severity of the situation.

5. CONCLUSION

We will demonstrate a method with which a power distribution authority can efficiently control the distribution of energy during energy imbalance scenarios. The scheme presented above ensures that a minimum adequate energy is supplied to all the consumers by the utility. It provides flexibility to the consumers to access electrical loads on priority basis during emergency. This paper covers part of the ongoing work, in which we are developing more dynamic, intelligent and fair energy distribution system to mitigate the problem of rolling blackout.

6. ACKNOWLEDGMENTS

We are thankful to Smart Energy Informatics Lab, IIT Bombay for their support in implementing system.

REFERENCES

[1] Ying. System for remotely controlling energy distribution at local sites, December 14 2004. US Patent 6,832,135. CHI '00. ACM, New York, NY, 526-531. DOI= http://doi.acm.org/10.1145/332040.332491.

UrJar: A Device to Address Energy Poverty using E-waste

Vikas Chandan[#1], Mohit Jain[#1], Harshad Khadilkar[#1], Zainul Charbiwala[#1*],
Anupam Jain[#1*], Sunil Ghai[#1*], Rajesh Kunnath[#2], Deva P Seetharam[#1*]
[#1]IBM Research India, [#2]Radio Studio India
{vchanda4, mohitjain, harshad.khadilkar}@in.ibm.com

ABSTRACT

A significant portion of the population in India does not have access to reliable electricity. At the same time, is a rapid penetration of Lithium Ion battery-operated devices such as laptops, both in the developing and developed world. This generates a significant amount of electronic waste (e-waste), especially in the form of discarded Lithium Ion batteries. In this work, we present *UrJar*, a device which uses re-usable Lithium Ion cells from discarded laptop battery packs to power low energy DC devices. We describe the construction of the device followed by findings from field deployment studies in India. The participants appreciated the long duration of backup power provided by the device to meet their lighting requirements. Through our work, we show that *UrJar* has the potential to channel e-waste towards the alleviation of energy poverty, thus simultaneously providing a sustainable solution for both problems. Mode details of this work are provide in [3].

Keywords

computing for development; e-waste; sustainability; discarded laptop battery; lighting device; energy poverty

Categories and Subject Descriptors

B.0 [**Hardware**]: General

1. INTRODUCTION

There is a significant portion of the world, where grid-based electricity has either not permeated down yet, or is unavailable for significant durations every day. For example, 44.7% of rural households in India do not have any access to electricity [6]. Most of these people cannot afford expensive power backup solutions, thus necessitating a dependence on kerosene oil which has adverse health, safety, economic and environmental implications [1]. On the other hand, a large amount of electronic waste (e-waste) is created around the world daily, both in developed and developing regions of the world. In India, it is estimated that more than 8,00,000 tons of e-waste is generated every year [2]. Lithium Ion (Li-Ion) batteries, which power portable devices such as laptops and mobile phones, form a key constituent of e-waste. In 2013, the India operations of just one large multinational IT company resulted in more than 10 tons of discarded laptop batteries[1]. Recycling of Li-Ion batteries is a complex, labour-intensive and costly process, and hence is not commercially viable.

Battery packs used in laptops consist of Li-Ion cells arranged in a series-parallel configuration. Studies undertaken by us reveal that some of the Li-Ion cells in discarded battery packs can still provide a satisfactory terminal voltage level, suggesting that when a battery pack is discarded, not all of its constituent cells are 'dead'. Also, a study on 32 discarded laptop batteries undertaken by us revealed that on average these batteries still had 64% of the design capacity remaining indicating that often, the complete battery pack can be reused directly after removing the battery conditioning circuit. Therefore, discarded laptop battery cells have reuse potential which potential has not been hitherto exploited. Used laptop battery collection services around the world and in India have had limited success so far, with an estimated collection rate of less than 5% [5]. Therefore, most discarded laptop batteries today end up in landfills or incinerators, which results in an adverse environmental impact. Novel use cases of discarded laptop batteries can alleviate their environmental impact by creating an ecosystem that has a demand for such batteries. We present one such attempt, a backup power device - called *UrJar* - that seeks to simultaneously address the problems of proliferation of laptop battery e-waste, and the prevalence of energy poverty in developing countries. It uses discarded but still usable laptop battery cells to power low energy DC appliances. The device is aimed at 'bottom-of-the-pyramid[2]' users, especially people in rural or semi-urban parts with access to intermittent power. The device is primarily aimed at powering a DC light bulb, since lighting represents an essential load for this population. Moreover, it also has provision to power secondary loads such as a DC fan and a mobile charger. To develop this device, we first conducted a survey of lighting solutions being used currently by our target end users in India based on which we identified the design considerations for *UrJar*. We then developed a few prototypes of *UrJar* and evaluated them through real world deployments. The key benefits offered by *UrJar* are: (i) a means to addess the proliferation of Li-Ion e-waste, (ii) a mechanism to meet the essential energy requirements of bottom-of-the-pyramid population in developing regions such as lighting, and (iii) enablement of an ecosystem to electrify rural areas.

* This work was done when the author was employed at IBM Research, India

[1]Data communicated through sources inside the organization.
[2]A country's poorest socio-economic group

e-Energy'15, July 14–17, 2015, Bangalore, India.
ACM 978-1-4503-3609-3/15/07.
http://dx.doi.org/10.1145/2768510.2770940.

2. DESCRIPTION OF URJAR

A few protypes of *UrJar* were built (Fig. 1) based on design considerations identified via a study involving 25 participants in India, belonging to the underprivileged community in India who do not have direct access to the grid. These considerations were derived by understanding the limitations of the current lighting solutions employed by these participants. Prototypes were built using the following steps:

Step 1: Source used laptop battery packs from e-waste.

Step 2: Disassemble packs to extract individual Li-Ion cells that can still deliver power.

Step 3: Connect re-usable cells to build a refurbished battery pack.

Step 4: Build a box which contains a charging circuit for the refurbished pack, step-up/step-down converters and other electronics to power extrenal devices such as a LED light bulb, a DC fan, and a mobile charger.

These prototypes have the following features:

Appliances: The prototypes power a DC light bulb (LED), a DC fan and a mobile charger.

Refurbished battery packs: Refurbished battery packs were built by extracting Li-Ion cells from discarded laptop batteries exhibiting terminal voltages of more than 3.7V. The cells were arranged in a 3S2P configutation, and the refurbished pack delivers DC power at around 12 V.

Battery charger: A 6W charger based on FSEZ1216 IC from Fairchild Semiconductor [4] is used as the off-line battery charger. The IC uses primary-side sensing which reduces the number of components enabling a compact design. The IC was chosen from a readily available inventory since it provides Constant Voltage and Constant Current control which is ideal for battery charging. The charging efficiency is close to 75%. Charging current is limited to 500 mA to ensure that batteries are not damaged due to higher charging currents. Since these batteries are not new, their ability to handle abuse is reduced and therefore, charging cut-off is kept between 4.0 to 4.1 V per cell.

Mobile charger: A sychronous DC-DC buck converter operating at 1 MHz is used for conversion from battery voltage to 5V needed for mobile charging. The output is a constant 5V output with a maximum current of 1A. Since the current is small, a sychronous regulator with internal MOSFETs is used. This reduced the footprint for the mobile charger. Operating at 1MHz reduced the power inductor size and current handling requirements. The efficiency of conversion was close to 90%.

Fan: Brushless DC motor based personal table fan is used. A similar buck converter topology, as above, with higher current is used.

Light: A buck regulator in continuous conduction mode is used for buck regulation. The regulator uses a current sense of 100 mV to precisely regulate LED current. High Power, high efficiency LEDs with 120 degree beam width is used. A frosted shell minimises glare. The regulator output drives three 1 W LED bulbs in series, housed in a 3 W LED bulb enclosure, at 100mA. A single LED driver at 350 mA could be used to lower costs further.

Cost: At a volume of 1000 pieces, we estimate the bill of material cost for each of these protoypes to be around INR 600. The pricing includes the enclosure, electronics, a 3 W LED light bulb, and a mobile charger but does not include a fan.

To understand the usability of *UrJar* in a real-world scenario, prototypes were handed to five participants to be used in unsupervised settings for one week or more. Overall, the participants mentioned that UrJar is safer, cheaper, and easier to use, compared to their existing solutions. The major benefit of UrJar mentioned by participants was long lighting hours after a single recharge.

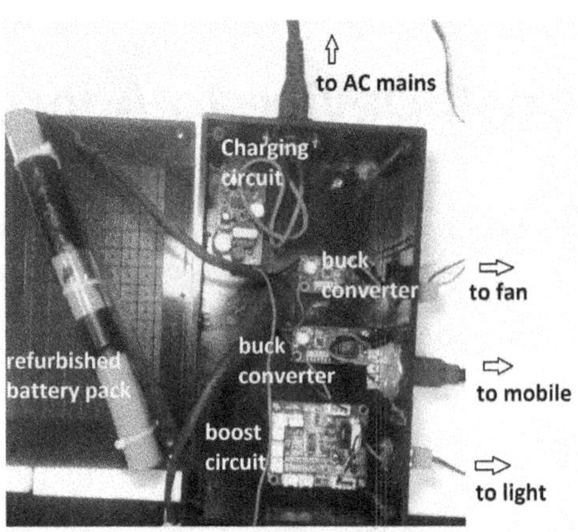

Figure 1: Component details of an *UrJar* prototype built using discarded laptop batteries.

3. CONCLUSIONS

In this work, we proposed a low-cost solution called *UrJar* to the problem of unreliable or unavailable electrical power in developing regions of the world. The novelty of this solution lies in the use of discarded lithium ion batteries as the source of energy. These batteries are employed to power lights, and additionaly fans and mobile chargers for the bottom-of-the-pyramid community in developing countries. We developed *UrJar* prototypes and conducted real world field deployments. We found that the participants were generally satisfied with *UrJar*. Future work shall focus on addition of other features such as direct solar charging, inclusion of other types of battery packs, e.g. cellphone batteries, and inclusion of additional DC devices.

4. ACKNOWLEDGMENTS

The authors acknowledge the assistance provided by the SELCO Foundation, India in conducting the field studies involved.

5. REFERENCES

[1] Solar Portable Projector - Selco Foundation. **http://timesofindia.indiatimes.com/india/11-lakh-households-have-no-electricity-85-of-rural-India-uses-firewood-as-fuel/articleshow/12256306.cms**.

[2] Workshop on E - waste - Designing Take Back System. **http://toxicslink.org/docs/E-Waste_Report-Designing-Take-Back-Systems.pdf**.

[3] Chandan, V., Jain, M., Khadilkar, H., Charbiwala, Z., Jain, A., Ghai, S., Kunnath, R., and Seetharam, D. Urjar: A lighting solution using discarded laptop batteries. In *Proceedings of the Fifth ACM Symposium on Computing for Development*, ACM (2014), 21–30.

[4] Fairchild Semiconductors. **http://www.fairchildsemi.com/pf/FS/FSEZ1216.html**.

[5] Georgi-Maschler, T., Friedrich, B., Weyhe, R., Heegn, H., and Rutz, M. Development of a recycling process for Li-ion batteries. *Journal of power sources 207* (2012), 173–182.

[6] Government of India. Census data - source of lighting. 2011.

Demo Abstract: Energy Optimization in Commercial Buildings: From Monitoring to Savings Realization

Amarjeet Singh[‡§], Shubham Saini[§], Sanchit Sharma[‡], Priyank Trivedi[‡]
[‡]Zenatix Solutions Pvt. Ltd. India [§]IIIT Delhi India
amarjeet.singh@zenatix.com

ABSTRACT

Commercial buildings such as office space, educational institutions and retail outlets consume more than 10% of total energy consumption in most countries. Major loads such as air conditioning and UPS together with diesel generator (used to provide backup power supply) constitute majority of energy expenses for such facilities, specifically in a developing economy like India. Lack of detailed monitoring for these subsystems results in several wasteful activities going unnoticed. Zenatix, an energy data analytics company, provides robust real time monitoring of energy and related data. Collected data is then analyzed to provide actionable insights in the form of SMS and Email based alerts leading to efficient manual control (preferred by facilities in India over automated control). In this paper, we present some examples of real world use cases of Zenatix's energy analytics that helped customers identify wasteful operations and reduce them to achieve up to 15% energy savings.

1. INTRODUCTION

Over the last two decades, from 1993 - 2011 while the world population has increased by 27%, global energy consumption per year has increased by 76%. Despite such a windfall increase in per capita energy generation, more than 1.5 billion people live without access to electricity[1]. Equitable and reliable access to electricity can only be achieved if each produced unit is consumed in the most optimal manner, eliminating wastage at each level from generation through distribution to consumption.

Office spaces, educational institutions and retail outlets account for more than 50% of the commercial building energy consumption in the USA. Ensuring optimal operations of such facilities that result in minimal wastage can free up useful energy units for consumption by other entities and reduce the overall energy burden. Often these facilities get a single monthly electricity bill that lack enough information for a facility manager to take energy reduction measures.

Some progressive facilities take personal initiative to install an energy monitoring system. However, the facilities team has little time and expertise to analyze the collected data and take appropriate control actions. Therefore, detailed and real time monitoring coupled with analytics (that convert data into actionable insights) are critical to help facilities team in minimizing wasteful operations. These insights can be delivered either through automated control (requiring additional investment) or through SMS/Email based alerts for optimal manual control (preferred by facilities in India). Zenatix, an energy data analytics company, provide robust systems for real time monitoring of energy and related parameters. Figure 1 illustrates the architecture of the solution deployed by Zenatix for commercial buildings. Data logger developed by Zenatix is capable of interfacing with diverse energy related sensors using open communication protocols (e.g. Modbus for energy meter and relays and 1-wire for temperature and humidity sensors). Collected data is then sent to a cloud platform through Ethernet, WiFi or Cellular network interface, depending on site availability. Cloud backend provides optimized storage and retrieval through storage in a time series database[2]. Analysis to develop actionable insights are also performed in the cloud and delivered in real time through email or SMS.

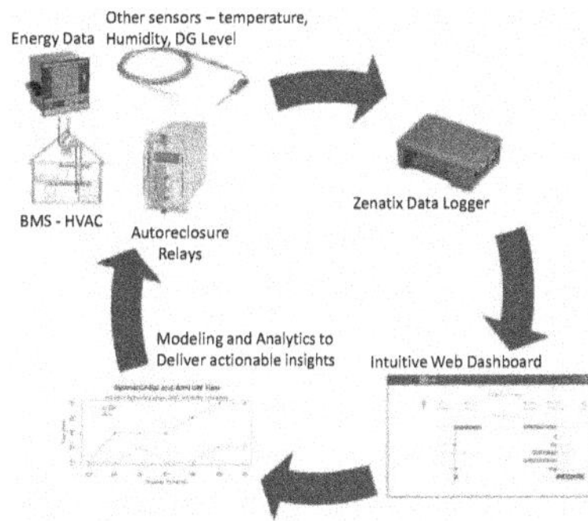

Figure 1: System Architecture for Zenatix Solutions

2. USE CASES

Zenatix has developed generalizable analytical use cases for three critical sub-systems that constitute majority of electricity expenses in a commercial building - Air Conditioning (AC), Uninterrupted Power Supply (UPS) and Diesel Generator (DG). Significant savings are possible with simple low hanging fruits such as identification of wasteful operations during non-working hours. Additional savings are obtained using sophisticated models like building specific empirical models correlating external weather and AC usage.

2.1 AC Optimization

AC optimization in any facility is achieved through the

e-Energy'15, July 14–17, 2015, Bangalore, India.

ACM 978-1-4503-3609-3/15/07.
http://dx.doi.org/10.1145/2768510.2770936.

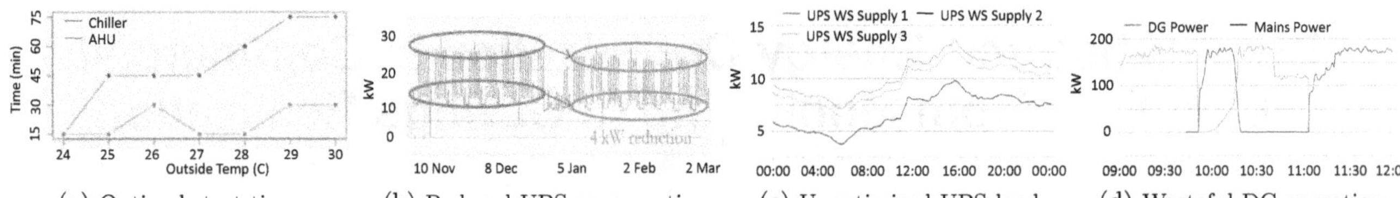

(a) Optimal start time (b) Reduced UPS consumption (c) Unoptimized UPS load (d) Wasteful DG operation

Figure 2: Illustration of HVAC, UPS and DG Optimization use case from several of Zenatix clients

following interventions:

1. **Reducing wasteful operations during non-working hours:** Simple alerts are set for operation of any AC sub-system (chillers, pumps, cooling tower and AHUs) during non-operational hours.
2. **Building specific optimal start time:** Energy data together with temperature data of occupied zones and external weather is analyzed to create an empirical model accounting for the building specific variations. This model is translated into a simple look-up table (for facility managers to act upon) that maps indoor temperature in the morning (at the time when AC is required) to the time required for the building to be cooled to a desired temperature (say 25°C). Such a mapping of indoor temperature to optimal start time for AHUs and Chillers for one of Zenatix's clients (Client-1) is shown in Figure 2(a). Working as per the calculated optimal start time had a potential saving of USD 2500 over 120 days from June to Oct'14.
3. **Building specific optimal stop time:** AC can be switched off a little earlier than the facility closing time if the desired temperature can be maintained until that time. Similar to optimal start time analysis, energy and temperature data from the facility is analyzed to calculate the optimal stop time. Operating as per the optimal stop time had potential savings of USD 1000 over 120 days from June to Oct'14. Overall 10% savings on chiller and 20% savings on AHU operation was identified with optimal start and stop times.
4. **Optimal usage of resources:** Empirical models are also used to determine optimal resources required at any instance. As an example, for a facility with 2 chillers with 2 compressors each, empirical model based on historical data is used to determine the number of compressors to use at any instance based on outside weather conditions, to achieve energy reductions without compromising on occupant comfort.
5. **Appropriate set points:** Chiller Leaving Water Temperature (LWT) is often set to 6°C as per manufacturer specification. When operating close to the LWT set-point, chiller at Client-1 was observed to consume 75% of the energy consumed otherwise. Based on historical data, it was observed that even for a LWT of 10°C, the inside temperature remained within the comfortable range. Changing the LWT setting from 6 to 10°C had 2.65% reduction potential in chiller energy consumption.

2.2 UPS Optimization

Following interventions lead to UPS Optimization:

1. **Reductions during non-working hours:** Often the IT load is kept running even after working hours. Figure 2(b) shows cyclic power consumption on one of the UPS serving the desktop IT load (for Client-2). High and low power consumption corresponds to working and non-working hours respectively. Based on the data, the client installed a utility that puts desktop into deep sleep mode after 30 minutes of inactivity, reducing consumption by 4 kW, as seen in Figure 2(b).
2. **Optimizing the efficiency throughput:** UPS sizing is often done to account for future addition of IT and allied load. However, running such system at reduced load (less than 30% load) puts UPS operation at the lower end of efficiency curve making it inefficient for 24x7 operation. Figure 2 (c) shows the running load for Client-3 for 3 UPS systems, each of 80 kVA capacity. Since the total load is less than 40% of the single UPS load, the client was advised to switch off one UPS of 80 kVA in rotation. This increased the load on each running UPS from 13% to 20% that improved its efficiency by 5%.

2.3 DG Optimization

Wasteful operations of Diesel Generator (DG) include:

1. **Running DG long after grid power is restored:** Figure 2(d) shows DG in operation for Client-4 from 10:20 to 10:40 when grid power was also available. With DG energy being three times costlier, alerts on such wasteful operations can save significant energy.
2. **Running DG on zero load:** Facilities often test run DG daily to ensure reliable operation during the times of need. However, this test operation (or no load condition) can be drastically reduced as well as operationalized in a regular pattern. For Client-2, such DG operation was worth USD 100 and 200 of diesel for the month of Dec'14 and Jan'15. An internal policy to rationalize the zero load DG operation can be created and implemented using the alerts feature.
3. **Inappropriate DG sizing:** Facilities are often equipped with DG of different sizing to cater to the varying load. DG efficiency depends on the percentage loading and hence running a DG at lower percentage loading results in significant fuel wastage. During grid failure Client-2 had a uniform policy of running 750 kVA and 500 kVA DG for working and non-working hours respectively. Real time monitoring provided an insight that beginning Oct'14, the working hours load never reached the critical limit of 400 kW (for which an alert was set in the system) and hence 500 kVA DG was sufficient for grid failure throughout the day. Running 500 kVA DG instead of 750 kVA DG during working hours saved Client-2 approx. 15% of their diesel consumption over Dec'14 - March'15.

3. REFERENCES

[1] World energy resources - 2013 survey. `http://www.worldenergy.org/wp-content/uploads/2013/09/Complete_WER_2013_Survey.pdf`, 2013.

[2] Stephen Dawson-Haggerty. readingdb. `https://github.com/stevedh/readingdb`, 2014.

Poster Abstract: Combining Multiple Forecast for Improved Day Ahead Prediction of Wind Power Generation

Milan Jain*
IIIT Delhi, India
milanj@iiitd.ac.in

Amarjeet Singh*
IIIT Delhi, India
amarjeet@iiitd.ac.in

ABSTRACT

Wind, a major alternative source of energy, provides dynamic output due to frequent weather changes, which introduces one of the biggest challenges in integrating it with the existing power system. Commercial wind power forecasters vary in their prediction accuracies both across the wind farms and for different time periods within a farm. Therefore, wind power generators (WPGs) employ multiple such forecasters and heuristically choose day-ahead-prediction from one of them (baseline model). In this work, we combine multiple forecasters to generate a superforecast for the day-ahead-prediction which is, expected to be better than individual forecasters in terms of penalty – the cost a WPG has to pay for inaccurate predictions. Performance evaluation using 6 months of SCADA and forecaster data, from a WPG, of a wind farm located in India, shows that superforecast reduced the penalty by 7% and 13% when compared with the least penalised forecaster for each month and the baseline model.

Categories and Subject Descriptors

H.4.2 [**Information Systems Applications**]: Types of Systems-Decision support (e.g. MIS)

Keywords

Wind forecasting, WPF, Wind Power, Renewable Energy

1. INTRODUCTION

Wind power production capacity reached 336GW (approx. 4% of the total electricity demand) by the end of June 2014 worldwide[1]. A single wind farm consists of multiple wind turbines that are expected to follow a standard power curve, as shown in Figure 1. However, each turbine deviates from the ideal power curve due to multiple reasons, including random variations in the wind, that are complex to model. Such deviations at the turbine level result in significant variation in power produced at the wind farm level complicating their integration with the existing power system.

Across the world, there exist regulations that require wind power generators to submit prediction for each 15-minute window (09:00-09:15, 09:15-09:30, so on) for the next day (day-ahead-prediction). These predictions are then used for appropriate supply side management by the electricity distribution centers. However, due to weather based deviations, even commercial wind power forecasters are not able to accurately perform day-ahead-prediction. For some countries, there exist incentives and penalties for correctly and incorrectly predicting the day-ahead-generation. To optimise on such incentives and penalties, often wind power generators employ multiple wind power forecasters to provide the day-ahead-predictions and then choose the best forecaster heuristically. In this paper, we present some initial insights from a real world wind farm dataset along with a basic model to generate superforecast, combining multiple commercial forecasters. Proposed model is evaluated using real data from a wind farm in south-east India that includes SCADA data from the farm and forecaster data from 4 commercial forecasters employed by the generator. We evaluate our approach in terms of the penalty that a generator would pay in comparison to the least penalised forecaster for each month and the baseline model (currently adopted by the generator to heuristically select one of the forecasters). Proposed model shows an improvement of approx. 7% and 13% (averaged over six months) in terms of penalty when compared to the monthly least penalised (MLP) forecaster and the baseline model, respectively.

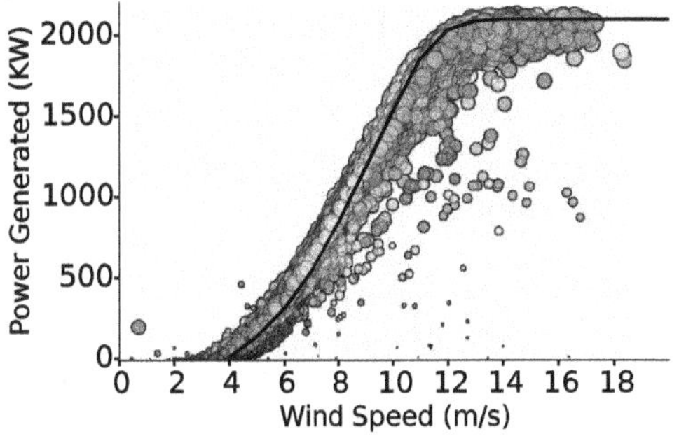

Figure 1: Power generated vs wind speed; Area of the circle represents average time per 10 minutes for which each turbine was operational; color indicates environmental temperature with darker shade representing higher temperature.

2. STATE OF THE ART

The current state of the art in wind power forecasting includes deterministic and probabilistic forecasting methods that can provide short, medium and long-term predictions. Deterministic forecasting methods generate spot predictions i.e. a single value of future wind output. In accordance with a survey by Zhang et al. [4], many of these prediction approaches have inherent and irreducible uncertainty. On the other hand, probabilistic forecasts usually take the form of a probability density function (PDF) and can be categorized into parametric (wherein the shape of PDF is assumed) and non-parametric (wherein PDF is estimated at a finite number of points and its full description is obtained by interpolation). Various wind power forecasters work on these existing techniques and generate predictions for wind power generators. Randomness in wind behavior leads to variations in their prediction accuracy, thus motivating research in hybrid approaches[2] and adaptive combination[3] of forecasts. Treating each of the forecasts as a time series, this work presents a simple

*This work was done while working with Zenatix Solutions Pvt. Ltd.

e-Energy'15, July 14–17, 2015, Bangalore, India.
ACM 978-1-4503-3609-3/15/07.
http://dx.doi.org/10.1145/2768510.2770953.

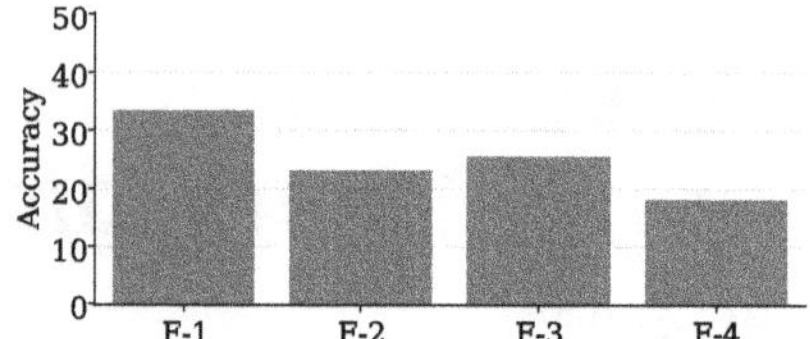

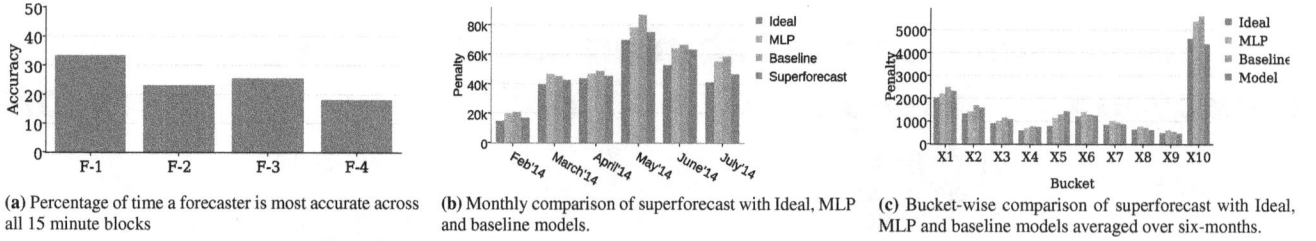

(a) Percentage of time a forecaster is most accurate across all 15 minute blocks

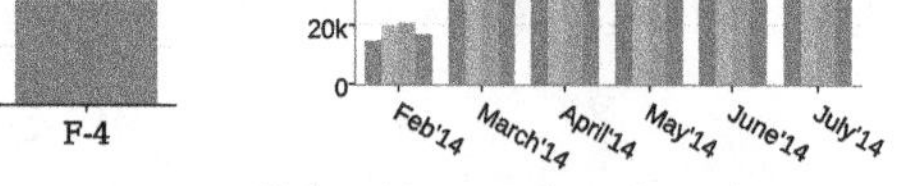

(b) Monthly comparison of superforecast with Ideal, MLP and baseline models.

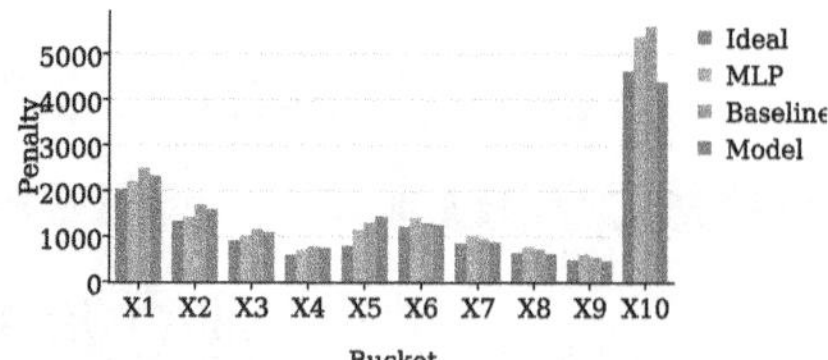

(c) Bucket-wise comparison of superforecast with Ideal, MLP and baseline models averaged over six-months.

Figure 2: Results showing reduction in penalty in comparison to MLP and baseline models.

Case	A	P	X_0	X_1	X_2	X_3	X_4	X_5	X_6	X_7	X_8	X_9	X_{10}
1	200	100	120	0	0	0	0	0	20	20	20	20	0
2	200	300	200	20	20	20	20	0	0	0	0	0	0

Table 1: Distribution of predicted power in buckets for two different scenarios

regression based approach to combine predictions from multiple forecasters and generate a superforecast.

3. MODELING AND EVALUATION

SCADA and forecaster data used for evaluation was spread over 6 months from Feb'14 to July'14 and was collected from a wind farm in south-east India, with power generation capacity of around 75 MW. SCADA data is collected from each turbine in the wind farm at a frequency of 1 (average) reading every 10 minutes. For this wind farm, wind power generator employed four wind power forecasters represented by F-1, F-2, F-3 and F-4 (names anonymized). Each forecaster provides day-ahead-prediction for each 15 minute window. Figure 2a presents the percentage of times each of these forecaster provided the best forecast across all the 15 minute windows over the evaluation period, demonstrating the absence of single accurate forecaster and thus motivating the need to generate a superforecast.

$$\begin{aligned}
X_0 &= \min(P + 0.1A, A), \text{if } P \in [0.9A, 1.1A] \\
X_1 &= \max(\min(P - 1.1A, 0.1A), 0.0), \text{if } P \in [1.1A, 1.2A] \\
X_2 &= \max(\min(P - 1.2A, 0.1A), 0.0), \text{if } P \in [1.2A, 1.3A] \\
X_3 &= \max(\min(P - 1.3A, 0.1A), 0.0), \text{if } P \in [1.3A, 1.4A] \\
X_4 &= \max(\min(P - 1.4A, 0.1A), 0.0), \text{if } P \in [1.4A, 1.5A] \\
X_5 &= \max(P - 1.5A, 0.0), \text{if } P \geq 1.5A \\
X_6 &= \max(\min(0.9A - P, 0.1A), 0.0), \text{if } P \in [0.8A, 0.9A] \\
X_7 &= \max(\min(0.8A - P, 0.1A), 0.0), \text{if } P \in [0.7A, 0.8A] \\
X_8 &= \max(\min(0.7A - P, 0.1A), 0.0), \text{if } P \in [0.6A, 0.7A] \\
X_9 &= \max(\min(0.6A - P, 0.1A), 0.0), \text{if } P \in [0.5A, 0.6A] \\
X_{10} &= \max(0.5A - P, 0.0), \text{if } P \leq 0.5A
\end{aligned} \tag{1}$$

Now we discuss the metric, *penalty*, used for the evaluation of our model. We divide predicted power into the 10 buckets, each of size 10% of the actual power generated. Table-1 shows two scenarios; Case-1: When predicted power (P) is less than actual power generated (A) and Case-2: When predicted power is greater than the actual power generated. Buckets start filling up in order $X_1 \rightarrow X_5$ and in order $X_6 \rightarrow X_{10}$ for Case-1 and Case-2 respectively. Values in each of these buckets are calculated using Equation 1. X_0 represents the exempted part of the predicted power, i.e. $[0.9A, 1.1A]$, corresponding to zero penalty ($p_0 = 0$). Total penalty for any prediction is calculated as weighted sum of power in each bucket (as shown in Equation 2) with weights (p_i) increasing as the predicted power deviates further away from the actual power. We simply assigned $p_i = i \, \forall_{i \in [0,5]}$.
The baseline model, currently used by the generator for selecting the best forecaster, selected the forecaster with least penalty from the previous week and used its day-ahead-prediction for the current week. Our simple regression-based model (Equation 3) learns weights for each forecaster from the last 15 days of SCADA and forecaster data for day-ahead-prediction. We also generate ideal scenario in which we select least penalised forecaster for a day and use prediction from the same forecaster for the same day. This gives us an idea of minimum penalty that we can achieve using our model (when using the same forecaster for the whole day).

$$penalty = p_0^* X_0 + \sum_{i=1}^{5} p_i^* (X_i + X_{i+5}) \tag{2}$$

$$y = \sum_{i=1}^{4} \mathbf{F}_{\mathbf{i}} \times w_i + \epsilon \tag{3}$$

Figure 2b presents monthly distribution of penalty for superforecast in comparison with least penalised forecaster for that month(MLP), baseline scenario and the ideal scenario. Our model reduced the average penalty by 7% and 13% when compared to most accurate forecaster for the month and baseline model, respectively. Figure 2c shows the average of monthly variation in buckets for superforecast, baseline and least penalised forecaster for the month.

4. CONCLUSIONS

Wind is one of the major renewable sources of energy and require accurate day-ahead-prediction for integration into the existing power systems. Wind power generators use multiple forecasters to generate day ahead predictions for their wind farms as their accuracy varies across the year, day and wind speed. In this work, we propose a basic model to generate superforecast using predictions from multiple forecasters to reduce penalty over wind power generators in comparison to their baseline model. We analysed six-month data from a wind farm located in the southern east part of India and results show a reduction of approx. 7% and 13% in terms of penalty when compared with least penalised forecaster for the month and the current heuristic for selecting the best forecaster respectively. We are working on developing improved models to generate superforecast with better accuracy than simple regression-based approach.

5. REFERENCES

[1] The World Wind Energy Association 2014 Half Year Report, year = 2015, note = `http://www.wwindea.org/webimages/WWEA_half_year_report_2014.pdf`.

[2] A. Haque, P. Mandal, H. Nehrir, A. Bhuiya, and R. Baker. A hybrid intelligent framework for wind power forecasting engine. In *Electrical Power and Energy Conference (EPEC), 2014 IEEE*, pages 184–189, Nov 2014.

[3] I. Sánchez. Adaptive combination of forecasts with application to wind energy. *International Journal of Forecasting*, 24(4):679–693, 2008.

[4] Y. Zhang, J. Wang, and X. Wang. Review on probabilistic forecasting of wind power generation. *Renewable and Sustainable Energy Reviews*, 32(0):255 – 270, 2014.

Online Energy Management Strategy for Hybrid Electric Vehicle

Lok To Mak
The Chinese University of Hong Kong

Minghua Chen
The Chinese University of Hong Kong

Guanglin Zhang
Donghua University

Longbo Huang
Tsinghua University

Haibo Zeng
Virginia Tech

ABSTRACT

In this paper, we present an online energy management strategy for parallel hybrid electric vehicle equipped with two power sources. The strategy orchestrates a fuel-based internal combustion engine and an electric motor to minimize total fuel consumption while meeting driving power demand. A unique feature of our proposed strategy is that it is proven to achieve near-optimal performance without the need of knowing any statistical information of the demand. Simulations based on real-world driving traces corroborate our theoretical findings.

1. INTRODUCTION

Hybrid Electric Vehicle (HEV) is a vehicle equipped with two power sources. One is fuel-based internal combustion engine (ICE) and the other is electric motor (EM) powered by battery. An important problem is to minimize the overall fuel consumption by orchestrating power supply from these two sources to meet the driving power demand, by designing intelligent energy management strategies [5].

Various strategies have been purposed; see [5] for a recent survey. A-ECMS [4] is arguably the state-of-the-art strategy that provides an online algorithm achieves decent performance without requiring any statistical information of the driving trace. However, it is known that A-ECMS does not provide any performance guarantee, the overall fuel consumption may be far from the optimal [3]. In this paper, we apply the Lyapunov drift-plus-penalty method [2] to design an easy-to-implement online energy management strategy with provable near-optimal performance and requires no statistical information of the driving power demand. Our proposed strategy is able to achieve average fuel consumption within $O(1/V)$ to the optimal with an $O(V)$ battery capacity, for any $V > 0$. In the following, we first formulate the problem of energy management strategy design and present our solution. We provide performance guarantee for the proposed solution and carry out simulations based on real-world traces to compare its performance against A-ECMS and an offline optimal assuming complete statistical knowledge.

e-Energy'15, July 14 - 17, 2015, Bangalore, India.
ACM 978-1-4503-3609-3/15/07.
http://dx.doi.org/10.1145/2768510.2770954.

2. PROBLEM FORMULATION

We consider parallel HEV, in which ICE and EM can operate in parallel to jointly meet the driving power demand.

Internal combustion engine (ICE): ICE can propel the vehicle and charge battery. $P_e(t)$ denotes the power to satisfy the driving power demand, and it is limited by its ramping constraint $|P_e(t+1)-P_e(t)| \leq P_e^{\max}$. $P_g(t)$ denotes the power to charge the battery. Let the total power output $P_{\text{ice}}(t)$ at time t formulated as $P_{\text{ice}}(t) = P_g(t) + P_e(t)$. We assume $P_{\text{ice}}(t) \leq P_{\text{ice}}^{\max}$. Upon generating $P_{\text{ice}}(t)$ amount of power, the ICE consumes $f(P_{\text{ice}}(t))$ amount of fuel, where $f(\cdot)$ is the fuel consumption function and is assumed to be convex.

Electric Motor (EM): EM draws $b_m(t)$ amount of electricity from battery and outputs power $P_m(t) = g(b_m(t))$ to meet the driving power demand, where $g(\cdot)$ is a power efficiency function and is assumed to be convex. $P_m(t)$ is limited by ramping constraint $|P_m(t+1) - P_m(t)| \leq P_m^{\max}$. We also assume $P_m(t) \leq P_m^{\max}$ for all t.

Power Demand and Braking Power: Given any driving traces, we can obtain the power demand for vehicle acceleration. Let this power demand at time t be $P_d(t)$. It must be jointly satisfied by ICE and EM at any time t; that is, $P_d(t) \leq P_e(t) + P_m(t)$. When the vehicle breaks, certain amount of braking power, denoted by $P_b(t)$, can be harvested to charge the battery.

Battery: State-of-charge of the battery at time t is defined as $q(t)$. Battery discharging power $b_m(t) \leq b_m^{max}$ can provide power to EM. Battery charging power $b_g(t) \leq b_g^{max}$ can charge the battery, which is upper-bounded by the sum of braking power and power from ICE $P_b(t) + P_g(t)$. Let the discharging and charging coefficients be η_m and η_g. The state-of-charge dynamics is then $q(t+1) = q(t) + \eta_g b_g(t) - \eta_m b_m(t)$.

We adopt a discrete-time model where time slot matches the timescale at which the management decisions can be updated. Without loss of generality, we assume there are totally T slots, and each has a unit length. We study the energy management strategy design problem as follows:

$$\min \quad \bar{J} = \frac{1}{T}\sum_{t=1}^{T} f\left(P_{\text{ice}}(t)\right) \tag{1}$$

$$\text{s.t.} \quad |P_{\text{ice}}(t) - P_{\text{ice}}(t-1)| \leq P_{\text{ice}}^{\max} \tag{2}$$

$$|P_m(t) - P_m(t-1)| \leq P_m^{\max} \tag{3}$$

$$b_g(t) \leq P_g(t) + P_b(t) \tag{4}$$

$$P_d(t) \leq P_e(t) + P_m(t) \tag{5}$$

$$0 \leq P_{\text{ice}}(t) \leq P_{\text{ice}}^{\text{ice}}, 0 \leq P_m(t) \leq P_m^{\max}$$
$$0 \leq b_m(t) \leq b_m^{\max}, 0 \leq b_g(t) \leq b_g^{\max} \quad (6)$$
$$q(t+1) = q(t) + \eta_g b_g(t) - \eta_m b_m(t) \quad (7)$$
$$\text{var} \quad P_{\text{ice}}(t), P_m(t), b_g(t), b_m(t), t \in [1, T]$$

The objective function in (1) represents the average fuel consumption in $[1, T]$. Constraints (2)-(3) capture the constraints of maximum changing rate. Constraint (4) states the maximum of battery charging power. Constraint (5) ensures driving power demand must be satisfied. Constraint (6) captures the upper and lower bounds of the power flow variables. Constraint (7) captures the state-of-charge dynamics. The goal is to minimize average fuel consumption, by controlling total ICE power output $P_{\text{ice}}(t)$, EM power output $P_m(t)$, battery charging power $b_g(t)$ and battery discharging power $b_m(t)$ to satisfy the driving power demand $P_d(t)$ in every time slot t, given driving power demand $P_d(t)$ and braking power $P_b(t)$ as inputs. We do not specify any battery constraints as our proposed strategy provides a safety value for battery capacity and ensures the battery will not underflow/overflow.

3. ALGORITHM DESIGN

To construct the energy management strategy, we adapt the Lyapunov drift-plus-penalty approach expounded in [2]. We first define two control parameters $\theta > 0$ and $V > 0$. V controls the performance optimality gap. θ will be specified later. We construct our energy management algorithm using the "min-drift" principle of Lyapunov optimization: at each time slot, choose a pair of feasible battery charging/discharging actions to minimize the cost. Our proposed **Energy Management Strategy** is as follows: at every time slot t,

1. Observe the state-of-charge $q(t)$ and power demand $P_d(t)$. Define the following weights:

$$W_g(t) = \eta_g(q(t) - \theta) + Vf(P_{\text{ice}}(t))$$
$$W_m(t) = \eta_m(q(t) - \theta) + Vf(P_{\text{ice}}(t))g(b_m(t))$$

2. Solve $\min_{b_g(t), b_m(t)} b_g(t)W_g(t) - b_m(t)W_m(t)$ subject to the constraints (2) - (6).

3. Update the battery according to (7) with the chosen $b_g(t), b_m(t)$, and calculate the corresponding fuel usage.

In the algorithm, we only have to solve a linear program with four variables, and it does not require any statistical knowledge of driving power demand. Hence, the algorithm can be easily implemented and the complexity is low.

4. PERFORMANCE ANALYSIS

We now provide performance guarantee for our proposed energy management strategy. Parameter θ is defined as:

$$\theta \triangleq \eta_m \min\left[P_d^{\max}, b_m^{\max}\right] + \frac{V f_{\max} g_{\max}}{\eta_g}$$

where $P_d^{\max}$, $f_{\max}$ and $g_{\max}$ are defined as the maximum driving power demand, maximum fuel consumption rate and maximum EM efficiency, respectively.

THEOREM 1. *(Determine Battery Capacity) Under our proposed energy management strategy, the battery state-of-charge is bounded by:*

$$0 \leq q(t) \leq \theta + \eta_g b_g^{\max}.$$

Theorem 1 shows the state-of-charge never go underflow and is upper bounded; thus we can size the battery capacity accordingly. Combining Theorem 1 and the definition of θ, we can see that a battery capacity of size $O(V)$ is sufficient.

We have the following performance guarantee on the average fuel consumption.

THEOREM 2. *(Performance guarantee) Let $\bar{J}$ be the average fuel consumption achieved by our strategy, and J^* be the optimal average fuel consumption by solving the problem with full statistical knowledge. We have*

$$\bar{J} \leq \frac{B}{V} + J^*$$

where B is a constant.

Theorem 2 guarantees that the fuel consumption is within $O(1/V)$ to the optimal. As we increase the value of V, the battery size increases and the gap to optimal decreases. It shows this strategy forms an $[O(1/V), O(V)]$ optimality gap-battery capacity tradeoff with performance guarantee.

5. SIMULATIONS

Using a real-world driving trace UDDS [1], we evaluate the performance of different algorithms under a reasonable range of battery sizes (0 to 2 kWh) in Fig. 1. We measure the performance of Dynamic Programming (DP), A-ECMS [4] and our proposed strategy. The DP solution with full driving demand knowledge achieve the optimal and serves as a benchmark. The results show that (i) our strategy saves more fuel as battery capacity increases, and (ii) it saves significant amount of fuel even when battery capacity is small. With one kWh battery capacity, our strategy saves about 10% fuel as compared to the state-of-the-art solution A-ECMS.

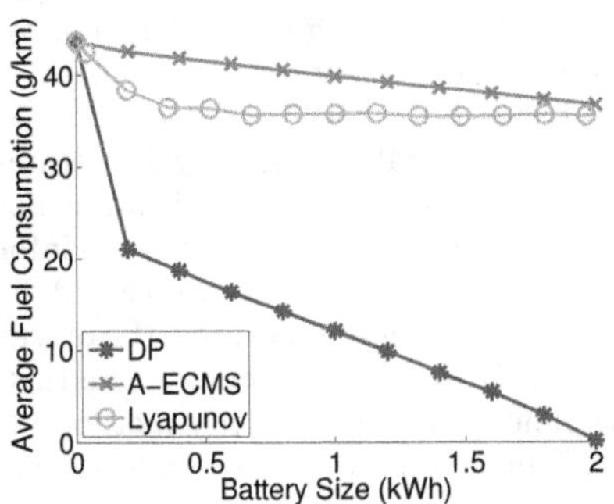

Figure 1: Fuel Efficiency vs. Battery Capacity.

6. REFERENCES

[1] Epa urban dynamometer driving schedule. `http://www.epa.gov/otaq/standards/light-duty/udds.htm`.

[2] L. Huang, J. Walrand, and K. Ramchandran. Optimal Demand Response with Energy Storage Management. In *IEEE SmartGridComm*, 2012.

[3] S. Kutter and B. Bäker. Predictive online control for hybrids: Resolving the conflict between global optimality, robustness and real-time capability. In *IEEE Vehicle Power and Propulsion Conference*, 2010.

[4] C. Musardo, G. Rizzoni, Y. Guezennec, and B. Staccia. A-ECMS: An adaptive algorithm for hybrid electric vehicle energy management. *European Journal of Control*, 11(4):509–524, 2005.

[5] A. Sciarretta and L. Guzzella. Control of hybrid electric vehicles. *IEEE Control Systems*, 27(2):60–70, 2007.

A Multi-objective Optimisation Approach for Energy Efficiency of Backhaul Traffic in Mobile Networks

Tao Lin
Centre for Energy-Efficient Telecommunications
Department of Electrical and Electronic Engineering
University of Melbourne, VIC 3010, Australia
t.lin10@student.unimelb.edu.au

Tansu Alpcan
Department of Electrical and Electronic Engineering
University of Melbourne, VIC 3010, Australia
tansu.alpcan@unimelb.edu.au

Kerry Hinton
Centre for Energy-Efficient Telecommunications
Department of Electrical and Electronic Engineering
University of Melbourne, VIC 3010, Australia
k.hinton@unimelb.edu.au

Arun Vishwanath
IBM Research
Melbourne, VIC 3000, Australia
arvishwa@au.ibm.com

1. INTRODUCTION AND SYSTEM MODEL

Improving the efficiency of mobile networks – in terms of energy consumption and traffic flow – is key to accommodating the growing traffic demand [2]. Prior work on energy efficiency of mobile networks focused on Radio Access Networks (RAN) because the energy consumption of base stations dominate the total energy consumption of current mobile networks [3]. However, this situation could change for next-generation mobile networks where large numbers of small cells will be deployed to meet the increasing demand for coverage and capacity. The move to smaller cells to augment existing macro mobile networks is widely viewed as a potential solution to the RAN congestion problem [4]. But it also creates a new one: that of backhaul capacity [1]. Backhaul requirements for small cells are expected to approach macro cell capacity requirements [1]. Innovations such as small base stations, Remote Radio Head and the GreenTouch consortium's technology "road-map" [2] means the proportion of energy consumed by the backhaul will increase significantly relative to the total energy consumption of the system.

In this paper, we propose an optimisation framework for distributing traffic across a mobile backhaul network in an energy efficient manner. A multi-objective optimisation scheme is developed to explore system power consumption and traffic load balancing tradeoffs. We implement a generic weighted-sum scheme to provide flexible controls over different optimisation objectives. Centralised solutions such as Mixed Integer Programming do not scale in general. We develop a distributed algorithm for mobile data traffic distribution, which requires no centralised information and has the benefit of distributing the computational load over the network. The main contributions of this paper are:

- We develop a general system model for next generation mobile backhaul networks that allows the performance of heterogeneous backhaul technologies to be evaluated and compared.
- The system model encompasses an optimisation framework along with a distributed algorithm to optimise both network power consumption and balancing of load over generic network elements. A layered Lyapunov stability analysis is also applied to illustrate the convergence of the proposed algorithm.
- Extensive simulations using various backhaul scenarios, e.g. fibre-optic, microwave and hybrid technologies, are performed to demonstrate the performance. The simulation results reveal the challenges and opportunities for network operators in planning and managing next generation mobile backhaul networks.

We consider a general system model, which consists of J evolved NodeBs (eNodeB), M virtualised intermediate multiplexing/aggregation (MUX) nodes, I virtualised Serving Gateway (S-GW) nodes and L links connecting those nodes as shown Fig. 1. The system has in sum $N = I + M + L$ *resources* for eNodeBs to share. Let $r \in \{1, \cdots, R\}$ (R number of routes from eNodeBs to S-GWs) label a predefined route carrying average traffic $\mathbf{d}_r$ from a eNodeB to a S-GW such that the traffic on all routes can be expressed as a vector $\mathbf{d} = [\mathbf{d}_1, \cdots, \mathbf{d}_R]^T$. An eNodeB is pre-allocated with a portion of $\mathbf{d}$. All traffic generated by eNodeBs can be expressed as a vector $\mathbf{d}^{\text{in}} = [\mathbf{d}_1^{\text{in}}, \cdots, \mathbf{d}_J^{\text{in}}]^T$. The topology of the system in Fig. 1 can be represented by a $N \times R$ matrix $\mathbf{A}$, which maps each *resource* to the route such that $\mathbf{A}_{n,r} = 1$ indicates route r is via *resource* n and $\mathbf{A}_{n,r} = 0$ indicates otherwise.

We formulate a traffic distribution problem in order to find the optimal traffic $\mathbf{d}$ for all eNodeBs such that the associated cost function is minimised. Currently, network equipment is always turned on to handle the peak time traffic, even

e-Energy'15, July 14–17, 2015, Bangalore, India.
ACM 978-1-4503-3594-2/15/06.
http://dx.doi.org/10.1145/2768510.2770941.

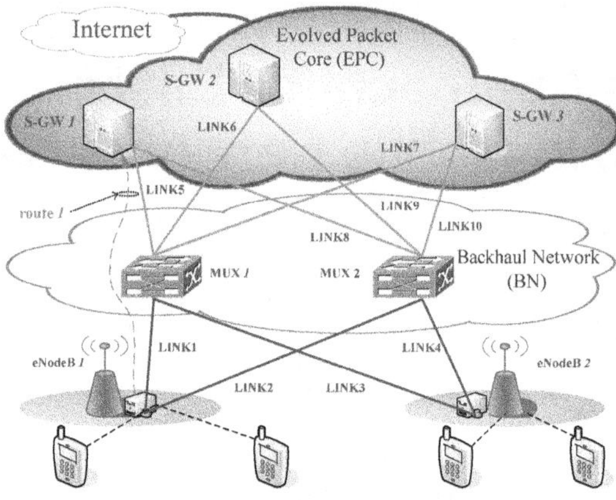

Figure 1: System model for mobile backhaul networks with 2 eNodeB, 2 MUX and 3 S-GW nodes.

if the carried traffic is nearly zero. To reduce power consumption, network resources are "switched-off" when they carry no traffic [5]. We apply the weighted sum method to construct a cost function where two potentially conflicting objectives are considered: (1) total system power consumption minimisation weighted by $(1-\omega)$ and (2) system traffic load balancing weighted by ω, where ω denotes the operator's preference. Two constraints are introduced: the first one governs the input traffic flow conservation (input traffic band width guarantee), and the second ensures that the aggregate traffic on each *resource* shall not exceed its corresponding processing capacity.

2. ALGORITHM AND RESULTS

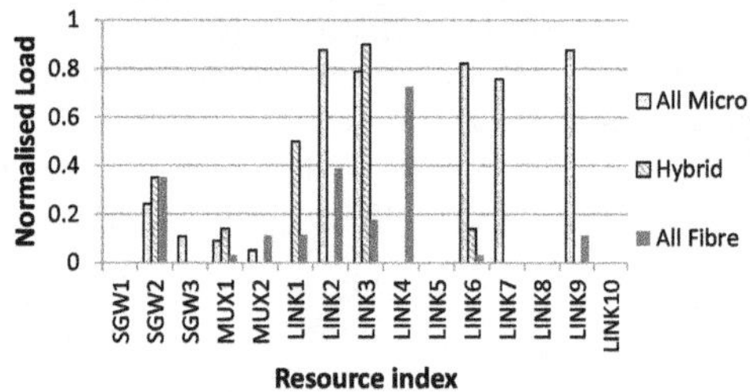

Figure 2: Resource normalised load with $\omega = 0.5$

First, we observe that the joint optimisation problem is convex with the associated linear constraints. This enables us to derive the equivalent Lagrangian for the joint optimisation problem and the constraints. The Lagrangian formulation is further decomposed into J sub-problems for each eNodeB, which are also convex problems. By applying an iterative "pricing" feedback mechanism, a discrete-time and distributed dynamic gradient method is used to derive the optimal $\mathbf{d}^*$. Each iteration comprises two steps: First the Lagrangian multipliers for constraints are adjusted based on the updates of traffic $\mathbf{d}$. Second each subproblem $j = 1, \cdots, J$ is solved by adjusting the subset of $\mathbf{d}$ for eNodeB j, given the updated Lagrangian multipliers. To discuss the stability of the proposed algorithm, we impose a time-scale separation between dynamics in the iterative algorithm and apply Lyapunov stability analysis for each step.

We use Matlab to simulate the proposed distributed solution for mobile backhaul traffic distribution considering a simple network shown in Fig. 1. In order to show the impact of different backhaul links on the network performance, we propose three different test cases: (1) all fibre backhaul links

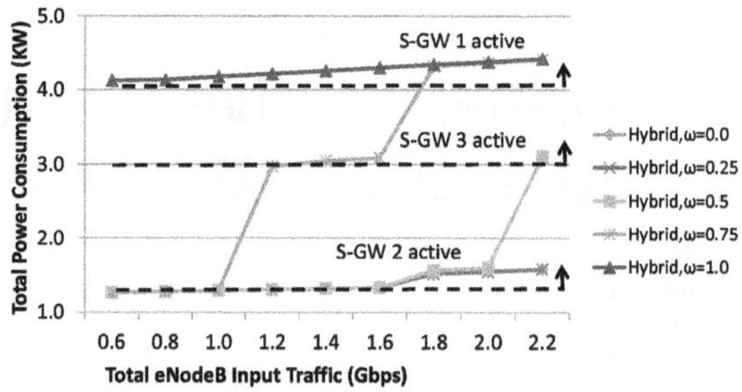

Figure 3: System power consumption

("All Fibre"), (2) hybrid backhaul links ("Hybrid") and (3) all microwave backhaul links ("All Micro"). Fig. 2 illustrates the impact of using different backhaul technologies on the normalised load over all *resources*. Fig. 3 shows the system power consumption as a function of $\mathbf{d}^{\text{in}}$ for different weighting factors ω for the "Hybrid" case. When $\omega = 0$, i.e. the operator wishes to minimise only the power consumption, all traffic is directed towards the least energy consuming gateway (in this case S-GW 2) via the most energy efficient links. As ω is increased, other gateways and links get activated. This increases the power consumption of the network but comes with the benefit of balancing the network load.

3. CONCLUSIONS

Improving the energy efficiency of mobile networks is an important problem for network operators. However, realising this objective should not be at the expense of undermining network performance. In this paper, we have developed a generalised framework that allows an operator to evaluate the tradeoff between energy efficiency and performance. Further, as part of network planning, it is important to decide which backhaul technology to use and where to implement it on the network topology. We have shown via the framework that changes to the backhaul technology links could result in very different performance (Fig. 2). In addition, handling dynamic network traffic in an energy efficient manner requires traffic-adaptive network management. The results in Fig. 3 shows that the diurnal characteristic of traffic – low during the night and high during the day – provides opportunities to improve network energy efficiency by changing the effective routing topology of the network. The network operator can choose the ω (dynamically) that is most suitable to their operating requirements.

4. REFERENCES

[1] Easy small cell backhaul an analysis of small backhaul requirement and comparision of solutions. `http://www.academia.edu/4402938/Easy_Small_Cell_Backhaul_v0_9_5`, Feb 2012.

[2] Greentouch green meter research study: Reducing the net energy consumption in communications networks by up to 90% by 2020. `http://www.greentouch.org/uploads/documents/GreenTouch_Green_Meter_Research_Study_26_June_2013.pdf`, Jan 2013.

[3] D. Feng et al. A survey of energy-efficient wireless communications. *Communications Surveys Tutorials, IEEE*, PP(99):1 –12, 2012.

[4] J. Hoydis, M. Kobayashi, and M. Debbah. Green small-cell networks. *Vehicular Technology Magazine, IEEE*, 6(1):37 –43, Mar 2011.

[5] Z. Niu. TANGO: traffic-aware network planning and green operation. *Wireless Communications, IEEE*, 18(5):25 –29, Oct 2011.

Towards Virtual Sensors for Estimating the Electricity Consumption of Networked Appliances

Patrick Lieser, Frank Englert, Alaa Alhamoud, Daniel Burgstahler, Doreen Boehnstedt
Multimedia Communications Lab
TU Darmstadt, Germany
firstname.lastname@kom.tu-darmstadt.de

ABSTRACT

In modern environments, more and more "smart appliances" exist. Those devices are equipped with sensors to measure their internal state and environmental variables, with processing power, and also with networking capabilities. To make these appliances aware of their own electricity expenditure we propose the concept of virtual electricity sensors. Instead of adding dedicated hardware sensors, we use the device integrated sensors in conjunction with an energy model to estimate the actual power draw based on the current device state. First results indicate that this approach leads to an accuracy of up to 98% for various smart appliances. Our approach leads to cost-efficient fine grained electricity metering for future smart appliances.

1. INTRODUCTION

According to recent studies, the electricity consumption of consumer electronics has grown by +18% over the last decade (cf. Residential Energy Consumption Survey 2009). With the rise of the Internet of things, we expect this growth to continue. While traditional electricity consumption monitoring systems could supervise these loads, their application is often not beneficial from a financial point of view. The cost for these metering systems often outweighs the potential savings [1]. Thus, we present an alternative approach which significantly reduces the cost of electricity metering by replacing hardware circuitry with software components.
So-called "smart appliances" are equipped with a variety of different sensors. The core idea of our work is to infer the electricity consumption of smart appliances solely from sensor data which is available by accessing the sensors already installed. This methodology leads to three main advantages:

1. A reduction of costs as no dedicated current sensors are required for monitoring the electricity consumption.
2. A reduction of complexity as the total number of sensors in an environment decreases.
3. The capability to implement novel feedback and interaction services on systems aware of their own consumption.

e-Energy'15, July 14–17, 2015, Bangalore, India
ACM 978-1-4503-3609-3/15/07.
http://dx.doi.org/10.1145/2768510.2770942

2. RELATED WORKS

Related works exist in two areas: First, our approach competes with load disaggregation methods and distributed electricity sensors in the area of smart homes. In this area a lot of effort has led to higher accuracies[2] and better scalability [3]. However, using this technology, it is impossible to influence the monitored environment. On the other hand, distributed electricity meters have a rather poor scalability of one sensor per appliance. Second, our work adopts techniques for system modeling from the field of energy efficient computing. In order to make computing machinery more energy efficient, models are used to determine the electricity consumption of different subtasks. E.g. Kansal [4] uses energy models to optimize the utilization of servers in data centers which leads to huge electricity savings. Zhang [5] enhances the battery life of smart phones by making the owner aware of energy consuming apps. What both approaches have in common is that manually fine-tuned models are used to express the power consumption based on the current system load.

3. VIRTUAL ELECTRICITY SENSORS

As illustrated in Figure 1, energy models consist of three major steps. First, the sensors with data relating to power consumption are selected from all available sensors for further processing. The selection of relevant sensors is either made manually by domain experts or automatically by calculating a correlation coefficient between the sensor data stream and the appliance's electricity consumption. Second, the omnipresent time-lag between each sensor data stream and the power consumption data stream is compensated for. Finding appropriate factors for the delay compensation is rather challenging if events indicated by the sensor data and their impact on the electricity consumption do not follow one another promptly. Finally, a regression algorithm is used to calculate the actual power consumption based on the selected and shifted sensor readings.
In order to adopt this rather general model to particular appliances, we developed a non-parametric training algorithm for energy models. This algorithm factors in time series of sensor data as well as the corresponding time series of power recordings for the appliances obtained from an externally connected power meter. Based on this input data, our algorithm selects relevant sensors, compensates for the time lag and inputs the data into an appropriate regression model. To do so, our training algorithm parametrizes the energy model with appropriate, non-zero default values and calculates the resulting accuracy on a subset of the training

Figure 1: Overview of components for the energy model.

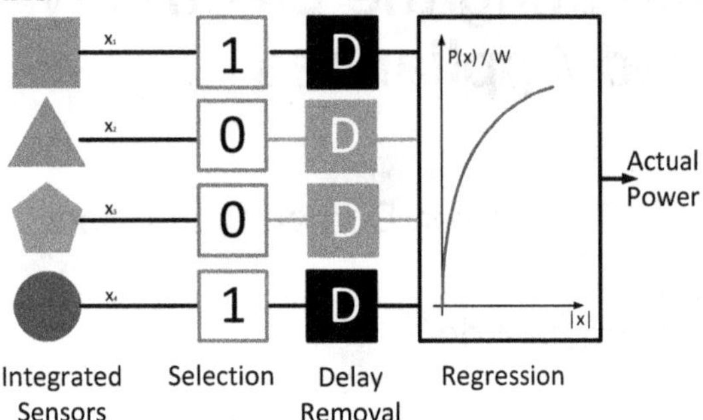

data. Based on that, our algorithm varies model parameters in order to maximize the resulting model accuracy. We use the mean squared error between the predicted instantaneous power draw and the measured power draw as fitness function for this optimization.

4. EVALUATION

In order to test the real world applicability of virtual electricity sensors, it is important to consider three important properties:

1. *Accuracy* of predictions.
2. *Adaptability* to different appliances.
3. *Consumption overhead* due to additional calculations.

To determine the *accuracy* of virtual electricity sensors we compare the predicted power demand with the actual power demand obtained from an external power meter. The *accuracy* should be as high as possible in each individual prediction step and over a long period of time the difference between the predicted and measured energies should be as low as possible. As shown in Table 1, our virtual electricity sensors already achieve good *accuracy*.
The property of *adaptability* states how well virtual electricity sensors generalize for arbitrary appliances without requiring manual fine-tuning during the fitting of the model parameters. Currently, we test for this property by applying energy models to different appliances and testing the *accuracy* of the resulting energy model (cf. Table 1). However, a more systematic approach would be desirable to quantify this property. Last but not least, the *consumption overhead* of the virtual electricity sensors themselves should be as low as possible. By running the calculations on embedded processors, the energy demand for those calculations should be as low as possible. Furthermore, embedded systems are often carefully optimized for low resource demand and thus low prices. The hardware requirements should not change due to the inclusion of virtual electricity sensors.

5. APPLICATION SCENARIO

Virtual electricity sensors can be applied in a wide spectrum of environments. The technology is useful in residential homes to estimate the electricity consumption of multimedia appliances. However, we expect this technology to have an even greater impact on office- and industrial environments with a multitude of different networked appliances. In this field, virtual electricity sensors offer deep insights into causes of high electricity consumption whilst requiring nearly no financial investment.

Table 1: Results of the Regression Algorithm with energy models for different networked appliances

Machine	Regressor	e_{tabs}	Class
Dell 1	ERFR	2.067 %	3
Lenovo 1	ERFR	0.683 %	3
Lenovo 2	KNNR	2.685 %	3
Macbook	LassoR	0.162 %	3
Gaming PC	LassoR	3.400 %	3
Philips Hue	KNNR	4.539%	2
Fan	RFR	1.322%	1
Canon Printer	ERFR	3.757%	1..2
Vending Machine	DTR	10.8%	1

6. CONCLUSION AND OUTLOOK

Our concept of virtual sensors for measuring the electricity demand of networked appliances has great potential to simplify the task of electricity metering with a high level of detail in a cost-efficient manner. Our current implementation is capable of determining the power draw of office appliances with an accuracy of up to 98% without adding additional hardware sensors. Furthermore, we have developed a non-parametric algorithm to train energy models for virtual sensors and showed its applicability for six different classes of office appliances. In the future, we plan to apply the technique of virtual electricity sensors to a much broader spectrum of electrical appliances.

7. ACKNOWLEDGEMENTS

This work was funded by the German Federal Ministry of Education and Research (Support Code: 01IS12054). Co-funding was provided by the Social Link Project within the Loewe Program of Excellence in Research, Hessen, Germany. The authors are fully responsible for the content of this work.

8. REFERENCES

[1] F. Englert, I. Diaconita, A. Reinhardt, A. Alhamoud, R. Meister, L. Backert, and R. Steinmetz, "Reduce the Number of Sensors - Sensing Acoustic Emissions to Estimate Appliance Energy Usage," in *BuildSys'13*. New York, New York, USA: ACM Press, 2013.

[2] O. Parson, S. Ghosh, M. Weal, and A. Rogers, "An Unsupervised Training Method for Non-Intrusive Appliance Load Monitoring," *Artificial Intelligence*, pp. 1–42, 2014.

[3] S. N. Patel, S. Gupta, and M. S. Reynolds, "The Design and Evaluation of an End-user-deployable, whole House, Contactless Power Consumption Sensor," in *CHI '10*. New York, NY, USA: ACM, 2010, pp. 2471–2480.

[4] A. Kansal, F. Zhao, and A. A. Bhattacharya, "Virtual Machine Power Metering and Provisioning Categories and Subject Descriptors," in *Proceedings of the 1st ACM symposium on Cloud computing*, 2010, pp. 39–50.

[5] L. Zhang, B. Tiwana, Z. Qian, Z. Wang, R. P. Dick, Z. M. Mao, and L. Yang, "Accurate Online Power Estimation and Automatic Battery Behavior Based Power Model Generation for Smartphones," in *CODES/ISSS '10*. New York, NY, USA: ACM, 2010, pp. 105–114.

Poster Abstract: Towards NILM for Industrial Settings

Emil Holmegaard
Center for Energy Informatics
The Maersk Mc-Kinney Moller Institute
University of Southern Denmark, Denmark
em@mmmi.sdu.dk

Mikkel Baun Kjærgaard
Center for Energy Informatics
The Maersk Mc-Kinney Moller Institute
University of Southern Denmark, Denmark
mbkj@mmmi.sdu.dk

ABSTRACT

Industry consumes a large share of the worldwide electricity consumption. Disaggregated information about electricity consumption enables better decision-making and feedback tools to optimize electricity consumption. In industrial settings electricity loads consist of a variety of equipment, which can be difficult to monitor individually due to cost restrictions. We believe that Non-Intrusive Load Monitoring (NILM) can ease the burden of such a monitoring infrastructure. This hypothesis has been preliminary evaluated by collecting a data set, from more than forty sensors, measuring power consumption for six months, at an industrial site. In this poster abstract we provide initial results for how industrial equipment challenge NILM algorithms. These results thereby open up for evaluating the use of NILM in industrial settings.

Categories and Subject Descriptors

H.4 [**Information Systems Applications**]: Miscellaneous

Keywords

Disaggregation; Energy Efficiency; Data Analysis; Smart Meters; Electricity; NILM; Industry

1. INTRODUCTION

Industry consumes a large share of the worldwide electricity consumption. In fact industries accounts for around 30% of the total electricity consumption in the US[1] and Denmark[2]. Therefore improvements in the electricity consumption can have a significant impact on a national and worldwide scale. For illustrating how much electricity industry consumes, we consider a real example; For a year the cold store, used as case in our work, consumes the same amount of electricity as 2040 average four-person households[3]. Carrie Armel *et al.* [2] argue that equipment augmented with feedback can reduce the electricity consumption with more than 12% in the residential sector, and Darby *et al.* [4] points to results in the range of 5-15%. The cold store case illustrates that it potentially could be more effective to apply saving efforts in one cold store, than trying to implement systems for reducing electricity consumption in 2040 residential houses. In addition to feedback tools with disaggregated information, one can provide knowledge for decision-making in general, e.g., for replacing inefficient equipment or optimization of work procedures.

Since Hart [5] introduced Non-Intrusive Load Monitoring (NILM) for disaggregation of electricity consumption, almost all research efforts have been focusing on the residential sector [7]. NILM in industrial settings require new assumptions as equipment, load levels and temporal patterns are different. This poster abstract present initial results for the challenges of using NILM in industrial settings.

[1]`http://goo.gl/1g4FzU`, accessed 01.05.15
[2]`http://goo.gl/iQ1UPy`, accessed 01.05.15
[3]`http://goo.gl/1XDQGI`, accessed 01.05.15

e-Energy'15 July 14-17, 2015, Bangalore, India

ACM 978-1-4503-3609-3/15/07
http://dx.doi.org/10.1145/2768510.2770943.

2. INDUSTRIAL SETTINGS

In this section we present an initial analysis of collected data from a cold store to characterize the electricity consumption of industrial equipment. The analysis focuses on characteristics relevant to the performance of NILM disaggregation including power level change events and power states. For the analysis we have collected electricity consumption data from a cold store located in the Danish city of Vejle. The data set covers forty electricity sensors in the cold store from the period 01-06-2014 to 01-12-2014 with a one minute resolution. The temperature inside a cold store is restricted to minimum $-18°C$ or lower. For the data collection forty sensors have been installed to sub-meter loads. The sensors sub-meter 16% of the total consumption in the cold store. The sensors are allocated to equipment with eighteen sensors for compressors, eight sensors for light, five for industrial fans, three for condensers and two for evaporators. The forty sensors monitor pure loads without influence of other equipment.

2.1 Power Changes

Power change events indicate how often equipment are going from one state to another. We define a power change event as a change of $\pm\Delta p$ W between two electricity consumption samples. The value of Δp is in the following set to 10W following previous research, eg., this is the minimum event value used by the open-source toolkit NILMTK [1]. For understanding the collected data set, we have analysed change events for each type of equipment. We have split the counts into hours of the day, to evaluate if there are any hourly patterns. Figure 1 shows histograms for the dominant equipment in the cold store, like compressors and condenser. For comparison the figure also includes a histogram for a residential house computed for the sockets of house one in the REDD data set [6].

From Figure 1 it is clear that the compressor has a high number of events, between 1800 and 2800 events, peaking in the afternoon. For most of the equipment there is an increase in events around 20-21 and 05-06, this increment most likely relates to day and

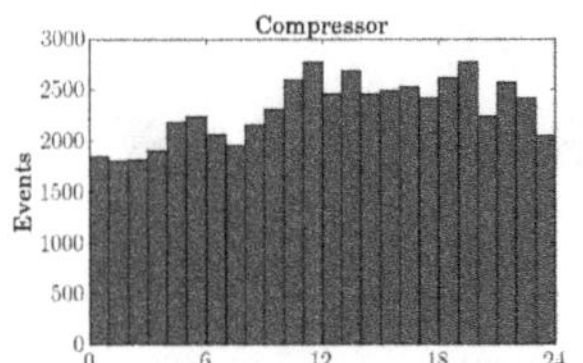

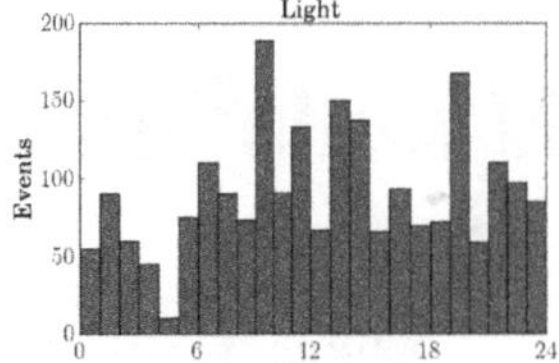

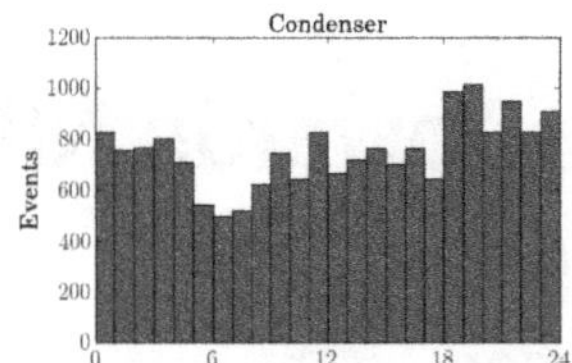

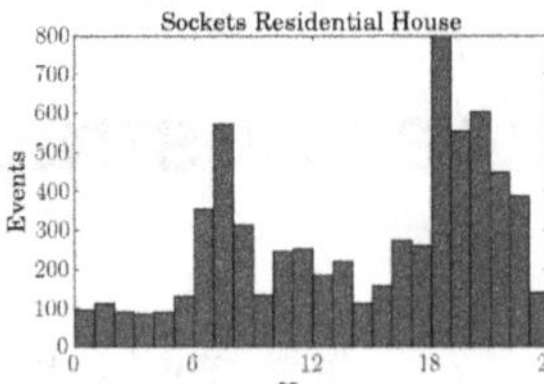

Figure 1: Events within a specific hour of the day for compressor, condenser, light and a residential household.

night temperature set points. One might expect an event pattern in relation to when the workers arrive and leave the cold store. However, no such pattern is present, as the influence of the workers are too small compared to the process loads. Furthermore, some of the equipment used directly by workers, e.g. electrical forklifts, has been left out of the study due to the sensor setup.

In comparison, the residential house data set, has a clear pattern of events in the morning(7-9) and in the evening(18-23). This pattern was expected as the occupants wake up and make breakfast, leave the house during the day, and then in the afternoon arrive, cook for dinner and use other electrical equipment.

2.2 Power States

The task of disaggregation depends on learning a model, of possible power states for each type of equipment. The equipment in a cold store is expected to have multiple states, as observed by Chang *et al.* [3] who have described load signatures of industry equipment. Compressors can be managed as a Variable Frequency Drive (VFD) and therefore potentially have infinite many operation levels. Other equipment might also be managed as a VFD using frequency converters. Figure 2 shows the distribution of electricity consumption in descending order for a condenser and a compressor. Figure 2 identify that the equipment do have several plateaus in the ordered power draw, indicating individual power states. We apply k-means clustering with $k=3$, which is also the clustering type used by NILMTK [1]. The clustering results are shown in Figure 2 by color codes.

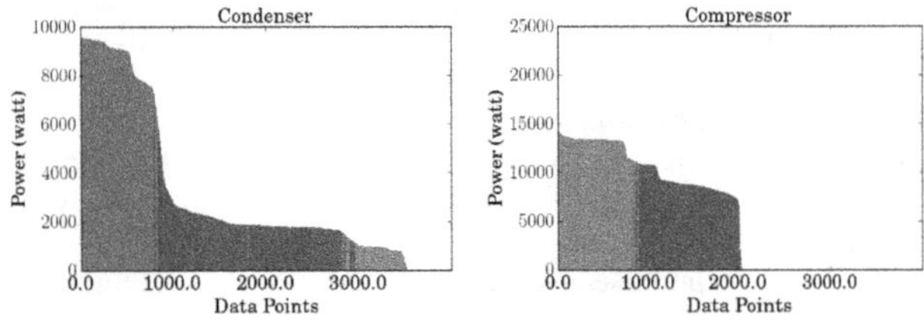

Figure 2: Ordered power draw for condenser and compressor.

The slope of the ordered power draw for the compressor in Figure 2 has several plateaus, indicating that the compressor is managed more like a on/off device than a VFD. The technical manager at the cold store, verified that they have minimized ramp times, to obtain higher efficiency of the equipment at specific operation levels. The clustering of the data identifies two major states and one ramp state for the compressor. However, for the condenser the clustering have found three states but six states can be visually identified by the plateaus in the ordered power draw.

3. NILM CHALLENGES

The study indicate that the industrial loads have significantly different usage patterns than residential households. Furthermore, the loads have a larger variety in consumption, as seen in Figure 1. The number of events in industrial settings, can make it very difficult to disaggregate, due to the Switch Continuity Principle [5]. Furthermore the industrial equipment, have multiple states, see Figure 2, which will make it a computational challenge.

Chang *et al.* [3] states that VFDs can be hard to disaggregate. We have studied a data set from a cold store, and found that some types of equipment have a characterization as VFDs, e.g., condenser. We have also found that several types of equipment excepted to be VFDs, are in practice managed like on/off devices, e.g., compressor. The condenser might be difficult to disaggregate, due to the number of states.

The work of this paper open up for further research on particular challenges for introduce NILM in industrial settings. Future work will include modification of standard NILM algorithms to take our findings into account.

Acknowledgment

The authors would like to thank European Regional Development Fund (The Region of Southern Denmark) for funding the Micro Grid Living Lab project.

4. REFERENCES

[1] BATRA, N., KELLY, J., PARSON, O., DUTTA, H., KNOTTENBELT, W., ROGERS, A., SINGH, A., AND SRIVASTAVA, M. Nilmtk: An open source toolkit for non-intrusive load monitoring.

[2] CARRIE ARMEL, K., GUPTA, A., SHRIMALI, G., AND ALBERT, A. Is disaggregation the holy grail of energy efficiency? the case of electricity. *Energy Policy 52* (2013), 213–234.

[3] CHANG, H.-H., YANG, H.-T., AND LIN, C.-L. Load identification in neural networks for a non-intrusive monitoring of industrial electrical loads. In *Computer Supported Cooperative Work in Design IV*. Springer, 2008, pp. 664–674.

[4] DARBY, S. The effectiveness of feedback on energy consumption. *A Review for DEFRA of the Literature on Metering, Billing and direct Displays 486* (2006).

[5] HART, G. W. Nonintrusive appliance load monitoring. *Proceedings of the IEEE 80*, 12 (1992), 1870–1891.

[6] KOLTER, J. Z., AND JOHNSON, M. J. Redd: A public data set for energy disaggregation research. In *In SustKDD* (2011).

[7] PARSON, O., GHOSH, S., WEAL, M., AND ROGERS, A. Non-intrusive load monitoring using prior models of general appliance types. In *AAAI* (2012).

The SPOT* System for Flexible Personal Heating and Cooling

Alimohammad Rabbani and S. Keshav
School of Computer Science, University of Waterloo
Waterloo, Ontario, Canada
{amrabban, keshav}@uwaterloo.ca

ABSTRACT

SPOT* is a cost-effective, legacy-compatible, flexible system for personalized heating and cooling. It senses occupancy and worker comfort uses the Predicted Mean Vote equation to determine worker comfort. It then actuates a fan or a heater to adjust the comfort level so that it lies between -0.5 and +0.5 in the ASHRAE comfort scale. SPOT* greatly reduces costs compared to our prior SPOT and SPOT+ systems by using the fewest possible sensors and a lightweight compute engine that can be located in the cloud. Moreover, SPOT* provides both cooling and heating using a speed-controlled desktop fan, rather than only controlling heating using a radiant heater. Finally, SPOT* is less intrusive in that it does not use a camera. The per-user cost for SPOT* is about $185 compared to $1000 for SPOT/SPOT+. We find that in a preliminary deployment, SPOT* is able to improve user comfort by 78% over legacy systems alone.

Categories and Subject Descriptors

H.4.0 [**Information Systems Applications**]: General

General Terms

Design, Human Factors

Keywords

HVAC, Personalization, Human Thermal Comfort, Energy Management

1. INTRODUCTION

SPOT* is a low-cost, flexible, legacy-compatible *personal thermal comfort system.* It bridges the gap between the comfort provided by a legacy central HVAC and individual worker preferences. By allowing the central HVAC to use higher temperature set points in summer and lower ones in winter, SPOT* can reduce energy usage. Thus SPOT* can reduce building energy use yet ensure that workers are always comfortable.

e-Energy'15, July 14-17, 2015, Bangalore, India
ACM 978-1-4503-2782-4/14/04.
http://dx.doi.org/10.1145/2768510.2770944.

This work extends prior work on the SPOT and SPOT+ personal thermal control systems [1, 2]. Both systems use the Predicted Personal Vote (PPV) model (described below) to automatically adjust room heating to maintain a desired comfort level. SPOT is *reactive*, in that it only heats the room when the worker is actually present, and SPOT+ is *pro-active*, pre-heating the workspace before the arrival of the worker, or turn off heating in anticipation of the worker's departure.

SPOT* differs from both systems in five significant ways. First, it controls *both* heating and cooling, so can be used both in winter and in summer. Second, it is about an order of magnitude *less expensive.* Third, it implements an innovative software architecture that allows *flexible tradeoffs* between cost, privacy, and data durability. Specifically, it allows most software components to execute either on the thermal controller, in the Internet cloud, or on the worker's smartphone. Fourth, the use of a fan instead of a radiant heater makes it possible to *rapidly react* to worker discomfort. Finally, it is far less intrusive than our two prior systems, because it does not use a camera.

Our work makes the following contributions:

- We have designed SPOT*, a low-cost, flexible personalized workspace thermal control system.
- We have built four SPOT* devices in two different configurations in a real testbed.
- We find that SPOT* improves average user comfort by 78% in our deployment.

2. DESIGN SKETCH

Our main design goal was to reduce costs and our secondary goals were to allow both heating and cooling and to keep office occupancy data private. We first outline SPOT*'s architecture, then discuss how these goals were met.

SPOT* is composed from five components: sensors, actuators, control logic, data store, and user interface (Figure 1). Each software component shown on the right hand side can be executed on a per-office embedded compute platform (a Raspberry Pi), in the cloud, or on a worker's smartphone.

Sensors detect worker occupancy (using the approach discussed by Hailemariam et al [3]) and comfort (using a temperature sensor and using default values for all other PMV parameters). Actuators turn on a fan or a fan as well as a heater to cool or heat the worker, respectively. Logic computes the PPV from sensed data and decides on actuation levels. The data store stores historical sensor data and system events. Finally, the user interface allows the user to correct for errors in the PPV model and to override control decisions.

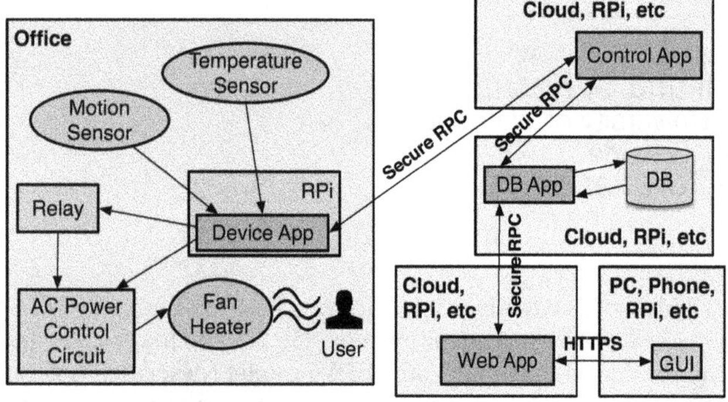

Figure 1: SPOT* has 5 main components. Actuation and sensing (left box), control application, data storage, web application, and graphical user interface. All software components communicate through RPC to allow easy deployment of different configurations.

To reduce costs, we replace the expensive Kinect sensor and the per-office PC-based processing unit with a simple motion sensor and a Raspberry Pi B+ (RPi). The RPi costs only about $40 compared to $500-PC used in SPOT. Without the Kinect, we are unable to automatically detect the worker's clothing level. Instead, we assume that the clothing insulation factor is 0.6*clo*, and provide a simple web-based user interface for workers to tune their comfort set-point to reflect a different clothing insulation factor. To further reduce costs, we also reduced the number of sensors: SPOT* measures air temperature using a temperature sensor and assumes that this temperature is identical to the background radiant temperature. It also computes air velocity as a function of the fan speed (which is known), and given that SPOT* is deployed in an HVAC-controlled office space, it assumes that the humidity is controlled to 50%, and that the worker's metabolic rate is 1.2*met*.

Most SPOT* software components can execute either on the RPi, in the cloud, or on the user's smartphone, using python's RPyC library in SSL mode for communications. By flexible composition and location of these elements, SPOT* allows tradeoffs between cost, privacy, and data durability. For instance, if all the elements are in the workspace, the system is expensive, but private. If software elements are in the cloud, instead, the cost is reduced but privacy can be compromised.

Thus, our system meets our design goals.

3. EVALUATION

We built four SPOT* devices and deployed them in offices at the University of Waterloo. At the time of writing this paper, we have data from this deployment for about 25 days.

We measured the effectiveness of SPOT* in maintaining user comfort using the average absolute discomfort[2] in the presence and absence of the SPOT* during the 25-day period. We calculate the average absolute discomfort of users with and without SPOT*. Instead of measuring this value after turning off control actions, note that SPOT* performs no control actions when the workspace is unoccupied. So, the average absolute discomfort when the workspace is unoccupied is identical to its expected value in the *absence* of SPOT*. Thus, to measure average discomfort in absence of SPOT*, we simply define:

$$\dot{d} = \frac{\Sigma_{t=0}^{T} d(t)m'(t)}{\Sigma_{t=0}^{T} m'(t)} \qquad (1)$$

where $m'(t)$ is 0 when the user is present and 1 when the the workspace is not occupied (i.e., $m' = 1 - m$).

The average $\hat{d}$ for all four users is 0.16 compared to 0.73 for $\dot{d}$. Therefore, SPOT* improves user comfort by 78% in this trial (see Figure 2 for details).

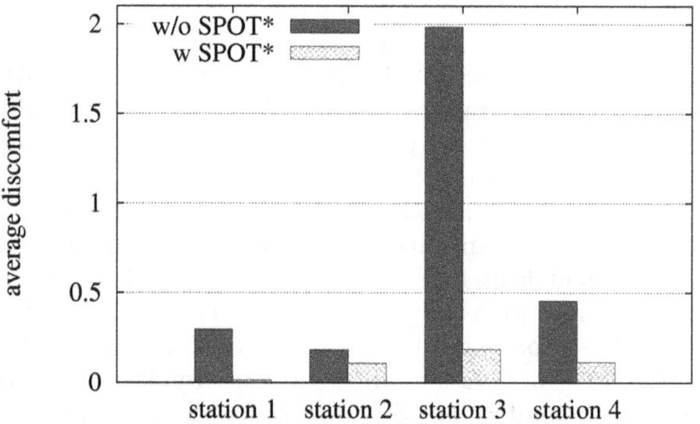

Figure 2: Average discomfort of users when SPOT* is being used, and when it is not being used. For each user, the average discomfort decreases significantly when SPOT* is maintaining comfort.

4. FUTURE WORK

We are currently in the process of deploying an additional 60 instances of SPOT* and will report on the results from this deployment in future work.

5. REFERENCES

[1] Peter Xiang Gao and Srinivasan Keshav. SPOT: a smart personalized office thermal control system. In *Proceedings of the fourth international conference on Future energy systems*, pages 237–246. ACM, 2013.

[2] Peter Xiang Gao and S Keshav. Optimal Personal Comfort Management Using SPOT+. In *Proceedings of the 5th ACM Workshop on Embedded Systems For Energy-Efficient Buildings*, pages 1–8. ACM, 2013.

[3] Ebenezer Hailemariam, Rhys Goldstein, Ramtin Attar, and Azam Khan. Real-time occupancy detection using decision trees with multiple sensor types. In *Proceedings of the 2011 Symposium on Simulation for Architecture and Urban Design*, pages 141–148. Society for Computer Simulation International, 2011.

Enabling Practical Demand Response in Highly-Stressed Grids using Aashiyana

Zohaib Sharani, Noman Bashir, Khushboo Qayyum, Affan A. Syed
National University of Computer & Emerging Sciences
Islamabad, Pakistan
first.last@sysnet.org.pk

ABSTRACT

This paper targets the unexplored problem of demand response in highly-stressed grids. We present here a novel building DLC system, Aashiyana, that can enforce several user-defined low-power states. We evaluate distributed and centralized load-shedding schemes using Aashiyana that can, compared to current load-shedding strategy, reduce the number of homes with *no* power by > 80% for minor change in the fraction of homes with full-power.

1. INTRODUCTION

Demand response (DR) is a smart-grid technology allowing grid to communicate a demand decrease request to meet supply, using indirect (pricing) or direct (through some control) signals. We however argue that most DLC work has focused on *over-provisioned* grid systems of developed countries, with a focus on increasing revenue and reliability [5], but remains largely blind to the unique characteristics of *highly-stressed grids* of countries (like Pakistan, Nepal, and India) with a very large and nearly continuous supply-demand gap. As an example, for Pakistan, this gap can be as high as 6GW during summers, but stays around 1.2GW even during the winter months (2011-2012). The (largely national) utilities in these countries enforce periodic events of controlled black-outs, or load-shedding, to relieve this stress. Existing DLC mechanisms allow for control events, like changing HVAC set-points, or possibly for controlling the AC for a few hours a day [3]. These mechanism are **inadequate in their magnitude as well as flexibility** for managing the large and continuous gaps that exist in highly-stressed grids.

We believe that the consumers in a highly-stressed grid — being acclimatized to frequent blackouts — are much more amenable to aggressive DLC mechanisms and thus willing to accept a wider-range of load-shedding policies. *We thus propose instrumenting homes with a system that provides utilities with transitions to several* ***low-power states*** *that map to user-specified appliances.*

In this paper we design and evaluate a novel and practical home-level DLC system solution, *Aashiyana*, that can implement several user-configurable power-states of a home. This system is practical as it can retrofit into the existing wiring scheme of homes; is of low cost while controlling most appliances in a home; provides home consumers a flexible way to describe these lower-power states as a compact disconnectivity matrix requiring one-time configuration.

e-Energy'15, July 14–17, 2015, Bangalore, India.
ACM ACM 978-1-4503-3609-3/15/07.
http://dx.doi.org/10.1145/2768510.2770945.

2. AASHIYANA: A PRACTICAL SYSTEM TO IMPLEMENT POWER CONTROL

Our major focus is to design a system that can enforce a consumption budget at each home, while allowing the users the ability to flexibly configure devices running at each demand reduction level. We next describe the major design decisions and the architectural components of our demand-management solution.

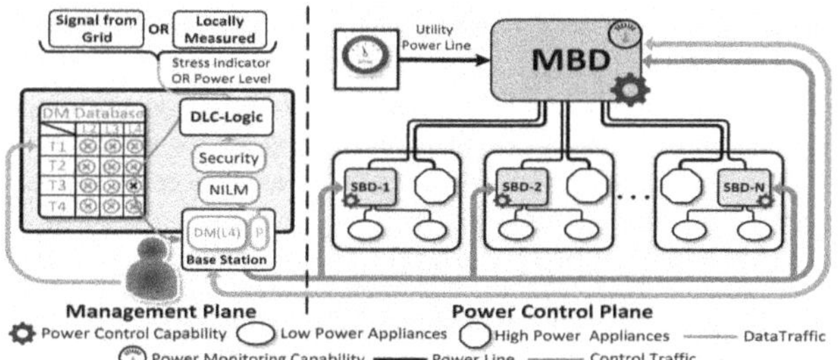

Figure 1: Aashiyana Architecture

2.1 Design Decisions for Aashiyana

We first decided on locating our two control components at the main distribution board and switch boards installed at each home, in light of the traditional wiring structure for Pakistan. These locations provide us sufficient control as the high-power device sockets are accessible from the main distribution board, while individual sockets as well as fixed appliances are accessible from a switch box.

We next decided to restrict the power consumption of our homes to **five levels**. *Level 5 and Level 1* represent the current two binary modes (unrestricted power and full disconnection). *Level 4-2* represent power consumption that is 75%, 50%, and 25% of full rated capacity. We restrict ourselves to just three configurable level, for each level user will provide a matrix of devices that will be disconnected (which we call a *Disconnectivity Matrix (DM)*). Finally, we also decide on using existing building automation and IoT frameworks, like [2] to enable an ease of application development and a robust rendezvous mechanism.

We split the architecture of Aashiyana into two planes (Figure 1): Management Plane and the Power Control Plane which we describe next.

2.2 Power Control Plane

The power control plane consists of two different control components, located at switch boards and main distribution board, that enable the enforcement of different power-states of a home.

Main Board Device (MBD), located at the main distribution box, is responsible for controlling room level power and all heavy appliances from one location. Another purpose of the MBD is to monitor the power consumption at each room level to provide monitoring ability to prevent overuse.

Switch Board Device (SBD) is located inside the switch board for each room, which terminates the direct line coming from the main distribution box. It is responsible, much like MBD, to control the wires distributing from this sockets.

Both these components communicate their data to the home management plane through some IoT-based communication technology. We describe this plane next.

2.3 Management Plane

The Management Plane, the brains behind the power-management of Aashiyana, consists of a DLC-logic module as well as Base-station component that enables the communication using the IoT technology (802.15.4, Z-wave, power-line) used by the MBD and SBD.

This plane is first responsible for saving user preferences in the form of a database of DMs for each power-state. A second, and most important, function is to appropriately respond to a grid-stress signal by selecting the appropriate power-state using the DLC-logic present within this plane. Once the power level is selected the appropriate DM is used to send commands to the control plane in order to switch off power to selected points.

The demand-reduction process initiated by the management plane requires an indication of grid-stress which can occur in a fully distributed manner at each home (by, for example, sensing frequency [4]).

3. DLC ALGORITHMS

We propose two different algorithms, one central and the other distributed which enforce reduction at an hour-long granularity.

In the iterative distributed algorithm, DLC signal will be stochastically generated within Aashiyana system when grid is under stress and a segment of Aashiyana homes will move to different lower power states. If the power reduction achieved by first iteration of Aashiyana homes is not enough, the utilities will move a segment of non-Aashiyana homes to no power state.

In centralized approach, the utilities refine the current loadshedding scheme by picking a feeder-level group and computing the savings by shutting-off all non-Aashiyana homes. The utility then computes the power savings by reducing the consumption level of Aashiyana homes one at a time, given the demand-supply gap is still positive and move to the next group until the demand is met. Once this decision is made centrally, the control decisions are then communicated directly (and at once) to every home.

4. EVALUATION SETUP AND RESULTS

We evaluated the benefits of our proposed large-scale DLC algorithms using Aashiyana, employing a custom event-driven simulator implemented in C++ having 40,000 home agents. We used REDD and Uk-DALE datasets to stochastically model the power consumption of appliances in a home.

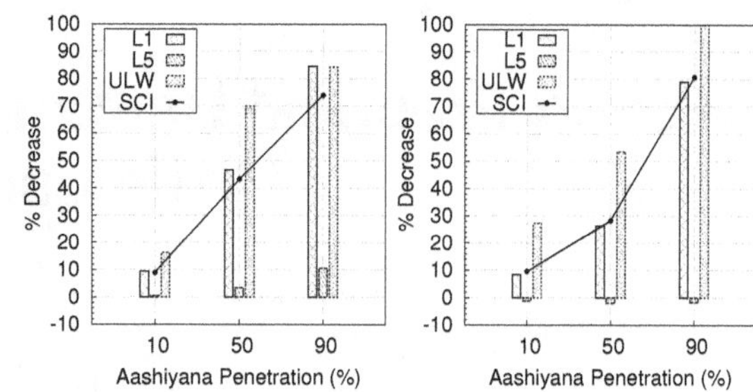

(a) Distributed 20% gap (b) Centralized 20% gap

Figure 2: DLC Algorithm Results: Change (from no AP) in distribution of home-levels with 20% demand supply gap

We limit the generation at 80% of total demand of all homes, which results into a supply-demand gap of 20%

Figure 2 shows the results for our centralized and distributed algorithm averaged over 10 simulation runs. Our fine-grading DLC schemes allow not only a decrease in the number of homes with no power (L1) for a slight decrease, sometime even increase, in homes with full-power (L5). As is quite evident, the fractional decrease of homes in L1 is *always* greater than (by more than 100%) the corresponding decrease in L5. This difference, corresponding to increase in social comfort, is understandably greatest at the highest Aashiyana Penetration (AP) level with the **social comfort index** (SCI[1]) $\approx$ 80 percentage points for 90% AP, thus clearly indicating the benefit of wide-scale adoption. The details evaluation setup and results can be found at a companion tech-report[1]).

5. CONCLUSIONS

We present here a novel and practical DLC system, Aashiyana, that enables several different low-power states for homes within the context of highly stressed grids. We design and evaluate this with practical incentives for the utilities (decreasing social unrest) as well as consumers (low-cost, lower hours with no-power, greater utility), *all without* having to increase the supply side equation. We show that, compared to current load-shedding strategy, for the same supply-demand gap, we can reduce homes with *no* power by $> 80\%$ while not significantly impacting the fraction of homes with full power.

6. REFERENCES

[1] N. Bashir, Z. Sharani, K. Qayyum, and A. A. Syed. Aashiyana: Design and evaluation of a smart demand-response system for highly-stressed grids. *arXiv preprint arXiv:1504.06975*, 2015.

[2] C. Dixon, R. Mahajan, S. Agarwal, A. J. Brush, B. Lee, S. Saroiu, and P. Bahl. An operating system for the home. NSDI'12. USENIX Association.

[3] S. C. Edison. Summer discount plan. web site `https://www.sce.com/wps/portal/home/residential/rebates-savings/summer-discount-plan/`.

[4] T. Ganu, J. Hazra, D. P. Seetharam, S. A. Husain, V. Arya, L. C. D. Silva, R. Kunnath, and S. Kalyanaraman. nplug: a smart plug for alleviating peak loads. In *e-Energy'12*, pages 30–30, 2012.

[5] S.Keshav and C.Rosenberg. Direct adaptive control of electricity demand. Technical report, University of Waterloo, 2010.

[1]SCI is defined as the magnitude of difference between the fractional decrease in L1 and fractional decrease in L5.

E-Adivino: A Novel Framework for Electricity Consumption Prediction based on Historical Trends

Shubham Saini[§], Pandarasamy Arjunan[§], Amarjeet Singh[§], Ullas Nambiar[‡]

[§]Indraprastha Institute of Information Technology Delhi, India
{shubhams,pandarasamya,amarjeet}@iiitd.ac.in

[‡]EMC Corporation Bangalore, India
ullas.nambiar@emc.com

ABSTRACT

Electricity demand prediction is important for several real world applications such as Demand Response (DR) program for peak demand management. For utilities with many customers, learning a best fit baseline for every consumer may be time consuming. We propose E-Adivino: an electricity forecasting framework that first clusters customers based on their consumption pattern followed by forecasting for each cluster using a generalized baseline projection approach. E-Adivino allows for selection of appropriate models for different consumers based on their demand patterns rather than using a uniform model for all the consumers, as is the practice today. E-Adivino is evaluated for its real world applicability using data from a university campus in India spanning over a year.

1. INTRODUCTION

To address energy supply and demand mismatch and in order to shed the peak hour energy usage, various Demand Response (DR) models have been put in place by utilities [1, 2]. However, success of DR programs is primarily based on the accuracy of baseline energy estimation at the demand side.

Consider two food chains A and B, both participating in a DR program. Individual outlets of the food-chains are identical in terms of capacity, business hours, electrical equipment and geographical location. Consequently, daily energy usage patterns for the outlets of the same chain are likely to be similar. In contrast, different food chains have different load profiles and energy usage behavior. Based on this observation, we identify two limitations in the baseline estimation methods in current DR programs: (1) Same baseline estimation technique is used by a DR program for both the food chains irrespective of the variation in their daily load consumption patterns [3], and (2) Wherever modeling (such as regression) on historical data is performed, different parameters are learned for each outlet separately while these could be learned jointly for the outlets within a food chain.

e-Energy'15, July 14–17, 2015, Bangalore, India.

ACM 978-1-4503-3609-3/15/07.
http://dx.doi.org/10.1145/2768510.2770946.

To address these shortcomings, we present E-Adivino, a novel framework for estimating baseline electricity consumption based on historical trends.

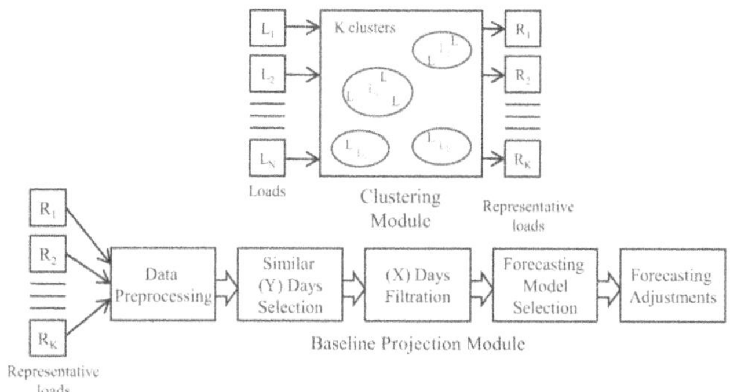

Figure 1: E-Adivino: A multi-stage forecasting framework which consists of load clustering and baseline projection modules.

2. E-ADIVINO

We now present E-Adivino- our multi-stage baseline estimation framework, illustrated in Figure 1. It is a multi-stage modular framework with flexible components that allow for efficient selection and application of appropriate forecasting models for different consumers based on their consumption profile.

2.1 Clustering Module

Learning the best fit baseline projection instance, that may also vary based on seasonality and other temporal characteristics of the consumption, would require high computation time for a large number of consumers. We use clustering techniques to group similar loads together and apply a unique (the best-fit) baseline projection instance for all the loads within a cluster. Clustering of loads can either be done using external information like geographical location, weather information, or intrinsic characteristics of the load i.e. actual data points or features extracted using the data points. *Evaluation using Partitioning Around Medoids with DTW and Temporal Features*

2.2 Generalized Baseline Projection Module

Each cluster, after the clustering phase, represents a consumption pattern that is similar for loads within the cluster and different for loads belonging to different clusters. Accordingly, a separate best-fit projection model needs to be learned for different clusters.

2.2.1 Dataset Preprocessing

Granularity: A certain period of time for which individual data inputs are gathered and summarized statistically describes the granularity of the time series. It should neither be too high so as to avoid the impact of power transients lasting for a small duration nor too low so as to ignore a prominent consumption pattern. For baseline projection, usage of mean hourly interval data is a commonplace.

Forecasting Horizon: Forecasting Horizon implies the number of data points a model forecasts into the future. If consumption follows a specific pattern for a time interval across all chosen days, probability of accurate forecast for that particular interval will be high. The accuracy of baseline projection can be increased by forecasting consumption for different intervals independently. *Evaluation using {8,24} Hours*

2.2.2 Similar (Y) Days Selection

Days prior to the DR event day are considered as Y similar days. While the use of recent data can give us a better approximation of the consumer load during an event, such short look-back windows can also be susceptible to manipulation in the case of DR with long events and advanced notification. *Evaluation using {4,7,10} Previous Business Days and Previous Same Days*

2.2.3 (X) Days Filtration

Selecting just a range of days prior to the event day for baseline calculation may not be sufficient. Most programs consider only a fixed number (X) of load days from the (Y) similar days, selected based on criteria such as total consumption or weather. Further, the number of X days with respect to the number of Y days is an important parameter that can drastically affect the accuracy of a model. *Evaluation using {60% and 80%} High X and Middle X*

2.2.4 Forecasting Model Application

Forecasting models such as ARIMA and BATS [4] are in use for a long time. Models based on AI algorithms like Neural Networks have recently gained popularity in the community due to its flexible non-linear modeling capability. However, due to the complexity argument of a sophisticated statistical model that is hard for the participants to understand, most utilities choose to use a simple averaging approach. *Evaluation using ARIMA+ANN and Simple Average models*

2.2.5 Forecast Adjustments

Despite all the similarities between the subset X days and the event day, conditions on the event day are very often different, even though in a subtle way. An appropriate adjustment mechanism is necessary to accurately reflect prediction day condition.

3. EMPIRICAL EVALUATION

Test Data: The IIIT Delhi campus is instrumented with over 200 smart meters spread across 7 buildings. The smart meters measure 8-12 different electrical parameters including power, energy, frequency, power factor and current at every 30 second. The sensing infrastructure was deployed incrementally since July 2013, and more than 2.5 billion data points have been archived till the time of writing this paper. The average daily total electricity consumption across the campus is more than 2500 KWh. In practice, power utilities have customers with diverse consumption pattern. In order to emulate different loads, top 18 of the highest consumption loads that contribute to 90% of commercial consumption were selected. Consumption pattern of the 18 loads used for evaluation at a granularity of 5 minutes for the overall duration of 1 year is released publicly[1].

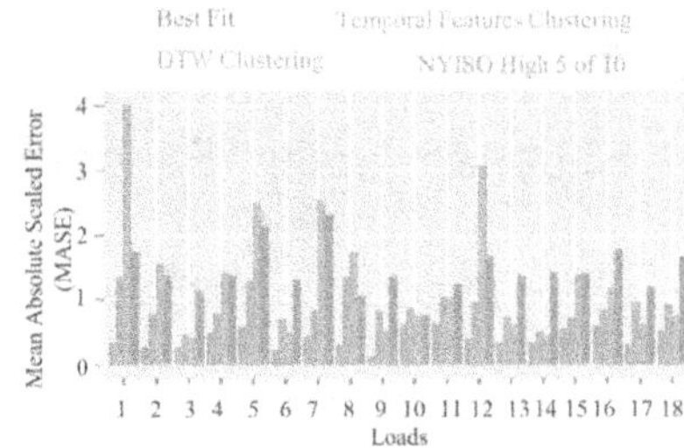

Figure 2: MASE achieved across the selected loads using different methods

Accuracy measure: We use Mean Absolute Scaled Error (MASE) [5] as a measure of prediction accuracy. MASE makes comparison of forecast accuracy across different loads and models easier to interpret. Thus, comparison of E-Adivino with best fit instance and standard NYISO baseline projection method, is better presented using this metric.

The average MASE achieved using the best fit instance was 0.41. Average *INCREASE* in MASE when the temporal features based clustering parameters were used was observed to be 0.47. Further, average *INCREASE* in MASE when the DTW based clustering parameters were used was observed to be 0.54.

In order to evaluate the need of different baseline estimation parameters, MASE achieved across the selected loads using E-Adivino was compared with the parameters used by NYISO *(High 5 of 10 days with simple averaging)*. While a MASE of 1.46 was achieved using NYISO parameters across the selected IIIT Delhi loads, average MASE of 0.88 and 0.95 was achieved after clustering with temporal features and DTW respectively.

4. CONCLUSIONS

In this paper, we presented E-Adivino - an electricity forecasting framework, that allows for accurate estimation of baseline consumption. An analysis of the proposed framework, using two diverse datasets from two different countries, highlights the need for the proposed generalized framework. We believe that the release of IIIT Delhi dataset will help further the research in this space by providing an interesting mix of consumption patterns.

5. REFERENCES

[1] Clifford Grimm and DTE Energy. Evaluating baselines for demand response programs. In *2008 AEIC Load Research Workshop*, 2008.

[2] Peter Cappers, Charles Goldman, and David Kathan. Demand response in us electricity markets: Empirical evidence. *Energy*, 35(4):1526–1535, 2010.

[3] Miriam L Goldberg and G Kennedy AgnewâĂŤDNV KEMA Energy. Measurement and verification for demand response. *DNV KEMA Energy and Sustainability, Tech. Rep*, 2013.

[4] Volkan Ş Ediger and Sertac Akar. Arima forecasting of primary energy demand by fuel in turkey. *Energy Policy*, 35(3):1701–1708, 2007.

[5] Rob J Hyndman and Anne B Koehler. Another look at measures of forecast accuracy. *International journal of forecasting*, 22(4):679–688, 2006.

[1]`https://www.iiitd.edu.in/~amarjeet/Datasets/eadivino/`

Poster Abstract: Towards a Categorization Framework for Occupancy Sensing Systems

Mikkel Baun Kjærgaard, Sanja Lazarova-Molnar and Muhyiddine Jradi
Center for Energy Informatics
Mærsk McKinney Møller Institute
University of Southern Denmark
mbkj,slmo,mjr@mmmi.sdu.dk

ABSTRACT

A large share of the energy consumption of buildings is driven by occupancy behavior. Means to minimize this share of consumption depend upon accurate information about occupant behavior. Therefore, it is important to improve sensing systems for gathering such information. However, as research on occupancy sensing systems goes beyond *basic methods*, there is an increasing need for better comparison of proposed occupancy sensing systems. Developers of occupancy sensing systems are also lacking good frameworks for understanding different options when building occupancy sensing systems. This poster abstract motivates the need for working towards a better categorization framework to address both of these problems. For researchers, the categorization framework is also an aid when scoping out future research in the area of occupancy sensing systems.

Categories and Subject Descriptors

H.4 [**Information Systems Applications**]: Miscellaneous

1. INTRODUCTION

Improving the energy performance of buildings is an important goal towards realizing a more sustainable society. An important challenge for improving the energy performance is the impact of occupancy behavior [4]. Occupancy behavior here refers to *all actions of occupants (including presence) that affect building energy consumption* [2]. Occupancy behavior affects both individual equipment in buildings and building-wide infrastructures. Three scenarios have been established towards addressing the impact of occupancy behavior: A) replace equipment and infrastructures in buildings with more efficient ones resulting into less energy consumption while maintaining the occupancy behavior, B) involve occupants in changing their behaviors towards less energy consuming behaviors, and C) improve the intelligence of equipment and infrastructures to better adapt to occupancy behavior to only spend energy for providing the needed utility and comfort to occupants. In all three cases it is important to gather quantitative information about occupants behavior to document savings related to occupancy behavior in case A, to provide feedback to support behavior change in case B and to use occupancy behavior to optimize control in case C.

To gather occupancy information, a wide range of occupancy sensing systems have been proposed, developed and commercialized. Here, we define occupancy behavior sensing systems as sensing systems that measure, estimate, model and predict occupancy behavior based on inputs from sensing infrastructures. Examples include systems for presence detection using PIR sensors, visual, stereo and thermal camera-based systems for people counting and systems based on sensor-instrumented spaces to recognize activities of individuals. Development of occupancy sensing systems has also been supported by developments in related areas, including, among others, the areas of location tracking, pervasive computing and sensor networks. These areas together have established many different forms of occupancy sensing systems. When surveying occupancy sensing systems, one has to answer a number of different questions. How do systems differ in types of occupancy information provided? What is the relationship between the system and occupants? What is the spatial and temporal coverage; do the system allow for prediction of future occupancy situations? What types of sensor strategies are applied for monitoring and data gathering; is the environment, objects or persons augmented? What types of modeling strategies are utilized? These questions are not only important for researchers surveying occupancy sensing systems, but also developers of occupancy sensing systems who have to understand different design options. We believe that a categorization framework will aid developers and researchers to better survey, compare, and design occupancy sensing systems. Being able to better survey and compare existing work also makes it possible to use the categorization framework as a reference when scoping out future research. This is especially important as research more and more moves from understanding basic mechanisms to combining different sensor strategies and modalities to provide information on complex behavioral patterns of occupants. Existing surveys on occupancy sensing systems [4, 3] have so far not presented a comprehensive categorization framework for the area.

2. TOWARDS A FRAMEWORK

In this poster abstract we motivate the need for developing a categorization framework for occupancy sensing sys-

e-Energy'15, July 14 - 17, 2015, Bangalore, India.
Copyright © 2015 ACM 978-1-4503-3609-3/15/07 ...$15.00.
http://dx.doi.org/10.1145/2768510.2770947

tems. In order to put this in context through documentation, we are currently conducting a comprehensive literature survey of existing work on occupancy sensing systems taking into account various features and characteristics. Our initial categorization framework is based on nine categories. These were partly inspired by earlier work on surveys on occupancy behavior in general, and from our literature study. The literature study is conducted by searching for key terms in relevant journals and conferences of the area. The categories of our initial framework are as follows: *Information Type* describes types of occupancy information. *Occupant relation* describes the relationship between the system and occupants. *Spatial granularity and temporal granularity* provides a characterization of resolution of occupancy information. *Spatial coverage and temporal coverage* provides a characterization of the spatial and temporal extent of coverage. *Sensing strategy and sensing modality* describe how sensors are applied and the types of sensor modalities. *Modeling strategy* describes how models of occupant behavior are used to clean, combine, estimate and predict occupancy information from sensor measurements.

Earlier surveys have only considered a subset of these dimensions. Christensen et al. [3] discuss the three dimensions *occupancy resolution, temporal resolution and spatial resolution* mapping to our dimensions *information type, spatial granularity and temporal granularity*, respectively. Nguyen et al. [4] introduce the dimensions of *Activities, technologies and methodologies* that maps to our dimensions *information type combined with temporal coverage, sensing modality and modeling strategy*, respectively. In this work we do not consider the type of building, e.g. , residential, commercial, public or industrial buildings, that a system is used in. However, system goals including privacy protection, needed maintenance, acceptable cost of cause differ among different building types.

We are developing the categorization framework including both subcategories and categorization of systems in parallel. In regards to the outlined nine categories, one can for example categorize two existing occupancy sensing systems as follows:

Agarwal et al. [1] propose a system for detecting the *information type* of occupancy *presence-boolean* with a *system relationship* that is *anonymous.* The system has a *spatial granularity* of *spaces* corresponding to rooms and an *event-based temporal granularity.* The system's *spatial coverage* is spaces considered as individual rooms and the *temporal covarage* is the *now.* The system applies the *sensor modalities* of *Infrared Light-PIR* and *Magnetic Fields-REED Switch* using the *sensing strategy* of *augmenting the environment.* The system apply the *modeling strategy* of conditional rules to model the relationship between sensor input and occupancy information.

Ruiz et al. [5] propose a system for detecting the *information type* of occupancy *presence-counts* with a *system relationship* that is *anonymous.* The system has a *spatial granularity* of *spaces* mapping to zones of interest and an *event-based temporal granularity.* The system's *spatial coverage* is at the *building* level and the *temporal covarage* is the *now* or the *past.* The system applies the *sensor modality* of *EM Waves-Radio-based Communication* using the *sensing strategy* of *repurpose infrastructure.* The system apply the *modeling strategy* of machine learning to compute the occupancy information.

As illustrated above, with a categorization framework we can start to analyze existing work. Such analysis can help scope out future research by mapping the coverage of system design choices. The analysis can for instance be preformed by grouping systems by their design choices and by providing statistics calculated from the categorizations.

3. CONCLUSIONS

In this poster abstract we have argued for the need to develop a comprehensive categorization framework for occupancy sensing systems. We are currently developing the framework based on an extensive literature study. By publishing this poster abstract we hope to gather initial feedback from the community in regards to the development of the categorization framework. Valuable categorization frameworks can account for everything that is known so far and they can predict things to come based on future scenarios, as variations of parameters accounted for and enumerated in the framework. A categorization framework first and foremost shows both depth and breadth of our understanding of the field of research. We would like others to join and, based on inputs from the community, further improve the proposed categorization framework.

Acknowledgment

This work is supported by the Innovation Fund Denmark for the project COORDICY (4106-00003B).

4. REFERENCES

[1] Y. Agarwal, B. Balaji, R. E. Gupta, J. Lyles, M. Wei, and T. Weng. Occupancy-driven energy management for smart building automation. In *BuildSys'10*, pages 1–6, 2010.

[2] A. Caucheteux, A. Es Sabar, and V. Boucher. Occupancy measurement in building: A litterature review, application on an energy efficiency research demonstrated building. *International Journal of Metrology and Quality Engineering*, 4:135–144, 1 2013.

[3] K. Christensen, R. Melfi, B. Nordman, B. Rosenblum, and R. Viera. Using existing network infrastructure to estimate building occupancy and control plugged-in devices in user workspaces. *Int. J. Commun. Netw. Distrib. Syst.*, 12(1):4–29, Nov. 2014.

[4] T. A. Nguyen and M. Aiello. Energy intelligent buildings based on user activity: A survey. *Energy and Buildings*, 56(0):244 – 257, 2013.

[5] A. J. R. Ruiz, H. Blunck, T. S. Prentow, A. Stisen, and M. B. Kjærgaard. Analysis methods for extracting knowledge from large-scale wifi monitoring to inform building facility planning. In *IEEE PerCom 2014*, pages 130–138, 2014.

Curtailment Estimation Methods for Demand Response

Lessons Learned by Comparing Apples to Oranges

Charalampos Chelmis, Muhammad Rizwan Saeed, Marc Frincu, Viktor K. Prasanna
Ming Hsieh Electrical Engineering Department
University of Southern California
{chelmis, saeedm, frincu, prasanna}@usc.edu

ABSTRACT

Accurate estimation and evaluation of consumption reduction achieved by participants during Demand Response is critical to Smart Grids. We perform an in-depth study of popular estimation methods used to determine the extent of consumption shedding during DR, using a real-world Smart Grid dataset from the University of Southern California campus microgrid. We provide insights to the process of selecting a reasonable baseline with respect to potential misinterpretation of the estimation of electricity consumption reduction during DR.

Categories and Subject Descriptors

G.3 [**Probability and Statistics**]: Time Series Analysis; H.4.m [**Information Systems Applications**]: Miscellaneous

Keywords

Baseline Models; Reduced Consumption; Load Forecasting

1. INTRODUCTION

In this work, we statistically analyze the effect of Baseline Load Profile (BLP) models on the interpretation of consumption reduction as a result of Demand Response (DR) [6, 10] using real-world data from the University of Southern California (USC) microgrid, with the objective of improving the accuracy of estimating electricity demand reduction due to participation in DR programs. Accurate estimation and evaluation of consumption reduction achieved by participants during curtailment is critical to DR programs [6], particularly when participation is voluntary [1]. The amount of computed curtailment depends on the accuracy of the baseline model used. As many baseline models exist, different curtailment estimates can be derived. The problem with calculating BLP model accuracy, lies mainly in the fact that there is no actual reference value to compare against. We argue that without careful consideration, utility providers can end up with erroneous data on the actual curtailment which can in turn lead to billing or rewarding issues. We show that choosing a good baseline depends on both intrinsic (e.g., DR strategy, day of week) and extrinsic (e.g., temperature, human behavior) factors. To the best of our knowledge, our work is the first to provide an in-depth comparative analysis of the effect of BLP models for post DR analysis in a real-world, large-scale setting.

e-Energy'15, July 14–17, 2015, Bangalore, India.
ACM 978-1-4503-3609-3/15/07.
http://dx.doi.org/10.1145/2768510.2775332 .

2. REAL-WORLD CASE STUDY

We consider a real-world Smart Grid dataset from the University of Southern California campus microgrid[1]. The dataset comprises of a collection of observed electricity consumption values (measured in kWh at every 15 minutes) from 35 diverse buildings, collected over a one year period (November 2012 - December 2013) [3]. Using our real-world dataset, we benchmark a set of BLPs: Auto Regressive Integrated Moving-Average (ARIMA) [5], New York ISO (NYISO) [8], Southern California Edison ISO (CASCE) [9], California ISO (CAISO) [2] and a modified version that introduces a morning adjustment factor (CAISOm) [6], and Fixed Value (i.e., the consumption value just prior to the beginning of the DR event is used as the predictor).

We examine the performance of a baseline in terms of *bias*, i.e., dominance of positive or negative predictions, and *accuracy*, i.e., average absolute percent error. To measure model bias, we measure the median of the distribution of errors. Intuitively, the closest to zero the median of the error is, the more unbiased the model. We measure average deviance between predicted consumption, fc_t^{15}, and actual consumption, ac_t^{15}, on non-DR days (between 1-5pm, for consistency with DR days), as $MPE = \frac{100}{n}\sum_{t=1}^{n}\frac{fc_t^{15}-ac_t^{15}}{ac_t^{15}}$. We found CASCE to perform the best among all BLPs, achieving good MAPE values while at the same time being the least biased.

3. ACHIEVING A CURTAILMENT GOAL

To shed light on the effect of baseline selection on the interpretation of consumption reduction estimation and evaluation due to DR programs, we consider DR events in which all buildings participate, each following a random DR strategy (e.g., Duty Cycling, Variable Frequency Drive [7], Global Temperature Reset [7]). In order to ensure that randomly selecting a strategy for each building does not affect our findings, we repeated the experiment, with the difference that the "best" strategy per building was used. Evidently, curtailment estimation is highly correlated to the baseline selected

[1]The dataset is available upon request for academic use from the USC Facility Management Services (FMS).

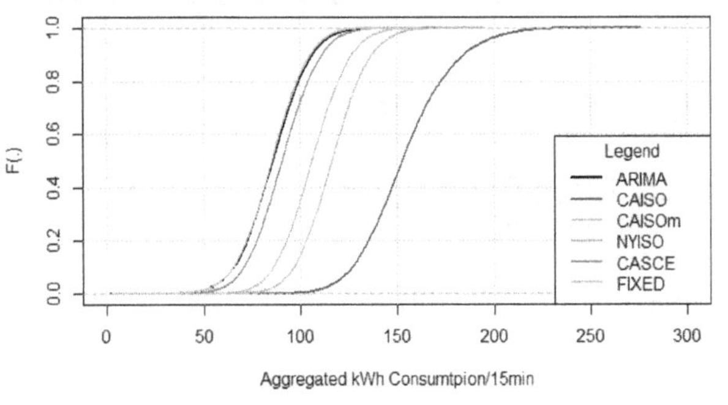

(a) Probability density function

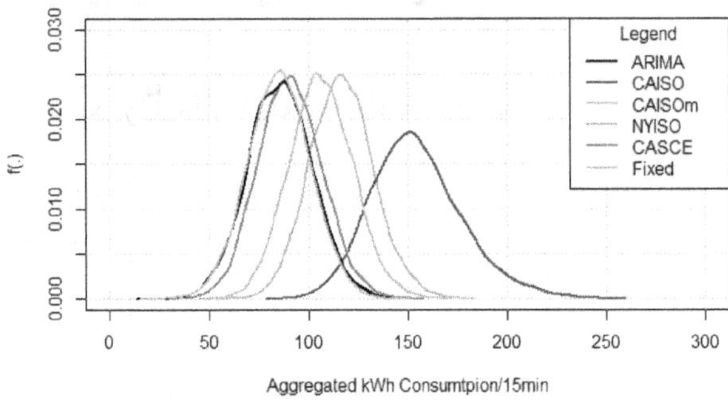

(b) Cumulative density function

Figure 1: Aggregate curtailment over all buildings.

for analysis. Therefore more effort should be allocated in the following areas of research. First, better baseline methods that can be applied to all customers without exhibiting volatility to external factors would be highly desirable. If a "one solution fits all" is not possible, developing a framework that would adapt to individual household attributes so as to select the "best" performing baseline method for each individual customer would be advisable. Learning to switch between baselines as time progresses to adapt to customers (changing) behavior would also be beneficial, but at the same time computationally expensive.

Instead of estimating what the consumption would have been in the absence of DR (i.e., baseline consumption), and then calculating the difference between such estimate and the actual consumption during DR, computational methods for reduced consumption prediction would be beneficial. The advantage of such an approach is twofold. First, reduced consumption prediction does not require a baseline calculation. Instead, observed curtailed consumption from past events could be used to predict future curtailed consumption. Second, predicted values would be directly comparable against observed consumption during DR for a fair performance evaluation. Some works [4] have already proposed solutions towards this direction. Our findings motivate an exploration of promising future work.

The drawback of our work is that it only considers a single regional scenario, even though our analysis involves a heterogeneous collection of buildings with diverse functions and purpose, covering a wide percentage of consumer demographics. Considering scenarios on a per-household basis, as well as including more diverse customer types (e.g. industrial or residential) would strengthen our study.

Acknowledgments

This material is based upon work supported by the United States Department of Energy under Award Number number DE-OE0000192, and the Los Angeles Department of Water and Power (LA DWP). The views and opinions of authors expressed herein do not necessarily state or reflect those of the United States Government or any agency thereof, the LA DWP, nor any of their employees.

4. REFERENCES

[1] S. Aman, Y. Simmhan, and V. K. Prasanna. Energy management systems: state of the art and emerging trends. *IEEE Communications Magazine*, 51(1):114–119, 2013.

[2] CaliforniaISO. Caiso demand response resource user guide. Technical report, 2007. http://www.caiso.com/1ca6/1ca67a5816ee0.pdf.

[3] C. Charalampos, S. Muhammad Rizwan, F. Marc, and P. Viktor K. Curtailment estimation methods for demand response. Technical report, University of Southern California, 2015.

[4] C. Chelmis, S. Aman, M. R. Saeed, M. Frincu, and V. K. Prasanna. Estimating reduced consumption for dynamic demand response. In *Proceedings of the Twenty-Ninght AAAI Conference on Artificial Intelligence*. AAAI Press, 2015.

[5] B. George E. P. and J. Gwilym M. *Time series analysis, forecasting and control*. Holden-Day, 1970.

[6] C. Katie, P. Mary Ann, G. Charles A., and K. Sila. Statistical analysis of baseline load models for non-residential buildings. *Energy and Buildings*, 41(4):374–381, 2009.

[7] N. Motegi, M. A. Piette, D. S. Watson, S. Kiliccote, and P. Xu. Introduction to commercial building control strategies and techniques for demand response. Technical report, Lawrence Berkely National Laboratory, 2006. http://gaia.lbl.gov/btech/papers/59975.pdf.

[8] NewYorkISO. Emergency demand response program manual. Technical report, 2013. `http://www.nyiso.com/public/webdocs/markets\_operations/documents/Manuals\_and\_Guides/Manuals/Operations/edrp\_mnl.pdf`.

[9] SouthernCaliforniaEdison. 10 day average baseline and "day-off" adjustment. Technical report, 2011. http://asset.sce.com/Documents/Business - Energy Management Solutions/10DayAvgBaselineFS.pdf.

[10] A. Veit, C. Goebel, R. Tidke, C. Doblander, and H. Jacobsen. Household electricity demand forecasting: benchmarking state-of-the-art methods. In *The Fifth International Conference on Future Energy Systems, e-Energy '14, Cambridge, United Kingdom - June 11 - 13, 2014*, pages 233–234. ACM, 2014.

On the Utility of Occupancy Sensing for Managing HVAC Energy in Large Zones

Srinarayana Nagarathinam, Shiva R. Iyer, Arunchandar Vasan, Venkata Ramakrishna P, Venkatesh Sarangan
Innovation Labs, Tata Consultancy Services, India
venkataramakrishna.p@tcs.com

Anand Sivasubramaniam
Dept. of Comp. Sci. & Eng.
Pennsylvania State University
University Park, PA 16802, USA
anand@cse.psu.edu

ABSTRACT

HVAC control strategies that exploit temporal variations in zone occupancy have been well studied. Occupancy can also vary spatially within a zone, especially during off-design operating conditions. We complement prior work by studying the usefulness of sensing occupancy information at different spatial resolutions in large zones served by multiple AHUs. As conventional PID controllers cannot utilize this information effectively, we propose a new control strategy and study the usefulness of sensing. We observe that utility of sensing occupancy at finer spatial resolutions is higher when the actual spatial heterogeneity in occupancy is higher.

Categories and Subject Descriptors

G.1.6 [**Mathematics of computing**]: Numerical analysis—*Optimization*; I.2.8 [**Computing Methodologies**]: AI—*Problem Solving, Control Methods, & Search*

Keywords

Energy; HVAC; Optimization; Occupancy sensing

1. INTRODUCTION

The raison d'être of HVAC systems is to condition a building's indoor space so that its occupants feel comfortable. Understanding when and where people are present inside a building can help to control the HVAC systems in a better way. Occupancy based control strategies are useful when there is skewness in occupancy, so that the instances of lean occupancy can be exploited. The skewness can occur in *space* or *time*; if the information is sensed at appropriate *resolution*, with sufficient *fidelity*, it can be utilized with a suitable *control*. The usefulness of sensing depends on how dynamic the occupancy variations are in space/time; and on the ability of the controller to consume the information.

Researchers have proposed various HVAC control strategies that exploit temporal variations in zone occupancy to reduce energy consumption with little or no negative impact on occupant comfort [1, 3, 4]. Apart from time, occupancy can be skewed across space as well – i.e., different areas within a zone can have different occupancy levels at the same time. This skewness can become more pronounced as the zone size increases. Large zones can be typically found in office buildings with open floor workspaces, airports, and large restaurants. In such cases, the large zone will be served by several VAVs or AHUs. We refer to the large zone as a super-zone and this configuration where Multiple AHUs serve a Super-zone as an MAS configuration. Henceforth, within a MAS, the primary regions of influence of individual AHUs will be referred to as *zones*; and sub-divisions of a zone will be referred to as sub-zones. The key distinguishing feature of the MAS is that *the zones served by individual AHUs are thermally coupled* – this is because there is no partition that separates the areas served by individual AHUs.

In such MASes, significant spatial variations in occupancy can occur across individual zones, especially during off-design operating conditions such as weekend shifts in offices. This spatial non-uniformity gives an opportunity to condition different zones (with different occupancy densities) differently. The zones in which people are present can be maintained at desired set-point temperatures while the temperatures in the vacant zones can be allowed to drift. Such a skewed set-point strategy could potentially conserve energy without compromising on occupant comfort. This potential to save energy in MAS configurations and its linkage to occupancy sensing resolution (in spatial terms) has not been investigated previously. Exploiting spatial heterogeneity in MAS configurations is not trivial for the following reasons:

- In a MAS, the air mass and heat across different zones mix due to lack of partitions between them; this limits the ability to achieve desired temperature skewness in the super-zone. Therefore the extent to which the zone temperatures can drift (and hence the energy savings) during lean occupancy is also limited.

- The conditioned temperature within a zone not only depends on the air flow setting of that zone's AHU but also on the settings of the AHUs serving the neighboring zones. In other words, AHUs of different zones remain thermally coupled and are not independent. Therefore the individual AHUs cannot be operated in isolation by dividing the MAS into individual zones.

Given these observations the following questions arise:

- Knowing the spatial occupancy distribution in a MAS, can we determine appropriate flow settings for the con-

e-Energy'15, July 14–17, 2015, Bangalore, India.
ACM 978-1-4503-3594-2/15/06.
http://dx.doi.org/10.1145/2768510.2770948.

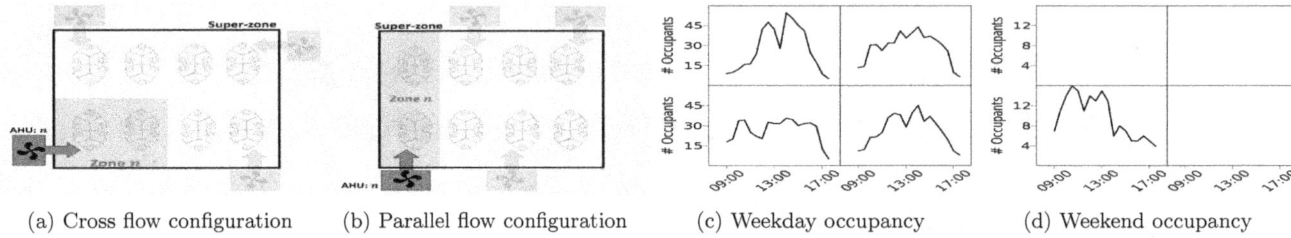

(a) Cross flow configuration (b) Parallel flow configuration (c) Weekday occupancy (d) Weekend occupancy

Figure 1: AHU configurations and occupancy patterns observed in real world MASes.

tributing AHUs which will reduce the HVAC energy consumption without compromising occupant comfort?

- What level of occupancy information (in terms of the spatial resolution – MAS, zone, or sub-zone) is necessary to achieve these savings? In other words, what will be the *marginal utility* of sensing occupancy at different spatial resolutions? (in terms of energy savings or improved comfort)?

2. OPTIMAL AHU CONTROL FOR MAS

We design a physical *model based reactive control strategy* that uses occupancy information to determine the optimum fan speeds for the AHUs serving a MAS. The control strategy works in tandem with a fixed point iteration based approach to estimate the state of the thermally coupled zones.

Given the current state of the MAS, the control strategy searches through the space of AHU flow rate vectors $\mathbf{M}$. It identifies an optimal flow setting $\mathbf{M}_{opt}$ for the AHUs that can meet the comfort while minimizing the HVAC energy consumption. For a given flow rate, the energy consumed by the AHU system is obtained from the power models of the AHU fans and chiller as a continuous function $P(\mathbf{M})$. This continuous function is minimized using sequential quadratic programming technique by constraining the search-space to include only those regions where occupant comfort is met.

The question of whether a particular flow vector $\mathbf{M}$ meets the comfort requirement of the occupants in the MAS is answered as follows. Given the system state at time t, we pick a flow vector $\mathbf{M}$ for the interval $[t, t+\Delta t]$. For this flow rate setting, we determine the new system state – defined in terms of zone temperatures and relative humidities at time $(t+\Delta t)$. We use a zone thermal model, that gives the zone temperature $(T_{z,i})$ and humidity ratio $(W_{z,i})$ of a zone i at $(t+\Delta t)$ as a function of the following: (i)$T_{z,i}$ and $W_{z,i}$ at t, (ii) zone temperatures and humidity ratios of its neighboring zones at $(t+\Delta t)$, and (iii) the new flow-rate vector $\mathbf{M}$ of the AHUs serving these zones at $(t+\Delta t)$. The coupling between the new system state and the new flow value yields a system of non-linear equations in the zone-temperatures and humidity ratios that we solve using a fixed point iteration. In our study, we assume that the supply air temperature of the AHUs remain constant. Once we obtain the new system state, we can evaluate if the comfort levels of the occupants in the MAS will be met at time $(t+\Delta t)$ in a straight forward manner.

3. PERFORMANCE

We collected occupancy traces and HVAC configuration from *large multi-AHU zones found in real-world office buildings*. We used this real-world data and our optimal AHU control strategy to study the marginal utility of having occupancy information through co-simulations involving MLE+ [2] and EnergyPlus. We used calibrated models of the real world MASes in our simulations. The studied MAS is of size $20,000$ ft^2, rectangular in shape with an aspect ratio of 2.0, and served by four AHUs. Each AHU has a capacity of 20 TR and is capable of delivering a flow rate of 11000 cfm. The AHU system is sized for an occupancy of 200 people (100 ft^2 per person). The office hours are 09:00 to 18:00 on Monday through Saturday. The region of influence of each AHU is obtained from the actual air-flow ducting in the floor and the location of the supply diffusers from each AHU. The MAS configuration and sample occupancy traces are shown in Figure 1. Important findings are as follows:

- The proposed AHU control strategy exploits spatial-skewness in MAS occupancy better than conventional PID control. Independent PID control of AHUs which uses MAS design occupancy was taken as the baseline. With respect to this, PID control of AHUs with sub-zone occupancy information saved 9% of energy while our proposed control saved 18%.

- The utility of sensing occupancy at finer resolutions varies with the spatial heterogeneity in occupancy and the MAS configuration. For weekday occupancy – which is less skewed spatially, the utility of sensing occupancy at the finest resolution (in terms of energy savings) was around 9% under a cross flow configuration. For weekend occupancy – which is highly skewed, the utility of sensing occupancy at the finest resolution was 18%. The utility under a parallel flow configuration decreased by $2-3\%$ from the cross flow values.

- The marginal utility of sensing occupancy decreases with the sensing resolution. We observed 9%, 6%, and 4% as the marginal utilities of sensing occupancy at aggregate MAS, zone, and sub-zone levels respectively.

We are at present working towards developing a model based predictive control strategy to control the AHUs in a MAS.

4. REFERENCES

[1] Y. Agarwal, B. Balaji, R. Gupta, J. Lyles, M. Wei, and T. Weng. Occupancy-driven energy management for smart building automation. In *ACM BuildSys*, 2010.

[2] W. Bernal, M. Behl, T. Nghiem, and R. Mangharam. MLE+: A Tool for Integrated Design and Deployment of Energy Efficient Building Controls. *SIGBED Rev.*, 10(2):34–34, July 2013.

[3] J. R. Dobbs and B. M. Hencey. Model predictive HVAC control with online occupancy model. *Energy and Buildings*, 82(0):675 – 684, 2014.

[4] V. L. Erickson and A. E. Cerpa. Occupancy based demand response HVAC control strategy. In *ACM BuildSys*, pages 7–12, 2010.

A Framework for Evaluating the Costs and Benefits of Instrumentation in Smart Home Systems

Seema Nagar[I], Sandhya Aneja[U], Harshad Khadilkar[I], Sampath Dechu[I], Zainul Charbiwala[I]
[I]IBM Research [U]Universiti Brunei Darussalam
senagar3@in.ibm.com

ABSTRACT

The goal of this paper is to establish a framework for *evaluating the marginal utility of adding smart sensing and metering hardware to residential premises*, in terms of efficiency improvement (reduction in energy consumption) and economic benefits (reduction in energy cost). A simulation procedure is developed for experimenting with different types of hardware architectures. In-house analysis algorithms suitable to the installed suite of sensing and metering hardware are applied, which take into account realistic practical constraints. The proposed methodology allows us to perform a cost-benefit analysis of several potential smart home solutions. This analysis is meant to enable home owners to evaluate *a priori* the real cost saving potential of these solutions, when applied to their home.

1. INTRODUCTION

The residential sector consumes a significant fraction of the world's energy supply, the establishment of *smart homes* is seen to be an important step towards limiting or reversing the growth in residential energy demand. A smart home typically utilises a combination of appliance-level energy meters, context sensing equipment, automated relays, and user interfaces for detecting and curtailing energy waste. The cost of a 'smart home system' naturally increases with the increasing number of sensors and meters, as well as with the sophistication of the analytical algorithms employed for recommending changes to energy consumption patterns. Off-the-shelf solutions for residential energy management tend to assume that additional sensing, metering and actuation infrastructure will deliver proportionally higher benefits to consumers. In this paper, we explicitly address the issue of cost effectiveness of smart home systems. We do this by (i) considering two types of smart home systems, one with relatively fewer sensing and metering components, and another with a more thorough set of hardware components, (ii) developing a simulator that allows us to evaluate different types of hardware architectures. A cost-benefit analysis is carried out for each option, with a view to estimate their return on investment.

e-Energy'15, July 14–17, 2015, Bangalore, India.
ACM 978-1-4503-3609-3/15/07
http://dx.doi.org/10.1145/2768510.2770949.

Table 1: List of appliances in the two-bedroom apartment model, for the basic architecture. Room tags correspond to Bedroom 1, Bedroom 2, Kitchen, and Living room.

Appliance	Loc.	Energy	Context	Cost (USD)
AC	BR-1	Yes	Yes	100
AC	BR-2	Yes	Yes	100
WM	KN	Yes	No	50
FR	KN	Yes	Yes	100
TV	LR	Yes	Yes	100
User display	LR	No	No	200
Home meter	LR	No	No	200
			Total:	850

Table 2: List of appliances in addition to the basic architecture in the two-bedroom apartment model, for the advanced architecture.

Appliance	Loc.	Energy	Context	Cost (USD)
Oven	KN	Yes	No	50
Elec. stove	KN	Yes	No	50
Computer	BR-1,BR-2	Yes	No	100
User display	LR,KN,BR-1,BR-2	No	No	800
Home meter	LR	No	No	200
Basic			Total:	850
			Total:	1650

2. SYSTEM ARCHITECTURE

2.1 Basic hardware installation

Basic hardware installation is comprise of (i) energy measurement plugs for major appliances, (ii) one set of context sensors for each room, (iii) one interactive display in a central location in the home for communicating information and alerts, and (iv) one home level smart meter for capturing energy consumption of non-instrumented loads. The context data to be measured includes temperature and motion detection. The full list of appliances is given in Table 1.

2.2 Advanced hardware installation

The appliance layout in the advanced instrumentation case includes three additional user displays. These additional displays are placed in the three remaining rooms in the house, and messages/alerts can be independently sent to each display. This allows us to (i) direct messages to rooms where activity is detected, in order to ensure message delivery, and (ii) avoid annoyance to residents by ensuring

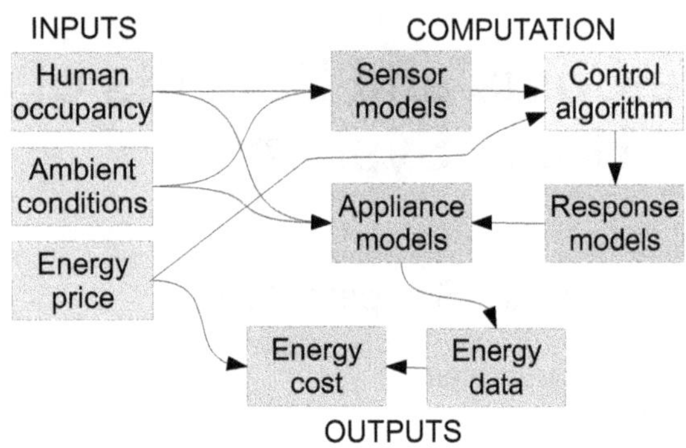

Figure 1: Logical flowchart of the simulator.

selective delivery of messages and alerts. For example, we can avoid sending alerts to bedrooms when a combination of appliance usage and context information indicates that occupants might be asleep. The revised list of appliances and sensors is given in Table 2.

3. SIMULATION RESULTS AND INSIGHTS

In this section, we present the simulation procedure for estimating the benefits of installing smart home technologies in residences.

3.1 Simulation procedure

We simulate 7 days of residential energy consumption for (i) the default case, (ii) with the basic architecture, and (iii) with the advanced architecture. We employ the simulation architecture depicted in Figure 1. Human occupancy is picked up from the ATUS data set[1]. The variable time of use tariff is based on data published in prior work [2]. Ambient temperature is generated through a random process. The results of this simulation are depicted in Figure 2 and are summarised in Table 3.

The simulation estimated that the default energy consumption for the 2-bedroom apartment was 200 kWh per month, and the monetary cost of this energy (as per the assumed tariff) was INR 1440, or USD 24. Table 3 shows that loads such as the washing machine (WM) and computers (included in Others) show no reduction in energy consumption when moving from the default case to the basic or advanced architecture. However, they show a reduction in energy cost, realised by deferring these loads to times of low tariff. Reduction in energy consumption is achieved by implementing efficiency measures for the television (TV), refrigerator (FR), and the two air conditioners (AC-1, AC-2). Since the two bedrooms have different levels of simulated activity, AC-1 and AC-2 show different levels of energy consumption and savings. The energy savings delivered by the basic and advanced architectures are 11.5% and 19.0% respectively, while the cost savings are 18.6% and 26.3%.

3.2 Insights into simulation results

Added instrumentation provides the advantage of better classification of user activities, thus increasing the potential for energy saving. However, major deferrable loads such as washing machines (which deliver the highest cost savings) are only loosely correlated with human activities. Therefore, additional instrumentation does not improve cost saving in the same proportion as energy saving.

Since there is a fixed hardware cost for any architecture, instrumentation of only one or two major appliances is also

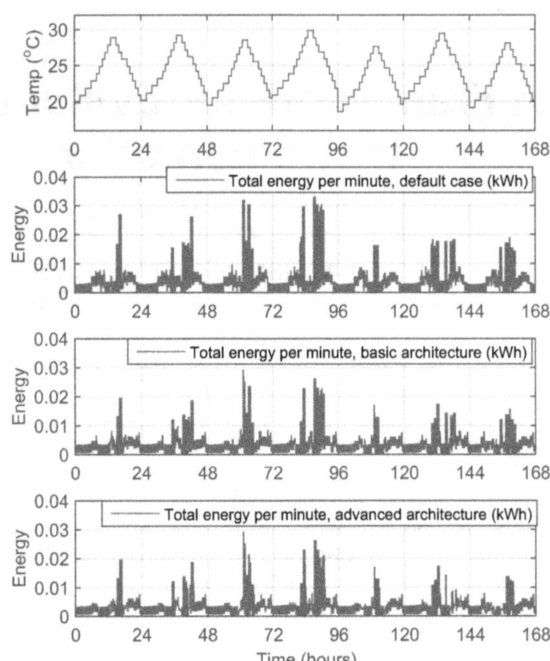

Figure 2: Ambient temperature and energy consumption in the three simulated cases. The period of simulation is 7 days.

Table 3: Contribution of appliances in terms of energy consumed and cost, over 7 simulated days.

	Default		Basic		Advanced	
App.	Cons.	Cost	Cons.	Cost	Cons.	Cost
WM	5.8	7.3	5.8	3.4	5.8	3.4
TV	3.7	5.0	3.1	4.1	3.1	4.1
FR	37.5	33.8	35.4	32.1	30.3	26.8
AC1	11.2	10.0	8.2	7.3	7.6	6.8
AC2	20.9	19.5	15.1	13.9	13.3	12.0
KN	4.3	4.5	4.3	4.5	4.3	4.5
Others	16.6	19.9	16.6	16.1	16.6	16.1
Savings	0	0	11.5	18.6	19.0	26.3
Total	100	100	100	100	100	100

not cost effective. Neither is instrumenting every single appliance in the home. In conclusion, the best returns are obtained by instrumenting a well chosen subset of appliances in the home.

3.3 Recommendations

Automated actuation of appliances. The simulations described in Section 3.1 showed that approximately 70% of all messages and alerts that were delivered to occupied rooms, were responded to. The energy savings would increase to 25% for a full response rate during times of occupancy, and to approximately 30% for a fully automated system.

4. REFERENCES

[1] US Department of Labor, Bureau of Labor Statistics, "American Time Use Survey," 2013. [Online]. Available: http://www.bls.gov/tus/#data

[2] H. Khadilkar, V. Chandan, S. Kalra, S. Ghai, Z. Charbiwala, T. Ganu, R. Kunnath, C. Lim, and D. Seetharam, "DC picogrids as power backups for office buildings," in *International Conference on Smart Grid Communications*, Venice, Italy, November 2014.

Locating and Sizing Smart Meter Deployment in Buildings

Anand Krishnan Prakash, Uddhav Arote, Vivek Chil Prakash, Pallab Kumar Sahu, Bhavin Doshi, Krithi Ramamritham

Department of Computer Science and Engineering
Indian Institute of Technology, Bombay

ABSTRACT

The use of smart-meters is proliferating, they are now being deployed without asking the obvious question: Do we really need each of them? Beyond the cost of smart-meters, there are overheads related to installation, wiring, etc. To formally tackle this question, we first define the notion of observability that one or more pieces of information (including that from smart-meters) enable. This notion allows us to compare two different deployments of sensors with respect to their information content and their usefulness. We then examine some commonly available information from which one can infer power consumption of devices in a given space. We show how we have applied this approach to systematically decide the optimal number and location of smart-meters to ensure observability of consumption by different parts of a building.

General Terms

Smart Energy

Keywords

Smart metering; Energy consumption; Optimal location

1. INTRODUCTION

Figure 1 shows the power consumption pattern for a typical week for our building as collected by the smart-meter attached to our building. The total energy consumption during this observation period is dominated by the base power consumption – the minimum power consumption present at any given time, which was 80KW. Concerned by the fact that (a) the instantaneous base consumption is about 50% of the peak and (b) the base energy consumption is about 80% of the aggregate consumed during this period, we wanted to develop the necessary tools to analyze and determine the reasons and also try to reduce the consumption. This case study motivated our research and we were interested in finding the answers to the following questions:

i) Where should we locate a tranche of smart-meters for maximum visibility of a building's power consumption? ii) How can we capitalize on different areas having the same profile? iii) What are the other readily available information which can be used to infer consumption? iv) Can we develop an incremental approach of installation in which the building manager is not burdened with huge initial investments?

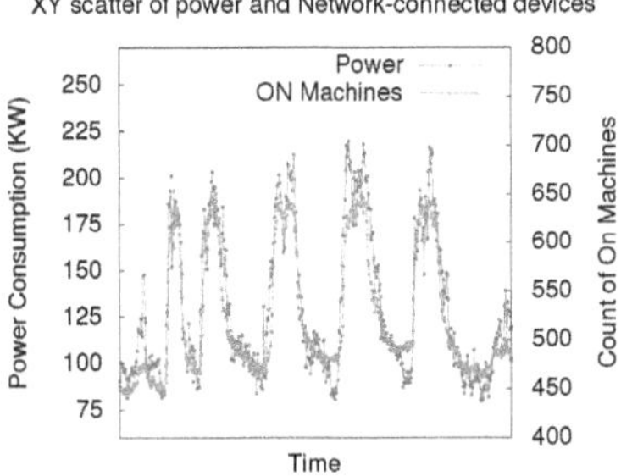

Figure 1: Plot of Power Consumption and Network-Connected Device in our building

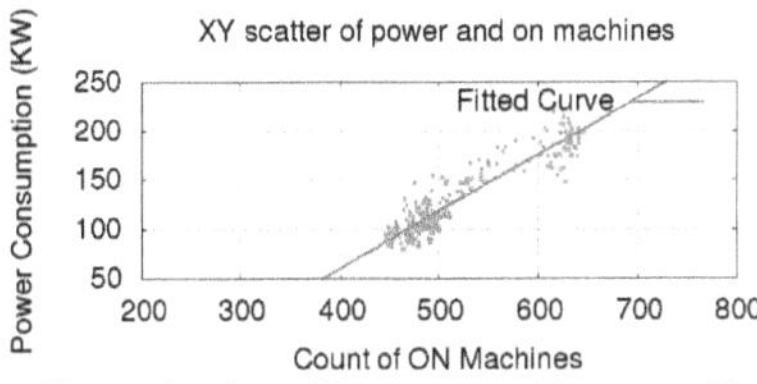

Figure 2: Correlation Between Power Consumption and Network-Connected Device in our building

On further diagnosis, we found that 13KW of the 80KW is attributed to on-but-idle desktop computers. This motivated us to reduce the base consumption by focusing on such machines. By running an arp-scan every 15 minutes, we determined the total number of connected devices which had a strong correlation with power consumption of the building as shown in Figure 1 and Figure 2. Hence data sources like arp-scan, calendar data, biometric attendance etc, along with parameterized consumption models can help infer power consumption of the observed space.

2. THE FORMAL BUILDING BLOCKS

2.1 The Notion of Observability

A node is any location in a building which is required to be monitored (eg: room, floor). The user defines a notion of observability as per his requirement which can be in terms of number of appliances or occupants or the power consumption observed by the node. Meters are placed in the decreasing order of the notion to ensure maximum observability.

e-Energy'15, July 14–17, 2015, Bangalore, India.
ACM 978-1-4503-3609-3/15/07.
http://dx.doi.org/10.1145/2768510.2770950.

2.2 Soft Sensors

Soft Sensors are other readily available information which we can use to infer power consumption of a node. They have to be initialized and tuned with the real power measurement data. Once tuned, the soft-sensor can replace a smart-meter for all practical purposes. For example, from Figure 2, it can be seen that we use number of ON machines as a soft sensor to infer power consumption via the equation:
Power (in KW) = 0.577 x Machines - 170.611

3. RULES AND ALGORITHMS

3.1 Rules for Determining Observability

If a node is observable, *Observable(N)* = True, else False.
Rule 1: A node is observable if it has either a physical meter or soft-sensors installed. It measures the aggregate consumption of appliances present in the node (if it is a leaf node) or the leaf nodes in its subtree (if it is a non-leaf node).
Rule 2: If all the children of a node N are observable, then that node becomes observable.
Rule 3: For a node M, if the parent node and all its siblings are observable, then it is observable. $Parent(M) = N$

3.2 Identifying Observable States of Nodes

Initialization: From Rule 1, Observable(N) is true if it has a smart-meter or a soft-sensor installed at that node.
Bottom Up Pass: From Rule 2, $\forall\ C \in Children(N)$ Observable(C) $\implies$ Observable(N).
Top Down Pass: From Rule 3, if $Parent(M) = N$, Observable(N) $\wedge\ \forall\ C \in Siblings(M)$ Observable(C) $\implies$ Observable(M).

3.3 Algorithm for Locating Smart-meters

When we have sufficient number of smart-meters, place them at each of the leaf nodes. Otherwise follow Algorithm 1 for maximizing the observability.

Algorithm 1: Meter Placement Algorithm

```
Install soft-sensors where applicable
Apply state identification
for each level of the tree (from root)
    while more unobserved node at current level
        Select an unobserved node with maximum
        observability
        if more metering instruments available
            if current node is unobserved and is not
            the last unobserved child of its parent
                put a meter on the current node
            else
                continue to next level of tree
```

3.4 Errors

As with every measuring device, smart-meter outputs also have an error component. When the consumption readings of one node is derived from other nodes, this error adds up. If it exceeds the error bound on that particular node, install a smart-meter there. A larger error would have to be dealt with in the case of soft-sensors. Different error bounds would produce different placements.

4. METER PLACEMENT IN A BUILDING

Figure 3 depicts the electrical distribution of our CSE Department building and shows the result of applying the meter placement algorithm. From the source, the electrical

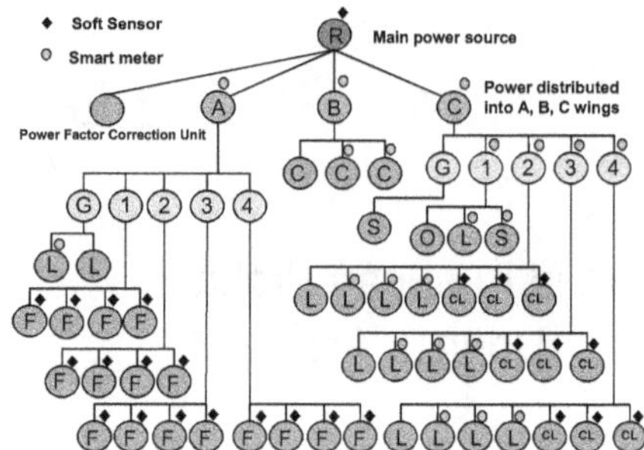

Figure 3: Meter placement with soft-sensors

system at the main power supply divides into three lines (each line with 3 phases), which supplies to the three wings A, B and C. A wing houses the Faculty offices (F), B wing conference rooms (C) and C wing classrooms (CL), office (O), server rooms (S) and labs (L).

Number of Meters at each node	61
Number of Meters at leaf node	47
Number of Meters given soft-sensors	21

Table 1: Number of meters required with various deployment techniques

When we have sufficient meters, we place them directly at each of the leaf nodes. In the case of insufficient meters, we start placement from root node R and follow the Algorithm 1 for meter placement. Soft-sensors can be used at faculty offices and classrooms. An occupancy detector sensor is sufficient because if the faculty/class is present, it has a more or less constant consumption. As can be inferred from Figure 2, number of ON machines is used as a soft sensor instead of placing smart-meter at the root node. This further reduces the number of meters required. As it can be seen from Table 1, the number of meters required for the full observability reduces significantly with the use of soft-sensors and optimal placement algorithm.

5. CONCLUSIONS AND APPLICATIONS

In this paper, we present an algorithm to optimally place smart-meters in a building without compromising on the observability using minimum number of smart-meters. We also show that by using soft-sensors this number can be reduced even further, albeit with lesser accuracy. Following are few of the applications of such a placement of meters:

- **Detecting and locating anomalies**: After anomaly detection in the root node meter, with multiple smart-meters, we can follow this anomaly upto the leaf nodes and localize the anomalous appliance, without requiring any occupant information as in [1].
- **Theft location**: Smart-meter deployments aid in detection of possible theft of power. An abnormally high consumption that cannot be accounted for in any node points to theft.

6. REFERENCES

[1] K. Palani, N. Nasir, V. C. Prakash, A. Chugh, R. Gupta, and K. Ramamritham. Putting smart meters to work: Beyond the usual. In *Proceedings of the 5th International Conference on Future Energy Systems*, e-Energy '14, pages 237–238, New York, NY, USA, 2014. ACM.

The Energy Cost of Your Netflix Habit

Oche Ejembi
School of Computer Science
University of St Andrews, UK
ooe@st-andrews.ac.uk

Saleem N. Bhatti
School of Computer Science
University of St Andrews, UK
saleem@st-andrews.ac.uk

ABSTRACT

Through measurements on our testbed, we show how users of Netflix could make energy savings of up to 34% by adjusting video quality settings. By using Netflix as a case study, we aim to assess the impact of energy usage in Video-on-demand (VoD) services. We estimate the potential impact of video quality settings on energy usage on a global scale.

1. INTRODUCTION

Video-on-Demand (VoD) is by far the most popular type of traffic on the Internet today (April 2015). The Sandvine Global Internet Phenomena report for H1/2014 [1], reports that VoD was responsible for 64%|40% of all the downstream traffic experienced on fixed|mobile networks in the US. Cisco estimates that by 2018, 79% of all Internet traffic in the world will be some form of video. Video consumes more resources – network capacity, device CPU utilisation, memory, I/O, disk space etc. – than the other Internet media, such as text, audio and still images. So, it follows that video also consumes more energy and has a larger carbon footprint than other application flows.

Netflix is the world's largest *premium* VoD service, available to over 50 million users in almost 50 countries. It is responsible for 34% of the downstream traffic in the US [1]. In August 2014, Plusnet, a major ISP in the UK, announced that Netflix had become the largest single source of traffic on their networks during peak hours.

2. EXPERIMENT METHODOLOGY

We performed an empirical investigation of the CPU, energy, and network bandwidth consumption of Netflix video playback on a desktop client system. Our focus was investigating the client side energy usage of video on desktops: globally, the energy usage at the client is at least the same as that of datacentres [2].

Using a simple testbed, we made measurements of system resource usage for over 200 unique video titles from Netflix UK. Users may select one of three preferred quality levels (LOW, MEDIUM and HIGH), or allow Netflix to automatically choose, as shown in Figure 1.

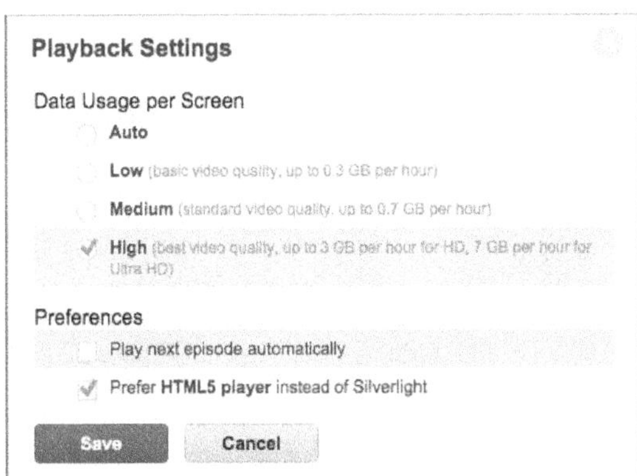

Figure 1: Netflix playback quality settings for selection by the user.

3. RESULTS

We captured the CPU utilisation, memory usage, network usage and power consumption at 1 second intervals during video playback. Figure 2 has summary results.

Previously, we defined an energy metric for video P_{dv} [3]:

$$\begin{aligned} P_{dv} &= \frac{\text{energy usage for video decoding/playback}}{t_v} \\ &= P_a - P_{idle} \end{aligned} \qquad (1)$$

where P_{dv} is the mean energy usage per second of video decoding / playback, P_{dv} (units (J/s_v)), and t_v is the duration of the video stream in seconds. P_a is the mean measured power of the system during decoding (or encoding) of the video. P_{idle} is the mean power when the system is idle.

In Figure 2, each data point used for the boxplot is the mean of 5 runs from a 2-minute clip of video from the chosen video title. Figure 2a is energy usage as given by equation 1). We obtain average values of 10.8 J/s_v, 12.7 J/s_v and 14.5 J/s_v for the respective quality levels. This corresponds to a difference of 34% between LOW and HIGH quality levels. We observe significant variability in the energy and system resource usage over the entire corpus, even at the same quality levels.

We measured system resources (CPU and memory utilisation), with the Unix program *top*, and the network utilisation, with the program *tshark*. In Figure 2b and 2c, we show boxplots summarising the CPU utilisation and network bitrate for the entire corpus, grouped by Netflix quality level.

e-Energy'15, July 14–17, 2015, Bangalore, India.
ACM 978-1-4503-3609-3/15/07
http://dx.doi.org/10.1145/2768510.2770951.

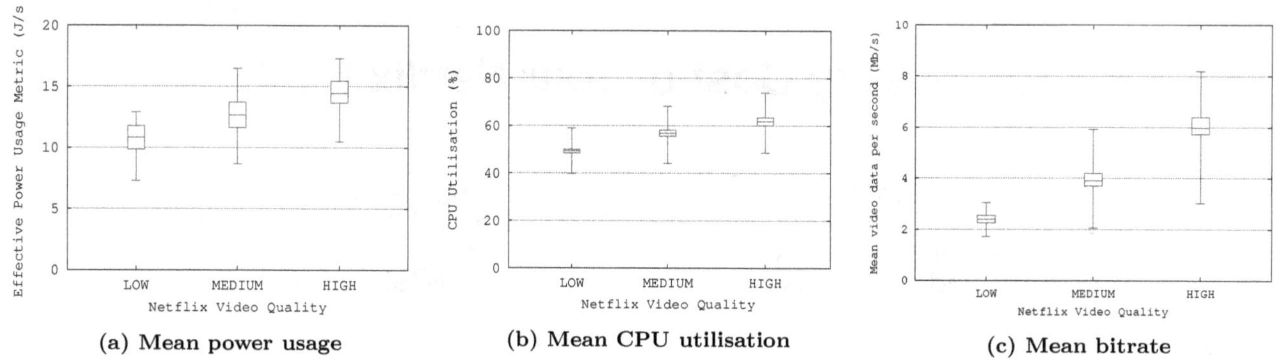

(a) Mean power usage (b) Mean CPU utilisation (c) Mean bitrate

Figure 2: Summary of the resource usage (energy, CPU and network) for playback of the entire corpus of Netflix videos at the available quality levels. The corpus consisted of 202 videos. Each data point is the mean of 5 runs, each of 120 seconds in duration.

4. ENERGY SAVINGS AND TRADE-OFFS

A simple Fermi estimate based on our observations gives a view of energy usage by VoD at global scales, showing the significant cumulative impact from even small savings at individual client systems. Netflix claim they have over 50 million subscribers, and Nielsen Research[1] suggests that roughly 60% (~30 million) of Netflix subscribers watch via a personal computer. Netflix have further claimed that 2 billion hours of video are streamed from their servers every month. Assuming savings as we have measured of 3.7 J/s_v by watching all video at LOW quality instead of HIGH, this would be a total of ~7.4 million KWh a month or 88.8 Million KWh a year. To appreciate the scale of these savings, 88.8 Million KWh is enough energy required to power 21,382 homes in the United Kingdom or 114,138 homes in India for a year (based on available estimates[2]).

Our Fermi estimate is not an authoritative or comprehensive estimate: we wish only to show the sheer scale of the energy savings potentially possible, and raise awareness of the amount of energy consumed by video streaming. Our assumptions that all users will see similar savings as our testbed and chose lower quality will not hold generally – some equipment may have greater energy usage, some may have less; while users may chose different quality levels based on personal preferences and costs. There are several other VoD services which have very significant numbers of users and viewing hours, so our numbers are likely to be an underestimate of the true overall impact of VoD. Users need to be informed of energy usage and incenitivised to make energy-efficient choices, an issue of ongoing research in the wider community. In Figure 3, we propose a modification to the Netflix user interface of Figure 1.

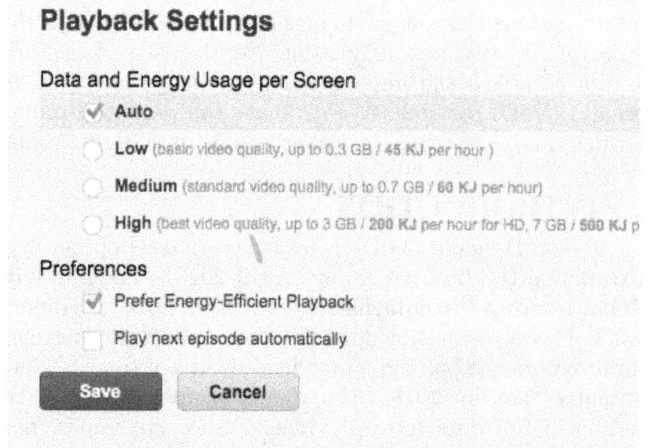

Figure 3: A mock-up of modified Netflix quality selection page with very simple energy usage information. This information could be based on a system specific benchmark or crowdsourced usage data.

5. CONCLUSION AND FUTURE WORK

Small energy savings on video playback for a single client can sum to significant energy savings when considered for a global population of users. Our experiments and estimates show there is the potential to save many millions of KWh of energy if users can be incentivised to make appropriate choices in video streaming.

Items for future work include: finer-grained analyses of the energy usage of video playback across genres / spatio-temporal classification; studies on mobile and other devices (e.g Smart TVs); exploring green quality of experience (QoE) metrics and energy usage feedback for video; and incentives for saving energy while using digital video. A benchmark tool for video energy usage, based partly on the work presented here is currently under development [4].

Acknowledgements

This work was partly supported by the IU-ATC project, funded by grant EP/J016756/1 from the Engineering and Physical Sciences Research Council (EPSRC). Oche Ejembi is funded by the Scottish Informatics and Computer Science Alliance (SICSA).

6. REFERENCES

[1] "Global Internet Phenomena Report 1H 2014," Jul 2014. [Online]. Available: http://goo.gl/Lb33Wf

[2] P. Somavat, S. Jadhav, and V. Namboodiri, "Accounting for the Energy Consumption of Personal Computing Including Portable Devices," in *e-Energy2010 - 1st ACM Intl. Conf. Energy-Efficient Computing and Networking*, 2010.

[3] O. Ejembi and S. N. Bhatti, "Help save the planet: Please do adjust your picture," in *MM2014 - 22nd ACM Intl. Conf. on Multimedia*, Nov 2014.

[4] ——, "Towards Energy Benchmarking for Green Video," in *SustainIT2015 - 4th IFIP Conf. on Sustainable Internet*, Apr 2015.

[1] http://www.nielsen.com

[2] http://www.wec-indicators.enerdata.eu/household-electricity-use.html

Poster Abstract: "Let There be Light: Unveiling how PRIME Networks Actually Work"

Miguel Seijo,
Jose Ignacio Moreno,
Gregorio López
Universidad Carlos III
Leganés, Spain
name.surname@uc3m.es

Fernando Martín
Unión Fenosa Distribución
Madrid, Spain
fmartins@gasnatural.com

Javier Matanza,
Sadot Alexandres,
Carlos Rodríguez
ICAI School of Engineering
Madrid, Spain
jmatanza@comillas.edu
sadot@comillas.edu
carlos.rodriguez@comillas.edu

Categories and Subject Descriptors

C.2.2 [**Network Protocols**]: Protocol verification; C.2.3 [**Network Operations**]: Network monitoring

Keywords

Advanced Metering Infrastructure; Narrowband Power Line Communications; PoweRline Intelligent Metering Evolution; Smart Grid; Traffic Analysis

1. PROBLEM STATEMENT

Advanced Metering Infrastructures (AMI) represent the first steps towards a fully operational Smart Grid. Narrow Band Power Line Communications (NB-PLC) technologies, such as PoweRline Intelligent Metering Evolution (PRIME), are winning momentum in the last-mile of current AMI deployments, mainly due to the benefits that using the low voltage cables as communications medium brings to Distribution System Operators (DSOs) [3].

PRIME specification is open, which promotes its implementation by the major smart meter manufacturers. However, as in many other communications standards, PRIME specification just sets the maximum values of certain communications parameters that may influence overall network performance, thus leaving them up to the manufacturer.

So, how do communications in PRIME networks actually work? Are all the manufacturers setting such parameters to the same values or not? Are such parameters being set based on network conditions? The main goal of this study is to shed some light, for the very first time, on this issue. In order to achieve this goal, we develop a novel tool to automatically process PRIME traffic traces and we use it to analyze an actual PRIME network involving smart meters and concentrators from the main manufacturers of the market.

e-Energy'15, July 14-17 2015, Bangalore, India
ACM 978-1-4503-3609-3/15/07
http://dx.doi.org/10.1145/2768510.2770952.

2. RESOURCES AND METHODOLOGY

This study is based on data gathered from actual tests carried out in the Network Integration Laboratory (LINTER) of Unión Fenosa Distribución [1]. Notably, the main files used as input to the analysis are: "S11 Report", "Results", and "Traffic Trace".

"S11 Report" is a standard report obtained from the concentrator that includes information about the network topology in eXtensible Markup Language (XML) format. By processing it, we obtained that there were 88 smart meters, 3 of them working as switches, with 4, 3 and 2 nodes reaching the concentrator through each of them.

"Results" is a Comma Separated Values (CSV) file also obtained from the concentrator including miscellaneous information about the smart meters of the network. By processing it, we unveiled that the PRIME network under study was composed of devices from 9 different manufacturers.

"Traffic Trace" is a log of all the messages exchanged between the smart meters and the concentrators. The log provided by the Circutor concentrator used in this analysis includes CSV for the PRIME layer and hexadecimal representation of the application layer (Device Language Message Specification/COmpanion Specification for Energy Metering (DLMS/COSEM)). From this log we extracted relevant information such as: physical layer parameters like the modulation in use or the Signal to Noise Ratio (SNR) values for the uplink communication between the meters directly connected to the concentrator and the concentrator; link and upper layer parameters like the Medium Access Control (MAC) Maximum Transfer Unit (MTU) or the effective Window Size (WS); and high-level quality indicators such as the time to read a standard 24-hours consumption report (so-called "S02") from each meter (TTR_i).

The data from the traffic trace was extracted using regular expressions in MATLAB. One of the main challenges of this procedure was to deal with the optional headers that the frame might contain [2]. The MTU value was extracted from all the PRIME frames starting a DLMS/COSEM *GetResponse* block and set to the maximum of all these values. The effective WS was calculated as the number of PRIME frames sent without acknowledge during the data response. TTR_i was calculated as the time between the first DLMS/COSEM *GetRequest* and the first PRIME frame that belongs to the DLMS/COSEM superframe with flag *LastBlock* sets to true.

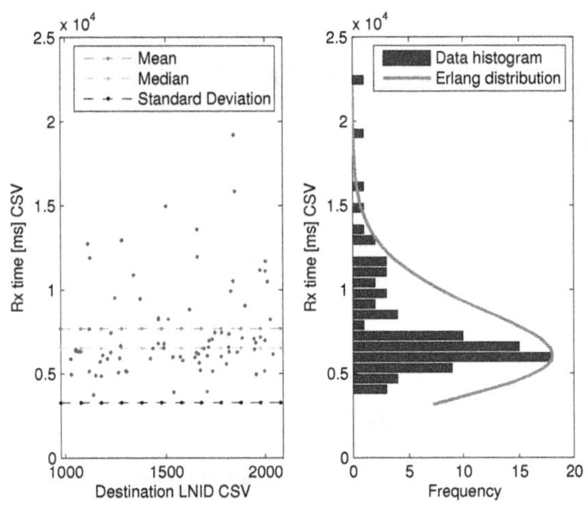

Figure 1: TTR_i - LNID vs Time and Histogram

Table 1: Number of different configurations

# meters	Effective WS	MTU (Bytes)
7	6	47
2	1	211
33	4	67
5	4	64
4	2	67
2	1	67
18	1	115
4	4	68
3	3	65
1	1	178
2	3	52
1	1	79
1	1	178

3. MAIN FINDINGS

Regarding the physical parameters, it was observed that manufacturers are currently only implementing the most robust communication mode, namely Differential Binary Phase Shifting Keying (DBPSK) with Forward Error Correction (FEC) ON, which allows raw data rate up to 21.4 Kbps. The evolution of SNR with time was also obtained, which can be very useful to diagnose potential communications problems.

Analyzing the number of different WS/MTU configurations, we obtain the 13 groups shown in Table 1. Comparing groups based on WS/MTU configurations in Table 1 with the 9 different vendors obtained from the "Results" file, we can conclude that these parameters take different values depending on the manufacturer and even on the firmware (both PRIME and DLMS/COSEM) version.

The results from the TTR_i analysis are shown in Figure 1. It can be observed that most of the smart meters need the same amount of time to be read, as their TTR values are close to the median. Nevertheless, there are also some outliers. Based on the histogram of the measured TTR also shown in Figure 1, it can be seen that such a random variable may be modeled using an Erlang distribution, which may be interesting for potential simulations.

4. DISCUSSION

Traffic analysis, such as the one presented in this study, is of capital importance to DSOs, since it allows for network forensics and diagnosis, helping them to identify and solve communications problems they are facing on their day-to-day operation.

This kind of analysis is also specially relevant to appropriately configure communications network simulators [4] based on cross-validation, which allows increasing their reliability when simulating novel scenarios. Simulation tools are indeed critical for DSOs since they support network design and planning while mitigating the investment costs.

A similar approach to the one presented in this paper can be also followed to characterize typical scenarios (e.g., urban, rural, semi-urban) by applying data mining and machine learning techniques to analyze large datasets of traffic traces.

5. CONCLUSIONS

This study unveils that in a multi-vendor network with devices from 9 manufacturers, there are 13 different configurations of certain communications parameters related to network performance, such as the MTU or the effective WS. The heterogeneity of configurations invites to conclude that the problem of the optimum configurations of the communications parameters that are left up to implementation by the PRIME standard is still unsolved (since indeed it will not actually have one single solution). This inspires carrying out research on optimal parameter configurations depending on the specific constraints of given scenarios in order to propose the results to smart meter manufacturers and DSOs. Taking into account that AMI represents such a huge and competitive market and that Power Line Communications (PLC) use such a harsh communications medium, the paper sets the foundation of a certain hot research topic in Smart Grids in the coming years.

6. ACKNOWLEDGMENTS

The research leading to these results has been partly funded by the Spanish Ministry of Economy and Competitiveness through the project OSIRIS (RTC-2014-1556-3).

7. REFERENCES

[1] U. F. Distribución. Linter official website. `http://www.unionfenosadistribucion.com/en/smart+grids/1297137260045/find+out+about+our+laboratory.html`. [Online; accessed 8-January-2015].

[2] ITU-T. G.9904 : Narrowband orthogonal frequency division multiplexing power line communication transceivers for PRIME networks. Technical report, 2012.

[3] G. Lopez, J. I. Moreno, H. Amaris, and F. Salazar. Paving the road toward smart grids through large-scale advanced metering infrastructures. *Electric Power Systems Research*, 120:194–205, March 2015.

[4] J. Matanza, S. Alexandres, and C. Rodríguez-Morcillo. Advanced metering infrastructure performance using european low-voltage power line communication networks. *IET Communications*, May 2014.

Enabling Automated Dynamic Demand Response: From Theory to Practice

Marc Frincu, Charalampos Chelmis, Rizwan Saeed, Viktor Prasanna
Electrical Engineering Department
University of Southern California
{frincu, chelmis, saeedm, prasanna}@usc.edu

Saima Aman, Vasilis Zois
Computer Science Department
University of Southern California
{saman, vzois}@usc.edu

ABSTRACT

Demand response (DR) is used in smart grids to shape customer load during peak hours. Automated DR offers utilities a fine grained control and a high degree of confidence in the outcome. However the impact on the customer's comfort means this technique is more suited for industrial and commercial settings than for residential homes. In this paper we present a real-life system for achieving automated controlled DR in a heterogeneous environment. The system is integrated with the USC microgrid. Results show that while on a per building per event basis the accuracy of our prediction and customer selection techniques varies, it performs well on average when considering several events and buildings.

Categories and Subject Descriptors

H.4 [**Information Systems**]: Information Systems Applications; J.m [**Computer Applications**]: Miscellaneous

General Terms

Smart Grid; Automated direct demand response platform;

1. INTRODUCTION

With the increasing presence of smart appliances, smart grids have a great opportunity to become ubiquitous in our society. Their unique advantages driven by the bidirectional smart meter communication channel between providers and customers make them suited for energy consumption optimization. Demand Response (DR) is a well known technique used by utilities to shape customers load especially during peak hours when the generation capacity is in danger of being exceeded. Utilities have at their disposal a variety of techniques including direct control , incentives , or voluntary programs to reduce peak demand.

Direct control is a technique which lets utilities control the customers' appliances directly without relying on incentives or voluntary participation. For this reason it can be seen as intrusive and having a considerable impact on the customer lifestyles. Hence, it seems more suited for offices and industrial complexes than for residential customers. Nonetheless its advantages including fine grained control of the amount of energy to curtail and the ability to efficiently target specific areas and time periods make it suited for further research into how it can be easily and with minimal impact integrated in complex microgrid environments consisting of heterogeneous buildings (e.g., offices, residential apartments, libraries, lecture rooms).

To achieve a customer-tolerated and utility-efficient directly controlled DR numerous factors need to be taken into consideration including: data privacy, customer satisfiability, reliability of the controlled DR action, and fast turnaround time of the decision process. To make things more complicate the DR model widely used nowadays needs to consider more realistic scenarios on when, for how long, by how much, and how (whom to pick) to reduce electricity consumption. We call this decision making process Dynamic DR (D^2R). We have addressed all the above in numerous papers that can be found on our group's website[1].

2. EXPERIMENTAL TESTBED

The USC microgrid, peaking at around 27 MW, is a unique environment to study the impact of direct control in complex social and cultural environments by offering a state-of-the-art control center capable of managing 170 buildings spread across two campuses and totaling more than 50,000 sensors. This makes the USC campus a truly "living laboratory" for advancing Smart Grid research and technology [5]. The USC Facility Management Services (FMS) owns and operates the campus electrical infrastructure which includes two substations and a 3 million gallon Thermal Energy Storage (TES) system complementing the existing chilled water system. FMS has more than 6 years worth of historical and real-time kWh consumption data, gathered from 33 DR enabled buildings, aggregated at 15 minute intervals. Combined with

[1] http://ganges.usc.edu/wiki/Smart_Grid

e-Energy'15, July 14–17, 2015, Bangalore, India.
ACM 978-1-4503-3609-3/15/07.
http://dx.doi.org/10.1145/2768510.2775333.

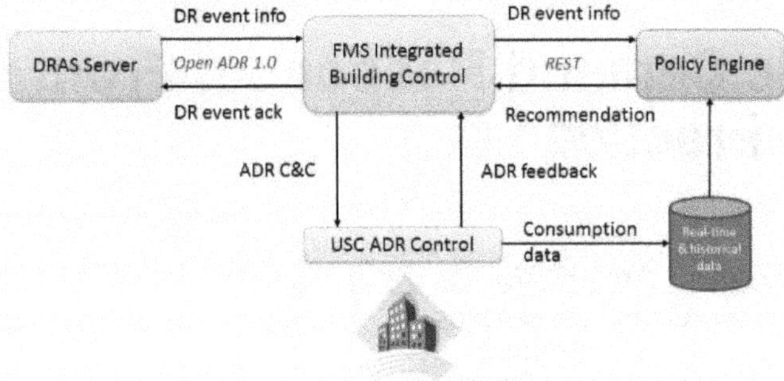

Figure 1: Overview of the complete automated D^2R system.

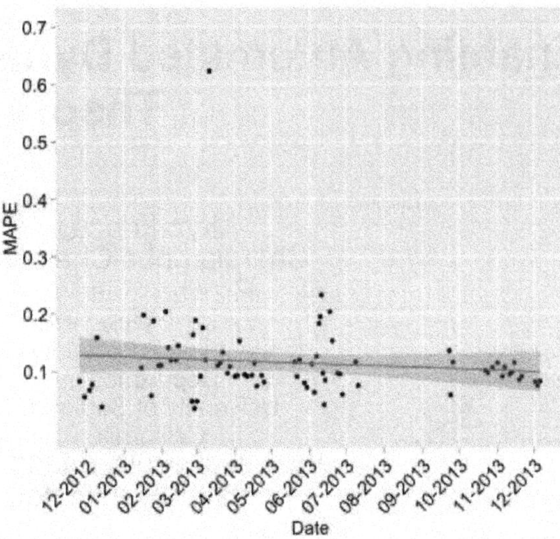

Figure 2: Average MAPE error per event across buildings.

detailed information on the classes' schedule, buildings' occupancy, and weather data, it offers a unique opportunity to investigate the main challenges and possible solutions to adopting an efficient and reliable controlled DR program in complex dynamic environments. Currently FMS's focus is on HVAC based DR (through Duty Cycling, Variable Frequency Drive, Global Temperature Reset) but upgrades to extend it to other DR techniques such as those based on the lighting system are planned.

The USC microgrid is also a test bed for the LA DWP Smart Grid Demonstration Project (SGRDP) [3] which involves more than 50,000 residential customers in voluntary and controlled (through smart home appliances) DR.

3. SYSTEM REALIZATION

We have bundled our consumption and prediction methods as well as customer and DR strategy selection algorithms in a Demand Decision Support (DDS) API module integrated with FMS's infrastructure.

The USC microgrid communicates with the LA DWP DRAS server [4] through OpenADR [1] messages. Internally, the software infrastructure consists of two main components: the Integrated Building Control (IBC) and our DDS. The former is in charge of controlling buildings through the BACnet protocol [2], while the latter is responsible for the building-strategy selection during each DR event. Figure 1 gives an overview of the system's main components. A typical workflow begins with an LA DWP OpenADR message containing the request details for a DR event (e.g., datetime, duration, curtailment target). For the USC microgrid the duration is always set between 1:00PM and 5:00PM due to the specific LA climate. Once it has received the request, the IBC forwards the details to DDS including additional details such as the list of buildings and associated DR strategies for the given event. DDS then processes the message, performs consumption and curtailment predictions based on historical and real-time data (i.e., consumption, weather, occupancy, etc.), and recommends the building-strategy pairs to be used in DR. This list is sent back to IBC which puts the selected buildings into DR by using the suggested strategies. Information on the achieved curtailment and estimated achievable target is sent back to the LA DWP DRAS every 15 minutes. To ensure a sustainable D^2R a building-strategy reselection is performed hourly. Finally, the outcome of the DR event is sent 15 minutes after its completion, by providing LA DWP with information on the achieved curtailment and the deviation from the initial estimate.

Analysis of over 400 DR events run between 1:00PM and 5:00PM from Nov 2012 to Dec 2014 have shown that our system is capable of achieving low MAPE error per event (cf. Figure 2). Individually, around 49% of buildings had an error less than 10% while 6% were greater than 20%.

4. ACKNOWLEDGMENTS

This material is based upon work supported by the United States Department of Energy under Award Number number DE-OE0000192, and the Los Angeles Department of Water and Power (LA DWP). The views and opinions of authors expressed herein do not necessarily state or reflect those of the United States Government or any agency thereof, the LA DWP, nor any of their employees.

5. ADDITIONAL AUTHORS

Carol Fern (Facility Management Services, email: `carol.fern@usc.edu`) and Aras Akbari (Smart Utility Systems and LA DWP Contractor, email: `Aras.Akbari@ladwp.com`).

6. REFERENCES

[1] O. A. Alliances. Open automated demand response, 2014. URL: http://www.openadr.org/ (accessed May 23, 2014).

[2] ASHRAE. Bacnet, 2015. URL: http://www.bacnet.org/ (accessed Jan 3, 2015).

[3] L. DWP. Los angeles department of water and power smart grid regional demonstration, 2014. URL: `https://www.smartgrid.gov/project/los\_angeles\_department\_water\_and\_power\_smart\_grid\_regional\_demonstration` (accessed Dec 16, 2014).

[4] E. Koch and M. A. Piette. Architecture concepts and technical issues for an open, interoperable automated demand response infrastructure. *Lawrence Berkeley National Laboratory*, 2008.

[5] U. of Southern California. Usc living lab and smart grid, 2014. URL: `http://losangeles.usc.edu/` (accessed Dec 16, 2014).

The Pervasive Data Center and the Elusive Negawatt

Amod Ranade
Schneider Electric India
amod.ranade@schneider-electric.com

ABSTRACT

Data Centers today are everywhere. Its becoming increasingly difficult to imagine any service or interaction today; that does not involve Information Technology. The IT landscape is fast evolving, introducing new technologies, architectures and consumption models.

Traditionally, critical infrastructure like Data centers have not been looked at from an agility and innovation perspective. Tools like the internet-of-things, BIG Data & analytics hold a lot of promise in evolving the infrastructure design and operation and making it "smart".

Our infrastructures today are smarter, machine to machine communication is becoming common place. The resulting BIG Data is creating opportunities for leveraging the analytics to help support the IT environments in becoming more nimble, agile, and efficient.

The Energy consumed by IT is only half the story, there exists an equally large opportunity to reduce energy consumption in the infrastructure space. The presentation will discuss some of the trends in technology and architecture that are helping the industry capture the elusive Negawatt in the Data Center infrastructure.

Categories and Subject Descriptors

E.0 [General]

Keywords

Data Center, Energy Efficiency.

e-Energy'15, July 14-17, 2015, Bangalore, India.
ACM 978-1-4503-3609-3/15/07.
http://dx.doi.org/10.1145/2768510.2775331

BIO

Amod Ranade is General Manager - Data Center Business Development at Schneider Electric. He focuses on business development of the Data Center portfolio from Schneider Electric.

He comes with a rich experience in Data Center offerings having held Product/Program management positions for Site and Facilities Services at IBM India. He was involved in driving various Programs for Data Center infrastructure services offerings; in different stages of the Data Center infrastructure lifecycle (Design, Build, Assessment & Audits).

Amod also comes with a strong background with respect to Data Center technologies with respect to Power, Cooling and Management software having held Product Management positions in APC by Schneider Electric for Data Center Solutions. He has also managed Data Center related product lines (Racks and Power distribution systems, High Density cooling systems, etc).

Amod is an MBA and an Engineering graduate from University of Pune.

Data Center Energy Efficiency Standards in India: Preliminary Findings from Global Practices

Sanyukta Raje, Hemant Maan, Suprotim Ganguly, Tanvin Singh, and Nisha Jayaram
Confederation of Indian Industry (CII)
New Delhi, India 110003
+91 11 45771000, 24629994/7 (Ext: 403)
Suprotim.Ganguly@cii.in

Girish Ghatikar, Steve Greenberg, Satish Kumar, and Dale Sartor
Lawrence Berkeley National Laboratory (LBNL)
Berkeley, CA 94608 United States
+1 510-486-5988
DASartor@lbl.gov

ABSTRACT

Global data center energy consumption is growing rapidly. In India, information technology industry growth, fossil-fuel generation, and rising energy prices add significant operational costs and carbon emissions from energy-intensive data centers. Adoption of energy-efficient practices can improve the global competitiveness and sustainability of data centers in India. Previous studies have concluded that advancement of energy efficiency standards through policy and regulatory mechanisms is the fastest path to accelerate the adoption of energy-efficient practices in the Indian data centers. In this study, we reviewed data center energy efficiency practices in the United States, Europe, and Asia. Using evaluation metrics, we identified an initial set of energy efficiency standards applicable to the Indian context using the existing policy mechanisms. These preliminary findings support next steps to recommend energy efficiency standards and inform policy makers on strategies to adopt energy-efficient technologies and practices in Indian data centers.

Categories and Subject Descriptors

D.2.8 [**Software Engineering**]: Metrics – *Performance measures,* H.3.4 [**Information Storage and Retrieval**]: Systems and Software – *Performance evaluation (efficiency and effectiveness)*

General Terms

Design, Documentation, Economics, Measurement, Performance, Standardization, Verification

Keywords

Best Practices; Data Centers; Energy Efficiency; Technologies; Standards and Codes; Evaluation Metrics; Carbon Emissions; Energy Consumption

1. INTRODUCTION

Data centers are energy-intensive facilities that support a diverse set of services such as Web, e-mail, data storage, and processing. They are operated around the clock, and are energy intensive. It has been reported that global data center emissions will grow 7% year-on-year through 2020 [1]. Over the last decade India has witnessed increased demand in data because of explosive growth in smartphones and widespread use of social media apps, banking and e-commerce transactions, and multimedia storage needs, providing an impetus to the large growth in data center markets in India. According to studies, Indian data center spending on storage, server, and network equipment reached USD 2.2 billion in 2012, and this market is expected to grow at a compound annual growth rate of 8.5% to reach USD 3 billion by 2016 [2]. Energy represents one of the most significant operating costs in data centers. Rising energy costs increase their operational expenses. In India, where coal is the primary source of electricity generation, it is necessary for data centers to adopt sustainable operations. In power-deficit India, energy efficiency offers the following benefits to data centers: (a) increased reliability of electricity supply; (b) reduction in operating costs; and (c) enhanced efficiency in design and operations.

It is estimated that achieving just half of the technologically feasible savings by adopting best practices could cut electric use in data centers by 40% [3]. In India, the increased focus on data center efficiency, reliability, and cost optimization has led to the identification of challenges such as: (a) lack of integrated building design approach; (b) lack of technical awareness, exposure to best practices, and energy-efficient solutions; (c) identification of information technology (IT) infrastructure needs to keep up with evolving technologies; and (d) lack of regulatory measures and an institutional framework to promote energy efficiency. The industry has noted these challenges, and efficiency practices in data centers are high on the agenda. But it is not enough to simply recognize the need to save energy and improve efficiency; one must quantify key benefits associated with energy efficiency practices and prioritize the actions to achieve them. This quantification has been a key outcome from the collaborative U.S.– India activities since 2009 [4].

This paper outlines preliminary findings from a joint study supported by the United States (U.S.) and India. It presents a review of various global practices to provide data center energy efficiency in their respective countries and beyond. We propose energy efficiency evaluation metrics and application of these global practices to the Indian context. We review existing energy efficiency practices in India and show the key similarities that these measures share with global practices. These preliminary findings will aid next steps to recommend energy efficiency standards and inform policy makers on strategies to adopt energy-efficient technologies and practices in Indian data centers. Both public- and private sector stakeholders in India will review the recommendations from this study and specific recommendations for energy efficiency practices will be proposed following this exercise.

e-Energy'15, July 14-17, 2015, Bangalore, India.

ACM 978-1-4503-3609-3/15/07…$15.00.
DOI: http://dx.doi.org/10.1145/2768510.2768524

2. METHODOLOGY

Adoption practices and success stories from different countries are the stepping-stone to devising appropriate energy efficiency *guidelines* or *standards* (the terms used interchangeably in our study) for Indian data centers. Our effort focuses on a detailed review of energy efficiency guidelines or standards and assessment of their appropriateness for India. The initial step was to identify existing and relevant global energy efficiency practices for data centers. The following step was to list key evaluation metrics for these energy efficiency practices. Finally, energy efficiency practices were proposed and evaluation metrics were identified for each selected energy efficiency mechanism, to determine its relevancy to the India context.

3. EVALUATION OF GLOBAL ENERGY EFFICIENCY PRACTICES

The following global energy efficiency practices for data centers were reviewed for this study: *Energy Star Rating (U.S.)* [5], *Leadership in Energy and Environment Design (U.S)* [6], *American Society of Heating, Refrigerating and Air-Conditioning Engineers (U.S)* [7], *California Title 24 Standards (U.S)* [8], *National Australian Built Environment Rating System (Australia)* [9], *Green Mark (Singapore)* [10], *Green Building Index (Malaysia)* [11], *Certified Energy Efficient Data Center Audit (U.K)* [12], *Building Research Establishment Environmental Assessment Method (U.K)* [13], *European Code of Conduct* [14], *Blue Angel Eco-Label (Germany)* [15], *and International Standards Organization 50001: 2011 (Europe)* [16]. The following section describes these global practices.

- **ENERGY STAR Rating by Environment Protection Agency (EPA):** The score, expressed as a number on a 1-to-100 scale, such that one point represents 1% of the population. Performance ratings given on a percentile basis.
- **Leadership in Energy and Environmental Design (LEED):** The certification recognizes a best-in-class data center based on the score achieved on a scale of 110 points.
- **American Society of Heating, Refrigerating and Air-Conditioning Engineers (ASHRAE) 90.1:** This standard establishes the minimum energy efficiency requirements of buildings, including Data Centers and Telecommunications Buildings, for design, construction, and a plan for operation and maintenance, as well as utilization of on- or off-site renewable energy resources.
- **California Title 24 Standards:** The standard focuses on key areas to improve the energy efficiency of new data centers, additions, and major alterations to existing data centers.
- **National Australian Built Environment Rating System (NABERS):** This is a tool to measure environmental performance on a scale of 1 to 6 stars. Rating is done across three categories.
- **Green Mark:** This Singapore performance-based rating system awards points for green features, energy efficiency, and best practices.
- **Green Building Index (GBI):** This is derived from existing rating tools, including the Green Mark, but extensively modified for relevance to the Malaysian tropical weather, environmental context, and cultural and social needs.
- **Certified Energy Efficient Datacenter Audit (CEEDA):** This U.K-based award assesses the implementation of energy efficiency best practices within a data center.
- **Building Research Establishment Environmental Assessment for Data Centers (BREAM):** This U.K-based rating, also practiced by Hong Kong, is based on the total score achieved by a data center across ten categories.
- **European Code of Conduct by the European Commission:** This promotes data center energy efficiency by setting targets, understanding of energy demand, raising awareness, and recommending energy-efficient best practices.
- **Blue Angel Eco-Label:** This label may be awarded to any resource-conscious company committed to the implementation of a long-term strategy to improve the energy and resource efficiency of its data center with respect to the IT services to be delivered and conducting regular monitoring to optimize its data center operations.
- **International Organization for Standardization (ISO) 50001 Standard for Energy Management Systems (EMS):** This international standard specifies EMS requirements upon which data centers can develop and implement an energy policy, and establish objectives, targets, and action plans which take into account legal requirements and information related to significant energy use.

Additional practices reviewed include: energy efficiency programmes such as *Building Energy Rating (Ireland)* [17], *Green Star Rating System (Australia)* [18], and *German Sustainable Building Certificate* [19]. Two other important mechanisms to determine resource availability are *Uptime Institute (U.S.)* [20] and *Data Center Star Audit (Germany)* [21]. *The Green Grid* has developed the *Data Center Maturity Model* [22].

All these countries have varied approaches for data center energy efficiency practices. To normalize these global practices against the existing energy efficiency mechanisms in India, we classify them under four broad categories and provide descriptions.

i. *Point-Based (Whole-Building) Ratings*
ii. *Best Practices/Guidelines-Oriented Ratings*
iii. *Comparative-Scale Ratings*
iv. *Performance-Based Relative Benchmarking*

A few basic common characteristics are described to establish the similarities in approach and other basic characteristics between existing energy efficiency mechanisms in India and some of the global energy efficiency methods.

i. Point-Based (Whole-Building) Rating systems reward design excellence through specifications of building components, systems, and processes in a quantifiable fashion by allocating credits or points to achieve different levels of environmental performance. Points are awarded against each of these parameters, and the cumulative sum of these points is categorized to define the level of energy efficiency achieved. These awards are usually time bound and need reassessment after fixed time tenures. Most of them also address other aspects of sustainable design and operation (such as water use, energy and water sources, materials, and indoor environment) in an attempt to achieve a holistic rating for environmental sustainability. Energy efficiency mechanisms that follow this approach are *Leadership in Energy and Environmental Design (LEED), Certified Energy Efficient Data Center Audit (CEEDA), Building Research Establishment Environmental Assessment Method (BREEAM), Green Building Index (GBI),* and *Green Mark.*

ii. Best Practices/Guidelines-Oriented Ratings define energy efficiency targets, which must be achieved through a defined action plan, based on the guidelines defined in the policy document. The successful achievement of these targets leads to the certification of the data center as an "Energy Efficient Data Center." Standards/Policies based on this approach are the *European Code of Conduct*, *ISO 50001*, and *Blue Angel Eco-Label*.

iii. Comparative-Scale Ratings emphasize a relative rating system, wherein a peer group of buildings with similar characteristics and services are defined, and the rating is awarded based on a relative percentile. Energy efficiency data center mechanisms based on this rating are the *ENERGY STAR* rating and the *National Australian Built Environment Rating System (NABERS)*.

iv. Performance-Based Relative Benchmarking focuses on energy efficiency related to building envelope; heating, ventilation, and air-conditioning (HVAC); lighting; water; gas; etc. It offers compliance through a prescriptive whole-building performance method using a simulation model to assess energy performance. Standards based on this approach include American Society of Heating, Refrigerating and Air-Conditioning Engineers (ASHRAE) 90.1 and California Title 24 standards. The standard ASHRAE 90.4, *Energy Standard for Data Centers and Telecommunication Buildings,* is proposed and under review.

Most of the short-listed energy efficiency data center practices have adopted *Power Usage Effectiveness (PUE)* and *Data Center Infrastructure Efficiency (DCiE),* introduced by The Green Grid [23], as an evaluation metric or criteria to rate data center energy efficiency. While PUE is the ratio of a facility's total power drawn to the amount of power used solely by the data center's IT equipment, DCiE is its inverse. The PUE and DCiE gauge the efficiency of a data center by focusing mostly on the support infrastructure (e.g., cooling).

4. EVALUATION AND METRICS FOR ENERGY EFFICIENCY PRACTICES

Evaluation metrics for energy efficiency are the instruments used to accurately capture the efficiency of a data center or its components. Evaluation metrics can be used to capture unique requirements for the Indian data centers. For e.g., data centers in India operate in hot and humid weather, and poor outdoor air quality conditions with less opportunity for water and airside free cooling technologies. Poor power quality and reliability also leads to increased use of power systems and backups. Many such metrics have evolved over the years to simplify the evaluation procedure and increase the efficiency of data capture for calculations. Attempts have been made to categorize and summarize the evaluation metrics. The evaluation metrics have been grouped into two categories: (a) ***Basic Metrics:*** *Cooling System Efficiency (CSE), Airflow Efficiency (AE), Cooling System Sizing (CSS), Air Economizer Utilization (AEU), Water Economizer Utilization (WEU), Data Center Infrastructure Efficiency (DCiE)* [23], *Power Usage Effectiveness (PUE)* [24] [23] [25] [26], *HVAC Effectiveness, Data Center Energy Productivity (DCeP)* [27] [23], and *Space, Watts and Performance (SWaP),* and (b) ***Extended Metrics:*** *Storage Utilization (Storage-U), Network Utilization (Network-U), and Server Utilization (Server-U)* [28]. The basic metrics define the level of efficiency of a data center and extended metrics are defined as functions of basic metrics that give an in-depth efficiency practices. There are many other metrics used around the world, typically to characterize sub-systems. For example, for infrastructure, cooling plant overall and component efficiencies, power distribution efficiency, and fan-specific power are used. For IT, utilization, virtualization, and power management are used. Several such metrics are covered in [26] and [27]. Others include: *Data Center Energy Efficiency and Productivity (DC-EEP)* [29], *Carbon* [27] [26], *Water Usage Effectiveness (Site) (WUE)* [30], and *Electronics Disposal Efficiency (EDE)* [31]. These evaluation metrics are also defined as "Green Performance Indicators" (GPIs) to assess a data center's environmental performance; in particular energy, greenhouse gas emissions, and resource efficiency. Further, the GPIs or metrics are classified as Data Center Level GPIs, SI system Level GPIs, IT system Level GPIs, and IT Benchmarks [32]. Among the standards/policies considered in this paper, seven standards/policies use PUE to provide a scoring or rating. The Green Mark rating system has benchmarked PUE in the range of 2.2–1.5 for existing data centers and 2.0–1.4 for new constructions. Malaysia's Green Building Index rating system [11] has benchmarked PUE in the range of 1.3–1.9. The PUE metric drives the need to minimize power used by anything other than IT. However, there are concerns that the metric does not consider the actual productivity or efficiency of the IT equipment [23]. Metrics that evaluate energy use by the generation sources are, Energy Reuse Effectiveness (ERE) and Green Energy Coefficient (GEC). The ERE [33] quantifies the amount of energy reused outside of the data center, and GEC looks at the amount of renewable energy used. SI-EER is similar to PUE. The DCeP is the ratio of work produced in the data center to the energy used in producing it [34].

5. OPPORTUNITIES FOR INDIA

With the introduction of the Energy Conservation Act 2001, the Government of India (GOI) started the efforts to institutionalize and mainstream energy efficiency, starting with the formation of the Bureau of Energy Efficiency (BEE) under the Ministry of Power. There are no dedicated energy efficiency data center standards/policies in India. However, there are a few mechanisms available for rating the energy efficiency of buildings (such as the *Indian Green Building Council* [35], *Energy Conservation Building Code (ECBC)* [36], *Star Rating – Standards and Labeling* [37], *Green Rating for Integrated Habitat Assessment* [38], and Star Rating for equipment. Additionally the Perform, Achieve and Trade (PAT) scheme of the GOI assigns mandatory emission reduction targets for the high energy-consuming industries, known as *Designated Consumers* [39]. Due to the page limit for this paper, Appendix A summarizes these energy efficiency initiatives, including the assessment criteria, compliance criteria, and award criteria.

These identified energy efficiency programmes have also been categorized across each of the four categories mentioned above in Section 3. This categorization shows that although India has no standards or policies specifically for energy efficiency in Indian data centers, it does have overall energy efficiency mechanisms that share a similar approach and the basic characteristics as some of the international standards/policies. The IGBC Rating System is based on a framework similar to other international point-based rating systems (e.g., LEED, BREEAM, GBI, Green Mark), which evaluates building performance against set criteria and points are assigned accordingly. Star Labeling of buildings by the BEE demonstrates certain similarities with the EPA ENERGY STAR rating scheme in terms of evaluation of energy performance. It is based on actual performance (metered data), and it provides a peer-group-based comparison (applicable to offices, hotels, retail malls, IT parks, and hospitals) that accounts operational characteristics of the building such as climatic zone, hours of operation, etc. It also provides a simple metric to evaluate energy performance of the building—i.e., Energy Performance Index (EPI). ECBC by BEE follows the same structure as the ASHRAE 90.1 standard and California T-24, and it covers building envelope, HVAC, service hot water and pumping, lighting, electric power, etc. Similar to ASHRAE 90.1 and California Title 24, there are three compliance options: Prescriptive, Trade-Off, and Whole-Building Performance Method. Due to the page limit for this paper, Appendix B compares the key characteristics of global energy efficiency practices with the Indian standards.

6. CONCLUSIONS AND NEXT STEPS

Enhancing energy efficiency through standards has been recognized as an appropriate strategy to reduce energy consumption in Indian data centers. Though India has well-established energy efficiency standards and practices in its non-data center sectors —commercial and industrial facilities—there are no dedicated standards for data centers. In this context, the review of global practices can aid the development of a "composite policy structure" for data center energy efficiency and help leapfrog India to embrace the concept of "Green IT" for sustained growth. This study established that existing energy efficiency programmes in India share certain similarities with some of the international policies/mechanisms reviewed in this study. The new policy framework for data centers can be a blend of existing energy efficiency programmes rather than a single mechanism to encompass the holistic rating of data centers in India. Indian policy makers can use the review of global practices to develop energy efficiency standards/guidelines specific to the Indian data centers and not reinvent the wheel.

Due to the necessity to engage both public- and private sector stakeholders when determining sustainability practices for the Indian context, specific recommendations will follow this process. The next steps includes consultative discussions with relevant public-private stakeholders in India, a survey capturing the views of various categories of data center stakeholders—technology providers, data center owners, hosting providers, policy makers, and academic and industry experts—on different energy efficiency practices, metrics, and technologies. The collaboration between the U.S. and India should lead to the formulation and implementation of a robust and impactful energy efficiency policy for the Indian data centers.

7. ACKNOWLEDGMENTS

The U.S. Department of Energy's Office of Energy Efficiency and Renewable Energy, under Contract No DE-AC02-05CH11231, funded LBNL activities, and managed under the auspices of the U.S.–India Energy Dialogue and the Power and Energy Efficiency Working Group. The U.S. Department of State partially funded the CII activities. The authors acknowledge the support from DOE and Energy Efficiency and Renewable Energy International Program staff, Rob Sandoli and Elena Berger. We are grateful to the Indian Bureau of Energy Efficiency's Director General, Dr. Ajay Mathur, and its staff for guidance. We extend our thanks to all the stakeholders for the continued support.

8. REFERENCES

[1] National Resources Defence Council. 2014. *Data Center Efficiency Assessment.*

[2] NASSCOM. 2012. *Data Center Landscape in India.*

[3] Whitney, P. D. Josh. 2014. *Data Center Efficiency Assessment.* NRDC.

[4] Ghatikar, G., Sartor, D., Kumar, S., and Kamath, M. 2011. *Opportunities and Challenges for Indian Data Center Energy Efficiency: Findings from Focus Groups.*

[5] Environmental Protection Agency. 2013. *ENERGY STAR Score for Data Centers in the United States.*

[6] U.S. Green Building Council. 2014. *LEED v4 Building Design and Construction Addenda.*

[7] ANSI/ASHRAE Standard 90.1. 2010.

[8] California Energy Commission. 2013. *Title 24, Building Efficiency Standards 2013.*

[9] State of NSW and Office of Environment and Heritage. 2011. *A guide to the NABERS Energy for data centres rating tools.*

[10] BCA-IDA. No date. *Green Mark for New Data Centres.*

[11] GBI. 2012. *GBI Assessment criteria NRNC: Data Centre.*

[12] British Computing Society - The Chartered Institute for IT. 2011. *Certified Energy Efficient Data Centre Award (CEEDA).*

[13] BRE Global. 2010. *BREEAM Scheme Document SD 5068.*

[14] European Commission. 2008. *Code of Conduct on Data Centres Energy Efficiency.*

[15] RAL gGmbH. 2012. *Basic Criteria for Award of the Environmental Label.*

[16] International Standard Organization. 2011. *Win the energy challenge with ISO 50001.*

[17] Sustainable Energy Authority of Ireland. No date. *A Guide to Building Energy Rating for Homeowners.*

[18] Green Building Council of Australia. DATE? *Australian Green Star Rating.*

[19] German Sustainable Building Council. 2008. *German Building Sustainable Certificate.*

[20] Uptime Institute. 2012. *Data Center Site Infrastructure Standard: Topology.*

[21] eco — Association of the German. 2013. *Eco Data Center Star Audit Version 3.*

[22] Singh. H. 2011. *Green Grid: Data Center Maturity Model.*

[23] The Green Grid. 2009. *Usage and public reporting guidelines for the green grid's infrastructure metrics PUE/DciE.*

[24] The Green Grid. 2007. *Green grid metrics: describing datacenter power efficiency.*

[25] The Green Grid. 2010. *Recommendations for measuring and reporting overall data center efficiency. Version 1e measuring PUE at dedicated data centers.*

[26] T. Geen. 2010. *The Green Grid Introduces Data Center Sustainabilty Metrics.*

[27] The Green Grid. 2014. *Harmonizing Global Metrics for Data Center Energy Efficiency Global Taskforce Reaches Agreement Regarding Data Center Productivity.*

[28] Wang, L., and Khan, S. 2011. *Review of performance metrics for green data centers: a taxonomy study.*

[29] K. Brill. 2007. *Data Center Energy Efficiency and Productivity.*

[30] T. G. Grid. 2011. *Water Usage Effectiveness: a green grid data center sustainability metric.*

[31] T. G. Grid. 2012. *Electronic Disposal Efficiency: An IT Recycling Metric for Enterprises and Data Centers.*

[32] Schödwell, B., Erek, K., and Zarnekow, R. 2013. "Data Center Green Performance Measurement: State of the Art and Open Research Challenges," in *Proceedings of the Nineteenth Americas Conference on Information Systems*, Chicago, Illinois.

[33] T. G. Grid. 2010. *ERE: a metric for measuring the benefit of reuse energy from a data center.*

[34] T. G. Grid. 2009. *Proxy Proposals for Measuring Data Center Productivity.*

[35] Indian Green Building Council. 2010. *IGBC Green SEZ Rating.* October.

[36] Bureau of Energy Efficiency. 2009. *Energy Conservation Building Code: User Guide.*

[37] Jose, N. *Star Labelling Programme in India.*

[38] MNRE-BEE. 2010. *Introduction to National Rating System – GRIHA.*

[39] BEE. Perform, Achieve and Trade (PAT).

Appendix A: Assessment and Certification Criteria of India's Energy Efficiency Practices

EXISTING STANDARDS	ASSESSMENT and CERTIFICATION CRITERIA
Indian Green Building Council (IGBC) Green Rating System	This tool enables the designer to apply green concepts and criteria, so as to reduce the environmental impacts, which are measurable. **Assessment Criteria:** The assessment is carried out through certain credit points using a prescriptive approach and other credits on a performance-based approach. The credit points are awarded for the following parameters: Site Preservation and Restoration (16 Points), Site Planning and Design (25 Points), Water Efficiency (15 Points), Energy Efficiency (30 Points), Materials and Resources (10 Points), and Innovation and Design (4 Points). **Award Criteria:** The certifications received are Certified (51–60), Silver (61–70), Gold (71–80), and Platinum (81–100).
Energy Conservation Building Code (ECBC) by the Bureau of Energy Efficiency (BEE)	The ECBC by the Indian Bureau of Energy Efficiency aims to provide minimum requirements for energy-efficient design and construction of buildings and their systems. ECBC encourages energy-efficient design or retrofit of buildings so that it does not constrain the building function, comfort, health, or the productivity of the occupants, and has appropriate regard for economic considerations. **Assessment Criteria:** ECBC follows the same structure as the ASHRAE 90.1 standard and covers the following areas: Building Envelope, HVAC, Service Hot Water and Pumping, Lighting, Electric Power, and more. The code allows a Prescriptive path or Simulated (baseline building) Calculation to show compliance. **Compliance Criteria:** Energy performance is regulated through prescriptive requirements for the thermal envelope and performance requirements for HVAC, hot water and pumping, lighting, and auxiliary systems.
GRIHA – Green Rating for Integrated Habitat Assessment National Green Building Rating System	GRIHA is a guiding and performance-oriented system where points are earned for meeting the design and performance intent of the criteria. Each criterion has a number of points assigned to it, and a maximum of 100 points can be achieved regarding the building's environmental performance in each category. **Assessment Criteria:** The rating is given on the basis of the total score achieved by the building across 34 criteria categorized under various sections such as Site Selection and Site Planning, Conservation and Efficient Utilization of Resources, Building Operation and Maintenance, and Innovation points. Eight of these 34 criteria are mandatory; four are partly mandatory; the rest are optional. **Award Criteria:** 1 star: 50–60 points; 2 stars: 61–70 points; 3 stars: 71–80 points; 4 stars: 81–90 points; 5 stars: 91–100 points.
Perform, Achieve and Trade (PAT) by Bureau of Energy Efficiency (BEE)	PAT is a market-based mechanism to enhance cost effectiveness of improvements in energy efficiency in energy-intensive large industries and facilities, through certification of energy savings that could be traded. **Assessment Criteria:** The scheme imposes mandatory Specific Energy Consumption (SEC) targets on the covered facilities with less-energy-efficient facilities having a greater reduction target than the more-energy-efficient ones. A facility's baseline is determined by its historic specific energy consumption. **Compliance Criteria:** Facilities making greater reductions than their targets receive "EsCerts" or "energy saving certificates" which can be traded with facilities that have trouble meeting their targets. Facilities can also bank them for future use.
Standards and Labeling Program by Bureau of Energy Efficiency (BEE)	The Objectives of Standards and Labelling Program is to provide the consumer an informed choice about the energy-saving and thereby the cost-saving potential of the marketed energy-consuming equipment. **Assessment Criteria:** The amount of electricity consumed per unit amount of appropriate service delivered by the equipment over a period of time. **Award Criteria:** The energy performance of the equipment is rated on a 1- to 5-star scale. A higher star rating means better energy efficiency.
Star Rating for Buildings by Bureau of Energy Efficiency	This standard is based on the actual performance of a building in terms of its specific energy usage in $kWh/m^2/year$. Buildings have been categorized into two categories: (1) having air-conditioned area greater than 50% of built up area or (2) less than 50% of built-up area. **Assessment Criteria:** Rating is given on the basis of Energy Performance Index (EPI) in $kWh/m^2/year$. Only those buildings having a connected load of 100 kW and above are considered for assessment. **Award Criteria:** This programme rates office buildings on a 1- to 5-star scale, with 5-star labelled buildings being the most efficient.

Appendix B: Comparing Global Practices With Indian Standards

POINT-BASED (WHOLE BUILDING) RATING APPROACH

COUNTRY	STANDARD	BROAD KEY CHARACTERISTICS	CURRENT INDIAN STANDARDS
USA	**LEED (Leadership in Energy and Environmental Design) for Data Centers**	1. Point-based rating process usually considers energy and environmental performance criteria. It highly emphasizes energy efficiency but also considers other factors such as environment, reliability, water efficiency, etc. 2. Each section includes credit points for a set of minimum requirements, which are mandatory. 3. This type of rating is mostly applicable to all data centers. 4. The assessment identifies the specific energy-efficient and environment-friendly features and practices that have been incorporated in the projects. 5. Additional innovation points are awarded for incorporating environment-friendly features, which are better than normal practices. 6. The rating achieved for a facility in its design phase may not be reflected in its actual performance. 7. In a point-based rating system, an applicant seeking a certification is more concerned about scoring higher points than actually improving building performance. 8. Though it gives more weight to energy efficiency, it does not focus on specific technologies, which impact overall efficiency. 9. It focuses only on reducing the environmental effects of the building and does not consider criticality of operation/performance of data centers.	1. The BEE Star Rating for Office Buildings determines the Energy Performance Index (EPI) but it only focuses on kWh/m^2/year. 2. The Indian Green Building Council (IGBC) Green SEZ Rating System is based on a framework similar to other point-based rating systems addressing various important factors such as sustainable sites, water efficiency, energy efficiency, materials resources, innovation, and design.
UK	**BREAM (Building Research Establishment Environmental Assessment) For Data Centers**		
Malaysia	**Green Building Index (GBI) for Data Centers**		
Singapore	**Green Mark for Data Centers**		

BEST PRACTICES/GUIDELINES-ORIENTED APPROACH

COUNTRY	STANDARD	BROAD KEY CHARACTERISTICS	CURRENT INDIAN STANDARDS
GLOBAL STANDARD (Across 44 ISO member countries)	**IS/ ISO 50001 Standard: Energy Management Systems**	1. Key performance parameters such as DCiE, IT Productivity, and Total Data Center Energy Consumption are the basis on which energy efficiency is measured for any data center. 2. Percentage targets for yearly energy efficiency improvements (which are voluntary) are set, depending on type and services of the data centers. 3. It involves a continual improvement process through an energy management program. 4. It includes assessment and implementation of best practices and new technologies. 5. In most cases it involves third-party validation and certification. 6. This type of approach offers too much of flexibility to data center owners/operators in terms of setting their own targets for improving energy efficiency. 7. Being a purely voluntary programme, there are no penalties incurred if compliance with these standards are not achieved, and resignation from the programme is permitted at any time.	The **Perform, Achieve, and Trade (PAT) Mechanism,** an initiative by BEE to improve energy efficiency of energy-intensive industries in India, shares some similarities with this approach. Energy-saving targets (mandatory) and subsequently the compliance period to achieve the targets are set on the basis of specific energy consumption for any industry. A third party authorized by BEE conducts the validation. Non-compliance to the given targets will attract penalties.
Europe	**European Code of Conduct by The European Commission for Data Centers**		
	The Blue Angel eco-label for Data Centers - Germany		

PERFORMANCE-BASED RELATIVE BENCHMARKING APPROACH

COUNTRY	STANDARD	KEY CHARACTERISTICS	CURRENT INDIAN STANDARDS
USA	**California T-24: Building Energy Efficiency Standards for Data Centers**	1. Provides flexibility in choosing a compliance method: Prescriptive, Trade-Off, Performance or Energy Cost Budgeting Method. 2. After fulfillment of the minimum requirements, in some sections (e.g., HVAC, Infrastructure Designing, etc.), excess credit points may be extended to the other sections to achieve a trade-off to achieve an overall rating/compliance. 3. These standards focus on energy efficiency related to building HVAC, lighting, water, etc., and do not consider energy efficiency of equipment in the facility (e.g., energy-efficient IT technologies in data centers).	The **Energy Conservation Building Code** by BEE follows a similar structure as the ASHRAE 90.1 standard and covers the following areas: building envelope, HVAC, service hot water and pumping, lighting, electric power, etc. Similar to **ASHRAE 90.1 and California T-24** there are three compliance options: **Prescriptive, Trade-Off and Whole-Building Performance Method.**
	ASHRAE-90.1 for Data Centers		

COMPARATIVE SCALE RATING APPROACH			
COUNTRY	**STANDARD**	**KEY CHARACTERISTICS**	**CURRENT INDIAN STANDARDS**
USA	**ENERGY STAR Rating for Data Centers by the U.S. Environmental Protection Agency (EPA)**	1. The EPA star rating allow users to compare the energy performance of one data center with others and also enables them to compare energy performance with the national average. (The peer group used for comparison is identified through nationally representative survey data.) 2. It is based on "actual as-billed" energy data. 3. It involves tracking, measurement, and improving energy consumption on a regular basis. 4. Unit of analysis is being carried out in terms of (Total Energy / IT Energy). It measures infrastructure efficiency (i.e., it captures impact of cooling and support systems but does not capture IT equipment efficiency). 5. This certification process requires data for 11 months of continuous operation of the facility before the rating can be evaluated. 6. The rating determines the rank of a data center in its peer group of data centers, which essentially does not reflect the implementation of best practices and new energy-efficient technologies in that data center.	**Star Labeling of Buildings** by BEE demonstrates following similarities to this standard: 1. Evaluation of energy performance of a building is based on **Actual Performance** in terms of specific energy use (kWh/m^2/year) 2. Provides **Peer Group-Based Energy Performance Comparison Mechanism** (applicable to offices, hotels, retail malls, IT parks, and hospitals). 3. Accounts for **Operational Characteristics** of the building (e.g., climatic zone, hours of operation). 4. Provides a simple metric to evaluate energy performance of the building (i.e., **Energy Performance Index (EPI)** measured in kWh/m^2/year).
AUSTRALIA	**National Australian Built Environment Rating System (NABERS) for Data Centers**	1. It offers the ability to separately rate the building infrastructure, whole building, and tenancy of a data center and gives flexibility to the applicants to choose rating for any one of the three in form of an Infrastructure Rating, IT Equipment Rating, and Whole Facility Rating. 2. It measures actual performance of the data center as it uses metered data of actual energy consumption. 3. The number of stars is calculated by benchmarking the energy consumption and by comparing it against a list of data centers with similar attributes. 4. It requires 12 months of building operation before the rating can be evaluated.	

Increasing Data Centre Renewable Power Share via Intelligent Smart City Power Control

Florian Niedermeier
University of Passau
Computer Networks and
Computer Communications
Innstrasse 43
Passau, Germany
florian.niedermeier@uni-passau.de

Wolfgang Duschl
University of Passau
Computer Networks and
Computer Communications
Innstrasse 43
Passau, Germany
wolfgang.duschl@uni-passau.de

Torben Möller
Software Engineering Group
University of Mannheim
B6, 26
Mannheim, Germany
moeller@informatik.uni-mannheim.de

Hermann de Meer
University of Passau
Computer Networks and
Computer Communications
Innstrasse 43
Passau, Germany
hermann.demeer@uni-passau.de

ABSTRACT

Urbanization has been an increasing trend that has lead to higher population densities in cities worldwide. Providing these large amounts of citizens with a high quality of living is one of the main goals of future smart cities. A high quality of living requires the smart city to offer several services, many of them supported by a sophisticated, power-intensive IT infrastructure. We present a cooperation scheme between smart city and data centres that allows for an effective use of power flexibilities inherently available in data centres. By adapting the power demand of data centres to the availability of renewable energy, smart city goals like a low carbon emission of its IT infrastructure become achievable. To this end, a demand side management scheme under orchestration of a central control system is proposed. The concrete guidelines on power use for data centres are calculated by a component named "Ideal Power Planner", based on smart city goals and renewable power availability forecasts. The effectiveness of the developed approach has been validated in three testbeds.

Categories and Subject Descriptors

J.7 [**Computer Applications**]: Computers in Other Systems

e-Energy'15, July 14–17, 2015, Bangalore, India.

ACM 978-1-4503-3609-3/15/07 ...$15.00.
DOI: http://dx.doi.org/10.1145/2768510.2768527.

Keywords

Smart City; Data Centre; Renewable Energy

1. INTRODUCTION

To provide a more sustainable and eco-friendly energy supply, the integration of renewable energy into the power grid has been a major factor in the recent years. Especially for smart cities, which strive to provide a high quality of living to its citizens, a green power grid is a key goal. However, power generation based on renewable sources may be volatile, especially for wind and solar. In turn, the fraction of renewably generated power inside the electricity grid is varying over time. To gain a maximum benefit from renewable generation, power demand should coincide with times of maximum renewable availability in the power grid. Simultaneously, situations of supply surplus or scarcity should be avoided to ensure grid stability and avoid high costs for peak load coverage. Prognosis of weather conditions can help, but this is not always as precise as necessary, especially if weather conditions fluctuate massively during the day. One further approach is using batteries to store electrical energy to even fluctuations in the electricity grid and provide a need oriented return of energy. However, this technology is mostly not considered beneficial enough from an economic point of view to be used at large scale in deployments yet [4]. Considering the problem that volatile energy resources cannot be controlled directly without wasting resources like traditional fossil fuel based power plants, there is a need for an alternative approach to handle this situation.
We propose a demand side management scheme under orchestration of a central control system which is able to perform a higher level optimization compared to autonomous demand side management approaches. The proposed system is based on a two-stage calculation of desired power values for the participating consumers. In the first stage, the high level goals of the smart city are divided into con-

crete objectives. In the second stage, these objectives serve as an input to the Ideal Power Planner, which derives a time series of power values to be followed by the demand side participants to the system. In the following, it is assumed that the demand side participants to the system are data centres with a certain amount of flexibility regarding their power demand. Additionally, we assume that forecasts regarding the availability of renewable energy are either readily available or easily derivable using information shared by Energy Related Data Suppliers (ERDS). This work contributes three major points:

1. A system architecture description of a cooperation scheme between smart city and data centres
2. The Ideal Power Planner, a component that translates high level goals of the smart city into concrete power values to be followed by a data centre
3. The communication scheme to share smart city goals and objectives with data centres

The remainder of this paper is structured as follows: Section 2 gives an overview of the proposed system. Section 3 introduces the Ideal Power Planner, a central component in the system. Section 4 briefly discusses the influence of metrics. In Section 5, the communication between smart city and data centres is explained. Section 6 presents first results gathered at three trial sites. After positioning our work in relation to previously conducted research in Section 7, the paper is concluded in Section 8.

2. SMART ARCHITECTURE

Through the high concentration of users on the demand side in cities, the energy consumption fluctuates significantly during a day. On the other hand it is important to consider that photovoltaic (PV) and wind power are not necessarily available over a whole day. At least for PV power, it is evident that it is not available during the night. To deal with this situation, it would be best to use renewable power peaks to satisfy the demand side. To cope with volatilities on both demand and generation side, we propose an intelligent control mechanism for demand side management based on the cooperation of smart city and large power consumers [14]. To this end, suitable grid participants are needed, which can provide a certain level of adaptiveness. Adaptiveness means in this context that the particular power demand can be shifted to another point in time, if necessary. Although the proposed scheme can be applied to different types of consumers, this work focuses on data centres. They seem promising candidates to provide the previously discussed adaptiveness as automation frameworks are usually already in place and several mechanisms exist to gracefully scale power demand at the expense of service performance (e.g., dynamic voltage and frequency scaling (DVFS)).

To integrate DCs in a suitable way, the following factors should be fulfilled to the highest possible extent:

- A sufficient amount of non-time critical jobs, whose execution schedule can be adjusted on demand
- Available power saving mechanisms (e.g., p-states) to exploit differences in machine load patterns
- Localized in (or close to) a city and connected to the same power grid or micro grid

2.1 Suitable DC types

The capability of data centres to adapt to a changing amount of available renewably generated power depends on several factors, however for the proposed system the most important are those impacting flexibility [13]. From the perspective of business models two criteria are taken as an example: First, the so-called "Outsourcing Factor". It depends on the business model of a data centre and is defined as the amount of operation control the DC may exert on its hosted services. This also includes control possibilities to increase flexibility. As the proposed system relies on DC flexibilities, DCs with high Outsourcing Factors should be preferred. Second, the suitability depends on the flexibility of service level agreements (SLAs). SLAs determine constraints of a data centre regarding, e.g., response time of services or generation rate of documents. If a SLA allows for a more flexible approach, it also improves possibilities for adaptation. Figure 1 shows the relationship between SLA flexibility, Outsourcing Factor and DC suitability (color of the circles). Data centres offering software as a service are very flexible, for example, their SLAs guarantee high flexibility and their high Outsourcing Factor allows for high control through the data centre administration. Best suitable data centres offer SaaS and are bound to a flexible SLA. From

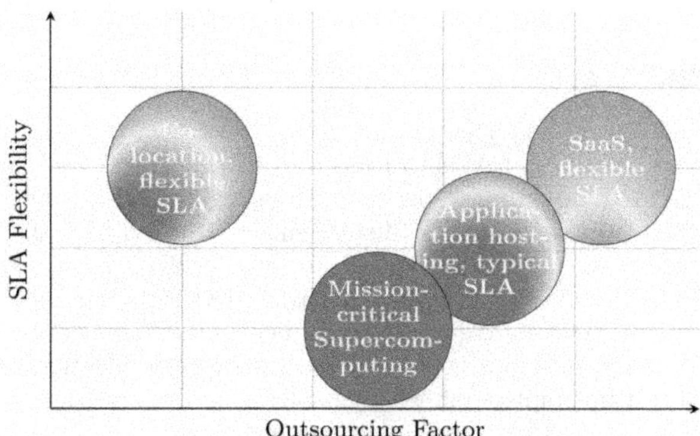

Figure 1: SLA flexibility (based on [13])

a technical perspective, there are different levels at which data centers may offer adaptation. Depending on where the adaptation is performed, adaptation time, amount of power adaption, and other characteristics of the created flexibility may change drastically. This also has a significant impact on the response time that can be provided and in turn on the adaptation requests which can be fulfilled. On a qualitative level, adaptations which are based on "silicon only", i.e. no mechanical operations are involved, and are performable at runtime qualify for very rapid execution (< 1s). Examples include DVFS, application internal changes or virtual machine resource capping. On the other hand, there are flexibilities which cannot be provided instantaneously. Amongst others, these are virtual machine live migration, switching machines on/off or any change that is usually only performed after manual review.

2.2 System interactions

Many different stakeholders are interacting in a smart city environment. These include bulk generation like nuclear or coal power and so called "Distributed Energy Resources" [3] like solar and wind power generation in a power range of

100kW to 10MW. Further, there are grid operators which take care of transporting and distributing electricity to the consumers, an electrical energy market and end users. The central role in a future smart city environment is a management authority which deals with different grid situations. It is called "Energy Management Authority of the Smart City" (EMA-SC). Tasks of an EMA-SC include, amongst others, monitoring of all available producers and consumers as well as their regulation and balancing by creating power plans for the demand side, especially for DCs. Additionally, an EMA-SC has a management role if problems arise during the regulation process. Besides the provision of the required energy to DCs, it is also important for an EMA-SC to have information on directly or locally installed renewable generation, which can be used for own consumption. Additionally, the expected energy mix in the grid or micro grid and the guidelines of the EMA-SC are taken into account. In the course of its task of calculating power plans (a kind of an energy budget) for DCs in the smart city, an EMA-SC makes use of a component named Ideal Power Planner (cf. Section 3), which bases its calculations on metered and forecasted values of energy generation and constraints imposed by an EMA-SC. All this information is used to generate a suitable power plan, which should be followed as closely as possible by the respective DC by splitting and shifting its tasks accordingly. The result is a maximum usage of renewable energy under the constraints of the EMA-SC. The goals for creating power plans are:

- Maximum usage of renewable (especially volatile) energy
- Provide enough energy to DCs to maintain an acceptable quality of service
- Support the implementation of smart city goals by taking them into account during power plan calculation

It is still important to mention that the generation of these power plans is improved by incorporating a city-wide view, which includes all large generation and demand participants. This allows for the creation of a more sustainable power infrastructure under the conditions of optimal use of renewables and provision of enough energy for the demand side.

3. THE IDEAL POWER PLANNER

For a data centre to be able to comply with smart city regulations, the high-level goals that drive a smart city have to be translated into concrete technical terms that can be implemented. To this end, a software component called Ideal Power Planner (IPP) translates the constraints from smart city side and forecasts on renewable energy availability into bounds on power consumption that should be followed by a data centre.

3.1 Tasks and attributes of the IPP

The IPP is a stateless component that provides to a DC an upper bound regarding its power demand. The upper bound in this case means the maximum power amount that may be used while still complying with the constraints set by an EMA-SC.

- Input values: Basically, the IPP takes two kinds of input data: On the one hand, it needs forecasts on future renewable power availability. This may be provided directly by the distribution system operator (DSO) or computed independently by monitoring the respective environmental parameters. On the other hand, the constraints set by an EMA-SC on power, energy, and energy properties have to be communicated.
- Output values: The output produced by the IPP is an upper bound on power use for a certain time into the future (e.g., 24 hours) in a resolution of e.g., 15 minutes. The concrete values may vary and depend mostly on the prediction accuracy and computing resources available. A DC participating in the system should try to not exceed this limits to be in line with the constraints set by the respective EMA-SC. Of course, a DC has to fulfill its SLAs at the same time. Rewards and penalties for keeping/breaking the power plan may be defined in a contract between an EMA-SC and a DC.
- Internal working process: To calculate power bounds, the IPP has to translate constraints set by an EMA-SC to concrete power values. This can be quite easy (e.g., for a simple constraint on max. power use) or complex (e.g., a constraint on min. % of renewable energy and multiple energy sources). Internally, the IPP can solve these tasks by employing, e.g., a constraint solving engine. For a more detailed description on how objectives are set, please refer to Section 5.1.

3.2 IPP location

The IPP may be located at two different points in the envisioned system: Either centrally on smart city side or locally at each participating DC. The choice of location has several implications on the system.

3.2.1 *EMA centrally on smart city side*

In a future smart city, calculating a power plan may be performed centrally by an EMA-SC. As an EMA-SC has more detailed information on the power grid state, it may be able to perform a higher level optimization. All data related to power generation and demand are gathered, processed and orchestrated at EMA-SC side. It collects all forecasts and after consolidation it may calculate power budgets that can be distributed among data centres in order to make use of their flexibility. In this case, DCs are relieved completely from having to calculate power values. DCs directly receive power budgets per time slot from an EMA-SC. Figure 2 shows a scenario with central power planning.

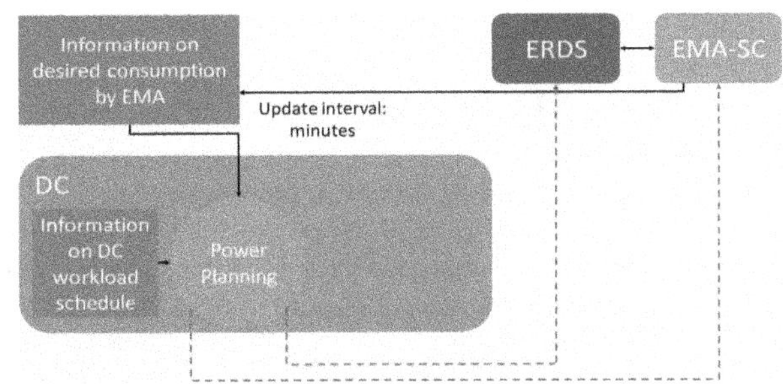

Figure 2: The envisioned future integration with smart cities

3.2.2 EMA locally on DC side

However, with current smart cities, it is highly likely that there is no way to directly give restrictions on power use to a DC. The future scenario described above is not currently in place. To be applicable even in absence of a strong EMA-SC and to support legacy systems in the future, the system also offers the possibility to run without a central power planning service. In this case, the system gathers forecasts of renewable energy availability and/or environmental data that is used to create needed forecasts locally. Power is then adapted using power availability information and goals set by the respective EMA-SC. The minimum required functionality from EMA side is therefore limited to setting at least one objective for each DC. Figure 3 shows the architecture with locally calculated power plans.

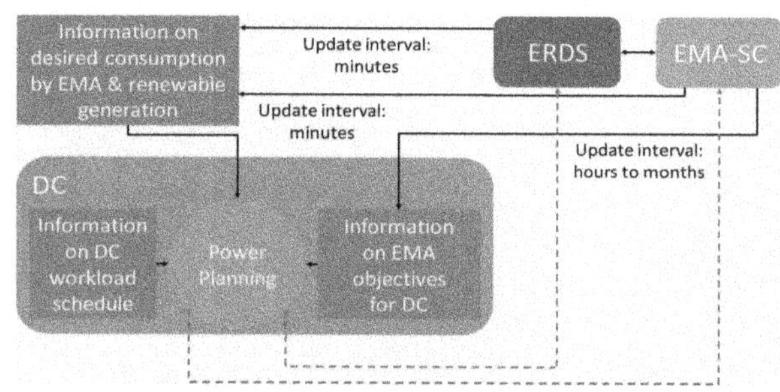

Figure 3: An architecture not depending on power planning capabilities on smart city side

4. METRICS

Metrics are a very important utility to measure and evaluate the results of an adaption process. As an essential requirement, a single metric should be as generically applicable as possible. In case of DCs, it is obvious that the measurement of utility or adaptiveness is specific to certain classes of applications offering different services. The quality of service (QoS) of a web server, for example, may be measured by the number of served websites or response time. In contrast, a backup system has to perform a lot of I/O operations and handle network traffic. If a specific environment is considered, it is possible to measure, e.g., power demand vs. received utility of a service. To find the correct constraints in CPU time, I/O etc. without creating a single-resource bottleneck for the service is however a complex task which required further investigation. Another useful application of metrics would be to quantify the overall flexibility of a DC while still fulfilling its SLAs.

5. COMMUNICATION

An EMA-SC and a data centre communicate with each other in two ways. First, an EMA-SC sets objectives a data centre should accomplish. A data centre tries to shift its workload to accomplish these objectives. If this is not possible, it will escalate the process by sending a message to the EMA-SC so the organization can try to find further solutions.

5.1 Setting objectives

The objectives communicated to a DC are derived from high level goals of the respective smart city. A goal may be very abstract, like a certain percentage of renewable energy used. This goal is subdivided into objectives, which are more concrete and easier to implement. These objectives are further specified into targets. The relationship of goals, objectives and targets is shown in Figure 5.

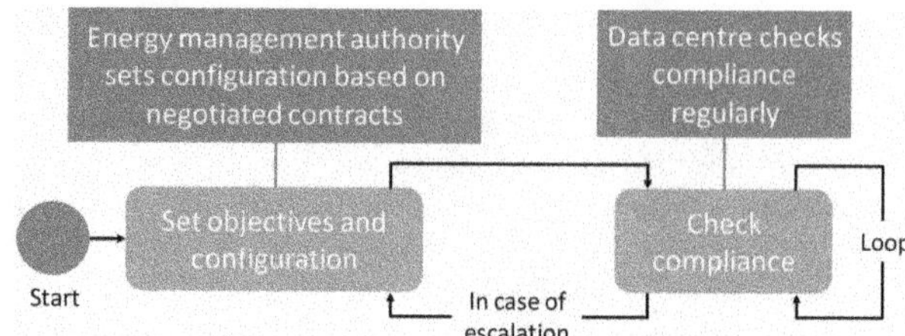

Figure 4: State diagram of EMA-SC and DC interaction (based on [6])

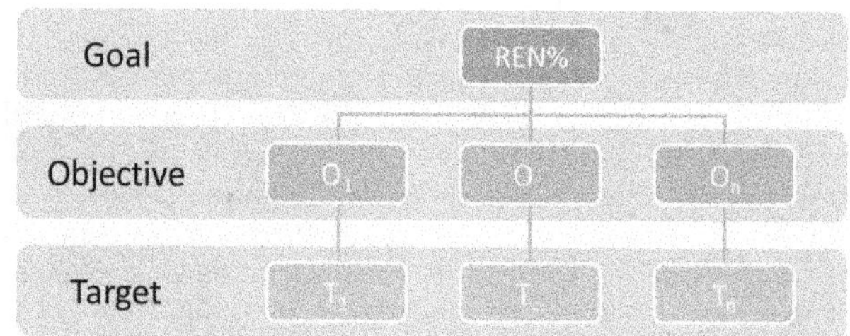

Figure 5: Goals, objectives and targets (based on [6])

In order to set objectives, an EMA-SC negotiates with the owner of a data centre and notes agreed on objectives in a contract. Objectives are set with respect to the local context (e.g., local renewable supply). To enable technical enforcement of objectives, they are modeled by three different types of constraints:

- Energy property constraints, like the renewable energy ratio and CO_2 emissions can be used for long term goals. E.g., to reach at least a renewable energy percentage of 80%.
- Energy constraints are used to limit the energy used in a certain time frame while retaining a certain flexibility regarding the exact time of power use.
- Power constraints work in a similar way to energy constraints. They are however limited to power, i.e. instantaneous demand.

These objectives are fixed for a given time frame. It is also possible to define recurrence of objectives, in case they are expected to happen again in certain intervals. E.g., weekends can be handled similarly every week by using an interval of one week.

5.2 Deriving objectives

Objectives are based on metrics that are expressive and can be applied to every data centre. Energy-related information like terms fixed in already existing energy supply contracts or energy bill details can be taken into account. This information can be used to generate a prediction of future energy needs. From data centre side the workload based on size or customer amount can be used for predictions. It should be noted that all this data has to be used in the local energy context and time-dependent consumption in mind. For example, workload can depend on day-night or season cycles.

5.3 Escalation

If one or more of the objectives agreed on are not possible to accomplish, the respective data centre starts an escalation process. A determined person is informed via a negotiated communication channel on important information the data centre can provide to determine the affected objective, time frame and possible solutions. An EMA-SC may react in multiple ways: Usually one of the solutions applied to the data centre is, e.g., migrating services to other data centres participating in the system. The objectives, SLAs or the contract could be changed to avoid violations. If none of these steps can be applied the EMA-SC is left with two possibilities: Either incur a penalty according to the contract or allow the data centre to break the contract once.

6. TRIALS

The proposed system was evaluated in the course of the EU project "DC4Cities" in three different data centers. The trial sites have different core workloads and therefore exhibit different load patterns. In the following, more details on the trials will be given. Afterwards, first results are discussed.

6.1 Test setup

Trial site 1 was built upon two independent data centres. These data centres host several services like web crawling or backup. The focus was put on a compute and I/O intensive video transcoding batch job, to which privileged users can upload videos, which are converted to save storage space. Since the SLA requires a certain amount of videos to be transcoded every 24h, it is possible to shift the jobs intra-day to times of high renewable energy availability. The trials at trial site 2 are executed in collaboration with a local health agency. The local health agency needs a report generation application, which generates high load on the systems. This report generation can be shifted to time frames with high renewable energy availability. Shifting is possible, since there is no need for on-demand generation. The generation can be scheduled and executed ahead. Trial site 3 hosts a web application e-learning platform in its trial. This platform is available 24/7. During the trial the number of backend servers available to the web application is adapted to the availability of renewable energy while keeping SLA requirements.

6.2 Current results

The key performance indicator of success of the trials is the percentage of renewable energy of the total amount of consumed energy.

$$RenPercent = \frac{\sum_{i=1}^{N}(E_{DCgrid_i} \cdot \frac{E_{ren_i}}{E_{sys_i}} + E_{DCself-cons_i})}{\sum_{i=1}^{N} E_{DC_i}} \quad (1)$$

The calculation of RenPercent is explained in equation 1. For each time period i the DC energy consumption from grid is multiplied with the percentage of renewable energy in the whole energy system plus the energy produced and consumed locally. The result is divided by the total DC energy consumption. A more detailed description of the trials, formula and results can be found in [9].

Trial site 1 shows an increase from 40.09% to 41.78%. The biggest increase on one day of the trial was from 38.75% to 47.76%, which is an improvement of 23.25%. The second data centre of trial site 1 has shown an improvement of 10.11% (from 41.74% to 45.96%). This was reached by tuning the start and stop times of services and batch jobs. In trial site 2 the data centre was tuned by using parallelism and adjusting start and stop times of the jobs. The difference is that in this trial the SLAs define a stringent timing. In trial site 2 two configurations were tested. The first one did not show any improvement due to the high idle power of the legacy servers used in this trial. The second configuration was set to shut down idle servers and increased the percentage of renewable energy from 43.13% up to 57.88%. That is an improvement of 34.20%.
Trial site 3 has shown an average improvement of 4.63% in the first run (from 57.45% to 60.11%) and 4.47% in the second run (from 62.40% to 65.19%). The improvements of trial sites 1 and 3 are significantly lower compared to those of trial site 2 as their infrastructure features more up-to-date hardware and was already tuned for energy efficiency before the trials.

7. RELATED WORK

This work has connections to many research fields, amongst others energy efficiency, power flexibility and smart city control. In the following, previous work in the most significant areas is discussed.

Extensive research has been performed in the area of data centre energy efficiency. In this field, both software and hardware approaches are discussed. The work [2] aims to improve DC energy efficiency by measures like improving the cooling system efficiency, usage of variable frequency drivers, or using direct current power systems. Also, management techniques like virtualization and consolidation of servers are considered. [7] researches the possibility of using power management policies (consolidating, P-states, etc.) to design a power management plan that matches the supply of power with the demand for power in DCs. In [5] the SESAMES architecture is presented, aiming to reduce energy demand while reducing both cost and environmental impact in future supercomputing (HPC) environments.

The work of [12] introduces a green wide-area testbed. The focus is on reducing greenhouse gas emissions. In [1] the authors propose an approach to negotiate flexibility between energy suppliers and energy consumers. By an increased flexibility the supplier can react easier to changes in renewable energy supply. DC4Cities uses the gained knowledge of All4Green for contracts between smart city and data centre owners.

Regarding the adaptation of workload, [8] propose a combination of electrical storage and workload adaptation to power DCs by renewable energy. The work also considers the cost implications of peak power management, storing energy on the grid, and the ability to delay the MapReduce jobs. In [10] the GreenCassandra system is introduced. It uses a combination of prediction (workload and energy availability) and modeling (performance and power) to improve the use of self-generated solar power while keeping SLAs in distributed structured storage systems.

Other work also takes SLAs between DC and its customers into account. In [11] the authors state that the environmental impact of a service offered to a user should have an influence on its cost. Therefore, a collaboration between DSO, DC and its customers is suggested, called Green SLAs. The work of [15] investigates how to dynamically distribute service requests among data centres in different geographical locations, based on the local weather conditions, to maximize the use of renewable energy. The authors introduce the middleware system "GreenWare", that conducts dynamic request dispatching to maximize the percentage of renewable energy used to power a network of distributed DCs.

Our work differs from all stated approaches in the respect that it specifically aims at integrating DCs better into future smart cities. Additionally, in contrast to other approaches, we consider an optimization that builds on a cooperation of smart city and DCs, which we believe will increase the effectiveness of our work and enable a higher level of optimization.

8. CONCLUSION AND FUTURE WORK

In this work we presented a novel cooperation scheme between smart city and data centres aimed at achieving a better integration of data centers into future urban environments. At its core, the proposed system relies on predictions of future renewable energy availability and guidance by a smart city energy management authority. The system may operate both in a tight coupling with a smart city or, if a strong EMA-SC is not available, in a more autonomous mode relying only on objectives given by an EMA-SC. The effectiveness of the approach has been validated in a first set of trials, which show promising results. Future work will include further improvements to the power planner algorithm and research on including data centre federation in the system.

9. ACKNOWLEDGMENTS

This work was carried out within the European Project DC4Cities (FP7-ICT-2013.6.2).

10. REFERENCES

[1] R. Basmadjian, G. Lovász, M. Beck, H. de Meer, X. Hesselbach-Serra, J. Botero, S. Klingert, M. Perez Ortega, J. Lopez, A. Stam, R. van Krevelen, and M. di Girolamo. A generic architecture for demand response: The All4Green approach. In *Cloud and Green Computing (CGC), 2013 Third International Conference on*, pages 464–471, Sept. 2013.

[2] M. Bramfitt, A. Bard, R. Huang, and M. McNamara. Understanding and designing energy-efficiency programs for data centers, Nov. 2012.

[3] J. Bruinenberg, L. Colton, E. Darmois, J. Dorn, J. Doyle, O. Elloumi, H. Englert, R. Forbes, J. Heiles, P. Hermans, et al. Smart grid coordination group technical report reference architecture for the smart grid version 1.0 (draft) 2012-03-02. *CEN, CENELEC, ETSI, Tech. Rep*, 2012.

[4] P. Denholm, J. Jorgenson, M. Hummon, T. Jenkin, D. Palchak, B. Kirby, O. Ma, and M. O'Malley. The value of energy storage for grid applications. *Contract*, 303:275–3000, 2013.

[5] M.-M. Diouri, O. Gluck, and L. Lefevre. SESAMES: a smart-grid based framework for consuming less and better in extreme-scale infrastructures. In *Green Computing and Communications (GreenCom), 2013 IEEE and Internet of Things (iThings/CPSCom), IEEE International Conference on and IEEE Cyber, Physical and Social Computing*, pages 187–194. IEEE, 2013.

[6] Florian Niedermeier et al. DC4Cities - D4.1: First results on renewable energy generation and smart city authority coordination of single DCs. `http://www.dc4cities.eu/en/wp-content/uploads/2014/12/D4.1-First-results-on-renewable-energy-generation-and-smart-city-authority-coordination-of-single-DCs.pdf`, 2014. Acccessed: 2015-03-25.

[7] D. Gmach, J. Rolia, C. Bash, Y. Chen, T. Christian, A. Shah, R. Sharma, and Z. Wang. Capacity planning and power management to exploit sustainable energy. In *Network and Service Management (CNSM), 2010 International Conference on*, pages 96–103. IEEE, 2010.

[8] I. Goiri, W. Katsak, K. Ley, T. D. Nguyen, and R. Bianchini. Parasol and greenswitch: managing datacenters powered by renewable energy. *ASPLOS '13 Proceedings of the eighteenth international conference on Architectural support for programming languages and operating systems*, pages 51–64, 2013.

[9] Jordi Guijarro et al. DC4Cities - D6.2: Description on the experimentation phase 1, 2015.

[10] W. Katsak, Í. Goiri, R. Bianchini, and T. D. Nguyen. Greencassandra: Using renewable energy in distributed structured storage systems. Technical report, Rutgers University, 2015.

[11] S. Klingert, A. Berl, M. Beck, R. Serban, M. di Girolamo, G. Giuliani, H. de Meer, and A. Salden. Sustainable energy management in data centers through collaboration. In *Energy Efficient Data Centers*, volume 7396 of *Lecture Notes in Computer Science*, pages 13–24. Springer Berlin Heidelberg, 2012.

[12] K.-K. Nguyen, M. Cheriet, M. Lemay, M. Savoie, and B. Ho. Powering a data center network via renewable energy: A green testbed. *IEEE Internet Computing*, 17(1):40–49, 2013.

[13] Sonja Klingert et al. DC4Cities - D2.2: First market analysis. `http://www.dc4cities.eu/en/wp-content/uploads/2014/12/D2.2-First-market-analysis.pdf`, 2014. Acccessed: 2015-03-25.

[14] U.S. Department of Energy. Energy Efficiency & Renewable Energy. The importance of flexible electric supply. Technical Report 1 of 3, NREL National Renewable Energy Laboratory, May 2011.

[15] Y. Zhang, Y. Wang, and X. Wang. Greenware: Greening cloud-scale data centers to maximize the use of renewable energy. *Lecture Notes in Computer Science*, 7049:143–164, Dec. 2011.

Next Generation Data Centers Business Models Enabling Multi-Resource Integration for Smart City Optimized Energy Efficiency

Massimo Bertoncini,
Diego Arnone
Engineering Ingegneria Informatica
Via S. M. della Battaglia 56,
Rome, Italy
massimo.bertoncini@eng.it

Tudor Cioara, Ionut Anghel,
Ioan Salomie
Technical University of Cluj-Napoca
Baritiu 26, Cluj-Napoca, Romania
tudor.cioara@cs.utcluj.ro

Terpsichori-Helen Velivassaki
Singular Logic
Al. Panagouli & Siniosoglou, Athens,
Greece
tvelivassaki@ep.singularlogic.eu

ABSTRACT
An innovative approach for increasing the energy efficiency of Data Centers is discussed. This approach views Data Centers as active load resources, integrated in the context of the smart city and operated in a coordinated manner. Data Centers can thus contribute to establishing sustainable, local, energy management ecosystems on a smart city level, while enabling optimized operation of the involved energy grids. To that end, the development of local marketplaces will allow for trading surplus of energy, both electricity and thermal, and provide local balancing flexibility as ancillary services. Reinforcing this vision, innovative business models are proposed that enable next generation of smart Net-zero Energy Data Centers acting as energy prosumers at the interface with smart energy grids within a smart city environment. Simulation experiments are conducted using the GEYSER defined Data Centers flexibility models and non-linear optimization techniques. Such simulations are used to evaluate the Data Centers energy demand flexibility in meeting various network level goals.

Categories and Subject Descriptors
G.1.6 [**Optimization**]: Nonlinear programming, Global optimization; D.4.8 [**Performance**]: Simulation

General Terms
Experimentation; Verification; Economics.

Keywords
Data center, business models, smart grid, energy efficiency, optimization, demand response.

1. INTRODUCTION
Nowadays, power costs have been identified as primary contributors to the operational Data Center (DC) expenses, comparable to initial facilities investment. Amazon considers that power and power distribution and cooling account for 13% and 18% respectively of the total capital investment for constructing a DC and the according operational expenses [1]. Operational expenses are naturally of great concern for DC owners and operators, increasingly seeking for energy efficient and cost effective solutions. To address such concerns, within the FP7 GEYSER European R&D project [2], we are developing a framework for Net-zero Energy DCs acting as energy-centered multi-resource hubs at the interplay between smart energy grids (electricity, district heating/cooling, or both) and telecommunication networks.

Currently there are limited active links between on one hand, DCs and, in general, ICT networks and, on the other hand, smart cities and resource grid operators; practically, no energy or information exchange exist among them. Exacerbating such situation, urban DCs are operated in an uncoordinated way and their energy efficiency has been so far addressed in an isolated way. Nevertheless, urban DCs have large, yet mostly unexploited, potential regarding their energy demand flexibility. Through this potential they can contribute to efforts for managing more efficiently energy at a local, smart city level, while enabling optimized energy grids operation. To that end, DCs can elicit their latent flexibility by considering non-electrical cooling devices such as thermal storage, IT workload temporal and spatial migration through data networks, and dynamic usage of electrical storage devices and diesel generators as shown in Figure 1.

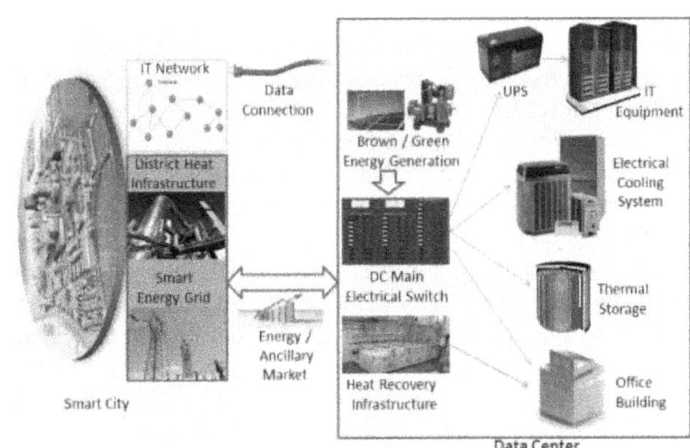

Figure 1. DCs at the intersection of smart power grids, district heating, and IT network

At the heart of this innovative approach lies the modeling of a smart city as a network of interconnected resource infrastructures; the latter make the necessary resources available to citizens for carrying out their daily activities. Nowadays, the major bottleneck preventing smart city level energy efficiency and carbon footprint reduction lies in the decoupled planning and operation of the individual resources infrastructures. Hence, our conceptual model considers urban resource infrastructures connected with each other through physical hubs, where local generation, consumption, or conversion of one resource to another takes place. Accordingly,

e-Energy'15, July 14 - 17, 2015, Bangalore, India
© 2015 ACM. ISBN 978-1-4503-3609-3/15/07…$15.00
DOI: http://dx.doi.org/10.1145/2768510.2768522

DCs can become physical hubs of integrated energy (electricity, thermal, or a combination) and data networks.

Indeed DCs can be seen as conceptual and technological hubs which enact the exploitation of synergies and integration with other resources infrastructures, such as telecommunication networks. In doing so, they can provide larger flexibility to the local energy networks and accordingly achieve a major holistic smart city-level efficiency of urban energy networks. Energy grid companies must trade with commercial players to a far greater extent than is currently the case, in order to use flexibility products as a more cost-effective and more reactive alternative to grid reinforcements. Accordingly, DCs are expected to be transformed into flexible energy players providing different levels and type of flexibility to the interested stakeholders (Distribution System Operator (DSO), district heating) with a view to become adjustable, adaptive power consumers able to participate in Demand Response (DR) programs. Hence, various levels of integration are envisioned enabled by diverse technology stack. In doing so, diverse "multi-utility" business models can be designed; (i) a "lighter" multi-service deployment where the DC collaborates with smart energy grids by exchanging information related to resources infrastructures, with no technical integration (e.g. service/business integration), or (ii) a coupled optimization operation of different DCs hardware resources, which builds on a hub-based integration among the different infrastructures.

Reinforcing the vision of DCs acting as flexible, load resources, suitable innovative business models are developed enabling next generation of smart Net-zero Energy DCs to act as energy prosumers at the interface with smart energy grids within a smart city environment. Such business models are enabled within the GEYSER project by the novel combination of monitoring system, DC-level resource demand flexibility management practices, with marketplaces as tools for DC integration in the smart city holistic energy optimization matter and nonlinear optimized control [3].

So far typical *energy saving solutions* considered DCs in isolation, including actions on hardware and software, as well as IT and non-IT infrastructure. As such, energy losses due to faulty or legacy hardware can be identified via frequent monitoring and optimized control of the infrastructure. Within the framework of this emerging vision, the key concept for DCs business models moves away from investigating practices and technologies aimed at achieving isolated energy savings towards **demand flexibility optimized management**, in which sub-optimal DC-level energy savings can be offset by appropriate valuation of DC contribution to system-level smart city resource (energy and beyond) savings. Accordingly data center participation via marketplaces to the smart city locally generated resources exploitation (when and where they become available) and optimized usage is expected to provide larger scale system-level resource consumption savings, which, despite may not achieve DC-level energy savings, however bring effective contributions to the overall smart city optimized energy and beyond consumption. Within such holistic framework GEYSER has been making them available a comprehensive set of technologies to fully implement the DC-effective integration with smart city, which will enable innovative cooperative multi-layered business models to take place.

Recent developments do exist on data center integration with smart electricity distributors [15], however there is no system-level smart city integration perspective. Other on-going initiatives [16] address the smart city holistic vision, but are mostly tailored to the DC exploitation of local renewable energy generation when available, however systemic integration with other resource infrastructure is limited to the case of electricity network. Moreover some works are focused on emphasizing how the DC exploitation of onsite or nearby generated renewable energy could provide DCs with a unique opportunity to reduce their operational energy costs, thanks to the self-consumption of locally generated renewable energy and/or the additional financial benefits related to greenhouse gas emissions [4]. However the above mentioned approaches are focused on how DCs may reconfigure internally for adapting to the surplus of available renewable generation (either onsite generated either available along the same medium voltage power network branch), which would allow DC energy savings from the self-generation.

To enable the increasing renewable generation and exploit the green energy to the largest extent possible, flexible resources are required in the power system, such as flexible generation systems, storage and demand-side management [5]. As renewable generation takes place on an unplanned basis, the system should be capable of consuming as much energy as possible at generation time, which is addressed by flexibly matching of energy demand to supply [6] [7]. Along these approaches DCs are seen as energy prosumers, potentially providing flexibility services to individual power grid operators, whereas the usual business model will be to participate to DR programs by workload "flexibilization" [8].

Currently, few DCs participate in such programs mainly due to lack of trusted technologies for optimizing their capacity planning [9]. Under certain conditions, energy surplus from the DCs renewable sources may be fed back to the grid while recovered heat may also be used for heating. Advanced storage systems, diesel generators, and IT workload migration may also be exploited to shift peak demand away from high peak periods [10]. In this context the potential benefits of the GEYSER approach for DCs and energy marketplaces is revealed from DCs participation in DR in UK [11]. The potential savings are derived from the pure DR participation in the lower demand charges, and the automated testing of diesel generator. As a consequence there is no overarching approach in which DCs are able uniquely to combine "nature-based" local resource exploitation (e.g. onsite renewable geothermal cold water for DC cooling and thermal storage subsystem optimized management or intermittent power generation from nearby non co-located RES sources) and DC IT workload shifting and thermal storage management to provide effective flexibility to the smart city integrated infrastructures (from electricity grid to district heating to IT/telco infrastructure).

2. GEYSER MARKETPLACES

A variety of energy flexibility marketplaces has been explored within the GEYSER project as an effective way for integrating urban DCs with smart energy grids. Major beneficiaries for such marketplaces are electricity stakeholders, primarily DSOs, but also energy retailers and sellers, including DCs, while spill over to the heating stakeholders is possible as well. Flexibility products targeted at grid companies are, initially, expected to be traded via bilateral agreements, followed by participation to, simple at first and formal at a later stage, marketplaces for flexibility products; introducing new ways for grid companies to procure flexibility products as alternative to grid reinforcements.

The envisioned GEYSER marketplaces allow for: (i) trading surplus of energy of different types, such as electricity generated from renewable energy sources (RES), heat, etc., among green DCs and the Smart City, also supported by the local DSO, with a view to match higher systemic smart city/district energy demand; and (ii) providing local balancing flexibility as ancillary services at local level, enacting an effective local way to achieve congestion relief and security of supply for DSOs.

Market variants introduced may ideally be applied to any energy carrier, either electricity, district heating or natural gas. In that respect, smart metering technologies for real-time monitoring and control of heating and natural gas generation and distribution have been recently started, although respective technologies are lagging behind in comparison to the electricity grid. However, the concept of Energy and Ancillary Services Market continues to be valid also for the district heating case. There are indeed some preliminary experiments in the region of Amsterdam, in which DCs have been cooperating with district heating and water network operators, with the objective of managing and absorbing heat power to alleviate the district heating network and release the surplus of heat when the network operator risks incurring in lower pressure heat. In such an example, DCs are acting as energy prosumers to alleviate district heating network congestion.

2.1 Smart City Green Energy Marketplace

It allows GEYSER-enabled DCs to offer flexibility for deploying energy management services, energy services (load management services) and network services (voltage management).

Energy management services are provided to energy sellers/traders, energy service companies and municipal utilities for anticipated energy contracting and provisioning (energy services in intra-day or real time markets). Main stakeholder would be the Smart City/District Energy Manager who will be in charge for procuring energy to meet the demands of the city. The interested DCs will interact with energy operators either responding to a bid (network-driven optimization) to provide the requested mix of energy, or through time-scaled adaptation of their internal operations. The marketed flexibility here is energy.

Energy services (load management services) and/or **network services** (voltage management services) are offered to energy network distributors (DSO or district heating operators), with a view to call for a given reduction of energy demand at peak times. Here, flexibility is offered to network operators aimed at alleviating peak shaving, or providing a firm load diagram (load leveling) or a generation load profile, while reducing the demand and supply fluctuations, which may be known in advance (for example, hot summer days). In this scenario only network-driven optimization makes sense. The marketed flexibility may be expressed by energy or power. For example, follow-the-sun strategies or following load profiles suggested by DSO could be conveniently adopted by DCs if appropriate signals are captured from the city-level DSO or district heating operator, such as maximization of local consumption or usage of district generated fluctuating RES respectively. Based on the follow-the sun strategy, local generation combined with thermal storage could be used for temporary thermal storage with a view to subsequently alleviate later thermal (and power) peak demand.

This marketplace is related to the management of the near real-time unexpected energy availability fluctuations. It implements and realizes the principal features of Intra-Day and Real-Time Energy Markets enabling the direct interaction of GEYSER-enabled DCs (and other energy prosumers) with Smart City/Smart District. The market rules for both intra-day and real-time markets are very similar, the only differentiation mostly arising from the time operational framework (from few hours to one hour for the Intra-Day Market, while from one hour to the next 15 minutes for the real-time market). Due to their large flexibility potential, DCs may participate to the smart city energy marketplaces directly, without any aggregators' intermediation. Participating stakeholders are the Smart City/District Energy Manager, Energy Retailers/Traders, and Energy Prosumers including DCs, while the object transacted consists of energy flexibility offered by DCs.

2.2 Local Balancing Marketplace

This marketplace is tailored to **real-time network service provisioning** to DSO to alleviate their specific operational problems. For example, DCs could provide flexibility services to DSO to manage peak shaving in the DSO network, or local balancing service systems, like voltage regulation or reactive power regulation. Ancillary Services Markets are currently used by Transmission System Operators (TSOs) to procure flexibility for system-level demand-supply balance. No direct involvement of DSO is planned at the moment within the current regulatory framework. However, thanks to the continuous sprawl of Smart Grid technology there is an emerging possibility for creating a Local Balancing Market in which DSOs become active players, being in charge of procuring the necessary resources in a near real-time way to optimally operate their own network. Within this new scenario, a new local balancing market is about to appear in which fluctuating RES generators and suppliers, after preventive registration in a suitable repository, could directly participate to a geographically-limited market. Real-time procurement of the necessary power for the DSO stability would be possible from those registered RES generators which in given times would be available to offer the requested power. No planning phase, if not a registration one, will be necessary, due to the unpredictability of stochastic RES generation. The Local Balancing Market becomes then the venue where the DSO procures the resources that it requires for managing, operating, monitoring, and controlling the power system (relief of intra-zonal congestions, creation of energy reserve, real-time balancing). Temporal operating framework for this market is within fifteen minutes ahead of physical delivery.

The GEYSER Local Balancing Market overlaps with the Ancillary Services Market in which power (i.e. electricity) instantaneously generated by decentralized stochastic RES is offered to DSOs as Ancillary Services. Thus, contributing to alleviate and mitigate local grid networks security and stability problems. Local strategies prevent the propagation of the security, congestion, and stability problems to the upper layers of the electricity network (i.e. High Voltage), with a view to eliminate the need for committing TSOs to sorting out these problems. In this DSO-oriented marketplace, the participating entities are DCs, other Distributed Generation providers and DSOs in a bilateral way without any retailer/supplier intermediation. Rewarding should be managed in a different way, possibly using models like marginal contribution to reduce congestion or peak shaving.

3. GEYSER BUSINESS MODELS

In this context, near real-time energy flexibility service provisioning would aim at either alleviating local power grid - medium voltage (MV) and low voltage (LV) - network constraints at real time as caused by imbalances due to the stochastic nature of RES; or optimizing energy management at city/district level with a view to prioritize green, locally produced energy.

GEYSER builds its flexibility offer to interested stakeholders through uniquely combining and optimizing internal generation capability (backup and intermittent RES) along with energy storage (either thermal or electric), smart cooling system usage, and computational workload shifting techniques. In particular, local power generation (i.e. RES management) and thermal storage combined with workload management has a significant potential to shed the peak load and reduce energy costs, provided that adaptation, responsiveness, and latency time will match real-time requirements from local utility operator(s). The optimal combination of the various available strategies allows the GEYSER-enabled DCs to become active stakeholders in the energy market and smart city/local energy optimization affair.

Business models have been specifically designed for valuing and rewarding DC prospects for timely combining its internal flexibility strategies, using time based Service Level Agreements (SLAs), intended as major or minor capability (responsiveness) of DCs to offer the required flexibility with different latency times. For instance, DCs may deploy a premium, more expensive, service with a very low latency and highest responsiveness in the range of 1 to 5 minutes; otherwise, make available cheaper, less responsive computational services in combination with ancillary services tailored to DSOs, in the range of 5 to 15 minutes.

To better identify synergistic opportunities, diverse yet increasing integration levels among urban resource infrastructures have been defined. As such, Cross-network Integration of Services (Business or Service Integration) breaks existing organizational barriers and provides cross-infrastructures services (Integrated Service Delivery Model). The integrated delivery model is based on the IT cross-infrastructure interoperability and integration (lighter integration, cooperation business models). On the other hand, System-level Integration (Technical Integration), promotes further optimized and cost-effective, multi-resource operations. The deployment method at smart city level along with the respective service delivery and business models strictly depend on the tailored integration level.

The envisioned GEYSER business models focus on DCs acting as multi-resource integration hubs for optimized management of energy and ICT networks. In that respect, such business models fall within the System-level Integration family:

GEYSER-enabled DCs acting as Independent Players (generation-optimized management). Based on a market signal (e.g. real-time price) for potential flexibility, DCs are self-configured to match the requested flexibility; to that end, they exploit the strategies available to them such as IT workload, electricity/thermal storage, back-up generation, or a combination.

GEYSER-enabled DCs responding to energy or beyond-energy distributors bids (network-optimized management):

- **Individual energy network level optimization (smart city optimization)**, where the optimized amount of energy, or generally flexibility, is set at network level and the DC node exploits its internal flexibility potential to provide the requested level of service;
- **City-level multi-network optimization**, where optimization of energy (electricity/thermal) and IT infrastructure (considering data transmission cost) takes place. DC is presented with given quantity of energy and computation costs to follow up. This is the business model which allows larger smart-city level, holistic, energy efficiency.

4. USE CASES SIMULATION

To demonstrate the viability of our proposed approach, early simulations have been carried out, with a view to subsequently apply and validate in the coming months these models and strategies to the four GEYSER pilot DCs. To that end, we have developed a simulation environment in which characteristics (see Table 1) and operation of DC hardware systems are modeled [12].

Table 1. Modeled DC components characteristics

Component	Characteristics
Electrical Cooling System	Cooling Capacity = 4000 kWh, Minimum Cooling Load = 200 kWh, Maximum Cooling Load = 2000 kWh, COP Coefficient = 3.5
IT Computing Resources	P_MAX = 325 W, Memory, Processor, Hard Drive = RAM 8 GB, CPU 2.4 GHz, HDD 1Tb
Electrical Storage System	Charge Loss Rate = 1.2, Discharge Loss Rate = 0.8 Energy Loss Rate = 0.995, Max Charge & Discharge Rate = 1000 kWh, Max Capacity = 1000 kWh
Thermal Storage System	Charge Loss Rate = 1.1, Discharge Loss Rate = 0.99, Energy Loss Rate = 0.999, Max Charge & Discharge Rate = 1000 kWh, Maximum Capacity = 3000 kWh
Diesel Gen.	Max Capacity = 3000 kWh

The DC workload energy demand was taken from the IT power consumption logs of a real DC [13] considering 5 minutes samples normalized using the maximum power consumption of the modeled DC. The source used for the energy price data is [14].

Following upon the GEYSER vision and approach, the optimization methodology exploits high demand flexibility of DCs to provide an optimal near real-time capacity / operational planning. Such planning aims at shaping their power consumption profile to meet various objectives and thus allowing them to participate in DR programs.

The core of our optimization methodology and simulation is the DC power consumption and generation flexibility model along with the non-linear programing algorithms described in [3]. The proposed model allows us to estimate the DC's energy demand flexibility and the impact of systems' operation on its energy profile adaptation. The *Electrical Cooling System Demand Flexibility* is based on dynamically using non-electrical cooling mechanisms, such as thermal energy storage, available at DC sites to cool down the DC for certain periods of time. Thus, the electrical cooling systems are expected to be utilized at smaller capacity when energy is being discharged from the thermal storage and in consequence the DC's energy demand is reduced. Similarly, when the electrical cooling system is used at greater capacity to overcool the thermal storage tanks the DC's energy demand is increased. The *IT Computing Resources Demand Flexibility* is based on shifting the delay-tolerant IT workload at different timeslots. Thus, the DC's energy demand at timeslot t_1, is reduced with the amount of energy needed to execute the delay-tolerant load that is shifted at timeslot t_2, while the DC energy demand from timeslot t_2 is increased. The *Energy Storage Components Flexibility* is based on dynamically charging /discharging the DC's installed batteries. Thus, the DC's energy demand is lowered with the amount of energy discharged from the batteries and is increased with the amount of energy charged back. The *Diesel Generators Flexibility* is based on planning their periodic maintenance in moments of energy production deficits or in case of high energy prices.

The result of the simulation process is a plan of actions to optimize and adapt the DC's energy consumption profile. The estimated impact of such actions was also estimated using the proposed energy consumption flexibility model.

4.1 DCs as Independent Players

In this scenario the DC will act as an energy player aiming at maximizing the usage of locally generated renewable energy (no renewable co-location, but district-scale RES generation), which means pushed by more real time energy convenient tariffs for injecting energy when there is a surplus available (energy services, like load leveling, peak shaving).

Figure 2 presents the DC's energy demand profile without GEYSER, highlighting the major elements which generate this demand (timeslot of one hour). As shown, the DC's energy profile is not compatible with the situation shaped by the local marketplace considering the RES generation as driving factor. Using GEYSER the DC will be enacted with the following possibilities. Firstly, increase its power demand at noon where there is the surplus of energy generation, by executing additional load and adapting the computational workload scheduling to anticipate as much as possible the work and/or make use of thermal storage for pre-cooling the data center. Secondly reduce its power demand in the morning and afternoon through workload shifting (time migration, considering cost for data transmission) and surplus of heating provisioning to alleviate cooling requirements or running diesel backup generator. In this situation the DC will buy energy from the local marketplace when it is generated at low prices thus consuming to the possible extent the available renewable energy from grid.

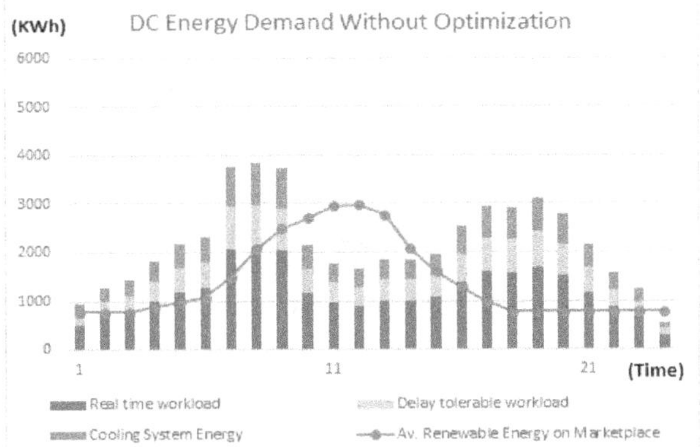

Figure 2. DC Energy demand profile without optimization

Figure 3 presents the DC's energy profile generated as a result of enacting the GEYSER defined DC energy flexibility models and non-linear programming algorithms.

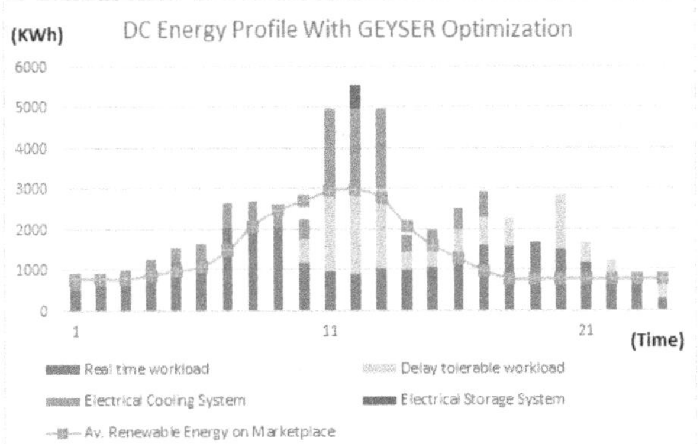

Figure 3. DC Energy Consumption after optimization

From the above we infer that the execution of delay-tolerant workload, initially scheduled between timeslots 1 - 9 and 15 - 21, is now shifted to timeslots between 11 and 13, thus matching the high RES generation in the local marketplace. In addition, during the renewable energy production peak, actions to overcool the thermal storage systems are executed; in doing so the electrical cooling system energy demand will be increased (see blue column). After the renewable energy peak (i.e. after timeslot 13) actions to cool down the DC using the cold stored in the thermal storage are executed; thus the electrical cooling system demand is reduced, contributing to the decrease of energy consumption.

4.2 Individual Energy Network level Optimization

In this case we simulate multi-energy generation scenario in which GEYSER will allow the DC to make use of optimized thermal storage enacted internal conversion of energy with the overall goal of optimizing its own economic performance.

Figure 4 shows the DC energy demand and the optimization goals set at the level of electricity and thermal networks (timeslot of half hour). The DC is requested to decrease its energy consumption to an optimized value set at electricity network level for the timeslots 4-6 and to consume more electricity between time slots 1-2 to provide a certain amount of thermal energy internally converted and accumulated during that period to the district heating.

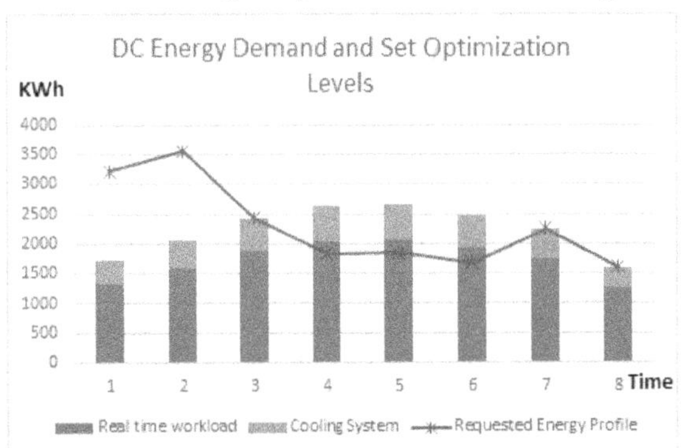

Figure 4. Energy optimization goals and DC energy demand

As a result of the GEYSER optimization actions, Figure 5 energy profile was achieved. Leveraging on the DC energy flexibility, actions are decided and executed to shift the demand from timeslots 4-6. To that end the electrical cooling is used between timeslots 1-2 to overcool the thermal storage which will in turn be used to cool down the DC during timeslots 4-6; thus reducing the energy consumption of the electrical cooling. At the same time thermal energy is stored at timeslots 1 and 2 enabling DC to feed it by means of heat recovery infrastructure to the district heating.

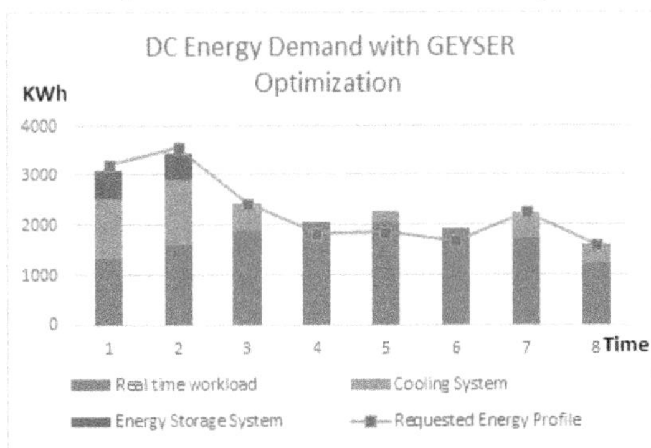

Figure 5. DC energy profile to meet the request

4.3 City level Multi-network Optimization

In this scenario the DC is provided with a mix of energy (thermal and electrical) profile and computation costs to follow up. GEYSER will allow the DC to reconfigure and optimize internally in order to make available the requested flexibility. The grid is seen as a collection of interconnected and cross-network energy (thermal and electric) consumption objects. In this context the GEYSER enabled DC is a large flexibility load resource placed at the intersection of major city networks (i.e. electricity, thermal, and data). Figure 6 shows such a profile generated and used in our simulation (timeslot of one hour); in this case the DC's energy demand profile does not match the requested one. E.g. between timeslots 9 - 15 the DC energy demand is much lower than requested. Thus the DC has to shift its energy profile, by exploiting its electricity, thermal and data flexibility.

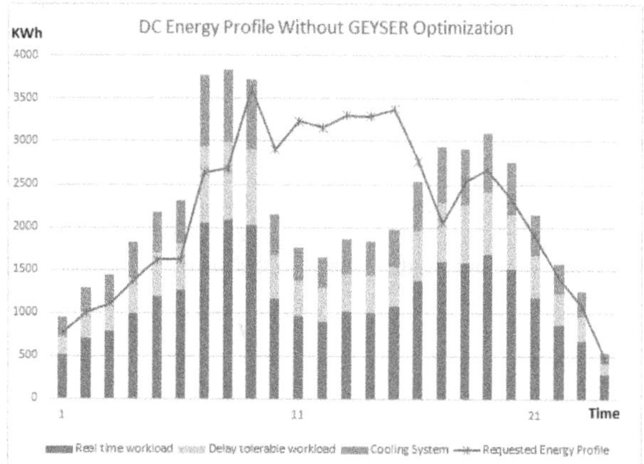

Figure 6. Requested energy profile and DC energy demand without optimization

Figure 7 presents the DC's energy profile as a result of the suggested GEYSER optimization actions. The DC energy demand is shifted to follow the requested energy profile by using less the electrical cooling system and leveraging on the thermal storage to cool down the DC between timeslots 1 – 9; in addition delay-tolerant workload is shifted from timeslots 1-9 to timeslots 10 – 15 while considering its established computational deadline. Also, during peak timeslots 10-15 the electrical cooling system is used to overcool the thermal storage, while the DC's energy storage system is charged to optimally meet the required profile and eventually feed energy (electrical/thermal) to the grid.

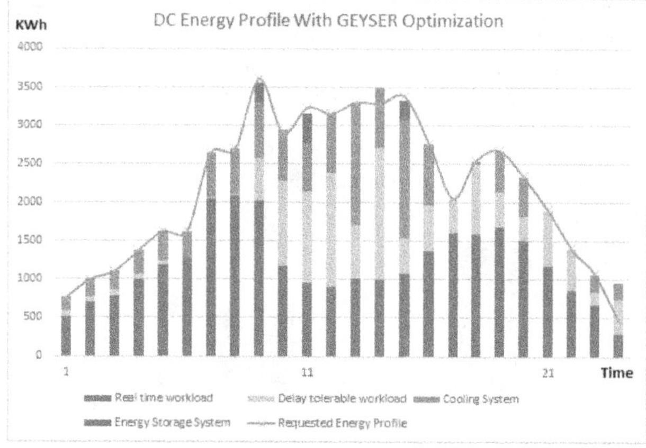

Figure 7. DC energy profile using GEYSER optimization

5. CONCLUSIONS

This paper presented novel business models and strategies where urban DCs are active load resources integrated in the context of the smart city and contributing to optimized operations of local grids. To that end local marketplaces are designed tailored to offer flexibility for deploying energy management, load management and voltage management services. Simulation results validate the DC's potential for shaping its energy profile to meet goals of diverse energy networks, by leveraging on energy storage devices, workload migration, dynamic usage of cooling system, etc. Such promising approach is about to be validated within the context of four operational data centers (Pont Saint Martin and Terni in Italy, Alticom in the Netherlands and RWTH Aachen in Germany).

6. ACKNOWLEDGMENTS

This work has been conducted within the GEYSER project Grant number 609211 [2], co-funded by the European Commission as part of the 7th Research Framework Programme (FP7-SMARTCITIES-2013).

Special thanks to Marcel Antal, Dan Valea, and Claudia Pop from the Technical University of Cluj-Napoca and Vasiliki Georgiadou from Green IT Amsterdam for their valuable contributions.

7. REFERENCES

[1] Critical Factors: The Data Center Location Decision, 2012, http://www.areadevelopment.com/siteSelection/April2012/data-center-location-decision-criteria-26255554.shtml

[2] GEYSER FP7 project, www.geyser-project.eu

[3] Cioara T., Anghel I., et. al. Data Center Optimization Methodology to Maximize the Usage of Locally Produced Renewable Energy, SustainIT 2015, pp.1,8, http://dx.doi.org/10.1109/SustainIT.2015.7101363

[4] The EU Emissions Trading System (EU ETS), 2014, Online: http://ec.europa.eu/clima/policies/ets/index_en.htm

[5] Energy Roadmap 2050, 2012, Online at: http://ec.europa.eu/energy/publications/doc/2012_energy_roadmap_2050_en.pdf

[6] Li Y., Chiu D., Liu C., et.al., Towards Dynamic Pricing-Based Collaborative Optimizations for Green Data Centers: 2nd Int. Workshop on Data Management in the Cloud, 2013.

[7] Liu Z., Chen Y., Bash C., et. al., Renewable and cooling aware workload management for sustainable data centers: SIGMETRICS Perform. Eval. Rev. 40, 1, 175-186, 2012.

[8] Aksanli B., Rosing T., Providing Regulation Services and Managing Data Center Peak Power Budgets, DATE14

[9] Wierman A., Liu Z., Opportunities and Challenges for Data Center Demand Response, Green Computing Conf., 2014

[10] Janacek S., Schomaker G., Data Center Smart Grid Integration Considering Renewable Energies and Waste Heat Usage: Energy-Efficient Data Centers LNCS 8343, 2014.

[11] ABB Review: Data Centers, The corporate technical journal, 4/13, 2013.

[12] Zheng W., Ma K., Exploiting Thermal Energy Storage to Reduce Data Center Capital and Operating Expenses, http://www2.ece.ohio-state.edu/~xwang/papers/hpca14.pdf

[13] Chen Y., et. al., The Case for Evaluating MapReduce Performance Using Workload Suites, MASCOTS, 2011.

[14] http://www.nordpoolspot.com/Market-data1/Elspot/Area-Prices/ALL1/Hourly/?view=table

[15] All4Green project, http://www.all4green-project.eu/

[16] DC4Cities project, http://www.dc4cities.eu/en/

Modeling Impact of Power- and Thermal-aware Fans Management on Data Center Energy Consumption

Wojciech Piatek
Poznan Supercomputing and Networking Center
Noskowskiego 10, Poznan, Poland
piatek@man.poznan.pl

Ariel Oleksiak
Poznan Supercomputing and Networking Center
Institute of Computing Science
Poznan University of Technology, Poland
ariel@man.poznan.pl

Micha vor dem Berge
Christmann Informationstechnik & Medien
Micha.vordemBerge@christmann.info

ABSTRACT

In this paper we study the power usage and thermal management of micro servers to analyze their impact on the overall data center energy consumption. We propose thermal models of micro servers based on analytical approach tuned with parameters derived from empirical tests. We demonstrate how fan management configuration affects the energy consumption of servers and the whole data center. We also apply the proposed model to predict temperature changes in a short time ahead and take advantage of these predictions to improve fan management. We show why PUE is not sufficient or can be even misleading in minimizing data center energy consumption. To mitigate this issue, we propose metrics that can be used to reflect correctly fans management impact on the overall energy consumption.

Categories and Subject Descriptors

I.6.4 [**Computing Methodologies**]: SIMULATION AND MODELING—*Model Validation and Analysis*

Keywords

energy-efficiency; data centers; fans management; power and thermal simulations; power leakage; microservers

1. INTRODUCTION

Recent rapid growth of data center capacities made the reduction of their energy consumption an important research topic. Both hardware vendors and data center managers aim at lowering data center cooling costs and Power Usage Effectiveness (PUE) metric values. One of the solutions recently used in data centers to limit raising carbon footprint and energy costs is the adoption of micro servers. This emerging class of servers is based on low-power architectures and enables space savings by packing a substantial number of computing units into a single enclosure.

In this paper we study the use of micro servers, especially power usage and thermal management, to analyze their impact on the overall data center energy consumption.

To this end, we propose thermal models of micro servers based on analytical approach tuned with parameters derived from empirical tests. This approach enables fast calculation of temperature changes (without the use of complex Computational Fluid Dynamics methods) that can be applied to simulations of whole data centers, including transient simulations of workload execution. We use this holistic simulation model to analyze the comprehensive impact of heat dissipation and fans operation of micro servers on the total data center energy consumption. We do this by taking into account (often neglected) impact of CPU temperature on its power usage and fans operation on data center cooling system.

We demonstrate how fan management configuration can be used to minimize overall energy consumption and high temperature excesses (that may cause failures and shorten server exploitation) in a data center. Based on the proposed model, we are able to predict temperature changes in a short time ahead and take advantage of these predictions to improve fan management techniques.

To assess the impact on the whole data center we also show why PUE is not sufficient or can be even misleading in minimizing data center energy consumption. To mitigate this issue we propose metrics that can be used to reflect correctly fans management impact on the overall energy consumption.

We conduct our studies on the RECS systems being developed by Christmann company [5] within the EU FiPS project [7], [11]. The RECS compute box, a high density computing system with embedded power meters for each of its computing nodes, can host from 6 up to 18 servers (24 to 72 in the case of ARM-based systems) within one rack unit. FiPS goal is to deliver energy-efficient servers based on lower power processors used in mobile/embedded market and reconfigurable hardware along with the methodology that facilitates mapping applications on these servers as well as server customization.

e-Energy'15, July 14–17, 2015, Bangalore, India.
© 2015 ACM. ISBN 978-1-4503-3609-3/15/07 ...$15.00.
DOI: http://dx.doi.org/10.1145/2768510.2768525.

The remaining part of this paper is organized as follows. In Section 2 we give a brief overview of the current state of the art. Section 3 highlights the models we use in the simulation of energy consumption and temperature of computing systems together with the experiments performed on real hardware. In Section 4 we demonstrate the application of these models to a few types of resource management policies in the DCworms simulator. Final conclusions and directions for future work are given in Section 5.

2. RELATED WORK

Issues related to energy-efficiency of computing system are gaining more and more interest due to the rapid growth of the system scale and related energy costs. For now, lots of effort has been put on managing the IT infrastructure [14], cooling equipment [3] and workload management [16]. However, many studies ignore the impact of fans located inside a rack on the system performance and its power efficiency.

In [17] authors presented a fan controller that utilizes thermal models to manipulate the operation of fans. Taking into account the prediction of server temperatures, controller adjusts the speed of particular fans. Similarly, Kim et al. [9] proposed stable fan speed control scheme allowing to reduce the performance degradation and power usage up to 19%. In [2] authors studied the impact of fan speed on the disk throughput and finally on overall system performance. They tuned the fan speed with respect to the disk activity, while maintaining the given thermal constraints.

Both Moore [8] and Tang [15] omitted the impact of fans in their thermal considerations. Although they noticed the effect of airflow on the outlet temperature, they do not use fan speed control as a mean to improve energy-efficiency. They put their attention on reducing the heat recirculation, and thus increasing the temperature of air supplied by the cooling system.

Zapater et al. [18] studied leakage and temperature tradeoffs of a server and provided the empirical model. Based on it, they designed a controller that tunes the fan speed to minimize the energy consumption for a given workload. However, they did not expand their studies beyond a single server level to evaluate the energy-efficiency of the whole data center.

3. POWER AND THERMAL MODELING

In this section we present power and thermodynamic models used in our studies. We conclude with the verification of thermal models and identify the power leakage function.

3.1 Power

We assume that data center server room is composed by a cooling system and a hierarchy of IT resources with a rack on its top and a set of processors at the bottom.

Power usage at processor level is defined by the equation:

$$P_{cpu}(f, load) = (P_{cpu}(idle) + load * (P_{cpu}(f, 100) - P_{cpu}(idle))) * g(T_{cpu}) \quad (1)$$

where $P_{cpu}(f, load)$ is a power consumed by a processor operating at a given frequency f and utilized in *load* percent. $P_{cpu}(idle)$ and $P_{cpu}(f, 100)$ expresses the power drawn by an idle and fully loaded processor working at a given frequency, respectively. This form of equation corresponds to the one discussed in [1] with additional consideration of the processor frequency. Finally, $g(T_{cpu})$ is a function representing the power leakage of the processor due to the increase in its temperature [4].

Power usage characteristics for other levels of resources are presented in [3] and [13].

In terms of cooling system, apart from cooling infrastructure installed in and/or outside a server room, fans mounted within an enclosure may contribute significantly to overall energy consumption. Power usage of a single fan can be expressed as follows:

$$P_{fan} = k_p * V^3 \quad (2)$$

where P_{fan} is a power consumption of the fan, V defines the related airflow volume and k_p parameter that needs to be determined experimentally for specific hardware configuration (it covers fan efficiency and surrounding pressure drop).

To describe a power drawn by the cooling system for the whole data center we adopted the model introduced in [8]:

$$P_{cooling} = \frac{P_{load}}{CoP} \quad (3)$$

where $P_{cooling}$ is a power consumed by cooling equipment installed in a server room using P_{load} power and CoP (Coefficient of Performance) is the ratio of heat removal.

3.2 Thermal

In terms of thermal models we follow the ones presented in our recent studies [13]. Hence, the changes in temperature of the processor are characterized by:

$$T_{cpu}(t + \Delta t) = T_{cpu}^{\infty} + (T_{cpu}(t) - T_{cpu}^{\infty})e^{-\frac{\Delta t}{RC}} \quad (4)$$

with $T_{cpu}^{\infty} = P_{cpu}R + T_{amb}$, $R = R_{cond} + R_{conv}$, $R_{conv} = \frac{1}{k_n V^n}$ and $V = \sqrt[3]{k_p P_{fan}}$

where $T_{cpu}(t)$ defines a temperature at a given time t, Δt is a time step, T_{cpu}^{∞} is a steady temperature for a processor dissipating the given amount of heat, P_{cpu} is the processor power usage, T_{amb} is a temperature of ambient air, R defines thermal resistance and C is a thermal capacitance. Thermal resistance consists of conductive part R_{cond} and convective one R_{conv}, that can be defined by airflow volume V and k_v and n parameters that need to be determined experimentally as they are typical for a given equipment model.

Corresponding formula for the increase in outlet temperature (at the outlet of particular servers) is defined as:

$$T_{out}(t + \Delta t)) = T_{out}^{\infty} + (T_{out}(t) - T_{out}^{\infty})e^{-\frac{\Delta t}{RC}} \quad (5)$$

where $T_{out}^{\infty} = \frac{\sum_{i=1}^{n} P_{node_i} + P_{fan}}{K} + T_{in}$, $K = \rho V C_p$ and $R = R_{cond} + \frac{1}{k_n V^n}$ as previously.

where $T_{out}(t)$ defined an outlet temperature at a given time, T_{out}^{∞} is the steady temperature, P_{node} is the power consumed by the node, T_{in} is the temperature of inlet air, K refers to the heat absorption capacity of air specified by air density ρ, its volume V and specific heat capacity C_p.

3.3 Evaluation of thermal model

In this section we briefly present a comparison between the temperature derived on the basis of the above models and the measured values obtained within the real environment. Finally, we determine the power leakage function ($g(T_{cpu})$).

3.3.1 Testbed configuration

We carried out our experiments on the Christmann's RECS systems [5]. Figure 1 shows evaluated RECS architecture.

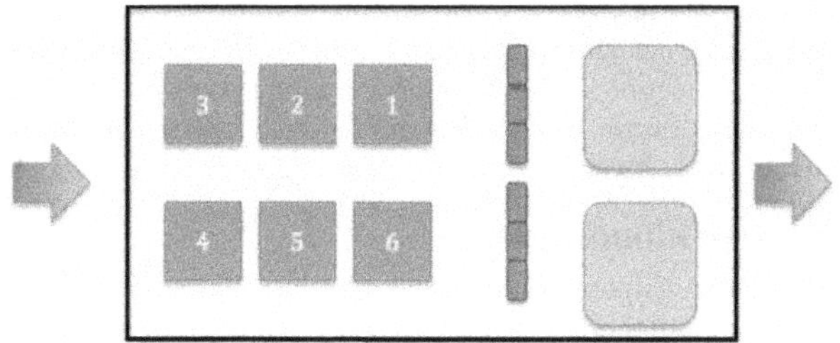

Figure 1: Illustration of RECS architecture

As presented, RECS system contains 6 baseboards that can be equipped with 6 x86- or up to 24 ARM CPU modules (6 baseboards x 4 CPU modules). Blue arrows indicate the direction of the airflow, while the dark-grey rectangles stand for the fans, which is 6 in total. To monitor temperature of processor we exploit internal CPU unit sensors and for temperature of input air we installed AKCP securityProbe 5ES sensor on inlets of the RECS. Moreover, we are able to adjust the speed of fans in a manual way within the range 0-100%. According to the vendor, each fan can blow $0.0112m^3/s$ of air drawing 6.6 W of power, while operating at full speed. We studied RECS system filled with i5-4400E and Toradex Apalis T30 with ARM processors. In both cases we observed similarities in terms of model accuracy and trends of power leakage function. For ARM nodes we noticed higher values of thermal resistance and capacitance and thus longer heating time. Due to the paper page limit constraints, we only present the results for i5 processors.

3.3.2 Methodology

In order to be able to extract the necessary parameters, we first ran a stress workload generator [6] on the given types of nodes. For simplification we evaluated only nodes placed within one column (from the inlet to the outlet of the RECS). Then, we monitored each second all the relevant values like: power usage and temperature of a processor, power usage of a node and inlet temperature. Moreover, as we were able to adjust the fan speed, we repeated our tests for the fans working at 30%, 70% and 100% of their maximum speed. Inlet temperature (T_{in}) oscillates between 19.5°C and 21.5°C. One should note that the inlet temperature for the nodes located closer to the outlet is equal to the temperature of air leaving the preceding node (outlet temperature calculated considering the preceding nodes). Based on our observations [13], we noticed that a good approximation of local ambient temperature (T_{amb}) is a weighted average of inlet and processor temperature, expressed as follows: $T_{amb} = (T_{cpu} + 2 * T_{in})/3$.

3.3.3 Obtained results

In this section we present the validation results obtained for the RECS system. Based on the measurements, we extracted the following values describing thermal characteristics of the system (Table 1).

The following picture presents comparison of temperatures obtained for the processor located on the outlet side with the fan working at full speed.

Parameter	Symbol	Value
Conductive thermal resistance	R_{cond}	1.06 °C/W
Convective thermal resistance	R_{conv}	0.28 - 0.7 °C/W
Heatsink constant	k_v	49 W s/°Cm^3
Heatsink airflow factor	n	0.77
Thermal capacitance	C	8 W s/°C

Table 1: Thermal characteristics for i5-4400E nodes

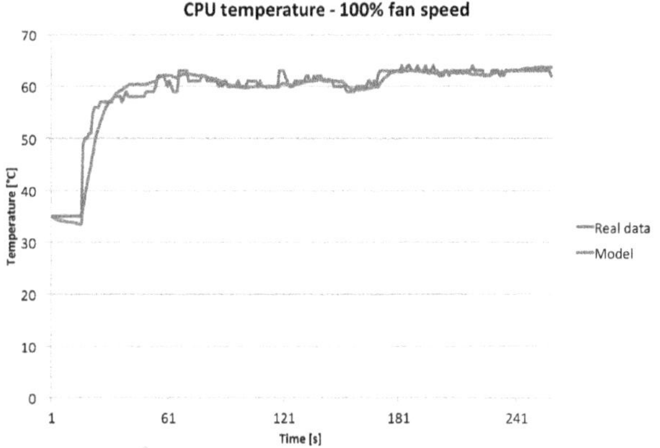

Figure 2: Measured and simulated values for processor temperature

Table 2 summarizes the accuracy of the proposed model for three levels of fan speed.

Fan speed	Avg. temperature difference	Avg. relative error
30%	1.91 °C	2.75%
70%	1.95 °C	3.14%
100%	1.04 °C	1.86%

Table 2: Accuracy of processor temperature model

Obtained results suggest high accuracy of the model. Both the values as well as the curve of temperature are reflected with satisfactory score.

To identify the power leakage function, we compared the power usage values for the processor operating at different temperatures (due to the differences in the fan speed). It can be described by a quadratic function (for processor temperatures higher than 59 °C):

$P_{leakage} = 0.0067 * (T_{cpu} - 59)^2 - 0.0482 * (T_{cpu} - 59)$

illustrated in Figure 3 together with the power drawn by the processor and compared to real measurements.

Accordingly, values of the power leakage may constitute even 30% of the processor power consumption, for the processor operating at temperatures above 90°C. Presented trend is consistent with the one presented in [4].

4. SIMULATION OF ENERGY EFFICIENCY

In this section we discuss, how the proposed models can be used in the simulations of resource management strategies, in particular management of cooling infrastructure. To this end we used the Data Center Workload and Resource Management Simulator (DCworms) [10] together with the power usage and thermodynamic models proposed in previous sections. We performed experiments in order to get insight into energy- and thermal-aware fans management policies.

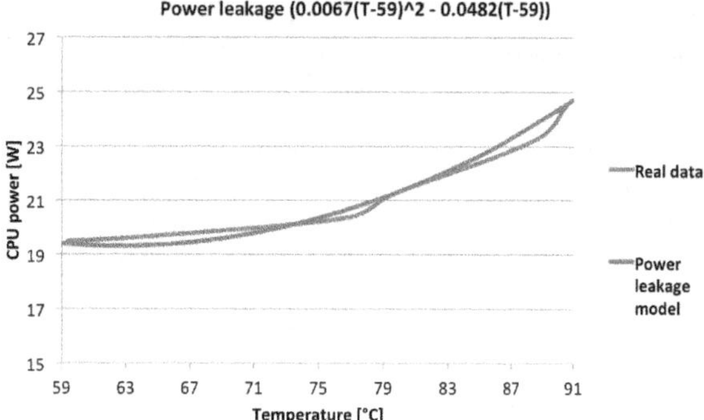

Figure 3: Power leakage impact on processor power

4.1 Resource characteristics

For our simulation purposes, we modeled a server room with 10 racks. Each rack contains 42 1-unit enclosures equipped with 6 nodes with a processor belonging to Intel Core i5-4400E family. As in the case of the evaluated system we are allowed to control only the group of 3 fans, we decided to model, for simplification, 1 fan per column of nodes reflecting the characteristics of three ventilators working together.

Below we give a short power characteristic of the particular components: processors (in Table 3), nodes (in Table 4) and fans (in Table 5). We adopted the cooling model [8], while power supply efficiency was assumed to be 87% and fan efficiency 60%. All these characteristics correspond to the power profiles created based on the taken measurements, as well as to the vendors' guidelines. Additionally, in Table 6 we summarized environmental conditions that were applied to our simulations.

State	Power
idle	5 W
fully loaded	26 W

Table 3: Processor characteristics

State	Power
idle	11 W
fully loaded	36 W

Table 4: Node characteristics

Speed	Airflow	Power	Up	Down
30%	0.01008 m^3/s	1.58 W	-	56 °C
70%	0.02352 m^3/s	9.36 W	58 °C	76 °C
100%	0.0336 m^3/s	19.8 W	78 °C	-

Table 5: Single fan characteristics

Parameter	Value
Room temperature	22 °C
Air heat capacity	1024 J/kg °C
Air density	1.168 m^3/s

Table 6: Environmental conditions

Finally, we modeled the thermal characteristics of the evaluated processor (introduced in Table 1) and assumed that fan has 3 working states (as presented in Table 5). Last two columns indicate the thresholds triggering fan speed adjustment. Increasing the fan speed is activated when the power level from the penultimate column is exceeded, while decreasing occurs if the temperature falls below the value in the last column. These thresholds were determined in an arbitrary way, based on the processor temperature ranges.

4.2 Workload profile

In our experiment we imposed the load, lasting for 7200 seconds, on all nodes in the system. Within this interval we identified 10 time periods determined using uniform distribution. These periods varies in terms of load levels that were generated according to the probability shown in Table 7, which resulted in the 46% overall system utilization.

Load	Probability	Load	Probability
0	0.3	60	0.05
10	0.02	70	0.05
20	0.03	80	0.1
30	0.05	90	0.1
40	0.05	100	0.2
50	0.05	-	-

Table 7: Load levels probabilities

4.3 Applying models to resource management strategies

The ultimate goal of our work is to improve energy efficiency of computing systems while maintaining system reliability. To achieve it, we study how energy- and thermal-aware fans management policies can benefit from the proposed models. We evaluated the following strategies:

Constant fan speed - 30% - This strategy keeps all fans working at 30% of their full speed.

Constant fan speed - 100% - In this policy all fans are working at their maximum speed.

Variable fan speed - We assume that fans may operate at 3 speed levels: 30%, 70% and 100%. The speed of fan is tuned according to the temperature levels in Table 5.

Dynamic fan speed control - As the current fans control systems provide means to manage their speed at a more fine-grained level (in case of evaluated RECS system speed of fans can be set with 1% granularity), we propose a strategy that tries to adjust it in a smoother way. Having the trend of the processor temperature, we tune the fan speed in advance. This approach also verifies whether increasing a fan speed gradually allows keeping the temperature at the desired level and thus reducing the cost of operating fans at higher speed. Details of proposed fan speed levels and corresponding temperature thresholds are introduced in Table 8.

4.4 Metrics

In addition to direct amount of energy consumed for particular workload there is a number of metrics that are used to assess various aspects of data center operation. So far PUE is the most commonly used. It was defined by The Green Grid as the ratio between energy used by the whole data center to the energy used by the IT equipment. The accuracy level of this metric depends on the point of measure-

Speed	Airflow	Power	Up	Down
30%	0.01008 m^3/s	1.58 W	-	56 °C
40%	0.01344 m^3/s	2.89 W	58 °C	60 °C
50%	0.0168 m^3/s	4.61 W	62 °C	64 °C
60%	0.02016 m^3/s	6.77 W	66 °C	70 °C
70%	0.02352 m^3/s	9.36 W	72 °C	76 °C
80%	0.02688 m^3/s	12.39 W	78 °C	80 °C
90%	0.03024 m^3/s	15.86 W	82 °C	84 °C
100%	0.0336 m^3/s	19.8 W	86 °C	-

Table 8: Fan speed control scheme

ment of IT power that can be: UPS (Uninterruptible Power Supply Unit), PDU (Power Distribution Unit) or the IT itself, behind PSU (Power Supply Unit). Depending on the measurement points, three levels of PUE are distinguished, for example for measurements done behind PSU the metric is referred as PUE Level 3.

However, even for PUE Level 3 the IT equipment includes fans responsible for server cooling. This fact may lead to the situation in which adoption of server with powerful fans improves the PUE as it increases the IT equipment share in total energy consumption. Consequently, application of such high performance fans can lead to lower PUEs while the energy consumption can stay the same or even increase. Thus, we proposed to also take into consideration the measurement of IT part only, excluding PSU and fans, and called this metric by analogy PUE Level 4 (even if it could be a separate metric focused more on IT impact on energy consumption) [3].

We included PUE Level 4 metric in Table 10. It can be easily seen that it differs from PUE even up to 50% reflecting more accurately whether energy is consumption in an effective way. Energy consumption and power usage effectiveness metrics are complemented by the Average temperature exceeded time metric, which denotes a time in which temperature exceeded certain value (in this case 90°C).

4.5 Results

Table 9 shows the results of simulations for the evaluated policies. Additionally, we investigated for how long the system (processors) works exceeding the given, hazardous temperature threshold. We set this level to 90°C, according to [12] and validated strategies against it.

One should note that running all fans (within the racks) at 30% of their maximum speed resulted in the lowest total energy consumption. However, this approach leads to long time intervals (more than 17% of the whole workload execution) in which temperature exceeds the given threshold. That may cause the deterioration of system reliability and, in the long term, system damage. This policy also precludes managing inlet air temperatures and potential savings on cooling equipment.

Figure 4 illustrates dependency between PUEs and total energy and the one consumed by fans. While energy costs of operating fans do not affect PUE much, they have substantial impact on PUE Level 4. Moreover, the increase in total energy consumed is not reflected by the PUE metric.

In the next set of experiments we increased inlet air temperature to 24°C to evaluate system performance. We decided to skip the policy with the fans operating at the lowest speed. Results are gathered in Table 10.

Metrics	Const = 30%	Const = 100%	Variable	Dynamic
Energy Leakage [kWh]	14.49	4.17	4.91	5.22
Avg temp. exceeded time (90°C) [s]	1311	0	0	0
Processors energy [kWh]	87.78	77.46	78.2	78.51
Enclosure fans energy [kWh]	2.7	33.27	17.86	14.26
Racks energy [kWh]	149.23	172.55	155.69	151.91
Cooling energy [kWh]	40.08	42.58	39.93	39.35
Total energy [kWh]	192.3	218.58	198.73	194.3
PUE	1.288	1.266	1.276	1.279
PUE Level 4	1.512	1.87	1.69	1.648

Table 9: Simulation results for $T_{in} = 22°C$

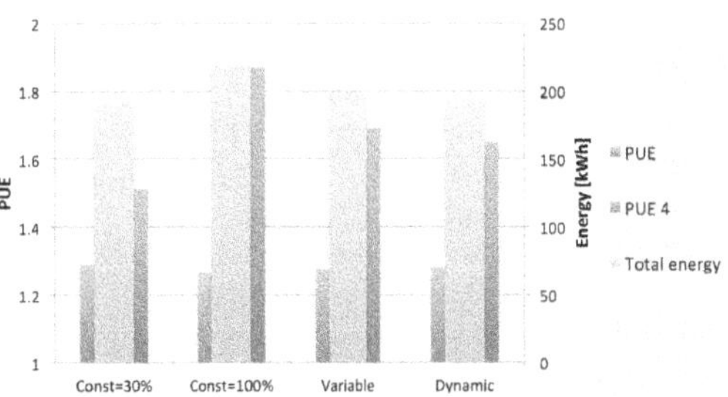

(a) Total energy consumption and PUEs

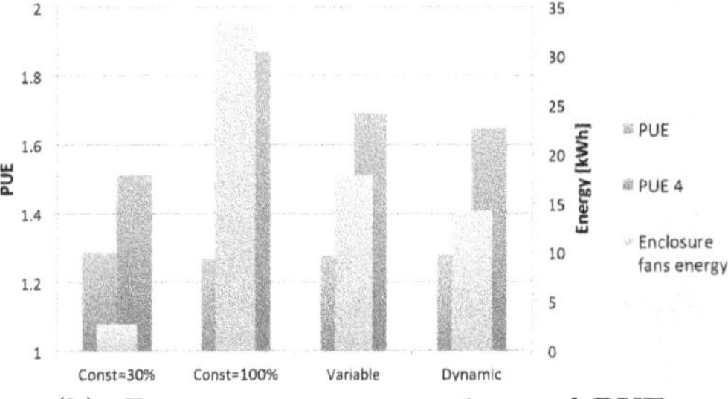

(b) Fans energy consumption and PUEs

Figure 4: Energy consumption and PUEs metrics

Metrics	Const = 100%	Variable	Dynamic
Energy Leakage [kWh]	4.91	5.37	5.88
Avg temp. exceeded time (90°C) [s]	0	0	0
Processors energy [kWh]	78.2	78.66	79.17
Enclosure fans energy [kWh]	33.28	21.37	15.25
Racks energy [kWh]	173.41	160.25	153.80
Cooling energy [kWh]	36.70	34.91	34.07
Total energy [kWh]	213.58	198.37	190.95
PUE	1.231	1.237	1.241
PUE Level 4	1.631	1.566	1.531

Table 10: Simulation results for $T_{in} = 24°C$

It is easy to see that applying fans control strategies (in particular Dynamic one) together with increasing temperature of air supplied by cooling system allows achieving even higher savings than running fans at 30%. Moreover, one should note again the significant dissimilarity in PUE and PUE Level 4 for all policies. PUE Level 4 is correlated with total energy consumption so it is better suited to anticipate the actual energy efficiency.

5. CONCLUSIONS AND FUTURE WORK

In this paper we presented the study on thermal management of micro servers to minimize energy consumption in data centers. We proposed thermal models of micro servers along with their validation showing that their accuracy reaches 1.85-3.14%. This approach enabled us to perform fast simulations of whole data centers for transient simulations of workload execution. The simulations were implemented within the DCworms simulation tool.

We showed that when changing the fan speed we should take into account their influence on CPU power usage (increase up to 15%) and the cooling system. We applied this holistic simulation model to find a trade-off between energy consumption of data center and server high temperature periods that may cause failures and shorten server exploitation.

We also proposed a fan management policy that helped to save additional 12% of energy (compared to running the fans at their full speed) by prediction of temperature changes in a short time ahead based on derived models.

Finally, we showed that PUE remains the same for very different scenarios or even its value can be favorable for worse solutions in terms of overall energy consumption. To distinguish between actual IT work and cooling (including server fans) better we applied another metric (PUE Level 4). This metric allowed us to evaluate more accurately the impact of fan management on energy consumption. Differences between PUE and PUE Level 4 reached even 50%.

In the future we would like to perform more comprehensive tests and to compare results obtained for ARM-based micro servers with typical high-end servers. Another step is modeling and analysis of denser and heterogeneous architectures. Future work also includes the method to optimize fan management in a whole data center in a more automated way in order to minimize the overall energy consumption dynamically. We also plan to find more precise models for the architecture of enclosures to enable better proactive fan management.

6. ACKNOWLEDGMENTS

The results presented in this paper are partially funded by the European Union Seventh Framework Programme (FP7/2007-2013) under grant agreement No 609757 (FiPS - Developing Hardware and Design Methodologies for Heterogeneous Low Power Field Programmable Servers) and a grant from Polish National Science Center under award number 2013/08/A/ST6/00296.

7. REFERENCES

[1] R. Basmadjian, N. Ali, F. Niedermeier, H. D. Meer, and G. Giuliani. A methodology to predict the power consumption of servers in data centres. In *Proc. of the ACM SIGCOMM 2nd Int'l Conf. on Energy-Efficient Computing and Networking (e-Energy)*, 2011.

[2] C. S. Chan, Y. Jin, Y.-K. Wu, K. C. Gross, K. Vaidyanathan, and T. S. Rosing. Fan-speed-aware scheduling of data intensive jobs. In *ISLPED*, pages 409–414, 2012.

[3] G. D. Costa, A. Oleksiak, W. Piatek, J. Salom, and L. Siso. Minimization of costs and energy consumption in a data center by a workload-based capacity management. In *3rd International Workshop on Energy-Efficient Data Centres Co-located with the ACM e-Energy*, 2014.

[4] F. Fallah and M. Pedram. Standby and active leakage current control and minimization in cmos vlsi circuits. In *IEICE Transactions on Electronics*, pages 509–519, 2005.

[5] http://christmann.info/show/57.

[6] http://people.seas.harvard.edu/ apw/stress/.

[7] https://www.fips project.eu. Fips project.

[8] J.Moore, J. Chase, P. Ranganathan, and R. Sharma. Making scheduling "cool": Temperature - aware workload placement in data centers. In *Proceedings of the 2005 USENIX Annual Technical Conference*, 2005.

[9] J. Kim, M. M. Sabry, D. Atienza, K. Vaidyanathan, and K. C. Gross. Global fan speed control considering non-ideal temperature measurements in enterprise servers. In *DATE*, pages 1–6, 2014.

[10] K. Kurowski, A. Oleksiak, W. Piatek, T. Piontek, A. Przybyszewski, and J. Weglarz. Dcworms - a tool for simulation of energy efficiency in distributed computing infrastructures. *Simulation Modelling Practice and Theory*, 39:135–151, December 2013.

[11] Y. Lhuillier, J. M. Philippe, A. Guerre, M. Kierzynka, and A. Oleksiak. Parallel architecture benchmarking: From embedded computing to hpc, a fips project perspective. In *Proceedings of the 2014 12th IEEE International Conference on Embedded and Ubiquitous Computing (EUC '14)*, pages 154–161, 2014.

[12] M. Patterson. The effect of data center temperature on energy. In *Proc. ITHERM*, pages 1167–1174, 2008.

[13] W. Piatek, G. D. Costa, and A. Oleksiak. Energy and thermal models for simulation of workload and resource management in computing systems. *Simulation Modelling Practice and Theory*, 2015.

[14] I. Rodero, H. Viswanathan, E. K. Lee, M. G. andDario Pompili, and M. Parashar. Energy-efficient thermal- aware autonomic management of virtualized hpc cloud infrastruc- ture. In *Journal of Grid Computing*, pages 447–473, 2012.

[15] Q. Tang, S. K. S. Gupta, D. Stanzione, and P. Cayton. Thermalaware task scheduling to minimize energy usage of blade server based datacen- ters. In *IEEE DASC*, 2006.

[16] L. Wang, G. von Laszewski, J. Dayal, and F. Wang. Towards energy aware scheduling for precedence constrained parallel tasks in a cluster with dvfs. In *Proceedings of the 10th IEEE/ACM International Symposium on Cluster, Cloud, and Grid Computing*, pages 368–377, 2010.

[17] Z. Wang, C. Bash, N. Tolia, M. Marwah, X. Zhu, and P. Ranganathan. Optimal fan speed control for thermal management of servers. In *Proceedings of the ASME*, 2009.

[18] M. Zapater, J. L. Ayala, J. M. Moya, K. Vaidyanathan, K. C. Gross, and A. K. Coskun. Leakage and temperature aware server control for improving energy efficiency in data centers. In *DATA*, pages 266–269, 2013.

GEYSER – A Data Centre Energy Simulation Prototype Enabling Future Hardware in the Loop Testing

Marco Cupelli, Lisette Cupelli, Antonello Monti
E.ON Energy Research Center – RWTH Aachen University
Mathieustrasse 10
52074 Aachen
{mcupelli, lcupelli, amonti}@eonerc.rwth-aachen.de

ABSTRACT

This paper focuses on modelling energy components within a Data Centre (DC) in a Smart City environment. This allows exploring the DC dynamics in a way that includes conditions that might be difficult or too risky to recreate in the real world, e.g. the impact of a large power injection from renewable energy sources and its influence on the DC operation. The DC components' models execution in real-time will enable Hardware in the Loop (HiL) testing of real DC equipment under fully controlled conditions.

Categories and Subject Descriptors

I.6.4 [**SIMULATION AND MODELING**]: Model Validation and Analysis – PROSPECTOR.

General Terms

Algorithms, Management, Measurement, Performance, Design, Economics, Reliability, Experimentation, Theory, Verification.

Keywords

Data Centre; Demand Response Management; Energy Simulation; Component Test; Smart City Interaction; Renewables; Simulation Scenarios; Simulation Architecture; Hardware in the Loop.

1. INTRODUCTION

The rising energy demand of DCs is both associated with increasing operational costs and a detrimental environmental impact in terms of high CO_2 emissions [1]. These facts put pressure on DC operators to take steps towards reducing their energy consumption while improving their energy efficiency.

The FP7 project GEYSER addresses this challenge by considering the DCs as active participants in Smart City environments and developing a software framework, which aims at improving DCs' energy efficiency and reducing their carbon footprint while managing their energy consumption and local energy generation in response to the Smart City needs.

Related work is performed in frame of the ICT-2013.6.2 FP7 call on Data Centre Sustainability, where 6 research projects (RenewIT, GreenDataNet, DC4Cities , GENiC, Dolfin, GEYSER) aim to significantly improve the energy efficiency of DCs and simultaneously stabilizing the Smart Grid. In these projects dynamic simulation models of DCs are developed in combination with different workload scheduling, consolidation and migration techniques. Those are combined with an optimization framework and advanced control algorithms which should enable the matching of the DC energy demand with the energy supply of brown and green energy source.

e-Energy'15, July 14 - 17, 2015, Bangalore, India
© 2015 ACM. ISBN 978-1-4503-3609-3/15/07…$15.00
DOI: http://dx.doi.org/10.1145/2768510.2768523

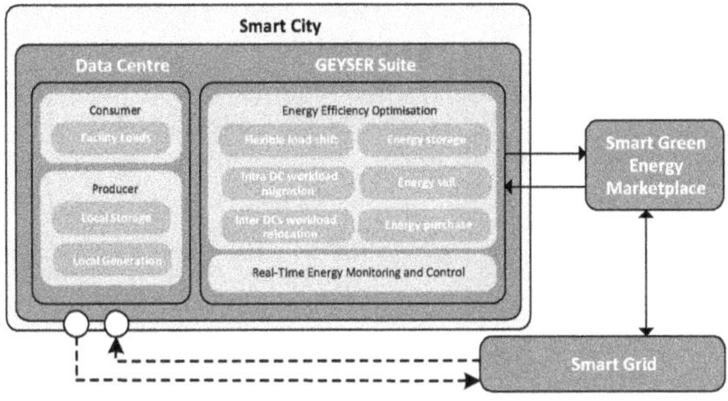

Figure 1. Smart City - Data Centre Operation Context

In order to manage effectively the energy demand of DCs, the GEYSER Suite can initiate several flexibility mechanisms, for example load migration to process IT workload at the lowest cost and thus can trigger the DC to provide surplus electricity to the grid. Other example is shifting load associated with cooling purposes to satisfy the DC's demand at the lowest cost by operating a thermal storage. The operation context of the GEYSER framework is depicted in Figure 1.

Naturally, the decision-making process of the GEYSER Suite requires measuring the internal energy of the DC. To this aim, a sophisticated, real-time and minute-level monitoring and control is designed as part of the GEYSER Suite, including information of consumed, reused or stored energy by the DC, and the energy produced by the renewable sources in the DC and its proximate areas (e.g., photovoltaic, wind power, geothermal, cool air). This information is used in the formulation of a multi-criteria energy efficiency optimisation problem, described in [2][3].

Having access to a local smart green marketplace, the suggested optimisation engine, provides the optimal schedules for the DC's flexible energy loads, maximises the renewable energy usage, and adjusts the DC interaction with the Smart Grid.

Prior to the laboratory testing and validation period, the GEYSER project develops an Energy Simulation Prototype (ESP) to obtain detailed understanding of the DC energy dynamics and its interaction with the Smart City. The ESP is compiled based on the guidelines presented in [4]. The ESP is the main scope of this paper and comprises the models of different energy components of the DC where multiple, simultaneous, physical phenomena are incorporated, including the different natures of local sources of energy (brown/green), energy storage (electrical/thermal), and energy sinks (IT/non-IT).

The ESP integrates a subset of the GEYSER optimiser actions [2][3], and allows exploring the DC behaviour in a way that includes futuristic scenarios and extreme testing conditions that might be difficult or too risky to recreate in the real world, e.g. large infeed of renewable energy sources and its influence on the DC operation. The ESP execution in real-time will enable Hardware in the Loop (HiL) testing of various components in a DC within a Smart City environment.

2. DESCRIPTION OF THE ENERGY SIMULATION PROTOTYPE

In this section the GEYSER ESP and its components are described. This prototype comprises the models of several energy production and consumption components in the DC, as shown in Table 1, whose functionalities and energy transformations have been previously analysed in [5]. The methodology chosen in this work consists of a component validation to assure the desired dynamics and consistent behaviour, followed by the execution of a set of integrated simulation scenarios.

Table 1. Data Centre Energy Production and Consumption Components

Energy Production Components					
Green Energy Sources		Brown Energy Sources		Energy Storage Components	
Photovoltaic		Diesel Generator		Batteries	
Wind Power					
Geothermal		Combined Heat and Power		Thermal Storage	
Energy Consumption Components					
Cooling System	Heat Recovery	Lighting System	Electrical System	IT Components	Smart City Load Profiles

The ESP models corresponding to brown energy generation, green energy generation, electrical storage, thermal storage, and electrical system components are implemented in SimulationX [6] using the commercial library "GreenBuilding" and the standard "Modelica" library. The GEYSER ESP models for cooling system and heat recovery are implemented in Dymola [7], for the thermal components a zone room model is used.

To better match the DC unique modelling and simulation needs, custom-made models were developed for the Power Supply Unit (PSU), IT components power consumption, household power consumption, industrial power consumption, and lighting system power consumption. These components will be explained in detail in the following subsections.

2.1 Power Supply Unit (PSU)

The PSU provides electric energy to several electrical loads of the IT equipment. The PSU model transforms 3-phase or 1-phase alternating current power to direct current power, which is the power consumed by the IT components in the DC; the voltage level is regulated by the PSU at a constant level and the current varies according to the usage of each IT component. The PSU model incorporates the efficiency versus load characteristic according to the "80 PLUS" certification, in which PSUs are typically most efficient between 50% and 75% load, and less efficient at minimum and maximum load [8].

2.2 IT Components

IT components like servers, networking devices, and storage devices, are typically responsible for 50% of the power consumption of the DC during its operational cycle [9].

The power consumption of IT components at the PSU level can be simplified as shown in Table 2. For the simulation, IT loads are simplified as a fixed part corresponding to idle power consumption and a variable part which depends on the usage rate or workload of the IT component.

The model developed here contains information like the number of IT components present in the DC, workload, and idle power consumption. The output signal is the instantaneous workload-dependent current value of all IT components, which enables the modelling of the total IT power consumption. In order to control the IT power demand, the user can enable workload migration in combination with shutting down of the components [11].

For compute nodes, the IT components' power consumption model is a more complex model where the energy relationship is determined by the processor family, architecture, generation and the processor. For the scope of this paper, the simplified power consumption characteristic described in Table 2 is used.

Table 2. IT components power consumption characteristic

$P_{server} = P_{idle} + (P_{max} - P_{idle}) \cdot u$ [10]	P_{server}:Estimated power consumption P_{idle}:Power consumed by an idle server P_{max}:Power consumed by the server at full load u: CPU usage at the current load
$P_{switch} = \begin{cases} P_{fixed} + C \cdot x, \text{if } x > 0 \\ P_{idle}, \text{otherwise} \end{cases}$ [11]	Where: P_{switch}:Estimated power consumption P_{fixed}:Fixed power consumed by a network device C:bandwidth capacity x:utilisation of the device ($0 < x < 1$) P_{idle}:Power consumed by an idle switch
$P_{drive} = P_{idle} + P_{active}$ [12]	Where: P_{drive}:the power consumed by the drive of interest P_{idle}:the power consumed by the drive of interest at idle state P_{active}:the power consumed by the drive of interest at active state

2.3 Smart City Load Profiles

The Smart City and Smart Grid industrial and commercial loads are represented with standard energy consumption profiles defined by the Bundesverband der Energie- und Wasserwirtschaft (BDEW) in Germany [10][13]. Likewise, the corresponding households load profile was used. The aforementioned profiles are accessible on the webpages of the utilities in Germany and represent the load demand in a 15-minute resolution over the whole year.

3. SIMULATION SCENARIOS

In this section the integrated simulation of the GEYSER ESP is presented; several scenarios have been defined aiming at simulating highly probable future interactions of the DC in a Smart Grid/Smart City context while aligned with scenarios described in [2]. This context poses the requirement on the ESP of adapting dynamically to the renewable energy production while covering the DC's electrical, thermal and hydraulic domains. Thus, the dynamic models of the DC have to be multi-physics and cover the interdependencies between electrical consumption and thermal cooling.

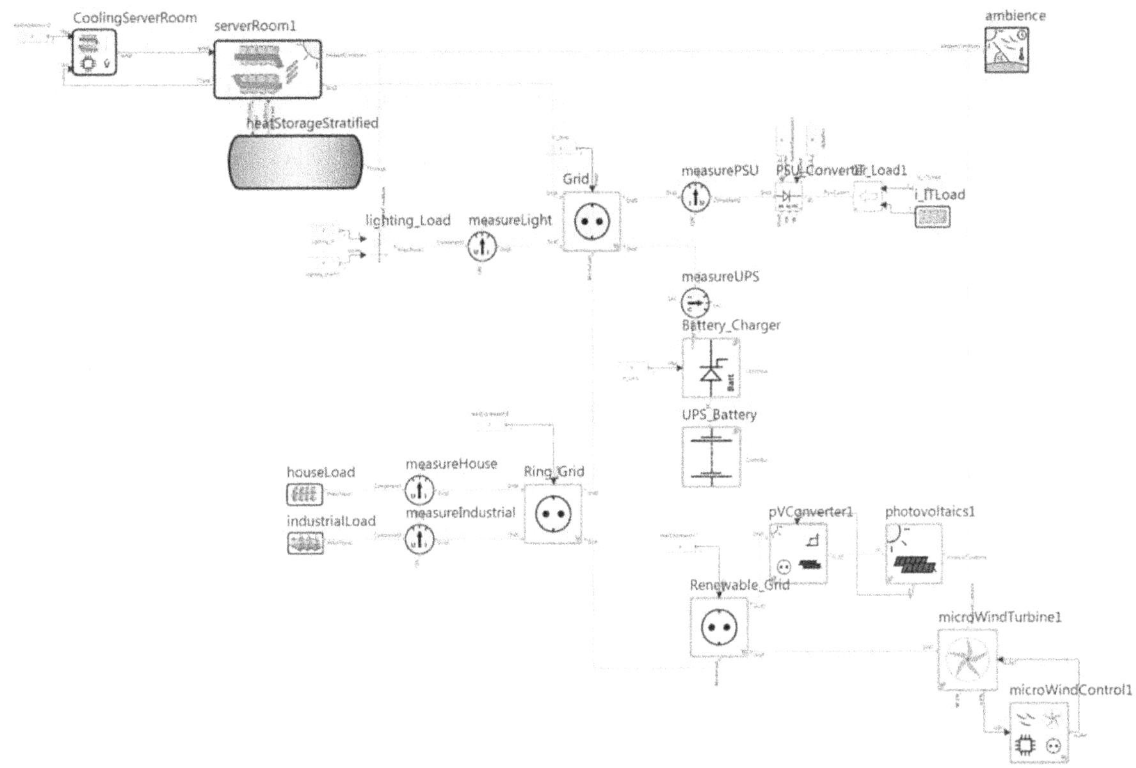

Figure 2. SimulationX Implementation of the Data Centre, the Renewables, Industrial and Residential Loads

The ESP relates to the following subset of the GEYSER optimiser objectives:

- Optimising the DC energy consumption through flexible energy loads
- Using renewable energy sources
- Integrating DC with the Smart Grid

The presented simulation scenarios share the following assumptions:

- The DC operates at a base load condition of 30% from the computational standpoint, which is a high value referring to the study performed in 2011 on Amazon EC2 clouds where there is only a 7% usage on the servers [14]. Data from Google shows that on average over a 3month period the base load lies between 20%-40% [16].
- The aggregated load demands (households, industrial, etc.) of the smart city also form a baseline condition.
- In the vicinity of the data centre a large renewable installation is present (either Photovoltaic or Wind generation).
- The DC aims to minimise variable energy costs, while maximizing computational load while increasing two Key Performance Indicators (KPIs) referenced in FP7-SMARTCITIES-2013 Objective ICT-2013.6.2.-Cluster Activities Task 3 Report [17]:
    - Renewable Energy Factor (REF): is the ratio of local renewable energy over the total DC energy consumption.
    - DCAdapt (DCA): measures how much the DC energy profile has shifted from a baseline energy consumption after the implementation of flexibility mechanisms (e.g. workload shifting).

3.1 Scenario A

The objective of this scenario is to evaluate how an active controlled DC behaves on the under the impact of large photovoltaic power generation, where the control goal is to optimise the REF and DCAdapt metrics. The DC is operated under the GEYSER software stack in a near real time control loop. The DC is part of a network of DCs which are operated by the same owner. In all these DCs spatial load migration techniques are present. Each DC is in different geographical region, which has own weather data. The load profiles are taken from [13]. Those are standard load profiles for Germany which can be scaled. In this case a city with relative low industrial presence was chosen, as the industrial load can be assumed to be nearly constant as depicted in Figure 3.

The weather conditions of this scenario feature high solar irradiation, thus yielding to a large photovoltaic power generation that decreases the local energy price. The date centre is part of a DC network and has spatial load migration enabled. The scenario implementation in terms of the model described above is schematically shown in Figure 2 and the parameters used are given in Table 3. The variables that were controlled to meet the objective are the computational workload and the DC power consumption.

The large infeed of photovoltaic power generation is shown in Figure 3 (purple curve). This surplus of power triggers a reduction of the local energy price. As a consequence, the DC power consumption curve, in green colour, increases (noticeably for a simulation time from 8:30am to 4:40pm). The other loads of the MVAC grid, such as, households (red curve) and industry (blue curve) follow their expected load curve.

The increase of DC power consumption was triggered by using the spatial load migration inter DCs, the computational jobs

Table 3. Scenarios Simulation Parameters

Component	Parameter	Value
serverRoom1 (Server Room model simulating Cooling/Heating behaviour)	Maintenance Personal (average day)	4
	Net floor space of the zone	100 [m²]
	Height of zone	2.5 [m]
	Electrical power of ventilation system	2500 [W.s/m3]
	Power factor of ventilation system	0.8
	Body heat dissipation per person	80 [W]
	Air leak of zone	0.5 [1/h]
CoolingServer Room (Ventilation System controller)	Specific heat capacity of Ventilation medium	4.177 [kJ/(kg·K)]
	Density of heating medium	1000 [kg/m³]
	Maximum volume flow for Ventilation system	0.1 [m³/s]
heatStorageStratified (Thermally stratified heat storage)	Heat storage volume	750 [l]
	Diameter of heat storage	0.75[m]
	Heat conductance of isolation	3.16 [W/K]
	Number of heat storage layers	5
	Maximum layer temperature	41 [°C]
	Heat transmission coefficient of layers	465 [W/(m²·K)]
lighting_Load (Lighting load model)	Number of Lights (LED Fixtures) in Data Centre	15
	Wattage per Light used	72 [W]
PSU_Converter (3-ph AC to DC)	Efficiency Kind (etaCurve)	Max.[50%-75%]
IT Load (servers, network and storage)	Number of IT Components	120
	Base Workload per IT Component	30 [%]
	average Idle Power	70[W]
	Voltage level (direct current)	12[V]
UPS Li-Ion_Battery + Battery_Charger (Line interactive power converter)	Charge efficiency of battery charger	90 [%]
	Maximum charge/discharge power	22 [kW]
	Maximum SOC of battery for charging	95 [%]
	Minimum SOC of battery for discharging	5 [%]
	Module capacity	40 [Ah]
Photovoltaics + PV_Converter	Efficiency of PV-Converter	0.95
	Number PV modules in series	10
	Number PV modules in parallel	2
	Effective surface area of PV module	1.312 [m²]
	Module efficiency	12.6 [%]
	Nominal operation cell temp.	47.1 [°C]
	Nominal radiation into module plane	800 [W]
microWindTurbine + microWindControl	Number of turbines (pitch controlled)	5
	Efficiency gear box	97 [%]
	Effective rotor cross-section-area	5.72 [m²]
	Airflow effective surface area	9 [m²]
	Moment of inertia of rotor	3.06 [kgm²]
	Switch-on wind speed	2.5 [m/s]
	Switch-off wind speed	20 [m/s]
	Nominal wind speed	11 [m/s]
	Moment of inertia of generator	1.3 [kgm²]
	Power factor of wind generator	0.98
	Nominal generator power	3500 [W]
House Standard Load profile	Number of houses	100
	Power factor	0.9
Industrial Standard Load profile	Number of Industrial Loads	10
	Power factor	0.8

moved towards this DC increase the IT power consumption and the electrical power demand; in turn these are both responsible for an increase in the cooling power demand as the thermal control has to keep the server room temperature constant. Therefore an increase in IT workload took place. In this way the total power demand of the DC tries to match the renewable generation curve by adapting the IT workload.

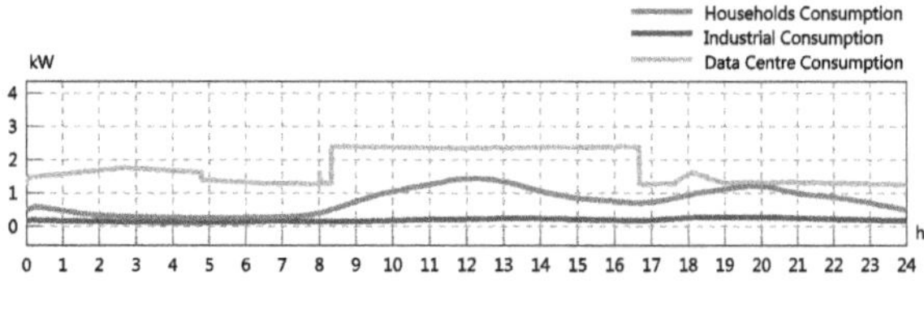

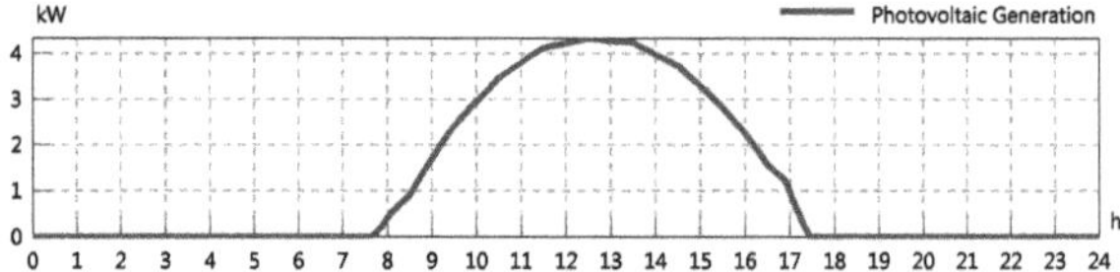

Figure 3. Scenario A Results

3.2 Scenario B

The objective of this scenario is to evaluate how an active controlled DC behaves on the under the impact of fluctuating wind power generation, where the control goal is to optimise the REF and DCAdapt metrics and simultaneously minimising the cost of energy. The minimisation of the cost of energy is based on the general assumption that in situations of high renewable feed in the energy price will be lower level, while when there is a low renewable feed in the energy price will be at a higher level. The pricing is not part of the simulator.

The DC is operated under the GEYSER software stack in a near real time control loop.

In the vicinity of the DC a large wind park is present. The DC is standalone and has therefore no access to spatial load migration; the thermal storage equipment is in service. The computational workload condition is kept constant during the complete simulation. The implementation of scenario B is the same as in Figure 2 and the parameters used are given in Table 3.

The variables that were controlled to meet the objective are the temperature set-point of the server room, the State of Charge (SoC) of the thermal storage, and the cooling power required to maintain the desired temperature set-point.

3.2.1 High Wind Speed and precooling of DC

The weather conditions of this scenario offer high wind speed. The large wind power generation decreases the local energy price.

The generated power, measured at the wind park, is depicted in magenta colour in Figure 4. The wind power generation follows the actual wind speed level (blue curve), saturating when the nominal speed is exceeded to protect the turbines due to the pitch power control. The surplus of wind power triggers a reduction of the local energy price. The SoC of the available thermal storage in the DC (orange curve) aims to follow the wind power surplus. The temperature set-point of the server room (light blue) is enforced to its lower bound of 18°C, as consequence of the renewable infeed. This action increases the DC cooling power demand; its active and reactive power are shown in green and red colour, respectively. This DC operation condition is feasible as long as there is a surplus of wind power. After t=11h the wind speed drops; hence, the energy price increases. As a result a new temperature set-point is chosen which is on the upper boundary of the temperature room control and it can be observed that the temperature rises slowly until the end of the simulation time.

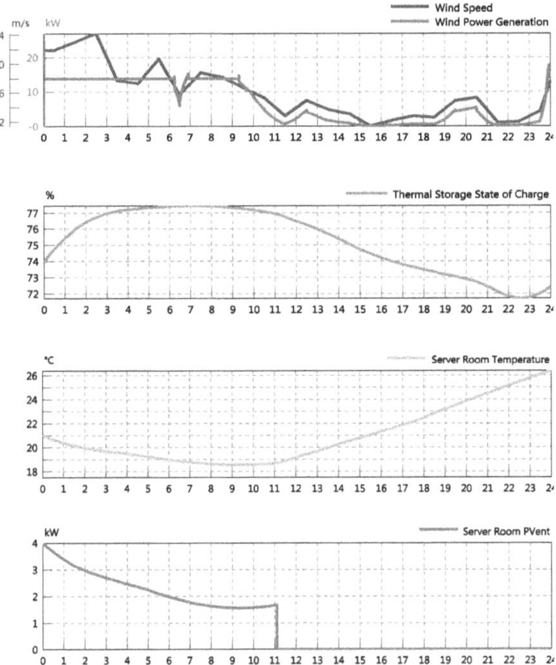

Figure 4. Scenario B-1 Results

From this scenario it can be concluded that, enforcing more cooling in the DC' server rooms during a surplus of green energy sources, i.e. by purchasing energy when there is a local reduction in the energy price, can be used to reduce the DC operational costs and CO_2 emissions.

Furthermore, an action like switching-off the cooling equipment will be noticed in terms of temperature rise in the server room several minutes later, due to the inherent inertia of heat/cooling systems. This inertia enables to use a server room with several m³ of size as a thermal storage element. Thus, charging this thermal storage element means pre-cooling the room to reach the lower range of the normal operating conditions as indicated by ASHRAE [15][18], while reducing the cooling power represents discharging the thermal storage. As a conclusion the DC' cooling capacity can be used in a demand side management context while following a renewable generation curve [12].

3.2.2 Low wind speed and cooling power reduction

The simulation parameters of this simulation run are the same as in 3.2.1 except by the weather conditions, which offer low wind speed. The low wind power generation increases the local energy price.

An increment of the room temperature set-point implies that less cooling power is required, as the thermal balance will take place at a higher temperature; in this case the action is to switch-off the cooling system until the temperature' upper bound according to the ASHRAE standard is reached [10][15][18].

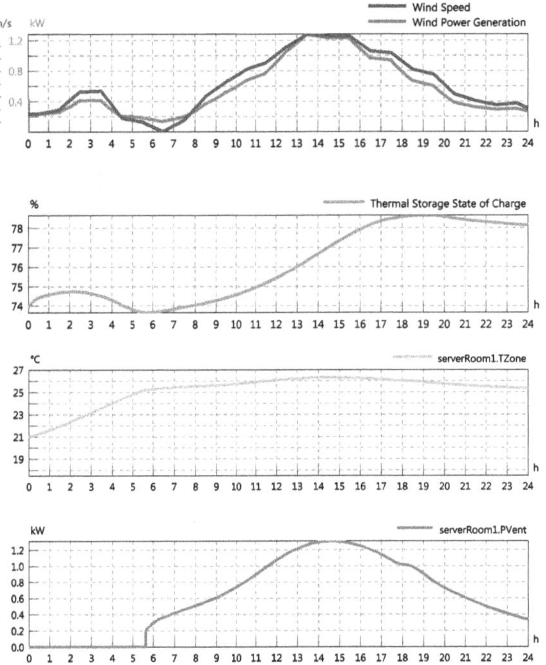

Figure 5. Scenario B-2 Results

The simulation graphs in Figure 5 depict wind power generation, wind speed and thermal storage SOC in the colours magenta, blue and orange correspondingly. The server room temperature set-point, in light blue colour, indicates an increment, reaching its upper bound as a reaction to the small renewable power generation. This translates in a lower cooling power demand at the DC, observed in the active and reactive power of the cooling system, in red and green colour, respectively.

The conclusions of this scenario are, that using the server rooms of the DC as thermal storage is possible and enables to cover periods of times where a drop in the renewable generation occurs. The DC power consumption is able to follow this renewable generation curve; hence it offers beneficial demand side management options.

3.3 Future Scenario - HiL implementation

This scenario will verify the interaction among the IT-subsystem, the electrical, and the thermal-hydraulic subsystem. A future objective of this scenario will also be the evaluation of the HiL implementation where one or more server racks are evaluated in HiL tests to assess the cooling efficiency.

For the GEYSER HiL implementation, the C-Code Export functionality of SimulationX is used to convert the GEYSER ESP code into an executable. The compiled C binary makes the GEYSER ESP execution possible in real-time on Linux under a small time step (1 ms) conductive to testing the cooling efficiency of the computational racks, as presented in Figure 6.

The scenario will consist of a server room equipped with various servers and air-conditioning, heat-pump cooling equipment. The closed control loop of the server room would maintain the temperature at a predefined set-point and the variable that could be influenced during runtime would be the computational workload intensity. The setup of the scenario power interfaces is specified in [19] and [20].

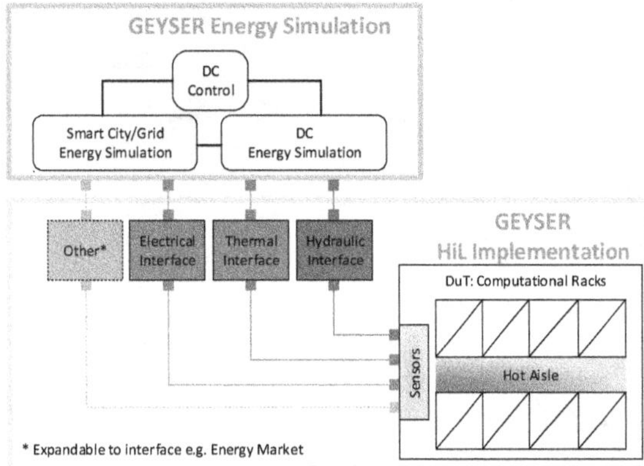

Figure 6. HiL Implementation Overview

4. CONCLUSIONS

We have presented the modelling of certain components of DCs (IT, power, thermal/cooling) and others related to energy generation and energy load profiles in the Smart City environment, our simulation results validate these models since they reflect the physical behaviour of their real-life counterparts. The integration scenarios were chosen to mimic the flexibility of the high-level optimisation logic. A focus was also given on two scenarios which directly influence KPIs referenced in [17]. The goal of the selected Smart City testing scenarios was to test the functionality and the proper logical behaviour of the GEYSER ESP. These goals were indeed reached with the test cases A, B and C. Further work on the simulation prototype is planned for the future HiL scenario, which is highly dependent on coherent data from a DC operator.

5. ACKNOWLEDGMENTS

GEYSER (Grant No: 609211) is co-funded by the European Commission as part of the 7th Research Framework Programme (FP7-SMARTCITIES-2013). The authors wish to acknowledge the Commission for its support, the efforts of all consortium partners, and the contributions of all experts involved in GEYSER. The GEYSER consortium is: Engineering - Ingegneria Informatica Spa (IT), ASM Terni Spa (IT), Green IT Amsterdam (NL), ABB Limited (IE), Zuericher Hochschule fur Angewandte Wissenschaften (CH), SingularLogic (GR), Wattics Limited (IE), Rheinisch-Westfaelische Technische Hochschule Aachen (DE), Universitatea Tehnica Cluj-Napoca (RO).

6. REFERENCES

[1] Schulz, G. 2009. The Green and Virtual Data Center, Printed by CRS Press, Taylor & Francis Group, p8-139

[2] Salomie, I., Cioara, T., Anghel, I., 2014, GEYSER – D4.2 Multi-Criteria Data Centre Energy Efficiency Optimiser, http://www.geyser-project.eu/downloads

[3] Cioara, T.; Anghel, I.; Antal, M.; Crisan, S.; Salomie, I.; "Data Center Optimization Methodology to Maximize the Usage of Locally Produced Renewable Energy", *Sustainable Internet and ICT for Sustainability (SustainIT), 2015* , Apr. 2015

[4] Anghel, I., Bertoncini, M., Cioara, T., Cupelli, M., Georgiadou, V., Jahangiri, P., Monti, A., Murphy, S., Schoofs, A., Velivassaki, T., 2015. "GEYSER: Enabling Green Data Centres in Smart Cities." In *Energy Efficient Data Centers*, edited by Sonja Klingert, Marta Chinnici, and Milagros Rey Porto, 8945:71–86. Cham: Springer International Publishing. http://dx.doi.org/10.1007/978-3-319-15786-3_5

[5] Cupelli, M., Hernandez, L., Jahangiri. P., Shanahan, J., Schoofs, A., Holthues, P., Velivassaki, T., 2014, GEYSER – D3.1 Energy consumption and production monitoring subsystem design. http://www.geyser-project.eu/download/geyser-d3-1-rwth-wp3-v1-1.pdf

[6] http://www.simulationx.com/

[7] http://www.3ds.com/products-services/catia/capabilities/modelica-systems-simulation-info/dymola

[8] "80 Plus PSU List". Plug load solutions. Retrieved 31 October 2011.

[9] Seidl, H., Noster, R., Blank, S., "Leistung steigern, Kosten senken: Energieeffizienz im Rechenzentrum". Deutsche Energie-Agentur (DENA). (2012, February). [Online].

[10] Beloglazov, A., Buyya, R., Lee, Y. C., Zomaya, A.,"A Taxonomy and Survey of Energy-Efficient Data Centers", Advances in Computers, Vol. 82, Elsevier, 2011.

[11] Mandal, U.; Habib, M. F.; Zhang, S.; Mukherjee, B.; Tornatore, M., "Greening the Cloud Using Renewable-Energy-Aware Service Migration", IEEE Network, Vol.27, No. 6, pp.36-43, 2013.

[12] Allalouf, M., Arbitman, Y., Factor, M., Kat, R. I., Meth, K. M.; Naor, D., "Storage modeling for power estimation". SYSTOR 2009.

[13] https://www.bdew.de/.

[14] Huan Liu, "A Measurement Study of Server Utilization in Public Clouds," *Dependable, Autonomic and Secure Computing (DASC), 2011 IEEE Ninth International Conference on* , vol., no., pp.435,442, 12-14 Dec. 2011 doi: 10.1109/DASC.2011.87

[15] American Society of Heating, Refrigerating and Air-Conditioning Engineers, ed. 2012. *Thermal Guidelines for Data Processing Environments*. 3rd ed. ASHRAE Datacom Series, bk. 1. Atlanta, GA: ASHRAE.

[16] Barroso, L. A., Clidaras, J, Hölzle, U., 2013. "The Datacenter as a Computer: An Introduction to the Design of Warehouse-Scale Machines, Second Edition." *Synthesis Lectures on Computer Architecture* 8 (3): 1–154. doi:10.2200/S00516ED2V01Y201306CAC024.

[17] https://ec.europa.eu/digital-agenda/en/news/cluster-fp7-projects-proposes-new-environmental-efficiency-metrics-data-centres

[18] "Thermal guidelines for Data Processing environments," ASHRAE Datacom Series 1 - Third Edition, 2012.

[19] Hernandez, L., Cupelli, M., Jahangiri.P , 2015, GEYSER – D6.2 Energy simulation and Hardware in the Loop simulation, http://www.geyser-project.eu/downloads

[20] Chen, K., Molitor, C., Streblow, R., Benigni, A., Müller, D., Monti, A., 2012, Hardware-in-the-Loop Test Bed for Home Energy Systems, E.ON Energy Research Center Series, Volume 4, Issue 2

Energy-Minimal Scheduling of Divisible Loads

Pragati Agrawal
IIIT Bangalore
Bangalore, India
pragati.a.in@ieee.org

Shrisha Rao
IIIT Bangalore
Bangalore, India
shrao@ieee.org

ABSTRACT

It is known that energy-minimal scheduling is strictly harder than minimal-makespan scheduling, but it is not well understood. This paper is a study of the problems of scheduling to minimize the energy consumed by a system of dissimilar machines (with no restriction on the makespan). The different system types considered are for machines with identical speeds but different power ratings, and for machines with different speeds and power ratings but no idle power consumption. The results give insights for further studies classifying various types of energy-minimal scheduling problems, and for deriving algorithms for exact or approximate solutions for such problems.

Categories and Subject Descriptors

D.4 [**Operating Systems**]: Process Management—*Scheduling*; C.2.4 [**Computer-Communication Networks**]: Distributed Systems; D.4.8 [**Operating Systems**]: Performance—*Modeling and prediction*

General Terms

Theory, Algorithms, Performance

Keywords

scheduling; energy minimization; distributed systems; divisible loads

1. INTRODUCTION

Energy is a precious resource, and it is a desideratum in the current industrial economy that every system be as energy efficient as possible.

e-Energy'15, July 14–17, 2015, Bangalore, India.

ACM 978-1-4503-3609-3/15/07...$15.00.
DOI: http://dx.doi.org/10.1145/2768510.2768528.

In this scenario, though the energy efficiency of individual machines of a system is important, greater energy efficiencies can be achieved by proper scheduling of jobs over the system of machines. Clearly, scheduling jobs in such a way that the total energy consumption of the system is minimal, or at least low, is of the essence. Computing schedules given input conditions including the energy specifications of machines in a given system, such that the energy consumption is reduced, is of importance.

Our work focuses on systems whose machines are similar in their capabilities but may have different working and idle power ratings and working speeds. Based on different types of machines cooperatively running similar loads, we classify the problems of energy-minimal offline scheduling with non-identical interconnected machines and independent jobs, as follows:

1. *Identical speeds, divisible loads*:
   We have discussed this class of problem in Section 3.1.

2. *Identical speeds, non-divisible loads*:
   Our results for the previous case show that all working machines should have equal working time. But in the case of non-divisible jobs, this problem is an instance of the k-partition problem [2]. Hence we can say that energy-minimal scheduling in this case is an NP-hard problem. We give a detailed proof and approximation algorithm for the same in later work.

3. *Different speeds, divisible loads*:
   In Section 3.2 we have discussed a special case of this class of problem, where the idle power consumption of the machines is zero.

4. *Different speeds, non-divisible loads*:
   Scheduling for non-divisible loads, even on a system with identical-speed machines, is NP-hard. So this is also a hard problem, and only approximation algorithms can be given.

Since one has to take other parameters into account, energy-minimal scheduling is much more complex than the classical makespan problem. Agrawal and Rao [1] show that scheduling to minimize energy consumption is strictly harder (more general) than makespan scheduling. They present a model for scheduling considering the working power and idle power of each machine, which is a step in the direction of developing a generic theory (one not specific to a particular domain) for scheduling under energy constraints. They propose three heuristic algorithms for energy-aware scheduling.

Surprisingly, there is relatively little literature by the engineering and scientific community on scheduling for minimizing or reducing energy. The prime focus of general works on scheduling [5, 9] has been to optimize on objectives related to time—such as makespan, earliness, and avoidance of tardiness. Some literature focuses on energy reduction in specific domains, particularly high-performance computing or embedded systems, and communication networks. Such work invariably relies on specific features and technologies of those domains [12], such as DVFS. One branch of scheduling which is relatively closer is multi-objective scheduling, but works dealing with it [4, 7, 10] do not offer a general solution to energy minimal scheduling.

In the present paper we derive results that can guide the design of scheduling algorithms for systems which deal with independent jobs on interconnected machines. The results indicate conditions that, if satisfied, mean that such a schedule will be energy-minimal.

There is of course a lot of work on scheduling divisible or non-divisible loads in general, and even in the context of data centers, such approaches are seen in some recent work; e.g., Wang *et al.* [11] consider both divisible job and non-divisible jobs in the context of profit optimization for a data center, and Lin *et al.* [8] consider divisible load scheduling and given a bandwidth-aware algorithm for cloud computing to obtain better performance.

In our system model we consider divisible and independent jobs to develop a theory and this theory can be applied to any domain. We can use this theory to solve other, more complex classes of problems.

The novelty of this work is in considering an energy-specific objective with completely generic machine specifications. No other theoretical work until now has considered energy consumption of machines while idle, which is known to be significant from real life; e.g., in data centers [3, 6]. Our system model also shows the absolute limits of energy-minimal scheduling for specific types of systems. We have derived results (for divisible jobs) which serve as an upper-bound to maximum achievable efficiency—because a system with divisible jobs can always have higher efficiency as compared to system with non-divisible jobs [9].

In the system as we have considered it, machines are connected to one another and execute similar jobs, so that a job from one machine can be transferred to any other machine. There is no set limit to the number of machines in a system. Machines and jobs to be executed are independent, and hence any job can be executed in any order on any machine.

Our model and approach are extensible and hence can be developed to include systems having timing or precedence constraints or machines with different capabilities. Based on our results and algorithms, the theory of energy-minimal scheduling can be further developed.

The remainder of the paper is organized as follows. The system model, classification of energy-minimal scheduling problems, and notation used are presented in Section 2. The proposed method along with relevant results are explained in Section 3. Finally, Section 4 describes the conclusion and scope for future work.

2. PROBLEM FORMULATION

In this section we formally introduce our system model and define the energy-minimal scheduling problem. We also describe the type of systems we have worked upon in this paper. In the first subsection we describe the system model along with the notations used in this paper, and then the scheduling problem in the second subsection.

2.1 System Model

Consider machines numbered 1 to m. The working power of machine i is denoted as μ_i, and the idle power as γ_i. The sum of the idle powers of all the machines is given by Γ. The speed of machine i is denoted as v_i. The speed (throughput of work per unit time) of a machine is fixed throughout its working tenure.

When $v_i = 1$, with $1 \leq i \leq m$, then we can say that the machines are identical in their working capacities or speed, implying that they can execute and complete any job given to them in equal time. And if in that case all jobs are executed sequentially on one machine, then that time taken is W.

All machines in the system work in parallel, and the maximum working time of the system to execute a given set of jobs is T, which is the makespan of the system for that set of jobs. If machine i works only for time t_i, then the idle time of machine i is given by $T - t_i$. The amount of work done by machine i is represented by w_i.

$$w_i = t_i v_i \tag{1}$$

The sum of the work done by all machines is equal to the total work to be done, i.e., $\sum_{i=1}^{m} w_i = W$. E represents the energy consumption of the complete system.

Since we consider the energy consumption in working as well as idle states, the energy consumed by machine i is the sum of the energy consumed in the working state and that consumed in the idle state. The energy consumed by machine i in the working state is given by $\mu_i t_i$, and the energy consumed in the idle state by $\gamma_i(T - t_i)$.

We assume the following of our system:

1. All jobs are independent. It means a job need not wait for completion of any other particular job to start its execution. This implies that

$$T = \max t_i, \forall i, 1 \leq i \leq m \tag{2}$$

2. Jobs are divisible, so that jobs can be arbitrarily divided.

3. All machines stay on for the duration of the makespan of the whole set of jobs. (This is reasonable considering that in many systems the cycle time to stop/restart a machine is large; stopping idle machines can be covered by setting idle power to zero.)

4. In the identical-speed model, all machines are arranged in increasing order of the differences of their working and idle powers. For the different-speed but zero idle power consumption model, all machines are arranged in increasing order of the ratios of their working powers and speeds.

5. In the identical-speed model, one unit of work takes one unit of time for execution, irrespective of the machine on which it is executed.

2.2 Problem Definition

We deal with two classes of energy-minimal scheduling problems:

1. *Identical speeds, divisible loads*:
   The machines have different working and idle power consumption. All machines have equal speeds in execution of jobs. The aim for this type of system is to minimize E given by,

$$E = \sum_{i=1}^{m} [\mu_i t_i + \gamma_i (T - t_i)] \quad (3)$$

2. *Different speeds, divisible loads*:
   Machines can have different working power consumptions as well as different speeds, but power consumptions of all machines is zero. The energy equation for this type of problem can be formed by replacing t_i with $\frac{w_i}{v_i}$ (from (1))and dropping the term associated with γ in (3). The objective in this type of problem is to minimize E given by (4).

$$E = \sum_{i=1}^{m} \mu_i \frac{w_i}{v_i} \quad (4)$$

After formulating the problems, we now proceed to solve them in the following sections.

3. ENERGY MINIMIZATION PROBLEM

Here we derive the basic results that govern energy-minimal scheduling. We have first derived results for the case where machines have identical speeds. Though any scheduling algorithm which fulfills the criteria arrived at in these results will provide optimal schedules, we give an algorithm which does so. Later on, we deal with the case where machines have different speeds but zero idle power consumptions.

3.1 Identical Speed

In this subsection we consider the energy-minimal scheduling of machines with identical speeds and address two questions in relation to expending the least energy in a system: (i) Given the set of m machines, which subset of machines should be allowed to work and which should remain idle for all times during the makespan? and (ii) What should be the distribution of work among the working machines?

As indicated previously, we assume that all machines are arranged in the increasing order of the differences between their working and idle powers. We claim that when the machines are arranged in such an order, then the loading of machines should be such that the working times of these machines are in non-increasing order.

LEMMA 3.1. *Given $\mu_k - \gamma_k \leq \mu_l - \gamma_l$, then for energy optimality of the system, $t_k \geq t_l \; \forall k, l$, where $1 \leq k \leq l \leq m$.*

PROOF. We prove this by contradiction. Given $\mu_k - \gamma_k \leq \mu_l - \gamma_l$, then let us say that for minimal energy consumption, $t_k < t_l$.

With a little rearrangement of (3) and expanding it, we get,

$$\begin{aligned} E =& \sum_{i=1}^{k-1} [(\mu_i - \gamma_i)t_i + \gamma_i T] + [(\mu_k - \gamma_k)t_i + \gamma_k T] \\ &+ \sum_{i=k+1}^{l-1} [(\mu_i - \gamma_i)t_i + \gamma_i T] + [(\mu_l - \gamma_l)t_i + \gamma_l T] \\ &+ \sum_{i=l+1}^{m} [(\mu_i - \gamma_i)t_i + \gamma_i T] \end{aligned} \quad (5)$$

There are two possible cases to be considered: when $t_k \geq t_l$, and when $t_k < t_l$. We derive the energy equations for both cases and then compare them. By comparing the energy equations in both, we arrive at a condition under which the energy consumed in one case is less, and find a contradiction.

Case 1: $t_k \geq t_l$. Take $t_k = t + \epsilon_1$ and $t_l = t - \epsilon_1$, where $\epsilon_1 \geq 0$. Putting these values in (5) we get,

$$\begin{aligned} E =& \sum_{i=1}^{k-1} [(\mu_i - \gamma_i)t_i + \gamma_i T] + [(\mu_k - \gamma_k)(t + \epsilon_1) + \gamma_k T] \\ &+ \sum_{i=k+1}^{l-1} [(\mu_i - \gamma_i)t_i + \gamma_i T] + \sum_{i=l+1}^{m} [(\mu_i - \gamma_i)t_i + \gamma_i T] \\ &+ [(\mu_l - \gamma_l)(t - \epsilon_1) + \gamma_l T] \end{aligned} \quad (6)$$

Case 2: $t_k < t_l$. Take $t_k = t - \epsilon_2$ and $t_l = t + \epsilon_2$, where $\epsilon_2 > 0$. Putting these values in (5) we get,

$$\begin{aligned} E' =& \sum_{i=1}^{k-1} [(\mu_i - \gamma_i)t_i + \gamma_i T] + [(\mu_k - \gamma_k)(t - \epsilon_2) \\ &+ \gamma_k T] + \sum_{i=k+1}^{l-1} [(\mu_i - \gamma_i)t_i + \gamma_i T] + [(\mu_l - \gamma_l)(t \\ &+ \epsilon_2) + \gamma_l T] + \sum_{i=l+1}^{m} [(\mu_i - \gamma_i)t_i + \gamma_i T] \end{aligned} \quad (7)$$

If we say that in Case 2 the energy consumed is less, then using (6) and (7), we get,

$$(\mu_k - \gamma_k) > (\mu_l - \gamma_l) \quad (8)$$

Clearly (8) is in contradiction to our assumption. QED. □

We have shown which machines should be given comparatively more work then others. For energy optimality it may well be suitable to give work to only some of the machines while letting others run completely idle. We now state the condition showing which machines should be used when using only a subset of all the machines is beneficial.

LEMMA 3.2. *If we give work to only some r machines, where $1 \leq r \leq m$, then, for reduced energy consumption, these are the r machines that form the set $\{1, 2, \ldots, r\}$.*

PROOF. For the r machines working, $t_i > 0$, and for the other $m - r$ machines $t_i = 0$. If $t_{r+1} > 0$ then there must be any t_i from the set $\{t_1, t_2, \ldots, t_r\}$ which is equal to 0. But by Lemma 3.1, $t_1 \geq t_2 \geq t_3 \geq \ldots \geq t_r > 0$ since $t_{r+1} > 0$. Clearly these two statements are contradictory and so it is not possible that $t_{r+1} > 0$. Hence it stands proved that for energy optimality, if we give work to only some r machines where $1 \leq r \leq m$, then these r machines are of the set $\{1, 2, \ldots, r\}$. □

Using Lemma 3.2, given the number of machines to be used, we can find which machines should be assigned jobs. We now state and prove the condition which decides how many machines should be used so that energy consumption of the system is minimal.

Let the energy consumption of a system of m machines, when jobs are distributed to r machines, be given by $E_{m,r}$. In the next theorem, we use a term s_i which represents the amount of work taken away from machine i and given to other machine(s).

THEOREM 3.3. *When $r-1$ machines are working, for machine r to be given work (i.e., $t_r \neq 0$) and result in reduced energy consumption, the following must hold.*

$$\sum_{i=1}^{r-1}[(\mu_i - \gamma_i - \mu_r + \gamma_r)s_i] + s_1 \sum_{i=1}^{m} \gamma_i > 0 \quad (9)$$

PROOF. We prove this by construction. If it is known that only r of the m machines are used and the rest remain idle all the time, the above energy equation can be re-written as follows, where E is replaced by $E_{m,r}$:

$$\begin{aligned} E_{m,r} =& \sum_{i=1}^{r-1}[\mu_i t_i + \gamma_i(T - t_i)] + \mu_r t_r \\ &+\gamma_r(T - t_r) + T \sum_{i=r+1}^{m} \gamma_i \end{aligned} \quad (10)$$

Putting $T = t_1$, [by (2), Lemma 3.1 and Lemma 3.2] and $t_r = W - \sum_{i=1}^{r-1} t_i$ in (10), we get,

$$E_{m,r} = \sum_{i=1}^{r-1}[(\mu_i - \gamma_i - \mu_r + \gamma_r)t_i] + (\mu_r - \gamma_r)W + t_1\Gamma \quad (11)$$

This is a general equation for the energy of a system with m machines, with jobs given to r machines, where $1 \leq r \leq m$. If we give jobs to $r-1$ machines in a m machine system, its energy can be derived by putting $r = r-1$ in (11). Also the t_is are changed to t_i's as in the following:

$$\begin{aligned} E_{m,r-1} =& \sum_{i=1}^{r-2}[\mu_i - \gamma_i - \mu_{r-1} + \gamma_{r-1}]t_i' \\ &+ (\mu_{r-1} - \gamma_{r-1})W + t_1'\Gamma \end{aligned} \quad (12)$$

If $E_{m,r-1} > E_{m,r}$, then only we should give work to r machines, else we give to $r-1$ machines only. Using (11) and (12) in this condition and putting $s_i = t_i' - t_i$, we get,

$$\sum_{i=1}^{r-1}[(\mu_i - \gamma_i - \mu_r + \gamma_r)s_i] + s_1\Gamma > 0 \quad (13)$$

QED. □

Having derived the condition describing which machines to use for doing jobs, all we need to know now for scheduling is the amount of work to be given to each of these machines. We now state a result governing the distribution of amount of work among machines.

THEOREM 3.4. *When we give jobs to r number of machines, then the distribution of jobs on all r machines should be equal and given by $\frac{W}{r}$.*

PROOF. We prove this by contradiction. Consider two cases, one in which the distribution of work among the machines which qualify to work according to Theorem 3.3 is equal, and the other in which the work distribution is unequal. We claim, to show the contradiction, that in the case in which the distribution is unequal, the energy consumption is greater as compared to the other, and that such is hence a non-optimal distribution.

Case 1: Equal distribution, $t_i = \frac{W}{r}, \forall i, 1 \leq i \leq r$.

Case 2: Unequal distribution, $t_1 = \frac{W}{r} + \epsilon$, $t_2 = t_3 = \ldots = t_{r-1} = \frac{W}{r}$ and $t_r = \frac{W}{r} - \epsilon$.

Here we assign more work to machine 1 compared to that required by equal distribution of work among r machines (by Lemma 3.1, a bias has to favor smaller-numbered machines, and therefore machine 1 most of all). We have chosen only to alter the work distributions of machines 1 and r to keep the proof simple. We could have chosen any machine k for doing extra work and any machine l for doing lesser work, where $k > l$. But for allotting extra work ϵ to machine k, we have to increase the amount of work assigned to all machines in the set $\{1, 2, \ldots, k\}$ by at least ϵ, so that Lemma 3.1 is satisfied.

Similarly for reducing the work of machine l by ϵ, we have to reduce the amount of work assigned to all machines in the set $\{l+1, l+2, \ldots, r\}$ by at least ϵ so that Lemma 3.1 is satisfied. Hence if we want to alter the amount of work of just two machines (to keep the proof simple) from an equal distribution, then we have alter it for machine 1 and r. It may be noted that our proof is generalizable for imbalances involving any numbers of machines.

Let the energy in Case 1 be denoted by $E'_{m,r}$ and the energy in Case 2 be $E''_{m,r}$. Then according to our proposition:

$$E''_{m,r} - E'_{m,r} < 0 \quad (14)$$

Putting the respective values of t_i's in (11) to derive $E'_{m,r}$,

$$\begin{aligned} E'_{m,r} =& (\mu_1 - \gamma_1 - \mu_r + \gamma_r)(\frac{W}{r}) + \sum_{i=2}^{r-1}[(\mu_i - \gamma_i \\ &-\mu_r + \gamma_r)(\frac{W}{r})] + (\mu_r - \gamma_r)W + (\frac{W}{r})\Gamma \end{aligned} \quad (15)$$

Similarly, we may derive $E''_{m,r}$ as:

$$\begin{aligned} E''_{m,r} =& (\mu_1 - \gamma_1 - \mu_r + \gamma_r)(\frac{W}{r} + \epsilon) + \sum_{i=2}^{r-1}[(\mu_i - \gamma_i \\ &-\mu_r + \gamma_r)(\frac{W}{r})] + (\mu_r - \gamma_r)W + (\frac{W}{r} + \epsilon)\Gamma \end{aligned} \quad (16)$$

Using (14), (15) and (16) we get

$$(\mu_1 - \gamma_1 - \mu_r + \gamma_r) + \Gamma < 0 \quad (17)$$

Re-writing (9) from Theorem 3.3, we get,

$$(\mu_1-\gamma_1-\mu_r+\gamma_r)s_1+\sum_{i=2}^{r-1}[(\mu_i-\gamma_i-\mu_r+\gamma_r)s_i]+s_1\Gamma > 0 \quad (18)$$

Now $s_i \geq 0, \forall i \in \{1, 2, \ldots, r\}$ and according to our assumption 4 in Section 2.1, $(\mu_i-\gamma_i-\mu_r+\gamma_r) \leq 0, \forall i \in \{1, 2, \ldots, r\}$. Hence the first and the second term of (18) are negative, and the third term is positive. So for the condition in (18) to hold, the following is necessary:

$$(\mu_1 - \gamma_1 - \mu_r + \gamma_r) + \Gamma > 0. \quad (19)$$

But (17) is in contradiction with (19). Hence, $E''_{m,r} - E'_{m,r} < 0$ is false, which means, $E'_{m,r} < E''_{m,r}$. Hence it stands proved that we should give equal fractions of jobs to all the machines to get minimum energy. QED. □

Thus, for energy-minimal scheduling in this setting, work has to be divided equally among r machines, where r is chosen to satisfy (9). If the energy consumption overhead due to division/breaking of jobs overhead is null or negligible, then any schedule which complies with Theorems 3.3 and 3.4 is energy-optimal.

Algorithm 1 finds out machines which should be assigned work for the energy-minimal scheduling when the machines of the system are of identical speed.

Algorithm 1: Find the minimum energy consumption of the system when the speeds of machine are identical

```
input  : m, μ_i, γ_i, W
output: r, T, E
for i = 1 to m do
  | calculate μ_i − γ_i
end
sort (μ_i − γ_i);
low ← 1, high ← m;
while low ≤ high do
    mid ← low + (high−low)/2;
    Calculate E(mid − 1), E(mid), E(mid + 1);
    if
    (E(mid − 1) > E(mid))&&(E(mid) ≤ E(mid + 1))
    then
        r ← mid;
        return r;
    else
        if E(mid − 1) > E(mid) then
          | low ← mid;
        else
          | high ← mid;
        end
    end
end
T ← W/r;
E ← T[Σ_{i=1}^{r} μ_i + Σ_{i=r+1}^{m} γ_i];
```

Algorithm 1 takes the number of machines, the working power and idle power of the machines, and the total work to be done as input, and gives the value of r, i.e., the number of working machines, as output. Along with the number of working machines, it also calculates the value of makespan and total energy consumption of the system. The algorithm is based on the previously given results in a way that should be absolutely clear.

We now proceed to we analyse the case when the speed of machines are also different.

3.2 Different Speeds When Idle Power is Zero

We now consider the scheduling problem in a system where machines can have different speeds of working, i.e. different machines can execute the same job over different durations. In this model, the idle power consumptions of all the machines are zero, i.e. $\gamma_i = 0, \forall i$, as would happen if idle machines were switched off. Finding energy-minimal schedule in this case can be solved in polynomial time, as we now show.

We start with a lemma for prioritization of work among machines.

LEMMA 3.5. *Given $\frac{\mu_k}{v_k} \leq \frac{\mu_l}{v_l}$, then for minimal energy, $w_k \geq w_l$ $\forall k, l$, where $1 \leq k \leq l \leq m$.*

PROOF. We prove this by contradiction. Given $\frac{\mu_k}{v_k} \leq \frac{\mu_l}{v_l}$, then by contradiction, $w_k < w_l$.

Rearranging (4), we get,

$$E = \mu_k \frac{w_k}{v_k} + \mu_l \frac{w_l}{v_l} + \sum_{i \neq k,l} \mu_i \frac{w_i}{v_i} \tag{20}$$

To analyze just the two machines k and l, assume that the work distribution among the rest of the machines is constant. Since the idle power consumptions of all the machines is zero, the power consumed by a machine completely depends only upon the amount of work it is doing. We thus take the amount of work done by all machines other than k and l be equal to w' and the power dissipated by them be C, i.e.,

$$C = \sum_{i \neq k,l} \mu_i \frac{w_i}{v_i} \tag{21}$$

Substituting C in (20), we get,

$$E = \frac{\mu_k w_k}{v_k} + \frac{\mu_l w_l}{v_l} + C \tag{22}$$

Clearly $w_k + w_l + w' = W$. Now there are two cases to be considered: when $w_k \geq w_l$, and when $w_k < w_l$.

Case 1: $w_k \geq w_l$. Take $w_k = w + \epsilon_1$ and $w_l = w - \epsilon_1$, where $\epsilon_1 \geq 0$. Putting these values in (22), we get,

$$E = \frac{\mu_k w}{v_k}(1 + \epsilon_1) + \frac{\mu_l w}{v_l}(1 - \epsilon_1) + C \tag{23}$$

Case 2: $w_k < w_l$. Take $w_k = w - \epsilon_2$ and $w_l = w + \epsilon_2$, where $\epsilon_2 > 0$. Putting these values in (22) we get,

$$E' = \frac{\mu_k w}{v_k}(1 - \epsilon_2) + \frac{\mu_l w}{v_l}(1 + \epsilon_2) + C \tag{24}$$

If we say that in Case 2 the energy consumed is less, this means $E - E' > 0$. Using (23) from (24) in this condition, we get,

$$\frac{\mu_k}{v_k} > \frac{\mu_l}{v_l} \tag{25}$$

(25) is in contradiction to our assumption 4. QED. □

As for the identical-speed machine case, here also it is possible that just giving work to a subset of machines might prove more energy efficient than all the machines. Our next lemma tells which subset of machines should be working.

LEMMA 3.6. *If we give work to only some r machines, where $1 \leq r \leq m$, then, for minimal energy consumption, these are the r machines that form the set $\{1, 2, \ldots, r\}$.*

This lemma is the analog of Lemma 3.2 and the proof is similar. Now we proceed to the main theorem which indicates the set of machines to be used.

THEOREM 3.7. *When the speeds of all machines are different, and their idle power consumption is zero, to minimize the energy, we give all the load to the machine whose $\frac{\mu_i}{v_i}$ is minimum.*

PROOF. We prove this by contradiction. Since we have arranged the machines in increasing order of $\frac{\mu_i}{v_i}$, the first machine has minimum $\frac{\mu_i}{v_i}$. We denote the energy spent when first i machines are working as $E_{m,i}$. From Lemma 3.6, we know that if $E_{m,i} > E_{m,i-1}$ then $E_{m,i+1} > E_{m,i-1}$. Hence if we prove that $E_{m,1} < E_{m,2}$, then it is implicit that $E_{m,1} < E_{m,i}, \forall i, 1 < i \leq m$. Consider two cases:

Case 1: When all the work is given to first machine, i.e. $w_1 = W$. Using (4), the energy consumed by system is given by:

$$E_{m,1} = \frac{\mu_1 W}{v_1} \tag{26}$$

Case 2: When work is given to machines 1 and 2. Using (4), the energy consumed by system is given by:

$$E_{m,2} = \frac{\mu_1 w_1}{v_1} + \frac{\mu_2 w_2}{v_2} \tag{27}$$

As a contradiction to our theorem, we try to prove that $E_{m,1} > E_{m,2}$. Using (26) and (27), and substituting $w_1 = W - w2$ we get,

$$\frac{\mu_1}{v_1} > \frac{\mu_2}{v_2} \tag{28}$$

Here (28) is in contradiction to our assumption 4. QED. □

It is shown that only one machine has to be given all work and this machine can easily be identified. Clearly the solution to the problem of energy-minimal scheduling for machines with different speeds and zero idle power can be found in polynomial time. Algorithm 2 gives the makespan and the energy consumption for the same.

Algorithm 2: Find the minimum energy consumption of the system with variable speeds but when idle power consumption of machines is not considered

---

input : m, μ_i, v_i, W
output: r, T, E

for $i = 1$ *to* m **do**
| calculate $\frac{\mu_i}{v_i}$
end
$\min(\frac{\mu_i}{v_i})$;
$(\frac{\mu_1}{v_1}) \leftarrow min(\frac{\mu_i}{v_i})$;
$r \leftarrow 1$;
$T \leftarrow \frac{W}{v_1}$;
$E \leftarrow \mu_1 T$;

This algorithm is based on the result given above. The output of the theorem is the total energy consumption of the system, and the makespan. The complexity for Algorithm 2 is $\mathcal{O}(m)$, where m is the number of machines in the system.

4. CONCLUSIONS

This paper provides a generic formulation of energy-minimal scheduling of divisible jobs. We have derived results which govern the work distribution among machines of different energy specifications, for keeping overall energy consumption to a minimum. We have also suggested algorithms in line with our theoretical findings. Though energy-minimal scheduling of non-divisible loads is NP-hard, we can strive to achieve a close to ideal performance, using approximation algorithms. Our results also give insights to how many machines are actually useful for doing assigned work in an energy-optimal manner, and can be combined with constraints on the system such as timing constraints to derive energy-minimal schedules for the problem in hand. Our aim is for this work to serve as a building block for a generalized theory of energy-minimal and energy-aware scheduling.

5. REFERENCES

[1] P. Agrawal and S. Rao. Energy-aware scheduling of distributed systems. *IEEE Trans. Autom. Sci. Eng.*, 11(4):1163–1175, Oct. 2014.

[2] L. Babel, H. Kellerer, and V. Kotov. Thek-partitioning problem. *Mathematical Methods of Operations Research*, 47(1):59–82, 1998.

[3] J. L. Berral, I. Goiri, R. Nou, F. Juliá, J. Guitart, R. Gavaldá, and J. Torres. Towards energy-aware scheduling in data centers using machine learning. In *e-Energy '10: Proceedings of the 1st International Conference on Energy-Efficient Computing and Networking*, pages 215–224, 2010.

[4] M. Drozdowski, J. M. Marszałkowski, and J. Marszałkowski. Energy trade-offs analysis using equal-energy maps. *Future Generation Computer Systems*, 36:311–321, 2014.

[5] J. W. Herrmann, editor. *Handbook of Production Scheduling*, volume 89 of *(International Series in Operations Research & Management Science)*. Springer, 2006.

[6] T. Hirofuchi, H. Nakada, H. Ogawa, S. Itoh, and S. Sekiguchi. Eliminating datacenter idle power with dynamic and intelligent VM relocation. In *Distributed Computing and Artificial Intelligence*, volume 79 of *Advances in Intelligent and Soft Computing*, pages 645–648. Springer Berlin Heidelberg, 2010.

[7] K. Lee, J. Y. Leung, Z.-h. Jia, W. Li, M. L. Pinedo, and B. M. Lin. Fast approximation algorithms for bi-criteria scheduling with machine assignment costs. *European Journal of Operational Research*, 238(1):54–64, 2014.

[8] W. Lin, C. Liang, J. Z. Wang, and R. Buyya. Bandwidth-aware divisible task scheduling for cloud computing. *Software: Practice and Experience*, 44(2):163–174, 2014.

[9] M. L. Pinedo. *Scheduling: theory, algorithms, and systems.* Springer, 2012.

[10] H. Shi, W. Wang, and N. Kwok. Energy dependent divisible load theory for wireless sensor network workload allocation. *Mathematical Problems in Engineering*, 2012. doi:10.1155/2012/235289.

[11] W. Wang, P. Zhang, T. Lan, and V. Aggarwal. Datacenter net profit optimization with deadline dependent pricing. In *Information Sciences and Systems (CISS), 2012 46th Annual Conference on*, pages 1–6. IEEE, 2012.

[12] A. Y. Zomaya and Y. C. Lee, editors. *Energy-Efficient Distributed Computing Systems.* Wiley-IEEE Computer Society, 2012.

Discovering the Right Incentives for Demand Response Programs

Marilena Minou, Eugenia Kaskantiri, George D. Stamoulis,
Department of Informatics, Athens University of Economics and Business, Greece
{minou, kaskantiri, gstamoul} @aueb.gr

ABSTRACT

A Demand Response (DR) program can only be effective if it offers to users the proper incentives to participate and thus to modify their energy consumption patterns. In this paper, we focus on DR for residential environments. We propose a learning algorithm that helps the energy provider explore iteratively and discover for each user the minimum acceptable incentives that can motivate him to participate in DR on the basis of DR participation history and of profiling information possibly available. The provider can thus allocate incentives in the way that ensures the highest participation rate with the least possible total incentives, even when little information is available. We also deal with assessing, by means of a simple model, the effect of the provision of recommendations on users' participation in DR. We evaluate our algorithms for incentives' allocation and learning by means of simulations. Our results reveal interesting insights on the impact of profiling information on the allocation of the incentives for DR. The proposed algorithms and the environment implemented, when fed with appropriate values for certain parameters, can be employed to provide approximate evaluation of the performance of DR in practical cases.

Categories and Subject Descriptors

H.4 [**Information Systems Applications**]: Miscellaneous

Keywords

Demand Response, Incentives, Consumption Pattern, Budget Allocation, Learning Algorithm.

1. INTRODUCTION

DR programs constitute an efficient way to alleviate the peak demand problem in smart electrical-power grids. They encourage electricity end-users to adjust their consumption in response to DR events and signals issued by the energy provider. DR programs have been implemented both in industrial and commercial environments. Their successful penetration, particularly in the residential sector, can result in considerable savings, due to the fact that such environments account for a large portion of the total energy demand. However, the real success of such programs depends on offering adequate incentives for the participation and timely response of users to DR events, especially for critical peak rebate DR programs. Results from DR pilots indicate that the level of discomfort/inconvenience caused to users during a DR event due to modifications in their consumption pattern is a key factor that shapes DR participation; e.g. see the work of project WATTALYST available in [1] and references therein. In principle, users are assumed to follow a particular consumption pattern according to their preferences. To be encouraged to participate in DR, energy providers offer various types of incentives to compensate users for the inconvenience caused to them. However, estimating the appropriate amount of the incentives needed to engage them to actively participate in DR is considered a major challenge. This is due to the type and amount of information that is necessary for the provider to carry out such an estimation, particularly information relating to demographic and consumption characteristics, such as profile of the household, its total consumption or consumption at the appliance level etc. The analysis of users' consumption patterns to obtain such information is a critical issue. Any request for reduction and/or shifting of power load in order to be successful should be consistent with the type of loads arising in each household, i.e. with the appliances used by each user and the constraints imposed by their operation. This of course implies that the provider, in order to acquire more detailed information on appliance usage and preferences, either employs the appropriate equipment, additionally to the smart meters, e.g. appliance level meters, or invests in different non-intrusive load monitoring (NILM) or load disaggregation systems and algorithms. These algorithms allow for the derivation of detailed information on appliance usage from data on the total consumption that is collected by a smart meter [2] and also for avoiding the additional cost of installing new infrastructure in both the provider and the user sides. While this profiling grants for a better and at once realisation as well as for a possibly accurate assessment of users' participation probability, users cannot be obliged to participate in DR and modify their consumption patterns, but can only be incentivized to reduce or defer consumption. The importance of incentives for successful DR programs is recognized and in fact has motivated several theoretical works in the literature; e.g. [3] deals with a similar problem with that addressed in the present paper. In this context, we propose a learning algorithm that helps the provider discover how to allocate DR incentives to ensure the highest participation rate (even when little information is available) while offering the least possible total incentives for achieving this participation rate.

Our algorithm utilises the available information in order to discover for each user the minimum acceptable incentives that motivate him to participate in DR. Indeed, to stimulate users' participation and/or incite them to follow the provider's requests for load curtailment or shifting, the provider is willing to dedicate a budget for providing incentives. In essence, the provider offers each user a reimbursement for his inconvenience in the form of monetary incentives. We assume that the provider aims to achieve the highest participation rate, which may amount to 100%. We develop a learning approach aiming to iteratively explore and exploit at the same time (in successive DR events) which incentive to offer in the next event based on the current estimates of users' participation probability, so that the highest participation rate is achieved and the least possible incentives for achieving this participation rate are offered by the provider. In fact, in the course of this process the provider may prefer to choose attaining a lower DR participation rate if this is considered more beneficial for him, e.g. according to

e-Energy'15, July 14 - 17, 2015, Bangalore, India

DOI: http://dx.doi.org/10.1145/2768510.2768519

the required number of users participating in DR (or to the load that should be curtailed) or to the trade-off between the participation achieved and the total incentives offered. We also develop a simple model to study the impact in users' participation of recommendations. The recommendations are based on the information about users' consumption patterns and can address either the total consumption or the consumption of specific monitored appliances in each household. The evaluation of our work is done by means of simulations. To this end, we also develop a parameterized environment, which (when fed with appropriate values for certain parameters) can be employed for the approximate evaluation of DR performance in practical cases.

2. RELATED WORK

From the very broad literature on DR, our work is related mainly to learning of the DR incentives that should be offered per user and to a smaller extent to non-intrusive load monitoring (NILM). The literature on NILM is already extensive; e.g. see [2] (which was one of the first related articles), and [4] and [5] for some recent works. In this paper, we do not develop an approach for NILM, but we deal with how the provider can benefit from knowledge of consumption data (obtained through NILM) and/or profiling information in order to design more effective DR programs and allocate efficiently the DR incentives' budget. Regarding learning of the necessary DR incentives, [3] develops a related Multi-Armed Bandit (MAB) approach. The objective of that work is very similar to ours. However, in our work we only do learning without resorting to MAB, since at each DR event we offer some incentive to each of the users. Moreover, both in the model of [3] and in ours the user is characterized by a minimum incentive parameter, referred to as cost per unit reduction in [3]. The authors of [3] assume that the DR participation probability of a user is fixed provided that the offered incentive exceeds this threshold, while it equals 0 otherwise. In our model we assume that this probability varies with the incentive offered to the user according to a sigmoid function; see equation (3).

In this paper, we develop a methodology for an energy provider to exploit already available profiling data in order to dynamically discover for each user the minimum monetary incentives that should be offered to him to participate in DR, as well as to assess the impact of recommendations. These are proposed to users based on knowledge extracted from load disaggregation methods, or simply from profiling based on demographic data (see below). Thus, our methodology offers the provider a way of exploring a set of possible incentive allocations to choose from, each of which ensures specific levels of participation attained by offering the minimum total DR incentives using also the available profiling information. Our learning algorithm is iterative; each iteration corresponds to a DR event with simultaneous exploration and exploitation. Our methodology can be easily modified into a budget-limited problem, whereby the budget constraint is satisfied in all iterations.

3. THE MODEL

Consider a set of N users (and corresponding households) that are served by a single energy provider and are eligible for participation in DR. Each user $i \in N$ is characterised by i) a set of demographic characteristics, e.g. size of family, age, etc., ii) a consumption pattern, which is formed according to his needs and preferences and iii) the price of electricity. To simplify our analysis, we assume that each user $i \in N$ can only belong to one of two categories, to which users are categorized on the basis of the above profiling information; the categories are i) elastic (N_1), those who are willing to modify their consumption in order to benefit from a discount and/or reduced energy prices and ii) inelastic (N_2), those who are reluctant to participate in a DR program. How exactly this categorization is done, falls beyond the scope of our work. Therefore, the provider should offer a higher incentive to inelastic users than to the elastic ones in order to engage them in DR if this is necessary due to the load that should be curtailed. To model user response to the incentives offered for DR, we assume that for each user i there is a minimum incentive value $t_{min,i,j}$ that triggers the user to participate in DR, yet not always, as explained later in detail. Moreover, for each user belonging to category $N_j, j = \{1,2\}$, this minimum incentive is drawn separately from the uniform distribution in the interval $[a_j, b_j], j = \{1,2\}$, which is the same for all users in $N_j, j = \{1,2\}$, while its expected value equals $\overline{inc}_{N_j} = mean\left(t_{min,N_j}\right) = \frac{a_j+b_j}{2}$. If the provider knows the classification of users by means of profiling information, then he can offer initially a different DR incentive $inc_{N_j}$to each category $N_j, j = \{1,2\}$. All users of N_j are then offered inc_{N_j}, which is expressed as

$$inc_{N_j} = \alpha * \overline{inc}_{N_j} \quad (1),$$

where the parameter α is an economic scaling factor that is used to relate the initial incentives to the average of the minimum incentive per category. This case is henceforth referred to as Approach 2. If the provider does not know the classification of users, then he is assumed to offer the same initial incentive to all users. This case is referred to as Approach 1. However, even under Approach 1, we take that the provider does have an estimate of the average $\overline{inc}$ of the minimum incentive over both categories (e.g. by means of some profiling or historical information regarding user DR behaviour), which in fact equals $\frac{\sum_{j=1}^{2} \overline{inc}_{N_j} * N_j}{N}$, where $N = N_1 + N_2$ is the total number of users. Although this assumption is non-trivial, it is employed so that the provider makes a meaningful choice of initial incentives offered per user. Alternatively, if the provider does not have any estimate of the average $\overline{inc}$, then he can start with an arbitrary value of the initial incentives and employ the learning algorithm as is. Thus, in our model, after scaling $\overline{inc}$ by the economic factor α, the provider offers the following initial incentive to all users of both categories:

$$inc = \alpha * \overline{inc} = \alpha * \frac{\sum_{j=1}^{2} \overline{inc}_{N_j} * N_j}{N} \quad (2).$$

We have assumed that $t_{min,i,j}$ expresses the elasticity of users and in association with the incentives offered, this parameter can be used for the assessment of users' participation probability. In particular, when the incentive exceeds $t_{min,i,j}$ the participation probability p_i of this user should be close to 1; of course, the larger the incentive, the higher the participation probability. On the contrary, when the incentive is lower than $t_{min,i,j}$ this probability should be close to zero. Moreover, when provider gives recommendations to the user, the participation probability is considered to be higher than when no recommendations are used. Indeed, for a given amount of incentives a successful recommendation facilitates the user's planning of the consumption schedule based on the proposed reduction. Thus, the user can achieve the corresponding DR objective more easily and therefore more often than in the case when no recommendation is given. In the sequel, we assume that the participation probability of the users is given by the following formula:

$$p_i = \frac{e^{5(y_i-1)}}{e^{5(y_i-1)} + e^{5(1-y_i)}} * \gamma \quad (3)$$

The parameter γ accounts for the fact that the maximum participation probability is higher in the case when recommendations are offered. It is assumed to take the indicative, values $\gamma = 1$ and $\gamma = 0.8$ for DR programs with and without recommendations respectively. These values are considered as representative of the positive impact of recommendations in the DR participation probability, The parameter y_i is the ratio of the incentive to the elasticity parameter of this user $i \in N$, i.e. $y_i = \frac{incentive}{t_{min,i,j}}$, where the variable $incentive$ varies according to the approach implemented in each case. Therefore, the participation probability given by equation (3) has a sigmoid shape with a considerable increase from low to high values when the incentive offered to a user exceeds his elasticity parameter $t_{min,i,j}$. We choose to multiply $y_i - 1$ in the exponent by 5, as the resulting curve is steep but not very much, meaning that the participation probability does not increase or decrease very sharply. We have not taken $t_{min,i,j}$ as a strict threshold, to allow for some uncertainty in user participation. However, we still refer to this parameter as the minimum incentive.

4. EFFECTIVE INCENTIVE ALLOCATION

We present below three approaches $k = \{1,2,3\}$ each following a different strategy for providing incentives. The third approach is a learning algorithm aiming to assist the energy provider in deducing information about users' preferences in a dynamic manner and thus increasing the participation rate, by effectively allocating the incentives to be offered. The purpose of this algorithm is to grant the provider with additional knowledge concerning the trade-off between the amount of money used for incentives and the DR participation that can be achieved accordingly. We distinguish two cases with regard to the exploitation of the available information in the implementation of DR. In the first case, the provider applies a DR program without offering any recommendations on the actions to be taken by the users, while in the second case utilising the knowledge originating from the load disaggregation and profiling the provider offers recommendations regarding the load curtailment/shifting of certain of the appliances deduced, with the aim to examine to what extent the introduction of such recommendations leads to better results on user participation. Overall, the basic idea of the algorithm is to gradually exploit the available information in order to attain an efficient participation rate in conjunction with an efficient incentives allocation scheme. The approaches begin with the minimum information available to the provider. After each approach, the provider is assumed to enrich his knowledge of the monetary incentive preferences of each user, so that the maximum participation rate is achieved.

4.1 DR without recommendations

In this section, we consider the deployment of DR program without any recommendation and we run three distinct approaches.

4.1.1 Approach 1: DR with a single unified incentive

In this approach we consider that any prior information about the participation of users is either unknown to the provider, or ignored. Hence, the implemented DR program utilises the incentive defined in (2). The objective of the provider is to extract knowledge of the users' elasticity from their participation. After the DR program is executed, the provider identifies the set of users that participated in DR as $Z_1, Z_1 \subset N$ and estimates the total participation rate $PAR_1 = Z_1/N$.

4.1.2 Approach 2: DR using participation information and common incentive per category

Suppose that the provider by leveraging the demographic characteristics of users and the participation information from the previous approach generates better users' profiles with regard to their elasticity characteristics. Thus, utilising this information, the provider deploys DR offering to each category the same incentive as in (1). In this case, we denote as $Z_{2,j}$ the set of users that participated in the DR and as $Par_{2,j} = Z_{2,j}/N_j$ the participation rate for each category. The total participation rate equals $PAR_2 = \sum_{j=1}^{2} Z_{2,j}/N$.

Table 1. Mining the minimum threshold $t_{min,i,j}$ for $k = 3$

Step 1: Define the initial incentive to be offered either according to Approach 1 or according to Approach 2.
Step 2: Sort all users (Approach 1) and users in each category (Approach 2) in ascending order of $t_{min,i,j}$.
For each iteration r: ***Step 3:*** Examine users one by one (for more details refer to the text of Subsection 4.1.3). ***Step 3a***: Reduce the incentive value for each of the participating users by δ: $inc_{new,3,r,1} = incentive - \delta$ ***Step 3b***: Increase the incentive value for each of the non-participating users by δ': $inc_{new,3,r,2} = incentive + \delta'$
Step 4: Set $inc_{3,i,j} = inc_{new,3,r,j}$ and mark user i as "Discovered". The algorithm terminates, when changes in the $inc_{3,i,j}, \forall j = \{1,2\}$ do not affect users' state, i.e. users do not change from participating to non-participating.
Step 5: Compute for each category $j = \{1,2\}$ the percentage of participation $Par_{3,r,j} = \frac{Z_{3,r,j}}{N_{3,j}}$ and total participation rate $PAR_{3,r,j} = \frac{\sum_{j=1}^{2} Z_{3,r,j}}{N}$, where $Z_{3,r,j}$ is the set of users that participated in the DR.

4.1.3 Approach 3: Effective incentive allocation using learning of customized incentives

This approach can be defined as an extension of both the first and the second approach. We refer to them as Approach 3.1 and 3.2 respectively. The provider utilises the rate of participating users as input. The aim is to extract information concerning the minimum incentive $t_{min,i,j}$ of each user $i \in N_j$ in a dynamic way and employ it in a subsequent DR event. In particular, the approach consists of independent runs, each r corresponding to a DR event. (The first iteration is essentially an execution of either the first or the second approach.) We introduce two parameters δ and δ' that denote the amount of decrease and increase in the incentives offered. Their values are chosen to be quite small and fixed, so that there is limited dispersion of the resulting incentive values to be offered between the participating and non-participating users with similar values of $t_{min,i,j}$. Table 1 describes briefly the steps followed. In particular, given the outcomes of the previous approaches as starting points, at each subsequent r, the provider sorts the set of users (and in each category) in ascending order, so that users with the lowest thresholds to be investigated first, and the total amount of money spent to not increase rapidly. Then he reduces (resp. increases) the amount of incentives by δ to the participating users resp. (resp. δ' to the non-participating users). Reducing gradually the incentive of the users that participated in the first and second approach resp. allows for exploring (learning) their minimum incentive $t_{min,i,j}$ without affecting their participation. If in some iteration a user is not engaged with the new reduced incentive, then he is offered the same incentive for the next iteration as well, in order to confirm whether non-participation depends on the randomness of (3) or is due to the low incentive offered. In such a case, users that do not participate for two subsequent times are marked as "Discovered" and in following iteration they are offered the incentive by which they participated the last time. Each initially non-participating user is given an incentive increased by $\delta' = 2\delta$ in order for the provider to gradually approach this user's $t_{min,i,j}$. The process continues until $t_{min,i,j}$ is indeed reached and the user is marked as "Discovered". However, if a user does not participate when given the new incentive, we keep this incentive for next iteration. If this user still does not participate for this iteration, we increase his incentive by $\delta' = 2\delta$. Therefore, under this approach, the provider observes dynamically users' response to DR incentives offered until each user is given roughly the minimum amount of incentives that can lead him to a high participation probability. Thus, the algorithm both ensures consistently successful DR events in the intermediate iterations and improves gradually the participation rate, until the maximum participation is reached with the minimum total amount of DR incentives. Note that to maintain consistently successful DR events, we are more conservative in reducing an incentive value that proved to be effective than in increasing one that was not, for which a larger step is employed.

4.2 DR using recommendations

In this case, we consider DR programs, for which the provider utilises the consumption profiles stemming from load disaggregation (the details of such an algorithm are out of the scope of our paper) and offers recommendations regarding the load curtailment or shifting of specific appliances. The objective is to investigate whether the use of specific recommendations influences the participation rate of a DR program and to what extent. We employ again three such approaches that build on the same basis in terms of input data, methodology followed and the objectives to be served, as the approaches introduced in Section 4.1 albeit with minor differences. For this reason, we only describe them briefly, highlighting their differences.

4.2.1 Approach 1: DR with a single unified incentive

Again, as in Section 4.1.1, we assume that the provider has no information about users' participation. The DR program applied uses a single incentive that is unified for all users $inc_{1,i} = inc$. The difference lies in the fact that the provider can additionally offer recommendations regarding the actions of curtailment and/or shifting of the load for specific appliances. We evaluate the approach by means of independent runs, where each run is mapped to a DR event.

4.2.2 Approach 2: DR using profiling information and common incentive

Given the profiling information obtained by the demographic characteristics of users, the provider applies DR program and offers to all users of each category the average incentive as defined in (2), both when using recommendations and when not, aiming to examine whether the introduction of such recommendations has positive impact on the overall user participation and the participation in each type of users. Again the approach is evaluated by means of independent runs.

4.2.3 Approach 3: Effective incentive allocation using learning of customised incentives

The difference of this approach with the corresponding one of Section 4.1.3 lies in the fact that the provider wishes to discover the $t_{min,i,j}$ of each user but also the optimal choice of recommendation to accompany the DR message and achieve the highest participation rate. The approach is executed following the same methodology as described in Table 1. At Step 3a, if a user does not participate in the DR event, at the next iteration, he is offered the same incentive $inc_{new,3,r,1}$ but supposedly with some other different recommendation. If he does not still participate for this iteration, he is categorised as non-participating and the new incentive offered is calculated according to Step 3b. Otherwise, we assume that the reason for his behaviour is an inappropriate recommendation. The same logic is followed at Step 3b.

5. EXPERIMENTAL EVALUATION

This section presents our evaluation results. We assume a set $N = 60$ users. N_1, N_2 are the subsets of elastic and inelastic users, for each of which the parameter $t_{min,i,j}$ is drawn from the uniform distribution within the range of $[2,6]$ and $[6,10]$ resp. For the decrement δ a small value of 0.1 is taken, while the increment δ' is taken $\delta' = 2\delta$. When evaluating the various approaches, we should keep in mind that users' behaviour in terms of participation is not fully predictable and depends on the probability defined in (3). Therefore, for all approaches, we measure the average participation rate for each of several iterations over a set of multiple independent runs of the experiment.

5.1 DR without recommendations

To experimentally evaluate our approaches, we study three cases of users' partition in the two categories, i.e. symmetric partition, asymmetric partition with more elastic users and asymmetric partition with more inelastic users. For conciseness, we present results for only one of the cases, namely the asymmetric partition with more inelastic users (75% of total users), as it is considered more challenging to identify $t_{min,i,j}$ for those users and achieve higher participation. However, the same evaluation approach is used for the other two cases and similar conclusions apply. Figure 1 depicts the results of the two static Approaches 1 and 2 resp. for a broad range of values of the economic scaling factor α, for each of which the average participation from 35 independent runs is depicted. We observe that in general the lower the value α and thus the initially offered incentives the less the (average) participation. Note that despite the stochastic modelling of users' participation in (3), the average participation rate is monotonic as intuitively expected.

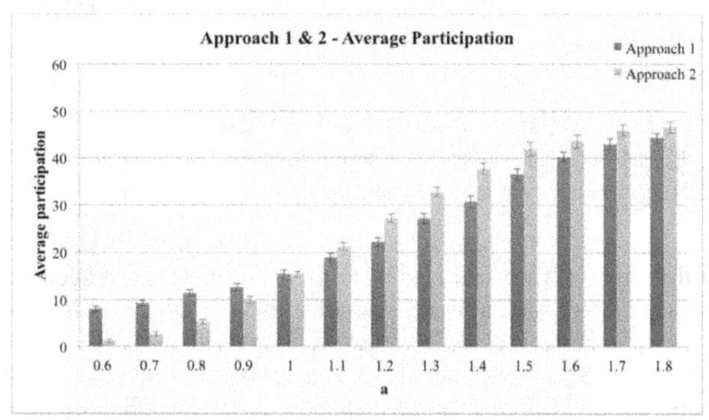

Figure 1. Approaches 1 & 2: Participation for each value of α.

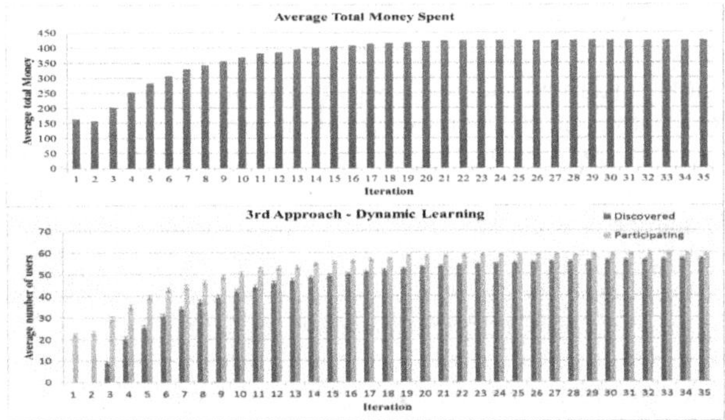

Figure 2. Approach 3.1, for $\alpha = 1.1$ and 35 iterations

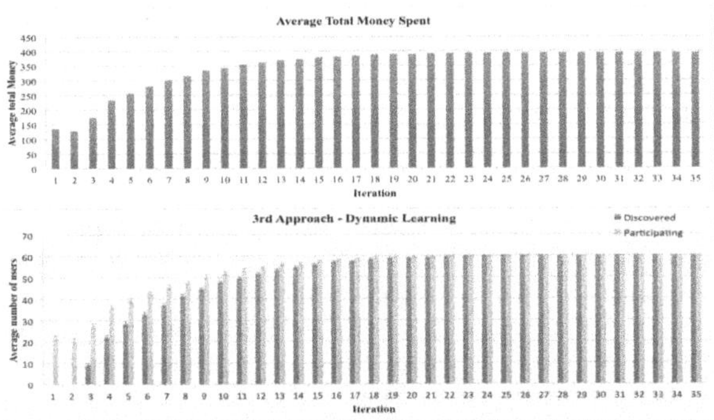

Figure 3. Approach 3.2 for $\alpha = 1.1$ and 35 iterations

The use of profiling information in Approach 2 in general leads to higher levels of participation than for Approach 1. Somewhat surprisingly though this does not apply for low values of the factor α, for which Approach 1 attains a higher average participation. This can be attributed to the fact that by offering the same incentives to all users, Approach 1 succeeds in inciting all elastic users. Approach 2 offers different incentives per category of users. Hence, for low values of a, these incentives may be lower than most users' thresholds, thus resulting in lower participation probability for Approach 2. Additional evidence for the above comparisons of participation under Approaches 1 and 2 is provided by also observing the associated confidence intervals, all constituting a small portion of the respective average participation; see Figure 1.

For the dynamic Approach 3, we examine and compare both possible ways of its implementation, i.e. as extension of the static Approaches 1 and 2. Thus, for both Approaches 3.1 and 3.2 we simulate 30 independent runs, with 35 iterations each for $\alpha = 1.1$. Figure 2 and Figure 3 indicate that both variations of Approach 3 converge to high average participation; Approach 3.2 achieves the highest possible participation (100%). The confidence intervals vary with the approach and the iteration but in general are relatively small. In addition, users are being discovered gradually as the algorithm converges. Actually, Approach 3.1 does not discover all users in contrast to Approach 3.2. However, the key difference lies in the total amount of money spent. For attaining a specific number of participating users, Approach 3.2, which employs classification in setting the initial incentives, utilises less money than Approach 3.1. This can be justified by the fact that the initial incentive per category of users in Approach 3.2 is closer to $t_{min,i,j}$; hence the participating users are offered from the start incentives that are more likely to be both effective and close to their real values of $t_{min,i,j}$. Therefore, it is really beneficial for the provider to utilize profiling information under Approach 3, enabling him to offer an appropriate initial incentive per category. In addition, by sorting users in ascending order of $t_{min,i,j}$, under both Approaches 3.1 and 3.2, the algorithm avoids selecting at the beginning the inelastic users requiring a higher incentive to participate. In essence, in this manner the learning algorithm attempts to minimise the amount of money to be spent for incentives at each given level of participation rate. Thus, in its successive iterations, the algorithm produces a set of possible incentive allocations that attain different participation rates with nearly the minimum possible total amount of money for DR incentives. The provider can decide on when to stop trying to learn the required incentives of more users depending on his objectives for participation rate and/or total money to be spent.

5.2 DR using recommendations

In this case, users are again considered to be asymmetrically distributed with 75% of them being inelastic. For the two first approaches we perform again simulations of 35 independent runs for a broad range of values of the economic scaling factor α. Figure 4 reveals that with the use of recommendations too when the value of a increases the average participation raises similarly as in the results of Section 5.1. In the present case, the use of profiling information in Approach 2 leads to lower levels of participation compared to the Approach 1. We observe that the stochastic modelling in (3) results in smaller confidence intervals. Regarding Approach 3, we have run a set of 30 independent runs each with 35 iterations for each run for $a = 1.1$ and for both variations of the approach. Figure 5 and Figure 6 indicate that the algorithm, either as Approach 3.1 or 3.2 converges really fast and thus reaches in a few iterations a very high average participation. It is noteworthy that Approach 3.2 results in discovering almost all users as opposed to Approach 3.1. Similarly to the outcomes described in Section 5.1, the use of the profiling information plays a key role also when combined with the use of recommendations, since it results in the extraction of more detailed and accurate knowledge of users' threshold and in a faster manner.

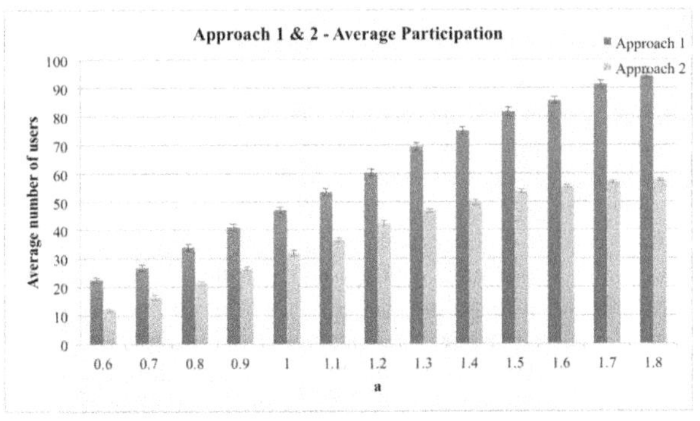

Figure 4. Approaches 1 & 2: Participation for each value of α.

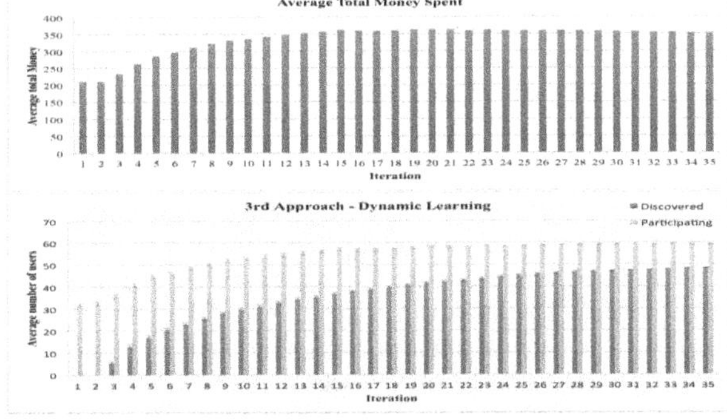

Figure 5. Approach 3.1 for $\alpha = 1.1$ and 35 iterations

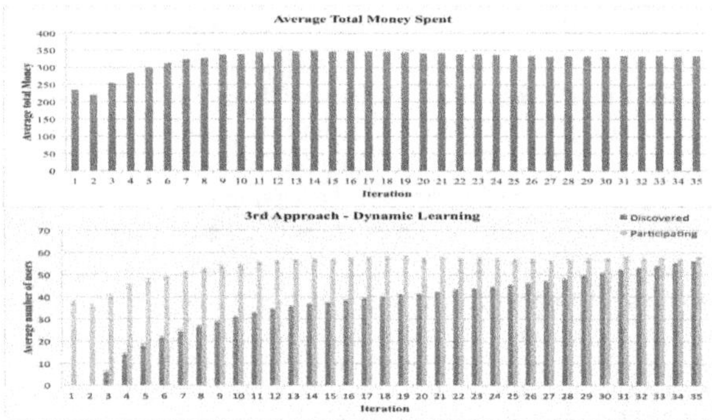

Figure 6. Approach 3.2 for $\alpha = 1.1$ and 35 iterations

We observe here as well the trade-off between the participation rate and the total money spent for this level of participation with Approach 3.2 ultimately requiring a smaller total amount for incentives than 3.1. Again, the appropriate selection rests with the provider given his objectives. For example, assume that the provider wishes to achieve participation only 58 out of 60 users, so he seeks to select the DR program that requires the least money. In general, we observe that both Approaches 3.1 and 3.2, either without or when using recommendations can fulfil the provider's objective. However, Approach 3.2 outperforms Approach 3.1 in both scenarios of applied DR with regard to the total amount of money spent. Thus, the provider should choose to implement Approach 3.2. In a practical case, the provider should estimate the value of the parameter γ in equation (3) for DR programs with and without recommendations respectively, and assess whether the DR budget reduction when he uses recommendations is worth the additional cost for deriving them.

6. CONCLUDING REMARKS

In this paper, we have introduced and evaluated three approaches (two static ones and a learning approach) that help the energy provider perform DR effectively exploiting information that are available from profiling and/or result from load disaggregation. In particular, the learning approach is applied in successive DR events and aims to explore and at the same time exploit the minimum acceptable incentives that motivate each user to participate in DR. Our study focused on two basic types of incentive-based DR programs offered to residential environments; namely, critical peak rebate DR programs with and without accompanying recommendations regarding the curtailment or shifting of the load of specific appliances. We have assumed two categories of users, namely elastic and inelastic. We have investigated different users' distributions between the two categories, but due to space limitations we have presented in detail the results for only one distribution; the conclusions for other distributions are similar. Our simulations reveal interesting insights on the impact of the use of profiling information on users' participation in DR programs and on the effective allocation of provider's budget for DR incentives.

In particular, in the case of the static Approaches 1 and 2, it turns out that using profiling information to offer customized incentives per category of users is beneficial except if the initial incentives are rather low. This implies that, in a practical case, if the budget for DR incentives offered to a specific set of users is relatively low, then a unified DR incentive should be offered to all users. Moreover, Approach 3 employs a learning algorithm in order to discover the minimum acceptable incentive for each user. After the first two iterations, and by starting with those users that are characterised by the lowest incentives accepted so far, the learning algorithm explores and discovers the lowest acceptable incentives for an increasing subset of the users until the maximum participation is attained. Thus, after a few iterations, in each DR event the algorithm attains a DR participation rate by dedicating in DR incentives nearly the minimum of the corresponding amount of money required for achieving this rate. The specific DR program to be applied in subsequent events depends on the DR participation rate that the provider aims to achieve and on the amount of money he wishes to spend for this purpose. Thus, this selection depends on the significance for the provider of the participation of additional users in conjunction with the total incentives to be offered, given the provider's objectives on the load to be curtailed and operational constraints, if any. One should keep in mind, though, that applying DR by using Approach 3.2 and recommendations leads to better results concerning the total amount of money spent. Also, that for the static Approaches 1 and 2, the provider's budget plays a significant role on users' participation, since in general the higher the value of incentives offered the higher the participation. Under Approach 3, in all cases considered for the mix of users (elastic vs. inelastic) and the value of a, the participation raises in each DR event (iteration). Also, for all cases of user mix, the introduction of specific recommendations in the DR programs (made possible by means of using profiling information) leads to noticeable improvement of the convergence rate of the algorithm to the maximum participation. This should have been reasonably expected because we have assumed that the maximum participation probability γ in equation (3) is higher for DR programs with recommendations. Consequently, the total money that is spent in each run of a DR program is less in the case of using recommendations, and especially when employing Approach 3.2. It should also be noted that the introduction of parameter γ in our model offers an interesting new possible use of our algorithm. Indeed, by employing different values of γ close to real life conditions, the algorithm can serve as a tool for assessing the impact on the improvement of participation and of the trade-offs arising when recommendations are provided. This can be considered as an interesting direction of future work based on the results stemming from real-life trials, such as those conducted in the context of the WATTALYST project [1], through which the provider can appraise whether and to what extent the provision of more specific recommendations leads to higher participation of users in DR.

7. ACKNOWLEDGEMENTS

This research has been partly funded from the European Union's Seventh Framework Programme (FP7/2007-2013) under grant agreement n° 288322 WATTALYST [1].

REFERENCES

[1] WATTALYST project: www.wattalyst.org

[2] Hart, G. W. 1992. Nonintrusive appliance load monitoring. *Proceedings of the IEEE*, 80(12), 1870-1891.

[3] Jain, S., Narayanaswamy, B., & Narahari, Y. 2014. A Multiarmed Bandit Incentive Mechanism for Crowdsourcing Demand Response in Smart Grids. *In Twenty-Eighth AAAI Conference on Artificial Intelligence.*

[4] Marceau, M. L., & Zmeureanu, R. 2000. Nonintrusive load disaggregation computer program to estimate the energy consumption of major end uses in residential buildings. *Energy Conversion and Management*, 41(13), 1389-1403.

[5] Ardakanian, O., Keshav, S., & Rosenberg, C. 2011, August. Markovian models for home electricity consumption. In *Proceedings of the 2nd ACM SIGCOMM workshop on Green networking* (pp. 31-36). ACM.

Optimization of Solar PV System and Analysis of Tilt Angle

Pooja Jain
M.E. Scholar
Electrical Engineering Department
Sec-12, PEC University of Technology
Chandigarh, India
poojajain9219@gmail.com

Dr. Tarlochan Kaur
Assoc. Professor
Electrical Engineering Department
Sec-12, PEC University of Technology
Chandigarh, India
tarlochankaur@pec.ac.in

ABSTRACT

This paper presents feasibility study of a standalone solar PV System in a remote village. The key to optimum energy output from Solar PV panels is the tilt angle of the PV panels.The Solar panels are most efficient when they are perpendicular to solar irradiations.The Sun's path and altitude vary throughout the year.The focus of this paper is to maximize PV power generation while minimizing the total system cost. Simulation of the system has been done using HOMER. Case study of Sanoder village, Bhavnagar district, Gujarat in India has been undertaken.

Keywords

Solar Photovoltaic panel; Tilt Angle; Optimization; HOMER software

1. INTRODUCTION

Renewable Energy sources present unique opportunities for greater fuel diversity and security. As a result of rapid pace of the technical and commercial development of renewable energy systems, the cost is decreasing. Rapid depletion of fossil-fuels and increasing environmental concern about global warming has necessitated research on renewable energy sources. Among renewable energy sources, solar photovoltaic (PV) energy is widely used in small-sized applications.

The tilt angle of solar panels has a major effect on the capture of solar irradiations impinging on solar panels.The amount of solar power available per unit area is known as irradiance. Irradiance is a radiometric term for the power of electromagnetic radiation at a surface per unit area. The position of the earth relative to the sun changes with time.The change must be monitored adequately in order to increase the amount of energy received by solar panels.Thus, to optimize solar insolation, appropriate method is required.

As the sun is higher in summers and lower in winters, more energy can be captured throughout the year by adjusting the tilt of the panels according to the season. Panel's tilt angle can be changed regularly according to sun's position. But it is most economical to mount the solar panels at some fixed tilt angle as the tracking systems connected to Solar system highly increases the cost of system. Our main aim is to determine the optimum tilt angle to maximize the solar PV production with the help of HOMER Software. HOMER simulates the operation of a system by making energy balance calculations for each of the 8,760 hours (365x24) in a year.

2. LITERATURE REVIEW

Over the last few years, many authors have presented models to predict solar radiation on inclined surfaces. Some of these models apply to specific cases, some require special measurements, and some are limited in their scope. These models use the same methods of calculating beam and ground reflected radiation on a tiltedsurface. The only difference exists in the treatment of the diffuse radiation. [1–3]. Extensive research was made in the field of Solar PV system. Moghadam Hamid, et. al. [4] estimated solar global radiation on a horizontal surface using a mathematical model and the results were compared. Ibrahim D. [5] examined for selection of optimum tilt angle of Cyprus. Indradip Mitra and S.P.Gon Chaudhuri [6] have given a plan for remote village electrification through Renewable Energy in the Islands of Indian Sundarbans. A technical report was prepared by T. Givler and P. Lilienthal using HOMER Software, NREL's Micro power Optimization Model, to explore the role of gen-sets in small solar power systems in Sri Lanka [7]. Anagreh et al [8], investigated the potential of solar energy for seven sites in Jordan and created a motivation of use of solar PV based power system. Yousif El-Tous [9] also performed a case study on the effect of the incentive tariff on the economic feasibility of a grid-connected PV household system in Amman. Li et al [10], presented a study of a grid-connected PV system in Hong Kong, and showed that the payback period was estimated as 8.9 years. On the other hand, various mathematical models of the elements that make up these systems have been used, as well as various design and simulation models. For maximum radiation the results were calculated by varying tilt angle form 0° to 90° with the increment of 10°.

3. METHODOLOGY

In order to design a PV system, typical information required for the selected location is the load profile of that location, solar radiation for PV generation, initial cost of various component (renewable energy generators, battery, converter), project lifetime, etc. Using this data one can perform the simulations to obtain the best PV grid connected power system configuration. HOMER software from NREL has been used for the optimization process.

e-Energy'15, July 14-17, 2015, Bangalore,India.
 ISBN 978-1-4503-3609-3/15/07...$15.00
DOI: http://dx.doi.org/10.1145/2768510.2768517

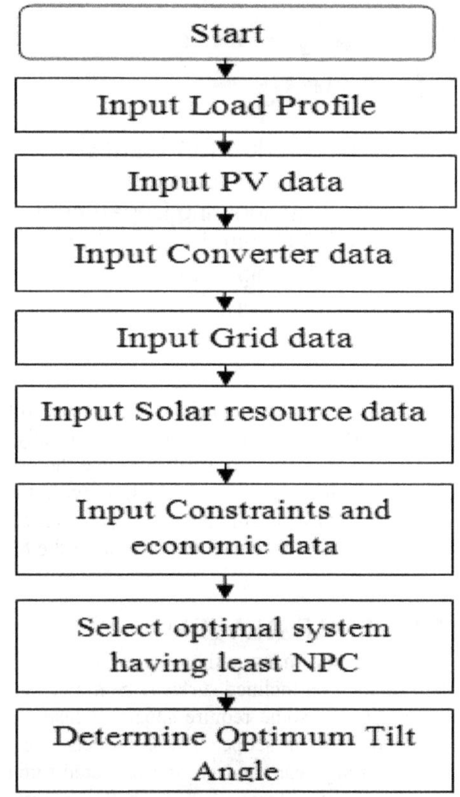

Figure 1. Flow Chart for Sizing of system

The analysis of the hourly surplus renewable power is done by comparing the available renewable power to the electric load. Then the system configuration is changed, so that little or no renewable surplus exists. After completion ofcalculation for one year, it is determined whether the system configuration fulfills the constraints imposed by the modeler. If it follows the constraints, life-cycle cost is estimated. The total net present cost (NPC) is used as the measurement to represent the life-cycle cost of a particular system. The NPC includes investment costs, operation, maintenance and replacement costs that for a particular project lifetime.

When the simulation process is completed to search for viable system configurations, the optimization process determined the best possible system configuration. The best possible, or optimal solutions, were those who satisfy user's specified constraints and having the lowest possible NPC. The system with the lowest NPC is considered as the optimal system configuration. From design point of view, the optimization of the size of plant is very important, and generates good ratio between cost and performances. Before system sizing, load profile and available insolation should also be evaluated.

For the most optimal system, monthly PV production is analyzed to determine monthly adjustment of tilt angle. After that optimum tilt angle is found such that yearly production is maximized, for an economical and efficient production.

In sensitivity analysis, the aim is to analyze how outputs of the problem will change with changes in input. A range of values were entered for sensitivity variables like the tilt angle values of PV panel, solar irradiation values, the grid power price, among others. The systems are optimized once again for a better long term knowing of systems behavior, permitting the user to deal with uncertainties and thus making better design decisions. [11]

In this work, the following factors were analyzed:

i. Effect of change of tilt angle of solar panel on PV production.
ii. Comparison of solar PV-battery storage system, solar PV -diesel generator system, diesel generator only system and grid connected PV system.

4. SYSTEM DESCRIPTION

4.1 Site description

India receives on an average 4-7kWh/m^2 of solar energy daily with an average of 250-300 sunny days in a year. The states of Rajasthan and Gujarat in western India receive maximum radiation in the range of 6–6.6 kWh per square meter.

Among the several districts of Gujarat, Sanodar village(latitude is 21° 56' N, and longitude is 72°59'E in GMT + 5:30 time zone, altitude : 892.7 m above sea level) located in Bhavnagar district was selected. It is located 27 Km towards South from District headquarters Bhavnagar. It is located 20 km from Ghogha and 224 km from State capital Gandhinagar [12]. As per the census of 2001, there were 798 inhabited villages in Bhavnagar district. Sanoder is one of the rural and remote village.72% of India's population is rural based and agriculture dependent. As electrification of rural areas has become an important instrument for sustainable development of a country, Sanoder village having abundant solar energy was chosen for study.

4.2. Input Data

4.2.1. Solar Radiation Data

Fig. 2 gives the monthly average daily solar radiation of 5.212 (kWh/m^2). Data is taken from NREL site.

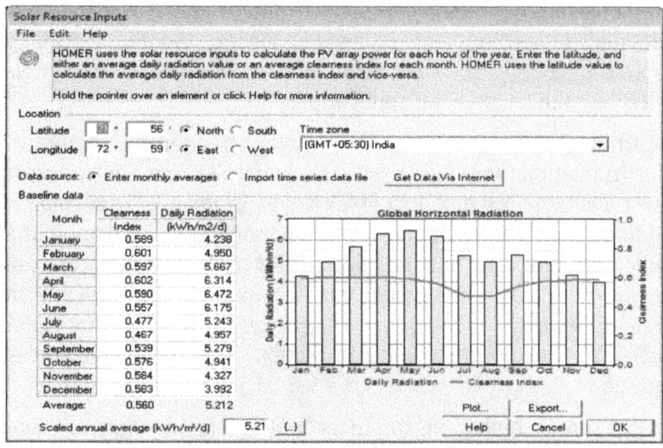

Figure 2. Solar Resource Inputs

4.2.2. Load Profile

An important consideration of any power generating system is load. As a case study and as a representation of remote village which lacks access to the utility grid, the measured annual average energy consumption was considered to be small at 10kW for a group of 50 households in Sanodar village of Gujarat. The load was scaled to 6 (kWh/d) in the present study. The peak requirements of the load dictate the system size. In this study 796 (W) was considered to scale peak load.

Considering the low income status of the residents of this village, the electrical appliances possessed by each household of the village comprises of the following:

1. 2 CFLs (20W each)
2. 1 Fan (80 W)
3. 1 Electric Pump for irrigation (60W)
4. 1 Television (80W)

Monthly load profile is shown in Figure 3.

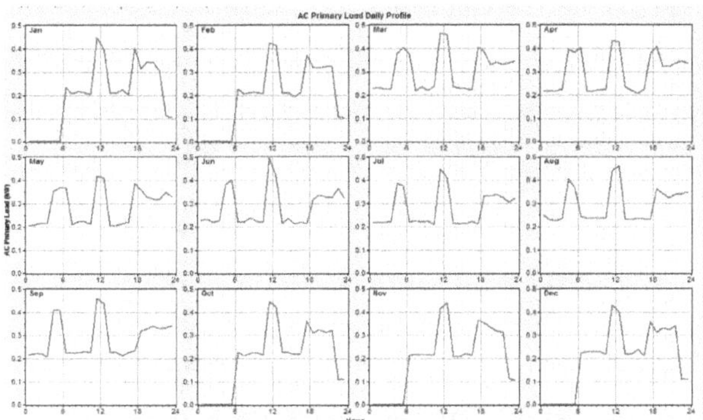

Figure 3.Monthly Load Profile

5. HOMER SIMULATION MODEL

In the present work, the selection and sizing of components of hybrid power system was done using NREL's HOMER software. HOMER is general purpose hybrid system design software that facilitates design of electric power systems for stand-alone applications. Input information to be provided to HOMER designs an optimal power system to serve the desired loads. [13]

The model, developed using HOMER, consists of a PV, a battery and converter. The proposed model is shown in Fig.4. The goal of the optimization process is to determine the optimal value of each decision variable that interests the modeler.

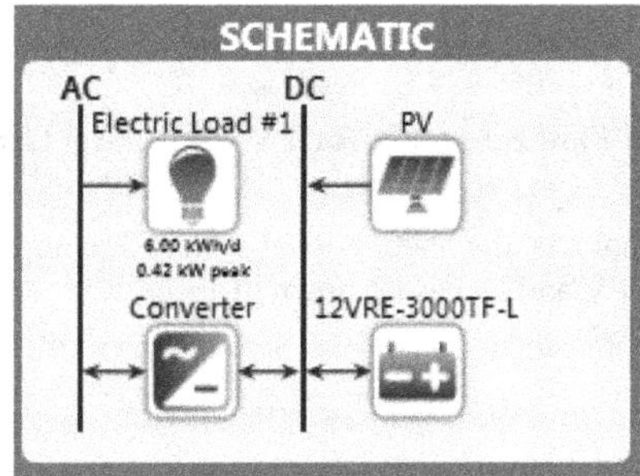

Figure 4.Case System 1 – Solar PV System with batteries

Following case systems have been studied:

i. Case System 1: Solar PV system with batteries
ii. Case System 2: Solar PV with DG
iii. Case System 3 : Diesel Generator Only
iv. Case System 4: Solar PV Grid connected system

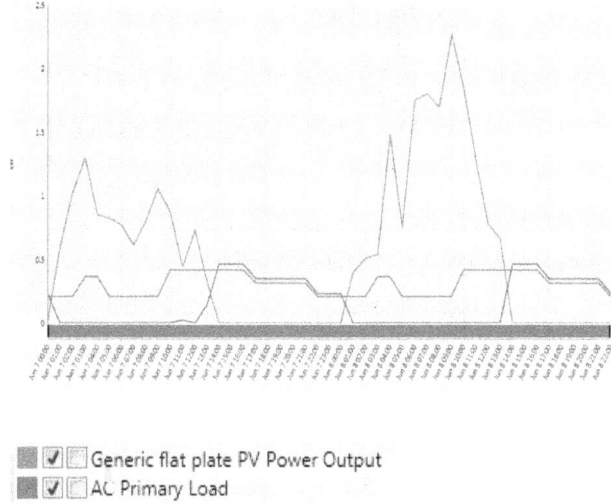

Figure 5. Load profile, PV and battery power output for a typical day of June

Figure 5 depicts the load profile, PV power output for a typical day.It is observed that during some hours of day there is deficit of electricity and at other times, PV power is produced in excess. To mitigate this deficit, grid can supply power or batteries/DG can be used. The batteries can be charged with excess power produced during off peak hours.

Since the village under study is not connected to grid, therefore following options are considered: (i) battery integration with solar PV (ii) installing a D.G (iii) exploring if other renewable resource potential like wind resource exist so as to have a hybrid system to create a standalone energy source that is both dependable and consistent. In this work option (i) and (ii) were analyzed and option (iii) will be analyzed in future work.

6. OPTIMIZATION RESULTS

Solar PV with batteries, PV with DG, DG only and PV with Grid systems were optimized. The results are tabulated inTable 1.

It was observed that PV with battery system need 3kW solar panel along with 10 batteries and 1 kW converter to meet the total load requirement . The results of the simulation program indicate that the lowest COE obtained is 0.29 $/kWh is achieved at 100% PV contribution.

To meet the full load through renewable source (0% capacity shortage), the system is such that high amount of excess electricity is produced. The excess electricity in this case is 52%. To utilize this excess energy and to feed the load during non-PV hours, battery storage is used. Battery storage is most important component in anoff grid systems. Also it accounts for major portion of cost or economics for systemconfiguration. COE($/kWh) for PV is 0.065 and COE($/kWh) for batteries is 0.22. So most of cost of system is incorporated by batteries.To reduce the cost of batteries, diesel generator can be used in place of batteries.

Table 1. Comparison of different optimized systems

System	NPC ($)	C.O.E ($/kWh)	Production (kWh/yr)	Excess Electricity (%)	CO_2 Emissions (Kg/yr)
PV with battery	8,165	0.29	5,556	52%	0
PV with DG	13,089	0.49	4,918	53.30	1,486
DG	14,911	0.62	2,190	0%	3,390
PV Grid	3,509	0.08	3,186	0%	1,300

In the 2nd scenario, PV with diesel generator configuration was considered. The optimized system consist of 2kW PV,1kW DG set and 1kW converter. It produces 4918 kWh/year of energy. COE for the system is 0.49$/kWh and COE for PV is 0.065$/kWh.So COE for generator is approximately 0.425$/kWh. It is observed that per unit cost for DG set is high for lower loads. Excess electricity in this system is 53.30%.

Diesel generator only configuration consists of 1kW DG set and 1kW converter and has production of 2190 kWh/year. COE for system is 0.62$/kWh. Excess electricity in this system is Zero. Therefore DG sets are economical for higher loads.

Figure 6 shows possible cost scenario of batteries and DG set. Series 1 shows cost due to diesel generator and Series 2 shows cost due to batteries. This scenario is typical, in that, the battery's cost of energy exceeds that of the diesel. But because the diesel generator has fixed cost, the battery can supply small amounts of ac power more cheaply than the diesel. In this case the crossover point is around 7kWh/d.Therefore, if the net load is less than 7kWh/d, HOMER will serve the load by discharging the battery. If the net load is greater than 7kWh/d, HOMER will serve the load with the generator instead of the battery, even if the battery is capable of supplying the load.

It appears that a hybrid system consisting of PV, batteries and diesel will be the best option. But any system configuration which incorporates DG, high CO_2 emissions are present as is also evident from Table 1, mitigating which would entail cost, therefore PV with battery for Sanoder village is the best system configuration.

Scenario 4 i.e. PV Grid connected System, assuming village is electrified, was also analysed. It required 1kW PV panel,1kW converter connected with 1000 kW grid with no battery. This system configuration has production of 3186 kWh/year with no excess electricity. COE ($/kWh) for system is 0.08. COE($/kWh) for PV is 0.065. Hence this configuration account for least NPC and COE. This is because energy deficit between PV production and load is met by Grid, which is cheaper in rates because of subsidies. However, as this village is yet not electrified, this scenario is not a viable at present. Also it emits pollutants in environment. So it is not environmental friendly.

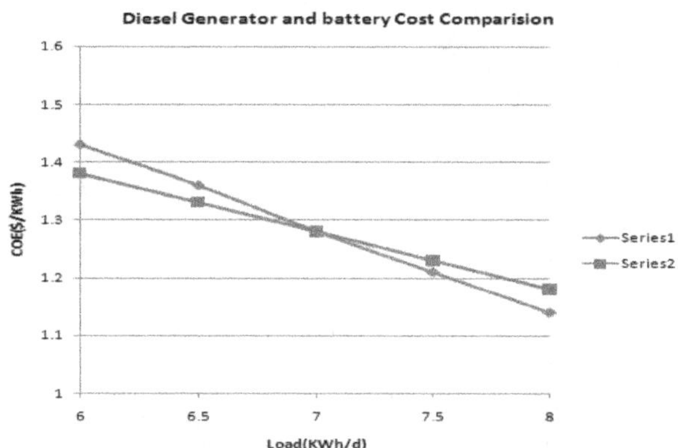

Figure 6.Cost comparison between batteries and DG set

Tables 2 - 5 shows the cash flow summary of the systems. Case System 1 has its cost mainly due to PV panels and batteries as given in Table 2.

Component	Capital ($)	Replacem	O&M ($)	Fuel ($	Salvage ($)	Total ($)
Generic flat plate PV	$4,500.00	$0.00	$193.91	$0.00	$0.00	$4,693.90
Discover 12VRE-3000TF-L	$2,000.00	$714.83	$646.38	$0.00	($292.79)	$3,068.40
Converter	$300.00	$127.28	$0.00	$0.00	($23.96)	$403.33
System	$6,800.00	$842.12	$840.29	$0.00	($316.75)	$8,165.70

Table 2. Cash Flow Summary for PV with batteries System

Component	Capital ($)	Replacem	O&M ($)	Fuel ($	Salvage ($)	Total ($)
Generic flat plate PV	Rs. 1,500.00	Rs. 0.00	Rs. 0.00	Rs. 0.00	Rs. 0.00	Rs. 1,500.00
10kW Genset	Rs. 250.00	Rs. 1,285.90	Rs. 2,065.20	Rs. 7,297.10	Rs. -20.96	Rs. 10,877.00
Converter	Rs. 350.00	Rs. 127.28	Rs. 258.55	Rs. 0.00	Rs. -23.96	Rs. 711.88
System	Rs. 2,100.00	Rs. 1,413.20	Rs. 2,323.70	Rs. 7,297.10	Rs. -44.92	Rs. 13,089.00

Table 3. Cash Flow Summary for PV with Diesel Generator System

DG set incorporates the major cost of system 2 comprising of PV and DG as is shown in Table 3.

Component	Capital ($)	Replacem	O&M ($)	Fuel ($	Salvage ($)	Total ($)
10kW Genset	Rs. 250.00	Rs. 1,643.10	Rs. 2,538.30	Rs. 10,534.00	Rs. -54.50	Rs. 14,911.00
System	Rs. 250.00	Rs. 1,643.10	Rs. 2,538.30	Rs. 10,534.00	Rs. -54.50	Rs. 14,911.00

Table 4. Cash Flow Summary for Diesel Generator System

Component	Capital (Rs.)	Replacemer	O&M (Rs.)	Fuel (Rs.)	Salvage (Rs	Total (Rs.)
Generic flat plate PV	Rs. 1,500.00	Rs. 0.00	Rs. 0.00	Rs. 0.00	Rs. 0.00	Rs. 1,500.00
Grid	Rs. 0.00	Rs. 0.00	Rs. 1,297.10	Rs. 0.00	Rs. 0.00	Rs. 1,297.10
Converter	Rs. 350.00	Rs. 127.28	Rs. 258.55	Rs. 0.00	Rs. -23.96	Rs. 711.88
System	Rs. 1,850.00	Rs. 127.28	Rs. 1,555.70	Rs. 0.00	Rs. -23.96	Rs. 3,509.00

Table 5. Cash Flow Summary for PV Grid connected System

Table 4 shows the cost of DG set, the main component of system 3. While in system 4, PV panels incorporate for the major cost factor, grid adds to less cost value as shown in Table 5.

7. OPTIMUM TILT ANGLE

Sensitivity Analysis is done to determine optimum tilt angle for maximum PV production. Sun's position changes with time, therefore irradiations impinging on panel changes continuously, which affect solar production. Monthly optimum tilt angles are determined [14] and yearly average PV production iscorresponding to these tilt angles is given in Table 6.

Table 6. Monthly optimum Tilt angles and PV production

Month	Optimum Tilt Angle	Yearly PV Production for different tilt angles(kWh/yr)
Jan	38	4,712
Feb	30	4,806
March	21	4,834
April	24	4,833
May	6	4,686
June	4	4,648
July	6	4,794
August	14	4,522
September	22	4,834
October	30	4,806
November	38	4,712
December	46	4,522

However if tracking system is not used and average yearly production is analysed, then it is observed that max PV production is obtained at tilt angle of 21 degree which is approximately equals to latitude of the place.

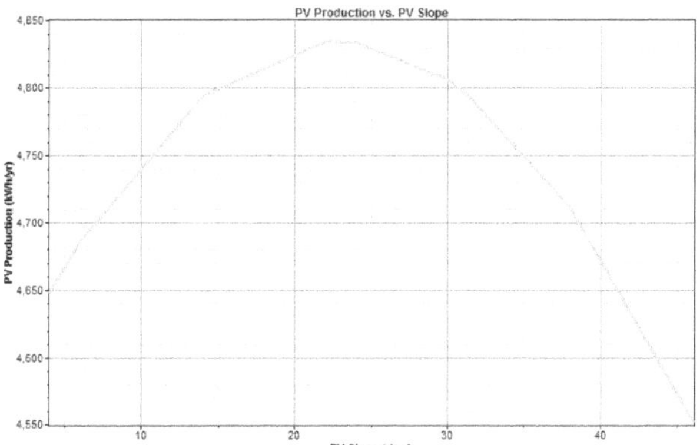

Figure 7a. Effect of tilt angle variation on PV generated energy

Figure 7a illustrates the effect of tilt angle on PV energy generated. For Sanodar village corresponding to tilt angle equal to 21 degrees, maximum PV energy is generated. Figure 7b gives the monthly average production at this optimum tilt angle of 21 degree, which is 4,834 kW. Maximum production is obtained in March and April months.

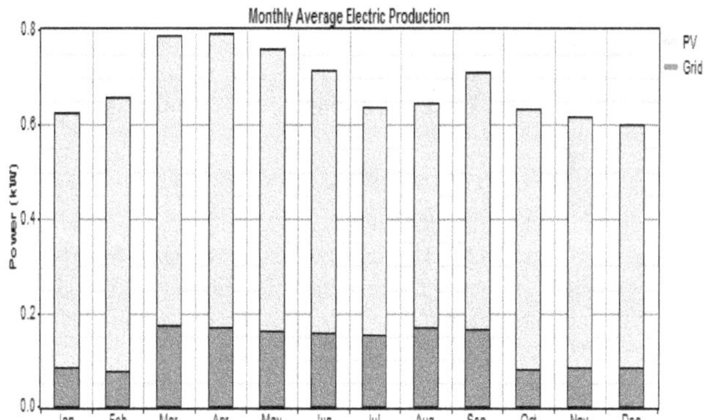

Figure 7b. Monthly Average Energy Production at optimum

8. CONCLUSION:

Solar radiation data analysis for the location of the study shows that the yearly average is 5.21 kWh/m^2 day while tilting the PV modules at the optimized angle results in yearly average to 5.66 kWh/m^2 day. The maximum solar production is obtained at optimum tilt angle of the panel. It is observed that yearly fixed optimum tilt angle for a location is approximately same at its latitude value. This angle is found to be 21 °. However, optimum tilt angle is lesser than latitude for winter months and higher than latitude value for summer months.

For feasibility studies, four scenarios are analyzed in this paper. For off grid application, the most economic scenario is the one that includes in addition to the PV panels, the battery system. The COE for this scenario is found to be the least at 0.29 $/kWh and happens at 100% PV contribution. The scenario which is dependent on standalone PV and diesel, give results of COE greater than this value. For the diesel only scenario, both, the COE and amount of CO_2 produced is greater. The amount of produced CO_2 is about 2 times greater compared to the hybrid one. This is an important environmental issue. Considering Sanodar village which is a remote area far away from the grid, PV with battery solution is the most feasible. As battery adds to a major project cost so instead of using battery bank, a back-up diesel generator can also be used when energy demanded by the load is high than that supplied by the solar PV. A complete renewable solution like PV-Wind Hybrid System is also an option to reduce use of batteries and will be an area of future work.

Penetration of renewable sources reduces CO_2 emission significantly which reduces global warming as well as plays a key role in developing climate-friendly sustainable power systems for future.

REFERENCES

[1] Manes A, and Ianetz A., On the optimum exposure of flat-plate fixed solar collectors‖ Sol Energy, 1983;31:1,65–73.

[2] Ahmad M. Jamil and Tiwari G.N., ―Optimization of Tilt Angle for Solar Collector to Receive Maximum Radiation‖, The Open Renewable Energy Journal, 2009; 2: 19-24.

[3] Bekker, B. (2004). Methods to extract maximum electrical energy from PV panels on the earth's surface. University of Stellenbosch

[4] Moghadam Hamid, Farshchi T. F. and Sharak A. Z., ―Optimization of solar flat collector inclination‖, Desalination, 2011; 265: 107–111.

[5] Pooja and Dr.Tarlochan kaur, 'Optimal Sizing of Solar Photovoltaic Wind Hybrid System' International Journal Of Innovative Research In Electrical, Electronics, Instrumentation And Control Engineering, Vol. 3, Issue 1, January 2015;99-103

[6] Ibrahim D., —Optimum tilt angle for solar collectors used in Cyprus Renewable Energy‖ 1995; 6:813 -819.

[7] IndradipMitra and S. P. Gon Chaudhuri, "Remote Village Electrification Plan through Renewable Energy in the Islands of Indian Sundarbans". „homerenergy.com webcast-downloads ises-remic2-v2.pdf

[8] T. Givler and P. Lilienthal, "Using HOMER Software, NREL's Micropower Optimization Model, to Explore the Role of Gen-sets in Small Solar Power Systems in Sri Lanka".

[9] Y. Anagreh, A. Bataineh and M. Al- Odat, solar energy potential in Jordan, ICEGES 2009.

[10] Yousif El-Tous, „International Journal of Applied Science and Technology Vol. 2 No. 2; February 2012

[11] Danny Li, K.L. Cheung, T. Lam and W. Chan, a study of grid-connected photovoltaic PV system in Hong Kong. Applied Energy, 2011

[12] "Design Optimization of Stand-Alone Hybrid Energy Systems" ,Francisco Gonçalves Goiana Mesquita

[13] http://www.eei.org/issuesandpolicy/generation/NetMetering/Documents.pdf

[14] http://www.gogreensolar.com/pages/solar-panel-tilt-calculator

[15] Satish Kumar Ramoji1, B. Jagadish Kumar2, 'Optimal Economical sizing of a PV-Wind Hybrid Energy System using Genetic Algorithm and Teaching Learning Based Optimization', International Journal of Advanced Research in Electrical, Electronics and Instrumentation Engineering ,Vol. 3, Issue 2, pp.7352-67.February 2014.

[16] National Renewable Energy Laboratory. Available at: http://www.nrel.gov/international/tools/HOMER/homer.html

A Compendious Study on Demand Side Management- An Indian Perspective

Shivani Garg
Student
Electrical Engg. Deptt.
MANIT, Bhopal
shivaanigarg@gmail.com

Anoop Arya
Asstt. Professor
Electrical Engg. Deptt.
MANIT, Bhopal
anooparya.nitb@gmail.com

Priyanka Paliwal
Asstt. Professor
Electrical Engg. Deptt.
MANIT, Bhopal
priyanka_manit@yahoo.com

Abstract

This review provides an overview of available techniques used for Demand side Management. Demand side management techniques used are classified into three categories direct load control, peak load management, and time of use (TOU). The different DSM techniques comprehend reasonable savings to both utility and consumers simultaneously, while reducing the system peak. This paper also gives a small review on demand response and energy efficiency. Demand Response plays an important role in the electricity market for maintaining the balance between supply and demand by introducing load flexibility instead of only adjusting generation levels, at almost all operational time scales. Demand Response is going to become a part of the system operations in smart grid driven restructured power system around the world in near future. India has initiated the National Mission for Enhanced Energy Efficiency under National Action Plan for Climate Change which addresses various aspects of energy efficiency such as technology, financing, fiscal incentive and also creation of energy efficiency as a market instrument. However, even though energy efficiency has substantial scope in the Indian subcontinent, the market for energy efficiency has been limited. This paper also provides an illustration of the concept of DSM Power Plant model through some case studies in different states of India.

Key words

Demand Side Management, Energy Efficiency, Demand Response, Direct Load Control and OpenADR.

1. INTRODUCTION

Electricity is something most of us take for granted, but still almost 1.3 billion of people are without access to electricity (IEA 2013) and demand for electricity is expected to increase significantly over coming years. A limited number of large power plants feed into the grid and try to keep demand and supply balanced at all times [1]. In order to increase efficiency and hold the line on costs, utilities are now controlling, directly and indirectly, when and how the electric energy is used-shifting from a supply-side-only viewpoint to an integrated demand- and supply-side viewpoint. They are including the customer as a new utility planning option [2].

e-Energy'15, July 14-17, 2015, Bangalore, India.
 ISBN 978-1-4503-3609-3/15/07…$15.00.
DOI: http://dx.doi.org/10.1145/2768510.2768515

In spite of continued growth in power generation over years, gap between demand and generation is growing every year [3]. DSM is an important function in energy management of future smart grid, which provides support towards smart grid functionalities in various areas such as electricity market control, and management, infrastructure construction, and management of decentralized energy resources and electric vehicles [4]. DSM refers to technologies, actions and programmes on the demand-side of energy metres that seek to manage or decrease energy consumption, in order to reduce total energy system expenditures or contribute to the achievement of policy objectives such as emissions reduction or balancing supply and demand [5]. The methods utilized for DSM are gone for attaining valley filling, peak clipping and strategic conservation of electrical frameworks. There are also more exotic means such as power wheeling, the installation of energy efficient processes and equipment, the use of energy storage devices, co-generation, use of renewable energy and reactive power control [6].

2. DSM PROGRAMS

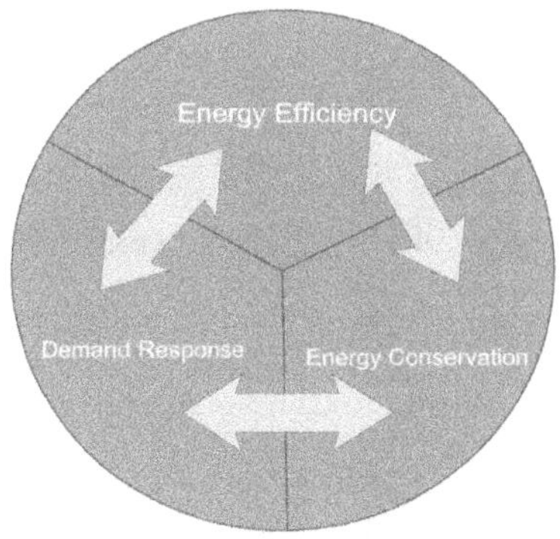

Figure 1. DSM Concept Integration [7]

As shown in Fig. 1, DSM Programs can be classified into: Energy Efficiency (EE), Demand Response (DR) and Energy Conservation (EC). It is clear that all three types of activities are complementary and relevant for saving energy [7].

2.1 Energy Efficiency

Essentially, every user site has shrouded issues that waste energy, for e.g. compressed air leakages, dirty filters, broken equipment, etc. Energy efficient technologies are structured application of a range of management techniques that enables an organization to identify and implement measures for reducing energy consumption and costs. Sometimes seen as a separate category of DSM, Energy Conservation (EC) [8] shall be seen as a part of EE [12]. Improvement in efficiency of energy use will lead to a reduction in national energy consumption, and hence is an effective policy for reducing national CO_2 emissions.

However, economists of all persuasions are united in their belief that opposite will occur. They argue that effect of improving efficiency of a factor of production, like energy, is to lower its implicit price and hence make its use more affordable, thus leading to greater use. Thus energy efficiency is not as 'environmental friendly' as many claims. Its promotion will not necessarily lead to a reduction in energy use and hence reduced CO_2 emissions. It will, however, save consumers money, promote a more efficient and prosperous economy, and allow the financing of move towards fossil-free energy future [9]. To reduce energy consumption and improve energy efficiency in enterprises and other organizations measures are divided into three basic categories [10]:

- No-cost and low-cost measures;
- Measures requiring moderate levels of investment;
- Measures requiring significant investment

Additional gains in EE are possible through technologies that can provide targeted education or real time verification of customer demand reduction [11].

2.2 Demand Response

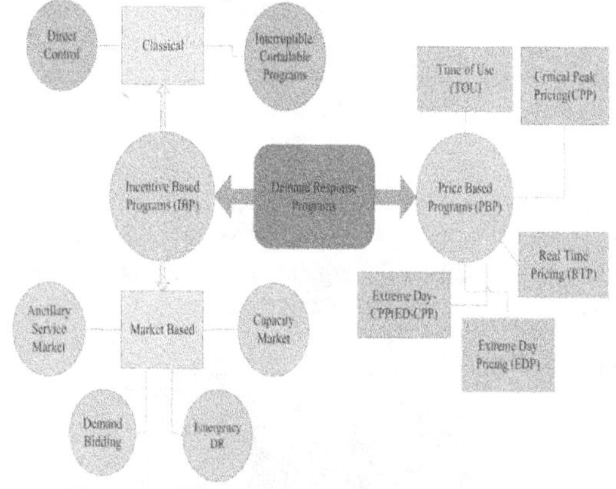

Figure 2. Demand Response Classification

According to the U.S. Department of Energy (DOE) report, Demand Response (DR) is: "Changes in electric usage by end-use customers from their normal consumption patterns in response to changes in the price of electricity over time or to incentive payment designed to induce lower electricity use at times of high wholesale market prices or when system reliability is jeopardized" [13, 15]. One of the basic comprehensive DR definitions, as a subsequent part of DSM programs, announced by Federal Energy Regulatory Commission (FERC) says that DR is the ability of customers to respond to either a reliability trigger or a price trigger from their utility system operator, load-serving entity, regional transmission organization (RTO)/ISO, or the demand response provider by lowering their power consumption [15]. As what can be inferred from recent definition, DR includes incentive payment actions in addition to peak clipping actions [16]. DR includes all intentional electricity consumption pattern modifications by end-use customers that are intended to alter the timing, level of instantaneous demand, or total electricity consumption [17].

Different DR programs are shown in Figure 2 these programs can be classified into two main categories: Incentive-Based Programs (IBP) [18] and Price-Based Programs (PBP) [19, 20]. IBP are further divided into classical programs and market-based programs. Classical IBP incorporates Direct Load Control programs and Interruptible/Curtailable Load programs. Market based IBP include Emergency DR Programs, Demand Bidding, Capacity Market, and the Ancillary services market. PBP programs are based on dynamic pricing rates in which electricity tariffs are not flat; the rates fluctuate following the real time cost of electricity. DR can reduce system peak load in the long term and therefore postpone the need for building new power plants, leading to considerable environmental impacts [21]. The short term impacts of DR on electricity markets leads to financial benefits of both the utility and the consumers. Sugihara et al. [22] made an attempt to evaluate the effects of implementing demand response on system variables like total cost of energy and market clearing price by formulating a unit commitment problem. Ferreira et al. [23] proposed a method of load control based on the price elasticity of consumers.

3. DSM TECHNIQUES

There are many DSM techniques proposed in different literatures some of which are reviewed in this paper as:

3.1 Load Reduction: Dynamic Voltage Management

As cumulative load or distance along a circuit increases, voltage begins to diminish on distribution feeder lines. To make up for this loss, utilities typically raise the level of voltage to customers at the beginning of the circuit. However, this practice can create significant line losses and inefficient equipment loading. Dynamic voltage management, or adaptive voltage control, is a DSM solution that offers substantial opportunities for utilities to lower net energy consumption by customers and reduce distribution losses between the distribution feeder and the customer site. Dynamic voltage management (DVM) algorithms reduce energy consumption by changing processor speed and voltage at run time depending on the needs of the applications running and Dynamic power management (DPM) policies trade off the performance for the power consumption by selectively placing components into low-power states [24].

3.2 Peak Load Management: Direct Load Control

One approach in residential load management is direct load control (DLC) [25]–[28]. In DLC programs, based on an agreement between the utility company and the customers, the utility or an aggregator, which is managed by the utility, can remotely control the operations and energy consumption of certain appliances in a household. Authors of [29] have made a good survey of the literature on LM techniques for direct load control, communication systems and economic evaluation. Reed et al [30] have demonstrated the techniques used to monitor load control by high speed monitoring equipment. Author of [31] presented DLC for agricultural pumps and commercial air conditioners.

Backer [32] introduced the DLC carried by the Pacific Gas and Electric Company. Author proposed classification of customers loads according to the size of load. Tools for evaluation of end-use monitoring DLC programs were described by Nancy et al. [33] namely as a duty cycle model (DCM) and demand side planning. During the last three decades, DLC programmes received much more attention from researchers than others. Most DLC programmes have been analysed from the supply side, offering schemes to achieve single or multiple objectives, such as minimising the system operation costs [34, 35], maximising the reduction of system peak load, maximising utility's profit [36], minimising system peak load [37] and minimising the discomfort caused to customers [38]. A method for scheduling the load control using dynamic programming is based on an analytical model of the load under control [39], which gives it the advantage of allowing any length of time for the control periods and any cycle rates.

3.3 Load management by price based demand response (PBDR)

The PBDR programmes are based on dynamic pricing rates in which the electricity tariffs are not flat. They are designed to lower system costs for utilities and bring down customer bills by offering high price during expensive hours and lower prices during inexpensive hours. According to reference [39], the rates include Time of Use (TOU), Critical Peak Pricing (CPP), Extreme Day Pricing (EDP), Extreme Day CPP (ED-CPP), and Real Time Pricing (RTP). CPP rate contains a pre-specified higher electricity price superimposed on TOU rate or normal flat rate. Similar to CPP, EDP rate [32] has a higher price of electricity and differs from CPP in the fact that the price is in effect for the whole 24 hours of the extreme day, which is unknown until a day-ahead. ED-CPP rate [39] contains two types of rate, which are invoked under different conditions. During extreme days, the CPP rate is called for peak and off-peak periods. Whilst for other days, a flat rate is being used. RTP is hourly fluctuating prices reflecting the real cost of electricity in the wholesale market [40]. Customers are informed about the prices on a day-ahead or hour-ahead basis.

3.4 Open Automated Demand Response

Open Automated Demand Response (OpenADR) is a research and standards development effort for energy management led by North American research labs and companies. The typical use is to send information and signals to cause electrical power-using devices to be turned off during periods of high demand [41]. OpenADR is a family of specifications and standards driving progress in automated demand response. It provides an open and standardized way for electricity providers and system operators to communicate demand response signals with each other and with their customers using a common language over any existing IP-based communication network, such as Internet. As the most comprehensive standard for automated demand response, OpenADR has achieved widespread support throughout the industry [42]. Automated demand response connects utility needs with customers' resources and is a win-win for both parties. Peak loads are being shaved, grid reliability is being enhanced, the share of renewable generation footprints is increasing, and utility costs are dropping, and customers-commercial, industrial and residential-are seeing reductions in cost as well. Meanwhile, a comprehensive standard for ADR is rapidly gaining popularity.

3.5 nPlug: Peak load controller

nPlug is situated between the wall socket and shift-able loads (for example, water warmers, clothes washers, PHEV and iron etc. nPlugs combine local sensing and analytics to infer peak periods as well as supply demand imbalance conditions. They schedule these appliances in a manner such that to reduce peak load whenever possible without disturbing the requirements of consumers. Although cellular communication is inexpensive in India, existing infrastructure will need a capacity upgrade to support household appliances as well. An Internet based solution may not be widely applicable as only 11.3% of Indian households have access to Internet [43]. nPlugs do not require any manual intervention by the end consumer nor any communication infrastructure nor any enhancements to the appliances or the power grids [44]. Ganu et al [44] presented a decentralized DSM system based on smart plugs called nPlugs that sit between deferrable loads and wall sockets. An nPlug senses line voltage and frequency to infer the load level and supply-demand imbalance in the grid respectively.

4. DSM programs in Indian perspective

The Ministry of Power (MoP) is the nodal agency for energy conservation in the country. The Bureau of Energy Efficiency (BEE), an autonomous body under the MoP, was set up in 1989 to coordinate initiatives and activities on energy conservation. There are various agencies which are responsible for undertaking energy conservation activities in the country. In line with the ECAct2001, BEE has initiated various schemes for promoting energy efficiency in India. The schemes of BEE include Standard and Labeling programme (S&L), Energy Conservation and Building Code (ECBC), Bachat Lamp Yojana (BLY), Agriculture DSM and Perform, Achieve and Trade (PAT)[45].

4.1 Case study 1- Maharashtra State Electricity Distribution Company Ltd (MSEDCL)

Replacement of 5000 Old Ceiling Fans by 5-Star Rated Ceiling Fans [46].

- Old 1200 mm and above ceiling fans with over 7 years vintage typically have a power consumption of approximately 80 watts.
- While the 5 Star ceiling fans consume only 50 Watts of energy which is 30% less than the conventional ceiling fans.
- Reduced costly power purchase will reduce overall tariffs of substation.
- Further the pilot aims for annual saving of 0.30 MUs at user end and expected 125 kW demand savings.
- EE Fan Cost: Rs. 1135 per fan
- MSEDCL Potential Money saving : utility perspective: Rs.575/ year/fan (pay back < 2 years)

Some more DSM initiatives by MSEDCL are as listed in [47]:

- Akshya Prakash Yojana (APY): This is a scheme under which a village (Goathan) can avoid load shedding in the evening by reducing the load voluntarily to 20% of the existing load.
- Single Phase Supply in Villages: Main suffering of the public due to load shedding is in the evening hours. In order that at least basic lighting is available in the households, single phase transformers are being fixed in village.
- Municipal Water Pumping Scheme: encouraging efficient pump system operation during off peak hours to help reduce peak demand and energy demand.

Outcomes:

- Energy efficient fans result in 25 watts saving & 11 hrs/day use, results in 0.4 M kWh reductions.
- Till date about 5,548 villages and 5 towns have been covered leading to 1,260MW of load relief through APY.
- These villages are now free from planned load shedding of 14 hours. They now receive 21 hours of uninterrupted power supply.
- MSEDCL has contributed to reduction of the Maharashtra system demand by 1260 MW in the system demand over 14700 MW and thereby improving the power situation in the state [47].

4.2 Case study 2- BESCOM efficient Light Program (BELP)

For the first time in India, BESCOM started DSM activity on 05.11.2007. International Institute for Energy Conservation (IIEC), Washington was consultants for BESCOM. It was based on replacement of incandescent bulbs by Compact Fluorescent Lights (CFLs) [48].

- Goal: To promote efficient lighting among Indian domestic consumers by facilitating removal of price and quality barriers.
- Program targeted design of utility-driven CFL branding exercise in India with potential replication.
- Technology used: Lighting retrofit- replacing 300,000 incandescent lamps with CFLs.
- Investment cost: BESCOM invested in this program around Rs. 1.5 million
- Demand savings: 13.5 MW
- Energy savings: 24.3 Million Units
- Cost savings: Rs. 0.7 million

Outcomes:

- It was estimated that about 1.81 Lakhs additional CFLs were sold during the scheme implementation.
- About 100% increase in sales of CFLs was observed compares to the previous year which resulted in reduction in residential demand to an extent of 10.46MWs.
- This Pilot Project encouraged in formulation of Bachat Lamp Yojana in the country. It enforced manufacturers to give one year warranty to the customers. This scheme lead to regulation stipulating a minimum power factor of 0.85 for CFLs.

4.3 Case study 3: JUSCO Tata steel authority

- Light Emitting Diodes (LED), the technology has been around for a while, but the strongest associations were with television or a laptop and mobile screen.
- The newly installed LED lights did not emit any heat which led to a reduction in air-conditioning loads.
- LED lights are expected to last 5-10 times longer than the usual CFL lights.
- This not only reduced the replacement costs of tube lights by 80% but also reduced the associated manpower costs by 70%.
- Jamshedpur Utilities and Services Company (JUSCO) is India's only comprehensive urban infrastructure service provider [49].
- Recognizing the advantages that LED street lighting can offer in terms of lower operating and energy costs coupled with low vertical light distribution and better colour rendering qualities, JUSCO decided to upgrade their street lighting from conventional sources to energy efficient LED lighting and started the 'Green City' initiative.
- In place of the existing 250 w high pressure sodium vapour lamp (HPSV) conventional light source, JUSCO upgraded 400 No's of 130 W LED Street Lights.

Outcomes:

- With innovative Technology being used by GE for manufacturing LED, it brings down the energy consumption by over 54% as compared to conventional lights.
- It is estimated that almost 20% of a town's electricity consumption can be attributed to street lighting.
- Hence this is a great energy saver which is of national interest.

4.4 SELCO India

Solar Electricity Light Company (SELCO) India makes solar lighting technology accessible to the economically impoverished people in India. Most of India's rural population does not have access to electricity. However, given an average rural income of less than US$50 per month, upfront investment in solar lighting, ranging from US$200 to US$500, can be expensive. To remove this barrier, SELCO made sustained efforts to persuade state-owned rural banks to lend money to households so that they can make the purchase. They worked extensively with these state-owned banks to ensure that the repayment pattern matched the cash flow that would be generated as a result of the additional income facilitated by the purchase of solar lights [50]. Over 14 years, SELCO has established 21 energy service centers across Karnataka and Gujarat and is mobilized by a workforce of 140 employees catering to more than 1,00,000 customers[51].

Founder of SELCO India, Harish found that solar lights were not novel in rural India. Almost every year in the month of March, Indian government would install solar-powered street lights to utilize funds devoted to non-conventional energy. However, very little effort was subsequently put in for proper maintenance of these lights. By the time, many of the lights would stop functioning, thereby creating a perception among villagers that solar lights were fragile and unlikely to function for more than three to four months. Harish thus realized that he would have to change this negative perception about solar technology and decided to take the responsibility of maintaining some of the solar street lights in rural Karnataka [50]. He also trained some of the local villagers, typically those involved in television or cycle repair, on how to maintain these lights. For this, he started creating a pool of technicians who could take on the responsibility of maintaining and repairing solar lights as and when SELCO would install them in future.

Outcomes:

Till date, SELCO has sold solar lighting to more than 110,000 rural homes and to 4,000 institutions such as orphanages, clinics, seminaries and schools in the Indian state of Karnataka. An impact assessment study by World Resources Institute in 2007 [52] reported that 86% of SELCO's poor customers cited significant savings in energy costs as their primary benefit of using SELCO products, while the rest pointed to their children's education as the primary benefit. Being a non-polluting source of energy, solar lights contribute to environmental benefits as and when they replace other energy sources such as firewood and kerosene [50]. Moreover, SELCO's inclusive business model has led to the creation of employment not only for its own employees but also for several rural entrepreneurs who rent out solar lights to vendors and institutions.

4.5 Global DSM Programs and Lessons Learned for India

In different parts of the world there have been implemented a large number of DSM programs. A brief review from some of international experience has been undertaken to understand the different approaches being adopted to implement DSM Models in different countries. Table 1 briefly compares the global DSM programs in various countries and also suggests the lessons that can be learnt by India for large scale implementation of DSM program in India.

Table 1. Global DSM programs and lessons learnt for India

Country	Responsible Agency	Reasons for Success	Barriers and Lessons Learnt for India
New York Model	• Programme administered by New York State Energy Research and Development Agency (NYSERDA) and investor owned utilities. • The New York Public Service Commission issued EE portfolio standard (EEPS) under which several EE schemes have been implemented [54].	• One of the reasons for the successful implementation of EE programs was the creation of adequate funds through the levy of tariff surcharge in terms of the 'system benefit charge'.	• In India, the government already levies electricity duty; but in most cases this fund is not transferred to state due to weak financial situation of utilities or is adjusted against the electricity subsidies with no real outflow of such funds. • The DSM Program model cannot be entirely dependent on the resource constrained government owned utility for implementation.
Guangdong Model (China)	• Implementing agency for model is an existing or newly created government agency which is responsible for administering the programme [55].	• EE programs have been dependent upon the availability of funds from large development banks such as ADB.	• Access to such resources may or may not be available in India. • Promotion of private sector participation and ESCOs will be a key to garnering funds and other resources for effective implementation.
Hebei Model (China)	• Joint venture (JV) or a special purpose vehicle (SPV) between a government-created public sector agency (super ESCO) and a private sector partner to take on the implementation responsibility for implementation of the DSM Power Plant projects [55].	• This model provides for public private partner-ship and combines the strengths and capabilities of the public and private partners through the creation of super ESCO.	• In case of India, Energy Efficiency Services Ltd. (EESL) a super ESCO has already been created by GoI but the adequate utilization of the strength of a super ESCO to attract private sector investments for DSM implementation has not been initiated.

5. CONCLUSION

In this paper, techniques of demand side management have been reviewed. This review gave an assessment of current methods of managing loads. These methods were developed on the supply side and implemented on the demand side, aiming at a reduction of system peak demand and improving the reliability of power supply. Load management initiated by customers was based on implementation of strategies that lead to reduction of electrical energy consumption. With limited generation capacity, some form of DSM Strategy or technology is required to maintain reliable electricity service and ensure equitable sharing of the resource among users. Foremost, the use of efficient appliances can greatly improve the overall efficiency of the system. By both encouraging conservation and reducing peak loads, these measures can allow an existing grid to serve more households and reduce the required initial investment in generation and distribution capacity for a new grid.

The paper has given a brief introduction to the demand response programmes reported in the literature. It is observed that DR can play a major role in the smart grid implementations and the end-consumer participation in the energy management can be promoted by the means of DR programmes. The design of DR programmes is dependent on the prevailing market conditions of a particular region.

The paper also reviewed some case studies based on Indian perspective. Though there is a limited experience with DSM in India, demand management has an enormous potential which is yet to be tapped. Innovative concepts of managing demand are yet to be tried out in the various sectors. For a country where the agricultural load dominates consumption, such measures can deliver significant benefits.

6. REFERENCES

[1] Peter Palensky, Dietmar Dietrich, 20011, Demand Side Management: Demand Response, Intelligent Energy Systems, and Smart Loads. *IEEE Trans. on Ind. Informatics*, vol. 7, no. 3(Aug. 2011), 381-388

[2] Gellings C. W, 1981, Demand-side load management, *IEEE Spectrum*, vol. 18(Dec. 1981) 49-52.

[3] Nandkishor Kinhekar, Narayana Prasad Padhy, Hari Om Gupta, 2014, *Multiobjective demand side management solutions for utilities with peak demand deficit, Electrical Power System*, vol. 55, 612-619.

[4] Thillainathan Logenthiran, Dipti Srinivasan, and Tan Zong Shun, 2012, Demand,Side Management in Smart Grid Using Heuristic Optimization, *IEEE Trans. on Smart Grid*, vol. 3, no. 3(Sep. 2012) 1244-1252.

[5] Peter Warren, 2014, *A review of demand-side management policy in the UK, Renewable and Sustainable Energy Reviews*, vol. 29, 941–951.

[6] Afua Mohamed, Mohamed Tariq Khan,2009, A review of electrical energy management techniques: supply and consumer side (industries), *Journal of Energy in Southern Africa*, Vol. 20, No. 3(Aug. 2009), 14-21.

[7] Boshell F., Veloza O.P., 2008, Review of Developed Demand Side Management Programs Including Different Concepts and their Results, *IEEE transaction on Transmission and Distribution*, 1-7.

[8] Boshell F, Veloza O, 2008, Review of developed demand side management programs including different concepts and their results, *in Proc. IEEE Transmission and Distrib. Conf. Expo. Latin America*, PES, 1–7.

[9] Horace Herring, 2006, *Energy efficiency-a critical view, Energy*, vol. 31, no. 1.

[10] *Report of Sustainable Energy Regulation and Policymaking for Africa on Demand Side Management.* http://africa-toolkit.reeep.org/modules/Module14.pdf

[11] Prüggler N, Prüggler W, Wirl F.,2011, Storage and Demand Side Management as power generator's strategic instruments to influence demand and prices, *Energy*, Vol. 36, 6308–6317.

[12] Gellings CW, Chamberlin JH., 1993, *Demand-side management: concepts and methods, in 2nd ed. USA: The Fairmont Press.*

[13] *DOE Report on Benefits of demand response,* 2006. DOI= http://westvirginia.sierraclub.org/.

[14] Albert Chiu, Ali Ipakchi, Angela Chuang, Bin Qiu, Brent Hodges, Dick Brooks, 2009, *Frame work for integrated demand response(DR) and distributed energy resources (DER) models*. DOI= http://www.neopanora.com/.

[15] National action plan on demand response, 2010, *The federal energy regulatory commission*.

[16] Jamshid Aghaei, Mohammad-Iman Alizadeh, 2013, Demand response in smart electricity grids equipped with renewable energy sources: *A review, Renewable and Sustainable Energy Reviews*, vol. 18, 64–72.

[17] International Energy Agency, 2003, *The Power to Choose—Demand Response in Liberalized Electricity Markets, OECD, Paris*.

[18] Albadi MH, El-Saadany E F, 2008, A summary of demand response in electricity markets, *Electric Power Systems Research*, vol. 78, 1989–1996.

[19] US Department of Energy, Benefits of Demand Response, *Report to the United States Congress*, February 2006. DOI= http://eetd.lbl.gov/.

[20] Albadi MH, 2007, Demand response in electricity markets: an overview, *in IEEE PES GM, Montreal*,1–5.

[21] V. S. K. Murthy Balijepalli, Vedanta Pradhan, S. A. Khaparde, and R. M. Shereef, 2011, Review of Demand Response under Smart Grid Paradigm, *in IEEE PES Innovative Smart Grid Technologies – India*.

[22] Behrangrad M, Sugihara H, Funaki T, 2010, Analysing the system effects of optimal demand response utilization for reserve procurement and peak clipping, *in Proc. of IEEE Power and Energy Society General Meeting*, 1-7.

[23] Faria P, Vale Z, Soares J, Ferreira J, 2011, Demand response management in power systems using a particle swarm optimization approach, *IEEE Intelligent System*, no. 99(Apr 2011), 1-9.

[24] Simunic T, Benini L, Acquaviva A, Glynn P, De Micheli G, 2001, Dynamic voltage scaling and power management for portable systems, *in Proc. of IEEE Design Automation Conference*, 524-529.

[25] N. Ruiz, I. Cobelo, and J. Oyarzabal, 2009, A direct load control model for virtual power plant management, *IEEE Trans. Power Syst.*, no. 2(May 2009), 959–966.

[26] A. Gomes, C. H. Antunes, and A. G. Martins, 2007, A multiple objective approach to direct load control using an interactive evolutionary algorithm, *IEEE Trans. Power Syst.*, no. 3(Aug. 2007), 1004–1011.

[27] D. D. Weers and M. A. Shamsedin, 1987, Testing a new direct load control power line communication system, *IEEE Trans. Power Del.*, no. 3(July 1987), 657–660.

[28] C. M. Chu, T. L. Jong, and Y. W. Huang, 2005, A direct load control of air-conditioning loads with thermal comfort control, in *Proc. IEEE PES Gen. Meet.*, San Francisco, CA.

[29] Morgan G.M., and Talukdar, N.S., 1979, Electric Power Load Management, Some Technical, Regulatory and Social Issues, *IEEE proceedings*, Vol.67, No. 2(Feb 1979), 241-313.

[30] Reed H.J, Nelson R.W, Wetherington R.G, Broadaway R.E., 1980, Monitoring Load Control at the Feeder Level Using High Speed Monitoring Equipment, *IEEE Trans. Power Delivery*, No.1, 694-703.

[31] Banerjee R, 1998, *Load management in the Indian power sector using US experience*, *Energy*, Vol.23, No. 11, 961-972.

[32] Backer D. L, 1986, Load Management direct control fact or simulation, *IEEE transaction on Power system*, Vol. 1, No. 1, 82-88.

[33] Nancy E. Ryan, John T. Power, 1989, Generalizing direct load program analysis: Implementation of the duty cycle approach, *IEEE transactions on power systems*, Vol. 4, No. 1, 293-299.

[34] Chen J., Lee F. N., Breipohl A. M., and Adapa R., 1995, Scheduling direct load control to minimize system operational cost, *IEEE Transactions on Power Systems*, vol. 10, no. 4, 1994-2001.

[35] Hsu Y. Y. and Su, C. C., 1991, Dispatch of direct load control using dynamic programming, *IEEE Transactions on Power Systems*, vol. 6, no. 3, 1056-1061.

[36] Ng, K. H. and Sheble, G. B. 1998, Direct load control-A profit-based load management using linear programming, *IEEE Transactions on Power Systems*, vol. 13, no. 2, 688-694.

[37] Cohen, A. I. and Wang, C. C., 1998, An optimization method for load management scheduling, *IEEE Transactions on Power Systems*, vol. 3, no. 2, 612-618.

[38] Bhattacharya, K. and Crow, M. L., 1996, Fuzzy logic based approach to direct load control, *IEEE Transactions on Power Systems*, vol. 11, no. 2, 708-714.

[39] Charles River Associates, 2005, Primer on "Demand-Side Management with an Emphasis on Price-Responsive Programs," *Report prepared for The World Bank, Washington, DC, CRA*, No. D06090. DOI= http://www.worldbank.org/

[40] Moholkar A, Klinkhachorn P, and Feliachi A, 2004, Effects of dynamic pricing on residential electricity bill, *IEEE Power systems conference and exposition*, vol. 2, 1030–1035.

[41] http://newscenter.lbl.gov/press-releases/2009/04

[42] K. Edward, S. Tariq, 2013, Power Industry is Embracing Automated Demand Response Standard, *IEEE PES. Smart Grid.*

[43] Juxt Consulting. Internet usage behavior & preferences of indians. http://www.juxtconsult.com/, 2011.

[44] T. Ganu, D. P. Seetharam, V. Arya. J. Hazra, D. Sinha, R. Kunnath, L. C. De Silva, Saiful A. Husain, S. Kalyanaraman,2013, nPlug: An Autonomous Peak Load Controller, IEEE Journal on Selected Areas In Communications, no. 7.

[45] Gupta S., Bhattacharya T., 2013, DSM Power Plants in India, Renewable and Sustainable Energy Reviews, 1-11.

[46] DOI=http://www.mahadiscom.in/DSM%20Activities%20in%20MSEDCLJan14.pdf

[47] Sonavane V. L, Vaishnav R., 2008, DSM Initiatives – A Case Study from Maharashtra, IEEE, 1-4.

[48] DOI= https://cp.tatapower.com/CP_HINDI/save-energy/pdf/bescom.pdf

[49] DOI=http://www.gelighting.com/LightingWeb/ind/images/JUSCO_tcm288-87982.pdf

[50] S. Mukharji, SELCO: Solar Lighting for Poor, case study.

[51] DOI= http://www.selco-india.com.

[52] N. M. Koppa, S. Willoughby, 2007, Base of Pyramid Impact Assessment, World Resource Institute.

[54] http://www.ieadsm.org/Files/AdminUpload/(1)RAP_IEADSM%20Best%20Practices%20in%20Designing%20and%20Implementing%20Energy%20Efficiency%20Obligation%20Schemes%202012 %20June(6).pdfS.

[55] Developing the energy efficient power plant: Policy and Regulatory initiatives, USAID, 2012.

Operating Power Grids with Few Flow Control Buses*

Thomas Leibfried[1] Tamara Mchedlidze[2] Nico Meyer-Hübner[1]
Martin Nöllenburg[2] Ignaz Rutter[2] Peter Sanders[2]
Dorothea Wagner[2] Franziska Wegner[2†]

[1] Institute of Energy Systems and High Voltage Technology / [2] Institute of Theoretical Informatics
Karlsruhe Institute of Technology, Karlsruhe, Germany
firstname.lastname@kit.edu

ABSTRACT

Future power grids will offer enhanced controllability due to the increased availability of power flow control units (FACTS). As the installation of control units in the grid is an expensive investment, we are interested in using few controllers to achieve high controllability. In particular, two questions arise: How many flow control buses are necessary to obtain best possible power flows? And if fewer flow control buses are available, what can we achieve with them?

Using steady state IEEE benchmark data sets, we explore experimentally that already a small number of controllers placed at certain grid buses suffices to achieve best possible power flows. We present a graph-theoretic explanation for this behavior. To answer the second question we perform a set of experiments that explore the existence and costs of feasible power flow solutions at increased loads with respect to the number of flow control buses in the grid. We observe that adding a small number of flow control buses reduces the flow costs and extends the existence of feasible solutions at increased load.

Categories and Subject Descriptors

G.2.2 [**Discrete Mathematics**]: Graph Theory; G.2.3 [**Discrete Mathematics**]: Applications; J.2 [**Computer Applications**]: Physical Sciences and Engineering—*Engineering*

General Terms

Experimentation, Theory

Keywords

Hybrid Power Flow Model, FACTS, Transmission Network Control

†Corresponding author

*This work was funded (in part) by the Helmholtz Program Storage and Cross-linked Infrastructures, Topic 6 Superconductivity, Networks and System Integration.

e-Energy'15, July 14–17, 2015, Bangalore, India.

DOI: http://dx.doi.org/10.1145/2768510.2768521.

1. INTRODUCTION

The central task of any electrical power infrastructure is the reliable and cost-efficient supply of electrical energy to industry and population on a national or even continental scale. Future power grids and their usage are subject to fundamental changes due to the shift towards renewable distributed energy production and the installation of new power flow control units, which offer increased control, but make the grid operation more demanding. Not only do these changes lead to a much larger number of independent power producers (IPP), which are highly distributed in the network, but they also cause very different patterns of energy flow. For example, regions with off-shore wind farms may sometimes produce enough energy to supply remote consumers, but at other times they are consumers themselves. In particular, this may require long-distance energy transmission and frequent flow direction changes. Most of the existing power grids, however, were not designed for such transmission patterns. The current strategy to cope with these changes is to either extend the grid with additional transmission lines, or to install advanced control units to facilitate better utilization of the existing infrastructure.

We consider the latter option and study the effects of making selected buses of a power grid controllable. We investigate both the minimum number of controllable buses needed for achieving maximum flow control and the effect of a fixed number of controlled buses on the operation costs and the existence of feasible power flows at critical line loads.

In abstract terms, we assume that a *flow-control bus* is able to flexibly distribute the entire power flow at this bus among the incident edges, as long as Kirchhoff's current law (or the *flow-conservation property*) is satisfied, i.e., the inflow to the bus equals its out-flow. These flow control buses can be realized using power electronics devices known as *flexible AC transmission systems* (FACTS), which are a class of power systems that have the capabilities to control various electrical bus parameters [11]. More specifically, since we are interested in controlling the real power flow on the branches incident to a particular bus, we can realize our flow control buses by installing on each (but one) incident branch a *unified power flow controller* (UPFC), which is a FACTS that is able to control the voltage magnitude and angle and consequently has control of the real and reactive power flow on the particular branch [15].

One of the most important tasks in operating a power grid is to decide the energy production of each power generator such that supply and consumption are balanced and the resulting power flow does not exceed the thermal limits of the power lines. Among all solutions we are interested in one that minimizes the total cost of energy production and transmission. This is called *Economic Dispatch Problem* (EDP). The main approach for solving this problem in power grids without FACTS is the optimal power flow (OPF) method, a numerical method that was introduced in 1962 by Carpentier [4] and has subsequently been refined and generalized, see the recent surveys by Frank et al. [6,7]. However, OPF is not designed for hybrid power grids with flow control buses and cannot exploit the extended flow control possibilities to improve solutions.

Hence, we propose in Section 3 a new hybrid DC-based model for power flows in power grids that combine traditional grid buses with some flow control buses. In order to answer our questions on the effects of installing flow control buses, we solve the EDP in our hybrid model using a linear programming (LP) formulation. Our LP combines a standard graph-theoretical network flow model, which already includes Kirchhoff's current law at all buses, with additional constraints for Kirchhoff's voltage law in those parts of the grid that are not equipped with flow control buses. Thus we are able to obtain electrically feasible power flows that minimize, similarly to OPF, the overall flow costs in terms of generation and transmission costs.

Using the well-known IEEE power systems test cases, we performed simulation experiments related to two key questions, which take into account that the FACTS needed for realizing our flow control buses in reality constitute a significant and expensive investment and hence their number should be as small as possible.

1. How many flow control buses are necessary to obtain globally optimal power flows and which buses need to be controlled?
2. If the number of available flow control buses is given, do we still see a positive effect on the flow costs and on the operability of the grid when approaching its capacity limits?

In Section 4 we address the first question. In our experiments we determine the minimum number of flow control buses necessary to achieve the same solution quality as in a power grid in which each bus is controllable and which clearly provides an upper bound on what can be achieved with the network topology. Interestingly, it turns out that a relatively small number of flow control buses are sufficient for this. In fact, we can prove a theorem stating a structural graph-theoretic property, which, if met by the placement of flow control buses, implies the optimality of the power flow and serves as a theoretical explanation of the observed behavior. Section 5 deals with the second question of operating a power grid close to its capacity limits, which becomes increasingly relevant as the consumption of electrical energy grows faster than the grid capacities. Our experiments indicate that installing few flow control buses in a power grid is sufficient not only to achieve lower costs compared to an OPF solution, but also allows to operate the grid at capacities for which no feasible OPF solution exists any more.

Due to space restrictions we refer to the full paper [13] for omitted details.

2. RELATED WORK

With the increasing availability and technological advancement of FACTS researchers began to study the possible benefits of their installation in power grids from different perspectives.

From an economic perspective, it is of interest to support investment decisions in power grid expansion planning by considering alternative investment strategies that either focus on new transmission lines or allow mixed approaches including FACTS placement [2,19].

From the perspective of operating a power grid, the main question is how many and where FACTS should be placed in order to optimize a certain criterion, where Cai et al. [3] and Gerbex et al. [8] evaluate a genetic algorithm, and Ongsakul and Jirapong [16] use evolutionary programming. In contrast to these heuristic approaches Lima et al. [14] use mixed-integer linear programming to optimally increase the loadability of a system by placing FACTS subject to limits on their number or cost. Similar to our approach, they do not distinguish different types of FACTS but rather assume "ideal" FACTS that can control all transmission parameters of a branch. In contrast to our work, they focus only on loadability and do not consider generation costs and line losses.

All related work mentioned so far considers the DC model for electrical networks as an approximation to the AC model and aims at providing a preliminary step in an actual planning process, where this approximation is sufficient. There are also a few attempts to solve the placement problem for FACTS in the more realistic but also more complicated AC model. Sharma et al. [18] develop an evaluation whether transmission lines are critical and propose to place FACTS at critical lines in order to improve voltage stability in the grid. Ippolito and Siano [12] present a genetic algorithm for FACTS placement in AC networks and experimentally evaluate it in a case study. In contrast to these heuristic approaches, Farivar and Low [5] consider exact OPF evaluation in a relaxed AC-model. In this context, they place phase shifters to exploit structural characteristics that are similar to our approach.

3. MODEL

In this section we introduce three graph-theoretic flow models for optimal power flows. Our models are based on the DC power grid model [21], which is commonly used as an approximation of AC grids [17]. We model a power grid as a graph $G = (V, E)$, where V is the set of vertices and $E \subseteq \binom{V}{2}$ is the set of edges. The vertices represent the buses, some of which may be generator and consumer buses, and the edges represent the branches, which may be transmission lines between the incident buses or transformers. By $V_G \subseteq V$ we denote the set of generator buses. Each generator $g \in V_G$ has a maximum supply $x_g \in \mathbb{R}^+$ and is equipped with a convex cost function $\gamma_g > 0$ that is assumed to be piecewise linear with

$$\gamma_g(x) = \max\{a_i x + c_i \mid (a_i, c_i) \in F_g\}, \qquad (1)$$

where F_g is the set of all piecewise linear functions of γ_g and $a_i \leq a_{i+1}$. Further, by $V_C \subseteq V \setminus V_G$ we denote the set of consumer buses. Each consumer $u \in V_C$ has a power demand $d_u \in \mathbb{R}$.

Each branch $e \in E$ has a thermal limit, which is modeled as a capacity function $c\colon E \to \mathbb{R}$ restricting the real power. Further, each branch causes a certain loss of power depending on the physical branch parameters and the actual power flow on the branch. These losses are again approximated as a convex, piecewise linear function ℓ_e for each edge $e \in E$ with

$$\ell_e(x) = \max\{a_i x + c_i \mid (a_i, c_i) \in F_e\}, \quad (2)$$

where F_e is the set of all piecewise linear functions of ℓ_e and $a_i \leq a_{i+1}$.

A *flow* f in the power grid G is a function $f\colon V \times V \to \mathbb{R}$ with the property that

$$f(u, v) = -f(v, u) \quad \forall u, v \in V. \quad (3)$$

For every vertex u in G, we define its *net out-flow* $f_{\text{net}}(u) = \sum_{\{u,v\}\in E} f(u, v)$. For a flow f, we further define two types of costs, the *generator costs* $c_g(f) = \sum_{g\in V_G} \gamma_g(f_{\text{net}}(g))$ and the *line losses* $c_\ell(f) = \sum_{\{u,v\}\in E} \ell_{\{u,v\}}(|f(u, v)|)$. To obtain the overall cost for the flow f, we weight these two terms as

$$c_\lambda(f) = \lambda \cdot c_g(f) + (1 - \lambda) \cdot c_\ell(f), \quad (4)$$

where $\lambda \in [0, 1]$. Our goal is to minimize this objective function in several different power flow models.

3.1 Power Flow Models

The most basic model is the *flow model*, where f has to satisfy the following constraints.

$$-c(e) \leq f(u, v) \leq c(e) \qquad \forall e = \{u, v\} \in E \quad (5)$$

$$f_{\text{net}}(v) = 0 \qquad v \in V \setminus (V_G \cup V_C) \quad (6)$$

$$f_{\text{net}}(v) = -d_v \qquad v \in V_C \quad (7)$$

$$0 \leq f_{\text{net}}(v) \leq x_v \qquad v \in V_G \quad (8)$$

We call a flow satisfying these constraints *feasible*. Equation (5) models the thermal limits or real power capacities of all branches and is called *capacity constraint*. Equation (6) models that vertices that are neither generators nor consumers have zero net out-flow and is called *flow conservation constraint*. Equation (7) models that all consumer demands are satisfied and is called *consumer constraint*. Finally, Equation (8) models that all generators respect their production limits and is called *generator constraint*.

The flow model neglects some physical properties of electrical flows, in particular Kirchhoff's voltage law. Thus, the computed power flows can only be applied to power grids where every vertex is a flow control bus (FCB). In contrast, the *electrical flow model*, e.g., according to Zimmerman et al. [21], models the power flow via the same set of constraints as the flow model, but additionally requires the existence of a suitable voltage angle assignment $\Theta\colon V \to \mathbb{R}$ such that for each branch $\{u, v\}$ the following equation holds

$$f(u, v) = B(u, v)(\Theta(u) - \Theta(v)). \quad (9)$$

Here $B(u, v)$ is the *susceptance* of the branch (u, v). This is equivalent to restricting the model to feasible flows that also satisfy Kirchhoff's voltage law, or, in other words, no FCBs are used. This yields a model that matches the situation in the traditional power grids existing today. We call a feasible flow f *electrically feasible* if there exists a voltage angle assignment Θ satisfying (9).

Recall from the introduction that FCBs can be technically realized by UPFCs, which is a FACTS. Ideal FACTS as introduced by Griffin et al. [10] are often used to simplify the modeling of FACTS by using a linear model and assuming a complete and independent control of the real and reactive power. Our FCBs are ideal FACTS that control the power flow to all incident edges. The flow model—in contrast to the electrical model—assumes FCBs at each vertex, whereas the electrical model assumes no immediate control of the power flow. Instead, the grid is balanced by changing the generator outputs only. In the following we propose a *hybrid model* that combines the flow model and the electrical flow model in order to handle power grids with FCBs at a subset of selected vertices.

case	nb	nl	ng	p_d
case6	6	11	3	210.00
case9	9	9	3	315.00
case14	14	20	5	259.00
case30	30	41	6	189.20
case39	39	46	10	6254.23
case57	57	78	7	1250.80
case118	118	179	54	4242.00

Table 1: IEEE benchmark set with nb, nl, ng and p_d representing number of buses, number of transmission lines, number of generators and total power demand, respectively.

Let $F \subseteq V$ be a subset of vertices of G. We denote by G_F the power grid obtained from G by considering all vertices in F as FCBs. We call any subgraph $G' = G[V']$ induced by a subset $V' \subseteq V \setminus F$ of the vertices without controllers a *native power grid* of G. A flow of G is *electrically feasible* for a native power grid $G' \subseteq G$ if there exists a voltage angle assignment $\Theta\colon E \to \mathbb{R}$ such that every edge in G' satisfies Equation (9). In this case we call Θ *feasible (voltage) angle assignment* for G'.

A feasible flow f is *electrically feasible for* G_F if and only if f is electrically feasible for the *maximal native power grid* $G - F = G[V \setminus F]$. Intuitively, this models the fact that a power flow in G_F must be a feasible flow and that it satisfies the second Kirchhoff law in the maximum native power grid.

Obviously, if $F \subseteq F'$ and f is an electrically feasible flow for G_F, then f is also electrically feasible for $G_{F'}$. Hence the minimum value of the cost c_λ does not increase when adding more FCBs.

We note that each of the models can easily be expressed as a linear program (LP), and thus in all three models an optimal solution can be computed efficiently [1]. However, the flow model can be reduced to a special minimum cost network flow problem, for which efficient exact optimization algorithms exist [9].

4. PLACING FLOW CONTROL BUSES

In this section we seek to answer the question of how many FCBs are necessary to obtain a globally optimal solution. Recall that the flow model is a relaxation of the physical model and uses fewer constraints. Therefore, optimal solutions in the flow model are at least as good as in the physical model. Given a power grid $G = (V, E)$, we say that making the vertices in F FCBs achieves *full control* if the objective value of an optimal power flow for the grid G_F is the same as the objective value of an optimal solution in the flow model (or equivalently in the hybrid network G_V, where every vertex is an FCB). Our experiments indicate that in the IEEE instances often a small fraction of the vertices is sufficient to achieve full control. Afterwards we give a graph-theoretical explanation of this behavior.

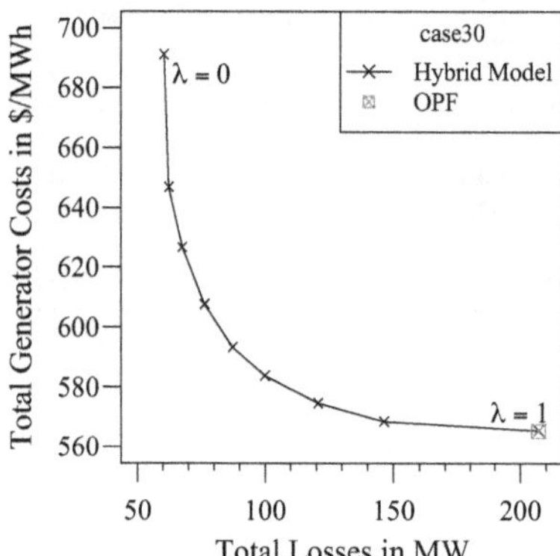

Figure 1: Trade-off of generator costs and losses depending as λ varies from 0 to 1. The square cross marks the solution computed by OPF.

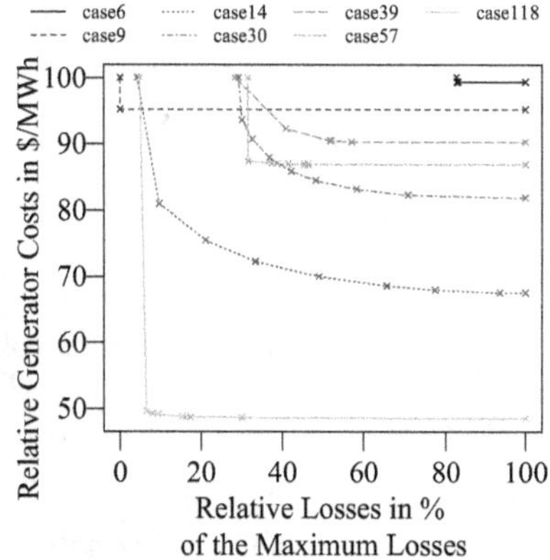

Figure 2: Trade-off of generator costs and losses normalized to the maximum generator cost ($\lambda = 0$) and the maximum loss ($\lambda = 1$) as λ varies from 0 to 1.

4.1 Experiments

For our evaluation we use the IEEE benchmark data sets[1] shown in Table 1. There each case is named accordingly to the number of buses *nb*. The number of generators and the number of edges are denoted by *ng* and *nl*, respectively.

To obtain piecewise linear functions for generator costs and line losses, we simply sample the cost functions using a specified number of sampling points. Note further that our approach requires convex cost functions, but this is fine in practice [20]; in particular the functions are convex for the IEEE benchmark instances.

We performed our experiments on an AMD Opteron processor 6172 running openSUSE 12.2. Our implementation is written in Python 2.7.3 and uses PYPOWER[2], a Python port of MATPOWER [21], for computing OPF solutions. For computing solutions and minimizing the number of FCBs in our hybrid model we use the (integer) linear programming solver Gurobi 6.0.0[3].

First, we observe that the value of λ, which controls the weighting of costs and losses in the objective value has a significant effect on the objective values of generator costs and line losses. Figure 1 shows the trade-off for the IEEE instance `case30`. The OPF solution, which ignores losses, is typically at the far end of the spectrum with high losses and is comparable to our solution with $\lambda = 1$. As can be seen in Figure 2, where the costs and losses are normalized to the maximum cost and the maximum loss per instance, the same trade-off behavior is present in all instances. It thus makes sense to allow the operator of a power grid to choose the value of λ in order to model the true operation costs.

[1]data sources `http://www.pserc.cornell.edu/matpower/` and `http://www.ee.washington.edu/research/pstca/`
[2]`https://pypi.python.org/pypi/PYPOWER/4.0.0`
[3]`www.gurobi.com`

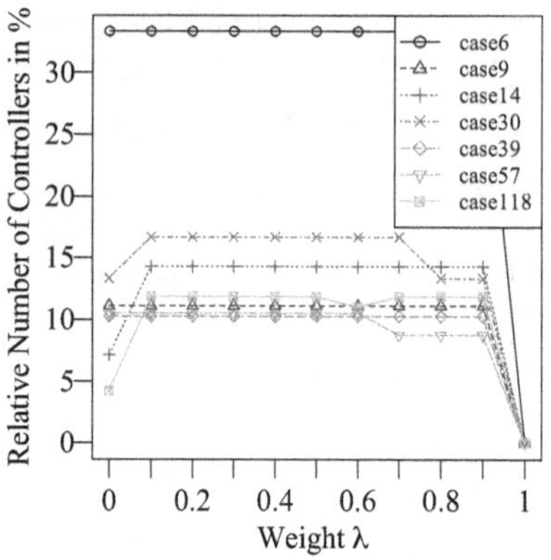

Figure 3: Relative number of controllers for achieving full control in the IEEE instances as λ varies from 0 to 1.

On the other hand, it may then be the case that the number of FCBs to achieve full control of the network varies depending on the choice of λ. Figure 3 shows the relative number of FCBs necessary to achieve full control in each of the instances for different values of λ. In most cases less than 15% of all buses need to be controllers to achieve full control. For the cases with 6 buses and 14 buses this percentage is slightly bigger, which is mainly an artifact stemming from the small total size. As can be seen, the required number of units is relatively stable but drops to zero for $\lambda = 1$, i.e., when only the generator costs are considered. This is due to the fact that all IEEE instances have basically unlimited line capacities and thus do not restrict the possible flows. In order to make a useful prediction on the number of vertices required for full control that applies to all choices of λ, in the following we take for each instance the maximum of the smallest possible number of vertices to achieve full control over all values of λ and refer to this as the number of vertices for achieving full control of the instance. This conservative choice ensures that the numbers we compute are certainly an upper bound for achieving full control, independent of the actual choice of λ.

4.2 Structure of Optimal Solutions

As we have seen in our experimental evaluation, often a small number of FCBs is sufficient to ensure that solutions in the hybrid model are the same as in the flow model. In the following we provide a theoretical explanation of this property and link it to structural properties of power grids. Farivar and Low [5] give similar structural results on spanning trees, but using a different model.

A first observation is that FCBs influence all incident edges. Thus, if every edge is incident to an FCB, i.e., the set F is a *vertex cover* of G, no edge in the network is affected by constraint (9). Then the flow model and the hybrid model

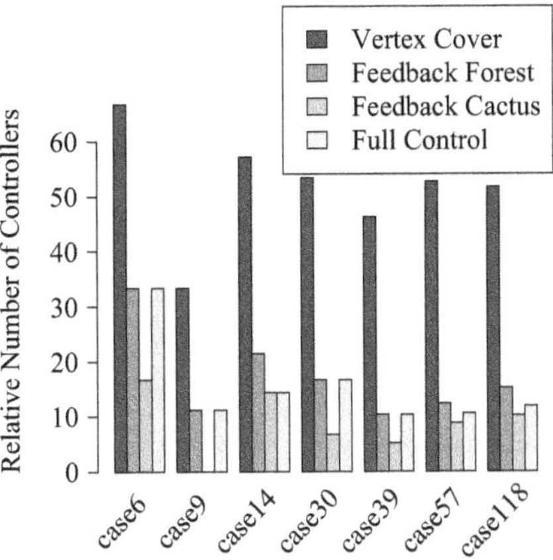

Figure 4: Comparison of the number of vertices which need to be removed from the network to get a tree (Feedback Vertex Set) or a cactus, with the worst number of controller to have full control in the network.

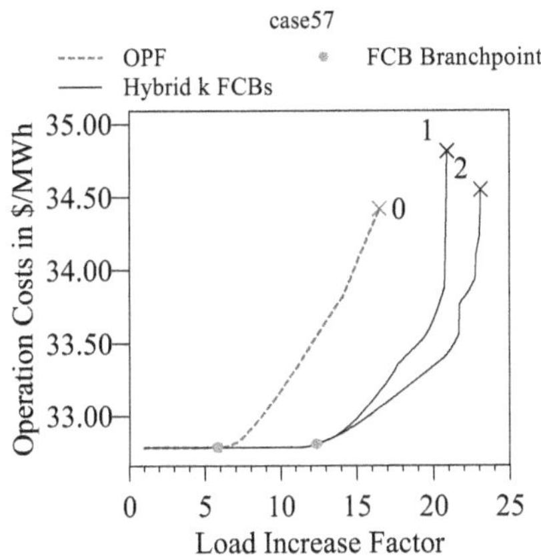

Figure 5: Operation costs of `case57` for OPF and the hybrid model with one and two FCBs with respect to the load factor ρ.

are equivalent and full control is achieved. However, it is generally not true that power grids admit small vertex covers; as shown in Figure 4, all instances require more than 40% of their vertices for a vertex cover. In the following we state (the proofs can be found in [13]) a much stronger result, namely that it suffices for becoming independent of Equation (9) that the native power grid $G - F$ is an acyclic network, i.e. the set F is a *forest feedback set*. Moreover, if $\lambda = 1$, (line losses are neglected) and edge capacities are ignored, it even suffices that $G - F$ is a so-called *cactus* graph, in which every edge is part of at most one cycle and F is called *cactus feedback set*.

THEOREM 4.1. *Let $G - F$ be a forest. Then every flow f is electrically feasible on G_F.*

THEOREM 4.2. *Let G_F be a power grid with FCBs at the vertices in F such that the maximum native power grid $G - F$ is a cactus and every edge of $G - F$ that lies on a cycle has infinite capacity. For any feasible flow f there exists a feasible flow f' with identical cost that is electrically feasible for G_F.*

We can actually give a finite upper bound on the edge capacities for which Theorem 4.2 still holds, see [13]. In Figure 4, in all cases the number of vertices for full control is between the size of feedback vertex sets with respect to forests and cacti. For the cases 14, 57 and 118, the minimum number of FCBs for achieving full control indeed result in native power grids that form cacti, although they do not necessarily achieve the smallest feedback number due to some influence of line capacities.

5. GRID OPERATION UNDER INCREASING LOADS

In the previous section we have seen that typically selecting a small fraction of the buses as FCBs suffices to achieve full control in the network. In this section we study what happens when even fewer FCBs are available and whether few FCBs allow a better utilization of the existing infrastructure in the presence of increasing loads.

To measure the controllability in the presence of very few FCBs, we simulate a load increase by a factor ρ in the power grid by decreasing all line capacities by the factor $1/\rho$. This has the effect that the overall demand remains constant and thus any change of costs is due to flow redirections. It is then expected that, once the load increases, the network without FCBs will require significantly higher operating costs, since the main criterion for determining the generator outputs becomes the overall feasibility of the flow rather than the cost-efficient generation of the energy. At some point, the load increases to a level where, by means of changing only the generator outputs, a feasible energy flow cannot be found. We compare the operation costs to solutions in power grids with a small number of FCBs. Specifically, our plots show two things. First, they show the operation costs for various small numbers of FCBs and, second, the operation costs and the number of FCBs for achieving full control in the network with respect to the load increase factor ρ.

Of course these operation costs again vary depending on the value of λ. Since most related work ignores line losses, we consider only the case $\lambda = 1$, i.e., only generation costs are taken into account. Varying λ changes the objective value, but it does not influence the existence of solutions with a certain number of FCBs. Recall from the plot in Figure 3 that, if the load increase ρ is small, full control can be achieved without FCBs for $\lambda = 1$. In the IEEE instances all lines have very large flow capacities, often much larger than even the total demand in the network, e.g., 9900 MW in `case14` and `case57`. To better highlight the interesting parts, similarly to the work by Lima et al. [14], we first scale all line capacities such that the smallest capacity is equal to the total demand of the consumers as given in Table 1. This changes neither the existence nor the cost of solutions. We increase the load until the flow model becomes infeasible; at this point a feasible solution cannot be achieved by adding FCBs and adding additional lines to the network becomes unavoidable.

Figure 5 shows the results of our experiment for the power grid `case57`. To improve readability, all costs have been rescaled by the total demand in the network, and thus give the cost per MWh. The black curve labeled 2 shows the operation cost with sufficiently many (here: $k = 2$) FCBs for full control. In fact, the FCB branchpoints indicate at which values of ρ an additional FCB becomes necessary for achieving full control. Moreover, for each number of FCBs from 1 up to the number required at the point when further load increase makes the instance infeasible, we show the optimal operation costs with this number of FCBs (solid black curves). Finally, the dashed curve shows the operation cost with OPF, i.e., without any FCBs.

As expected, increasing loads result in increasing operation costs. Interestingly, in Figure 5 two FCBs suffice for extending the maximal feasible operation point from 17.27 to 23.09. When using FCBs, the costs start increasing much later and more moderately. Interestingly, the solution with one FCB remains mostly equivalent to the solution with two FCBs until shortly before the end of its feasibility range. This example shows that FCBs indeed extend the feasible operation point and also decrease the corresponding operation costs even if there are only very few controllers available.

6. CONCLUSION

Assuming the existence of special buses that control the flow on all their incident transmission lines, we have presented a hybrid model for including some flow control buses. In this model, we have shown that relatively few control buses suffice for achieving full control. Further, we scaled the load of the network and showed that even fewer flow control buses improve the loadability and have a lower cost increase compared to OPF.

Our work shows the benefits of augmenting power grids with flow control devices. Using our theoretical model, we were able to explain our empirical observations on controller placement with graph-theoretical means. While this also explains previous observations of Gerbex et al. [8], the main drawback is that the model is based on several strong, simplifying assumptions.

Future work should consider more realistic power grid models both in terms of the control units, which are placed on transmission lines rather than buses, and using the AC power grid model.

7. REFERENCES

[1] M. S. Bazaraa, J. J. Jarvis, and H. D. Sherali. *Linear Programming and Network Flows*. Wiley-Interscience, 2004.

[2] G. Blanco, F. Olsina, F. Garces, and C. Rehtanz. Real option valuation of FACTS investments based on the least square monte carlo method. *IEEE Transactions on Power Systems*, 26(3):1389–1398, 2011.

[3] L. J. Cai, I. Erlich, and G. Stamtsis. Optimal choice and allocation of FACTS devices in deregulated electricity market using genetic algorithms. In *Power Systems Conference and Exposition. IEEE PES*, volume 1, pages 201–207, 2004.

[4] J. Carpentier. Contribution to the Economic Dispatch Problem. *Bull. Sac. France Elect.*, 8(-):431–437, 1962.

[5] M. Farivar and S. Low. Branch flow model: Relaxations and convexification – part II. *IEEE Transactions on Power Systems*, 28(3):2565–2572, 2013.

[6] S. Frank, I. Steponavice, and S. Rebennack. Optimal power flow: a bibliographic survey I. *Energy Systems*, 3(3):221–258, 2012.

[7] S. Frank, I. Steponavice, and S. Rebennack. Optimal power flow: a bibliographic survey II. *Energy Systems*, 3(3):259–289, 2012.

[8] S. Gerbex, R. Cherkaoui, and A. Germond. Optimal location of multi-type FACTS devices in a power system by means of genetic algorithms. *IEEE Transactions on Power Systems*, 16(3):537–544, 2001.

[9] A. V. Goldberg. An efficient implementation of a scaling minimum-cost flow algorithm. *Journal of Algorithms*, 22(1):1–29, 1997.

[10] J. Griffin, D. Atanackovic, and F. D. Galiana. A study of the impact of flexible AC transmission system devices on the economic-secure operation of power systems. In *12th Power Syst. Comput. Conf.*, pages 1077–1082, 1996.

[11] N. Hingorani. Flexible AC transmission. *IEEE Spectrum*, 30(4):40–45, 1993.

[12] L. Ippolito and P. Siano. Selection of optimal number and location of thyristor-controlled phase shifters using genetic based algorithms. *IEE Proceedings Generation, Transmission and Distribution*, 151(5):630–637, 2004.

[13] T. Leibfried, T. Mchedlidze, N. Meyer-Hübner, M. Nöllenburg, I. Rutter, P. Sanders, D. Wagner, and F. Wegner. Operating power grids with few flow control buses. *CoRR*, abs/1505.05747, 2015.

[14] F. Lima, F. Galiana, I. Kockar, and J. Munoz. Phase shifter placement in large-scale systems via mixed integer linear programming. *IEEE Transactions on Power Systems*, 18(3):1029–1034, 2003.

[15] M. Noroozian, L. Angquist, M. Ghandhari, and G. Andersson. Use of UPFC for optimal power flow control. *IEEE Transactions on Power Delivery*, 12(4):1629–1634, 1997.

[16] W. Ongsakul and P. Jirapong. Optimal allocation of FACTS devices to enhance total transfer capability using evolutionary programming. In *IEEE International Symposium on Circuits and Systems (ISCAS '05)*, volume 5, pages 4175–4178.

[17] K. Purchala, L. Meeus, D. Van Dommelen, and R. Belmans. Usefulness of DC power flow for active power flow analysis. In *IEEE Power Engineering Society General Meeting*, pages 2457–2462, 2005.

[18] N. Sharma, A. Ghosh, and R. Varma. A novel placement strategy for FACTS controllers. *IEEE Transactions on Power Delivery*, 18(3):982–987, 2003.

[19] C. Y. Tee and M. Ilic. Optimal investment decisions in transmission expansion. In *North American Power Symposium (NAPS '12)*, pages 1–6.

[20] A. Wood and B. Wollenberg. *Power Generation, Operation, and Control.* A Wiley-Interscience publication. Wiley, 1996.

[21] R. D. Zimmerman, C. E. Murillo-Sanchez, and R. J. Thomas. MATPOWER: Steady-state operations, planning, and analysis tools for power systems research and education. *IEEE Transactions on Power Systems*, 26(1):12–19, 2011.

A Comprehensive Review on Micro grid Operation, Challenges and Control Strategies

Romi Jain, Student
Electrical Engg. Department
M.A.N.I.T, BHOPAL
romijain210@gmail.com

Anoop Arya
Electrical Engg. Department
M.A.N.I.T, BHOPAL
anooparya.nitb@gmail.com

ABSTRACT
The world is observing a transition from its present centralized generation paradigm to a future with increased share of renewable energy sources (RES). Renewable energy sources (RES) based microgrids are seen as a solution to decrease reliance on depleting fossil fuel reserves provide an environment friendly solution to growing power demand. This paper put forwards a comprehensive review on controlling techniques. An overview of different control strategies of microgrid has been presented. The microgrids have been critically reviewed with respect to conventional and droop based control strategies. This paper presents a complete description, advantages and challenges of a microgrid and following a brief survey on the conventional voltage/frequency droop control, a generalized droop control (GDC) scheme and ANFIS control scheme. Finally, visualizing the wide scope of research in the micro grid; an attempt has been made to identify future research avenues.

Keywords
Microgrid, Droop control, Distributed generation.

1. INTRODUCTION
A microgrid is a group of interconnected loads, energy storage and generation systems within clearly defined boundaries that act as a single controllable entity with respect to the grid [8]. Future distribution networks will require completely novel smart grid concepts [1–3].In this regard, flexible microgrids (MGs) that are capable of intelligently operating in both grid-connected and island modes are required [4–6]. The basic concept of microgrid was invented in 1998 by the Consortium for Electric Reliability Technology Solutions (CERTS) [7]. A microgrid presents several advantages in relation to the current electric model paving the way for a future definitive deployment and they are reliability and security of the system [10],power system efficiency increase up to 90% if CHP is applied in microgrid to utilize heat for local use[11],the line congestion can be reduced, alleviate the immediate needs for generation augmentation, environment friendliness [12], emergence of new ancillary markets and exploitation of excess of energy from distributed generation [13].

2. MICRO GRIDS CHALLENGES AND OPERATION
Immense technical challenges associated with Micro Grids are summarized here — [14]:

e-Energy'15, July 14-17, 2015, Bangalore, India.
© 2015 ACM. ISBN 978-1-4503-3609-3/15/07…$15.00.
DOI: http://dx.doi.org/10.1145/2768510.2768514

- Coordinated control of a large number of RES.
- Limited communication imposes the adoption of distributed intelligence techniques
- Management of instantaneous active and reactive power balances, power flow and network voltage profiles
- Micro Grids are dominated by inverter interfaced distributed sources that are inertia-less.
- Instable operation during faults and various network disturbances may occur if Storage components are not there.
- Maintaining stability and power quality in the islanding mode of operation requires the development of sophisticated control strategies which need to be included on both generation and demand sides.
- Transitions from interconnected to islanding mode of operation are likely to cause large mismatches between generation and loads, posing a severe frequency and voltage control problem.
- Resistance to reactance ratio of the low voltage networks are high.[15].

A microgrid is a cluster of DGs, storage system and local loads that can offer many advantages to the current power grid and future power grid in terms of power autonomy and the ability to incorporate renewable and non-renewable energy sources. The MG is intended to operate in the following two different operating conditions.

✓ Normal Interconnected Mode—the MG is connected to a main MV networks either being supplied by it or injecting some amount of power into the main system.
✓ Emergency Mode—the MG operates autonomously, in a similar way to physical islands, when the disconnection from the upstream MV network occurs.

3. HIERARCHICAL CONTROL OF MICROGRIDS
The high penetration of distributed generators, linked to the grid through highly controllable power processors based on power electronics, together with the incorporation of electrical energy storage systems, communication technologies, and controllable loads, opens new horizons to the effective expansion of microgrid applications integrated into electrical power systems. Different islanding detection methods have been proposed by many researchers [16-17].The objectives and control strategies are different in two modes [26]. In the islanded mode of a microgrid, dynamics are strongly dependent on the connected sources and on the power regulation control of the converter interfaces [27]. An overview about microgrid control techniques at different hierarchical levels is considered [18]. In order to adapt ISA-95(international standard from the International Society of Automation) to the control of a microgrid, zero to three levels can be adopted as follows (see Fig.3) [19-25]. These control levels

differ in their: Speed of response and the time frame in which they operate, and Infrastructure requirements (e.g., communication requirements)[22]. A control method is required to control power quality indices at sensitive load buses while it does not disturb the desired coordination among power sources.The first control theory was initially introduced in 1993 The power sharing accuracy was enhanced by employing a virtual power frame transformation or virtual impedance [31]-[33]. In [34-35], an angle controller was proposed to minimize frequency variation by drooping the inverter output voltage angle instead of the frequency. [28].

Table 1. Important Microgrid Contributing Elements

Area EPS	System	The EPS that normally supplies the microgrid through their PCC.
EMS	System	EMS acting at the interface between loads and the microgrid. It communicates with smart devices and to the outside with the microgrid control center. It aggregates the services of the smart devices and provides further services to the microgrid. Furthermore, it can implement some level of intelligence to fulfill the services.
Grid Control Center	System	Control center from which the grid is operated. All required supervision and control functions are carried out here.
Market Operator (MO)	System	The system that procures energy and ancillary services and ensures reliability for the area EPS. The MO may be part of the area EPS or may be a separate entity.
Microgrid Control Center	System	The control system comprising different microgrid operator subsystems that ensures the control & management tasks of the microgrid and the aggregation of supply and demand.
Microgrid Controller	System	A control system able to dispatch the microgrid assets, e.g., opening/closing switches, changing control reference points, changing generation/consumption levels, etc. Other than the microgrid functions specifically referenced below, this use case does not specify the objective of any of the microgrid controller functions. This use case does not specify how the control signals are transferred or implemented in the microgrid assets.
Consumer	Person/ Org	A consumer of electricity, e.g., a private house, business building, large industrial/manufacturing industry or transportation system. The consumer acts as a customer. The consumer may operate smart appliances (an electric load with some intelligence to control it) that are flexible in demand.
DER Owner	Person/ Org	The distributed energy resource (DER) owner (or DG owner) operates a DER (or DG) that is connected to the microgrid.
Service Provider	Person/ Org	The service provider provides different kinds of services to the microgrid operator to support him in the operation of the microgrid, e.g., weather forecasts or energy market analysis.
Storage Owner	Person/ Org	Provider of storage capacity for storing and delivering energy.
Aggregator	Org	Market participant that purchases/sells electricity products on behalf of two or more consumers/generators/DERs. In a small microgrid, the microgrid operator could act also as aggregator. In a large microgrid, the aggregator might be a legal entity and the microgrid operator contracts with this entity.
Grid Operator	Org	The grid operator is the operator of the grid to which the microgrid has a connection point. The term "grid operations" refers to the undertakings of operating, building, maintaining, and planning electric power transmission and distribution.
Microgrid Operator	Org	The microgrid operator acts as system operator in the microgrid and is responsible for operating, maintaining, and, if necessary, developing the microgrid's distribution system. In some use cases, e.g., running the microgrid in an islanding mode, the microgrid should take over the roles of the energy retailer and/or the aggregator to ensure system stability.
Retailer	Org	Entity selling electrical energy to consumers. Could also be a grid user who has a grid connection and access contract with the transmission system operator or distribution system operator (DSO)
DER Unit	Device	DER including DG (small photovoltaic [PV], wind, etc.) connected to the microgrid. The device provides some degree of intelligence to facilitate monitoring and control.
Network Smart	Device	An intelligent electrical device in the microgrid that can be supervised and controlled (e.g., sensors, circuit breakers, or switches)
Storage Unit	Device	A storage unit provides an electricity reserve to the microgrid. The device provides some degree of intelligence to facilitate monitoring and control.

Source: NIST Smart Grid Interoperability Panel, Subgroup C – microgrids

4. DROOP CONTROL THEORY

Droop control also enables the system to disconnect smoothly and reconnect routinely to the complex power system [36].The role of droop control in power sharing is that it controls the real power on the basis of frequency droop control and it controls the reactive power on the basis of voltage control [37] Consider a simple MG as shown in Fig. 1. The DG is connected to the load, with line impedance Z .At point S, as represented in Fig.5.The real and reactive power are designed as:

$$P=|V||V|\frac{COS\phi}{|Z|}-|V||E|\frac{COS(\phi+\delta)}{|Z|} \quad (1)$$

$$Q=|V||V|\frac{\sin\phi}{|Z|}-|V||E|\frac{\sin(\phi+\delta)}{|Z|} \quad (2)$$

In equation (1) and (2) ϕ is the angle of line impedance Z, where $Z=R+jX$. Resistance (R) is neglected for an overhead:

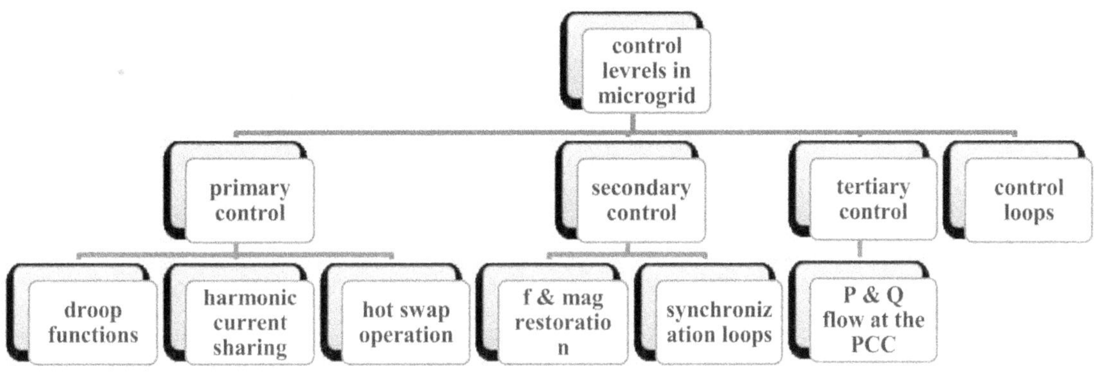

Fig 1. Hierarchical control levels of a microgrid

transmission lines as it is much lower than inductance (L). So the equations can be approximated as

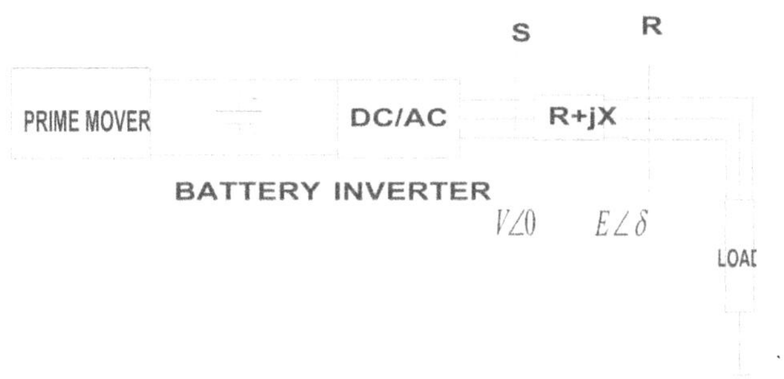

Fig 2. Simple MG with an interfaced inverter system

$$P=\frac{|V|}{|X|}|E|\sin\delta \quad (3) \quad Q=|V|\frac{|V|}{|X|}-|V||E|\frac{COS\delta}{|X|} \quad (4)$$

Also the power angle δ is very small. Equation (3) and (4) can further simplified by assuming cos δ = 1 and sin δ = δ

$$\delta=\frac{PX}{VE} \quad (5) \quad \Delta V=\frac{QX}{V} \quad (6)$$

From eq (5), it is clear that the real power transferred from bus S in fig 5 is proportional to $\sin\delta=\delta$. Therefore the power angle δ can be controlled by regulating real power P. In eq (6), reactive power is proportional to the magnitude of the voltage drop across the line. The voltage V can be controlled through reactive power Q. Dynamically, the frequency control leads to regulate the power angle and this in turn controls the real power flow [38]. Finally, the frequency and voltage amplitude of the microgrid are manipulated by adjusting the real and reactive power autonomously. As a result, the frequency and voltage droop regulation can be determined as:

$$f-f_0=K_p(P-P_0) \quad (7)$$

$$V-V_0=K_q(Q-Q_0) \quad (8)$$

Where, f_0 and V_0 are rated frequency and voltage of the microgrid. The K_p and K_q are droop coefficient of DG's active and reactive power. The amount of suitable frequency and voltage deviation can be achieved through the droop characteristics. This primary control provides a fast control action to keep the instantaneous balance between system production and consumption [39], [40].

5.1 TYPES OF DROOP CONTROL

Droop control is categorized on the basis of regulating the system parameters. They are:

5.1.1 Conventional droop control

This is a common type of droop control. Equations (7&8) show a strong linkage between active power and power angle, as well as between reactive power and voltage. Hence forth the power sharing in microgrid is attained by the output power generation according to its DG's power rating. The conventional droop control is further classified as[41]:a) Real power–frequency (P–F) droop control b) Reactive power–voltage magnitude (Q–V) droop control. Main advantages of conventional droop control are [42-44]:great flexibility, high reliability, avoid communication and free laying. The drawbacks [44-46] of conventional droop control are: tradeoff between voltage regulation and load sharing, poor harmonic sharing in case of non linear loads, slow dynamic response, poor performance while integration of more DG's and the necessity to maintain the same per unit impedance and voltage set points of the inverter for proper power sharing [47].

5.1.2 Modified droop control

In the case of conventional droop control, the resistance is taken as negligible quantity because L >>> R in high voltage lines. Whereas this assumption is not suitable for microgrid as it operates at low and medium voltage. Hence modified droop controls arise by changing the parameters of the conventional droop control as per their system requirement. The modified droop control [41] referred in this work are :P-V and Q-F droop control, angle droop control and generalized droop control.

5.1.2.1 P-V and Q-F droop control

The method of proper power sharing in an inverter interfaced microgrid by means of P-V & Q-F droop control was given by Qing-Chang Zhong and Charles K [47], [48].Microgrid operates at low and medium voltage, R>>X then equation 1 and 2 are modified as (9&10): From eq (10), it is clear that the active power is proportional to voltage drop across the microgrid.

$$\delta=-\frac{RQ}{VE}$$

$$\Delta V=\frac{PR}{V} \quad (9\ \&\ 10)$$

Therefore the voltage V can be controlled by regulating real power P.In eq (11), reactive power Q is proportional to the power angle. Dynamically, the frequency control leads to regulate the power angle and this in turn controls the reactive power flow [47, 48]. Finally, the frequency and voltage amplitude of the microgrid are manipulated by adjusting the reactive and active power autonomously. As a result, the frequency and voltage droop regulation can be determined as:

$$f - f_0 = K_q(Q - Q_0) \tag{11}$$

$$V - V_0 = K_p(P - P_0) \tag{12}$$

5.1.2.2 Angle Droop Control

Ritwik Majumder et al. [49], investigated the droop control of converters coupled with microsources in rural distribution generation with the help of angle droop control. The signal from global positioning system controls the angle droop. Their compilation includes the aim of satisfactory power sharing under a weak system conditions and high resistive network. They discussed two control methods where the first one shares power between DGs with no communication. However the second one is less communication based output feedback controller. With this technique, the power sharing was proper and economical with the web based communication.

5.1.2.3 Generalized droop control

In general case, both X and R should be considered a [50].The drawback of above droop control is that those methodology are based on independency of voltage variations and frequency deviation. In this type of droop control, voltage variations and frequency deviation has been taken in account and modified equation of active power and reactive power were developed.

$$P' = \frac{XP}{Z} - \frac{RQ}{Z}$$

$$Q' = \frac{RP}{Z} - \frac{XQ}{Z} \tag{13 \& 14}$$

Now, defining the index as $K_R = -\frac{R}{X}$, and applying eq (7&8)to P' and Q' and where $K_f = -\frac{1}{K_p}$, $K_V = -\frac{1}{K_q}$ .The Δf and ΔV are inverter frequency and voltage deviations, respectively.

$$P' = \frac{X}{Z}[K_f\Delta f + P_0 - K_R K_V \Delta V - K_R Q_0]$$

$$Q' = \frac{X}{Z}[K_R K_f \Delta f + K_R P_0 + K_V \Delta V + Q_0] \tag{15\& 16}$$

These equations can also be written as:

$$\Delta f = \frac{1}{K_f}\left(\frac{ZP'}{X} - P_0\right) + K_R K_V \Delta V + K_R Q_0 \tag{17}$$

$$\Delta V = \frac{1}{K_V}\left(\frac{ZQ'}{X} - Q_0\right) - K_R K_f \Delta f - K_R P_0 \tag{18}$$

The generalized droop control based frequency and voltage control, stabilize the microgrid frequency and voltage following the step load change.

5.1.3 ANFIS based GDC

In most of microgrid more than one DG are used, then there will be more line parameters will be present and all line parameters should be calculated. This becomes difficult and virtual parameters used will increase calculation time and also probabilities of converging of evolutionary algorithm in local minima. These are the drawbacks of generalized droop control based frequency and voltage control. Hassan Bevrani et.al [51] proposed ANFIS control strategy so as to resolve GDC based frequency and voltage control drawback. In ANFIS based GDC, the training ability of the ANN to the FL creates a new hybrid technique, known as ANFIS [51]. The ANFIS provides an adaptive modeling procedure to learn data set information. It creates an appropriate input/output (I/O) mapping with membership functions (MFs) based on fuzzy If-Then rules to generate the I/O pairs. The MFs parameters can be changed through the learning process. The ANFIS is trained by a desired I/O data set o the GDC, and then it is applied to the inverter interfaced DG control structure.To design the ANFIS-based controller, the GDC structure, which is used in the simple MG, might be modeled by the ANFIS. Then, after ensuring about the model validity, the ANFIS-based controller could be used instead of the GDC block diagram (Fig.3). Design steps can be summarized as follows [51]:

i) By applying and testing the GDC on the system shown in Fig. 3, and then saving the controller inputs/outputs, the training data for the ANFIS controller synthesis are collected. To obtain an accurate model, the training data under violent changes of active and reactive loads are considered.

ii) After obtaining the training dataset, the ANFIS structure to be completed. The MFs of input and output are considered in form of linear and Gaussian functions.

Following creating the controller structure, using the optimal hybrid method (combination of the LSE and BP), the ANFIS is trained for 5 iterations with a small error tolerance (i.e., 0.00001 ms) Using the developed intelligent GDC synthesis, one does not need more to know the MG structure and line parameters. Thus, this approach is applicable for a wide range of MGs [51].

5. CONCLUSION

In this paper a comprehensive review on challenges related to microgrid has been presented. Droop control strategies have been discussed with their associated merits and demerits. The assessment of popularity of benefits helps in formulating controlling problem more efficiently. When controlling is inappropriate, DG can have negative effect on system performance in terms of increased losses and degraded voltage profile. The techniques used for controlling problem have been investigated and a comparison of different approaches has also been presented. It has been found from literature survey that the research is mostly focused on control techniques using conventional drooping method. However owing to growing environmental concerns, countries across the world are resorting to stable and better voltage and frequency regulation. The authors' critical comments from literature survey have been summarized in Table 2. This review found that ANFIS is most promising control technique due to applicability for a wide range of MGs.An ANFIS Controller enables faster computational time for large power systems by optimizing the steady-state and the mathematical problems separately. ANFIS control structure carefully tracks the GDC dynamic behavior, and exhibits high performance and desirable response for different load change scenarios. . In the researcher's perception, this literature survey will be valued as a reference to work in the area of droop control application to meet the challenges of the power sharing challenges in microgrid.

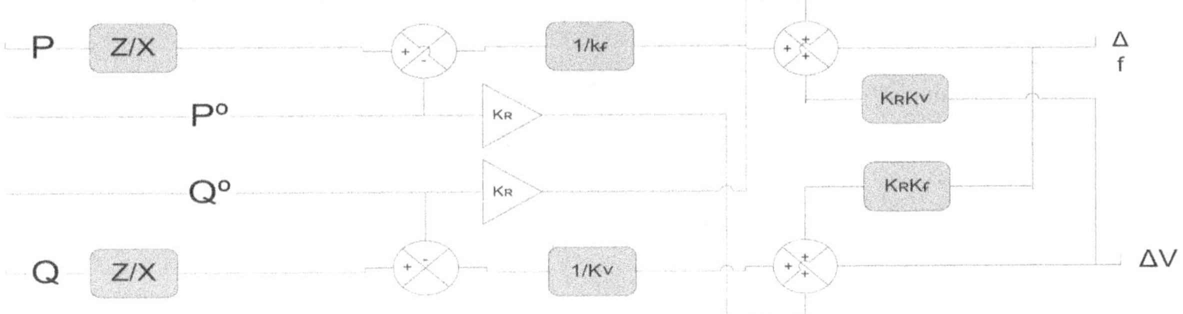

Fig 3. Block diagram of the GDC

TABLE.2 SUMMARY OF LITERATURE

Inference drawn from literature survey	Authors' critical comments
Microgrid is focused on controlling using Conventional droop control[41-46]	Due to trade off between voltage regulation and load sharing, Poor harmonic sharing in case of non linear loads, Coupling inductance, Influence of system impedance, Slow dynamic response and Poor performance while integration of more DG's, modified droop control methods had been researched.
P-V and Q-F droop control[47-48]	The methodology is based on independency of voltage variations and frequency deviation.
Angle droop control[34-35,49]	This strategy is better than above but the methodology is still based on independency of voltage variations and frequency deviation.
Generalized droop control[50]	The voltage variations and frequency deviation is taken into consideration. The generalized droop control based frequency and voltage control, stabilize the microgrid frequency and voltage following the step load change. The virtual parameters used in this droop control will increase calculation time and also probabilities of converging of evolutionary algorithm in local minima.
ANFIS based GDC[51]	ANFIS control strategy proposed by Hassan Bevrani et.al [51] as to resolve GDC based frequency and voltage control drawback. This approach is applicable for a wide range of MGs.

6. REFERENCES

[1] Farhangi, H. (2010, January 14). The path of the smart grid. *Power and Energy Magazine, IEEE*, 18-28

[2] Siano, P. (2014). Demand response and smart grids—A survey. *Renew Sustain Energy Rev, 30*, 461–478.

[3] Siano, J., Spaargaren, G., Van Vliet, B., & Van der Horst, H. (2014). Smart grids, information flows and emerging domestic energy practices. *Energy Policy*.

[4] Kyriakarakos, G., Piromalis, D., Dounis, A., Arvanitis, K., & Papadakis, G. (2013, March 31). Intelligent demand side energy management system for autonomous polygeneration microgrids. *Applied Energy, 103*, 39-51.

[5] Firestone, Ryan, Marnay, & Chris. (2005). *Energy Manager Design for Microgrids* (p. 58). LBNL.

[6] Kim, J., M Guerrero, J., Rodriguez, P., Teodorescu, R., & Nam, K. (2011). Mode adaptive droop control with virtual output impedances for an inverter-based flexible AC microgrid. *Power Electronics, IEEE Transactions*.

[7] Lasseter, R. (1998, August 23). Control of distributed resources. *Bulk Power Systems Dynamics and Control IV, Restructuring*, 323–329.

[8] Hatziargyriu, N., Asano, H., Iravani, R., & Marnay, C. (2007, August 18). Microgrids, an overview of ongoing research, development and demonstration projects. *Power and Energy Magazine, IEEE*, 78-94.

[9] Sanz, J., Matute, G., & Alonso, M. (2014). Analysis of European policies and incentives for microgrids. *International Conference on Renewable Energies and Power Quality, 12*.

[10] Dohn, R. (2011). *The business case for microgrids. White paper: The new face of energy modernization*. Siemens AG.

[11] *Unesa - Asociacion Españoladela Industrial Electrical. (n.d.). Retrieved 2015, from http://www.unesa.es/*

[12] Bustos, C., Watts, D., & Ren, H. (2012). Optimal Sizing of DGs for a CHP-Based Agro-Industrial Microgrid with a Priority Criteria Operational Strategy. *IEEE Latin America Trans, 9*(2).

[13] Madureira, A.& Lopes, J. (2012).Ancillary services market framework for voltage control in distribution networks with microgrids. *Electric Power Systems Research, 86*, 1-7.

[14] Hatziargyriou, N. (2002). MICROGRIDS – Large Scale Integration of Micro-Generation to Low Voltage Grids. *Technical Annex*.

[15] Agrawal, M., & Mittal, A. (2011). Microgrid technological activities across the globe a review. *IJRRAS*.

[16] Lin, C., Cao, C., Cao, Y., Kuang, Y., Zeng, L., & Fang, B. (2014). A review of islanding detection methods for microgrid. *Renewable and Sustainable EnergyReviews*.

[17] Kim, J., Kim, J., Ji, Y., Jung, Y., & Won, C. (2011). An Islanding Detection Method for a Grid-Connected System Based on the Goertzel Algorithm. *IEEE Transactions on Power Electronics, 26*(4), 1049-1055.

[18] Rocabert, J., Luna, A., Blaabjerg, F., & Rodríguez, P. (2012, Nov). Control of Power Converters in AC Microgrids. *IEEE Transactions on Power Electronics, 27*(11), 4734-4749.

[19] Technical Paper – Requirements to Generating Units. (2008). *UCTE,* 1-21.

[20] Guerrero, J., Vasquez, & Vicuna, L. (2009, March). Control Strategy for Flexible Microgrid Based on Parallel Line-Interactive UPS Systems. *IEEE Transactions on Industrial Electronics, 56*(3), 726-736.

[21] Guerrero, J., Vásque, J., & Teodorescu. (2009). Hierarchical Control of Droop-Controlled DC and AC Microgrids - A General Approach Towards Standardization. *Proceedings of the 35th Annual Conference of the IEEE Industrial Electronics Society.*

[22] Cañizare, C. (2014). Trends in Microgrid Control. *IEEE Transactions on smart grid, 5*(4).

[23] Karimi, H., Nikkhajoei, H., & Iravani, R. (2008). Control of an Electronically-Coupled Distributed Resource Unit Subsequent to an Islanding Event. *IEEE Transactions on Power delivery, 23*(1), 493-501.

[24] Katiraei, F., Iravani, M., & Lehn, P. (2005). Micro-Grid Autonomous Operation During and Subsequent to Islanding Process. *IEEE Transactions on Power delivery.*

[25] Cells, P. (2009). *IEEE application guide for IEEE Std 1547, IEEE standard for interconnecting distributed resources with electric power systems.* New York, NY: Institute of Electrical and Electronics Engineers.

[26] Jiang, Q.& Geng, G. (2013). Energy Management of Microgrid in Grid-Connected and Stand-Alone Modes. *IEEE Transactions on Power Systems.*

[27] Green, T., & Prodanović, M. (2007). Control of inverter-based micro-grids. *Electric Power Systems Research.*

[28] Chandorkar, M. & Adapa, R. (1998). Control of parallel connected inverters in standalone AC supply systems. *IEEE Transactions on Industry Applications, 29*(1)

[29] Guerrero, J., Garciadevicuna, L., Matas, J., Castilla, M., & Miret, J. (2004). A Wireless Controller to Enhance Dynamic Performance of Parallel Inverters in Distributed Generation Systems. *IEEE Transactions on Power Electronics, 19*(5), 1205-1213.

[30] Brabandere, K., Bolsens, B., Keybus, J., Woyte, A., Driesen, J., & Belmans, R. (2007). A Voltage and Frequency Droop Control Method for Parallel Inverters. *IEEE Transactions on Power Electronics, 22*(4).

[31] Vásquez, J., Guerrero, J., Luna, A., Rodríguez, P., & Teodorescu, R. (2009). Adaptive droop control applied to voltage-source inverter operating in gridconnected and islanded modes. *IEEE Trans. Ind. Electron, 56*(10).

[32] Li, Y., & Kao, C. (2009). An Accurate Power Control Strategy for Power-Electronics-Interfaced Distributed Generation Units Operating in a Low-Voltage Multibus Microgrid. *IEEE Transactions on Power Electronics.*

[33] Guerrero, J., Hang, L., & Uceda, J. (2008). Control of Distributed Uninterruptible Power Supply Systems. *IEEE Transactions on Industrial Electronics, 55*(8).

[34] Majumder, R., Chaudhuri & Zare, F. (2010). Improvement of Stability and Load Sharing in an Autonomous Microgrid Using Supplementary Droop Control Loop. *IEEE Transactions on Power Systems.*

[35] Hua, M., Hu, H., Xing, Y., & Guerrero, J. (2012). Multilayer Control for Inverters in Parallel Operation without Intercommunications. *IEEE Transactions on Power Electronics, 27*(8).

[36] Zamora, R., & Srivastava, A. (2010). Controls for microgrids with storage: Review, challenges, and research needs. *Renewable and Sustainable Energy Reviews, 14.*

[37] Dou, C., Liu, D., Jia, X., & Zhao, F. (2011). Management and Control for Smart Microgrid Based on Hybrid Control Theory. *Electric Power Components and Systems, 39*(8).

[38] Llaria, A., Curea, O., Jiménez, J., & Camblong, H. (2011). Survey on microgrids: Unplanned islanding and related inverter control techniques. *Renewable Energy.*

[39] Bevrani, H., Hiyama, T., Mitani, Y., & Tsuji, K. (2011). Automatic Generation Control: A Decentralized Robust Approach. *Intelligent Automation & Soft Computing..*

[40] Sheble, G. (2009). Power systems (review of "Robust Power System Frequency Control" by Bevrani, H.; 2009) [Book reviews]. *IEEE Power and Energy Magazine,*77-80

[41] Natesan, C., Ajithan, S., Mani, S., & Kandhasamy, P. (2014). Applicability of Droop Regulation Technique in Microgrid - A Survey. *Engineering Journal,* 23-36.

[42] Chandrokar, M., Divan, D., & Banerjee, B. (1994). Control of distributed UPS systems. *PESC '94 Record., 25th Annual IEEE, 1.*

[43] Chandorkar, M., & Divan, D. (1996). Decentralized operation of distributed UPS systems. *Power Electronics, Drives and Energy Systems for Industrial Growth, 1996.*

[44] Guerrero, J., Berbel, N.& Matas, J. (2006). Droop control method for the parallel operation of online uninterruptible power systems using resistive output impedance. *APEC '06. Twenty-First Annual IEEE.*

[45] Guerrero, J., De Vicuña, L & Miret, J. (2005). Output Impedance Design of Parallel-Connected UPS Inverters With Wireless Load-Sharing Control. *IEEE Transactions on Industry Applications, 52*(4).

[46] Chiang,, S., & Chang, J. (2001). Droop control method for the parallel operation of online uninterruptible power systems using resistive output impedance. *Power Electronics Specialists Conference, 2,* 957-961.

[47] Zhong, Q. (2011). Robust Droop Controller for Accurate Proportional Load Sharing among Inverters Operated in Parallel. *IEEE Transactions on Industrial Electronics.*

[48] Sao, C., & Lehn, P. (2008). Control and Power Management of Converter Fed Microgrids. *IEEE Transactions on Power Systems, 23*(3), 1088-1098.

[49] Majumder, R., Ledwich, G., Ghosh, A., Chakrabarti, S., & Zare, F. (2010). Droop Control of Converter-Interfaced Microsources in Rural Distributed Generation. *IEEE Transactions on Industry Applications, 25*(4).

[50] Brabandere, K., Bolsens, B., Keybus, J., Woyte, A., Driesen, J., & Belmans, R. (2007). A Voltage and Frequency Droop Control Method for Parallel Inverters. *IEEE Transactions on Power Electronics, 22.*

[51] Bevrani, H., & Shokoohi, S. (2013). An Intelligent Droop Control for Simultaneous Voltage and Frequency Regulation in Islanded Microgrids. *IEEE Transactions on Smart Grid, 4*(3), 1505-1513.

A Smarter Grid with the Internet Of Energy

Giampaolo Fiorentino
Research & Development Lab
Engineering - Ingegneria Informatica,
Rome, Italy
giampaolo.fiorentino@eng.it

Antonello Corsi
Research & Development Lab
Engineering - Ingegneria Informatica,
Rome, Italy
antonello.corsi@eng.it

Pietro Fragnito
Research & Development Lab
Engineering - Ingegneria Informatica
Rome, Italy
pietro.fragnito@eng.it

ABSTRACT

The increasing share of electricity generation from renewable sources creates several issues on power electricity system especially as regards demand and generation balance. In order to maintain power system stable new framework are now available. On key idea is based upon the participation on demand side management of smart and intelligent appliances as flexibility providers. The high penetration of intelligent appliances turns the whole buildings into effective and efficient prosumers. These distributed and autonomous intelligent Commercial Prosumer Hubs, constituted of Distributed Energy Resources clusters raising an actual decentralized Demand Side Management, behave like Smart Virtual Power Plants that an aggregator can manages using a portfolio of commercial buildings composed of flexible device to deliver services to the electricity grid. This new infrastructure maximizes the response capacity of the vast, small-commercial prosumer base (e.g., tertiary buildings, offices, etc.), presenting incentives and delivering benefits through their automated active participation in the energy market, aligning consumption by asking consumers to reduce their power usage rather than increasing the power generation facilities. Under this approach, prosumers that cooperate might receive incentive payments from the power company. In this respect, an overlay smart network for efficient grid control, running on top of the existing energy grid and incorporating high levels of distributed intelligence within autonomous and semantically enhanced Prosumer Hubs will bring to the new concept of Internet of Energy through widespread use of smart devices, bi-directional communication and proper software infrastructure.

General Terms

Management, Measurement, Performance, Design, Human Factors, Standardization

Keywords

Internet Of Things, Energy of Things, Smart Grid, Demand Side Management , Energy Flexibility

1. INTRODUCTION

The efforts to reduce greenhouse gases emissions related to electricity generation have been leading to a fast increase in the deployment of renewable generation [1]. As a result, the proper integration of renewables into the electric grid presents a major challenge and new tools are required to ensure the grid reliability.

e-Energy'15, July 14 - 17, 2015, Bangalore, India.
© 2015 ACM. ISBN 978-1-4503-3609-3/15/07...$15.00 DOI: http://dx.doi.org/10.1145/2768510.2768518

At the same time, the energy consumption in European Union (EU) households has been steadily growing due to the widespread utilization of new types of loads and the requirement of higher levels of comfort and services. The electricity consumption breakdown in EU households was recently characterized recognizing that several end-use loads present some kind of flexibility; therefore, if properly controlled these loads can be used as a demand side resource capable of offering a responsive behavior [2]. As far as security of supply is concerned, the most severe problems due to power intermittence occur in peak load hours, since most system resources are already in use and a sudden reduction of power generation can have critical consequences on the system reliability. Thus, instead of acting on the supply side, Demand Response (DR) programs and technologies have the potential to contribute to optimize consumption and reduce peak loads, in (near) real-time. In this way, DR is an enabling strategy for the successful integration of renewable energy sources in the electric system, in a perspective of integrated energy resource management, involving controlling flexible loads according to (price and/or emergency) signals from the grid and end-users' preferences. In addition, DR can become a new source of revenue for entities that *aggregate* this load flexibility. Therefore, the involving of the end-user, in no intrusive way, knowing her behavior and how she uses the electrical devices became essential in the flexibility supply. So, it's very important to apply three best practices for energy customer-communications shows in Figure 1.

Figure 1 - Three best practices for energy customer-communications

Knowing and predicting both users and electrical devices behavior help to tackle frequency fluctuations and voltage imbalances, due to the rising energy and complexity of energy demand, originating from the increasing usage of decentralized renewables resources. This paper depicts a new strategy to take on this big issue. This new strategy aims at extending DSM strategies by incorporating a new entity: an enhanced Distributed Energy Resources (DER). This new entity includes local generation and consumption capacity as well as the flexibility that is provided by the same DER within comfort boundaries. This DER, semantically enhanced (generation, consumption and flexibility), ware the core of our solution and constitute an active and flexible knot equipped with local information based on environmental, occupancy, and historical data. The adopted solution enables a mechanism that allows consumers to actively participate in the Demand Side Management without affecting the customer's comfort level, as well as turning the customer into an active and proactive prosumer. According to this approach, every DER has a computational model and a communication part in embedded systems, paving the way towards highly sophisticated networked devices that will be able to carry out a variety of tasks not in a standalone mode, as usually today, but taking into fully account dynamic and context specific information. These *Virtual* DERs are able to cooperate, share information, act as part of communities and generally be active elements of a more complex system. Our solution is a real instance of the so called Ubiquitous Computing: different systems and subsystems (each having its computational capacity) are driven simultaneously to cooperate with each other as in Figure 2.

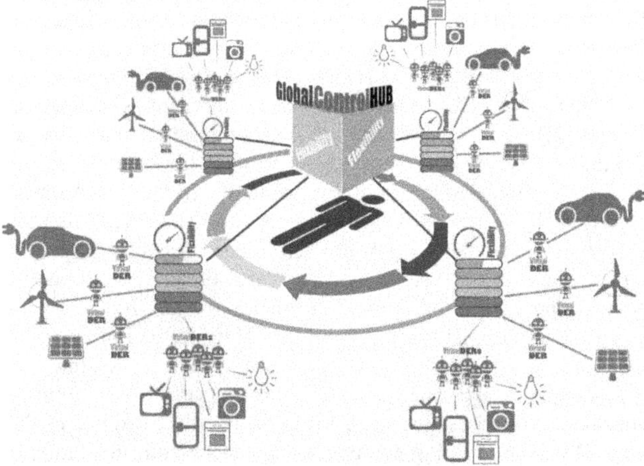

Figure 2 – Decentralized architecture

Eventually, this paper learns from the progress of the existing efforts in demand side management and using the approach of IoT leads naturally to the definition of an Internet Of Energy.

2. LITERATURE REVIEW

Many empirical and experimental studies have estimated the impact of the inelasticity of demand along with the continuously increasing presence of distributed intermittent energy sources has on the overall grid balance.

Recent studies proposed the development of an advanced and integrated, management system [4], which enables energy efficiency in buildings and special infrastructures from a holistic perspective in order to connect the subsystems with facilities allowing to respond to emergency situations without rough old tool as interrupting the service. Many studies have aimed at making the end-use an active player in the DSM[5]. The active participation of domestic and small commercial consumers in power system markets and in provision of services to the different power system stakeholders characterizes precisely in advance the services and flexibilities that they can provide. Domestic consumers are not likely to "offer" services. Therefore, the services they can provide will be "requested" through the developed price and/or volume signal mechanisms and will be provided on a voluntary and contractual basis. Furthermore, managing distributed generation and to enhance its valorization within electrical distribution systems the concept of virtual power plant (VPP) is developed. It consists in aggregating various small size generating units of commercial virtual power plant (CVPP) that tackles the aggregation of small generating units with respect to market integration and the technical virtual power plant (TVPP) that tackles aggregation of these units with respect to services that can be offered to the grid.

However, all aforementioned studies deem the price as balancing *indicator* and they are based on highly centralized control frameworks and heavily depend on the continuous interaction with consumers [8], thus exhibiting considerable complexity on the central level and significant drawbacks in terms of real-time applicability and response capacity on specific grid events. Finally, no study has addressed local generation and demand as intertwined parameters co-existing within typical prosumer profiles, towards establishing service oriented prosumer portfolios and flexible *energy on demand* services [9]. An effective DR requires the integration of many sub-initiatives conducted at peak and off peak times, utilizing customer pro-activeness, load efficient control and high levels of automation.

This paper applies the Internet of Things (IoT) concept into Energy network, providing an overlay coordination and grid management framework, which on top of the grid and consisting of distributed and autonomous intelligent Commercial Prosumer Hubs (Tertiary Buildings). and also at the Aggregated Control Hubs

3. INTERNET OF THINGS REVOLUTION FOR ENERGY EFFICENCY IN SMART GRID

The Internet of Energy (IoE) is a new conception of the power grid that allows promoting a transition from the current energy system to a new modulated one. IoE provides architecture with distributed embedded systems to implement a real-time interface between the smart grid (which depends of electrical generating energy sources as well as flexibility concept) and a cloud of devices (electric vehicles, commercial and residential buildings, offices, electrical devices, appliances, etc).

This innovation needs all network elements of a physical model instantly connected and able to contribute actively to the network to the purpose of DSM, feeding to the Local Control Hub (LCH) with the real-time information. The LCH gathers information, in an anonymous way, in order to calculate the flexibility degree. The flexibility degree indicates the trustworthiness of the LCH. The flexibility degree is based on the robust modeling of individual behavior and their incorporation to the prosumer load flexibility profiles as well as energy device models.

In this respect, introducing an overlay virtual network for efficient grid control, running on top of the existing energy grid and incorporating high level distributed intelligence within autonomous and semantically enhanced things, the apparent structural inertia of the Distribution Grid becomes smart.

Therefore with the proliferation of Internet enabled devices and the visions for an Internet of People and Things, ubiquitous computing and cloud computing, this new Smart Grid manages, using also flexibility degree, active elements, which coupled with the necessary control and distributed coordination mechanisms, in order to balance the grid.

3.1 Flexibility Models

The Flexibility Model is the heart of the solution depicted in Figure 1. There, the LCH gathers information and using its Flexibility Model to create the Flexibility degree.

The LCH periodically collects information asking its Virtual Distributed Energy Resources both their consumption/production and forecast of the immediate future regarding consumption/production, including a certain flexibility obtained from User Profiling. The LCH sends the GCH this information, so the GCH, through some holistic mechanisms as well as basing on this information (and the aggregation thereof) the GCH may decide on committing to a requested change in the overall forecast which in turn is based on the provided flexibility, in order to keep balancing the Grid.

So the flexibility comes from individual devices that may shift some of their power consumption or production through time without their users noticing. Flexibility forecasts may be further refined when combined with the human factor under the form of an user profiling mechanism that is an indispensable part because occupant's individual and group preferences affects and often define DER operations, performance and therefore overall DER flexibility (both generation and consumption). So, it's very important to assert that the flexibility is aggregated at two levels, firstly within the LCH and then the GCH forming clusters of the LCHs. The exact amount of flexibility is provided by means of DER model and the control actions that are possible to simulate.

For this purpose, it is useful emphasize that a DER model consisting of two main parts:

1 The first part contains the mathematical formulation defining the electric demand (consumption, generation and storage) of the DER in function of dynamic and static input parameters.
2 The second part defines control models used to calculate and offer available flexibility.

The importance of control models lies in the fact that power modification (increase/decrease) signals received by the LCH are executed by means of them. These control models are categorized following three typologies:

1 *Control based on occupancy.* The controller turns off the associated DER is empty and it turns on the DER if an occupant gets in the DER area.
2 *Lighting Control.* Controllers operate by adjusting the dimming of the lighting devices in the building according to the external natural light provided by lighting sensors.
3 *Schedule Control.* Prefixed set point schedules are previously set up. Some set point can act on some DERs, such as lighting on/offs and temperatures for HVAC systems and can be predefined according to some predefined operator logic

3.1.1 Holistic component

The Virtual DER provides the lowest kind of available flexibility. The aggregation of some Virtual DERs allows managing of more flexibility amount, which is essential for balancing the grid. Furthermore, the Virtual DER Clusters along with context and environmental information are handled by an holistic component in order to be able to face the DSO's flexibility request. The holistic component uses several algorithms, for elaborating a plenty of information in order to building up some strategies based on several KPIs able to response the unbalancing of the grid. Moreover, the holistic component feeds its-self with useful information for a self-learning that improves the quality of the forecasting to reflect actual DER behaviors.

In this respect, the intertwine interactions among several tiers forming a learning loop: from sensors upstream up to the DSO and vice versa. The learning loop continuously updates and calibrates model based on incoming observations, improving the accuracy (minimizing the error) as more observation data comes in.

3.1.2 Calibration

The calibration is an important action that allows refining both the DER model and the User Profile. The Fitness Evaluator component and an Optimization Algorithm are the tools in charge of making the calibration. In fact the interaction between the Fitness Evaluator and the Optimization Algorithm components constitutes the learning loop by which the respective DER Models are calibrated. The Fitness Evaluator provides the *forecast error* describing the distance between the expected power consumption from the DER model and the observed power consumption from the actual DER.

The general steps of aforementioned Optimization Algorithm is the following:

1	Initialize the search space model
2	While not optimal or updated training data (in this case continuously true)
2.1	Generate a candidate solution point using the search space model
2.2	Obtain the solution point's actual reward or fitness (in this case the match between forecast and historic power consumption)
2.3	Update the search space model

Table 1 - Optimization Algorithm

This algorithm calibrates the DER model of a specific smart appliance that typically runs in four phases, each with its own power consumption level, duration and maximum delay. Depending on the kind of DER device, varying amounts of model parameters need to be calibrated. For instance, lighting devices may have only a few model parameters to set (dimmer control setting, power consumption level, luminance level) whereas HVAC installations have many parameters. The search space or landscape to explore for minimizing the forecast error typically grows exponentially with the number of parameters (dimensions) to be calibrated or trained.

3.1.3 Key Performance indicators

The flexibility computation is done through the Holistic Component using a system of key performance indicators. This whole system aims at defining of the appropriate metrics allowing to quantify the particular requirements posed by different groups of occupants and identify points of optimal balance among conflicting interests to the purpose of well balanced energy infrastructure. The KPIs are groped in four categories: Flexibility, Comfort, Business and Energy.

3.1.4 Sensor and Occupancy in LCH

The behavior of occupant has been shown to have large impact on LCH. Consequently, user activity and presence is considered as a key element and has been used for control of various devices. The innovative approach of this paper consists on bring occupancy related information in the DER models through an Occupancy and Flow Model. It refers to both the occupants as a group (Overall), and specific individuals (Individual). Using RFID equipment for some occupants improve prediction accuracy and user profiling, as it is possible to track occupants' location at any time having more specific information concerning their habits and schedules. The data provided by occupancy allows forecasting short-term (near real time) and mid-term (next day) demand at LCH level taking into account the comfort parameter expressed as a discomfort probability

3.2 User Interface system in IoT context

The User Interface system of an application based on IoT is the synthesis of active entities interconnection. It is represent in a human friendly mode, designed following the guidelines of the Figure 1, the modeling behind these entities and these interconnections. So in IoT we have a lot of active elements and the User Interface system should connects all these active elements with the last and probably most important active element one: the final user. For this reason the User Interface system should not only merely shows entity's data but also especially gives to user the possibility of being an active actor of its IoT world. A personalized UI, reporting real-time information, allows sharing user habits and preferences about devices and comfort.

3.2.1 View – functionalities

The end-user can interact with system, knowing DERs status, setting his preferences and arranging an appointment. Using following described views:

- HOME view: user monitors status and consumption of all DERs (personal and zonal), taking under control his comfort status. He also monitors his position in the building;
- PREFERENCES view: user submits to system his preferences about his devices, such as for example, HVAC winter or summer temperature, electrical vehicle time-in and SoC, personal devices start and stop;
- CALENDAR view: user submits to system his habits and commitments such as for example "surgery in operating room from 11:00 am to 3:00 pm" or "training every Monday from 6:00 pm to 9:00 pm in the workout room";
- HISTORICAL view: user monitors the historical data about consumption at different time;

Figure 4. User Interface in iPhone

4. APPROACH

The new approach tackling DSM issues thus far described, introduces an intelligent and autonomous Virtual Layer on the actual Electricity Grid. This new Virtual Layer, based on the Internet of Things principles, gathers active and flexible components carrying contextual knowledge of their local and global environment in order to extend the DSM strategies by incorporating various types of DER going beyond simple consumer loads, and treats both local generation and consumption under a single unified framework. At this layer each DER gets Virtual DER. As already said, the concept of Virtual DER, which affects DER operation and performance, as well as potential capacity of DER to provide flexible services to the Distribution Grid. So, the Virtual Layers, aggregating the Virtual DER is be able to form dynamic clusters comprising self-organized networks of active nodes that efficiently distribute and balance global and local intelligence. The Cyber DERs are aggregated at two hierarchical levels: building or LCH level and District or GCH level.

4.1 Local Control and Automation hub

A whole tertiary building can be represented by a building automation system named Local Control Hub (LCH). Thanks to Building Automation Systems, all individual building subsystems DER can become part of a single central system, also able to learn users' needs and behavior, to anticipate solutions or provide recommendations. These systems make use of forecasting, optimization and evaluation algorithms that acquire real-time data from smart sensors and meters, placed in strategic points of the building, capable of detecting internal microclimate parameters, space and ICT infrastructure use, attendance, weather data and energy quality. Based on the input data analysis, the system suggests actions to support building management optimizing energy consumption; users, on the other hand, as an active part of the system can monitor consumption instant by instant, by tablet or smartphone, and improve their behavior accordingly.

In this respect, the objects become self-recognizable and acquire intelligence due to the ability to communicate information about them and gain access to aggregate information from any other devices, allowing these systems to operate in real time. Some ambient user interfaces (AUIs) is to continuously collect data resulting from the occupant's interaction with existing traditional building hub devices and provide the necessary incentives through different interaction UIs (Section 3.2), driving them to more energy efficient choices. The specific user interface - e.g. tablet, smartphone - delivers to the end user - mainly building hub occupants and building managers - personalized services to fully support a high level overview of the energy consumption in the current building zone, as well as more detailed information on the energy consumption for efficient demand side management. Therefore, the UIs offer different interaction modalities according to the involved users and roles in the local hub level (occupants, group of occupants or facility managers).

4.2 Global Control and Automation hub

One or more LCHs arranges a GCH. In energy universe a new stakeholder is arising: the Aggregator. This paper lays the Aggregator on GCH level. The Aggregator in a scale of aggregation following immediately the building and therefore manages different clusters of buildings (LCHs) using their portfolio, trading with the market stakeholders on behalf of small customers. Aggregators gather, analyze and efficiently organize their customer flexibility portfolios and define specific active demand (AD) strategies and services based on market needs. They act as an intermediary between suppliers and network operators and the different commercial and industrial (C&I) prosumers belonging to their portfolios. A User Interface is also provided at this level. It mainly gathers and analyses aggregated information in order to balance the network using the flexibility provided by the LCH. This Global User Interface can foresee the energy demand flow analyzing the information coming from LCHs, so it can better handle both critical and unforeseen situations creating virtual LCH clusters dynamically accordingly their flexibility degree.

4.3 Privacy, Data Protection and Cyber-Security

The designed solution is supported by a communications network that collects and processes an increasingly high quantity of sensing data and makes it available to entitled stakeholders and systems. The next section shows the delivery of our solution, this section is immediate realizing that the nascent Smart Grid is an electricity network that can cost efficiently integrate the behavior and actions of all users connected to it – generators, consumers and those that do both – in order to ensure an economically efficient, sustainable power system with low losses and high levels of quality and security of supply and safety. In our solution the data is collected from everywhere including consumers' homes and possibly, electric vehicles handling high quantity of sensing data and makes it available to entitled stakeholders and systems, which leads toward the creation of new risks for data subjects with potential impact in different areas (e.g. price discrimination, profiling for behavioral advertisement, taxation, law enforcement access, household security).

So, our solution applies some of principles of Privacy by Design both for final prototype and during the whole lifecycle project, when it could also happen that personal data of potential users have been processed. Privacy by Design principles allow us to work in accordance with Directive 95/46/EC [12], which obliges EU Member States to introduce compulsory notification to National Data Protection Authorities (DPA). Furthermore, following EG2.P.7 and EG2.P.6 some principles are applied for the purpose of data retention:

data minimization – in the data collection and data retention not exceed what is necessary to achieve specific and lawful purpose,

transparency – i.e. who, when and in what circumstances collects, processes and retains personal data for what purposes, and what data and where is stored;

Moreover, the data coming from the LCH toward GCH are sent in an anonymous way making unworkable to go back to the original personal data, even though this anonymous aggregated data are inferred.

Finally, our solution guarantees the privacy and security of data harnessing Privacy-Enhancing Technologies (PET) for protecting informational privacy by eliminating or minimizing personal data thereby preventing unnecessary or unwanted processing of personal data, without the loss of the functionality of the information system.

5. CASE STUDY

The idea thus far discussed is the basis of the concept behind the INERTIA project **Error! Reference source not found.**. Analyzing our system performance in large-scale setups beyond the available pilot sites, virtual LCHs are added in the evaluation framework. Virtual LCHs come in two forms: simulators with meso-level and with micro-level realism. The meso-level LCH simulators reproduce LCH behaviors (flexibility forecasting and adaption) based on historical data of the overall LCH interaction. The micro-level LCH simulators contain virtual representatives for every individual LCH component. They are largely descried in [13].

5.1.1 Case Imbalance risk reduction

Reducing the risk of power imbalances is a one of the major issues to solve. In this solution the aggregator plays the role of a Balancing Responsible Party. The aggregator aims at matching the real time aggregated power consumption/generation of the LCHs in its portfolio with the power schedule agreed in the wholesale electricity market. If there is a deviation from the planned schedule, the system operator (TSO) will need to use available generation reserves in order to compensate for the deviations and the extra costs of using these reserves will be finally paid among those BRPs that caused the deviation.

The GCH, as depicted in the simulator user interface's ecosystem graph **Error! Reference source not found.**), undertakes the *Mitigator* role. This user agrees to a certain Service Level Agreement (SLA) with the whole sale Market Operator-TSO and is in charge to actually realizing its long-term power consumption predictions in order to avoid the penalties applied by the TSO if deviations occur between scheduled and actual aggregated power consumption/generation. The *Mitigator* user relies on the GCH to achieve the SLA commitments in the face of any local deviations and even larger disruptions as it applies available load flexibility across the set or pool of energy resources successfully, as long as the pool is large enough. Otherwise, should committed levels be exceeded, the *Mitigator* faces penalties as defined by national regulations and applied by the responsible TSO.

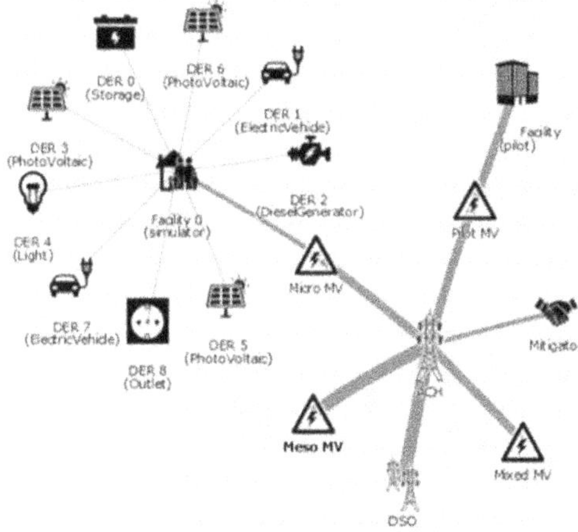

Figure 3 - A Graph visualization of the INERTIA ecosystem

The Imbalance Risk Reduction (IRR) scenario tests the sensitivity of the proposed solution with respect to the size of the pool of flexibility. The extent of exposure to imbalance risk is determined by the size of potential disruptions given the available pool of flexibility. Flexibility pools in the INERTIA system are aggregated over several levels, range from the Aggregator and the MV-point representative Portfolio Manager, down to the Holistic Component, each representing a heterogeneous pool of DERs with their respective individual amounts of flexibility.

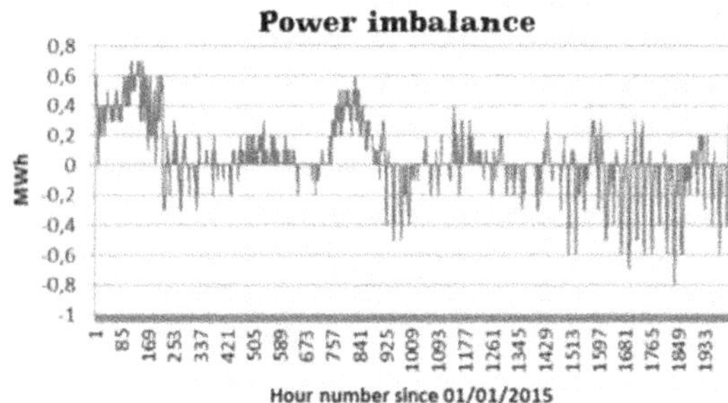

Figure 4: small TSO client: Realistic hourly power imbalance

The charts in **Error! Reference source not found.** shows realistic power imbalances for two clients of a Swedish transmission system operator (TSO): one smaller client with typical power demand varying between 1.48MW and 7.23MW (**Error! Reference source not found.**), one larger client with typical power demand varying between 74MW and 3.2GW. The charted power imbalance is the deviation between power supply contracted from the TSO in day-ahead and intra-day markets and the actual power consumed: positive imbalance means consumption was more than contracted, negative imbalance means consumption was less.

The test results provide valuable insight into the service level that may be safely agreed upon by the *Mitigator* role, if any, in return for energy cost savings. Basically, they are demonstrated that the Aggregator system is able to balance the energy of the LCHs in its portfolio in order to match a predefined aggregated power profile and therefore avoiding imbalance. This test can be split in different step to fulfill in order test is passed.

1 The tester obtains the aggregated forecasted demand profile corresponding to the set of LCHs (simulated + real) in the lab test-bed. This forecast is the one applicable to the day of the test
2 The tester feeds the Aggregator with the aggregated forecasted demand profile
3 The tester switches the operating mode of the GCH to *Imbalance Risk Reduction* operating mode
4 After a period lasted at least 12 hours the tester obtains the historical aggregated demand data from the Aggregator and for the period when the GCH was running in the *Imbalance Risk Reduction* operating mode.
5 The tester subtracts the forecasted profile with the stored profile and obtains the difference between both of them for each hour of the testing period

The difference between power profiles forecasted and simulated in imbalance risk reduction mode can be represented quantitatively by means of KPI, giving a system performance measurement.

$$Kpi_1 = \frac{Demand\ flexibility}{Baseline\ energy\ consumption}$$

Equation 1 - System performance measurement

5.1.2 Pilot

In order to test the whole framework, the aforementioned case studies are implemented in different premises throughout Europe. The various parts of the system have been divided in the following countries:

Greece's premises accommodate the basic LCH and ACH software components. In addition, the selected sites comprise the basic Real Local Hub infrastructures where diverse sensors, actuators and DERs are allocated for the realization of the actual real-case testing scenarios. Moreover, the PV Park located at there is included representing one of the energy production elements that will be part of the test suite.

Spain pilot sites host the DSO component infrastructure, which is in charge of requesting demand flexibility for operating the electricity distribution network and the PC installations facilitating the simulated Local Control Hub environment. Furthermore, within the pilots several DERs (Diesel generators) are attached to the Real Local Control Hub at Greece premises via the Semantic Based Middleware.

In Sweden, the Pilot site provides real-time measurements from PV energy production and EV charging stations, integrated to the other pilot sites

6. CONCLUSION

Currently, the majority of the DSM capacity stems large customers, failing to capture the vast amount of small residential and commercial consumers. Ineffective programmer design and low consumer interest are major barriers on the DSM vast exploitation. Thus, all DSM approaches are based on highly centralized control frameworks and heavily depend on continuous interaction with consumers, exhibiting significant drawbacks in terms of real-time applicability and response capacity on specific grid events. The proposed solution has provided an IoT approach in overcoming the existing barriers to DSM and offers a distributed solution for the vast implementation of DR strategies. Our solution introduces efficiently coordinated active DER clusters, which collectively behave more reliably and in a more controlled manner. Decentralized DSM is considered a part of future active grid control systems, comprising various automated DR strategies. Within future the IoT paradigm enables the active grid management frameworks, distributed local generation sources, distributed storage (when available) and DR will be equally treated and all resources will be treated in a unified way for optimal coordination and integration to the active grid.

7. REFERENCES

[1] H. Farhangi, "The path of the smart grid." Power and Energy Magazine, IEEE 8.1, 2010

[2] H. Lund, A. N. Andersen, P. A. Østergaard, and B. V. Mathiesen, "From electricity smart grids to smart energy systems–a market operation based approach and understanding." Energy.

[3] European Commission, "Energy 2020: A Strategy for Competitive, Sustainable and Secure Energy", SEC (2010).

[4] Karfopoulos, E., Tena, L., Torres, A., Salas, P., Jorda, J. G., Dimeas, A., & Hatziargyriou, N. 2015. A multi-agent system providing demand response services from residential consumers.

[5] http://www.addressfp7.org

[6] de Almeida, A., Fonseca, P., Schlomann, B., Feilberg, N., (Characterization of the Household Electricity Consumption in the EU, Potential Energy Savings and Specific Policy Recommendations. Energy & Buildings, Gross, G., (2010).

[7] Kowli, A., Negrete-Pincetic, M., Gross, G., (2010). A successful implementation with the Smart Grid: Demand response resources, 2010

[8] Ganu, T.; Seetharam, D.P.; Arya, V.; Hazra, J.; Sinha, D.; Kunnath, R.; De Silva, L.C.; Husain, S.A.; Kalyanaraman, S., "nPlug: An Autonomous Peak Load Controller," Selected Areas in Communications, IEEE Journal, July 2013

[9] Mohsenian-Rad, A. H., Wong, V. W., Jatskevich, J., Schober, R., & Leon-Garcia, A. 2010. Autonomous demand side management based on game-theoretic energy consumption scheduling for the future smart grid. .

[10] Biegel, B., Andersen, P., Stoustrup, J., Madsen, M. B., Hansen, L. H., & Rasmussen, L. H. 2014. Aggregation and Control of Flexible Consumers–A Real Life Demonstration. *In Proceedings of the 19th IFAC World Congress, Cape Town, South Africa.*

[11] Karnouskos, S., Ilic, D., & Silva, P. G. D. 2012. Using flexible energy infrastructures for demand response in a smart grid city. *IEEE.*

[12] EU Directive 95/46/EC - The Data Protection Directive https://www.dataprotection.ie/docs/EU-Directive-95-46-EC-Chapter-1/92.htm

[13] http://www.inertia-project.eu/

[14] http://www.inertia-project.eu/inertia/results/publications.html

Encouraging Energy Conservation in Campus Dormitory via Monitoring and Policies

Lei Zhan, Dah Ming Chiu
Department of Information Engineering
The Chinese University of Hong Kong
zl011, dmchiu@ie.cuhk.edu.hk

ABSTRACT

Promoting and practicing energy conservation requires a cost-effective system for monitoring electricity usage and a well-designed incentive policy to induce energy-saving habits. In this paper, we describe our experiences in building a smart meter system in campus dormitories and the design of an incentive policy. The smart meter system captures different types of electricity usage in each dormitory room, and allows the students to see their usage and then to pay as necessary. The policy is to assign credit to students based on their long-term usage averages, and to make students pay if they go above that, but to rebate them for any unused balance. The system allows us to log the usage behavior on a continuous basis, and we can thereafter analyze the measurement data in order to report the effectiveness of such a scheme.

1. INTRODUCTION

Energy conservation is an important attitude to living that we try to promote and practice on our university campus. The challenge is how to set up a cost-effective way of monitoring energy usage and to design incentive systems to encourage energy-savings behaviors. The monitoring system measures and extracts energy usage patterns, which helps in designing effective policies to motivate lodgers to save energy. In this paper, we describe a practical system which we recently deployed in the student dormitories on our campus that allowed us to monitor and experiment with incentive policies. The results were positive and the experience is worth relating.

The Chinese University of Hong Kong [1] runs a College system. While academic study mostly happens in the faculties and departments, many other aspects of a student's life are supported by the College to which the student belongs. The Colleges provide the dormitories and dining halls for students, organize social and sporting activities, and offer various general education programs. The study reported here is based on a collaboration with Lee Woo Sing (LWS) College [3] for which "Green Life" is a motto. One of the projects at the College is to set up a smart meter system to encourage energy conservation.

e-Energy'15, July 14–17, 2015, Bangalore, India
© 2015 ACM. ISBN 978-1-4503-3609-3/15/07 ...$15.00
DOI: http://dx.doi.org/10.1145/2768510.2768516.

The smart meter system includes the functionalities of: (a) electricity consumption measurement using smart sensors; (b) a prepayment system based on quota; (c) an interface for administrators to allocate quota; and (d) an interface for students to add payment. Electricity measurement is based on pulse counting. In each room in the dormitory, multiple smart units are deployed to separately collect the electricity consumption of Air Conditioner (AC), Power Socket, and Lighting & Fan. The collected values are periodically reported to a central server via TCP/IP. With the ability to monitor the electricity consumption of each dormitory room, the college designed and applied a pricing scheme for charging students as an incentive policy to conserve energy. The pricing scheme is progressive and it motivates students to save energy because it charges higher unit prices for more usage quotas and it refunds the unused quota balances.

Based on the measurement data exported from the smart meter system, we conducted a detailed analysis of the electricity consumption of the dormitory rooms as well as the quota value adding behavior of the students. The results validate the effectiveness of the pricing scheme on positively encouraging the students to conserve energy. Besides, we report some interesting observations in terms of energy usage, such as the influences from the gender factor and the weather factor. Other important findings include the potential policy adjustments to further encourage energy conservation, including modifying the current pricing scheme and encouraging energy conservation in the public areas of the dormitory.

The rest of this paper is organized as follows. In Section 2, we first briefly review the related work; this is followed by a description of the smart meter system in Section 3. In Section 4, we introduce the student dormitory setting and the incentive scheme design. In Section 5 and Section 6, we show our analysis of the measurement data and discuss its implications and our future plans. In Section 7, we draw our conclusions.

2. RELATED WORK

In previous studies, there are various approaches for measuring and monitoring the electricity consumption in buildings. In some early studies [12, 8], the data of electricity consumption were collected manually and periodically. In [11], the authors presented an approach for selecting a set of sensors for capturing energy events in buildings. In our study, the electricity consumption is measured by deploying smart meters in dormitory rooms. Although our measurement approach is different, the experiences reported in the earlier studies suggested several good ideas, such as how to conserve energy in public areas.

There are some other studies concerning the design of effective policies to motivate energy conservation. Both [5] and [8] illustrate that feedback on electricity consumption may provide a tool for customers to better control their consumption and to thereby save energy. The authors of [5] have extracted the features of successful feedbacks and emphasized that successful feedback has to capture the attention of consumers. Their ideas suggest one direction for our future study: to develop interfaces for students to better compare their electricity consumption with that of others so as to further encourage energy conservation.

There are also some works which illustrate possible applications of the data collected in our smart meter system. For example, [10] evaluated the forecasting of household electricity demand by using three realistic datasets of geospatial and lifestyle diversity. Another example is the Grand Challenge of DEBS 2014 [6], which seeks the design of an event-based system to provide scalable, real-time analytics over high-volume sensor data. The dataset used is the recordings originating from smart plugs, which are deployed in private households to measure electricity consumption.

3. THE SMART METER SYSTEM

3.1 System Framework

Figure 1 shows the framework of the smart meter system. In each bedroom of the dormitory, we deployed a Single Room Unit (SRU) to measure the electricity consumption of the room in realtime. Each SRU periodically reports the measured values to the System Server via TCP/IP over the local Ethernet. Upon receiving a measured value, the System Server processes and stores it in a local database.

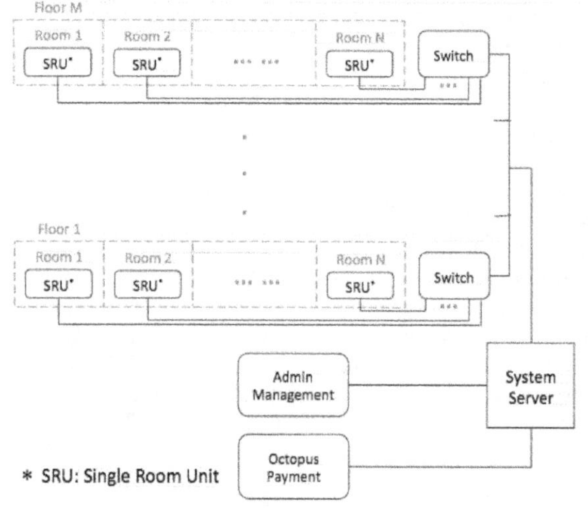

Figure 1: The Framework of Smart Meter System

Besides, the System Server is responsible for handling requests from the Admin Management Platform and the Octopus Payment System. These systems are provided for the college administrator and the students, respectively. The Admin Management Platform allows the dormitory administrator: (1) to check the electricity consumption of any room during a customized period; (2) to manage the usage quota for each room; and (3) to generate customized reports of electricity consumption and quota adding records. The Octopus Payment System provides the interface for students: (1) to check their quota adding history, and (2) to get additional quotas by payment when necessary.

3.2 Single Room Unit

The SRU is the core component of the smart meter system. Basically, it is responsible for measuring the electricity consumption from the different sources in a room. Meanwhile, it periodically sends the measured values to the System Server via TCP/IP for data aggregation. There are several components in the SRU: the Power Control Unit; the Network Panel; and the Power Calculating Circuit (PCC). Figure 2 illustrates the structure of the SRU.

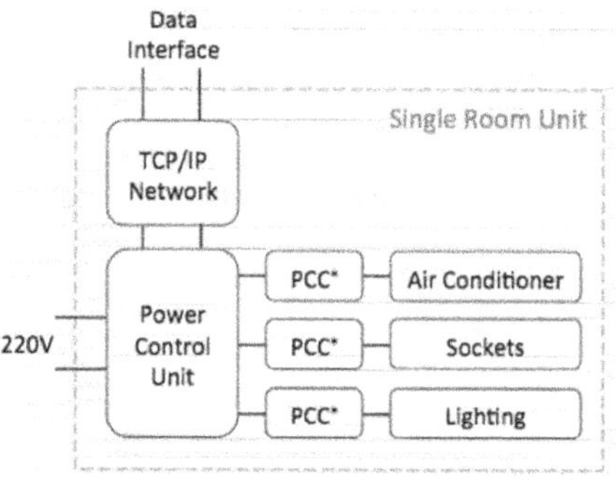

Figure 2: The Structure of Single Room Unit

The measurement of electricity consumption is based on pulse counting at the PCC. Pulses are generated at a rate proportional to the corresponding electricity consumption [7, 9]. Therefore, the frequency of such pulses indicates the power demand, while the number of pulses indicates the energy metered [13]. The number of pulses is convertible into the commonly used electricity consumption in kWh, and the conversion is given in the following formula.

$$Electricity\ Consumption\ in\ kWh = \frac{\#\ of\ Pulses}{3200}$$

At the beginning of each hour, the SRU reports the number of pulses counted in the previous hour. The reporting is done via the Network Panel. The Network Panel is an embedded system that is equipped with a TCP/IP connection for remote updating and monitoring. Through this connection, the measurement results are reported to the System Server in realtime. In the other direction, the configuration is downloadable to the panel for updating the equipments.

In the smart meter system, the electricity consumption of each dormitory room is divided into three parts: (1) Air Conditioner (AC); (2) Power Socket; and (3) Lighting & Fan. For each part, there exists a PCC for measuring the electricity consumption. Therefore, we can separately monitor the electricity consumption of each dormitory room in terms of AC, Power Socket, and Lighting & Fan. The Power Control Unit consists of several Solid State Relays, which cut off the power supply of the corresponding room when the quota balance reaches zero.

With the measurement results, we can infer the electricity usage profile for different consumption sources. For example, Figure 3 illustrates the hourly electricity consumption of AC, Power Socket, and Lighting & Fan in the same room during one week (2014/09/01 to 2014/09/07). Apparently, different consumption sources show great differences in terms of usage pattern.

Figure 3(a) shows the strong daily usage pattern of AC during weekdays: the student usually use AC from midnight to noon as well as for several hours in the afternoon. However, he or she might leave their room during the weekend as there is no electricity consumption of AC after midday on Saturday. Compared to AC, Power Socket consumes a relatively lower amount of power, but the consumption is continuous over time. While for Lighting & Fan, most of the electricity consumption is generated during the night, and zero values over the weekend are consistent with the usage of AC.

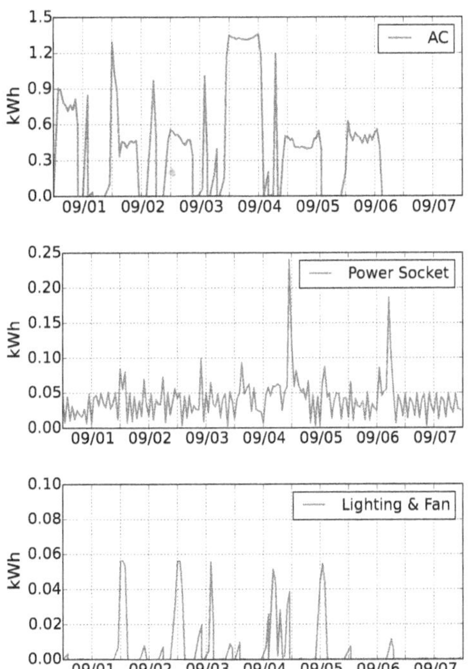

Figure 3: Hourly Electricity Consumption of AC, Power Socket, and Lighting & Fan in a Room during One Week

4. SYSTEM OPERATION

4.1 Overview

LWS College is a new and medium-sized college of the Chinese University of Hong Kong, which was founded in 2006. It promotes green life among students in order to raise their concerns about the environment, and to help develop a sustainable campus. The smart meter system was built into LWS College's new dormitory buildings when they were being constructed more than two years ago, so there were no retrofitting costs. Actually, the system is the first deployment of such a system in Hong Kong.

The dormitory building of LWS College has two blocks: North Block and South Block. Both of them have 155 dormitory rooms for students. Table 1 lists the detailed information of the college dormitory, including the number of rooms, the gender of the lodgers, and the room type.

We deployed a SRU in each of the total 310 rooms and

Block	Floor	Room #	Gender	Room Type
North	G	10	M	Triple
	01	22	F	Double
	02	21	F	
	03	22	F	
	04	21	F	
	05	22	M	
	06	21	M	
	07	16	M	Mixed
South	03	22	F	Double
	04	22	M	
	05	21	M	
	06	22	M	
	07	21	M	
	08	12	F	Mixed
	09	12	F	
	10	12	F	
	11	11	F	

Table 1: Detailed Information of Dormitory Rooms in LWS College

connected all SRUs to the central System Server. Meanwhile, the System Server runs as a server of TeamViewer so that the college administrator can remotely access the Admin Management Platform via TeamViewer.

4.2 The Pricing Scheme

The pricing scheme for the students is semester-based. For a normal semester, at a fixed date in each month, the college administrator manually allocates some free quotas for all rooms. The amount value is calculated by referencing the average electricity consumption of the previous year and it varies for different room types: 95 units for a single room; 105 units for a double room; and 115 units for a triple room.

Whenever a room runs out of its quotas in the middle of a semester, its lodgers have to buy additional quotas. Otherwise, the power supply in that room will be unavailable till the next free quota releasing date. The lodgers get warning signals well before power supply is cut off. Between two consecutive free quota releasing dates, the unit price of the additional quota follows the rule in Table 2. Such rule is progressive and it means the more additional quotas are bought, the more expensive is the unit price.

Payment ($)	First 50	Next 50	Next 50	Next 50+
Unit Price	$0.92	$1.61	$2.07	$2.87

Table 2: Progressive Pricing Scheme of Additional Usage Quota in LWS College

At the end of a semester, the balance of unused quotas of a room can be refunded to the corresponding lodgers of that room. Therefore, the charge of electricity consumption is directly linked to student consumption levels, and this motivates students to save energy.

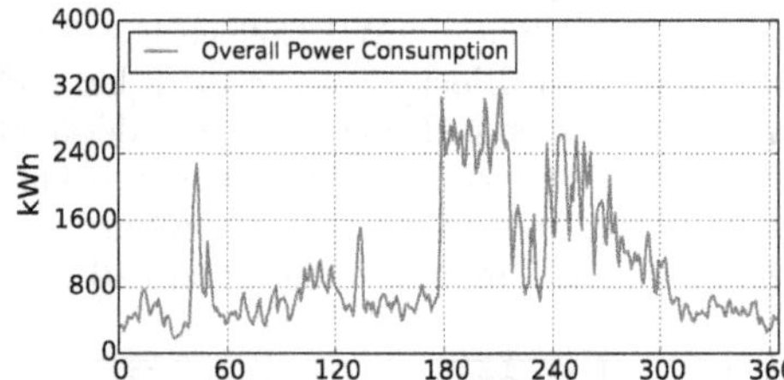

Figure 4: Daily Overall Electricity Consumption of All Dormitory Rooms in 2014

5. MEASUREMENT DATA ANALYSIS

5.1 Electricity Consumption

Figure 4 gives the daily overall electricity consumption of all dormitory rooms in 2014. As we explained in Section 3.2, the electricity consumption of each dormitory room is divided into three components: AC; Power Socket; and Lighting & Fan. Figure 5 shows the daily overall electricity consumption of each component during the whole of 2014. There exist great disparities in consumption amount and usage pattern between the three components.

According to Figure 5, the electricity consumption of

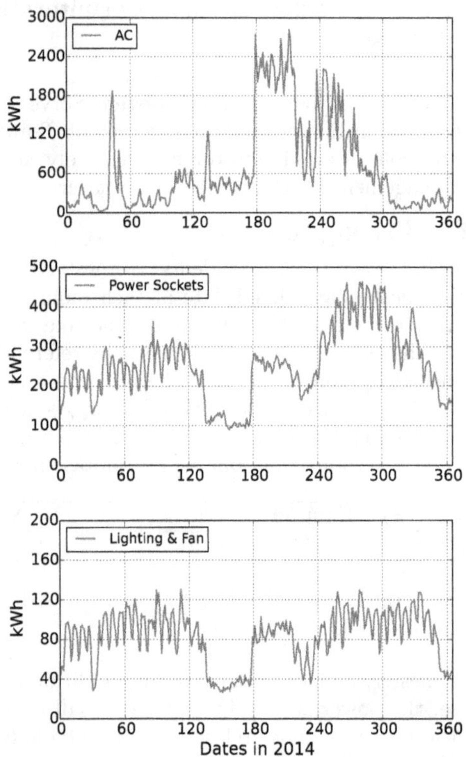

Figure 5: Daily Overall Electricity Consumption of All Rooms for AC, Power Socket, and Lighting & Fan in 2014

AC represents the largest portion of overall consumption, and the usage pattern of AC is highly related to time. The electricity consumption of Power Socket and that of Lighting & Fan share similar usage patterns and distribute more uniformly over time, even the usage amounts are not comparable. Table 3 shows the absolute electricity consumption value and the corresponding percentage of the three components, which suggests that the primary target of energy saving is AC.

Component	Consumption Value	Percentage
AC	251429 kWh	67.24%
Power Socket	92419 kWh	24.72%
Lighting & Fan	30053 kWh	8.04%

Table 3: Overall Electricity Consumption of AC, Power Socket, and Lighting & Fan in 2014

5.2 The Effect of Pricing Scheme

For LWS College, the motivation for deploying the smart meter system and setting up the pricing scheme is to encourage the students to be responsible for their own electricity consumption, thereby promoting a reduction in energy waste. Actually, the pricing scheme described in Section 4.2 is applied only to dormitory rooms during the normal semesters. There is no separate charge for electricity consumption when the rooms are rented to guests during summer holidays. Therefore, we can compare the electricity consumption during a normal semester with that during a summer holiday to validate the effect of the pricing scheme.

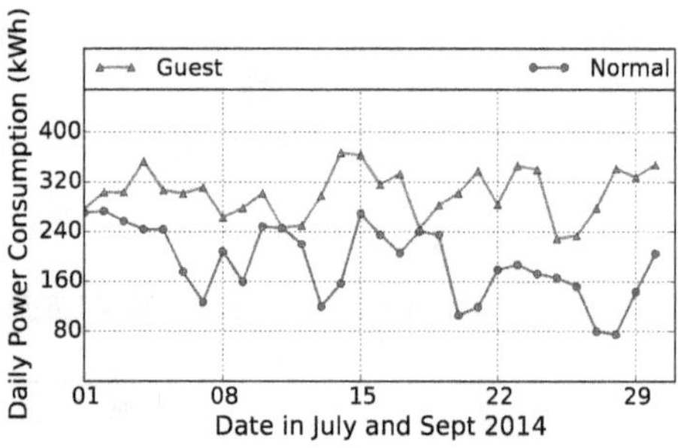

Figure 6: Effect of Pricing Scheme on Electricity Consumption

We selected the daily total electricity consumption of the same floor (6th) in two different months for comparison: July 2014, and September 2014. During July, the lodgers were visitors and there is no pricing scheme of electricity consumption for them. The pricing scheme was, however, applied to students during September. We chose September for comparison to minimize the influence of the weather; this is because the weather in Hong Kong in July and in September is similar both in temperature and humidity.

Figure 6 illustrates the comparison results. Apparently, the consumption under the pricing scheme is smaller than that without usage limitation. The overall electricity consumption in September is only around 63% of that in July. Therefore, the pricing scheme shows a positive effect on motivating students to save energy.

On the other hand, Figure 6 proves the different energy usage patterns for visitors and students. For example, compared with weekdays, students usually spend less time in their dormitory room during weekends. The visitors, however, have the opposite behavior: that is, they spend more time in their room during the weekends.

5.3 Value Adding Behavior

As we described in Section 4.2, students are allowed to buy additional usage quotas, and the pricing scheme follows the rule in Table 2. The behavior of value adding helps us to understand the usage pattern of students so as to enhance the pricing scheme.

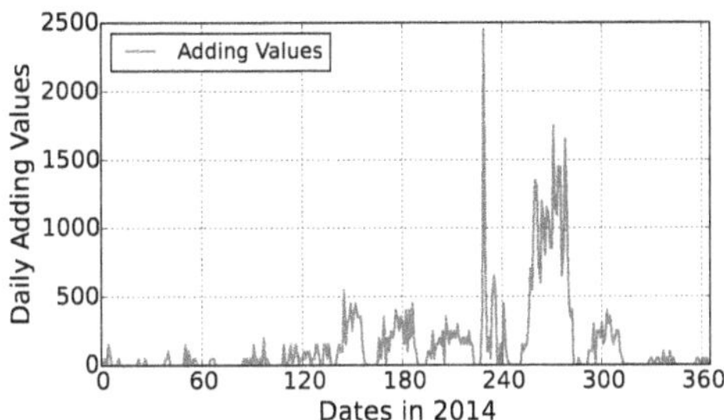

Figure 7: Daily Overall Adding Amounts in 2014

The daily value adding amount of 2014 is shown in Figure 7. Apparently, the majority of value adding occurs from August to October, which is consistent with the results shown in Figure 4. There are only two amount options for students to select when paying additional quotas: 50HKD, and 100HKD. Therefore, we can infer the amount of value adding behavior of a student from the history records of his or her value adding amount.

According to the daily electricity consumption shown in Figure 4, the demands placed on the power supply are distributed in a non-uniform way. The pricing scheme formulated by the College determines that the free quotas are assigned uniformly for each month. Students have to buy additional quotas once their quota balance runs out. Even though the unused quotas are refundable at the end of each semester, the unit price of an additional quota is much higher than the refund price.

5.4 Other Observations

5.4.1 Gender Effect

Another interesting observation which we made from the measurement results is the influence of gender on electricity consumption. The College assigns the dormitory rooms to male or female students based on floor. We chose two adjacent floors to extract the gender effect. Both floors have 21 rooms with the same room type. We compared the electricity consumption of the two floors during the same period.

Figure 8 illustrates the daily electricity consumption in September for both floors. Basically, male students and female students share similar consumption patterns, while the female students on average consume less energy than the male students. For this reason, the college administrator might consider normalizing the free usage quota for the male students and the female students separately.

5.4.2 Weather Effect

According to Figure 5(a), the usage pattern of AC is highly related to time. A possible explanation is the influence of the weather. The hourly measurement of AC usage

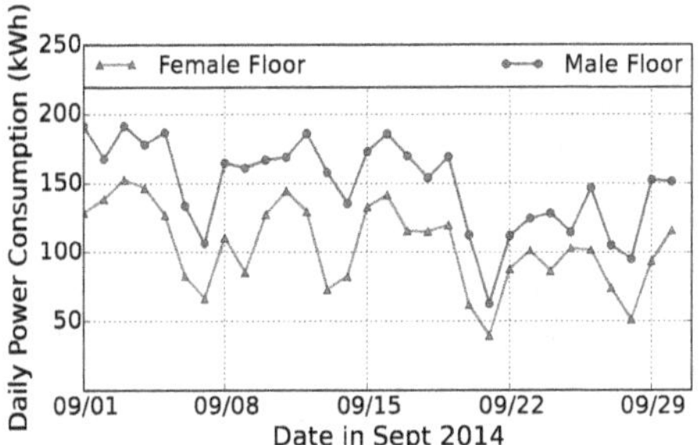

Figure 8: Electricity Consumption Comparison Between Male and Female Students in September 2014

for dormitory rooms allows us to study the correlation between the weather and the AC usage. We retrieved the daily average temperature of Hong Kong in 2014 from [2] and then calculated the Pearson correlation coefficient between the daily temperature and the daily AC usage (electricity consumption) of overall rooms. The coefficient value is 0.5867, and it proves the strong positive correlation between the weather and the AC usage.

6. POTENTIAL POLICIES

6.1 Free Quotas Allocation

According to the daily value adding amount shown in Figure 7, the values are somewhat different for the two semesters. For the spring semester (from January to May), there are only a few records of value adding, although there are many records of value adding in the autumn semester (from September to December). This is a reasonable observation because the average temperature is much higher in the autumn semester than in the spring semester, and this leads to heavy electricity consumption on AC in the autumn semester. This observation suggests that there should be a review of whether or not the uniform allocation of free quotas for each month is reasonable, given that the electricity consumption distributes non-uniformly over the year.

6.2 Continuous AC Usage

Another observation which we made from the measurement data relates to the AC usage pattern of the students. A large portion of AC usage is in a continuous mode. Table 4 gives the distribution of AC operating time for the AC usage in September 2014. More than half of the AC usage is with an operating time longer than three hours. A possible reason is that the AC used in the dormitory rooms of LWS College is Window-Mounted Air Conditioner (WM-AC), which is the most commonly used AC for single rooms. In this type of AC, all the components are enclosed in a single box, which is fitted into a slot made in the wall of the room, or more commonly onto a window sill [4].

Time	1 Hour	2 Hours	3 Hours	> 3 Hours
Percent	16.33%	19.28%	9.70%	54.69%

Table 4: Distribution of Continuous AC Usage Time

The WM-AC provides several control functions for its users; these functions are limited to the ON/OFF Switching, the Fan Speed, and the Cooling Level. Users can hardly control the operation of WM-AC is in a smart way, such as setting the auto-switching on and off at a preferred time. The continuous operating of AC might be easily neglected by users, especially during the night. According to the results in Section 5.1, AC use is the greatest part of overall electricity consumption, and hence it should be the primary target of energy conservation. Therefore, it should help conserve energy by fixing the problem of continuous AC usage.

The problem can be improved in two dimensions: (1) by encouraging students to switch AC to a lower Cooling Level for continuous operating; and (2) by developing additional features for the smart control of AC. Approach (1) strongly depends on the promotion and education by the College; this should result in increased efficiency. Whereas for approach (2), the deployment might only involve in software adjustments. As we introduced in Section 3, the existing Solid State Relay connected to AC helps in upgrading to more advanced control.

6.3 Energy Conservation in Public Areas

The smart meter system of LWS College monitors the electricity consumption of student bedrooms, but does not cover the public areas. However, according to the College's electricity consumption report, the electricity consumption of the public areas represents an even larger proportion than that of the students' bedrooms. Therefore, we are working on ways to encourage energy conservation in the public areas as part of our future study.

Actually, energy conservation in the public areas is considerably more difficult. Firstly, compared to the student bedrooms, the structure of the electricity transmission line in the public areas is quite complicated. It is challenging and costly to deploy smart meters for different components of electricity consumption. We are investigating how many meters need to be installed and at which locations so as to make the system cost-effective. Secondly, it is not clear who is responsible for the power usage in the public areas at any given time. In some cases, it makes sense to make all students responsible for the cost in the public areas, whereas in other cases (for example, at times when most students are not present), it makes more sense to use a system which identifies the student(s) responsible. In any case, we cannot simply apply the same pricing scheme in the public areas as in the student bedrooms.

Understanding the main challenges, we have started the work by using some commonly used approaches for energy conservation in the public areas. For example, we have done delamping for lightings in the public areas, especially in the corridors of the students' bedrooms. With regard to the usage of AC in the public areas, we plan to deploy a central system to control it.

7. CONCLUSIONS

In this paper, we reported our experience in deploying a smart meter system in a university campus for measuring and monitoring the electricity consumption in the dormitory rooms. Setting up such a system allows the College's administrators to adopt incentive policies to manage demand and to encourage energy-saving practices. We show that such policies are effective. From our study, it is also clear that there is much room for improvement. In particular, we discuss the need to implement incentive policies for public areas as well, and the challenges facing this problem.

Compared to other studies of electricity consumption in buildings, we focused on the consumption in campus dormitories. In such a scenario, the lodgement usually lasts for a short period, and this requires stronger incentives to encourage energy conservation. On the other hand, promoting energy conservation in campus dormitories is profound and it will influence students in their future lives. We believe that our experiences are useful for many similar efforts in campuses worldwide.

8. ACKNOWLEDGMENTS

This work was conducted with the strong support of LWS College. We would like to thank Samuel Yeung and Terence Yip, the project coordinators of LWS College, for providing us with continuous help. The project also benefited from a Theme-based Research Grant from the Research Grants Council of the Hong Kong government: Project No. T23-407/13-N.

9. REFERENCES

[1] The Chinese University of Hong Kong. http://www.cuhk.edu.hk/.

[2] Hong Kong Weather. http://www.accuweather.com/en/hk/hong-kong-weather.

[3] Lee Woo Sing College, CUHK. http://www.ws.cuhk.edu.hk/.

[4] Types of air conditioning systems. http://www.brighthubengineering.com/hvac/897-types-of-air-conditioning-systems/.

[5] Feedback on household electricity consumption: a tool for saving energy? *Energy Efficiency*, 2008.

[6] Grand challenge. In *ACM International Conference on Distributed Event Based Systems*, 2014.

[7] B. A. Corp. What are kyz pulses? *Solid State Instruments*, March 2011.

[8] A. L. Gwendolyn Brandon. Reducing household energy consumption: A qualitative and quantitative field study. *Journal of Environmental Psychology*, 1999.

[9] T. E. E. Institute. Handbook for electricity metering. August 2014.

[10] C.-Y. Kuo, M.-F. Lee, C.-L. Fu, Y.-H. Ho, and L.-J. Chen. An in-depth study of forecasting household electricity demand using realistic datasets. In *Proceedings of the 5th International Conference on Future Energy Systems*, e-Energy '14, 2014.

[11] T. Lovett, E. Gabe-Thomas, S. Natarajan, M. Brown, and J. Padget. Designing sensor sets for capturing energy events in buildings. In *Proceedings of the 5th International Conference on Future Energy Systems*, e-Energy '14, 2014.

[12] J. B. Shi-Ming Deng. A study of energy performance of hotel buildings in Hong Kong. *Energy and Buildings*, 2000.

[13] Wikipedia. Electricity meter. http://en.wikipedia.org/wiki/Electricity_meter/.

A Novel IoT- Based Energy Management System for Large Scale Data Centers

Sharad S
Dept. of Computer Science & Engineering
Amrita Vishwa Vidyapeetham
Coimbatore, India
0422 - 268 5000
sharad.sriram@gmail.com

Bagavathi Sivakumar P.
Dept. of Computer Science & Engineering
Amrita Vishwa Vidyapeetham
Coimbatore, India
0422 - 268 5000
pbsk@cb.amrita.edu

V. Anantha Narayanan
Dept. of Computer Science & Engineering
Amrita Vishwa Vidyapeetham
Coimbatore, India
0422 - 268 5000
v_ananthanarayanan@cb.amrita.edu

ABSTRACT

The high energy consumption in data centers is becoming a major concern because it leads to increased operating costs and also, pollution, as fuel is burnt to produce the required energy. While many techniques and methods have been proposed by various organizations and researchers to minimize the energy consumption, there has been considerably less work done in making a smart-energy management system that is capable of collecting the data available and make decisions based on the energy consumption patterns. In this work, a smart system is proposed that uses Internet of Things to gather data and a machine learning algorithm for decision making.

Categories and Subject Descriptors

B.1.3 **[Hardware]:** *Control Structure and Microprogramming - Control Structure Reliability, Testing, and Fault-Tolerance*

Keywords

Large Data Centers, High Energy Consumption, IoT, wireless communication, Cloud; Beagle Bone Black, CC2500.

1. INTRODUCTION

In the information age, we have more data that is generated than ever in history. These data are stored and served by data centers. These data centers are the back-bone of the growing economy of the world. The number of data centers across the world is growing very fast and these data centers consume electricity as much as the amount needed for a small town. This high consumption has lead data centers be called as "polluters" - because of the large amounts of fuel is burnt to produce electricity which results in higher CO2 Emissions. Thus, an efficient system [2,3] is needed to manage and monitor the electricity consumed. The proposed system uses efficient algorithms and protocols that not only saves power, optimizes the trust and reliability but also enables real-time data sharing and also make a co-existing ecosystem of different devices within a single network - Internet of Things [1,5], ready.

e-Energy'15, July 14-17, 2015, Bangalore, India.

 ISBN 978-1-4503-3609-3/15/07 $15.00.

DOI: http://dx.doi.org/10.1145/ 2768510.2768520

The paper is organized as follows : Secion II, is a study on the energy consumption at data centers. In section III, the scope and related works are discussed. In Section IV, we discuss the application of IoT and Machine Learning. In Section V, we dicuss our proposed solution. The hardware and software implementation with pseudo codes and algorithms are discussed in section VI. Results are discussed in Section VII. Conclusion and the scope for further work are presented in Section VIII.

2. A STUDY ON ENERGY CONSUMPTIONS IN DATA CENTERS

Data centers face under-utilization of servers as a major hurdle to better energy efficiency. There is a loss of about 13% in the conversion from AC to DC. Moreover, the servers need to be kept in an air-conditioned environment, which are known to consume more power. Thus, we need a system to smartly monitor and manage the power consumed and minimize the loss and wastage [8]. The growing footprint of data centers with respect to electricity consumption is shown in figure1 [7].

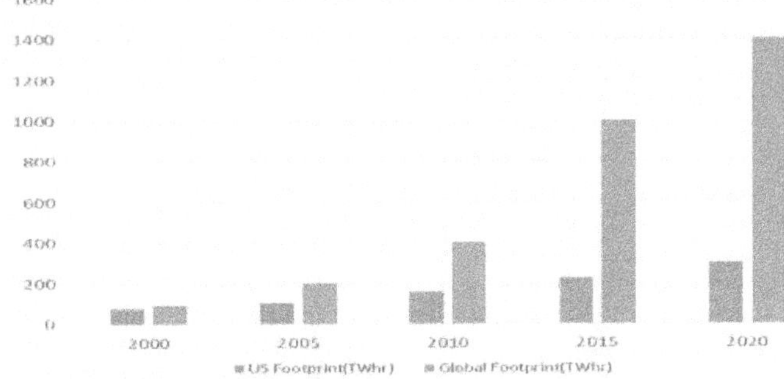

Figure 1. Projected data center electricity usage.

Natural Resource Defense Council (NRDC), is an international enivronment advocacy group which is based in the USA[11]. They have conducted a study on the energy consumed by data centers in the US and the details are shown in Table 1. Their study shows the estimated increase in terms of End-use Energy, Electricity Bill, the number of power plants needed and the carbon dioxide emissions.

Table 1. Study done by NRDC on the energy consumed by data centers in the US [6]

Year	End-Use Energy (B kWh)	Electric Bill (US ,$B)	Power Plants(in 500MW)	CO2 Emission (in million MT)
2013	91	9.0	34	97
2020	139	13.7	51	147
2013-2020 increase	47	4.7	17	50

3. SCOPE and RELATED WORK

There are many methods that are employed by organizations to minimize the energy consumptions at data centers and many researchers have also contributed with efficient ways to minimize energy consumptions [12-14]. The most common methods include using energy-efficient power supplies and fans, optimizing the data center layout and use optimized compilers, etc. [10]. The following are the practices that are suggested by Google [9] to reduce the energy consumption at datacenters.

1. Manage PUE (Power Usage Effectiveness):

The PUE, is an industrial measure used to reduce the energy consumed by non- computing functions like cooling systems, etc.

$$PUE = \frac{\text{IT Equiment Energy+Facility Overhead Energy}}{\text{IT Equipment Energy}}$$

Where:

- IT Equipment Energy – energy consumed by the servers, storage & networking devices and devices where the actual work is done
- Facility Overhead Energy – energy consumed by the lighting, cooling units and power distribution systems

2. Manage Airflow:

Good air flow management is crucial for the data center to operate efficiently. A well designed containment minimizes the mixing of hot and cold air. Furthermore, one can use Computational Fluid Dynamics to characterize and optimize air flow.

3. Adjust Thermostat:

Many manufacturers now allow servers to be run at 26 C, or more. The use of economizer allows you to run elevated cold aisle temperatures and offers higher savings.

4. Use free cooling:

"Free Cooling", refers to the process of removing the heat without a chiller. The proposed methods here are using low temperature ambient air, evaporating water, etc. It is seen water and air-side economizers can also be used.

5. Optimize power distribution:

Power distribution losses can be minimized by eliminating as many power conversion steps as possible by using efficient transformers & power distribution units. The UPS results in the largest loss of power, so an efficient model is to be used.

As discussed above, there is a need for monitoring the energy consumption over a long period of time. In Google's case the energy consumed is measured quarterly and trailing – 12 month performance of the data center. In our implementation, we can measure every fortnight, as the measurement taken few hours once may not be useful for decision making. Even though, we compute the energy consumptions every fortnight, we still continue to monitor our devices and their respective sensor values to identify and assure that the devices are functioning properly. This will use only minimal energy and since we send only a few bytes of data, this method has a very low resource overhead.

4. USE of IoT and Machine Learning

This work aims to use the benefits of two research areas namely, Machine Learning and Internet of Things. We use the concepts of IoT to collect the data and cloud for storage. The data thus collected is used as inputs to our machine learning algorithm. The machine learning algorithm can crunch the data and provide the necessary optimizations in the settings to manage and minimize energy consumption in data centers. The novelty lies with the concept of using our algorithm on the data which is acquired from the cloud and take necessary actions in real-time frame. The inputs to the algorithm are the real-time data from the sensors measuring temperature, humidity, power consumption, etc. This enables the proposed system, to provide a very efficient energy management.

5. PROPOSED SOLUTION

Our proposed system provides an audio- visual indication to the administrator when there is a sudden rise or unnecessary usage of energy in the data center. Generally, the primary appliances that consume a lot of energy are air-conditioner, cooling system, etc. This system senses the energy consumption at each point (where the appliance is present), and based on the usage and the input energy, it makes a decision whether or not that appliance requires more energy. This decision is based on the sensor values from that point and also from the nearby points.

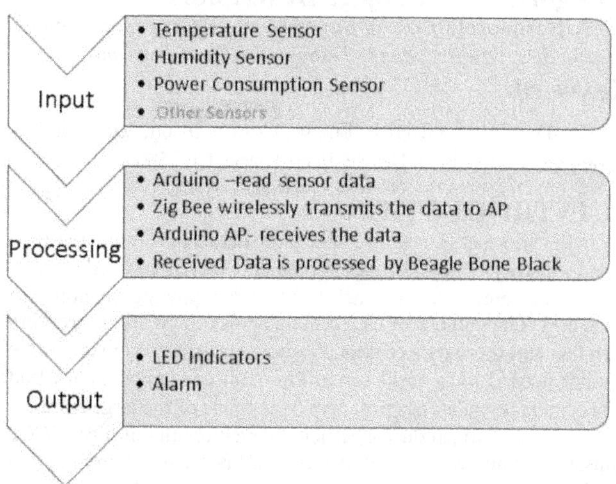

Figure 2. Top-Level Design

The proposed solution is to have an automated Energy Monitoring system. This top level design is shown in Fig.2. This system will have a set of micro-controllers that uses sensors to measure the temperature, humidity, power consumption, etc. These data are sent to a common access-point, another micro-controller, wirelessly [4] using the ZigBee protocol. The data from the access-point is sent to the decision hub, a single-board computer (SBC).

The SBC is configured as a cloud server as well as a decision hub. The Beagle Bone Black (BBB) acts as a local server and uploads all sensor data to a cloud and also a database. The cloud database is created using Owncloud, a Linux package. This database is populated with the sensor data using a python script. The functions of the SBC as a decision hub are as follows:

- Control the parameters
- Monitor the parameters at regular intervals
- Alert the administrator at critical scenarios
- Log the data into a cloud-based database
- Use the inputs for Machine Learning

In a large-scale data center where there is a vast area to be covered with a lot of servers and appliances to be sensed we propose the following hierarchy as shown in figure 3. The description is that, the number of end-devices is proportional to the number of columns of servers in the data centers. The number of access-points is less than the number of end-devices, this also depends on the area of the data center. The bigger the area, we may use more acces points to ensure realiable data transfers.There will be a single SBC, BeagleBone Black in this case to gather the incoming data and upload it into the cloud.

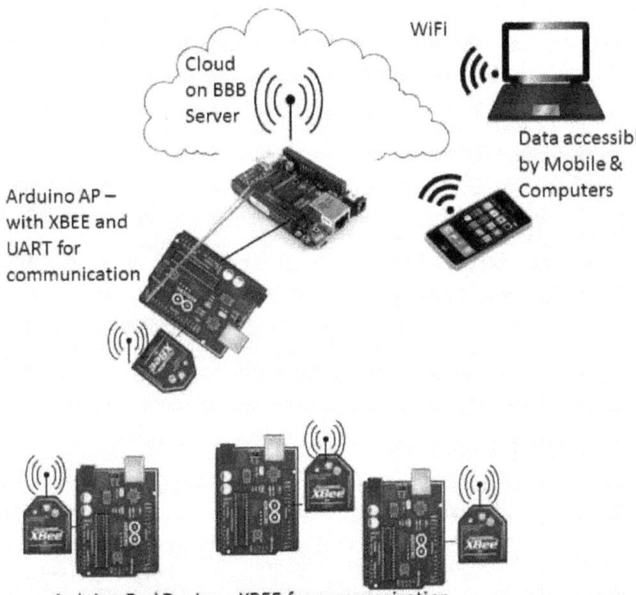

Figure 3.The hierarchy of devices in large-scale deployment

6. IMPLEMENTATION

6.1 Hardware Implementation

The proposed solution has two devices namely the base system and the end device. The proposed model is a warning system that uses sensory inputs from various points across the data center and sounds an alarm. The sensors are controlled by a micro-controller (Arduino) which is in turn controlled by a Beagle Bone Black. The Beagle Bone controls all the micro-controllers and is in constant communication with the administrator of the data center and, this forms the base system as shown in figure 4. This is to give some control to the administrator and also report any damages or failures. The communication between the Beagle Bone and Arduino micro controllers is wireless and is encrypted for security purposes. The AES or XXTEA may be the cryptographic support in the setup.

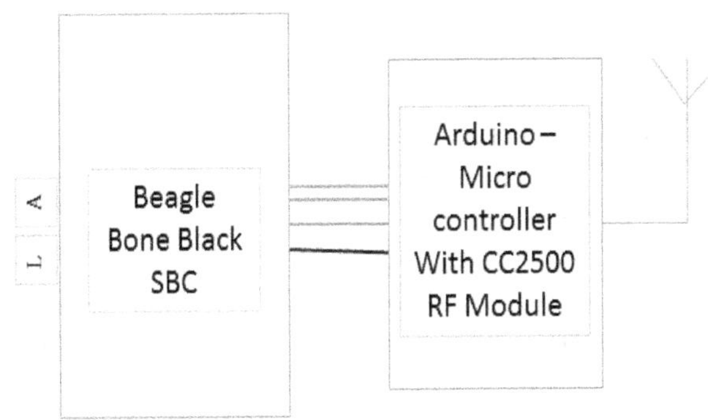

Figure 4. Design of the Base System

The **Base- System:** this is the decision hub along with the Access Point. This device has LED to provide visual indications and an alarm to indicate and alert the operator when the system reaches a critical level. This is also the system which acts as a local server and hosts all the sensor data in a cloud. The communication is wireless between the end-devices and the access-point. The access point is an Arduino board interfaces with a ZigBee wireless module. The design also features a complementing set of sustainable power sources like Battery and Solar Cells that can be used in case of a power failure. The administrator is warned of abnormal energy consumptions by audio (an alarm (A)) and visually by a set of LEDs (L) as shown in figure.4. The communication between the Arduino – Access Point and the Beagle Bone Black is done using the hardware UART. The Access Point receives data from the various end-devices, decrypts it and then sends to Beagle Bone Black.

The other device is the end-device. This is also an Arduino board which is interfaced with a Zigbee module for wireless communication to the access-point, in addition to that this also has sensors(S1,S2,S3) attached to it as shown in figure 5. We use Texas Instrumnets' CC2500 Wireless Modules, for communication between the End Device and Access Point. The CC2500, operates in SPI mode which saves a lot of power and extends the battery life of the device.

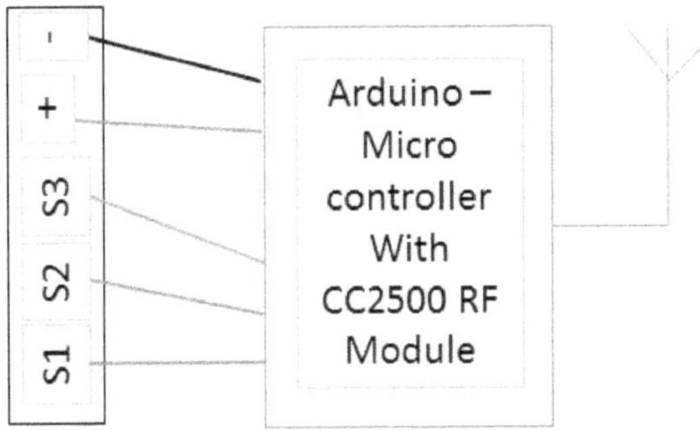

Figure 5. The design of the end device

The sensor values are read and is clubbed to form a packet with the device ID . This packet is sent to the access point. These sensors are controlled by the micro-controller.

The functionality of these two devices can be summarized as follows: the Arduino board transmits the sensor inputs and also about the state/working condition of the sensors. Beagle Bone Black acts like a hub interacting with the administrator and the micro-controller. Thus, BBB receives data/instructions from the administrator and sends usage reports, sensor readings and also triggers alerts in case of any mishaps or failure in the vicinity of the device setup by uploading the data to a secure cloud.

6.2 Data Organization and Data Flow

The data which is collected by the end devices is uploaded to the cloud server that is created using beagle bone black. This data is uploaded every 30 minutes. The data is processed using a python script which appends the received data to a local data base and the data is also appended to a comma separated value (.csv) file which is maintained at the cloud server. Thus, we get the proposed outputs - the graph - generated using the google graphs API and a .csv file which can be accessed from the cloud server by the administrator or the authorized personnel in the network. The .csv file forms the basis for the learning and prediction. The data extracted from the .csv file contains the details of the sensor reading from all the sensors along with a timestamp, each in separate columns. The columns contain the values measured by the temperature, humidity, power consumption sensors.

We are presently conducting system tests in the data center at Amrita University, Coimbatore to analyze the implementation costs and performance of our proposed system. The threshold value can be computed from this pilot work and then this can be scaled up to large data centers.

6.3 Software Implementation

This section gives the details of the software implementation. The algorithm or pseudo steps are shown below.

6.3.1. End Device – Arduino

a) Read sensor values from sensors.

b) Store the read ADC values into a variable.

c) Add precision with desired representation for values.

d) Push these into an array of characters

e) Array [0] = '*' and array [n-1] = '#' where n is the array size.

f) Array [1:2] => the device ID assigned to the end device.

g) Encrypt the data using the XXTEA algorithm.

h) Send the data Via SPI using ZigBee.

6.3.2. Access Point – Arduino

a) Receive the data via SPI from different End Devices.

b) Store the data in a buffer

c) Serially send the buffer contents to Beagle Bone Black

d) Sleep for 500 ms.

6.3.3. Data Processing at Beagle Bone Black

a) Open a Serial port and always listen.

b) Read the incoming serial data

c) Decrypt the data and append it to the database.

d) Also write the data into a csv file

e) Sleep for 10ms

6.4. HARDWARE HEALTH MONITORING

The scenarios which indicate that the system is not functioning and when the administrator is needed to take the decision are as follows:

1. When a sensor fails - this is detected when the packet has a null value for a consistent time period, then the End Device alerts the SBC which in turn alerts the administrator using an alarm
2. When an End Device fails – this is detected at the access point, when data is not received over a long time (time in terms of hours), then the access point alerts the SBC which in turn alerts the administrator.

6.5. APPLICATION OF MACHINE LEARNING ALGORITHM

For further analysis we plan to use the csv file generated as discussed in section 6.2. This forms a training set for our machine learning algorithm. But, in real-time implementation of this work, the administrator has an option to set the frequency at which the energy consumption is to be measured.

Once the data set is ready, our proposal is to implement and try with machine learning algorithms. The algorithm aims to learn and find a pattern for the energy consumption in the data center. We get a distribution curve, from the gathered data; this curve will help us to find out the servers that are operated at max-load or are shut-down or throttled. We are still working on how to use the data available from the distribution function mentioned above and to further optimize the power consumption. Furthermore, we can use the learned function to find the pattern of energy consumption, analyze the energy consumption with the past and present consumptions and make suitable decisions or prediction.

7. RESULTS

This section discusses the results obtained from the implementation methods discussed in section 6. The first task, was to read the sensor data and make a simple comma-separated packet. In 6, the sensor read data is shown. This packet is sent for encryption and then will be sent wirelessly as discussed in section 6.3.1.

The encryption module, used in our proposed module is the XXTEA encryption algorithm. The reason for choosing XXTEA is that it uses less resources for the encryption process which makes it suitable for embedded devices. For ensuring that there is no ambiguity with the data that is received we send them as packets. Each packet is made with certain conventions like:

- Each packet begins with a '*'.
- This is followed by a 2 digit number – which is the device ID which is user assigned
- Following the device id, we have the sensor values each separated by some special characters. These characters are useful to extract the data in the later stages

The need for security is to prevent data loss, bit errors in data during the communication and also to prevent intruder attacks like phishing, etc. The encryption takes place at the Arduino -End Device soon after the packet is formed and just before sending it. The decryption takes place at the Arduino – access point, right after a packet is received. The packet when received by Beagle Bone Black, is split into variables as device Id, timestamp, and sensor data which are then uploaded to a cloud created using Owncloud, as discussed in Section 6.2. The data are also uploaded into a local database which is used with a web page to give a graphical plot of the sensor values for each end-device, and is used for maintenance and monitoring.

```
*01 , 0304 , 0227 , 0196 , 0168#
*01 , 0122 , 0107 , 0115 , 0120#
*01 , 0115 , 0102 , 0113 , 0115#
*01 , 0113 , 0100 , 0110 , 0113#
*01 , 0130 , 0120 , 0132 , 0128#
*01 , 0113 , 0099 , 0110 , 0113#
*01 , 0116 , 0102 , 0113 , 0115#
*01 , 0111 , 0098 , 0109 , 0111#
*01 , 0112 , 0098 , 0109 , 0111#
*01 , 0111 , 0098 , 0109 , 0111#
*01 , 0109 , 0096 , 0108 , 0110#
*01 , 0110 , 0097 , 0108 , 0110#
*01 , 0111 , 0097 , 0108 , 0111#
*01 , 0111 , 0097 , 0109 , 0111#
*01 , 0110 , 0097 , 0108 , 0110#
*01 , 0107 , 0093 , 0104 , 0106#
*01 , 0110 , 0097 , 0108 , 0110#
*01 , 0108 , 0094 , 0105 , 0108#
*01 , 0109 , 0096 , 0107 , 0109#
*01 , 0109 , 0096 , 0107 , 0109#
```

Figure 6. Read data made as packets

Table 2 shows the data at the end-device after encryption. Table 3 shows the data at the access point after decryption.

Table 2. Data in the End Device

Plain Text –from End Device	Encrypted Text – Sent from End Device
*01@310$236%204^179#	Ïk(f{"r+Ý Ïk(f{"r+
*01@136$121%127^132#	Ž‡R¯Wûñ^XšU Ž‡R¯Wûñ^Xš
*01@127$114%122^125#	¿íÉ1ð[˜‹r‹å ¿íÉ1ð[˜‹r‹
*01@126$113%121^124#	²viR¢ˆ£l* N ²viR¢ˆ£l*
*01@126$113%121^124#	8ó…bjkêL€K 8ó…bjkêL€K

Table 3. Data in the Access Point

Received Text at Access Point	Decrypted Text – at Access Point
Ïk(f{"r+Ý Ïk(f{"r+	*01@310$236%204^179#
Ž‡R¯Wûñ^XšU Ž‡R¯Wûñ^Xš	*01@136$121%127^132#
¿íÉ1ð[˜‹r‹å ¿íÉ1ð[˜‹r‹	*01@127$114%122^125#
²viR¢ˆ£l* N ²viR¢ˆ£l*	*01@126$113%121^124#
8ó…bjkêL€K 8ó…bjkêL€K	*01@126$113%121^124#

The data stored as a .csv file is shown in figure 7. This file is downloaded from the cloud server, which we created using BBB. This file can be downloaded by the administrator and personnel with the correct user name & password.

	A	B	C	D
1	time_stamp	Temperature	Humidity	Current
2	15-01-2015 13:01	18.8717896	41.79128373	241.9353437
3	16-01-2015 13:01	19.69651585	41.2914899	238.7431818
4	17-01-2015 13:01	19.0062998	41.1550225	238.9108178
5	18-01-2015 13:01	18.41751864	41.15060604	239.3359684
6	19-01-2015 13:01	18.67465577	40.61333002	238.9756181
7	20-01-2015 13:01	19.02040625	40.50230712	239.6869579
8	21-01-2015 13:01	18.98470534	40.93267361	238.4867019
9	22-01-2015 13:01	18.99363854	40.99504336	238.1661016
10	23-01-2015 13:01	18.95953329	40.77795314	238.5597949
11	24-01-2015 13:01	18.64115868	41.23134922	240.3600644
12	25-01-2015 13:01	19.32267255	40.42835616	241.604791
13	26-01-2015 13:01	19.3480558	40.56397824	239.5538768
14	27-01-2015 13:01	18.8863302	40.7438205	240.8735028
15	28-01-2015 13:01	19.77388424	41.28753091	239.584819
16	29-01-2015 13:01	19.90835456	40.77785043	240.7926488
17	30-01-2015 13:01	18.27005139	41.79245728	240.7296895
18	31-01-2015 13:01	18.94560186	40.88807274	241.3729795
19	01-02-2015 13:01	19.95808706	41.96150349	239.173598
20	02-02-2015 13:01	19.51452019	40.45662065	242.2580277
21	03-02-2015 13:01	19.45350944	41.60946641	242.827221
22	04-02-2015 13:01	19.74062943	41.04452311	241.7174744
23	05-02-2015 13:01	19.11399226	40.27400162	241.354964

amrita_dc

Figure 7. The .csv file, downloaded from the cloud

Currently this work is in progress in the data center at Amrita University, Coimbatore. The end device is kept on the server rack as shown in figure 8. The base system (BBB + Arduino AP), is kept close to the controlling system, shown in figure 9. Figure 10 shows the data center.

Figure 8. End Device on a Server Rack

Figure 9. Access Point with SBC along with Client System

Figure 10 the data center at Amrita University, Coimbatore

8. CONCLUSION AND FUTURE WORK

In this paper, we introduce the prototype of a smart energy management system for large scale data centers that uses IoT and machine learning concepts. Our implementation in the data center at a university environment shows that the overall system works perfectly & consumes minimal energy. The results reported in section (implementation), forms the basic test bench with the data being accumulated in a cloud. In future, this will be used as the dataset for the proposed machine learning algorithm to predict future energy consumptions and also the estimate the amount of energy required to cater the demand. The proposed design can be scaled up to optimize energy consumptions in various other domains like: hospital, home and office –based energy management systems by modifying the sensors used, and a minor modification to the proposed algorithm.

ACKNOWLEDGMENTS

We would like to extend our heartfelt gratitude to the Mobile and Wireless Networks Lab, Dept. of CSE, Amrita School of Engineering, Coimbatore and the ICTS Department, Amrita Vishwa Vidyapeetham, Coimbatore for the support extended in carrying out this work.

9. REFERENCES

[1] Gubbi, Jayavardhana, Rajkumar Buyya, Slaven Marusic, and Marimuthu Palaniswami. "Internet of Things (IoT): A vision, architectural elements, and future directions." Future Generation Computer Systems 29, no. 7 (2013): 1645-1660.

[2] Chase, Jeffrey S., Darrell C. Anderson, Prachi N. Thakar, Amin M. Vahdat, and Ronald P. Doyle. "Managing energy and server resources in hosting centers." In ACM SIGOPS Operating Systems Review, vol. 35, no. 5, pp. 103-116. ACM, 2001.

[3] Younis, Mohamed, Moustafa Youssef, and Khaled Arisha. "Energy-aware routing in cluster-based sensor networks." In Modeling, Analysis and Simulation of Computer and Telecommunications Systems, 2002. MASCOTS 2002. Proceedings. 10th IEEE International Symposium on, pp. 129-136. IEEE, 2002.

[4] Baronti, Paolo, Prashant Pillai, Vince WC Chook, Stefano Chessa, Alberto Gotta, and Y. Fun Hu. "Wireless sensor networks: A survey on the state of the art and the 802.15. 4 and ZigBee standards." Computer communications 30, no. 7 (2007): 1655-1695.

[5] Kortuem, Gerd, Fahim Kawsar, Daniel Fitton, and Vasughi Sundramoorthy. "Smart objects as building blocks for the internet of things." Internet Computing, IEEE 14, no. 1 (2010): 44-51.

[6] Patrick Thibodeau, Data Centers are the new polluters,http://www.computerworld.com/article/2598562/data-center/data-centers-are-the-new-polluters.html, accessed: 5.4.2015

[7] Jason Verge, NRDC: Multi-Tenant Data Centers need to play a bigger energy efficiency role, http://www.datacenterknowledge.com/archives/2014/08/26/data-center-energy-efficiency-role/, accessed: 5.4.2015

[8] America's Data Centers Consuming and Wasting Growing amounts of energy,http://www.nrdc.org/energy/data-center-efficiency-assessment.asp, accessed: 6.4.2015

[9] Google's Green Data Centers: Network POP Case Study, Google Inc., Available: http://static.googleusercontent.com/external_content/untrusted_dlcp/www.google.com/en/us/corporate/datacenter/dc-best-practices-google.pdf ,2011, accessed: 24.4.2015.

[10] Reducing Data Center Energy Consumption, Intel, Available: http://www.cs.berkeley.edu/~istoica/classes/cs294/09/CERN_Whitepaper_r04.pdf, accessed: 30.4.2015.-

[11] Natural Resources Defense Council, http://www.nrdc.org/about/, [accessed] 07.04.2015.

[12] Rahman, A.; Xue Liu; Fanxin Kong, "A Survey on Geographic Load Balancing Based Data Center Power Management in the Smart Grid Environment," Communications Surveys & Tutorials, IEEE , vol.16, no.1, pp.214,233, First Quarter 2014

[13] Junwei Cao; Keqin Li; Stojmenovic, I., "Optimal Power Allocation and Load Distribution for Multiple Heterogeneous Multicore Server Processors across Clouds and Data Centers," Computers, IEEE Transactions on, vol.63, no.1, pp.45,58, Jan. 2014

[14] Liang Yu; Tao Jiang; Yang Cao, "Energy Cost Minimization for Distributed Internet Data Centers in Smart Microgrids Considering Power Outages," Parallel and Distributed Systems, IEEE Transactions on , vol.26, no.1, pp.120,130, Jan. 2015

Author Index

www.ingramcontent.com/pod-product-compliance
Lightning Source LLC
Chambersburg PA
CBHW082106220326
41598CB00066BA/5642
* 9 7 8 1 4 5 0 3 3 8 8 4 4 *